CASES AND MATERIALS ON

ENVIRONMENTAL LAW

Fifth Edition

By

Roger W. Findley

Fritz B. Burns Chair of Real Property
Loyola Law School, Los Angeles

Daniel A. Farber

Henry J. Fletcher Professor of Law
University of Minnesota

AMERICAN CASEBOOK SERIES®

WEST GROUP

ST. PAUL, MINN., 1999

 TEXT IS PRINTED ON 10% POST CONSUMER RECYCLED PAPER

Preface

Almost exactly twenty years before the publication date for this edition, we began work on the original version of this casebook. Environmental law has seen many changes in the meantime: new statutes such as CERCLA, new Supreme Court rulings such as *Lucas* and *Sweet Home*, and new challenges such as the greenhouse effect. In addition, the legal frameworks that were put in place during the 1970s have become far more elaborate and fully developed. In succeeding editions of this casebook, we have attempted to maintain continuity but have not hesitated to revamp the book in light of new developments. For instance, in the midst of the energy crisis, it seemed highly appropriate to have a chapter dedicated to energy issues; as the focus has shifted, that chapter has been dismantled and some of its components used elsewhere.

This edition is no exception. Much will be familiar to those with a knowledge of previous editions. We continue to believe that a basic working knowledge of the key federal statutes and judicial doctrines is just as necessary as an understanding of environmental policy. Many of the same materials appear in their familiar places. But there have also been changes. We have expanded the materials on international environmental law in Chapter I, and have added a new section on transboundary pollution in Chapter III. We have also augmented the coverage of other topics, such as RCRA, the Endangered Species Act, and the increasingly important overlap between environmental and criminal law. In the meantime, we have streamlined the coverage of the basic pollution statutes to eliminate extraneous and distracting details. Our goal is to provide not just a survey of the environmental statutes, but insights into the process of environmental decisionmaking and the difficult policy choices involved.

As in previous editions, we are indebted to Mell Bañez and Laurie Newbauer for their assistance in wordprocessing, and to our families for their understanding and support during the writing process.

ROGER W. FINDLEY
DANIEL A. FARBER

Los Angeles, California
Minneapolis, Minnesota
February, 1999

*

Summary of Contents

Table of Contents

*

Table of Cases

The principal cases are in bold type. Cases cited or discussed in the text are roman type. References are to pages. Cases cited in principal cases and within other quoted materials are not included.

CASES AND MATERIALS ON

ENVIRONMENTAL LAW

Fifth Edition

*

Chapter I

ENVIRONMENTAL PROBLEMS
IN PERSPECTIVE

Before a detailed examination of the legal responses to environmental issues, some general background material is useful. This chapter is intended to introduce you to the problem of environmental disruption and to the major policy perspectives on this problem.

A. THE ECOLOGICAL PERSPECTIVE

A. LEOPOLD, A SAND COUNTY ALMANAC[a]
202–205, 214–217, 220 (Oxford University Press paperback, 1970).

An ethic, ecologically, is a limitation on freedom of action in the struggle for existence. An ethic, philosophically, is a differentiation of social from anti-social conduct. These are two definitions of one thing. The thing has its origin in the tendency of interdependent individuals or groups to evolve modes of co-operation. The ecologist calls these symbioses. Politics and economics are advanced symbioses in which the original free-for-all competition has been replaced, in part, by co-operative mechanisms with an ethical content.

The complexity of co-operative mechanisms has increased with population density, and with the efficiency of tools. It was simpler, for example, to define the anti-social uses of sticks and stones in the days of the mastodons than of bullets and billboards in the age of motors.

The first ethics dealt with the relation between individuals; the Mosaic Decalogue is an example. Later accretions dealt with the relation between the individual and society. The Golden Rule tries to integrate the individual to society; democracy to integrate social organization to the individual.

There is as yet no ethic dealing with man's relation to land and to the animals and plants which grow upon it. Land, like Odysseus' slave-girls, is still property. The land-relation is still strictly economic, entailing privileges but not obligations.

The extension of ethics to this third element in human environment is, if I read the evidence correctly, an evolutionary possibility and an ecological necessity. It is the third step in a sequence. The first two have already been taken. Individual thinkers since the days of Ezekiel and Isaiah have asserted that the despoliation of land is not only inexpedient but wrong. Society, however, has not yet affirmed their belief. I regard the present conservation movement as the embryo of such an affirmation.

An ethic may be regarded as a mode of guidance for meeting ecological situations so new or intricate, or involving such deferred reactions, that the path of social expediency is not discernible to the average individual. Animal instincts are modes of guidance for the individual in meeting such situations. Ethics are possibly a kind of community instinct in-the-making.

The Community Concept

All ethics so far evolved rest upon a single premise: that the individual is a member of a community of interdependent parts. His instincts prompt him to compete for his place in that community, but his ethics prompt him also to co-operate (perhaps in order that there may be a place to compete for).

The land ethic simply enlarges the boundaries of the community to include soils, waters, plants, and animals, or collectively: the land.

This sounds simple: do we not already sing our love for and obligation to the land of the free and the home of the brave? Yes, but just what and whom do we love? Certainly not the soil, which we are sending helter-skelter downriver. Certainly not the waters, which we assume have no function except to turn turbines, float barges, and carry off sewage. Certainly not the plants, of which we exterminate whole communities without batting an eye. Certainly not the animals, of which we have already extirpated many of the largest and most beautiful species. A land ethic of course cannot prevent the alteration, management, and use of these "resources," but it does affirm their right to continued existence, and, at least in spots, their continued existence in a natural state.

In short, a land ethic changes the role of *Homo sapiens* from conqueror of the land-community to plain member and citizen of it. It implies respect for his fellow-members, and also respect for the community as such.

In human history, we have learned (I hope) that the conqueror role is eventually self-defeating. Why? Because it is implicit in such a role that the conqueror knows, *ex cathedra,* just what makes the community clock tick, and just what and who is valuable, and what and who is worthless, in community life. It always turns out that he knows neither, and this is why his conquests eventually defeat themselves.

In the biotic community, a parallel situation exists. Abraham knew exactly what the land was for: it was to drip milk and honey into Abraham's mouth. At the present moment, the assurance with which we regard this assumption is inverse to the degree of our education.

The ordinary citizen today assumes that science knows what makes the community clock tick; the scientist is equally sure that he does not. He knows that the biotic mechanism is so complex that its workings may never be fully understood.

* * *

THE LAND PYRAMID

An ethic to supplement and guide the economic relation to land presupposes the existence of some mental image of land as a biotic mechanism. We can be ethical only in relation to something we can see, feel, understand, love, or otherwise have faith in.

The image commonly employed in conservation education is "the balance of nature." For reasons too lengthy to detail here, this figure of speech fails to describe accurately what little we know about the land mechanism. A much truer image is the one employed in ecology: the biotic pyramid. I shall first sketch the pyramid as a symbol of land, and later develop some of its implications in terms of land-use.

Plants absorb energy from the sun. This energy flows through a circuit called the biota, which may be represented by a pyramid consisting of layers. The bottom layer is the soil. A plant layer rests on the soil, an insect layer on the plants, a bird and rodent layer on the insects, and so on up through various animal groups to the apex layer, which consists of the larger carnivores.

The species of a layer are alike not in where they came from, or in what they look like, but rather in what they eat. Each successive layer depends on those below it for food and often for other services, and each in turn furnishes food and services to those above. Proceeding upward, each successive layer decreases in numerical abundance. Thus, for every carnivore there are hundreds of his prey, thousands of their prey, millions of insects, uncountable plants. The pyramidal form of the system reflects this numerical progression from apex to base. Man shares an intermediate layer with the bears, raccoons, and squirrels which eat both meat and vegetables.

The lines of dependency for food and other services are called food chains. Thus soil-oak-deer-Indian is a chain that has now been largely converted to soil-corn-cow-farmer. Each species, including ourselves, is a link in many chains. The deer eats a hundred plants other than oak, and the cow a hundred plants other than corn. Both, then, are links in a hundred chains. The pyramid is a tangle of chains so complex as to seem disorderly, yet the stability of the system proves it to be a highly organized structure. Its functioning depends on the co-operation and competition of its diverse parts.

In the beginning, the pyramid of life was low and squat; the food chains short and simple. Evolution has added layer after layer, link after link. Man is one of thousands of accretions to the height and complexity of the pyramid. Science has given us many doubts, but it has given us at least one certainty: the trend of evolution is to elaborate and diversify the biota.

Land, then, is not merely soil; it is a fountain of energy flowing through a circuit of soils, plants, and animals. Food chains are the living channels which conduct energy upwards; death and decay return it to the soil. The circuit is not closed; some energy is dissipated in decay, some is added by absorption from the air, some is stored in soils, peats, and long-lived forests; but it is a sustained circuit, like a slowly augmented revolving fund of life. There is always a net loss by downhill wash, but this is normally small and offset by the decay of rocks. It is deposited in the ocean and, in the course of geological time, raised to form new lands and new pyramids.

The velocity and character of the upward flow of energy depend on the complex structure of the plant and animal community, much as the upward flow of sap in a tree depends on its complex cellular organization. Without this complexity, normal circulation would presumably not occur. Structure means the characteristic numbers, as well as the characteristic kinds and functions, of the component species. This interdependence between the complex structure of the land and its smooth functioning as an energy unit is one of its basic attributes.

When a change occurs in one part of the circuit, many other parts must adjust themselves to it. Change does not necessarily obstruct or divert the flow of energy; evolution is a long series of self-induced changes, the net result of which has been to elaborate the flow mechanism and to lengthen the circuit. Evolutionary changes, however, are usually slow and local. Man's invention of tools has enabled him to make changes of unprecedented violence, rapidity, and scope.

* * *

The combined evidence of history and ecology seems to support one general deduction: the less violent the man-made changes, the greater the probability of successful readjustment in the pyramid.

Note

For more about Aldo Leopold and ecological values, see the article by Charles Meyers and related notes, pages 728–739 infra. See also H. Rolston, *Environmental Ethics: Duties to and Values in the Natural World* (1988).

G. LEDEC AND R. GOODLAND, WILDLANDS: THEIR PROTECTION AND MANAGEMENT IN ECONOMIC DEVELOPMENT[b]

5–15 (1988).

"The land is one organism," wrote the American naturalist Aldo Leopold over forty years ago. "Its parts, like our own parts, compete with each other and cooperate with each other * * *. If the biota, in the course of aeons, has built something we like but do not understand, then who but a fool would discard seemingly useless parts?" Wildlands, kept in their natural state and properly managed, provide a refuge for plant and animal species that may prove to have direct economic uses and that, more important, form part of the vast and still inadequately understood web of connections among all living things and their environment. Wildlands are also essential for the maintenance of environmental services—water control, soil conservation, and the like—most of them unpriced public goods that are indispensable for meeting human needs and supporting sustainable development.

Because wildlands make significant and even unique long-term contributions to human welfare, prudent development should minimize or mitigate damages from wildland conversion. Indeed, the timely management of strategically important wildlands often prolongs or improves the effectiveness of development projects. Conversely, the unnecessary or short-sighted destruction of wildlands can lead to unanticipated and costly consequences, such as the rapid siltation of reservoirs and waterways, the loss of topsoil and of economically important species, and even the spread of disease. By incorporating wildland management in their projects and other activities, development organizations can improve the prospects for sustainable economic development.

* * *

BIOLOGICAL DIVERSITY

Biological diversity usually refers to three elements: (1) the number of different ecosystems (communities of plants and animals and the environments that sustain them) and their relative frequencies in a country or in the world; (2) the number of species of animals and plants and their relative frequencies; and (3) the genetic variation within each species.

The variability we see in the life forms on Earth is primarily a result of variations in DNA (deoxyribonucleic acid), as expressed in genes—the blueprints for life. Genetic variability is greatest among species, but variability among isolated populations of a species or among individuals in a population is also important. A rare species is a genetically vulnerable species. If the number of individuals is small, the probability of advantageous genetic variations occurring is reduced, and inbreeding may perpetuate disadvantageous characteristics. Preserving biological diversity, then, entails preserving not only species but also different populations of species and the largest feasible number of individuals within those populations.

Most of the world's wild plant and animal species depend on wildlands for their existence, as they cannot survive in areas that have been significantly modified by human beings. Moreover, most species depend on specific types of wildland habitats and have limited geographic ranges. * * * The elimination of a unique wildland habitat therefore causes the summary extinction of all the species that are completely dependent on that habitat for their survival. Appropriate wildland management is the only method of preserving large and distinct populations of most species, thereby ensuring species survival and biological diversity. Conservation measures other than wildland management (such as the establishment of plantation forests) preserve some environmental services but cannot by themselves maintain diversity.

The Modern Loss of Biological Diversity

Human activities in the last quarter of the twentieth century are reducing biological diversity at a rate that may be unprecedented in the history of life on Earth. It is impossible to assess, with our limited knowledge, the consequences of the disappearance of species for the stability of Earth's environment or the economic value lost because of extinctions. The best available estimates indicate that if current trends continue, some 15–20 percent of the estimated 10 million to 30 million species of plants and animals alive in 1980 may become extinct by 2000, and many more species could be lost in the early decades of the twenty-first century. Development activities can be modified to help reduce these disturbing trends. * * *

The most striking difference between natural and human-induced extinctions is in the rates. Over the millennia the rate of natural extinction of species has usually been slightly less than the rate of formation of new species through evolutionary processes. Human activity is greatly accelerating extinction rates; several hundred species *a day* may become extinct over the next twenty to thirty years. More species of the Earth's flora and fauna may disappear in the next several decades than were lost in the mass extinction that wiped out whole taxonomic groups of animals, including the dinosaurs, 65 million years ago.

Another difference is that whereas in the course of evolution a species that becomes extinct is often replaced by a better-adapted successor or group of successors, human-induced extinctions are evolutionary dead ends. Furthermore, although human beings are not the first species to have caused the extinction of other species, they are the first to be aware of the implications of their actions and to be capable of controlling them.

The reduction of wildland habitats to less than the critical amount necessary for the survival of a species is by far the greatest cause of modern extinctions. Although many endangered species live in temperate areas, the problem is most severe in tropical regions, where at least two-thirds of the world's species of plants and animals are found. Appropriate, low-cost wildland management can significantly reduce current extinction rates to much lower—perhaps almost "natural"—levels. * * *

* * *

The Case for Preserving Biological Diversity

There are compelling economic, scientific, aesthetic, and ethical reasons for preserving biological diversity. All of them are grounded in the view that because species extinctions are completely irreversible, preserving biological diversity keeps open important options for the future.

The *economic* justification for preserving biological diversity is that many species of wild plants and animals are undeveloped resources—that is, they have significant economic potential that is currently undiscovered, undervalued, or underutilized. Biological resources are essential to human existence, and the preservation of biological diversity is important to the maintenance and improvement of agriculture, forestry, ranching, fisheries, medicine, industry, and tourism.

The importance of genetic diversity for sustaining and increasing agricultural production is increasingly acknowledged. Without a diverse genetic base for plant breeding, the development of high-yielding crop varieties probably could not be sustained. The disappearance of many domesticated crop varieties and their wild relatives has made many of the world's productive farming areas increasingly susceptible to catastrophic attacks by pests and diseases. Despite efforts to preserve crop germplasm, many domestic varieties and wild relatives of crop plants remain threatened.

An example of the benefits of genetic diversity is a perennial wild maize (*Zea diploperennis*) which has been preserved almost accidentally. It may have seemed to be "just another weed" when it was discovered growing on a few hectares of land in Jalisco, Mexico, but it may become important for higher food production. Perennial maize could be grown in "maize orchards" that would not have to be plowed and seeded each year; the advantages for soil and energy conservation are obvious. In addition, cross-breeding with *Zea diploperennis* may significantly improve the resistance of annual varieties of maize to a number of serious diseases and insect pests. * * *

* * *

Wild plant species have even greater potential as completely new crops. Of the world's approximately 240,000 species of plants, only about 3,000 have even been used as food, only 150 have been cultivated on any scale, and a mere 20 account for over 85 percent of present human consumption. Population growth, rising per capita consumption, and shortages of arable land may make it important in future years to cultivate new species of crops that can produce calories, protein, specific mineral nutrients, vitamins, or fibers more efficiently than many of the species currently used.

Many otherwise obscure animal species, particularly insects, should also be protected to maintain or enhance agricultural output. For example, the oil palm (*Elaeis guineensis*) is pollinated in the wild in Africa by a weevil, *Elaeidobius kamerunicus*. The oil palm was introduced in what is now Malaysia in 1917 without the weevil and required costly, inefficient, labor-intensive hand pollination. In 1980–81 the pollinator was collected from its native habitat in the forests of Cameroon and brought to Malaysia; it promptly boosted fruiting in oil palm trees by 40–60 percent. This improvement was worth approximately $57 million in foreign exchange in the first year alone.

* * *

Wild plants and animals are also fundamentally important for modern medicine and offer even greater future applications. Over 40 percent of all prescriptions written in the United States contain one or more drugs that originate from wild species (fungi, bacteria, higher plants, and animals); annual sales of such drugs in this one country are over $8 billion. In many cases it is still impossible to synthesize these compounds or more costly to synthesize them than to obtain them from living sources; in any case it would not have been possible to know what compound to synthesize without first having the natural model.

Wild plant and animal species are of great and increasing importance to industry as sources of tannins, resins, gums, oils, dyes, and other commercially useful compounds. Until about 1850 even the rubber tree (*Hevea brasiliensis*) was just another Amazonian tree species of unknown economic value. The potential for new industrial products from currently unknown or poorly known plant and animal species is significant but impossible to quantify. Such products may even include hydrocarbons for an oil-short world. For example, *Copaifera langsdorfii,* a tree that grows only in northern Brazil, produces 20 liters of sap per tree every six months, and this sap, it has recently been discovered, can be used directly as a fuel in diesel engines. * * *

* * *

The *scientific* reason for species preservation is that we cannot understand the interactions of life forms and their environments unless we can observe how they function in the absence of significant human intervention. It is therefore necessary to conserve comprehensive samples of ecological systems in an undisturbed state. Moreover, each species has unique physiological, biochemical, and population characteristics, the study of which can help us to understand basic life processes. In addition to the direct economic applications of research on poorly known species, eventual economic payoffs are likely to emerge from more basic scientific research.

* * *

The *aesthetic* justification is that many wild species of plants and animals are an irreplaceable source of wonder, inspiration, and joy to human beings because of their beauty, intriguing appearance, variety, or fascinating behavior. * * * Millions of people who may never actually encounter many wild species derive enrichment and vicarious satisfaction from reading and learning about them; are our descendants to be denied these pleasures?

The *ethical,* or moral, justification, espoused by a significant and growing number of people, is that human beings should not exercise their power to obliterate other species at will—even species not known to have any practical value to humankind. From this perspective nonhuman species have their own intrinsic value independent of any practical or utilitarian value they may have for human beings. This ethical viewpoint has been called the "Noah principle." A related, perhaps more traditional, view is that to eradicate other species is to deprive future generations of options and thus to fail in the duty of stewardship. For a couple of generations of human beings to eliminate unnecessarily a sizable proportion of the diversity of life on Earth can be construed as an act of considerable arrogance.

All of these considerations argue that human beings should exercise great care to avoid inadvertent extinctions. A leading biologist, Edward O. Wilson, has said:

> The worst thing that can happen—will happen—in the 1980s is not energy depletion, economic collapse, limited nuclear war, or conquest by a totalitarian government. As terrible as these catastrophes would be for us, they can be repaired within a few generations. The one process ongoing in the 1980s that will take millions of years to correct is the loss of genetic and species diversity by the destruction of natural habitats. This is the folly our descendants are least likely to forgive us.

Notes

1. The authors sketch four types of reasons for preserving diversity: economic, scientific, aesthetic, and ethical. Depending on what priority we give to these reasons, we might structure our efforts differently. For example, some species have more aesthetic appeal than others. Should this play a role in our preservation decisions? Moreover, some of the justifications focus more on individual species, while others focus on distinctive ecosystems, which might also influence the choice of methods for preserving biodiversity. How much of the rationale for preservation should turn on utilitarian considerations, and how much on the intrinsic value that a species might be thought to have? Suppose, for example, that it were determined that some species of whale had little potential economic value, little impact on the oceanic ecosystem (perhaps because it is quite rare anyway), and limited

aesthetic beauty. Should we preserve it anyway? In terms of priorities, should we be willing to make greater sacrifices to save such a species or a less appealing but potentially useful type of fern?

2. As we will see in Chapter VIII, the Endangered Species Act is drafted in terms of preserving individual species rather than ecosystems, and gives little attention to costs. Is this legal structure consistent with the rationales for preserving biodiversity?

3. Some of the interests involved in protecting an endangered species involve some immediate interaction with the species by scientists or others. Other interests involve unknown possibilities for future economic or scientific uses, or a desire to preserve the species for the possible benefit of future generations. Yet our litigation system was originally designed to settle concrete disputes over existing harms. What kind of connection with a biodiversity issue should the law require as the basis for bringing a claim? Should anyone be allowed to sue, or only someone with a more definite short-term interest? Should some legal mechanism be created to help protect the rights of future generations?

RUHL, "THINKING OF ENVIRONMENTAL LAW AS A COMPLEX ADAPTIVE SYSTEM: HOW TO CLEAN UP THE ENVIRONMENT BY MAKING A MESS OF ENVIRONMENTAL LAW"[c]

34 *Houston Law Review* 933, 954–958 (1997).

Biological evolution is one of the most studied topics in science, and yet the amount we do not know about evolution far exceeds the amount we do know. The part we do not even begin to understand is associated with the contribution ecological forces make to evolutionary dynamics. As the eminent biologist Edward O. Wilson puts it, "[w]hat we understand best about evolution is mostly genetic, and what we understand least is mostly ecological.... [T]he major remaining questions of evolutionary biology are ecological rather than genetic in content."[84]

The emergence in environmental biology of the concept of ecosystems as unpredictable, dynamically changing systems has injected a heightened awareness of the role of indeterminacy and randomness into evolutionary theory.[85] The mix of species in an ecosystem depends largely on the timing of introduction and the location. But how are the assembly rules[87] for an ecosystem determined, and how do they contribute to

---

c. Copyright 1997 by *Houston Law Review*. Reprinted by permission.

84. Edward O. Wilson, The Diversity of Life 93 (1992).

85. The past 30 years of research in biology have spawned a "new paradigm of ecology, mothballing the old notion of a 'balance of nature' and unveiling a vibrant new replacement focusing on flux." William Stolzenburg, Building a Better Refuge, Nature Conservancy, Jan.-Feb. 1996, at 18, 21.

The new focus on dynamic change has led scientists to reevaluate the premises upon which many legal and policy decisions have been based, such as the size, location, and operation of wildlife refuges.

87. Wilson explains that "[a]ssembly rules determine which species can coexist in a community of organisms (such as the bird species occupying a forest patch). The rules also determine the sequence in which species are able to colonize the habitat." Wilson, supra note 84, at 171.

evolution of species across time? These are the questions of the future for evolutionary biologists.

Questions about ecosystems not only are relevant to evolutionary biologists, but also go to the heart of environmental law and policy at all levels. Here again, we find that we know less than we do not know, but we do know the following:

> *1. The connections between species within an ecosystem are often poorly understood,[88] or understood too late to do any good.*

> *2. Little is known, particularly for large carnivores, about how much habitat and how many species individuals are needed to support a species as a long-term viable population.[90]*

> *3. One of the most pernicious and least understood threats to ecosystems involves the "invasion," often unwittingly assisted by human activities, by particularly adaptable species that prey upon or out-compete the "native" species of the ecosystem.[91]*

> *4. Evidence of more direct adverse effects of human activities on ecosystems is abundant but difficult to understand in terms of causal effect, source of the problem, and possible solution.[92]*

> *5. It cannot be assumed that human influence always presents a negative for ecosystem dynamics.[93]*

> *6. Human efforts to conserve species may sometimes actually do more damage to ecosystems than good.[94]*

---

88. The extinct dodo, for example, is now believed to have had a mutualistic relationship with the endangered tambalacoque tree: the tree's seed evolved to resist crushing in a dodo's gizzard, resulting in a pit too thick to germinate without abrasion of its outer wall. See Sally Valdes–Cogliano, A Lost Piece of the Puzzle, Endangered Species Bull., Nov.-Dec. 1996, at 11, 11. But, while passing through the birds' system, the seeds underwent sufficient abrasion to promote germination once expelled from the bird. The dodo's extinction over 300 years ago only recently was identified as a major cause of the tree's decline. Now that the connection is understood, the tree's seed can be germinated artificially.

90. For example, a single wolverine may travel 60 miles in one day; a Rocky Mountain wolf pack uses about 500 square miles as its home base; and a population of 1,000 grizzly bears might require an area 20 times larger than Yellowstone National Park. See William Stolzenburg, The Jaguar's Umbrella, Nature Conservancy, Mar.-Apr. 1997, at 8, 9.

91. For example, the zebra mussel, which entered North American waters in the ballast of ships, has disrupted the algae and nutrient components of many ecosys-

tems on its way to becoming a dominant mollusk species. See Peter M. Vitousek et al., Biological Invasions as Global Environmental Change, 84 Am. Scientist 468, 468 (1996).

92. For example, recently a cyberspace conference was held in which researchers exchanged papers and hypotheses, with no clear consensus, regarding the increase in amphibian deformities that has been experienced around the world. See Sasha Nemecek, Amphibians On-line, Sci. Am., Mar. 1997, at 18, 18. Possible explanations offered included parasitic flatworms, water pollution, and increased ultraviolet radiation.

93. Ohio's largest single bat colony lives in an abandoned mine. See Bruce A. Stein & Stephanie R. Flack, Conservation Priorities: The State of U.S. Plants and Animals, Environment, May 1997, at 6, 37.

94. For example, efforts to restore duck and goose habitats in the United States have resulted in a snow goose population explosion that threatens the snow goose habitat as well as the habitat of other species, some already endangered, that nest in the same arctic region. See United States Fish and Wildlife Service, United States

These sources of uncertainty make societal decisions all the more difficult, as we are unsure what effects our behavior will have on the environment. A growing effort to explain these properties through complexity theory and the depiction of ecosystems as complex adaptive systems promises to improve our understanding of their origins and inevitability.[96]

Notes

1. Ruhl stresses the high level of scientific uncertainty surrounding environmental issues. In Chapter V, we will focus on this problem as it relates specifically to the regulation of toxic chemicals, but the problem is broader. How can we regulate in a sensible way when we are unsure about the causes of a problem and unclear about the appropriate cure? Would it help to use presumptions, and if so, what presumptions would be appropriate–"leave nature alone until you have enough information to know what you're doing" or "don't interfere with the free economy until you have enough information to justify regulation"? Who should have the burden of proof, regulators or industry?

2. Accompanying our initial uncertainty about environmental problems is the likelihood that new information will change our initial strategy. As a matter of institutional design, what institutions can best deal with shifting information: Congress, federal agencies such as EPA, or local governments? Chapters II and III explore how the legal system has allocated authority over environmental problems, but sensitivity to the issue of scientific uncertainty might suggest some different choices.

B. SOME DIMENSIONS OF ENVIRONMENTAL PROBLEMS

"IN A DELUGE OF PROBLEMS, WHERE ARE THE WORST THREATS?"[d]

Conservation Foundation Letter, December 1983.

[H]alf a dozen recent studies have sought to identify and, to some extent, rank the major environmental threats.[e] They have done this principally by surveying scientists and other knowledgeable people for

Department of Interior, News Release, Report Warns that Snow Goose Population Explosion Threatens Arctic Ecosystems (April 1, 1997) <www.fws.gov>.

96. Robert Costanza et al., Modeling Complex Ecological Economic Systems, 43 BioScience 545, 545 (1993) (noting new ways for modeling interactions between anthropogenic and natural systems); Douglas S. Robertson & Michael C. Grant, Feedback and Chaos in Darwinian Evolution, Complexity, Nov.-Dec. 1996, at 18 (applying chaos theory to develop a numerical model depicting Darwinian natural selection); Karl Sigmund, Darwin's "Circles of Com-

plexity": Assembling Ecological Communities, Complexity, Jan. 1995, at 40 (applying complexity theories to analyze the stability of ecosystems).

d. Copyright © 1983. The Conservation Foundation. Reprinted with permission.

e. The studies were conducted by the Royal Swedish Academy of Sciences, the United States EPA, the French Ministry of Environment and Ministry of Urban Planning and Housing, the University of Michigan's Program in Technology Assessment, the Congressional Clearinghouse for the Future, and The Conservation Foundation.

their expert, albeit fairly subjective, opinions. This issue is devoted to assessing the results of these surveys and discussing environmental problems in the context of criteria related to their seriousness, their controllability, and the irreversibility of their effects. * * *

* * *

The surveys reflect a recognition that, in some respects, the conventional or "standard" air and water pollutants either no longer present the problems they once did or will not remain serious problems much longer. It is true, of course, that significant progress has been made in controlling such pollutants, at least in developed countries. At the same time, the traditional pollutants are by no means satisfactorily regulated everywhere. The air pollution in cities such as Mexico City is evidence enough of that. There are new manifestations of pollution that keep the issues alive, such as indoor air pollution. Success in dealing with point sources of water pollution contrasts with the unsolved problem of nonpoint sources.

In any case, many experts have noted that, by and large, the newer environmental problems tend to involve more "second generation" pollutants—small amounts of organic chemicals, trace metals, and the like— that typically are transported over long distances and either escape or are transferred from one medium to another. These pollutants produce more transboundary problems, more chronic effects, longer latency periods, more long-term pressures on resources.

The environmental issues can be placed in four general categories:

1.   War, accidents, and natural disasters.

2.   Population growth and distribution.

3.   Contaminants—including those of a physical, chemical or biological nature.

4.   Natural resource depletion.

Forty-seven serious environmental threats were identified in the six surveys. However, these threats do not comprise a complete enumeration of all the issues cited. Rather, they make up a consolidated list [below].

* * *

It should be noted that the issues listed are substantive problems— *not* those involving "institutional" difficulties. They deal with the effects of, say, acid rain and what methods of control are available; they do not deal with the political difficulties of reaching international or interstate agreements on a solution, or meeting the costs of control. Many institutional problems—involving the political, social, and economic aspects— were cited in the surveys and clearly they can be very daunting.

To put it another way, it can be said of many, perhaps most, of the major substantive problems that society already has adequate scientific information on causes and effects *and* has adequate knowledge to apply the necessary control techniques. What remains is the necessary political will, leadership, management ability, diplomacy, funding, and so forth.

47 ISSUES

War

Nuclear accidents, terrorism

Chemical plant explosions

Failure of aging infrastructure

Intentional weather modification (unintentional effects)

Drought

Floods

Earthquakes, volcanoes, and other natural disasters

Population growth

Crowding and impacts of urbanization

Sprawl problems

Mass migration, immigration

Radioactive waste disposal

Debris from space

Microwave radiation

Electronic pollution

Solid waste disposal

Noise

Pathogens from human waste

Proliferation of biological organisms, bioengineering wastes and mistakes

Mutagens

Carbon dioxide accumulation in the atmosphere

Acid deposition

Depletion of the ozone layer

Hazardous waste management

Conventional pollutants, ambient air

Toxic pollutants in air

Indoor air pollution

Conventional pollutants in water, from point sources

Nonpoint source water pollution

Toxic pollutants in surface water

Groundwater, drinking water contamination

Pesticides

Chemical fertilizers

Chemicals in food chains

Water scarcity

Loss of agricultural land due to salinization, desertification, or urbanization

Soil erosion and overexploitation of agricultural soils

Ocean fisheries depletion

Plant and animal species loss

Energy scarcity

Critical materials scarcity

Damage to the marine environment

Loss of tropical forests

Coastal area degradation

Loss of wetlands

Wilderness and wild and scenic rivers degradation

---

* * *

[O]ne should have criteria by which to assess and compare problems—yet criteria can be chosen and interpreted in widely different ways.

The simplest possible approach would involve only two general criteria: the severity of the effects and the likelihood of the threat occurring. A problem could then be categorized, for example, as a severe threat that is highly unlikely to occur or as a threat of low severity that is highly likely to occur.

* * *

Following is a more detailed, comprehensive set of criteria for characterizing the gravity of environmental problems in a more analytical way.

A. *Severity of effects.* The seriousness of the effects to people/environment exposed to them, assuming a worst-case situation.

B. *Extent of population/environment likely to be affected.* The number of people or amount of area likely to be affected if threat occurs.

C. *Geographic extent.* The amount of area likely to be threatened by several distinct manifestations or occurrences of the threat.

D. *Special populations or areas affected.* Specific population subgroups or unique natural areas at particularly high risk.

E. *Nature of effects.* Types of effects that the threat might create—for example, damage to amenities, ecological stability, human economic and social welfare, or human health.

F. *Certainty of effects.* The extent of scientific evidence that effects of concern will in fact occur if threat is manifested.

G. *Indirect effects.* Whether the threat and its effects are likely to generate indirect additional threats and effects that are of significant concern.

H. *Benefits associated with threat.* The extent to which society benefits from the activities that may create the threat.

I. *Immediacy of threat.* The extent to which this is a problem that is being faced now or that may only appear in the long term.

J. *Probability of threat occurring.* The likelihood that the threat which would cause the effects of concern will actually occur, assuming the current situation or trend or if no new action is taken.

K. *Controllability of threat—technological.* The extent to which physical or technological methods for controlling the threat are currently known and can be technologically adopted.

L. *Controllability of threat—political, social, economic.* The extent to which high costs and social or political constraints may interfere with adoption of controls if the technology is available.

M. *Irreversibility of effects—physical.* The ability to physically reverse or undo the effects if they occur.

N. *Irreversibility of effects—economic, political, social.* The feasibility of reversing effects if there are technological means available.

O. *Adequacy of existing institutions.* The ability of existing institutions to effectively implement any programs needed to control or respond to the threat.

These criteria fall into three prime categories: (1) the severity of the effects associated with the threat, including offsetting benefits (criteria A through H fall into this category); (2) the possibilities of avoiding the threat (I through L); and (3) the possibilities of reversing or mitigating the effects (M through O).

Notes

1. A glance at the Table of Contents will confirm that this casebook does not, nor could it, attempt to deal with the full range of environmental threats mentioned in the foregoing article. Of the four general categories identified at the beginning of the article, we shall focus on numbers 3 and 4, contaminants and resource depletion.

2. In 1999, the Ecological Risks Subcommittee of the U.S. EPA's Science Advisory Board's Integrated Risk Project generated a relative ranking of ecological risks at the national level, using a "scientifically sound weighting system." The highest risk categories included:

Hydrologic alteration;

Harvesting marine living resources;

Habitat conversion;

Climate change;

Introduction of exotic species;

Turbidity/sedimentation;

Habitat fragmentation; and

Pesticides.

The subcommittee also concluded that management of the sources of these ecological risks was "not adequately addressed by any level of government." 28 *Env't Rptr.* 2743 (1998).

MYERS, "ENVIRONMENTAL UNKNOWNS"[f]

269 *Science* 358, 358–360 (July 21, 1995).

It might seem fruitless to speculate about seemingly unknown problems in the environmental field. But recall that at the time of the first major international conference on the environment in Stockholm in 1972, there was next to no mention of what have now become established as front-rank problems: global warming, acid rain, and tropical deforestation. Environmental scientists could have gone at least partway toward anticipating these problems. They had had 100 years of warning from the Swedish scientist Arrhenius about the possibility of global warming. For decades acid rain impacts were accumulating unseen and unsuspected; could we not have asked whether all of those SO_2 and NO_x pollutants would eventually have an adverse effect on biotas? We could readily have alerted ourselves to tropical deforestation through remote-sensing surveys if only we had thought to identify it as a problem. So does the difficulty lie with "ignorance" or "ignore-ance"?

In the midst of much scientific uncertainty about our world—a world on which we are imposing multitudes of simultaneous new insults—we can be all but certain that there are environmental processes at work, or waiting in the wings, with the capacity to generate significant problems and to take us by ostensible surprise. Of course a true surprise is, by definition, beyond our purview. But is it truly beyond our scientific scope to identify a few likely candidates for semisurprises, especially those that could develop into outsize problems? . . .

Recent portents of environmental problems include the decline of amphibians, the bleaching of coral reefs, the appearance of phytoplankton blooms, the decline of sea urchins, mass mortality among seals and dolphins, and cancer epizootics in fish. All these share several characteristics. First they are regional or even global phenomena. Second, they are unprecedented in our scientific experience and in our general ecological understanding. Third, there is no immediate or obvious explanation, although a primary or contributory cause is probably widespread pollution. Fourth, this pollution seems to cause the most harm when it works in conjunction with other stresses such as aquatic eutrophication, other forms of habitat disruption, and whatever else can induce immunosuppression, all operating in possibly reinforcing unison. Most important of all, they may add up to a whole flock of miners' canaries singing.

DISCONTINUITIES

One category of impending problems for environmental processes comprises discontinuities. The classic instance of a discontinuity is when liquid water suddenly changes to ice or steam. Environmental discontinuities occur when ecosystems absorb stresses over long periods without much outward sign of injury, then reach a disruption threshold at which the cumulative consequences finally reveal themselves in critical proportions. For instance, when forest ecosystems undergo "creeping degradation" through acid rain, they manifest slow decline and chronic stress before finally and suddenly displaying severe injury.

Such discontinuities are especially pertinent to climate change , notably global warming. The most advanced climate models are largely unable, because of their very structure, to encompass the possibility of nonlinear interactions. We scarcely know how to identify and define these interactions, let alone describe their workings across the board. Yet we know that Earth's past climate has often responded in a manner far from smooth, gradual, and hence predictable. It has frequently reacted through sharp changes "which involve large-scale reorganization of Earth's system." What if such jump effects were to be triggered, perhaps in multiple forms, by global warming? For instance, what if the Gulf Stream were to be significantly disrupted, even diverted southward, rather than flowing northeastward to warm northwestern Europe? More important for the present analysis, what further discontinuities could ensue if that outcome were to interact with potential further disruptions such as soil erosion on croplands, pervasive pollution [for example, low-level ozone, acid precipitation, ultraviolet (UV)B radiation] on crops, and increased pests and diseases—all at a time when we will be trying to feed far larger numbers of people?

* * *

We encounter a nonlinear relationship between resource exploitation and population growth (the latter is but one possible variable) with respect to many other natural resource stocks, notably fisheries, soil, and fresh water. As soon as the sustainable yield is slightly exceeded, the debacle of resource depletion is precipitated with surprising rapidity. The same applies to environmental services such as the pollution-absorbing capacity of the atmosphere. Whereas the increase in fossil fuel consumption can be linear, the atmospheric pollution's response often is not.

SYNERGISMS

A second category of "anticipatable surprises" comprises environmental synergisms—literally, a uniting of energies. These synergisms arise when two or more environmental processes interact in such a way that the outcome is not additive but multiplicative. For instance, a biota's tolerance of one stress tends to be lower when other stresses operate at the same time. A plant that experiences reduced sunlight, and hence less photosynthesis, is unduly prone to the adverse effects of cold weather, water shortage, insect pests, or diseases. Similarly, plants already injured by one of these factors are exceptionally susceptible to the trauma of reduced sunlight. The compounding impact of the relationship can be so powerful that the result may be a whole order of magnitude greater that the simple sum of the components. Despite their obvious importance, however, we know all too little about synergisms. Ecologists cannot even identify and define their main manifestations in nature, let alone document their more important impacts.

Consider the potential for mutually reinforcing interactions between global warming and ozone layer depletion. By cooling the stratosphere through buildup of ice clouds, global warming accentuates ozone layer depletion. Conversely, ozone layer depletion, by increasing UVB radiation, poses an aggravated threat to phytoplankton in the upper ocean layer, as these organisms are unusually susceptible to the radiation. Phytoplankton serve as a sink for roughly half of all anthropogenic emissions of carbon dioxide. Ozone layer depletion could readily reduce phytoplankton populations to an extent where they sequester less carbon dioxide, thus accentuating global warming—leading to greater ozone layer depletion, more phytoplankton die-off, and so compoundingly forth.

* * *

Policy Responses

Policy interventions can sometimes constitute constructive dislocations and synergisms. For example, grand-scale tree planting in the humid tropics, undertaken to generate a sink for atmospheric carbon dioxide and thus counter global warming could supply many spin-off benefits through, for example, commercial forestry plantations that relieve excessive logging pressure on remaining natural forests. In turn, reduced deforestation helps to safeguard the uniquely abundant stocks of species and genetic resources in tropical forests (sometimes with large agricultural benefits, as when the disease resistance of a wild rice in India's forests saved much of the Asian rice crop from a pandemic blight). Tree plantations and surviving natural forests both supply many hydrological functions with multiplier effects—for example, through their capacity in upland catchments to regulate water flow and thus reduce downstream flooding—and with advantages for irrigation agriculture and domestic water needs.

Notes

1. Like the Ruhl excerpt above, the Myers article highlights the problem of uncertainty. In the face of such uncertainty, how much should we invest in preventative measures? Is it reasonable to expect society to make

major investments in forestalling possible hazards that may never material-ize anyway?

2. Given the possible development of new hazards, one challenge is to design institutions that will foster innovative responses. Can we expect more innovation to come from the "top" (EPA) or from the bottom (industry and local government)? If from the bottom, consider how we might best encourage innovation without at the same time inviting bad performance; if from the top, consider how to allow EPA to innovate without opening it to political pressure to relax standards.

WORLD RESOURCES INSTITUTE, WORLD RESOURCES 1990–91[g]

24–25 (1990).

The responses of human societies to global warming can take several approaches. First, prevention strategies can be employed to reduce the quantities of greenhouse gases being emitted. Mitigation mechanisms strategies can attempt to compensate for emissions that do occur; for example, through reforestation policies that increase the uptake of CO_2 from the air by trees and other plants. Lastly, strategies can be employed that help communities and nations adapt to changes in climate and their consequences. In practice, all three types of policies are likely to be important. . . .

* * *

. . . The highest potential lies with policies targeted at the energy and industrial sectors. Nevertheless, virtually all elements of human activity contribute to greenhouse gas emissions. The fact that nearly one quarter of the potential warming arises from the forestry and agricultural sectors suggests that each of these sectors should be examined on a country-by-country basis to determine which strategies are most readily implementable at local and national levels. By the nature of the patterns of greenhouse gas emissions, reducing these emissions will be an incremental process.

* * *

While work should proceed simultaneously on mitigation and adaptation strategies, prevention deserves the highest priority. Preventing the emission of greenhouse gases that would be released into the atmosphere not only delays the onset of significant global warming, but also slows its advance and reduces its ultimate magnitude.

To reduce greenhouse gas emissions or even to slow their rate of growth on a global scale will require an extraordinary degree of political consensus. [N]o one country or even one region can prevent the buildup of greenhouse gases by itself, although leadership by individual countries will be important in achieving global consensus. To be broadly acceptable, ideally, prevention policies should confer other local benefits on their adopting countries in addition to the worldwide benefit of reducing the risk of a global warming.

Many policies have been proposed and are under study. It seems clear, however, that any successful prevention strategy will include five key elements:

> increasing the efficiency of energy production and use,

> switching from carbon-intensive fuels such as coal to hydrogen-intensive fuels such as natural gas, where possible,

> encouraging the rapid development and use of solar and other carbon-free energy sources,

> eliminating the production of most CFCs and developing the means to recapture those now in use,

> reducing the rate of deforestation.

Note on the Prisoner's Dilemma

The greenhouse effect may be an apt example of what game theorists call a prisoner's dilemma. This scenario gets its name from the following illustrative story. Consider two prisoners, charged with being involved in the same crime but held in different rooms. The prosecutor gives each of them the following information: "(a) If neither of you confesses, I will charge you both with a lesser crime that I can easily prove, resulting in two-year sentences for each. (b) If you both confess, you will each get a three-year sentence. (c) If only one of you confesses, that person will get a one-year sentence and the other will get a four-year sentence." Each prisoner reasons as follows: "Either the other person will confess or not. If the other person does confess, I will get a three-year sentence if I confess but a four-year sentence if I don't. So if the other person confesses, I should do the same. If the other person doesn't confess, I will get a one-year sentence if I do confess and a two-year sentence if I don't, so the best move is to confess. Thus, no matter what the other person does, I will be better off if I confess." Following the same reason, the other prisoner also confesses, and they both get three-year sentences. This is the "rational" outcome. But notice that if the prisoners could somehow count on each other, neither would confess, and they would get only two-year sentences. So the individually rational set of actions leads to an inferior outcome in terms of their group welfare.

What does this have to do with the greenhouse effect? Consider the situation of Freedonia, a hypothetical average country. If the rest of the world fails to address the greenhouse effect, Freedonia can do little on its own, and therefore shouldn't bother. If everyone else does take action to control the greenhouse effect, Freedonia can contribute only slight additional help but will have to spend a lot of money to do so. So if everyone else "does the right thing," Freedonia should take a "free ride" on their efforts rather than wasting its own resources to minimal effect. Thus, no matter what the rest of the world does, Freedonia is better off to do nothing. Reasoning the same way, every country in the world decides to take no action.

Yet, all might be better off if they could somehow make an enforceable deal to cooperate. But such deals are difficult to negotiate and enforce on the international level, because the prisoner's dilemma takes hold again: each individual country has an incentive to sit out the negotiations and let everyone else make a deal; once a deal is made, each country has an incentive to breach the agreement and allow others to bear the costs of carrying it out.

The upshot is that, in the absence of some mechanism for making and enforcing cooperative agreements, each nation may find inaction to be the only sensible individual choice, though everyone also knows that collective inaction will only lead to disaster. Within individual nations, the central government can lead the way out of prisoners' dilemmas by forcing a cooperative solution. (As we will see at the end of Chapter III, however, even a strong central government, like that in the United States, may find practical and legal obstacles to solving the prisoner's dilemma). In the international sphere, the problem is more difficult, but as we will see in the following note, some progress has been made.

Note on International Environmental Treaties

The foregoing report, *World Resources 1990–91*, at page 363, presents this summary—as of 1990—of major environmental treaties and their places and dates of adoption:

Nuclear Test Ban: Treaty Banning Nuclear Weapon Tests in the Atmosphere, in Outer Space, and Under Water (Moscow, 1963); to prohibit atmospheric and underwater nuclear weapons tests and other nuclear explosions and prohibit tests in any other environment if radioactive debris would be present outside the territory of the country conducting the test.

Wetlands (Ramsar): Convention on Wetlands of International Importance Especially as Waterfowl Habitat (Ramsar, 1971); to stem the encroachment on and loss of wetlands, by establishing a List of Wetlands of International Importance, and providing that parties will establish wetland nature reserves and consider their international responsibilities for migratory waterfowl.

World Heritage: Convention Concerning the Protection of the World Cultural and Natural Heritage (Paris, 1972); to establish a system to protect cultural and natural heritage sites of outstanding value.

Ocean Dumping: Convention on the Prevention of Marine Pollution by Dumping of Wastes and Other Matter (London, Mexico City, Moscow, Washington, D.C., 1972); to control pollution of the seas by dumping, by prohibiting the dumping of certain materials and regulating ocean disposal of others, authorizing regional agreements, and establishing a mechanism for assessing liability and settling disputes.

Biological and Toxin Weapons: Convention on the Prohibition of the Development, Production, and Stockpiling of Bacteriological (Biological) and Toxin Weapons, and on their Destruction (London, Moscow, Washington, D.C., 1972); to prohibit acquisition and retention of biological agents and toxins that are not justified for peaceful purposes and of the means of delivering them for hostile purposes or armed conflict.

Endangered Species (CITES): Convention on International Trade in Endangered Species of Wild Fauna and Flora (CITES) (Washington, D.C., 1973); to protect endangered species from over-exploitation by tightly controlling trade in live or dead animals and in animal parts through a system of permits.

Ship Pollution (MARPOL): Protocol of 1978 Relating to the International Convention for the Prevention of Pollution from Ships, 1973 (London, 1978); a modification of the 1973 convention to eliminate international pollution by oil and other harmful substances and to minimize accidental discharge of such substances.

Migratory Species: Convention on the Conservation of Migratory Species of Wild Animals (Bonn, 1979); to protect wild animal species that cross international borders, by promoting international agreements.

Law of the Sea: United Nations Convention on the Law of the Sea (Montego Bay, 1982); to establish a comprehensive legal regime for the seas and oceans, establish rules for environmental standards and enforcement provisions, and develop international rules and national legislation to prevent and control marine pollution.

Ozone Layer: Vienna Convention for the Protection of the Ozone Layer (Vienna, Austria, 1985); to protect human health and the environment by conducting research on ozone layer modification and its effects and on alternative substances and technologies, monitoring the ozone layer, and taking measures to control activities that produce adverse effects.

CFC Control: Protocol on Substances That Deplete the Ozone Layer (Montreal, 1987); to require a 50 percent reduction in production of chlorofluorocarbons (CFCs) by 1999, with allowances for consumption increases in developing countries.

Hazardous Waste Movement: Convention on the Control of Transboundary Movements of Hazardous Wastes and their Disposal (Basel, 1989); to restrict and control the international traffic in hazardous wastes.

Regional Seas: A series of conventions and their associated protocols addressing region-specific marine-related environmental issues. Areas of seas or ocean zones included under Regional Sea conventions are the Mediterranean, west and central Africa, eastern Africa, the Red Sea and the Gulf of Aden, the Caribbean, the South Pacific, the Southeast Pacific, and the Kuwait region.

The 1990 London Amendments to the Montreal Protocol accelerated the phase-out of CFCs (to 50 percent by 1995 and 100 percent by 2000), added other ozone-depleters to the ban list, and established a fund to assist developing countries in complying with the agreement. This was the first time that the national governments of developed countries had voted to provide developing countries financial assistance to meet environmental goals.

Two additional treaties were signed by more than 150 nations at the 1992 United Nations Conference on Environment and Development (UNCED) in Rio de Janeiro:

The *Convention on Biological Diversity* aims to preserve the diversity of animal and plant species and their natural habitats. Developed countries agree to provide "new and additional financial resources to enable developing country Parties to meet the agreed full incremental costs to them of implementing measures which fulfill the obligations of this Convention and to benefit from its provisions." Article 20. The convention recognizes the "sovereign rights of states over their natural resources" but provides that each party "shall endeavor to create conditions to facilitate access to genetic resources for environmentally sound uses" by other parties, "on mutually agreed terms" and "subject to prior informed consent" of the party providing the resources. Each party agrees to take appropriate legislative, administrative or policy measures to further the "aim of sharing in a fair and equitable way the results of research and development and the benefits arising from the commercial and other utilization of genetic resources with the Contracting Party providing such resources." Article 15.

President Bush declined to sign the convention, primarily on the ground that it would not protect the patents of American biotechnology firms, which prospect in tropical forests for plants, animals, insects and microorganisms useful in making drugs and other products. The convention obligates parties to take appropriate legislative, administrative or policy measures "with the aim that Contracting Parties, in particular those that are developing countries which provide genetic resources, are provided access to and transfer of technology [including biotechnology] which makes use of those resources, on mutually agreed terms, including technology protected by patents and other intellectual property rights, where necessary through the [financial assistance] provisions of Articles 20 and 21." Access to and transfer of technology are to be provided or facilitated "under fair and most favorable terms, including concessional and preferential terms where mutually agreed." In the case of technology subject to patents or other intellectual property rights, access and transfer shall be provided "on terms which recognize and are consistent with the adequate and effective protection of intellectual property rights." Article 16.

In April 1993, President Clinton announced that the United States would sign the convention. To reassure biotechnology firms, he said that an "interpretative statement" on patent protection would qualify the approval. See *New York Times,* April 22, 1993, p. A1, col. 6. On June 4, 1993, the U.S. Ambassador to the United Nations signed the convention, saying that the administration would submit to the Senate simultaneously the treaty (for ratification) and a statement addressing intellectual property rights protection and explaining "what we think relatively ambiguous language in the treaty means." See *BNA Int'l Envt. Daily,* June 9, 1993.

In November 1993, President Clinton transmitted the convention for the advice and consent of the Senate to ratification, recommending favorable consideration subject to certain "understandings" described in an accompanying report by the Secretary of State. Senate Treaty Doc. 103–20 (Nov. 20, 1993). One understanding, regarding access to and transfer of technology under Article 16, was that "fair and most favorable terms" means "terms that are voluntarily agreed to by all parties to the transaction." As of January 1999, the Senate had not voted to ratify the convention.

The *Convention on Climate Change* aims at "stabilization of greenhouse gas concentrations in the atmosphere at a level that would prevent dangerous anthropogenic interference with the climate system. Such a level should be achieved within a time frame sufficient to allow ecosystems to adapt naturally to climate change to ensure that food production is not threatened and to enable economic development to proceed in a sustainable manner." Article 2. Like the Montreal Protocol on Substances That Deplete the Ozone Layer and the Convention on Biological Diversity, the Convention on Climate Change provides that developed countries shall provide financial resources and transfers of technology to assist the developing countries in complying with their obligations to inventory and control greenhouse gas emissions. Resources are to be channeled, at least initially, through the Global Environment Facility (GEF), a fund created by the World Bank. The Climate Convention is a "framework" treaty requiring further protocols to spell out the specific emission limitations and timetables necessary for implementation. The United States did sign this convention at Rio, but the Senate has not yet ratified it. In Kyoto, Japan, in December 1997, most if not all of the parties to the convention signed the *Kyoto Protocol*, which specifies for developed nations the amount by which each of them agrees to reduce its emissions (from 1990 levels) by the year 2012. The protocol is discussed in the excerpt from *World Resources 1998–99* at page 35 infra.

Delegates to UNCED also approved three other documents in 1992:

The *Rio Declaration on Environment and Development*, a set of 27 principles outlining the rights and responsibilities of countries toward the environment. This nonbinding declaration reflects concern about the ability of the deteriorating environment to sustain life as well as awareness that long-term economic progress and the need for environmental protection must be seen as interdependent.

Agenda 21, a comprehensive plan to guide national and international action toward sustainable development. The 40–chapter plan covers many environmental and development program areas, defining problems and objectives, outlying specific steps for implementation, and giving estimates for funding.

The *Declaration on Forests*, a statement of 15 principles for the sustainable management of forests as the basis for further negotiations on an international forestry agreement. A nonbinding declaration, this document consists of general principles rather than a specific program of action, reflecting wide differences between industrialized and developing countries.

In October 1994, in Paris, more than one hundred nations signed a *Convention on Desertification* stemming from UNCED. The treaty focuses on the world's arid and semiarid lands, which are steadily yielding less because of overgrazing, excessive planting, poor irrigation, and deforestation related to population pressures. Erosion and exhaustion of the soil are most serious in Africa, where almost 75 percent of the arid land has been degraded. Worldwide, arid and semiarid lands make up one-fourth of the earth's land mass and support 900 million people.

The Desertification Convention, which became legally binding for the signers in October 1996, establishes a "Global Mechanism" to coordinate projects to protect and rehabilitate lands and to find money for those purposes. It urges governments to provide such funds through the Global Environment Facility. Initially, however, wealthy nations pledged only modest amounts of new money.

One part of the Convention on Desertification commits donee governments to a "bottom-up" approach which will involve local communities and nongovernmental organizations (NGOs) in designing and implementing projects. Donors believe this will ensure use of traditional knowledge and local practices and improve the chances for honest use of the money. See *New York Times,* Oct. 16, 1994, p. 11, col. 5.

———

The substantive text of the *Rio Declaration* is as follows.

RIO DECLARATION ON ENVIRONMENT AND DEVELOPMENT

Adopted by the U.N. Conference on Environment and Development
(UNCED) at Rio de Janeiro, 13 June 1992.

PRINCIPLE 1

Human beings are at the centre of concerns for sustainable development. They are entitled to a healthy and productive life in harmony with nature.

PRINCIPLE 2

States have, in accordance with the Charter of the United Nations and the principles of international law, the sovereign right to exploit their own resources pursuant to their own environmental and developmental policies, and the responsibility to ensure that activities within their jurisdiction or control do not cause damage to the environment of other States or of areas beyond the limits of national jurisdiction.

PRINCIPLE 3

The right to development must be fulfilled so as to equitably meet developmental and environmental needs of present and future generations.

PRINCIPLE 4

In order to achieve sustainable development, environmental protection shall constitute an integral part of the development process and cannot be considered in isolation from it.

PRINCIPLE 5

All States and all people shall cooperate in the essential task of eradicating poverty as an indispensable requirement for sustainable development, in order to decrease the disparities in standards of living and better meet the needs of the majority of the people of the world.

PRINCIPLE 6

The special situation and needs of developing countries, particularly the least developed and those most environmentally vulnerable, shall be given special priority. International actions in the field of environment and development should also address the interests and needs of all countries.

PRINCIPLE 7

States shall cooperate in a spirit of global partnership to conserve, protect and restore the health and integrity of the Earth's ecosystem. In view of the different contributions to global environmental degradation, States have common but differentiated responsibilities. The developed countries acknowledge the responsibility that they bear in the international pursuit of sustainable development in view of the pressures their societies place on the global environment and of the technologies and financial resources they command.

PRINCIPLE 8

To achieve sustainable development and a higher quality of life for all people, States should reduce and eliminate unsustainable patterns of production and consumption and promote appropriate demographic policies.

PRINCIPLE 9

States should cooperate to strengthen endogenous capacity-building for sustainable development by improving scientific understanding through exchanges of scientific and technological knowledge, and by enhancing the development, adaptation, diffusion and transfer of technologies, including new and innovative technologies.

PRINCIPLE 10

Environmental issues are best handled with the participation of all concerned citizens, at the relevant level. At the national level, each individual shall have appropriate access to information concerning the environment that is held by public authorities, including information on hazardous materials and activities in their communities, and the opportunity to participate in decision-making processes. States shall facilitate and encourage public awareness and participation by making information widely available. Effective access to judicial and administrative proceedings, including redress and remedy, shall be provided.

PRINCIPLE 11

States shall enact effective environmental legislation. Environmental standards, management objectives and priorities should reflect the environmental and developmental context to which they apply. Standards applied by some countries may be inappropriate and of unwarranted economic and social cost to other countries, in particular developing countries.

PRINCIPLE 12

States should cooperate to promote a supportive and open international economic system that would lead to economic growth and sustainable development in all countries, to better address the problems of environmental degradation. Trade policy measures for environmental purposes should not constitute a means of arbitrary or unjustifiable discrimination or a disguised restriction on international trade. Unilateral actions to deal with environmental challenges outside the jurisdiction of the importing country should be avoided. Environmental measures addressing transboundary or global environmental problems should, as far as possible, be based on an international consensus.

PRINCIPLE 13

States shall develop national law regarding liability and compensation for the victims of pollution and other environmental damage. States shall also cooperate in an expeditious and more determined manner to develop further international law regarding liability and compensation for adverse effects of environmental damage caused by activities within their jurisdiction or control to areas beyond their jurisdiction.

PRINCIPLE 14

States should effectively cooperate to discourage or prevent the relocation and transfer to other States of any activities and substances that cause severe environmental degradation or are found to be harmful to human health.

PRINCIPLE 15

In order to protect the environment, the precautionary approach shall be widely applied by States according to their capabilities. Where there are threats of serious or irreversible damage, lack of full scientific certainty shall not be used as a reason for postponing cost-effective measures to prevent environmental degradation.

PRINCIPLE 16

National authorities should endeavor to promote the internalization of environmental costs and the use of economic instruments, taking into account the approach that the polluter should, in principle, bear the cost of pollution, with due regard to the public interest and without distorting international trade and investment.

PRINCIPLE 17

Environmental impact assessment, as a national instrument, shall be undertaken for proposed activities that are likely to have a significant adverse impact on the environment and are subject to a decision of a competent national authority.

PRINCIPLE 18

States shall immediately notify other States of any natural disasters or other emergencies that are likely to produce sudden harmful effects on the environment of those States. Every effort shall be made by the international community to help States so afflicted.

PRINCIPLE 19

States shall provide prior and timely notification and relevant information to potentially affected States on activities that may have a significant adverse transboundary environmental effect and shall consult with those States at an early stage and in good faith.

PRINCIPLE 20

Women have a vital role in environmental management and development. Their full participation is therefore essential to achieve sustainable development.

PRINCIPLE 21

The creativity, ideals and courage of the youth of the world should be mobilized to forge a global partnership in order to achieve sustainable development and ensure a better future for all.

PRINCIPLE 22

Indigenous people and their communities and other local communities have a vital role in environmental management and development because of their knowledge and traditional practices. States should recognize and duly support their identity, culture and interests and enable their effective participation in the achievement of sustainable development.

PRINCIPLE 23

The environment and natural resources of people under oppression, domination and occupation shall be protected.

PRINCIPLE 24

Warfare is inherently destructive of sustainable development. States shall therefore respect international law providing protection for the environment in times of armed conflict and cooperate in its further development, as necessary.

PRINCIPLE 25

Peace, development and environmental protection are interdependent and indivisible.

PRINCIPLE 26

States shall resolve all their environmental disputes peacefully and by appropriate means in accordance with the Charter of the United Nations.

PRINCIPLE 27

States and people shall cooperate in good faith and in a spirit of partnership in the fulfilment of the principles embodied in this Declaration and in the further development of international law in the field of sustainable development.

Note

The two most prominent "sources" of international law are (a) international *conventions*, or treaties, establishing rules expressly recognized by the parties thereto, and (b) "international *custom*, as evidence of a general practice accepted as law." Article 38, Statute of the International Court of Justice, 1976 Y.B. U.N. 1052, 59 Stat. 1031, T.S. No. 993. See L. Guruswamy et al., *International Environmental Law and the World Order* 46, 75 (1994). Although the Rio "Declaration," unlike the Rio Conventions on Biological Diversity and Climate Change, is not an international agreement intended to "bind" the parties, some of the principles recited therein were previously well established as *customary* international law. For example, the duty in Principle 2 "to ensure that activities within [a State's] jurisdiction . . . do not cause damage to the environment of other States" stems from the famous *Trail Smelter Arbitration* (United States v. Canada), 3 U.N. Rep. Int'l Arb. Awards 1911 (1941), reprinted in 35 *Am.J. Int'l L.* 684 (1941). In that case, half a century before the Rio Earth Summit, the arbitral tribunal concluded that " 'under the principles of international law, . . . no State has the right to use or permit the use of its territory in such a manner as to cause injury by fumes [sulfur dioxide air pollutants from a smelter] in or to the territory of another or the properties or persons therein, when the case is of serious consequence and the injury is established by clear and convincing evidence.' " Since *Trail Smelter*, this principle has been the fundamental rule of international law governing transboundary air and water pollution.

Some of the "principles" of the Rio Declaration are merely aspirational goals, while others constitute what is known as "soft law," principles which are on the way to likely eventual acceptance as "hard" or "binding" customary law.

WORLDWATCH INSTITUTE, STATE OF THE WORLD 1997
3–12 (1997).[h]

Five years after the historic U.N. Conference on Environment and Development in Rio de Janeiro, the world is falling well short of achieving its central goal—an environmentally sustainable global economy. Since the Earth Summit in 1992, human numbers have grown by roughly 450 million, which exceeds the combined populations of the United States and Russia. Annual emissions of carbon, which produce carbon dioxide, the leading greenhouse gas, have climbed to a new high, altering the very composition of the atmosphere and the earth's heat balance.

During these past five years, the earth's biological riches have also been rapidly and irreversibly diminished. Huge areas of old-growth forests have been degraded or cleared—in temperate as well as tropical regions—eliminating thousands of species of plants and animals. Biologically rich wetlands and coral reefs are suffering similar fates....

.... Unfortunately, few governments have even begun the policy changes that will be needed to put the world on an environmentally sustainable path. Only a half-dozen countries, for example, have levied environmental taxes to discourage the unsustainable use of materials and energy. And many nations continue to subsidize clear-cutting of forests, inefficient energy and water use, and mining.

One of the signal accomplishments of Rio was the official linking of environment and development issues, including an explicit recognition that poverty itself is a driving force behind a large share of environmental degradation....

.... Yet most governments still pursue economic growth as an end in itself, neglecting the long-term sustainability of the course they chart. In many developing countries, rapid growth has led to a sharp deterioration in air and water quality in the nineties, and undermined the natural resources on which people depend

* * *

THE ROAD FROM RIO

The broad goals of the Earth Summit were laid out in Agenda 21, the 40–chapter plan of action for achieving sustainable development that was signed by the leaders gathered in Rio. This landmark document concludes that "an environmental policy that focuses mainly on the conservation and protection of resources without consideration of the livelihoods of those who depend on the resources in unlikely to succeed."

The goals included in Agenda 21 range from protecting wetlands and deserts to reducing air and water pollution, improving energy and agricultural technologies, managing toxic chemicals and radioactive wastes more effectively, and reducing the incidence of disease and malnutrition....

The most important institution to emerge from the Earth Summit was the United Nations Commission on Sustainable Development (CSD), set up to review national implementation of Agenda 21 and to provide high-level coordination among various U.N. environment and development programs....

* * *

The one major financial initiative dedicated to the Rio agenda is the Global Environment Facility (GEF), a specialized fund managed by the World Bank, UNEP [United Nations Environment Programme] and

UNDP [United Nations Development Programme]. Started in pilot form in 1991, the GEF was envisioned in Agenda 21 as a means to support developing-country projects that mitigate global environmental problems. Since Rio, the GEF has also become the interim funding arm of the climate and biodiversity conventions.

Following these mandates, the GEF has provided support for several dozen worthwhile projects, including efforts to set up national parks, protect endangered species, and promote solar energy, energy efficiency, and other alternatives to fossil fuels. . . .

The World Bank, which loans roughly $20 billion to developing countries each year, has a far greater impact on environmental trends around the world. Since Rio, the Bank has strengthened its environmental review process and has withdrawn support from some high-profile environmental projects that critics denounced as wasteful or destructive. . . .

These symbolic changes have highlighted a growing gulf between the new environmentally concerned senior management and the hundreds of task managers and country directors that wield the Bank's real power. These individuals remain focused on narrow financial goals, and so far the Bank has failed even to develop an adequate environmental screening process for their loans, according to internal assessments. Consequently, it continues to lend large sums for projects that add to global carbon emissions, destroy natural ecosystems, and undermine the livelihoods of poor people, say outside critics, while the broader vision of a more sustainable economy is largely ignored.

The failure to fulfill the legacy of Rio during these past five years can be attributed in part to the inevitable time lags that mark any new policy initiatives—particularly at the international level. In fact, the fastest progress is now occurring on those issues that were first identified decades ago. In most industrial countries, for example, air and water pollution are now less severe than they were during the Stockholm Conference on the Human Environment in 1972. And many developing countries have begun to implement stringent air pollution laws and to phase lead out of gasoline. At the global level, efforts to end production of the chemicals that deplete the atmosphere's protective ozone layer are already well under way, and have led to a 76–percent reduction in the manufacture of the most damaging ones.

In other areas, the world still seems to be moving in reverse. Lack of clean water, for example, has permitted a resurgence of infectious disease in many developing nations, while human and animal immune and reproductive systems are being disrupted by chlorine-based chemicals that have become ubiquitous in ecosystems. More seriously, three global problems still stand in the way of achieving a sustainable world: human-induced climate change, the loss of biodiversity, and expanding human population and consumption levels. As recognized in three separate agreements—the 1992 Framework Convention on Climate Change, the 1992 Convention on Biological Diversity, and the 1994 Population

Plan of Action—a stable atmosphere, a rich biological world, and a steady human population are essential to humanity's future prospects. Failure to achieve these goals would complicate a range of other problems and lead to an almost inevitable decline in the human condition.

EIGHT ENVIRONMENTAL HEAVYWEIGHTS

In assessing progress on these three global issues since the Earth Summit, it is clear that all countries are not created equal. Global environmental trends are dominated by just a few nations. This chapter looks at eight countries—four industrial and four developing—that together account for 56 percent of the world's population, 59 percent of its economic output, 58 percent of its carbon emissions, and 53 percent of its forests. (See Table 1–1.) These eight environmental powers included the country with the largest population—China; the one with the largest economy and carbon emissions—the United States; and the nation that arguably claims the richest array of biodiversity—Brazil. Together with Germany, Japan, India, Indonesia, and Russia, these countries constitute what could be called the E8—eight nations that disproportionately shape global environmental trends.

Table 1—1. Eight Environmental Heavyweights

Country	Share of World Population, 1996	Share of Gross World Product, 1994	Share of World Carbon Emissions, 1995	Share of World Forest Area, 1990	Share of World Flowering Plant Species, 1990
			(percent)		
United States	5	26	23	6	8
Russia	3	2	7	21	9
Japan	2	17	5	0.7	2
Germany	1	8	4	0.3	1
China	21	2	13	4	12
India	17	1	4	2	6
Indonesia	4	0.7	1	3	8
Brazil	3	2	1	16	22
E8 Total	56	59	58	53	—

Even more than the Group of Seven (G7)—the industrial nations that have dominated the global economy since World War II—the E8 will help shape the future of the entire world. The political systems of the E8 range from communist to democratic, and their experience with capitalism varies from five years to two centuries. But in terms of environmental impact, these eight nations are in a league of their own. Their post-Rio record provides a revealing picture of the progress being made by the world as a whole.

The industrial countries in the E8 shape global trends in part because of their economic strength, their high levels of material consumption and social trend-setting, and their dominance of technology. The developing countries' influence, in contrast, is determined in part by their large populations, their rapid economic development and their rich diversity of wildlife. . . .

* * *

STABILIZING THE CLIMATE

One of the centerpieces of the Earth Summit was the Framework Convention on Climate Change signed by the world leaders gathered in Rio. In the five years since, the urgency of the climate problem has grown, according to scientists. With the atmospheric concentration of carbon dioxide at its highest level in 150,000 years—and still increasing—the world is projected to face a rate of climate change in the next several decades that exceeds natural rates by a factor of 10. Scientists believe that the rapid climate change ahead is likely to be erratic, disruptive, and unpredictable. Local weather patterns may shift suddenly. The incidence of floods, droughts, fires, and heat outbreaks will probably increase as global temperature rise.

Between 1990 and 1995, annual fossil-fuel-related emissions of carbon, which produce carbon dioxide, rose by 113 million tons, reaching 6 billion tons in 1995. They would have risen an additional 400–500 million tons if not for the collapse of fossil-fuel-dependent industries in Central and Eastern Europe. An estimated 1.6 billion tons of additional carbon are released annually from forest clearing, primarily in tropical regions. Emissions of CFCs, another important greenhouse gas, are falling sharply as a result of efforts to protect the ozone layer, while emissions of hydrofluorocarbons and methane—both potent greenhouse gases—are still increasing.

Greenhouse gas emission levels vary widely among nations, as seen in figures for the E8. Per capita carbon emissions from fossil fuels range from 5.3 tons in the United States to 2.4 tons in Japan and 0.3 tons in India. This more-than-twentyfold range in emission rates reflects many differences, including stages of industrial development and personal lifestyles and consumption levels. But even among countries at similar stages of economic development, the situation varies widely: per capita emissions in China are 75 percent higher than they are in Brazil, for instance, while those in the United States are 120 percent higher than in Japan.

* * *

Carbon emissions have soared in developing countries in the first half of the nineties. Emissions rose 20 percent in Brazil between 1990 and 1995, 28 percent in China and India, and 30 percent in Indonesia. Growth in energy demand, which was restrained by high oil prices and economic stagnation in the eighties, is now surging. Such growth is hardly surprising, given that emissions per person in India and Indonesia are only one tenth the European level, while Brazil's are one seventh and China's one fourth as high.

WORLD RESOURCES INSTITUTE, WORLD RESOURCES 1998–99[i]

174–176 (1998).

How can the international community strike the necessary balance between expanding the pace of economic development—and resultant higher energy use—and responding adequately to concerns about climate change? How can nations gradually but substantially reduce their emissions of greenhouse gases without stalling their economies? And how can we ensure that the burden of protecting the climate is shared most equitably among nations? These are the questions the 167 nations that ratified the 1992 Framework Convention on Climate Change have been grappling with since before they first initialed the treaty at the Rio Earth Summit.

In December 1997, these nations began to address these questions by forging the Kyoto Protocol, which was a follow-on to the original climate treaty, and marks the first international attempt to place legally binding limits on greenhouse gas emissions from developed countries. In addition to CO_2, the primary greenhouse gas, the Protocol focuses on five other greenhouse gases: methane (CH_4), nitrous oxide (N_2O), hydrofluorocarbons (HFCs), perfluorocarbons (PFCs), and sulfur hexafluoride (SF_6). Specifically, the Protocol aims to cut the combined emissions of greenhouse gases from developed countries by roughly 5 percent from their 1990 levels by the 2008–2012 time frame, and it specifies the amount each industrialized nation must contribute toward meeting that reduction goal. Nations with the highest CO_2 emissions—the United States, Japan, and most European nations—are expected to reduce emissions by a range of 6 to 8 percent. By 2005, all industrialized nations that ratify the accord must show "demonstrable progress" toward fulfilling their respective commitments under the Protocol. To enter into force, at least 55 nations must ratify the treaty, including enough developed countries to account for 55 percent of the global CO_2 emissions in 1990.

The new treaty represents real progress in bringing to fruition the good intentions of the 1992 agreement. For the most part, developed nations have failed to attain the nonbinding emission reductions they committed to in the original climate treaty (i.e., they had agreed to voluntarily reduce greenhouse gas emissions back to 1990 levels by 2000), and have thus acknowledged the need for the binding emission targets represented in the Kyoto Protocol. Despite this progress, the new agreement contains complex issues to be resolved in future negotiations. One issue is that the Kyoto Protocol officially sanctions the concept of "emissions trading" between industrialized nations. In this scenario, a nation whose emissions fall below its treaty limit can sell credit for its remaining emissions allotment to another nation, which in turn can use the credit to meet its own treaty obligations. Proponents of this market-based approach to pollution control believe an emissions trading program will help curb the cost of controlling greenhouse gases by allowing emissions cuts to occur wherever they are least expensive. Such a trading scheme has been quite successful in the United States in lowering the cost of controlling SO_2 emissions from power plants—the primary source of acid rain. However, the details for implementing such a complex trading plan, involving six different gases across several national borders, will need to be worked out at the next negotiating session in 1998 in Buenos Aires. The plan will need to address how reductions are to be counted, verified, and credited.

Another problematic area is that the treaty is ambiguous regarding the extent to which developing nations will participate in the effort to limit global emissions. The original 1992 climate treaty made it clear that, while the developed nations most responsible for the current buildup of greenhouses gases in the atmosphere should take the lead in combating climate change, developing nations also have a role to play in protecting the global climate. However, the Kyoto Protocol does not set any binding limits on developing nation emissions, nor does it establish a mechanism or timetable for these countries to take on such limits voluntarily. On the other hand, the Protocol does establish a so-called Clean Development Mechanism, which allows developed countries to invest in projects in developing countries that reduce greenhouse gas emissions and receive credit for the reductions. The intent is to help developing nations minimize their emissions even as they develop their energy sectors and expand their economies.

* * *

The treaty negotiators in Kyoto acknowledged that the Kyoto Protocol represents only a first step toward achieving the goal set by the original climate treaty: to stabilize greenhouse gas concentrations in the atmosphere "at a level that would prevent dangerous interference with the climate system." Even if the Kyoto Protocol is ratified and nations abide by its terms, neither of which can be taken for granted, its effect will only slow—not halt—the buildup of greenhouse gases. Unlike the Montreal Protocol on Substances That Deplete the Ozone Layer, which will eventually "solve" the problem of Ozone depletion if adhered to, the Kyoto Protocol will not "solve" the problem of climate change, but only begin the long process of weaning the world away from heavy reliance on fossil fuels and other sources of greenhouse gases.

Notes

1. How many of the E8 have "signed on" to combat the greenhouse effect? What steps could be taken to obtain the cooperation of the others?

2. Note the use of the trading scheme to try to minimize the costs of compliance and introduce as much flexibility as possible. We will consider such trading schemes at the end of Chapter IV. Some environmentalists

object to such schemes on the ground that they undercut the moral imperative of environmental law by treating pollution as a marketable commodity
rather than an evil. They also worry about the difficulty of monitoring the
trades. In the Kyoto context, do you find these objections convincing?

3.   The prisoner's dilemma stands as a significant barrier to addressing
the greenhouse effect, as does the remaining scientific uncertainty about the
scope of the problem. What strategies could be used to overcome these
barriers to agreement?

U.S. COUNCIL ON ENVIRONMENTAL QUALITY, ENVIRONMENTAL QUALITY: TWENTY–FIFTH ANNIVERSARY REPORT, 1994–95

10–17, 129–132 (1996).

Population growth, economic activity, and rising per capita income
all tend to put pressures on the U.S. environment.

* * *

Rising [population] and wealth both result in rising consumption,
which shows up in a variety of forms, such as increased demand for
energy and natural resources, more cars on the road and a doubling in
vehicle-miles traveled, and more solid waste.

In the face of these pressures, the record of improvement in many
environmental, energy, and natural resource areas is impressive. . . .

AIR QUALITY

Overall, between 1970 and 1994 the combined emissions of the six
principal pollutants declined 24 percent.

Carbon monoxide (CO). From 1970 to 1994, emissions of carbon
monoxide declined from 128 to 98 million tons per year, or 23 percent.
During the 1985–94 period, national average CO concentrations were
down 28 percent and emissions were down 15 percent.

Lead (Pb). The transition to unleaded gasoline in automobiles has
resulted in a drastic decline in emissions, which are down 98 percent
over the 1970–94 period and 75 percent over the 1985–94 period.

Nitrogen oxides (NO_x), Over the 1970–94 period, emissions of
NOx are up 14 percent, from 20.6 to 23.6 million tons per year. Since
1985, emissions from highway vehicles decreased 7 percent while fuel
combustion emissions increased 8 percent.

Ozone. High levels of ozone persist in many heavily populated
areas, including much of the Northeast, the Texas Gulf Coast, and Los
Angeles. It is estimated that about 50 million people lived in counties
with ozone levels above the national standard in 1994.

Particulate Matter (PM). Over the 1970–94 period, particulate
emissions declined about 78 percent. During the 1988–94 period, emissions were down 12 percent and concentrations down 20 percent. Emis-

sions from sources such as fuel combustion, industrial processes, and transportation declined by 17 percent during the 1985–94 period.

Sulfur Dioxide (SO$_2$). Over the 1970–94 period, emissions of sulfur dioxide are down 32 percent. During the 1985–94 period, emissions were down 9 percent and concentrations were down 25 percent.

TRI Air Emissions. Data on annual air emissions, starting with the 1987 reporting year, have been collected annually for the Toxics Release Inventory (TRI). The reports have been submitted annually since 1987 by manufacturing facilities with 10 or more employees. Not all chemicals are listed under TRI reporting requirements, although chemical coverage was greatly expanded for the 1995 reporting year and now includes almost 650 chemicals and chemical categories.

Over the 1988–1994 period, total TRI reported air emissions declined by over 40 percent, from about 2.3 billion pounds in 1988 to about 1.3 billion pounds in 1994. Of the TRI listed chemicals, 10 account for over half of all reported releases to air. Of these chemicals, all but hydrochloric acid have declined since 1988.

* * *

WATER QUALITY AND AQUATIC RESOURCES

Since passage of the Clean Water Act in 1972, most of the conspicuous water pollution from point sources has been eliminated. More than 57,000 industrial facilities now operate under a pollution control permit.

During the 1972–92 period, population and pollutant loads arriving at treatment plants each rose about 30 percent, yet biochemical oxygen demand (BOD) and total suspended solids (TSS) from treatment plants declined by 36 percent. Direct industrial discharges of toxic pollutants are down dramatically since 1972.

EPA's 1994 National Water Quality Inventory is based on surveys conducted during 1992 and 1993. The inventory included 17 percent of the nation's total river miles, 42 percent of the nation's total lake area, and 78 percent of the national's total estuarine area.

The survey of rivers found that 57 percent of all river miles showed good water quality and broadly met the standards associated with their designated use, while 7 percent were in good condition but threatened by future degradation. About 22 percent were in fair condition, partially supporting their designated uses. Another 14 percent showed poor quality. Bacteria and siltation were the problems most often found, each affecting 34 percent of all impaired rivers. Pollutants from agricultural activities were identified in 60 percent of all impaired miles.

The lake survey found 50 percent of the nation's lake area in good condition, 13 percent in good condition but threatened, 28 percent in fair condition, and 9 percent in poor condition. Leading pollutants included nutrients, which were found in 43 percent of all impaired lake acres, followed by siltation (28 percent), oxygen-depleting substances (24 percent), and metals (21 percent).

The survey of the nation's total estuarine area found 57 percent in good condition, 6 percent in good condition but threatened, 27 percent in fair condition, and 9 percent in poor condition. Nutrients and bacteria were the pollutants most often found in impaired estuaries.

In all three cases, less than 1 percent of rivers, lakes, and estuaries had such poor water quality that use support was not attainable due to various biological, chemical, physical, or economic/social conditions.

The conversion of wetlands (both federal and nonfederal) to other uses has slowed considerably over the past several decades, dropping from an average of 690,000 acres per year in the 1954–74 period to about 423,000 acres annually in the 1974–83 period. During the 1982–92 period, it is estimated that 156,000 acres were lost annually on nonfederal lands (estimates for federal lands during this period are not yet available).

Of the 1.56 million acres of nonfederal wetlands lost over the 1982–92 period, about 1.4 million acres became uplands and about 200,000 acres became deepwater habitat. During the same period, about 769,000 acres of deepwater or upland habitat became wetland. Thus, though absolute losses were estimated at 156,000 acres annually, the average "net" loss of wetlands on nonfederal lands averaged 70,000 to 90,000 acres annually.

Solid and Hazardous Waste

In absolute terms, municipal waste generation has grown steadily and is expected to continue to grow. From 1960 to 1994, waste generation increased from 88 million tons to 209 million tons, and projections indicate that it will rise to 262 million tons by the year 2010. Per capita generation, which rose from 2.7 pounds per day in 1960 to 4.4 pounds per day in 1994, is projected to hold steady at 4.4 pounds through the year 2000, but increase to 4.7 pounds by the year 2010.

By September 1995 EPA had identified 40,094 potentially hazardous waste sites across the nation, including sites potentially contaminated with radioactive waste. About 94 percent of these sites have been assessed by EPA to determine if further action is needed. To clear the way for the economic redevelopment of sites that are not of federal concern, the Clinton Administration by 1995 had removed more than 24,000 sites from the Superfund inventory, leaving 15,622 remaining in the inventory.

The Superfund law's National Priorities List (NPL) identifies the nation's most seriously contaminated hazardous waste sites, which are given highest priority for Superfund cleanup. By September 1995, a total of 1,374 sites had been listed or proposed for listing. Work was underway at 93 percent of these sites and permanent cleanup construction was in process or complete at 60 percent.

* * *

ECOSYSTEMS AND BIODIVERSITY

The Nature Conservancy and state agency-based Natural Heritage Network maintain databases with information on more than 28,000 U.S. species and an additional 11,000 subspecies and varieties. In 1996, the Conservancy reported on the conservation status of 20,481 native U.S. species. This represents 13 major groups of plants and animals that have been classified and studied in sufficient detail to allow a status assessment for each of their species.

Based on their global rarity, the report found that almost one third (32 percent) of the species surveyed were in some danger. About 1.3 percent were presumed or possibly extinct, 6.5 percent were classified as critically imperiled, another 8.9 percent imperiled, and 15 percent were classified as vulnerable.

* * *

CATEGORIES AND CURRENT STATUS OF ECOSYSTEMS

The National Biological Service of the Interior Department organizes ecosystems into four broad categories: terrestrial, aquatic, coastal and marine, and riparian. The following paragraphs summarize the current status of these ecosystems.

Terrestrial Ecosystems. Chance has been a natural part of terrestrial ecosystems throughout history; in recent years, human intervention has been the principal agent of change. Disease, fire suppression, pollution, conversions to other uses, exotic species, noxious weeds, harvesting activities such as logging, and global climate change are among the numerous variables that can affect terrestrial ecosystems.

Aquatic Ecosystems. Aquatic ecosystems have been severely degraded in the last century in the United States. Natural aquatic systems have been altered for transportation, diverted for agricultural and municipal needs, straightened, dammed, and polluted.

Coastal and Marine Ecosystems. The quantity and health of the nation's coastal and marine resources have declined over time at the species, community, and ecosystem levels. Urbanization, shoreline modifications, overfishing, high-density recreational use, and other human activities have been the major factors contributing to this decline.

Riparian Ecosystems. Stream bank and floodplain ecosystems, particularly in the West, have been greatly altered over the last 200 years, largely as a result of water development projects, clearing of trees, overgrazing by livestock, agricultural conversion, urban growth, and invasions of nonnative plants.

ASSESSING ECOSYSTEMS

Within these four broad categories are many smaller ecological units. The relative condition of these units has been examined recently by Defenders of Wildlife, the World Wildlife Fund, and The Nature Conservancy.

In its 1995 report, Defenders of Wildlife listed the 21 "most-endangered" ecosystems in the United States (see Table 7.1). The three highest ranking ecosystems were the South Florida landscape, Southern Appalachian spruce-fir forest, and longleaf pine forest and savana. The sources of threat to these ecosystem types vary, ranging from human population growth in Florida to acid fog and an insect pest in the Southern Appalachians; the longleaf pine and savanna communities have been replaced by agriculture, tree farms, and by the invasion of hardwood forests.

The ranking used by Defenders of Wildlife was based on four criteria: decline in original area since European settlement, present area (rarity), imminence of threat, and number of federally listed threatened and endangered species. But the report acknowledges that there may be a need to supplement risk with other criteria, including ecological value, scientific value, and the economic and political feasibility of conservation.

Table 7.1

The 21 Most Endangered

Ecosystems of the United States

South Florida Landscape

Southern Appalachian Spruce–Fir Forest

Longleaf Pine Forest and Savanna

Eastern Grasslands, Savannas, and Barrens

Northwestern Grasslands and Savannas

California Native Grasslands

Coastal Communities in the Lower 48 States and Hawaii

Southwestern Riparian Forests

Southern California Coastal Sage Shrub

Hawaiian Dry Forest

Large Streams and Rivers in the Lower 48 States and Hawaii

Cave and Karst Systems

Tallgrass Prairie

California Riparian Forests and Wetlands

Florida Scrub

Ancient Eastern Deciduous Forest

Ancient Forest of Pacific Northwest

Ancient Red and White Pine Forest, Great Lakes States

Ancient Ponderosa Pine Forest

Midwestern Wetlands

Southern Forested Wetlands

Notes

1. Some of the sources of environmental problems, such as the number of automobiles, the amount of municipal waste, and the size of the population, have increased, often limiting and sometimes reversing improvements due to regulations or new control technologies. Is there an inherent conflict between the environment and growth?

2. Whether the environmental laws are considered a failure or a success depends on two factors: (a) whether we focus on improvements over the past or on the significant remaining problems, and (b) whether we consider the environmental improvements to have been purchased at an acceptable cost. Not surprisingly, as we will see in the next section, economists have given the latter question considerable thought.

C. ECONOMIC PERSPECTIVES

HARDIN, "THE TRAGEDY OF THE COMMONS"[a]

162 *Science* 1243, 1244–45 (1968).

The tragedy of the commons develops in this way. Picture a pasture open to all. It is to be expected that each herdsman will try to keep as many cattle as possible on the commons. Such an arrangement may work reasonably satisfactorily for centuries because tribal wars, poaching, and disease keep the numbers of both man and beast well below the carrying capacity of the land. Finally, however, comes the day of reckoning, that is, the day when the long-desired goal of social stability becomes a reality. At this point, the inherent logic of the commons remorselessly generates tragedy.

As a rational being, each herdsman seeks to maximize his gain. Explicitly or implicitly, more or less consciously, he asks, "What is the utility to me of adding one more animal to my herd?" This utility has one negative and one positive component.

(1) The positive component is a function of the increment of one animal. Since the herdsman receives all the proceeds from the sale of the additional animal, the positive utility is nearly–1.

(2) The negative component is a function of the additional overgrazing created by one more animal. Since, however, the effects of overgrazing are shared by all the herdsmen, the negative utility for any particular decision-making herdsman is only a fraction of–1.

Adding together the component partial utilities, the rational herdsman concludes that the only sensible course for him to pursue is to add another animal to his herd. And another; and another * * *. But this is the conclusion reached by each and every rational herdsman sharing a commons. Therein is the tragedy. Each man is locked into a system that compels him to increase his herd without limit in a world that is limited. Ruin is the destination toward which all men rush, each pursuing his own best interest in a society that believes in the freedom of the commons. Freedom in a commons brings ruin to all.

* * *

In an approximate way, the logic of the commons has been understood for a long time, perhaps since the discovery of agriculture or the invention of private property in real estate. But it is understood mostly only in special cases which are not sufficiently generalized. Even at this late date, cattlemen leasing national land on the western ranges demonstrate no more than an ambivalent understanding, in constantly pressuring federal authorities to increase the head count to the point where overgrazing produces erosion and weed-dominance. Likewise, the oceans of the world continue to suffer from the survival of the philosophy of the commons. Maritime nations still respond automatically to the shibboleth of the "freedom of the seas." Professing to believe in the "inexhaustible resources of the oceans," they bring species after species of fish and whales closer to extinction.

The National Parks present another instance of the working out of the tragedy of the commons. At present, they are open to all, without limit. The parks themselves are limited in extent—there is only one Yosemite Valley—whereas population seems to grow without limit. The values that visitors seek in the parks are steadily eroded. Plainly, we must soon cease to treat the parks as commons or they will be of no value to anyone.

What shall we do? We have several options. We might sell them off as private property. We might keep them as public property, but allocate the right to enter them. The allocation might be on the basis of wealth, by the use of an auction system. It might be on the basis of merit, as defined by some agreed upon standards. It might be by lottery. Or it might be on a first-come, first-served basis, administered to long queues. These, I think, are all the reasonable possibilities. They are all objectionable. But we must choose—or acquiesce in the destruction of the commons that we call our National Parks.

* * *

In a reverse way, the tragedy of the commons reappears in problems of pollution. Here it is not a question of taking something out of the commons, but of putting something in—sewage, or chemical, radioactive, and heat wastes into water; noxious and dangerous fumes into the air; and distracting and unpleasant advertising signs into the line of sight. The calculations of utility are much the same as before. The rational man finds that his share of the cost of the wastes he discharges into the commons is less than the cost of purifying his wastes before releasing them. Since this is true for everyone, we are locked into a system of "fouling our own nest," so long as we behave only as independent, rational, free-enterprisers.

The tragedy of the commons as a food basket is averted by private property, or something formally like it. But the air and waters surrounding us cannot readily be fenced, and so the tragedy of the commons as a cesspool must be prevented by different means, by coercive laws or taxing devices that make it cheaper for the polluter to treat his pollutants than to discharge them untreated. We have not progressed as far with the solution of this problem as we have with the first. Indeed, our particular concept of private property, which deters us from exhausting the positive resources of the earth, favors pollution. The owner of a factory on the bank of a stream—whose property extends to the middle of the stream—often has difficulty seeing why it is not his natural right to muddy the waters flowing past his door. The law, always behind the times, requires elaborate stitching and fitting to adapt it to this newly perceived aspect of the commons.

Notes

1. Hardin suggests the need for social control or intervention in situations where individually rational decisions eventually will produce collectively irrational results. Important economic concepts in the excerpt include marginal utility (the benefits and costs to a producer of one additional unit of production) and external costs (costs of production borne by persons other than the producer). Why may different types of remedies be necessary to protect the commons as a food basket or source of minerals, and as a cesspool? To what extent do the forms of public intervention mentioned by Hardin rely on private market forces to help allocate scarce resources?

2. One effort to fence the commons was the Magnuson Fishery Conservation and Management Act, enacted in 1976 and extending the territorial limits of the United States from 6 to 200 miles into the oceans. 16 U.S.C.A. § 1801 et seq. After opposing such claims by other nations for years, the U.S. joined the trend in 1976 because fisheries off our Atlantic and Pacific coasts had been seriously depleted by foreign trawlers.

The Magnuson Act not only established a 200–mile exclusive economic zone of the United States, but also created regional fishery councils and charged them with rebuilding depleted fish stocks. The eight regional councils were dominated by local fishing interests and authorized to allocate to boat owners transferable rights to catch specified amounts of fish. In effect, collective fishing rights were privatized and distributed as windfalls to current boat owners, rather than, for example, being auctioned off to the highest bidders with proceeds going to the federal treasury.

The intent was that the councils would limit fishing rights sufficiently so that stocks would have the opportunity to recover. In some regions, at least, it did not work out that way. Excessive numbers of rights were allocated. The result was a catastrophic decline in the numbers of salmon in the Pacific Northwest and of cod, haddock and flounder off the New England coast. See *New York Times,* March 7, 1994, p. A1, col. 1. Late in 1994, upon recommendation of the New England Fishery Council, the U.S. Department of Commerce issued an emergency order closing three prime Atlantic fishing grounds, encompassing about 6,600 square miles of ocean, to virtually all commercial fishing. The order also banned the use, in other New England waters, of nets with mesh sizes smaller than six inches. See *Los Angeles Times,* Dec. 8, 1994, p. A18, col. 4.

The Magnuson Act was reauthorized and amended by the 1996 Sustainable Fisheries Act, Pub. L. No. 104–297, 110 Stat. 3559 (1996). For an illuminating analysis of reasons for the failure of the 1976 Magnuson Act, and an explanation of some of the improvements and shortcomings of the 1996 Act, see David Dana, "Overcoming the Political Tragedy of the Commons: Lessons Learned from the Reauthorization of the Magnuson Act," 24 *Ecology L.Q.* 833 (1997). See also Shi–Ling Hsu and James Wilen, "Ecosystem Management and the 1996 Sustainable Fisheries Act," 24 *Ecology L.Q.* 799 (1997); Allison Rieser, "Property Rights and Ecosystem Management in U.S. Fisheries: Contracting for the Commons?" 24 *Ecology L.Q.* 813 (1997).

For a thoughtful discussion about different forms of public intervention to protect common resources generally, and fisheries in particular, see Carol Rose, "Rethinking Environmental Controls: Management Strategies for Common Resources," 1991 *Duke L.J.* 1, 5–23.

3.   In another part of his article Hardin suggests that increased population is the major cause of the environmental problem. However, Barry Commoner, in *The Closing Circle* (1971), argues that misuse of new technologies and chemicals is mainly to blame. Others have emphasized modern man's ethical notions of his relationship to the environment. One writer concluded that the root of the problem is the Judeo–Christian conception of man as a dominator and exploiter of nature. White, "The Historical Roots of Our Ecologic Crisis," 155 *Science* 1203 (1967).

ROYAL COMMISSION ON ENVIRONMENTAL POLLUTION, FIRST REPORT
Cmnd. No. 4585, pp. 4–6 (1971).

WHY THERE IS A POLLUTION PROBLEM

It may well be asked why it is that there should be a growing conflict between economic and technological advance on the one hand, and the quality of the environment on the other. There are two main reasons. One is rooted in a basic law of nature: it is impossible to add to the material resources with which the world is endowed and impracticable to dispose of waste materials outside the world and its envelope of air. * * * The second reason for the growing conflict is largely economic. Little can be done about the first reason, for even the most powerful legislatures cannot change the laws of nature; but many things can be done about the second. Governments can protect the environment through legal and institutional arrangements.

The economic reason why society may not strike the right balance between economic output and the quality of the environment is that the

46 PROBLEMS IN PERSPECTIVE Ch. 1

costs of many kinds of pollution are borne not by the polluters, but by somebody else. As a result these "external" costs will not, in general, be taken fully into account by firms, individuals or other bodies who cause pollution. The other side of the coin is that those who spend money on reducing pollution may not always be the people who gain from the resulting improvement in the environment. This applies both to "tangible" pollution, such as the poisoning of fish in polluted waters, and to "intangible" pollution, such as unpleasant smells or ugly landscapes.

This characteristic of pollution has three main consequences:

(a) Output of goods and services which give rise to pollution tends to be pushed beyond the socially optimum point. Also, expenditure to reduce pollution will often be inadequate. This is true not only for private firms or individuals: it is true also for public authorities. For example, it is hardly surprising that a large proportion of the many sewage works in this country are inadequate, since it may well be that the benefits from better installations—in the form of cleaner effluent and hence cleaner rivers—would be enjoyed only by communities living further downstream. In such cases all the benefits are external to the sewage authority, which therefore has little inducement to improve its plant.

(b) There is generally not enough incentive to reduce the amount of pollution per unit of output of the goods and services responsible, so that not enough resources and effort are devoted to this objective. For example, if it becomes cheaper to distribute milk in plastic containers instead of glass bottles, this will be done whether or not the production and disposal of plastic containers impose higher pollution costs per unit of milk consumed than does the use of glass bottles. We cannot rely on technological innovation automatically to reduce environmental pollution.

(c) Insofar as pollution costs are not borne by those who cause pollution or by the purchasers of their products, but by people who happen to be the victims of the pollution, some of the total welfare resulting from the economic activity of the community is being redistributed away from the victims of pollution in favour of other groups in the community. Manufacturers whose production gives rise to pollution make greater profits than they would if they were obliged to bear the full social costs of their production, and purchasers of their goods buy them at a lower price than they would if the price had to cover the full social costs involved. * * *

POLLUTION ABATEMENT VERSUS OTHER CLAIMS ON RESOURCES

None of this implies—as is often believed to be the case—that all forms of pollution must cease. All production involves some costs, whether they are borne by the polluter or are external costs borne by others; but this is not a reason for stopping all production * * *. [T]he fact that airline operators do not have to pay to soundproof the homes of people who live near airports, is merely the result of particular legal and institutional arrangements and does not mean that the costs to society of the necessary soundproofing are any greater. Alternative legal or institutional arrangements could, in principle, be made to ensure that the costs of pollution caused by noise did enter into the calculations of the polluters like any other production costs. These costs would then play their full part in determining how far society should go in reducing pollution, and would no doubt lead to less pollution, other things being equal. But the costs to society of any given reduction in pollution would not necessarily be affected.

Thus, the problem which has to be faced often is not how to stop pollution altogether, but how far it should be reduced.

* * * Ideally we might all like to have pure water and complete freedom from noise and dirty air; but in practice we might tolerate some shortcomings in the environment in the interests of having, say, better schools, or better health or cultural facilities than we now enjoy. So long as resources are limited, choices have to be made between alternative ways of using them. There is no social merit in making exaggerated claims for one particular form of expenditure to the detriment of others which, to many people, may be more important.

Note on Economic Analysis

Economics is concerned with society's allocation of scarce resources. Many economists prefer a competitive market as the means of allocating resources among consumers in an "efficient" manner, that is, so as to maximize the total value of production, or total welfare. Externalization of costs can result in overproduction of the commodity in question and inefficient allocation of resources, since the sale price to consumers need not reflect all production costs.

Is "efficiency" the only criterion that should govern the allocation of scarce resources? What about "equity" or "justice" among different segments of society, or among different generations? How can such distributional criteria be implemented? See J. Rawls, *A Theory of Justice* 274–298 (1971).

The economic reason why society may not strike a proper balance between economic output and the quality of the environment is that the costs of many kinds of pollution are borne not by the polluters but by somebody else. As a result, these "externalized" costs will not, in general, be taken fully into account by those who cause pollution. An example of economic activity which confers external *benefits* is the renovation of a deteriorated building, with resultant upgrading of aesthetic and property values for nearby landowners. Because the neighbors rarely pay for these benefits, they (the benefits), like external costs, usually are not reflected in the producer's profits or losses. Closely related to the concept of external benefits is that of collective or public goods, commodities which cannot readily be supplied to one person without also enabling many other persons to enjoy them. Examples are national defense and the clean air "produced" by installing emission control equipment at large power plants or on all motor vehicles. Consumption of such goods is collective, and within limits enjoyment by any one person does not diminish the enjoyment available to others. The nonexcludability which characterizes collective goods tends to cause them to be underproduced by the market system, even though their value to all consumers may substantially exceed the production costs.

The economic analysis of pollution implicitly assumes that in the absence of externalities and other imperfections, the free market will lead to optimal results. A full understanding of the basis for this assumption would require a course in microeconomic theory, but the following excerpt should give you at least some idea of the rationale for economists' belief in the free market:

> Assuming that trades between parties are both voluntary and are made with full knowledge, every trade logically must be to the benefit of both parties. Even if every trade benefits both parties, however, the cumulative effect of these trades conceivably might not be beneficial. Both real life and game theory present numerous situations in which individually rational choices lead to social catastrophe. Furthermore, even if trades are beneficial, government intervention might produce even better results than trade among individuals. As the following discussion will explain in more detail, the two fundamental theorems of neoclassical economics preclude the possibility that society as a whole might not benefit by individually rational choices and the possibility that government intervention might create even better results than unimpeded exchanges.

* * *

> [In a state of economic equilibrium], no one has any incentive to engage in any further trades. General equilibrium theory leads to the important conclusion that such an equilibrium does indeed exist. This equilibrium can be described by a set of prices at which, for each good, the quantities supplied and the quantities demanded are equal.

> The fundamental theorems of welfare economics describe some important characteristics of this competitive equilibrium state. The first fundamental theorem of welfare economics asserts that, given certain assumptions, the competitive equilibrium is Pareto-optimal. A state of affairs is Pareto-optimal when any one individual's welfare can be improved only at someone else's expense. Thus, the first theorem asserts that a competitive equilibrium is economically efficient.

> The problem with using Pareto-optimality as a normative guide is that infinitely many Pareto-optimal states may exist, each corresponding with a different initial endowment of goods. For example, a state in which one individual owns all the goods is Pareto-optimal because no other individual can be helped without decreasing the welfare of this individual. Hence, calling a state Pareto-optimal or economically efficient is not necessarily much of an endorsement for that state, even if it is economically efficient. One might well ask whether competitive equilibria restrict the range of possible distributions of wealth. For example, one might wonder whether individuals always have unequal incomes in a competitive equilibrium. If so, some forms of egalitarianism and the free market might be considered incompatible. The second fundamental theorem asserts that given any Pareto-optimal allocation of goods, a set

of prices and initial endowments exists for which that allocation is an equilibrium. This means that, through the political process, society can choose the Pareto-optimal allocation that corresponds to its preferences about the distribution of wealth. By rearranging individuals' initial endowments through an appropriate system of taxes and transfer payments, the government could assure that a competitive equilibrium having the desired distributional characteristics would be reached.

Together, the two fundamental theorems make a strong case for the free market. The first theorem says that the free market will reach economically efficient results. The second theorem says that these results can be squared with society's preferences about the distribution of income without interfering with the competitive process; the government need only change the initial allocation of goods and then let the market go to work. To the extent that any rigorous, theoretical basis exists for economists' general preference for the free market, it is to be found in these two theorems.

* * *

[S]ome of the important limitations on these theorems should be noted. First, the equilibrium state may never actually be reached. A difficult analysis is required to determine whether equilibrium eventually will result if the economy begins in a state of disequilibrium. Second, some of the assumptions underlying the theorems are clearly unrealistic. Not all markets are competitive. Many economic actors lack the perfect information postulated by the theory. * * * Third; these results are inherently keyed to general equilibrium analysis. In other words, they are keyed to the economy as a whole rather than to some individual market. If the assumptions fail for some sectors of the economy, free markets in other sectors may not be optimal. Despite these limitations, many economists believe that the two theorems provide appropriate guidance for formulating social policy.

Farber, "Contract Law and Modern Economic Theory". 78 *Nw.U.L.Rev.* 303, 310–314 (1983).

BOULDING, "THE ECONOMICS OF THE COMING SPACESHIP EARTH"[b]

H. Jarrett (ed.), *Environmental Quality in a Growing Economy* 3–11 (1966).

We are now in the middle of a long process of transition in the nature of the image which man has of himself and his environment. Primitive men, and to a large extent also men of the early civilizations, imagined themselves to be living on a virtually illimitable plane. There was almost always somewhere beyond the known limits of human habitation. * * * That is, there was always some place else to go when things got too difficult, either by reason of the deterioration of the natural environment or a deterioration of the social structure in places where people happened to live. The image of the frontier is probably one of the oldest images of mankind, and it is not surprising that we find it hard to get rid of.

Gradually, however, man has been accustoming himself to the notion of the spherical earth and a closed sphere of human activity. * * *

* * *

The closed earth of the future requires economic principles which are somewhat different from those of the open earth of the past. For the sake of picturesqueness, I am tempted to call the open economy the "cowboy economy," the cowboy being symbolic of the illimitable plains and also associated with reckless, exploitative, romantic, and violent behavior, which is characteristic of open societies. The closed economy of the future might similarly be called the "spaceman" economy, in which the earth has become a single spaceship, without unlimited reservoirs of anything, either for extraction or for pollution, and in which, therefore, man must find his place in a cyclical ecological system which is capable of continuous reproduction of material form even though it cannot escape having inputs of energy. The difference between the two types of economy becomes most apparent in the attitude towards consumption. In the cowboy economy, consumption is regarded as a good thing and production likewise; and the success of the economy is measured by the amount of the throughput. * * *

By contrast, in the spaceman economy, throughput is by no means a desideratum, and is indeed to be regarded as something to be minimized rather than maximized. The essential measure of the success of the economy is not production and consumption at all, but the nature, extent, quality, and complexity of the total capital stock, including in this the state of the human bodies and minds included in the system. In the spaceman economy, what we are primarily concerned with is stock maintenance, and any technological change which results in the maintenance of a given total stock with a lessened throughput (that is, less production and consumption) is clearly a gain. This idea that both production and consumption are bad things rather than good things is very strange to economists, who have been obsessed with the income-flow concepts to the exclusion, almost, of capital-stock concepts.

* * *

It may be said, of course, why worry about all this when the spaceman economy is still a good way off (at least beyond the lifetimes of any now living), so let us eat, drink, spend, extract and pollute, and be as merry as we can, and let posterity worry about the spaceship earth. It is always a little hard to find a convincing answer to the man who says, "What has posterity ever done for me?" and the conservationist has always had to fall back on rather vague ethical principles postulating identity of the individual with some human community or society which extends not only back into the past but forward into the future. Unless the individual identifies with some community of this kind, conservation is obviously "irrational." Why should we not maximize the welfare of this generation at the cost of posterity? *"Apres nous, le deluge"* has been the motto of not insignificant numbers of human societies.

Note

Writing in 1966, Professor Boulding was an unusually perceptive and farsighted economist. More recently, a prestigious international group of policymakers expanded upon his theme in an eloquent call for "sustainable development." World Commission on Environment and Development, *Our Common Future* (1987). Focusing especially on the relationships between environmental resources and economic development, and on the growing economic gap between industrialized and less developed nations, the Commission demonstrated that many forms of development in both groups of nations erode the environmental resources upon which continued economic growth must be based. *Our Common Future* provided the factual and intellectual foundation for UNCED, the 1992 "Earth Summit" in Rio de Janeiro.

RUHL, "THINKING OF ENVIRONMENTAL LAW AS A COMPLEX ADAPTIVE SYSTEM: HOW TO CLEAN UP THE ENVIRONMENT BY MAKING A MESS OF ENVIRONMENTAL LAW[c]

34 Houston Law Review 933, 992–999 (1997).

There has been no dominant organizing policy principle for the last two decades of environmental law. Rather, environmental policy has been decided on an ad hoc basis worked out through an ongoing struggle between two policy poles: preservationism and resourcism. Contemporary preservationism is guided by a consequentialist philosophy directed toward eliminating human interference with the environment. Resourcism might be thought of as the nihilist opposite of preservationism—eliminating environmental barriers to human pursuits. Because each principle in its polar form marginalizes either environment or humanity, neither is particularly useful in addressing environmental problems of the future, the common characteristic of which is the existence of intricate feedback cycles between the human and environmental conditions. For example, it will do little good to talk of protecting endangered species in highly-populated, poverty-stricken areas where basic daily human survival depends on extraction of water, fuelwood, and other resources from the environment. On the other hand, it will do little good in such areas to fail to address resource protection if the collapse of the resource base only worsens the human condition. By each focusing on only one side of that feedback cycle, preservationism and resourcism are fundamentally reductionist and thus doomed to miss the point more times than not.

A policy principle is needed that transcends the preservationism-resourcism dichotomy to address such complicated problems in an adaptive manner. The theme that is emerging, known as sustainable development, holds much promise in that respect. The literature attempting to define what sustainable development means and how to implement it as a coordinating policy principle is burgeoning.[238] The prevailing definition of sustainable development at the international level comes from the 1987 Brundtland Report of the World Commission on Environment and Development: "[A] process of change in which the exploitation of resources, the direction of investments, the orientation of technological development and institutional change are all in harmony and enhance both current and future potential to meet human needs and aspirations."[239]

Further, we have learned from the President's Commission on Sustainable Development what these international ideals mean for the United States:

> A sustainable United States will have a growing economy that provides equitable opportunities for satisfying livelihoods and a safe, healthy, high quality of life for current and future generations. Our nation will protect its environment, its natural resource base, and the functions and viability of natural systems on which all life depends.[240]

It is no accident that these definitions eschew alignment with either the preservationism or resourcism orientations—terms such as sustainable growth and sustainable environment would not have transcended the debate. Sustainable development, however, implies that an economy can thrive and meet human needs without necessarily growing in the sense of increased throughput of resources. But it also implies that economic prosperity matters and that resources must be used to maintain social equity. Indeed, many diehard capitalists and environmentalists alike have begun to realize that the best business opportunity of the future is environmental sustainability and that the best environmental protection opportunity of the future is economic sustainability.

Sustainable development, the combination of economic and environmental sustainability, has always been a necessity. Usually, however, the reality of the need to practice sustainable development has only become apparent in advanced cases of localized unsustainable development. Cases of social collapse caused by unsustainable development abound in history.[246] Today's movement to define sustainable development as an

238. *See* World Future Soc'y, Environmental Issues and Sustainable Futures (Michael Marien ed., 1996) (abstracting 450 books and identifying 170 periodicals dealing with sustainable development and related topics). Information about international efforts to implement and coordinate sustainable development is available from the United Nations Division for Sustainable Development's home page, <http://www.un.org/dpcsd/dsd.htm>

239. World Comm'n on Env't & Dev., Our Common Future 46 (1987).

240. President's Council on Sustainable Development, Sustainable America at i (1996) (quoting the Council's Vision Statement).

246. *See* Clayton & Radcliffe, SUSTAINABILITY: A SYSTEMS APPROACH (1996), at 3 (providing "the Old Kingdom of Egypt around 1950 BC, the Sumerians in 1800 BC, the Maya at about 600 AD and

explicit policy tool is merely a reflection of the mounting reality that unsustainable development is becoming more likely in more settings, even to the point of being a global possibility. Sustainable development, in other words, must be a deliberate practice in today's world—a guiding principle for all social decisions.

* * *

The emerging measure of environmental sustainability, known as biological diversity or biodiversity, has galvanized both the scientific and policy communities. The relatively new discipline of conservation biology[261] tells us that biodiversity is the building block of conservation policy as the basic measure of ecosystem health. Regardless of whatever debate might exist over the rate of loss of biodiversity, it appears widely accepted that biodiversity provides a strong index of ecological sustainability and that we are generally experiencing more losses than gains globally. Accordingly, programs such as the National Biological Information Infrastructure[265] and the Gap Analysis Program[266] are now used as means of improving environmental decision making by increasing the availability, uniformity, and scope of information regarding biodiversity. The new policy model that has emerged from the combination of those efforts is known as "ecosystem management"....[267]

In order to make information about biological diversity most useful to [ecosystem] management..., a number of researchers have embarked on an effort to translate biological diversity information into hard data on the value of nature to the goal of sustainable development.... [They] are discovering that we can translate nature into its service values, such as the value of wild honeybee pollination to agriculture, of water filtering by wetlands, of carbon cycling by forests, and so on.[269]

the Polynesians of Easter Island at about 1600 AD" as examples of civilizations that collapsed due to environmental degradation).

261. Conservation biology has emerged as a biological sciences discipline largely in the past decade, as traced by its chief literature and research outlet, the journal *Conservation Biology*.

265. The National Biological Information Infrastructure ("NBII") began in 1993 as a distinct bureau of the Department of the Interior known as the National Biological Survey. The program name later was changed to National Biological Service ("NBS"), and subsequent to that the program was merged into the United States Geological Survey ("USGS") as the Biological Resources Division ("BRD"). The NBII is a BRD led initiative. The BRD was created by consolidating the biological research, inventory and monitoring, and information transfer programs of seven different Department of the Interior bureaus.

266. The Gap Analysis Program ("GAP") refers to a state-based cooperative program using Geographic Information Systems ("GIS") technology to map major indicators of biodiversity over states, along with the existing network of conservation lands. See A. Ross Kiester et al., *Conservation Prioritization Using GAP Data*, 10 Conservation Biology 1332, 1333 (1996).

267. For excellent overviews of the ecosystem management philosophy, including its application through adaptive management techniques, see The Keystone Ctr., THE KEYSTONE NATIONAL POLICY DIALOGUE ON ECOSYSTEM MANAGEMENT 5–22; Steven L. Yaffee et al., Ecosystem Management in the United States 35–38 (1996); R. Edward Grumbine, *Reflections on "What is Ecosystem Management?"*, 11 Conservation Biology 41, 41–42 (1997); R. Edward Grumbine, *What Is Ecosystem Management?*, 8 Conservation Biology 27, 28, 31 (1994).

269. *See* Center for Resources Econs., Nature's Services 177–254 (Gretchen C. Daily ed., 1997) (providing a comprehensive review from various authors of what is al-

Note

The final paragraph of the foregoing excerpt introduces the concept of "ecosystem services." The services supplied by *soil*, for example, include: (1) buffering and moderation of the hydrological cycle, e.g., soaking up precipitation and gradually releasing it to plant roots and into underground aquifers and surface streams; (2) physical support of plants; (3) retention and delivery of nutrients to plants; (4) disposal of wastes and dead organic matter; (5) renewal of soil fertility, i.e., processing of wastes and dead organic matter by soil organisms to replenish nutrients necessary for plant production; and (6) regulation of major element cycles, e.g., of carbon, nitrogen and sulfur. G. Daily (ed.), *Nature's Services: Societal Dependence on Natural Ecosystems* 117 (1997).

The following table, from Worldwatch Institute, *State of the World 1994*, at 33 (1994), identifies valuable services provided on a continuing basis by forest ecosystems.

Economic Services Provided by Intact Forest Ecosystems

Service	Economic Importance
Gene pool	Forests contain a diversity of species, habitats, and genes that is probably their most valuable asset; it is also the most difficult to measure. They provide the gene pool that can protect commercial plant strains against pests and changing conditions of climate and soil and can provide the raw material for breeding higher-yielding strains. The wild relatives of avocado, banana, cashew, cacao, cinnamon, coconut, coffee, grapefruit, lemon, paprika, oil palm, rubber, and vanilla—exports of which were worth more than $20 billion in 1991—are found in tropical forests.
Water	Forests absorb rainwater and release it gradually into streams, preventing flooding and extending water availability into dry months when it is most needed. Some 40 percent of Third World farmers depend on forested watersheds for water to irrigate crops or water livestock. In India, forests provide water regulation and flood control valued at $72 billion per year.
Watershed	Forests keep soil from eroding into rivers. Siltation of reservoirs costs the world economy about $6 billion per year in lost hydroelectricity and irrigation water.
Fisheries	Forests protect fisheries in rivers, lakes, estuaries, and coastal waters. Three fourths of fish sold in the markets of Manaus, Brazil, are nurtured in seasonally flooded *varzea* forests, where they feed on fruits and plants. The viability of 112 stocks of salmon and other

ready known about ecosystem services, how the information can be transformed into valuation estimations that can be used to better understand human impact on ecosystems, and the monumental research agenda that will need to be implemented to create a sufficient information source upon which to base reliable decisions).

	fish in the Pacific Northwest depends on natural, old-growth forests; the region's salmon fishery is a $1–billion industry.
Climate	Forests stabilize climate. Tropical deforestation releases the greenhouse gases carbon dioxide, methane, and nitrous oxide, and accounts for 25 percent of the net warming effect of all greenhouse gas emissions. Replacing the carbon storage function of all tropical forests would cost an estimated $3.7 trillion—equal to the gross national product of Japan.
Recreation	Forests serve people directly for recreation. The U.S. Forest Service calculates that in eight of its nine administrative regions, the recreation, fish, wildlife, and other nonextractive benefits of national forests are more valuable than timber, grazing, mining, and other commodities.

SALZMAN, "VALUING ECOSYSTEM SERVICES"[d]

24 *Ecology Law Quarterly* 887, 888–896 (1997).

... The primary reason that ecosystem services are taken for granted ... is that they are free. We explicitly value and place dollar figures on "ecosystem goods" such as timber and fish. Yet the services underpinning these goods generally have to market value—not because they are worthless, but rather because there is no market to capture and express their value directly.

Although awareness of ecosystem services dates back to Plato, only recently have ecologists and economists begun systematically examining the contribution of ecosystem services to social welfare. An important synthesis, entitled *Nature's Services: Societal Dependence on Natural Ecosystems*, has just been written for the general public. Edited by Stanford biologist Gretchen Daily, the book presents one of the first rigorous attempts to identify the range of ecosystem services and to value objectively the services in dollars. . . .

... The tough decisions revolve not around whether protecting ecosystems is a good thing but, rather, how much we should protect and at what cost. For example, how would the flood control and water purification services of a particular forest be diminished by the clearcutting or selective logging of 10%, 20% or 30% of its area? At what point does the ecosystem's net value to humans diminish, and by how much? Can the degradation of these services (in addition to ecosystem goods) be accurately measured? And, if so, how can partial loss of these services be balanced against benefits provided by development or pollution?

One might argue that ecosystem services cannot be evaluated, but this is clearly incorrect. We implicitly assess the value of these services every time we choose to protect or degrade the environment. The fundamental question is whether our implicit valuation of ecosystem services is accurate, and if not, what should be done about it. Indeed, studies such as *Nature's Services* indicate that our valuations are grossly and systematically understated....

* * *

So how does one value an ecosystem? Assume our object of study is a wetland along the banks of the Potomac. The first step lies in defining the ecosystem's contribution to human well-being. An ecosystem may be characterized by its physical features (site-specific characteristics such as landscape context, vegetation type, salinity), its goods (vegetation, fish), its services (nutrient cycling, water retention) or its amenities (recreation, bird-watching). These four aspects may not be complementary. For example, one could manage a wetland for cranberry production at the expense of primary productivity and services. Furthermore, the location determines the distribution of goods and services. An ecosystem's carbon sequestration and biodiversity will be valuable even if distant from human populations, but its role in pollination and flood control likely will not. Thus two identical ecosystems may have very different values depending on their landscape context.

Economists classify these characteristics using four categories. The most obvious category includes consumable ecosystem goods such as cranberries and crabs that are exchanged in markets and easily prices (direct market uses). Activities such as hiking and fishing (direct non-market uses) as well as more intangible existence and option values (non-market, non-use) are not exchanged in markets. As a result, their values must be determined indirectly by shadow pricing techniques such as hedonic pricing, travel-cost methodologies, or contingent valuation. Ecosystem services are categorized as indirect non-market uses, for while they provide clear benefits to humans they are neither directly "consumed" nor exchanged in markets. These are also classic public goods because their use cannot be exclusively controlled.

How does one measure dollar figures for indirect non-market resources—ecosystem services—which may have the greatest value of all the economic categories? A recent investment choice made by the city of New York provides one elegant example. The watershed of the Catskills mountains provides New York City's primary source for drinking water. Water is purified as it percolates through the watershed's soil and vegetation. Recently, however, this water failed EPA standards for drinking water, due both to habitat degradation in the Catskills from development, and to increased sewage, pesticides, and fertilizers. New York faced two starkly different choices as to how to obtain large quantities of clean water. It could invest in physical capital, building a water purification plant with a capital cost of $4 billion plus operating expenses. Or, it could invest in natural capital at a much lower cost, restoring the integrity of the Catskills watershed through land acquisition and restoration. Choosing the latter option, last year New York floated an "environmental bond issue" to raise just over $660 million. The cost of restoring the ecosystem service of water purification provided a payback period of five to seven years as well as increased flood protection at no extra charge. The lesson: investments in natural capital can be more financially profitable than those in physical capital.

In many ways, the Catskills example offers an ideal measure of the worth of an ecosystem service. Replacement cost provides an effective method for valuing services because one can compare dollar investments in natural capital and physical capital to determine payback periods and overall costs. Unfortunately, ecosystem services rarely are identified so easily or valued at a local scale. Direct comparisons between manufactured services and ecosystem services break down very quickly as one moves from supplying clean water for New Yorkers to services that are not discretely purchased, such as nutrient cycling or climate regulation. Although functioning markets do not exist for these services, one could imagine calculating the value of an ecosystem service such as carbon sequestration through payments for joint implementation [e.g., under the Climate Change Convention, payments by CO_2 emitters in the U.S. to finance reforestation in Costa Rica]. Similarly, one could imagine insurance companies funding conservation of forest habitat for its flood prevention qualities. Each of these would provide a lower-bound dollar figure for services, but such market developments seem unlikely anytime soon.

Currently, there are three challenges to incorporating benefits of ecosystem services more directly into decisionmaking: identifying services on a local scale, measuring the value of these services, and projecting their future value. First, ecologists must understand the services provided by a specific ecosystem.... But in most cases, our scientific knowledge is inadequate to predict with any certainty how specific local actions affecting these factors will impact the local ecosystem services themselves.

* * *

As noted above, ecosystem services rarely are exchanged in functioning markets or have readily determined replacement costs. As a result, ecologists face a second challenge in deducing the monetary value of these services from non-market valuation techniques. Contingent valuation (CV), also known as willingness-to-pay, is an important valuation method in the regulations that implement the Oil Pollution Act's provisions for natural resource damages.[18] In the context of ecosystem services, CV suffers from a number of serious shortcomings. Most important, polling people's willingness to pay to preserve specific ecosystems assumes a knowledge of the services provided. Given the difficulties ecologists face in quantifying services provided by discrete ecosystems, it is specious to assume John and Mary Doe have an informed idea of

18. See Final Rule, 61 Fed. Reg. 440, 470, 499 (NOAA 1996). [See also pages 666–671 and 804–806 infra.]

ecosystem services, much less in a site-specific context. This information gap limits the application of CV to ecosystem services. Alternative shadow pricing techniques such as hedonic pricing and travel cost methods are equally inapt in valuing ecosystem services. The EPA is currently wrestling with this problem and has requested counsel from its Science Advisory Board.[19]

* * *

Despite these difficulties, let us assume we understand fully the ecosystem service and have determined its current value. Even then, we face a third challenge when we try to determine in dollars the *future stream* of services flowing from the current biophysical features and landscape of the ecosystem. This figure is important because the net present value of most proposed actions that will degrade an ecosystem, such as shopping mall developments, take into account future streams of income.[21] To ensure a full accounting of costs and benefits, the future "income" flow of the ecosystem service should be factored into its current value as well, since that value may change over time due to land-use patterns, weather, pollution, etc.

Notes

1. Does translating ecosystem services into dollar terms carry the risk of encouraging people to think of the environment as just another commodity to be exploited? What about the alternative method of contingent valuation, also described in the excerpt? On the other hand, if we don't find some way of attaching a dollar value to the environment, how do we go about deciding how much of an economic sacrifice to make in order to preserve the environment? We will return to the question of cost-benefit analysis repeatedly, most notably in Chapter III in connection with pollution control, Chapter V in connection with toxics regulation, and Chapter VIII in connection with preserving natural areas.

2. Also note the problem of computing the "present value" of environmental services by "discounting." Since the costs of resolving environmental problems are often incurred today, while important benefits may be decades or more in the future, the temporal mismatch is often a crucial problem in making policy determinations. Discounting in effect treats future benefits (especially those long in the future, such as those to future generations) as being much less important than current ones. Is this ethically appropriate? If not, what is the alternative?

19. See Notification of Public Advisory Committee Meetings, 62 Fed. Reg. 10, 853 (EPA 1997) (in response to request by EPA Deputy Administrator, the Valuation Subcommittee of the Scientific Advisory Board is holding hearings "to propose a new framework for assessing the value of ecosystems to humans, including ecological services and environmentally mediated health and quality of life values").

21. The Office of Management and Budget's traditional use of a 10% discount rate in cost-benefit analyses greatly diminishes the present value of future benefits. While beyond the scope of this essay, there are persuasive reasons to choose much lower discount rates which would, therefore, take greater account of future income streams in net present value calculations. At a minimum, the discount rate of a proposed development's future benefits should be no less than that applied to future ecosystem services. [OMB's standard discount rate was reduced to 7% in 1998—eds.

REPETTO, "ACCOUNTING FOR ENVIRONMENTAL ASSETS"[e]

Scientific American, June 1992, at 94–96.

Natural scientists frequently seem baffled and dismayed when economists display little appreciation of the gravity of environmental degradation. One reason for this seeming indifference is that economists' accounting framework, and the models built on it, assigns no economic value to changes in natural resource stocks. This basic measuring instrument must be recalibrated if policymakers are to recognize and be held accountable for the wholesale disruption of natural systems now under way.

The 50–year-old framework, standardized in the United Nations System of National Accounts (SNA), completely ignores the crucial environmental changes of our times: the marked degradation of natural resources in much of the developing world and the growing pressures on global life-support systems such as climate and biological diversity. These changes may shape the future development of the world economy. But by failing to recognize the asset value of natural resources, the accounting framework that underlies the principal tools of economic analysis misrepresents the policy choices nations face.

Fortunately, at a time when more and more countries are adopting the policies and institutions of the market economy, this methodological model is under revision, for the first time in 20 years. The situation presents an opportunity, not to be missed, to correct a fundamental flaw.

Whatever their shortcomings and however little their construction is understood by the general public, the national income accounts are undoubtedly one of the most significant social inventions of the 20th century. It is no coincidence that since these measures have become available governments in all major countries have taken responsibility for the growth and stability of their economies, and enormous investments of talent and energy have been made to understand how economies can be better managed. Their political and economic impact can scarcely be overestimated. In the U.S., should quarterly gross domestic product (GDP, the sum of all goods and services produced in the country) be even marginally lower than in the preceding three months, a recession is declared, the administration's competence is impugned and public debate ensues. Throughout the world the rate of GDP growth is the primary measure of economic progress.

The current system of national accounts reflects the Keynesian macro-economic model that was dominant when the system was developed. The great aggregates of Keynesian analysis—consumption, savings and investment—are carefully defined and measured. But Keynes and his contemporaries were preoccupied with the Great Depression and the business cycle. Because commodity prices were at an all-time low, natural resource scarcity was the least of their worries. Unfortunately, as Keynesian analysis for the most part ignored the productive role of natural resources, so does the current system of national accounts.

In fact, scarcity of natural resources was of little concern to 19th-century neoclassical economics, from which most contemporary economic theories are derived. In 19th-century Europe, food grains and raw materials were flooding in from America, Australia, Russia and the colonies, while steamships and railroads were lowering transport costs. Forgotten were the dismal predictions of Ricardo, Malthus, Marx and other earlier classical economists that industrial economies would stagnate or collapse because of rising land rents and subsistence wages. What mattered to England and other industrializing nations was the pace of investment and technological change.

The classical economists had regarded income as the return on three kinds of assets: natural resources, human resources and invested capital. Neoclassical economists virtually dropped natural resources from their model and concentrated on labor and invested capital. When these theories were applied after World War II to problems of economic development in the Third World, human resources were also left out on the grounds that labor was always "surplus," and development was seen almost entirely as a matter of savings and investment in physical capital.

As a result, there is a dangerous asymmetry in the way economists measure, and hence the way they think about, the value of natural resources. Buildings, equipment and other manufactured assets are valued as income-producing capital, and their depreciation is written off as a charge against the value of production. This practice recognizes that consumption cannot be maintained indefinitely simply by drawing down the stock of capital without replenishing it. Natural resource assets, however, are not so valued. Their loss, even though it may lead to a significant decrease in future production, entails no charge against current income.

Although the model balance sheet in the U.N. SNA (which few countries actually compile) recognizes land, minerals and timber as economic assets to be included in a nation's capital stock, the SNA income and product accounts do not. This approach is fundamentally inconsistent. Logically, if a country's balance sheets at two different times indicate that an asset—say, a forest—has been depleted, then the income and product accounts for the intervening years should show a charge for the depreciation. This follows from perhaps the most fundamental identity of accounting: the difference in stocks between two temporal points equals the net flow in the intervening period. For example, the difference between a person's net worth at the start and end of a year equals his or her net savings (or dissavings) during the year.

The U.N. System of National Accounts violates this basic identity with respect to natural resource assets. Ironically, low-income countries, which are typically most dependent on natural resources for employment, revenues and foreign-exchange earnings, are instructed to use a national accounting system that almost completely ignores their principal assets.

Behind this anomaly is the mistaken assumption that natural resources are so abundant that they have no marginal value. In fact, whether they enter the marketplace directly or not, natural resources make important contributions to long-term economic productivity. Another misunderstanding is that natural resources are "free gifts of nature," so that there are no investment costs to be written off per se. The value of an asset, however, is not its investment cost but the present value of its income potential. Common formulas for calculating depreciation by writing off investment costs are just convenient rules of thumb. The true measure of depreciation is the capitalized present value of the reduction in future income from an asset because of its decay or obsolescence. In the same way that a machine depreciates as it wears out, soils depreciate as their fertility is diminished, since they can produce the same crop yield only at higher cost.

Codified in the U.N. SNA, the bias against natural resource assets gives false signals to policymakers. It reinforces the illusion that a dichotomy exists between the economy and the environment and so leads policymakers to ignore or destroy the latter in the name of economic growth. It confuses the depletion of valuable assets with the generation of income. The result can be illusory gains in income and permanent losses in wealth.

There is nothing wrong with drawing on natural resources to finance economic growth, especially in resource-dependent countries. The revenues derived from resource extraction can finance productive investments in industrial capacity, infrastructure and education. A reasonable accounting representation of the process, however, should recognize that one kind of asset has been exchanged for another. Should a farmer cut and sell the timber in his woods to raise money for a new barn, his private accounts would reflect the acquisition of a new income-producing asset, the barn, and the loss of an old one, the woodlot. He thinks himself better off because the barn is worth more to him than the timber. In the national accounts, however, income and investment rise as the barn is built, and income also rises as the wood is cut. Nowhere is the loss of a valuable asset reflected. Even worse, if the farmer used the proceeds from his timber sale to finance a winter vacation, he would be poorer on his return and unable to afford the barn. But national income would still register a gain.

The true definition of income encompasses the notion of sustainability. It is similar to the definition of sustainable development given by the World Commission on Environment and Development (the Brundtland Commission): that which meets the needs of the present generation without sacrificing the welfare of the future. This income concept encompasses not only current earnings but also changes in asset positions: capital gains are equivalent to an increase in income, and capital losses are a reduction in income.

Notes

1. The ultimate purpose of any accounting system is to provide decisionmakers with useful information. What decisionmakers would be assisted by a more "environmentally sensitive" way of keeping national accounts?

2. Consider whether the concept of "sustainable development" has any analytical content, or whether as some critics contend it is merely a pious platitude used to paper over fundamental disagreements between environmentalists and advocates of economic growth. Do Ruhl, Salzman, and Repetto agree on how they define sustainability?

3. Once information is developed, the question is what to do with it. Would it be useful to require agencies to perform an asset-based analysis in connection with all decisions? Is this a requirement that courts could usefully police? In Chapter II, we consider in some depth the role of the courts in forcing agencies to make environmental disclosures under NEPA. There is considerable dispute about how useful these disclosures have been, though the principle of environmental disclosure has now been endorsed in the Rio Declaration and elsewhere. We will also discuss disclosure requirements relating to toxics in Chapter VI.

D. POLITICAL PERSPECTIVES

FARBER, "POLITICS AND PROCEDURE IN ENVIRONMENTAL LAW"[a]

8 *Journal of Law, Economics & Organization* 59, 59–61, 65–72 (1992).

Economists often take a jaundiced view of environmental legislation. They are generally skeptical of most current regulatory strategies and favor other mechanisms like marketable permits and emission fees. Yet, from the perspective of positive political theory, the puzzle is not that Congress produces public goods such as clean air so inefficiently, but that Congress manages to produce any public goods at all.

Despite their flaws, environmental statutes have produced genuine improvements in environmental quality. For instance, between 1970 and 1987, lead emissions declined 96 percent and sulfur dioxide emissions dropped 28 percent. Emissions of other air and water pollutants improved or remained relatively constant despite substantial economic growth. This record is especially impressive because GNP increased by 72 percent in the same period (and automobile use increased by about 50 percent). Although these improvements might have been obtained at lower cost, environmental statutes clearly have created important public benefits.

As Mancur Olson pointed out, the dynamics of collective action are actually quite adverse to the passage of statutes such as these, which involve the production of public goods. For example, almost everyone presumably benefits from improved air quality. An individual's support for pollution regulation, however, normally can have only an infinitesimal effect. Hence, a rational individual would usually "free ride" on the efforts of others, contributing nothing to environmental protection while benefiting from other people's actions. Because of this "free rider" problem, it should be relatively difficult to organize large groups of individuals to seek broadly dispersed public goods. Politics should instead be dominated by the rent-seeking activities of special-interest groups.

* * *

Yet the reality is quite different. Environmental groups manage to organize quite effectively. As of 1985, for example, the Sierra Club had 368,941 members, while the National Wildlife Federation had 853,000. Environmental groups also have substantial budgets (as high as $50 million) and staff that run into the hundreds, including economists, lawyers, and other professionals. Nor, obviously, is there any dearth of federal environmental legislation.

* * *

* * * The core prediction of interest-group theory (the dominance of "special interests") does not depend on the absolute weakness of broad, diffuse groups. Rather it depends on their relative weakness compared to smaller, more concentrated groups with equivalent total stakes. Even apart from the free-rider problem, smaller groups would be easier to organize simply because of lower transaction costs. Moreover, the free-rider problem itself is likely to be less severe for smaller groups, because group members begin with relatively larger individual shares of expected benefits. Thus, we would expect the more concentrated group to muster greater political resources in such forms as campaign contributions and professional lobbying. Indeed, this appears to be true: while the budgets of environmental groups are substantial, they certainly do not compare with the resources available to the major corporations, which typically suffer the costs of regulation. Yet, environmental legislation is enacted anyway. * * *

In this article, I seek not to "debunk" interest-group theory, but to explain how the political system manages to overcome the inherent advantages of special interests. Synthesizing prior scholarship on the subject, I identify a symbiotic relationship between legislators and environmental groups. Briefly, the passage of environmental laws is attributable to strong public demand, coupled with exploitation of that demand by ideological and credit-seeking politicians. Environmental groups serve legislators by acting as information brokers during the enactment process, and by invoking procedural control mechanisms during the implementation phase. In return, environmental legislation promotes the growth of the environmental groups themselves.

* * *

* * * In 1989, 80 percent of the population agreed that "[p]rotecting the environment is so important that regulations and standards cannot be too high, and continuing environmental improvements must be made regardless of cost."[9] It is doubtful that voters would really support environmental regulation "regardless of cost," but their willingness to endorse this statement does show that they place a high value on the environment. Other studies of public opinion characterize environmentalism as a "consensual" value in American society. * * *

* * *

Classical public-choice theory tends to cut any link between public opinion and legislation, giving center stage to special-interest groups, with more widely dispersed preferences having only a peripheral role. Indeed, public-choice theory has some well-known difficulties accounting for the fact that people vote at all. Given the small chance of any individual vote influencing the outcome, voting seems irrational as an instrumental activity. In short, we would expect to see very little public attention to or influence on legislation.

An alternative tradition of political thought, that of civic republicanism,[10] is represented in a recent article by James Pope:

> Our history has from the outset been characterized by periodic outbursts of democratic participation and ideological politics. And if history is any indicator, the legal system's response to these "republican moments" may be far more important than its attitude toward interest group politics. The most important transformations in our political order * * * were brought on by republican moments.

As Pope defines these republican moments, their major features are (a) widespread public participation, taking the form of social movements and voluntary associations; and (b) utilizing a moral discourse appealing to concepts of the common good. For present purposes, it is the first of these characteristics that is most significant.

Putting aside the normative aspects of this theory, it adds a significant temporal dimension to the analysis. The implication is that politics

9. *New York Times,* July 2, 1989, p. 1. See also *New York Times,* April 17, 1990, p. 1 ("The environment * * * has reached the forefront of American politics, with candidates for one political office after another proclaiming themselves environmentalist.").

10. Background on republicanism may be helpful for some readers. Philosophical liberalism has been the dominant strain in current American thought. In the 18th century, however, another political tradition was also highly influential, a tradition that stressed civic virtue—the willingness of individuals to sacrifice private interests to the public good. Modern reconstructions of republicanism are based on the allure of civic virtue. They view political life not merely as an effort to use the machinery of government to further the ends of private life, but as a distinct and in some respects superior sphere in which citizens rise above their merely private concerns to join in a public dialogue to define the common good.

alternates between normal periods, in which public attention to an issue is weak, and extraordinary periods, in which the issue has high salience for the public. In those extraordinary periods when broad segments of the public are intensely involved with an issue, legislators find themselves in the spotlight, and their positions shift closer to those of the public at large. During republican moments, voters acquire information about legislative positions, but they also acquire information about the state of the world that may lead to a change in their own expressed preferences. These periods are likely to be attended by new legislative initiatives responding to this public demand, which is less likely than legislation passed in other periods to be responsive to the demands of conventional interest groups.

The original 1970 Earth Day looks very much like a "republican moment." As estimated 20 million Americans participated in a variety of public events that day. More than 2,000 colleges, 10,000 high schools and elementary schools, and 2,000 communities took part. Some 20 years later, the reverberations were still being felt, as millions of people took part in a celebration of the 20th anniversary of Earth Day. * * *

The observation that environmental legislation has been driven by broad public opinion is not necessarily tied to republicanism or any normative political theory; it is ultimately an empirical assertion. Positive theory confirms that in periods of heightened public attention, legislative "shirking" will diminish, and legislative outcomes will be pushed in the direction preferred by the median voter.

* * *

The term "republican moment" is perhaps misleading, to the extent that it suggests that very short periods of high-pitched public interest alternate with periods of nearly total public apathy. Rather, there is a continuum. Earth Day of 1970 represented a peak, but there have been lesser peaks of public pressure sparked by events such as Love Canal or Three Mile Island. In between these peaks, public attention is lower, but not nonexistent.

Popular enthusiasm cannot by itself produce federal legislation; the Constitution provides no mechanism for direct democracy. If popular enthusiasm is to be translated into legislation, then legislators have to be actively involved. What is their motivation?

[One]   powerful motivation is the desire to earn a public reputation by taking credit for major reform legislation. This incentive is especially strong in the Senate, where a significant number of members have presidential aspirations. For example, one driving force behind the Clean Air Act was Senator Muskie's desire to establish himself as "Mr. Environment." Once the legislative leadership defined the "environmentally sound" position, other legislators had a strong incentive to "get on board" or risk the wrath of an aroused public; the leadership proposal became the minimum measure of environmentally sound policy.

The combination of republican moments and legislative credit-seeking provides a convincing explanation for the passage of environmental legislation. As the reference to republican "moments" itself suggests, however, waves of popular mobilization are usually intense but short. The rational strategy for legislators is, in the language of Roger Noll and James Krier, "to 'lash themselves to the mast' while waiting out the temporary siren calls for immediate overreaction"; the politicians then delegate to an agency on terms that will allow the "agency to 'strike when the iron is cold,' after the issue has lost its political salience." Thus, as Noll and Krier say, we would expect to find a temporal instability, in which apparently bold legislative measures result in little actual implementation.

* * *

Environmental legislation often does have a strongly symbolic nature and is rarely implemented to the full extent promised by the statutory language. Perhaps the most notorious example was the promise of the 1972 Clean Water Act to eliminate all pollution by 1985. Yet, this is hardly the full story. * * *

* * *

Why do legislatures enact real as opposed to symbolic legislation? Part of the motivation for environmental legislation may be ideological. For example, Earth Day was the brainchild of Senator Gaylord Nelson, who had previously demonstrated his environmental allegiance as governor of Wisconsin. Ideological legislators seek to screen legislation for substance as well as symbolism, since they care about policy outcomes.

* * *

Credit-seeking legislators also have good reason to seek effective legislation. Typically, they will not be able to establish their positions as leaders on particular issues overnight. Rather, only a series of legislative initiatives can convince the media of their leadership role. Because of this delay factor, however, information will become available on the implementation of the legislator's earlier proposals. If these earlier proposals were purely symbolic, the media will dismiss the legislator as a lightweight. To be an effective credit seeker, it is important to avoid the appearance of pure credit seeking—to show that one is not "all hat and no cattle" or "all sizzle and no steak." Yet it is difficult to develop an image as a substantive player without actually delivering some substance.

Political parties * * * (as ongoing enterprises) have incentives like those of individual legislators to demonstrate ideological commitments on highly topical issues and to engage in credit-seeking behavior. These incentives are especially strong on issues like the environment, which are salient but nonconflictual among voters. Like individual legislators, parties also have some incentive to demonstrate that their commitment on particular issues is substantive rather than merely symbolic. Thus, party organizations may attempt to pressure individual legislators toward more substantive stands, although the extent of the pressure they can exert is unclear.

What we have established so far is that some key political actors have incentives to do more than pass symbolic legislation—rather, they wish to be recognized as supporting substantive, durable regulation. The remaining issue is the role of environmental groups in this scenario.

The impetus for environmental legislation seems to be popular pressure rather than lobbying by environmental groups. Nevertheless, these groups are prominent features in the political landscape. This raises two questions: What role do these groups play in environmental law? And what factors account for the formation and growth of these groups?

* * *

Politicians gain from the existence of groups that can provide voters with endorsements of a politician's environmentalist credentials. * * *

Environmental groups also play other incidental roles within the legislature. As recent studies of the legislative process emphasize, one role played by policy advocates is to generate an inventory of proposals. Legislators cannot readily generate new regulatory ideas and therefore depend on others for proposals. * * *

Because environmental legislation is so complex, it is often difficult for legislators to be sure of just what they are voting for or what its effects will be. Because of the environmental group's incentives as a "repeat player" to maintain its reputation for reliability, such information may be relatively unbiased despite the group's status as an advocate. The availability of this information source is especially valuable to legislators because it offers a check on their other major source of such information, the executive branch. Particularly for legislators who are hoping to build reputations for themselves as policy players, it is crucial not to be completely dependent on the president and his underlings for information. Environmental groups are one of the sources of this information.

Notably, all of these roles involve the provision of information. As compared with the ability to generate large campaign funds or other financial rewards, mere control over information may seem relatively inconsequential. But recall that in the Olson model, the entire political process is ultimately driven by information costs. In particular, the reason that legislators are free to respond to special interests is that information costs lead to rational voter ignorance. For this reason, information brokers such as public-interest groups can exercise important influence in the legislative process.

Once legislation is passed, its effectiveness depends on the implementation process. Legislators face serious problems in obtaining vigorous implementation by administrative agencies. Agencies may be captured by interest groups; they may be subordinate to presidents who are hostile to the legislation; or they may have their own bureaucratic agendas. Oversight hearings give the legislature some leverage, but the ability of legislators to monitor the agency's performance is limited. Moreover, the agency may be unresponsive to the sanctions available to the oversight committee, and procedural obstacles may make corrective legislation impractical.

One set of solutions to these problems is procedural. * * * [S]everal procedural strategies are available to the legislature. First, procedural obstacles to agency action may create sufficient delay for legislative oversight to mobilize. * * * Second, the beneficiaries of regulation can be given access to agency procedures. Among other benefits, this allows the beneficiaries to act as "fire alarms," alerting the legislature to agency misbehavior. It also broadens the information base available to Congress in assessing the agency's decisions. Third, the beneficiaries may be allowed to litigate against adverse agency decisions. [This role is played by trade associations on behalf of conventional interest groups and by environmental groups on behalf of the environment.]

LAZARUS, "PURSUING 'ENVIRONMENTAL JUSTICE': THE DISTRIBUTIONAL EFFECTS OF ENVIRONMENTAL PROTECTION"[b]

87 *Northwestern University Law Review* 787, 792–796, 808, 812 (1993).

Environmental protection confers benefits and imposes burdens in several ways. To the extent that the recipients of related benefits and burdens are identical, no problem of discrimination is presented (there may, of course, be other problems with the tradeoff). But identical recipients are rarely, if ever, the result. Hardly any laws provide pareto optimality in the classic sense of making everyone better off and no one worse off. Virtually all laws have distributional consequences, including those laws designed to further a particular conception of the public interest. Problems of discrimination, therefore, may arise in the disparities between the distribution of benefits and their related burdens.[23]

The benefits of environmental protection are obvious and significant. A reduction in pollution decreases the public health risks associated with exposure to pollution. It also enhances public welfare by allowing greater opportunity for enjoyment of the amenities associated with a cleaner natural environment. Many would also contend that environmental protection furthers the human spirit by restoring balance between humankind and the natural environment. More pragmatically,

23. Of course, the perception among developing nations of just such a disparity is what prompted many of them, during the recent United Nations Conference on the Environment and Development held in Rio De Janeiro, to demand monies from wealthier nations. The justification for these payments was to compensate the developing nations for the costs associated with their taking action (for example, greater protection of tropical rain forests) that would provide environmental benefits to the entire world, including industrialized nations.

environmental protection laws are the source of new jobs in pollution control industries. EPA recently estimated, for instance, that the recently amended Clean Air Act would result in the creation of 30,000 to 45,000 full-time equivalent positions during 1996–2000.

The burdens of environmental protection range from the obvious to the more subtle. They include the economic costs borne by both the producer and the consumer of goods and services that become more expensive as a result of environmental legislation. For consumers, product and service prices may increase; some may become unavailable because the costs of environmental compliance renders their production unprofitable; while other goods and services may be specifically banned because of their adverse impact on the natural environment. For those persons who produce goods and services made more costly by environmental laws, personal income may decrease, employment opportunities may be reduced or displaced, and certain employment opportunities may be eliminated altogether. Finally, environmental protection requires governmental expenditures, the source of which varies from general personal and corporate income taxes to special environmental taxes. These expenditures necessarily decrease public monies available for other social welfare programs.

The burdens of environmental protection, however, also include the redistribution of the risks that invariably occur with pollution control techniques that treat pollution following its production. For instance, air pollution scrubbers and municipal wastewater treatment facilities reduce air and water pollution, but only by creating a sludge that, when disposed, will likely impose risks on a segment of the population different than the segment which would have been exposed to the initial pollution in the air or water. Additionally, the incineration of hazardous wastes stored in drums and tanks converts a land disposal problem into an air pollution issue (leaving, of course, a sludge residue that presents a different land disposal problem), and thereby may change the identity of those in the general population exposed to the resulting pollution. Just transporting solid and hazardous wastes from one geographic area to another for treatment or storage results in a major redistribution of the risks associated with environmental protection. Indeed, such transportation, and the resulting shift of environmental risks, has been the recent subject of massive litigation, as various jurisdictions have sought to export their wastes or prevent the importation of waste from elsewhere.

Nor does the purported prevention of pollution, as opposed to its treatment, necessarily eliminate the distributional issue. "Pollution prevention" frequently depends upon production processes that reduce one kind of pollution by increasing another. For example, water pollution may increase as air pollution is decreased, or a decrease in the mining of one kind of natural resource may be limited or completely offset by the increase in mining of another. Such shifts in the type of pollution or activity allowed will almost invariably shift those risks arising with the "new" pollution or activity to different persons. Hence, pollution may decrease for society as a whole, yet simultaneously increase for certain subpopulations.

Racial minorities could therefore be disproportionately disadvantaged by environmental laws in a number of ways. For example, with regard to the benefits of environmental protection, the natural environments that are selected for protection may be less accessible, or otherwise less important, to minorities. This may be the result of priorities expressly established by statute, or by agency regulations or enforcement agenda.

Inequities in the ultimate distribution of environmental protection benefits may also result, paradoxically, from environmental improvement itself. A cleaner physical environment may increase property values to such an extent that members of a racial minority with fewer economic resources can no longer afford to live in that community. Indeed, the exclusionary impact of environmental protection can be more than just an incidental effect; it can be the *raison d'etre,* with environmental quality acting as a socially acceptable facade for attitudes that cannot be broadcast.

Minorities may at the same time incur a share of the burdens of environmental protection that are disproportionate to those benefits that they receive. Higher product and service prices may be regressive, as may some taxes depending on their form. Although whites are poorer in greater absolute numbers than nonwhites, the latter group is disproportionately poorer in terms of population percentages. Minorities may also more likely be the victims of reduced or eliminated job opportunities. Similarly, they may be less likely to enjoy the economic, educational, or personal positions necessary to exploit the new job opportunities that environmental protection creates. Finally, minorities may receive an unfair share of the environmental risks that are redistributed by environmental protection. Elimination of the risks in one location may result in the creation or increase of risks in another location where the exposure to minorities is greater.

* * *

* * * As a result of racist laws and attitudes extending back to slavery itself, racial minorities today possess significantly less power both in the marketplace and in the political fora, particularly at the national level. This absence of economic and political clout makes it much more probable that racial minorities will receive an unfavorably disproportionate share of the benefits (less) and burdens (more) of living in society, including those associated with environmental protection. * * * Because those with fewer economic resources are disproportionately affected adversely by across-the-board price increases, such individuals are also more likely to suffer greater economic harm when prices rise because of environmental protection. The economic plight of many minority communities also confines its members as a practical matter to the less healthy residential areas which are, for that reason, less expensive to live in.* * *

* * *

* * * Minority interests have traditionally had little voice in the various points of influence that strike the distributional balances necessary to get environmental protection laws enacted, regulations promulgated, and enforcement actions initiated. The interest groups historically active in the environmental protection area include a variety of mainstream environmental organizations representing a spectrum of interests (conservation, recreation, hunting, wildlife protection, resource protection, human health), as well as a variety of commercial and industrial concerns. Until very recently, if at all, the implications for racial minorities of environmental protection laws have not been a focal point of concern for any of these organizations.

SALEEM, "OVERCOMING ENVIRONMENTAL DISCRIMINATION: THE NEED FOR A DISPARATE IMPACT TEST AND IMPROVED NOTICE REQUIREMENTS IN FACILITY SITING DECISIONS"[c]

19 *Columbia Journal of Environmental Law* 211, 213–219 (1994).

In 1982, a predominately African–American community in Warren County, North Carolina, became the proposed site for a polychlorinated biphenyl (PCB) disposal facility. The decision to site the facility in Warren County ushered forth the first national African–American protest against hazardous waste siting practices. The local community, along with civil rights leaders, protested the siting of the facility. Despite efforts by the National Association for the Advancement of Colored People (NAACP) to secure a preliminary injunction to prohibit the siting of the facility—on the ground of racial discrimination—the facility was approved. The protest, however, led to a statewide review of hazardous waste siting procedures. North Carolina then passed a law barring additional sites in Warren County.

GAO REPORT

In response to the siting of the proposed facility in Warren County, Congressman Walter E. Fauntroy asked the Government Accounting Office (GAO) to determine the correlation between the location of hazardous waste landfills and the racial and economic status of the surrounding communities.[10] The GAO did so and found in pertinent part:

> There are four off-site hazardous waste landfills in [EPA] Region IV's eight States. Blacks make up the majority of the population in three of the four communities where the landfills are located. At

c. Copyright © 1994 by the Columbia Journal of Environmental Law. Reprinted with permission.

10. U.S. General Accounting Office, *Siting of Hazardous Waste Landfills and Their Correlation With Racial and Economic Status of Surrounding Communities, GAO/RCED–83–168* (June 1, 1983).

least 26 percent of the population in all four communities have income below the poverty level and most of this population is Black.

An unrelated 1983 study presented similar data on the siting of solid waste facilities in Houston, Texas. The findings revealed solid waste facilities tended to be located in predominantly African–American neighborhoods.[12] Four years after the GAO report, the United Church of Christ Commission for Racial Justice (CRJ) published the report on Toxic Wastes and Race in the United States.[13] The CRJ report, similar to the GAO report, examined the correlation between the location of hazardous waste landfills and the racial and economic status of surrounding communities. While the GAO report examined only the southeastern United States, the CRJ report examined the entire nation. The CRJ report concluded: "Race proved to be the most significant among variables tested in association with the location of commercial hazardous waste facilities. This represented a consistent national pattern." * * *

The GAO and CRJ reports nurtured a burgeoning movement that has been examining the functional relationship between race, poverty, and environmental hazards. The movement is called the "environmental justice movement." The term denotes an effort to broaden the goals of environmental protection to include providing a clean and safe environment where racial minorities and low-income people live and work. The movement seeks to identify and address "environmental racism" which has been defined to include "any policy, practice, or directive that differentially affects or disadvantages (whether intended or unintended) individuals, groups, or communities based on race or color [as well as] exclusionary and restrictive practices that limit participation by people of color in decision-making boards, commissions, and regulating bodies."[20]

EPA ACTIONS AND REPORTS

As part of their efforts, members of the environmental justice movement met with William K. Reilly, the U.S. Environmental Protection Agency [EPA] Administrator, in September 1990.[21] * * * As a result of this meeting the EPA subsequently formed the "Environmental Equity Workgroup" to "assess the evidence that racial minority and low-income communities bear a higher environmental burden than the general population, and consider what EPA might do about any identified disparities." The Workgroup consisted of senior-level officials from EPA regional offices and EPA headquarters * * *.

* * *

12. Robert D. Bullard, "Solid Waste and the Black Houston Community," 53 *Soc. Inquiry* 273 (1983).

13. United Church of Christ Commission for Racial Justice, *Toxic Wastes and Race in the United States: A National Report on the Racial and Socio–Economic Characteristics of Communities With Hazardous Waste Sites* (1987).

20. Robert Bullard, "The Threat of Environmental Racism," 7 *Nat. Resources & Env't* 23 (1993).

21. 1 U.S. EPA, *Environmental Equity—Reducing Risk for All Communities* 2 (June 1992).

Although the GAO and CRJ reports were focal points, the movement is not limited to the siting of hazardous waste facilities. Other areas of concern include proposals to site incinerators, landfills, and nuclear waste facilities on Indian lands; farmworkers' exposure to pesticides; discharges from chemical plants; air pollution problems in minority communities; lead poisoning; workplace conditions; the exportation of hazardous waste to developing countries; placement of homes for the homeless; and international trade. * * *

In mid–1992 the EPA released its finding, which stated:

1. There are clear differences between racial groups in terms of disease and death rates. There are also limited data to explain the environmental contribution to these differences * * *. The notable exception is lead poisoning.

2. Racial minority and low-income populations experience higher than average exposures to selected air pollutants, hazardous waste facilities, contaminated fish, and agricultural pesticides in the workplace. Exposure does not always result in an immediate or acute health effect. High exposures, and the possibility of chronic effects, are nevertheless a clear cause for health concerns.

3. Environmental and health data are not routinely collected and analyzed by income and race. Nor are data routinely collected on health risks posed by multiple industrial facilities, cumulative and synergistic effects, or multiple and different pathways of exposure * * *. However, risk assessment and risk management procedures can be improved to better take into account equity considerations.

4. Great opportunities exist for EPA and other government agencies to improve communication about environmental problems with members of low-income and racial minority groups * * *.

5. Since they have broad contact with affected communities, EPA's program and regional offices are well suited to address equity concerns * * *.

6. Native Americans are a unique racial group that has a special relationship with the federal government and distinct environmental problems.[29]

NATIONAL LAW JOURNAL *FINDINGS*

Beside government agencies, others were sparked into action by the efforts and advocacy of the environmental justice movement. For example, the *National Law Journal* examined the correlation between race and income and the EPA's enforcement of environmental laws. The resulting report revealed that not only are a disproportionate number of hazardous waste facilities located in low-income racial minority communities, but in addition, the EPA discriminates against minority communi-

29. *Environmental Equity*, supra note 21.

ties in enforcing all federal environmental laws.[30] According to the *National Law Journal* report: 1) Penalties under hazardous waste laws at sites having the greatest proportion of white residents are 500% higher than penalties at sites with the greatest minority population, averaging $335,566 for white areas compared to $55,318 for minority areas. 2) The disparity under the toxic waste laws occurs by race alone, not income. 3) For all the federal environmental laws aimed at protecting citizens from air, water, and waste pollution, penalties in white communities are 46% higher than in minority communities. 4) Under the giant Superfund cleanup program, abandoned hazardous waste sites in minority areas take 20% longer to be placed on the national priority list than those in white areas. 5) In more than half of the ten autonomous regions that administer EPA programs around the country, action on cleanup at superfund sites begins 12% to 42% later at minority sites than at white sites. 6) At sites in minority communities, the EPA chooses "containment," the capping or walling off of a hazardous waste dump site, 7% more frequently than the cleanup method preferred under the law permanent "treatment"—to eliminate the waste or rid it of toxins. At sites in white neighborhoods, the EPA orders treatment 22% more often than containment.

Notes

1.   In response to articles like this one, another scholar has noted:

To support the * * * charge—that the siting of waste dumps, polluting factories, and other locally undesirable land uses (LULUs) has been racist and classist—advocates for environmental justice have cited more than a dozen studies analyzing the relationship between neighborhoods' socioeconomic characteristics and the number of LULUs they host. The studies demonstrate that those neighborhoods in which LULUs are located have, on average, a higher percentage of racial minorities and are poorer than non-host communities.

That research does not, however, establish that the host communities were disproportionately minority or poor at the time the sites were selected. Most of the studies compare the *current* socioeconomic characteristics of communities that host various LULUs to those of communities that do not host such LULUs. This approach leaves open the possibility that the sites for LULUs were chosen fairly, but that subsequent events produced the current disproportion in the distribution of LULUs. In other words, the research fails to prove environmental justice advocates' claim that the disproportionate burden poor and minority communities now bear in hosting LULUs is the result of racism and classism in the *siting process* itself.

In addition, the research fails to explore an alternative or additional explanation for the proven correlation between the current demographics of communities and the likelihood that they host LULUs. Regardless of whether the LULUs originally were sited fairly, it could well be that

30. Marianne Lavelle & Marcia Loyle, "Unequal Protection—The Racial Divide in   Environmental Law," *Nat'l L.J.*, Sept. 21, 1992, at S1–S12.

neighborhoods surrounding LULUs became poorer and became home to a greater percentage of people of color over the years following the sitings. Such factors as poverty, housing discrimination, and the location of jobs, transportation, and other public services may have led the poor and racial minorities to "come to the nuisance"—to move to neighborhoods that host LULUs—because those neighborhoods offered the cheapest available housing. Despite the plausibility of that scenario, none of the existing research on environmental justice has examined how the siting of undesirable land used has subsequently affected the socioeconomic characteristics of host communities. Because the research fails to prove that the siting process causes any of the disproportionate burden the poor and minorities now bear, and because the research has ignored the possibility that market dynamics may have played some role in the distribution of that burden, policymakers now have no way of knowing whether the siting process is "broke" and needs fixing. Nor can they know whether even an ideal siting system that ensured a perfectly fair initial distribution of LULUs would result in any long-term benefit to the poor or to people of color.

Vicki Been, "Locally Undesirable Land Uses in Minority Neighborhoods: Disproportionate Siting or Market Dynamics?", 103 *Yale L.J.* 1383, 1384–1386 (1994). Reprinted by permission of The Yale Law Journal Company and Fred B. Rothman & Company.

The author also observed that, in addition to market dynamics, there could be yet other alternative explanations for the correlation between LULUs and current demographics. For example, siting decisionmakers may seek to distribute LULUs fairly but face constraints imposed by regulations over which they have no control, such as zoning regulations, which may underprotect the interests of the poor or people of color.

Professor Been reported the results of a follow-up study in Vicki Been and Francis Gupta, "Coming to the Nuisance or Going to the Barrios? A Longitudinal Analysis of Environmental Justice Claims," 24 *Ecology L.Q.* 1 (1997). The study looked at the demographics of the 544 communities which in 1994 hosted active commercial hazardous waste treatment, storage and disposal facilities (TSDFs). The authors looked first at the demographics of the communities at the time of the census taken immediately before they became hosts, then examined the demographic changes in each subsequent decade through the 1990 census. The authors summarized their findings as follows:

"[W]e found no substantial evidence that the facilities that began operating between 1970 and 1990 were sited in areas that were disproportionately African American. Nor did we find any evidence that these facilities were sited in areas with high concentrations of the poor; indeed, the evidence indicates that poverty is negatively correlated with sitings. We did find evidence that the facilities were sited in areas that were disproportionately Hispanic at the time of the siting. The analysis produced little evidence that the siting of a facility was followed by substantial changes in a neighborhood's socioeconomic status or racial or ethnic composition. Finally, the analysis shows that the areas surrounding TSDFs currently are disproportionately populated by African Americans and Hispanics." Id. at 9.

In another recent study, Thomas Lambert and Christopher Boerner, "Environmental Inequity: Economic Causes, Economic Solutions," 14 *Yale J. Reg.* 195 (1997), the authors analyzed demographic characteristics around three types of industrial facilities and waste sites in and around St. Louis, Missouri: TSDFs, permitted solid waste landfills and incinerators, and inactive hazardous waste (CERCLA) sites. There were 167 facilities and sites in all. The authors found "no significant difference in poverty rates and percentages of minority residents between census tracts with active facilities (TSDFs, landfills, and incinerators) and those tracts without such facilities. Including inactive CERCLA waste sites in the data set, however, uncovered weak evidence that the percentages of poor and minority residents living near industrial and waste sites are significantly higher than the corresponding percentages living in tracts without facilities." The authors believe that they have "empirical support for the theory that housing values are closely related to existing environmental inequities, raising the possibility that siting decisions caused an influx of minority and poor residents, as opposed to the contrary causation assumptions made by environmental discrimination theorists." Id. at 203–204. As a solution to falling real estate values around facilities the authors propose providing compensation to those who live near locally undesirable facilities so that, on balance, the surrounding property is not rendered less desirable. Possible forms of compensation include: (1) direct payments to affected landowners, (2) host fees which are paid into a community's general revenue fund to be used to finance a variety of public projects or to lower property taxes, (3) grants for improving local health-care delivery and education, and (4) the provision of parks and other recreational amenities. Id. at 214.

For an interesting case study of how the predominantly poor, African-American residents of Chester, Pennsylvania attempted to stop the clustering of waste facilities in their community, see Sheila Foster, "Justice from the Ground Up: Distributive Inequities, Grassroots Resistance, and the Transformative Politics of the Environmental Justice Movement," 86 *Calif. L Rev.* 775 (1998).

2.   In 1994, President Clinton signed Executive Order 12898 concerning "Federal Actions to Address Environmental Justice in Minority Populations and Low–Income Populations," 59 Fed.Reg. 7629 (Feb. 16, 1994). The order provided that each federal agency "shall make achieving environmental justice part of its mission by identifying and addressing, as appropriate, disproportionately high and adverse human health or environmental effects of its programs, policies, and activities on minority populations and low-income populations in the United States and its territories and possessions." The Administrator of the U.S. EPA was directed to convene an interagency Federal Working Group on Environmental Justice, to assist each agency to develop an agency-wide environmental justice strategy.

In 1995, EPA issued its environmental justice strategy, based on the principle that communities affected by decisions with environmental impacts should be actively involved in the decisionmaking process. The strategy calls for EPA to increase coordination with affected communities, state, tribal, and local governments, business, and nongovernmental organizations. To develop local knowledge bases necessary for effective participation in complex decisionmaking, EPA will promote technical assistance programs and grants for minority and low-income areas. The Agency also will focus enforcement activities on minority and low-income areas suffering disproportionate environmental and health impacts. See Terry Schnell and Kathleen Davis, "The Increased Significance of Environmental Justice in Facility Siting, Permitting," 29 *Env't Rptr.* 528, 529 (1998).

Pursuant to Executive Order 12898 and Title VI of the Civil Rights Act of 1964, as amended, 42 U.S.C. §§ 2000d to 2000d–7, which prohibits discrimination under any program receiving federal financial assistance, EPA has begun to include environmental justice as a factor in its review of state permits under federally delegated programs pursuant to the Clean Air and Clean Water Acts and the Resource Conservation and Recovery Act. In February 1998, EPA's Office of Enforcement and Compliance Assurance issued interim guidelines for processing complaints under Title VI relating to permit issuance. "Interim Guidance for Investigating Title VI Administrative Complaints Challenging Permits," available at http://es.epa.gov/oeca/oej/titlevi.html on EPA's World Wide Web site. The guidance was quickly criticized as too vague by a variety of industries, state and local regulators, and environmental justice advocates. Although the groups agreed that the guidance was not specific enough, they sharply diverged on almost everything else. See 29 *Env't Rptr.* 234–236 (1998). Revisions by EPA are likely.

3. For bibliographic materials on the subject generally, see Adam Schwartz, "The Law of Environmental Justice: A Research Pathfinder," 25 *Envt'l L. Rptr.* 10543 (1995).

Chapter II

THE JUDICIAL ROLE

In this chapter, we will be concerned with the role of the courts in reviewing environmental actions by other government bodies. The first section focuses on the general role of courts in limiting administrative agencies. It presents the highlights of federal administrative law, with special reference to environmental law. The second section deals with the special restrictions placed on federal agencies by the National Environmental Protection Act.

Environmental regulation is inseparable from administrative law. Regulatory statutes are administered by agencies, with the courts having only a supervisory role.[a] Thus, the problem of regulating private conduct has a strongly administrative orientation. The other major source of environmental disruption is the government itself. Here, the administrative agency is a part of the problem rather than a part of the solution. In both cases, the two key issues are the same: What are the agency's powers? To what extent may a court intervene?

The following article by a leading environmental litigator may help put these issues in historical perspective. Although it is now over twenty years old, it remains a useful introduction to some key features of litigation challenging agency decisions.

SIVE, "FOREWORD: ROLES AND RULES IN ENVIRONMENTAL DECISIONMAKING"[b]

62 Iowa Law Review 637, 638–41 (1977).

The environmentalists' crusade had the courts as its gods and agencies such as the Federal Power Commission and the Atomic Energy Commission as its devils. The opposition, too, viewed the environmental conflict as a holy war; they feared the imminent demise of the Republic. Predictably, the battleground became enshrouded in mist; the allies and

a. As we will see in Chapter VII, today there is also a considerable amount of litigation involving private liability rather than government regulation.

b. Copyright © 1979, University of Iowa (Iowa Law Review). Reprinted by permission.

enemies of both factions became less easily recognizable when *nonenvironmental agencies* began to take cognizance of environmental values, recently created *environmental agencies* (primarily EPA) began to dutifully discharge their missions, and the *developmental interests* began to seek expanded judicial review of agency action.

* * *

It requires no behaviorist theory of legal history to state that the narrowing gap between the standards of judicial review of environmental decisionmaking and other forms of agency decisionmaking is in part due to the changing fortunes of the contending parties. As the agencies respond to judicial directives there is less reason for the courts to interpose themselves in the administrative process. Consequently, the environmentalists are increasingly able to rely on the efficacy of agency decisionmaking while the developmental interests must appeal to the courts for relief. * * *

There are other distinctive features of environmental decisionmaking that have shaped it in ways which, while not readily visible, may provide further insights into administrative and judicial behavior. First, it is clear that a large fraction of all important environmental litigation, and thus of all judicial lawmaking pertaining to the environment, is at the instance of public interest law firms such as the Natural Resources Defense Council, the Environmental Defense Fund, and the Sierra Club Legal Defense Fund. These and other environmental and general public interest law firms are mission oriented rather than client oriented. The firms, generally acting as both client and lawyer, carefully choose the proceedings they bring, with their choices partially predicated on the probability of success. In addition, because the staffs of environmental public interest firms are among the most brilliant and highly motivated of all law firms, the body of law they have been instrumental in creating is different from that created out of the haphazard course of private litigation.

A second distinctive feature of environmental litigation is the severity of the challenges to agency decisionmaking and the attendant problems faced by the courts in attempting to review agency decisions that not only present sharp value conflicts, but that also must be made within stringent time limits and with incomplete scientific knowledge. * * * It is perhaps not too early to suggest that the courts, sensitive to some of these problems endemic to environmental law, have responded by lowering the requisite standard of proof when confronted with a risk of adverse environmental impact.[c]

Third, environmental decisionmaking is frequently *political* in nature. Environmental disputes often involve the interests of many people instead of one or a small number of private litigants. The parties to an environmental dispute clearly view litigation and its judicial resolution

---

   c. These issues are discussed in Chapter V. See also Sive, "The Litigation Process in the Development of Environmental Law," 12 *Pace Envt'l L.Rev.* 1 (1995).

as part of the political process. The advantages to be gained by using the judicial process as a tool for this political purpose are readily available. Litigation grants to its participants, generally without regard to the merits of their claims, the weapons of discovery. The issues that may be debated back and forth unendingly in the political process become subject in the judicial process to the discovery of documents, facts, and opinions underlying the adversaries' positions. Litigation thus serves to clarify and crystallize the political issues. Litigation also holds great drama for the public: points made in speeches about important controversies may attract little media notice, but achieve page-one status if set down in the language of a court-filed complaint. Controversy attracts journalists, and media attention attracts lawyers and litigants.

A. ACCESS TO THE COURTS

1. INJURY IN FACT

In a suit challenging action by a government agency, often the first issue raised is whether the plaintiff has the right to file the suit at all. It is quite possible to imagine a system in which any individual could bring suit to halt any government action that violated the law. American law has not, however, evolved along this line.[d] Instead, a plaintiff generally must have some specific connection with the controversy. At the federal level, the analysis is complicated by the constitutional limitation of federal jurisdiction to "cases and controversies." This limitation has been construed to prevent federal courts from hearing moot cases or issuing advisory opinions, and thus as giving at least limited constitutional status to the idea of "standing."

SIERRA CLUB v. MORTON

Supreme Court of the United States, 1972.
405 U.S. 727, 92 S.Ct. 1361, 31 L.Ed.2d 636.

[The Forest Service approved a plan by Walt Disney Enterprises, Inc., to build a $35 million resort in the Mineral King Valley, "an area of great natural beauty nestled in the Sierra Nevada Mountains." Construction of the huge resort-complex was opposed by the Sierra Club on the ground that the Forest Service had violated several federal statutes. The Sierra Club filed suit to enjoin approval of the Disney plan. It sued as a membership corporation with "a special interest in the conservation and the sound maintenance of the national parks, game refuges and forests of the country." As the Court noted, there was "no allegation in the complaint that members of the Sierra Club would be affected by the actions of [the respondents] other than the fact that the actions are personally displeasing or distasteful to them." The lower court had concluded: "We do not believe such club concern without a showing of

d. For a historical discussion, see L. Jaffe, *Judicial Control of Administrative* *Action* 327–35, 501–45 (1965).

l. enjoin: to legally prohibit or restrain by injunction

more direct interest can constitute standing in the legal sense sufficient to challenge the exercise of responsibilities on behalf of all the citizens by two cabinet level officials of the government acting under Congressional and Constitutional authority."]

JUSTICE STEWART delivered the opinion of the Court.

The first question presented is whether the Sierra Club has alleged facts that entitle it to obtain judicial review of the challenged action. Whether a party has a sufficient stake in an otherwise justiciable controversy to obtain judicial resolution of that controversy is what has traditionally been referred to as the question of standing to sue. Where the party does not rely on any specific statute authorizing invocation of the judicial process, the question of standing depends upon whether the party has alleged such a "personal stake in the outcome of the controversy," as to ensure that "the dispute sought to be adjudicated will be presented in an adversary context and in a form historically viewed as capable of judicial resolution." Where, however, Congress has authorized public officials to perform certain functions according to law, and has provided by statute for judicial review of those actions under certain circumstances, the inquiry as to standing must begin with a determination of whether the statute in question authorizes review at the behest of the plaintiff.[1]

The Sierra Club relies upon § 10 of the Administrative Procedure Act (APA) which provides:

> A person suffering legal wrong because of agency action, or adversely affected or aggrieved by agency action within the meaning of a relevant statute, is entitled to judicial review thereof.

Early decisions under this statute interpreted the language as adopting the various formulations of "legal interest" and "legal wrong" then prevailing as constitutional requirements of standing. But, in *Association of Data Processing Service Organizations, Inc. v. Camp,* 397 U.S. 150, 90 S.Ct. 827, 25 L.Ed.2d 184, and *Barlow v. Collins,* 397 U.S. 159, 90 S.Ct. 832, 25 L.Ed.2d 192, decided the same day, we held more broadly that persons had standing to obtain judicial review of federal agency action under § 10 of the APA where they had alleged that the challenged action had caused them "injury in fact," and where the alleged injury was to an interest "arguably within the zone of interests to be protected or regulated" by the statutes that the agencies were claimed to have violated.[2]

In *Data Processing,* the injury claimed by the petitioners consisted of harm to their competitive position in the computer-servicing market

---

1. Congress may not confer jurisdiction on Art. III federal courts to render advisory opinions, or to entertain "friendly" suits, because suits of this character are inconsistent with the judicial function under Art. III. But where a dispute is otherwise justiciable, the question whether the litigant is a "proper party to request an adjudication of a particular issue," is one within the power of Congress to determine.

2. In deciding this case we do not reach any questions concerning the meaning of the "zone of interests" test or its possible application to the facts here presented.

through a ruling by the Comptroller of the Currency that national banks might perform data-processing services for their customers. In *Barlow,* the petitioners were tenant farmers who claimed that certain regulations of the Secretary of Agriculture adversely affected their economic position vis-à-vis their landlords. These palpable economic injuries have long been recognized as sufficient to lay the basis for standing, with or without a specific statutory provision for judicial review. Thus, neither *Data Processing* nor *Barlow* addressed itself to the question, which has arisen with increasing frequency in federal courts in recent years, as to what must be alleged by persons who claim injury of a noneconomic nature to interests that are widely shared. That question is presented in this case.

The injury alleged by the Sierra Club will be incurred entirely by reason of the change in the uses to which Mineral King will be put, and the attendant change in the aesthetics and ecology of the area. Thus, in referring to the road to be built through Sequoia National Park, the complaint alleged that the development "would destroy or otherwise adversely affect the scenery, natural and historic objects and wildlife of the park and would impair the enjoyment of the park for future generations." We do not question that this type of harm may amount to an "injury in fact" sufficient to lay the basis for standing under § 10 of the APA. Aesthetic and environmental well-being, like economic well-being, are important ingredients of the quality of life in our society, and the fact that particular environmental interests are shared by the many rather than the few does not make them less deserving of legal protection through the judicial process. But the "injury in fact" test requires more than an injury to a cognizable interest. It requires that the party seeking review be himself among the injured.

The impact of the proposed changes in the environment of Mineral King will not fall indiscriminately upon every citizen. The alleged injury will be felt directly only by those who use Mineral King and Sequoia National Park, and for whom the aesthetic and recreational values of the area will be lessened by the highway and ski resort. The Sierra Club failed to allege that it or its members would be affected in any of their activities or pastimes by the Disney development. Nowhere in the pleadings or affidavits did the Club state that its members use Mineral King for any purpose, much less that they use it in any way that would be significantly affected by the proposed actions of the respondents.[3]

The Club apparently regarded any allegations of individualized injury as superfluous, on the theory that this was a "public" action

---

3. * * * In an *amici curiae* brief filed in this Court by the Wilderness Society and others, it is asserted that the Sierra Club has conducted regular camping trips into the Mineral King area, and that various members of the Club have used and continue to use the area for recreational purposes. These allegations were not contained in the pleadings, nor were they brought to the attention of the Court of Appeals. Moreover, the Sierra Club in its reply brief specifically declines to rely on its individualized interest, as a basis for standing.

Our decision does not, of course, bar the Sierra Club from seeking in the District Court to amend its complaint by a motion under Rule 15, Federal Rules of Civil Procedure.

involving questions as to the use of natural resources, and that the Club's longstanding concern with and expertise in such matters were sufficient to give it standing as a "representative of the public." This theory reflects a misunderstanding of our cases involving so-called "public actions" in the area of administrative law.

* * *

The trend of cases arising under the APA and other statutes authorizing judicial review of federal agency action has been toward recognizing that injuries other than economic harm are sufficient to bring a person within the meaning of the statutory language, and toward discarding the notion that an injury that is widely shared is *ipso facto* not an injury sufficient to provide the basis for judicial review. We noted this development with approval in *Data Processing,* in saying that the interest alleged to have been injured "may reflect 'aesthetic, conversational, and recreational' as well as economic values." But broadening the categories of injury that may be alleged in support of standing is a different matter from abandoning the requirement that the party seeking review must himself have suffered an injury.

1st time Supreme Ct. said this.

Some courts have indicated a willingness to take this latter step by conferring standing upon organizations that have demonstrated "an organizational interest in the problem" of environmental or consumer protection. It is clear that an organization whose members are injured may represent those members in a proceeding for judicial review. But a mere "interest in a problem," no matter how longstanding the interest and no matter how qualified the organization is in evaluating the problem, is not sufficient by itself to render the organization "adversely affected" or "aggrieved" within the meaning of the APA. The Sierra Club is a large and long-established organization, with a historic commitment to the cause of protecting our Nation's natural heritage from man's depredations. But if a "special interest" in this subject were enough to entitle the Sierra Club to commence this litigation, there would appear to be no objective basis upon which to disallow a suit by any other bona fide "special interest" organization however small or short-lived. And if any group with a bona fide "special interest" could initiate such litigation, it is difficult to perceive why any individual citizen with the same bona fide special interest would not also be entitled to do so.

The requirement that a party seeking review must allege facts showing that he is himself adversely affected does not insulate executive action from judicial review, nor does it prevent any public interests from being protected through the judicial process.[4] It does serve as at least a

4. In its reply brief, after noting the fact that it might have chosen to assert individualized injury to itself or to its members as a basis for standing, the Sierra Club states:

"The Government seeks to create a 'heads I win, tails you lose' situation in which either the courthouse door is barred for lack of assertion of a private, unique injury or a preliminary injunction is denied on the ground that the litigant has advanced private injury which does not warrant an injunction adverse to a

rough attempt to put the decision as to whether review will be sought in the hands of those who have a direct stake in the outcome. That goal would be undermined were we to construe the APA to authorize judicial review at the behest of organizations or individuals who seek to do no more than vindicate their own value preferences through the judicial process. The principle that the Sierra Club would have us establish in this case would do just that.

JUSTICE DOUGLAS, dissenting.

The critical question of "standing" would be simplified and also put neatly in focus if we fashioned a federal rule that allowed environmental issues to be litigated before federal agencies or federal courts in the name of the inanimate object about to be despoiled, defaced, or invaded by roads and bulldozers and where injury is the subject of public outrage. Contemporary public concern for protecting nature's ecological equilibrium should lead to the conferral of standing upon environmental objects to sue for their own preservation. See Stone, "Should Trees Have ← Standing? Toward Legal Rights for Natural Objects," 45 *S.Cal.L.Rev.* 450 (1972). This suit would therefore be more properly labeled as *Mineral King v. Morton.*

Inanimate objects are sometimes parties in litigation. A ship has a legal personality, a fiction found useful for maritime purposes. The corporation sole—a creature of ecclesiastical law—is an acceptable adversary and large fortunes ride on its cases. The ordinary corporation is a "person" for purposes of the adjudicatory processes, whether it represents proprietary, spiritual, aesthetic, or charitable causes.

So it should be as respects valleys, alpine meadows, rivers, lakes, estuaries, beaches, ridges, groves of trees, swampland, or even air that feels the destructive pressures of modern technology and modern life. The river, for example, is the living symbol of all the life it sustains or nourishes—fish, aquatic insects, water ouzels, otter, fisher, deer, elk, bear, and all other animals, including man, who are dependent on it or who enjoy it for its sight, its sound, or its life. The river as plaintiff speaks for the ecological unit of life that is part of it. Those people who have a meaningful relation to that body of water—whether it be a fisherman, a canoeist, a zoologist, or a logger—must be able to speak for the values which the river represents and which are threatened with destruction.

* * *

Mineral King is doubtless like other wonders of the Sierra Nevada such as Tuolumne Meadows and the John Muir Trail. Those who hike it, fish it, hunt it, camp in it, frequent it, or visit it merely to sit in solitude and wonderment are legitimate spokesmen for it, whether they may be a

competing public interest. Counsel have shaped their case to avoid this trap." The short answer to this contention is that the "trap" does not exist. The test of injury in fact goes only to the question of standing to obtain judicial review. Once this standing is established, the party may assert the interests of the general public in support of his claims for equitable relief.

few or many. Those who have that intimate relation with the inanimate object about to be injured, polluted, or otherwise despoiled are its legitimate spokesmen.

JUSTICE BLACKMUN, dissenting.

* * * I would permit an imaginative expansion of our traditional concepts of standing in order to enable an organization such as the Sierra Club, possessed, as it is, of pertinent, bona fide, and well-recognized attributes and purposes in the area of the environment, to litigate environmental issues.[e] This incursion upon tradition need not be very extensive. Certainly, it should be no cause for alarm. It is no more progressive than was the decision in *Data Processing* itself. It need only recognize the interest of one who has a provable, sincere, dedicated, and established status. We need not fear that Pandora's box will be opened or that there will be no limit to the number of those who desire to participate in environmental litigation. The courts will exercise appropriate restraints just as they have exercised them in the past. Who would have suspected 20 years ago that the concepts of standing enunciated in *Data Processing* and *Barlow* would be the measure for today?[f]

Notes

1. Is the *Sierra Club* decision realistic in light of Sive's description of environmental litigation, page 78 supra? How does Justice Douglas' position differ from the majority's?

2. In extending standing only to users of Mineral King, the Court seems implicitly to grant a higher constitutional status to the pleasures derived from physical presence than to those derived from other forms of contact, such as photographs, literature, and television. More fundamentally, the underlying assumption seems to be that natural areas are only important to the hikers and campers who "use" them, and that their existence adds nothing to the lives of the rest of the population. (Justice Blackmun seemingly rejected this view by ending his dissent with an allusion to John Dunne's statement that "[n]o man is an Island, intire of itselfe. * * *" 405 U.S. at 760 n. 2, 92 S.Ct. at 1378 n. 2, 31 L.Ed.2d at 657 n. 2.) Having expanded the scope of "injury in fact" to include intangible, aesthetic values, is the Court justified in ignoring these broader forms of injury?

3. In addition to the "injury in fact" requirement, the *Data Processing* test includes a "zone of interests" requirement. This requirement is illustrated in *Churchill Truck Lines, Inc. v. United States*, 533 F.2d 411 (8th Cir.1976). *Churchill Truck* involved a challenge by competitors to an ICC order authorizing another carrier to perform certain services. The court held that, because their injury was purely pecuniary, they lacked standing to argue that the ICC action had violated NEPA. We will consider the "zone of interests" requirement in depth in the next subsection.

e. Justice Brennan noted his agreement with this part of Justice Blackmun's opinion.

f. Historical note: In 1978, Congress ended a renewed controversy over develop-

ment by making the Mineral King Valley a part of Sequoia National Park. See 16 U.S.C.A. § 45f.

4. *Problem.* An environmental organization wishing to challenge the construction of a high-voltage power line offers the following evidence on standing: (a) the organization's articles of incorporation mention the affected geographic area as one of its special concerns, and (b) the organization's president testified that she went fishing approximately a half-mile from the proposed line. Is this enough to confer standing upon the organization? See *Save Our Wetlands, Inc. v. Sands,* 711 F.2d 634, 634–40 (5th Cir.1983). You may wish to reconsider your answer after reading *Lujan v. National Wildlife Federation,* infra, p. 88.

UNITED STATES v. STUDENTS CHALLENGING REGULATORY AGENCY PROCEDURES (SCRAP I)

Supreme Court of the United States, 1973.
412 U.S. 669, 93 S.Ct. 2405, 37 L.Ed.2d 254.

JUSTICE STEWART delivered the opinion of the Court.

[The plaintiffs filed suit to challenge the ICC's refusal to suspend a railroad rate increase. The railroads were seeking an across-the-board increase to augment revenue. The plaintiffs contended that the increase would discourage recycling of various goods by magnifying existing distortions in the rate structure.]

The appellants challenge the appellees' standing to sue, arguing that the allegations in the pleadings as to standing were vague, unsubstantiated, and insufficient under our recent decision in *Sierra Club v. Morton,* supra. The appellees respond that unlike the petitioner in *Sierra Club,* their pleadings sufficiently alleged that they were "adversely affected" or "aggrieved" within the meaning of § 10 of the Administrative Procedure Act (APA). They point specifically to the allegations that their members used the forests, streams, mountains, and other resources in the Washington metropolitan area for camping, hiking, fishing, and sightseeing, and that this use was disturbed by the adverse environmental impact caused by the nonuse of recyclable goods brought about by a rate increase on those commodities. The District Court found these allegations sufficient to withstand a motion to dismiss. We agree.

* * *

Unlike the specific and geographically limited federal action of which the petitioner complained in *Sierra Club,* the challenged agency action in this case is applicable to substantially all of the Nation's railroads, and thus allegedly has an adverse environmental impact on all the natural resources of the country. Rather than a limited group of persons who used a picturesque valley in California, all persons who utilize the scenic resources of the country, and indeed all who breathe its air, could claim harm similar to that alleged by the environmental groups here. But we have already made it clear that standing is not to be denied simply because many people suffer the same injury. Indeed some of the cases on which we relied in *Sierra Club* demonstrated the patent fact that persons across the Nation could be adversely affected by major governmental actions. * * * To deny standing to persons who are in fact injured simply because many others are also injured, would mean that the most injurious and widespread Government actions could be questioned by nobody. We cannot accept that conclusion.

But the injury alleged here is also very different from that at issue in *Sierra Club* because here the alleged injury to the environment is far less direct and perceptible. The petitioner there complained about the construction of a specific project that would directly affect the Mineral King Valley. Here, the Court was asked to follow a far more attenuated line of causation to the eventual injury of which the appellees complained—a general rate increase would allegedly cause increased use of nonrecyclable commodities as compared to recyclable goods, thus resulting in the need to use more natural resources to produce such goods, some of which resources might be taken from the Washington area, and resulting in more refuse that might be discarded in national parks in the Washington area. The railroads protest that the appellees could never prove that a general increase in rates would have this effect, and they contend that these allegations were a ploy to avoid the need to show some injury in fact.

Of course, pleadings must be something more than an ingenious academic exercise in the conceivable. A plaintiff must allege that he has been or will in fact be perceptibly harmed by the challenged agency action, not that he can imagine circumstances in which he could be affected by the agency's action. And it is equally clear that the allegations must be true and capable of proof at trial. But we deal here simply with the pleadings in which the appellees alleged a specific and perceptible harm that distinguished them from other citizens who had not used the natural resources that were claimed to be affected.[5] If, as the railroads now assert, these allegations were in fact untrue, then the appellants should have moved for summary judgment on the standing issue and demonstrated to the District Court that the allegations were sham and raised no genuine issue of fact. We cannot say on these pleadings that the appellees could not prove their allegations which, if proved, would place them squarely among those persons injured in fact by the Commission's action, and entitled under the clear import of

5. The Government urges us to limit standing to those who have been "significantly" affected by agency action. But, even if we could begin to define what such a test would mean, we think it fundamentally misconceived. "Injury in fact" reflects the statutory requirement that a person be "adversely affected" or "aggrieved," and it serves to distinguish a person with a direct stake in the outcome of a litigation—even though small—from a person with a mere interest in the problem. We have allowed important interests to be vindicated by plaintiffs with no more at stake in the outcome of an action than a fraction of a vote, a $5 fine and costs, and a $1.50 poll tax.

* * * While these cases were not dealing specifically with § 10 of the APA, we see no reason to adopt a more restrictive interpretation of "adversely affected" or "aggrieved." As Professor Davis has put it: "The basic idea that comes out in numerous cases is that an identifiable trifle is enough for standing to fight out a question of principle; the trifle is the basis for standing and the principle supplies the motivation." Davis, "Standing: Taxpayers and Others," 35 *U.Chi.L.Rev.* 601, 613.

Sierra Club to seek review. The District Court was correct in denying the appellants' motion to dismiss the complaint for failure to allege sufficient standing to bring this lawsuit.

Notes

1. One commentator has suggested that the *SCRAP* Court should have focused more carefully on the nature of the statutory claim before it:

> The issue in *SCRAP* was whether under NEPA an EIS had to be prepared before the rate increase could be implemented. The standing question was whether plaintiffs were entitled to insist that NEPA be followed. * * * A perfectly plausible—and I believe the best—reading of NEPA is that anyone who can make a colorable claim that the proposed actions may possibly affect her should have standing, even if the effect is remote or speculative and even if the person's sense of what constitutes injury is somewhat idiosyncratic. This should be so because of the nature of the remedy plaintiff is seeking. She wishes to compel an investigation and the preparation of a report that spells out in detail what she has claimed will be the likely environmental consequences of the proposed federal action. To require a greater showing by plaintiff of actual effect would be to require, as a condition of bringing suit, that plaintiff show much of what she claims should be investigated.

Fletcher, "The Structure of Standing," 98 *Yale L.J.* 221, 259 (1988). The Supreme Court, however, later referred to *SCRAP* as "[p]robably the most attenuated injury" conferring standing, and added that the SCRAP decision "surely went to the very outer limit of the law." *Whitmore v. Arkansas*, 495 U.S. 149, 159, 110 S.Ct. 1717, 1725, 109 L.Ed.2d 135 (1990).

2. For a survey of standing cases under NEPA, see chapter 4 of D. Mandelker, NEPA Law and Litigation (2d ed. 1994). With a few notable exceptions, courts have usually followed *SCRAP* by requiring plaintiffs to allege some possible injury to their own environment. But, as we will see later, NEPA has been construed as a disclosure statute, requiring the agency to provide information about its decisions rather than providing direct protection for the environment. Since the statute, strictly speaking, creates only a duty to provide information, it would be logical to construe it as conferring a right to that information on members of the public. Should standing be based on the right to obtain information, instead of an interest in the substance of the agency's decision? For an elaboration of this argument, see Comment, "Informational Standing Under NEPA: Justiciability and the Environmental Decisionmaking Process," 93 *Colum.L.Rev.* 996 (1993).

LUJAN v. NATIONAL WILDLIFE FEDERATION

Supreme Court of the United States, 1990.
497 U.S. 871, 110 S.Ct. 3177, 111 L.Ed.2d 695.

[As discussed in Chapter VIII, certain federal lands have been withdrawn from resource development by executive order. In 1976, as part of a comprehensive statute governing the Bureau of Land Management, Congress directed BLM to review existing withdrawals in eleven

respondent = defendant
petitioner = plaintiff

western states. BLM was ordered to decide whether the lands should be reopened for development by being reclassified or placed in the public domain. The plaintiff alleged that BLM violated the required statutory procedures in numerous respects, and that BLM's action would open up the lands involved to mining activities. The complaint alleged that plaintiff's members used the lands involved. The government moved for summary judgment based on plaintiff's lack of standing. To establish standing, plaintiff submitted affidavits by two members, Peterson and Erman. After the district court ruled for the government, plaintiff submitted four additional affidavits. The D.C.Circuit reversed. The issue before the Court was whether plaintiff was entitled to review under the APA.]

JUSTICE SCALIA delivered the opinion of the Court.

We turn * * * to whether the specific facts alleged in the two affidavits considered by the District Court raised a genuine issue of fact as to whether an "agency action" taken by petitioners caused respondent to be "adversely affected or aggrieved * * * within the meaning of a relevant statute." We assume, since it has been uncontested, that the allegedly affected interests set forth in the affidavits—"recreational use and aesthetic enjoyment"—are sufficiently related to the purposes of respondent association that respondent meets the requirements of § 702 if any of its members do.

As for the "agency action" requirement, we think that each of the affidavits can be read, as the Court of Appeals believed, to complain of a particular "agency action" as that term is defined in § 551. The parties agree that the Peterson affidavit, judging from the geographic area it describes, must refer to that one of the BLM orders listed in the appendix to the complaint that appears at 49 Fed.Reg. 19904–19905 (1984), an order captioned W–6228 and dated April 30, 1984, terminating the withdrawal classification of some 4500 acres of land in that area. The parties also appear to agree, on the basis of similar deduction, that the Erman affidavit refers to the BLM order listed in the appendix that appears at 47 Fed.Reg. 7232–7233 (1982), an order captioned Public Land Order 6156 and dated February 18, 1982.

We also think that whatever "adverse effect" or "aggrievement" is established by the affidavits was "within the meaning of the relevant statute"—*i.e.,* met the "zone of interests" test. The relevant statute, of course, is the statute whose violation is the gravamen of the complaint—both the FLPMA and NEPA. We have no doubt that "recreational use and aesthetic enjoyment" are among the *sorts* of interests those statutes were specifically designed to protect. The only issue, then, is whether the facts alleged in the affidavits showed that those interests *of Peterson and Erman* were actually affected.

The Peterson affidavit averred [*declared*]:

My recreational use and aesthetic enjoyment of federal lands, particularly those in the vicinity of South Pass–Green Mountain, Wyoming, have been and continue to be adversely affected in fact by the unlawful actions of the Bureau and the Department. In particular, the South Pass–Green Mountain area of Wyoming has been opened to the staking of mining claims and oil and gas leasing, an action which threatens the aesthetic beauty and wildlife habitat potential of these lands.

Erman's affidavit was substantially the same as Peterson's, with respect to all except the area involved; he claimed use of land "in the vicinity of Grand Canyon National Park, the Arizona Strip (Kanab Plateau), and the Kaibab National Forest."

[The District Court had found the affidavits flawed because they referred to activities "in the vicinity" of the land that was subject to the government action, rather than actually on that land. The Court of Appeals found the affidavits ambiguous and said that any ambiguities should be resolved by assuming the plaintiffs used the affected lands.]

That is not the law. In ruling upon a Rule 56 motion, "a District Court must resolve any factual issues of controversy in favor of the nonmoving party" only in the sense that, where the facts specifically averred by that party contradict facts specifically averred by the movant, the motion must be denied. That is a world apart from "assuming" that general averments embrace the "specific facts" needed to sustain the complaint. * * *

At the margins there is some room for debate as to how "specific" must be the "specific facts" that Rule 56(e) requires in a particular case. But where the fact in question is the one put in issue by the § 702 challenge here—whether one of respondent's members has been, or is threatened to be, "adversely affected or aggrieved" by Government action—Rule 56(e) is assuredly not satisfied by averments which state only that one of respondent's members uses unspecified portions of an immense tract of territory, on some portions of which mining activity has occurred or probably will occur by virtue of the governmental action. It will not do to "presume" the missing facts because without them the affidavits would not establish the injury that they generally allege. That converts the operation of Rule 56 to a circular promenade: plaintiff's complaint makes general allegation of injury; defendant contests through Rule 56 existence of specific facts to support injury; plaintiff responds with affidavit containing general allegation of injury, which must be deemed to constitute averment of requisite specific facts since otherwise allegation of injury would be unsupported (which is precisely what defendant claims it is).

Respondent places great reliance, as did the Court of Appeals, upon our decision in *SCRAP* [supra p. 86]. The *SCRAP* opinion, whose expansive expression of what would suffice for § 702 review under its particular facts has never since been emulated by this Court, is of no relevance here, since it involved not a Rule 56 motion for summary judgment but a Rule 12(b) motion to dismiss on the pleadings. The latter, unlike the former, presumes that general allegations embrace those specific facts that are necessary to support the claim.

We turn next to the Court of Appeals' alternative holding that the four additional member affidavits proffered by respondent in response to the District Court's briefing order established its right to § 702 review of agency action.

It is impossible that the affidavits would suffice, as the Court of Appeals held, to enable respondent to challenge the entirety of petitioners' so-called "land withdrawal review program." That is not an "agency action" within the meaning of § 702, much less a "final agency action" within the meaning of § 704. The term "land withdrawal review program" (which as far as we know is not derived from any authoritative text) does not refer to a single BLM order or regulation, or even to a completed universe of particular BLM orders and regulations. It is simply the name by which petitioners have occasionally referred to the continuing (and thus constantly changing) operations of the BLM in reviewing withdrawal revocation applications and the classifications of public lands and developing land use plans as required by the FLPMA. It is no more an identifiable "agency action"—much less a "final agency action"—than a "weapons procurement program" of the Department of Defense or a "drug interdiction program" of the Drug Enforcement Administration. As the District Court explained, the "land withdrawal review program" extends to, currently at least, "1250 or so individual classification terminations and withdrawal revocations."

Respondent alleges that violation of the law is rampant within this program—failure to revise land use plans in proper fashion, failure to submit certain recommendations to Congress, failure to consider multiple use, inordinate focus upon mineral exploitation, failure to provide required public notice, failure to provide adequate environmental impact statements. Perhaps so. But respondent cannot seek *wholesale* improvement of this program by court decree, rather than in the offices of the Department or the halls of Congress, where programmatic improvements are normally made. Under the terms of the APA, respondent must direct its attack against some particular "agency action" that causes it harm. Some statutes permit broad regulations to serve as the "agency action," and thus to be the object of judicial review directly, even before the concrete effects normally required for APA review are felt. Absent such a provision, however, a regulation is not ordinarily considered the type of agency action "ripe" for judicial review under the APA until the scope of the controversy has been reduced to more manageable proportions, and its factual components fleshed out, by some concrete action applying the regulation to the claimant's situation in a fashion that harms or threatens to harm him. (The major exception, of course, is a substantive rule which as a practical matter requires the plaintiff to adjust his conduct immediately. Such agency action is "ripe" for review at once, whether or not explicit statutory review apart from the APA is provided.)

In the present case, the individual actions of the BLM identified in the six affidavits can be regarded as rules of general applicability (a "rule" is defined in the APA as agency action of "general or particular applicability *and future effect*," 5 U.S.C. § 551(4) (emphasis added)) announcing, with respect to vast expanses of territory that they cover, the agency's intent to grant requisite permission for certain activities, to decline to interfere with other activities, and to take other particular action if requested. It may well be, then, that even those individual actions will not be ripe for challenge until some further agency action or inaction more immediately harming the plaintiff occurs.[6] But it is at least entirely certain that the flaws in the entire "program"—consisting principally of the many individual actions referenced in the complaint, and presumably actions yet to be taken as well—cannot be laid before the courts for wholesale correction under the APA, simply because one of them that is ripe for review adversely affects one of respondent's members.

The case-by-case approach that this requires is understandably frustrating to an organization such as respondent, which has as its objective across-the-board protection of our Nation's wildlife and the streams and forests that support it. But this is the traditional, and remains the normal, mode of operation of the courts. Except where Congress explicitly provides for our correction of the administrative process at a higher level of generality, we intervene in the administration of the laws only when, and to the extent that, a specific "final agency action" has an actual or immediately threatened effect. Such an intervention may ultimately have the effect of requiring a regulation, a series of regulations, or even a whole "program" to be revised by the agency in order to avoid the unlawful result that the court discerns. But it is assuredly not as swift or as immediately far-reaching a corrective process as those interested in systemic improvement would desire. Until confided to us, however, more sweeping actions are for the other Branches.

JUSTICE BLACKMUN, with whom JUSTICE BRENNAN, JUSTICE MARSHALL, and JUSTICE STEVENS join, dissenting. to disagree

In my view, the affidavits of Peggy Kay Peterson and Richard Loren Erman, in conjunction with other record evidence before the District Court on the motions for summary judgment, were sufficient to establish the standing of the National Wildlife Federation (Federation or NWF) to bring this suit. I also conclude that the District Court abused its discretion by refusing to consider supplemental affidavits filed after the

---

6. Contrary to the apparent understanding of the dissent, we do not contend that no "land withdrawal review program" exists, any more than we would contend that no weapons procurement program exists. We merely assert that it is not an identifiable "final agency action" for purposes of the APA. If there is in fact some specific order or regulation, applying some particular measure across-the-board to all individual classification terminations and withdrawal revocations, and if that order or regulation is final, and has become ripe for review in the manner we discuss subsequently in text, it can of course be challenged under the APA by a person adversely affected—and the entire "land withdrawal review program," insofar as the content of that particular action is concerned, would thereby be affected. But that is quite different from permitting a generic challenge to all aspects of the "land withdrawal review program," as though that itself constituted a final agency action.

hearing on the parties' cross-motions for summary judgment. I therefore would affirm the judgment of the Court of Appeals.

* * *

As the Court points out, the showing (whether as to standing or the merits) required to overcome a motion for summary judgment is more extensive than that required in the context of a motion to dismiss. The principal difference is that in the former context *evidence* is required, while in the latter setting the litigant may rest upon the allegations of his complaint. In addition, Rule 56(e) requires that the party opposing summary judgment "must set forth *specific* facts showing that there is a genuine issue for trial" (emphasis added). Thus, Courts of Appeals have reiterated that "conclusory" allegations unsupported by "specific" evidence will be insufficient to establish a genuine issue of fact.

The requirement that evidence be submitted is satisfied here: the Federation has offered the sworn statements of two of its members. There remains the question whether the allegations in these affidavits were sufficiently precise to satisfy the requirements of Rule 56(e). The line of demarcation between "specific" and "conclusory" allegations is hardly a bright one. But, to my mind, the allegations contained in the Peterson and Erman affidavits, in the context of the record as a whole, were adequate to defeat a motion for summary judgment. * * *

No contrary conclusion is compelled by the fact that Peterson alleged that she uses federal lands "in the vicinity of South Pass–Green Mountain, Wyoming," rather than averring that she uses the precise tract that was recently opened to mining. The agency itself has repeatedly referred to the "South Pass–Green Mountain area" in describing the region newly opened to mining. Peterson's assertion that her use and enjoyment of federal lands *have been* adversely affected by the agency's decision to permit more extensive mining is, as the Court of Appeals stated, "meaningless, or perjurious" if the lands she uses do not include those harmed by mining undertaken pursuant to termination order W–6228. To read particular assertions within the affidavit in light of the document as a whole is, as the majority might put it, "a world apart" from "presuming" facts that are neither stated nor implied simply because without them the plaintiff would lack standing. The Peterson and Erman affidavits doubtless could have been more artfully drafted, but they definitely were sufficient to withstand the Government's summary judgment motion.

* * *

* * * The Administrative Procedure Act permits suit to be brought by any person "adversely affected or aggrieved by agency action." 5 U.S.C. § 702. In some cases the "agency action" will consist of a rule of broad applicability; and if the plaintiff prevails, the result is that the rule is invalidated, not simply that the court forbids its application to a particular individual. Under these circumstances a single plaintiff, so long as he is injured by the rule, may obtain "programmatic" relief that affects the rights of parties not before the court. On the other hand, if a generally lawful policy is applied in an illegal manner on a particular occasion, one who is injured is not thereby entitled to challenge other applications of the rule.

Application of these principles to the instant case does not turn on whether, or how often, the Bureau's land-management policies have been described as a "program." In one sense, of course, there is no question that a "program" exists. Everyone associated with this lawsuit recognizes that the BLM, over the past decade, has attempted to develop and implement a comprehensive scheme for the termination of classifications and withdrawals. The real issue is whether the actions and omissions that NWF contends are illegal are themselves part of a plan or policy. For example: if the agency had published a regulation stating that an Environmental Impact Statement should never be developed prior to the termination of a classification or withdrawal, NWF could challenge the regulation (which would constitute an "agency action"). If the reviewing court then held that the statute required a pre-termination EIS, the relief (invalidation of the rule) would directly affect tracts other than the ones used by individual affiants. At the other extreme, if the applicable BLM regulation stated that an EIS *must* be developed, and NWF alleged that the administrator in charge of South Pass/Green Mountain had inexplicably failed to develop one, NWF should not be allowed (on the basis of the Peterson affidavit) to challenge a termination in Florida on the ground that an administrator there made the same mistake.

The majority, quoting the District Court, characterizes the Bureau's land management program as "§ 1250 or so individual classification terminations and withdrawal revocations.'" The majority offers no argument in support of this conclusory assertion, and I am far from certain that the characterization is an accurate one. Since this issue bears on the scope of the relief ultimately to be awarded should the plaintiff prevail, rather than on the jurisdiction of the District Court to entertain the suit, I would allow the District Court to address the question on remand.[16]

Notes

1.   The Court's first holding is that the Peterson and Erman affidavits are inadequate. How serious a problem will this holding pose for environmental groups in the future? To what extent can it be avoided by offering more detailed affidavits?

16.   The majority also suggests that the agency actions challenged in this suit may not be ripe for review. Since the issue of ripeness has not been briefed or argued in this Court, nor passed on by the courts below, I need not address it. I do note, however, that at the outset of this case the Government made precisely the opposite argument, asserting that a preliminary injunction should be denied on the ground that NWF's claims were barred by laches. The Government contended: "[T]he Federation offers no explanation why, despite its detailed knowledge of BLM's revocation and termination activities, it has waited so long to institute litigation."

Some more recent cases have grappled with the question of geographic specificity. In *Resources Limited, Inc. v. Robertson*, 35 F.3d 1300 (9th Cir.1993), an organization challenged a forest management plan. The organization alleged that its members visited the forest on a regular basis and that their enjoyment of the forest would be decreased by adoption of the plan. The government argued that these allegations were inadequate because they failed to specify more precisely the locations within the forest which were used. The court held that it was unnecessary for the organization to "point to the precise area of the park where their injury will occur." Id. at 1303. In *Committee to Save the Rio Hondo v. Lucero*, 102 F.3d 445 (10th Cir.1996), an environmental organization challenged the decision to allow summer use of a ski area in a national forest. Two members of the group lived twelve to fifteen miles downstream and alleged that the decision would affect water quality. Another member alleged that the summertime use of the ski area would "disturb the recreational and aesthetic value of the land in and around the Ski Area because summertime use of the Ski Area increases development and mechanization." The court found these allegations sufficient. Id. at 450.

2. The Court's second holding is that the BLM program cannot be challenged as a whole because it is not an "agency action" under the APA. We will later consider a similar question under NEPA involving when a program constitutes a "proposal" and requires a single environmental impact statement. A closely related issue is that of "ripeness," which holds that a suit is premature because the plaintiff's injury has not yet sufficiently crystalized. A recent illustration is provided by *Ohio Forestry Ass'n v. Sierra Club*, 523 U.S. 726, 118 S.Ct. 1665, 140 L.Ed.2d 921 (1998). The plaintiff filed an action challenge a Forest Service management plan for allowing too much logging and clearcutting in the Wayne National Forest. In an opinion for a unanimous Court, Justice Breyer held the suit to be premature. The issuance of the plan did not impose any legal obligation on anyone or modify anyone's legal rights. Nor, the Court said, did the plan in itself "inflict significant practical harm upon the interests that the Sierra Club advances." Before any logging could take place, additional steps would take place, providing an opportunity to challenge the legality of the plan if that issue was ultimately relevant to the logging decision. "Nor," Justice Breyer added, "has the Sierra Club pointed to any other way in which the Plan could now force it to modify its behavior in order to avoid future adverse consequences, as, for example, agency regulations can sometimes force immediate compliance through fear of future sanctions." Having found no hardship to Sierra Club in delaying review, the Court then turned to three additional factors: (1) immediate judicial review could hinder the agency's ability to refine its policies by revising the plan or through site-specific proposals correcting defects in the plan; (2) immediate review would "require time-consuming judicial consideration of the details of an elaborate, technically based plan," which "would lack the focus that a particular logging proposal could provide"; and (3) Congress had not specifically provided for pre-implementation judicial review of forest plans. Justice Breyer distinguished NEPA claims, which can be brought without waiting for the agency to take any concrete action, because NEPA only guarantees a particular procedure, not a particular result, and the procedural failure "can never get riper."

3. Ripeness standards prevent a plaintiff from bringing suit "too early." The doctrine of laches, which is discussed in footnote 16 of the dissent, may bar the plaintiff from suing "too late." The consequences of laches doctrine are much more severe: the plaintiff can remedy a ripeness problem by waiting, but without the use of a time machine, the plaintiff has no way of curing laches. Courts have been reluctant to apply laches in environmental litigation, on the ground that the public's interest in enforcing environmental statutes should not be sacrificed because a plaintiff has been dilatory. For a rare exception, see *Apache Survival Coalition v. United States,* 21 F.3d 895 (9th Cir.1994).

4. Justice Scalia seems particularly skeptical of the idea of basing standing on procedural injury. Consider the following criticism of his view:

> Justice Scalia's position ignores the value of the basic principles of informal rulemaking and judicial review under the APA. He seeks to rule out just the sort of judicial review that the courts are best able to perform without taking on a policymaking role. Under the APA the ultimate policymaking decision is in the hands of the bureaucracy, but administrative discretion is constrained by the need for public notice, a hearing, and a statement of reasons. Thus, the process is open to opinions and information from outside groups, but it is not under the control of these groups. * * * To follow Justice Scalia's line would be to overlook the important role courts have to play in ensuring the democratic legitimacy of bureaucratic procedures under the American separation-of-powers doctrine.

Rose–Ackerman, "American Administrative Law Under Siege: Is Germany a Model?," 107 *Harv.L.Rev.* 1279, 1287 (1994).

LUJAN v. DEFENDERS OF WILDLIFE

Supreme Court of the United States, 1992.
504 U.S. 555, 112 S.Ct. 2130, 119 L.Ed.2d 351.

JUSTICE SCALIA delivered the opinion of the Court with respect to Parts I, II, III–A, and IV, and an opinion with respect to Part III–B in which THE CHIEF JUSTICE, JUSTICE WHITE, and JUSTICE THOMAS join.

[As discussed in Chapter VIII, the Endangered Species Act seeks to protect species of animals and plants against threats to their continuing existence caused by humans. Endangered or threatened species are identified by a periodic list compiled by the Secretary of the Interior. Section 7(a)(2) of the Act provides that each federal agency must, in consultation with the Secretary of Interior, ensure that "any action authorized, funded, or carried out by such agency * * * is not likely to jeopardize the continued existence of any endangered species or threatened species or result in the destruction or adverse modification of the habitat of such species." The Secretary by regulation determined that § 7 applies only to species and habitats within the United States or on the High Seas. The statute authorizes "citizen suits" to halt violations of the Act. The plaintiffs obtained an injunction requiring the Secretary to promulgate a revised regulation applying § 7 extraterritorially.]

II

While the Constitution of the United States divides all power conferred upon the Federal Government into "legislative Powers," Art. I, § 1, "[t]he executive Power," Art. II, § 1, and "[t]he judicial Power," Art. III, § 1, it does not attempt to define those terms. To be sure, it limits the jurisdiction of federal courts to "Cases" and "Controversies," but an executive inquiry can bear the name "case" (the Hoffa case) and a legislative dispute can bear the name "controversy" (the Smoot–Hawley controversy). Obviously, then, the Constitution's central mechanism of separation of powers depends largely upon common understanding of what activities are appropriate to legislatures, to executives, and to courts. In The Federalist No. 48, Madison expressed the view that "[i]t is not infrequently a question of real nicety in legislative bodies whether the operation of a particular measure will, or will not, extend beyond the legislative sphere," whereas "the executive power [is] restrained within a narrower compass and * * * more simple in its nature," and "the judiciary [is] described by landmarks still less uncertain." One of those landmarks, setting apart the "Cases" and "Controversies" that are of the justiciable sort referred to in Article III C "serv[ing] to identify those disputes which are appropriately resolved through the judicial process"—is the doctrine of standing. Though some of its elements express merely prudential considerations that are part of judicial self-government, the core component of standing is an essential and unchanging part of the case-or-controversy requirement of Article III.

Over the years, our cases have established that the irreducible constitutional minimum of standing contains three elements: First, the plaintiff must have suffered an "injury in fact"—an invasion of a legally-protected interest which is (a) concrete and particularized, and (b) "actual or imminent, not 'conjectural' or 'hypothetical.'" Second, there must be a causal connection between the injury and the conduct complained of—the injury has to be "fairly * * * trace[able] to the challenged action of the defendant, and not * * * th[e] result [of] the independent action of some third party not before the court." Third, it must be "likely," as opposed to merely "speculative," that the injury will be "redressed by a favorable decision."

III

We think the Court of Appeals failed to apply the foregoing principles in denying the Secretary's motion for summary judgment. Respondents had not made the requisite demonstration of (at least) injury and redressability.

A

Respondents' claim to injury is that the lack of consultation with respect to certain funded activities abroad "increase[s] the rate of extinction of endangered and threatened species." * * * To survive the Secretary's summary judgment motion, respondents had to submit affidavits or other evidence showing, through specific facts, not only that listed species were in fact being threatened by funded activities abroad, but also that one or more of respondents' members would thereby be "directly" affected apart from their " 'special interest' in th[e] subject."

[The affidavits] alleged that two members, Kelly and Skilbred, had visited two project areas in the past and intended to return in the future to observe endangered species.

[The affidavits] plainly contain no facts * * * showing how damage to the species will produce "imminent" injury to Mss. Kelly and Skilbred. That the women "had visited" the areas of the projects before the projects commenced proves nothing. As we have said in a related context, " '[p]ast exposure to illegal conduct does not in itself show a present case or controversy regarding injunctive relief * * * if unaccompanied by any continuing, present adverse effects.' " And the affiants' profession of an "inten[t]" to return to the places they had visited before—where they will presumably, this time, be deprived of the opportunity to observe animals of the endangered species—is simply not enough. * * *

Besides relying upon the Kelly and Skilbred affidavits, respondents propose a series of novel standing theories. The first, inelegantly styled "ecosystem nexus," proposes that any person who uses *any part* of a "contiguous ecosystem" adversely affected by a funded activity has standing even if the activity is located a great distance away. This approach, as the Court of Appeals correctly observed, is inconsistent with our opinion in *National Wildlife Federation,* which held that a plaintiff claiming injury from environmental damage must use the area affected by the challenged activity and not an area roughly "in the vicinity" of it. It makes no difference that the general-purpose section of the ESA states that the Act was intended in part "to provide a means whereby the ecosystems upon which endangered species and threatened species depend may be conserved." To say that the Act protects ecosystems is not to say that the Act creates (if it were possible) rights of action in persons who have not been injured in fact, that is, persons who use portions of an ecosystem not perceptibly affected by the unlawful action in question.

Respondents' other theories are called, alas, the "animal nexus" approach, whereby anyone who has an interest in studying or seeing the endangered animals anywhere on the globe has standing; and the "vocational nexus" approach, under which anyone with a professional interest in such animals can sue. Under these theories, anyone who goes to see Asian elephants in the Bronx Zoo, and anyone who is a keeper of Asian elephants in the Bronx Zoo, has standing to sue because the Director of AID did not consult with the Secretary regarding the AID-funded project in Sri Lanka. This is beyond all reason. Standing is not "an ingenious academic exercise in the conceivable," but as we have said, requires, at the summary judgment stage, a factual showing of perceptible harm. It is clear that the person who observes or works with a particular animal threatened by a federal decision is facing perceptible harm, since the very subject of his interest will no longer exist. It is even plausible—though it goes to the outermost limit of plausibility—to think that a person who observes or works with animals of a particular species in the very area of the world where that species is threatened by a federal decision is facing such harm, since some animals that might have been the subject of his interest will no longer exist. It goes beyond the limit, however, and into pure speculation and fantasy, to say that anyone who observes or works with an endangered species, anywhere in the world, is appreciably harmed by a single project affecting some portion of that species with which he has no more specific connection.

B

The most obvious problem in the present case is redressability. Since the agencies funding the projects were not parties to the case, the District Court could accord relief only against the Secretary: He could be ordered to revise his regulation to require consultation for foreign projects. But this would not remedy respondents' alleged injury unless the funding agencies were bound by the Secretary's regulation, which is very much an open question. [Although the Secretary of Interior thought his regulation binding upon other federal agencies, the Solicitor General opined that it was not, and the other agencies agreed with him. Since these other agencies were not parties to the lawsuit, no relief could be entered against them, according to Justice Scalia.]

IV

The Court of Appeals found that respondents had standing for an additional reason: because they had suffered a "procedural injury." The so-called "citizen-suit" provision of the ESA provides, in pertinent part, that "any person may commence a civil suit on his own behalf (A) to enjoin any person, including the United States and any other governmental instrumentality or agency * * * who is alleged to be in violation of any provision of this chapter." The court held that, because § 7(a)(2) requires interagency consultation, the citizen-suit provision creates a "procedural righ[t]" to consultation in all "persons"—so that *anyone* can file suit in federal court to challenge the Secretary's (or presumably any other official's) failure to follow the assertedly correct consultative procedure, notwithstanding their inability to allege any discrete injury flowing from that failure. To understand the remarkable nature of this holding one must be clear about what it does *not* rest upon: This is not a case where plaintiffs are seeking to enforce a procedural requirement the disregard of which could impair a separate concrete interest of theirs (*e.g.*, the procedural requirement for a hearing prior to denial of their license application, or the procedural requirement for an environmental impact statement before a federal facility is constructed next door to them). Nor is it simply a case where concrete injury has been suffered by many persons, as in mass fraud or mass tort situations. Nor, finally, is it the unusual case in which Congress has created a concrete private interest in the outcome of a suit against a private party for the government's benefit, by providing a cash bounty for the victorious plaintiff.

Rather, the court held that the injury-in-fact requirement had been satisfied by congressional conferral upon *all* persons of an abstract, self-contained, noninstrumental "right" to have the Executive observe the procedures required by law. We reject this view.

* * * "The province of the court," as Chief Justice Marshall said in *Marbury v. Madison*, "is, solely, to decide on the rights of individuals." Vindicating the *public* interest (including the public interest in government observance of the Constitution and laws) is the function of Congress and the Chief Executive. The question presented here is whether the public interest in proper administration of the laws (specifically, in agencies' observance of a particular, statutorily prescribed procedure) can be converted into an individual right by a statute that denominates it as such, and that permits all citizens (or, for that matter, a subclass of citizens who suffer no distinctive concrete harm) to sue. If the concrete injury requirement has the separation-of-powers significance we have always said, the answer must be obvious: To permit Congress to convert the undifferentiated public interest in executive officers' compliance with the law into an "individual right" vindicable in the courts is to permit Congress to transfer from the President to the courts the Chief Executive's most important constitutional duty, to "take Care that the Laws be faithfully executed," Art. II, § 3. It would enable the courts, with the permission of Congress, "to assume a position of authority over the governmental acts of another and co-equal department," and to become " 'virtually continuing monitors of the wisdom and soundness of Executive action.' " We have always rejected that vision of our role.

JUSTICE KENNEDY, with whom JUSTICE SOUTER joins, concurring in part and concurring in the judgment.

[I] join Part IV of the Court's opinion with the following observations. As government programs and policies become more complex and far-reaching, we must be sensitive to the articulation of new rights of action that do not have clear analogs in our common-law tradition. Modern litigation has progressed far from the paradigm of Marbury suing Madison to get his commission, or Ogden seeking an injunction to halt Gibbons' steamboat operations. *Gibbons v. Ogden*, 9 Wheat. 1 (1824). In my view, Congress has the power to define injuries and articulate chains of causation that will give rise to a case or controversy where none existed before, and I do not read the Court's opinion to suggest a contrary view. In exercising this power, however, Congress must at the very least identify the injury it seeks to vindicate and relate the injury to the class of persons entitled to bring suit. The citizen-suit provision of the Endangered Species Act does not meet these minimal requirements, because while the statute purports to confer a right on "any person * * * to enjoin * * * the United States and any other governmental instrumentality or agency * * * who is alleged to be in violation of any provision of this chapter," it does not of its own force establish that there is an injury in "any person" by virtue of any "violation."

[JUSTICE STEVENS concurred in the judgment; he rejected the plurality opinion's analysis of standing but found the Secretary's regulation a correct interpretation of the statute and so concurred in the reversal of the lower courts' orders. JUSTICE BLACKMUN, joined by JUSTICE O'CONNOR, dissented from the Court's holding that there was no standing.]

Note on Defenders and the Concept of Injury

How far does *Defenders* go in restricting standing? Consider *NRDC v. Watkins,* 954 F.2d 974 (4th Cir.1992), in which the plaintiff organization sought to block reopening of a nuclear reactor until the building of a cooling tower. Affidavits filed by two of the plaintiff's members alleged that they had formerly used the section of the river in question, had not done so for at least three years, but would do so again if the river were not so polluted. According to the court, these allegations were sufficient to create standing, even though there were probably other major sources of pollution that would prevent the river from being used by the plaintiffs anyway. In a Clean Water Act citizen's suit, the court said, the plaintiffs need not show that the defendant's actions were the but-for cause of the poor water quality, but only that the defendant's actions *contributed* to the pollution. Is *Watkins* still good law after *Defenders?* Can plaintiffs avoid *Defenders* by careful drafting of the affidavits? See James McElfish, "Drafting Standing Affidavits after Defenders: In the Court's Own Words," 23 *Env.L.Rep.* 10026 (1993). Several more recent cases have confronted the causation issue.

In *NRDC v. Texaco Refining & Marketing Co.,* 2 F.3d 493 (3d Cir.1993), the court considered the scope of the "fairly traceable" requirement after *Defenders.* In a Clean Water Act citizen suit, the NRDC alleged that a Texaco refinery had violated its permit restrictions. According to the court, NRDC was required to show only that Texaco had violated its permit with respect to some pollutant, that the pollutant "may" adversely affect a waterway in which plaintiffs have an interest, and that this pollution "contributes to the kinds of injuries alleged by the plaintiffs." The plaintiffs testified that they disliked the sight and smell of pollution in the vicinity of the refinery, that they didn't eat local fish because of concern about toxic chemicals, and that the river had an oily sheen in some places. An expert witness testified that the kinds of pollutants discharged by Texaco can cause these types of ill effects. He did not testify, however, that the specific oil compounds causing slicks were compounds found in Texaco's discharges. The court held that further specificity was unnecessary, and that NRDC had made an adequate showing that their injuries were fairly traceable to Texaco's permit violations. Would Justice Scalia agree? Would Justices Kennedy and Souter (the "swing voters" in *Defenders*)?

In *Friends of the Earth, Inc. v. Crown Central Petroleum Corp.,* 95 F.3d 358 (5th Cir.1996), the court denied standing to plaintiffs who birdwatched and fished at a lake eighteen miles (and three tributaries) away from the pollution source. The plaintiffs offered no evidence that the pollution actually made its way to the lake or otherwise affected the lake:

> When asked whether they know that [the discharges] ended up in Lake Palestine, the members replied they did not know but assumed it to be the case because "that's the way water runs." In short, FOE and its

members relied solely on the truism that water flows downstream and inferred therefrom that any injury suffered downstream is "fairly traceable" to unlawful discharges upstream. At some point this common sense observations becomes little more than surmise. At that point certainly the requirements of Article III are not met.

Id. at 361. Although there was no evidence in the record that the pollutants evaporate, dilute, or sink to the bottom before reaching the lake, the court held that the burden of proof was on the plaintiffs to establish standing, and this burden was not met "by pointing to the absence of evidence showing that it lacks standing."

The court apparently did not intend the ruling as a major restriction on standing in pollution cases:

> We emphasize the narrow scope of our holding. We do not impose a mileage or tributary limit for plaintiffs proceeding under the citizen suit provision of the CWA. To the contrary, plaintiffs who use "waterways" far downstream from the source of unlawful pollution may satisfy the "fairly traceable" element by relying on alternative types of evidence. For example, plaintiffs may produce water samples showing the presence of a pollutant of the type discharged by the defendant upstream or rely on expert testimony suggesting that pollution upstream contributes to a perceivable effect in the water that the plaintiffs use. At some point, however, we can no longer assume that an injury is fairly traceable to a defendant's conduct solely on the basis of the observation that water runs downstream. Under such circumstances, a plaintiff must produce some proof; here, that proof was lacking.

Id. at 362.

Satisfying the "fairly traceable" requirement may be more difficult when the causation is behavioral rather than physical. In *Florida Audubon Society v. Bentsen*, 94 F.3d 658 (D.C.Cir.1996)(en banc), the plaintiffs claimed that an environmental impact statement was required on the effects of a tax credit for a fuel additive. The plaintiffs alleged that the tax credit would increase corn and sugar production, resulting in increased agricultural cultivation and accompanying environmental harms in regions that border wildlife areas used by the plaintiffs. The court found this line of reasoning far too speculative.

One might question what constitutional values are advanced by denying Congress a free hand in creating citizen standing. Justice Scalia's answer would seem to be that, if the plaintiff has suffered no concrete injury, the suit merely operates to force administrators to obey the law, and that the "take care" clause vests this responsibility in the President rather than the courts. Hence, allowing the citizen suit essentially violates the "take care" clause. This is a highly novel interpretation of the "take care" clause. For a critique of Justice Scalia's argument, and an attack on the idea that Article III requires injury-in-fact, see Sunstein, "What's Standing After Lujan? Of Citizens Suits, 'Injuries,' and Article III," 91 *Mich.L.Rev.* 163 (1992). For further discussion of Sunstein's critique, see Krent & Shenkman, "Of Citizens Suits and Citizen Sunstein," 91 *Mich.L.Rev.* 1793 (1993); Sunstein, "Article II Revisionism," 92 *Mich.L.Rev.* 131 (1993).

Defenders seems to apply the injury-in-fact test fairly aggressively, but is at least on solid precedential ground in insisting that some such injury be shown. The problem here is that the traditional function of law suits—that of vindicating private rights—is really not central to the modern function of judicial review, which operates more to uphold the public interest than to protect private rights. This mismatch between current function and traditional model clearly creates some intellectual tensions, which Justice Scalia seeks to resolve by endorsing the traditional model and branding the current function as illegitimate. Yet, unless the traditional model is applied very restrictively indeed, overturning *Sierra Club* and related cases, it may be impossible for the Court to return judicial review to its older function. At least Justices Kennedy and Souter, who held the balance of power in *Defenders,* seem averse to such a radical change in standing law.

Judge Patricia Wald of the D.C. Circuit has questioned whether the increasingly baroque law of standing has become dysfunctional. In *Humane Soc. of United States v. Babbitt,* 46 F.3d 93 (1995), for example, the court rejected an effort by the Humane Society to prevent the transfer of Lota, an Asian elephant, from the Milwaukee Zoo. The transfer allegedly violated the Endangered Species Act. The court held that no one had standing to raise the question—not zoo visitors who claimed emotional harm, nor a visitor who wanted to learn about endangered elephants (there were others at the zoo), nor those who wanted to see her in a conservation setting (not precisely enough defined). And besides, the court said, the government certificate only covered the transfer to the ultimate destination (an exhibition farm) rather than the departure from the Milwaukee Zoo (though it seems unlikely that the elephant would have left the zoo without any permission for a final destination). Hence, the Court said, the elephant's departure from the zoo was not "fairly traceable" to the government certificate for the transfer to the farm. Judge Wald is skeptical of the usefulness of this analysis:

> I ask you: Is this work for sophisticated adult jurists? There was a real dispute here, whether Lota's transfer to the animal exhibition in Illinois was in violation of the Endangered Species Act; and who was more qualified to raise it than those whose concern about animal welfare had caused them to join a professional organization dedicated to that cause, including members who had personally viewed and visited Lota, and yes, by golly, missed her and worried about her survival in her new environment? The descent in Talmudic refinements about whether one must be a student of the animal in that particular environment to bring suit, and whether the disputed permit covered the transport away from the zoo as well as to the animal exhibition would strike an ordinary person as the essence of caprice. More than most subjects of lawsuits, the use of our natural resources is a communitarian matter. Why then must a genuine dispute over an acknowledged injury to the environment stemming from a violation of law be judgeable only when one individual can show a minutely particularized use of the resource that is threatened, down to the last square inch of hiked soil, or the date of the next planned visit to the zoo? I believe it is truly time to reconceptualize environmental standing. Whether our substantive environmental law changes or remains the same, surely the incorporation into our law of more realistic notions of which affected persons or

communities have the right to protest environmental violations is subject to rethinking. But in the meantime, as practical men and women of the law, I can only tell you to consult your zoology manual for details of the specialty fields of your putative plaintiffs and have them make their appointments well ahead of time at the local zoo. "Gotcha" is still the name of the standing game.

Patricia Wald, "Environmental Postcards from the Edge: The Year That Was and the Year That Might Be," 26 *Env. L. Rep.* 10182 (1996).

Defenders may create an imbalance in administrative law. The regulated parties will always have standing to protest overregulation, since they are the direct targets of the regulation. But the intended beneficiaries of regulation will sometimes have standing and sometimes be denied standing. As a result, agencies will face more of a litigation threat if they overregulate than if they underregulate. This conclusion may not concern Justice Scalia, but it does highlight the tension between *Defenders* and the modern role of judicial review as a guarantee of administrative fidelity to the legislative mandate.

Although *Defenders* is in part a technical ruling on standing law, it also reflects broader conceptual issues. The heart of the decision is the Court's conception of what kind of connection with an environmental problem is necessary to support a claim of legitimate harm. Economists distinguish between "use" and "non-use" values. Non-use values include the amount that people would be willing to pay for the option of using a resource in the future and the amount they would be willing to pay simply to ensure the existence of an animal or area even if they never plan to use it at all. A technique called "contingent valuation," which is discussed in Chapter 7, is used to attach monetary amounts to these non-use values, and this technique has been used for a variety of purposes including tort awards for damages to natural resources. But in *Defenders*, the Court seems to consider these values insufficient to attain constitutional recognition as "injury in fact." For further discussion of the general problem of identifying legitimate interests in geographically remote environmental events, see Daniel Farber, "Stretching the Margins: The Geographic Nexus in Environmental Law," 48 *Stan. L. Rev.* 1247 (1996).

Suppose that the plaintiff has indeed suffered an injury in fact, but one that a Court is powerless to remedy. Is there standing? Consider the following case:

STEEL CO. v. CITIZENS FOR A BETTER ENVIRONMENT

Supreme Court of the United States, 1998.
523 U.S. 83, 118 S.Ct. 1003, 140 L.Ed.2d 210.

[An environmental group brought suit against a steel manufacturer under the Emergency Planning and Community Right-to-Know Act (EPCRA) by failing to file timely reports about toxic-chemicals. By the time the suit was filed, however, the company had brought all of its reports up to date. The complaint requested a declaratory judgment, authorization to inspect the company's facilities and records, copies of the company's future compliance reports, civil penalties to be paid to the government, reimbursement of litigation costs, including attorney's fees, and a blanket plea for any other appropriate relief.]

JUSTICE SCALIA delivered the opinion of the Court.

[After reviewing the facts, the Court first determined after a lengthy discussion that it was required to consider the issue of standing before turning to the statutory issue of whether EPCRA allowed citizen suits for wholly past violations. It then turned to the issue of standing.]

Having reached the end of what seems like a long front walk, we finally arrive at the threshold jurisdictional question: whether respondent, the plaintiff below, has standing to sue. Article III, § 2 of the Constitution extends the "judicial Power" of the United States only to "Cases" and "Controversies." We have always taken this to mean cases and controversies of the sort traditionally amenable to and resolved by the judicial process. Such a meaning is fairly implied by the text, since otherwise the purported restriction upon the judicial power would scarcely be a restriction at all. Every criminal investigation conducted by the Executive is a "case," and every policy issue resolved by congressional legislation involves a "controversy." These are not, however, the sort of cases and controversies that Article III, § 2, refers to, since "the Constitution's central mechanism of separation of powers depends largely upon common understanding of what activities are appropriate to legislatures, to executives, and to courts." Standing to sue is part of the common understanding of what it takes to make a justiciable case. The "irreducible constitutional minimum of standing" contains three requirements. First and foremost, there must be alleged (and ultimately proven) an "injury in fact"—a harm suffered by the plaintiff that is "concrete" and "actual or imminent, not 'conjectural' or 'hypothetical.'" Second, there must be causation—a fairly traceable connection between the plaintiff's injury and the complained-of conduct of the defendant. And third, there must be redressability—a likelihood that the requested relief will redress the alleged injury. This triad of injury in fact, causation, and redressability comprises the core of Article III's case-or-controversy requirement, and the party invoking federal jurisdiction bears the burden of establishing its existence.

We turn now to the particulars of respondent's complaint to see how it measures up to Article III's requirements. This case is on appeal from a Rule 12(b) motion to dismiss on the pleadings, so we must presume that the general allegations in the complaint encompass the specific facts necessary to support those allegations.* * * [R]espondent asserts petitioner's failure to provide EPCRA information in a timely fashion, and the lingering effects of that failure, as the injury in fact to itself and its members. We have not had occasion to decide whether being deprived of information that is supposed to be disclosed under EPCRA—or at least being deprived of it when one has a particular plan for its use—is a concrete injury in fact that satisfies Article III. And we need not reach that question in the present case because, assuming injury in fact, the complaint fails the third test of standing, redressability.

The complaint asks for (1) a declaratory judgment that petitioner violated EPCRA; (2) authorization to inspect periodically petitioner's facility and records (with costs borne by petitioner); (3) an order requiring petitioner to provide respondent copies of all compliance reports submitted to the EPA; (4) an order requiring petitioner to pay civil penalties of $25,000 per day for each violation of §§ 11022 and 11023; (5) an award of all respondent's "costs, in connection with the investigation and prosecution of this matter, including reasonable attorney and expert witness fees, as authorized by Section 326(f) of [EPCRA]"; and (6) any such further relief as the court deems appropriate. None of the specific items of relief sought, and none that we can envision as "appropriate" under the general request, would serve to reimburse respondent for losses caused by the late reporting, or to eliminate any effects of that late reporting upon respondent.

The first item, the request for a declaratory judgment that petitioner violated EPCRA, can be disposed of summarily. There being no controversy over whether petitioner failed to file reports, or over whether such a failure constitutes a violation, the declaratory judgment is not only worthless to respondent, it is seemingly worthless to all the world.

Item (4), the civil penalties authorized by the statute, see § 11045(c), might be viewed as a sort of compensation or redress to respondent if they were payable to respondent. But they are not. These penalties-the only damages authorized by EPCRA—are payable to the United States Treasury. In requesting them, therefore, respondent seeks not remediation of its own injury—reimbursement for the costs it incurred as a result of the late filing—but vindication of the rule of law—the "undifferentiated public interest" in faithful execution of EPCRA. This does not suffice. JUSTICE STEVENS thinks it is enough that respondent will be gratified by seeing petitioner punished for its infractions and that the punishment will deter the risk of future harm. * * * But although a suitor may derive great comfort and joy from the fact that the United States Treasury is not cheated, that a wrongdoer gets his just deserts, or that the nation's laws are faithfully enforced, that psychic satisfaction is not an acceptable Article III remedy because it does not redress a cognizable Article III injury. Relief that does not remedy the injury suffered cannot bootstrap a plaintiff into federal court; that is the very essence of the redressability requirement.

Item (5), the "investigation and prosecution" costs "as authorized by Section 326(f)," would assuredly benefit respondent as opposed to the citizenry at large. Obviously, however, a plaintiff cannot achieve standing to litigate a substantive issue by bringing suit for the cost of bringing suit. The litigation must give the plaintiff some other benefit besides reimbursement of costs that are a byproduct of the litigation itself. An "interest in attorney's fees is * * * insufficient to create an Article III case or controversy where none exists on the merits of the underlying claim." Respondent asserts that the "investigation costs" it seeks were incurred prior to the litigation, in digging up the emissions and storage information that petitioner should have filed, and that respondent needed for its own purposes. The recovery of such expenses unrelated to litigation would assuredly support Article III standing, but the problem is that § 326(f), which is the entitlement to monetary relief that the complaint invokes, covers only the "costs of litigation." Respondent finds itself, in other words, impaled upon the horns of a dilemma: for the expenses to be reimbursable under the statute, they must be costs of litigation; but reimbursement of the costs of litigation cannot alone support standing.

The remaining relief respondent seeks (item (2), giving respondent authority to inspect petitioner's facility and records, and item (3), compelling petitioner to provide respondent copies of EPA compliance reports) is injunctive in nature. It cannot conceivably remedy any past wrong but is aimed at deterring petitioner from violating EPCRA in the future. The latter objective can of course be "remedial" for Article III purposes, when threatened injury is one of the gravamens of the complaint. If respondent had alleged a continuing violation or the imminence of a future violation, the injunctive relief requested would remedy that alleged harm. But there is no such allegation here—and on the facts of the case, there seems no basis for it. Nothing supports the requested injunctive relief except respondent's generalized interest in deterrence, which is insufficient for purposes of Article III.

The United States, as <u>amicus curiae</u>, argues that the injunctive relief does constitute remediation because "there is a presumption of [future] injury when the defendant has voluntarily ceased its illegal activity in response to litigation," even if that occurs before a complaint is filed. This makes a sword out of a shield. The "presumption" the Government refers to has been applied to refute the assertion of mootness by a defendant who, when sued in a complaint that alleges present or threatened injury, ceases the complained-of activity. It is an immense and unacceptable stretch to call the presumption into service as a substitute for the allegation of present or threatened injury upon which initial standing must be based. To accept the Government's view would be to overrule our clear precedent requiring that the allegations of future injury be particular and concrete. "Past exposure to illegal conduct does not in itself show a present case or controversy regarding injunctive relief * * * if unaccompanied by any continuing, present adverse effects." Because respondent alleges only past infractions of EPRCA, and not a continuing violation or the likelihood of a future violation, injunctive relief will not redress its injury.

* * *

Having found that none of the relief sought by respondent would likely remedy its alleged injury in fact, we must conclude that respondent lacks standing to maintain this suit, and that we and the lower courts lack jurisdiction to entertain it.

JUSTICE STEVENS [joined in part by JUSTICE SOUTER and by JUSTICE GINSBURG] concurring in the judgment.

[Justice Stevens initially argued that the Court should dispose of the case on the ground that the statute did not provide a cause of action for past violations. He then turned to the standing question.]

[T]he Court fails to specify why payment to respondent—even if only a peppercorn—would redress respondent's injuries, while payment to the Treasury does not. Respondent clearly believes that the punishment of the Steel Company, along with future deterrence of the Steel Company and others, redresses its injury, and there is no basis in our previous standing holdings to suggest otherwise.

When one private party is injured by another, the injury can be redressed in at least two ways: by awarding compensatory damages or by imposing a sanction on the wrongdoer that will minimize the risk that the harm-causing conduct will be repeated. Thus, in some cases a tort is redressed by an award of punitive damages; even when such damages are payable to the sovereign, they provide a form of redress for the individual as well.

History supports the proposition that punishment or deterrence can redress an injury. In past centuries in England, in the American colonies, and in the United States, private persons regularly prosecuted criminal cases. The interest in punishing the defendant and deterring violations of law by the defendant and others was sufficient to support the "standing" of the private prosecutor even if the only remedy was the sentencing of the defendant to jail or to the gallows. Given this history, the Framers of Article III surely would have considered such proceedings to be "Cases" that would "redress" an injury even though the party bringing suit did not receive any monetary compensation.

The Court's expanded interpretation of the redressability requirement has another consequence. Under EPCRA, Congress gave enforcement power to state and local governments. 42 U.S.C. § 11046(a)(2). Under the Court's reasoning, however, state and local governments would not have standing to sue for past violations, as a payment to the Treasury would no more "redress" the injury of these governments than it would redress respondent's injury. This would be true even if Congress explicitly granted state and local governments this power. Such a conclusion is unprecedented.

Notes

1. Although the majority opinion was written by Justice Scalia, one of the Court's leading advocates of relying on the original understanding of the Constitution, the majority did not respond to Justice Stevens' historical evidence, perhaps viewing the issue as settled by precedent.

Is Justice Stevens correct that the implication of *Steel Co.* is to foreclose suits by state and local governments to enforce federal statutes? Might one argue that the state has a quasi-sovereign interest in law enforcement (even as to federal laws) that a private party lacks?

2. If we conceive of standing as relating to each remedy sought by the plaintiff, then *Steel Co.* casts some doubt about the constitutionality of

statutes authorizing the collection of civil penalties in citizen suits. (After all, if the civil penalties don't redress the plaintiff's injury, one might wonder how the plaintiff has standing to seek the penalties at all even if the plaintiff does have standing to obtain other remedies.) But it probably makes more sense to think of all three parts of the standing inquiry as relating to a single inquiry: does the "harm" alleged by the plaintiff qualify under Article III by (1) falling into the category of "injury in fact", (2) stemming from the defendant's conduct, and (3) providing a basis for some possible remedy? (In fact, we could incorporate ripeness and mootness into the inquiry by asking whether the "harm" has crystalized sufficiently or has evaporated by the time of the suit.) On this "harm" based analysis of standing, *Steel Co.* does not pose any threat to statutes authorizing citizen suits to collect penalties. Once we find that the plaintiff's harm qualifies, we have crossed the standing threshold for Article III purposes, so we need not reapply the "redress" test to each remedy sought by the plaintiff so long as the law entitles the plaintiff to that remedy. (Thus, for example, if a state tort law entitled the plaintiff not only to damages but an apology, a federal court in a diversity case could also mandate the apology, even though the plaintiff's interest in obtaining an apology might not be enough to create Article III standing by itself.) Often, of course, substantive rules of law will require the remedy to redress the plaintiff's injury, with varying degrees of specificity, but these substantive rules of law can be changed by Congress (unlike Article III).

2. ZONE OF INTERESTS

In this section, we consider another issue about standing. We can imagine a plaintiff who has an injury in fact, clearly caused by the defendant's illegal conduct, and redressable by the court–yet the injury might be only coincidentally related to the reasons why the conduct is illegal. For instance, suppose the suit in *Sierra Club v. Morton* had been brought by a nearby ski resort, which wanted to keep Mineral King from being developed because the new resort would reduce its business. While satisfying the requirements of injury-in-fact (dollars out of pocket), causation (easily proved with expert witnesses), and redressability (no new resort, no competitive injury), still there seems to be something fishy about this law suit. After all, the environmental statutes aren't designed to protect competitors; they're designed to protect the environment. Is such a "coincidental" connection between the plaintiff's harm and a law designed for entirely different purposes enough to create standing?

DUKE POWER CO. v. CAROLINA ENVIRONMENTAL STUDY GROUP, INC.

Supreme Court of the United States, 1978.
438 U.S. 59, 98 S.Ct. 2620, 57 L.Ed.2d 595.

CHIEF JUSTICE BURGER delivered the opinion of the Court.

[Plaintiffs challenged the constitutionality of the Price–Anderson Act, 42 U.S.C.A. § 2210. The Act included a $560 million limit on the total liability of the nuclear industry for damages resulting from a single nuclear accident.[g] The plaintiffs contended that without this protection, reactors would not be built, and that this in turn would spare them immediate environmental injuries. The district court held the Act unconstitutional. The Supreme Court began by raising *sua sponte* the issue of subject-matter jurisdiction. Over a strong dissent from Justice Rehnquist, it held that jurisdiction existed. It then turned to the issues of standing and ripeness. The Court based its conclusion on the trial judge's factual conclusions following four days of hearings on these issues.]

A

We turn first to consider the kinds of injuries the District Court found the appellees suffered. It discerned two categories of effects which resulted from the operation of nuclear power plants in potentially dangerous proximity to appellees' living and working environment. The immediate effects included: (a) the production of small quantities of non-natural radiation which would invade the air and water; (b) a "sharp increase" in the temperature of two lakes presently used for recreational purposes resulting from the use of the lake waters to produce steam and to cool the reactor; (c) interference with the normal use of the waters of the Catawba River; (d) threatened reduction in property values of land neighboring the power plants; (e) "objectively reasonable" present fear and apprehension regarding the "effect of the increased radioactivity in the air, land and water upon [appellees] and their property, and the genetic effects upon their descendants"; and (f) the continual threat of "an accident resulting in uncontrolled release of large or even small quantities of radioactive material" with no assurance of adequate compensation for the resultant damage. * * * Into a second category of potential effects were placed the damages "which may result from a core melt or other major accident in the operation of a reactor * * *." * * *

For purposes of the present inquiry, we need not determine whether all the putative injuries identified by the District Court, particularly those based on the possibility of a nuclear accident and the present apprehension generated by this future uncertainty, are sufficiently concrete to satisfy constitutional requirements. It is enough that several of the "immediate" adverse effects were found to harm appellees. Certainly the environmental and aesthetic consequences of the thermal pollution of the two lakes in the vicinity of the disputed power plants is the type of harmful effect which has been deemed adequate in prior cases to satisfy the "injury in fact" standard [citing *SCRAP I* and *Sierra Club*]. And the emission of non-natural radiation into appellees' environment would also seem a direct and present injury, given our generalized concern about

g. [Ed. note: The statute expired on August 1, 1987. See 17 *Envir.L.Rep.* 10379 (1987). A modified version of the statute was reenacted in 1988. P.L. 100–408, 102 Stat. 1066 (1988), now codified at 42 U.S.C.A. § 2210. The ceiling on liability is now about $7 billion. See Note, "How the Price–Anderson Act Failed the Nuclear Industry," 15 *Colum.J.Env.L.* 121, 128 (1990). For a more recent application of the statute, see *O'Conner v. Commonwealth Edison Co.*, 13 F.3d 1090 (7th Cir.1994).]

exposure to radiation and the apprehension flowing from the uncertainty about the health and genetic consequences of even small emissions like those concededly emitted by nuclear power plants.[8]

The more difficult step in the standing inquiry is establishing that these injuries "fairly can be traced to the challenged action of the defendant," or put otherwise, that the exercise of the Court's remedial powers would redress the claimed injuries. The District Court discerned a "but for" causal connection between the Price–Anderson Act, which appellees challenged as unconstitutional, "and the construction of the nuclear plants which the [appellees] view as a threat to them." Particularizing that causal link to the facts of the instant case, the District Court concluded that "There is a substantial likelihood that Duke would not be able to complete the construction and maintain the operation of the McGuire and Catawba Nuclear Plants but for the protection provided by the Price–Anderson Act." * * *

These findings * * * are challenged on two grounds. First, it is argued that the evidence presented at the hearing, contrary to the conclusion reached by the District Court, indicated that the McGuire and Catawba Nuclear Plants would be completed and operated without the Price–Anderson Act's limitation on liability. And second, it is contended that the Price–Anderson Act is not, in some essential sense, the "but for" cause of the disputed nuclear power plants and resultant adverse effects since if the Act had not been passed Congress may well have chosen to pursue the nuclear program as a government monopoly as it had from 1946 until 1954. We reject both of these arguments.

The District Court's finding of a "substantial likelihood" that the McGuire and Catawba Nuclear Plants would be neither completed nor operated absent the Price–Anderson Act rested in major part on the testimony of corporate officials before the Joint Committee on Atomic Energy (JCAE) in 1956–1957 when the Price–Anderson Act was first considered and again in 1975 when a second renewal was discussed. * * *

Nor was the testimony at the hearing in this case, evaluation of which is the primary responsibility of the trial judge, at odds with the impression drawn from the legislative history. * * * Considering the documentary evidence and the testimony in the record, we cannot say we are left with "the definite and firm conviction that" the finding by the trial court of a substantial likelihood that the McGuire and Catawba Nuclear Power Plants would be neither completed nor operated absent the Price–Anderson Act is clearly erroneous and hence we are bound to accept it. [The court also rejected as speculative the argument that "if Price–Anderson had not been passed, the Government would have un-

8. It is argued that the District Court's findings on the question of injury in fact upon which we rely are clearly erroneous and should not be accepted as a predicate for standing. "A finding is 'clearly erroneous' when, although there is evidence to support it, the reviewing court on the entire evidence is left with the definite and firm conviction that a mistake has been committed." Application of this standard to the factual findings of the District Court does not persuade us that [this standard is met].

dertaken development of nuclear power on its own and the same injuries would likely have accrued to appellees from such government operated plants as from privately operated ones."]

B

It is further contended that in addition to proof of injury and of a causal link between such injury and the challenged conduct, appellees must demonstrate a connection between the injuries they claim and the constitutional rights being asserted. * * * Since the environmental and health injuries claimed by appellees are not directly related to the constitutional attack on the Price–Anderson Act, such injuries, the argument continues, cannot supply a predicate for standing. * * *

* * * [We] cannot accept the contention that, outside the context of taxpayers' suits, a litigant must demonstrate anything more than injury in fact and a substantial likelihood that the judicial relief requested will prevent or redress the claimed injury to satisfy the "case and controversy" requirement of Art. III.

Our prior cases have, however, acknowledged "other limits on the class of persons who may invoke the court's decisional and remedial powers," which derive from general prudential concerns "about the proper—and properly limited—role of the courts in a democratic society." Thus, we have declined to grant standing where the harm asserted amounts only to a generalized grievance shared by a large number of citizens in a substantially equal measure. We have also narrowly limited the circumstances in which one party will be given standing to assert the legal rights of another. "[E]ven when the plaintiff has alleged injury sufficient to meet the 'case or controversy' requirement, this Court has held that the plaintiff generally must assert his own legal rights and interests, and cannot rest his claim to relief in the legal rights or interests of third parties." * * * This limitation on third party standing arguably suggests a connection between the claimed injury and the right asserted bearing some resemblance to the nexus requirement now urged upon us.

There are good and sufficient reasons for this prudential limitation on standing when rights of third parties are implicated—the avoidance of the adjudication of rights which those not before the Court may not wish to assert, and the assurance that the most effective advocate of the rights at issue is present to champion them. We do not, however, find these reasons a satisfactory predicate for applying this limitation or a similar nexus requirement to all cases as a matter of course. Where a party champions his own rights, and where the injury alleged is a concrete and particularized one which will be prevented or redressed by the relief requested, the basic practical and prudential concerns underlying the standing doctrine are generally satisfied when the constitutional requisites are met.

We conclude that appellees have standing to challenge the constitutionality of the Price–Anderson Act.

C

The question of the ripeness of the constitutional challenges raised by appellees need not long detain us. To the extent that "issues of ripeness involve, at least in part, the existence of a live 'Case or Controversy,'" our conclusion that appellees will sustain immediate injury from the operation of the disputed power plants and that such injury would be redressed by the relief requested would appear to satisfy this requirement.

The prudential considerations embodied in the ripeness doctrine also argue strongly for a prompt resolution of the claims presented. Although it is true that no nuclear accident has yet occurred and that such an occurrence would eliminate much of the existing scientific uncertainty surrounding this subject, it would not, in our view, significantly advance our ability to deal with the legal issues presented nor aid us in their resolution. However, delayed resolution of these issues would foreclose any relief from the present injury suffered by appellees—relief that would be forthcoming if they were to prevail in their various challenges to the Act. Similarly, delayed resolution would frustrate one of the key purposes of the Price–Anderson Act—the elimination of doubts concerning the scope of private liability in the event of a major nuclear accident. In short, all parties would be adversely affected by a decision to defer definitive resolution of the constitutional validity *vel non* of the Price–Anderson Act. Since we are persuaded that "we will be in no better position later than we are now" to decide this question, we hold that it is presently ripe for adjudication.

[On the merits, the Court upheld the constitutionality of the Act.]

BENNETT v. SPEAR

Supreme Court of the United States, 1997
520 U.S. 154, 117 S.Ct. 1154, 137 L.Ed.2d 281

[The Endangered Species Act calls upon the Secretary of the Interior to identify "critical habitat" for threatened or endangered species. Although final decisionmaking authority rests with the Secretary, he is required to consult the Fish and Wildlife Service, which must provide a written "Biological Opinion." The Biological Opinion explains how a proposed action might affect the species and provides for mitigation measures. (The ESA is discussed in detail in Chapter VIII.) The Bureau of Reclamation informed the Service that the operation of the Klamath Irrigation Project might harm two endangered species of fish (Lost River and shortnose suckers). The Service issued a Biological Opinion agreeing with the concern and recommending that the Bureau maintain minimum water levels in reservoirs. The Bureau then agreed to do so. The plaintiffs were irrigation districts and ranchers who claimed that the Biological Opinion violated various provisions of the ESA and the Administrative Procedure Act. The Ninth Circuit held that they lacked standing because their economic interests did not lie within the "zone of interests" protected by the ESA.]

Justice Scalia delivered the opinion of the Court.

We first turn to the question the Court of Appeals found dispositive: whether petitioners lack standing by virtue of the zone-of-interests test. Although petitioners contend that their claims lie both under the ESA and the APA, we look first at the ESA because it may permit petitioners to recover their litigation costs, see 16 U.S.C. § 1540(g)(4), and because the APA by its terms independently authorizes review only when "there is no other adequate remedy in a court," 5 U.S.C. § 704.

The question of standing "involves both constitutional limitations on federal-court jurisdiction and prudential limitations on its exercise." To satisfy the "case" or "controversy" requirement of Article III, which is the "irreducible constitutional minimum" of standing, a plaintiff must, generally speaking, demonstrate that he has suffered "injury in fact," that the injury is "fairly traceable" to the actions of the defendant, and that the injury will likely be redressed by a favorable decision. [*Lujan v. Defenders of Wildlife*] In addition to the immutable requirements of Article III, "the federal judiciary has also adhered to a set of prudential principles that bear on the question of standing." Like their constitutional counterparts, these "judicially self-imposed limits on the exercise of federal jurisdiction," are "founded in concern about the proper—and properly limited—role of the courts in a democratic society," but unlike their constitutional counterparts, they can be modified or abrogated by Congress. Numbered among these prudential requirements is the doctrine of particular concern in this case: that a plaintiff's grievance must arguably fall within the zone of interests protected or regulated by the statutory provision or constitutional guarantee invoked in the suit.

The "zone of interests" formulation was first employed in *Association of Data Processing Service Organizations, Inc. v. Camp*, 397 U.S. 150, 90 S.Ct. 827, 25 L.Ed.2d 184 (1970). There, certain data processors sought to invalidate a ruling by the Comptroller of the Currency authorizing national banks to sell data processing services on the ground that it violated, inter alia, § 4 of the Bank Service Corporation Act of 1962, which prohibited bank service corporations from engaging in "any activity other than the performance of bank services for banks." The Court of Appeals had held that the banks' data-processing competitors were without standing to challenge the alleged violation of § 4. In reversing, we stated the applicable prudential standing requirement to be "whether the interest sought to be protected by the complainant is arguably within the zone of interests to be protected or regulated by the statute or constitutional guarantee in question." *Data Processing*, and its companion case, *Barlow v. Collins*, 397 U.S. 159, 90 S.Ct. 832, 25 L.Ed.2d 192 (1970), applied the zone-of-interests test to suits under the APA, but later cases have applied it also in suits not involving review of federal administrative action, and have specifically listed it among other prudential standing requirements of general application. We have made clear, however, that the breadth of the zone of interests varies according to the provisions of law at issue, so that what comes within the zone of interests of a statute for purposes of obtaining judicial review of administrative action under the " 'generous review provisions' " of the APA may not do so for other purposes.

Congress legislates against the background of our prudential standing doctrine, which applies unless it is expressly negated. The first question in the present case is whether the ESA's citizen-suit provision, * * * negates the zone-of-interests test (or, perhaps more accurately, expands the zone of interests). We think it does. The first operative portion of the provision says that "any person may commence a civil suit"—an authorization of remarkable breadth when compared with the language Congress ordinarily uses. Even in some other environmental statutes, Congress has used more restrictive formulations, such as "[any person] having an interest which is or may be adversely affected," 33 U.S.C. § 1365(g) (Clean Water Act).

Our readiness to take the term "any person" at face value is greatly augmented by two interrelated considerations: that the overall subject matter of this legislation is the environment (a matter in which it is common to think all persons have an interest) and that the obvious purpose of the particular provision in question is to encourage enforcement by so-called "private attorneys general"—evidenced by its elimination of the usual amount-in-controversy and diversity-of-citizenship requirements, its provision for recovery of the costs of litigation (including even expert witness fees), and its reservation to the Government of a right of first refusal to pursue the action initially and a right to intervene later. Given these factors, we think the conclusion of expanded standing follows a fortiori from our decision in *Trafficante v. Metropolitan Life Ins. Co.*, 409 U.S. 205, 93 S.Ct. 364, 34 L.Ed.2d 415 (1972), which held that standing was expanded to the full extent permitted under Article III by a provision of the Civil Rights Act of 1968 that authorized "[a]ny person who claims to have been injured by a discriminatory housing practice" to sue for violations of the Act. There also we relied on textual evidence of a statutory scheme to rely on private litigation to ensure compliance with the Act. The statutory language here is even clearer, and the subject of the legislation makes the intent to permit enforcement by everyman even more plausible.

It is true that the plaintiffs here are seeking to prevent application of environmental restrictions rather than to implement them. But the "any person" formulation applies to all the causes of action authorized by § 1540(g)—not only to actions against private violators of environmental restrictions, and not only to actions against the Secretary asserting underenforcement under § 1533, but also to actions against the Secretary asserting overenforcement under § 1533. As we shall discuss below, the citizen-suit provision does favor environmentalists in that it covers all private violations of the Act but not all failures of the Secretary to meet his administrative responsibilities; but there is no textual basis for saying that its expansion of standing requirements applies to environmentalists alone. The Court of Appeals therefore erred in concluding that petitioners lacked standing under the zone-of-interests test to bring their claims under the ESA's citizen-suit provision.

[The Court concluded that the citizen-suit provision did extend to the claim that the government had in effect designated critical habitat without considering economic factors at all, but not to the plaintiff's other claims. The Court then considered whether these other claims could be brought under the APA.]

No one contends (and it would not be maintainable) that the causes of action against the Secretary set forth in the ESA's citizen-suit provision are exclusive, supplanting those provided by the APA. The APA, by its terms, provides a right to judicial review of all "final agency action for which there is no other adequate remedy in a court," 5 U.S.C. § 704, and applies universally "except to the extent that—(1) statutes preclude judicial review; or (2) agency action is committed to agency discretion by law," § 701(a). Nothing in the ESA's citizen-suit provision expressly precludes review under the APA, nor do we detect anything in the statutory scheme suggesting a purpose to do so. And any contention that the relevant provision of 16 U.S.C. § 1536(a)(2) is discretionary would fly in the face of its text, which uses the imperative "shall."

In determining whether the petitioners have standing under the zone-of-interests test to bring their APA claims, we look not to the terms of the ESA's citizen-suit provision, but to the substantive provisions of the ESA, the alleged violations of which serve as the gravamen of the complaint. The classic formulation of the zone-of-interests test is set forth in *Data Processing*: "whether the interest sought to be protected by the complainant is arguably within the zone of interests to be protected or regulated by the statute or constitutional guarantee in question." The Court of Appeals concluded that this test was not met here, since petitioners are neither directly regulated by the ESA nor seek to vindicate its overarching purpose of species preservation. That conclusion was error.

Whether a plaintiff's interest is "arguably * * * protected * * * by the statute" within the meaning of the zone-of-interests test is to be determined not by reference to the overall purpose of the Act in question (here, species preservation), but by reference to the particular provision of law upon which the plaintiff relies. It is difficult to understand how the Ninth Circuit could have failed to see this from our cases. In *Data Processing* itself, for example, we did not require that the plaintiffs' suit vindicate the overall purpose of the Bank Service Corporation Act of 1962, but found it sufficient that their commercial interest was sought to be protected by the anti-competition limitation contained in § 4 of the Act—the specific provision which they alleged had been violated. As we said with the utmost clarity in *National Wildlife Federation*, "the plaintiff must establish that the injury he complains of ... falls within the 'zone of interests' sought to be protected by the statutory provision whose violation forms the legal basis for his complaint."

In the claims that we have found not to be covered by the ESA's citizen-suit provision, petitioners allege a violation of § 7 of the ESA, which requires, inter alia, that each agency "use the best scientific and commercial data available." Petitioners contend that the available scientific and commercial data show that the continued operation of the Klamath Project will not have a detrimental impact on the endangered suckers, that the imposition of minimum lake levels is not necessary to protect the fish, and that by issuing a Biological Opinion which makes unsubstantiated findings to the contrary the defendants have acted arbitrarily and in violation of § 1536(a)(2). The obvious purpose of the requirement that each agency "use the best scientific and commercial data available" is to ensure that the ESA not be implemented haphazardly, on the basis of speculation or surmise. While this no doubt serves to advance the ESA's overall goal of species preservation, we think it readily apparent that another objective (if not indeed the primary one) is to avoid needless economic dislocation produced by agency officials zealously but unintelligently pursuing their environmental objectives. That economic consequences are an explicit concern of the Act is evidenced by § 1536(h), which provides exemption from § 1536(a)(2)'s no-jeopardy mandate where there are no reasonable and prudent alternatives to the agency action and the benefits of the agency action clearly outweigh the benefits of any alternatives. We believe the "best scientific and commercial data" provision is similarly intended, at least in part, to prevent uneconomic (because erroneous) jeopardy determinations. Petitioners' claim that they are victims of such a mistake is plainly within the zone of interests that the provision protects.

* * *

The Court of Appeals erred in affirming the District Court's dismissal of petitioners' claims for lack of jurisdiction. Petitioners' complaint alleges facts sufficient to meet the requirements of Article III standing, and none of their ESA claims is precluded by the zone-of-interests test. Petitioners' § 1533 claim is reviewable under the ESA's citizen-suit provision, and petitioners' remaining claims are reviewable under the APA.

The judgment of the Court of Appeals is reversed, and the case is remanded for further proceedings consistent with this opinion.

It is so ordered.

Notes

1. *Duke Power* and *Bennett* both make it clear that the "zone of interests" test is not part of Article III standing. Instead, it is either a prudential requirement imposed by the courts or a consequence of specific statutory language, such as that used in the APA. Still, if "zone of interests" is a prudential requirement, one might wonder why it did not bar the suit in *Duke Power*. The answer is probably found in the portion of the *Duke Power* opinion dealing with ripeness, where the Court found that delaying the suit would be imprudent because of the adverse effect on the nuclear industry of

continued uncertainty about the constitutionality of the Price–Anderson Act. Presumably, the same argument would justify an exception to the prudential "zone of interests" test.

2. *Duke Power* created some doubt about the continuing vitality of the "zone of interests" concept, but the *Bennett* Court may have given it renewed vitality despite the lack of success of the standing challenge in the case. Consider whether the following claims are within the "zone of interests" of the relevant legal provision:

(a) Consumers bring an action challenging an environmental regulation by their local government under the dormant commerce clause, claiming that it discriminates against interstate commerce and results in higher prices. See *Oehrleins v. Hennepin County*, 115 F.3d 1372 (8th Cir. 1997) (no standing).

(b) State governments contend that a ban on logging in a national forest reduces local industry and thereby impairs their tax bases.

(c) A competing firm alleges that its competitor is shaving costs by illegally disposing of toxic chemicals.

3. In an omitted portion of the opinion, *Bennett* addressed the government's claim that the plaintiff's injury (the ultimate water allocation by one agency) was not "fairly traceable" to the contested government action (issuance of the Biological Opinion by another agency). The Court found that as a practical matter the Biological Opinion would have a major, probably decisive influence, on the ultimate decision. In the course of this discussion, however, the Court only added to the confusion about the requirements of standing to challenge "procedural" decisions, such as an EIS or a Biological Opinion. Courts are divided about the extent to which the plaintiff must show that the alleged procedural error would impact the ultimate decision. See William Buzbee, "Expanding the Zone, Tilting the Field: Zone of Interests and Article III Standing Analysis After *Bennett v. Spear*," 49 *Admin.L.Rev.* 763 (1997). Is this best considered as part of the "fairly traceable" inquiry under the second prong of standing, as going to the "concreteness" of the injury under the first prong of standing, or as a ripeness problem? As the caselaw about justiciability becomes ever more intricate, such problems provide increasingly interesting technical puzzles— which may, however, become increasingly frustrating to those who are not experts on the law of federal jurisdiction. Reconsider Judge Wald's plea (page 103 *supra*) for a reconsideration of the law of environmental standing. Does current doctrine advance the goals of government regulation? Protect individual rights? Maintain necessary boundaries on judicial authority?

B. THE SCOPE OF REVIEW

The question whether a particular plaintiff has standing must be distinguished from the question whether the issues raised in the lawsuit are within the power of a court to decide. The discussion so far has assumed that, given the proper plaintiff, the court has the power to determine the legality of government action. Some of the qualifications that must be placed on this assumption are explored in the following case. The case also raises an entirely new set of issues: Once a court has decided it has the power to decide a case, what does it do next? What degree of deference does it give a decision by a federal agency?

CITIZENS TO PRESERVE OVERTON PARK, INC. v. VOLPE → Secretary of Transportation

Supreme Court of the United States, 1971.
401 U.S. 402, 91 S.Ct. 814, 28 L.Ed.2d 136.

Opinion of the Court by JUSTICE MARSHALL, announced by JUSTICE STEWART. The growing public concern about the quality of our natural environment has prompted Congress in recent years to enact legislation designed to curb the accelerating destruction of our country's natural beauty. We are concerned in this case with '4(f) of the Department of Transportation Act of 1966, as amended, and § 18(a) of the Federal–Aid Highway Act of 1968, 82 Stat. 823, 23 U.S.C.A. § 138 (hereafter § 138). These statutes prohibit the Secretary of Transportation from authorizing the use of federal funds to finance the construction of highways through public parks if a "feasible and prudent" alternative route exists. If no such route is available, the statutes allow him to approve construction through parks only if there has been "all possible planning to minimize harm" to the park.

[The plaintiffs contended that the Secretary violated these restrictions in approving the construction of an interstate highway through Overton Park, a 342–acre city park in Memphis.]

A threshold question—whether petitioners are entitled to any judicial review—is easily answered. Section 701 of the Administrative Procedure Act, 5 U.S.C.A. § 701, provides that the action of "each authority of the Government of the United States," which includes the Department of Transportation, is subject to judicial review except where there is a statutory prohibition on review or where "agency action is committed to agency discretion by law." In this case there is no indication that Congress sought to prohibit judicial review and there is most certainly no "showing of 'clear and convincing evidence' of a * * * legislative intent" to restrict access to judicial review. * * *

Similarly, the Secretary's decision here does not fall within the exception for action "committed to agency discretion." This is a very narrow exception. The legislative history of the Administrative Procedure Act indicates that it is applicable in those rare instances where "statutes are drawn in such broad terms that in a given case there is no law to apply."

Section 4(f) of the Department of Transportation Act and § 138 of the Federal–Aid Highway Act are clear and specific directives. Both the Department of Transportation Act and the Federal–Aid Highway Act provide that the Secretary "shall not approve any program or project" that requires the use of any public parkland "unless (1) there is no feasible and prudent alternative to the use of such land, and (2) such

program includes all possible planning to minimize harm to such park
* * *." This language is a plain and explicit bar to the use of federal
funds for construction of highways through parks—only the most unusual situations are exempted.

Despite the clarity of the statutory language, respondents argue that
the Secretary has wide discretion. They recognize that the requirement
that there be no "feasible" alternative route admits of little administrative discretion. For this exemption to apply the Secretary must find that
as a matter of sound engineering it would not be feasible to build the
highway along any other route. Respondents argue, however, that the
requirement that there be no other "prudent" route requires the Secretary to engage in a wide-ranging balancing of competing interests. They
contend that the Secretary should weigh the detriment resulting from
the destruction of parkland against the cost of other routes, safety
considerations, and other factors, and determine on the basis of the
importance that he attaches to these other factors whether, on balance,
alternative feasible routes would be "prudent."

But no such wide-ranging endeavor was intended. It is obvious that
in most cases considerations of cost, directness of route, and community
disruption will indicate that parkland should be used for highway
construction whenever possible. * * * Thus, if Congress intended these
factors to be on an equal footing with preservation of parkland there
would have been no need for the statutes.

Congress clearly did not intend that cost and disruption of the
community were to be ignored by the Secretary. But the very existence
of the statutes indicates that protection of parkland was to be given
paramount importance. The few green havens that are public parks were
not to be lost unless there were truly unusual factors present in a
particular case or the cost or community disruption resulting from
alternative routes reached extraordinary magnitudes. If the statutes are
to have any meaning, the Secretary cannot approve the destruction of
parkland unless he finds that alternative routes present unique problems.

Plainly, there is "law to apply" and thus the exemption for action
"committed to agency discretion" is inapplicable.

* * *

But the existence of judicial review is only the start: the standard
for review must also be determined. For that we must look to § 706 of
the Administrative Procedure Act, 5 U.S.C.A. § 706, which provides that
a "reviewing court shall * * * hold unlawful and set aside agency action,
findings, and conclusions found" not to meet six separate standards. In
all cases agency action must be set aside if the action was "arbitrary,
capricious, an abuse of discretion, or otherwise not in accordance with
law" or if the action failed to meet statutory, procedural, or constitutional requirements. In certain narrow, specifically limited situations, the
agency action is to be set aside if the action was not supported by

"substantial evidence." And in other equally narrow circumstances the reviewing court is to engage in a *de novo* review of the action and set it aside if it was "unwarranted by the facts." * * *

[The Court rejected the plaintiff's arguments that either the "substantial evidence" test or the "*de novo* review" requirement applied.]

Even though there is no *de novo* review in this case and the Secretary's approval of the route of I–40 does not have ultimately to meet the substantial evidence test, the generally applicable standards of § 706 require the reviewing court to engage in a substantial inquiry. Certainly, the Secretary's decision is entitled to a presumption of regularity. * * * But that presumption is not to shield his action from a thorough, probing, indepth review.

The court is first required to decide whether the Secretary acted within the scope of his authority. * * * This determination naturally begins with a delineation of the scope of the Secretary's authority and discretion. As has been shown, Congress has specified only a small range of choices that the Secretary can make. Also involved in this initial inquiry is a determination of whether on the facts the Secretary's decision can reasonably be said to be within that range. The reviewing court must consider whether the Secretary properly construed his authority to approve the use of parkland as limited to situations where there are no feasible alternative routes or where feasible alternative routes involve uniquely difficult problems. And the reviewing court must be able to find that the Secretary could have reasonably believed that in this case there are no feasible alternatives or that alternatives do involve unique problems.

Scrutiny of the facts does not end, however, with the determination that the Secretary has acted within the scope of his statutory authority. Section 706(2)(A) requires a finding that the actual choice made was not "arbitrary, capricious, an abuse of discretion, or otherwise not in accordance with law." To make this finding the Court must consider whether the decision was based on a consideration of the relevant factors and whether there has been a clear error of judgment.

* * * Although this inquiry into the facts is to be searching and careful, the ultimate standard of review is a narrow one. The court is not empowered to substitute its judgment for that of the agency.

* * * The lower courts based their review on the litigation affidavits that were presented. These affidavits were merely "*post hoc*" rationalizations * * * which have traditionally been found to be an inadequate basis for review. * * * And they clearly do not constitute the "whole record" compiled by the agency: the basis for review required by § 706 of the Administrative Procedure Act. * * *

Thus it is necessary to remand this case to the District Court for plenary review of the Secretary's decision. That review is to be based on the full administrative record that was before the Secretary at the time he made his decision. But since the bare record may not disclose the factors that were considered or the Secretary's construction of the evidence it may be necessary for the District Court to require some explanation in order to determine if the Secretary acted within the scope of his authority and if the Secretary's action was justifiable under the applicable standard.

The court may require the administrative officials who participated in the decision to give testimony explaining their action. Of course, such inquiry into the mental processes of administrative decisionmakers is usually to be avoided. *United States v. Morgan,* 313 U.S. 409, 422, 61 S.Ct. 999, 85 L.Ed. 1429 (1941). And where there are administrative findings that were made at the same time as the decision, as was the case in *Morgan,* there must be a strong showing of bad faith or improper behavior before such inquiry may be made. But here there are no such formal findings and it may be that the only way there can be effective judicial review is by examining the decisionmakers themselves. * * *

The District Court is not, however, required to make such an inquiry. It may be that the Secretary can prepare formal findings including the information required by DOT Order 5610.1 that will provide an adequate explanation for his action. Such an explanation will, to some extent, be a *"post hoc* rationalization" and thus must be viewed critically. If the District Court decides that additional explanation is necessary, that court should consider which method will prove the most expeditious so that full review may be had as soon as possible.

Notes

1.   The Secretary ultimately decided to disapprove the highway, and this decision was upheld on appeal. See *Citizens to Preserve Overton Park, Inc. v. Brinegar,* 494 F.2d 1212 (6th Cir.1974). For a critique of the outcome in *Overton Park,* see Strauss, "Considering Political Alternatives to 'Hard Look' Review," 1989 *Duke L.J.* 538, 544–47. More recently, Professor Strauss has written a detailed history of section 4(f) of the Transportation Act and the events leading up to *Overton Park.* He concludes that the Court misinterpreted the statute:

> Political controls, so far as one can tell, were the only controls Congress had considered; and in the instance, they were working well. A fuller appreciation for the Overton Park controversy, whether viewed from Washington, D.C., or Memphis, Tennessee, shows wide and effective engagement of a variety of political actors in the controversy. The effect of the Court's action * * * was to empower one of those actors to an extent that had not been contemplated. * * *

P. Strauss, "Revisiting *Overton Park:* Political and Judicial Controls Over Administrative Actions Affecting the Community," 39 *UCLA L.Rev.* 1251 (1992).

2.   After *Overton Park,* what actions are "committed to agency discretion"? *Heckler v. Chaney,* 470 U.S. 821, 105 S.Ct. 1649, 84 L.Ed.2d 714 (1985), holds that an agency's decision to eschew enforcement action is unreviewable. The Court considered enforcement decisions generally unsuitable for judicial review. See also *Arnow v. United States Nuclear Regulatory*

Com'n, 868 F.2d 223 (7th Cir.1989) (applying *Chaney* to an NRC enforcement decision). For a critique of *Chaney,* see Sunstein, "Reviewing Agency Inaction After *Heckler v. Chaney,* 52 *U.Chi.L.Rev.* 653 (1985).

3. The *Overton Park* approach to reviewing informal administrative action was strongly reconfirmed in *Motor Vehicle Mfrs. Ass'n v. State Farm Mutual Automobile Ins. Co.,* 463 U.S. 29, 103 S.Ct. 2856, 77 L.Ed.2d 443 (1983), in which the Court overturned an administrative decision through an application of the arbitrary and capricious test. The National Highway Traffic Safety Administration in 1981 rescinded a 1977 decision, which had required all new cars produced after September 1982 to be equipped with passive restraints such as airbags. After a detailed examination of the rulemaking record, the Court found the rescission to be arbitrary and capricious. The Court found that the agency failed to consider the possibility of modifying rather than rescinding the standard and had been too quick to dismiss the safety benefits of automatic seatbelts.

4. A major scholarly debate has arisen about the kind of "hard look" review endorsed by *Overton Park* and *State Farm.* The following statement is typical of the view of the critics:

> The predictable result of stringent "hard look" judicial review of complex rulemaking is ossification. Because the agencies perceive that the reviewing courts are inconsistent in the degree to which they are deferential, they are constrained to prepare for the worst-case scenario on judicial review. This can be extremely resource-intensive and time-consuming. Moreover, since the criteria for substantive judicial review are the same for repealing old rules as for promulgating new rules, the agencies are equally chary of revisiting old rules, even in the name of flexibility.

McGarity, "Some Thoughts on 'Deossifying' the Rulemaking Process," 41 *Duke L.J. 1419–20* (1992). For reviews of the scholarly debate on this point, see Glicksman & Schroeder, "EPA and the Courts: Twenty Years of Law and Politics," 54 *L. & Contemp.Problems* 249, 250, 273–74, 301–02 (1991); Mark Seidenfeld, "Demystifying Deossification: Rethinking Recent Proposals to Modify Judicial Review of Notice and Comment Rulemaking," 75 *Tex.L.Rev.* 483 (1997); Thomas McGarity, "The Courts and the Ossification of Rulemaking: A Response to Professor Seidenfeld," 75 *Tex.L.Rev.* 525 (1997); Mark Seidenfeld, "Hard Look Review in a World of Techno–Bureaucratic Decisionmaking: A Reply to Professor McGarity," 75 *Tex.L.Rev.* 559 (1997). In response to the critics of "hard look" review, Seidenfeld contends that his "experience as an agency lawyer leads me to believe that, without some external constraint on agency decisionmaking processes, staff members are apt to take shortcuts to avoid extra work, to yield to short-run political pressures that take time and energy to counter, or to alter a decision to make it easier to defend to their superiors." 75 *Tex.L.Rev.* at 564. McGarity counters that judicial discretion is "in fact so wide that a single unsympathetic or confused reviewing court can bring about a dramatic shift in focus or even the complete destruction of an entire regulatory program." 75 *Tex. L.Rev.* at 541. You should appraise the validity of the criticisms in light of the materials on EPA regulation in Chapters IV and VI.

Note on Administrative Procedure

The scope-of-review issue cannot be fully understood without an understanding of the basics of administrative procedure. Under the Administrative Procedure Act, there are three important categories of administrative actions. The first category consists of adjudications. This form of procedure applies (with some exceptions) whenever the specific statute governing the agency requires an issue to be "determined on the record after opportunity for an agency hearing." 5 U.S.C.A. § 554. The procedures required for an adjudication are essentially similar to those of a judicial trial. In reviewing the agency's ruling, courts must uphold the action unless it is unsupported by substantial evidence or violates substantive limits on the agency's powers. 5 U.S.C.A. § 706(2)(A)-(E).

The second category of administrative action is rulemaking. When an agency proposes to implement a "legislative" rule, it must follow a relatively simple procedure. The first step is the publication of a notice in the Federal Register describing the proposed rule. The agency must then allow interested parties an "opportunity to comment" for at least 30 days. Then, the agency must issue, in conjunction with its promulgation of the rule, a "concise general statement" of the rule's basis and purpose. These procedures do not apply to matters relating to public property, benefits, or contracts. See 5 U.S.C.A. § 553. The statute fails to specify clearly the scope of review for agency rules. (There is also another kind of rulemaking procedure known as "formal rulemaking" which has virtually no practical importance).

The final category consists of the vast number of government actions that neither impose sanctions on (or grant licenses to) individuals, nor impose rules governing future conduct. The Administrative Procedure Act has little to say about the procedures to be used in these cases.

In the early 1970s, a number of courts of appeals appeared to find the APA's dichotomy between adjudication and informal rulemaking too confining. In several cases involving rulemaking, they required agencies to adopt procedures going beyond the APA's simple notice-and-comment requirement. See, e.g., *Mobile Oil Corp. v. FPC,* 483 F.2d 1238, 1257 (D.C.Cir.1973); *Appalachian Power Co. v. EPA,* 477 F.2d 495 (4th Cir.1973). The primary reason for these "hybrid rulemaking" cases was apparently a belief that the basic APA procedures failed in complex cases to provide fairness to the parties and to compel reasoned decisionmaking by the agencies.

The hybrid rulemaking issue finally reached the Supreme Court in the following case. This case was part of the longstanding controversy over nuclear waste disposal. Critics argued that plants should not be built until the disposal problem was solved. The agency consistently rejected this and other concerns about the safety of nuclear power. The issue before the Court was whether the agency had employed the proper procedures to consider this issue. If the issue had been handled during the proceeding to license a specific plant, a full hearing would have been required. By shifting the issue to a rulemaking, could the agency escape all but the minimal "notice and comment" requirements?

VERMONT YANKEE NUCLEAR POWER CORP. v. NATURAL RESOURCES DEFENSE COUNCIL, INC.

petitioner

respondent

Supreme Court of the United States, 1978.
435 U.S. 519, 98 S.Ct. 1197, 55 L.Ed.2d 460.

JUSTICE REHNQUIST delivered the opinion of the Court.

In December 1967, after the mandatory adjudicatory hearing and necessary review, the Commission granted petitioner Vermont Yankee a permit to build a nuclear power plant in Vernon, Vt. Thereafter, Vermont Yankee applied for an operating license. Respondent Natural Resources Defense Council (NRDC) objected to the granting of a license, however, and therefore a hearing on the application commenced on August 10, 1971. Excluded from consideration at the hearings, over NRDC's objection, was the issue of the environmental effects of operations to reprocess fuel or dispose of wastes resulting from the reprocessing operations.[9] This ruling was affirmed by the Appeal Board in June 1972.

In November 1972, however, the Commission, making specific reference to the Appeal Board's decision with respect to the Vermont Yankee license, instituted rulemaking proceedings "that would specifically deal with the question of consideration of environmental effects associated with the uranium fuel cycle in the individual cost-benefit analyses for light water cooled nuclear power reactors." * * *

Much of the controversy in this case revolves around the procedures used in the rulemaking hearing which commenced in February 1973. In a supplemental notice of hearing the Commission indicated that while discovery or cross-examination would not be utilized, the Environmental Survey would be available to the public before the hearing along with the extensive background documents cited therein. All participants would be given a reasonable opportunity to present their position and could be represented by counsel if they so desired. Written and, time permitting, oral statements would be received and incorporated into the record. All persons giving oral statements would be subject to questioning by the Commission. At the conclusion of the hearing, a transcript would be made available to the public and the record would remain open for 30 days to allow the filing of supplemental written statements. More than 40 individuals and organizations representing a wide variety of interests submitted written comments. On January 17, 1973, the Hearing Board

---

9. The nuclear fission which takes place in light water nuclear reactors apparently converts its principal fuel, uranium, into plutonium, which is itself highly radioactive but can be used as reactor fuel if separated from the remaining uranium and radioactive waste products. Fuel reprocessing refers to the process necessary to recapture usable plutonium. Waste disposal, at the present stage of technological development, refers to the storage of the highly and very long-lived radioactive waste products until they detoxify sufficiently that they no longer present an environmental hazard. There are presently no physical or chemical steps which render this waste less toxic, other than simply the passage of time.

held a planning session to schedule the appearance of witnesses and to discuss methods for compiling a record. The hearing was held on February 1 and 2, with participation from a number of groups, including the Commission's staff, the United States Environmental Protection Agency, a manufacturer of reactor equipment, a trade association from the nuclear industry, a group of electric utility companies, and a group called Consolidated National Intervenors who represented 79 groups and individuals including respondent NRDC.

After the hearing, the Commission's staff filed a supplemental document for the purpose of clarifying and revising the Environmental Survey. Then, the Hearing Board forwarded its report to the Commission without rendering any decision.

[The Commission approved the procedures used, issued a final rule concluding that "the environmental effects of the uranium fuel cycle have been shown to be relatively insignificant," and issued the license requested by Vermont Yankee].

Respondents appealed from both the Commission's adoption of the rule and its decision to grant Vermont Yankee's license to the Court of Appeals for the District of Columbia Circuit.

* * *

* * * [B]efore determining whether the Court of Appeals reached a permissible result, we must determine exactly what result it did reach, and in this case that is no mean feat. Vermont Yankee argues that the court invalidated the rule because of the inadequacy of the procedures employed in the proceedings. Respondent NRDC, on the other hand, labeling petitioner's view of the decision a "straw man," argues to this Court that the court merely held that the record was inadequate to enable the reviewing court to determine whether the agency had fulfilled its statutory obligation. But we unfortunately have not found the parties' characterization of the opinion to be entirely reliable; it appears here, as in *Orloff v. Willoughby,* 345 U.S. 83, 87, 73 S.Ct. 534, 537, 97 L.Ed. 842 (1953), that "in this Court the parties changed positions as nimbly as if dancing a quadrille."

[The Court concluded, however, that the court of appeals had reversed the NRC on procedural grounds, because the agency failed to allow cross-examination of the fairly conclusory evidence presented by the key expert witness on whom it relied].

In prior opinions we have intimated that even in a rulemaking proceeding when an agency is making a "quasi-judicial" determination by which a very small number of persons are " 'exceptionally affected, in each case upon individual grounds,' " in some circumstances additional procedures may be required in order to afford the aggrieved individuals due process. *United States v. Florida East Coast R. Co.,* 410 U.S. at 242–245, 93 S.Ct. at 819–821, quoting from *Bi-Metallic Investment Co. v. State Board of Equalization,* 239 U.S. 441, 446, 36 S.Ct. 141, 142, 60 L.Ed. 372 (1915). It might also be true, although we do not think the issue is presented in this case and accordingly do not decide it, that a totally unjustified departure from well settled agency procedures of long standing might require judicial correction.

But this much is absolutely clear. Absent constitutional constraints or extremely compelling circumstances "the administrative agencies 'should be free to fashion their own rules of procedure and to pursue methods of inquiry capable of permitting them to discharge their multitudinous duties.' " *Federal Communications Comm'n v. Schreiber,* 381 U.S. at 290, 85 S.Ct. at 1467. Indeed, our cases could hardly be more explicit in this regard. The Court has, as we noted in *FCC v. Schreiber,* upheld this principle in a variety of applications, including that case where the District Court, instead of inquiring into the validity of the FCC's exercise of its rulemaking authority, devised procedures to be followed by the agency on the basis of its conception of how the public and private interest involved could best be served. Examining § 4(j) of the Communications Act, the Court unanimously held that the Court of Appeals erred in upholding that action. And the basic reason for this decision was the Court of Appeals' serious departure from the very basic tenet of administrative law that agencies should be free to fashion their own rules of procedure.

* * *

Respondent NRDC argues that § 553 of the Administrative Procedure Act merely establishes lower procedural bounds and that a court may routinely require more than the minimum when an agency's proposed rule addresses complex or technical factual issues or "issues of great public import." We have, however, previously shown that our decisions reject this view. We also think the legislative history, even the part which it cites, does not bear out its contention. The Senate Report explains what eventually became § 533(c) thusly:

> "This subsection states * * * the minimum requirements of public rule making procedure short of statutory hearing. Under it agencies might in addition confer with industry advisory committees, consult organizations, hold informal 'hearings,' and the like. Considerations of practicality, necessity, and public interest * * * will naturally govern the agency's determination of the extent to which public proceedings should go. Matters of great import, or those where the public submission of facts will be either useful to the agency or a protection to the public, should naturally be accorded more elaborate public procedures."

The House Report is in complete accord. * * *

There are compelling reasons for construing § 553 in this manner. In the first place, if courts continually review agency proceedings to determine whether the agency employed procedures which were, in the Court's opinion, perfectly tailored to reach what the court perceives to be the "best" or "correct" result, judicial review would be totally unpredictable. And the agencies, operating under this vague injunction to employ the "best" procedures and facing the threat of reversal if they did not, would undoubtedly adopt full adjudicatory procedures in every instance. Not only would this totally disrupt the statutory scheme, through which Congress enacted "a formula upon which opposing social and political forces have come to rest," but all the inherent advantages of informal rulemaking would be totally lost.

Secondly, it is obvious that the court in this case reviewed the agency's choice of procedures on the basis of the record actually produced at the hearing, and not on the basis of the information available to the agency when it made the decision to structure the proceedings in a certain way. This sort of Monday morning quarterbacking not only encourages but almost compels the agency to conduct all rule-making proceedings with the full panoply of procedural devices normally associated only with adjudicatory hearings.

Finally, and perhaps most importantly, this sort of review fundamentally misconceives the nature of the standard for judicial review of an agency rule. The court below uncritically assumed that additional procedures will automatically result in a more adequate record because it will give interested parties more of an opportunity to participate and contribute to the proceedings. But informal rulemaking need not be based solely on the transcript of a hearing held before an agency. Indeed, the agency need not even hold a formal hearing. See 5 U.S.C.A. § 553(c). Thus, the adequacy of the "record" in this type of proceeding is not correlated directly to the type of procedural devices employed, but rather turns on whether the agency has followed the statutory mandate of the Administrative Procedure Act or other relevant statutes. If the agency is compelled to support the rule which it ultimately adopts with the type of record produced only after a full adjudicatory hearing, it simply will have no choice but to conduct a full adjudication prior to promulgating every rule. In sum, this sort of unwarranted judicial examination of perceived procedural shortcomings of a rulemaking proceeding can do nothing but seriously interfere with that process prescribed by Congress.

Respondent NRDC also argues that the fact that the Commission's inquiry was undertaken in the context of NEPA somehow permits a court to require procedures beyond those specified in § 553 when investigating factual issues through rulemaking. The Court of Appeals was apparently also of this view, indicating that agencies may be required to "develop new procedures to accomplish the innovative task of implementing NEPA through rulemaking." But we search in vain for something in NEPA which would mandate such a result. We have before observed that "NEPA does not repeal by implication any other statute." [quoting *SCRAP II, infra* page 159]. In fact, just two Terms ago, we emphasized that the only procedural requirements imposed by NEPA are those stated in the plain language of the Act. *Kleppe v. Sierra Club,* [infra page 161]. Thus, it is clear NEPA cannot serve as the basis for a substantial revision of the carefully constructed procedural specifications of the APA.

In short, nothing in the APA, NEPA, the circumstances of this case, the nature of the issues being considered, past agency practice, or the statutory mandate under which the Commission operates permitted the court to review and overturn the rulemaking proceeding on the basis of the procedural devices employed (or not employed) by the Commission so long as the Commission employed at least the statutory *minima,* a matter about which there is no doubt in this case.

Notes

1. As the Court explains at the beginning of its opinion and in footnote 6, the issue of the environmental effects of fuel reprocessing was excluded from the individual plant licensing (adjudicatory) proceeding and treated as a "generic" issue to be handled through rulemaking. This treatment of the issue effectively denied NRDC the advantages of cross-examination, discovery, and other procedures available in an adjudicatory proceeding under section 554 of the Administrative Procedure Act. For the further history of the *Vermont Yankee* litigation, see *Baltimore Gas & Electric Co. v. NRDC,* p. 190 infra.

2. The courts of appeals have generally held that, despite *Vermont Yankee,* additional procedural restrictions can be imposed on agencies through a liberal construction of the APA itself. These courts appear to find *Vermont Yankee* a barrier only to the creation of avowedly nonstatutory procedural requirements. See, e.g., *United States Lines, Inc. v. FMC,* 584 F.2d 519 (D.C.Cir.1978); *National Crushed Stone Association v. EPA,* 601 F.2d 111 (4th Cir.1979), reversed on other grounds 449 U.S. 64, 101 S.Ct. 295, 66 L.Ed.2d 268 (1980). Do you agree with these courts? For further discussion of *Vermont Yankee,* see the symposium by Professors Stewart, Byse, and Breyer in 91 *Harv.L.Rev.* 1804 (1978); and Rodgers, "A Hard Look at Vermont Yankee: Environmental Law Under Close Scrutiny," 67 *Geo.L.J.* 699 (1979). For a critique of the Court's interpretation of legislative intent, see Nathanson, "The *Vermont Yankee* Nuclear Power Opinion: A Masterpiece of Statutory Misinterpretation," 16 *San Diego L.Rev.* 183 (1979).

3. Congress is perhaps less persuaded than the Court of the sufficiency of minimal APA rulemaking procedures. See § 307(d)(3)-(7) of the Clean Air Act, which provides detailed procedures for certain rulemaking proceedings. See also section 307(a)(2) of the Clean Water Act. For an important discussion about the political forces behind such procedural provisions, see McCubbins, Noll & Weingast, "Structure and Process, Politics and Policy: Administrative Arrangements and the Political Control of Agencies," 75 *Va.L.Rev.* 431 (1989). See also Spence, "Administrative Law and Agency Policymaking: Rethinking the Positive Theory of Political Control," 14 *Yale J.on Reg.* 407 (1997).

4. There may be a point of diminishing returns in imposing procedural requirements, where the effect of increased procedural requirements is to divert the agency from engaging in explicit rulemaking at all. Instead, the agency may make rules in the form of informal policy pronouncements or use adjudication or other procedures to announce rules. If, as in California, the legislature seeks to cut off these informal methods as well, the result may be to stymie needed regulations or to encourage agencies to ignore or

evade the procedural requirements. See Asimow, "California's Underground Regulations," 44 *Admin.L.Rev.* 43 (1992). Somewhat similar developments have occurred at the federal level. Richard Lazarus reports:

> Another adverse effect of excessive oversight of EPA is that it has caused the agency to go "underground" in its lawmaking. To avoid overseers, EPA has increasingly resorted to less formal means of announcing agency policy determinations. Instead of promulgating rules pursuant to the Administrative Procedure Act, EPA now frequently issues guidance memoranda and directives. Also, many important agency rulings are not reflected in generic rulemaking, but in individual permit decisions. OMB oversight is thereby avoided, and judicial review of agency action is limited.

Lazarus, "The Tragedy of Distrust in the Implementation of Federal Environmental Law," 54 *L. & Contemp. Problems* 311, 356 (1991). One unfortunate effect of this development is that it diminishes the public accountability of the agency, because it becomes increasingly difficult for outsiders to appraise the agency's activities.

Another way of short-circuiting procedural requirements, as well as heading off possible judicial review, is to continue issuing formal regulations, but to do so only after reaching a consensus among all interested parties about the content of the regulations. After all the major "players" have reached an agreement, the rulemaking procedures become only a formality; judicial review is not a risk because everyone who might be likely to attack the regulation in court has already "signed on" in advance. This approach has become known as regulatory negotiation or "reg-neg." In 1990, Congress provided an explicit statutory basis for reg-neg, and EPA has now used it several times with success. See Sigler, "Regulatory Negotiations: A Practical Perspective," 22 *Env.L.Rep.* 10647 (1992). For concerns about the widespread application of reg-neg, see Cary Loglianese, "Assessing Consensus: The Promise and Performance of Negotiated Rulemaking," 46 *Duke L.J.* 1255 (1997); Rose–Ackerman, "Consensus Versus Incentives: A Skeptical Look at Regulatory Negotiations," 42 *Duke L.J.* 1206, 1208–1212 (1994).

5. Was the Court too quick to dismiss the impact of NEPA on agency procedures? Consider this question in connection with the materials on NEPA later in this chapter. See also sections 102(A) and (B) of NEPA, which seem to call for some modifications in agency procedure.

6. As the next case illustrates, *Vermont Yankee* does not necessarily give the executive branch a free hand in procedural matters.

NATURAL RESOURCES DEFENSE COUNCIL, INC. v. ENVIRONMENTAL PROTECTION AGENCY

United States Court of Appeals, Third Circuit, 1982.
683 F.2d 752.

[The Clean Water Act requires EPA to promulgate regulations requiring that industry pretreat pollutants before releasing them into public treatment works. In 1978, EPA issued such regulations. On January 24, 1981, EPA promulgated in "final form" a set of amendments to the regulations. EPA designated March 13 as the effective date of the amendments. On January 29, President Reagan ordered a 60–day postponement in the effective dates of all regulations that were final but not yet effective. On February 17, a second Presidential order required cost benefit analysis of all "major" rules (with certain exceptions). Rules that had not yet become effective were to have their effective dates postponed indefinitely, unless "good cause" was shown. Pursuant to this Presidential order, EPA indefinitely postponed the effective date of the pretreatment regulations. NRDC then filed suit. EPA responded on October 13, 1981 by terminating the indefinite postponement and making the amendment effective January 31, 1982. In the meantime, it began a rulemaking proceeding to determine whether to further postpone the effective date. Ultimately, it decided to postpone some but not all of the pretreatment regulations.]

HUNTER, CIRCUIT JUDGE:

In this petition, NRDC challenges the failure of EPA to comply with APA notice and comment procedures when it indefinitely postponed the amendments. "[R]eview of an agency's procedural compliance with statutory norms is an exacting one." The exacting standard applicable in determining whether an agency has failed to comply with the procedural requirements for its action contrasts with the deferential standard applicable to substantive challenges to agency action. However, even though substantive agency actions are entitled to deference, and the scope of review of such actions is narrow, "sharp changes of agency course constitute 'danger signals' to which a reviewing court must be alert."

Where an agency has sharply changed its substantive policy, then, judicial review of its action, while deferential, will involve a scrutiny of the reasons given by the agency for the change. Here, NRDC has mounted a procedural attack on an agency's action. Review of the procedural aspects of an agency decision is more broad in any event than review of the substantive contents of an agency action. As with substantive review, however, it makes sense to scrutinize the procedures employed by the agency all the more closely where the agency has acted, within a compressed time frame, to reverse itself by the procedure under challenge. In this case, the agency, without notice and the opportunity for comment, abrogated rules which had been proposed, which had undergone years of notice and comment procedures, and which had been promulgated, with an effective date, in final form. By postponing the effective date of the amendments, EPA reversed its course of action up to the postponement. That reversal itself constitutes a danger signal. Where the reversal was accomplished without notice and an opportunity for comment, and without any statement by EPA on the impact of that postponement on the statutory scheme pursuant to which the amendments had been promulgated, the reviewing court must scrutinize that action all the more closely to insure that the APA was not violated.

* * *

In this case, EPA postponed the effective date of the amendments indefinitely, after those amendments had undergone notice and comment procedures, had been published in final form (including a "final" effective date), and had become final for purposes of judicial review. Both Ford and the Chemical Manufacturers' Association (but *not* EPA) contend that the indefinite postponement was not a rule, and therefore was not subject to the rulemaking requirements of the APA. Thus, the first question we must confront in ascertaining the legality of EPA's action is whether the APA rulemaking procedures apply at all in this case. In other words, where a rule has been published in final form after undergoing the notice and comment procedures required by the APA, and has become final for all purposes, may the agency promulgating the rule postpone it indefinitely without subjecting that indefinite postponement to the notice and comment procedures of the APA?

We conclude that, under the facts of this case, EPA's action in indefinitely postponing the effective date of the amendments fit the definition of "rule" in the APA, and, as such, was subject to the APA's rulemaking requirements. In general, an effective date is "part of an agency statement of general or particular applicability and of future effect." It is an essential part of any rule: without an effective date, the "agency statement" could have no "future effect," and could not serve to "implement, interpret, or prescribe law or policy." In short, without an effective date a rule would be a nullity because it would never require adherence.

If the effective date were not "part of an agency statement" such that material alterations in that date would be subject to the rulemaking provisions of the APA, it would mean that an agency could guide a future rule through the rulemaking process, promulgate a final rule, and then effectively repeal it, simply by indefinitely postponing its operative date. The APA specifically provides that the repeal of a rule is rulemaking subject to rulemaking procedures. Thus, a holding that EPA's action here was not a rule subject to the rulemaking procedure of the APA would create a contradiction in the statute where there need be no contradiction: the statute would provide that the repeal of a rule requires a rulemaking proceeding, but the agency could (albeit indirectly) repeal a rule simply by eliminating (or indefinitely postponing) its effective date, thereby accomplishing without rulemaking something for which the statute requires a rulemaking proceeding. By treating the indefinite postponement of the effective date as a rule for APA purposes, it is possible to avoid such an anomalous result.

* * *

We have ruled that the indefinite postponement of the effective date of the amendments required notice and comment procedures prior to becoming effective, and that EPA did not have good cause for dispensing with the APA's requirements. The final question we must face is the remedy. [The Court concluded that EPA's later actions could not cure its failure to use the proper rulemaking procedures in connection with the initial postponement. Consequently, it held that all of the pretreatment amendments went into effect on March 30, 1981.]

Notes

1. For a more recent example of procedural review, see *Ober v. U.S. EPA*, 84 F.3d 304 (9th Cir.1996). EPA had approved Arizona's implementation plan for controlling airborne particulates. After the comment period had expired, Arizona submitted an additional 300 pages of documentation to justify its rejection of some control measures. The court reversed because opponents did not have notice or an opportunity to comment on this submission. Also, EPA had given Arizona credit for more reductions than the state itself had claimed, in connection with a determination that the plan met the statutory requirement of "reasonable further progress." Again, the court found a lack of opportunity for comment. Are *Ober* and the main case consistent with *Vermont Yankee?* With the *spirit* of Justice Rehnquist's opinion?

2. The subject of cost-benefit analysis is increasingly important in environmental law. When it was promulgated, the Executive Order involved in the main case was called President Reagan's "most significant step yet in his administration's campaign to relieve the private sector of the burden of complying with federal regulations." Comment, "Reagan Orders Cost–Benefit Analysis of Regulations, Confers Broad Powers on OMB and Regulatory Task Force," 11 *ELR* 10044 (1981). OMB oversight was further strengthened in 1985. 46 *Fed.Reg.* 1036 (1985). OMB's role in environmental rulemaking has remained controversial but was largely reaffirmed by President Clinton in E.O. 12866. For further discussions of the proper limits of that role, see Percival, "Rediscovering the Limits of the Regulatory Review Authority of the Office of Management and Budget," 17 *Envir.L.Rep.* 10017 (1987); Strauss & Sunstein, "The Role of the President and OMB in Informal Rulemaking," 38 *Admin.L.Rev.* 181 (1986). For a thoughtful appraisal by an economist, see Rose–Ackerman, "Deregulation and Reregulation: Rhetoric and Reality," 6 *J.L. & Politics* 287, 293–296 (1990). We discuss cost-benefit analysis further in Chapter IV.

3. So far, we have considered how courts review an agency's determination on factual and procedural matters. How do courts review an agency's views on a legal issue? As we shall see at numerous points throughout this casebook, the process of statutory construction is hardly a straightforward one. The student who has not previously studied the interpretation of federal statutes should become aware of at least three points.

First, in the 1960s, federal courts begin to rely heavily on legislative history. Committee reports were given particular weight (especially the report of the conference committee); statements by a bill's sponsor were less important but still significant. In recent years, Justice Scalia has campaigned against use of legislative history. So far, he has failed to persuade a majority to exclude the use of legislative history, but he has succeeded in reducing reliance on this material.

Second, courts tend to defer to the construction adopted by the agency that administers the statute. Among the reasons for this deference are the complexity and technical nature of many environmental statutes and the subjects they regulate, the obscurity of much of the statutory language, and the agency's unique experience in dealing with these problems. There is also a need to give agency rules enough credibility so that industry will rely on them immediately, rather than waiting for years while the courts independently determine the legal issues.

Third, despite these doctrines, the final decision on statutory construction is made by the court after an independent consideration of the merits. In making this determination, statutory language and policy are both given weight; different judges vary in the relative weight they give these two factors.

These considerations are all rather abstract, but hopefully will become more meaningful to the reader after seeing how courts analyze the statutory questions considered in the remainder of the book. For a comprehensive treatment of statutory interpretation, see W. Eskridge & P. Frickey, *Cases and Materials on Legislation* (2d ed. 1995). For more specific discussions of statutory interpretation in the context of environmental law, see "Symposium on Statutory Interpretation and Environmental Law," 5 *NYU Env.L.J.* 292 (1996); Bradford Mank, "Is a Textualist Approach to Statutory Interpretation Pro–Environmentalist?: Why Pragmatic Agency Decisionmaking Is Better than Judicial Literalism," 53 *Washington & Lee L.Rev.* 1231 (1996).

C. THE NATIONAL ENVIRONMENTAL POLICY ACT

In addition to general principles of administrative law, judicial review and agency procedures in environmental cases are also heavily affected by NEPA. The provisions of the statute are well-summarized in Judge Skelly Wright's opinion in *Calvert Cliffs' Coordinating Committee v. United States AEC,* 449 F.2d 1109 (D.C.Cir.1971), one of the earliest major cases involving NEPA. Although the specific holdings of the case have been largely superseded by later developments, the opinion has been the foundation for much of the later judicial construction of NEPA. Judge Wright's opinion summarizes the main features of the statute as follows:

> The relevant portion of NEPA is Title I, consisting of five sections. Section 101 sets forth the Act's basic substantive policy: that the federal government "use all practicable means and measures" to protect environmental values. Congress did not establish environmental protection as an exclusive goal; rather, it desired a reordering of priorities, so that environmental costs and benefits will assume their proper place along with other considerations. In Section 101(b), imposing an explicit duty on federal officials, the Act provides that "it is the continuing responsibility of the Federal Government to use all practicable means, consistent with other essential considerations of national policy," to avoid environmental degradation, preserve "historic, cultural, and natural" resources, and promote "the widest range of beneficial uses of the environment without * * * undesirable and unintended consequences."

Thus the general substantive policy of the Act is a flexible one. It leaves room for a responsible exercise of discretion and may not require particular substantive results in particular problematic instances. However, the Act also contains very important "procedural" provisions—provisions which are designed to see that all federal agencies do in fact exercise the substantive discretion given them. These provisions are not highly flexible. Indeed, they establish a strict standard of compliance.

NEPA, first of all, makes environmental protection a part of the mandate of every federal agency and department. The Atomic Energy Commission, for example, had continually asserted, prior to NEPA, that it had no statutory authority to concern itself with the adverse environmental effects of its actions. Now, however, its hands are no longer tied. It is not only permitted, but compelled, to take environmental values into account. Perhaps the greatest importance of NEPA is to require the Atomic Energy Commission and other agencies to *consider* environmental issues just as they consider other matters within their mandates. This compulsion is most plainly stated in Section 102. There, "Congress authorizes and directs that, to the fullest extent possible: (1) the policies, regulations, and public laws of the United States shall be interpreted and administered in accordance with the policies set forth in this Act * * *." Congress also "authorizes and directs" that "(2) all agencies of the Federal Government shall" follow certain rigorous procedures in considering environmental values. Senator Jackson, NEPA's principal sponsor, stated that "[n]o agency will [now] be able to maintain that it has no mandate or no requirement to consider the environmental consequences of its actions." He characterized the requirements of Section 102 as "action-forcing" and stated that "[o]therwise, these lofty declarations [in Section 101] are nothing more than that."

The sort of consideration of environmental values which NEPA compels is clarified in Section 102(2)(A) and (B). In general, all agencies must use a "systematic, interdisciplinary approach" to environmental planning and evaluation "in decisionmaking which may have an impact on man's environment." In order to include all possible environmental factors in the decisional equation, agencies must "identify and develop methods and procedures * * * which will insure that presently unquantified environmental amenities and values may be given appropriate consideration in decisionmaking along with economic and technical considerations." "Environmental amenities" will often be in conflict with "economic and technical considerations." To "consider" the former "along with" the latter must involve a balancing process. In some instances environmental costs may outweigh economic and technical benefits and in other instances they may not. But NEPA mandates a rather finely tuned and "systematic" balancing analysis in each instance.

To ensure that the balancing analysis is carried out and given full effect, Section 102(2)(C) requires that responsible officials of all agencies prepare a "detailed statement" covering the impact of particular actions on the environment, the environmental costs which might be avoided, and alternative measures which might alter the cost-benefit equation. The apparent purpose of the "detailed statement" is to aid in the agencies' own decision making process and to advise other interested agencies and the public of the environmental consequences of planned federal action. Beyond the "detailed statement," Section 102(2)(D) requires all agencies specifically to "study, develop, and describe appropriate alternatives to recommended courses of action in any proposal which involves unresolved conflicts concerning alternative uses of available resources." This requirement, like the "detailed statement" requirement, seeks to ensure that each agency decision maker has before him and takes into proper account all possible approaches to a particular project (including total abandonment of the project) which would alter the environmental impact and the cost-benefit balance. Only in that fashion is it likely that the most intelligent, optimally beneficial decision will ultimately be made. Moreover, by compelling a formal "detailed statement" and a description of alternatives, NEPA provides evidence that the mandated decision making process has in fact taken place and, most importantly, allows those removed from the initial process to evaluate and balance the factors on their own.

Of course, all of these Section 102 duties are qualified by the phrase "to the fullest extent possible." We must stress as forcefully as possible that this language does not provide an escape hatch for footdragging agencies; it does not make NEPA's procedural requirements somehow "discretionary." Congress did not intend the Act to be such a paper tiger. Indeed, the requirement of environmental consideration "to the fullest extent possible" sets a high standard for the agencies, a standard which must be rigorously enforced by the reviewing courts.

* * *

Thus the Section 102 duties are not inherently flexible. They must be complied with to the fullest extent, unless there is a clear conflict of *statutory* authority. Considerations of administrative difficulty, delay or economic cost will not suffice to strip the section of its fundamental importance.

We conclude, then, that Section 102 of NEPA mandates a particular sort of careful and informed decision making process and creates judicially enforceable duties. The reviewing courts probably cannot reverse a substantive decision on its merits, under Section 101, unless it be shown that the actual balance of costs and benefits that was struck was arbitrary or clearly gave insufficient weight to environmental values. But if the decision was reached procedurally without individualized consideration and balancing of environmental factors—conducted fully and in good faith—it is the responsibility of the courts to reverse. * * *

For further discussion of the background and purposes of NEPA, see Andreen, "In Pursuit of NEPA's promise: The Role of Executive Oversight in the Implementation of Environmental Policy," 64 *Ind.L.J.* 205 (1989); W. Rodgers, *Environmental Law* § 9.1 (1994). D. Mandelker, *NEPA Law and Litigation* (2d ed. 1994), provides a comprehensive treatment of NEPA issues.

At the risk of being simplistic, the following observations may help make the development of NEPA law more understandable. The early decisions under NEPA were strongly influenced by activist judges such as Skelly Wright, who creatively used the statute to further environmental values. As time has gone on, however, the courts (and particularly the Supreme Court) have tended to "domesticate" NEPA by integrating it into the fabric of administrative law. See W. Rodgers, supra, at § 9.3. As we saw in the preceding section, post-*Overton Park* administrative law requires agencies to compile fairly elaborate records and explanations of their actions. The EIS can be reconceptualized as merely a specialized application of this general concept.

The integration of NEPA into administrative law has had some interesting technical consequences. First, as we will see, after a great deal of initial uncertainty, courts ended up applying the *Overton Park* standard of review to NEPA (namely, the "arbitrary and capricious" test). Second, technical APA concepts such as "final action" (which we saw used by Justice Scalia in *National Wildlife Fed.*, supra page 88) are now used under NEPA. An important recent example was *Public Citizen v. U.S. Trade Rep.*, 5 F.3d 549 (D.C.Cir.1993), in which the court refused to review a NEPA challenge to the NAFTA trade agreement, on the ground that the Trade Representative merely made a recommendation to the President, which was not a "final action." (The President's own actions, on the other hand, are not covered by the APA, so no judicial review was possible.) Third, courts have been increasingly cautious about allowing NEPA plaintiffs to go outside the administrative record. Rather, they normally must establish from the record compiled by the agency itself that the agency failed to investigate or consider important information. See French, "Judicial Review of the Administrative Record in NEPA Litigation," 81 *Cal.L.Rev.* 929 (1993). See also *National Audubon Society v. Hoffman*, 132 F.3d 7, 14–16 (2d Cir. 1997); *Greenpeace Action v. Franklin*, 14 F.3d 1324, 1334 (9th Cir.1992).

Despite this trend, NEPA still retains its own special flavor as an aspect of administrative law. The statutory text has made it difficult for courts to eliminate completely the idea that NEPA heightens the agency's normal duty to consider relevant factors. Perhaps more importantly, the CEQ has played a crucial role in implementing NEPA. Its regulations governing the production of the EIS have often served the function of preserving early judicial doctrines, which might otherwise have been expunged by later rulings.

1. THRESHOLD REQUIREMENTS

NEPA requires the filing of an environmental impact statement in connection with "legislation and other major Federal actions significantly affecting the quality of the human environment."[h] Thus, an EIS is needed only when a project is "major," constitutes a "federal action," and has a "significant environmental impact." The following materials involve the scope of these threshold requirements.

HANLY v. MITCHELL [HANLY I]

United States Court of Appeals, Second Circuit, 1972.
460 F.2d 640, cert. denied 409 U.S. 990, 93 S.Ct. 313, 34 L.Ed.2d 256 (1972).

FEINBERG, CIRCUIT JUDGE.

* * * The basic issue before us is whether [NEPA] was complied with in the planning for a nine-story federal jail in back of the United States Court House in Manhattan, just across the street from two large apartment buildings. Plaintiffs, who include some owners of these apartments, allege that defendants violated the Act. [The agency, GSA, had concluded that no impact statement was needed because the project would not have a substantial environmental impact.]

* * *

There is no doubt that the Act contemplates some agency action that does not require an impact statement because the action is minor and has so little effect on the environment as to be insignificant. * * * There is, however, a further question of statutory construction. Plaintiffs argue that if a federal action is "major," as defendants now concede this one is, it must have a "significant" effect on the environment and call for an impact statement. Defendants claim that the term "major Federal action" refers to the cost of the project, the amount of planning that preceded it, and the time required to complete it, but does not refer to the impact of the project on the environment. We agree with defendants that the two concepts are different and that the responsible federal agency has the authority to make its own threshold determination as to each in deciding whether an impact statement is necessary. * * *

* * *

GSA's entire determination regarding the Courthouse Annex—including both office building and jail—is found principally in a memorandum dated February 23, 1971, of George M. Paduano, who was then Regional Director of the Public Buildings Service of GSA, and, according

h. There are a few explicit exclusions from NEPA, ranging from the important (the Alaska oil pipeline) to the bizarre (the San Antonio Freeway). See Anderson, "The National Environmental Policy Act," in Environmental Law Inst., *Federal Environmental Law 273* (1974). Note that many EPA actions are also exempt. See § 511(c) of the Clean Water Act and 15 U.S.C.A. § 793. There is considerable dispute about whether the government's actions under the Endangered Species Act are covered by NEPA. See *Catron County Bd. v. U.S. FWS,* 75 F.3d 1429 (10th Cir.1996).

to defendants, the proper official to make such a decision under GSA's regulations. [The court then quotes the document.]

This document is terse, to say the least. Nonetheless, for the purpose of supporting GSA's determination that the proposed office building portion of the Courthouse Annex will have "no adverse effects on the environment," we believe, as did the district judge, that the document is sufficient. True, the memorandum fails to mention aesthetic and architectural considerations, but in a neighborhood such as this with public buildings of wildly varying architecture, we cannot say that failure to mention explicitly such considerations is a vital flaw. Further, as [another] memorandum makes clear, * * * "[t]he building will house 357 people, most of whom are already employed in the same general area." * * *

The proposed jail, however, stands on a different footing. The Paduano memorandum does adequately discuss problems of water, heat, sewage and garbage. But those considerations apply to virtually any building. The memorandum contains no hard look at the peculiar environmental impact of squeezing a jail into a narrow area directly across the street from two large apartment houses. Indeed, there is not even a word about those apartment houses or the others located nearby. If GSA were planning a missile base on that site, a compact discussion of sewage, garbage, water and heat would hardly be adequate. Additional factors would have to be considered, and the same principle holds true here. Plaintiffs claim that the living environment of all the families in this area will be adversely affected by the presence of the jail and by the fears of "riots and disturbances" so generated. In particular, plaintiffs argue that the city prison formerly located at Sixth Avenue and Eighth Street has been vacated because the noise of the inmates, their demonstrations, and the beckoning and signaling between them and their visitors caused disturbances in the neighborhood. The Paduano memorandum contains no hint that such possible disturbances were considered. Nor is there any mention of the potential dangers of housing an out-patient treatment center in this area. * * *

* * * The National Environmental Policy Act contains no exhaustive list of so-called "environmental considerations," but without question its aims extend beyond sewage and garbage and even beyond water and air pollution. The Act must be construed to include protection of the quality of life for city residents. Noise, traffic, overburdened mass transportation systems, crime, congestion and even availability of drugs all affect the urban "environment" and are surely results of the "profound influences of * * * high-density urbanization [and] industrial expansion." Section 101(a). Thus, plaintiffs do raise many "environmental considerations" that should not be ignored. We believe the record in this case indicates that, as to the proposed jail, they were.

* * *

We hasten to point out that we do not suggest plaintiffs are correct in claiming that the jail requires a section 102(2)(C) impact statement.

The area in back of the Court House may not be a residential area in the usual sense and the entire Courthouse Annex may actually be an improvement in the area—jail and all. Also, GSA is obviously not required to give the same weight to plaintiffs' concerns as plaintiffs do. But the essential point is that GSA must actually consider them.

Notes

1. Do you agree with the *Hanly* court's expansion of the "environmental impact" concept to include general "quality of life"? Do the general policies established in section 101 of NEPA shed any light on this question? Don't all major government actions have some effect on the quality of someone's life? In this connection, consider *Image of Greater San Antonio v. Brown*, 570 F.2d 517 (5th Cir.1978). The issue in that case was whether an EIS was required for a managerial decision to eliminate a number of jobs at an Air Force base. The former employees argued, not without justification, that the decision would have an adverse effect on the quality of their lives and those of their families. The court rejected this argument on the ground that:

> Although the language and legislative history of NEPA are somewhat less than clear, we are convinced that Congress did not intend that a managerial decision to discharge a number of employees would require preparation of an EIS. NEPA was enacted in recognition of the effect that man's activities—his technological advances, industrial expansion, resource exploitation, and urban development—have on the "natural environment." The primary concern was with the physical environmental resources of the nation. * * *

> We do not mean to say that socio-economic effects can never be considered under NEPA. When an action will have a primary impact on the natural environment, secondary socio-economic effects may also be considered. But when the threshold requirement of a primary impact on the physical environment is missing, socio-economic effects are insufficient to trigger an agency's obligation to prepare an EIS.

Id. at 522.[i] Do you agree with the court? Is there any basis in the statutory language for this distinction? How much weight should be given to the CEQ's adoption of this distinction in its regulations? (See 40 CFR § 1508.14)

2. Recall that in *Sierra Club v. Morton*, the Court held that an aesthetic interest was enough to confer standing. Should an aesthetic injury be considered environmental for NEPA purposes, for example when a historic building is demolished or a group of artists is evicted? See *Goodman Group, Inc. v. Dishroom*, 679 F.2d 182 (9th Cir.1982); *Preservation Coalition, Inc. v. Pierce*, 667 F.2d 851, 859–860 (9th Cir.1982). How about health

i. Similarly, *Nucleus of Chicago Homeowners Association v. Lynn*, 524 F.2d 225, 231 (7th Cir.1975), rejected the suggestion that a scattered-site public housing project involved a substantial environmental impact. (The plaintiffs had argued that an EIS was needed because of the anti-social conduct supposedly characteristic of public housing tenants.) Does this holding conflict with *Hanly*? Under *Hanly*, is an allegation that a project would cause "urban blight" sufficient to justify an impact statement? See *City of Rochester v. United States Postal Service*, 541 F.2d 967 (2d Cir.1976). See generally, Ackerman, "Impact Statements and Low Cost Housing," 46 *So.Cal.L.Rev.* 754 (1973).

effects? Is the risk that a packaging change will increase the chances of tampering with liquor bottles an "environmental" risk? See *Glass Packaging Institute v. Regan,* 737 F.2d 1083 (D.C.Cir.1984). If *Hanly* is correct that the risk of increased criminal activity in a neighborhood is environmental, why not the risk of another "Tylenol episode"?

3. The *Hanly* court's distinction between the "major action" and "significant impact" requirements received a mixed reception. It was criticized by other courts,[j] and by commentators.[k] The CEQ Regulations state that "[m]ajor reinforces but does not have a meaning independent of significantly." 40 CFR § 1508.18 (1980). See also *Fund for Animals v. Thomas,* 127 F.3d 80 (D.C.Cir.1997) (action with small geographic scope and "negligible" environmental effects is not "major").

Note that even if an action is not "major" and therefore does not require an EIS, § 102(2)(E) of NEPA generally still requires agency consideration of alternatives.

METROPOLITAN EDISON CO. v. PEOPLE AGAINST NUCLEAR ENERGY

Supreme Court of the United States, 1983.
460 U.S. 766, 103 S.Ct. 1556, 75 L.Ed.2d 534.

JUSTICE REHNQUIST delivered the opinion of the Court.

The issue in these cases is whether petitioner Nuclear Regulatory Commission (NRC) complied with the National Environmental Policy Act, when it considered whether to permit petitioner Metropolitan Edison Co. to resume operation of the Three Mile Island Unit 1 nuclear power plant (TMI–1). The Court of Appeals for the District of Columbia Circuit held that the NRC improperly failed to consider whether the risk of an accident at TMI–1 might cause harm to the psychological health and community well-being of residents of the surrounding area. We reverse.

Metropolitan owns two nuclear power plants at Three Mile Island near Harrisburg, Pennsylvania. Both of these plants were licensed by the NRC after extensive proceedings, which included preparation of Environmental Impact Statements (EIS). On March 28, 1979, TMI–1 was not operating; it had been shut down for refueling. TMI–2 was operating, and it suffered a serious accident that damaged the reactor * * *.

After the accident, the NRC ordered Metropolitan to keep TMI–1 shut down until it had an opportunity to determine whether the plant could be operated safely. The NRC then published a notice of hearing specifying several safety related issues for consideration. The notice stated that the Commission had not determined whether to consider

j. See, e.g., *Minnesota Public Interest Research Group v. Butz,* 498 F.2d 1314, 1321–22 (8th Cir.1974) (en banc); *Davis v. Morton,* 469 F.2d 593 (10th Cir.1972).

k. See W. Rodgers, *Environmental Law* 873 (2d ed. 1994).

psychological harm or other indirect effects of the accident or of renewed operation of TMI–1.

* * *

All the parties agree that effects on human health can be cognizable under NEPA, and that human health may include psychological health. The Court of Appeals thought these propositions were enough to complete a syllogism that disposes of the case: NEPA requires agencies to consider effects on health. An effect on psychological health is an effect on health. Therefore, NEPA requires agencies to consider the effects on psychological health asserted by PANE. PANE, using similar reasoning, contends that because the psychological health damage to its members would be caused by a change in the environment (renewed operation of TMI–1), NEPA requires the NRC to consider that damage. Although these arguments are appealing at first glance, we believe they skip over an essential step in the analysis. They do not consider the closeness of the relationship between the change in the environment and the "effect" at issue.

* * *

To paraphrase the statutory language in light of the facts of this case, where an agency action significantly affects the quality of the human environment, the agency must evaluate the "environmental impact" and any unavoidable adverse environmental effects of its proposal. The theme of § 102 is sounded by the adjective "environmental": NEPA does not require the agency to assess *every* impact or effect of its proposed action, but only the impact or effect on the environment. If we were to seize the word "environmental" out of its context and give it the broadest possible definition, the words "adverse environmental effects" might embrace virtually any consequence of a governmental action that someone thought "adverse." But we think the context of the statute shows that Congress was talking about the physical environment—the world around us, so to speak. NEPA was designed to promote human welfare by alerting governmental actors to the effect of their proposed actions on the physical environment.

To determine whether § 102 requires consideration of a particular effect, we must look at the relationship between that effect and the change in the physical environment caused by the major federal action at issue. For example, if the Department of Health and Human Services were to implement extremely stringent requirements for hospitals and nursing homes receiving federal funds, many perfectly adequate hospitals and homes might be forced out of existence. The remaining facilities might be so limited or so expensive that many ill people would be unable to afford medical care and would suffer severe health damage. Nonetheless, NEPA would not require the Department to prepare an EIS evaluating that health damage because it would not be proximately related to a change in the physical environment.

Some effects that are "caused by" a change in the physical environment in the sense of "but for" causation, will nonetheless not fall within § 102 because the causal chain is too attenuated. For example, residents of the Harrisburg area have relatives in other parts of the country. Renewed operation of TMI–1 may well cause psychological health problems for these people. They may suffer "anxiety, tension and fear, a sense of helplessness," and accompanying physical disorders, because of the risk that their relatives may be harmed in a nuclear accident. However, this harm is simply too remote from the physical environment to justify requiring the NRC to evaluate the psychological health damage to these people that may be caused by renewed operation of TMI–1.

Our understanding of the congressional concerns that led to the enactment of NEPA suggests that the terms "environmental effect" and "environmental impact" in § 102 be read to include a requirement of a reasonably close causal relationship between a change in the physical environment and the effect at issue. This requirement is like the familiar doctrine of proximate cause from tort law.[10] The issue before us then is how to give content to this requirement. This is a question of first impression in this Court.

The federal action that affects the environment in this case is permitting renewed operation of TMI–1. The direct effects on the environment of this action include release of low-level radiation, increased fog in the Harrisburg area (caused by operation of the plant's cooling towers), and the release of warm water into the Susquehanna River. The NRC has considered each of these effects in its EIS, and again in the EIA. Another effect of renewed operation is a risk of a nuclear accident. The NRC has also considered this effect.[11]

PANE argues that the psychological health damage it alleges "will flow directly from the risk of [a nuclear] accident." But a *risk* of an accident is not an effect on the physical environment. A risk is, by definition, unrealized in the physical world. In a causal chain from renewed operation of TMI–1 to psychological health damage, the element of risk and its perception by PANE's members are necessary middle links.[12] We believe that the element of risk lengthens the causal chain beyond the reach of NEPA.

10. In drawing this analogy, we do not mean to suggest that any cause-effect relation too attenuated to merit damages in a tort suit would also be too attenuated to merit notice in an EIS; nor do we mean to suggest the converse. In the context of both tort law and NEPA, courts must look to the underlying policies or legislative intent in order to draw a manageable line between those causal changes that may make an actor responsible for an effect and those that do not.

11. The NRC concluded that the risk of an accident had not changed significantly since the EIS for TMI–1 was prepared in 1972.

We emphasize that in this case we are considering effects caused by the risk of an accident. The situation where an agency is asked to consider effects that will occur if a risk is realized, for example, if an accident occurs at TMI–1, is an entirely different case. The NRC considered, in the original EIS and in the most recent EIA for TMI–1, the possible effects of a number of accidents that might occur at TMI–1.

12. This risk can be perceived differently by different people. Indeed, it appears that the members of PANE perceive a much greater risk of another nuclear accident at

Risk is a pervasive element of modern life; to say more would belabor the obvious. Many of the risks we face are generated by modern technology, which brings both the possibility of major accidents and opportunities for tremendous achievements. Medical experts apparently agree that risk can generate stress in human beings, which in turn may rise to the level of serious health damage. For this reason among many others, the question whether the gains from any technological advance are worth its attendant risks may be an important public policy issue. Nonetheless, it is quite different from the question whether the same gains are worth a given level of alteration of our physical environment or depletion of our natural resources. The latter question rather than the former is the central concern of NEPA.

* * *

This case bears strong resemblance to other cases in which plaintiffs have sought to require agencies to evaluate the risk of crime from the operation of a jail or other public facility in their neighborhood. The plaintiffs in these cases could have alleged that the risk of crime (or their dislike of the occupants of the facility) would cause severe psychological health damage.[13] The operation of the facility is an event in the physical environment, but the psychological health damage to neighboring residents resulting from unrealized risks of crime is too far removed from that event to be covered by NEPA. The psychological health damage alleged by PANE is no closer to an event in the environment or to environmental concerns.

The Court of Appeals thought that PANE's contentions are qualitatively different from the harm at issue in the cases just described. It thought PANE raised an issue of health damage, while those cases presented questions of fear or policy disagreement. We do not believe this line is so easily drawn. Anyone who fears or dislikes a project may find himself suffering from "anxiety, tension, fear, [and] a sense of helplessness." Neither the language nor the history of NEPA suggest that it was intended to give citizens a general opportunity to air their policy objections to proposed federal actions. The political process, and not NEPA, provides the appropriate forum in which to air policy disagreements.[14]

JUSTICE BRENNAN, concurring.

Three Mile Island than is perceived by the NRC and its staff.

13. Although these cases involved similar facts, they presented different legal issues. They did not consider allegations that risk of crime would lead to psychological health damage. They did hold that the risk of crime, or the plaintiffs' concern about crime do not constitute environmental effects. Of course, these holdings are not at issue in this case.

14. PANE's original contention seems to be addressed as much to the symbolic significance of continued operation of TMI–1 as to the risk of an accident. NEPA does not require consideration of stress caused by the symbolic significance individuals attach to federal actions. Psychological health damage caused by a symbol is even farther removed from the physical environment, and more closely connected with the broader political process, than psychological health damage caused by risk.

I join the opinion of the Court. There can be no doubt that psychological injuries are cognizable under NEPA. As the Court points out, however, the particular psychological injury alleged in this case did not arise, for example, out of the direct sensory impact of a change in the physical environment, but out of a perception of risk. In light of the history and policies underlying NEPA, I agree with the Court that this crucial distinction "lengthens the causal chain beyond the reach" of the statute.

Notes

1. Does *Metropolitan Edison* overrule *Hanly I*, supra page 138? After *Metropolitan Edison*, can the term "environmental" ever extend beyond direct effects on the physical environment? See W. Rodgers, *Environmental Law* 942–946 (2d ed. 1994). At least one court of appeals has expressed serious doubts about whether socio-economic effects can ever be considered, even if some physical effects are also present. See *Olmsted Citizens for a Better Community v. United States,* 793 F.2d 201, 206 (8th Cir.1986) (no impact statement required for conversion of a mental hospital into a prison hospital). Also, Judge Posner has argued that aesthetic effects should rarely compel the completion of an impact statement, since they can be adequately described in the environmental assessment. *River Road Alliance, Inc. v. Corps of Engineers of U.S. Army,* 764 F.2d 445 (7th Cir.1985), cert. denied 475 U.S. 1055, 106 S.Ct. 1283, 89 L.Ed.2d 590 (1986). But other courts continue to require discussion in the EIS of socioeconomic effects that are "interrelated" with physical effects. See, e.g., *Tongass Conserv. Soc. v. Cheney,* 924 F.2d 1137 (D.C.Cir.1991) (R. Ginsburg, J.). For a summary of the post-*PANE* cases, see Smith, "Consideration of Socioeconomic Effects Under NEPA and the EC Directive on Environmental Impact Assessment, 1992 *U.Chi.L.F.* 355, 363.

2. Note the use of the causation concept in the Supreme Court's opinion. Is the causation requirement more or less onerous than the causation requirement for standing? What is the Court's rationale for adopting its causation requirement?

3. Prior to *Metropolitan Edison*, the Court had decided two cases dealing with NEPA's threshold requirements. The first case was *Flint Ridge Development Co. v. Scenic Rivers Association,* 426 U.S. 776, 96 S.Ct. 2430, 49 L.Ed.2d 205 (1976). *Flint Ridge* involved a statute requiring certain real estate developers to file a disclosure statement with HUD. The issue before the Court was whether HUD was required to file an EIS. The Court held that no EIS was required, but without reaching the question of whether there was a major federal action significantly affecting the environment. Instead, the Court held that NEPA was inapplicable because HUD faced a statutory 30–day deadline in responding to disclosure statements. This deadline was too short to allow an EIS. Hence, requiring an EIS "would create an irreconcilable and fundamental conflict with the Secretary's duties under the Disclosure Act."

The second case was *Andrus v. Sierra Club,* 442 U.S. 347, 99 S.Ct. 2335, 60 L.Ed.2d 943 (1979). In *Andrus*, the Court held that appropriations requests are neither "proposals for legislation" nor major federal actions.

The only aspect of *Andrus* destined to have broader significance was the Court's reliance on CEQ regulations. Unlike the regulations discussed in *Hanly II* below, these regulations were issued pursuant to an executive order which makes them binding on all federal agencies. The Court held that these regulations were entitled to "substantial deference."

4. Once "environmental effects" are defined, the question still remains how to determine whether such effects are major and significant. This question was the focus of another Second Circuit opinion later in the *Hanly* litigation.

HANLY v. KLEINDIENST [HANLY II]

United States Court of Appeals, Second Circuit, 1972.
471 F.2d 823, cert. denied 412 U.S. 908, 93 S.Ct. 2290, 36 L.Ed.2d 974 (1973).

MANSFIELD, CIRCUIT JUDGE.

Following the remand a new threshold determination in the form of a 25–page "Assessment of the Environmental Impact" ("Assessment" herein) was made by the GSA and submitted to the district court on June 15, 1972. This document (to which photographs, architect's renditions and a letter of approval from the Director of the Office of Lower Manhattan Development, City of New York, are attached) reflects a detailed consideration of numerous relevant factors. Among other things, it analyzes the size, exact location, and proposed use of the MCC; its design features, construction, and aesthetic relationship to its surroundings; the extent to which its occupants and activities conducted in it will be visible by the community; the estimated effects of its operation upon traffic, public transit and parking facilities; its approximate population, including detainees and employees; its effect on the level of noise, smoke, dirt, obnoxious odors, sewage and solid waste removal; and its energy demands. It also sets forth possible alternatives, concluding that there is none that is satisfactory. Upon the basis of this Assessment the Acting Commissioner of the Public Building Service Division of the GSA, who is the responsible official in charge, concluded on June 7, 1972, that the MCC was not an action significantly affecting the quality of the human environment.

* * *

[The court first considered the proper standard of review.]

Where the court's interpretation of statutory language requires some appraisal of facts, a neat delineation of the legal issues for the purpose of substituted judicial analysis has sometimes proven to be impossible or, at least, inadvisable. Furthermore, in some cases a complete *de novo* analysis of the legal questions, though theoretically possible, may be undesirable for the reason that the agency's determination reflects the exercise of expertise not possessed by the court. * * * Accordingly, with respect to review of such mixed questions of law and fact the Supreme Court has authorized a simpler, more practical standard, the "rational basis" test, whereby the agency's decision will be accepted where it has "warrant in the record" and a "reasonable basis in law."

Notwithstanding the possible availability of the "rational basis" standard, we believe that the appropriate criterion in the present case is the "arbitrary, capricious" standard established by the Administrative Procedure Act, since the meaning of the term "significantly" as used in § 102(2)(C) of NEPA can be isolated as a question of law. This was the course taken by the district court and is in accord with the Supreme Court's decision in [*Overton Park,* supra page 119]. * * *

* * *

Guidelines issued by the CEQ, which are echoed in rules for implementation published by the Public Buildings Service, the branch of GSA concerned with the construction of the MCC, suggest that a formal impact statement should be prepared with respect to "proposed actions, the environmental impact of which is likely to be highly controversial." However, the term "controversial" apparently refers to cases where a substantial dispute exists as to the size, nature or effect of the major federal action rather than to the existence of opposition to a use, the effect of which is relatively undisputed. This Court in *Hanly I,* for instance, did not require a formal impact statement with respect to the office building portion of the Annex despite the existence of neighborhood opposition to it. The suggestion that "controversial" must be equated with neighborhood opposition has also been rejected by others. See *Citizens for Reid State Park v. Laird,* 336 F.Supp. 783 (D.Me.1972).

In the absence of any Congressional or administrative interpretation of the term, we are persuaded that in deciding whether a major federal action will "significantly" affect the quality of the human environment the agency in charge, although vested with broad discretion, should normally be required to review the proposed action in the light of at least two relevant factors: (1) the extent to which the action will cause adverse environmental effects in excess of those created by existing uses in the area affected by it, and (2) the absolute quantitative adverse environmental effects of the action itself, including the cumulative harm that results from its contribution to existing adverse conditions or uses in the affected area. Where conduct conforms to existing uses, its adverse consequences will usually be less significant than when it represents a radical change. Absent some showing that an entire neighborhood is in the process of redevelopment, its existing environment, though frequently below an ideal standard, represents a norm that cannot be ignored. For instance, one more highway in an area honeycombed with roads usually has less of an adverse impact than if it were constructed through a roadless public park.

Although the existing environment of the area which is the site of a major federal action constitutes one criterion to be considered, it must be recognized that even a slight increase in adverse conditions that form an existing environmental milieu may sometimes threaten harm that is significant. One more factory polluting air and water in an area zoned for industrial use may represent the straw that breaks the back of the environmental camel. Hence the absolute, as well as comparative, effects of a major federal action must be considered.

Chief Judge Friendly's thoughtful dissent, while conceding that we (and governmental agencies) face a difficult problem in determining the meaning of the vague and amorphous term "significantly" as used in § 102(2)(C), offers no solution other than to suggest that an impact statement should be required whenever a major federal action might be "arguably" or "potentially" significant and that such an interpretation would insure the preparation of impact statements except in cases of "true" insignificance. In our view this suggestion merely substitutes one form of semantical vagueness for another. * * *

* * *

* * * Now that the GSA has made and submitted its redetermination in the form of a 25–page "Assessment," our task is to determine (1) whether it satisfies the foregoing tests as to environmental significance, and (2) whether GSA, in making its assessment and determination, has observed "procedure required by law" as that term is used in § 10 of the APA, 5 U.S.C.A. § 706(2)(D).

* * *

Appellants offer little or no evidence to contradict the detailed facts found by the GSA. For the most part their opposition is based upon a psychological distaste for having a jail located so close to residential apartments, which is understandable enough. It is doubtful whether psychological and sociological effects upon neighbors constitute the type of factors that may be considered in making such a determination since they do not lend themselves to measurement. However we need not decide that issue because these apartments were constructed within two or three blocks of another existing jail, The Manhattan House of Detention for Men, which is much larger than the proposed MCC and houses approximately 1,200 prisoners. Furthermore the area in which the MCC is located has at all times been zoned by the City of New York as a commercial district designed to provide for a wide range of uses, *specifically including "Prisons."*

Despite the GSA's scrupulous efforts the appellants do present one or two factual issues that merit further consideration and findings by the GSA. One bears on the possibility that the MCC will substantially increase the risk of crime in the immediate area, a relevant factor as to which the Assessment fails to make an outright finding despite the direction to do so in *Hanly I.* Appellants urge that the Community Treatment Program and the program for observation and study of nonresident out-patients will endanger the health and safety of the immediate area by exposing neighbors and passersby to drug addicts visiting the MCC for drug maintenance and to drug pushers and hangers-on who would inevitably frequent the vicinity of a drug mainte- nance center. If the MCC were to be used as a drug treatment center, the potential increase in crime might tip the scales in favor of a mandatory detailed impact statement. * * *

Appellants further contend that they have never been given an opportunity to discuss the MCC with any governmental agency prior to GSA's submission of its Assessment, which raises the question whether the agency acted "without observance of procedure required by law," — [citing *Overton Park*]. We do not share the Government's view that the procedural mandates of § 102(A), (B), and (D), apply only to actions found by the agency itself to have a significant environmental effect. While these sections are somewhat opaque, they are not expressly limited to "major Federal actions significantly affecting the quality of the human environment." Indeed if they were so limited § 102(D), which requires the agency to develop appropriate alternatives to the recommended course of action, would be duplicative since § 102(C), which does apply to actions "significantly affecting" the environment, specifies that the detailed impact statement must deal with "alternatives to the proposed action."

* * *

A more serious question is raised by the GSA's failure to comply with § 102(2)(B), which requires the agency to "identify and develop methods and procedures * * * which will insure that presently unquantified environmental amenities and values may be given appropriate consideration in decisionmaking along with economic and technical considerations." Since an agency, in making a threshold determination as to the "significance" of an action, is called upon to review in a general fashion the same factors that would be studied in depth for preparation of a detailed environmental impact statement, § 102(2)(B) requires that some rudimentary procedures be designed to assure a fair and informed ← preliminary decision. Otherwise the agency, lacking essential information, might frustrate the purpose of NEPA by a threshold determination that an impact statement is unnecessary. Furthermore, an adequate record serves to preclude later changes in use without consideration of their environmental significance as required by NEPA.

* * *

Notwithstanding the absence of statutory or administrative provisions on the subject, this Court has already held in *Hanly I* that federal agencies must "affirmatively develop a reviewable environmental record * * * even for purposes of a threshold section 102(2)(C) determination." We now go further and hold that before a preliminary or threshold determination of significance is made the responsible agency must give notice to the public of the proposed major federal action and an opportunity to submit relevant facts which might bear upon the agency's threshold decision. We do not suggest that a full-fledged formal hearing must be provided before each such determination is made, although it should be apparent that in many cases such a hearing would be advisable for reasons already indicated. The necessity for a hearing will depend greatly upon the circumstances surrounding the particular proposed action and upon the likelihood that a hearing will be more effective than other methods in developing relevant information and an understanding of the proposed action. The precise procedural steps to be adopted are better left to the agency, which should be in a better position than the court to determine whether solution of the problems faced with respect to a specific major federal action can better be achieved through a hearing or by informal acceptance of relevant data.

FRIENDLY, CHIEF JUDGE (dissenting):

The learned opinion of my brother Mansfield gives these plaintiffs, and environmental advocates in future cases, both too little and too much. It gives too little because it raises the floor of what constitutes "major Federal actions significantly affecting the quality of the human environment," higher than I believe Congress intended. It gives too much because it requires that before making a threshold determination that no impact statement is demanded, the agency must go through procedures which I think are needed only when an impact statement must be made. The upshot is that a threshold determination that a proposal does not constitute major Federal action significantly affecting the quality of the human environment becomes a kind of mini-impact statement. The preparation of such a statement under the conditions laid down by the majority is unduly burdensome when the action is truly minor or insignificant. On the other hand, there is a danger that if the threshold determination is this elaborate, it may come to replace the impact statement in the grey area between actions which, though "major" in a monetary sense, are obviously insignificant (such as the construction of the proposed office building) and actions that are obviously significant (such as the construction of an atomic power plant). We would better serve the purposes of Congress by keeping the threshold low enough to insure that impact statements are prepared for actions in this grey area and thus to permit the determination that no statement is required to be made quite informally in cases of true insignificance.

* * *

It is not readily conceivable that Congress meant to allow agencies to avoid this central requirement by reading "significant" to mean only "important," "momentous," or the like. One of the purposes of the impact statement is to insure that the relevant environmental data are before the agency and considered by it prior to the decision to commit Federal resources to the project; the statute must not be construed so as to allow the agency to make its decision in a doubtful case without the relevant data or a detailed study of it. * * *

* * *

I thus reach the question whether, with the term so narrowed, the GSA's refusal to prepare an impact statement for the MCC can be supported. Accepting the majority's standard of review, I would think that, even with the fuller assessment here before us, the GSA could not reasonably conclude that the MCC does not entail potentially significant environmental effects. I see no ground for the majority's doubt "whether psychological and sociological effects upon neighbors constitute the type of factors that may be considered in making such a determination [of significant environmental effect] since they do not lend themselves to measurement." The statute speaks of "the overall welfare and development of man," and makes it the responsibility of Federal agencies to "use all practicable means * * * to * * * assure for all Americans safe, healthful, productive, and esthetically and culturally pleasing surroundings." Moreover, § 102(2)(B) directs that "presently unquantified environmental amenities and values * * * be given appropriate consideration in decisionmaking along with economic and technical considerations." I cannot believe my brothers would entertain the same doubt concerning the relevance of psychological and sociological factors if a building like the MCC were to be constructed at Park Avenue and East 72nd Street, assuming that zoning allowed it.

Notes on NEPA Threshold Issues

1. Note the court's comment that "[a]bsent some showing that an entire neighborhood is in the process of redevelopment, its existing environment, though frequently below an ideal standard, represents a norm that cannot be ignored." This observation seems innocuous enough, and a similar view is echoed by courts that view compliance with local zoning as evidence against any significant impact. See D. Mandelker, *NEPA Law and Litigation* § 8.08[3] (2d ed. 1994). But the implications are potentially troubling. Recall the discussion of environmental justice in Chapter I. Poor and minority neighborhoods are more likely to suffer already from a lack of environmental amenities, and from an excess of environmental disamenities. Hence, any given project is less likely to be considered significant if it is located in such a neighborhood, rather than in a more affluent area. (Is it unfair to suggest that the *Hanly* court would have been less troubled by a proposed jail in Harlem?) Because performing an EIS involves both expense and delay, there is consequently an incentive (other things being equal) to locate environmentally questionable projects in "bad" neighborhoods. Is this "environmental racism" or merely realistic urban planning?

2. Was the majority's creation of procedural requirements consistent with *Vermont Yankee,* page 125 supra? Can it be defended on the basis of § 102(2)(B)? (Section 102(2)(B) requires agencies to develop procedures to "insure that presently unquantified environmental amenities and values may be given appropriate consideration in decisionmaking along with economic and technical consideration.") See *Cross-Sound Ferry Services, Inc. v. United States,* 573 F.2d 725 (2d Cir.1978). For a survey of procedural requirements under NEPA, see W. Rodgers, Environmental Law § 9.2A (1998 Supp.).

The CEQ regulations now contain detailed procedural requirements for the entire EIS process, which are binding on all federal agencies. See 40 CFR § 1500.3.[1] The process normally begins with an "environmental assess-

---

1. See also, *United States ex rel. Accardi v. Shaughnessy,* 347 U.S. 260, 74 S.Ct. 499, 98 L.Ed. 681 (1954); *United States v. Nixon,* 418 U.S. 683, 94 S.Ct. 3090, 41 L.Ed.2d

ment," 40 CFR §§ 1501.3–1501.4, which is to be prepared under procedures the agencies were required to develop themselves. § 1507.3. The environmental assessment is to be "a concise public document" that "[b]riefly provide[s] sufficient evidence and analysis" for deciding whether to produce an EIS, and that also considers alternatives to the proposed action, as required by § 102(2)(E) of NEPA. 40 CFR § 1508.9. If the agency decides not to prepare an EIS, it must make a "finding of no significant impact" (FONSI) available to the public. § 1501.4(e)(1).

The first step in the EIS process is called "scoping." Scoping is intended: (a) to obtain early participation by other agencies and the public in planning the EIS, (b) to determine the scope of the EIS, and (c) to determine the significant issues to be discussed in the EIS. § 1501.7(a).

The actual preparation of the EIS itself involves a draft EIS, a comment period, and a final EIS. §§ 1503.1, 1503.4. Agencies with jurisdiction or special expertise relating to the project are required to comment. § 1503.2. Major interagency disagreements are to be referred to CEQ, which can then take a variety of actions, including publication of recommendations or referral to the President. §§ 1504.1, 1504.3(f). When an agency reaches a final decision on the project, it must prepare a "record of decision" summarizing its actions, and explaining why it rejected environmentally preferable alternatives and mitigation measures. § 1503.3.

3. The problem of defining "substantial" impact has not proved easy. Professor Mandelker views the judicial opinions on this subject as ad hoc. See D. Mandelker, *NEPA Law and Litigation* § 8.08[3] (2d ed. 1994). The CEQ Regulations provide a helpful list of the relevant factors:

"Significantly" as used in NEPA requires considerations of both context and intensity:

(a) *Context.* This means that the significance of an action must be analyzed in several contexts such as society as a whole (human, national), the affected region, the affected interests, and the locality. Significance varies with the setting of the proposed action. For instance, in the case of a site-specific action, significance would usually depend upon the effects in the locale rather than in the world as a whole. Both short-and long-term effects are relevant.

(b) *Intensity.* This refers to the severity of impact. Responsible officials must bear in mind that more than one agency may make decisions about partial aspects of a major action. The following should be considered in evaluating intensity:

(1) Impacts that may be both beneficial and adverse. A significant effect may exist even if the Federal agency believes that on balance the effect will be beneficial.

(2) The degree to which the proposed action affects public health or safety.

1039 (1974) (both holding agency procedural regulations to be judicially enforceable). Many agencies have supplemented the CEQ regulations with EIS regulations of their own.

(3) Unique characteristics of the geographic area such as proximity to historic or cultural resources, park lands, prime farmlands, wetlands, wild and scenic rivers, or ecologically critical areas.

(4) The degree to which the effects on the quality of the human environment are likely to be highly controversial.

(5) The degree to which the possible effects on the human environment are highly uncertain or involve unique or unknown risks.

(6) The degree to which the action may establish a precedent for future actions with significant effects or represents a decision in principle about a future consideration.

(7) Whether the action is related to other actions with individually insignificant but cumulatively significant impacts. Significance exists if it is reasonable to anticipate a cumulatively significant impact on the environment. Significance cannot be avoided by terming an action temporary or by breaking it down into small component parts.

(8) The degree to which the action may adversely affect districts, sites, highways, structures, or objects listed in or eligible for listing in the National Register of Historic Places or may cause loss or destruction of significant scientific, cultural, or historical resources.

(9) The degree to which the action may adversely affect an endangered or threatened species or its habitat that has been determined to be critical under the Endangered Species Act of 1973.

(10) Whether the action threatens a violation of Federal, State, or local law or requirements imposed for the protection of the environment.

40 CFR § 1508.27.

Judge Posner has offered another interesting test for whether an impact is significant:

> The statutory concept of "significant" impact has no determinate meaning, and to interpret it sensibly in particular cases requires a comparison that is also a prediction: whether the time and expense of preparing an environmental impact statement are commensurate with the likely benefits from a more searching evaluation than an environmental assessment provides.

River Road Alliance, supra, 764 F.2d at 445. Do you find this test helpful?

The *Hanly* court attached little importance to the existence of a public controversy regarding the project. In *Jones v. Gordon,* 792 F.2d 821 (9th Cir.1986), the court held that public comments arguing that the project would have adverse environmental effects required the agency to prepare an EIS. On the other hand, another court found 120 letters and a petition signed by 558 people insufficient to constitute "a substantial number of persons" opposing the project, which would have required an environmental assessment under agency regulations. *West Houston Air Committee v. FAA,* 784 F.2d 702 (5th Cir.1986). See also *Greenpeace Action v. Franklin,* 14 F.3d

1324, 1333–34 (9th Cir.1992). What role should public controversy play in determining the need for an EA or EIS?

4.   Another troublesome problem considered in *Hanly II* is the scope of judicial review on threshold determinations. The lower courts were sharply divided on this issue. See Hoskins, "Judicial Review of an Agency's Decision Not to Prepare an Environmental Impact Statement," 18 *Envir.L.Rep.* 10331 (1988).

The issue now appears to have been mostly resolved by *Marsh v. Oregon Natural Resources Council* [infra p. 172], in which the Court adopted the arbitrary and capricious standard. *Marsh* involved a somewhat different issue—whether to supplement an existing EIS rather than whether to prepare an EIS at all. Nevertheless, the Court's language in *Marsh* seems quite applicable to review of threshold issues. See Mandelker, "NEPA Alive and Well: The Supreme Court Takes Two," 19 *Envir.L.Rep.* 10385, 10386 (1989).

Despite *Marsh*, some lack of clarity may still linger regarding the scope of review for threshold requirements. The majority position is that *Marsh* applies, see *Sierra Club v. Lujan*, 949 F.2d 362 (10th Cir.1991) (citing cases); *Greenpeace Action v. Franklin*, 14 F.3d 1324, 1331 (9th Cir.1992). At least one opinion continues to endorse a reasonableness standard, *Goos v. ICC*, 911 F.2d 1283, 1292 (8th Cir.1990) (applying "arbitrary and capricious" to the significant impact issue, but using a reasonableness test for determining whether there was a major federal action). See also *Village of Grand View v. Skinner*, 947 F.2d 651 (2d Cir.1991) (asking whether agency took a "hard look" at issuance of an SIP, then applying the "arbitrary and capricious" test as a second stage in the inquiry); *National Audubon Soc. v. Hoffman*, 132 F.3d 7, 13–14 (2d Cir.1997) (similar two-step analysis; EIS should be prepared when significance of action is a "close call").

Note on the "Federal Action" Requirement

Besides the issues considered in the *Hanly* cases, an additional threshold issue sometimes also arises: Is there a *federal* action? The CEQ Regulations provide a good synthesis of the case law:

> "Major Federal action" includes actions with effects that may be major and which are potentially subject to Federal control and responsibility. Major reinforces but does not have a meaning independent of significantly (§ 1508.27). Actions include the circumstance where the responsible officials fail to act and that failure to act is reviewable by courts or administrative tribunals under the Administrative Procedure Act or other applicable law as agency action.
>
> (a) Actions include new and continuing activities, including projects and programs entirely or partly financed, assisted, conducted, regulated, or approved by federal agencies; new or revised agency rules, regulations, plans, policies, or procedures; and legislative proposals (§§ 1506.8, 1508.17). Actions do not include funding assistance solely in the form of general revenue sharing funds, distributed under the State and Local Fiscal Assistance Act of 1972, 31 U.S.C.A. § 1221 et seq., with no Federal agency control over the subsequent use of such funds. Actions

do not include bringing judicial or administrative civil or criminal enforcement actions.

40 CFR § 1508.18. For a survey of the earlier cases, see Ellis & Smith, "The Limits of Federal Environmental Responsibility and Control Under the National Environmental Policy Act," 18 *Envir.L.Rep.* 10055 (1988). Under the so-called "small handle" doctrine, if only a minor part of a project is under federal control, only impacts from that portion of the project need be considered. See, e.g., *Macht v. Skinner*, 916 F.2d 13 (D.C.Cir.1990).

A closely related problem is posed by attempts to "de-federalize" a project in order to avoid NEPA. Courts have generally been inhospitable to such attempts. See *San Antonio Conservation Society v. Texas Highway Department*, 446 F.2d 1013 (5th Cir.1971), cert. denied 406 U.S. 933, 92 S.Ct. 1775, 32 L.Ed.2d 136 (1972); *Scottsdale Mall v. State of Indiana*, 549 F.2d 484 (7th Cir.1977), cert. denied 434 U.S. 1008, 98 S.Ct. 717, 54 L.Ed.2d 750 (1978).

Still another related problem is posed when the federal government has failed to exercise its power to prevent actions by others. Courts have generally (but not always) held NEPA inapplicable. See *Defenders of Wildlife v. Andrus*, 627 F.2d 1238 (D.C.Cir.1980); Comment, "Inaction as Action Under NEPA: EIS Not Required for Interior's Failure to Halt Alaskan Wolf Hunt," 10 *Envir.L.Rep.* 10055 (1980). For instance, where a valid contract with a private party did not leave the agency with any discretion to object to a logging road on environmental grounds, neither NEPA nor the ESA applied, according to the Ninth Circuit. See *Sierra Club v. Babbitt*, 65 F.3d 1502 (9th Cir.1995). Likewise, the Forest Service's advice to a logging company on how to avoid violating the ESA was not an agency action requiring an EIS, since the agency was in effect explaining the conditions under which it would decline to take enforcement action. See *Marbled Murrelet v. Babbitt*, 83 F.3d 1068 (9th Cir.1996).

When a project is undertaken by others, but with sufficient federal involvement to trigger NEPA, may an injunction be issued against the nonfederal defendants? In an important case requiring an EIS for outdoor genetic engineering experiments, the court upheld an injunction against a university on the ground that "judicial power to enforce NEPA extends to private parties where 'non-federal action cannot lawfully begin or continue without the prior approval of a federal agency.' " *Foundation on Economic Trends v. Heckler*, 756 F.2d 143, 155 (D.C.Cir.1985).

2. SCOPE AND TIMING OF THE IMPACT STATEMENT

SCIENTISTS' INSTITUTE FOR PUBLIC INFORMATION, INC. v. AEC

United States Court of Appeals, District of Columbia Circuit, 1973.
481 F.2d 1079.

J.   SKELLY WRIGHT, CIRCUIT JUDGE.

[The issue in this case was whether the AEC's Liquid Metal Fast Breeder Reactor program, which is described below, required an environmental impact statement.]

I. FACTUAL BACKGROUND: THE LIQUID METAL
FAST BREEDER REACTOR PROGRAM

Although more than a superficial understanding of the technology underlying this case is beyond the layman's ken, a brief summary will prove helpful. Nuclear reactors use nuclear fission—the splitting of the atom—to produce heat which may be used to generate electricity in nuclear power plants. Only a few, relatively rare, naturally occurring substances—primarily Uranium–235—can maintain the nuclear fission chain reaction necessary for operation of these reactors. There are thus severe constraints on the long run potential of nuclear energy for generating electricity unless new nuclear fuel is "artificially" produced. Such fuel can be produced through the process of "breeding" within a "fast breeder reactor." The fast breeder reactor differs from the now common light water nuclear reactor in that the neutrons which split atoms in the fuel (thereby releasing new neutrons and heat energy) travel much faster than the neutrons in ordinary reactors. The reactor breeds new fuel through what has aptly been termed "a sort of modern alchemy." Some neutrons leave the inner core of the reactor, which is made up of fissionable Uranium–235, and enter a blanket of nonfissionable Uranium–238. When atoms in this blanket are struck by neutrons, they are transmuted into Plutonium–239, itself a fissionable fuel which can be removed from the reactor and used in other installations. It is estimated that after about 10 years of operation the typical fast breeder reactor will produce enough fissionable Plutonium–239 not only to refuel itself completely, but also to fuel an additional reactor of comparable size. The Liquid Metal Fast Breeder Reactor (henceforth LMFBR) is simply a fast breeder reactor that uses a liquid metal, sodium, as a coolant and heat transfer agent.

Because the breeding principle makes possible vast expansion of fuel available for nuclear reactors (Uranium–238 is many times more common than Uranium–235), it has been the subject of considerable interest since the earliest days of atomic energy. * * * In sum, the Commission came to see its program as serving "as the key to effecting the transition of the fast breeder program from the technology development stage to the point of large-scale commercial utilization."

* * *

The LMFBR's prospects are sufficiently bright to have led President Nixon to say: "Our best hope today for meeting the Nation's growing demand for economical clean energy lies with the fast breeder reactor." And the Commission has recently predicted that by the year 2000 LMFBR capacity will equal total electrical generating capacity in the United States today.

II. APPLICATION OF NEPA TO TECHNOLOGY DEVELOPMENT PROGRAMS

* * * That the Commission must issue a detailed statement for each of the major test facilities and demonstration plants encompassed by the LMFBR program is conceded by the Commission * * *. The question

raised, instead, is basically twofold: whether at some point in time the Commission must issue a statement for the research and development program as a whole, rather than simply for individual facilities, and, assuming an affirmative answer to this question, whether a statement covering the entire program should be drafted now.

* * *

* * * The Commission's basic position seems to be that NEPA requires detailed statements only for particular facilities, and that no separate NEPA analysis of an entire research and development program is required. [The cumulative effect of the whole program would apparently be discussed in these individual impact statements, and perhaps also in an "environmental survey."]

The Commission takes an unnecessarily crabbed approach to NEPA in assuming that the impact statement process was designed only for particular facilities rather than for analysis of the overall effects of broad agency programs. Indeed, quite the contrary is true. * * *

We think it plain that at some point in time there should be a detailed statement on the overall LMFBR program. The program comes before the Congress as a "proposal for legislation" each year, in the form of appropriations requests by the Commission. And as the Council on Environmental Quality has noted in its NEPA Guidelines, the statutory phrase "recommendation or report on proposals for legislation" includes "[r]ecommendations or favorable reports relating to legislation *including that for appropriations.*" In addition, the program constitutes "major Federal action" within the meaning of the statute.

* * *

It is apparent, however, that the Commission seeks to avoid issuing its forthcoming "environmental survey" as an impact statement under Section 102, not out of any desire to circumvent NEPA's procedural requirements, but rather because of a fear that Section 102's requirements as to the contents of an impact statement are so strict, particularly as to the need for "detail" in the statement, that any Commission attempt to issue its environmental survey as a NEPA statement would be doomed to failure. While we do not altogether understand the Commission's fears, we feel they are based on certain misapprehensions as to what NEPA requires.

[In an omitted portion of the opinion, the court attempts to assuage the agency's fears by explaining that NEPA requires reasonable forecasts, not "crystal ball inquiry."]

* * *

III.   TIMING THE NEPA STATEMENT

Whether a statement on the overall LMFBR program should be issued now or at some uncertain date in the future is the most difficult question presented by this case. * * *

In our view, the timing question can best be answered by reference to the underlying policies of NEPA in favor of meaningful, timely information on the effects of agency action. In the early stages of research, when little is known about the technology and when future application of the technology is both doubtful and remote, it may well be impossible to draft a meaningful impact statement. * * * NEPA requires predictions, but not prophecy, and impact statements ought not to be modeled upon the works of Jules Verne or H.G. Wells. At the other end of the spectrum, by the time commercial feasibility of the technology is conclusively demonstrated, and the effects of application of the technology certain, the purposes of NEPA will already have been thwarted. Substantial investments will have been made in development of the technology and options will have been precluded without consideration of environmental factors. Any statement prepared at such a late date will no doubt be thorough, detailed and accurate, but it will be of little help in ensuring that decisions reflect environmental concerns. Thus we are pulled in two directions. Statements must be written late enough in the development process to contain meaningful information, but they must be written early enough so that whatever information is contained can practically serve as an input into the decision making process.

Determining when to draft an impact statement for a technology development program obviously requires a reconciliation of these competing concerns. Some balance must be struck, and several factors should be weighed in the balance. How likely is the technology to prove commercially feasible, and how soon will that occur? To what extent is meaningful information presently available on the effects of application of the technology and of alternatives and their effects? To what extent are irretrievable commitments being made and options precluded as the development program progresses? How severe will be the environmental effects if the technology does prove commercially feasible?

Answers to questions like these require agency expertise, and therefore the initial and primary responsibility for striking a balance between the competing concerns must rest with the agency itself, not with the courts. At the same time, however, some degree of judicial scrutiny of an agency's decision that the time is not yet ripe for a NEPA statement is necessary in order to ensure that the policies of the Act are not being frustrated or ignored. Agency decisions in the environmental area touch on fundamental personal interests in life and health, and these interests have always had a special claim to judicial protection.

* * *

* * * Our examination of this record leads us to conclude that the Commission could have no rational basis for deciding that the time is not yet ripe for drafting an impact statement on the overall LMFBR program. * * *

* * *

* * * [I]t is evident that the program presents unique and unprecedented environmental hazards. The Commission itself concedes it is expected that by the year 2000 some 600,000 cubic feet of high-level concentrated radioactive wastes will have been generated. These wastes will pose an admitted hazard to human health for hundreds of years, and will have to be maintained in special repositories. The environmental problems attendant upon processing, transporting and storing these wastes, and the other environmental issues raised by widespread deployment of LMFBR power plants, warrant the most searching scrutiny under NEPA.

ABERDEEN & ROCKFISH RAILROAD v. STUDENTS CHALLENGING REGULATORY AGENCY PROCEDURES (SCRAP II)

Supreme Court of the United States, 1975.
422 U.S. 289, 95 S.Ct. 2336, 45 L.Ed.2d 191.

[This case is a sequel to *SCRAP I,* page 86 supra, in which the Court granted the plaintiffs standing. On remand, the district court held that the ICC had failed to comply with NEPA in determining the environmental impact of the proposed general rate increase. The district court found three deficiencies in the agency procedure. First, the agency did not hold any hearings before adopting its final EIS. Second, the court found that the EIS analyzed only the impact of the rate increase, rather than the problems caused by the underlying rate structure. Third, the EIS was lacking in rigor.

On appeal, the Supreme Court began by noting that the reviewability of ICC approval of a general rate increase was unclear. However, the Court held that compliance with NEPA was a severable procedural issue. "When agency or departmental consideration of environmental factors in connection with [a] 'federal action' is complete, notions of finality and exhaustion do not stand in the way of judicial review of the adequacy of such consideration, even though other aspects of the rate increase are not ripe for review."

Justice White's opinion for the Court then turned to the NEPA issues.]

We agree with appellants that the District Court erred in deciding that the oral hearing which the ICC chose to hold prior to its October 4, 1972, order was an "existing agency review process" during which a final draft environmental impact statement (i.e., the one circulated in March 1973) should have been available. * * *

NEPA provides that "such statement * * * shall accompany *the proposal* through the existing agency review processes" (emphasis added). This sentence does not, contrary to the District Court opinion, affect the time when the "statement" must be prepared. It simply says what must be done with the "statement" once it is prepared—it must accompany the "proposal." The "statement" referred to is the one required to be included "in every recommendation or report on proposals for * * * major Federal actions significantly affecting the quality of the human environment" and is apparently the final impact statement, for no other kind of statement is mentioned in the statute. Under *this* sentence of the statute, the time at which the agency must prepare the final "statement" is the time at which it makes a recommendation or report on a *proposal* for federal action. Where an agency initiates federal action by publishing a proposal and then holding hearings on the proposal, the statute would appear to require an impact statement to be included in the proposal and to be considered at the hearing. Here, however, until the October 4, 1972, report, the ICC had made no proposal, recommendation, or report. The only proposal was the proposed new rates filed by the railroads. Thus, the earliest time at which the *statute* required a statement was the time of the ICC's report of October 4, 1972—some time after the oral hearing.

* * *

In order to decide what kind of an environmental impact statement need be prepared, it is necessary first to describe accurately the "federal action" being taken. The action taken here was a decision—entirely nonfinal with respect to particular rates—not to declare unlawful a *percentage increase* which on its face applied equally to virgin and some recyclable materials and which on its face limited the increase permitted on other recyclables. As in most general revenue proceedings, the "action" was taken in response to the railroads' claim of a financial crisis; and the inquiry * * * was primarily into the question whether such a crisis—usually thought to entitle the railroads to the general increase—existed, leaving *primarily* to more appropriate future proceedings the task of answering challenges to rates on individual commodities or categories thereof. The point is that it is the latter question—usually involved in a general revenue proceeding only to a limited extent—which may raise the most serious environmental issues. The former question—the entitlement of the railroads to some kind of a general rate increase—raises few environmental issues and none which is claimed in this case to have been inadequately addressed in the impact statement.

The appellees insist that the decision not to prevent the facially neutral increases itself involves an impact on the environment when superimposed on an underlying rate structure which discriminates against recyclables.

[The Court rejects this argument on the grounds that (1) the fairness of the underlying rate structure is not at issue in a general rate proceeding and (2) the ICC had begun a separate proceeding to consider that issue.]

The decision of the lower court, therefore, to deem the "federal action" involved [in this case] to include an implicit approval of the underlying rate structure was inaccurate and led it to an entirely unwarranted intrusion into an apparently sensible decision by the ICC to take much more limited "action" in that proceeding and to undertake the larger action in a *separate* proceeding better suited to the task.

Having defined the scope of the "federal action" being taken * * * our decision of this case becomes easy. The lower court held that the environmental impact statement inadequately explored the underlying rate structure and the *extent* to which the use of recyclables will be affected by the rate structure. Whatever the result would have been if the ICC had been approving the entire rate structure * * *, given the nature of the action taken by the ICC, the lower court was plainly incorrect.

Note

The Court in *SCRAP II* seems to adopt a fairly mechanistic test. Once the "proposal" and the "federal action" are correctly identified, the scope and timing problems are solved almost automatically under the Court's approach. The *SIPI* court, on the other hand, used a more policy-oriented approach. Which approach is more faithful to the legislative intent? To the judicial role? The following case is the Court's definitive word on the issues of timing and scope.

KLEPPE v. SIERRA CLUB

Supreme Court of the United States, 1976.
427 U.S. 390, 96 S.Ct. 2718, 49 L.Ed.2d 576.

JUSTICE POWELL delivered the opinion of the Court.

Respondents, several organizations concerned with the environment, brought this suit in July 1973 in the United States District Court for the District of Columbia. The defendants in the suit, petitioners here, were the officials of the Department and other federal agencies responsible for issuing coal leases, approving mining plans, granting rights-of-way and taking the other actions necessary to enable private companies and public utilities to develop coal reserves on land owned or controlled by the Federal Government. Citing widespread interest in the reserves of a region identified as the "Northern Great Plains region," and an alleged threat from coal-related operations to their members' enjoyment of the region's environment, respondents claimed that the federal officials could not allow further development without preparing a "comprehensive environmental impact statement" under § 102(2)(C) [of NEPA] on the entire region. They sought declaratory and injunctive relief.

* * *

The record and the opinions of the courts below contain extensive facts about coal development and the geographic area involved in this suit. The facts that we consider essential, however, can be stated briefly.

The "Northern Great Plains region" identified in respondents' complaint encompasses portions of four States—northeastern Wyoming, eastern Montana, western North Dakota and western South Dakota.

There is no dispute about its richness in coal, nor about the waxing interest in developing that coal, nor about the crucial role the federal petitioners will play due to the significant percentage of the coal to which they control access. The Department has initiated, in this decade, three studies in areas either inclusive of or included within this region. The North Central Power Study was addressed to the potential for coordinated development of electric power in an area encompassing all or part of 15 States in the north central United States. It aborted in 1972 for lack of interest on the part of electric utilities. The Montana–Wyoming Aqueducts Study, intended to recommend the best use of water resources for coal development in southeastern Montana and northeastern Wyoming, was suspended in 1972 with the initiation of the third study, the Northern Great Plains Resources Program (NGPRP).

While the record does not reveal the degree of concern with environmental matters in the first two studies, it is clear that the NGPRP was devoted entirely to the environment. It was carried out by an inter-agency, federal-state task force with public participation, and was designed "to assess the potential social, economic and environmental impacts" from resource development in five States—Montana, Wyoming, South Dakota, North Dakota, and Nebraska. Its primary objective was "to provide an analytical and informational framework for policy and planning decisions at all levels of government" by formulating several "scenarios" showing the probable consequences for the area's environment and culture from the various possible techniques and levels of resource development. The final interim report of the NGPRP was issued August 1, 1975, shortly after the decision of the Court of Appeals in this case.

In addition, since 1973 the Department has engaged in a complete review of its coal leasing program for the entire Nation. * * * The purpose of the program review was to study the environmental impact of the Department's entire range of coal-related activities and to develop a planning system to guide the national leasing program. The impact statement, known as the "Coal Programmatic EIS," went through several drafts before issuing in final form on September 19, 1975— shortly before the petition for certiorari was filed in this case. * * *

* * *

The major issue remains the one with which the suit began: whether NEPA requires petitioners to prepare an environmental impact statement on the entire Northern Great Plains region. Petitioners, arguing the negative, rely squarely upon the facts of the case and the language of § 102(2)(C) of NEPA. We find their reliance well placed.

* * * Respondents can prevail only if there has been a report or recommendation on a proposal for major federal action with respect to the Northern Great Plains region. Our statement of the relevant facts shows there has been none; instead, all proposals are for actions of either local or national scope.

The local actions are the decisions by the various petitioners to issue a lease, approve a mining plan, issue a right-of-way permit, or take other action to allow private activity at some point within the region identified by respondents. Several courts of appeals have held that an impact statement must be included in the report or recommendation on a proposal for such action if the private activity to be permitted is one "significantly affecting the quality of the human environment" within the meaning of § 102(2)(C). The petitioners do not dispute this requirement in this case, and indeed have prepared impact statements on several proposed actions of this type in the Northern Great Plains during the course of this litigation. Similarly, the federal petitioners agreed at oral argument that § 102(2)(C) required the Coal Programmatic EIS that was prepared in tandem with the new national coal leasing program and included as part of the final report on the proposal for adoption of that program. Their admission is well made, for the new leasing program is a coherent plan of national scope, and its adoption surely has significant environmental consequences.

But there is no evidence in the record of an action or a proposal for an action of regional scope. The District Court, in fact, expressly found that there was no existing or proposed plan or program on the part of the Federal Government for the regional development of the area described in respondents' complaint. It found also that the three studies initiated by the Department in areas either included within or inclusive of respondents' region—that is, the Montana–Wyoming Aqueducts Study, the North Central Power Study, and the NGPRP—were not parts of any plan or program to develop or encourage development of the Northern Great Plains. That court found no evidence that the individual coal development projects undertaken or proposed by private industry and public utilities in that part of the country are integrated into a plan or otherwise interrelated. These findings were not disturbed by the Court of Appeals, and they remain fully supported by the record in this Court.

* * *

The Court of Appeals, in reversing the District Court, did not find that there was a regional plan or program for development of the Northern Great Plains region. It accepted all of the District Court's findings of fact, but concluded nevertheless that the petitioners "contemplated" a regional plan or program. * * *

* * *

Even had the record justified a finding that a regional program was contemplated by the petitioners, the legal conclusion drawn by the Court of Appeals cannot be squared with the Act. The court recognized that the mere "contemplation" of certain action is not sufficient to require an impact statement. But it believed the statute nevertheless empowers a court to require the preparation of an impact statement to begin at some point prior to the formal recommendation or report on a proposal. The

Court of Appeals accordingly devised its own four-part "balancing" test for determining when, during the contemplation of a plan or other type of federal action, an agency must begin a statement. The factors to be considered were identified as the likelihood and imminence of the program's coming to fruition, the extent to which information is available on the effects of implementing the expected program and on alternatives thereto, the extent to which irretrievable commitments are being made and options precluded "as refinement of the proposal progresses," and the severity of the environmental effects should the action be implemented.

* * *

The Court's reasoning and action find no support in the language or legislative history of NEPA. The statute clearly states when an impact statement is required, and mentions nothing about a balancing of factors. Rather, as we noted [in *SCRAP II*] last Term, under the first sentence of § 102(2)(C) the moment at which an agency must have a final statement ready "is the time at which it makes a recommendation or report on a *proposal* for federal action." The procedural duty imposed upon agencies by this section is quite precise, and the role of the courts in enforcing that duty is similarly precise. A court has no authority to depart from the statutory language and, by a balancing of court-devised factors, determine a point during the germination process of a potential proposal at which an impact statement *should be prepared*. Such an assertion of judicial authority would leave the agencies uncertain as to their procedural duties under NEPA, would invite judicial involvement in the day-to-day decision making process of the agencies, and would invite litigation. As the contemplation of a project and the accompanying study thereof do not necessarily result in a proposal for major federal action, it may be assumed that the balancing process devised by the Court of Appeals also would result in the preparation of a good many unnecessary impact statements.

* * *

Our discussion thus far has been addressed primarily to the decision of the Court of Appeals. It remains, however, to consider the contention now urged by respondents. They have not attempted to support the Court of Appeals' decision. Instead, respondents renew an argument they appear to have made to the Court of Appeals, but which that court did not reach. Respondents insist that, even without a comprehensive federal plan for the development of the Northern Great Plains, a "regional" impact statement nevertheless is required on all coal-related projects in the region because they are intimately related.

There are two ways to view this contention. First, it amounts to an attack on the sufficiency of the impact statements already prepared by the petitioners on the coal-related projects that they have approved or stand ready to approve. As such, we cannot consider it in this proceeding, for the case was not brought as a challenge to a particular impact statement and there is no impact statement in the record. It also is possible to view the respondents' argument as an attack upon the decision of the petitioners not to prepare one comprehensive impact statement on all proposed projects in the region. This contention properly is before us, for the petitioners have made it clear they do not intend to prepare such a statement.

We begin by stating our general agreement with respondents' basic premise that § 102(2)(C) may require a comprehensive impact statement in certain situations where several proposed actions are pending at the same time. NEPA announced a national policy of environmental protection and placed a responsibility upon the Federal Government to further specific environmental goals by "all practicable means, consistent with other essential considerations of national policy." NEPA § 101(b). Section 102(2)(C) is one of the "action-forcing" provisions intended as a directive to "all agencies to assure consideration of the environmental impact of their action in decision-making." By requiring an impact statement Congress intended to assure such consideration during the development of a proposal or—as in this case—during the formulation of a position on a proposal submitted by private parties. A comprehensive impact statement may be necessary in some cases for an agency to meet this duty. Thus, when several proposals for coal-related actions that will have cumulative or synergistic environmental impact upon a region are pending concurrently before an agency, their environmental consequences must be considered together.[15] Only through comprehensive consideration of pending proposals can the agency evaluate different courses of action.[16]

* * *

Respondents conceded at oral argument that to prevail they must show that petitioners have acted arbitrarily in refusing to prepare one comprehensive statement on this entire region, and we agree. The determination of the region, if any, with respect to which a comprehensive statement is necessary requires the weighing of a number of relevant factors, including the extent of the interrelationship among proposed actions and practical considerations of feasibility. Resolving these issues requires a high level of technical expertise and is properly

---

15. At some points in their brief respondents appear to seek a comprehensive impact statement covering contemplated projects in the region as well as those that already have been proposed. The statute, however, speaks solely in terms of *proposed* actions; it does not require an agency to consider the possible environmental impacts of less imminent actions when preparing the impact statement on proposed actions. Should contemplated actions later reach the stage of actual proposals, impact statements on them will take into account the effect of their approval upon the existing environment; and the condition of that environment presumably will reflect earlier proposed actions and their effects.

16. Neither the statute nor its legislative history contemplates that a court should substitute its judgment for that of the agency as to the environmental consequences of its actions. The only role for a court is to insure that the agency has taken a "hard look" at environmental consequences; it cannot "interject itself within the area of discretion of the executive as to the choice of the action to be taken." *Natural Resources Defense Council v. Morton,* 148 U.S.App.D.C. 5, 16, 458 F.2d 827, 838 (1972).

left to the informed discretion of the responsible federal agencies. Absent a showing of arbitrary action, we must assume that the agencies have exercised this discretion appropriately. Respondents have made no showing to the contrary.

Respondents' basic argument is that one comprehensive statement on the Northern Great Plains is required because all coal-related activity in that region is "programmatically, geographically, and environmentally" related. Both the alleged "programmatic" relationship and the alleged "geographic" relationship resolve, ultimately, into an argument that the region is proper for a comprehensive impact statement because the petitioners themselves have approached environmental study in this area on a regional basis. Respondents point primarily to the NGPRP, which they claim—and petitioners deny—focused on the region described in the complaint. The precise region of the NGPRP is unimportant, [because it was only a background study]. As for the alleged "environmental" relationship, respondents contend that the coal-related projects "will produce a wide variety of cumulative environmental impacts" throughout the Northern Great Plains region. They described them as follows: diminished availability of water, air and water pollution, increases in population and industrial densities, and perhaps even climatic changes. Cumulative environmental impacts are, indeed, what require a comprehensive impact statement. But determination of the extent and effect of these factors, and particularly identification of the geographic area within which they may occur, is a task assigned to the special competency of the appropriate agencies. Petitioners dispute respondents' contentions that the interrelationship of environmental impacts is regionwide[17] and, as respondents' own submissions indicate, petitioners appear to have determined that the appropriate scope of comprehensive statements should be based on basins, drainage areas, and other factors. We cannot say that petitioners' choices are arbitrary. Even if environmental interrelationships could be shown conclusively to extend across basins and drainage areas, practical considerations of feasibility might well necessitate restricting the scope of comprehensive statements.

In sum, respondents' contention as to the relationships between all proposed coal-related projects in the Northern Great Plains region does not require that petitioners prepare one comprehensive impact statement covering all before proceeding to approve specific pending applications.[18] As we already have determined that there exists no proposal for

17. For example, respondents assert that coal mines in the region are environmentally interrelated because opening one reduces the supply of water in the region for others. Petitioners contend that the water supply for each aquifer or basin within the region—of which there are many—is independent.

Moreover, petitioners state in their reply brief that few active or proposed mines in respondents' region are located within 50 miles of any other mine, and there are only 30 active or proposed mines in the entire 90,000 square miles of the region.

18. Nor is it necessary that petitioners always complete a comprehensive impact statement on all proposed actions in an appropriate region before approving any of the projects. As petitioners have emphasized, and respondents have not disputed, approval of one lease or mining plan does not commit the Secretary to approval of any others; nor, apparently, do single approvals

regionwide action that could require a regional impact statement, the judgment of the Court of Appeals must be reversed, and the judgment of the District Court reinstated and affirmed.

Notes

1.   For further information on the factual background of the case, see Tiefer, "NEPA and Energy Supply: A Case Study of the Effects of *Sierra Club v. Morton* on Coal Production in the Northern Great Plains," *Env.Rep. Monograph No. 22* (1976). One fact of interest is that the Sierra Club made a deliberate decision not to challenge the sufficiency of the individual EISs, in part because to do so would require litigation in dozens of cases as additional leases were issued. See Johnston, "*Kleppe v. Sierra Club:* An Environmental Planning Catch–22," 1 *Harv.Env.L.J.* 182, 187–188 (1976).

2.   *Kleppe* was given a rather critical reception. See W. Rodgers, *Environmental Law* 924–28 (2d ed. 1994); Comment, "The Scope of the Program EIS Requirement: The Need for a Coherent Judicial Approach," 30 *Stan. L.Rev.* 767 (1978); Note, "Program Environmental Impact Statements," 75 *Mich.L.Rev.* 107, 117–118 (1976); Tiefer, supra note 1, at 195–196, 202. Two criticisms of *Kleppe* seem most prevalent. First, it is argued that the *Kleppe* test is both too mechanical and unhelpful, because it assumes that the presence or absence of a "proposal" is self-evident. (How would the *Kleppe* Court decide which, if any, of the hundreds of documents generated by the breeder reactor program in *SIPI* constituted a "proposal"?) Second, it is argued that the Court was overly deferential to agency decisions and ignored the overriding policies of NEPA. Do you agree?

Note on Proposal Definition, Scope, and Timing

The CEQ regulations address both the timing and scope issues. On the timing issue, the most important provision is 40 CFR § 1508.23, which defines the term "proposal" as follows:

> "Proposal" exists at that stage in the development of an action when an agency subject to the Act has a goal and is actively preparing to make a decision on one or more alternative means of accomplishing that goal and the effects can be meaningfully evaluated. Preparation of an environmental impact statement on a proposal should be timed (§ 1502.5) so that the final statement may be completed in time for the statement to be included in any recommendation or report on the proposal. A proposal may exist in fact as well as by agency declaration that one exists.

Section 1508.23 must be read together with two other sections. Section 1502.5 provides:

> An agency shall commence preparation of an environmental impact statement as close as possible to the time the agency is developing or is presented with a proposal (§ 1508.23) so that preparation can be com-

by the other petitioners commit them to subsequent approvals. Thus an agency could approve one pending project that is fully covered by an impact statement, then take into consideration the environmental effects of that existing project when preparing the comprehensive statement on the cumulative impact of the remaining proposals. Cf. n. 20, supra.

pleted in time for the final statement to be included in any recommendation or report on the proposal. The statement shall be prepared early enough so that it can serve practically as an important contribution to the decisionmaking process and will not be used to rationalize or justify decisions already made * * *.

This section is reinforced by § 1501.2, which provides that "[a]gencies shall integrate the NEPA process with other planning at the earliest possible time to insure that planning and decisions reflect environmental values, to avoid delays later in the process, and to head off potential conflicts." These regulations suggest a need to construe the definition of "proposal" in favor of early application. Courts, however, have continued to have difficulty in defining "proposal." For a review of the cases, see D. Mandelker, *NEPA Law and Litigation* § 8.03[4] (2d ed. 1994).

The Regulations also provide explicit criteria on the scope issue:

Scope consists of the range of actions, alternatives, and impacts to be considered in an environmental impact statement. The scope of an individual statement may depend on its relationships to other statements (§§ 1502.20 and 1508.28). To determine the scope of environmental impact statements, agencies shall consider 3 types of actions, 3 types of alternatives, and 3 types of impacts. They include:

(a) Actions (other than unconnected single actions) which may be:

(1) Connected actions, which means that they are closely related and therefore should be discussed in the same impact statement. Actions are connected if they:

(i) Automatically trigger other actions which may require environmental impact statements.

(ii) Cannot or will not proceed unless other actions are taken previously or simultaneously.

(iii) Are interdependent parts of a larger action and depend on the larger action for their justification.

(2) Cumulative actions, which when viewed with other proposed actions have cumulatively significant impacts and should therefore be discussed in the same impact statement.

(3) Similar actions, which when viewed with other reasonably foreseeable or proposed agency actions, have similarities that provide a basis for evaluating their environmental consequences together, such as common timing or geography. An agency may wish to analyze these actions in the same impact statement. It should do so when the best way to assess adequately the combined impacts of similar actions or reasonable alternatives to such actions is to treat them in a single impact statement.

(b) Alternatives, which include: (1) No action alternative. (2) Other reasonable courses of actions. (3) Mitigation measures (not in the proposed action).

(c) Impacts, which may be: (1) Direct. (2) Indirect. (3) Cumulative.

40 CFR § 1508.25.

Despite *Kleppe,* the courts of appeals have continued to require agencies to take a "hard look" at cumulative impacts. See *Resources Limited v. Robertson,* 35 F.3d 1300, 1305 (9th Cir.1993). As one court said in a case involving one of a series of dams, the "synergistic impact of the project should be taken into account at some stage, and certainly before the last dam is completed." *Oregon Natural Resources Council v. Marsh,* 832 F.2d 1489, 1498 (9th Cir.1987). The lower courts have taken the CEQ regulations seriously, see *Thomas v. Peterson,* 753 F.2d 754 (9th Cir.1985); *LaFlamme v. FERC,* 852 F.2d 389, 401 (9th Cir.1988); *Fritiofson v. Alexander,* 772 F.2d 1225, 1246–47 (5th Cir.1985). They have looked to factors like the extent of the current commitment and the specificity of future impacts in determining the need for an impact statement, much like the test used in *SIPI.* See *Sierra Club v. Marsh,* 769 F.2d 868, 878 (1st Cir.1985). On the other hand, a mere allegation that various federal actions have the same general purpose will not suffice as a basis for requiring a programmatic impact statement. See *Foundation on Economic Trends v. Lyng,* 817 F.2d 882 (D.C.Cir.1987).

A related issue is that of "segmentation." In considering whether to grant a permit for a river crossing by a 67–mile transmission line, should the Corps of Engineers consider the environmental impact of only the river crossing or the whole line? Does *Kleppe* provide any guidance? Do the CEQ regulations? See *Winnebago Tribe of Nebraska v. Ray,* 621 F.2d 269 (8th Cir.1980) (holding that only the river crossing need be considered). Similar issues arise in highway construction cases. For example, in *Maryland Conservation Council, Inc. v. Gilchrist,* 808 F.2d 1039, 1042 (4th Cir.1986), the court required an impact statement for a highway segment because other segments would inevitably cross a state park. The already-proposed segments, the court said, would "stand like gun barrels pointing into the heartland of the park * * *." See also *Save the Yaak Committee v. Block,* 840 F.2d 714, 721 (9th Cir.1988). Of course, the need to prevent such abuses must be balanced against the importance of allowing planning to remain flexible on long-term projects. See *Taxpayers Watchdog, Inc. v. Stanley,* 819 F.2d 294 (D.C.Cir.1987) (allowing segmentation of a mass transit project where the record contained no suggestion of any potential environmental abuse).

For a more recent segmentation decision, see *Preserve Endangered Areas v. U.S. Army Corps,* 87 F.3d 1242 (11th Cir.1996). The plaintiffs sought to block the construction of a five mile highway which would run through a historic district and impact several acres of wetlands. According to the court, "by far the most important" factor in segmentation decisions is whether the proposed project has independent utility apart from other proposals. Here, the county had shown that the new road would connect residents in the western part of the county to businesses in the east, and some of the other east-west roads in the area were already overloaded. The court seemed impressed with the fact that the county had "support[ed] its position with over fifty exhibits."

As the following case indicates, sometimes the scope and timing issue can merge into the issue of whether any impact statement will *ever* be required.

WEINBERGER v. CATHOLIC ACTION OF HAWAII

Supreme Court of the United States, 1981.
454 U.S. 139, 102 S.Ct. 197, 70 L.Ed.2d 298.

JUSTICE REHNQUIST delivered the opinion of the Court.

The facts relevant to our decision are not seriously controverted. Pursuant to a decision by the Navy to transfer ammunition and weapons stored at various locations on the island of Oahu, Hawaii, to the West Loch branch of the Lualualei Naval Magazine, the Navy prepared an Environmental Impact Assessment (EIA) concerning how the plan would affect the environment. The assessment concluded that the necessary construction of 48 earth-covered magazines and associated structures would have no significant environmental impact, and therefore no Environmental Impact Statement (EIS) was prepared at the construction stage. Construction contracts were let in March 1977 and in April 1978. Construction of the West Loch facilities has been completed and the magazines are now in use. It is stipulated that the magazines are capable of storing nuclear weapons. Because the information is classified for national security reasons, the Navy's regulations forbid it either to admit or deny that nuclear weapons are actually stored at West Loch.

* * *

We have previously noted that "[t]he thrust of § 102(2)(C) is * * * that environmental concerns be integrated into the very process of agency decisionmaking. The 'detailed statement' it requires is the outward sign that environmental values and consequences have been considered during the planning stage of agency actions." *Andrus v. Sierra Club,* 442 U.S. 347, 350, 99 S.Ct. 2335, 2337, 60 L.Ed.2d 943 (1979). Section 102(2)(C) thus serves twin aims. The first is to inject environmental considerations into the federal agency's decisionmaking process by requiring the agency to prepare an EIS. The second aim is to inform the public that the agency has considered environmental concerns in its decisionmaking process. Through the disclosure of an EIS, the public is made aware that the agency has taken environmental considerations into account. Public disclosure of the EIS is expressly governed by FOIA. 42 U.S.C. § 4332(2)(C) (1976).

The decisionmaking and public disclosure goals of § 102(2)(C), though certainly compatible, are not necessarily coextensive. Thus, § 102(2)(C) contemplates that in a given situation a federal agency might have to include environmental considerations in its decisionmaking process, yet withhold public disclosure of any NEPA documents, in whole or in part, under the authority of a FOIA exemption. That the decisionmaking and disclosure requirements of NEPA are not coextensive has been recognized by the Department of Defense's regulations, both at the time the West Loch facility was constructed and today.

[One of the exemptions from public disclosure under FOIA relates to classified information, such as that relating to storage of nuclear weapons.]

Since the public disclosure requirements of NEPA are governed by FOIA, it is clear that Congress intended that the public's interest in ensuring that federal agencies comply with NEPA must give way to the Government's need to preserve military secrets. In the instant case, an EIS concerning a proposal to store nuclear weapons at West Loch need not be disclosed. As we indicated earlier, whether or not nuclear weapons are stored at West Loch is classified information exempt from disclosure to the public under Exemption 1.

If the Navy proposes to store nuclear weapons at West Loch, the Department of Defense's regulations can fairly be read to require that an EIS be prepared solely for internal purposes, even though such a document cannot be disclosed to the public. The Navy must consider environmental consequences in its decisionmaking process, even if it is unable to meet NEPA's public disclosure goals by virtue of FOIA Exemption 1.

It does not follow, however, that the Navy is required to prepare an EIS in this case. The Navy is not required to prepare an EIS regarding the hazards of storing nuclear weapons at West Loch simply because the facility is "nuclear capable." As we held in *Kleppe v. Sierra Club* [*supra* page 161], an EIS need not be prepared simply because a project is *contemplated,* but only when the project is *proposed.* To say that the West Loch facility is "nuclear capable" is to say little more than that the Navy has contemplated the possibility that nuclear weapons, of whatever variety, may at some time be stored there. It is the proposal to *store* nuclear weapons at West Loch that triggers the Navy's obligation to prepare an EIS. Due to national security reasons, however, the Navy can neither admit nor deny that it proposes to store nuclear weapons at West Loch. In this case, therefore, it has not been and cannot be established that the Navy has proposed the only action that would require the preparation of an EIS dealing with the environmental consequences of nuclear weapons storage at West Loch.

Ultimately, whether or not the Navy has complied with NEPA "to the fullest extent possible" is beyond judicial scrutiny in this case. In other circumstances, we have held that "public policy forbids the maintenance of any suit in a court of justice, the trial of which would inevitably lead to the disclosure of matters which the law itself regards as confidential, and respecting which it will not allow the confidence to be violated." *Totten v. United States,* 92 U.S. 105, 107, 23 L.Ed. 605 (1876). We confront a similar situation in the instant case.

Notes

1.   Note the Court's reasoning: (a) if the Navy proposes to store nuclear weapons it must issue a secret EIS, (b) since the proposal is also secret, the plaintiffs cannot prove whether it exists, therefore (c) the plaintiffs cannot prove the need for an EIS. Thus, the Navy can escape legal scrutiny by making its noncompliance with the law classified information. See also *Hudson River Sloop Clearwater v. Department of the Navy,* 891 F.2d 414 (2d Cir.1989) (applying *Catholic Action*).

2. If the government's actions are classified, *Catholic Action* creates a considerable barrier to applying NEPA. Nevertheless, it should not be inferred that there is a "national security" exception to NEPA. Even with respect to important military projects like a major missile program, NEPA still applies. See *Romer v. Carlucci*, 847 F.2d 445 (8th Cir.1988) (en banc). On the other hand, a NEPA suit is not the proper forum for debating whether a proposed action will increase the chances of nuclear war. *No GWEN Alliance of Lane County, Inc. v. Aldridge*, 855 F.2d 1380 (9th Cir.1988).

3. So far, we have been concerned with the timing of the initial EIS. Because of the long delays often involved in major projects (and in part fostered by NEPA itself), new information may well appear after the EIS is released. The question then is whether a supplementary EIS is required. The Supreme Court's view on the question is found in the following case.

MARSH v. OREGON NATURAL RESOURCES COUNCIL

Supreme Court of the United States, 1989.
490 U.S. 360, 109 S.Ct. 1851, 104 L.Ed.2d 377.

JUSTICE STEVENS delivered the opinion of the Court.

[This case involved the construction of the Elk Creek Dam. The EIS concluded that the dam would have no major effect on fish production, but that its effect on turbidity might occasionally impair fishing. The plaintiffs argued that a supplemental EIS was required because of two new documents: (1) the "Cramer Memorandum," an Oregon Fish & Wildlife document suggesting that the dam would have a greater effect on downstream fishing, and (2) a U.S. Soil Conservation Service soil survey that implied greater downstream turbidity than the EIS suggested. Applying a "reasonableness" standard, the Ninth Circuit held that these documents brought significant new information to light and that the Corps failed to evaluate that information with sufficient care.]

The subject of post-decision supplemental environmental impact statements is not expressly addressed in NEPA. Preparation of such statements, however, is at times necessary to satisfy the Act's "action-forcing" purpose. NEPA does not work by mandating that agencies achieve particular substantive environmental results. Rather, NEPA promotes its sweeping commitment to "prevent or eliminate damage to the environment and biosphere" by focusing government and public attention on the environmental effects of proposed agency action. 42 U.S.C. § 4321. By so focusing agency attention, NEPA ensures that the agency will not act on incomplete information, only to regret its decision after it is too late to correct. Similarly, the broad dissemination of information mandated by NEPA permits the public and other government agencies to react to the effects of a proposed action at a meaningful time. It would be incongruous with this approach to environmental protection, and with the Act's manifest concern with preventing uninformed action, for the blinders to adverse environmental effects, once unequivocally removed, to be restored prior to the completion of agency action simply because the relevant proposal has received initial approval. As we explained in *TVA v. Hill,* [infra p. 581], although "it would make sense to hold NEPA inapplicable at some point in the life of a project, because the agency would no longer have a meaningful opportunity to *weigh* the benefits of the project versus the detrimental effects on the environment," up to that point, "NEPA cases have generally required agencies to file environmental impact statements when the remaining governmental action would be environmentally 'significant.'"

This reading of the statute is supported by Council on Environmental Quality (CEQ) and Corps regulations, both of which make plain that at times supplementation is required. The CEQ regulations, which we have held are entitled to substantial deference, impose a duty on all federal agencies to prepare supplements to either draft or final EIS's if there "are significant new circumstances or information relevant to environmental concerns and bearing on the proposed action or its impacts."[19] Similarly, the Corps' own NEPA implementing regulations require the preparation of a supplemental EIS if "new significant impact information, criteria or circumstances relevant to environmental considerations impact on the recommended plan or proposed action."

The parties are in essential agreement concerning the standard that governs an agency's decision whether to prepare a supplemental EIS. They agree that an agency should apply a "rule of reason," and the cases they cite in support of this standard explicate this rule in the same basic terms. These cases make clear that an agency need not supplement an EIS every time new information comes to light after the EIS is finalized. To require otherwise would render agency decisionmaking intractable, always awaiting updated information only to find the new information outdated by the time a decision is made. On the other hand, and as the Government concedes, NEPA does require that agencies take a "hard look" at the environmental effects of their planned action, even after a proposal has received initial approval. Application of the "rule of reason" thus turns on the value of the new information to the still pending decisionmaking process. In this respect the decision whether to prepare a supplemental EIS is similar to the decision whether to prepare an EIS in the first instance: If there remains "major Federal actio[n]" to occur, and if the new information is sufficient to show that the remaining action will "affec[t] the quality of the human environment" in a significant manner or to a significant extent not already considered, a supplemental EIS must be prepared.

19. The CEQ regulation provides, in part:

"Agencies:

'(1) Shall prepare supplements to either draft or final environmental impact statements if:

"(i) The agency makes substantial changes in the proposed action that are relevant to environmental concerns; or

"(ii) There are significant new circumstances or information relevant to environmental concerns and bearing on the proposed action or its impacts.

"(2) May also prepare supplements when the agency determines that the purposes of the Act will be furthered by doing so." 40 CFR § 1502.9(c) (1987).

The parties disagree, however, on the standard that should be applied by a court that is asked to review the agency's decision. The Government argues that the reviewing court need only decide whether the agency decision was "arbitrary and capricious," whereas respondents argue that the reviewing court must make its own determination of reasonableness to ascertain whether the agency action complied with the law. In determining the proper standard of review, we look to § 10(e) of the Administrative Procedure Act (APA), 5 U.S.C. § 706, which empowers federal courts to "hold unlawful and set aside agency action, findings, and conclusions" if they fail to conform with any of six specified standards. We conclude that review of the narrow question before us of whether the Corps' determination that the FEISS need not be supplemented should be set aside is controlled by the "arbitrary and capricious" standard of § 706(2)(A).

Respondents contend that the determination of whether the new information suffices to establish a "significant" effect is either a question of law or, at a minimum, a question of ultimate fact and, as such, "deserves no deference" on review. Apparently, respondents maintain that the question for review centers on the legal meaning of the term "significant" or, in the alternative, the predominantly legal question of whether established and uncontested historical facts presented by the administrative record satisfy this standard. Characterizing the dispute in this manner, they posit that strict review is appropriate under the "in accordance with law" clause of § 706(2)(A) or the "without observance of procedure required by law" provision of § 706(2)(D). We disagree.

The question presented for review in this case is a classic example of a factual dispute the resolution of which implicates substantial agency expertise. Respondents' claim that the Corps' decision not to file a second supplemental EIS should be set aside primarily rests on the contentions that the new information undermines conclusions contained in the FEISS, that the conclusions contained in the ODFW memorandum and the SCS survey are accurate, and that the Corps' expert review of the new information was incomplete, inconclusive, or inaccurate. The dispute thus does not turn on the meaning of the term "significant" or on an application of this legal standard to settled facts. Rather, resolution of this dispute involves primarily issues of fact. Because analysis of the relevant documents "requires a high level of technical expertise," we must defer to "the informed discretion of the responsible federal agencies." *Kleppe v. Sierra Club,* [supra p. 161]. Under these circumstances, we cannot accept respondents' supposition that review is of a legal question and that the Corps' decision "deserves no deference." Accordingly, as long as the Corps' decision not to supplement the FEISS was not "arbitrary or capricious," it should not be set aside.[20]

20. Respondents note that several Courts of Appeals, including the Court of Appeals for the Ninth Circuit as articulated in this and other cases, have adopted a "reasonableness" standard of review, and argue that we should not upset this well-settled doctrine. This standard, however, has not been adopted by all of the Circuits. Moreover, as some of these courts have recognized, the difference between the "ar-

As we observed in [*Overton Park*], in making the factual inquiry concerning whether an agency decision was "arbitrary or capricious," the reviewing court "must consider whether the decision was based on a consideration of the relevant factors and whether there has been a clear error of judgment." This inquiry must "be searching and careful," but "the ultimate standard of review is a narrow one." *Ibid.* When specialists express conflicting views, an agency must have discretion to rely on the reasonable opinions of its own qualified experts even if, as an original matter, a court might find contrary views more persuasive. On the other hand, in the context of reviewing a decision not to supplement an EIS, courts should not automatically defer to the agency's express reliance on an interest in finality without carefully reviewing the record and satisfying themselves that the agency has made a reasoned decision based on its evaluation of the significance—or lack of significance—of the new information. A contrary approach would not simply render judicial review generally meaningless, but would be contrary to the demand that courts ensure that agency decisions are founded on a reasoned evaluation "of the relevant factors."

* * *

The significance of the Cramer Memorandum and the SCS survey is subject to some doubt. Before respondents commenced this litigation in October 1985, no one had suggested that either document constituted the kind of new information that made it necessary or appropriate to supplement the FEISS. Indeed, the record indicates that the Corps was not provided with a copy of the Cramer Memorandum until after the lawsuit was filed. Since the probative value of that document depends largely on the expert qualification of its authors, the fact that they did not see fit to promptly apprise the Corps of their concern—or to persuade ODFW to do so—tends to discount the significance of those concerns. Similarly, the absence of any pretrial expression of concern about the soil characteristics described in the 1982 SCS survey is consistent with the view that it shed little, if any, new light on the turbidity potential of the dam. Yet, even if both documents had given rise to prompt expressions of concern, there are good reasons for concluding that they did not convey significant new information requiring supplementation of the FEISS.

The Court of Appeals attached special significance to two concerns discussed in the Cramer Memorandum: the danger that an increase in water temperature downstream during fall and early winter will cause an early emergence and thus reduce survival of spring chinook fry and the danger that the dam will cause high fish mortality from an epizootic disease. Both concerns were based partly on fact and partly on speculation.

* * *

bitrary and capricious" and "reasonableness" standards is not of great pragmatic consequence. Accordingly, our decision to-day will not require a substantial reworking of long-established NEPA law.

The Corps' response to [the first] concern in SIR [Supplemental Information Report] acknowledged that the "biological reasoning is sound and has been recognized for some time," but then explained why the concern was exaggerated. The SIR stressed that because the model employed by ODFW had not been validated, its predictive capability was uncertain. Indeed, ODFW scientists subsequently recalculated the likely effect of a one degree centigrade increase in temperature, adjusting its estimate of a 60 to 80 percent loss downward to between 30 and 40 percent. Moreover, the SIR supplied a variable missing in the Cramer Memorandum, suggesting that the Elk Creek Dam would, in most cases, either reduce or leave unchanged the temperature of the Rogue River. Discernible increases were only found in July, August, and December of the study year, and even during those months the maximum temperature increase was only 0.6 degrees centigrade. Finally, the SIR observed that the Cramer Memorandum failed to take into account the dam's beneficial effects, including its ability to reduce peak downstream flow during periods of egg incubation and fry rearing and its ability to reduce outflow temperature through use of the multiport structure. Given these positive factors, the Corps concluded that any adverse effects of the 0.6 degree temperature increase can be offset.

With respect to the second concern emphasized by the Court of Appeals, the Cramer Memorandum reported the fact that "an unprecedented 76% of the fall chinook in 1979 and 32% in 1980 were estimated to have died before spawning" and then speculated that the Lost Creek Dam, which had been completed in 1977, was a contributing cause of this unusual mortality. The Corps responded to this by pointing out that the absence of similar epizootics after the closure of the Applegate Dam and the evidence of pre-spawning mortality in the Rogue River prior to the closing of the Lost Creek Dam were inconsistent with the hypothesis suggested in the Cramer Memorandum. In addition, the Corps noted that certain diseased organisms thought to have been the cause of the unusually high mortality rates were not found in the outflow from the Lost Creek Dam.

In thus concluding that the Cramer Memorandum did not present significant new information requiring supplementation of the FEISS, the Corps carefully scrutinized the proffered information. Moreover, in disputing the accuracy and significance of this information, the Corps did not simply rely on its own experts. Rather, two independent experts hired by the Corps to evaluate the ODFW study on which the Cramer Memorandum was premised found significant fault in the methodology and conclusions of the study. We also think it relevant that the Cramer Memorandum did not express the official position of ODFW. In preparing the memorandum, the authors noted that the agency had "adopted a neutral stand on Elk Creek Dam" and argued that new information raised the question whether "our agency should continue to remain neutral." The concerns disclosed in the memorandum apparently were not sufficiently serious to persuade ODFW to abandon its neutral position.

The Court of Appeals also expressed concern that the SCS survey, by demonstrating that the soil content in the Elk Creek watershed is different than assumed in the FEISS, suggested a greater turbidity potential than indicated in the FEISS. In addition, the court observed that ODFW scientists believe that logging and road-building in the Elk Creek watershed has caused increased soil disturbance resulting in higher turbidity than forecast by the FEISS. As to this latter point, the SIR simply concluded that although turbidity may have increased in the early 1980's due to logging, "watershed recovery appears to have occurred to reduce the turbidity levels back to those of the 1970's." The implications of the SCS soil survey are of even less concern. As discussed in the FEISS, water quality studies were conducted in 1974 and 1979 using computer simulation models. The 1974 Study indicated that turbidity in the Rogue River would increase by no more than one to three JTU's as a result of the Elk Creek Dam, and the 1979 study verified this result. These studies used water samples taken from Elk Creek near the proposed dam site and from near the Lost Creek Dam, and thus did not simply rely on soil composition maps in drawing their conclusions. Although the SIR did not expressly comment on the SCS survey, in light of the in-depth 1974 and 1979 studies, its conclusion that "the turbidity effects are not expected to differ from those described in the 1980 FEISS" surely provided a legitimate reason for not preparing a supplemental FEISS to discuss the subject of turbidity.

There is little doubt that if all of the information contained in the Cramer Memorandum and SCS survey was both new and accurate, the Corps would have been required to prepare a second supplemental EIS. It is also clear that, regardless of its eventual assessment of the significance of this information, the Corps had a duty to take a hard look at the proffered evidence. However, having done so and having determined based on careful scientific analysis that the new information was of exaggerated importance, the Corps acted within the dictates of NEPA in concluding that supplementation was unnecessary. Even if another decisionmaker might have reached a contrary result, it was surely not "a clear error of judgment" for the Corps to have found that the new and accurate information contained in the documents was not significant and that the significant information was not new and accurate. As the SIR demonstrates, the Corps conducted a reasoned evaluation of the relevant information and reached a decision that, although perhaps disputable, was not "arbitrary or capricious."

Notes

1. On remand after the Supreme Court's decision, the district court enjoined completion of the dam pending a supplemental impact statement, but denied attorney's fees under the Equal Access to Justice Act. The Court of Appeals remanded for an explanation of the fee denial. *Oregon Natural Resources Council v. Marsh*, 959 F.2d 241 (9th Cir.1992). For further developments, see *Oregon Natural Resources Council v. Harrell*, 52 F.3d 1499 (9th Cir.1995).

2.   For conflicting appraisals of *Marsh,* see Rossman, "NEPA: Not So Well At Twenty," 20 *Envir.L.Rep.* 10174 (1990); Mandelker, "NEPA Alive and Well: The Supreme Court Takes Two," 19 *Envir.L.Rep.* 10385 (1989). *Marsh* clearly endorses the rule of reason as the standard for agency implementation under NEPA and "arbitrary or capricious" as the test on judicial review. The combination would seem to give the agency a great deal of leeway. And yet, the Court appraised the record very carefully to ensure that the agency took a "hard look" at the issue. On balance, does *Marsh* strengthen or weaken NEPA?

3.   Lower courts do not appear to have interpreted *Marsh* as a directive for lax judicial review. For instance, in *City of Carmel–By–The–Sea v. U.S. DOT*, 95 F.3d 892 (9th Cir.1996), the court considered a plan to expand California Highway 1. The court found the EIS inadequate for several reasons. First, the EIS relied on wetlands studies that were several years old, and the 1989 Loma Prieta earthquake might have created new wetlands. "Reliance on stale scientific evidence," the court said, "is sufficient to require re-examination of an EIS." Other federal agencies sharply criticized mitigation measures as well. In addition, the EIS failed to provide sufficient detail about other possible cumulative impacts to allow the court to evaluate the project. According to the court, the study should have described the area and expected impacts, other actions ("past, proposed, and reasonably forseeable") that might impact the same area, and a description of the individual and cumulative impacts. Moreover, the description of the project's purposes was changed in midstream in a way that eliminated all of the proposed alternatives from consideration, violating the agency's duty to consider relevant alternatives. In dissent, Judge Trott compared the agency's efforts since the 1940s to deal with the traffic congestion to the torture of Sisyphus, struggling to lift a stone which comes rolling back upon him the minute he lets ago.

Similarly, in *Hughes River Watershed Conservancy v. Glickman*, 81 F.3d 437 (4th Cir.1996), the Court held that the Corps of Engineers violated NEPA by failing to take a sufficiently hard look at the problem of zebra mussel infestation before deciding not to prepare an SEIS. The court also faulted the agency for using distorted economic assumptions to overinflate the benefits of the project. The agency had used a study which estimated gross rather than net benefits—that is, included benefits from recreational uses which would simply shift from other locations. Because this estimate had played an integral role in the evaluation of the project, the court considered the EIS inadequate:

> Misleading economic assumptions can defeat the first function of an EIS [ensuring a hard look by the agency] by impairing the agency's consideration of the adverse environmental effects of a proposed project. NEPA requires agencies to balance a project's economic benefits against its adverse environmental effects. The use of inflated economic benefits in this balancing process may result in approval of a project that otherwise would not have been approved because of its adverse environmental effects. Similarly, misleading economic assumptions can also defeat the second function of an EIS [public information] by skewing the public's evaluation of a project.

Id. at 446.

3. CONTENT OF THE IMPACT STATEMENT

So far, we have been largely concerned with what documents the agency must produce and when. We now turn to the question of what those documents must contain.

NATURAL RESOURCES DEFENSE COUNCIL, INC. v. MORTON

United States Court of Appeals, District of Columbia Circuit, 1972.
458 F.2d 827.

LEVENTHAL, CIRCUIT JUDGE.

This appeal raises a question as to the scope of the requirement of the National Environmental Policy Act (NEPA) that environmental impact statements contain a discussion of alternatives. Before us is the Environmental Impact Statement filed October 28, 1971, by the Department of Interior with respect to its proposal, under § 8 of the Outer Continental Shelf Lands Act, for the oil and gas general lease sale, of leases to some 80 tracts of submerged lands, primarily off eastern Louisiana. The proposal was finally structured so as to embrace almost 380,000 acres, about 10% of the offshore acreage presently under Federal lease. Opening of bids for the leases was scheduled for December 21, 1971, and three conservation groups brought this action on November 1, to enjoin the proposed sale. * * *

* * *

Adjacent to the proposed lease area is the greatest estuarine coastal marsh complex in the United States, some 7.9 million acres, providing food, nursery habitat and spawning ground vital to fish, shellfish and wildlife, as well as food and shelter for migratory waterfowl, wading birds and fur-bearing animals. This complex provides rich nutrient systems which make the Gulf of Mexico, blessed also with warm waters and shallow depths, the most productive fishing region of the country. It yielded $71 million of fish and shellfish to Louisiana and Mississippi commercial fishermen in 1970, and some 9 million man-days of sport fishing.

* * *

Oil pollution is the problem most extensively discussed in the [Environmental Impact] Statement and its exposition of unavoidable adverse environmental effects. The Statement acknowledges that both short and long term effects on the environment can be expected from spillage, including in that term major spills (like that in the Santa Barbara Channel in 1969); minor spills from operations and unidentified sources; and discharge of waste water contaminated with oil.

These adverse effects relate both to the damage to the coastal region—beaches, water areas and historic sites; and the forecast that oil pollution "may seriously damage the marine biological community"—both direct damage to the larger organisms, visible more easily and sooner, and to smaller life stages which would lead one step removed to damage later in the food chain.

* * *

The Statement asserted that while past major spills in the Gulf resulted in minimal damage, this was due to a fortunate combination of offshore winds and surface currents. The Statement rates blocks in the sale on an estimated probability of impact basis, calculated principally on proximity to high value/critically vulnerable area.

* * *

Congress contemplated that the Impact Statement would constitute the environmental source material for the information of the Congress as well as the Executive, in connection with the making of relevant decisions, and would be available to enhance enlightenment of—and by—the public. The impact statement provides a basis for (a) evaluation of the benefits of the proposed project in light of its environmental risks, and (b) comparison of the net balance for the proposed project with the environmental risks presented by alternative courses of action.

NEED TO DISCUSS ENVIRONMENTAL CONSEQUENCES OF ALTERNATIVES

We reject the implication of one of the Government's submissions which began by stating that while the Act requires a detailed statement of alternatives, it "does not require a discussion of the environmental consequences of the suggested alternative." A sound construction of NEPA, which takes into account both the legislative history and contemporaneous executive construction, requires a presentation of the environmental risks incident to reasonable alternative courses of action. The agency may limit its discussion of environmental impact to a brief statement, when that is the case, that the alternative course involves no effect on the environment, or that their effect, briefly described, is simply not significant. A rule of reason is implicit in this aspect of the law as it is in the requirement that the agency provide a statement concerning those opposing views that are responsible.

ALTERNATIVE AS TO OIL IMPORT QUOTAS

We think the Secretary's Statement erred in stating that the alternative of elimination of oil import quotas was entirely outside its cognizance. Assuming, as the Statement puts it, that this alternative "involves complex factors and concepts, including national security, which are beyond the scope of this statement," it does not follow that the Statement should not present the environmental effects of that alternative. While the consideration of pertinent alternatives requires a weighing of numerous matters, such as economics, foreign relations, national security, the fact remains that, as to the ingredient of possible adverse environmental impact, it is the essence and thrust of NEPA that the pertinent Statement serve to gather in one place a discussion of the relative environmental impact of alternatives.

The Government also contends that the only "alternatives" required for discussion under NEPA are those which can be adopted and put into effect by the official or agency issuing the statement. * * *

While we agree with so much of the Government's presentation as rests on the assumption that the alternatives required for discussion are those reasonably available, we do not agree that this requires a limitation to measures the agency or official can adopt. This approach would be particularly inapposite for the lease sale of offshore oil lands hastened by Secretary Morton in response to the directive which President Nixon set forth in his message to Congress on the Supply of Energy and Clean Air, as part of an overall program of development to provide an accommodation of the energy requirements of our country with the growing recognition of the necessity to protect the environment. The scope of this project is far broader than that of other proposed Federal actions discussed in impact statements, such as a single canal or dam. The Executive's proposed solution to a national problem, or a set of interrelated problems, may call for each of several departments or agencies to take a specific action; this cannot mean that the only discussion of alternatives required in the ensuing environmental impact statements would be the discussion by each department of the particular actions it could take as an alternative to the proposal underlying its impact statement.

When the proposed action is an integral part of a coordinated plan to deal with a broad problem, the range of alternatives that must be evaluated is broadened. While the Department of the Interior does not have the authority to eliminate or reduce oil import quotas, such action is within the purview of both Congress and the President, to whom the impact statement goes. The impact statement is not only for the exposition of the thinking of the agency, but also for the guidance of these ultimate decision-makers, and must provide them with the environmental effects of both the proposal and the alternatives, for their consideration along with the various other elements of the public interest.

An evaluation of the environmental effects of all the alternatives in the area of the energy crisis might have been provided by an impact statement issued by an officer or agency with broad responsibility. * * * The impact statement function could have been assigned to the group designated by the President to coordinate and analyze overall energy questions for the executive branch—the Energy Subcommittee of the Domestic Council. In the absence of assignment of the impact statement function to an agency with broader responsibility, the implementation of the statutory requirement of the environmental review mandated by NEPA fell on the Interior Department when it took the first step in carrying out the broader energy program.

* * *

OTHER "ALTERNATIVES"

The foregoing establishes that we cannot grant the Government's motion for summary reversal. We discuss other aspects of the case in anticipation that the Secretary may choose to supplement or modify the Statement—perhaps even, assuming approval by the District Court, in an effort to open the sealed bids without a new offering.

We think there is merit to the Government's position insofar as it contends that no additional discussion was requisite for such "alternatives" as the development of oil shale, desulfurization of coal, coal liquefaction and gasification, tar sands and geothermal resources.

The Statement sets forth * * * that while these possibilities hold great promise for the future, their impact on the energy supply will not likely be felt until after 1980, and will be dependent on environmental safeguards and technological developments. Since the Statement also sets forth that the agency's proposal was put forward to meet a near-term requirement, imposed by an energy shortfall projected for the mid–1970's, the possibility of the environmental impact of long-term solutions requires no additional discussion at this juncture. We say "at this juncture" for the problem requires continuing review, in the nature of things, and these alternatives and their environmental consequences may be more germane to subsequent proposals for OCS leases, in the light of changes in technology or in the variables of energy requirements and supply.

Furthermore, the requirement in NEPA of discussion as to reasonable alternatives does not require "crystal ball" inquiry. Mere administrative difficulty does not interpose such flexibility into the requirements of NEPA as to undercut the duty of compliance "to the fullest extent possible." But if this requirement is not rubber, neither is it iron. The statute must be construed in the light of reason if it is not to demand what is, fairly speaking, not meaningfully possible, given the obvious, that the resources of energy and research—and time—available to meet the Nation's needs are not infinite.

Still different considerations are presented by the "alternatives" of increasing nuclear energy development, listed in the Statement, and the possibilities, identified by the District Court as a critical omission, of federal legislation or administrative action freeing current offshore and state-controlled offshore production from state market demand pro-rationing, or changing the Federal Power Commission's natural gas pricing policies.

The mere fact that an alternative requires legislative implementation does not automatically establish it as beyond the domain of what is required for discussion, particularly since NEPA was intended to provide a basis for consideration and choice by the decisionmakers in the legislative as well as the executive branch. But the need for an overhaul of basic legislation certainly bears on the requirements of the Act. We do not suppose Congress intended an agency to devote itself to extended discussion of the environmental impact of alternatives so remote from reality as to depend on, say, the repeal of the antitrust laws.

In the last analysis, the requirement as to alternatives is subject to a construction of reasonableness, and we say this with full awareness that this approach necessarily has both strengths and weaknesses. Where the environmental aspects of alternatives are readily identifiable by the agency, it is reasonable to state them—for ready reference by those concerned with the consequences of the decision and its alternatives. * * *.

There is reason for concluding that NEPA was not meant to require detailed discussion of the environmental effects of "alternatives" put forward in comments when these effects cannot be readily ascertained and the alternatives are deemed only remote and speculative possibilities, in view of basic changes required in statutes and policies of other agencies—making them available, if at all, only after protracted debate and litigation not meaningfully compatible with the time-frame of the needs to which the underlying proposal is addressed.

A final word. In this as in other areas, the functions of courts and agencies, rightly understood, are not in opposition but in collaboration, toward achievement of the end prescribed by Congress. So long as the officials and agencies have taken the "hard look" at environmental consequences mandated by Congress, the court does not seek to impose unreasonable extremes or to interject itself within the area of discretion of the executive as to the choice of the action to be taken.

Notes

1.   In Chapter VIII, we will return to the subject of offshore oil drilling and its potential environmental effects.

2.   The requirement that an EIS discuss, and the preparing agency actively "consider," alternatives which the agency is not authorized to implement means that it may have to employ staff or consultants with expertise beyond that needed to carry out its own "mission." Full compliance with NEPA also should involve agency officials at all levels in consideration of issues and values not necessarily conducive to expansion of the agency's programs. This, of course, is not the usual inclination of bureaucracies.

3.   According to one survey of the cases, courts attach considerable importance to the comments of other agencies regarding the draft EA or EIS. Judicial intervention is much more likely when other agencies disagree with the ultimate decision. See Blumm & Brown, "Pluralism and the Environment: The Role of Comment Agencies in NEPA Litigation," 14 *Harv.Env.L.Rev.* 277 (1990).

VERMONT YANKEE NUCLEAR POWER CORP. v. NATURAL RESOURCES DEFENSE COUNCIL, INC.

Supreme Court of the United States, 1978.
435 U.S. 519, 98 S.Ct. 1197, 55 L.Ed.2d 460.

[This is another aspect of the case on page 125 supra. This portion of the opinion involves a reactor-license application by Consumers Power Company. A group called Saginaw intervened and submitted 119 environmental contentions, of which 17 related to the general topic of energy conservation. Saginaw participated in none of the hearings in the final stage of the proceedings. The licensing board declined to consider energy conservation issues. At about the time the administrative proceedings ended, CEQ issued guidelines calling for agency consideration of energy conservation issues. The AEC refused to reopen the case, in part because of Saginaw's procedural default. The court of appeals reversed, holding that the AEC should have explored these issues *sua sponte*.]

JUSTICE REHNQUIST delivered the opinion of the Court.

There is little doubt that under the Atomic Energy Act of 1954 state public utility commissions or similar bodies are empowered to make the initial decision regarding the need for power. The Commission's prime area of concern * * * is public health and safety. * * *

NEPA, of course, has altered slightly the statutory balance, requiring "a detailed statement by the responsible official on * * * alternatives to the proposed action." But as should be obvious even upon a moment's reflection, the term "alternatives" is not self-defining. To make an impact statement something more than an exercise in frivolous boilerplate the concept of alternatives must be bounded by some notion of feasibility. As Court of Appeals for the District of Columbia Circuit has itself recognized:

> "There is reason for concluding that NEPA was not meant to require detailed discussion of the environmental effects of 'alternatives' put forward in comments when these effects cannot be readily ascertained and the alternatives are deemed only remote and speculative possibilities, in view of basic changes required in statutes and policies of other agencies—making them available, if at all, only after protracted debate and litigation not meaningfully compatible with the time-frame of the needs to which the underlying proposal is addressed."

Common sense also teaches us that the "detailed statement of alternatives" cannot be found wanting simply because the agency failed to include every alternative device and thought conceivable by the mind of man. Time and resources are simply too limited to hold that an impact statement fails because the agency failed to ferret out every possible alternative, regardless of how uncommon or unknown that alternative may have been at the time the project was approved.

With these principles in mind we now turn to the notion of "energy conservation," an alternative the omission of which was thought by the Court of Appeals to have been "forcefully pointed out by Saginaw in its comments on the draft EIS." Again, as the Commission pointed out, "the phrase 'energy conservation' has a deceptively simple ring in this context. Taken literally, the phrase suggests a virtually limitless range of possible actions and developments that might, in one way or another, ultimately reduce projected demands for electricity from a particular proposed plant." Moreover, as a practical matter, it is hard to dispute the observation that it is largely the events of recent years that have emphasized not only the need but also a large variety of alternatives for energy conservation. Prior to the drastic oil shortages imposed upon the United States in 1973, there was little serious thought in most government circles of energy conservation alternatives. Indeed, the Council on Environmental Quality did not promulgate regulations which even remotely suggested the need to consider energy conservation in impact statements until August 1, 1973. And even then the guidelines were not made applicable to draft and final statements filed with the Council before January 28, 1974. The Federal Power Commission likewise did not require consideration of energy conservation in applications to build hydroelectric facilities until June 19, 1973. And these regulations were not made retroactive either. All this occurred over a year and a half after the draft environmental statement for Midland had been prepared, and over a year after the final environmental statement had been prepared and the hearings completed.

We think these facts amply demonstrate that the concept of "alternatives" is an evolving one, requiring the agency to explore more or fewer alternatives as they become better known and understood. This was well understood by the Commission, which, unlike the Court of Appeals, recognized that the Licensing Board's decision had to be judged by the information then available to it. And judged in that light we have little doubt the Board's actions were well within the proper bounds of its statutory authority. Not only did the record before the agency give every indication that the project was actually needed, but there was nothing before the Board to indicate to the contrary.

We also think the court's criticism of the Commission's "threshold test" displays a lack of understanding of the historical setting within which the agency action took place and of the nature of the test itself. In the first place, while it is true that NEPA places upon an agency the obligation to consider every significant aspect of the environmental impact of a proposed action, it is still incumbent upon intervenors who wish to participate to structure their participation so that it is meaningful, so that it alerts the agency to the intervenors' position and contentions. This is especially true when the intervenors are requesting the agency to embark upon an exploration of uncharted territory, as was the question of energy conservation in the late '60's and early '70's.

* * *

We have also made it clear that the role of a court in reviewing the sufficiency of an agency's consideration of environmental factors is a limited one, limited both by the time at which the decision was made and by the statute mandating review.

Neither the statute nor its legislative history contemplates that a court should substitute its judgment for that of an agency as to the environmental consequences of its actions. * * * [citing *Kleppe v. Sierra Club,* supra p. 161].

We think the Court of Appeals has forgotten that injunction here and accordingly its judgment in this respect must also be reversed.

Notes

1. In *Vermont Yankee,* did the Court go beyond *NRDC v. Morton* in diluting the scope of review of the EIS? Is the agency required only to consider *obvious* alternatives? (Under *Marsh* [supra p. 172], could the NRC have been required to prepare a supplemental EIS after energy conservation emerged as an alternative?) In applying *Vermont Yankee,* one problem is determining how obvious an alternative must be in order for the agency to have a duty to consider that alternative on its own initiative. One court has indicated that the alternative must be "reasonably apparent." *Roosevelt Campobello International Park Commission v. United States EPA,* 684 F.2d 1041, 1047 (1st Cir.1982). Is this a helpful formulation?

2. When the project in question is proposed by a nonfederal party, the question arises whether that party can control the range of possible alternatives. In *Citizens Against Burlington, Inc. v. Busey,* 938 F.2d 190 (D.C.Cir. 1991), then-Judge Clarence Thomas wrote an opinion giving the project applicant considerable leeway. The case involved a decision by the city of Toledo to expand one of its airports. A NEPA suit was brought against the FAA, challenging the agency's approval of the project. The agency considered only the alternatives of approving the plan and doing nothing, rather than the possibilities of expanding the airport in other ways, changing flight patterns, or expanding other airports. FAA defined the goal for its action as "helping to launch a new cargo hub in Toledo and thereby helping to fuel the Toledo economy." It then eliminated all alternatives that did not promote that goal. Justice Thomas upheld this very narrow definition of alternatives under NEPA. In dissent, Judge Buckley said:

> By sanctioning the FAA's approach, the majority in effect allows a non-federal party to sort out alternatives based entirely on economic considerations, and then to present its preferred alternative as a take-it-or-leave-it proposition. If allowed to stand, today's decision will undermine the NEPA aim of "inject[ing] environmental considerations into the federal agency's decisionmaking process." The discussion of reasonable alternatives—"the heart of the environmental impact statement"—becomes an empty exercise when the only alternatives addressed are the proposed project and inaction.

For further discussion of this issue, see Kirsch and Rippy, "Defining the Scope of Alternatives in an EIS After Citizens Against Burlington," 21 *Env.L.Rep.* 10701 (1991); Lackey, "Misdirecting NEPA: Leaving the Definition of Reasonable Alternatives in the EIS to the Applicants," 60 *Geo. Wash.L.Rev.* 1232 (1992) (student note).

3.   The rule of reason does not always operate to the advantage of the agency involved. In *Alaska Wilderness Rec. & Tourism Ass'n v. Morrison*, 60 F.3d 647 (9th Cir.1995), the court held that the Forest Service had improperly failed to reconsider alternatives to a proposed project when cancellation of an existing contract unexpectedly broadened the range of possibilities. Similarly, in *Dubois v. U.S. Dept. of Agriculture*, 102 F.3d 1273 (1st Cir.1996), the court held that the Service had failed to explore all reasonable alternatives for the proposed expansion of a ski facility, including the possibility of using an artificial pond rather than a natural one to store water for snowmaking. The agency had failed to discuss this option in the EIS, even though similar ponds had been used elsewhere in the vicinity. The lower court had been convinced by counsel for the Forest Service that the alternative was not practical, but the appellate court said "[s]uch *post hoc* rationalizations are inherently suspect, and in any event are no substitute for the agency's following statutorily mandated procedures. * * * [E]ven if the agency's actual decision was a reasoned one, the EIS is insufficient if it does not properly discuss the required issues." "After a searching and careful review of the record in the instant case," the court concluded, "we are not convinced that the Forest Service's decision was founded on a reasoned evaluation of the relevant factors, or that it articulated a rational connection between the facts found and the choice made." Id. at 1289. Hence, the Forest Service's decision was arbitrary and capricious.

4.   Another important issue in many NEPA cases is whether the agency has ignored important environmental impacts. The next case is instructive on this point. The petitioners sought review of the issuance of a construction license to build two reactors about 17 miles from Charlotte, North Carolina. The issue was whether the EIS should have discussed the risk of a major nuclear accident.

CAROLINA ENVIRONMENTAL STUDY GROUP v. UNITED STATES

United States Court of Appeals, District of Columbia Circuit, 1975.
510 F.2d 796.

MARKEY, CIRCUIT JUDGE:

The A.E.C. has classified hypothetical reactor accidents from Class 1 (trivial incidents with high occurrence probability) to Class 9 (ultimate severity with occurrence highly unlikely). The Class 9 accident, known as a breach-of-reactor containment accident, involves concurrent rupture of the three-foot thick concrete containment vessel and the several inches of steel surrounding the reactor core, resulting in the exposure of the radioactive core to the atmosphere. Such an accident would necessarily involve simultaneous malfunction of all safety systems.

The A.E.C.'s Final Environmental Statement, section 7, page 3, included this comment:

> The postulated occurrences in Class 9 involve sequences of successive failures more severe than those required to be considered

in the design bases of protective systems and engineered safety features. The consequences could be severe. However, the probability of their occurrence is so small that their environmental risk is extremely low. * * *

What the A.E.C. means by the small probability of such accidents is seen in its report that

some experts held that numerical estimates of a quantity [of major accidents] so vague and uncertain as the likelihood of occurrence of major reactor accidents have no meaning. They declined to express their feeling about this probability in numbers. Others, though admitting similar uncertainty, nevertheless ventured to express their opinions in numerical terms. Estimations so expressed of the probability of reactor accidents having major effects on the public ranged from a chance of one in 100,000 to one in a billion per year for each large reactor. However, whether numerically expressed or not, there was no disagreement with the opinion that the probability of major reactor accidents is exceedingly low.

Focusing on the degree of possible damage resulting from the occurrence of a Class 9 accident,[21] the Study Group argues that the risk is very real, thus tending to equate damage with risk. At the same time, the Study Group accuses the A.E.C. of equating probability with risk. We agree with neither equation.

The A.E.C. is required by NEPA to set forth the factors involved, to the end that the ultimate decision on a proposed course of action shall be enlightened by prior recognition of its impact on the quality of human environment. Viewing the record as a whole, we cannot say that the A.E.C.'s general consideration of the probabilities and severity of a Class 9 accident amounts to a failure to provide the required detailed statement of its environmental impact. That the probability of a Class 9 accident is remote and that its consequences would be catastrophic are undisputed. Neither the A.E.C.'s finding of low probability, nor its methodology or basis for that finding, are challenged here by appellant.

Because each statement on the environmental impact of a proposed action involves educated predictions rather than certainties, it is entirely proper, and necessary, to consider the probabilities as well as the consequences of certain occurrences in ascertaining their environmental impact. There is a point at which the probability of an occurrence may be so low as to render it almost totally unworthy of consideration. Neither we, nor the A.E.C. on this record, would treat lightly the horrible consequences of a Class 9 accident. Recognition of the minimal probability of such an event is not equatable with non-recognition of its consequences. We find nothing in the instant record which would indicate that the A.E.C. findings regarding Class 9 accidents are clearly

21. A.E.C. report WASH—740, pg. viii, estimated that a Class 9 accident in a reactor approximately one-seventh the size of one of Duke's reactors would result in up to 3,400 deaths, 43,000 injuries, and $7 billion property damage.

erroneous or that the A.E.C.'s compliance with NEPA Section 102(2)(C)(i) in this case was inadequate.

Notes

1. There is a certain irony to the preceding decision, in light of the later Three Mile Island episode (which was classified as a class 9 accident). Despite the TMI incident, one court held that the NRC still did not have to consider the possibility of class 9 accidents:

> As we have discussed above, the Commission did not conclude in its Statement of Interim Policy that its original assumption regarding Class Nine accidents was scientifically incorrect. Rather, it recognized the need for renewed study of the issue. The clear import of the Commission's Statement is that, until such time as its research yields a contrary result, the Commission continues to regard Class Nine accidents as highly improbable events.

> We do not consider that conclusion unreasonable. Neither the 1978 study by the Risk Assessment Review Group nor the accident at Three Mile Island established that the probability of a Class Nine accident with significant environmental consequences is anything but very small * * * Because the environmental consequences of Three Mile Island were scientifically and legally inconsequential, the fact that the accident occurred does not establish that accidents with significant environmental impacts will have significant probabilities of occurrence.

> NEPA, therefore, does not require the consideration of Class Nine accidents in future EISs, nor does it require that final EISs be supplemented to take account of the Class Nine risk. The approach adopted in the Statement of Interim Policy—to include discussion of such accidents in future EISs—was a discretionary policy choice of the Commission. Because it need not have imposed upon itself the burden it did, the Commission was perfectly free to deny its new policy retroactive effect. We conclude that the Commission did not violate its obligations under NEPA by declining to supplement the Diablo Canyon EIS with a discussion of the environmental impacts of a Class Nine accident.

San Luis Obispo Mothers for Peace v. NRC, 751 F.2d 1287, 1301 (D.C.Cir. 1984), vacated in part 760 F.2d 1320 (D.C.Cir.1985) (en banc). But see *Limerick Ecology Action, Inc. v. U.S. Nuclear Regulatory Com'n,* 869 F.2d 719, 739–40 (3d Cir.1989) (rejecting *San Luis Obispo*).

2. For a description of a similar example of judicial optimism see W. Rodgers, *Environmental Law* 734 n. 87 (1977) (court considered likelihood of collapse of Grand Teton dam too unlikely to require mention in EIS; dam later collapsed). Such experiences have shown that the common human tendency to assume that the worst will not happen applies as much to environmental impact statements as to people smoking cigarettes or refusing to wear seatbelts.

3. As *Carolina Study Group* illustrates, a recurring issue under NEPA has been how to treat uncertain but highly adverse outcomes. The following two cases are the Supreme Court's response to the problem. The first case is a sequel to *Vermont Yankee* [supra p. 125].

BALTIMORE GAS & ELECTRIC CO. v. NATURAL RESOURCES DEFENSE COUNCIL, INC.

Supreme Court of the United States, 1983.
462 U.S. 87, 103 S.Ct. 2246, 76 L.Ed.2d 437.

JUSTICE O'CONNOR delivered the opinion of the Court.

Section 102(2)(C) of the National Environmental Policy Act requires federal agencies to consider the environmental impact of any major federal action. As part of its generic rulemaking proceedings to evaluate the environmental effects of the nuclear fuel cycle for nuclear power plants, the Nuclear Regulatory Commission (Commission) decided that licensing boards should assume, for purposes of NEPA, that the permanent storage of certain nuclear wastes would have no significant environmental impact and thus should not affect the decision whether to license a particular nuclear power plant. We conclude that the Commission complied with NEPA and that its decision is not arbitrary or capricious within the meaning of § 10(a) of the Administrative Procedure Act (APA), 5 U.S.C. § 706.

I

The environmental impact of operating a light-water nuclear power plant[22] includes the effects of offsite activities necessary to provide fuel for the plant ("front end" activities), and of offsite activities necessary to dispose of the highly toxic and long-lived nuclear wastes generated by the plant ("back end" activities). The dispute in these cases concerns the Commission's adoption of a series of generic rules to evaluate the environmental effects of a nuclear power plant's fuel cycle. At the heart of each rule is Table S–3, a numerical compilation of the estimated resources used and effluents released by fuel cycle activities supporting a year's operation of a typical light-water reactor. The three versions of Table S–3 contained similar numerical values, although the supporting documentation has been amplified during the course of the proceedings.

The Commission first adopted Table S–3 in 1974, after extensive informal rulemaking proceedings. This "original" rule, as it later came to be described, declared that in environmental reports and impact statements for individual licensing proceedings the environmental costs of the fuel cycle "shall be as set forth" in Table S–3 and that "[n]o further discussion of such environmental effects shall be required." The original Table S–3 contained no numerical entry for the long-term environmental effects of storing solidified transuranic and high-level wastes, because the Commission staff believed that technology would be developed to isolate the wastes from the environment. The Commission and the parties have later termed this assumption of complete repository integrity as the "zero-release" assumption: the reasonableness of this assumption is at the core of the present controversy.

* * *

22. A light-water nuclear power plant is one that uses ordinary water H₂O), as opposed to heavy water (D₂O), to remove the heat generated in the nuclear core. The bulk of the reactors in the United States are light-water nuclear reactors.

While *Vermont Yankee* was pending in this Court, the Commission proposed a new "interim" rulemaking proceeding to determine whether to adopt a revised Table S-3. The proposal explicitly acknowledged that the risks from long-term repository failure were uncertain, but suggested that research should resolve most of those uncertainties in the near future. After further proceedings, the Commission promulgated the interim rule in March 1977. Table S-3 now explicitly stated that solidified high-level and transuranic wastes would remain buried in a federal repository and therefore would have no effect on the environment. Like its predecessor, the interim rule stated that "[n]o further discussion of such environmental effects shall be required." The NRDC petitioned for review of the interim rule, challenging the zero-release assumption and faulting the Table S-3 rule for failing to consider the health, cumulative, and socioeconomic effects of the fuel cycle activities. The Court of Appeals stayed proceedings while awaiting this Court's decision in *Vermont Yankee.* In April 1978, the Commission amended the interim rule to clarify that health effects were not covered by Table S-3 and could be litigated in individual licensing proceedings.

In 1979, following further hearings, the Commission adopted the "final" Table S-3 rule. Like the amended interim rule, the final rule expressly stated that Table S-3 should be supplemented in individual proceedings by evidence about the health, socioeconomic, and cumulative aspects of fuel cycle activities. The Commission also continued to adhere to the zero-release assumption that the solidified waste would not escape and harm the environment once the repository was sealed. It acknowledged that this assumption was uncertain because of the remote possibility that water might enter the repository, dissolve the radioactive materials, and transport them to the biosphere.

* * *

In its Table S-3 Rule here, the Commission has determined that the probabilities favor the zero-release assumption, because the Nation is likely to develop methods to store the wastes with no leakage to the environment. The NRDC did not challenge and the Court of Appeals did not decide the reasonableness of this determination, and no party seriously challenges it here. The Commission recognized, however, that the geological, chemical, physical and other data it relied on in making this prediction were based, in part, on assumptions which involve substantial uncertainties. Again, no one suggests that the uncertainties are trivial or the potential effects insignificant if time proves the zero-release assumption to have been seriously wrong. After confronting the issue, though, the Commission has determined that the uncertainties concerning the development of nuclear waste storage facilities are not sufficient to affect the outcome of any individual licensing decision.

It is clear that the Commission, in making this determination, has made the careful consideration and disclosure required by NEPA. The sheer volume of proceedings before the Commission is impressive. Of far greater importance, the Commission's Statement of Consideration announcing the final Table S–3 Rule shows that it has digested this mass of material and disclosed all substantial risks. The Statement summarizes the major uncertainty of long-term storage in bedded-salt repositories, which is that water could infiltrate the repository as a result of such diverse factors as geologic faulting, a meteor strike, or accidental or deliberate intrusion by man. The Commission noted that the probability of intrusion was small, and that the plasticity of salt would tend to heal some types of intrusions. The Commission also found the evidence "tentative but favorable" that an appropriate site could be found. Table S–3 refers interested persons to staff studies that discuss the uncertainties in greater detail. Given this record and the Commission's statement, it simply cannot be said that the Commission ignored or failed to disclose the uncertainties surrounding its zero-release assumption.

Congress did not enact NEPA, of course, so that an agency would contemplate the environmental impact of an action as an abstract exercise. Rather, Congress intended that the "hard look" be incorporated as part of the agency's process of deciding whether to pursue a particular federal action. It was on this ground that the Court of Appeals faulted the Commission's action, for failing to allow the uncertainties potentially to "tip the balance" in a particular licensing decision. As a general proposition, we can agree with the Court of Appeals' determination that an agency must allow all significant environmental risks to be factored into the decision whether to undertake a proposed action. We think, however, that the Court of Appeals erred in concluding the Commission had not complied with this standard.

As *Vermont Yankee* made clear, NEPA does not require agencies to adopt any particular internal decisionmaking structure. Here, the agency has chosen to evaluate generically the environmental impact of the fuel cycle and inform individual licensing boards, through the Table S–3 rule, of its evaluation. The generic method chosen by the agency is clearly an appropriate method of conducting the hard look required by NEPA. The environmental effects of much of the fuel cycle are not plant specific, for any plant, regardless of its particular attributes, will create additional wastes that must be stored in a common long-term repository. Administrative efficiency and consistency of decision are both furthered by a generic determination of these effects without needless repetition of the litigation in individual proceedings, which are subject to review by the Commission in any event.

The Court of Appeals recognized that the Commission has discretion to evaluate generically the environmental effects of the fuel cycle and require that these values be "plugged into" individual licensing decisions. The court concluded that the Commission nevertheless violated NEPA by failing to factor the uncertainty surrounding long-term storage into Table S–3 and precluding individual licensing decisionmakers from considering it.

The Commission's decision to affix a zero value to the environmental impact of long-term storage would violate NEPA, however, only if the

Commission acted arbitrarily and capriciously in deciding generically that the uncertainty was insufficient to affect any individual licensing decision. In assessing whether the Commission's decision is arbitrary and capricious, it is crucial to place the zero-release assumption in context. Three factors are particularly important. First is the Commission's repeated emphasis that the zero-risk assumption—and, indeed, all of the Table S–3 rule—was made for a limited purpose. The Commission expressly noted its intention to supplement the rule with an explanatory narrative. It also emphasized that the purpose of the rule was not to evaluate or select the most effective long-term waste disposal technology or develop site selection criteria. A separate and comprehensive series of programs has been undertaken to serve these broader purposes. In the proceedings before us, the Commission's staff did not attempt to evaluate the environmental effects of all possible methods of disposing of waste. Rather, it chose to analyze intensively the most probable long-term waste disposal method—burial in a bedded-salt repository several hundred meters below ground—and then "estimate its impact conservatively, based on the best available information and analysis." The zero-release assumption cannot be evaluated in isolation. Rather, it must be assessed in relation to the limited purpose for which the Commission made the assumption.

Second, the Commission emphasized that the zero-release assumption is but a single figure in an entire Table, which the Commission expressly designed as a risk-averse estimate of the environmental impact of the fuel cycle. It noted that Table S–3 assumed that the fuel storage canisters and the fuel rod cladding would be corroded before a repository is closed and that all volatile materials in the fuel would escape to the environment. Given that assumption, and the improbability that materials would escape after sealing, the Commission determined that the overall Table represented a conservative (i.e., inflated) statement of environmental impacts. It is not unreasonable for the Commission to counteract the uncertainties in post-sealing releases by balancing them with an overestimate of pre-sealing releases. A reviewing court should not magnify a single line item beyond its significance as only part of a larger Table.

Third, a reviewing court must remember that the Commission is making predictions, within its area of special expertise, at the frontiers of science. When examining this kind of scientific determination, as opposed to simple findings of fact, a reviewing court must generally be at its most deferential. See, e.g., *Industrial Union Department v. American Petroleum Institute* [infra page 439].

With these three guides in mind, we find the Commission's zero-release assumption to be within the bounds of reasoned decisionmaking required by the APA. * * *

                              * * *

As we have noted, Table S–3 describes effluents and other impacts in technical terms. The Table does not convert that description into tangible effects on human health or other environmental variables. The original and interim rules declared that "the contribution of the environmental effects of * * * fuel cycle activities * * * shall be as set forth in the following Table S–3 [and] no further discussion of such environmental effects shall be required." Since the Table does not specifically mention health effects, socioeconomic impacts, or cumulative impacts, this declaration does not clearly require or preclude their discussion. The Commission later amended the interim rule to clarify that health effects were not covered by Table S–3 and could be litigated in individual licensing proceedings. In the final rule, the Commission expressly required licensing boards to consider the socioeconomic and cumulative effects in addition to the health effects of the releases projected in the Table.

The Court of Appeals held that the original and interim rules violated NEPA by precluding licensing boards from considering the health, socioeconomic, and cumulative effects of the environmental impacts stated in technical terms. As does the Commission, we agree with the Court of Appeals that NEPA requires an EIS to disclose the significant health, socioeconomic and cumulative consequences of the environmental impact of a proposed action. We find no basis, however, for the Court of Appeals' conclusion that the Commission ever precluded a licensing board from considering these effects.

Notes

1.   The Court says that the NRC is entitled to maximum deference here because its finding of no risk was made in a context "at the frontiers of science." It cites in support of this statement a case involving toxic substances. Are the two situations really equivalent? Is the Court saying that under NEPA, the greater the scientific uncertainty, the more the Court should defer to an agency decision to ignore uncertainty?

2.   To the extent that NEPA is intended to force agencies to take a hard look at the environmental consequences of their actions, has it achieved this result? Is there *any* way to get an agency like the NRC, which is institutionally structured around a given program, to consider seriously the desirability of terminating the program? If not, how can the government obtain objective expert advice on key policy issues? Would a report from the National Academy of Sciences be more useful than an EIS by the NRC?

3.   As described in the next case, a CEQ regulation formerly dealt with the issue of risk by requiring a discussion of the "worst case" scenario. Would that regulation have lead to a more useful EIS in *Baltimore Gas*?

ROBERTSON v. METHOW VALLEY CITIZENS COUNCIL

Supreme Court of the United States, 1989.
490 U.S. 332, 109 S.Ct. 1835, 104 L.Ed.2d 351.

[The plaintiffs challenged the Forest Service's issuance of special use permits for a ski resort on national forest land. The EIS (entitled the

Early Winters Alpine Winter Sports Study and referred to in the Court's opinion as the "Early Winters Study") considered the effect of the resort on wildlife and outlined possible mitigation measures. [The Court of Appeals found the EIS inadequate for two reasons.] First, the state game department had predicted a 50% loss in the mule deer herd. The EIS adopted a 15% estimate, but admitted that the off-site effects of the resort were uncertain because they depended on the extent of private development. The EIS relied on mitigation measures to reduce the impact, but those measures had not been fully developed or tested. In light of this uncertainty, the Court of Appeals held that the EIS should have included a worst-case analysis. Second, the Court of Appeals held that the EIS was inadequate because it did not contain a complete mitigation plan to protect wildlife (and it lacked a plan to protect air quality).]

JUSTICE STEVENS delivered the opinion of the Court.

Simply by focusing the agency's attention on the environmental consequences of a proposed project, NEPA ensures that important effects will not be overlooked or underestimated only to be discovered after resources have been committed or the die otherwise cast. Moreover, the strong precatory language of § 101 of the Act and the requirement that agencies prepare detailed impact statements inevitably bring pressure to bear on agencies "to respond to the needs of environmental quality." 115 Cong.Rec. 40425 (1969) (remarks of Sen. Muskie).

Publication of an EIS, both in draft and final form, also serves a larger informational role. It gives the public the assurance that the agency "has indeed considered environmental concerns in its decision-making process," [Baltimore Gas & Electric Co.], and, perhaps more significantly, provides a springboard for public comment. Thus, in this case the final draft of the Early Winters Study reflects not only the work of the Forest Service itself, but also the critical views of the Washington State Department of Game, the Methow Valley Citizens Council, and Friends of the Earth, as well as many others, to whom copies of the draft Study were circulated. Moreover, with respect to a development such as Sandy Butte, where the adverse effects on air quality and the mule deer herd are primarily attributable to predicted off-site development that will be subject to regulation by other governmental bodies, the EIS serves the function of offering those bodies adequate notice of the expected consequences and the opportunity to plan and implement corrective measures in a timely manner.

The sweeping policy goals announced in § 101 of NEPA are thus realized through a set of "action-forcing" procedures that require that agencies take a " 'hard look' at environmental consequences," and that provide for broad dissemination of relevant environmental information. Although these procedures are almost certain to affect the agency's substantive decision, it is now well settled that NEPA itself does not mandate particular results, but simply prescribes the necessary process. * * *

If the adverse environmental effects of the proposed action are adequately identified and evaluated, the agency is not constrained by NEPA from deciding that other values outweigh the environmental costs. In this case, for example, it would not have violated NEPA if the Forest Service, after complying with the Act's procedural prerequisites, had decided that the benefits to be derived from downhill skiing at Sandy Butte justified the issuance of a special use permit, notwithstanding the loss of 15 percent, 50 percent, or even 100 percent of the mule deer herd. Other statutes may impose substantive environmental obligations on federal agencies, but NEPA merely prohibits uninformed—rather than unwise—agency action.

To be sure, one important ingredient of an EIS is the discussion of steps that can be taken to mitigate adverse environmental consequences.[23] The requirement that an EIS contain a detailed discussion of possible mitigation measures flows from both the language of the Act and, more expressly, from CEQ's implementing regulations. Implicit in NEPA's demand that an agency prepare a detailed statement on "any adverse environmental effects which cannot be avoided should the proposal be implemented," is an understanding that the EIS will discuss the extent to which adverse effects can be avoided. More generally, omission of a reasonably complete discussion of possible mitigation measures would undermine the "action-forcing" function of NEPA. Without such a discussion, neither the agency nor other interested groups and individuals can properly evaluate the severity of the adverse effects. An adverse effect that can be fully remedied by, for example, an inconsequential public expenditure is certainly not as serious as a similar effect that can only be modestly ameliorated through the commitment of vast public and private resources. Recognizing the importance of such a discussion in guaranteeing that the agency has taken a "hard look" at the environmental consequences of proposed federal action, CEQ regulations require that the agency discuss possible mitigation measures in defining the scope of the EIS, 40 CFR § 1508.25(b) (1987), in discussing alternatives to the proposed action, § 1502.14(f), and consequences of that action, § 1502.16(h), and in explaining its ultimate decision, § 1505.2(c).

There is a fundamental distinction, however, between a requirement that mitigation be discussed in sufficient detail to ensure that environmental consequences have been fairly evaluated, on the one hand, and a substantive requirement that a complete mitigation plan be actually

---

23. CEQ regulations define "mitigation" to include:

"(a) Avoiding the impact altogether by not taking a certain action or parts of an action.

"(b) Minimizing impacts by limiting the degree or magnitude of the action and its implementation.

"(c) Rectifying the impact by repairing, rehabilitating, or restoring the affected environment.

"(d) Reducing or eliminating the impact over time by preservation and maintenance operations during the life of the action.

"(e) Compensating for the impact by replacing or providing substitute resources or environments." 40 CFR § 1508.20 (1987).

formulated and adopted, on the other. In this case, the off-site effects on air quality and on the mule deer herd cannot be mitigated unless nonfederal government agencies take appropriate action. Since it is those state and local governmental bodies that have jurisdiction over the area in which the adverse effects need be addressed and since they have the authority to mitigate them, it would be incongruous to conclude that the Forest Service has no power to act until the local agencies have reached a final conclusion on what mitigating measures they consider necessary. Even more significantly, it would be inconsistent with NEPA's reliance on procedural mechanisms—as opposed to substantive, result-based standards—to demand the presence of a fully developed plan that will mitigate environmental harm before an agency can act. Cf. *Baltimore Gas & Electric Co.,* [supra p. 190] ("NEPA does not require agencies to adopt any particular internal decisionmaking structure").

We thus conclude that the Court of Appeals erred, first, in assuming that "NEPA requires that 'action be taken to mitigate the adverse effects of major federal actions,'" and, second, in finding that this substantive requirement entails the further duty to include in every EIS "a detailed explanation of specific measures which *will* be employed to mitigate the adverse impacts of a proposed action."

The Court of Appeals also concluded that the Forest Service had an obligation to make a "worst case analysis" if it could not make a reasoned assessment of the impact of the Early Winters project on the mule deer herd. Such a "worst case analysis" was required at one time by CEQ regulations, but those regulations have since been amended. Moreover, although the prior regulations may well have expressed a permissible application of NEPA, the Act itself does not mandate that uncertainty in predicting environmental harms be addressed exclusively in this manner. Accordingly, we conclude that the Court of Appeals also erred in requiring the "worst case" study.

In 1977, President Carter directed that CEQ promulgate binding regulations implementing the procedural provisions of NEPA. Pursuant to this presidential order, CEQ promulgated implementing regulations. Under § 1502.22 of these regulations—a provision which became known as the "worst case requirement"—CEQ provided that if certain information relevant to the agency's evaluation of the proposed action is either unavailable or too costly to obtain, the agency must include in the EIS a "worst case analysis and an indication of the probability or improbability of its occurrence." 40 CFR § 1502.22 (1985). In 1986, however, CEQ replaced the "worst case" requirement with a requirement that federal agencies, in the face of unavailable information concerning a reasonably foreseeable significant environmental consequence, prepare "a summary of existing credible scientific evidence which is relevant to evaluating the * * * adverse impacts" and prepare an "evaluation of such impacts based upon theoretical approaches or research methods generally accepted in the scientific community." 40 CFR § 1502.22(b) (1987). The amended regulation thus "retains the duty to describe the consequences of a remote, but potentially severe impact, but grounds the duty in evaluation of scientific opinion rather than in the framework of a conjectural 'worst case analysis.' " 50 Fed.Reg. 32237 (1985).

The Court of Appeals recognized that the "worst case analysis" regulation has been superseded, yet held that "[t]his rescission * * * does not nullify the requirement * * * since the regulation was merely a codification of prior NEPA case law." This conclusion, however, is erroneous in a number of respects. Most notably, review of NEPA case law reveals that the regulation, in fact, was not a codification of prior judicial decisions. The cases cited by the Court of Appeals ultimately rely on the Fifth Circuit's decision in *Sierra Club v. Sigler,* 695 F.2d 957 (1983). *Sigler,* however, simply recognized that the "worst case analysis" regulation codified the "judicially created principl[e]" that an EIS must "consider the probabilities of the occurrence of any environmental effects it discusses." *Id.,* at 970–971. As CEQ recognized at the time it superseded the regulation, case law prior to the adoption of the "worst case analysis" provision did require agencies to describe environmental impacts even in the face of substantial uncertainty, but did not require that this obligation necessarily be met through the mechanism of a "worst case analysis." CEQ's abandonment of the "worst case analysis" provision, therefore, is not inconsistent with any previously established judicial interpretation of the statute.

Nor are we convinced that the new CEQ regulation is not controlling simply because it was preceded by a rule that was in some respects more demanding. In *Andrus v. Sierra Club,* 442 U.S., at 358, 99 S.Ct., at 2341, we held that CEQ regulations are entitled to substantial deference. In that case we recognized that although less deference may be in order in some cases in which the " 'administrative guidelines' " conflict " 'with earlier pronouncements of the agency,' " substantial deference is nonetheless appropriate if there appears to have been good reason for the change. Here, the amendment only came after the prior regulation had been subjected to considerable criticism. Moreover, the amendment was designed to better serve the twin functions of an EIS—requiring agencies to take a "hard look" at the consequences of the proposed action and providing important information to other groups and individuals. CEQ explained that by requiring that an EIS focus on reasonably foreseeable impacts, the new regulation "will generate information and discussion on those consequences of greatest concern to the public and of greatest relevance to the agency's decision," rather than distorting the decisionmaking process by overemphasizing highly speculative harms. In light of this well-considered basis for the change, the new regulation is entitled to substantial deference. Accordingly, the Court of Appeals erred in concluding that the Early Winters Study is inadequate because it failed to include a "worst case analysis."

Notes

1. *Robertson,* like *Marsh* [supra p. 172], stresses the importance of the CEQ regulations. Are the current CEQ regulations adequate as a means of dealing with low-probability disasters? Would a worst-case requirement be

more useful, as a way of preventing the agency from sugar-coating its predictions? We will return in Chapter V to the problem of how the law should respond to scientific uncertainty and low-probability disasters.

2. Note that the *Robertson* Court refers to section 101 as "precatory" and says that "NEPA itself does not mandate particular results, but simply prescribes the necessary process." *Robertson* seems to make it clear that NEPA is purely procedural and imposes no substantive restraint on the government. The courts of appeals had divided on the issue of substantive review under NEPA. In *Strycker's Bay Neighborhood Council, Inc. v. Karlen,* 444 U.S. 223, 100 S.Ct. 497, 62 L.Ed.2d 433 (1980), the Second Circuit had held that an agency's choice of a site for a housing project was unjustifiable under NEPA. The Supreme Court reversed. The opinion contained broad language about the procedural nature of NEPA, such as the following:

> [I]n the present case there is no doubt that [the agency] considered the environmental consequences of its decision to designate the proposed site for low-income housing. NEPA requires no more.

444 U.S. at 228, 100 S.Ct. at 500.

A footnote, however, seemed to leave some possible room for substantive judicial review:

> If we could agree with the dissent that the Court of Appeals held [the agency] had acted "arbitrarily" * * * we might also agree that plenary review is warranted. But the District Court expressly concluded that [the agency] had not acted arbitrarily or capriciously and our reading of the opinion of the Court of Appeals satisfies us that it did not overturn that finding. Instead, the Appellate Court required [the agency] to elevate environmental concerns over other, admittedly legitimate considerations. Neither NEPA nor the APA provides any support for such a reordering of priorities by review in court.

444 U.S. at 228 n. 2, 100 S.Ct. at 500 n. 2.

3. The *Robertson* Court did not refer to the *Stryker* footnote, but its description of section 101 as "precatory" seems to leave little room for substantive judicial review under NEPA. In adopting this view of NEPA, hasn't the Court overlooked the language of § 102(1)? How can the section 101 policies be completely precatory, when § 102 "directs that, to the fullest extent possible: (1) the policies, regulations, and public laws of the United States shall be interpreted and administered in accordance with the policies set forth in this chapter. * * * ?"

The Supreme Court's resolution of this issue seems unjustifiable in principle, given the language of § 102(2). See Yost, "NEPA's Promise—Partially Fulfilled," 20 *Env.L.* 553 (1990). This is particularly ironic, given the stress placed by Justice Scalia and others on the need for fidelity to statutory texts. Nevertheless, it probably does not make much practical difference. Apart from the Second Circuit's ill-fated decision in *Strycker's Bay,* no court of appeals had ever actually reversed an agency decision on the merits under NEPA. One reason may be that NEPA's procedural standard overlaps considerably with the arbitrary and capricious standard anyway. Recall that the arbitrary and capricious test requires a "reasoned explanation" of the agency's decision. An EIS that fails to meet this "substantive" test can probably be faulted for its discussion of the impact of the action or of alternatives, and thus will be found inadequate. Moreover, most government actions are subject to some restrictions under other statutes, which will usually provide a basis for judicial correction of egregious agency decisions.

Note: Appraising NEPA After Thirty Years

Do you see any overall pattern in the outcomes in the Supreme Court's NEPA decisions? (Hint: Which side always won?) See Farber, *Nat'l L.J.*, May 4, 1987, at 20 (arguing that the Court's consistent rejection of NEPA claims reflects disdain for the statute). For a contrary view, see Shilton, "Is the Supreme Court Hostile to NEPA? Some Possible Explanations for a 12–0 Record," 20 *Env.L.* 551 (1990). In any event, the Court's reading of the statute has not been an expansive one.

NEPA's reception in other quarters, however, has been more favorable. If "imitation is the sincerest form of flattery," as the saying goes, then NEPA has received its share of praise. Fifteen states have adopted their own versions of NEPA, including California. More notably, EIS-type requirements have now been adopted in over thirty countries. For further details, see chapters 13 and 14 of D. Mandelker, *NEPA Law and Litigation* (2d ed. 1994). See also Michael Jeffrey, "The Canadian Environmental Assessment Act," 24 *Urban Lawyer* 775 (1992).

How effective has NEPA been? According to the *Robertson* Court, NEPA's procedures are "almost certain to affect the agency's substantive decision." Among those who have studied NEPA, there have been a variety of opinions about the statute's effectiveness. After a review of early airport runway-extension controversies, Professor Sax concluded that NEPA was simply ineffectual.[q] Other early commentators concluded that NEPA puts useful pressure on agencies to consider environmental issues, but is ultimately incapable of forcing them to do so.[r]

On the other hand, clear instances exist of agencies substantially changing their actions in light of NEPA. Perhaps the best example is the Corps of Engineers' decision to broaden consideration of whether to issue dredge-and-fill permits to include full consideration of environmental factors, despite substantial opposition.[s] The CEQ attempted in 1978 to discover the effects of NEPA litigation. A survey of 938 NEPA cases indicated the following results: (1) NEPA filings peaked in 1974; (2) a total of 202 cases were delayed by a NEPA injunction, almost half of them for longer than one year; (3) none of the projects were halted by a permanent injunction; (4) 60 of the projects were abandoned after the NEPA action was filed. A more recent CEQ study found that NEPA has had a highly beneficial effect on EPA's construction grant program for waste water treatment. See CEQ, *Twentieth Annual Report* 31–37

q. Sax, "The (Unhappy) Truth about NEPA," 26 *Okla.L.Rev.* 239 (1973).

r. Cramton & Berg, "On Leading a Horse to Water: NEPA and the Federal Bureaucracy," 71 *Mich.L.Rev.* 511, 536

(1973) ("[y]ou can lead a horse to water but * * *").

s. See *Zabel v. Tabb,* 430 F.2d 199 (5th Cir.1970), cert. denied 401 U.S. 910, 91 S.Ct. 873, 27 L.Ed.2d 808 (1971).

(1990). CEQ also reported that after 1978 the number of NEPA cases filed and the number of injunctions issued was highest in 1982–1983. In 1988, only half as many NEPA complaints were filed as in 1974. *Id.* at 392. Moreover, in 1987, only a third as many EISs were prepared by federal agencies as ten years earlier. See Montange, "NEPA in an Era of Economic Deregulation," 9 *Va.Env'l L.J.* 1, 7 n. 44 (1989). For further discussion of NEPA's effects, see S. Taylor, *Making Bureaucracies Think: The Environmental Impact Statement Strategy of Administrative Reform* (1984); Bear, "NEPA at 19," 19 *Envir.L.Rep.* 10062 (1989); Liroff, "NEPA Litigation in the 1970s: A Deluge or a Dribble?," 21 *Nat.Res.J.* 315, 325 (1981); Strelow, Book Review, 9 *Ecology L.Q.* 777, 779 (1981).

It is perhaps apt to close our discussion of NEPA with the following observation:

> Environmental law casebooks almost always include a few in-conclusive pages wondering whether NEPA has accomplished anything. If after twenty years of EISs there is still no conclusive empirical evidence as to whether NEPA has in fact influenced agency decisions, such evidence is unlikely to appear. * * * Nonetheless, a large body of both anecdotal and more scientific evidence indicates that NEPA has had a significant effect on substantive outcomes and has made an important contribution to environmental protection.

Herz, "Parallel Universes: NEPA Lessons for the New Property," 93 *Colum.L.Rev.* 1668, 1704 (1993).

Chapter III

ENVIRONMENTAL FEDERALISM

Environmental protection is complicated by the division of the world into political subunits. Environmental problems themselves recognize no such boundaries. As we saw in Chapter I, where the units of government are nation states, existing institutions for environmental cooperation are primitive. As we will see in this chapter, the same is not true today within the U.S., though some significant gaps and friction points remain.

Spillover effects can be economic as well as environmental. Efforts to solve environmental problems may have economic repercussions elsewhere. Environmental regulations may, for example, have the intended or unintended effect of acting as barriers to trade. Besides their direct economic impacts, such trade barriers can lead to further polarization between units of government, making cooperation even more difficult. Given the dramatic expansion of world trade since World War II, the relationship between trade and the environment has substantial practical significance.

In this chapter, we will explore these important topics. We will begin by considering a key mechanism created by the U.S. Constitution in response to the difficulty of obtaining cooperation between states: empowering the federal government to take action on a national basis. We will then turn to the American experience with the problem of regulatory trade barriers. As we will see, state environmental regulations are increasingly challenged as violations of the Supreme Court's "dormant commerce clause" doctrine. We will also examine the analogous problem at the international level, where GATT may impose similar restraints on environmental regulation by individual nations. Having considered these mechanisms for dealing with economic conflicts between jurisdictions, we turn in the last section to conflicts between jurisdictions caused by physical spillovers.

A. THE SCOPE OF FEDERAL POWER

The federal government was formed to deal with problems that could not be solved without centralized intervention. Under the Articles of Confederation, federal action could only be taken with unanimous agreement of all states, which severely hindered the government's role. Thus, the Constitution is a solution to what economists call a collective action problem. One of the basic assumptions of American constitutional law is that the federal government is a government of limited, delegated powers. Its authority was defined by the issues that at the time seemed to require a collective response. It does not have, at least in theory, the power even today to take any action it deems in the public interest. Instead, the federal government has a collection of specific powers: the power to regulate interstate commerce, the power to tax and spend, the power to enter treaties, etc. In this section, we will explore the scope of these federal powers and the extent to which they are limited by "states' rights." We begin with three cases involving the government's power to protect wildlife and wilderness—a goal not at the forefront in 1789.

KLEPPE v. NEW MEXICO

Supreme Court of the United States, 1976.
426 U.S. 529, 96 S.Ct. 2285, 49 L.Ed.2d 34.

JUSTICE MARSHALL delivered the opinion of the Court.

At issue in this case is whether Congress exceeded its powers under the Constitution in enacting the Wild Free-roaming Horses and Burros Act.   *Issue*

[The Act protects all unbranded horses and burros on public lands from capture. If the animals stray on to private land, the owner may require the government to retrieve them. In this case, state game officers entered public land to remove wild horses.]

The Property Clause of the Constitution provides that "Congress shall have Power to dispose of and make all needful Rules and Regulations respecting the Territory or other Property belonging to the United States." U.S. Const., Art. IV, § 3, cl. 2. In passing the Wild Free-roaming Horses and Burros Act, Congress deemed the regulated animals "an integral part of the natural system of the public lands" of the United States * * * and found that their management was necessary "for achievement of an ecological balance on the public lands." * * * According to Congress, these animals, if preserved in their native habitats, "contribute to the diversity of life forms within the Nation and enrich the lives of the American people." * * * Indeed, Congress concluded, the wild free-roaming horses and burros "are living symbols of the historic and pioneer spirit of the West." * * * Despite their importance, the Senate committee found:

> [These animals] have been cruelly captured and slain and their carcasses used in the production of pet food and fertilizer. They have been used for target practice and harassed for "sport" and profit. In spite of public outrage, this bloody traffic continues unabated, and it

is the firm belief of the committee that this senseless slaughter must be brought to an end.

For these reasons, Congress determined to preserve and protect the wild free-roaming horses and burros on the public lands of the United States. The question under the Property Clause is whether this determination can be sustained as a "needful" regulation "respecting" the public lands. In answering this question, we must remain mindful that, while courts must eventually pass upon them, determinations under the Property Clause are entrusted primarily to the judgment of Congress.

Appellees argue that the Act cannot be supported by the Property Clause. They contend that the Clause grants Congress essentially two kinds of power: (1) the power to dispose of and make incidental rules regarding the use of federal property; and (2) the power to protect federal property. According to appellees, the first power is not broad enough to support legislation protecting wild animals that live on federal property; and the second power is not implicated since the Act is designed to protect the animals, which are not themselves federal property, and not the public lands. As an initial matter, it is far from clear that the Act was not passed in part to protect the public lands of the United States or that Congress cannot assert a property interest in the regulated horses and burros superior to that of the State. But we need not consider whether the Act can be upheld on either of these grounds, for we reject appellees' narrow reading of the Property Clause.

Appellees ground their argument on a number of cases that, upon analysis, provide no support for their position. Like the District Court, appellees cite *Hunt v. United States,* 278 U.S. 96, 49 S.Ct. 38, 73 L.Ed. 200 (1928), for the proposition that the Property Clause gives Congress only the limited power to regulate wild animals in order to protect the public lands from damage. But *Hunt,* which upheld the Government's right to kill deer that were damaging foliage in the national forests, only holds that damage to the land is a sufficient basis for regulation; it contains no suggestion that it is a necessary one.

* * *

Camfield v. United States, 167 U.S. 518, 17 S.Ct. 864, 42 L.Ed. 260 (1897), is of even less help to appellees. Appellees rely upon the following language from *Camfield:*

> While we do not undertake to say that Congress has the unlimited power to legislate against nuisances within a State, which it would have within a Territory, we do not think the admission of a Territory as a State deprives it of the power of legislating for the protection of the public lands, though it may thereby involve the exercise of what is ordinarily known as the police power, *so long as such power is directed solely to its own protection.* Id., at 525–526, 17 S.Ct. at 867 (emphasis added).

Appellees mistakenly read this language to limit Congress' power to regulate activity on the public lands; in fact, the quoted passage refers to the scope of congressional power to regulate conduct on *private* land that affects the public lands * * *.

Lastly, appellees point to dicta in two cases to the effect that, unless the State has agreed to the exercise of federal jurisdiction, Congress' rights in its land are "only the rights of an ordinary proprietor * * *." *Fort Leavenworth R. Co. v. Lowe,* 114 U.S. 525, 527, 5 S.Ct. 995, 996, 29 L.Ed. 264 (1885). See also *Paul v. United States,* 371 U.S. 245, 264, 83 S.Ct. 426, 437, 9 L.Ed.2d 292 (1963). In neither case was the power of Congress under the Property Clause at issue or considered and * * * these dicta fail to account for the raft of cases in which the Clause has been given a broader construction.

In brief, beyond the *Fort Leavenworth* and *Paul* dicta, appellees have presented no support for their position that the Clause grants Congress only the power to dispose of, to make incidental rules regarding the use of, and to protect federal property. This failure is hardly surprising, for the Clause, in broad terms, gives Congress the power to determine what are "needful" rules "respecting" the public lands. And while the furthest reaches of the power granted by the Property Clause have not yet been definitively resolved, we have repeatedly observed that "[t]he power over the public land thus entrusted to Congress is without limitations."

* * * In short, Congress exercises the powers both of a proprietor and of a legislature over the public domain. Although the Property Clause does not authorize "an exercise of a general control over public policy in a State," it does permit "an exercise of the complete power which Congress has over particular public property entrusted to it." In our view, the "complete power" that Congress has over public lands necessarily includes the power to regulate and protect the wildlife living there.

Notes

1. *Kleppe* makes it clear that the federal government has the combined power of a proprietor and a sovereign over activities taking place on federal land. Thus, as to public lands, the United States is not a government of limited powers, but rather has the plenary legislative power enjoyed by the states within their own territories. See also *State of Nevada v. Watkins,* 914 F.2d 1545 (9th Cir.1990) (designation of federal land in Nevada as sole nuclear waste site permissible under property clause and does not violate 10th Amendment).

2. The scope of federal legislative power over private lands adjoining the public lands is less clear. In *Camfield v. United States,* 167 U.S. 518, 17 S.Ct. 864, 42 L.Ed. 260 (1897), an adjoining landowner had built fences on his own land in such a way as to enclose government land. The Court held that the fence constituted a nuisance, and Congress had the power to order its removal. Some of the language of the opinion seems to go beyond allowing Congress a simple power to abate nuisances:

The general Government doubtless has a power over its own property analogous to the police power of the several States, and the extent to which it may go in the exercise of such power is measured by the exigencies of the particular case. * * * A different rule would place the public domain of the United States completely at the mercy of the state legislature.

Id. at 525–526, 17 S.Ct. at 867, 42 L.Ed. at 262.

3. The scope of Congressional power under the Property Clause has given rise to scholarly debate. For a sampling of the views, see Gaetke, "Congressional Discretion Under the Property Clause," 33 *Hastings L.J.* 381 (1981); Wilkinson, "The Field of Public Land Law: Some Connecting Threads and Future Directions," 1 *Public Land L.Rev.* 1 (1980); Engdahl, "State and Federal Power over Federal Property," 18 *Ariz.L.Rev.* 282 (1976).

MINNESOTA v. BLOCK

United States Court of Appeals, Eighth Circuit, 1981.
660 F.2d 1240, cert. denied 455 U.S. 1007, 102 S.Ct. 1645, 71 L.Ed.2d 876 (1982).

BRIGHT, CIRCUIT JUDGE.

The challenged portion of the statute, section 4, prohibits the use of motorboats in the BWCAW in all but a small number of lakes. [The Boundary Waters Canoe Area (BWCA) is a wilderness area located on the border between Canada and Minnesota.]

The Act also limits snowmobiles to two routes. The United States owns ninety percent of the land within the borders of the BWCAW area. The State of Minnesota, in addition to owning most of the remaining ten percent of the land, owns the beds of all the lakes and rivers within the BWCAW.

* * *

* * * In a recent unanimous decision, the Supreme Court upheld an expansive reading of Congress' power under the property clause. See *Kleppe v. New Mexico,* [supra]. The Court concluded that

the Clause in broad terms, gives Congress the power to determine what are "needful" rules "respecting" the public lands. * * * And while the furthest reaches of the power granted by the Property Clause have not yet been definitively resolved, we have repeatedly observed that "[t]he power over the public lands thus entrusted to Congress is without limitations."

With this guidance, we must decide the question left open in *Kleppe*—the scope of Congress' property clause power as applied to activity occurring off federal land. Without defining the limits of the power, the Court in *Kleppe,* relying on its decision in *Camfield v. United States,* 167 U.S. 518, 17 S.Ct. 864, 42 L.Ed. 260 (1897), acknowledged that "it is clear the regulations under the Property Clause may have some effect on private lands not otherwise under federal control." In *Camfield,* the Court concluded that Congress possessed the power to control conduct occurring off federal property through its "power of legislating for the protection of the public lands, though it may thereby involve the exercise of what is ordinarily known as the police power, so long as such power is directed solely to [the public lands'] own protection."

Under this authority to protect public land, Congress' power must extend to regulation of conduct on or off the public land that would threaten the designated purpose of federal lands. Congress clearly has the power to dedicate federal land for particular purposes. As a necessary incident of that power, Congress must have the ability to insure that these lands be protected against interference with their intended purposes. As the Supreme Court has stated, under the property clause "[Congress] may sanction some uses and prohibit others, and *may forbid interference with such as are sanctioned.*"

This court has previously held that Congress, under the property clause, could prohibit hunting on waters within the boundaries of the Voyagers National Park in Minnesota, even though the waters were subject to state jurisdiction. *United States v. Brown*, 552 F.2d 817, 821 (8th Cir.), cert. denied, 431 U.S. 949, 97 S.Ct. 2666, 53 L.Ed.2d 266 (1977). In *Brown*, the purpose of the challenged regulations extended beyond the mere protection of the federal land from physical harm. This court, in effect, affirmed the district court's approval of the regulations as necessary because "hunting on the waters in the park could 'significantly interfere with the *use of the park and the purposes for which it was established.*'"

Having established that Congress may regulate conduct off federal land that interferes with the designated purpose of that land, we must determine whether Congress acted within this power in restricting the use of motorboats and other motor vehicles in the BWCAW. In reviewing the appropriateness of particular regulations, "we must remain mindful that, while courts must eventually pass upon them, determinations under the Property Clause are entrusted primarily to the judgment of Congress." [citing *Kleppe*]. Thus, if Congress enacted the motorized use restrictions to protect the fundamental purpose for which the BWCAW had been reserved, and if the restrictions in section 4 reasonably relate to that end, we must conclude that Congress acted within its constitutional prerogative.

Hearings and other evidence provided ample support for Congress' finding that use of motorboats and snowmobiles must be limited in order to preserve the area as a wilderness. Testimony established that the sight, smell, and sound of motorized vehicles seriously marred the wilderness experience of canoeists, hikers, and skiers and threatened to destroy the integrity of the wilderness.

As a result of considerable testimony and debate and a series of compromises, Congress enacted section 4 in an attempt to accommodate all interests, determining the extent of motorized use the area might tolerate without serious threat to its wilderness values.

The motor use restrictions form only a small part of an elaborate system of regulation considered necessary to preserve the BWCAW as a wilderness. The United States owns close to ninety percent of the land surrounding the waters at issue. Congress concluded that motorized vehicles significantly interfere with the use of the wilderness by canoeists, hikers, and skiers and that restricted motorized use would enhance and preserve the wilderness values of the area. From the evidence presented, Congress could rationally reach these conclusions. We hold, therefore, that Congress acted within its power under the Constitution to pass needful regulations respecting public lands.

Conclusion →

Notes

1. Why should the federal government, rather than the state in which the land is located, be assigned the task of preserving wilderness? Are the interests of citizens of other states implicated? Is interstate cooperation required?

2. Under *Block,* are there any limits to the use of the federal property power over nonfederal property? Note that the *Block* court's basic rationale is that if Congress can dedicate public lands to a particular purpose, it can pass any appropriate legislation to ensure that this purpose is effectuated. But how is a court to assess what legislation is "appropriately" related to the Congressional goal? For further discussion of the federal government's power over adjoining nonfederal lands, see Gaetke, "The Boundary Waters Canoe Area Wilderness Act of 1978: Regulating Nonfederal Property Under The Property Clause," 60 *Ore.L.Rev.* 157 (1981); Sax, "Helpless Giants: The National Parks and the Regulation of Private Lands," 75 *Mich.L.Rev.* 239 (1976).

3. In *Stupak-Thrall v. United States,* 70 F.3d 881 (6th Cir.1995), the court upheld a federal regulation prohibiting use of houseboats and sailboats on a lake bordering a wilderness area. The regulation also discouraged use of electronic fish-finders, boom-boxes, and other mechanical or electronic devices. Almost all of the lake, except for the portion owned by the plaintiffs, was actually within the wilderness area. Under state law, all riparian owners (including both the federal government in this case and the private owners) have a common riparian right to reasonable use of the water. The court found the regulation to be well within congressional power under the Property Clause:

> [T]he management prescriptions at issue are clearly tailored toward protecting federal property. The avowed purpose of the prohibition against sailboats, houseboats, and "nonburnable" food containers is "to protect and perpetuate wilderness character and values." * * * Certainly Congress could rationally conclude that certain forms of mechanical transport should be excluded from the Sylvania Wilderness in order to preserve the "wilderness character" of the property. * * * Just as Congress's authority may sometimes extend to purely private property in order to provide adequate protection of private property, so in this instance may federal regulations encompass shared property rights between the United States and private owners, at least to the extent that the regulations are designed to govern the portion of the water

bill in equity: on equitable pleading where claimant brings a claim in a court of equity.

Sec. A   THE SCOPE OF FEDERAL POWER   **209**

surface contained completely within the borders of government-owned land.

Id. at 886. One unusual wrinkle is that the federal action was taken under a statute that explicitly preserved existing private rights. The court held that under state law, the private landowner's riparian rights were subject to the action of adjoining sovereigns such as townships, and that the federal government stood in the same position.

plaintiff   defendant

MISSOURI v. HOLLAND, Sec. of Agriculture

Supreme Court of the United States, 1920.
252 U.S. 416, 40 S.Ct. 382, 64 L.Ed. 641.

MR. JUSTICE HOLMES delivered the opinion of the Court.

This is a bill in equity brought by the State of Missouri to prevent a game warden of the United States from attempting to enforce the Migratory Bird Treaty Act of July 3, 1918, and the regulations made by the Secretary of Agriculture in pursuance of the same. The ground of the bill is that the statute is an unconstitutional interference with the rights reserved to the States by the Tenth Amendment, and that the acts of the defendant done and threatened under that authority invade the sovereign right of the State and contravene its will manifested in statutes. * * *

On December 8, 1916, a treaty between the United States and Great Britain was proclaimed by the President. It recited that many species of birds in their annual migrations traversed certain parts of the United States and of Canada, that they were of great value as a source of food and in destroying insects injurious to vegetation, but were in danger of extermination through lack of adequate protection. It therefore provided for specified close seasons and protection in other forms, and agreed that the two powers would take or propose to their law-making bodies the necessary measures for carrying the treaty out. The above mentioned Act of July 3, 1918, entitled an act to give effect to the convention, prohibited the killing, capturing or selling of any of the migratory birds included in the terms of the treaty except as permitted by regulations compatible with those terms, to be made by the Secretary of Agriculture. Regulations were proclaimed on July 31, and October 25, 1918. It is unnecessary to go into any details, because, as we have said, the question *issue* raised is the general one whether the treaty and statute are void as an interference with the rights reserved to the States.

To answer this question it is not enough to refer to the Tenth Amendment, reserving the powers not delegated to the United States, because by Article II, § 2, the power to make treaties is delegated expressly, and by Article VI treaties made under the authority of the United States, along with the Constitution and laws of the United States made in pursuance thereof, are declared the supreme law of the land. If the treaty is valid there can be no dispute about the validity of the statute under Article I, § 8, as a necessary and proper means to execute the powers of the Government. The language of the Constitution as to

Issue

the supremacy of treaties being general, the question before us is narrowed to an inquiry into the ground upon which the present supposed exception is placed.

* * *

* * * [W]hen we are dealing with words that also are a constituent act, like the Constitution of the United States, we must realize that they have called into life a being the development of which could not have been foreseen completely by the most gifted of its begetters. It was enough for them to realize or to hope that they had created an organism; it has taken a century and has cost their successors much sweat and blood to prove that they created a nation. The case before us must be considered in the light of our whole experience and not merely in that of what was said a hundred years ago. The treaty in question does not contravene any prohibitory words to be found in the Constitution. The only question is whether it is forbidden by some invisible radiation from the general terms of the Tenth Amendment. We must consider what this country has become in deciding what that Amendment has reserved.

The State as we have intimated founds its claim of exclusive authority upon an assertion of title to migratory birds, an assertion that is embodied in statute. No doubt it is true that as between a State and its inhabitants the State may regulate the killing and sale of such birds, but it does not follow that its authority is exclusive of paramount powers. To put the claim of the State upon title is to lean upon a slender reed. Wild birds are not in the possession of anyone; and possession is the beginning of ownership. The whole foundation of the State's rights is the presence within their jurisdiction of birds that yesterday had not arrived, tomorrow may be in another State and in a week a thousand miles away. If we are to be accurate we cannot put the case of the State upon higher ground than that the treaty deals with creatures that for the moment are within the state borders, that it must be carried out by officers of the United States within the same territory, and that but for the treaty the State would be free to regulate this subject itself.

As most of the laws of the United States are carried out within the States and as many of them deal with matters which in the silence of such laws the State might regulate, such general grounds are not enough to support Missouri's claim. Valid treaties of course "are as binding within the territorial limits of the States as they are elsewhere throughout the dominion of the United States." No doubt the great body of private relations usually fall within the control of the State, but a treaty may override its power. * * *

Here a national interest of very nearly the first magnitude is involved. It can be protected only by national action in concert with that of another power. The subject-matter is only transitorily within the State and has no permanent habitat therein. But for the treaty and the statute there soon might be no birds for any powers to deal with. We see nothing in the Constitution that compels the Government to sit by while a food supply is cut off and the protectors of our forests and our crops are destroyed. It is not sufficient to rely upon the States. The reliance is vain, and were it otherwise, the question is whether the United States is forbidden to act. We are of the opinion that the treaty and statute must be upheld.

Conclusion

Notes

1.   The Tenth Amendment states:

The powers not delegated to the United States by the Constitution, nor prohibited by it to the States, are reserved to the States respectively, or to the people.

Is this anything more than a "truism," that "all is retained which has not been surrendered," as the Court said in *United States v. Darby,* 312 U.S. 100, 124, 61 S.Ct. 451, 462, 85 L.Ed. 609, 622 (1941)? Does Justice Holmes give it any more meaning than this?

2.   Does federalism place any limit on the treaty power? As part of an air pollution treaty with Canada, could the federal government require officials in the State of Washington to engage in an extensive program of automobile inspections?

3.   Perhaps the most important Congressional power is the power to regulate interstate commerce, as the next case illustrates. As we will see, the issue remains controversial even today.

HODEL v. INDIANA

Supreme Court of the United States, 1981.
452 U.S. 314, 101 S.Ct. 2376, 69 L.Ed.2d 40.

JUSTICE MARSHALL delivered the opinion of the Court.

[In the Surface Mining Control and Reclamation Act of 1977, 30 U.S.C.A. §§ 1201–1328, Congress adopted a program of nationwide environmental standards for stripmining, with enforcement primarily in the hands of the states if they elect to exercise the authority. Generally, no person may conduct surface coal mining without a permit issued under a state or federal program. The Act specifies environmental protection performance standards which every permit must require. The coal mining operation must "restore the land affected to a condition capable of supporting the uses which it was capable of supporting prior to any mining, or higher or better uses of which there is reasonable likelihood," and use the best technology currently available to minimize environmental impacts. The statute also contains special provisions strictly regulating mining on "prime farmland." The issue before the Court in the following case was whether the surface mining statute exceeded the federal government's constitutional powers.]

The District Court gave two rationales for its decision on the Commerce Clause issue. The court first held that the six "prime farmland" provisions are beyond congressional power to regulate interstate commerce because they are "directed at facets of surface coal mining which have no substantial and adverse effect on interstate commerce."

The court reached this conclusion by examining statistics in the *Report of the Interagency Task Force on the Issue of a Moratorium or a Ban on Mining in Prime Agricultural Lands (Interagency Report)* (1977). These statistics compared the prime farmland acreage being disturbed annually by surface mining to the total prime farmland acreage in the United States. The *Interagency Report* stated that approximately 21,800 acres of prime farmland were being disturbed annually and that this acreage amounted to .006% of the total prime farmland acreage in the Nation. This statistic and others derived from it, together with similar comparisons for Indiana, persuaded the court that surface coal mining on prime farmland has "an infinitesimal effect or trivial impact on interstate commerce."

With respect to the other 15 substantive provisions which apply to surface mining generally, the District Court reasoned that the only possible adverse effects on interstate commerce justifying congressional action are air and water pollution and determined that these effects are adequately addressed by other provisions of the Act. The court therefore concluded that these 15 provisions as well as the six prime farmland provisions "are not directed at the alleviation of water or air pollution, to the extent that there are any such effects, and are not means reasonably and plainly adapted to the legitimate end of removing any substantial and adverse effect on interstate commerce." We find both of the District Court's rationales untenable.

It is established beyond peradventure that "legislative Acts adjusting the burdens and benefits of economic life come to the Court with a presumption of constitutionality * * *." A court may invalidate legislation enacted under the Commerce Clause only if it is clear that there is no rational basis for a congressional finding that the regulated activity affects interstate commerce, or that there is no reasonable connection between the regulatory means selected and the asserted ends. * * *

In our view, Congress was entitled to find that the protection of prime farmland is a federal interest that may be addressed through Commerce Clause legislation. The *Interagency Report* provides no basis for the District Court's contrary view. That report dealt only with the question whether a complete moratorium or ban on surface coal mining on prime farmland was advisable as a matter of policy. The report neither purported to examine the full impact of surface mining on interstate commerce in agricultural commodities, nor concluded that the impact is too negligible to warrant federal regulation. More important, the court below incorrectly assumed that the relevant inquiry under the rational basis test is the volume of commerce actually affected by the regulated activity. * * *

* * *

We also conclude that the court below erred in holding that the prime farmland and 15 other substantive provisions challenged by appellees are not reasonably related to the legitimate goal of protecting interstate commerce from adverse effects attributable to surface coal mining. The court incorrectly assumed that the Act's goals are limited to preventing air and water pollution. * * *

Congress adopted the Surface Mining Act in order to ensure that production of coal for interstate commerce would not be at the expense of agriculture, the environment, or public health and safety, injury to any of which interests would have deleterious effects on interstate commerce. * * * The statutory provisions invalidated by the District Court advance these legitimate goals and we conclude that Congress acted reasonably in adopting the regulatory scheme contained in the Act.

The District Court also held that the 21 substantive statutory provisions discussed above violate the Tenth Amendment because they constitute "displacement or regulation of the management structure and operation of the traditional governmental function of the States in the area of land use control and planning * * *." * * *

* * * [T]he sections of the Act under attack in this case regulate only the activities of surface mine operators who are private individuals and businesses, and the District Court's conclusion that the Act directly regulates the States as States is untenable. * * *

Notes

1. The Court applied a rational basis test to assess the validity of the statute. As a practical matter, does this test impose any significant constraints on Congress?

2. Why should environmental regulation cut across jurisdictional lines? Why not allow each jurisdiction to pursue independently its own preferred environmental policies? One reason is that environmental problems themselves may cross jurisdictional lines. As Richard Revesz has pointed out, the economic argument for a coordinated solution in this situation is undeniable. Revesz, "Federalism and Interstate Environmental Externalities," 144 *U. Pa.L.Rev.* 2341 (1996). In Part D, we will examine the problem of physical spillovers in more detail.

Another type of spillover is economic rather than environmental. In a world of capital mobility, regulatory efforts may be stymied by capital flight. In order to attract and retain industry, a jurisdiction may lower its environmental standards, only to spark a round of similar responses from other jurisdictions. The result is a race to the bottom, in which jurisdictions compete by progressively lowering their environmental standards until they hit rock bottom. For discussions of the race to the bottom, see David L. Shapiro, *Federalism: A Dialogue* 42–43, 81–82 (1995); Revesz, "Rehabilitating Interstate Competition: Rethinking the ' "Race-to-the-Bottom' Rationale for Federal Environmental Regulation," 67 *NYU L. Rev.* 1210 (1992). In the trade context, see Hudec, "Differences in National Environmental Standards: The Level–Playing–Field Dimension," 5 *Minn. J. Global Trade* 1 (1996). Only the intervention of a centralized authority can halt this destructive competition between jurisdictions. As Revesz explains, under this model, local jurisdictions would face a prisoner's dilemma, so that federal regulation can be seen "not as an intrusion on the autonomy of states, as it is often portrayed, but rather as a mechanism by which states can improve the welfare of their citizens."

Considerable dispute exists among scholars regarding the "race to the bottom" rationale. Under many conditions, just as competitive markets for goods can produce efficient results, so interstate competition can produce economically efficient environmental regulation. However, economic theory does suggest the following list of circumstances in which the race to the bottom might occur, justifying some multi-jurisdictional solutions:

a.   Local governments may be forced to use flawed methods of taxation, leading to distortions in other regulations in an effort to attract business.

b.   Competition in product or capital markets may be imperfect, leading to efforts by states to capture firms or monopoly profits, or to avoid unemployment.

c.   Public choice problems may distort local decisions, leading to capture of the regulatory process by industry.

d.   Jurisdictions may be large enough to affect global prices, leading to protectionist policies.[a]

3.   It may be helpful to consider how these various theories apply in a specific case such as *Hodel*. On which of the following theories, if any, is federal regulation to protect prime farmland from stripmining justified: interstate environmental effects of stripmining such as water pollution, the economic impact of such stripmining on agricultural production, the potential for a "race to the bottom" among state regulators of stripmining, or the greater expertise available to federal regulatory agencies than to state governments? On the other hand, are there any reasons why, at least as a policy matter, we might prefer to leave the matter to state governments. (For instance, are people in different states likely to have conflicting views about the importance of preserving prime farmland? Is it better for land use regulation to take place at a level of government more accessible to ordinary people?)

✳ *Note on the Recent Revival of Limits on the Commerce Clause*

As *Hodel* illustrates, Congress has not been shy about exercising the commerce power. Between 1965 and 1980, Richard Stewart reports, "Congress adopted sweeping new environmental, health, safety, and antidiscrimination regulatory statutes. There are at present over sixty major federal programs regulating business and non-profit organizations." Richard B. Stewart, "Madison's Nightmare," 57 *U.Chi.L.Rev.* 335, 339 (1990). In particular, Congress took the lead on environmental issues. See Buzbee, "Brown-

---

a. Since Revesz's influential article debunking naive theories of the race to the bottom, efforts to rehabilitate the argument often stress the third factor, defects in local governments. See Farber, "Environmental Federalism in a Global Economy," 83 *Va. L.Rev.* 1283 (1997). For Revesz's defense of his theory, see Richard Revesz, "The Race to the Bottom and Federal Environmental Legislation: A Response to Critics," 82

Minn.L.Rev. 535 (1997). A recent comprehensive survey of the relevant economic literature seems to suggest that the race to the bottom is a genuine possibility though by no means inevitable. See Bratton & McCahery, "The New Economics of Jurisdictional Competition: Devolutionary Federalism in a Second–Best World," 86 *Geo.L.J.* 201 (1997).

fields, Environmental Federalism, and Institutional Determinism," 21 *Wm. & Mary L.Rev.* 1 (1997) (federal government's "first mover" status).

By the later 1980s, however, some conservative theorists were beginning to lay the groundwork for a retreat from this expansive view of federal power. Raoul Berger continued his campaign on behalf of unadulterated originalism with a book on federalism. Raoul Berger, *Federalism: The Founders' Design* (1987). He argued that the commerce clause extends only to trade across state lines, id at 125, and that the Supreme Court's commerce clause doctrines are ripe for reevaluation, id. at 170–80. Richard Epstein argued the doctrinal point in more detail. Notably, he endorsed the view that "the Ford Motor Company did not manufacture goods in interstate commerce, but the Northern Pacific Railroad shipped them in interstate commerce." Richard Epstein, "The Proper Scope of the Commerce Power," 73 *Va. L. Rev.* 1387, 1442 (1987). Epstein concluded in no uncertain terms: "The affirmative scope of the commerce power should be limited to those matters that today are governed by the dormant commerce clause: interstate transportation, navigation and sales, and the activities closely incident to them. All else should be left to the states." Id. at 170–80.

This debate seemed entirely "academic" until the Supreme Court unexpectedly put its weight behind the effort to limit federal legislative power in *United States v. Lopez*, 514 U.S. 549, 115 S.Ct. 1624, 131 L.Ed.2d 626 (1995). Chief Justice Rehnquist's opinion invalidated a federal ban on possession of firearms in the vicinity of schools (a subject on which the need for federal regulation does seem less than obvious.) At the outset, Rehnquist invoked Madison's characterization of federal powers as "few and defined" while state powers are "numerous and indefinite." Id. at 1626. Admittedly, he added, the scope of federal power had greatly increased in the post-New Deal era, partly because of the "great changes" in the economy and partly because of a desire to eliminate "artificial" restraints on federal power. Id. at 1628. Rehnquist concluded, however, that the school gun law did not fall squarely within the post-New Deal judicial holdings, and he declined to further expand the scope of the commerce power.

Justice Thomas argued that the majority had not gone nearly far enough. Like Epstein and Berger, he argued that modern commerce clause jurisprudence is almost wholly illegitimate. His analysis rests on two premises. First, commerce consists only of sales transactions and transportation in connection with those transactions. 115 S. Ct. at 1643. Second, most areas of life should be subject only to state regulation, "even many matters that would have substantial effects on commerce": "[D]espite being well aware that agriculture, manufacturing, and other matters substantially affected commerce, the founding generation did not cede authority over all these activities to Congress. Hamilton, for instance, acknowledged that the Federal Government could not regulate agriculture and like concerns* * *." Id. at 1645. Epstein and Berger, who had seemed so far outside the mainstream a few years before, now had the solid support of at least one Justice.

It remains to be seen how much *Lopez* will actually affect the scope of federal regulatory power. Justice Kennedy's concurrence (joined by Justice O'Connor) is more tentative than the majority opinion, and repeatedly suggests that the Court's role is to protect the *current* balance of power between the states and the federal government, rather than to begin a rollback of federal power. See 115 S. Ct. at 1638 (citizens need to be able to identify responsibility for government action, making use of traditional boundaries between the activities of those governments); id. at 1640 (gun control act objectionable because it invades traditional area of state regulation of education). Taking the Rehnquist and Kennedy opinions together, *Lopez* seems unlikely to fulfill Justice Thomas's hope for a major rollback of federal power. The scholarly response to *Lopez* has on the whole been negative, and most lower courts have not seen *Lopez* as signaling a major shift of power back to the states.[b]

Congress has used the commerce power as the basis for regulating air and water pollution, hazardous waste disposal, and a host of other environmental problems. For the present, at least, the massive body of federal environmental statutes resting on the commerce power seems safe from constitutional attack. See *United States v. Olin Corp.*, 107 F.3d 1506 (11th Cir.1997) (upholding application of CERCLA without proof that any off-site damage had occurred). But *Lopez* does seem to leave open the possibility of attacking some peripheral federal environmental regulations. Such attacks might be mounted against environmental laws that govern noncommercial activity in a traditional area of state concern and lack any evident interstate impact.

John Dwyer has suggested two possible areas where *Lopez* might have a significant impact:

> The SDWA establishes drinking water standards for public water systems, which normally deliver drinking water intrastate. Given that many of these systems are state or municipally owned, a court may conclude that their activities are "noncommercial" (one problem with *Lopez* is that it does not carefully define commercial and noncommercial activities). On the other hand, a court may conclude that public water systems are commercial because they sell water and that they substantially affect interstate commerce because they use equipment purchased from other states or because some water users are directly engaged in interstate commerce * * *.

> Arguably, another potentially vulnerable statute is the ESA, which prohibits the taking and possession of endangered species. Takings normally occur entirely intrastate and may well be the product of noncommercial activity. A cursory review of cases under the ESA, however, strongly suggests that takings of endangered species on private

b. For commentary on *Lopez*, see Herbert Hovenkamp, "Judicial Restraint and Constitutional Federalism: The Supreme Court's Lopez and Seminole Tribe Decisions," 96 *Colum. L. Rev.* 2213 (1996); Philip Frickey, "The Fool on the Hill: Congressional Findings, Constitutional Adjudication, and United States v. Lopez," 46 *Case W. L. Rev.* 695 (1996); Lawrence Lessig, "Translating Federalism: United States v. Lopez," 1996 *Sup. Ct. Rev.* 125; Daniel A. Farber, "The Constitution's Forgotten Cover Letter: An Essay on the New Federalism and the Original Understanding," 94 *Mich. L. Rev.* 615 (1995). For a sample of judicial responses, see *United States v. Genao*, 79 F.3d 1333 (2d Cir. 1996); *United States v. Bishop*, 66 F.3d 569 (3d Cir.1995); *United States v. McMasters*, 90 F.3d 1394 (8th Cir.1996); *United States v. McAllister*, 77 F.3d 387 (11th Cir.1996). See generally, Andrew Weis, "Commerce Clause in the Cross–Hairs: The Use of *Lopez*-Based Motions to Challenge the Constitutionality of Federal Criminal Statutes," 48 *Stan. L. Rev.* 1431 (1996) [student note].

land normally occur in the course of commercial or other economic activity. Thus, the regulation of noncommercial intrastate activities under the ESA might well be a small part of a larger scheme of economic regulation substantially affecting interstate commerce, in which case the ESA probably would survive a Commerce Clause challenge.

John Dwyer, "The Commerce Clause and the Limits of Congressional Authority to Regulate the Environment," 25 *Env. L. Rep.* 10421, 10427–28 (1995). See also John Nagle, "The Commerce Clause Meets the Delhi–Sands Flower–Loving Fly," 97 *Mich.L.Rev.* 174 (1998). Another possible area of concern involves federal regulation of isolated wetlands. See *Hoffman Homes, Inc. v. EPA*, 999 F.2d 256 (7th Cir.1993) (en banc) (pre-*Lopez* case upholding federal regulation of isolated wetlands); Comment, "The Birds: Regulation of Isolated Wetlands and the Limits of the Commerce Clause," 28 *U. Cal. of Davis L. Rev.* 1237 (1995). But see *United States v. Wilson*, 133 F.3d 251 (4th Cir.1997) (construing statute governing wetlands more narrowly to avoid constitutional doubt). So far, however, it is unclear that even those peripheral attacks on federal environmental statutes will be successful.

Note on the Tenth Amendment and Environmental Law

For a long time, the Tenth Amendment was considered to be nothing more than a reminder that the states retained whatever powers had not been given to the federal government. In 1976, however, the Court resurrected the Amendment in *National League of Cities v. Usery*, 426 U.S. 833, 96 S.Ct. 2465, 49 L.Ed.2d 245 (1976), striking down a law that extended the federal minimum wage to cover state employees.

Partly as a result of *National League of Cities*, the Tenth Amendment caused a good deal of litigation in the environmental area. For instance, the lower courts disagreed about whether Congress could force the states to administer inspection programs for automobiles. *National League of Cities* also led to a flurry of Supreme Court opinions. For example, in *Hodel* [supra page 211] the Court upheld the federal Surface Mining Act, rejecting the claim that land use regulation is an inherently state concern beyond federal power under the Tenth Amendment. Then, in *FERC v. Mississippi*, 456 U.S. 742, 102 S.Ct. 2126, 72 L.Ed.2d 532 (1982), a sharply divided Court upheld portions of a 1978 energy conservation act, even though the statute imposed affirmative duties on state administrative agencies.

Justice Blackmun had been the swing vote in *National League of Cities*. In *Garcia v. San Antonio Metropolitan Transit Authority*, 469 U.S. 528, 105 S.Ct. 1005, 83 L.Ed.2d 1016 (1985), he changed his mind, and became the decisive vote to overrule *National League of Cities*. Like the earlier case, *Garcia* involved the federal minimum wage law, this time as applied to public transit workers. Despairing of the effort to distinguish integral state functions from other state activities, the Court held that the political process is the primary shield of the states against Congress. At least in the absence of a clear breakdown in the political process, courts should not intervene. The dissenters in *Garcia* predicted a rapid demise for that case, however, so only time will tell whether *National League of Cities* is gone for good. If the *National League of Cities* rule is revived, the pre-*Garcia* cases suggest that environmental laws will be at risk only if they impose affirmative duties on state officers, rather than regulating individuals or offering state governments an incentive to adopt certain regulations voluntarily.

The following case focuses on the narrower problem posed by statutes that target *only* state governments. It may represent the first step toward resurrecting *National League of Cities.*

NEW YORK v. UNITED STATES

Supreme Court of the United States, 1992.
505 U.S. 144, 112 S.Ct. 2408, 120 L.Ed.2d 120.

JUSTICE O'CONNOR delivered the opinion of the Court.

[This case involves three provisions of the Low–Level Radioactive Waste Policy Amendments Act of 1985. Since 1979, only three disposal sites for low-level waste have been in operation. The statute is designed to create incentives for states to take responsibility for the waste they produce. Based largely upon a proposal of the National Governors' Association, the 1985 statute was a compromise between sited and unsited states (those containing or not containing disposal sites). The sited states agreed to accept waste for another seven years, and the unsited states agreed to handle their own waste by 1992. The statute provides several incentives to encourage states to tackle this problem. First, the sited states are authorized to charge gradually increasing fees for waste from unsited states. Second, states that miss certain deadlines may be charged higher surcharges and, eventually, may be denied access to disposal facilities altogether. Third, the so-called "take title" provision tells states that eventually they will literally own the problem themselves if they don't cooperate.

[New York joined no regional compact. It complied with the initial requirements of the statute by enacting legislation providing for the siting of a facility in the state. Residents of the two counties containing potential sites opposed the state's choice of location—a classic example of the NIMBY ("Not In My Back Yard") syndrome. Fearing that it could not comply with the statutory deadlines, New York and these two counties brought suit, contending that the statute is inconsistent with the Tenth Amendment and with the guarantee of a republican form of government in Article IV.]

Most of our recent cases interpreting the Tenth Amendment have concerned the authority of Congress to subject state governments to generally applicable laws. The Court's jurisprudence in this area has traveled an unsteady path. [Citing *National League of Cities* and *Garcia.*] This case presents no occasion to apply or revisit the holdings of any of these cases, as this is not a case in which Congress has subjected a State to the same legislation applicable to private parties.

This case instead concerns the circumstances under which Congress may use the States as implements of regulation; that is, whether

Congress may direct or otherwise motivate the States to regulate in a particular field or a particular way. * * *

* * * While Congress has substantial powers to govern the Nation directly, including in areas of intimate concern to the States, the Constitution has never been understood to confer upon Congress the ability to require the States to govern according to Congress' instructions. The Court has been explicit about this distinction. "Both the States and the United States existed before the Constitution. The people, through that instrument, established a more perfect union by substituting a national government, acting, with ample power, *directly upon the citizens,* instead of the Confederate government, which acted with powers, greatly restricted, only upon the States."

This is not to say that Congress lacks the ability to encourage a State to regulate in a particular way, or that Congress may not hold out incentives to the States as a method of influencing a State's policy choices. Our cases have identified a variety of methods, short of outright coercion, by which Congress may urge a State to adopt a legislative program consistent with federal interests. Two of these methods are of particular relevance here.

First, under Congress' spending power, "Congress may attach conditions on the receipt of federal funds." Such conditions must (among other requirements) bear some relationship to the purpose of the federal spending; otherwise, of course, the spending power could render academic the Constitution's other grants and limits of federal authority. Where the recipient of federal funds is a State, as is not unusual today, the conditions attached to the funds by Congress may influence a State's legislative choices. * * *

Second, where Congress has the authority to regulate private activity under the Commerce Clause, we have recognized Congress' power to offer States the choice of regulating that activity according to federal standards or having state law pre-empted by federal regulation. This arrangement, which has been termed "a program of cooperative federalism," is replicated in numerous federal statutory schemes. * * *

By either of these two methods, as by any other permissible method of encouraging a State to conform to federal policy choices, the residents of the State retain the ultimate decision as to whether or not the State will comply. If a State's citizens view federal policy as sufficiently contrary to local interests, they may elect to decline a federal grant. If state residents would prefer their government to devote its attention and resources to problems other than those deemed important by Congress, they may choose to have the Federal Government rather than the State bear the expense of a federally mandated regulatory program, and they may continue to supplement that program to the extent state law is not preempted. Where Congress encourages state regulation rather than compelling it, state governments remain responsive to the local electorate's preferences; state officials remain accountable to the people.

By contrast, where the Federal Government compels States to regulate, the accountability of both state and federal officials is diminished. If the citizens of New York, for example, do not consider that making provision for the disposal of radioactive waste is in their best interest, they may elect state officials who share their view. That view can always be preempted under the Supremacy Clause if it is contrary to the national view, but in such a case it is the Federal Government that makes the decision in full view of the public, and it will be federal officials that suffer the consequences if the decision turns out to be detrimental or unpopular. But where the Federal Government directs the States to regulate, it may be state officials who will bear the brunt of public disapproval, while the federal officials who devised the regulatory program may remain insulated from the electoral ramifications of their decision. Accountability is thus diminished when, due to federal coercion, elected state officials cannot regulate in accordance with the views of the local electorate in matters not pre-empted by federal regulation.

[The Court upheld the Act's provision authorizing sited states to impose a surcharge on waste received from other states. These charges are intended to provide financial incentives for states to cooperate with the waste disposal scheme. The Court called this provision "an unexceptional exercise of Congress' power to authorize the states to burden interstate commerce." The Court upheld the provision under which the federal government collects a portion of this surcharge and places it into an escrow account, calling it "no more than a federal tax on interstate commerce." Also held valid was the provision under which states reaching a series of milestones in combating radioactive waste receive portions of these federally collected funds, which was considered an appropriate "conditional exercise of Congress' authority under the Spending Clause." The Court also upheld a provision authorizing states and regional compacts with disposal sites to increase the costs of access to those sites, and deny access altogether, to waste generated in states that do not meet federal guidelines. This was viewed as a "conditional exercise of Congress' commerce power." The Court then turned to the remaining provision, requiring states to take title to the waste if they fail to meet the 1996 deadline.]

The take title provision is of a different character. [It] offers States, as an alternative to regulating pursuant to Congress' direction, the option of taking title to and possession of the low level radioactive waste generated within their borders and becoming liable for all damages waste generators suffer as a result of the States' failure to do so promptly. In this provision, Congress has crossed the line distinguishing encouragement from coercion.

The take title provision appears to be unique. No other federal statute has been cited which offers a state government no option other than that of implementing legislation enacted by Congress. Whether one views the take title provision as lying outside Congress' enumerated powers, or as infringing upon the core of state sovereignty reserved by the Tenth Amendment, the provision is inconsistent with the federal structure of our Government established by the Constitution.

* * *

JUSTICE WHITE, with whom JUSTICE BLACKMUN and JUSTICE STEVENS join, concurring in part and dissenting in part.

Curiously absent from the Court's analysis is any effort to place the take title provision within the overall context of the legislation. * * * Congress could have pre-empted the field by directly regulating the disposal of this waste pursuant to its powers under the Commerce and Spending Clauses, but instead it *unanimously* assented to the States' request for congressional ratification of agreements to which they had acceded. * * * [T]he States wished to take the lead in achieving a solution to this problem and agreed among themselves to the various incentives and penalties implemented by Congress to insure adherence to the various deadlines and goals. The chief executives of the States proposed this approach, and I am unmoved by the Court's vehemence in taking away Congress' authority to sanction a recalcitrant unsited State now that New York has reaped the benefits of the sited States' concessions.

Ultimately, I suppose, the entire structure of our federal constitutional government can be traced to an interest in establishing checks and balances to prevent the exercise of tyranny against individuals. But these fears seem extremely far distant to me in a situation such as this. We face a crisis of national proportions in the disposal of low-level radioactive waste, and Congress has acceded to the wishes of the States by permitting local decisionmaking rather than imposing a solution from Washington. New York itself participated and supported passage of this legislation at both the gubernatorial and federal representative levels, and then enacted state laws specifically to comply with the deadlines and timetables agreed upon by the States in the 1985 Act. For me, the Court's civics lecture has a decidedly hollow ring at a time when action, rather than rhetoric, is needed to solve a national problem. * * *

[The opinion of JUSTICE STEVENS, concurring in part and dissenting in part, is omitted.]

Notes

1. *New York* seems to create something of a dilemma. On the one hand, individual states are clearly subject to a NIMBY problem. See Hamilton, "Political and Social Costs: Estimating the Impact of Collective Action on Hazardous Waste Facilities," 24 *RAND J.Econ.* 101 (1993). They wish to have the benefits of using low-level radioactive materials for medical and other purposes, but would prefer to have the burden (political and otherwise) of disposing of the waste fall elsewhere. This is a classic collective action problem of the kind that motivated the formation of the national government.

One solution would be for each state to establish a quarantine, so that states would not be able to export their waste problems to each other. As we will see in the next section, however, this solution probably violates the dormant commerce clause. This leaves the states in what game theorists call a prisoner's dilemma; every state needs a place to dispose of the waste, but it is rational for each state to impose a ban on such sites, fearing that it will be flooded with waste from other states. See McGreal, "The Flawed Economics of the Dormant Commerce Clause," 39 *Wm. & Mary L.Rev.* 1191 (1998).

Another method of solving this problem would be for the states to agree to behave responsibly in establishing disposal sites, rather than trying to free ride on each other. Obviously, there is an incentive for states to default on such an agreement. In order to avoid default, the states requested that Congress make the agreement legally binding on them. But the Court says that this violates federalism. Is there any way to resolve this dilemma of federalism? What would Justice O'Connor suggest?

Query: Suppose that the states had embodied their agreement in an interstate compact, which would have required congressional approval to be enforceable. Would using this mechanism have avoided the *New York* holding? Could Congress simply replace its direct mandate with draconian funding cut-offs? Is some other mechanism available? Or is this dilemma simply an inescapable price of our federalist constitutional scheme?

2. In *Board of Natural Resources v. Brown*, 992 F.2d 937 (9th Cir. 1993), the state of Washington challenged portions of the 1990 Forest Resources Conservation and Shortage Relief Act, 16 U.S.C.A. §§ 620–620(j), which restricts the export of unprocessed timber from federal and state public lands in western states. The purpose of the restrictions is to preserve jobs at domestic sawmills in the face of reduced cutting in old-growth forests, due in part to efforts to protect the habitat of the Western Spotted Owl, an endangered species. The statute provides that "[e]ach state shall determine the species, grade, and geographic origin of unprocessed timber to be prohibited from export * * * and shall administer such prohibitions consistent with the intent of sections 620 to 620(j)," and that "the Governor * * * shall * * * issue regulations to carry out the purposes" of the Act. The court held that these provisions violate the Tenth Amendment as interpreted in *New York*.

Note that *Brown* expanded *New York* from a protection of the state legislature to a protection of state administrative officials. Although there is some reason to question whether this expansion is consistent with the original understanding of the Constitution, see Prakash, "Field Office Federalism," 79 *Va.L.Rev.* 1957 (1993), the Supreme Court ultimately ruled that Congress has no more power to commandeer state administrators than state legislators. See *Printz v. United States*, 521 U.S. 98, 117 S.Ct. 2365, 138 L.Ed.2d 914 (1997) (striking down portions of a federal gun control statute on this basis). Note, however, that while *New York* prohibits direct commandeering, it does allow Congress to use a battery of incentives to obtain state cooperation. As we will see in the next chapter, both the Clean Air Act and the Clean Water Act rely heavily on state agencies to implement the federal programs, providing various incentives for states to participate.

3. The problem of federal power discussed in this section has an analogue in the European Union. Unlike our federal government, however, the Maastricht treaty contains an explicit grant of power over environmental

matters. This environmental authority is created by Article 130. The EU can also use its other regulatory powers, such as the general power to eliminate barriers to a unified economy, as a basis for environmental protection. (There are, however, some subtle differences in the legislative procedures involved with these various powers). The EU also recognizes a general principle of "subsidiarity," under which regulatory action where possible should take place at the national rather than community level. See J. Shaw, *Law of the European Union*, 82–90 (2d ed. 1996), Bermann, "Taking Subsidiarity Seriously: Federalism in the European Community and the United States," 94 *Colum.L.Rev.* 331 (1994).

B.   COMMERCE CLAUSE RESTRICTIONS ON STATE POWER

In a unified national economy, the existence of a multitude of differing state pollution laws can impede the free flow of commerce. Yet the states have often taken the lead in the environmental area because of pressing local problems. This section deals with the need to accommodate these conflicting interests, which takes place under the auspices of the commerce clause.

The dormant commerce clause, like the grants of federal regulatory power discussed in the previous section, can be considered the solution to a collective action problem. Because out-of-state residents are not represented in the state legislature, the state may attempt to export the costs of regulation, while retaining the benefits. While the strategy makes sense for each state individually, it may leave the states worse off collectively. The federal courts step in to prevent this regulatory equivalent of the NIMBY syndrome. For a thorough review of the scholarly literature about the dormant commerce clause, see Winkfield Twyman, "Beyond Purpose: Addressing State Discrimination," 46 *S.Car.L.Rev.* 381 (1995).

The Commerce Clause, on its face, is a grant of power to Congress, not a restriction on state legislation. Yet, beginning with the period of the Marshall Court, the Supreme Court has always construed the Commerce Clause as preventing certain kinds of state regulation even when Congress has not spoken. Despite some indications to the contrary in the earliest cases, however, the states are not completely disabled from regulating interstate commerce. For instance, in *Huron Portland Cement Co. v. Detroit*, 362 U.S. 440, 80 S.Ct. 813, 4 L.Ed.2d 852 (1960), the Court upheld the application of an anti-smoke ordinance to ships that were temporarily docked in Detroit while engaged in transporting cement on the Great Lakes. Finding the ordinance "a regulation of general application," which did not discriminate against interstate commerce, the Court found no evidence that the regulation placed an "impermissible burden" on interstate commerce. *Huron Cement* illustrates one aspect of commerce clause doctrine, the undue burden test, which applies to *nondiscriminatory* state regulations. In applying this test, the Court will uphold a statute which effectuates a valid local purpose "unless the burden imposed on [interstate] commerce is clearly excessive in relation to the putative local benefits." *Pike v. Bruce Church, Inc.,* 397 U.S. 137, 142, 90 S.Ct. 844, 847, 25 L.Ed.2d 174, 178 (1970).

The next three cases involve the application of the *Pike* balancing test to environmental regulations. We will then turn to some categories of cases where different tests apply.

PROCTER AND GAMBLE CO. v. CHICAGO

United States Court of Appeals, Seventh Circuit, 1975.
509 F.2d 69, cert. denied 421 U.S. 978, 95 S.Ct. 1980, 44 L.Ed.2d 470 (1975).

SWYGERT, CHIEF JUDGE.

This appeal presents the question of whether an ordinance of the City of Chicago that bans the use of detergents containing phosphates is unconstitutional on the ground that it results in an impermissible interference with interstate commerce. The district court decided that the ordinance is unconstitutional. We disagree.

The ordinance was adopted by the City Council after its Committee on Environmental Control had held public meetings for three days. The measure provided that the sale of detergents containing any phosphorous after June 30, 1972 constituted a criminal offense. Most detergents sold in this country contain phosphates which are compounds containing the element phosphorous.

* * *

The plaintiffs unquestionably showed that the ordinance has had an adverse effect upon their businesses which admittedly are national in scope. Procter and Gamble was unable to sell any detergents in the Chicago area for five months after June 30, 1972 and lost $4,700,000 in sales as a result. FMC lost $500,000 worth of sales of phosphates as a result of the ordinance. Further, whereas before the ordinance Procter's Chicago plant was able to supply over 96 percent of the requirements for the six-state "Chicago Plant Area," after the ordinance became effective the plant could supply only 51 percent, which necessitated shipments to this area from other Procter plants in Louisiana, Missouri, and Kansas. The result was the establishment of a different and, from the company's viewpoint, a less efficient interstate system of distribution of its products.

Evidence was also introduced concerning the warehousing practices of the retail grocery chains serving Chicago and the surrounding area. These chains, which include chains of independents, warehouse their products on an area-wide basis as opposed to a city-wide basis. Goods are purchased from the manufacturer and stored in warehouses for eventual distribution to the individual retail stores. In the Chicago area, the same warehouses also service stores in northern Illinois, northern Indiana, southern Wisconsin, and Michigan. At the warehouses, each product is stored in its own particular area called a slot. There was testimony that these warehouses will not "double slot" a product and thus refused to carry both phosphate and non-phosphate versions of the same product. The explanation is that there is not sufficient space in the warehouses and there would be the possibility of a violation of the ordinance if phosphate formulas were accidently shipped to Chicago stores. Of the seventeen major Chicago area customers of Procter and Gamble, fifteen chose to carry only non-phosphate detergents. The result has been that consumers in areas of Illinois or the other adjacent states where the sale of phosphate detergents is legal can purchase only non-phosphate formulas of the major detergents from stores which are part of these fifteen chains. Thus, the Chicago ordinance affected Procter and Gamble's ability to sell its phosphate detergents in other states.

* * *

The ordinance's most direct effect is on the Illinois Waterway because the City's sewage effluent flows into it. This Waterway, which includes the Illinois River, is a water source for some communities, but not for Chicago. The Waterway has a very high percentage of phosphorous. The district court determined that before the passage of the ordinance the amount of phosphorous present in this Waterway was at least twenty-five times as much as is necessary to sustain nuisance algae. Still, there is a question of whether there is any nuisance algae problem in the Illinois River. Although the City introduced photographs showing the presence of such algae, the district court concluded "that there was no significant amount of nuisance algae in the Illinois River." Explanations offered for this lack of growth included the excessive turbidity of the river which prevents needed sunlight, periodic flushing, and possibly some undefined trace elements which inhibit such growth. Also, the district court found that the elimination of Chicago phosphates alone would not result in reaching the "limiting factor" level, though a 66 percent reduction did result in at least part of the Waterway after the ordinance had been in effect.

Finally, there is the evidence concerning Lake Michigan which is the source of Chicago's water supply. The danger of nuisance algae is more pronounced with regard to Lake Michigan because it does not have the flushing quality of a river. Moreover, the phosphorous concentration is at about the "limiting factor" of .02 milligrams per liter. But unlike some of the other communities along the lake, Chicago's sewage does not normally flow into the lake; only during excessively heavy rainstorms is one of two rivers reversed so that sewage flows into Lake Michigan. The district court determined that such reversals occurred only four times within a ten year period, though there was also testimony that the frequency of such reversals is increasing. As to the amount of phosphates entering the lake during a year in which a backflow resulted, the conclusion of the district court was that detergents contributed only 250 tons or about three percent of the total entering the lake each year.

* * *

We are now at the stage where we must determine whether the ordinance is a reasonable means of reaching the end desired. * * * We hold that the burden is so slight compared to the important and properly local objective that the presumption we discussed earlier should apply. We will accept the City Council's determination that this phosphate ban is a reasonable means of achieving the elimination and prevention of nuisance algae unless we find that the plaintiffs have presented clear and convincing proof to the contrary.

* * *

The crux of the matter is actually the question of whether the phosphorous level in the Waterway will ever be relevant to the control or removal of nuisance algae. We do not believe that the plaintiffs have met their burden of showing convincingly that limiting the quantity of phosphorous can never be the key to the problem. Admittedly, the evidence seems clear that phosphorous is not the "limiting factor" in the Waterway at this time. Moreover, even with the elimination of detergent phosphates from the Chicago sewage effluent, the phosphorous level would not reach the limiting point. The Chicago ordinance, by itself, would have no immediate effect on the Waterway. This does not indicate, however, that the ordinance is not a means of dealing with nuisance algae. The plaintiffs introduced evidence to show that the amount of phosphorous in the Illinois River could greatly increase without increasing nuisance algae. Even if this is true, it only proves that phosphorous is presently not the "limiting nutrient." It does not prove that phosphorous might not be the "limiting nutrient" at some point in time. Indeed, Chicago's ordinance appears to be a significant first step toward that goal. We do not agree with the district court that it can only be enacted on a stand-by basis. If this were the law, all programs aimed at eliminating phosphorous from the Waterway would have to be enacted at the same time. We can assume that other communities might follow Chicago's lead and prevent phosphate detergents. Nor do we think that there was clear evidence that if all phosphorous from detergents were eliminated there would still be other uncontrollable sources that would keep the level above the limiting point. There was testimony that indicated that agricultural run-off of phosphorous can be controlled. For Commerce Clause purposes the City Council was justified in believing that eventually its phosphate ban, in conjunction with other actions, would result in eliminating and preventing nuisance algae in the Illinois Waterway.

The effectiveness of the legislation is also shown, to some extent, by the evidence concerning Lake Michigan. There is no question that both eutrophication and phosphorous are serious problems in regard to Lake Michigan. Though Chicago might contribute relatively little phosphorous to the lake, the phosphorous level is at such a precarious point that even this minimal amount takes on added importance. Further, contrary to the district court's view, we find that Chicago has a legitimate interest in banning phosphate detergents as an example for other communities presently releasing their sewage into Lake Michigan.

Notes

1. Was the court sufficiently intensive in its scrutiny of the ordinance? If the court had been reviewing an EPA order based on the same record, should it have affirmed or remanded for further proceedings? Should the standards for commerce clause cases be the same as used in reviewing agency action? Stricter? More lenient?

2. Suppose the court had found both a substantial burden on commerce and proof that the ordinance would clearly decrease algae growth. Should it then have balanced these two objectives? Compare *Raymond Motor Transp., Inc. v. Rice,* 434 U.S. 429, 443, 98 S.Ct. 787, 795, 54 L.Ed.2d 664, 676 (1978), with id. at 450, 98 S.Ct. at 798–799, 54 L.Ed.2d at 680–681 (Blackmun, J., concurring). How can judges balance two such disparate goals? Yet, if the Court doesn't balance, how should it resolve such a case?

MINNESOTA v. CLOVER LEAF CREAMERY CO.

Supreme Court of the United States, 1981.
449 U.S. 456, 101 S.Ct. 715, 66 L.Ed.2d 659.

JUSTICE BRENNAN delivered the opinion of the Court:

In 1977, the Minnesota Legislature enacted a statute banning the retail sale of milk in plastic nonreturnable, nonrefillable containers, but permitting such sale in other nonreturnable, nonrefillable containers, such as paperboard milk cartons. Respondents contend that the statute violates the Equal Protection and Commerce Clauses of the Constitution.

* * *

Since the statute does not discriminate between interstate and intrastate commerce, the controlling question is whether the incidental burden imposed on interstate commerce by the Minnesota Act is "clearly excessive in relation to the putative local benefits." We conclude that it is not.

The burden imposed on interstate commerce by the statute is relatively minor. Milk products may continue to move freely across the Minnesota border, and since most dairies package their products in more than one type of containers, the inconvenience of having to conform to different packaging requirements in Minnesota and the surrounding States should be slight. Within Minnesota, business will presumably shift from manufacturers of plastic nonreturnable containers to producers of paperboard cartons, refillable bottles, and plastic pouches, but there is no reason to suspect that the gainers will be Minnesota firms, or the losers out-of-state firms. Indeed, two of the three dairies, the sole milk retailer, and the sole milk container producer challenging the statute in this litigation are Minnesota firms.

Pulpwood producers are the only Minnesota industry likely to benefit significantly from the Act at the expense of out-of-state firms.

Respondents point out that plastic resin, the raw material used for making plastic nonreturnable milk jugs, is produced entirely by non-Minnesota firms, while pulpwood, used for making paperboard, is a major Minnesota product. Nevertheless, it is clear that respondents exaggerate the degree of burden on out-of-state interests, both because plastics will continue to be used in the production of plastic pouches, plastic returnable bottles, and paperboard itself, and because out-of-state pulpwood producers will presumably absorb some of the business generated by the Act.

Even granting that the out-of-state plastics industry is burdened relatively more heavily than the Minnesota pulpwood industry, we find that this burden is not "clearly excessive" in light of the substantial state interest in promoting conservation of energy and other natural resources and easing solid waste disposal problems, which we have already reviewed in the context of equal protection analysis. We find these local benefits ample to support Minnesota's decision under the Commerce Clause. Moreover, we find that no approach with "a lesser impact on interstate activities," is available. Respondents have suggested several alternative statutory schemes, but these alternatives are either more burdensome on commerce than the Act (as, for example, banning all nonreturnables) or less likely to be effective (as, for example, providing incentives for recycling).

In *Exxon Corp. v. Governor of Maryland,* 437 U.S. 117, 98 S.Ct. 2207, 57 L.Ed.2d 91 (1978), we upheld a Maryland statute barring producers and refiners of petroleum products—all of which were out-of-state businesses—from retailing gasoline in the State. We stressed that the Commerce Clause "protects the interstate market, not particular interstate firms, from prohibitive or burdensome regulations." A nondiscriminatory regulation serving substantial state purposes is not invalid simply because it causes some business to shift from a predominantly out-of-state industry to a predominantly in-state industry. Only if the burden on interstate commerce clearly outweighs the State's legitimate purposes does such a regulation violate the Commerce Clause.

The judgment of the Minnesota Supreme Court is reversed.

Notes

1.   To what extent should a court probe behind the face of a statute to determine whether legislators' true motives were protectionist? What kind of fact-finding procedures would be appropriate in such an inquiry?

2.   To what extent is the *Clover Leaf* case consistent with the Seventh Circuit's approach in *Procter & Gamble* supra?

3.   Interestingly enough, the Minnesota statute was repealed after the Court's decision upholding it.

NORFOLK SOUTHERN CORPORATION v. OBERLY

United States Court of Appeals, Third Circuit, 1987.
822 F.2d 388.

[This case involved a challenge to part of Delaware's coastal management plan. The provision in question banned product transfer facilities in the coastal zone. The plaintiffs sought unsuccessfully to obtain approval for a "coal lightering service." Ports on the east coast are too shallow to allow full loading of coal supercolliers. A lightering service would allow these partially loaded ships to be "topped off." The Big Stone Anchorage in Delaware Bay is the only naturally suitable anchorage between Maine and Mexico, and is already used for oil lightering. The court concluded that the Delaware plan was not discriminatory for three reasons: (1) because it also blocked many kinds of local industry from locating in the coastal zone, (2) a general decision to favor certain industries over others cannot be considered constitutionally suspect, and (3) the exceptions to the specific ban on product transfer facilities were reasonable grandfather provisions. The court also rejected the argument that the involvement of foreign commerce called for a higher level of scrutiny. It then turned to the application of the balancing test for nondiscriminatory laws.]

STAPLETON, J.

Given that we have found the heightened scrutiny and deferential standards inapplicable, we hold that a balancing analysis is appropriate in this case. This holding is consistent with *Clover Leaf Creamery,* in which the Supreme Court held that the balancing test articulated in [*Pike*] is the appropriate tool for evaluating environmental statutes which impose incidental burdens on interstate commerce:

> [I]f a statute regulates "evenhandedly" and imposes only "incidental" burdens on interstate commerce, the courts must nevertheless strike it down if "the burden imposed on such commerce is clearly excessive in relation to the putative local benefits." [quoting *Pike*]

* * * The putative benefits of the § 7003 ban on offshore solid bulk transfer facilities are the protection of the coastal environment from transfer facility pollutant emissions and the industrial development that might result from the presence of such transfer operations. The district court found a material dispute of fact with respect to the "putative benefits" side of the balance, pointing to disputes over the magnitude and environmental consequence of predicted coal spills and dust emissions. We conclude that it is unnecessary to review this conclusion because the record reveals no legally relevant burden on interstate commerce that could be found to be "excessive."

The "incidental burden on interstate commerce" appropriately considered in Commerce Clause balancing is the degree to which the state action incidentally discriminates against interstate commerce relative to intrastate commerce. It is a comparative measure. There concededly is language suggesting that any increased costs imposed on out-of-state interests, in an absolute sense, are relevant burdens regardless of whether the same costs are imposed on in-state interests. However, we find that the holdings of the Supreme Court case law, consistent with the anti-protectionism purpose of the Commerce Clause, apply the much narrower comparative burden concept. As earlier noted, virtually all state regulation involves increased costs for those doing business within the state, including out-of-state interests doing business in the state as well as in-state interests. In this absolute sense, virtually all state regulation "burdens" interstate commerce. Where the "burden" on out-of-state interests is no different from that placed on competing in-state interests, however, it is a burden on *commerce* rather than a burden on *interstate* commerce. In such cases, nothing in Commerce Clause jurisprudence entitles out-of-state interests to more strict judicial review than that to which the in-state interests are entitled, i.e., arbitrary and capricious review under the Due Process Clause and rational basis review under the Equal Protection Clause, neither of which involves the kind of social value balancing that Norfolk Southern urges us to undertake. To the contrary, the case law makes clear that the Commerce Clause is concerned with protectionism and the need for uniformity and the holdings of the cases demonstrate that legislation will not be invalidated under the *Pike* test in the absence of *discriminatory* burdens on interstate commerce. Thus, as this court noted in *American Trucking Associations, Inc. v. Larson,* 683 F.2d at 791, when the need for uniformity is not at issue, "it is those measures that are discriminatory which are the focus of the Commerce Clause." In the *Pike* case itself, the "incidental" burden found to be excessive in relation to the "putative benefits" was the requirement that Bruce Church must relocate cantaloupe packing operations from the existing California location into Arizona, a clearly discriminatory measure. * * *

The necessity of a discriminatory burden is dispositive of this case. The burden identified by Norfolk Southern "is the total prevention of a new mode of export that may achieve undeniable commercial significance and that furthers national objectives." This alleged burden, at base, is that the CZA precludes coal exporters from lowering their average transportation costs. This kind of burden is not, however, a legally relevant incidental burden. * * *

We find this case virtually on all fours with *Huron Portland Cement Co. v. Detroit* [supra p. 223].* * * In *Huron Cement,* as in this case, the challenged regulation imposed significant additional costs upon a party desiring to engage in interstate commerce. The Supreme Court nevertheless rejected the Commerce Clause attack on the Code. * * * Finding no burden that discriminates against out-of-state interests or in favor of in-state interests, we conclude that the defendants are entitled to summary judgment.

In essence, Norfolk Southern's arguments reduce to an assertion that increasing coal exports is in the national interest and that Delaware, in seeking to protect its own environment, has struck an unwise balance between these competing interests. In our view, the dormant Commerce Clause does not authorize a federal court to engage in the kind of broad-based "national interest balancing" requested by Norfolk Southern. Balancing the societal value of decreasing unemployment in the Eastern coal mines and shrinking the size of the trade deficit against the societal value of protecting the coastal zone is within the province of Congress. In contrast, the Commerce Clause, as applied by the judiciary, acts as a limitation on the authority of the states designed to preclude the establishment of protectionist state barriers that would threaten the operation of the federal union.

Notes

1. For support for the court's view that the commerce clause should not be construed to prohibit nondiscriminatory burdens see Justice Scalia's concurring opinion in *CTS Corp. v. Dynamics Corp. of America,* 481 U.S. 69, 107 S.Ct. 1637, 95 L.Ed.2d 67 (1987), as well as Redish & Nugent, "The Dormant Commerce Clause and the Constitutional Balance of Federalism," 1987 *Duke L.J.* 569; Regan, "The Supreme Court and State Protectionism: Making Sense of the Dormant Commerce Clause," 84 *Mich.L.Rev.* 1091 (1986); Farber, "State Regulation and the Dormant Commerce Clause," 3 *Const. Comm.* 395 (1986). The latter article also suggests that the commerce clause should not apply where a federal administrative agency has the power to preempt state laws that disserve the national interest. Given the pervasive federal regulation found in many environmental areas, this suggestion would sharply limit the application of the dormant commerce clause to state environmental statutes.

2. The preceding cases involve the use of some variety of balancing test. As the next three cases show, however, the Supreme Court has not always found balancing to be appropriate in commerce clause cases.

HUGHES v. ALEXANDRIA SCRAP CORP.

Supreme Court of the United States, 1976.
426 U.S. 794, 96 S.Ct. 2488, 49 L.Ed.2d 220.

JUSTICE POWELL delivered the opinion of the Court.

[Maryland enacted a bounty system for old, abandoned cars ("hulks"). Prior to 1974, no title certificate was needed by the scrap processor in order to claim the bounty. After 1974, Maryland processors needed only to submit an indemnity agreement in which suppliers certify their own rights to the hulks. Out-of-state processors had to submit a title certificate or police certificate for each car. The appellee, a Virginia processor, challenged the amended statute as a violation of the Commerce Clause.]

The District Court accepted appellee's analysis, and concluded that the 1974 amendment failed the *Pike* test. First, the court found that the amendment did impose "substantial burdens upon the free flow of interstate commerce." Moreover, it considered the disadvantage suffered by out-of-state processors to be particularly suspect under previous decisions of this Court, noting that to avoid the disadvantage those processors would have to build new plants inside Maryland to carry on a business which, prior to the amendment, they had pursued efficiently outside the State. Maryland's principal argument in support of the amendment was that, by making it difficult for out-of-state processors to claim bounties on hulks delivered by unlicensed suppliers, the amendment tends to reduce the amount of state funds paid for destruction of Maryland-titled hulks abandoned in the States where those processors are located instead of in Maryland. The District Court acknowledged the validity of this interest, but considered the means employed inappropriate under *Pike* because the same interest could have been furthered, with less impact upon interstate commerce, by amending the statute to condition the bounty upon a hulk's abandonment in Maryland instead of its previous titling there.

This line of reasoning is not without force if its basic premise is accepted. That premise is that every action by a State that has the effect of reducing in some manner the flow of goods in interstate commerce is potentially an impermissible burden. But we are not persuaded that Maryland's action in amending its statute was the kind of action with which the Commerce Clause is concerned.

The situation presented by this statute and the 1974 amendment is quite unlike that found in the cases upon which appellee relies.

* * *

The common thread of all these cases is that the State interfered with the natural functioning of the interstate market either through prohibition or through burdensome regulation. By contrast, Maryland has not sought to prohibit the flow of hulks, or to regulate the conditions under which it may occur. Instead, it has entered into the market itself to bid up their price. There has been an impact upon the interstate flow of hulks only because, since the 1974 amendment, Maryland effectively has made it more lucrative for unlicensed suppliers to dispose of their hulks in Maryland rather than take them outside the State.

* * *

We do not believe the Commerce Clause was intended to require independent justification for such action. Maryland entered the market for the purpose, agreed by all to be commendable as well as legitimate, of protecting the State's environment. As the means of furthering this purpose, it elected the payment of state funds—in the form of bounties—to encourage the removal of automobile hulks from Maryland streets and junkyards. It is true that the state money initially was made available to licensed out-of-state processors as well as those located within Maryland, and not until the 1974 amendment was the financial benefit channeled, in practical effect, to domestic processors. But this chronology does not distinguish the case, for Commerce Clause purposes, from one in which a State offered bounties only to domestic processors from the start. Regardless of when the State's largesse is first confined to domestic processors, the effect upon the flow of hulks resting within the State is the same: they will tend to be processed inside the State rather than flowing to foreign processors. But no trade barrier of the type forbidden by the Commerce Clause, and involved in previous cases, impedes their movement out of State. They remain within Maryland in response to market forces, including that exerted by money from the State. Nothing in the purposes animating the Commerce Clause prohibits a State, in the absence of congressional action, from participating in the market and exercising the right to favor its own citizens over others.

JUSTICE STEVENS, concurring.

The dissent creates the impression that the Court's opinion, which I join without reservation, represents a significant retreat from its settled practice in adjudicating claims that a state program places an unconstitutional burden on interstate commerce. This is not the fact. There is no prior decision of this Court even addressing the critical Commerce Clause issue presented by this case.

It is important to differentiate between commerce which flourishes in a free market and commerce which owes its existence to a state subsidy program. Our cases finding that a state regulation constitutes an impermissible burden on interstate commerce all dealt with restrictions that adversely affected the operation of a free market. This case is unique because the commerce which Maryland has "burdened" is commerce which would not exist if Maryland had not decided to subsidize a portion of the automobile scrap-processing business.

By artificially enhancing the value of certain abandoned hulks, Maryland created a market that did not previously exist. The program which Maryland initiated in 1969 included subsidies for scrapping plants located in Virginia and Pennsylvania as well as for plants located in Maryland. Those subsidies stimulated the movement of abandoned hulks from Maryland to out-of-state scrapping plants and thereby gave rise to the interstate commerce which is at stake in this litigation.

That commerce, which is now said to be burdened, would never have existed if in the first instance Maryland had decided to confine its subsidy to operators of Maryland plants. A failure to create that commerce would have been unobjectionable because the Commerce Clause surely does not impose on the States any obligation to subsidize out-of-state business. Nor, in my judgment, does that Clause inhibit a State's power to experiment with different methods of encouraging local industry. Whether the encouragement takes the form of a cash subsidy, a tax credit, or a special privilege intended to attract investment capital, it should not be characterized as a "burden" on commerce. * * *

Note

1. Suppose a state paid a bounty to factories burning Illinois coal. Would such a bounty scheme be constitutional after *Hughes?* Would it matter if the state used a tax deduction instead of a bounty to achieve the

same result? How about an increased tax on users of out-of-state coal? Is there any constitutional limit on state economic incentives after *Hughes?*

2. *Hughes* was decided the same day as *National League of Cities,* [discussed on p. 217, supra]. Both cases hold that certain state activities have unusual status under the commerce clause. *Hughes* arguably holds that a state's regulatory programs are subject to judicial scrutiny under the commerce clause, but that its proprietary activities are immune from judicial control. *National League of Cities* reached just the opposite conclusion about congressional power: state proprietary activities are subject to federal control, nonproprietary activities are not.

CITY OF PHILADELPHIA v. NEW JERSEY

Supreme Court of the United States, 1978.
437 U.S. 617, 98 S.Ct. 2531, 57 L.Ed.2d 475.

JUSTICE STEWART delivered the opinion of the Court.

[A New Jersey statute prohibited the import of most waste originating out of the State. After a remand on a preemption issue, the case returned to the Supreme Court. The Court agreed with the lower court that the New Jersey statute was not preempted.[c] It disagreed, however, on the commerce clause issue].

Before it addressed the merits of the appellants' claim, the New Jersey Supreme Court questioned whether the interstate movement of those wastes banned by ch. 363 is "commerce" at all within the meaning of the Commerce Clause. Any doubts on that score should be laid to rest at the outset.

* * *

The state court reached this conclusion in an attempt to reconcile modern Commerce Clause concepts with several old cases of this Court holding that States can prohibit the importation of some objects because they "are not legitimate subjects of trade and commerce." *Bowman v. Chicago & Northwestern R. Co.,* 125 U.S. 465, 489, 8 S.Ct. 689, 700, 31 L.Ed. 700. These articles include items "which, on account of their existing condition, would bring in and spread disease, pestilence, and death, such as rags or other substances infected with the germs of yellow fever or the virus of small-pox, or cattle or meat or other provisions that

c. The preemption discussion is contained in footnote 4 of the opinion. The Court's analysis was as follows:

[W]e find no "clear and manifest purpose of Congress," to pre-empt the entire fields of interstate waste management or transportation, either by express statutory command, or by implicit legislative design. To the contrary, Congress expressly has provided that "the collection and disposal of solid wastes should continue to be primarily the function of State, region-

al, and local agencies * * *." 42 U.S.C.A. § 6901(a)(4). Similarly, ch. 363 is not preempted because of a square conflict with particular provisions of federal law or because of general incompatibility with basic federal objectives. In short, we agree with the New Jersey Supreme Court that ch. 363 can be enforced consistently with the program goals and the respective federal-state roles intended by Congress when it enacted the federal legislation.

are diseased or decayed, or otherwise, from their condition and quality, unfit for human use or consumption." * * *

We think the state court misread our cases, and thus erred in assuming that they require a two-tiered definition of commerce. In saying that innately harmful articles "are not legitimate subjects of trade and commerce," the *Bowman* Court was stating its conclusion, not the starting point of its reasoning. All objects of interstate trade merit Commerce Clause protection; none is excluded by definition at the outset. In *Bowman* and similar cases, the Court held simply that because the articles' worth in interstate commerce was far outweighed by the dangers inhering in their very movement, States could prohibit their transportation across state lines. Hence, we reject the state court's suggestion that the banning of "valueless" out-of-state wastes by ch. 363 implicates no constitutional protection. Just as Congress has power to regulate the interstate movement of these wastes, States are not free from constitutional scrutiny when they restrict that movement.

* * *

The opinions of the Court through the years have reflected an alertness to the evils of "economic isolation" and protectionism, while at the same time recognizing that incidental burdens on interstate commerce may be unavoidable when a State legislates to safeguard the health and safety of its people. Thus, where simple economic protectionism is effected by state legislation, a virtually *per se* rule of invalidity has been erected. The clearest example of such legislation is a law that overtly blocks the flow of interstate commerce at a State's borders. But where other legislative objectives are credibly advanced and there is no patent discrimination against interstate trade, the Court has adopted a much more flexible approach * * *. The crucial inquiry, therefore, must be directed to determining whether ch. 363 is basically a protectionist measure, or whether it can fairly be viewed as a law directed to legitimate local concerns, with effects upon interstate commerce that are only incidental.

* * * The state court * * * found that New Jersey's existing landfill sites will be exhausted within a few years; that to go on using these sites or to develop new ones will take a heavy environmental toll, both from pollution and from loss of scarce open lands; that new techniques to divert waste from landfills to other methods of disposal and resource recovery processes are under development, but that these changes will require time; and finally, that "the extension of the lifespan of existing landfills, resulting from the exclusion of out-of-state waste, may be of crucial importance in preventing further virgin wetlands or other undeveloped lands from being devoted to landfill purposes." [The appellants argued, on the other hand, that the statute's real purpose was economic.]

This dispute about ultimate legislative purpose need not be resolved, because its resolution would not be relevant to the constitutional issue to be decided in this case. Contrary to the evident assumption of the state court and the parties, the evil of protectionism can reside in legislative means as well as legislative ends. Thus, it does not matter whether the ultimate aim of ch. 363 is to reduce the waste disposal costs of New Jersey residents or to save remaining open lands from pollution, for we assume New Jersey has every right to protect its residents' pocketbooks as well as their environment. And it may be assumed as well that New Jersey may pursue those ends by slowing the flow of *all* waste into the State's remaining landfills, even though interstate commerce may incidentally be affected. But whatever New Jersey's ultimate purpose, it may not be accomplished by discriminating against articles of commerce coming from outside the State unless there is some reason, apart from their origin, to treat them differently. Both on its face and in its plain effect, ch. 363 violates this principle of nondiscrimination.

* * *

The New Jersey law at issue in this case falls squarely within the area that the Commerce Clause puts off-limits to state regulation. On its face, it imposes on out-of-state commercial interests the full burden of conserving the State's remaining landfill space. It is true that in our previous cases the scarce natural resource was itself the article of commerce, whereas here the scarce resource and the article of commerce are distinct. But that difference is without consequence. In both instances, the State has overtly moved to slow or freeze the flow of commerce for protectionist reasons. It does not matter that the State has shut the article of commerce inside the State in one case and outside the State in the other. What is crucial is the attempt by one State to isolate itself from a problem common to many by erecting a barrier against the movement of interstate trade.

The appellees argue that not all laws which facially discriminate against out-of-state commerce are forbidden protectionist regulations. In particular, they point to quarantine laws, which this Court has repeatedly upheld even though they appear to single out interstate commerce for special treatment. * * *

It is true that certain quarantine laws have not been considered forbidden protectionist measures, even though they were directed against out-of-state commerce. But those quarantine laws banned the importation of articles such as diseased livestock that required destruction as soon as possible because their very movement risked contagion and other evils. Those laws thus did not discriminate against interstate commerce as such, but simply prevented traffic in noxious articles, whatever their origin.

The New Jersey statute is not such a quarantine law. There has been no claim here that the very movement of waste into or through New Jersey endangers health, or that waste must be disposed of as soon and as close to its point of generation as possible. The harms caused by waste are said to arise after its disposal in landfill sites, and at that point, as New Jersey concedes, there is no basis to distinguish out-of-state waste from domestic waste. If one is inherently harmful, so is the other. Yet New Jersey has banned the former while leaving its landfill sites open to the latter. The New Jersey law blocks the importation of waste in an obvious effort to saddle those outside the State with the entire burden of slowing the flow of refuse into New Jersey's remaining landfill sites. That legislative effort is clearly impermissible under the Commerce Clause of the Constitution.

Today, cities in Pennsylvania and New York find it expedient or necessary to send their waste into New Jersey for disposal, and New Jersey claims the right to close its borders to such traffic. Tomorrow, cities in New Jersey may find it expedient or necessary to send their waste into Pennsylvania or New York for disposal, and those States might then claim the right to close their borders. The Commerce Clause will protect New Jersey in the future, just as it protects her neighbors now, from efforts by one State to isolate itself in the stream of interstate commerce from a problem shared by all.

JUSTICE REHNQUIST, with whom THE CHIEF JUSTICE joins, dissenting.

A growing problem in our Nation is the sanitary treatment and disposal of solid waste. For many years, solid waste was incinerated. Because of the significant environmental problems attendant to incineration, however, this method of solid waste disposal has declined in use in many localities, including New Jersey. "Sanitary" landfills have replaced incineration as the principal method of disposing of solid waste. In Chapter 363 of the Laws of 1973, the State of New Jersey legislatively recognized the unfortunate fact that landfills also present extremely serious health and safety problems. First, in New Jersey, "virtually all sanitary landfills can be expected to produce leachate, a noxious and highly polluted liquid which is seldom visible and frequently pollutes * * * ground and surface waters." The natural decomposition process which occurs in landfills also produces large quantities of methane and thereby presents a significant explosion hazard. Landfills can also generate "health hazards caused by rodents, fires, and scavenger birds" and, "needless to say, do not help New Jersey's aesthetic appearance nor New Jersey's noise or water or air pollution problems."

The health and safety hazards associated with landfills presents appellees with a currently unsolvable dilemma. Other, hopefully safer, methods of disposing of solid wastes are still in the development stage and cannot presently be used. But appellees obviously cannot completely stop the tide of solid waste that its citizens will produce in the interim. For the moment, therefore, appellees must continue to use sanitary landfills to dispose of New Jersey's own solid waste despite the critical environmental problems thereby created.

The question presented in this case is whether New Jersey must also continue to receive and dispose of solid waste from neighboring States, even though these will inexorably increase the health problems discussed above. The Court answers this question in the affirmative. New Jersey must either prohibit *all* landfill operations, leaving itself to cast about for a presently nonexistent solution to the serious problem of disposing of the waste generated within its own borders, or it must accept waste from every portion of the United States, thereby multiplying the health and safety problems which would result if it dealt only with such wastes generated within the State. Because past precedents [the quarantine cases] establish that the Commerce Clause does not present appellees with such a Hobson's choice, I dissent.

Notes

his guess: no state could not do it. bc it would not be commercial, it would be regulatory.

1. Would it matter if all available landfill areas were owned by the state? Suppose the state refused to accept waste from out-of-state. Would the market participant exception apply? In this connection, consider *Reeves, Inc. v. Stake,* 447 U.S. 429, 100 S.Ct. 2271, 65 L.Ed.2d 244 (1980), in which a closely divided Court held that South Dakota could refuse to sell cement from a state-owned factory to out-of-state buyers during a shortage. See Note, "The Commerce Clause and Federalism: Implications for State Control of Natural Resources," 50 *Geo.Wash.L.Rev.* 601, 614–623 (1982). On the other hand, the Court has also held that a state's theoretical title in wild animals does not justify discrimination against out-of-state businesses. *Hughes v. Oklahoma,* 441 U.S. 322, 99 S.Ct. 1727, 60 L.Ed.2d 250 (1979). See also, *South–Central Timber Development v. Wunnicke,* 467 U.S. 82, 104 S.Ct. 2237, 81 L.Ed.2d 71 (1984) (striking down an Alaska law requiring that timber taken from state lands be processed in Alaska before shipment elsewhere); *GSW, Inc. v. Long County,* 999 F.2d 1508 (11th Cir.1993) (county cannot require company, which it earlier hired to build and operate a landfill, to reject waste originating more than 150 miles away). *Hughes v. Oklahoma* also holds that the definition of "commerce" is "the same when relied on to strike down or restrict legislation as when relied on to support some exertion of federal control or regulation." Does this mean that the state program at issue in *Hughes v. Alexandria Scrap Corp.* is immune from congressional regulation?

2. As the Court noted, the New Jersey statute was consistent with the federal-state roles intended by Congress in RCRA. The Act gave the primary responsibility for control of solid wastes to state and local authorities. Apparently, this statute was not considered sufficient to override the commerce clause problem. (Congress clearly has the power to do so. *Prudential Insurance Co. v. Benjamin,* 328 U.S. 408, 66 S.Ct. 1142, 90 L.Ed. 1342 (1946).) Should this congressional policy have been given more weight in the commerce clause analysis? Is it clear that free trade in garbage is in the national interest? See Kirsten Engel, "Reconsidering the National Market in Solid Waste," 73 N.C.L.Rev. 1481 (1995).

3. The Supreme Court strongly reaffirmed the *City of Philadelphia* rule in two 1992 decisions. *Fort Gratiot Sanitary Landfill, Inc. v. Michigan Department of Natural Resources,* 504 U.S. 353, 112 S.Ct. 2019, 119 L.Ed.2d 139 (1992), involved regulations prohibiting landfills from accepting waste from outside a county unless authorized by the county's solid waste management plan. The Court considered the restriction on out-of-county waste to be equivalent to a restriction on out-of-state waste. Because the state regulations "discriminate against interstate commerce, the State bears the burden of proving that they further health and safety concerns that cannot be adequately served by nondiscriminatory alternatives." The state was unable to carry that burden of proof. In a companion case, *Chemical Waste Manage-*

ment, Inc. v. Hunt, 504 U.S. 334, 112 S.Ct. 2009, 119 L.Ed.2d 121 (1992), the Court struck down an Alabama statute which imposed an additional fee on all out-of-state hazardous waste disposed of within the state. The Court found no basis for the state's exemption of in-state waste from this charge. (The Court distinguished *Maine v. Taylor,* 477 U.S. 131, 106 S.Ct. 2440, 91 L.Ed.2d 110 (1986). In that case, Maine had banned out-of-state baitfish upon a showing that these fish would introduce new parasites and that no less-discriminatory method of protection existed.) In dissent, Chief Justice Rehnquist discussed a number of methods that Alabama might use to accomplish the same result, such as providing in-state generators with tax breaks, or opening its own facility. "But certainly we have lost our way," he added, "when we require States to perform such gymnastics." For a critique of these decisions, see Healy, "The Preemption of State Hazardous and Solid Waste Regulations: The Dormant Commerce Clause Awakes Once More," 43 *J.Urb. & Contemp.L.* 177 (1993).

In *Chemical Waste Management,* the Court left open the possibility that a differential surcharge could be imposed on out-of-state hazardous waste if the state could show that it was more expensive to dispose of out-of-state waste. This issue was resolved in *Oregon Waste Systems, Inc. v. Department of Environmental Quality,* 511 U.S. 93, 114 S.Ct. 1345, 128 L.Ed.2d 13 (1994). Oregon imposed a surcharge on out-of-state waste in 1989 and instructed the implementing agency to figure the charge from the costs of disposal. The agency imposed a $2.25 surcharge per ton of out-of-state waste, almost three times the $0.85 charge per ton of in-state waste. The Supreme Court, per Justice Thomas, held that this was a clear discrimination against interstate commerce, which triggers strict scrutiny under the dormant commerce clause. The state justified the discrimination as a "compensatory tax" necessary to ensure that out-of-staters paid their "fair share" of the total costs imposed by such waste. But Justice Thomas found no extra burden imposed on the state by the interstate waste that would justify a surcharge ($2.25) so much higher than the charge for comparable intrastate waste ($0.85).

Chief Justice Rehnquist, joined by Justice Blackmun, dissented. He objected to the Court's "nonchalant" analysis for slighting the fact that in-state producers of waste support Oregon's waste-disposal program through *both* their payment of direct charges ($0.85) *and* their payment of state income taxes and fees on landfill operations. Chief Justice Rehnquist found the Court's holding perverse, for it would allow other states to export their costs of waste-disposal to Oregon.

4.   Applying *Philadelphia v. New Jersey,* the Ninth Circuit struck down a Washington State prohibition against disposal of infectious medical wastes generated outside of the state. Since the facility did accept medical waste generated inside the state, the court held that the "quarantine" exception was inapplicable. *BFI Medical Waste Systems v. Whatcom County,* 983 F.2d 911 (9th Cir.1993). On the other hand, a burdensome but non-discriminatory regulatory scheme for hazardous waste was upheld in *Old Bridge Chemicals v. New Jersey Dept. of Environ. Protection,* 965 F.2d 1287 (3d Cir.1992).

5.   In *Philadelphia* and its progeny, the state was attempting to control the import of waste. In the following case, in contrast, the state had imposed an export ban.

C & A CARBONE, INC. v. TOWN OF CLARKSTOWN, NEW YORK

Supreme Court of the United States, 1994.
511 U.S. 383, 114 S.Ct. 1677, 128 L.Ed.2d 399.

JUSTICE KENNEDY delivered the opinion of the Court.

We consider a so-called flow control ordinance, which requires all solid waste to be processed at a designated transfer station before leaving the municipality. The avowed purpose of the ordinance is to retain the processing fees charged at the transfer station to amortize the cost of the facility. Because it attains this goal by depriving competitors, including out-of-state firms, of access to a local market, we hold that the flow control ordinance violates the Commerce Clause.

The town of Clarkstown, New York, lies in the lower Hudson River valley, just upstream from the Tappan Zee Bridge and by highway minutes from New Jersey. Within the town limits are the village of Nyack and the hamlet of West Nyack. In August 1989, Clarkstown entered into a consent decree with the New York State Department of Environmental Conservation. The town agreed to close its landfill located on Route 303 in West Nyack and build a new solid waste transfer station on the same site. The station would receive bulk solid waste and separate recyclable from nonrecyclable items. Recyclable waste would be baled for shipment to a recycling facility; nonrecyclable waste, to a suitable landfill or incinerator.

The cost of building the transfer station was estimated at $1.4 million. A local private contractor agreed to construct the facility and operate it for five years, after which the town would buy it for one dollar. During those five years, the town guaranteed a minimum waste flow of 120,000 tons per year, for which the contractor could charge the hauler a so-called tipping fee of $81 per ton. If the station received less than 120,000 tons in a year, the town promised to make up the tipping fee deficit. The object of this arrangement was to amortize the cost of the transfer station: The town would finance its new facility with the income generated by the tipping fees.

The problem, of course, was how to meet the yearly guarantee. This difficulty was compounded by the fact that the tipping fee of $81 per ton exceeded the disposal cost of unsorted solid waste on the private market. The solution the town adopted was the flow control ordinance here in question, Local Laws 1990, No. 9 of the Town of Clarkstown. The ordinance requires all nonhazardous solid waste within the town to be deposited at the Route 303 transfer station.

* * *

The central rationale for the rule against discrimination is to prohibit state or municipal laws whose object is local economic protectionism, laws that would excite those jealousies and retaliatory measures the Constitution was designed to prevent. We have interpreted the Commerce Clause to invalidate local laws that impose commercial barriers or discriminate against an article of commerce by reason of its origin or destination out of State.

Clarkstown protests that its ordinance does not discriminate because it does not differentiate solid waste on the basis of its geographic origin. All solid waste, regardless of origin, must be processed at the designated transfer station before it leaves the town. Unlike the statute in Philadelphia, says the town, the ordinance erects no barrier to the import or export of any solid waste but requires only that the waste be channeled through the designated facility.

Our initial discussion of the effects of the ordinance on interstate commerce goes far toward refuting the town's contention that there is no discrimination in its regulatory scheme. The town's own arguments go the rest of the way. As the town itself points out, what makes garbage a profitable business is not its own worth but the fact that its possessor must pay to get rid of it. In other words, the article of commerce is not so much the solid waste itself, but rather the service of processing and disposing of it.

With respect to this stream of commerce, the flow control ordinance discriminates, for it allows only the favored operator to process waste that is within the limits of the town. The ordinance is no less discriminatory because in-state or in-town processors are also covered by the prohibition. In *Dean Milk Co. v. Madison,* 340 U.S. 349, 71 S.Ct. 295, 95 L.Ed. 329 (1951), we struck down a city ordinance that required all milk sold in the city to be pasteurized within five miles of the city lines. We found it "immaterial that Wisconsin milk from outside the Madison area is subjected to the same proscription as that moving in interstate commerce."

In this light, the flow control ordinance is just one more instance of local processing requirements that we long have held invalid. The essential vice in laws of this sort is that they bar the import of the processing service. Out-of-state meat inspectors, or shrimp hullers, or milk pasteurizers, are deprived of access to local demand for their services. Put another way, the offending local laws hoard a local resource—be it meat, shrimp, or milk—for the benefit of local businesses that treat it.

The flow control ordinance has the same design and effect. It hoards solid waste, and the demand to get rid of it, for the benefit of the preferred processing facility. The only conceivable distinction from the cases cited above is that the flow control ordinance favors a single local proprietor. But this difference just makes the protectionist effect of the ordinance more acute. In *Dean Milk,* the local processing requirement at least permitted pasteurizers within five miles of the city to compete. An out-of-state pasteurizer who wanted access to that market might have built a pasteurizing facility within the radius. The flow control ordinance at issue here squelches competition in the waste-processing service altogether, leaving no room for investment from outside.

Discrimination against interstate commerce in favor of local business or investment is per se invalid, save in a narrow class of cases in which the municipality can demonstrate, under rigorous scrutiny, that it has no other means to advance a legitimate local interest. A number of amici contend that the flow control ordinance fits into this narrow class. They suggest that as landfill space diminishes and environmental clean-up costs escalate, measures like flow control become necessary to ensure the safe handling and proper treatment of solid waste.

The teaching of our cases is that these arguments must be rejected absent the clearest showing that the unobstructed flow of interstate commerce itself is unable to solve the local problem. The Commerce Clause presumes a national market free from local legislation that discriminates in favor of local interests. Here Clarkstown has any number of nondiscriminatory alternatives for addressing the health and environmental problems alleged to justify the ordinance in question. The most obvious would be uniform safety regulations enacted without the object to discriminate. These regulations would ensure that competitors like Carbone do not underprice the market by cutting corners on environmental safety.

Nor may Clarkstown justify the flow control ordinance as a way to steer solid waste away from out-of-town disposal sites that it might deem harmful to the environment. To do so would extend the town's police power beyond its jurisdictional bounds. States and localities may not attach restrictions to exports or imports in order to control commerce in other states.

The flow control ordinance does serve a central purpose that a nonprotectionist regulation would not: It ensures that the town-sponsored facility will be profitable, so that the local contractor can build it and Clarkstown can buy it back at nominal cost in five years. In other words, as the most candid of amici and even Clarkstown admit, the flow control ordinance is a financing measure. By itself, of course, revenue generation is not a local interest that can justify discrimination against interstate commerce. Otherwise States could impose discriminatory taxes against solid waste originating outside the State.

Clarkstown maintains that special financing is necessary to ensure the long-term survival of the designated facility. If so, the town may subsidize the facility through general taxes or municipal bonds. But having elected to use the open market to earn revenues for its project, the town may not employ discriminatory regulation to give that project an advantage over rival businesses from out of State.

Though the Clarkstown ordinance may not in explicit terms seek to regulate interstate commerce, it does so nonetheless by its practical effect and design. In this respect the ordinance is not far different from the state law this Court found invalid in *Buck v. Kuykendall*, 267 U.S. 307, 45 S.Ct. 324, 69 L.Ed. 623 (1925). That statute prohibited common carriers from using state highways over certain routes without a certificate of public convenience. Writing for the Court, Justice Brandeis said of the law: "Its primary purpose is not regulation with a view to safety or to conservation of the highways, but the prohibition of competition. It determines not the manner of use, but the persons by whom the highways may be used. It prohibits such use to some persons while permitting it to others for the same purpose and in the same manner."

State and local governments may not use their regulatory power to favor local enterprise by prohibiting patronage of out-of-state competitors or their facilities. We reverse the judgment and remand the case for proceedings not inconsistent with this decision.

JUSTICE O'CONNOR, concurring in the judgment.

In my view, the majority fails to come to terms with a significant distinction between the laws in the local processing cases discussed above and Local Law 9. Unlike the regulations we have previously struck down, Local Law 9 does not give more favorable treatment to local interests as a group as compared to out-of-state or out-of-town economic interests. Rather, the garbage sorting monopoly is achieved at the expense of all competitors, be they local or nonlocal. That the ordinance does not discriminate on the basis of geographic origin is vividly illustrated by the identity of the plaintiff in this very action: petitioner is a local recycler, physically located in Clarkstown, that desires to process waste itself, and thus bypass the town's designated transfer facility. Because in-town processors—like petitioner—and out-of-town processors are treated equally, I cannot agree that Local Law 9 "discriminates" against interstate commerce. Rather, Local Law 9 "discriminates" evenhandedly against all potential participants in the waste processing business, while benefiting only the chosen operator of the transfer facility.

* * *

That the ordinance does not discriminate against interstate commerce does not, however, end the Commerce Clause inquiry. Even a nondiscriminatory regulation may nonetheless impose an excessive burden on interstate trade when considered in relation to the local benefits conferred. Indeed, we have long recognized that "a burden imposed by a State upon interstate commerce is not to be sustained simply because the statute imposing it applies alike to . . . the people of the State enacting such statute." Moreover, "the extent of the burden that will be tolerated will of course depend on the nature of the local interest involved, and on whether it could be promoted as well with a lesser impact on interstate activities." Judged against these standards, Local Law 9 fails.

The local interest in proper disposal of waste is obviously significant. But this interest could be achieved by simply requiring that all waste disposed of in the town be properly processed somewhere. For example,

the town could ensure proper processing by setting specific standards
with which all town processors must comply.

In fact, however, the town's purpose is narrower than merely
ensuring proper disposal. Local Law 9 is intended to ensure the financial
viability of the transfer facility. I agree with the majority that this
purpose can be achieved by other means that would have a less dramatic
impact on the flow of goods. For example, the town could finance the
project by imposing taxes, by issuing municipal bonds, or even by
lowering its price for processing to a level competitive with other waste
processing facilities. But by requiring that all waste be processed at the
town's facility, the ordinance "squelches competition in the waste-
processing service altogether, leaving no room for investment from
outside."

JUSTICE SOUTER, with whom THE CHIEF JUSTICE and JUSTICE BLACKMUN
join, dissenting.

The majority may invoke "well-settled principles of our Commerce
Clause jurisprudence," but it does so to strike down an ordinance unlike
anything this Court has ever invalidated. Previous cases have held that
the "negative" or "dormant" aspect of the Commerce Clause renders
state or local legislation unconstitutional when it discriminates against
out-of-state or out-of-town businesses such as those that pasteurize milk,
hull shrimp, or mill lumber, and the majority relies on these cases
because of what they have in common with this one: out-of-state processors are excluded from the local market (here, from the market for
trash processing services). What the majority ignores, however, are the
differences between our local processing cases and this one: the exclusion
worked by Clarkstown's Local Law 9 bestows no benefit on a class of
local private actors, but instead directly aids the government in satisfying a traditional governmental responsibility. The law does not differentiate between all local and all out-of-town providers of a service, but
instead between the one entity responsible for ensuring that the job gets
done and all other enterprises, regardless of their location. The ordinance thus falls outside that class of tariff or protectionist measures that
the Commerce Clause has traditionally been thought to bar States from
enacting against each other, and when the majority subsumes the
ordinance within the class of laws this Court has struck down as facially
discriminatory (and so avails itself of our "virtually per se rule" against
such statutes, see *Philadelphia v. New Jersey* [supra p. 234]), the
majority is in fact greatly extending the Clause's dormant reach.

* * *

[M]ost of the local processing statutes we have previously invalidated imposed requirements that made local goods more expensive as they
headed into the national market, so that out-of-state economies bore the
bulk of any burden. * * * Courts step in through the dormant Commerce Clause to prevent such exports because legislative action imposing
a burden " 'principally upon those without the state * * * is not likely to
be subjected to those political restraints which are normally exerted on

legislation where it affects adversely some interests within the state.' "
Here, in contrast, every voter in Clarkstown pays to fund the benefits of
flow control, however high the tipping fee is set. Since, indeed, the
mandate to use the town facility will only make a difference when the
tipping fee raises the cost of using the facility above what the market
would otherwise set, the Clarkstown voters are funding their benefit by
assessing themselves and paying an economic penalty. Any whiff of
economic protectionism is far from obvious.

* * *

[F]low control offers an additional benefit that could not be gained
by financing through a subsidy derived from general tax revenues, in
spreading the cost of the facility among all Clarkstown residents who
generate trash. The ordinance does, of course, protect taxpayers, including those who already support the transfer station by patronizing it,
from ending up with the tab for making provision for large-volume trash
producers like Carbone, who would rely on the municipal facility when
that was advantageous but opt out whenever the transfer station's price
rose above the market price. In proportioning each resident's burden to
the amount of trash generated, the ordinance has the added virtue of
providing a direct and measurable deterrent to the generation of unnecessary waste in the first place. And in any event it is far from clear that
the alternative to flow control (i.e., subsidies from general tax revenues
or municipal bonds) would be less disruptive of interstate commerce
than flow control, since a subsidized competitor can effectively squelch
competition by underbidding it.

Notes

1. As this case illustrates, the Supreme Court's three-part scheme for
the dormant commerce clause is less tidy than it seems. See Farber &
Hudec, "Free Trade and the Regulatory State: A GATT's—Eye View of the
Dormant Commerce Clause," 47 *Vand.L.Rev.* 1401 (1994). In *Carbone,* the
Court divided 5–4 over whether to apply the *Philadelphia v. New Jersey* test
or the *Pike* test—and the four favoring the *Pike* test could not agree on the
test's result. Should the Court attempt to reformulate its approach? For
instance, should it look only for evidence of protectionist intent?

2. *Carbone* heavily stresses what the Court considered the discriminatory effect of flow control, which triggers an almost per se rule of invalidity.
On the other hand, cases such as *Oberly* [supra p. 229] suggest that no
significant judicial scrutiny is appropriate in the absence of a discriminatory
effect. Are the courts moving toward a binary approach, in which the validity
of the statute turns entirely on whether or not a discriminatory effect is
present? Would this be an improvement over the current scheme?

3. Note the majority's statement that Clarkstown does not have jurisdiction to steer waste away from out-of-town disposal sites that have inferior
environmental standards. We will consider later whether the United States
as a nation can legitimately take action to protect the environment outside
its boundaries. *Carbone,* by analogy, suggests that the answer is "no."

4. *Carbone* gave rise to a new rash of litigation in the lower courts because of the widespread use of flow control ordinances by municipalities. In the meantime, local governments struggled to find ways to meet their goals without violating the Commerce Clause. Consider the following effort to avoid *Carbone*.

USA RECYCLING, INC. v. TOWN OF BABYLON

United States Court of Appeals, Second Circuit, 1995.
66 F.3d 1272

JOSE A. CABRANES, CIRCUIT JUDGE:

For ninety years, it has been settled law that garbage collection and disposal is a core function of local government in the United States. At their option, cities may provide garbage pick-up to their citizens directly (that is, through town employees or an independent contractor), or they may rely on a closely regulated private market to provide those services. In 1905, the Supreme Court turned away two challenges, brought on takings and due process grounds, to city ordinances in San Francisco and Detroit that gave a single scavenger firm the exclusive right to collect and dispose of city garbage. Although in neither of these cases did the Court address whether the municipal waste systems comported with the Commerce Clause, we squarely face that question today.

The Town of Babylon, New York, has elected to take over the local commercial garbage market. Rather than assemble a municipal waste disposal bureaucracy and purchase directly the necessary equipment, the Town has hired one private company to pick up all commercial garbage, and another to operate an incinerator where that garbage is burned. Businesses and commercial property owners finance this system by paying the Town flat property taxes and user fees tied to the amount of garbage they generate. No private companies, local or out-of-state, may collect commercial garbage in Babylon.

The plaintiffs in these consolidated cases argue that the Supreme Court's decision has stripped local governments of their long-settled authority to collect and dispose of town garbage. In *Carbone*, the Supreme Court struck down a municipal ordinance that required private garbage haulers to process all town garbage at a single, privately owned local transfer station. Likewise, the present plaintiffs argue, Babylon has in effect created monopolies in the waste collection and disposal markets by taking over both markets and then hiring independent contractors to provide services on the Town's behalf. This system, they contend, discriminates against interstate commerce and therefore violates the Commerce Clause.

We disagree. Babylon's waste management plan * * * neither discriminates against, nor imposes any incidental burdens on, interstate commerce. In reaching that conclusion, we reject the plaintiffs' contention that the *Carbone* decision fashioned from the "dormant" Commerce Clause a new, and unprecedentedly sweeping, limitation on local government authority to provide basic sanitation services to local residents and businesses, on an exclusive basis and financed by tax dollars. Such a limitation, to borrow the words of the Supreme Court, "would interfere significantly with a State's ability to structure relations exclusively with its own citizens. It would also threaten the future fashioning of effective and creative programs for solving local problems and distributing governmental largesse. A healthy regard for federalism and good government renders us reluctant to risk these results."

* * *

At the heart of the dispute is the relationship between the Town of Babylon, an incinerator built in Babylon at the behest of the Town ("Incinerator"), and a private garbage hauler hired by the Town (Babylon Source Separation Commercial, Inc., or "BSSCI"). * * * Three aspects of Babylon's waste management plan merit special attention. First, the Town has licensed and hired BSSCI to collect all garbage within the district and has refused to renew the licenses of any other private haulers to collect garbage pursuant to individual contracts with town businesses. Second, the Town permits BSSCI to dispose of town waste at no charge at the Incinerator. Third, the Town finances its commercial garbage collection and disposal system by charging a flat $1500 benefit assessment to commercial property owners, plus a schedule of user fees to individual businesses for garbage they generate beyond a fixed base amount.

* * *

Although the Town's decision to eliminate the commercial garbage collection market constitutes "market regulation" rather than "market participation," we find that it does not discriminate in any way against interstate commerce. The Town has not favored in-state garbage haulers over out-of-state competitors. Nor has the Town handicapped other in-state and out-of-state businesses from competing against a group of local proprietors. The plaintiffs argue, however, that Babylon is favoring a single local garbage hauler to the detriment of both in-state and out-of-state competitors. In essence, they argue that the Town's exclusion of private garbage haulers and the hiring of a single garbage hauler—whether that hauler is BSSCI or some other company—is nothing more than a crude facade for a flow control ordinance like the one struck down by the Supreme Court in *Carbone*. Babylon, they claim, has conferred on BSSCI the same favored status that Clarkstown bestowed on its local, privately owned transfer station. We disagree.

No one enjoys a monopoly position selling garbage collection services in Babylon's commercial garbage market, because the Town has eliminated the market entirely. Not even the Town itself remains as a seller in the market. Although the Town is now the lone provider of garbage collection services in the District, it does so as a local government providing services to those within its jurisdiction, not as a business selling to a captive consumer base. * * *

In Babylon, the Town chose to replace private commercial garbage hauling with public garbage collection—provided not by trucks and employees of the Babylon Department of Public Works, but by an independent contractor (BSSCI) hired by the Town. The Town's decision to hire an outside firm to provide services on the Town's behalf is quite unremarkable. State governments have turned to the private sector to "contract out" or "outsource" numerous governmental functions, including services in correctional facilities, the management of concessions in public parks, the operation of mental health facilities, the training of displaced workers, and the operation of toll roads. The same is true of local governments, including in the field of waste disposal. As environmental regulations proliferate, towns may find that their staffs lack the requisite expertise to provide sanitation services in compliance with state and federal mandates. Such expertise may be more readily available in the private sector, from firms that specialize in waste removal. * * *

* * *

This case boils down to two simple propositions. First, towns can assume exclusive responsibility for the collection and disposal of local garbage. Second, towns can hire private contractors to provide municipal services to residents. In neither case does a town discriminate against, or impose any burden on, interstate commerce. The local interests that are served by consolidating garbage service in the hands of the town—safety, sanitation, reliable garbage service, cheaper service to residents—would in any event outweigh any arguable burdens placed on interstate commerce.

Notes

1. *SSC Corp. v. Town of Smithtown*, 66 F.3d 502 (2d Cir.1995), was a companion case to *Babylon*. Smithtown passed a flow control ordinance (which was struck down), but also created a garbage collection district, in which it contracted with private haulers to pick up all of the garbage in town and dispose of the garbage at the municipal incinerator. Users of the incinerator were charged a tipping fee, which was refunded to the private haulers under the contract. The court found that Smithtown itself was the consumer of the incinerator services, so that the arrangement was protected by the market participant exception. The court said that "Smithtown has a very real interest in both the collection and disposal services, since it pays for both." Thus, "[i]f the town wished, it could perform these traditional municipal services itself (with public employees), or it could contract for each service separately."

2. In another post-*Carbone* case, the Third Circuit recognized a novel defense for a flow control scheme: "We believe, in fact, that a local authority could choose a single provider—without impermissibly discriminating against inter-state commerce—so long as the selection process was open and competitive, and offered truly equally opportunities to in-and out-of-state businesses." The court warned, however, that "a seemingly neutral bid specification with an entirely legitimate purpose, such as a specified proximity requirement, may have the effect of giving instate interests an advan-

tage." Also, the court said, "there may be aspects of a flow control regime that appear to be so unnecessarily restrictive that a factfinder reasonably could include that their real purpose was to entrench the local interest once selected by a neutral designation process." As examples, the court cited excessively long periods of exclusive service rights or the absence of any real possibility for future designation of additional sites. *Harvey & Harvey, Inc. v. County of Chester*, 68 F.3d 788, 802 (3d Cir.1995).

3. Are *Smithtown*, *Babylon*, and *Harvey & Harvey* consistent with *Carbone*, or do they simply allow municipalities to accomplish indirectly what the Supreme Court has said they may not do directly? Consider the following comment on the *Smithtown* case:

> The court's holding regarding the waste hauling contracts at issue in *SSC* allows the town to "have it both ways" by simultaneously escaping *Carbone* Commerce Clause scrutiny and enjoying antitrust immunity. In essence, what the court precluded the town from pursuing on a broad basis in the form of the flow control ordinance, it enabled the town to undertake on a cumulative, piecemeal basis in the form of the waste hauling contracts. The *SSC* decision could send a dangerous message to municipalities in the solid waste management field by encouraging them to enter into waste hauling contracts with individual private contractors as market participants to achieve anticompetitive results. This would allow them to make an "end run" around what they otherwise would be prohibited from achieving as market regulators.

Abate & Bennett, "Constitutional Limitations on Anticompetitive State and Local Solid Waste Management Schemes: A New Frontier in Environmental Regulation,"14 *Yale J. on Reg.* 165, 192 (1997). On the other hand, perhaps these cases are signs of dissatisfaction with the whole post-*Philadelphia* line of waste-disposal decisions which have themselves been sharply criticized, see Verchick, "The Commerce Clause, Environmental Justice, and Interstate Garbage Wars," 70 *S.Cal.L.Rev.* 1239 (1997).

4. The combined effect of *Carbone* and the market participant exception may be to push states into taking over markets rather than regulating them. Is this a sensible interpretation of the commerce clause?

Dormant Commerce Clause Problem

In order to finance a $200 million incinerator, Maxwell County (a composite of several Minnesota counties) enacted a flow control ordinance. The incinerator was chosen because at the time it was considered to be environmentally preferable to landfills. At the time the ordinance was passed, no waste was being shipped out of the state for disposal, although some waste was being shipped to landfills in other counties within the state. After another county's flow control ordinance was declared unconstitutional, Maxwell County formally announced that it would not enforce the flow control ordinance as to waste being shipped out-of-state. Because the tipping fee at the incinerator was initially set quite high, a significant amount of waste began to be shipped to a neighboring state. The waste still could not be shipped to closer sites within Minnesota. Maxwell County then adopted another ordinance, placing a tax on garbage generators within the county. The tax, which was collected by garbage haulers, was set at 15% of the cost of disposal. The tax moneys were placed in the general revenue fund, but the haulers claim that the same amount of money was appropriated to subsidize the incinerator and lower the tipping fee to a competitive level.

Is the county now in compliance with the requirements of the commerce clause? If not, are there other means it might use to achieve its goals without creating constitutional problems?

Consider, in this connection, a recent case regarding subsidies. In *West Lynn Creamery, Inc. v. Healy,* 512 U.S. 186, 114 S.Ct. 2205, 129 L.Ed.2d 157 (1994), the Court struck down a combination tax-subsidy scheme as a violation of the commerce clause. Massachusetts imposed a nondiscriminatory tax on wholesale milk sales and used the result to fund cash payments to the state's economically struggling dairy farmers. The Court held that this scheme had the same economic effect as a tariff:

> Its avowed purpose and its undisputed effect are to allow higher cost Massachusetts dairy farmers to compete with lower cost dairy farmers in other States. The "premium payments" are effectively a tax which makes milk produced out of State more expensive. Although the tax also applies to milk produced in Massachusetts, its effect on Massachusetts producers is entirely (indeed more than) offset by the subsidy provided exclusively to Massachusetts dairy farmers. Like an ordinary tariff, the tax is thus effectively imposed on only out-of-state products [resulting, the Court added, in increased market share for local producers]. This effect renders the program unconstitutional, because it, like a tariff, "neutralize[s] advantages belonging to the place of origin."

In a concurring opinion, Justice Scalia, joined by Justice Thomas, reiterated his view that dormant commerce clause jurisprudence is illegitimate. Feeling obligated to follow existing precedent, however, he would hold that a subsidy can be financed out of general revenue but not through an earmarked tax. Chief Justice Rehnquist and Justice Blackmun dissented. Is the Maxwell County tax scheme distinguishable from *West Lynn?*

Note on Federal Preemption

The preceding material dealt with the validity of state regulation in the absence of federal regulation. Here we are concerned with the validity of state regulations in areas where Congress has acted. It is clear, of course, that in cases of direct conflict, the state statute must give way. The Supremacy Clause of the Constitution provides:

> This Constitution, and the Laws of the United States which shall be made in Pursuance thereof; and all Treaties made, or which shall be made, under the authority of the United States, shall be the Supreme Law of the Land; and the Judges in every State shall be bound thereby, any Thing in the Constitution or Laws of any State to the Contrary not withstanding.

The presence of a conflict between federal and state law, however, is often less than obvious.

The Supreme Court has set forth various factors which are to be considered in preemption cases. First, the federal regulatory scheme may be so pervasive and detailed as to suggest that Congress left no room for the state to supplement it. Or the statute enacted by Congress may involve a field in which the federal interest is so dominant that enforcement of state laws is precluded. Other aspects of the regulatory scheme imposed by Congress may also support the inference that Congress has completely foreclosed state legislation in a particular area. Even where Congress has not completely foreclosed state regulation, a state statute is void to the extent that it actually conflicts with a valid federal statute. Such a conflict can be found where compliance with both the federal and state regulations is impossible, or more often, where the state law interferes with the accomplishment of the full objectives of Congress.

These factors are obviously rather vague and difficult to apply. The Supreme Court has done little to create any more rigorous framework for analysis. Therefore, the only way to get some degree of understanding of the field is to examine particular cases in order to see what kinds of situations have been found appropriate for application of the preemption doctrine.

Perhaps the area in which preemption is most likely to be found is interstate transportation. Many of the same arguments supporting federal power under the commerce clause also suggest that state regulation is inappropriate in this area. Such state regulation might well be struck down under the commerce clause even if Congress had not spoken, but where Congress has addressed a regulatory problem, the argument against state regulation is even stronger. For instance, the Supreme Court held in *City of Burbank v. Lockheed Air Terminal Inc.,* 411 U.S. 624, 93 S.Ct. 1854, 36 L.Ed.2d 547 (1973), that a local municipality may not impose a night curfew on commercial jet flights at a privately owned airport. The *Burbank* Court concluded that the widespread imposition of such local restrictions would interfere with flight scheduling and navigational patterns nationwide, thus hindering federal management of the national air traffic network. (The *Burbank* Court did not impose similar restrictions on the rights of a municipality which owns a local airport. The lower courts have generally held that regulations by a municipal owner are not necessarily forbidden by *Burbank,* but are subject to a requirement of reasonableness.)

Another important preemption issue involves nuclear energy. In a 1971 case, *Northern States Power Co. v. Minnesota,* 447 F.2d 1143 (8th Cir.1971), affirmed 405 U.S. 1035, 92 S.Ct. 1307, 31 L.Ed.2d 576 (1972), the Court held that the state lacked the authority to impose conditions on nuclear waste releases stricter than those imposed by the Atomic Energy Commission. The court relied heavily on a provision of the Atomic Energy Act allowing the federal government to delegate regulatory authority to the states with respect to certain categories of nuclear materials. Radioactive releases from nuclear power plants did not fall within any of these categories, which the court considered the exclusive areas in which states may regulate regarding radiation hazards. The court concluded that state regulation would interfere with the Congressional objectives expressed in the 1954 Act:

Thus, through direction of the licensing scheme for nuclear reactors, Congress vested the AEC with the authority to resolve the proper balance between desired industrial progress and adequate health and safety standards. Only through the application and enforcement of uniform standards promulgated by a national agency will these dual objectives be assured. Were the states allowed to impose stricter standards on the level of radioactive waste releases discharged from nuclear power plants, they might conceivably be so overprotective in the area of health and safety as to unnecessarily stultify the industrial development and use of atomic energy for the production of electric power.

In contrast, the Supreme Court upheld a California nuclear moratorium in a later decision, *Pacific Gas & Electric Co. v. State Energy Resources Conservation & Development Commission,* 461 U.S. 190, 103 S.Ct. 1713, 75 L.Ed.2d 752 (1983). In an opinion by Justice White, the Court upheld a California statute prohibiting nuclear plant operation until the federal government approved a permanent method of waste disposal. The Court found that the state statute was aimed not at radiation hazards but instead at economic problems posed by the failure of the federal government to approve a permanent method of waste disposal. The Court concluded that Congress had not intended to promote nuclear power at all costs, but rather had decided to leave the choice as to the necessity or economic benefits of a nuclear plant to the state through its utility regulatory powers. Thus, it appears that if the state casts its legislation in the form of utility regulation, it may indirectly accomplish what federal law would not allow it to do directly—that is, impose its own views as to the safety of nuclear reactors under various circumstances. So long as it can reasonably be argued that a possible safety risk would have repercussions on the economic desirability of nuclear energy, the Supreme Court would apparently allow the state to regulate.

A year after the *PG & E* case, the Court again displayed a permissive attitude toward state laws dealing with the nuclear industry. In *Silkwood v. Kerr–McGee Corp.,* 464 U.S. 238, 104 S.Ct. 615, 78 L.Ed.2d 443 (1984), the Court upheld an award of punitive damages against a utility for an employee's radiation injuries. As the dissent pointed out, the jury was told it could impose punitive damages even if the defendant had complied with all federal regulations. Thus, the state was allowed to hold the defendant to higher standards of conduct in the handling of radioactive materials than those imposed by the federal government. Together with *PG & E, Silkwood* made it clear that the Court's enthusiasm for preemption in the nuclear area had waned considerably since it affirmed *Northern States Power* in 1972.

Every preemption case in a sense is unique. Apart from some vague and usually unhelpful maxims, little can be said about this area of law that is of much help in deciding individual cases. The question before the court in each case is whether Congress in passing a particular statute would have been willing to allow the state to impose certain kinds of regulations in the same area. This is essentially an issue of statutory construction. It can only be resolved by close attention to the language of the federal statute, to its legislative history, and to its purposes. Thus, the best advice in analyzing preemption problems is to carefully consider the legislative materials and the extent to which the state statute would have a practical effect on the implementation of the federal statute.

Even when a federal statute itself does not preempt state law, the federal administrative agency implementing the statute may issue a regulation that preempts state law. The Court is reluctant to infer preemption merely from the existence of comprehensive federal regulations. The state law will stand unless it directly conflicts with the federal regulation. This reluctance to infer preemption makes sense, because the agency can readily adopt an express preemption regulation. Congress, on the other hand, must overcome considerably more inertia to respond to a state law that interferes with a federal statute. Hence, there is less reason for courts to apply preemption doctrines expansively when agency regulations are involved. Indeed, the ability of an agency to issue a preemptive regulation suggests that the courts perhaps should require all preemption issues to be presented initially to the agencies, subject to ultimate judicial review. This would give agencies "primary jurisdiction" over preemption matters.

C. ENVIRONMENTAL REGULATION AND INTERNATIONAL TRADE

The primary subject of the preceding section was how to reconcile state environmental regulation and an open national economy. This issue is not unique to the United States. For example, the European Court of Justice has evolved its own set of doctrines analogous to the dormant commerce clause. Based on Articles 30 and 36 of the EEC Treaty, the ECJ has struck down regulations of member nations that act as trade barriers. The best-known case is *Commission v. Kingdom of Denmark,* 1988 ECJ Rep. 4607, which is better known as the "Danish beer case." Denmark had imposed rigorous requirements that beverage containers be not only recyclable but actually reused. The ECJ applied a balancing test not unlike *Pike* to uphold much of the measure, while invalidating provisions that were unnecessarily burdensome for foreign manufacturers. The ECJ has also sometimes reached results interestingly different from U.S. law. For instance, it has allowed member states to ban the import of solid waste, on the theory that waste disposal is a responsibility of the member generating the waste. For discussions of this case and other aspects of EU law, see Hunter and Muylle, "European Community Environmental Law: Institutions, Law Making, and Free Trade," 28 *Env.L.Rep.* 10477 (1998); Stewart, "International Trade and Environment: Lessons from the Federal Experience," 49 *Wash. & Lee L.Rev.* 1329, 1339 (1992); Hartwell & Bergkamp, "Environmental Trade Barriers and International Competitiveness," 24 *Env.L.Rep.* 10109 (1994).

For most American lawyers, let alone environmentalists and politicians, EU law is still an obscure subject. Other tensions between trade and the environment have become front-page news. Such conflicts featured heavily in the debate over NAFTA, which became an issue in the 1992 Presidential elections. Similarly, the Uruguay Round amendments to GATT were vocally opposed by some environmentalists. Trade liberalization inevitably raises questions about environmental regulations. Because different countries, even more than different American states, have widely varying approaches to environmental regulation, tensions of various kinds are bound to arise.

So far, the tensions seem to fall into two major categories. First, as under the dormant commerce clause, there are situations in which stringent domestic regulations are attacked as trade barriers. The next Note will discuss the complicated international trade provisions applying to this situation. Second, there are situations in which a nation adopts trade measures, not as part of domestic regulations, but because of concerns about environmental degradation abroad. For example, the U.S. imposed trade sanctions on Taiwan for refusing to halt the sale of tiger bones and rhinoceros horns. *New York Times,* April 12, 1994, at C1. Often, the reason for the trade measure is that the processes used to produce the goods, rather than the goods themselves, are environmentally questionable.

Because of space limitations, we cannot explore the complex (not to mention spirited) debate in detail. We will, however, try to present some of the main themes. We begin by considering the effect of trade law on domestic regulation.

Note on GATT and Domestic Regulations

Unlike the constraints imposed on state government under the dormant commerce clause, the GATT restrictions imposed on member governments rest on an explicit mandate. GATT is a formal international agreement containing explicit prohibitions of certain kinds of protectionist trade barriers. The basic structure of the GATT agreement begins with "tariff bindings" setting a maximum rate for tariffs on an item-by-item basis. Then, to protect against other measures that would subvert the commercial opportunity created by tariff bindings, the GATT agreement adds a rather detailed code of rules prohibiting most other forms of trade barriers.[d] Similar

---

d. The main provisions are the prohibition of non-tariff restrictions under GATT Article XI:1 and the prohibition of discriminatory internal taxes and regulations under the so-called "national treatment" rule of GATT Article III. The text of Article XI:1, which is subject to numerous exceptions, provides quite simply and broadly,

1. No prohibitions or restrictions other than duties, taxes or other charges, whether made effective through quotas, import or export licenses or other measures, shall be instituted or maintained by any contracting party on the importation of any product from the territory of any other contracting party or on the exportation or sale for export of any product destined for the territory of any other contracting party.

The two key provisions of the national treatment rule of GATT Article III are paragraphs 2 and 4:

2. The products of the territory of any contracting party imported into the territory of any other contracting party shall not be subject, directly or indirectly, to internal taxes or other internal charges of any kind in excess of those applied, directly or indirectly, to like domestic products. Moreover, no contracting party shall otherwise apply internal taxes or other internal charges in a manner contrary to the principles set forth in paragraph 1 [i.e., internal measures should not "afford protection to domestic production."]

4. The products of the territory of any contracting party imported into the territory of any other contracting party shall be accorded treatment no less favourable

provisions are contained in NAFTA, which applies to trade among the United States, Canada, and Mexico. Some environmentalists fear that the strict regulations of some countries may be struck down under these trade agreements. For example, in the U.S. the Delaney Clause (see pages 488–490 infra) bans some food additives simply because they cause cancer in animals, no matter how small the possible risk to humans. Efforts to apply this provision to imports might trigger a GATT challenge.

The threat of interference with strict regulations has been accentuated by recent changes in GATT. The two changes raising the most concern are the new code on the Application of Sanitary and Phytosanitary Measures,[e] and the new and expanded rule on trade-restricting technical measures in the GATT's Standards Code.[f] Both texts were adopted in the Uruguay Round negotiations. Both make explicit that differentially burdensome regulations that deviate from internationally accepted standards may be subject to legal challenge. The result has been to heighten environmentalist concerns.

The application of GATT rules ultimately raises the same type of legal issues confronted by U.S. courts in consumer claims cases. Like U.S. law, GATT allows consideration of the strength of a regulation's benefits. GATT's prohibitions are qualified by GATT Article XX, which authorizes exceptions whenever trade barriers are found to be required by other widely-accepted government regulatory objectives such as health, safety or law-enforcement.[g] Application of Article XX requires GATT tribunals to analyze the extent to which claimed regulatory objectives are served by a particular trade-restricting measure. Recent additions to GATT incorporate this analysis into the test for establishing a violation, rather than making it part of an affirmative defense. Such an analysis of regulatory objectives is built into certain supplemental GATT rules that deal with facially neutral measures, such as the 1994 Standards Code prohibition of measures that create "unnecessary obstacles to international trade."

Like the Standards Clause, GATT law imposes the greatest restraints on trade-restricting measures that explicitly discriminate between domestic and foreign goods. Under GATT, the main items in this category would be border

than that accorded to like products of national origin in respect of all laws, regulations and requirements affecting their internal sale, offering for sale, purchase, transportation, distribution or use. * * *

e. GATT Doc. MTN.TNC/W/FA at pages L.35 to L.52 (20 December 1991).

f. In particular, a new Article 2.2, contained in GATT Doc. MTN.TNC/W/FA (20 December 1991), at pages G.2 and G.3.

g. Article XX reads as follows:

Subject to the requirement that such measures are not applied in a manner which would constitute a means of arbitrary or unjustifiable discrimination between countries where the same conditions prevail, or a disguised restriction on international trade, nothing in this Agreement shall be construed to prevent the adoption or enforcement by any contracting party of measures:

(a) necessary to protect public morals;

(b) necessary to protect human, animal or plant life or health;

* * *

(f) imposed for the protection of national treasures of artistic, historic or archaeological value;

(g) relating to the conservation of exhaustible natural resources if such measures are made effective in conjunction with restrictions on domestic production or consumption;

* * *

measures such as quotas and other restrictions that limit the volume of foreign goods allowed to enter the national market, and "internal" taxes or regulations that explicitly provide more onerous treatment of foreign goods. The U.S. case law often suggests that such explicitly discriminatory measures are all but *per se* prohibited under the Commerce Clause, but in practice does recognize some exceptions. Under GATT, such discriminatory measures are *prima facie* outlawed by Article III. However, Article XX permits even explicitly discriminatory measures when such discrimination is necessary to legitimate regulatory objectives.

Like U.S. doctrine, the GATT law also deals with facially neutral measures that may have a trade-restricting effect. For example, a different tax or regulatory burden may be placed on products with certain characteristics; it "just happens" that all or most foreign products fall into the disadvantaged category. An example might be emission controls that impose less burdensome requirements for large-bore engines used in domestic automobiles than for small-bore engines normally used in foreign autos.

Almost by definition, facially neutral regulations are invariably "internal" measures—taxes or other regulatory measures that are imposed on imported goods (together with domestic goods) after the imported goods have cleared customs and entered domestic commerce. GATT Article III requires that internal taxes and internal regulations treat foreign goods "no less favorably" than the "like" domestic goods. This is the so-called "national treatment" rule. Any measure found in violation of Article III would be a *prima facie* violation, and thus in the same category as explicitly discriminatory measures. Any regulatory justification for such a measure would have to comply with the strict rules of GATT Article XX. As we will see, this situation has proved difficult for GATT tribunals to handle.

Both the Standards Code and the SPS Agreement avoid the seemingly bifurcated approach of Articles III and XX. Both permit tribunals to weigh a measure's trade-restricting effects and its regulatory justification at the same time. Article 2.2 of the Standards Code provides as follows:

> Members shall ensure that technical regulations are not prepared, adopted or applied with a view to or with the effect of creating unnecessary obstacles to international trade. For this purpose, technical regulations shall not be more trade-restrictive than necessary to fulfil a legitimate objective, taking account of the risks non-fulfillment would create. Such legitimate objectives are, *inter alia*, national security requirements; the prevention of deceptive practices; protection of human health or safety, animal or plant life or health, or the environment. In assessing such risks, relevant elements of consideration are, *inter alia*, available scientific and technical information, related processing technology or intended end use of products.

This text clearly calls for an analysis and evaluation of the regulatory purpose of the measure.

The SPS Agreement contains a rather lengthy and convoluted set of legal standards, but the basic provisions are similar to those of the Standards Code. Paragraphs 6 and 7 of the Agreement provide:

6.   Members shall ensure that any sanitary or phytosanitary measure is applied only to the extent necessary to protect human, animal or plant life or health, is based on scientific principles and is not maintained without sufficient scientific evidence [with some exceptions].

7.   * * * Sanitary and phytosanitary measures shall not be applied in a manner which would constitute a disguised restriction on international trade.

The concept of "disguised restriction" has been interpreted to refer to cases where a claimed regulatory purpose is found to be of so little importance, or so little served, that it can be called a disguise.[h]

Could a plausible argument be made that the Delaney Clause violates the SPS agreement? How would you go about defending the Clause? Compare a recent GATT decision invalidating an EU ban on certain beef hormones because no substantial evidence of a significant health risk existed. See EC Measures Concerning Meat and Meat Products, 1998 WL 25520 (WTO App. Body, Jan. 16, 1998). See also Australia—Measures Affecting Importation of Salmon, AB–1998–5 (WTO App. Body, Oct. 20, 1998).

The SPS Agreement and the Standards Code are like the *Pike* test under the dormant commerce clause: they allow a balancing of trade effects and regulatory benefits. But the basic GATT agreement is more awkwardly drafted: first trade effects are considered under Article III, then regulatory benefits are considered under Article XX, but the two are never compared with each other. For the past few years, as explained below, GATT tribunals have engaged in complicated maneuvers in an attempt to avoid this dilemma.

In one effort to escape this artificial bifurcation, some GATT panels experimented with an interpretation of Article III which allowed consideration of regulatory benefits at that stage, rather than waiting for the Article XX defense. The key idea was that whether two products–say a food containing a particular pesticide residue and a similar food without the residue–were "like products" depends on whether there is a reasonable regulatory ground for distinguishing the two. If such a ground existed, then the two products were not "like" and the regulation could not be accused of treating foreign and domestic "like products" differently. The advantage of this approach was that it eliminated the bifurcated Articles III/XX inquiry–but its disadvantage was that it did so only by ignoring the obvious two-part structure of the GATT text itself.

Recent decisions have moved away from this functional interpretation of Article III.[i] Rather than focusing on either the likeness concept of Article III

h. This interpretation was adopted by a dispute settlement panel convened under the U.S.–Canada Free Trade Agreement. *In the Matter of Canada's Landing Requirement for Pacific Coast Salmon and Herring*, BNA, 12 Int'l Trade Reporter Decisions 1026 (1991) at ¶ 7.11 and n. 20.

i. A recent panel decision (affirmed on another ground) opines that the "likeness" analysis relates only to objective product characteristics rather than regulatory objec-

tives. *United States: Standards for Reformulated and Conventional Gasoline*, WHO Doc. DS2/4 (Jan. 17. 1996), affirmed on other grounds, AB–1996–2 (April 29, 1996). In striking down a Japanese tax favoring sakura over vodka, the WTO's new Appellate Body steered away from the functional analysis of "like product," calling instead for a "narrowly squeezed" definition of likeness based on product characteristics. *Japan—Taxes on Alcoholic Beverages*, AB–

or the specific defenses of Article XX, these recent decisions seem to shift toward reliance on general anti-protectionism language in both provisions. Article III:1 states that taxes and regulations "should not be applied to imported or domestic products so as to afford protection to domestic production." The "chapeau" to Article XX states that taxes and regulations must not be applied "in a manner which would constitute a means of arbitrary or unjustifiable discrimination between countries where the same conditions prevail" or be "a disguised restriction on international trade." These recent decisions call for a "totality of the circumstances" analysis in applying such language. This "totality of the circumstance" test may ultimately provide a workable method for GATT tribunals to analyze facially nondiscriminatory regulations. But both decisions involved laws which clearly discriminated against foreign products, either by explicitly tying the regulation to the point of origin or by giving favored treatment to a distinctive local product. The implications regarding less discriminatory regulations remain unclear. Developing a workable doctrinal framework to address the issue is a major challenge facing the WTO.

Obviously, GATT law is at least as complex as U.S. doctrines protecting free trade. Indeed, because it is based on a rather complicated set of legal codes, it may be even less understandable to outsiders than the common law doctrines developed by the Supreme Court. It is also at a much earlier stage of its development. GATT is less than a third as old as the dormant commerce clause. Despite these differences, however, GATT tribunals do seem to be wrestling with the same basic difficulty as the U.S. courts. On the one hand, they have a mandate to protect free trade, a goal that could be rapidly undermined unless protectionist regulations are kept under control. Moreover, their professional training and experience emphasize free trade as a value. On the other hand, neither GATT tribunals nor the U.S. courts have any authority to decide broad issues of public policy at the expense of other organs of government. Moreover, the judges themselves, like other citizens, are likely to be concerned about maintaining the effectiveness of environmental regulation.

Most of the preceding discussion has been most directly relevant to the situation in which domestic regulations are attacked as trade barriers. The use of trade sanctions to deal with extraterritorial environmental problems is even more controversial. This topic is the primary focus of the following excerpt, which also discusses the best-known GATT decision on the subject.

Charnovitz, "The Environment vs. Trade Rules: Defogging the Debate"[j]

23 *Environmental Law* 475 (1993).

During the past two years, the conflict between international trade rules and environmental regulation has drawn increasing attention and concern not only among policy makers, but also from the general public.

1996–2 (Oct. 4, 1996), at 21. For a critique of this analysis see Steve Charnovitz, "New WTO Adjudication and Its Implications for the Environment," *Int. Env. Rep.*, Sept. 18, 1996, at 851.

Unfortunately, the debate has not been entirely edifying, and a great deal of fog surrounds the issues. This Article will cover most of the controversial points in the debate and attempt to clarify the issues involved, in particular those dealing with the General Agreement on Tariffs and Trade (GATT).

A commonly held viewpoint among trade specialists is that there is no conflict between the environment and trade because trade stimulates efficiency and economic growth, generating wealth essential to environmental protection and restoration. In addition, economic growth may engender consumer demand for reversing environmental degradation. Yet, there can be circumstances where economic growth not only fails to help the environment, but where indiscriminate growth, fueled by trade, can actually harm the environment and waste irreplaceable resources.

Whereas trade may have either positive or negative affects on the environment, protectionism is inherently destructive because it leads to economic inefficiency and thus deprives societies of the resources necessary for bettering the environment. While there may be instances where protectionism could forestall environmentally sensitive trade, virtually any assault on the environment that can be accomplished through international commerce can be carried out just as insidiously through domestic commerce.

Although there is no inherent conflict between the environment and trade, such conflicts do arise between environmental protection and GATT rules.[1] These conflicts occur in five areas. First, many potential tools for environmental protection, such as subsidies to assist environmental cleanup, can run afoul of basic GATT principles. Even "economically correct" policy instruments, such as taxes to internalize external costs, can collide with the GATT. Second, any measure that targets uncooperative countries that do not participate in environmental treaties is apt to violate the GATT's unconditional most-favored-nation (MFN) principle. Third, inconsistencies in environmental regulation can raise problems of trade fairness.[2] Fourth, the GATT and related trade agreements may lead to the downward harmonization of health and safety standards. This can occur when the countries enjoying relatively high standards have a burden of demonstrating that those standards are not unnecessary trade barriers. Fifth, the GATT imposes a discipline on the use of export controls to conserve resources. This discipline is consistent with the GATT preamble, which declares as a goal of the contracting

---

1. It should be noted that the GATT does not "govern" or regulate trade. It regulates statutory and administrative rules that restrict or distort trade. Thus, those environmentalists who want GATT to ban certain practices of dirty trade are figuratively barking up the wrong tree because the usual GATT perspective would be to forbid such banning of dirty trade.

2. For example, a country may attempt to boost exports or attract investment by specializing in environmentally harmful production. But counter action against such "unfair" trade is likely to violate the GATT because special taxes on imports from "unfair" countries would violate the MFN principle.

parties "developing the full use of the resources of the world and expanding the production and exchange of goods."[3]

Not every environmental action, however, raises problems of GATT consistency. As a GATT panel recently pointed out, the GATT "imposes few constraints on a contracting party's implementation of domestic environmental policies."[4] But while there may be a few serious environmental problems amenable to purely domestic responses, most problems call for broader solutions. As the interdependence of economies increases, more and more economic instruments could potentially be constrained by the GATT.[5]

* * *

[O]ne front of GATT activity was the conciliation panel for the United States–Mexico dispute regarding dolphins and tuna. This dispute concerned an import provision of the U.S. Marine Mammal Protection Act (MMPA). The MMPA bans the importation of fish caught using techniques which result in an incidental kill of ocean mammals in excess of U.S. practices. In 1990, following a court order, the National Oceanic and Atmospheric Administration (NOAA) imposed a ban on imports of yellowfin tuna and tuna products caught by Mexican vessels using purse seine nets in the Eastern Tropical Pacific (ETP). In response, Mexico lodged a complaint at the GATT, and in August 1991, a GATT panel ruled against the United States.

The panel reached three main conclusions. First, the U.S. import prohibition on tuna could not be considered an internal regulation under GATT Article III because it was concerned with the process of tuna harvesting rather than tuna as a product.[6] Second, the MMPA violated GATT Article XI as an import prohibition other than a duty, tax, or other charge.[7] Third, the MMPA did not qualify for the Article XX(b) or (g) exceptions because these exceptions do not have "extrajurisdictional" application.[8] Article XX(b) provides an exception for measures designed for protection of human, animal, or plant life or health. Article XX(g) provides an exception for measures taken to preserve exhaustible natural resources if taken in conjunction with domestic restrictions. In other words, the exceptions could only be invoked by a country to protect living organisms or natural resources within that country's borders.

---

3. The clause in the preamble is a bit ambiguous. "Full use" could mean anything ranging from overuse to sustainable use.

4. Dispute Settlement Panel Report on United States Restrictions on Imports of Tuna, Aug. 16, 1991, para. 6.2, 30 I.L.M. 1594 [hereinafter Tuna–Dolphin Report].

5. Others argue that these constraints contribute to a better environment. In this view, GATT is seen as positive for the environment because in restraining trade policies that are not "first best" in dealing with

environmental externalities, the GATT necessitates the search for more effective policies.

6. Tuna–Dolphin Report, supra note 11, paras. 5.8–5.16. Article III permits certain types of laws, regulations, and requirements affecting products "as such," but not ones affecting process, according to the panel deciding the Tuna–Dolphin case.

7. Id. para. 5.18.

8. Id. paras. 5.24–5.34.

At first, word of the panel's decision merely disappointed advocates of marine mammal conservation. But after the report was leaked and studied, it sent shock waves through the international environmental community. In addition to ruling that the MMPA violated international trade rules, the GATT panel implicitly dropped a wide net over decades of environmental treaties and laws protecting everything from deep sea whales to stratospheric ozone. Indeed, the panel seemed to go out of its way to validate the popular caricature of the GATT as an inflexible, myopic, moss-grown institution inherently indifferent, if not downright antagonistic, toward ecological protection.[9] There was also bitterness about the way in which the GATT operated. How could a secretive panel presume the right to issue such a sweeping ruling without any consultation with environmental institutions?[10] The fact that the panel had refused to hear the dolphin conservation experts who had come to Geneva for the oral arguments served to heighten the widespread view among environmentalists that the GATT was a hostile institution.[11]

The most straightforward course for the United States in this situation would have been to defend the validity of import prohibitions at the GATT Council, and to attack the panel's report for its weak evidence and reasoning. The United States also could have attempted to rally other countries to its side, particularly those with strong environmental records. But the Bush administration chose an entirely different course. Taking advantage of Mexico's eagerness for a trade agreement with the United States, the administration prevailed upon the Salinas Government not to seek adoption of the report by the GATT Council. Belatedly recognizing that allowing its fishing fleets to slaughter about sixty dolphins a day was not the best way to garner support from American environmentalists, the Mexican government took out full page ads in six major newspapers trumpeting new conservation measures and announcing postponement of the GATT case "as a further demonstration of our good faith effort to develop better protection for the dolphin."

By gaining an agreement with Mexico to delay the report's consideration, the administration headed off a domestic political backlash against both Mexico and the GATT. The administration also avoided putting itself in the position where it had to block adoption of the report by the GATT Council, a step which might have made it more difficult to

9. It remains unclear why the panel issued such a far-reaching decision rather than ruling against the U.S. law on more narrow grounds. Perhaps the panel may have been influenced by the unusually large number of contracting parties who appeared before it to argue against the United States. Eight nations or instrumentalities spoke against the MMPA and three offered neutral statements. No party sided with the United States. See Tuna–Dolphin Report, supra note 11, paras. 4.7–4.30.

10. GATT panels do occasionally consult with intergovernmental organizations as provided for in Article XXIII:2. No rule bars consultation with outside groups.

11. Had the panel listened to the marine mammal experts, it might have learned about the long history of U.S. government efforts to negotiate agreements to protect dolphins, as mandated by U.S. law in 1972. Instead, in apparent ignorance of this information, the panel suggests the option of "international cooperative arrangements which would seem to be desirable in view of the fact that dolphins roam the waters of many states and the high seas." Tuna–Dolphin Report, supra note 11, para. 5.28.

conclude the Uruguay Round. As a result, the Tuna–Dolphin Report was left in limbo. It seems doubtful that the Tuna–Dolphin Report will ever gain official GATT approval. In the meantime, the U.S. ban on Mexican tuna remains in effect.

In October 1992, Congress amended the MMPA so that an import ban on any country can be halted if that country agrees to implement a global moratorium by March 1994, to reduce dolphin mortality each year until then, and to require observers. But if the country fails to meet these commitments, the ban on tuna would be reinstated. If this ban is not successful within sixty days, then the U.S. government will impose a trade sanction by excluding forty percent of the normal level of fish and fish product imports from that country. The MMPA amendments also ban the sale or shipment in the United States of tuna that is not dolphin-safe beginning in June 1994.

* * *

The portrayal of the GATT as a serious ecological danger is an exaggeration. To date the only victims of the GATT are dolphins.[12] But the underlying concerns of the environmentalists are valid. There is too much secrecy in the GATT. The recent developments in the Tuna–Dolphin case and the new disciplines being devised in the Uruguay Round do threaten to undermine environmental and health rules in countries with high standards of protection. Indeed, the GATT has not taken even the basic steps to assure that its dispute panels have accurate environmental information.

Of course, the GATT can change its stance on the environment. The GATT has proven flexible enough to adapt to new political exigencies in the past, such as the creation of the European Common Market in the 1950s, a string of restrictive textile programs beginning in the 1960s, the Generalized System of Preferences (GSP) for developing countries in the 1970s, and new "voluntary" export restraints in the 1980s. Thus, it seems unlikely that the GATT would flirt with institutional suicide by directly challenging a major environmental treaty like the Montreal Protocol.

The latent threat to the world economy is not what GATT may do to the environment, but rather what the environmentalists may do to the GATT. As the Uruguay Round nears conclusion, the ability of governments—especially the United States—to implement it will require building a coalition of beneficiaries of trade liberalization. The support of environmentalists and consumer groups will be critical to the attainment of such a coalition. Yet, unless environmentalists are convinced that the GATT will change its stance toward the environment, such political support may not be forthcoming. This problem is especially serious in

12. Had the United States won the Tuna–Dolphin case, Mexico and Venezuela would probably have signed on to the new dolphin protection agreement as much as one year earlier.

the United States, largely because the American government leads the world in the use of trade instruments to achieve environmental goals.

The forward momentum of freer trade is important not just for economic growth, but for environmental quality as well. The usual argument, as noted above, is that trade liberalization enriches society and, therefore, empowers people to "demand" more environmental quality. A wealthier society may also devote greater resources to government, thus allowing more funding for public environmental programs. But, there is another important argument. By linking nations together in one of the most basic human activities—economic exchange—trade agreements establish an atmosphere for fruitful intergovernmental cooperation over a wide range of issues, the environment included.

* * *

The "extraterritoriality" of trade measures is an important and frequently misunderstood concept. For instance, critics of the MMPA charge that it is extraterritorial in effect because it attempts to control foreign behavior. This criticism is misguided because the concept of extraterritoriality refers to laws that extend legal jurisdiction to a foreign territory. U.S. laws regulating the activities of "American" companies on foreign soil are examples of extraterritoriality.[13] Customs laws are not extraterritorial because they do not purport to control behavior outside the United States.[14] Customs laws merely establish rules for importation. To be sure, any product standard can have the effect of changing foreign behavior. But there is a big difference between a law that mandates a change in behavior and a law which makes that change financially advantageous.

In 1906, when the United States prohibited the importation of any sponge taken by means of diving or diving apparatus, Congress hoped that foreign fishing practices would improve. That does not, however, make the 1906 law any more extraterritorial than the tariff schedule itself. In 1906, the United States was simply exercising its own right to establish import standards. It was asserting nothing "against the sovereignty of any other nation," but merely closing U.S. ports to everybody who harvested sponges in a "needlessly wasteful and destructive method." Fifty years later, Senator E.L. Bartlett also explained this distinction well when, in the course of Senate consideration of his amendment for trade sanctions against nations that fail to engage in fishery conservation negotiations, he declared that his amendment "did not place an American flag on every fish on the high seas * * *."

13. If the MMPA prohibited Canadian subsidiaries of American companies from buying Mexican tuna or if it prohibited foreign fishermen from fishing in a manner unsafe to dolphins, it would have extraterritorial effect.

14. It has been suggested that the MMPA is an attempt by the United States to regulate Mexico's production of tuna. But if that is true, then the filing of the GATT case by Mexico could be viewed as a Mexican attempt to deregulate U.S. consumption of tuna. Deregulation may be more in the spirit of the GATT, but requiring foreign deregulation is "extrajurisdictional."

Perhaps recognizing that the MMPA was not extraterritorial, the Tuna–Dolphin panel condemned it as "extrajurisdictional" instead.[15] Curiously, the panel did not offer any definition of an extrajurisdictional offense, even though the panel apparently invented this term. Moreover, the panel's argument that the Article XX(g) exception does not cover extrajurisdictional laws is casuistic, resting upon a 1988 GATT case rather than on any legislative history from the ITO Conference that wrote the GATT. In addition, the historical evidence on the Article XX(b) exception marshalled by the panel does not suggest, as the panel claims, that XX(b) does not apply to extrajurisdictional laws.

Even if extrajurisdictionality were GATT-illegal, the panel made no attempt to distinguish between import standards on products from foreign countries and standards on products from the high seas.[16] The panel seems to imply that since the high seas are beyond every nation's jurisdiction, they cannot be reached by any nation's import standards. Furthermore, the panel fails to address the thesis of environmentalists that "Mexican" dolphins are part of one ecosystem that transcends all jurisdictions. In defending its decision, the panel warns that extrajurisdictionality would undermine the multilateral trading system.[17] No doubt the panel is well-intentioned in its opinion,[18] but it comes about a century too late to "save" world commerce from national actions to protect the global environment, which began in the 1890s.

Finally, although this point goes beyond the panel's terms of reference, it should be noted that the sovereign rights of states over resources within their jurisdiction is not absolute. According to the Stockholm Declaration on the Human Environment, nations have a "responsibility to ensure that activities within their jurisdiction or control do not cause damage to the environment of other states or of areas beyond the limits of national jurisdiction." This tension between sovereign rights and international responsibilities underlies many of the difficult environmental problems the world faces. While dolphins may roam in and out of national territory and thus be a jurisdictional concern as well as an extrajurisdictional one, trees in tropical forests do not. But Brazil may still have an obligation not to chop down its trees because of the impact on global warming.

Notes

1. In a sequel to the decision discussed above, another GATT panel ruled on a different aspect of the U.S. tuna restrictions in June 1994. The decision primarily involved secondary restrictions on imports from countries

---

15. Tuna–Dolphin Report, supra note 11, paras. 5.26, 5.32.

16. Tuna–Dolphin Report, supra note 11, para. 6.4.

17. Tuna–Dolphin Report, supra note 11, para. 5.27, 5.32.

18. An alternative thesis is that the panel intentionally perpetrated a hoax against the environment by ignoring the history of Article XX. It is interesting to note that the panel had the time needed to do a thorough search of GATT's preparatory history. Indeed, the panel submitted its report nearly a month earlier than it was due.

buying tuna from Mexico. The panel rejected the extraterritoriality rationale of the first Tuna/Dolphin decision. It concluded that the Article XX defenses include actions taken to protect the environment outside of one's own borders. GATT panels are not subject to any strict rule of precedent, and the panel did not feel obligated to follow *Tuna/Dolphin I*. Nevertheless, the panel concluded that the U.S. tuna restriction was a GATT violation anyway. Although GATT allows trade measures to be used to regulate commercial activities taking place abroad, it does not allow trade sanctions to be used to coerce regulatory action by other governments. The U.S. was not willing to import "dolphin safe" tuna on a case by case basis. Instead, it was demanding that the Mexican government adopt protective regulations for dolphins. According to the panel, this was impermissible. Although the exact import of this decision is not yet clear, it seems to be an effort to take a more conciliatory attitude toward environmentalist concerns.

2. The WTO has recently decided another similar case, this time involving restrictions on shrimp imports. U.S. law requires shrimp trawlers to use "turtle exclusion devices" to prevent incidental killing of endangered sea turtles by shrimping vessels. Shrimp cannot be exported without a certification that the exporting country has a comparable regulatory program. A GATT panel held the U.S. ban illegal, on the ground that unilateral actions by individual member states would threaten to unravel the entire trade agreement, and thus violated the prohibition on "inappropriate" trade measures in the introductory section of Article XX (the "chapeau"). The panel limited its holding to measures requiring the exporting country to change its own production standards, and distinguished more limited trade measures, even if unilateral, and also trade measures taken pursuant to multilateral agreements. The Appellate Body invalidated the U.S. measure on narrower grounds relating to allegedly unfair methods of implementation. On the jurisdictional issue, it said simply that on the specific facts, "there is a sufficient nexus" between the U.S. and the turtles. United States (Shrimp), 1998 WL 716669, 720123, (WTO App. Body 1998).

3. Should measures like the shrimp and tuna restrictions be seen as simple refusals to consume goods that are considered morally tainted by the importing country? Or should they be considered efforts at coercion of other governments? And is coercion in this context justified or merely cultural imperialism? Consider, for example, the trade sanctions against Taiwan for allowing sale of products derived from endangered species. Eco-globalism or neo-imperialism?

For further discussion, see Daniel A. Farber, "Stretching the Margins: The Geographic Nexus in Environmental Law," 48 *Stan.L.Rev.* 1247 (1996); Howard Chang, "An Economic Analysis of Trade Measures to Protect the Global Environment," 83 *Geo.L.J.* 2131 (1995).

4. Another issue involving trade versus the environment relates to what some have called "environmental dumping." The question is whether firms which are allowed to pollute are thereby being given an unfair cost-advantage. A countervailing tariff might be used to cancel this advantage. For a critical discussion, see Stewart, "Environmental Regulation and International Competitiveness," 102 *Yale L.J.* 2039 (1993). See also D. Esty, *Greening the GATT: Trade, Environment, and the Future* (1994) (a balanced

but environmentally oriented discussion of this and other trade issues). Is allowing a firm to pollute freely the equivalent of a subsidy? If so, a countervailing duty might be consistent with the GATT treatment of subsidies. Consider this "subsidy" question in light of the materials on economics in the opening and final sections of the next chapter.

D. HORIZONTAL FEDERALISM AND PHYSICAL SPILLOVERS

Thus far, in this chapter, we have discussed two topics. The first was "vertical" federalism—the relationship between higher and lower levels of government, such as the federal government and the states. The second was "horizontal" federalism as it relates to economic spillovers— the rules that govern when environmental regulation by one unit of government has adverse economic effects on another unit at the same "level", such as a state regulation which hurts industries in another state or a U.S. regulation that hurts Mexican fishing companies. Our final topic also concerns horizontal federalism, but here the concern is with physical spillovers such as pollution rather than economic ones.

The basic problem is illustrated by a famous international law case, *Trail Smelter Arbitration (U.S. v. Canada)* (1941), 3 UNRIAA 1938 (1949). Sulfur dioxide fumes from a Canadian smelter were causing damage in Washington State. An agreement between Canada and the U.S. called for arbitration of disputes. The tribunal held that Canada was responsible for correcting the problem. "Under the principles of international law," the tribunal said, "no State has the right to use or permit the use of its territory in such a manner as to cause injury by fumes in or to the territory of another or the properties or persons therein, when the case is of serious consequence and the injury is established by clear and convincing evidence." A later case spoke more generally of "every State's obligation not to allow knowingly its territory to be used for acts contrary to the rights of other states." *Corfu Channel Case (U.K. v. Albania)*, 1949 I.C.J. 4. But international authority is sparse because of the relative weakness of the international legal system. Indeed, the *Train Smelter* tribunal relied mostly on U.S. Supreme Court decisions involving litigation between different American states.

Physical spillovers between states within the U.S. should provide the easiest setting for dealing with such problems, since both the discharging and receiving states are subject to the jurisdiction of the federal courts, and if necessary Congress can step in to control the pollution problem. Yet, as we will see, even in the domestic U.S. setting, physical spillovers have created knotty problems, as courts have struggled to find the right institutional mechanism for addressing the spillovers. At one time or another, the Supreme Court has endorsed each of the following approaches: (1) litigation in federal court based on a uniform body of federal common law; (2) litigation in federal court based on state rather than federal law; (3) use of the federal administrative process to prevent violations of the environmental standards of the downstream state. The untidiness of the ultimate solution probably reflects the difficulty of the problem. For an insightful economically based analysis of the issue, see Thomas Merrill, "Golden Rules for Transboundary Pollution," 46 *Duke L.J.* 931 (1997).

We will focus on interstate water pollution. In *Illinois v. Milwaukee,* 406 U.S. 91, 92 S.Ct. 1385, 31 L.Ed.2d 712 (1972) [*Milwaukee I*], the Supreme Court held that interstate pollution violated the federal common law and that nuisance actions could be brought in federal court to redress the violation. In the meantime, a new federal water pollution statute created an elaborate permit system. Permits can be issued by the states under federally approved programs, but remain subject to federal supervision and enforcement and must incorporate pollution limits established in EPA regulations. This raised obvious questions about how to coordinate the nuisance action with the extensive regulations contained in the 1972 statute, which are described in the opinion below and will be explored in detail in the next chapter.

MILWAUKEE v. ILLINOIS [MILWAUKEE II]

Supreme Court of the United States, 1981.
451 U.S. 304, 101 S.Ct. 1784, 68 L.Ed.2d 114.

JUSTICE REHNQUIST delivered the opinion of the Court.

When this litigation was first before us we recognized the existence of a federal "common law" which could give rise to a claim for abatement of a nuisance caused by interstate water pollution. *Illinois v. Milwaukee,* 406 U.S. 91, 92 S.Ct. 1385, 31 L.Ed.2d 712 (1972). Subsequent to our decision, Congress enacted the Federal Water Pollution Control Act Amendments of 1972. We granted certiorari to consider the effect of this legislation on the previously recognized cause of action.

* * *

Federal courts, unlike state courts, are not general common law courts and do not possess a general power to develop and apply their own rules of decision. The enactment of a federal rule in an area of national concern, and the decision whether to displace state law in doing so, is generally made not by the federal judiciary, purposefully insulated from democratic pressures, but by the people through their elected representatives in Congress.

When Congress has not spoken to a particular issue, however, and when there exists a "significant conflict between some federal policy or interest and the use of state law,"[19] the Court has found it necessary, in a "few and restricted" instances to develop a federal common law. Nothing in this process suggests that courts are better suited to develop national policy in areas governed by federal common law than they are

19. In this regard we note the inconsistency in Illinois' argument and the decision of the District Court that both federal and state nuisance law apply to this case. If state law can be applied, there is no need for federal common law; if federal common law exists, it is because state law cannot be used.

in other areas, or that the usual and important concerns of an appropriate division of functions between the Congress and the federal judiciary are inapplicable. * * *

* * *

Contrary to the suggestions of respondents, the appropriate analysis in determining if federal statutory law governs a question previously the subject of federal common law is not the same as that employed in deciding if federal law pre-empts state law. In considering the latter question "we start with the assumption that the historic police powers of the States were not to be superseded by the Federal Act unless that was the clear and manifest purpose of Congress." While we have not hesitated to find preemption of state law, whether express or implied, when Congress has so indicated, or when enforcement of state regulations would impair "federal superintendence of the field," our analysis has included "due regard for the presuppositions of our embracing federal system, including the principle of diffusion of power not as a matter of doctrinaire localism but as a promoter of democracy." Such concerns are not implicated in the same fashion when the question is whether federal statutory or federal common law governs, and accordingly the same sort of evidence of a clear and manifest purpose is not required. Indeed, as noted, in cases such as the present "we start with the assumption" that it is for Congress, not federal courts, to articulate the appropriate standards to be applied as a matter of federal law.[20]

We conclude that, at least so far as concerns the claims of respondents, Congress has not left the formulation of appropriate federal standards to the courts through application of often vague and indeterminate nuisance concepts and maxims of equity jurisprudence, but rather has occupied the field through the establishment of a comprehensive regulatory program supervised by an expert administrative agency. The 1972 amendments to the Federal Water Pollution Control Act were not merely another law "touching interstate waters" of the sort surveyed in *Illinois v. Milwaukee,* and found inadequate to supplant federal common law. Rather, the amendments were viewed by Congress as a "total restructuring" and "complete rewriting" of the existing water pollution legislation considered in that case. Congress' intent in enacting the amendments was clearly to establish an all-encompassing program of water pollution regulation. *Every* point source discharge is prohibited unless covered by a permit, which directly subjects the discharger to the administrative apparatus established by Congress to achieve its goals. The "major purpose" of the amendments was "to establish a *comprehensive* long-range policy for the elimination of water pollution." No Con-

20. Since the States are represented in Congress but not in the federal courts, the very concerns about displacing state law which counsel against finding pre-emption of *state* law in the absence of clear intent actually suggest a willingness to find congressional displacement of *federal* common law. Simply because the opinion in *Illinois v. Milwaukee* used the term "pre-emption," usually employed in determining if federal law displaces state law, is no reason to assume the analysis used to decide the usual federal-state questions is appropriate here.

gressman's remarks on the legislation were complete without reference to the "comprehensive" nature of the amendments. * * * The establishment of such a self-consciously comprehensive program by Congress, which certainly did not exist when *Illinois v. Milwaukee* was decided, strongly suggests that there is no room for courts to attempt to improve on that program with federal common law.

Turning to the particular claims involved in this case, the action of Congress in supplanting the federal common law is perhaps clearest when the question of effluent limitations for discharges from the two treatment plants is considered. The duly issued permits under which the city commission discharges treated sewage from the Jones Island and South Shore treatment plants incorporate, as required by the Act, see § 402(b)(1), the specific effluent limitations established by EPA regulations pursuant to § 301 of the Act. There is thus no question that the problem of effluent limitations has been thoroughly addressed through the administrative scheme established by Congress, as contemplated by Congress. This being so there is no basis for a federal court to impose more stringent limitations than those imposed under the regulatory regime by reference to federal common law, as the District Court did in this case. * * *

* * *

Respondents argue that congressional intent to preserve the federal common law remedy recognized in *Illinois v. Milwaukee* is evident in §§ 510 and 505(e) of the statute. Section 510 provides that nothing in the Act shall preclude States from adopting and enforcing limitations on the discharge of pollutants more stringent than those adopted under the Act. It is one thing, however, to say that States may adopt more stringent limitations through state administrative processes, or even that States may establish such limitations through state nuisance law, and apply them to in-state discharges. It is quite another to say that the States may call upon *federal* courts to employ *federal* common law to establish more stringent standards applicable to out-of-state dischargers. Any standards established under federal common law are federal standards, and so the authority of States to impose more stringent standards under § 510 would not seem relevant. Section 510 clearly contemplates state authority to establish more stringent pollution limitations; nothing in it, however, suggests that this was to be done by federal court actions premised on federal common law.

Subsection 505(e) provides:

"Nothing *in this section* shall restrict any right which any person (or class of persons) may have under any statute or common law to seek enforcement of any effluent standard or limitation or to seek any other relief (including relief against the Administrator or a state agency)" (emphasis supplied).

Respondents argue that this evinces an intent to preserve the federal common law of nuisance. We, however, are inclined to view the quoted provision as meaning what it says: that nothing in § 505, the citizen suit provision, should be read as limiting any other remedies which might exist.

Subsection 505(e) is virtually identical to subsections in the citizen suit provisions of several environmental statutes. The subsection is common language accompanying citizen suit provisions and we think that it means only that the provision of such suit does not revoke other remedies. It most assuredly cannot be read to mean that the Act as a whole does not supplant formerly available federal common law actions but only that the particular section authorizing citizen suits does not do so. No one, however, maintains that the citizen suit provision pre-empts federal common law.

* * *

We therefore conclude that no federal common law remedy was available to respondents in this case. The judgment of the Court of Appeals is therefore vacated, and the case remanded for proceedings consistent with this opinion.

JUSTICE BLACKMUN, with whom JUSTICE MARSHALL and JUSTICE STEVENS join, dissenting.

Nine years ago, this Court unanimously determined that Illinois could bring a federal common-law action against the city of Milwaukee, three other Wisconsin cities, and two sewerage commissions. At that time, Illinois alleged that the discharge of raw and untreated sewage by these Wisconsin entities into Lake Michigan created a public nuisance for the citizens of Illinois. The Court remitted the parties to an appropriate federal district court, "whose powers are adequate to resolve the issues."

Illinois promptly initiated the present litigation, and pursued it through more than three years of pretrial discovery, a six-month trial that entailed hundreds of exhibits and scores of witnesses, extensive factual findings by the District Court and an exhaustive review of the evidence by the Court of Appeals. Today, the Court decides that this nine-year judicial exercise has been just a meaningless charade, inasmuch as, it says, the federal common law remedy approved in *Illinois v. Milwaukee* was implicitly extinguished by Congress just six months after the 1972 decision. Because I believe that Congress intended no such extinction, and surely did not contemplate the result reached by the Court today, I respectfully dissent.

* * *

[The Clean Water Act] sets forth certain effluent limitations. As did the Court of Appeals, a court applying federal common law in a given instance may well decline to impose effluent limitations more stringent than those required by Congress, because the complainant has failed to show that stricter standards will abate the nuisance or appreciably diminish the threat of injury. But it is a far different proposition to pronounce, as does the Court today, that federal courts *"lack authority to impose more stringent effluent limitations under federal common law than those imposed"* under the statutory scheme. The authority of the federal courts in this area was firmly established by the decision in *Illinois v. Milwaukee.* In delineating the legitimate scope of the federal common law, the Court there expressly noted the relevance of state standards, adding that "a State with high water-quality standards *may well ask that its strict standards be honored* and *that it not be compelled to lower itself* to the more degrading standards of a neighbor." (Emphasis added.) The Act attributes comparable respect to the strict effluent limitation levels imposed by individual States. § 510. Since both the Court and Congress fully expected that neighboring States might differ in their approaches to the regulation of the discharge of pollutants into their navigable waters, it is odd, to say the least, that federal courts should now be deprived of the common law power to effect a reconciliation of these differences.

Notes

1. In *Milwaukee II,* the defendant was in compliance with the requirements of the Clean Water Act. In *Middlesex County Sewerage Authority v. National Sea Clammers Association,* 453 U.S. 1, 101 S.Ct. 2615, 69 L.Ed.2d 435 (1981), the Court extended *Milwaukee II* by holding that even a defendant who is violating the Act is immune from federal nuisance liability. The lower courts have also given *Milwaukee II* an expansive reading. See, e.g., *Conner v. Aerovox, Inc.,* 730 F.2d 835 (1st Cir.1984) (Clean Water Act preempts federal maritime law).

2. On remand, the Seventh Circuit held that application of Illinois nuisance law to the interstate pollution originating in Wisconsin was also preempted by the Clean Water Act. *State of Illinois v. Milwaukee,* 731 F.2d 403 (7th Cir.1984), cert. denied 469 U.S. 1196, 105 S.Ct. 979, 83 L.Ed.2d 981 (1985). This issue reached the Supreme Court in the next case.

INTERNATIONAL PAPER COMPANY v. OUELLETTE

Supreme Court of the United States, 1987.
479 U.S. 481, 107 S.Ct. 805, 93 L.Ed.2d 883.

[The defendant operated a pulp and paper mill on the New York side of Lake Champlain. Its discharge pipe ran from the mill through the water toward Vermont, ending just before the state line that divides the lake. The plaintiffs owned or rented land on the Vermont shore. They filed suit in state court for compensatory and punitive damages, as well as an injunction requiring the defendant to restructure part of its water treatment system. The action was removed to federal district court. The trial court held that Vermont nuisance law was applicable and was not preempted by the Clean Water Act. The Second Circuit affirmed, relying on the savings clauses in sections 505(e) and 510.]

JUSTICE POWELL delivered the opinion of the court.

To begin with, the plain language of the provisions on which respondents rely by no means compels the result they seek. Section

505(e) merely says that "nothing *in this section,*" i.e., the citizen-suit provisions, shall affect an injured party's right to seek relief under state law; it does not purport to preclude preemption of state law by other provisions of the Act. Section 510, moreover, preserves the authority of a State "with respect to the waters (including boundary waters) of such State[ ]." This language arguably limits the effect of the clause to discharges flowing *directly* into a State's own waters, i.e., discharges from within the State. The savings clause then, does not preclude preemption of the law of an affected State.

Given that the Act itself does not speak directly to the issue, the Court must be guided by the goals and policies of the Act in determining whether it in fact preempts an action based on the law of an affected State. After examining the CWA as a whole, its purposes and its history, we are convinced that if affected States were allowed to impose separate discharge standards on a single point source, the inevitable result would be a serious interference with the achievement of the "full purposes and objectives of Congress." Because we do not believe Congress intended to undermine this carefully drawn statute through a general saving clause, we conclude that the CWA precludes a court from applying the law of an affected State against an out-of-state source.

In determining whether Vermont nuisance law "stands as an obstacle" to the full implementation of the CWA, it is not enough to say that the ultimate goal of both federal and state law is to eliminate water pollution. A state law also is preempted if it interferes with the methods by which the federal statute was designed to reach this goal. In this case the application of Vermont law against IPC would allow respondents to circumvent the NPDES permit system, thereby upsetting the balance of public and private interests so carefully addressed by the Act.

By establishing a permit system for effluent discharges, Congress implicitly has recognized that the goal of the CWA—elimination of water pollution—cannot be achieved immediately, and that it cannot be realized without incurring costs. The EPA Administrator issues permits according to established effluent standards and water quality standards, that in turn are based upon available technology, and competing public and industrial uses. The Administrator must consider the impact of the discharges on the waterway, the types of effluents, and the schedule for compliance, each of which may vary widely among sources. If a State elects to impose its own standards, it also must consider the technological feasibility of more stringent controls. Given the nature of these complex decisions, it is not surprising that the Act limits the right to administer the permit system to the EPA and the source States.

An interpretation of the saving clause that preserved actions brought under an affected State's law would disrupt this balance of interests. If a New York source were liable for violations of Vermont law, that law could effectively override both the permit requirements and the policy choices made by the source State. The affected State's nuisance laws would subject the point source to the threat of legal and equitable penalties if the permit standards were less stringent than those imposed by the affected State. Such penalties would compel the source to adopt different control standards and a different compliance schedule from those approved by the EPA, even though the affected State had not engaged in the same weighing of the costs and benefits. This case illustrates the problems with such a rule. If the Vermont Court ruled that respondents were entitled to the full amount of damages and injunctive relief sought in the complaint, at a minimum IPC would have to change its methods of doing business and controlling pollution to avoid the threat of ongoing liability. In suits such as this, an affected-state court also could require the source to cease operations by ordering immediate abatement. Critically, these liabilities would attach even though the source had complied fully with its state and federal permit obligations. The inevitable result of such suits would be that Vermont and other States could do indirectly what they could not do directly—regulate the conduct of out-of-state sources.

Application of an affected State's law to an out-of-state source also would undermine the important goals of efficiency and predictability in the permit system. The history of the 1972 amendments shows that Congress intended to establish "clear and identifiable" discharge standards. As noted above, under the reading of the saving clause proposed by respondents, a source would be subject to a variety of common-law rules established by the different States along the interstate waterways. These nuisance standards often are "vague" and "indeterminate." The application of numerous States' laws would only exacerbate the vagueness and resulting uncertainty. * * *

* * *

Our conclusion that Vermont nuisance law is inapplicable to a New York point source does not leave respondents without a remedy. The CWA precludes only those suits that may require standards of effluent control that are incompatible with those established by the procedures set forth in the Act. The saving clause specifically preserves other state actions, and therefore nothing in the Act bars aggrieved individuals from bringing a nuisance claim pursuant to the law of the *source* State. By its terms the CWA allows States such as New York to impose higher standards on its own point sources, and in *Milwaukee II* we recognized that this authority may include the right to impose higher common-law as well as higher statutory restrictions.

An action brought against IPC under New York nuisance law would not frustrate the goals of the CWA as would a suit governed by Vermont law. First, application of the source State's law does not disturb the balance among federal, source-state, and affected-state interests. Because the Act specifically allows source States to impose stricter standards, the imposition of source-state law does not disrupt the regulatory partnership established by the permit system. Second, the restriction of suits to those brought under source-state nuisance law prevents a source from being subject to an indeterminate number of potential regulations.

Although New York nuisance law may impose separate standards and thus create some tension with the permit system, a source only is required to look to a single additional authority, whose rules should be relatively predictable. Moreover, States can be expected to take into account their own nuisance laws in setting permit requirements.

IPC asks the Court to go one step further and hold that all state-law suits also must be brought in source-state *courts*. As petitioner cites little authority or justification for this position, we find no basis for holding that Vermont is an improper forum. Simply because a cause of action is preempted does not mean that judicial jurisdiction over the claim is affected as well; the Act pre-empts laws, not courts. In the absence of statutory authority to the contrary, the rule is settled that a district court sitting in diversity is competent to apply the law of a foreign State.

Notes

1. If the Court had gone the other way regarding application of Vermont law, wouldn't we have come full circle? *Milwaukee I* established federal common law to replace state nuisance law; *Milwaukee II* preempted the federal common law; an affirmance in *Ouellette* would have resurrected the multitude of state laws the Court had buried in *Milwaukee I*. Of course, the answer may be that the mistake was made earlier in the chain—some of the Justices would have argued that the crucial mistake was *Milwaukee II*. But given the *Milwaukee* opinions, a contrary result in the final case of the trilogy would have been decidedly peculiar.

2. Professor Rodgers reports on the interesting settlement agreement reached in the *Ouellette* case:

> The settlement agreement in *Ouellette* shows that there is some room for creative plaintiffs even under the Supreme Court's extravagant notions of preemption. The agreement calls for payment in the nature of "permanent damages" (as the term is used in *Boomer* [p. 290 infra]) as "full compensation" for the granting of an "equitable servitude" for operations of the Ticonderoga Mill with respect to the lakeshore property of the Settlement Class. A Settlement Fund of $5 million is established, in "full settlement" of past, present, and future claims. Payable out of the Fund are attorney's fees not to exceed $1,633,333 plus reasonable expenses (estimated not to exceed $100,000). A single payment of $500,000 is made to the South Lake Champlain Charitable Trust, which is established "to promote the advancement of scientific knowledge with respect to the environment of the South Lake Champlain area through grant for research, scientific study, and education."

W. Rodgers, *Environmental Law* 288 (2d ed. 1994). Allocation among the over 250 plaintiffs was to be made using a point system.

3. Does *Ouellette* apply to air pollution? See *Her Majesty The Queen In Right of the Province of Ontario v. City of Detroit*, 874 F.2d 332 (6th Cir.1989) (allowing an action by Ontario under the Michigan Environmental Protection Act to enjoin the construction of Detroit's proposed garbage burner). A dissent argued that *Ouellette* allows state law injunctions if a

source's pollution causes damage, but not an injunction before the source is constructed. Id. at 346–347 (Boggs, J., dissenting).

4. Suppose New York responded by exempting paper mills from nuisance liability? Would this raise constitutional issues? See *Bormann v. Board of Supervisors*, 584 N.W.2d 309 (Iowa 1998) (similar exemption invalid).

5. *Milwaukee II* invokes attractive concepts of judicial competence, legislative supremacy, and federalism. In light of *Ouellette*, has the Court actually furthered any of these goals? For a negative answer, see Farber & Frickey, "In the Shadow of the Legislature: The Common Law in the Age of the New Public Law," 89 *Mich.L.Rev.* 875 (1991). Note that *Ouellette* provides a cause of action for violating the *source* state's standards but no forum for complaints based on a *receiving* state's desire to have higher water quality. But, as the next case shows, that claim may obtain a hearing elsewhere.

ARKANSAS v. OKLAHOMA

Supreme Court of the United States, 1992.
503 U.S. 91, 112 S.Ct. 1046, 117 L.Ed.2d 239.

JUSTICE STEVENS delivered the opinion of the Court.

[An Arkansas sewage treatment plant received an EPA permit to discharge into a stream that ultimately flows (via some creeks) into the Illinois River 22 miles upstream of the Oklahoma border. The state of Oklahoma challenged the permit before an EPA hearing officer, on the ground that the discharge violated Oklahoma's water quality standards, which allow no degradation of water quality in that portion of the Illinois River. EPA granted the permit after concluding that the discharge would cause no detectable change in water quality. The Court of Appeals ruled, however, that a permit cannot be issued if the proposed discharge would contribute to an existing violation of water quality standards.]

The parties have argued three analytically distinct questions concerning the interpretation of the Clean Water Act. First, does the Act require the EPA, in crafting and issuing a permit to a point source in one State, to apply the water quality standards of downstream States? Second, even if the Act does not require as much, does the Agency have the statutory authority to mandate such compliance? Third, does the Act provide, as the Court of Appeals held, that once a body of water fails to meet water quality standards no discharge that yields effluent that reach the degraded waters will be permitted?

In this case, it is neither necessary nor prudent for us to resolve the first of these questions. In issuing the Fayetteville permit, the EPA assumed it was obligated by both the Act and its own regulations to ensure that the Fayetteville discharge would not violate Oklahoma's standards. As we discuss below, this assumption was permissible and reasonable and therefore there is no need for us to address whether the Act requires as much. Moreover, much of the analysis and argument in the briefs of the parties relies on statutory provisions that govern not only federal permits issued pursuant to §§ 401(a) and 402(a), but also state permits issued under § 402(b). It seems unwise to evaluate those arguments in a case such as this one, which only involves a federal permit.

Our decision not to determine at this time the scope of the Agency's statutory obligations does not affect our resolution of the second question, which concerns the Agency's statutory authority. Even if the Clean Water Act itself does not require the Fayetteville discharge to comply with Oklahoma's water quality standards, the statute clearly does not limit the EPA's authority to mandate such compliance.

Since 1973, EPA regulations have provided that an NPDES permit shall not be issued "[w]hen the imposition of conditions cannot ensure compliance with the applicable water quality requirements of all affected States." Those regulations—relied upon by the EPA in the issuance of the Fayetteville permit—constitute a reasonable exercise of the Agency's statutory authority.

* * *

Notwithstanding this apparent reasonableness, Arkansas argues that our description in *Ouellette* [supra p. 271] of the role of affected States in the permit process and our characterization of the affected States' position as "subordinate," indicates that the EPA's application of the Oklahoma standards was error. We disagree. Our statement in *Ouellette* concerned only an affected State's input into the permit process; that input is clearly limited by the plain language of § 402(b). Limits on an affected State's direct participation in permitting decisions, however, do not in any way constrain the EPA's authority to require a point source to comply with downstream water quality standards.

Arkansas also argues that regulations requiring compliance with downstream standards are at odds with the legislative history of the Act and with the statutory scheme established by the Act. Although we agree with Arkansas that the Act's legislative history indicates that Congress intended to grant the Administrator discretion in his oversight of the issuance of NPDES permits, we find nothing in that history to indicate that Congress intended to preclude the EPA from establishing a general requirement that such permits be conditioned to ensure compliance with downstream water quality standards.

Similarly, we agree with Arkansas that in the Clean Water Act Congress struck a careful balance among competing policies and interests, but do not find the EPA regulations concerning the application of downstream water quality standards at all incompatible with that balance. Congress, in crafting the Act, protected certain sovereign interests of the States; for example, § 510 allows States to adopt more demanding pollution-control standards than those established under the Act. Arkansas emphasizes that § 510 preserves such state authority only as it is applied to the waters of the regulating State. Even assuming Arkansas's construction of § 510 is correct, that section only concerns state authority and does not constrain the EPA's authority to promulgate reasonable regulations requiring point sources in one State to comply with water quality standards in downstream States.

For these reasons, we find the EPA's requirement that the Fayetteville discharge comply with Oklahoma's water quality standards to be a reasonable exercise of the Agency's substantial statutory discretion.

The Court of Appeals construed the Clean Water Act to prohibit any discharge of effluent that would reach waters already in violation of existing water quality standards. We find nothing in the Act to support this reading.

The interpretation of the statute adopted by the court had not been advanced by any party during the agency or court proceedings. Moreover, the Court of Appeals candidly acknowledged that its theory "has apparently never before been addressed by a federal court." The only statutory provision the court cited to support its legal analysis was § 402(h), which merely authorizes the EPA (or a state permit program) to prohibit a publicly owned treatment plant that is violating a condition of its NPDES permit from accepting any additional pollutants for treatment until the ongoing violation has been corrected. Although the Act contains several provisions directing compliance with state water quality standards, the parties have pointed to nothing that mandates a complete ban on discharges into a waterway that is in violation of those standards. The statute does, however, contain provisions designed to remedy existing water quality violations and to allocate the burden of reducing undesirable discharges between existing sources and new sources. Thus, rather than establishing the categorical ban announced by the Court of Appeals—which might frustrate the construction of new plants that would improve existing conditions—the Clean Water Act vests in the EPA and the States broad authority to develop long-range, area-wide programs to alleviate and eliminate existing pollution. To the extent that the Court of Appeals relied on its interpretation of the Act to reverse the EPA's permitting decision, that reliance was misplaced.

* * *

In sum, the Court of Appeals made a policy choice that it was not authorized to make. Arguably, as that court suggested, it might be wise to prohibit any discharge into the Illinois River, even if that discharge would have no adverse impact on water quality. But it was surely not arbitrary for the EPA to conclude—given the benefits to the River from the increased flow of relatively clean water and the benefits achieved in Arkansas by allowing the new plant to operate as designed—that allowing the discharge would be even wiser. It is not our role, or that of the Court of Appeals, to decide which policy choice is the better one, for it is clear that Congress has entrusted such decisions to the Environmental Protection Agency.

Notes

1. The Court leaves open the question of whether state-issued permits (as opposed to the EPA permit in the case) must comply with the water

quality standards of downstream states. Given the Court's deference to EPA's regulations, however, there seems to be a strong case for extending the ruling to state permits.

Many states receive more than half of their water pollution from neighboring states, yet major differences exist between permit standards among states. For instance, Pennsylvania's criterion for arsenic was 2500 times more stringent than New York's. This situation has given rise to increasing concern about disparities, and may result in mounting efforts to take advantage of the *Arkansas* opinion to impose restraints on "underregulated" out-of-state sources. See GAO, "Water Pollution: Differences Among the States in Issuing Permits Limiting the Discharge of Pollutants" (Jan. 1996 Gao/RCED–96–42). For some doubts about the efficacy of the Clean Water Act as construed in *Arkansas v. Oklahoma*, see Glicksman, "Watching the River Flow: The Prospects for Improved Interstate Water Pollution Control," 43 *J.Urb. & Contemp.L.* 119 (1993).

Note on Interstate Spillovers under the Clean Air Act

Spillovers are most obvious in the case of water pollution: what is dumped into the Mississippi at St. Paul will probably eventually reach New Orleans. Air pollution was long considered a more localized problem, but spillover effects have increasingly become the focus of regulation there as well.

These spillover effects first gained widespread public attention in connection with the problem of acid rain. The dimensions of the transport problem were suggested in an article by an EPA official, discussing the clockwise movement of plumes from Ohio Valley power plants through Illinois, Iowa and Minnesota, over the Great Lakes and Canada, down through New England, and out over the Atlantic.[k] Naturally, transport is facilitated by use of tall smokestacks to meet standards near the source.

The EPA estimated that sulfur oxides and nitrogen oxides account for 14 percent (27.4 million metric tons) and 12 percent, respectively, of total air pollution in the United States. Although other pollutants also are precursors to acid rain, these two oxides are the major contributors. Sulfur oxides are emitted primarily from stationary sources, such as smelters and power plants, which burn coal as a fuel. Nitrogen oxides come from stationary sources using fossil fuels (56 percent) and from motor vehicles (40 percent). The most common sulfur and nitrogen oxides, sulfur dioxide (SO_2) and nitric oxide (NO), after being discharged into the atmosphere, can be chemically converted by oxidation into sulfuric and nitric acids, which may return to the earth as components of rain or snow.[l] Some of the effects were described by the EPA:

> Hundreds of lakes in North America and Scandinavia have become so acidic that they can no longer support fish life. More than 90 lakes in

k. Corrado, "Midwest 'in the soup'," *Environmental Midwest* (U.S.EPA, Region V), July 1979, p. 12. For recent information on regional transport, see Schwartz, "Acid Deposition: Unraveling a Regional Phenomenon," 243 *Science* 753 (1989).

l. U.S. EPA, *Acid Rain* 2 (Research Summary, 1979). For more recent scientific findings, see Hedin & Likens, "Atmospheric Dust and Acid Rain," *Scientific American*, Dec. 1996, at 88.

the Adirondack mountains in New York State are fishless because acidic conditions have inhibited reproduction. Recent data indicate that other areas of the United States, such as northern Minnesota and Wisconsin, may be vulnerable to similar adverse impacts.

While many of the aquatic effects of acid precipitation have been well documented, data related to possible terrestrial impacts are just beginning to be developed. Preliminary research indicates that the yield from agricultural crops can be reduced as a result of both the direct effects of acids on foliage, and the indirect effects resulting from the leaching of minerals from soils. The productivity of forests may be affected in a similar manner.

In addition, acid deposition is contributing to the destruction of stone monuments and statuary throughout the world. The 2500 year old Parthenon and other classical buildings on the Acropolis in Athens, Greece, have shown much more rapid decay in this century as a result of the city's high air pollution levels. Research is underway to clarify the role of acid rain in the destruction.[m]

The principal provisions of the Clean Air Act aimed at interstate pollution are §§ 110(a)(2)(E) and 126. Several states invoked these sections in petitions to and suits against the EPA, without tangible results. In *New England Legal Foundation v. Costle,* 475 F.Supp. 425 (D.Conn.1979), Connecticut plaintiffs sued the EPA Administrator and a New York public utility, seeking declaratory and injunctive relief from air pollution allegedly originating in New York and New Jersey. EPA was claimed to have failed in its statutory duty to revise New York and New Jersey air pollution plans, in order to abate transport of pollutants to Connecticut. (As we explore in detail in Chapter IV, the Clean Air Act directs EPA to establish national air quality standards and then to supervise state-issued plans to attain the standards.) The court held that EPA had no "mandatory duty at this time" and dismissed all causes of action against the Administrator.[n] *New England Legal Foundation v. Costle* was affirmed at 632 F.2d 936 (2d Cir.1980) and 666 F.2d 30 (2d Cir.1981). In another case, *Connecticut v. EPA,* 656 F.2d 902 (2d Cir.1981), New York had submitted for EPA approval a revision in its air pollution plan allowing a utility company to burn high sulfur oil for one year, and Connecticut and New Jersey had responded by filing protest petitions under section 126(b). With the court's approval, EPA approved the state plan revision before ruling on the § 126 petitions.

The Sixth Circuit commented on the difficulty of resolving interstate disputes under the 1977 statute:

In a most practical sense, [the plaintiff's] concerns are understandable. There would appear to be a patent unfairness in an Agency policy which would tolerate so much higher a level of SO_2 emissions in one area than in another, especially given the high costs which [plaintiff] has

---

m. Id. at 1.

n. 10 *Envir.Rep.* 1040–41 (1979). Subsequently Pennsylvania brought suit against EPA in the United States Court of Appeals for the Sixth Circuit, seeking to compel the Agency to revise the Ohio SIP and to stop what Pennsylvania called uncontrolled air pollution at two Ohio power plants, resulting in acid rain in Pennsylvania. 10 *Envir.Rep.* 2093 (1980).

already incurred to reduce its own pollution. Nevertheless, we believe that the construction placed upon the statute by the EPA appears to be literally correct, even though arguably at odds with the important policy values represented by the 1977 amendments. This conclusion, and our strong preference to achieve an interpretation of the Act which is consistent among the several circuits, compels us to agree with the Agency here.

It may be that the problem of interstate air pollution abatement requires an effective regional regulative scheme rather than the present unsatisfying reliance upon state boundaries as the basic unit for pollution control. However, we have neither the legislative authority to amend the statute nor the regulatory and technical expertise to set more specific technical standards. As long as the statute mandates that implementation plans be created and reviewed on the basis of state boundaries, there will be differences between the emission limitations imposed by neighboring states. * * * [W]e conclude that we do not possess the statutory or regulatory expertise to grant any relief.

Air Pollution Control District v. United States EPA, 739 F.2d 1071, 1088, 1094 (6th Cir.1984). Consequently, the court held that the emitting state had not been shown to "substantially contribute" to nonattainment in the receiving state. Note that the emitting state placed no emission limit at all on the main pollution source involved. See Comment, "Jefferson County's Lament, Clean Air Act Offers No Relief for Interstate Pollution," 14 *ELR* 10298 (1984).[o]

Under the Reagan Administration, acid rain became a highly controversial, heavily politicized issue. The Administration's position was that no action on the acid rain problem was advisable until a considerable amount of further study. Hence, the Administration opposed congressionally proposed control programs and refused to take action in cooperation with the Canadians on the problem. See 14 *Envir.Rep.,* 2205 (1984); "Canada Announces New Effort to Cut Acid Rain," *New York Times,* March 8, 1984.

The political deadlock was broken during the Bush Administration with the passage of the 1990 Clean Air Act. As we will see at the end of the next chapter where this provision is discussed in more detail, Congress entirely bypassed the existing mechanism for resolving interstate disputes and established a new system to reduce sulfur dioxide emissions nationwide.

In the meantime, Congress also made some changes to strengthen sections 110 and 126. As amended, the provisions allowed EPA to intervene if it found that an upwind state "significantly" contributed to a nonattainment or if it would prevent the maintenance of nationally required air standards. Congress also expanded the types of sources covered and allowed

o. The quest to obtain some legal remedy for interstate pollution continued despite these defeats. In *State of New York v. United States EPA,* 852 F.2d 574 (D.C.Cir.1988), *State of New York v. Administrator, United States EPA,* 710 F.2d 1200 (6th Cir.1983), and *New York v. EPA,* 716 F.2d 440 (7th Cir.1983), these later efforts were also rejected. Efforts to obtain relief from international acid rain were no more successful, see *Her Majesty the Queen in Right of Ontario v. United States EPA,* 912 F.2d 1525 (D.C.Cir.1990). It seems clear that, as construed by the courts, the Act allowed EPA to ignore the problem of interstate pollution as long as it wanted.

for aggregating emissions from multiple sources in determining the need for intervention. See Patton, "The New Air Quality Standards, Regional Haze, and Interstate Air Pollution Transport," 28 *Env.L.Rep.* 10155, 10179–80 (1998). Still, it seemed unclear that these provisions would ever see significant use, given the history of EPA reluctance to invoke them.

Congress also established a special forum for the affected states to deal with one major spillover effect: the long-range transfer of pollutants causing ozone problems in the Northeast. Nitrogen oxides (NOx) emissions in other regions resulted in the creation of ozone, which was transported hundreds of miles into the Northeast. This long-range transport made it impossible for the Northeast states to attain the federally mandated air quality standard for ozone. Under EPA's own interpretation of the statute, however, ozone transport was not really an excuse for nonattainment, see *Southwestern Penn. Growth Alliance v. Browner*, 121 F.3d 106 (3d Cir.1997). EPA dodged the compliance requirement, avoiding sanctions against the downwind states, but doing nothing to solve the problem.

The 1990 Amendments established a commission of the states in the transport area. Those states distrusted EPA, which was given the power to disapprove their recommendations only if it could carry a "heavy burden" of justification. The ozone commission voted to recommend that EPA impose extremely strict standards on car emissions throughout the region. Although EPA's effort to follow this recommendation was blocked by litigation,[p] it devised a voluntary program with much the same impact. This program was the result of complex negotiations between EPA, the states, and the auto industry. Patton, supra, at 10178–79.

Another effort to control ozone was made under the auspices of § 126. The downwind states filed petitions naming several hundred sources of nitrogen oxide in the East and Midwest. The petitions demanded 75% reduction in emissions from many of the sources. EPA's initial response was more favorable than had been the case with prior § 126 petitions. EPA was able to gain the support of an advisory group of state environmental officials, allowing it to claim broad state support for a more aggressive stance. Final EPA action is scheduled in mid–1999. See 26 *Env.Rep.* 2646 (Apr. 4, 1998).

As with water pollution, interstate air pollution has been handled only with great difficulty, because the statutory scheme is largely geared toward a state-by-state approach to achieving air standards. When air pollution fails to respect state lines, institutional innovation is required to deal with the spillover effects. These institutional innovations are particularly troublesome legislatively because it is clear in advance who will be the winners (downwind states) and losers (upwind states). This creates a "zero sum" political situation in which conflict is guaranteed, consensus is difficult, and deadlock is likely. Thus, even in the context of a federal union with strong centralized government, interjurisdictional spillovers are difficult to control.

On the international level, the problems are magnified, particularly when the spillovers involve the global commons as a whole. Thus, it is no surprise that negotiating and implementing the Kyoto Protocol for the greenhouse effect has been so difficult. The U.S. domestic experience with

p. See *Commonwealth of Virginia v. EPA*, 108 F.3d 1397 (D.C.Cir. 1997).

spillovers does not give rise to optimism about this process. See "Nations Now Must Focus on Details of Signing, Ratifying, Implementing Kyoro Protocol," 21 *Int'l Env.Rep.* 124 (1998); Campbell & Carpenter, "From Kyoto to Buenos Aires: Implementing the Kyoto Protocol on Climate Change," 21 *Int'l Env.Rep.* 748 (1998). On the other hand, the fact that the international community has managed to make even as much progress as it has, gains added significance once we appreciate the barriers to dealing with spillovers.

Chapter IV

POLLUTION CONTROL

As we saw in Chapter I, air and water pollution have caused significant health effects and other damage. Even putting aside the special difficulties posed by cross-boundary pollution, which we have already considered, controlling pollution is no simple challenge. This chapter will consider the regulatory schemes that have attempted to respond to this problem.

Those regulatory schemes are highly complex, and one purpose of the chapter is simply to convey a working knowledge of the major federal statutes. But the larger purpose is to explore the role of cost and technological feasibility in environmental protection. Pollution control would be easy if it were costless. Unfortunately, it almost always imposes costs on someone. A key policy issue in pollution law is how these costs should affect the level of pollution control. A closely related question involves institutional design. Apart from the ultimate question of how much control should be required at what price, there is also the question of process: who should make these decisions and with what procedures?

We will begin by considering these issues in the context of the common law of nuisance. We will then consider the two major regulatory methodologies used in federal pollution statutes.[a] One form of regulation sets a target for environmental quality and works backwards to determine the restrictions on individual sources. The other form focuses on the source's economic and technological capacity to control pollution. Finally, we will consider moves away from direct regulation toward market-based solutions, as well as other proposals for regulatory reform. Before examining these solutions in depth, we use some thought experiments to explore the problem in more depth.

a. We will defer two regulatory topics involving the major pollution statutes until later in the book: toxics regulation by the Clean Air Act will be discussed in Chapter VI and wetlands protection by the Clean Water Act is covered in Chapter VIII. In addition, Chapter VII covers a number of issues relating to enforcement actions under these pollution statutes.

Trade–Offs Between Environment and Economics: Three Scenarios

To give you a starting point in thinking about tradeoffs between cost and environmental protection, we will begin by sketching three alternative approaches to the issue. In order to provide a concrete context, we will present each approach in a scenario involving a fictional water pollutant, which we will call "kryptonia." All of the legislation and regulations discussed in these scenarios are also fictitious, though you will see later that they have some resemblance to actual statutes. We will use each scenario to explore the pros and cons of the major regulatory options.

Scenario #1: Protection at all Cost

The public was shocked by reports that kryptonia discharges from paper mills were endangering not only fish but birds such as eagles that live on fish. This concern turned into open alarm when the press reported the story of Corinth, a New York town that drew its drinking supply from the Ithaca River. Just upstream of the town, a large paper mill had operated in the 1940s and 1950s without any pollution control whatsoever, with the predictable result of causing extremely high kryptonia levels in the river. In the 1980s, the town reported a cluster of cases of a rare and highly fatal variety of stomach cancer. Calls for stringent legislation followed immediately.

In Congress, a bill was immediately introduced calling for the elimination of all kryptonia discharges within ten years. Supporters of the legislation argued that human life and the natural environment are both priceless: No one has the right to contaminate the public's water bodies for their own private profit. Our society, they said, needs to decide whether it values nature and human beings or the unfettered pursuit of profit; in the end, the health of the planet must come ahead of the balance sheet of industry.

In response, the paper industry and its sympathizers questioned the risks posed by kryptonia and argued that the proposed ban would close important segments of the paper industry, with the loss of thousands of jobs. "Isn't the right of communities and individuals to economic security an important value?" they asked. They contended that some of the scientific studies had flawed methodologies, and that the Corinth situation was probably a statistical fluke. They also argued that no technology exists for eliminating kryptonia discharges and complained that they were being asked to achieve the scientifically impossible.

Supporters of the bill replied by pointing out that technology is not static. As the Senate sponsor of the bill said:

> Given a sufficiently strong incentive to devote their research to the subject, the multi-billion dollar paper industry will succeed in finding new control technologies. True, the scientific studies about kryptonia's risks were not definitive. But society shouldn't have to wait for a body count—whether of people or bald eagles—to take

strong preventive action. Nor should such urgent legislation be side-tracked by the complaints of special interest groups. Business as usual just isn't good enough, given the ecological crisis faced by our society. Moreover, one of the major impacts of kryptonia is on Indian tribes that were heavily dependent on fishing as a source of revenue, so we must also face the issue of environmental racism.

In the end, Congress passed the "Freedom from Kryptonia Act of 1995." It required the complete elimination of all kryptonia discharges by 2005. As a concession to the fears of the paper industry, the industry was given the right to petition for a four-year extension if it could demonstrate by clear and convincing evidence that no control technology could be implemented by 2005 and that no imminent danger to human health or environment would be created by the extension.

Liberal commentators applauded the act as a victory for moral values over greed. Conservatives viewed it as an exercise in environmental zealotry. They also questioned whether, in the end, Congress would have the political will to destroy thousands of jobs or cripple an important industry. Industry immediately increased funding for research and development of control technologies—as well as funding for legal and lobbying challenges to the statute.

Scenario #2: Best Achievable Technology (BAT)

In this scenario, the kryptonia issue was more diffuse, with no cancer outbreak in upstate New York or eagle die-off to crystallize public opposition. Instead, concern about kryptonia built slowly over about a decade. Also, instead of being limited to a particular industry, kryptonia discharges came from a broad range of industrial sources, some of them discharging directly into rivers and lakes, and others into municipal sewage systems. Concern mounted, however, as growing evidence indicated that kryptonia might seriously impact the ecologies of some streams and posed at least a potential hazard to human health.

As in the first scenario, some environmentalists argued that a complete ban was needed, while many representatives of the industry argued against taking any regulatory action until more information was available. EPA argued for an intermediate course: requiring all kryptonia sources to install the best practical pollution control. Under the proposed legislation, EPA would issue regulations that would specify the best available pollution control (BAT) for each category of sources. Not surprisingly, some environmentalists attacked the legislation as a "sell out," while industry-sympathizers pointed to it as an example of the cancerous growth of government regulations and bureaucracy. They also expressed alarm about the effect of this burdensome regulation on the paper industry, which has been subject to increasingly severe competition from Canada because of free trade agreements.

Among the most articulate—though least politically powerful—opponents of the proposed legislation were economists. They had two major criticisms. First, they said, it makes no sense to require the use of the same control technology for each plant within an industrial category. Some plants might be polluting drinking-water supplies or discharging into small bodies of water where the ecological and health effects would be dramatic. These plants should be subject to stringent controls. But other plants might be discharging into large water bodies such as the Pacific with minimal effect, and they should not be required to spend as much on pollution control. Second, the economists argued, EPA really did not have the expertise to decide on the most appropriate level of pollution control, since most of the relevant information about costs and technologies was in the possession of the industry. The economists questioned whether EPA would be capable of effectively carrying out its assignment.

At the other end of the spectrum, "deep ecologists" argued that efforts to deal with pollution on a piecemeal solution are bound to fail. In this particular instance, kryptonia is only one of the environmental impacts of paper production, ranging from destruction of forests at one end of the process to massive solid waste at the other. Only a drastic decrease in the amount of paper produced and consumed can really address these issues.

The final legislation, known as the "Kryptonia Control Act of 1995," required the implementation of BAT by industry within ten years. Some concessions to critics were included, however. To quell environmentalist concerns, EPA was given the option of imposing a complete ban on kryptonia discharges by categories of sources that posed an imminent risk to health or environment. Also, in response to concerns that EPA would drag its feet, EPA was given one year to put regulations in place covering all industries. In response to industry concerns, a variance provision was included, whereby a particular plant could obtain a five year extension by showing that immediate compliance was unreasonably burdensome.

No changes were made in response to the economists or the deep ecologists. They were considered too politically insignificant to be worth placating. Also, EPA's pleas for a budget increase to cover its new responsibilities fell on deaf ears.

Scenario #3: Cost–Benefit Analysis

In this scenario, as in the last one, concerns about the risks of kryptonia grew gradually over a decade. Some studies indicated that in small lakes kryptonia might accumulate to the point of eliminating most fish. Also, some animal studies and a few statistical epidemiological studies suggested that stomach cancer rates in the general population might be elevated significantly as a result of kryptonia entering into the diet and drinking supply. Political pressure grew to take action regarding kryptonia, including some calls for new legislation.

EPA took the position that no new legislation was necessary. Instead, it took action under existing legislation providing it authority to regulate chemicals that pose "an unreasonable risk to health or environment." Under the EPA proposal, kryptonia levels would be reduced by 50% over a five-year period, at which point more stringent controls would be considered.

Because EPA's proposal was considered a major regulatory action, EPA produced a regulatory impact analysis, which was submitted to OMB (the Office of Management and Budget). OMB rejected EPA's analysis on three grounds. First, EPA had consistently used the highest possible estimates of risk, some of which were derived from studies that OMB considered methodologically weak. Second, in OMB's view, EPA had assigned arbitrary costs to environmental harms—$15 million per cancer fatality, and $5 million for serious ecological damage to each single small lake. OMB pointed out that rigorous economic methods were available and should have been used instead. With respect to the value of life, EPA should have looked to studies that estimate the increased wages demanded by workers in return for higher occupational risks. These increased wages measure the value workers place on their own lives. Using this methodology, OMB suggested using a value for human life of $1 million. With respect to the lakes, various techniques exist for measuring their recreational value. Finally, OMB pointed out, the benefits for reducing kryptonia levels would accrue over a period of at least 20–30 years, but EPA had treated those benefits as if they would be immediate. Instead, EPA should have used a methodology called discounting to reduce future benefits to their present values.

Combining all of its criticisms, OMB estimated that EPA's proposed measure would cost about $160 million to implement, but would save only about 6 lives per year, with a discounted present value of only $95 million. Even assigning what OMB considered a generous $15 million for total ecological damages to small lakes, the regulation was clearly unjustified. OMB suggested that a 15% reduction in kryptonia over ten years, focusing on the least controlled sources, might be warranted.

Sparked by an outcry in the press, public response to the OMB report was explosive. OMB was attacked for trying to put a price tag on human life, and for hiding anti-environmentalist attitudes behind incomprehensible economic technicalities. EPA challenged OMB's competence to review medical studies, and disagreed with the values assigned by OMB to health and environmental benefits of regulation (as well as to the 8% discount rate used by OMB). The President's chief of staff became involved in the negotiations between OMB and EPA regarding the regulation. The end result was a regulation requiring a 35% reduction in kryptonia over eight years.

Environmentalists had been less than thrilled by EPA's original proposal, and considered the watered-down final version even worse. They were also unhappy about the sheer delay caused by OMB's intervention. Industry felt that having expended significant political resources in the controversy, they had obtained a regulation that was still unreasonably burdensome (though better than the original proposal). Economists happily devoted themselves to studies of the technical issues raised in the debate, while other scholars debated the philosophical issues raised by cost-benefit analysis. In the meantime, both industry and environmental groups prepared to challenge the regulation in court.

* * *

The three hypotheticals demonstrate three different approaches to environmental regulation: cost-insensitivity, BAT, and cost–benefit. Which do you think is most effective in dealing with the scenario presented? As you read this chapter, consider how each of these approaches has worked in practice.

Note on Cost–Benefit Analysis in the Administrative Process

As suggested in our third scenario, cost-benefit analysis has attracted administrative, legislative, and scholarly attention. Shortly after taking office President Reagan signed Executive Order 12,291, 46 Fed.Reg. 13193 (1981), aimed at improving the efficiency of informal rulemaking by executive agencies. Section 2 directed that "major" regulations not be promulgated unless, "taking into account affected industries [and] the condition of the national economy," the potential benefits to society outweigh potential costs, and net benefits are at a maximum. Review of the cost-benefit analysis was conducted by the Office of Management and Budget.[b] In 1993, President Clinton issued an executive order maintaining the basic approach but attempting to streamline the process of OMB review. The rule was intended to reduce the number of regulations sent to OMB for approval and to make OMB's review more flexible. See Siegler, "Executive Order 12866: An Analysis of the New Executive Order on Regulatory Planning and Review," 24 *Env.L.Rep.* 10070 (1994). Debate about cost-benefit analysis and its limits continues among scholars.[c]

Whatever technique is used to consider the cost and benefits of a government action, it seems important that the government's analyses be exposed to public scrutiny. Although NEPA does not require the use of cost-benefit analysis, it may affect the use and presentation of that analysis. See *South Louisiana Environmental Council v. Sand,* 629 F.2d 1005 (5th Cir. 1980). The CEQ regulations provide:

> If a cost-benefit analysis relevant to the choice among environmentally different alternatives is being considered for the proposed action, it shall be incorporated by reference or appended to the statement as an aid in evaluating the environmental consequences. To assess the adequacy of compliance with section 102(2)(B) of the Act the statement shall, when a cost-benefit analysis is prepared, discuss the relationship between the analysis and any analyses of unquantified environmental

b. For further discussion of the executive order, see *NRDC v. EPA* [supra p. 130] and the accompanying notes. For critical examinations of the history of OMB oversight, see McGarity, "Some Thoughts on 'Deossifying' the Rulemaking Process," 41 *Duke L.J.* 1385, 1428–1434 (1992); Percival, "Checks Without Balance: Executive Office Oversight of the Environmental Protection Agency," 54 *L. & Contemp.Probs.* 127 (1991).

c. See, e.g., D. Farber, *Eco-Pragmatism: Making Sensible Environmental Decisions in an Uncertain World,* chs. 2 & 4 (1999); Heinzerling, "Regulatory Costs of Mythic Proportions," 107 *Yale L.J.* 1981 (1998); Rose, "Environmental Lessons," 27 *Loyola L.A. L.Rev.* 1023 (1994).

impacts, values, and amenities. For purposes of complying with the Act, the weighing of the merits and drawbacks of the various alternatives need not be displayed in a monetary cost-benefit analysis and should not be when there are important qualitative considerations. In any event, an environmental impact statement should at least indicate those considerations, including factors not related to environmental quality, which are likely to be relevant and important to a decision.

40 CFR 1502.23.

Whatever may be said one way or the other about cost-benefit analysis as a technique, there can be no doubt that we are spending large amounts of money for environmental quality. According to an EPA report, the United States spent $115 billion to clean up pollution in 1990; by the year 2000, the total may be about 60% of the defense budget and up to 2.8% of the GNP. See Roberts, "Costs of a Clean Environment," 251 *Science* 1182 (1991). See also, Carlin, Scordari & Garner, "Environmental Investments: The Cost of Cleaning Up," 34:2 *Environment* 12 (1992). Obviously, we should attempt to ensure that these expenditures are made in a way that provides the greatest degree of environmental quality. In reading the rest of this chapter, consider how well we have reached this goal.

Cost-benefit analysis has remained the subject of political controversy. In 1995, pursuant to the "Contract with America," the House passed a bill that would have required cost-benefit analyses for any rule that would increase annual costs by $25 million or more. A Senate bill introduced by Senator Dole would have imposed the same requirement with a $50 million "trigger level." The Dole bill would also have imposed a "super mandate" by making cost-benefit analysis the decisive consideration regardless of the standards previously imposed by an environmental statute. The Senate bill was killed by a fillibuster. Congress did succeed in passing some less significant regulatory reforms involving small businesses and unfunded mandates on state governments. See James Satterfield, "A Funny Thing Happened on the Way to the Revolution: The Environmental Record of the 104th Congress," 27 *Env. L. Rep.* 10019 (1997). The unfunded mandates legislation also contains a "sleeper" provision which requires use of the most cost-effective alternative unless doing so would be inconsistent with law or the agency explains its reasons for rejecting the alternative. 109 Stat. 48, 66 (1995).

Consider the following appraisal of the Contract with America proposals:

In fact, no one knows how regulation would be changed if legislation such as that discussed here were enacted. Its impact would depend not only on how the benefit-cost initially were interpreted and executed by the federal regulatory agencies, but also on the deference that appeals courts give to the agencies when regulations are challenged. If the appeals courts consistently overturned agencies' decisions, legal challenges would proliferate and the regulatory process could easily bog down.

On balance, however, my guess is that these fears would not be borne out. * * * To their credit, the architects of both H.R. 9 and S. 343 have explicitly directed that not every benefit or cost has to be quantified and expressed in dollar terms in the required analyses. Regulators should be able under such language to give these nonquantifiables appropriate weight in decisionmaking. In fact, as I read the language in both bills, it suggests to me that Congress is asking regulators to do no more than take action only when they can answer the following question in the affirmative: All things considered, will this regulation do the country more good than harm? If that is how the language comes to be interpreted (a big "if," admittedly), that seems to me to be a pretty reasonable test to apply to any and all proposed regulations, and one that would allow regulators more than enough latitude to consider consequences that do not lend themselves to quantification or monetization.

Paul Portney, "Cartoon Caricatures of Regulatory Reform," 121 *Resources* 21, 22 (Fall 1995). Portney finds it "very unlikely that judges would suddenly begin to overturn regulators' decisions on grounds that, for example, the regulators valued an asthma attack prevented at $100 rather than $50, that they used the wrong extrapolation technique in translating risks at high doses to those at lower levels, or that they failed to consider every possible alternative in formulating their regulatory strategy." Id. at 23. In his conclusion, he complains that the debate over cost-benefit analysis "has been dominated by false claims that regulation is strangling the economy or that popular safeguards will be wiped off the books by reform legislation. We deserve and should insist upon more, though the smart money is probably best wagered on more cartoon caricatures." Id. at 24.

Congressional debate continues on more modest proposals to require the agency to conduct and at least consider thoroughly the results of cost-benefit analysis. See 29 *Env.Rep.* 701 (July 31, 1998). See also Cass Sunstein, "Congress, Constitutional Moments, and the Cost–Benefit State," 48 *Stan. L. Rev.* 247 (1996) (endorsing a similar super-mandate for qualitative cost-benefit analysis).

A. NUISANCE LAW

The tort of nuisance dates back to the sixteenth century. An early case involved a complaint about free-running pigs; today's cases often involve air or water pollution. Essentially, a nuisance is defined as an unreasonable interference by another landowner with the plaintiff's use of his own land. Many forms of pollution fit this description. Once a nuisance is found, there remains the problem of fashioning the appropriate remedy, as the following case illustrates.

BOOMER v. ATLANTIC CEMENT CO.

Court of Appeals of New York, 1970.
26 N.Y.2d 219, 309 N.Y.S.2d 312, 257 N.E.2d 870.

BERGAN, JUDGE.

Defendant operates a large cement plant near Albany. These are actions for injunction and damages by neighboring land owners alleging injury to property from dirt, smoke and vibration emanating from the

tort: a civil wrong for which a remedy (in damages) may be obtained plant. A nuisance has been found after trial, temporary damages have been allowed but an injunction has been denied.

The public concern with air pollution arising from many sources in industry and in transportation is currently accorded ever wider recognition accompanied by a growing sense of responsibility in State and Federal Governments to control it. Cement plants are obvious sources of air pollution in the neighborhoods where they operate.

But there is now before the court private litigation in which individual property owners have sought specific relief from a single plant operation. The threshold question raised by the division of view on this appeal is whether the court should resolve the litigation between the parties now before it as equitably as seems possible; or whether, seeking promotion of the general public welfare, it should channel private litigation into broad public objectives.

A court performs its essential function when it decides the rights of parties before it. Its decision of private controversies may sometimes greatly affect public issues. Large questions of law are often resolved by the manner in which private litigation is decided. But this is normally an incident to the court's main function to settle controversy. It is a rare exercise of judicial power to use a decision in private litigation as a purposeful mechanism to achieve direct public objectives greatly beyond the rights and interests before the court.

Effective control of air pollution is a problem presently far from solution even with the full public and financial powers of government. In large measure adequate technical procedures are yet to be developed and some that appear possible may be economically impracticable.

It seems apparent that the amelioration of air pollution will depend on technical research in great depth; on a carefully balanced consideration of the economic impact of close regulation; and of the actual effect on public health. It is likely to require massive public expenditure and to demand more than any local community can accomplish and to depend on regional and interstate controls.

A court should not try to do this on its own as a by-product of private litigation and it seems manifest that the judicial establishment is neither equipped in the limited nature of any judgment it can pronounce nor prepared to lay down and implement an effective policy for the elimination of air pollution. This is an area beyond the circumference of one private lawsuit. It is a direct responsibility for government and should not thus be undertaken as an incident to solving a dispute between property owners and a single cement plant—one of many—in the Hudson River valley.

The cement making operations of defendant have been found by the court at Special Term to have damaged the nearby properties of plaintiffs in these two actions. That court, as it has been noted, accordingly found defendant maintained a nuisance and this has been affirmed at the Appellate Division. The total damage to plaintiffs' properties is, however, relatively small in comparison with the value of defendant's operation and with the consequences of the injunction which plaintiffs seek.

[The ground for the denial of injunction, notwithstanding the finding both that there is a nuisance and that plaintiffs have been damaged substantially, is the large disparity in economic consequences of the nuisance and of the injunction.] This theory cannot, however, be sustained without overruling a doctrine which has been consistently reaffirmed in several leading cases in this court and which has never been disavowed here, namely that where a nuisance has been found and where there has been any substantial damage shown by the party complaining an injunction will be granted.]

The rule in New York has been that such a nuisance will be enjoined although marked disparity be shown in economic consequence between the effect of the injunction and the effect of the nuisance.

* * *

* * * [T]o follow the rule literally in these cases would be to close down the plant at once. This court is fully agreed to avoid that immediately drastic remedy; the difference in view is how best to avoid it.*

One alternative is to grant the injunction but postpone its effect to a specified future date to give opportunity for technical advances to permit defendant to eliminate the nuisance;[another is to grant the injunction conditioned on the payment of permanent damages to plaintiffs which would compensate them for the total economic loss to their property present and future caused by defendant's operations.] For reasons which will be developed the court chooses the latter alternative.

If the injunction were to be granted unless within a short period— e.g., 18 months—the nuisance be abated by improved methods, there would be no assurance that any significant technical improvement would occur.

The parties could settle this private litigation at any time if defendant paid enough money and the imminent threat of closing the plant would build up the pressure on defendant. If there were no improved techniques found, there would inevitably be applications to the court at Special Term for extensions of time to perform on showing of good faith efforts to find such techniques.

Moreover, techniques to eliminate dust and other annoying by-products of cement making are unlikely to be developed by any research the defendant can undertake within any short period, but will depend on

* Respondent's investment in the plant is in excess of $45,000,000. There are over 300 people employed there.

the total resources of the cement industry nationwide and throughout the world. The problem is universal wherever cement is made.

For obvious reasons the rate of the research is beyond the control of defendant. If at the end of 18 months the whole industry has not found a technical solution a court would be hard put to close down this one cement plant if due regard be given to equitable principles.

On the other hand, to grant the injunction unless defendant pays plaintiffs such permanent damages as may be fixed by the court seems to do justice between the contending parties. All of the attributions of economic loss to the properties on which plaintiffs' complaints are based will have been redressed.

The nuisance complained of by these plaintiffs may have other public or private consequences, but these particular parties are the only ones who have sought remedies and the judgment proposed will fully redress them. The limitation of relief granted is a limitation only within the four corners of these actions and does not foreclose public health or other public agencies from seeking proper relief in a proper court.

It seems reasonable to think that the risk of being required to pay permanent damages to injured property owners by cement plant owners would itself be a reasonably effective spur to research for improved techniques to minimize nuisance.

The power of the court to condition on equitable grounds the continuance of an injunction on the payment of permanent damages seems undoubted. * * *

* * *

The judgment, by allowance of permanent damages imposing a servitude on land, which is the basis of the actions, would preclude future recovery by plaintiffs or their grantees * * *.

This should be placed beyond debate by a provision of the judgment that the payment by defendant and the acceptance by plaintiffs of permanent damages found by the court shall be in compensation for a servitude on the land.

JASEN, JUDGE (dissenting).

It has long been the rule in this State, as the majority acknowledges, that a nuisance which results in substantial continuing damage to neighbors must be enjoined. * * * To now change the rule to permit the cement company to continue polluting the air indefinitely upon the payment of permanent damages is, in my opinion, compounding the magnitude of a very serious problem in our State and Nation today.

* * *

I see grave dangers in overruling our long-established rule of granting an injunction where a nuisance results in substantial continuing damage. In permitting the injunction to become inoperative upon the payment of permanent damages, the majority is, in effect, licensing a continuing wrong. It is the same as saying to the cement company, you may continue to do harm to your neighbors so long as you pay a fee for it. Furthermore, once such permanent damages are assessed and paid, the incentive to alleviate the wrong would be eliminated, thereby continuing air pollution of an area without abatement.

It is true that some courts have sanctioned the remedy here proposed by the majority in a number of cases, but none of the authorities relied upon by the majority are analogous to the situation before us. In those cases, the courts, in denying an injunction and awarding money damages, grounded their decision on a showing that the use to which the property was intended to be put was primarily for the public benefit. Here, on the other hand, it is clearly established that the cement company is creating a continuing air pollution nuisance primarily for its own private interest with no public benefit.

This kind of inverse condemnation * * * may not be invoked by a private person or corporation for private gain or advantage. Inverse condemnation should only be permitted when the public is primarily served in the taking or impairment of property. * * * The promotion of the interests of the polluting cement company has, in my opinion, no public use or benefit.

Nor is it constitutionally permissible to impose servitude on land, without consent of the owner, by payment of permanent damages where the continuing impairment of the land is for a private use. * * * This is made clear by the State Constitution which provides that "[p]rivate property shall not be taken for public use without just compensation" (emphasis added). It is, of course, significant that the section makes no mention of taking for a private use.

* * *

I would enjoin the defendant cement company from continuing the discharge of dust particles upon its neighbors' properties unless, within 18 months, the cement company abated this nuisance.

* * *

I am aware that the trial court found that the most modern dust control devices available have been installed in defendant's plant, but, I submit, this does not mean that *better* and more effective dust control devices could not be developed within the time allowed to abate the pollution.

Moreover, I believe it is incumbent upon the defendant to develop such devices, since the cement company, at the time the plant commenced production (1962), was well aware of the plaintiffs' presence in the area, as well as the probable consequences of its contemplated operation. Yet, it still chose to build and operate the plant at this site.

Notes

1. Some additional facts about *Boomer* may be helpful in evaluating the case. The court's opinion focuses on air pollution, perhaps because the dissent stresses the public interest in pollution control. An examination of the appellate record, however, reveals that *Boomer* did not present simply a conventional pollution problem. Instead, the record suggests a severe but localized impact on neighboring lands, due less to the cement plant than to the operation of the quarry on the same site. In particular, neighbors complained of severe vibrations and heavy dust from blasting operations at the quarry. The main reason the trial judge declined to issue an injunction was not undue hardship to the cement company, but rather the central role of the plant in the local economy. Over half of the assessed value of the township involved the cement company's property, so closing the plant would have had a devastating effect on the local government and school system. On remand, the trial judge calculated that the amount of the decline in fair market value for one of the parcels was $140,000 and then added a "kicker" of $35,000 to arrive at the damage award. The cement company's liability, including its settlement of the other pending cases, came to $710,-000. For fuller details, see Farber, "Reassessing *Boomer:* Justice, Efficiency, and Nuisance Law," in *Essays on the Law of Property and Legal Education, in Honor of John E. Cribbet* (M. Hoeflich & P. Hay 1988).

2. Some statutes confer standing upon private persons to enforce publicly established pollution limitations. See, e.g., Ill.Rev.Stat. ch. 111½, § 31(b); Clean Air Act, § 304(a). If New York adopted such a law and promulgated a dust standard which was violated by defendant's emissions, should the courts "balance the equities" in determining whether to issue an injunction in such a case? We will return to that issue in Chapter VII.

3. It is a common remedy in nuisance cases to require the defendant to use the best available technology to control pollution. Many key pollution statutes now adopt similar standards as exemplified in our second "kryptonia" scenario in the introduction to this chapter. A recurring problem is what to do when existing technology is inadequate to control the problem. In *Boomer,* the court refused to require the defendant to develop new technology. But other courts have been somewhat more aggressive about using their equitable powers to force the development of new technology. As we will see later in this chapter, Congress has also pursued a strategy of "technology forcing," with mixed results.

4. It may seem obvious that the choice between a damage remedy and an injunctive remedy has enormous practical importance in a case like *Boomer.* Yet this is less clear on further reflection. If Mr. Boomer is entitled to an injunction but has relatively small damages, it might make sense for him to enter into a settlement. Thus, he might choose to forego his injunction in exchange for cash. If so, the pollution will continue. Some economists have suggested, on similar grounds, that even the existence or nonexistence of liability, quite apart from the remedy, may have no effect on pollution levels. At the very least, their work suggests that the problem is much more subtle than it appears. The following article is the leading work in this area.

COASE, "THE PROBLEM OF SOCIAL COST"[d]

3 *Journal of Law and Economics* 1–8, 15–19 (1960).

I propose to start my analysis by examining a case in which most economists would presumably agree that the problem would be solved in a completely satisfactory manner: when the damaging business has to pay for all damage caused *and* the pricing system works smoothly (strictly this means that the operation of a pricing system is without cost).

A good example of the problem under discussion is afforded by the case of straying cattle which destroy crops growing on neighbouring land. Let us suppose that a farmer and a cattle-raiser are operating on neighbouring properties. Let us further suppose that, without any fencing between the properties, an increase in the size of the cattle-raiser's herd increases the total damage to the farmer's crops. * * *

To simplify the argument, I propose to use an arithmetical example. I shall assume that the annual cost of fencing the farmer's property is $9 and that the price of the crop is $1 per ton. Also, I assume that the relation between the number of cattle in the herd and the annual crop loss is as follows:

Number in Herd (Steers)	Annual Crop Loss (Tons)	Crop Loss per Additional Steer (Tons)
1	1	1
2	3	2
3	6	3
4	10	4

Given that the cattle-raiser is liable for the damage caused, the additional annual cost imposed on the cattle-raiser if he increased his herd from, say, 2 to 3 steers is $3 and in deciding on the size of the herd, he will take this into account along with his other costs. That is, he will not increase the size of the herd unless the value of the additional meat produced (assuming that the cattle-raiser slaughters the cattle), is greater than the additional costs that this will entail, including the value of the additional crops destroyed. * * * Given that the annual cost of fencing is $9, the cattle-raiser who wished to have a herd with 4 steers or more would pay for fencing to be erected and maintained, assuming that other means of attaining the same end would not do so more cheaply. * * *

* * *

I now turn to the case in which, although the pricing system is assumed to work smoothly (that is, costlessly), the damaging business is not liable for any of the damage which it causes. * * * I propose to show that the allocation of resources will be the same [optimal] as it was when the damaging business was liable for damage causes. * * *

* * * Suppose that the size of the cattle-raiser's herd is 3 steers (and that this is the size of the herd that would be maintained if crop damage was not taken into account). Then the farmer would be willing to pay up to $3 if the cattle-raiser would reduce his herd to 2 steers, up to $5 if the herd were reduced to 1 steer and would pay up to $6 if cattle-raising was abandoned. The cattle-raiser would therefore receive $3 from the farmer if he kept 2 steers instead of 3. This $3 foregone is therefore part of the cost incurred in keeping the third steer. Whether the $3 is a payment which the cattle-raiser has to make if he adds the third steer to his herd (which it would be if the cattle-raiser was liable to the farmer for damage caused to the crop) or whether it is a sum of money which he would have received if he did not keep a third steer (which it would be if the cattle-raiser was not liable to the farmer for damage caused to the crop) does not affect the final result. In both cases $3 is part of the cost of adding a third steer, to be included along with the other costs. If the increase in the value of production in cattle-raising through increasing the size of the herd from 2 to 3 is greater than the additional costs that have to be incurred (including the $3 damage to crops), the size of the herd will be increased. Otherwise, it will not. The size of the herd will be the same whether the cattle-raiser is liable for damage caused to the crop or not.

* * *

It is necessary to know whether the damaging business is liable or not for damage caused since without the establishment of this initial delimitation of rights there can be no market transactions to transfer and recombine them. But the ultimate result (which maximizes the value of production) is independent of the legal position if the pricing system is assumed to work without cost.

* * *

The argument has proceeded up to this point on the assumption * * * that there were no costs involved in carrying out market transactions. This is, of course, a very unrealistic assumption. In order to carry out a market transaction it is necessary to discover who it is that one wishes to deal with, to inform people that one wishes to deal and on what terms, to conduct negotiations leading up to a bargain, to draw up the contract, to undertake the inspection needed to make sure that the terms of the contract are being observed, and so on. These operations are often extremely costly, sufficiently costly at any rate to prevent many transactions that would be carried out in a world in which the pricing system worked without cost.

* * * Once the costs of carrying out market transactions are taken into account it is clear that such a rearrangement of rights will only be undertaken when the increase in the value of production consequent upon the rearrangement is greater than the costs which would be involved in bringing it about. When it is less, the granting of an injunction (or the knowledge that it would be granted) or the liability to pay damages may result in an activity being discontinued (or may prevent its being started) which would be undertaken if market transactions were costless. In these conditions the initial delimitation of legal rights does have an effect on the efficiency with which the economic system operates. One arrangement of rights may bring about a greater value of production than any other. But unless this is the arrangement of rights established by the legal system, the costs of reaching the same result by altering and combining rights through the market may be so great that this optional arrangement of rights, and the greater value of production which it would bring, may never be achieved. * * *

* * *

* * * An alternative solution is direct Government regulation. Instead of instituting a legal system of rights which can be modified by transactions on the market, the government may impose regulations which state what people must or must not do and which have to be obeyed. Thus, the government (by statute or perhaps more likely through an administrative agency) may, to deal with the problem of smoke nuisance, decree that certain methods of production should or should not be used (e.g. that smoke preventing devices should be installed or that coal or oil should not be burned) or may confine certain types of business to certain districts (zoning regulations). * * *

* * * But the governmental administrative machine is not itself costless. It can, in fact, on occasion be extremely costly. Furthermore, there is no reason to suppose that the restrictive and zoning regulations, made by a fallible administration subject to political pressures and operating without any competitive check, will necessarily always be those which increase the efficiency with which the economic system operates. Furthermore, such general regulations, which must apply to a wide variety of cases will be enforced in some cases in which they are clearly inappropriate. From these considerations it follows that direct governmental regulation will not necessarily give better results than leaving the problem to be solved by the market * * *. But equally there is no reason why, on occasion, such governmental administrative regulation should not lead to an improvement in economic efficiency. This would seem particularly likely when, as is normally the case with the smoke nuisance, a large number of people are involved and in which therefore the costs of handling the problem through the market * * * may be high.

Notes

1. As an exercise, explain how Coase would argue that the result in *Boomer* is irrelevant to the amount of pollution produced, in the absence of transaction costs. Use these two sets of figures:

Case 1: The company's profit from polluting is $3,000,000 per year; the total damage caused is $4,000,000.

Case 2: The company's profit from polluting is $3,000,000 per year; the total damage caused is $2,000,000.

What is the economically efficient result in each case (i.e., the result that would be favored by a cost-benefit analyst)? How might that result be reached if (a) only damage liability exists, (b) injunctions can be obtained, or (c) no liability exists? What effects do the various liability rules have on the distribution of wealth between the company's shareholders and its neighbors?

2. The Coase Theorem has given rise to a considerable literature probing its validity and limitations. Some of the more important works are surveyed in Schwab, Book Review, 87 *Mich.L.Rev.* 1171 (1989); Cooter, "The Cost of Coase," 11 *J.Legal Studies* 1 (1982). For a more light-hearted look at Coase, see Farber, "The Case Against Brilliance," 70 *Minn.L.Rev.* 917, 918–20, 923–24 (1986). One particularly interesting (but fairly technical) critique of Coase can be found in Farrell, "Information and the Coase Theorem," 1 *J.Econ.Perspectives* 113 (1987). An important empirical test of Coase was undertaken by John Donahue. He found that the initial assignment of incentive payments between employers and employees had substantial behavioral consequences, contrary to the predictions of the Coase Theorem. Donahue, "Diverting the Coasean River: Incentive Schemes to Reduce Unemployment Spells," 99 *Yale L.J.* 549 (1989). The upshot of all this literature can probably be summarized by saying that people will often (but not always) negotiate their way around legal rules to economically efficient outcomes.

3. Although the "Coase Theorem" is one of the most famous results in law and economics, it is clear from "The Problem of Social Cost" itself that Coase regarded the zero-transaction-cost assumption as unrealistic. Indeed, his previous work made it clear that he regarded transaction costs as not only widespread but essential to understanding the structure of the economy. More recently, he has explained his view of the Coase Theorem more fully. In discussing what would happen in a world of zero transaction costs, he explains, his aim "was not to describe what life would be like in such a world but to provide a simple setting in which to develop the analysis and, what was even more important, to make clear the fundamental role which transaction costs do, and should, play in the fashioning of the institutions which make up the economic system." Ronald Coase, *The Firm, The Market, and the Law* 13 (1988).[e]

Little wonder that Coase was dismayed to find the world of zero transaction costs described as a Coasian world. Id. at 174. Instead, he says, "it is the world of modern economic theory, one which I was hoping to persuade economists to leave." Id. The failure of economists to consider transaction costs is, he believes, the major reason for their inability to account for the operation of the economy in the real world. As a result, their policy proposals are "the stuff that dreams are made of." Id. at 185. Given his actual views, the fame and impact of the Coase Theorem are at least a bit

e. Coase goes on to point out that a world without transaction costs "has very peculiar properties." For example, monopolies would act like competitors, insurance companies would not exist, and there would be no economic basis for the existence of firms. Id. at 14. Indeed, he points out that since transactions are costless, it also costs nothing to speed them up, "so that eternity can be experienced in a split second." Id. at 15. "It would not seem worthwhile," he concludes, "to spend much time investigating the properties of such a world." Id.

ironic. Indeed, in certain respects Coase has more in common with some of his critics than with many of his supporters. See Daniel Farber, "Parody Lost/Paradigm Regained: The Ironic History of the Coase Theorem," 83 *Va. L. Rev.* 397 (1997).

4. As Coase acknowledges, market transactions are not costless, and determination of the applicable liability rule therefore often does affect the ultimate allocation of resources as well as the distribution of income. Other authors have suggested, like Coase, that the courts might select liability rules with an eye toward the transaction costs that would be involved in negotiating changes (for the purpose of achieving economic efficiency) in the rights established by law. For example, in the case of a factory whose smoke damages many homeowners, what kinds of transaction costs (informational, organizational, negotiation, etc.) would be required to alter a legal rule under which: (a) the factory is not liable; (b) the factory is liable only to damage judgments; (c) the factory is liable to injunction at the behest of any injured homeowner? See Michelman, "Pollution as a Tort: A Non–Accidental Perspective on Calabresi's Costs," 80 *Yale L.J.* 647 (1971); Calabresi and Melamed, "Property Rules, Liability Rules, and Inalienability: One View of the Cathedral," 85 *Harv.L.Rev.* 1089 (1972). Michelman says that in applying a "decentralist or transaction-organizing" version of nuisance law, a court may decide to impose liability on the polluter because it believes the polluter is the "cheapest cost avoider" or because it believes that the polluter is the "best briber." However, if the court acts on the latter ground, it should be wary of "injunctions with their heavy negotiation costs which may prevent the polluter from bribing effectively."

Calabresi and Melamed suggest a fourth legal rule in addition to those mentioned in the preceding paragraph: (d) the factory is liable to injunction, but only if plaintiff homeowners compensate the factory for its costs attributable to the injunction. Is this closer to rule (a) or (c)? For an illustration of rule (d), see the next case. (A fifth rule, with seemingly limited practical application, has also been proposed: The factory decides whether or not to stay open, and if it closes, the neighbor pays damages measured by the social cost of the pollution. See Krier & Schwab, "Property Rules and Liability Rules: The Cathedral in Another Light," 70 *NYU L.Rev.* 440 (1995).)

SPUR INDUSTRIES, INC. v. DEL E. WEBB DEVELOPMENT CO.

Supreme Court of Arizona, In Banc. 1972.
108 Ariz. 178, 494 P.2d 700.

[In 1957 Del Webb began construction of a retirement community called Sun City, west of Phoenix. By 1967 the development had moved close to Spur's feedlot, which had been in operation for several years before Webb came into the area.]

CAMERON, VICE CHIEF JUSTICE.

Del Webb's suit complained that the Spur feeding operation was a public nuisance because of the flies and the odor which were drifting or being blown by the prevailing south to north wind over the southern portion of Sun City. At the time of the suit, Spur was feeding between 20,000 and 30,000 head of cattle, and the facts amply support the finding of the trial court that the feed pens had become a nuisance to the people who resided in the southern part of Del Webb's development. The testimony indicated that cattle in a commercial feedlot will produce 35 to 40 pounds of wet manure per day, per head, or over a million pounds of wet manure per day for 30,000 head of cattle, and that despite the admittedly good feedlot management and good housekeeping practices by Spur, the resulting odor and flies produced an annoying if not unhealthy situation as far as the senior citizens of southern Sun City were concerned. There is no doubt that some of the citizens of Sun City were unable to enjoy the outdoor living which Del Webb had advertised and that Del Webb was faced with sales resistance from prospective purchasers as well as strong and persistent complaints from the people who had purchased homes in that area.

* * *

The difference between a private nuisance and a public nuisance is generally one of degree. A private nuisance is one affecting a single individual or a definite small number of persons in the enjoyment of private rights not common to the public, while a public nuisance is one affecting the rights enjoyed by citizens as a part of the public. To constitute a public nuisance, the nuisance must affect a considerable number of people or an entire community or neighborhood.

Where the injury is slight, the remedy for minor inconveniences lies in an action for damages rather than in one for an injunction. Moreover, some courts have held, in the "balancing of conveniences" cases, that damages may be the sole remedy. See *Boomer v. Atlantic Cement Co.* [supra p. 290].

* * *

It is clear that as to the citizens of Sun City, the operation of Spur's feedlot was both a public and a private nuisance. They could have successfully maintained an action to abate the nuisance. Del Webb, having shown a special injury in the loss of sales, had standing to bring suit to enjoin the nuisance. The judgment of the trial court permanently enjoining the operation of the feedlot is affirmed.

* * *

In the so-called "coming to the nuisance" cases, the courts have held that the residential landowner may not have relief if he knowingly came into a neighborhood reserved for industrial or agricultural endeavors and has been damaged thereby. * * * Were Webb the only party injured, we would feel justified in holding that the doctrine of "coming to the nuisance" would have been a bar to the relief asked by Webb, and, on the other hand, had Spur located the feedlot near the outskirts of a city and had the city grown toward the feedlot, Spur would have to suffer the cost of abating the nuisance as to those people locating within the growth pattern of the expanding city * * *.

* * *

There was no indication in the instant case at the time Spur and its predecessors located in western Maricopa County that a new city would spring up, full-blown, alongside the feeding operation and that the developer of that city would ask the court to order Spur to move because of the new city. Spur is required to move not because of any wrongdoing on the part of Spur, but because of a proper and legitimate regard of the courts for the rights and interests of the public.

Del Webb, on the other hand, is entitled to the relief prayed for (a permanent injunction), not because Webb is blameless, but because of the damage to the people who have been encouraged to purchase homes in Sun City. It does not equitably or legally follow, however, that Webb, being entitled to the injunction, is then free of any liability to Spur if Webb has in fact been the cause of the damage Spur has sustained. It does not seem harsh to require a developer, who has taken advantage of the lesser land values in a rural area as well as the availability of large tracts of land on which to build and develop a new town or city in the area, to indemnify those who are forced to leave as a result.

Having brought people to the nuisance to the foreseeable detriment of Spur, Webb must indemnify Spur for a reasonable amount of the cost of moving or shutting down.

Notes

1. *Spur* raises some interesting questions of tort law: Should the residents be estopped from seeking relief against Spur because they moved into an area despite conditions of which they should have been aware? If the residents have any claim, should it be against the developer? Suppose the residents had obtained an injunction against Spur. Could Spur have filed an independent action against Webb for damages? If so, has the court in effect recognized a new tort: "wrongfully transforming a lawful use into a nuisance by changing neighboring uses?"

2. Do the ultimate results in *Boomer* and *Spur* make economic sense? Are they sound in light of the general policies of tort law? How do they differ from what Coase would expect if there was no liability for maintaining a nuisance?

B. COST AND FEASIBILITY IN SOURCE-ORIENTED REGULATORY SCHEMES

Today, common law remedies have largely been displaced by complex statutory schemes governing pollution. There are two basic types of statutory regulation. One type focuses on the individual pollution source. It attempts to determine what level of pollution control can feasibly be achieved. Normally, these statutes require the use of the "best available technology" (BAT) or some similar standard; occasionally, the statute itself may set the numerical level of pollution to be allowed. This type of regulation is central to the Clean Water Act, but also plays an important role in the Clean Air Act. The other type of regulation focuses on the level of pollution in the environment in a given locale and mandates formulation of a plan to reduce the pollution to a tolerable level. This kind of area planning is the backbone of the Clean Air Act, but plays only a secondary (though increasing) role in the Clean Water Act. In this section, we will consider source-oriented regulation in both statutes.

1. EMISSION STANDARDS IN THE CLEAN AIR ACT

The following background information about air pollutants and their sources is from The Environmental Working Group, *Smokestacks and Smoke Screens: Big Polluters, Big Profits, and the Fight for Cleaner Air* (May 1997) ["EWG"]. In addition to the direct emission of pollutants discussed below, ozone is produced by reactions between sunlight, nitrogen oxide and organic chemicals, resulting in smog. (For further information about air pollution, see the materials in Section B of Chapter I.)

Particulate pollution

Particulate pollution refers to a broad class of toxic air pollution made up of substances that exist as discrete particles, suspended in the air in either liquid or solid form. Particulate matter can include toxic metals (lead, copper, nickel, zinc, cadmium) and fine aerosol particles formed from sulfur and nitrogen oxides and volatile organic compounds (which are known as "particulate precursors"). (EWG 11). Particulate pollution causes the premature death of at least 35,000 people each year. (EWG 39). Particulate pollution shortens lives by several years for the average affected individuals. (EWG 13).

Seven of the top ten particulate polluters are either metal mining facilities or steel mills. Other significant sources of particulate matter include pulp and paper mills, chemical manufacturers, metal smelting and oil refining facilities. (EWG 4).

Sulfur Dioxide

All of the top 50, and 96 of the nation's top emitters are electric utilities; 45 of the top 50 are located east of the Mississippi. (EWG 4). The top four corporate SO_2 polluters account for one quarter of all SO_2 emissions from stationary sources. Just 20 electric power utilities account for nearly one half of all stationary SO_2 emissions. (EWG 6).

Nitrogen Oxides

All but two of the top 100 nitrogen oxide polluters are utilities. The top two stationary NOx polluters are power plants run by the Tennessee Valley Authority (TVA). (EWG 4). Nine out of the top ten NOx polluting corporations are electric power conglomerates; the ten corporations together account for one quarter of NOx pollution from stationary sources. (EWG 6). Nitric oxides contribute to ozone problems and also to acid rain.

Miscellaneous Facts

- While gas and diesel powered vehicles also contribute to air pollution, stationary sources account for 56% of particulate pollution, 96% of all SO_2 emissions, and 48% of all NOx emissions. (Vehicles are important sources of ozone precursors and of carbon monoxide).

- Polluters in just eight states account for half of all SO_2 pollution from stationary sources, while the top ten states account for 61 percent of all SO_2 pollution. (EWG 17).

- Five states—Texas, Indiana, Illinois, Ohio, and Pennsylvania—account for nearly one third of all nitrogen oxides emissions. Four of them—Indiana, Illinois, Ohio, and Pennsylvania—are also the top SO_2 polluting states in the nation, with the same power plants causing most of the pollution. (EWG 18).

- Six states account for one third, and ten states account for just over 50 percent of all direct particulate pollution. (EWG 18).

INTERNATIONAL HARVESTER
CO. v. RUCKELSHAUS

United States Court of Appeals, District of Columbia Circuit, 1973.
478 F.2d 615.

LEVENTHAL, CIRCUIT JUDGE.

The tension of forces presented by the controversy over automobile emission standards may be focused by two central observations:

(1) The automobile is an essential pillar of the American economy. Some 28 percent of the nonfarm workforce draws its livelihood from the automobile industry and its products.

(2) The automobile has had a devastating impact on the American environment. As of 1970, authoritative voices stated that "[a]utomotive pollution constitutes in excess of 60% of our national air pollution problem" and more than 80 percent of the air pollutants in concentrated urban areas.

* * *

On December 31, 1970, Congress grasped the nettle and amended the Clean Air Act to set a statutory standard for required reductions in levels of hydrocarbons (HC) and carbon monoxide (CO) which must be achieved for 1975 models of light duty vehicles. Section 202(b) of the Act added by the Clean Air Amendments of 1970, provides that, beginning with the 1975 model year, exhaust emission of hydrocarbons and carbon monoxide from "light duty vehicles" must be reduced at least 90 percent from the permissible emission levels in the 1970 model year. * * *

Congress was aware that these 1975 standards were "drastic medicine," designed to "force the state of the art." There was, naturally,
concern whether the manufacturers would be able to achieve this goal.
Therefore, Congress provided, in Senator Baker's phrase, a "realistic
escape hatch"; the manufacturers could petition the Administrator of
the EPA for a one-year suspension of the 1975 requirements, and
Congress took the precaution of directing the National Academy of
Sciences to undertake an ongoing study of the feasibility of compliance
with the emission standards. * * * Under section 202(b)(5)(D) of the
Act, the Administrator is authorized to grant a one-year suspension only
if he determines that (i) such suspension is essential to the public
interest or the public health and welfare of the United States, (ii) all
good faith efforts have been made to meet the standards established by
this subsection, (iii) the applicant has established that effective control
technology, processes, operating methods, or other alternatives are not
available or have not been available for a sufficient period of time to
achieve compliance prior to the effective date of such standards, and (iv)
the study and investigation of the National Academy of Sciences conducted pursuant to subsection (c) of this section and other information
available to him has not indicated that technology, processes, or other
alternatives are available to meet such standards.

* * *

At the outset of his Decision, the Administrator determined that the
most effective system so far developed was the noble metal oxidizing
catalyst. * * *

The problem the Administrator faced in making a determination
that technology was available, on the basis of these data, was that actual
tests showed only one car with actual emissions which conformed to the
standard * * *. No car had actually been driven 50,000 miles, the
statutory "useful life" of a vehicle and the time period for which
conformity to the emission standards is required. In the view of the EPA
Administrator, however, the reasons for the high test readings were
uncertain or ambivalent.

Instead, certain data of the auto companies were used as a starting
point for making a prediction, but remolded into a more usable form for
this purpose. * * * [T]he Administrator "adjusted" the data of the auto
companies by use of several critical assumptions.

First, he made an adjustment to reflect the assumption that fuel
used in 1975 model year cars would either contain an average of .03
grams per gallon or .05 grams per gallon of lead. This usually resulted in
an increase of emissions predicted, since many companies had tested
their vehicles on lead-free gasoline.

Second, the Administrator found that the attempt of some companies to reduce emissions of nitrogen oxides below the 1975 Federal
standard of 3.0 grams per vehicle mile resulted in increased emissions of

hydrocarbons and carbon monoxide. This adjustment resulted in a downward adjustment of observed HC and CO data, by a specified factor.

→ Third, the Administrator took into account the effect the "durability" of the preferred systems would have on the emission control obtainable. This required that observed readings at one point of usage be increased by a deterioration factor (DO) to project emissions at a later moment of use. The critical methodological choice was to make this adjustment from a base of emissions observed at 4000 miles. Thus, even if a car had actually been tested over 4000 miles, predicted emissions at 50,000 miles would be determined by multiplying 4000 mile emissions by the DO factor.

→ Fourth, the Administrator adjusted for "prototype-to-production slippage." This was an upward adjustment made necessary by the possibility that prototype cars might have features which reduced HC and CO emissions, but were not capable of being used in actual production vehicles.

→ Finally, in accord with a regulation assumed, as to substance, in the text of the Decision, but proposed after the suspension hearing, a downward adjustment in the data readings was made on the basis of the manufacturers' ability, in conformance with certification procedures, to replace the catalytic converter "once during 50,000 miles of vehicle operation," a change they had not used in their testing.

With the data submitted and the above assumptions, the Administrator concluded that no showing had been made that requisite technology was not available. The EPA noted that this did not mean that the variety of vehicles produced in 1975 would be as extensive as before. According to EPA, "Congress clearly intended to require major changes in the kinds of automobiles produced for sale in the United States after 1974" and there "is no basis, therefore, for construing the Act to authorizing suspension of the standards simply because the range of performance of cars with effective emission control may be restricted as compared to present cars." As long as "basic demand" for new light duty motor vehicles was satisfied, the applicants could not establish that technology was not available. * * *

[While the case was on appeal, the NAS completed a report on the issue. The report made by the AS, pursuant to its obligation under section 202(b)(5)(D) of the Clean Air Act, had concluded: "The Committee finds that the technology necessary to meet the requirements of the Clean Air Act Amendments for 1975 model year light-duty motor vehicles is not available at this time." After issuance of the report, the court had remanded to allow EPA to comment on it.]

The Administrator apparently relied, however, on the NAS Report to bolster his conclusion that the applicants had not established that technology was unavailable. The same NAS Report had stated:

> * * * the status of development and rate of progress made it possible that the larger manufacturers will be able to produce

vehicles that will qualify, provided that provisions are made for catalyst replacement and other maintenance, for averaging emissions of production vehicles, and for the general availability of fuel containing suitably low levels of catalyst poisons.

The Administrator pointed out that two of NAS's provisos—catalytic converter replacement and low lead levels—had been accounted for in his analysis of the auto company data, and provision therefor had been insured through regulation.

* * *

The most authoritative estimate in the record of the ecological costs of a one-year suspension is that of the NAS Report. Taking into account such "factors as the vehicle-age distribution among all automobiles, the decrease in vehicle miles driven per year, per car as vehicle age increases, the predicted nationwide growth in vehicle miles driven each year" and the effect of emission standards on exhaust control, NAS concluded that:

> * * * the effect on total emissions of a one-year suspension with no additional interim standards appears to be small. The effect is not more significant because the emission reduction now required of model year 1974 vehicles, as compared with uncontrolled vehicles (80 percent for HC and 69 percent for CO), is already so substantial.

* * *

On balance the record indicates the environmental costs of a one-year suspension are likely to be relatively modest. This must be balanced against the potential economic costs—and ecological costs—if the Administrator's prediction on the availability of effective technology is incorrect.

* * *

If in 1974, when model year 1975 cars start to come off the production line, the automobiles of Ford, General Motors and Chrysler cannot meet the 1975 standards and do not qualify for certification, the Administrator of EPA has the theoretical authority, under the Clean Air Act, to shut down the auto industry, as was clearly recognized in Congressional debate. We cannot put blinders on the facts before us so as to omit awareness of the reality that this authority would undoubtedly never be exercised. [More realistically, the court said, the standards would be later relaxed if they turned out to be wrong, but this too would cause problems.]

* * * The record before us suggests that there already exists a technological gap between Ford and General Motors, in Ford's favor. General Motors did not make the decision to concentrate on what EPA found to be the most effective system at the time of its decision—the noble metal monolithic catalyst. Instead it relied principally on testing the base metal catalyst as its first choice system. * * *

The case is haunted by the irony that what seems to be Ford's technological lead may operate to its grievous detriment, assuming the relaxation-if-necessary approach * * *. [If in 1974, when certification of production vehicles begins, any one of the three major companies cannot meet the 1975 standards, it is a likelihood that standards will be set to permit the higher level of emission control achievable by the laggard.] This will be the case whether or not the leader has or has not achieved compliance with the 1975 standards. Even if the relaxation is later made industry-wide, the Government's action, in first imposing a standard not generally achievable and then relaxing it, is likely to be detrimental to the leader who has tooled up to meet a higher standard than will ultimately be required.

In some contexts high achievement bestows the advantage that rightly belongs to the leader of high quality. In this context before us, however, the high achievement in emission control results, under systems presently available, in lessened car performance—an inverse correlation. The competitive disadvantage to the ecological leader presents a forbidding outcome—if the initial assumption of feasibility is not validated, and there is subsequent relaxation—for which we see no remedy.

* * *

This case inevitably presents, to the court as to the Administrator, the need for a perspective on the suspension that is informed by an analysis which balances the costs of a "wrong decision" on feasibility against the gains of a correct one. These costs include the risks of grave maladjustments for the technological leader from the eleventh-hour grant of a suspension, and the impact on jobs and the economy from a decision which is only partially accurate, allowing companies to produce cars but at a significantly reduced level of output. Against this must be weighed the environmental savings from denial of suspension. The record indicates that these will be relatively modest. * * *

Another consideration is present, that the real cost to granting a suspension arises from the symbolic compromise with the goal of a clean environment. We emphasize that our view of a one-year suspension, and the intent of Congress as to a one-year suspension, is in no sense to be taken as any support for further suspensions. This would plainly be contrary to the intent of Congress to set an absolute standard in 1976. * * *

We approach the question of the burden of proof on the auto companies with the previous considerations before us.

It is with utmost diffidence that we approach our assignment to review the Administrator's decision on "available technology." The legal issues are intermeshed with technical matters, and as yet judges have no scientific aides. Our diffidence is rooted in the underlying technical complexities, and remains even when we take into account that ours is a judicial review, and not a technical or policy redetermination. * * *

The Act makes suspension dependent on the Administrator's determination that:

> the applicant has established that effective control technology, processes, operating methods, or other alternatives are not available or have not been available for a sufficient period of time to achieve compliance prior to the effective date of such standards * * *.

* * *

Clearly this requires that the applicants come forward with data which showed that they could not comply with the contemplated standards. The normal rules place such a burden on the party in control of the relevant information. It was the auto companies who were in possession of the data about emission performance of their cars.

The submission of the auto companies unquestionably showed that no car had actually been driven 50,000 miles and achieved conformity of emissions to the 1975 standards. The Administrator's position is that on the basis of the methodology outlined, he can predict that the auto companies can meet the standards, and that the ability to make a prediction saying the companies can comply means that the petitioners have failed to sustain their burden of proof that they cannot comply.

* * *

[The number of unexplained assumptions used by the Administrator, the variance in methodology from that of the Report of the National Academy of Sciences, and the absence of an indication of the statistical reliability of the prediction, combine to generate grave doubts as to whether technology is available to meet the 1975 statutory standards.] We say this, incidentally, without implying or intending any acceptance of petitioners' substitute assumptions. These grave doubts have a legal consequence. This is customarily couched, by legal convention, in terms of "burden of proof." We visualize the problem in less structured terms although the underlying considerations, relating to risk of error, are related. As we see it the issue must be viewed as one of legislative intent. And since there is neither express wording nor legislative history on the precise issue, the intent must be imputed. The court must seek to discern and reconstruct what the legislature that enacted the statute would have contemplated for the court's action if it could have been able to foresee the precise situation. It is in this perspective that we have not flinched from our discussion of the economic and ecological risks inherent in a "wrong decision" by the Administrator. [We think the vehicle manufacturers established by a preponderance of the evidence, in the record before us, that technology was not available, within the meaning of the Act, when they adduced the tests on actual vehicles; that the Administrator's reliance on technological methodology to offset the actual tests raised serious doubts and failed to meet the burden of proof which in our view was properly assignable to him, in the light of accepted legal doctrine and the intent of Congress discerned, in part, by taking into account that the risk of an "erroneous" denial of suspension outweighed the risk of an "erroneous" grant of suspension. We do not use the burden of proof in the conventional sense of civil trials, but the [Administrator must sustain the burden of adducing a reasoned presentation supporting the reliability of EPA's methodology.]

* * *

[T]he parties should have opportunity on remand to address themselves to matters not previously put before them by EPA for comment * * *.

It is contemplated that, in the interest of providing a reasoned decision, the remand proceeding will involve some opportunity for cross-examination. In the remand proceeding—not governed by the same time congestion as the initial Decision process—we require reasonable cross-examination as to new lines of testimony, and as to submissions previously made to EPA in the hearing on a proffer that critical questions could not be satisfactorily pursued by procedures previously in effect. There is, however, still need for expedition, both by virtue of our order and the "lead time" problem, and the EPA may properly confine cross-examination to the essentials, avoiding discursive or repetitive questioning.

[Meanwhile] the Administrator may consider possible use of interim standards short of complete suspension. The statute permits conditioning of suspension on the adoption, by virtue of the information adduced in the suspension proceeding, of interim standards, higher than those set for 1974.

Notes

1.   Is the court's remand order consistent with *Vermont Yankee,* page 125 supra? Is the court's allocation of burden of proof consistent with the statute? For an argument that the court's decision flouted the statutory mandate, see Farber, "Statutory Interpretation and Legislative Supremacy," 78 *Geo.L.J.* 281, 298–300 (1989). For discussion of Judge Leventhal's use of burden of proof in another context, see pages 475–487, infra.

2.   You may find either of the following to be useful exercises: (a) Assume you are a member of the Supreme Court, which has granted certiorari in *International Harvester,* and write an opinion in the case. (b) Assume the court of appeals *upheld* EPA in *International Harvester* and that you are a member of a congressional committee overseeing EPA—what action would you take if it appeared that the industry could not meet the standards on time? Bear in mind Judge Leventhal's policy arguments about a simple postponement. Would the legislature have remedial options that would not be available to a court?

3.   Is the following a fair assessment of Judge Leventhal's opinion:

Reducing auto emissions 90% was, read literally, a rule statute. When read as if conditioned by the express commitment of the Act's authors to amend the requirements if the manufacturers made a real effort to comply, the section was not a rule because there was lacking an intention to apply the 90% requirement in the future; Congress was not about to shut down Detroit and had not concluded that accomplishing the 90% reduction was feasible. For these very reasons, the leading judicial interpretation of the 90% requirement dealt with the requirement primarily as a question of policy rather than one of rule interpretation.

Schoenbrod, "Goals Statutes or Rules Statutes: The Case of the Clean Air Act," 30 *U.C.L.A.L.Rev.* 740, 786 (1983). As you continue with this chapter, consider whether this is a fair description of the Clean Air Act as a whole.

Could it be argued that *International Harvester* is really a continuation of the common law tradition begun in the *Boomer* case, supra p. 290, of leniency toward polluters who claim better pollution control is technologically infeasible?

→ 4. The Clean Air Act contains a stringent preemption provision concerning state laws dealing with pollution control in new cars. Why do you suppose that Congress decided not to follow the usual pattern in federal pollution statutes, which has been that of giving states free rein to make their own regulations more stringent than the federal regulations? Note that an exception is made for California in light of the exceptional conditions in the L.A. area.

5. The ninety-percent emission reduction requirement imposed by the 1970 Clean Air Act was an example of "technology forcing" standards, that is, standards applicable at a later date, which can be met only through development of new technology not in existence at the time the standards are prescribed. (Compare the "cost-insensitive" scenario for kryptonia in the introduction of this chapter.) Whether the technology can be developed in time often is a matter of some uncertainty, and naturally depends to some extent on how hard the subject industry tries. Note that the vehicle manufacturers applied for suspensions at almost the earliest possible date (early in 1972), and that the EPA Administrator found against them on all four statutory points except the one concerning "good faith efforts" to meet the standard. In retrospect, wasn't it inevitable, given the language of the statute, that the companies would not meet the 1975 deadline and that either Congress, the Administrator or the court would forgive them? See Henderson and Pearson, "Implementing Federal Environmental Policies: The Limits of Aspirational Commands," 78 *Colum.L.Rev.* 1429, 1445–1453 (1978).

Note on Regulation of New Mobile and Stationary Sources

a.   Continuing Efforts to Control Car Emissions

International Harvester turned out to be only the first of a series of delays in meeting new car standards. [On remand in *International Harvester,* the Administrator granted the suspension and imposed interim emission standards more lenient than the ninety percent reduction, although allowing California to impose a more rigorous standard. In 1974 Congress amended the Act to postpone the final compliance deadlines until 1977, with another "escape hatch" to 1978. In 1975 the Administrator granted another one year suspension. In the 1977 Clean Air Act Amendments, Congress postponed final compliance until 1981, with provision for step reductions in the interim and for limited opportunities to obtain additional waivers. See Henderson and Pearson, cited in note 5 above, at 1447.] The 1981 standards were also the subject of waivers given to "financially troubled" automakers. *See* 12 *Envir.Rep.* 1398 (1981).

Title II of the 1990 Amendments to the Clean Air Act added extensive new provisions relating to mobile sources. One set of provisions tightened emission standards for 1998, cutting hydrocarbons 30% below the prior standard and nitrogen oxides 60%. Unless EPA determines that tougher standards are unnecessary or infeasible, a second tier of reductions will be required by 2003, cutting emissions by about another 50%. There is also a special carbon monoxide standard applicable to engine operation in low temperatures. States also have the option of adopting the even tougher California emission standards, which some have pursued (to great industry consternation). See *Motor Veh. Mfrs. Ass'n v. New York State Dept. of Env. Conserv.*, 17 F.3d 521 (2d Cir.1994).

In an unforeseen offshoot of the ozone transport problem discussed at the end of the previous chapter, EPA adopted the National Low Emission Vehicle (NLEV) program in March 1998. As noted above, the 1990 Amendments prohibited EPA from modifying the statutory standards until 2004, while still leaving intact California's special status. California adopted an ambitious program that required some zero emission cars. In the meantime, a majority of the ozone transport commission of northeastern and mid-Atlantic states, acting under § 184, pressed for uniform adoption of the California standards regionally. This proposal foundered in litigation, making it clear that state participation would be voluntary. See *Virginia v. EPA*, 108 F.3d 1397 (D.C.Cir.1997). Complex negotiations followed, involving California, the northeastern states, and EPA. The result was an agreement that substantially harmonized California and national requirements, allowing EPA to partially leapfrog the pre-2004 freeze on new national standards. See 62 Fed.Reg. 31, 191 (1997). Environmentalists were unhappy because California abandoned the proposed requirement for zero emissions.

In addition to these new emission standards, the 1990 amendments created an ambitious new program to change the composition of gasoline in heavily polluted cities. There seem to be two reasons for this program. First, the changed tailpipe standards have only a gradual impact on pollution levels, since they affect only new cars. Second, leaks from the system may defeat even the best exhaust treatment equipment. See "Gasoline: The Unclean Fuel?," 246 *Science* 199 (1989).

Reformulated gasoline must contain less volatile organic compounds and a higher amount of oxygen (in the form of alcohol or an ether compound). The changes in fuel composition should reduce ozone and carbon monoxide levels in the most smog-ridden cities. The sale of fuel exceeding the standards may earn credits, allowing sale of other fuel below the standards, thus providing flexibility. A recent scientific study suggests that some of the changes in gasoline composition will be helpful, such as the reduction in vapor pressure and light olefin, whereas the oxygenation will probably be less useful. See Calvert et al., "Achieving Acceptable Air Quality: Some Reflections on Controlling Vehicle Emissions," 261 *Science* 37 (1993). The next step may be to control the sulfur content of fuel. See "State Regulators Press for Sulfur Limit, Claim Oil Industry Obstructs Progress," 29 *Env.Rep.* 159 (May 15, 1998).

So long as gasoline-powered cars are used, emissions control will be essential. No matter how good the controls are when the car is manufactured, however, they will do little to reduce air pollution unless they remain effective over the life of the car. Increasingly strict inspection and maintenance (I & M) programs have been instituted for this reason. See Reitze & Needleman, "Control of Air Pollution from Mobile Sources Through Inspection and Maintenance Programs," 30 *Harv.J.Leg.* 411 (1993). Implementation of these programs has been plagued by delays. See GAO, "Delays in Motor Vehicle Inspection Programs Jeopardize Attainment of the Ozone Standard," (GAO/RCED 98–175, June 1998).

I & M programs, although politically unpopular, may be more effective than the alternatives. One study found that repairs to a single high-polluting car would reduce emissions more than fuel alterations in all eighty-four vehicles in the test group combined. Stuart Beaton et al., "On–Road Vehicle Emissions: Regulations, Costs, and Benefits," 268 *Science* 991, 992 (1995). Nevertheless, regulators are pressing ahead with fuel standards. One important rule was overturned in *American Petroleum Inst. v. U.S. EPA*, 52 F.3d 1113 (D.C.Cir.1995) (striking down a requirement that thirty percent of oxygen in reformulated fuel be derived from renewable sources such as ethanol). Manufacturers complain that some state fuel standards will in effect require stricter emissions standards for cars. See *Motor Vehicle Mfr. Ass'n v. New York State Dept. of Env. Conserv.*, 79 F.3d 1298 (2d Cir. 1996) (finding this claim to be unripe). In the meantime, there are snags in the program to design non-polluting cars by 2000, and the economics of non-gasoline cars remain unclear. See Marshall, "Slower Road for Clean–Car Program," 276 *Science* 194 (1997); Kazimi, "Valuing Alternative–Fuel Vehicles in Southern California," 87 *Amer.Econ.Rev.* 265 (1997).

Although eliminating smog has proved more difficult than anyone anticipated in 1970 when the Clean Air Act was passed, the stakes are high. One study suggests that in the L.A. area alone, attaining air pollution standards might save 1600 lives per year, and would produce an annual economic benefit of almost $10 billion. See Hall, et al., "Valuing the Health Benefits of Clean Air," 255 *Science* 812 (1992).

b. *Section 111 Standards for Stationary Sources*

Besides setting standards for new cars, the Clean Air Act also calls for standards governing new industrial facilities. Section 111 of the Clean Air Act directs EPA to promulgate "standards of performance" governing emissions by new stationary sources (i.e., not cars or trucks). Nationwide standards were apparently intended to prevent states from competing for new industry by lowering their pollution standards, and also to force industry to develop better pollution control technologies. Unlike the standards for new cars, the numerical limits for new plants were not set by Congress. Rather, this task was given to EPA.

The standards of performance are typical BAT regulations of the kind discussed in our second kryptonia scenario. In this case, the statutory formula is that the standards must reflect "the degree of emission limitation achievable through the application of the best system of emission reduction which (taking into account the cost of achieving such reduction and any nonair quality health and environmental impact and energy requirements) the Administrator determines has been adequately demonstrated." In *Portland Cement Ass'n v. Ruckelshaus,* 486 F.2d 375 (D.C.Cir.1973), cert. denied 417 U.S. 921, 94 S.Ct. 2628, 41 L.Ed.2d 226 (1974), industry challenged EPA's standard of performance for Portland cement plans—presumably including those of the Atlantic Cement Co., see p. 290 supra. The companies contended that EPA should have performed a cost-benefit analysis. Instead, EPA had estimated the total costs of the necessary control equipment and had concluded that those costs could be passed along to customers without much loss of business to substitutes such as steel, asphalt and aluminum. Because of the difficulties of performing a fuller cost-benefit analysis, the court held that EPA had given sufficient attention to costs. Notably, *Portland Cement* was written by Judge Leventhal, who also authored *International Harvester.*[f]

Significantly, the new source standards apply not only to brand-new facilities, but also to "modifications" of existing facilities. Section 111(a)(4) defines a modification to include any physical change in a facility, or any changed method of operations, that results in an increase in emissions. (Can you see why Congress wanted to extend the new source standards to these plant modifications?) The test is whether atmospheric emissions have increased, not whether pre-controlled emissions have done so. See *National–Southwire Aluminum Co. v. United States EPA,* 838 F.2d 835 (6th Cir.1988). Also, note that "routine" renovations are exempted. See *Wisconsin Electric Power Co. v. Reilly,* 893 F.2d 901 (7th Cir.1990).

Conventionally, best achievable technology is usually conceptualized as an "end of the pipeline" treatment method. But other forms of

---

f. Apparently in response to *Portland Cement,* § 317 was added to the Clean Air Act in 1977. It provides that before publishing notice of a proposal to adopt or revise any standard under section 111, the Administrator shall prepare "an economic impact assessment respecting such standard or regulation." This assessment, which shall be available to the public, is to analyze costs of compliance, potential inflationary or recessionary effects, effects on competition with respect to small business, effects on consumer costs, and effects on energy use. However, § 317(e) prohibits consideration of the adequacy of the economic impact statement in the course of judicial review of the ensuing regulation. Failure to prepare the statement is, however, subject to mandamus under § 317(f).

pollution reduction might be considered as possibilities, for example, recycling as an alternative to pollution control at an incinerator. See *Citizens for Clean Air v. U.S. EPA,* 959 F.2d 839 (9th Cir.1992) (rejecting recycling as BAT under the particular facts of the case). In general, integrated pollution control offers some intriguing possible advantages over "end-of-the-smokestack" controls.

Title V of the 1990 amendments established a permit program to strengthen enforcement of technology-based standards. [Permits are required for major sources and for sources that are covered by various technology-based standards such as § 111. (See § 502(a) for a complete listing of the sources covered by the permit requirement).] EPA can veto state permits, and if the state fails to meet EPA's objections within 90 days, EPA may then issue or deny the permit itself. § 505(b). While in effect, the permits will provide a shield against other requirements of the statute: compliance with the permit will be deemed compliance with all statutory requirements. § 504(f). Permits are limited to terms of five years or less. § 502(b)(5)(B). As we will see, a similar permit system has long been used under the Clean Water Act.

The permits may be particularly important because they simplify citizen suits. All that an environmental group will need to do is to verify the permit terms and then check state monitoring records to identify violations. (Note that the 1990 amendments to § 304 allow suit on repeated past violations, without requiring a showing of any threat of future violations). For further discussion of citizen suits, see p. 567 infra. Some of the other arguments for a permit system were explored in Pedersen, "Why the Clean Air Act Works Badly," 129 *U.Penn.L.Rev.* 1059 (1981). For a comprehensive analysis of the permit system, see Roady, "Permitting and Enforcement Under the Clean Air Act," 21 *Env.L.Rep.* 10179 (1991).

Implementation of the permit requirements has not been friction-free. One continuing issue has been the exception for small dischargers. In *Western States Petroleum Ass'n v. EPA*, 87 F.3d 280 (9th Cir.1996), the court overturned EPA's rejection of the Washington State permit program. Although the court did not find EPA's action to be inconsistent with the statute, it concluded that EPA had been so erratic in its decisions on the issue across the country that its rejection of Washington's program had to be considered an abuse of discretion. EPA had argued that it was impossible for it to fully coordinate decisions between various regional offices.

2. WATER POLLUTION

Water pollution law is an area with a long history. As Professor Rodgers puts it:

> Water pollution law today begins with an intimidating 90–page Act of Congress, the Federal Water Pollution Control Act Amendments of 1972, supplemented by a 45–pager in the form of the Clean Water Act of 1977 and an 82–page follow-up called the Water

Quality Act of 1987. Known either as the Federal Water Pollution Control Act or as the Clean Water Act, this colossal compilation is but a predictable convergence of several historical forces. In many ways a novel and remarkable legislative effort, the Clean Water Act, like the Clean Air Act before it, still is rooted deeply in the past, expressing principles well accepted for generations.

W. Rodgers, *Environmental Law* 247–248 (2d ed. 1994).

Prior to 1972 the Federal Water Pollution Control Act (FWPCA) prescribed a regulatory system consisting mainly of state-developed water quality standards for interstate or navigable waters. The standards for any particular locale depended upon the uses (e.g., agricultural, industrial, recreational) which the state wanted to facilitate. Enforcement was possible only where a discharge reduced the quality of the receiving water below the specified level. The system failed due to the lack, if not infeasibility, of enforcement. Multiple polluters discharging into the same stream or lake presented problems of proof similar to those encountered under nuisance law.

Seeking a more workable system in the late 1960s, the federal government turned to the little-known Refuse Act of 1899, 33 U.S.C.A. § 407, which prohibited the discharge of "refuse" into navigable waters without a permit from the Army Corps of Engineers. A new permit system was to be the means of establishing enforceable effluent limitations applicable to individual dischargers. However, implementation of this program was halted by an injunction, pending preparation of an environmental impact statement under the National Environmental Policy Act of 1969. Before the injunction was dissolved, Congress passed the FWPCA Amendments of 1972, completely revamping federal statutory authority over water pollution and displacing the permit program under the Refuse Act. We will limit our attention to the provisions covering industry, as opposed to municipal sewage systems.

The 1972 amendments established a system of standards, permits and enforcement aimed at a "goal" of eliminating all discharges into navigable waters by 1985. (Even today, the statute still contains this long-passed deadline!) Ambient water quality standards were to be supplemented by discharge standards in the form of effluent limitations applicable to all "point sources" ("any discernible, confined and discrete conveyance * * * from which pollutants are or may be discharged"). Under § 301, effluent limitations for all point sources except municipal treatment works were required to reflect "best practicable control technology currently available" (BPT) by July 1, 1977, and "best available technology economically achievable" (BAT) by July 1, 1983. Public treatment works were required to adopt "secondary treatment" by 1977 and "best practicable waste treatment over the life of the works" by 1983. Section 306 required that new sources in specified categories meet effluent limitations equivalent to the 1983 standards. Section 307 required that EPA maintain a list of toxic substances and establish separate limitations for them. These limitations were to be based mainly on protection of public health and water quality, rather than technological feasibility, and were to provide an "ample margin of safety."

Amended § 402 created a permit system, the National Pollutant Discharge Elimination System (NPDES), under which discharge permits could be granted by EPA or by states with EPA-approved programs. All discharges by point sources, except in compliance with the limitations imposed in a permit, were declared unlawful. Permits had to incorporate applicable effluent limitations established under §§ 301, 302, 306 and 307, including an enforceable schedule of compliance to meet the 1977 and 1983 deadlines.

The 1972 amendments contemplated that enforcement would be primarily by the states. However, the federal government was not constrained, as it had been under the previous FWPCA, from acting to enforce state or federal standards. Provisions allowing for inspection, entry and monitoring, federal enforcement (including emergency action), and citizen suits were all designed to facilitate enforcement of the new standards. Under § 505, citizens could sue to enforce effluent limitations in state or EPA permits and in orders issued by EPA. Citizens also could sue EPA for failure to perform nondiscretionary duties. Finally, states were left free to impose more rigorous standards.

The subsequent history of the FWPCA involved a complex series of adjustments to the deadlines established in 1972. Like the Clean Air Act, the FWPCA was substantially amended in 1977. It was renamed the Clean Water Act. EPA was authorized to grant case-by-case extensions of the 1977 deadline for adoption of "best practicable" control technology to industrial dischargers which had attempted in good faith to comply; however, full compliance was supposedly required by 1979.

Concerning the previous 1983 deadline for industry compliance with EPA effluent limitations reflecting "best available technology economically achievable," the revisions were more complex. Different requirements were adopted for three categories of pollutants: (1) "toxic" pollutants, including initially a list of 129 specific chemicals; (2) "conventional" pollutants of the kind commonly found in sewage, including BOD, fecal coliform, suspended solids, and pH; and (3) "nonconventional" pollutants, those not classified by the EPA as either toxic or conventional. Sections 301(b)(2), 304(a)(4) and (b)(4), and 307(a). The deadlines were set as follows:

> *For toxic pollutants,* BAT was supposed to be employed by July 1, 1984 (or, for pollutants not on the original list, within three years after EPA adoption of applicable effluent limitations), with no exceptions allowed. EPA may establish stricter toxic standards, including zero discharge, where necessary.

> *For conventional pollutants,* a new standard, "best conventional pollutant control technology" (BCT), was established. It was to be achieved by July 1, 1984. In establishing effluent limitations for conventional pollutants, EPA is to consider, among other things, "the reasonableness of the relationship between the costs of attain-

ing a reduction in effluents and the effluent reduction benefits derived." This factor is not considered in formulating BAT limitations for toxic and nonconventional pollutants.

For nonconventional pollutants, effluent limitations based on BAT were to be achieved within three years after the limitations are established or by July 1, 1984, whichever is later.

The Clean Water Act was extensively amended again in 1987, with more tinkering with deadlines.[g]

The bottom line of all of this reshuffling of deadlines was as follows. BPT (in theory) should have been achieved by 1979. For most pollutants, the deadline for the next tier of standards was "no later than 1989." We recount the complex history in part as an object lesson in the flexibility of statutory "deadlines."

These complicated phased standards may have limited real-world significance. In practice, the Act's elaborate system of phased standards may have virtually collapsed into a single stage of BPT. Oliver Houck observes:

> The attempt to set BAT for the organic chemicals, plastics, and synthetic materials category bottomed out, after years of administrative warfare, at a standard no better than BPT. Indeed, EPA concluded by proposing BAT for new sources in this industry, standards intended to be the toughest in the Clean Water Act, without consideration of recycling technologies that had already been adopted by thirty-six plants; twenty-six percent of the industry had already achieved *zero* discharge. These consequences are not unusual; one observer of the process concluded that, while the first-stage BPT inquiry was rigorous, subsequent BAT standards, in general, required little more.

Houck, "Of Bats, Birds, and B–A–T: The Convergent Evolution of Environmental Law," 63 *Miss.L.J.* 403, 452 (1994).

Problem on the Scope of the Permit Requirement

These facts are derived from an actual case. Geronimo Villegas operated a medical laboratory. On several occasions, he brought blood vials from the lab to his house, and then deposited them on a bulkhead along the Hudson River. Some of the vials were contaminated with hepatitis. He was prosecuted for discharging pollutants without a permit. Villegas claims not to be

g. As far as effluent limitations are concerned, the primary changes were as follows. First, the deadline for the conventional and toxic standards was set at "no later than March 31, 1989." Second, sources using "innovative production processes" or "innovative control techniques" that have the potential for attaining better effluent levels or attaining existing requirements more cheaply, could obtain an additional two years to comply "if it is also determined that such innovative system has the potential for industrywide application." (§ 301(k)). Third, a new "anti-backsliding" provision limits the ability of a source to obtain a new permit with weaker requirements than its old permit when subsequently issued effluent limitations are less stringent than those in the old permit. § 406(*o*).

subject to the permit requirement. The government points to the following legislative history. The Senate report stated:

> In order to further clarify the scope of the regulatory procedures in the Act the Committee had added a definition of point source to distinguish between control requirements where there are specific confined conveyances, such as pipes, and control requirements which are imposed to control runoff. The control of pollutants from runoff is applied pursuant to section 209 and the authority resides in the State or other authority.

Senator Dole added:

> Most of the problems of agricultural pollution deal with non-point sources. Very simply, a non-point source of pollution is one that does not confine its polluting discharge to one fairly specific outlet, such as a sewer pipe, a drainage ditch or conduit; thus, a feedlot would be considered to be a non-point source as would pesticides and fertilizers.

Taking into account the statutory language, legislative history, and whatever policy considerations are relevant, did Villegas violate the statute?

The following case, decided before the 1977 amendments, illustrates the process by which EPA establishes effluent limitations and the manner in which appellate courts review such rulemaking. It may give you a better "feel" for how pollution standards are actually established.

AMERICAN MEAT INSTITUTE v. EPA

United States Court of Appeals, Seventh Circuit, 1975.
526 F.2d 442.

TONE, CIRCUIT JUDGE.

This is a review of effluent limitations promulgated by the Administrator of the Environmental Protection Agency under the Federal Water Pollution Control Act Amendments of 1972 * * *. Petitioner is the American Meat Institute ("AMI"), whose members operate slaughterhouses and meat-packing plants throughout the country. The regulations under review limit the quantities of various pollutants which these plants can discharge into waterways. Our jurisdiction is invoked under § 509(b) of the Act.

* * *

The regulations before us cover the "Red Meat Processing Segment of the Meat Products Point Source Category." The common characteristic of the plants in this segment of the meat industry is that they all slaughter animals (but not poultry) and produce fresh meat, which may be sold as whole, half, or quarter carcasses, or as smaller meat cuts. Plants that produce only fresh meat are called slaughterhouses; those that also produce cured, smoked, canned, or other prepared meat products are called packinghouses. Both types of plants usually perform some by-product processing, such as rendering (separation of fats and water from tissue), blood processing, and hide processing.

EPA employed North Star Research Institute to study the industrial processes used by slaughterhouses and packinghouses, the wastes generated, and the treatment technologies in use or available to these plants, and to recommend, inter alia, effluent limitations under § 301(b). North Star proceeded to study relevant literature and information on the meat industry it had previously gathered for EPA. In conjunction with AMI, it prepared questionnaires which were distributed to slaughterhouses and packinghouses. From the responses to the questionnaires and information acquired from various other sources, North Star classified the plants into four subcategories and attempted to identify those in each subcategory having the most effluent control. To verify the questionnaire responses, selected plants from these groups were inspected and monitored to a very limited extent. In June 1973, North Star submitted to EPA a report in which the information North Star had gathered was collected and summarized, and analyses and recommendations were presented.

After reviewing the North Star report, distributing copies to industry representatives, and receiving their comments, EPA revised the report and published the revision as a Draft Development Document in October 1973. The standards recommended in this document were then incorporated into proposed regulations, which the agency published the same month. * * *

After publication of the proposed regulations, EPA received further comments. On February 28, 1974, it promulgated the final regulations which are the subject of this review proceeding. In addition, a revised version of the October 1973 Draft Development Document was published under date of February 1974 as the Final Development Document (hereinafter sometimes cited as FDD).

The regulations classify slaughterhouses and packinghouses into the following four subcategories:

    (1) simple slaughterhouses, which slaughter animals and perform a limited number, usually no more than two, by-product processing operations;

    (2) complex slaughterhouses, which slaughter animals and perform several, usually three or more, by-product processing operations; and

    (3) low-processing packinghouses, which not only slaughter animals but process meat from animals killed at that plant into cured, smoked, canned, and other prepared meat products, normally processing less than the total kill; and

    (4) high-processing packinghouses, which not only slaughter animals but process meat from both animals killed at the plant and animals killed elsewhere.

For existing sources in each subcategory, the regulations set forth "[e]ffluent limitations guidelines" for 1977, which are apparently intended to constitute both guidelines under § 304(b) and effluent limitations under § 301(b). * * * The same is true of the 1983 standards. * * *

The regulations limit the discharge of "BOD5," "TSS," and ammonia, in addition to other pollutants not involved in this proceeding. Two of these terms require explanation:

BOD5. The initials "BOD" stand for "biochemical oxygen demand" and describe pollutants which, when they decompose, deplete oxygen necessary to support aquatic life. BOD5 is BOD measured over a five-day period.

TSS. The initials "TSS" stand for "total suspended solids," which are particles of organic and inorganic matter suspended in the water or floating on its surface.

The regulations permit the discharge of certain amounts of BOD5 and TSS per 1,000 pounds (or per 1,000 kilograms) of live weight killed ("LWK"). The 1983 ammonia standard is set in terms of milligrams of ammonia per liter of effluent (mg/l), which shows the concentration of ammonia in the effluent. The regulations challenged in this case are the existing source limitations for 1977 and 1983 relating to BOD5 and TSS, and those for 1983 relating to ammonia. * * *

[The court then considered a jurisdictional issue and held that it had jurisdiction over the case. After resolving this issue, and discussing the standard of review, it turned to the merits.]

AMI's first challenge is directed at the 1977 effluent limitations, which require application of "the best practicable control technology currently available." For guidance in interpreting that term, EPA looks to Senator Muskie's written explanation to the Senate, * * * in which he stated as follows:

> In defining "best practicable" for any given industrial category, the Committee expects the Administrator to take a number of factors into account. These factors should include the age of the plants, their size, the unit processes involved, and the cost of applying such controls.

> The Administrator should establish the range of "best practicable" levels based upon the average of the best existing performance by plants of various sizes, ages, and unit processes within each industrial category. In those industrial categories where present practices are uniformly inadequate, the Administrator should interpret "best practicable" to require higher levels of control than any currently in place if he determines that the technology to achieve those higher levels can be practicably applied.

> "Best practicable" can be interpreted as the equivalent of secondary treatment for industry, but this interpretation should not be construed to limit the authority of the Administrator.

as long as you can show it can work. ⭐

This, we think, is a reasonable view of the Administrator's responsibility. The "best practicable technology" will normally be defined based on the average performance of the best existing plants. If, however, the Administrator concludes that present practices in an industrial category are uniformly inadequate, he may require levels of control based on technology not presently in use in the category (or, it would seem, technology in use only by a single plant), if he determines, by applying the criteria listed in § 304(b)(1)(B), that this technology can be practicably applied throughout the category. One of these criteria is the cost of applying the proposed technology in relation to the resulting effluent reduction. With these principles in mind, we turn to AMI's challenges to the 1977 standards.

It appears from EPA comments introducing the final regulation * * * that the 1977 effluent limitations are based primarily on the technology of biological treatment through a three-lagoon system. This is considered "secondary" treatment, that is, treatment which takes place after the waste water has passed through "primary," inplant treatment systems. In a three-lagoon system, waste water from the plant flows first into the anaerobic lagoon, where organic matter in the effluent is partially consumed by anaerobic bacteria (bacteria that do not require free oxygen). To increase oxygen levels in the waste water, it is then mechanically aerated in the aerated lagoon. The water then flows to the aerobic lagoon, where most of the remaining organic matter is consumed by aerobic bacteria (bacteria that do need oxygen). After being held there for a relatively long period, the waste water is discharged.

* * *

AMI's first argument, aimed at the 1977 effluent limitations for all four subcategories of plants, is that, while the proposed lagoon system qualifies as practicable, it cannot achieve the limitations on a year-round basis because of seasonal and climatic effects. Winter conditions, according to AMI, impair the efficiency of both anaerobic and aerobic lagoons, while algae growth in the summer increases BOD5 and TSS.

(1) THE EFFECT OF WINTER TEMPERATURES ON THE ANAEROBIC LAGOON

The optimum temperature for an anaerobic lagoon is approximately 90E F. Cold temperatures cause it to function less efficiently by slowing bacterial activity. The issue is the magnitude of this effect. AMI relies on an authority which says that removals are reduced to 70%. It conceded in its submittal to the agency, however, that the effect of winter temperatures on the anaerobic lagoon is small.

EPA argues that winter temperatures are counteracted by the heat of incoming waste water (80–100E F.) and by the insulating grease cover that forms over the pool. An article concerning the Wilson plant at Cherokee, Iowa, reports that the grease cover on the anaerobic pool, after taking some time to build up, insulated the effluent and maintained satisfactory temperatures. The anaerobic pond at that plant operated at a 92% level of efficiency in February 1970. EPA's conclusion is also supported by data on other plants supplied by the State of Iowa, which show, for example, that at one plant the anaerobic temperature on two dates in January 1972 was 77–78E F.

* * *

We conclude that there is firm record support for EPA's conclusion on the effect of cold weather on the efficiency of the anaerobic lagoon.

(2) The Effect of Winter Temperatures on the Aerobic Lagoon

Like anaerobic lagoons, aerobic lagoons operate less efficiently in winter. Cold temperatures inhibit aerobic microorganisms, and ice and snow covers reduce the oxygen content of water. EPA argues that these difficulties can be ameliorated by increasing detention time, thereby giving the microorganisms more time to work, by using additional aerobic ponds, or by using submerged aerators. We agree with AMI that EPA's argument as to these countermeasures is inadequately supported by the record.

The record does suggest, however, that winter conditions do not make compliance with the 1977 standards impossible, since some plants have succeeded in complying with the BOD5 standards in winter. One such plant was the Wilson plant at Cherokee, Iowa, which maintained a 45% level of aerobic removal of BOD5 in February. The American Beef plant at Oakland, Iowa, also met the BOD5 limitations during the winter months, as did several other plants. AMI's argument that some of these plants should be disregarded because they did not discharge in some winter months is unsound. As counsel for EPA pointed out during oral argument, a plant which does not discharge during a given period may be continuing its operations while storing its effluent. Our examination of the record confirms that the plants in question continued operations during periods when they did not discharge. The time of release is unimportant, so long as the effluent is successfully treated before release.

* * *

(3) The Effect of Summer Weather on Aerobic Lagoons

Warm weather promotes the growth of algae. On the basis of comments in the record by industry representatives, state pollution authorities, and others about the effect of algae on aerobic lagoons, AMI argues that algae growth increases TSS and BOD5 counts. Two of these comments refer in general terms to problems at individual plants without giving detailed supporting data; another comment is heavily qualified and inconclusive; and the others are purely conclusory.

EPA states that the Illini Beef plant at Genesco, Illinois, and the Swift plant at Glenwood, Iowa, were able to meet the standards during summer months, as was the Routh plant at Sandusky, Ohio. AMI does not respond directly to these assertions, and from our examination of the record we conclude that data from these plants fail to show the correlation between summer weather and TSS predicted by AMI.

With respect to BOD5, EPA cites data from five plants that complied with the 1977 effluent limitations during the summer. AMI does not contest the figures regarding summer performance for two of these plants (Wilson, Cherokee, and Swift, Glenwood) but argues that Illini Beef and another plant should be disregarded * * *. Nevertheless, the ability of even two plants using the proposed technology to meet the BOD5 and TSS standards in summer demonstrates that the standards are attainable in warm weather and is sufficient to overcome AMI's weakly supported position.

In summary, we find sufficient basis in the record for the Administrator's conclusion that temperature changes do not render the 1977 effluent limitations unattainable by the 1977 technology he designated.

Notes

1. *American Meat Institute* is a typical example of "hard look" judicial review. Indeed, it is not difficult to find some instances of much more intrusive judicial review of EPA decisions. See McGarity, "Some Thoughts on 'Deossifying' the Rulemaking Process," 41 *Duke L.J.* 1415–1422 (1992). In *Corrosion Proof Fittings v. EPA,* 947 F.2d 1201 (5th Cir.1991), page 501 infra, the Fifth Circuit overturned EPA's carefully considered asbestos regulations, effectively wrecking EPA's most serious effort to implement the Toxic Substances Control Act. Other judges have not hesitated to correct agencies on technical issues like choice of the proper computer model. See, e.g., *AFL–CIO v. OSHA,* 965 F.2d 962 (11th Cir.1992) (demanding that agency separately document health effects for each of 428 toxic substances, although OSHA argued that this was scientifically infeasible); *State of Ohio v. EPA,* 784 F.2d 224 (6th Cir.1986) (rejecting EPA computer model); *Gulf South Insulation v. Consumer Product Safety Comm'n,* 701 F.2d 1137 (5th Cir.1983) (second-guessing the agency on technical issues). Is intensive judicial scrutiny justified as a means of improving the objectivity and carefulness of EPA's decisionmaking? For some reflections on judicial review of EPA decisions, see Glicksman and Schroeder, "EPA and the Courts: Twenty Years of Law and Politics," 54 *L. & Contemp.Probs.* 249 (1991).

How suited are judges to deciding such issues? Would it be preferable to have a special "Science Court" to decide environmental cases?

2. The regulatory process has certainly been far more cumbersome, and exhausting, than Congress ever anticipated in 1972 when the statute was passed:

> The EPA's review of dozens of industrial categories, covering dozens of pollutants, hundreds of processes and affecting thousands of individual plants, was subject to intense lobbying from trade associations on the one hand and environmental organizations on the other. Each review was a prelude to litigation, frequent remands and the renewal of new rounds of battle. One lawsuit challenging BAT for one industrial category alone produced a 600,000 page administrative record, seventy legal claims, over 3,000 pages of briefs, and a 9,000 page joint appendix.

Twenty years after the CWA gave marching orders for BAT, EPA was still trying to promulgate these standards for industries as significant as offshore oil and gas production, pesticide manufacture, and plastics and organic chemicals.

Houck, "Of Bats, Birds, and B–A–T: The Convergent Evolution of Environmental Law," 63 *Miss.L.J.* 403, 456–57 (1994).

3.   When *American Meat Institute* was decided, there was a split among the lower federal courts concerning the basic mechanisms to be used in setting 1977 effluent limitations, particularly the respective roles to be played by federal regulations versus state permits. The following decision settled this controversy and remains the foundation for further interpretations of the Clean Water Act.

E.I. du PONT de NEMOURS & CO. v. TRAIN

Supreme Court of the United States, 1977.
430 U.S. 112, 97 S.Ct. 965, 51 L.Ed.2d 204.

MR. JUSTICE STEVENS delivered the opinion of the Court.

[EPA issued industry-wide effluent limitations for the organic chemicals industry, similar to the limitations for slaughterhouses issued in the *American Meat Institute* case. The Court began by reviewing the history of these regulations and described the statutory scheme. It then turned to the central issue in the case. Before reading the Court's discussion, you may wish to review the description of the statute on page 316 supra. Note that the *du Pont* opinion refers to the pre–1977 version of the statute.]

The broad outlines of the parties' respective theories may be stated briefly. EPA contends that § 301(b) authorizes it to issue regulations establishing effluent limitations for classes of plants. The permits granted under § 402, in EPA's view, simply incorporate these across-the-board limitations, except for the limited variances allowed by the regulations themselves and by § 301(c). The § 304(b) guidelines, according to EPA, were intended to guide it in later establishing § 301 effluent limitation regulations. Because the process proved more time consuming than Congress assumed when it established this two-stage process, EPA condensed the two stages into a single regulation.

In contrast, petitioners contend that § 301 is not an independent source of authority for setting effluent limitations by regulation. Instead, § 301 is seen as merely a description of the effluent limitations which are set for each plant on an individual basis during the permit-issuance process. Under the industry view, the § 304 guidelines serve the function of guiding the permit issuer in setting the effluent limitations.

The jurisdictional issue is subsidiary to the critical question whether EPA has the power to issue effluent limitations by regulation. Section 509(b)(1) provides that "[r]eview of the Administrator's action * * * (E) in approving or promulgating any effluent limitation * * * under section 301" may be had in the courts of appeals. On the other hand, the Act does not provide for judicial review of § 304 guidelines. If EPA is correct that its regulations are "effluent limitations under section 301," the regulations are directly reviewable in the Court of Appeals. If industry is correct that the regulations can only be considered § 304 guidelines, suit to review the regulations could probably be brought only in the District Court, if anywhere. Thus, the issue of jurisdiction to review the regulations is intertwined with the issue of EPA's power to issue the regulations.

We think § 301 itself is the key to the problem. The statutory language concerning the 1983 limitation, in particular, leaves no doubt that these limitations are to be set by regulation. Subsection (b)(2)(A) of § 301 states that by 1983 "effluent limitations for *categories and classes* of point sources" are to be achieved which will require "application of the best available technology economically achievable *for such category or class.*" (Emphasis added.) These effluent limitations are to require elimination of all discharges if "such elimination is technologically and economically achievable for a *category or class* of point sources." (Emphasis added.) This is "language difficult to reconcile with the view that individual effluent limitations are to be set when each permit is issued." *American Meat Institute v. EPA,* 526 F.2d 442, 450 (C.A.7 1975). The statute thus focuses expressly on the characteristics of the "category or class" rather than the characteristics of individual point sources. Normally, such class-wide determinations would be made by regulation, not in the course of issuing a permit to one member of the class.[1]

Thus, we find that § 301 unambiguously provides for the use of regulations to establish the 1983 effluent limitations. Different language is used in § 301 with respect to the 1977 limitations. Here, the statute speaks of "effluent limitations for point sources," rather than "effluent limitations for categories and classes of point sources." Nothing elsewhere in the Act, however, suggests any radical difference in the mechanism used to impose limitations for the 1977 and 1983 deadlines. For instance, there is no indication in either § 301 or § 304 that the § 304 guidelines play a different role in setting 1977 limitations. Moreover, it would be highly anomalous if the 1983 regulations and the new source standards were directly reviewable in the Court of Appeals, while the 1977 regulations based on the same administrative record were reviewable only in the District Court. The magnitude and highly technical character of the administrative record involved with these regulations makes it almost inconceivable that Congress would have required duplicate review in the first instance by different courts. We conclude

---

1. Furthermore, § 301(c) provides that the 1983 limitations may be modified if the owner of a plant shows "that such modified requirements (1) will represent the maximum use of technology within the economic capability of the owner or operator; and (2) will result in reasonable further progress toward the elimination of the discharge of pollutants." This provision shows that the § 301(b) limitations for 1983 are to be established prior to consideration of the characteristics of the individual plant. Moreover, it shows that the term "best technology economically achievable" does not refer to any individual plant. Otherwise, it would be impossible for this "economically achievable" technology to be beyond the individual owner's "economic capability."

that the statute authorizes the 1977 limitations as well as the 1983 limitations to be set by regulation, so long as some allowance is made for variations in individual plants, as EPA has done by including a variance clause in its 1977 limitations.[2]

* * *

The legislative history supports this reading of § 301. The Senate Report states that "pursuant to subsection 301(b)(1)(A), and Section 304(b)" the Administrator is to set a base level for all plants in a given category, and "[i]n no case * * * should any plant be allowed to discharge more pollutants per unit of production than is defined by that base level." The Conference Report on § 301 states that "the determination of the economic impact of an effluent limitation [will be made] on the basis of classes and categories of point sources, as distinguished from a plant by plant determination." In presenting the Conference Report to the Senate, Senator Muskie, perhaps the Act's primary author, emphasized the importance of uniformity in setting § 301 limitations. He explained that this goal of uniformity required that EPA focus on classes or categories of sources in formulating effluent limitations. [The Court then quotes extensively from Senator Muskie's explanation].

Our construction of the Act is supported by § 501(a), which gives EPA the power to make "such regulations as are necessary to carry out" its functions, and by § 101(d), which charges the agency with the duty of administering the Act. In construing this grant of authority, as Justice Harlan wrote in connection with a somewhat similar problem:

> "[C]onsiderations of feasibility and practicality are certainly germane" to the issues before us. We cannot, in these circumstances, conclude that Congress has given authority inadequate to achieve with reasonable effectiveness the purposes for which it has acted.

The petitioners' view of the Act would place an impossible burden on EPA. It would require EPA to give individual consideration to the circumstances of each of the more than 42,000 dischargers who have applied for permits and to issue or approve all these permits well in advance of the 1977 deadline in order to give industry time to install the necessary pollution control equipment. We do not believe that Congress would have failed so conspicuously to provide EPA with the authority needed to achieve the statutory goals.

Both EPA and petitioners refer to numerous other provisions of the Act and fragments of legislative history in support of their positions. We do not find these conclusive, and little point would be served by discussing them in detail. We are satisfied that our reading of § 301 is consistent with the rest of the legislative scheme.

Language we recently employed by another case involving the validity of EPA regulations applies equally to this case:

2. We agree with the Court of Appeals, that consideration of whether EPA's variance provision has the proper scope would be premature.

"We therefore conclude that the Agency's interpretation * * * was 'correct,' to the extent that it can be said with complete assurance that any particular interpretation of a complex statute such as this is the 'correct' one. Given this conclusion, as well as the facts that the Agency is charged with administration of the Act, and that there has undoubtedly been reliance upon its interpretation by the States and other parties affected by the Act, we have no doubt whatever that its construction was sufficiently reasonable to preclude the Court of Appeals from substituting its judgment for that of the Agency." *Train v. Natural Resources Defense Council,* [infra page 351].[3]

When as in this case, the Agency's interpretation is also supported by thorough, scholarly opinions written by some of our finest judges, and has received the overwhelming support of the courts of appeals, we would be reluctant indeed to upset the agency's judgment. In this case, on the contrary, our independent examination confirms the correctness of the Agency's construction of the statute.

Notes

1.   Note that the Court holds that a variance provision is required in connection with the 1977 effluent limitations. In footnote 19 of the opinion, the Court declines to consider the validity of the agency's restrictions on the availability of variances. We will return to this issue at page 334 infra.

The *du Pont* Court explained variances as a method of individually tailoring the BPT requirement to particular plants. An alternative method of tailoring the requirements would be to sub-categorize the industry when issuing effluent limitations. Because of the availability of FDF as an alternative, however, EPA's duty to sub-categorize is quite limited. See *Chemical Mfrs. Ass'n v. United States EPA,* 870 F.2d 177, 221–226 (5th Cir.1989). (The industry also argued that the regulations should be stayed with respect to those individual plants, pending EPA's decision on granting variances. The court declined to do so. Id. at 226.)

2.   For a critique of *du Pont,* see Currie, "Congress, The Court, and Water Pollution," 1977 *Sup.Ct.Rev.* 39. Note the *du Pont* Court's concern about the impracticality of overseeing 42,000 individual permit applications. This was a highly sensible concern at the time of the

---

3. Petitioners contend that the administrative construction should not receive deference because it was not contemporaneous with the passage of the Act. They base this argument primarily on the fact that EPA's initial notices of its proposed rulemaking refer to § 304(b), rather than § 301, as the source of authority. But, this is merely evidence that the Administrator originally intended to issue guidelines prior to issuing effluent limitation regulations. In fact, in a letter urging the President to sign the Act, the Administrator stated that "[t]he Conference bill fully incorporates as its central regulatory point the Administrator's proposal concerning *effluent limitations in terms of industrial categories and groups* ultimately applicable to individual dischargers through a permit system." Finally, the EPA interpretation would be entitled to some deference even if it was not contemporaneous, "having in mind the complexity and technical nature of the statutes and the subjects they regulate, the obscurity of the statutory language, and EPA's unique experience and expertise in dealing with the problems created by these conditions." *American Meat Inst.* [supra page 319].

Court's ruling, but may be less compelling today. True, it would be a daunting task to assess the technological and economic basis of each permit individually. But new methods of statistical quality control provide a possible alternative to uniform categorical standards or individualized permit review. Given the rapidly declining cost of computing power, it might be possible to analyze far more information, much more cheaply and efficiently, than it was in 1977 when the Court ruled.[h]

3. While *du Pont* established the basic mechanism for imposing the BPT standards, it did not directly address a number of questions about the content of the standards. These are addressed in the following opinion.

WEYERHAEUSER CO. v. COSTLE

United States Court of Appeals, District of Columbia Circuit, 1978.
590 F.2d 1011.

McGOWAN, CIRCUIT JUDGE.

EPA's consideration of the factors bearing on "the best practicable technology currently available" [for paper mills] has inspired several challenges from petitioners. Some of these challenges concern the Agency's refusal to consider receiving water quality, while others concern EPA's manner of assessing the factors that all agree must be considered: cost and nonwater environmental impacts. We uphold the Agency's interpretation and application of the statute against both sets of challenges.

1.

Some of the paper mills that must meet the effluent limitations under review discharge their effluent into the Pacific Ocean. Petitioners contend that the ocean can dilute or naturally treat effluent, and that EPA must take this capacity of the ocean ("receiving water capacity") into account in a variety of ways. They urge what they term "common sense," i.e., that because the amounts of pollutant involved are small in comparison to bodies of water as vast as Puget Sound or the Pacific Ocean, they should not have to spend heavily on treatment equipment, or to increase their energy requirements and sludge levels, in order to treat wastes that the ocean could dilute or absorb.[4]

---

h. For example, EPA might create a model to predict effluent limitations for plants having particular characteristics; the model could be based on economic or engineering theory, or it could incorporate statistical studies of actual permits from other states. Permits straying too far from the prediction could be automatically audited, as could a random sample of other permits. As an incentive, there could be a monetary penalty for rejected permits (with quick arbitration of any disputed claims). Would such a system have advantages over the current statutory scheme? Might it reduce the overall costs of regulation, or streamline the regulatory process? Or, on the contrary, would it simply allow states to evade federal environmental requirements? For an analysis of a similar proposal for the use of statistical claim profiles in tort cases, see Robinson and Abraham, "Collective Justice in Tort Law," 78 *Va.L.Rev.* 1481 (1992).

4. Apart from this simple "common sense" version of the argument, there is a more sophisticated economic version called

EPA's secondary response to this claim was that pollution is far from harmless, even when disposed of in the largest bodies of water. As congressional testimony indicated, the Great Lakes, Puget Sound, and even areas of the Atlantic Ocean have been seriously injured by water pollution. Even if the ocean can handle ordinary wastes, ocean life may be vulnerable to toxic compounds that typically accompany those wastes. In the main, however, EPA simply asserted that the issue of receiving water capacity could not be raised in setting effluent limitations because Congress had ruled it out. We have examined the previous legislation in this area, and the 1972 Act's wording, legislative history, and policies, as underscored by its 1977 amendments. These sources * * * fully support EPA's construction of the Act. They make clear that based on long experience, and aware of the limits of technological knowledge and administrative flexibility, Congress made the deliberate decision to rule out arguments based on receiving water capacity.

The earliest version of the Federal Water Pollution Control Act was passed in 1948 and amended five times before 1972. Throughout that 24 year period, Congress attempted to use receiving water quality as a basis for setting pollution standards. At the end of that period, Congress realized not only that its water pollution efforts until then had failed, but also that reliance on receiving water capacity as a crucial test for permissible pollution levels had contributed greatly to that failure.

Based on this experience, Congress adopted a new approach in 1972. Under the Act, "a discharger's performance is * * * measured against strict technology-based effluent limitations—specified levels of treatment—to which it must conform, rather than against limitations derived from water quality standards to which it and other polluters must collectively conform."

* * *

Moreover, by eliminating the issue of the capacity of particular bodies of receiving water, Congress made nationwide uniformity in effluent regulation possible. Congress considered uniformity vital to free the states from the temptation of relaxing local limitations in order to woo or keep industrial facilities. In addition, national uniformity made pollution cleanup possible without engaging in the divisive task of favoring some regions of the country over others.

More fundamentally, the new approach implemented changing views as to the relative rights of the public and of industrial

the "optimal pollution" theory. This economic theory contends that there is a level or type of pollution that, while technologically capable of being controlled, is uneconomic to treat because the benefit from treatment is small and the cost of treatment is large. These economic theories are premised on a view that we have both adequate information about the effects of pollution to set an optimal test, and adequate political and administrative flexibility to keep polluters at that level once we allow any pollution to go untreated. As discussed in this section, it appears that Congress doubted these premises.

polluters. Hitherto, the right of the polluter was pre-eminent, unless the damage caused by pollution could be proven. Henceforth, the right of the public to a clean environment would be pre-eminent, unless pollution treatment was impractical or unachievable. * * *

* * *

The Act was passed with an expectation of "mid-course corrections," and in 1977 Congress amended the Act, although generally holding to the same tack set five years earlier. Notably, during those five years, representatives of the paper industry had appeared before Congress and urged it to *change* the Act and to incorporate receiving water capacity as a consideration. * * * Except for a provision specifically aimed at discharges from "publicly owned treatment plants," section 301(h), Congress resolved in the recent amendments to continue regulating discharges into all receiving waters alike. [The court added, "Historically, the paper industry itself, and particularly the sulfite process sector, avoided the impact of regulation because of the difficulty of proving that its discharges adversely affected receiving water. Under the new statutory scheme, Congress clearly intended us to avoid such problems of proof so that a set of regulations with enforceable impact is possible."]

2.

Petitioners also challenge EPA's manner of assessing two factors that all parties agree must be considered: cost and non-water quality environmental impacts. They contend that the Agency should have more carefully balanced costs versus the effluent reduction benefits of the regulations, and that it should have also balanced those benefits against the non-water quality environmental impacts to arrive at a "net" environmental benefit conclusion. * * *

In order to discuss petitioners' challenges, we must first identify the relevant statutory standard. Section 304(b)(1)(B) identifies the factors bearing on BPCTCA ["best practicable control technology currently available"] in two groups. First, the factors shall

include consideration of the total cost of application of technology in relation to the effluent reduction benefits to be achieved from such application,

and second, they

shall also take into account the age of equipment and facilities involved, the process employed, the engineering aspects of the application of various types of control techniques, process changes, non-water quality environmental impact (including energy requirements), and such other factors as the Administrator deems appropriate[.]

The first group consists of two factors that EPA must compare: total cost versus effluent reduction benefits. We shall call these the "comparison factors." The other group is a list of many factors that EPA must "take into account": age, process, engineering aspects, process changes, environmental impacts (including energy), and any others EPA deems appropriate. We shall call these the "consideration factors." Notably, section 304(b)(2)(B), which delineates the factors relevant to setting 1983 BATEA limitations, tracks the 1977 BPCTCA provision before us except in one regard: in the 1983 section, *all* factors, including costs and benefits, are consideration factors, and no factors are separated out for comparison.

Based on our examination of the statutory language and the legislative history, we conclude that Congress mandated a particular structure and weight for the 1977 comparison factors, that is to say, a "limited" balancing test.[5] In contrast, Congress did not mandate any particular structure or weight for the many consideration factors. Rather, it left EPA with discretion to decide how to account for the consideration factors, and how much weight to give each factor. In response to these divergent congressional approaches, we conclude that, on the one hand, we should examine EPA's treatment of cost and benefit under the 1977 standard to assure that the Agency complied with Congress' "limited" balancing directive. On the other hand, our scrutiny of the Agency's treatment of the several consideration factors seeks to assure that the Agency informed itself as to their magnitude, and reached its own express and considered conclusion about their bearing. More particularly, we do not believe that EPA is required to use any specific structures such as a balancing test in assessing the consideration factors, nor do we believe that EPA is required to give each consideration factor any specific weight.

Notes

1. Why did the attempt to use receiving water quality as the basis for pollution standards fail? Under the present technology-based approach, what advantages do we get in exchange for surrendering the opportunity to make "efficient" use of our water resources? For an argument that technology-based standards have failed and that Congress would have done better to strengthen protection for water quality, see Pedersen, "Turning the Tide on Water Quality," 15 *Ecology L.Q.* 69 (1988). As we will see later in this chapter, water quality standards are beginning to play a renewed role today.

2. A later decision gave additional guidance concerning the role of cost in setting BPT and BCT. In *Chemical Mfrs. Ass'n v. United States EPA,* 870

---

5. Senator Muskie described the "limited" balancing test:

The modification of subsection 304(b)(1) is intended to clarify what is meant by the term "practicable." *The balancing test between total cost and effluent reduction benefits* is intended to limit the application of technology only where the additional degree of effluent reduction is *wholly out of proportion* to the costs of achieving such marginal level of reduction for any class or category of sources.

The Conferees agreed upon this limited cost-benefit analysis in order to maintain uniformity within a class and category of point sources subject to effluent limitations, and to avoid imposing on the Administrator any requirement to consider the location of sources within a category or to ascertain water quality impact of effluent controls, or to determine the economic impact of controls on any individual plant in a single community.

most conservative — most pro-industry court

F.2d 177 (5th Cir.1989), CMA argued that BPT should be governed by a "knee-of-the-curve" test, to determine the point at which the marginal cost of removal rises steeply. Increasing the removal of conventional pollutants for this industry from 96% to 99% would allegedly cost almost twice as much per pound of pollutant as current treatment methods. CMA argued that this shift went well beyond the knee of the curve, and was therefore impermissible. EPA countered that the knee-of-the-curve test applied only to increases in limitations beyond BPT (in this case, BCT). The Fifth Circuit agreed with the agency.

3. Section 301 effluent limitations continued to give rise to substantial litigation well after *Weyerhaeuser*. Perhaps in part because of this continued litigation, EPA fell far behind schedule in promulgating the regulations. For example, on November 5, 1987, EPA promulgated BPT regulations for the organic chemicals, plastics, and synthetic fibers industries. *Env.Rep.*, Nov. 13, 1987, at 1736. In 1988, EPA promulgated BPT regulations for placer mining operations, which were upheld in a 1990 decision. *Rybachek v. Alaska Miners Ass'n*, 904 F.2d 1276 (9th Cir.1990). Recall that the original *compliance* date for BPT limitations was over ten years earlier.

Because effluent limitation regulations have been so delayed, many permits have been issued without the benefit of § 301 regulations or § 304 guidelines. These are known as "best professional judgment" (or BPJ) permits. A recent article provides a critical view of these BPJ permits:

> Because there was legislative and public pressure for pollution control "progress," EPA issued many discharge permits before the applicable categorical standards had been promulgated. Congress wanted technology-based standards to apply uniformly to similar sources across the nation, but the permits were negotiated on an individualized basis incorporating whichever control measures and compliance schedules dischargers would accept. EPA characterized these permits as grounded on "best professional judgment;" but they often reflected simply the "best deal" the Agency could obtain in light of manpower and time constraints and its desire to demonstrate progress. These "professional judgments" were usually made by EPA regional personnel with water quality, not technology-based, orientations. Thus, many control measures imposed in the permits bore little resemblance to the technology-based requirements mandated by the statute.

Latin, "Regulatory Failure, Administrative Incentives, and the New Clean Air Act," 21 *Env.L.* 1647 (1991).

———

So far, we have been primarily concerned with the process of issuing industry-wide regulations. The next materials address the question of when variances are available from these regulations.

E.I. du PONT de NEMOURS & CO. v. TRAIN

Supreme Court of the United States, 1977.
430 U.S. 112, 97 S.Ct. 965, 51 L.Ed.2d 204.

[Earlier portions of this opinion by Justice Stevens appear at page 325 supra. The case involved challenges to EPA's water pollution regulations establishing industry-wide effluent limitations for inorganic chemical manufacturing plants. The text which follows concerns whether the "new source" standards must allow variances for individual plants.]

The remaining issue in this case concerns new plants. Under § 306, EPA is to promulgate "regulations establishing Federal standards of performance for new sources * * * "§ 306(b)(1)(B). A "standard of performance" is a "standard for the control of the discharge of pollutants which reflects the greatest degree of effluent reduction which the Administrator determines to be achievable through application of the best available demonstrated control technology, * * * including, where practicable, a standard permitting no discharge of pollutants." § 306(a)(1). In setting the standard, "[t]he Administrator may distinguish among classes, types, and sizes within categories of new sources * * * and shall consider the type of process employed (including whether batch or continuous)." § 306(b)(2). As the House Report states, the standard must reflect the best technology for "that category of sources, and for class, types and sizes within categories."

The Court of Appeals held that:

Neither the Act nor the regulations contain any variance provision for new sources. The rule of presumptive applicability applies to new sources as well as existing sources. On remand EPA should come forward with some limited escape mechanism for new sources.

The Court's rationale was that "[p]rovisions for variances, modifications, and exceptions are appropriate to the regulatory process."

The question, however, is not what a court thinks is generally appropriate to the regulatory process: it is what Congress intended for *these* regulations. It is clear that Congress intended these regulations to be absolute prohibitions. The use of the word "standards" implies as much. So does the description of the preferred standard as one "permitting *no* discharge of pollutants." (Emphasis added.) It is "unlawful for *any* owner or operator of *any* new source to operate such source in violation of any standard of performance applicable to such source." § 306(e) (emphasis added). In striking contrast to § 301(c), there is no statutory provision for variances, and a variance provision would be inappropriate in a standard that was intended to insure national uniformity and "maximum feasible control of new sources."

That portion of the judgment of the Court of Appeals requiring EPA to provide a variance procedure for new sources is reversed.

Notes

1. Section 301(n) now provides that FDF variances are available from § 301(b)(2) limitations (BAT and BCT) and § 307(b) pretreatment stan-

dards, which apply to discharges into public sewage systems as opposed to waterways. (Note that § 301(n) does not apply to BPT standards under § 301(b)(1) or new source standards under § 306.) Section 301(n) also places detailed restrictions on the FDF variances. The variance must be based on information presented during the original rulemaking or on newly discovered evidence. It cannot be any less stringent than required by the fundamentally different factor, and cannot result in markedly greater damage to other (non-water quality) environmental values. The application must be submitted within 180 days of the time when the standard is established or revised.

2.   Note that the language quoted by the *du Pont* Court makes it illegal for any plant to be operated without a new source permit. An EPA regulation prohibited the construction of new sources pending completion of the EIS and issuance of the permit, but the D.C. Circuit held this regulation invalid in *Natural Resources Defense Council, Inc. v. United States EPA,* 822 F.2d 104, 128–131 (D.C.Cir.1987). The court was unimpressed with the argument that allowing the construction to proceed first would render the EIS an exercise in futility.

3.   The next case explores the extent of the variance required in BPT standards for existing plants.

EPA v. NATIONAL CRUSHED STONE ASSOCIATION

Supreme Court of the United States, 1980.
449 U.S. 64, 101 S.Ct. 295, 66 L.Ed.2d 268.

JUSTICE WHITE delivered the opinion of the Court.

In April and July 1977, the Environmental Protection Agency promulgated pollution discharge limitations for the coal mining industry and for that portion of the mineral mining and processing industry comprising the crushed stone, construction sand, and gravel categories. Although the Act does not expressly authorize or require variances from the 1977 limitation, each set of regulations contained a variance provision. Respondents sought review of the regulations in various courts of appeals, challenging both the substantive standards and the variance clause. All of the petitions for review were transferred to the Court of Appeals for the Fourth Circuit [which] set aside the variance provision as "unduly restrictive" and remanded the provision to EPA for reconsideration.

To obtain a variance from the 1977 uniform discharge limitations a discharger must demonstrate that the "factors relating to the equipment or facilities involved, the process applied, or other such factors relating to such discharger are fundamentally different from the factors considered in the establishment of the guidelines." Although a greater than normal cost of implementation will be considered in acting on a request for a variance, economic ability to meet the costs will not be considered. A variance, therefore, will not be granted on the basis of the applicant's economic inability to meet the costs of implementing the uniform standard.

* * *

Section 301(c) of the Act explicitly provides for modifying the 1987 (BAT) effluent limitations with respect to individual point sources. A variance under § 301(c) may be obtained upon a showing "that such modified requirements (1) will represent the maximum use of technology within the economic capability of the owner or operator; and (2) will result in reasonable further progress toward elimination of the discharge of pollutants." Thus, the economic ability of the individual operator to meet the costs of effluent reductions may in some circumstances justify granting a variance from the 1987 limitations.

No such explicit variance provision exists with respect to BPT standards, but in [*du Pont*] we indicated that a variance provision was a necessary aspect of BPT limitations applicable by regulations to classes and categories of point sources. The issue in this case is whether the BPT variance provision must allow consideration of the economic capability of an individual discharger to afford the costs of the BPT limitation. For the reasons that follow, our answer is in the negative.

The plain language of the statute does not support the position taken by the Court of Appeals [which had relied on § 301(c)]. Section 301(c) is limited on its face to modifications of the 1987 BAT limitations. It says nothing about relief from the 1977 BPT requirements. Nor does the language of the Act support the position that although § 301(c) is not itself applicable to BPT standards, it requires that the affordability of the prescribed 1977 technology be considered in BPT variance decisions.[6] This would be a logical reading of the statute only if the factors listed in § 301(c) bore a substantial relationship to the considerations underlying the 1977 limitations as they do to those controlling the 1987 regulations. This is not the case.

The two factors listed in § 301(c)—"maximum use of technology within the economic capability of the owner or operator" and "reasonable further progress toward the elimination of the discharge of pollutants"—parallel the general definition of BAT standards as limitations that "require application of the best available technology economically achievable for such category or class, which will result in reasonable further progress toward * * * eliminating the discharge of all pollutants * * *." § 301(b)(2). A § 301(c) variance, thus, creates for a particular point source a BAT standard that represents for it the same sort of economic and technological commitment as the general BAT standard creates for the class. As with the general BAT standard, the variance assumes that the 1977 BPT has been met by the point source and that

---

6. It is true that in *du Pont* we said there "was no radical difference in the mechanisms used to impose limitations for the 1977 and the 198[7] deadlines" and that "there is no indication in either § 301 or § 304 that the § 304 guidelines play a different role in setting 1977 limitations." But our decision in *du Pont* was that the 1977 limitations, like the 1987 limitations, could be set by regulation and for classes of point sources. It dealt with the power of the Administrator and the procedures he was to employ. There was no suggestion, nor could there have been, that the 1977 BPT and the 1987 BAT limitations were to have identical purposes or content. It follows that no proper inference could be drawn from *du Pont* that the grounds for issuing variances from the 1987 limitations should also be the grounds for permitting individual point sources to depart from 1977 standards. * * *

the modification represents a commitment of the maximum resources economically possible to the ultimate goal of eliminating all polluting discharges. No one who can afford the best available technology can secure a variance.

There is no similar connection between § 301(c) and the considerations underlying the establishment of the 1977 BPT limitations. First, § 301(c)'s requirement of "reasonable further progress" must have reference to some prior standard. BPT serves as the prior standard with respect to BAT. There is, however, no comparable, prior standard with respect to BPT limitations. Second, BPT limitations do not require an industrial category to commit the maximum economic resources possible to pollution control, even if affordable. Those point sources already using a satisfactory pollution control technology need take no additional steps at all. The § 301(c) variance factor, the "maximum use of technology within the economic capability of the owner or operator," would therefore be inapposite in the BPT context. It would not have the same effect there that it has with respect to BAT's, i.e., it would not apply the general requirements to an individual point source.

More importantly, to allow a variance based on the maximum technology affordable by the point source, even if that technology fails to meet BPT effluent limitations, would undercut the purpose and function of BPT limitations. Rather than the 1987 requirement of the best measures economically and technologically feasible, the statutory provisions for 1977 contemplate regulations prohibiting discharges from any point source in excess of the effluent produced by the best practicable technology currently available in the industry. The Administrator was referred to the industry and to existing practices to determine BPT. He was to categorize point sources, examine control practices in exemplary plants in each category, and after weighing benefits and costs and considering other factors specified by § 304, determine and define the best practicable technology at a level that would effect the obvious statutory goal for 1977 of substantially reducing the total pollution produced by each category of the industry. Necessarily, if pollution is to be diminished, limitations based on BPT must forbid the level of effluent produced by the most pollution-prone segment of the industry, that segment not measuring up to "the average of the best existing performance." So understood, the statute contemplated regulations that would require a substantial number of point sources with the poorest performances either to conform to BPT standards or to cease production. To allow a variance based on economic capability and not to require adherence to the prescribed minimum technology would permit the employment of the very practices that the Administrator had rejected in establishing the best practicable technology currently in use in the industry.

To put the matter another way, under § 304, the Administrator is directed to consider the benefits of effluent reductions as compared to the costs of pollution control in determining BPT limitations. Thus, every BPT limitation represents a conclusion by the Administrator that the costs imposed on the industry are worth the benefits in pollution reduction that will be gained by meeting those limits. To grant a variance because a particular owner or operator cannot meet the normal costs of the technological requirements imposed on him, and not because there has been a recalculation of the benefits compared to the costs, would be inconsistent with this legislative scheme and would allow a level of pollution inconsistent with the judgment of the Administrator.

In terms of the scheme implemented by BPT limitations, the factors that the Administrator considers in granting variances do not suggest that economic capability must also be a determinant. The regulations permit a variance where "factors relating to the equipment or facilities involved, the process applied, or such other factors relating to such discharger are fundamentally different from the factors considered in the establishment of the guidelines." If a point source can show that its situation, including its costs of compliance, is not within the range of circumstances considered by the Administrator, then it may receive a variance, whether or not the source could afford to comply with the minimum standard.[7] In such situations, the variance is an acknowledgement that the uniform BPT limitation was set without reference to the full range of current practices, to which the Administrator was to refer. Insofar as a BPT limitation was determined without consideration of a current practice fundamentally different from those that were considered by the Administrator, that limitation is incomplete. A variance based on economic capability, however, would not have this character: it would allow a variance simply because the point source could not afford a compliance cost that is not fundamentally different from those the Administrator has already considered in determining BPT. It would force a displacement of calculations already performed, not because those calculations were incomplete or had unexpected effects, but only because the costs happened to fall on one particular operator, rather than 'on another who might be economically better off.

Because the 1977 limitations were intended to reduce the total pollution produced by an industry, requiring compliance with BPT standards necessarily imposed additional costs on the segment of the industry with the least effective technology. If the statutory goal is to be achieved, these costs must be borne or the point source eliminated. In

---

7. Respondents argue that precluding consideration of economic capability in determining whether to grant a variance effectively precludes consideration of the "total costs" for the individual point source. Respondents rely upon a statement by Representative Jones as to the meaning of "total cost" in § 304(b)(1)(B): "internal, or plant, costs sustained by the owner or operator and those external costs such as potential unemployment, dislocation and rural area economic development sustained by the community area, or region." Unless economic capability is considered, it is argued, it will be impossible to consider the potential external costs of meeting a BPT limitation, caused by a plant closing. Although there is some merit to respondent's contention, we do not believe it supports the decision of the Court of Appeals. The court did not hold that economic capability is relevant only if it discloses "fundamentally different" external costs from those considered by EPA in establishing the BPT limitation; rather, the court held that the factors included in § 301(c) *must* be taken into consideration. Section 301(c) makes economic capability, regardless of its effect on external costs, a ground for a variance. It is this position that we reject.

our view, requiring variances from otherwise valid regulations where dischargers cannot afford normal costs of compliance would undermine the purpose and the intended operative effect of the 1977 regulations.

The Administrator's present interpretation of the language of the statute is amply supported by the legislative history, which persuades us that Congress understood that the economic capability provision of § 301(c) was limited to BAT variances; that Congress foresaw and accepted the economic hardship, including the closing of some plants, that effluent limitations would cause; and that Congress took certain steps to alleviate this hardship, steps which did not include allowing a BPT variance based on economic capability.

* * *

As we see it, Congress anticipated that the 1977 regulations would cause economic hardship and plant closings: "[T]he question * * * is not what a court thinks is generally appropriate to the regulatory process; it is what Congress intended for *these* regulations." [Citing *du Pont*.]

It is by now a commonplace that "when faced with a problem of statutory construction, this Court shows great deference to the interpretation given the statute by the officers or agency charged with its administration." The statute itself does not provide for BPT variances in connection with permits for individual point sources, and we had no occasion in *du Pont* to address the adequacy of the Administrator's 1977 variance provision. In the face of § 301(c)'s explicit limitation and in the absence of any other specific direction to provide for variances in connection with permits for individual point sources, we believe that the Administrator has adopted a reasonable construction of the statutory mandate.

In rejecting EPA's interpretation of the BPT variance provision, the Court of Appeals relied on a mistaken conception of the relation between BPT and BAT standards. The court erroneously believed that since BAT limitations are to be more stringent than BPT limitations, the variance provision for the latter must be at least as flexible as that for the former with respect to affordability. The variances permitted by § 301(c) from the 1987 limitations, however, can reasonably be understood to represent a cost in decreased effluent reductions that can only be afforded once the minimal standard expressed in the BPT limitation has been reached.

We conclude, therefore, that the Court of Appeals erred in not accepting EPA's interpretation of the Act. EPA is not required by the Act to consider economic capability in granting variances from its uniform BPT regulations.

Notes

1. Under *National Crushed Stone*, variances may not be based on economic hardship. Can they be based on water quality considerations? *In re Louisiana–Pacific Corp.*, 10 ERC 1841 (Decision of the Administrator of the

EPA, 1977), involved requests for variances from effluent limitations for two paper mills in California. Petitioners urged that because the mills discharged directly into the Pacific Ocean with its vast dilution and regenerative capacity, EPA need not be concerned with pollution requirements designed to protect oxygen of pH levels of receiving waters. The Administrator ruled that the Act did not allow EPA to vary the technology-based effluent limitations solely because receiving water quality would not be measurably improved by compliance. The Administrator's decision was upheld in *Crown Simpson Pulp Co. v. Costle,* 642 F.2d 323 (9th Cir.1981), cert. denied 454 U.S. 1053, 102 S.Ct. 596, 70 L.Ed.2d 588 (1981). However, in December 1982, Congress enacted legislation exempting these plants (but no others) from the pH and BOD requirements. See § 301(m)(1) of the Clean Water Act. Congress did not, however, express any disapproval of the EPA's construction of the Act, but appeared to view this as a special case involving an exemption from the normal statutory requirements.

The basic rationale for rejecting water quality considerations was explained by the Fourth Circuit, which had taken a different position on the issue prior to *National Crushed Stone:*

> Because receiving water quality is clearly excluded in the setting of generic BPT limitations, it must also be excluded in determining whether to grant a variance from those general limitations. The purpose of the variance is to allow an individual determination of BPT for a particular point source where it is clear that the factors considered by EPA in setting the generic BPT limitations are so different for a particular point source as to make the generic BPT limitation unfair. By definition, the variance determination must be made on the same factors that controlled the generic determination. For purposes of decision here, that is the decisive point made in *National Crushed Stone.*

Appalachian Power Co. v. United States EPA, 671 F.2d 801 (4th Cir.1982). (Does the same reasoning hold for BAT and BCT variances under § 301(n)?)

Apparently, variances may consider neither hardship to the applicant nor harm (or lack thereof) to receiving waters. Aren't these the two obvious factors in any variance scheme? Why are these apparently relevant factors excluded from consideration?

Despite the extensive litigation about FDF variances, they seem to be sparse in practice. See Pedersen, "Turning the Tide on Water Quality," 15 *Ecology L.Q.* 69, 86 & n. 81 (1988).

2. One commentator questioned EPA's ability to give individualized attention to dischargers:

> A recent General Accounting Office (GAO) study of industry compliance with permit terms indicated that the EPA and the state made little attempt to identify the many polluters who did not even apply for permits, and that the agencies had not processed tens of thousands of existing permit applications in a timely manner. The GAO and the EPA itself attributed these deficiencies to the lack of administrative resources. The permit-issuing agencies depend almost entirely on monitoring and self-reporting by dischargers to identify violations of permit terms; yet the GAO study determined that over 40 percent of the

polluters examined failed to submit discharge monitoring reports or failed to provide all required data. * * * These experiences with individualized permit programs provide little reason for confidence about the accuracy of information in variance applications, or about the ability of agencies to review those applications in a carefully and timely fashion.

The implementation of variances based on individualized circumstances raises numerous problems: high decisionmaking costs, frequent litigation, inconsistent results, persistent delays, increased opportunities for manipulative behavior by applicants or administrators, and inadequate public participation.

Latin, "Ideal Versus Real Regulatory Efficiency," 37 *Stan.L.Rev.* 1267, 1322–23 (1985).

Serious concerns about CWA enforcement have continued since 1985. In 46 of 69 cases studied by the EPA Inspector General a decade later, penalties were insufficient to cover the economic benefits of non-compliance, and often penalties were reduced to a small fraction of the amounts originally calculated. States also had a tendency to limit their "sanctions" to warning calls even for repeat violators. A study of corporate environmental managers themselves found that about half considered the federal government's enforcement efforts inadequate, and EPA actually conducts only about 10% of the inspections of major dischargers. David Hodas, "Enforcement of Environmental Law in a Triangular Federal System: Can Three Not be a Crowd when Enforcement Authority is Shared by the United States, the States, and their Citizens?," 54 *Md. L. Rev.* 1552, 1604–05 (1995). A later GAO study found that about one in six of the nation's seven thousand major regulated facilities significantly violated their permits (and the study suggested that the actual number might be almost twice as high) GAO, Water Pollution: Many Violations Have Not Received Appropriate Enforcement Attention (GAO/RCED–96–23, March 20, 1996). See also Cushman, "EPA and States Found to be Lax on Pollution Law," NY Times, June 7, 1998, at 1, 17; Flatt, "A Dirty River Runs Through It (the Failure of Enforcement in the Clean Water Act," 25 *Env.Affairs* 1 (1997).

or maybe up to 3 times as high

Note on Regulation of Toxic Water Pollution

As originally enacted, § 307 required EPA to publish a list of toxic pollutants and to implement standards for these pollutants providing an "ample margin of safety." For various reasons, implementation of this section proved difficult. The agency lacked sufficient information about toxic pollutants and was not given enough time under the statutory timetable. Furthermore, because of the "ample margin of safety" requirement, the agency believed it had no leeway to consider feasibility. As a result, it feared that implementation of the statutory scheme would lead to widespread and politically unacceptable plant closures. When EPA was sued to force compliance with the statute, the result was a consent decree requiring BAT standards for a specified list of pollutants. This consent decree, with some modifications, was then incorporated into the 1977 amendments to § 307.[i]

i. Concerning the 1976 consent decree, one might ask if it was proper for the court to enter a decree that relaxed the statutory requirements. How desirable is "government by consent decree?" (For discussion, see Shane, "Federal Policy Making By Con-

Are variances available under § 307? The Supreme Court's decision in *Chemical Mfrs. Ass'n v. NRDC,* 470 U.S. 116, 105 S.Ct. 1102, 84 L.Ed.2d 90 (1985), involved § 301(*l*), which then said that EPA "may not modify any requirement of this section" as it applied to any toxic pollutant. The issue was whether this provision prohibited the agency from granting FDF variances from pretreatment standards. In a majority opinion by Justice White, the Court held that 301(*l*) does not prohibit FDF variances. The Court's rationale was that FDF variances do not excuse a discharger from complying with the applicable statutory standard, but only tailor the application of the standard to the polluter's exceptional circumstances. Thus, FDF variances are not "true" variances. There was a vigorous dissent by Justice Marshall, joined by Blackmun, Stevens, and (in part) O'Connor. The 1987 amendments, however, codified the majority's interpretation of § 301(*l*).

In addition to the toxics standards discussed above, § 307(b) provides for EPA establishment of pretreatment standards for wastes that are to be introduced into municipal treatment systems rather than being discharged directly into waters. These pretreatment standards are needed to prevent introduction of substances that cannot be adequately treated by public facilities or that might damage those facilities. Specifically, § 307(b)(1) requires that the standards "prevent the discharge of any pollutant through treatment works * * *, which pollutant interferes with, passes through, or otherwise is incompatible with such works." The need for this requirement arises from the fact that publicly owned treatment works (POTWs) generally are not designed to treat many industry-generated pollutants, particularly heavy metals and other toxic pollutants. If introduced into POTWs, such pollutants may impair the work's operation, pass through without effective treatment, or settle in and contaminate the POTWs' sludge, causing sludge disposal problems.

By 1987, Congress had become concerned that certain waters could not meet applicable water quality standards despite the imposition of BAT requirements. In particular, there were numerous "toxic hotspots" which needed more stringent controls. Section 304 of the Clean Water Act, added in 1987, established a comprehensive system for toxics control. States were directed to identify, within two years, such hotspots—waters where technology-based controls and existing water quality-based controls were not adequate to meet water quality standards because of toxic pollutants, even after implementation of BAT, new source performance standards, and standards requiring pretreatment of industrial wastes discharged into publicly owned treatment plants. The states then were to identify the specific point sources preventing the attainment of standards, and the amount of each toxic pollutant discharged by each source. Every state was then required to devise an individual control strategy to achieve standards at each hotspot within three years after the date of the establishment of the strategy.

sent Decree," 1987 *U.Chi.L.F.* 241; Rabbin & Devins, "Averting Government by Consent Decree," 40 *Stan.L.Rev.* 203 (1987).) On appeal it was held that Judge Flannery's decree was not superseded by the 1977 amendments, *Environmental Defense Fund v. Costle,* 636 F.2d 1229 (D.C.Cir. 1980); and the decree did not impermissibly infringe on the EPA Administrator's statutory discretion and could be enforced by the district court, *Citizens for a Better Environment v. Gorsuch,* 718 F.2d 1117 (D.C.Cir. 1983), cert. denied sub nom. *Union Carbide Corp. v. NRDC,* 467 U.S. 1219, 104 S.Ct. 2668, 81 L.Ed.2d 373 (1984).

Implementation of § 304(*l*) is discussed in detail in Houck, "The Regulation of Toxic Pollutants Under the Clean Water Act," 21 *Env.L.Rep.* 10528 (1991). As of that time, the BAT program for toxics was not considered successful; too few sources were covered, and many of the BAT standards were out-of-date. Id. at 10541. In contrast, the "toxic hotspots" program was considered more successful. By 1989, every state except Arizona had submitted the required lists and control strategies. Houck concludes:

> It is clear that [§ 304(*l*)] has had the effect intended of shifting attention from water quality standards for all pollutants to toxic standards on an accelerated basis. Whether that attention produces significant reductions, and consistent reductions, remains to be seen.

Id. at 10549. In a later report, Houck lauded the "hot spot" program for implementing "individual control strategies" in more than 675 permits, adding that the number of permits and "the vigor with which they were resisted" suggests that significant toxic reductions occurred. Houck, "TMDLs: The Resurrection of Water Quality Standards–Based Regulation Under the Clean Water Act," 28 *Env.L.Rep.* 10329, 10342 (1997).

Of special concern are toxic contaminants in water from underground sources. A 1984 report by the congressional Office of Technology Assessment identified more than 200 contaminants in groundwater used for drinking, many of them associated with cancer and damage to the central nervous system, liver, and kidneys. The report documented serious incidents of such contamination by toxic chemicals, including pesticides and wastes leaked from landfills or disposed of in underground injection wells, in at least 34 states. See 17 *Envir.Rep.*, No. 20, Part II, "Safe Drinking Water Act Amendments of 1986," at 20 (1986).

The Safe Drinking Water Act directs EPA to set health-based standards for contaminants in drinking water and to require water supply system operators to come as close as possible to meeting the standards by using the best available technology that is economically and technologically "feasible." See *Natural Resources Defense Council v. EPA*, 824 F.2d 1211 (D.C.Cir.1987) (upholding EPA rule establishing recommended maximum contaminant levels of zero for five known or probable carcinogens).

In 1996, Congress again amended the SDWA. The most important change is the repeal of a requirement that EPA regulate twenty-five new pollutants every three years. Under the new law, EPA is directed to regulate new substances when contaminants are found to actually occur in drinking water. Also, EPA has limited authority to engage in balancing where treatment for one pollutant may increase risks for another. If the agency finds that a regulation would not be cost-justified, it may issue a less stringent regulation that maximizes health benefits at a justified cost. The changes are intended to focus regulatory attention on the greatest threats to public health and to eliminate regulations whose benefits are dwarfed by their costs.

C. AREA PLANNING

The pollution control strategy we have just considered focuses on the pollution source, and attempts to determine the proper level of

Area planning technique

pollution control for an entire category of sources. This strategy lends itself to the use of nationwide regulations. The other possible control strategy is to determine the level of environmental quality desired for a given area and then work backwards to set the controls for each source. Although, as we have seen, the Clean Air Act makes some use of source-oriented controls, it relies primarily on this area-planning technique. In the Clean Water Act, area planning presently plays only a secondary role, as we will discuss below.

Because area planning is based on local conditions, it lends itself to heavy state involvement. One of the key issues to watch for is the division of authority between the states and the federal government.

1. STATE IMPLEMENTATION PLANS UNDER THE CLEAN AIR ACT

a. *The Statutory Scheme*

The development of federal air pollution control legislation through the mid–1970's was summarized by then–Justice Rehnquist in *Train v. Natural Resources Defense Council, Inc.,* 421 U.S. 60, 63–67, 95 S.Ct. 1470, 1474–1476, 43 L.Ed.2d 731, 737–738 (1975):

> Congress initially responded to the problem of air pollution by offering encouragement and assistance to the States. In 1955 the Surgeon General was authorized to study the problem of air pollution, to support research, training, and demonstration projects, and to provide technical assistance to state and local governments attempting to abate pollution. * * * In 1960 Congress directed the Surgeon General to focus his attention on the health hazards resulting from motor vehicle emissions. The Clean Air Act of 1963 authorized federal authorities to expand their research efforts, to make grants to state air pollution control agencies, and also to intervene directly to abate *interstate* pollution in limited circumstances. Amendments in 1965 broadened federal authority to control motor vehicle emissions and to make grants to state pollution control agencies.]

> The focus shifted somewhat in the Air Quality Act of 1967. It reiterated the premise of the earlier Clean Air Act "that the prevention and control of air pollution at its source is the primary responsibility of States and local governments." * * * Its provisions, however, increased the federal role in the prevention of air pollution, by according federal authorities certain powers of supervision and enforcement. But the States generally retained wide latitude to determine both the air quality standards which they would meet and the period of time in which they would do so.

> The response of the States to these manifestations of increasing congressional concern with air pollution was disappointing. Even by 1970, state planning and implementation under the Air Quality Act of 1967 had made little progress. Congress reacted by taking a stick

to the States in the form of the Clean Air Amendments of 1970. These Amendments sharply increased federal authority and responsibility in the continuing effort to combat air pollution. Nonetheless, the Amendments explicitly preserved the principle: "Each State shall have the primary responsibility for assuring air quality within the entire geographic area comprising such State * * *." § 107(a). The difference under the Amendments was that the States were no longer given any choice as to whether they would meet this responsibility. For the first time they were required to attain air quality of specified standards, and to do so within a specified period of time.

The Amendments directed that within 30 days of their enactment the Environmental Protection Agency should publish proposed regulations describing national quality standards for the "ambient air," which is the statute's term for the outdoor air used by the general public. After allowing 90 days for comments on the proposed standards, the Agency was then obliged to promulgate such standards. The standards were to be of two general types: "primary" standards, which in the judgment of the Agency were "requisite to protect the public health," § 109(b)(1), and "secondary" standards, those that in the judgment of the Agency were "requisite to protect the public welfare from any known or anticipated adverse effects associated with the presence of such air pollutant in the ambient air." § 109(b)(2).

Within nine months after the Agency's promulgation of primary and secondary air quality standards, each of the 50 States was required to submit to the Agency a plan designed to implement and maintain such standards within its boundaries. § 110(a)(1). The Agency was in turn required to approve each State's plan within four months of the deadline for submission, if it had been adopted after public hearings and if it satisfied eight general conditions set forth in § 110(a)(2). Probably the principal of these conditions, and the heart of the 1970 Amendments, is that the plan provide for the attainment of the national primary ambient air quality standards in the particular State "as expeditiously as practicable but * * * in no case later than three years from the date of approval of such plan." § 110(a)(2)(A). In providing for such attainment, a State's plan must include "emission limitations, schedules, and timetables for compliance with such limitations": it must also contain such other measures as may be necessary to insure both timely attainment and subsequent maintenance of national ambient air standards. § 110(a)(2)(B).

The 1970 Act seems to have been based on the premise that air pollution was a relatively straightforward problem, easily amenable to control. Hence, Congress apparently believed, five years would be enough to create and implement the necessary regulations. As it turned out, the problem was much more difficult. First, determining safe levels of air quality turned out to involve major scientific uncertainties about the health effects of various pollutants. Second, designing feasible plans of controlling pollution without eliminating economic growth turned out to be anything but straightforward. Third, in addressing both problems, EPA was handicapped by political resistance, inadequate budgets, staffing shortages, and incomplete information, compounded by competing regulatory demands involving new issues such as hazardous waste. In short, the deadlines set in the 1970 Act proved to be quite unrealistic.

Congress responded in 1977 with major amendments to the statute. Congress extended the deadlines for the primary air quality standards and added new measures dealing with nonattainment. The new deadlines were 1982 for most areas, and 1987 for areas with especially severe problems. These deadlines were also missed. As of 1989, 96 areas violated the ozone standard, and 41 failed to meet the carbon monoxide limit. *Env.Rep.*, August 24, 1990, at 815.

During the Reagan Administration, revisions of the air act foundered because of sharp philosophical differences between the White House and Congress, as well as some difficult problems in finding acceptable ways to deal with acid rain. President Bush, however, did not embrace the Reagan anti-environmentalist philosophy. In 1990, the political logjam was finally broken. The 1990 amendments contain extensive new provisions dealing with nonattainment, pollution from cars and trucks, and acid rain. As a result of the 1977 and 1990 amendments, the current statute is far more complex and detailed than the original 1970 version. The basic structure of the 1970 statute has, however, remained intact, and has provided the framework for these later elaborations.

Notes

1. Why did individual states, especially those with "dirty" industries, failed to adopt and enforce stringent air pollution standards prior to 1970? Bear in mind the materials in Chapter I on the politics of environmental law and those in Chapter III on multistate regulatory issues.

2. National ambient air quality standards are required for pollutants appearing on a list to be prepared by the EPA Administrator under § 108. The list is to include each air pollutant (1) which in his judgment has an adverse effect on public health and welfare and (2) which results from numerous or diverse mobile or stationary sources. *Natural Resources Defense Council, Inc. v. Train,* 545 F.2d 320 (2d Cir.1976), held that inclusion of a pollutant on the list was mandatory once the Administrator had made affirmative findings on points (1) and (2). Failure to list lead, despite having made the requisite findings, opened the Administrator to a citizens' suit under § 304, which permits "any person" to sue the Administrator for alleged failure to perform a nondiscretionary act or duty.

3. Once a substance is listed as a § 108 pollutant, what are the next steps in the regulatory process? See §§ 109(a)(2) and 110(a)(1). In general, EPA has been reluctant to revise the NAAQS. See *American Lung Ass'n v. EPA,* 134 F.3d 388 (D.C.Cir.1998) (reversing and remanding EPA's refusal to change sulfur dioxide standard to protect asthmatics from effects of "short-term bursts" after agency itself had found significant health effects); Oren, "Prevention of Significant Deterioration: Control–Compelling Versus

Site–Shifting," 74 *Iowa L.Rev.* 1, 64–67 (1988). If EPA revises the pollutant criteria based on later information, must it also revise the secondary NAAQS? See *EDF v. Thomas,* 870 F.2d 892 (2d Cir.1989) (NAAQS revision is discretionary). Suppose the state fails to take the necessary action? See § 110(c)(1). Is it reasonable to have uniform nationwide standards for air quality when the cost of achieving the standards may differ greatly from place to place?

4. One recent controversy involved changes to the ozone standard. There is clear evidence that "at the present standard, some people experience respiratory symptoms when exercising outdoors; there is less clarity about more severe and irreversible effects." On the other hand, control may be very difficult. Further reductions may require controls on people's travel, recreation, and lawns: "The City of Baltimore has calculated that motorboats and lawnmowers alone currently contribute more ozone to its air than all of its industry put together * * *." Alan Krupnick and J.W. Anderson, "Revising the Ozone Standard," *Resources* 6 (Fall 1996). An EPA study concluded that the costs of meeting a tighter ozone standard could easily outweigh its benefits, with the benefits ranging from zero to $1.5 billion per year depending on the form of the standard, while costs ranged from $600 million to $2.5 billion. See "Costs of Ozone Standard May Outweigh Benefits, EPA Impact Analysis Concludes," 27 *Env. Rep.* 1603 (1996). Ultimately, a new ozone standard was issued, but only after direct intervention by the White House. For further background on the ozone standard, and on a related change in the standard for small particulates, see Langworthy, "EPA's New Air Quality Standards for Particulate Matter and Ozone: Boon for Health or Threat to the Clean Air Act?," 28 *Env.L.Rep* 10502 (1998); Alex Zacaroli, "Revising the PM, Ozone Standards: Major Questions Remain on Major Projects," 27 *Env. Rep.* 929 (1996). The health problems caused by particulates are discussed in Hilts, "Dirty–Air Cities Far Deadlier Than Clean Ones, Study Shows," *N.Y. Times,* March 10, 1995, at A20.

5. The passage of the CAA in 1970 is the subject of an interesting article, which suggests that the statute was actually more stringent than its proponents really desired or than was warranted by the political power of environmental groups:

> These surprisingly tough provisions of the Clean Air Act of 1970 did not result from organized lobbying by environmentalists, at least not in the conventional sense. As a result of the Nader report, which threatened Muskie with the loss of his national reputation as "Mr. Clean," both Nixon and Muskie found themselves trapped in a Politicians' Dilemma. Both were forced to support legislation more stringent than either would have preferred.

> * * *

> It is important to recognize that the surprisingly strong environmental legislation in 1970 did not result from superior organization by environmentalists. Indeed, it is possible to speculate that if environmentalists had been more tightly organized as a conventional pressure group in 1970, as they later became, the Clean Air Act amendments might have been less, rather than more, stringent. Had there been a well-organized environmental lobby in 1970, Muskie could have deflected

Nader's charges by giving in to its demands. And it is quite likely that this lobby would have settled for far less than the Great Leap Forward achieved by the Clean Air Act. In 1970, however, no group yet existed with whom to bargain. In these circumstances, Muskie had no way of knowing how much would be enough. He did about all that he could have done to prove that he was more "pro-environmental" than Nixon: he proposed a bill which was essentially Nixon's, only more so on every point.

Elliott, Ackerman, & Millian, "Toward a Theory of Statutory Evolution: The Federalization of Environmental Law," 1 *J.L.Ec. & Org.* 313, 337–338 (1985). The fact that Congress in some sense "got ahead" of the political pressure from environmentalists may help to explain the later lack of momentum and delays in implementation.

The two cases in the next section establish the core legal principle governing the validity of state implementation plans.

b. *The Attainment Principle*

UNION ELECTRIC CO. v. EPA

Supreme Court of the United States, 1976.
427 U.S. 246, 96 S.Ct. 2518, 49 L.Ed.2d 474.

MR. JUSTICE MARSHALL delivered the opinion of the Court.

After the Administrator of the Environmental Protection Agency (EPA) approves a state implementation plan under the Clean Air Act, the plan may be challenged in a court of appeals within 30 days, or after 30 days have run if newly discovered or available information justifies subsequent review. We must decide whether the operator of a regulated emission source, in a petition for review of an EPA-approved state plan filed after the original 30–day appeal period, can raise the claim that it is economically or technologically infeasible to comply with the plan.

* * *

Petitioner is an electric utility company servicing the St. Louis metropolitan area, large portions of Missouri, and parts of Illinois and Iowa. Its three coal-fired generating plants in the metropolitan St. Louis area are subject to the sulfur dioxide restrictions in the Missouri implementation plan. Petitioner did not seek review of the Administrator's approval of the plan within 30 days, as it was entitled to do under § 307(b)(1) of the Act, * * * but rather applied to the appropriate state and county agencies for variances from the emission limitations affecting its three plants. Petitioner received one-year variances, which could be extended upon reapplication. The variances on two of petitioner's three plants had expired and petitioner was applying for extensions when, on May 31, 1974, the Administrator notified petitioner that sulfur dioxide emissions from its plants violated the emission limitations contained in

the Missouri plan. Shortly thereafter petitioner filed a petition in the
Court of Appeals for the Eighth Circuit for review of the Administrator's
1972 approval of the Missouri implementation plan.

Section 307(b)(1) allows petitions for review to be filed in an
appropriate court of appeals more than 30 days after the Administrator's
approval of an implementation plan only if the petition is "based solely
on grounds arising after such 30th day." Petitioner claimed to meet this
requirement by asserting, *inter alia,* that various economic and technological difficulties had arisen more than 30 days after the Administrator's approval and that these difficulties made compliance with the
emission limitations impossible. * * *

* * *

We reject at the outset petitioner's suggestion that a claim of
economic or technological infeasibility may be considered upon a petition
for review based on new information and filed more than 30 days after
approval of an implementation plan even if such a claim could not be
considered by the Administrator in approving a plan or by a court in
reviewing a plan challenged within the original 30-day appeal period.
* * * Regardless of when a petition for review is filed under § 307(b)(1),
the court is limited to reviewing "the Administrator's action in approving * * * [the] implementation plan * * *." Accordingly, if new
"grounds" are alleged, they must be such that, had they been known at
the time the plan was presented to the Administrator for approval, it
would have been an abuse of discretion for the Administrator to approve
the plan. To hold otherwise would be to transfer a substantial responsibility in administering the Clean Air Act from the Administrator and the
state agencies to the federal courts.

Since a reviewing court—regardless of when the petition for review
is filed—may consider claims of economic and technological infeasibility
only if the Administrator may consider such claims in approving or
rejecting a state implementation plan, we must address ourselves to the
scope of the Administrator's responsibility. The Administrator's position
is that he has no power whatsoever to reject a state implementation plan
on the ground that it is economically or technologically infeasible, and
we have previously accorded great deference to the Administrator's
construction of the Clean Air Act. After surveying the relevant provisions of the Clean Air Act Amendments of 1970 and their legislative
history, we agree that Congress intended claims of economic and technological infeasibility to be wholly foreign to the Administrator's consideration of a state implementation plan.

As we have previously recognized, the 1970 Amendments to the
Clean Air Act were a drastic remedy to what was perceived as a serious
and otherwise uncheckable problem of air pollution. The Amendments
place the primary responsibility for formulating pollution control strategies on the States, but nonetheless subject the States to strict minimum
compliance requirements. These requirements are of a "technology-
forcing character," * * * and are expressly designed to force regulated

sources to develop pollution control devices that might at the time appear to be economically or technologically infeasible.

This approach is apparent on the face of § 110(a)(2). The provision sets out eight criteria that an implementation plan must satisfy, and provides that if these criteria are met and if the plan was adopted after reasonable notice and hearing, the Administrator "shall approve" the proposed state plan. The mandatory "shall" makes it quite clear that the Administrator is not to be concerned with factors other than those specified, and none of the eight factors appears to permit consideration of technological or economic infeasibility. * * *

* * *

In sum, we have concluded that claims of economic or technological infeasibility may not be considered by the Administrator in evaluating a state requirement that primary ambient air quality standards be met in the mandatory three years. And, since we further conclude that the States may submit implementation plans more stringent than federal law requires and that the Administrator must approve such plans if they meet the minimum requirements of § 110(a)(2), it follows that the language of § 110(a)(2)(A) provides no basis for the Administrator ever to reject a state implementation plan on the ground that it is economically or technologically infeasible. Accordingly, a court of appeals reviewing an approved plan under § 307(b)(1) cannot set it aside on those grounds, no matter when they are raised.

Our conclusion is bolstered by recognition that the Amendments do allow claims of technological and economic infeasibility to be raised in situations where consideration of such claims will not substantially interfere with the primary congressional purpose of prompt attainment of the national air quality standards. Thus, we do not hold that claims of infeasibility are never of relevance in the formulation of an implementation plan or that sources unable to comply with emission limitations must inevitably be shut down.

Perhaps the most important forum for consideration of claims of economic and technological infeasibility is before the state agency formulating the implementation plan. So long as the national standards are met, the State may select whatever mix of control devices it desires, and industries with particular economic or technological problems may seek special treatment in the plan itself. Moreover, if the industry is not exempted from, or accommodated by, the original plan, it may obtain a variance, as petitioner did in this case; and the variance, if granted after notice and a hearing, may be submitted to the EPA as a revision of the plan.[8] Lastly, an industry denied an exemption from the implementation

---

8. A variance approved as a revision of a plan under § 110(a)(3)(A) will be honored by the EPA as part of an applicable implementation plan, § 110(d), a matter of no little import to those granted variances.

plan, or denied a subsequent variance, may be able to take its claims of economic or technological infeasibility to the state courts.

* * *

* * * Congress plainly left with the States, so long as the national standards were met, the power to determine which sources would be burdened by regulation and to what extent. Technology forcing is a concept somewhat new to our national experience and it necessarily entails certain risks. But Congress considered those risks in passing the 1970 Amendments and decided that the dangers posed by uncontrolled air pollution made them worth taking. Petitioner's theory would render that considered legislative judgment a nullity, and that is a result we refuse to reach.

Notes

1. The opinion stresses that there are several points in the SIP regulatory process, at both federal and state levels, where problems of economic and technological infeasibility may properly be considered. Among the most important adjustment mechanisms are variances and enforcement orders, discussed at pages 360–365 infra. Another important question is whether a defense of infeasibility can be raised in a federal enforcement proceeding. See § 307(b)(2) of the Clean Air Act; the *Getty* case, page 360 infra; and the *Weinberger* case, page 586 infra.

2. Is the *Union Electric* Court's approach to the feasibility issue consistent with Judge Leventhal's approach in *International Harvester?*

3. *Union Electric* holds the considerations of feasibility do not justify overturning a SIP as too harsh. Can a SIP be attacked as too lenient where more stringent regulation would be feasible? Consider the following case.

TRAIN v. NATURAL RESOURCES DEFENSE COUNCIL, INC.

Supreme Court of the United States, 1975.
421 U.S. 60, 95 S.Ct. 1470, 43 L.Ed.2d 731.

MR. JUSTICE REHNQUIST delivered the opinion of the Court.

No one can doubt that Congress imposed upon the Agency and States a comprehensive planning task of the first magnitude which was to be accomplished in a relatively short time. In the case of the States, it was soon realized that in order to develop the requisite plans within the statutory nine-month deadline, efforts would have to be focused on determining the stringent emission limitations necessary to comply with national standards. This was true even though compliance with the standards would not be necessary until the attainment date, which normally would be three years after Agency approval of a plan. The issue then arose as to how these stringent limitations, which often could not be satisfied without substantial research and investment, should be applied during the period prior to that date.

One approach was that adopted by Florida, under which the plan's emission limitations would not take effect until the attainment date. Under this approach, no source is subject to enforcement actions during the preattainment period, but all are put on notice of the limitations with which they must eventually comply. * * *

/Georgia chose the Agency's preferred approach. Its plan provided for immediately effective categorical emission limitations, but also incorporated a variance procedure whereby particular sources could obtain individually tailored relief from general requirements./ This variance provision was one of the bases upon which the Agency's approval of the Georgia plan was successfully challenged by respondents in the Court of Appeals. It is the only aspect of that court's decision as to which the Agency petitioned for certiorari.

The Agency's approval of Georgia's variance provision was based on its interpretation of § 110(a)(3), which provides that the Agency shall approve any revision of an implementation plan which meets the § 110(a)(2) requirements applicable to an original plan. The Agency concluded that § 110(a)(3) permits a State to grant individual variances from generally applicable emission standards, both before and after the attainment date, so long as the variance does not cause the plan to fail to comply with the requirements of § 110(a)(2). * * *

* * * [The position of respondent NRDC and] individual respondents who reside in affected air quality control regions within the State of Georgia, is that variances applicable to individual sources may be approved only if they meet the stringent procedural and substantive standards of § 110(f). This section permits one-year postponements of any requirement of a plan, subject to conditions which will be discussed below.

* * *

* * * Since a variance would normally implicate only the § 110(a)(2)(A) requirement that plans provide for attainment and maintenance of national ambient air standards,(treatment as revisions would result in variances being readily approved in two situations: first, where the variance does not defer compliance beyond the attainment date; and second, where the national standards have been attained and the variance is not so great that a plan incorporating it could not insure their continued maintenance.]Moreover, a § 110(a)(3) revision may be granted on the basis of hearings conducted by the State, whereas a § 110(f) postponement is available only after the Agency itself conducts hearings.

[There is thus considerable practical importance attached to the issue of whether variances are to be treated as revisions or as postponements] * * *. This practical importance reaches not merely the operator of a particular source who believes that circumstances justify his receiving a variance from categorical limitations. It also reaches the broader issue of whether Congress intended the States to retain any significant degree of control of the manner in which they attain and maintain national standards, at least once their initial plans have been approved * * *. To explain our conclusion as to Congress' intent, it is necessary that we consider the revision and postponement sections in the context of other provisions of the amended Clean Air Act, particularly those which distinguish between national ambient air standards and emission limitations.

* * *

The Agency is plainly charged by the Act with the responsibility for setting the national ambient air standards. Just as plainly, however, it is relegated by the Act to a secondary role in the process of determining and enforcing the specific, source-by-source emission limitations which are necessary if the national standards it has set are to be met. Under § 110(a)(2), the agency is *required* to approve a state plan which provides for the timely attainment and subsequent maintenance of ambient air standards, and which also satisfies that section's other general requirements. The Act gives the Agency no authority to question the wisdom of a State's choices of emission limitations if they are part of a plan which satisfies the standards of § 110(a)(2), and the Agency may devise and promulgate a specific plan of its own only if a State fails to submit an implementation plan which satisfies those standards. § 110(c). Thus, so long as the ultimate effect of a State's choice of emission limitations is in compliance with the national standards for ambient air, the State is at liberty to adopt whatever mix of emission limitations it deems best suited to its particular situation.

This analysis of the Act's division of responsibilities is not challenged by respondents insofar as it concerns the process of devising and promulgating an initial implementation plan. Respondents do, however, deny that the States have such latitude once the initial plan is approved. Yet the third paragraph of § 110(a), and the one immediately following the paragraphs which specify that States shall file implementation plans and that the Agency shall approve them if they satisfy certain broad criteria, is the section which *requires* the Agency to "approve any revision of an implementation plan" if it "determines that it meets the requirements" of § 110(a)(2). On its face, this provision applies to *any* revision, without regard either to its breadth of applicability, or to whether it is to be effective before or after the attainment date; rather, Agency approval is subject only to the condition that the revised plan satisfy the general requirements applicable to original implementation plans. Far from evincing congressional intent that the Agency assume control of a State's emission limitations mix once its initial plan is approved, the revision section is to all appearances the mechanism by which the States may obtain approval of their developing policy choices as to the most practicable and desirable methods of restricting total emissions to a level which is consistent with the national ambient air standards.

In order to challenge this characterization of § 110(a)(3), respondents principally rely on the contention that the postponement provision, § 110(f), is the only mechanism by which exceptions to a plan's requirements may be obtained, under any circumstances. Were this an accurate description of § 110(f), we would agree that the revision authority does not have the broad application asserted by the Agency. Like the Ninth Circuit, however, we believe that § 110(f) serves a function different from that of supervising state efforts to modify the initial mix of emission limitations by which they implement national standards.

In our view, § 110(f) is a safety valve by which may be accorded, under certain carefully specified circumstances, exceptions to the national standards themselves. That this is its role is strongly suggested by the process by which it became a part of the Clean Air Act. [The Court analyzed legislative history and other portions of the Act supporting its interpretation.]

* * *

We believe * * * that Congress, consistent with its declaration that, "Each State shall have the primary responsibility for assuring air quality" within its boundaries, § 107(a), left to the States considerable latitude in determining specifically how the standards would be met. This discretion includes the continuing authority to revise choices about the mix of emission limitations. We therefore conclude that the Agency's interpretation of §§ 110(a)(3) and 110(f) was "correct," to the extent that it can be said with complete assurance that any particular interpretation of a complex statute such as this is the "correct" one. * * *

Notes

1. *Train* and *Union Electric* establish the basic principle governing state implementation plans, which we have called the "attainment principle." The attainment principle requires EPA to approve a state plan that will attain the national air quality standards. It may not reject a plan because it is weaker than the agency thinks feasible or less rigorous than a previous state plan. Nor may it reject a plan because it is too stringent to be feasible. Thus, so long as the national standards are met, the state may use any mix of controls it wishes, no matter how lax or how strict. *Union Electric* illustrates the power the attainment principle gives states to seek cleaner air than the national standards require. *Train* illustrates the power the attainment principle gives states to readjust the burdens on individual sources.

2. Determining the degree of controls required for attainment necessitates construction of a model predicting the dispersion of air pollution. The validity of EPA's models has been attacked. See *State of Ohio v. United States EPA,* 784 F.2d 224 (6th Cir.1986) (holding EPA's reliance on a computer model arbitrary and capricious); *State of Ohio v. United States EPA,* 798 F.2d 880 (6th Cir.1986) (reaffirming earlier ruling; EPA's use of computer models to be subjected to "searching review"). Are judges likely to have much expertise about computer modeling?

3. The phrase "state implementation *plan* "may suggest a relatively coherent and well-organized document. The reality is quite different, as Professor Rodgers explains:

[T]he volume problem is notorious—the California SIP is measured in "truckloads"; Walter Barber, then acting EPA administrator and Director of the Office of Air Quality Planning and Standards had this to say in 1981: "I don't think I can lift this, but I will try. The box is full. The box is simply the 1979 amendment to the Illinois SIP. We couldn't bring the whole SIP. Nobody could read the whole SIP. Nobody even knows what is in one at this point."

W. Rodgers, *Environmental Law* 209 (2d ed. 1994).

c. Exceptions to the Attainment Principle

Understanding the Clean Air Act would be relatively simple if the attainment principle were universally applicable. For various reasons, however, several exceptions to the attainment principle limit the state's choice of implementation plans. In this section we will consider these exceptions.

(i) PSD and Related Rules

KENNECOTT COPPER CORP. v. TRAIN

United States Court of Appeals, Ninth Circuit, 1975.
526 F.2d 1149, cert. denied 425 U.S. 935, 96 S.Ct. 1665, 48 L.Ed.2d 176 (1976).

BROWNING, CIRCUIT JUDGE.

[Kennecott Copper Corporation petitions for review of an order of the Environmental Protection Agency (EPA) rejecting a portion of the State of Nevada's implementation plan under the Clean Air Act relating to control of sulfur dioxide (SO_2), and substituting provisions formulated by EPA.] The problem arises from a single source of SO_2 emissions in Nevada—Kennecott's copper smelter at McGill in White Pine County.[9]

[EPA based its order upon an interpretation of the Clean Air Act which requires that national air quality standards be met by continuous emission limitations to the maximum extent possible, and that intermittent controls and dispersion systems be used only when continuous emission controls are not economically feasible.] This court denied Ken-

---

9. For those not acquainted with the copper smelters' problem of controlling sulfur dioxide emissions, a few facts will help put the matter in perspective[.] Most copper produced in the U.S. is obtained from sulfide ores. The average copper concentrate contains about one ton of sulfur for each ton of copper, and in the smelting process this sulfur is driven off, largely in the form of sulfur dioxide. Each ton of sulfur produces two tons of sulfur dioxide which is emitted in gas streams of varying concentrations.

About 90% of the sulfur dioxide is captured by a smelter's gas collection system and is vented into the atmosphere through smokestacks. The remaining approximately 10% escapes the smelter as "fugitive emissions."

Senator Eagleton explained the importance of sulfur oxide emissions from copper smelters as follows:

In Clean Air Act implementation, the copper industry has a significant role. Smelters annually pour 4 million tons of sulfur oxide (SO_2) [sic] into the atmosphere. The SO_2 from copper smelters constitutes one-ninth of the total SO_2 problem with steam generators for electric power the largest source of SO_2 pollution—20 million tons annually. SO_2 causes about $8.5 billion damages annually.

necott's request for a temporary injunction against enforcement of the substitute plan promulgated by EPA but expedited Kennecott's appeal. We affirm EPA's order.

Section 109 of the Clean Air Act requires EPA to promulgate national primary and secondary air quality standards. Section 110, applicable to existing sources of pollutants such as Kennecott's McGill smelter, provides that the states must devise plans to implement, maintain, and enforce these national standards. EPA must approve state implementation plans if they are adopted after reasonable notice and hearing, and meet other specified requirements. EPA must disapprove any state plan that does not comply with the statute, and propose and adopt a plan of its own.

EPA approved the provisions of Nevada's implementation plan relating to control strategy except those involving control of SO$_2$ at Kennecott's McGill smelter, the sole stationary source of this pollutant in the Nevada Intrastate Air Quality Control Region. Nevada submitted an amended plan. EPA rejected the state's amendments, and proposed, and eventually adopted, a plan of its own.

The amended Nevada plan provided for a 60 percent reduction of SO$_2$ emissions from the McGill smelter by installation of a plant to convert SO$_2$ to sulfuric acid. When weather conditions are so adverse that the 60 percent reduction in emissions resulting from operation of the acid plant would not be sufficient to maintain national air quality standards, the Nevada plan provided for reducing the level of production at the smelter.

EPA rejected the Nevada plan on the ground that an 86 percent reduction of SO$_2$ emissions from the McGill smelter was required to achieve air quality standards. EPA recognized that it was not presently economically feasible to install an acid plant or other constant emission control that would reduce SO$_2$ emissions from the McGill smelter more than the 60 percent contemplated by the Nevada plan. The EPA plan therefore provided that, as an interim measure, Kennecott might use continuous emission reduction technology capable of reducing emissions by 60 percent, together with such other controls (including reducing production and use of a tall stack) as might be needed to maintain national air standards. However, EPA's plan also provided that, until full compliance with national air quality standards is achieved entirely by means of continuous emission reduction, Kennecott must undertake a research program to improve continuous emission control technology, and must adopt such improved technology as it becomes available for use at the McGill smelter on an economically feasible basis.

Kennecott's basic position is that EPA is not authorized to require continuous emission reduction techniques in preference to intermittent controls or other methods for dispersion, or dilution, of pollutants. Kennecott contends that EPA must approve a state implementation plan that provides for any combination of continuous emission controls and alternative control systems devised by the state, so long as the state plan will attain and maintain national air quality standards within the statutory time periods.]

This view of the statute underlies Kennecott's opposition to EPA's requirement that Kennecott engage in research to develop and apply constant emission control technology. It is also the principal source of Kennecott's objection to EPA's determination that an 86 percent reduction in SO_2 emissions from the McGill smelter is required to meet national air quality standards. EPA's calculation rests upon measurements made prior to the installation of a new 750–foot tall smokestack at McGill. Kennecott submitted data to EPA indicating that the new tall stack resulted in a 92 percent decrease in ground level SO_2 concentrations. EPA refused permanent credit for this reduction because, [in EPA's view, the statute requires use of continuous emission reduction technology, as opposed to dispersion techniques, whenever economically feasible.\

[EPA bases the requirement of constant emission controls upon § 110(a)(2)(B). This subsection provides that EPA shall approve a state implementation plan if "it includes emission limitations, schedules, and timetables for compliance with such limitations, and such other measures *as may be necessary* to insure attainment and maintenance of such primary or secondary standard, including, but not limited to, land-use and transportation controls; * * * " (emphasis added).

EPA reads the phrase "as may be necessary" as modifying only "such other measures," and not "emission limitations." In EPA's view, measures other than emission limitations are therefore permissible only if "necessary" to achieve applicable air quality standards; such "other measures" are not "necessary" if economically feasible emission limitation technology is available.

EPA supports its interpretation by references to the language and legislative history of the Clean Air Act Amendments of 1970. [EPA relies upon the fact that an option to utilize intermittent controls or tall stacks carries the potential for evasion of the intent of Congress that emission limitations be included in implementation plans.] EPA invokes the policy of nondegradation of the quality of the nation's air, implied from the Act.[10] EPA also draws support from the Supreme Court's decision in *Train v. Natural Resources Defense Council, Inc.* [supra p. 351], and from the provisions and legislative history of the Energy Supply and Environmental Coordination Act of 1974.

* * *

We agree * * * that *Train* adds significant support to EPA's interpretation of section [110](a)(2)(B) as expressing a preference for emission limitations. Intermittent control systems (such as those restricting production, or utilizing less polluting fuels, during periods of adverse weather) do limit the amount of pollutant emitted while such controls

---

10. The nondegradation policy requires that existing air quality be maintained even if degradation would not reduce the quality of the air below national standards. This court has recognized that the Clean Air Act intends such a policy.

are being applied. However, the reliability and enforceability of such controls is questionable; they may not be implemented when they are in fact needed. Moreover, there is no assurance that temporary reductions in emissions resulting from such controls will not be balanced, or even exceeded, by an increase in the amount of pollutant emitted when weather conditions improve and production is increased to make up for prior losses, or more polluting fuels are again used. Thus, intermittent controls, like tall stacks, may only disperse the pollutant rather than reduce it. Tall smokestacks disperse a pollutant through greater quantities of air; intermittent control systems disperse pollutant peaks through longer periods of time. Neither assures a reduction in the quantity of the pollutant eventually emitted. * * *

Notes

1. State agency determinations of technological infeasibility are not binding on the EPA, according to *Bunker Hill Co. v. EPA,* 572 F.2d 1286 (9th Cir.1977). The Idaho agency had determined that a maximum of 72 percent of lead and zinc smelters' SO_2 emissions could be captured under currently available continuous-control technology, and adopted a regulation to that effect. EPA refused to approve that part of the SIP and promulgated a substitute 82 percent limitation. Bunker Hill challenged EPA's action under section 307, contending that (a) EPA was bound by Idaho's determination on feasibility and (b) if not, EPA's determination was arbitrary and capricious. The court ruled in favor of EPA on the first issue, but against EPA on the second.

2. Section 123, also added in 1977, provides that the "degree of emission limitation required for control of any air pollutant" under an applicable implementation plan "shall not be affected in any manner" by (1) so much of the stack height of any source "as exceeds good engineering practice (as determined under regulations promulgated by the Administrator)," or (2) any other dispersion technique. "Good engineering practice" means the height necessary to insure that emissions from the stack do not result in "excessive concentrations of any air pollutant in the immediate vicinity of the source." Ordinarily, such height shall not exceed 2½ times the height of the source. EPA's implementing regulations were reviewed in *Sierra Club v. EPA,* 719 F.2d 436 (D.C.Cir.1983), cert. denied 468 U.S. 1204, 104 S.Ct. 3571, 82 L.Ed.2d 870 (1984); and *NRDC v. Thomas,* 838 F.2d 1224 (D.C.Cir.1988) (upholding most of the regulation but striking down some grandfather provisions).

It is not always easy to tell what constitutes a dispersion technique. In *Kamp v. Hernandez,* 752 F.2d 1444 (9th Cir.1985), opinion modified 778 F.2d 527 (9th Cir.1985), the court upheld use of a "multipoint" technique of determining emission standards, in which the calculation of the level of emissions allowed took into account the fact that the highest emissions may take place on days with favorable meteorological conditions.

Note on PSD Requirements

Among other reasons, *Kennecott Copper* relied on an anti-degradation policy that had been recognized by some courts. In 1977, Congress responded to litigation on the subject by adding special provisions intended to protect areas that already have especially clean air. Sections 160–169 provide a complicated regulatory scheme to prevent significant deterioration (otherwise known as "PSD" regulations). [Areas designated as having ambient air quality better than the applicable NAAQS are divided into three categories. Class I areas, for which very small increments apply, include international parks and large national parks and wilderness areas. Initially, all other areas were designated Class II, for which increments were set permitting moderate economic growth. However, some Class II areas could be redesignated Class III, to which only the NAAQS apply.]

No "major" stationary source may be constructed or modified in a PSD area without a permit setting forth emission limitations for the facility. The permit applicant must show that emissions will not cause or contribute to air pollution in excess of the allowable increment in the PSD area, and the facility must use "best available control technology" (BACT).

This regulatory scheme is complicated by the desire to retain state control over land use planning, while providing federal protection to areas with pristine air. Naturally, this complicated scheme raises equally complex interpretative issues. Suppose that a plant changes fuels or operating procedures in a way that increases emissions. Is this a "modification" requiring a PSD permit? See *Hawaiian Electric Co. v. United States EPA,* 723 F.2d 1440 (9th Cir.1984). Suppose the plant will emit less at the current operating level, but could emit more at a higher rate of production? See *Puerto Rican Cement Co. v. United States EPA,* 889 F.2d 292 (1st Cir.1989) (PSD applies).

[The actual operation of the PSD requirements diverged from what one might infer from reading the statute.] Reclassification was nearly a dead issue: virtually no area has been reclassified as either Class I or Class III. Except for national parks, essentially, the entire nation (except for nonattainment areas) was set at Class II. SIP revisions were problematic because of modeling difficulties: the best dispersion models are accurate only within a factor of two. About one hundred projects, mostly modifications, pass through the PSD permit process every year. Because PSD has had little effect on plant siting, the technology standards have become the focus of PSD policy. [This technology (BACT) has tended to be markedly stricter than the general new source standards, and has resulted in significant decreases in emissions as compared with those that would otherwise have been required by § 111.] For example, there has been over a 20% reduction in particulates and sulfur dioxide below new source standards. See Oren, "Prevention of Significant Deterioration: How to Decide Who is Allowed to Pollute," 74 *Iowa L.Rev.* 1, 20, 25, 30–32, 41–43 (1988). [EPA has implemented a "top down" review process, under which a source must use the most stringent control technology available unless it can demonstrate that use of that technology is infeasible based on "substantial and unique local factors."] Wilson, Martin & Friedland, "A Critical Review of the Environmental Protection Agency's Standards for 'Best Available Control Technology' Under the Clean Air Act," 20 *Env.L.Rptr.* 10067 (1990).[j]

no class I.

j. Most of the emphasis has been on the PSD policy for sulfur dioxide and particulates, but the statute also requires EPA to create PSD programs for other pollutants. Its efforts to do so got off to a bad start with the nitrogen oxides regulation, which

(ii) Nonattainment and Noncompliance Under the Clean Air Act

Thus far, we have been considering the requirements the Clean Air Act imposes on states and industries. How are these requirements enforced? And what happens if air quality standards are not attained?

The next case discloses some of the implications of our "cooperative" federal-state system of air pollution control. Note that when a state implementation plan (SIP) for attaining national ambient air quality standards is approved by the EPA, it can be enforced not only by state authorities but also by the Administrator (§ 113) and by private citizens (§ 304).

GETTY OIL CO. (EASTERN OPERATIONS)
v. RUCKELSHAUS

United States Court of Appeals, Third Circuit, 1972.
467 F.2d 349, cert. denied 409 U.S. 1125, 93 S.Ct. 937, 35 L.Ed.2d 256 (1973).

JAMES ROSEN, CIRCUIT JUDGE.

[After notice and public hearing on proposed state air pollution regulations, the Delaware pollution-control agency (WARC) had adopted Regulation VIII limiting the sulphur content of fuel burned by large plants in New Castle County. The only affected plant was a power station owned by Delmarva and specially designed to supply electricity and steam to the Getty refinery by burning fluid coke, a by-product of the refinery. Neither Getty nor Delmarva had sought judicial review of the action of the agency or of EPA's approval of the regulation as part of Delaware's implementation plan. Instead, the two firms sought from state authorities a "variance" which would extend the time for compliance. The firms also obtained an order from a state court restraining state enforcement of the regulation against Delmarva until the variance proceeding was concluded. However, before any final state decision on the variance application, the EPA, pursuant to § 113(a)(1) of the Clean Air Act, notified Delmarva that it was in violation of the implementation plan and ordered compliance. Getty thereupon filed this suit, seeking to enjoin the EPA Administrator from enforcing his order.]

A review of the tangled procedural history preceding Getty's institution of this suit convinces us that due process has been satisfied. First, Getty appeared at Delaware's hearing on the proposed implementation plan for attainment of air quality standards and argued against adoption of Regulation VIII. After approval by WARC Getty had an opportunity to appeal the adoption of the regulation to the state Superior Court. It

was held insufficiently stringent in *EDF v. Administrator of the United States EPA,* 898 F.2d 183 (D.C.Cir.1990). In *NRDC v. U.S. EPA,* 937 F.2d 641 (D.C.Cir.1991), the court upheld EPA's decision not to regulate fugitive dust from surface coal mining. EPA had decided not to regulate these emissions after a cost-benefit analysis; section 302(j) provides that sources of fugitive emissions constitute major sources only "as determined by rule by the Administrator." The court viewed EPA's approach as particularly reasonable given the fact that extractive industries must locate where their natural resources are found, so that there is no risk (as there is for manufacturing) that controls on urban emissions will lead to relocation in cleaner parts of the country.

vacate: to nullify or cancel

chose instead to seek a variance with the Secretary of Natural Resources and Environmental Control. The Secretary denied the application and Getty took an appeal to WARC. That appeal is still pending. The Administrator's adoption of Delaware's plan, and specifically Regulation VIII, received wide publicity in the media, and presumably came to Getty's attention in the fall of 1971. No appeal was taken from the Administrator's approval of the implementation plan to the Court of Appeals, as provided by the Clean Air Act. Instead, Getty chose to seek a restraining order in the Chancery Court of Delaware in December of 1971. Recently, that court denied a motion by the Delaware Secretary of Natural Resources and Environmental Control to vacate or modify the restraining order. Getty also took the opportunity to participate in the conference between EPA and Delmarva regarding possible violations of the regulations. In light of the above, Getty's protestations that the doctrines of ripeness and justiciability would have foreclosed it from obtaining meaningful review are frivolous. Furthermore, we reject Getty's attempt to establish the limited criteria for obtaining a variance contained in the Clean Air Act as a substitute for § 307 judicial review. Getty maintains that "[t]he adoption of the Regulation by the Commission involved the applicability of all the Regulations to the state as a whole and involved very different questions than are presented by the rather narrow question of a variance application which is made on the grounds of hardship to a Regulation which may be otherwise suitable for the entire state." However, the fact remains that the regulation in question quite possibly affects a single installation, i.e. Delmarva, in the designated area * * *. Getty could have raised the questions of economic hardship or lack of compelling necessity in a § 307 hearing that it sought to raise below. Its failure to do so cannot be contributed to any lack of sufficient notice or hearing.

* * *

Getty has sought to litigate the merits of its variance application on this appeal. It requested a postponement of argument before WARC pending a judicial determination by either the Chancery Court or the Court of Appeals. We decline to substitute our judgment for that of WARC. There is no constitutional or statutory authority which would allow us to make such a determination. The Clean Air Act authorizes approval of a revision of an implementation plan by the Administrator, after adoption by the state based upon reasonable notice and public hearings. [§ 110(a)(3).] Getty attempts an end run around the Act by seeking pre-enforcement judicial review before WARC has had an opportunity to pass upon Getty's application for a variance, and before the Administrator has had an opportunity to review any forthcoming state action. And here lies the crux of Getty's predicament: having failed to appeal the Administrator's approval of the Delaware plan, and faced as it is with the EPA's compliance order, Getty is presented with the choice of either compliance or breach, until such time as its application for a variance is favorably considered.

⌐The district court noted that when the issue concerns timing of judicial review rather than the existence of said review, the procedures which must be afforded to an individual further depends upon the governmental interest in summary enforcement.⌐ There can be no question that the primary and secondary air quality standards serve substantial governmental interests—in the case of primary standards, protection of the public health; in the case of secondary standards—protection of the public welfare from any known or anticipated adverse effects associated with the presence of a specified air pollutant in the ambient air. * * *

The Administrator has a responsibility to see that a state plan will meet the national standards. Because of that responsibility, he has a vital interest in determining whether a particular deferral will have the effect of preventing attainment or maintenance of the national standard. ⌐However, until the criteria of 40 CFR 51.32(a) through (f) are met, the Administrator is duty bound to enforce an approved implementation plan.⌐

Getty's protestations of good faith attempts to find suitable technology which would enable it to comply do not affect the Administrator's duty of enforcement. * * *

Appellant's efforts to establish the lack of necessity for early compliance due to the existence of primary air quality in Delaware must fail. ⌐Section 110 of the Clean Air Act requires that state air implementation plans attain primary standards. It does not preclude such standards from being exceeded. * * *

We conclude that Getty's belated effort to attack Regulation VIII in the guise of pre-enforcement review of the compliance order is precluded by § 307 of the Clean Air Act.

Notes

1. By refusing pre-enforcement judicial review of the regulation, the court created the "Getty dilemma": whether to spend money to comply with a standard from which Getty later might be at least partially excused, or to violate it and risk legal penalty if the standard ultimately is enforced. Is that a fair and economically sound situation?

Because *Train* requires that a variance (qua "plan revision") result in NAAQS compliance (or at least a move in that direction), these variances are theoretically unavailable in nonattainment areas. Nevertheless, in response to heavy demand from industry, states continue to issue such "variances" in large numbers, even though they are invalid under federal law. Only occasionally does the EPA exercise its power to enforce the SIP in these circumstances. For a fuller explanation, and two interesting case studies, see Melnick & Willes, "Watching the Candy Store: EPA Overfiling of Local Air Pollution Variances," 20 *Ecology L.Q.* 207 (1993).

2. Because § 307(b)(2) provides that actions of the Administrator reviewable under § 307(b)(1) "shall not be subject to judicial review in civil or criminal proceedings for enforcement," in most enforcement proceedings the

construe: to interpret

validity of governing standards or regulatory requirements will be immune from attack, and the only real issue will be whether the defendants in fact violated the standards or requirements.[k] Is that result consistent with the requirements of due process of law?

In *Sierra Club v. Indiana–Kentucky Electric Corp.*, 716 F.2d 1145 (7th Cir.1983), the Seventh Circuit construed § 307 narrowly to avoid foreclosing a later challenge. Indiana had adopted an SIP which was approved by EPA in 1972. In 1975, the state courts ruled that the plan was invalidly adopted because the state hearing officer had failed to submit written findings to the Indiana environmental board. In 1983, the Seventh Circuit held the plan unenforceable as a matter of federal law. Its reasoning was as follows:

> Sierra Club argues that, once EPA adopts a state implementation plan, that plan becomes federal law and only the federal government may alter that law. Sierra Club points out that [§ 307(b)(1)] provides that an approved plan may be invalidated only in the appropriate federal court of appeals. This assumes, however, that the plan is adopted initially in accordance with the Act. The state-federal partnership under the Act gave a place to the state and their reviewing courts in the initial plan formulation. That state's governmental bodies are entitled to review the procedures employed to adopt a state implementation plan. Once a plan is adopted by the state and it *withstands any subsequent procedural challenge,* then [§ 307] provides that invalidation may occur only in the federal appellate courts. Any other interpretation would destroy the meaningfulness of the review this circuit and others have held would be available in the state courts.

Id. at 1151–1152. But is allowing an SIP to be invalidated years after enactment consistent with the time limit for review under § 307? In that connection, consider *United States v. Ford Motor Co.*, 814 F.2d 1099 (6th Cir.1987). This case involved a Ford plant in Michigan which coats vinyl products, emitting ozone as a result. Ford sued the state environmental agency to enjoin enforcement of the SIP and entered into a consent decree, which it then contended was binding on the federal EPA. The court distinguished *Sierra Club:*

> The present suit, unlike *Sierra Club,* concerns invalidation of a SIP on technical grounds by a state court. Thus, even under the language of *Sierra Club,* such invalidation cannot be given effect, because invalidation of an EPA-approved SIP may only occur in the federal appellate

---

k. In *Harrison v. PPG Industries, Inc.*, 446 U.S. 578, 100 S.Ct. 1889, 64 L.Ed.2d 525 (1980) the Supreme Court adopted a broad interpretation of the scope of direct appellate review under § 307(b)(1) of the Clean Air Act, as amended in 1977. The case involved a chemical manufacturer's challenge to an informal determination by an EPA Regional Administrator, based only on an exchange of letters, that EPA's new source performance standards for major fossil fuel-fired steam generating units were applicable to petitioner's wasteheat boilers. Section 307(b)(1) provides for direct review in a federal court of appeals of certain ac- tions taken by the EPA Administrator under specifically enumerated provisions of the Act and of "any other final action of the Administrator under [the Act] * * * which is locally or regionally applicable." The Court acknowledged that its construction of the latter language, to include not only rulemaking of general applicability but also informal adjudicatory determinations concerning single plants, could entail a major jurisdictional shift from the district courts to the courts of appeals and pose procedural problems because fact-finding devices are limited at the appellate level.

(handwritten in left margin: SIP State Implementation Plan)

courts on direct appeal from the Administrator's decision under § 7607(b)(1), and revisions and variances of properly promulgated SIPs require EPA approval. This case, in short, does not concern a SIP found invalid on state procedural grounds by a state court, as was the case in *Sierra Club*. Nor does the fact that the consent decree in this case purported to vacate and modify the SIP as of its compliance date render it void *ab initio* in the sense described in *Sierra Club*. The mere fact that state authorities, through the discovery of subsequent technical data, or otherwise, change their views on the technological or economic feasibility of a properly adopted emission limit cannot in itself render the original emission limit unenforceable. As this court has stated, "the Act clearly envisions the possibility of continuous adjustments in the basic plan by the State and the EPA. If a plan became unenforceable every time such a revision became a possibility, the entire enforcement procedure of the Clean Air Act would be crippled." *Ohio Environmental Council v. United States District Court*, 565 F.2d 393, 398 (6th Cir.1977) (citations omitted). Instead, the original emission limit remains fully enforceable until a revision or variance is approved by both the State and EPA.

3. *Getty* involved efforts to use state law to escape the requirements of a SIP. Between 1977 and 1990, § 113 of the Clean Air Act also provided an express variance provision of sorts. Under the 1970 Act, EPA was authorized to issue administrative compliance orders. Those orders typically provided violators additional time in which to comply. In 1977, § 113 was amended to formalize this procedure. Section 113(d) provided a new mechanism, known as a "delayed compliance order" (DCO). After providing notice and an opportunity for public comment, EPA could issue an order providing up to three additional years to "any stationary source which is unable to comply with any requirement of an applicable implementation plan." The DCO was in effect a variance because it provided a shield against any other enforcement action. For an extensive discussion of DCO's, see Currie, "Relaxation of Implementation Plans Under the 1977 Clean Air Act Amendments," 78 *Mich.L.Rev.* 155 (1979).

The DCO provision was repealed in 1990. Section 113(a)(4) was amended to allow EPA enforcement orders to "specify a time for compliance which the Administrator determines is reasonable, taking into account the seriousness of the violation and any good faith efforts to comply with applicable requirements"; such an order may delay compliance "in no event longer than one year after the date the order was issued, and shall be nonrenewable." The order does not prevent collection of penalties or release the source from its obligation to comply with the SIP or any permit requirement.

4. The supposedly strict deadlines in the 1970 Act have instead turned into a long war of attrition between Congress and recalcitrant firms. Would Congress have done better to establish a more realistic mechanism in the first place? Or, was it important for Congress to begin by announcing a very tough stance, on the assumption that whatever Congress required in the statute would probably be eroded anyway?

Note on Nonattainment

The foregoing materials focus on the feasibility of individual polluters' complying with air pollution limits. But what if a *state* is unable to achieve timely attainment of a national ambient standard in one or more of its air quality control regions? Well before the 1975 deadline, it was clear that this situation would occur in many urban areas.

The 1977 Amendments. Section 172 of the Clean Air Act, as amended in 1977, effectively authorized postponement of the date for compliance with primary standards until 1982, or 1987 for oxidants and carbon monoxide. Subject to enumerated conditions, a revised state plan could relax requirements for existing stationary sources and allow construction of new ones. To obtain a construction or operation permit, a "major" new source—one with "potential to emit" 100 tons per year of any pollutant—was required by § 173 to comply with the "lowest achievable emission rate" (LAER) and to satisfy certain pollution "offset" requirements (discussed at page 388 infra). Section 171(3) defined LAER as "the most stringent emission limitation ... contained in the implementation plan of any State" (unless shown "not achievable") or "the most stringent emission limitation achieved in practice, ... whichever is more stringent." Since LAER could not be less stringent than standards of performance for new sources under § 111, it required at least "the best technological system of continuous emission reduction ... adequately demonstrated," considering cost.

The 1982 deadline for attainment of primary NAAQSs came and went, but many nonattainment areas remained. EPA made every effort to avoid imposing sanctions on the states. It is clear that some states, in their new SIPs, took credit for proposed emission reduction measures which state and local officials were never prepared to implement or which, if implemented, would provide less reductions than estimated. Many such unrealistic provisions were approved by EPA. Other submissions resulted in EPA's granting "conditional approval" of SIPs, subject to a requirement that the states revise them to assure attainment. The EPA Administrator's policy of granting conditional approval of inadequate SIPs, rather than disapproving unacceptable portions and himself promulgating implementation plans pursuant to § 110(c)(1), was upheld in *City of Seabrook v. EPA,* 659 F.2d 1349 (5th Cir.1981), cert. denied 459 U.S. 822, 103 S.Ct. 51, 74 L.Ed.2d 57 (1982), and in *Connecticut Fund for the Environment v. EPA,* 672 F.2d 998 (2d Cir.1982).

Under §§ 110(a)(2)(I), 172 and 173, the main sanction for nonattainment of primary NAAQSs by the statutory deadlines was a moratorium on construction and operation of new or modified major stationary sources. Section 176 also contemplated denial of federal grants for highway construction and various other purposes. EPA's policy was not to impose sanctions immediately. The Agency designated more than one hundred counties nationwide as "probable" noncompliance areas and announced procedures to be followed in making final determinations.

The arrival of the 1984 and 1987 deadlines for attainment placed EPA in an even more uncomfortable position. Over seventy cities missed the December 31, 1987 deadline for attainment of the ozone and carbon monoxide air quality standards. See 17 *Env.L.Rptr.* 10415 (Oct. 1987). One response to the attainment deadline was a series of attempts by states, with mixed results, to carve attainment areas out of larger nonattainment areas. See *State of Arizona v. Thomas,* 824 F.2d 745 (9th Cir.1987); Comment, "When is an Area that is in Attainment not an Attainment Area?" 16 ELR 10041 (1986). In *Abramowitz v. United States EPA,* 832 F.2d 1071 (9th Cir.1987), however, the court held that EPA could not approve the California SIP because it would not result in attainment of the standards by the statutory deadline. EPA had attempted to temporize by allowing California to take "reasonable extra efforts" to comply. In *Delaney v. EPA,* 898 F.2d 687 (9th Cir.1990), the court again rebuffed EPA's efforts to give states more time to comply.

The 1990 Amendments. Nonattainment was one of the central concerns of the 1990 amendments. Nonattainment areas now must include the entire metropolitan area unless the state can show that some sub-area does not contribute significantly to the nonattainment problem. The relatively simple noncompliance provisions of the 1977 amendments are replaced by a far more elaborate scheme.

The amendments require another round of SIP amendments to achieve compliance. In this connection, it is worth noting some changes in the general provisions governing plan revisions. EPA must issue minimum standards for a plan revision to qualify as a "complete" submission. Within sixty days of a plan submission, EPA must consider whether the submission is complete. If not, EPA may treat it in whole or in part as a nullity; if the submission is complete, EPA must approve or disapprove the plan within twelve months. EPA may issue a conditional approval if the state commits itself to adopt specific enforceable measures within a year.

If a SIP for a nonattainment area is inadequate, EPA must issue a federal implementation plan within two years. The amendments provide several other sanctions, including a cutoff of federal highway funds. Another important sanction is an upward adjustment of the "offset" requirements, which are discussed later at pages __ to __, infra. The effect of the adjustment is to limit economic growth in the offending region. Areas that fall behind schedule may be "bumped up" to higher categories, resulting in more stringent control requirements. Finally, depending on the severity of the non-attainment problem, the term "major source" is redefined to include smaller sources, with the result that those sources will have to implement technology-based standards such as LAER and RACT.

Apart from these general provisions, the amendments also contain a series of complex provisions relating specifically to ozone, NOx, CO, and particulates. The ozone provisions are illustrative. The statute divides ozone non-attainment areas into five classes, depending on the severity of the pollution. Only Los Angeles is in the worst class ("extreme" nonattainment.) Compliance requirements are keyed to this classification scheme. For example, "marginal" areas must achieve attainment within three years, while "serious" areas have nine years, and Los Angeles is given 20 years. Except for marginal areas, all ozone non-attainment areas were supposed to reduce emissions of volatile organic compounds (VOCs) by 15% by 1996, and further reductions of 3% must be achieved annually. Major sources are also defined differently for the different categories: 100 tons per year in the marginal and moderate areas, but only 50, 25, or 10 tons per year in the serious, severe, and extreme areas, respectively. Offset requirements also vary between these areas. The statute requires various specific control measures in different categories. For example, in areas ranked serious or worse, gas stations are required to install special hose-and-nozzle controls on gas pumps to capture fuel vapors. These areas are also required to have more stringent inspection and maintenance programs.

The ozone reduction measures have been predicted to have an annual cost of $9–12 billion after they are fully implemented in 2004. Benefits in the form of reductions in acute health effects and increased agricultural output were estimated at $5 billion. Other possible benefits include a possible (but conjectural) decrease in chronic respiratory disease, reductions in damage to forests, improved visibility, and incidental reductions in carcinogenic emissions. Portney, "Economics and the Clean Air Act," 4 *J.Econ.Persp.* 173, 176 (1990).

The provisions relating to nonattainment for other pollutants are also generally similar, but give EPA somewhat more discretion. One particularly interesting feature of the carbon monoxide provisions is that they require the use of oxygenated fuels (such as gasoline containing ethanol) in certain areas. These fuel additives increase the amount of oxygen available for combustion and thereby decrease emissions of carbon monoxide.

Congress has obviously learned a lot about the noncompliance problem in the two decades following the original enactment of the Clean Air Act. It remains to be seen whether this increased regulatory sophistication will be reflected in improved air quality, but the 1990 amendments do seem to promise significant further progress.

After 1990: "Deja Vu All Over Again?" There are considerable questions about whether the SIP process is working anymore (or whether it has ever worked very well). Delays have plagued the process and are expected to continue. See GAO, *Air Pollution: State Planning Requirements Will Continue to Challenge EPA and the States* (June 1993); Cushman, "State and Federal Agencies Lag in Meeting Clean Air Law," *New York Times,* July 16, 1993, at 1. Some critics contend that the entire process is fatally flawed:

> I believe there is a consensus among environmental analysts that the SIP process failed when the 1970 CAA was enacted, failed after the 1977 CAA Amendments, and was still failing to achieve attainment when the 1990 Amendments were enacted. Many states have produced "cheater SIPs" they never expected to implement. In the early years, EPA regional personnel or state officials issued hundreds of administrative orders and compliance schedules that diverged from SIP provisions and were more lenient than necessary to reach attainment. * * *

> * * * A 1989 EPA analysis noted with unusual candor: "It is clear that the process of reviewing and judging SIPs has been a constant struggle for EPA and the States and is a source of increasing tension." The EPA discussion cited conflicts in priorities between the agency and the states and between EPA regional and national offices. EPA also

acknowledged that its staff has been unwilling to impose strict deadlines or sanctions on state officials responsible for SIP implementation. * * *

Latin, "Regulatory Failure, Administrative Incentives, and the Clean Air Act," 21 *Env.L.* 1647, 1689–90 (1991).

Whether the states will succeed in meeting nonattainment requirements is unclear. A coalition of thirty-six states devised a plan that would impose new controls on industrial polluters in the midwest and south, which cause much of the smog problem in eastern cities. EPA threatened to propose its own air quality rules before the coalition has completed its work. See John Cushman, "Deadline Nears for States' Antismog Plan: A Coalition Tries to Avert Imposition of Federal Air Quality Rules," N.Y. Times, March 16, 1997 at 18. In the meantime, by using grandfather, transition, and de minimis rules, EPA continues to buy time for continued SIP revisions by the states. See *Env. Defense Fund v. EPA*, 82 F.3d 451 (D.C.Cir.1996). EPA also releases states from any obligation to make further progress once a factual showing of attainment is made, even without a formal redesignation as an attainment area. See *Sierra Club v. EPA*, 99 F.3d 1551 (10th Cir. 1996).

2. AREA PLANNING IN THE CLEAN WATER ACT

Although area planning does not play the same central role in the Clean Water Act as it does in the Air Act, the Clean Water Act does contain some significant area-planning provisions. Section 302 requires EPA to establish more stringent effluent limitations when the normal § 301 requirements would not achieve "water quality in a specific portion of the navigable waters which shall assure protection of public water supplies, agricultural and industrial uses, and the protection and propagation of a balanced population of shellfish, fish, and wildlife, and allow recreational activities in and on the water." Section 302(b) provides for the consideration of cost and feasibility in this process. Section 303 ratifies state water quality standards approved before 1972, calls for EPA to issue standards for states failing to submit their own, and requires states to periodically review their standards. States are also required to identify those waters within their boundaries for which the § 301 effluent limitations "are not stringent enough to implement any water quality standard applicable to such waters" and to establish a "total maximum daily load" for those waters at a level that will protect the water quality standards with a "margin of safety." This provision remained largely dormant until EPA was driven by lawsuits to activate it in 1996. See Houck, "TMDLs: Are We There Yet?," 27 *Env.L.Rep.* 10391, 10397 (1997). States are also required to put in place a "continuing planning process" as one requirement for obtaining approval of their permit programs under § 402.

The setting of water quality standards involves both federal and state governments, whose respective roles have not always been clear. In *Mississippi Comm'n on Natural Resources v. Costle*, 625 F.2d 1269 (5th Cir.1980), the court attempted to clarify EPA's relationship with the states. As the court understood the statute, the state's role is primarily to designate the appropriate use for a water body, while EPA sets the criteria appropriate for various levels of use (fishable, swimmable, etc.). The court also upheld EPA's contention that economic factors are not relevant to setting the criteria. The foregoing opinion has been sharply criticized:

> Only one appellate decision has addressed the extent of EPA's authority to review a state's criteria judgments and use designations. In *Mississippi Commission on Natural Resources v. Costle,* the court found that intensive review by EPA of state use designation would amount to federal exercise of the zoning power Congress explicitly denied it. By contrast, EPA's review of the technical accuracy of state criteria judgments was perfectly proper. The court claimed to be accepting an EPA argument. In fact, however, EPA's regulatory program is approximately the reverse of the court's prescription. EPA's water quality standards rules assert a broad federal power to circumscribe the uses a state may choose for its water. The regulations declare that EPA will not approve state standards that allow water quality in a lake or stream to decline, no matter how compelling an argument might be made concerning local preferences or circumstances. Even if a state simply wants to maintain existing levels of water quality, EPA insists on a showing that improved water quality is unattainable by reasonable control measures.

Pedersen, "Turning the Tide on Water Quality," 15 *Ecology L.Q.* 69, 93 (1988). Pedersen adds that the "legal soundness of these policies is highly debatable," and he contends that the current use designations often are arbitrary. Id. at 94–95.

As time goes on, progress using technology based standards may slow, because such standards may become more difficult to enforce as they become more burdensome, and because they may be insufficient to assure adequate water quality in some areas. It seems likely that water quality standards will attain greater significance as it becomes more difficult to make further progress using technology based standards. As we saw in Chapter III, EPA has also used water quality standards to deal with interstate pollution issues, requiring the upstream state's permit to be consistent with downstream water quality standards. See *Arkansas v. Oklahoma* [p. 275 supra]. See also *City of Albuquerque v. Browner,* 97 F.3d 415 (10th Cir.1996) (upstream state must respect water quality standards adopted by downstream Indian tribe acting under authority of § 518).

The following case illustrates the re-emerging role of water quality standards.

PUD NO. 1 OF JEFFERSON COUNTY
v. WASHINGTON DEPARTMENT
OF ECOLOGY

Supreme Court of the United States, 1994.
511 U.S. 700, 114 S.Ct. 1900, 128 L.Ed.2d 716.

JUSTICE O'CONNOR delivered the opinion of the Court.

Petitioners, a city and a local utility district, want to build a hydroelectric project on the Dosewallips River in Washington State. We must decide whether respondent, the state environmental agency, properly conditioned a permit for the project on the maintenance of specific minimum stream flows to protect salmon and steelhead runs.

The principal dispute in this case concerns whether the minimum stream flow requirement that the State imposed on the Elkhorn project [to preserve salmon and trout runs] is a permissible condition of a § 401 certification under the Clean Water Act. To resolve this dispute we must first determine the scope of the State's authority under § 401. We must then determine whether the limitation at issue here, the requirement that petitioners maintain minimum stream flows, falls within the scope of that authority.

There is no dispute that petitioners were required to obtain a certification from the State pursuant to § 401. Petitioners concede that, at a minimum, the project will result in two possible discharges—the release of dredged and fill material during the construction of the project, and the discharge of water at the end of the tailrace after the water has been used to generate electricity. Petitioners contend, however, that the minimum stream flow requirement imposed by the State was unrelated to these specific discharges, and that as a consequence, the State lacked the authority under § 401 to condition its certification on maintenance of stream flows sufficient to protect the Dosewallips fishery.

If § 401 consisted solely of subsection (a), which refers to a state certification that a "discharge" will comply with certain provisions of the Act, petitioners' assessment of the scope of the State's certification authority would have considerable force. Section 401, however, also contains subsection (d), which expands the State's authority to impose conditions on the certification of a project. Section 401(d) provides that any certification shall set forth "any effluent limitations and other limitations * * * necessary to assure that any applicant" will comply with various provisions of the Act and appropriate state law requirements. The language of this subsection contradicts petitioners' claim that the State may only impose water quality limitations specifically tied to a "discharge." The text refers to the compliance of the applicant, not the discharge. Section 401(d) thus allows the State to impose "other limitations" on the project in general to assure compliance with various provisions of the Clean Water Act and with "any other appropriate requirement of State law." Although the dissent asserts that this interpretation of § 401(d) renders § 401(a)(1) superfluous, we see no such anomaly. Section 401(a)(1) identifies the category of activities subject to certification—namely those with discharges. And § 401(d) is most reasonably read as authorizing additional conditions and limitations on the activity as a whole once the threshold condition, the existence of a discharge, is satisfied.

* * *

We agree with the State that ensuring compliance with § 303 is a proper function of the § 401 certification. Although § 303 is not one of the statutory provisions listed in § 401(d), the statute allows states to impose limitations to ensure compliance with § 301 of the Act, 33 U.S.C. § 1311. Section 301 in turn incorporates § 303 by reference. As a consequence, state water quality standards adopted pursuant to § 303 are among the "other limitations" with which a State may ensure compliance through the § 401 certification process. This interpretation is consistent with EPA's view of the statute. Moreover, limitations to assure compliance with state water quality standards are also permitted by § 401(d)'s reference to "any other appropriate requirement of State law." We do not speculate on what additional state laws, if any, might be incorporated by this language.[11] But at a minimum, limitations imposed pursuant to state water quality standards adopted pursuant to § 303 are "appropriate" requirements of state law. Indeed, petitioners appear to agree that the State's authority under § 401 includes limitations designed to ensure compliance with state water quality standards.

Having concluded that, pursuant to § 401, States may condition certification upon any limitations necessary to ensure compliance with state water quality standards or any other "appropriate requirement of State law," we consider whether the minimum flow condition is such a limitation. Under § 303, state water quality standards must "consist of the designated uses of the navigable waters involved and the water quality criteria for such waters based upon such uses." In imposing the minimum stream flow requirement, the State determined that construction and operation of the project as planned would be inconsistent with one of the designated uses of Class AA water, namely "[s]almonid [and other fish] migration, rearing, spawning, and harvesting." The designated use of the River as a fish habitat directly reflects the Clean Water Act's goal of maintaining the "chemical, physical, and biological integrity of the Nation's waters." Indeed, the Act defines pollution as "the man-made or man induced alteration of the chemical, physical, biological, and

---

11. The dissent asserts that § 301 is concerned solely with discharges, not broader water quality standards. Although § 301 does make certain discharges unlawful, it also contains a broad enabling provision which requires states to take certain actions, to wit: "In order to carry out the objective of this chapter [viz. the chemical, physical, and biological integrity of the Na-

tion's water] there shall be achieved * * * not later than July 1, 1977, any more stringent limitation, including those necessary to meet water quality standards * * * established pursuant to any State law or regulations." This provision of § 301 expressly refers to state water quality standards, and is not limited to discharges.

radiological integrity of water." Moreover, the Act expressly requires that, in adopting water quality standards, the State must take into consideration the use of waters for "propagation of fish and wildlife."

Petitioners assert, however, that § 303 requires the State to protect designated uses solely through implementation of specific "criteria." According to petitioners, the State may not require them to operate their dam in a manner consistent with a designated "use"; instead, say petitioners, under § 303 the State may only require that the project comply with specific numerical "criteria."

We disagree with petitioners' interpretation of the language of § 303(c)(2)(A). Under the statute, a water quality standard must "consist of the designated uses of the navigable waters involved and the water quality criteria for such waters based upon such uses." The text makes it plain that water quality standards contain two components. We think the language of § 303 is most naturally read to require that a project be consistent with both components, namely the designated use and the water quality criteria. Accordingly, under the literal terms of the statute, a project that does not comply with a designated use of the water does not comply with the applicable water quality standards.

* * *

Washington's Class AA water quality standards are typical in that they contain several open-ended criteria which, like the use designation of the River as a fishery, must be translated into specific limitations for individual projects. For example, the standards state that "[t]oxic, radioactive, or deleterious material concentrations shall be less than those which may affect public health, the natural aquatic environment, or the desirability of the water for any use." Similarly, the state standards specify that "[a]esthetic values shall not be impaired by the presence of materials or their effects, excluding those of natural origin, which offend the senses of sight, smell, touch, or taste." We think petitioners' attempt to distinguish between uses and criteria loses much of its force in light of the fact that the Act permits enforcement of broad, narrative criteria based on, for example, "aesthetics."

* * *

The State also justified its minimum stream flow as necessary to implement the "antidegradation policy" of § 303. When the Clean Water Act was enacted in 1972, the water quality standards of all 50 States had antidegradation provisions. These provisions were required by federal law. By providing in 1972 that existing state water quality standards would remain in force until revised, the Clean Water Act ensured that the States would continue their antidegradation programs. EPA has consistently required that revised state standards incorporate an antidegradation policy. And, in 1987, Congress explicitly recognized the existence of an "antidegradation policy established under [§ 303]."

* * *

Petitioners contend that we should limit the State's authority to impose minimum flow requirements because FERC has comprehensive authority to license hydroelectric projects pursuant to the FPA, 16 U.S.C. § 791a et seq. In petitioners' view, the minimum flow requirement imposed here interferes with FERC's authority under the FPA.

* * *

[T]he requirement for a state certification applies not only to applications for licenses from FERC, but to all federal licenses and permits for activities which may result in a discharge into the Nation's navigable waters. For example, a permit from the Army Corps of Engineers is required for the installation of any structure in the navigable waters which may interfere with navigation, including piers, docks, and ramps. Similarly, a permit must be obtained from the Army Corps of Engineers for the discharge of dredged or fill material, and from the Secretary of the Interior or Agriculture for the construction of reservoirs, canals and other water storage systems on federal land. We assume that a § 401 certification would also be required for some licenses obtained pursuant to these statutes. Because § 401's certification requirement applies to other statutes and regulatory schemes, and because any conflict with FERC's authority under the FPA is hypothetical, we are unwilling to read implied limitations into § 401. If FERC issues a license containing a stream flow condition with which petitioners disagree, they may pursue judicial remedies at that time.

In summary, we hold that the State may include minimum stream flow requirements in a certification issued pursuant to § 401 of the Clean Water Act insofar as necessary to enforce a designated use contained in a state water quality standard. The judgment of the Supreme Court of Washington, accordingly, is affirmed.

So ordered.

JUSTICE STEVENS, concurring.

While I agree fully with the thorough analysis in the Court's opinion, I add this comment for emphasis. For judges who find it unnecessary to go behind the statutory text to discern the intent of Congress, this is (or should be) an easy case. Not a single sentence, phrase, or word in the Clean Water Act purports to place any constraint on a State's power to regulate the quality of its own waters more stringently than federal law might require. In fact, the Act explicitly recognizes States' ability to impose stricter standards.

JUSTICE THOMAS, with whom JUSTICE SCALIA joins, dissenting.

The Court today holds that a State, pursuant to § 401 of the Clean Water Act, may condition the certification necessary to obtain a federal license for a proposed hydroelectric project upon the maintenance of a minimum flow rate in the river to be utilized by the project. In my view, the Court makes three fundamental errors. First, it adopts an interpretation that fails adequately to harmonize the subsections of § 401. Second, it places no meaningful limitation on a State's authority under

§ 401 to impose conditions on certification. Third, it gives little or no consideration to the fact that its interpretation of § 401 will significantly disrupt the carefully crafted federal-state balance embodied in the Federal Power Act. Accordingly, I dissent.

* * *

Although the Court notes in passing that "[t]he limitations included in the certification become a condition on any Federal license," it does not acknowledge or discuss the shift of power from FERC to the States that is accomplished by its decision. Indeed, the Court merely notes that "any conflict with FERC's authority under the FPA" in this case is "hypothetical" at this stage, because "FERC has not yet acted on petitioners' license application." We are assured that "it is quite possible * * * that any FERC license would contain the same conditions as the State § 401 certification."

The Court's observations simply miss the point. Even if FERC might have no objection to the stream flow condition established by respondents in this case, such a happy coincidence will likely prove to be the exception, rather than the rule. In issuing licenses, FERC must balance the Nation's power needs together with the need for energy conservation, irrigation, flood control, fish and wildlife protection, and recreation. State environmental agencies, by contrast, need only consider parochial environmental interests. Cf., e.g., Wash.Rev.Code § 90.54.010(2) (1992) (goal of State's water policy is to "insure that waters of the state are protected and fully utilized for the greatest benefit to the people of the state of Washington"). As a result, it is likely that conflicts will arise between a FERC-established stream flow level and a state-imposed level.

Notes

1. Note Justice Thomas's rather jaundiced view of environmental regulation by the states, which he considers to reflect only parochial local interests, as opposed to the national interests behind increased power generation. It remains to be seen whether this attitude toward the environment will be reflected in his positions on other legal issues.

2. Consider the following assessment of the majority opinion:

After reflecting about the Supreme Court decision in *PUD No. 1*, I recalled my high school chemistry teacher who, after observing my inelegant experimental techniques, stated that the Jesuits used an old Latin expression in such circumstances—*non disputandum resultatem* [sic]. He roughly translated this to mean you don't argue with good results. * * *

In the area of statutory interpretation, unlike high-school chemistry experiments however, good technique is at least as important as good results. A good interpretive approach requires that courts consider more than mere text; they must carefully consider context as well. In the legal dispute at the heart of *PUD No. 1*, that context is defined not only by the CWA, but also by the FPA, the Court's interpretations of that statute, and how FERC and the state agencies have exercised the powers they believe have been delegated them. In enacting the FPA, Congress gave FERC the power to balance a variety of interests, including aesthetic, wildlife protection, recreation, preservation, and economic interests, against the need for energy. Congress also carved out an exception to FERC's authority and gave states the power to ensure that projects do not violate WQSs. Because, in conducting its balancing, FERC's concerns about the economic, development, and electric power factors have largely overwhelmed all other factors, courts, when they consider the interaction of the CWA and FPA, need to safeguard the single consideration that Congress has identified as beyond FERC's ability to balance out of existence. When interpreting these statutes, courts must also not view the in-state water quality factor so broadly that it alone overwhelms all other factors, at least some of which will have out-of-state impacts unlikely to be considered by the state when identifying its WQSs.

Healy, "The Attraction and Limits of Textualism: The Supreme Court Decision in *PUD No. 1 of Jefferson County v. Washington Department of Ecology*," 5 *NYU Env. L.J.* 382, 441–43 (1996).

3. One might expect that water quality standards would be expressed in terms of concentrations of various pollutants. As shown by *P.U.D. No. 1*, however, EPA has found it desirable to take a variety of different approaches, including standards focusing on sediment, wildlife, and biological criteria relating to aquatic communities as a whole. EPA has provided states with three different methodologies for translating the criteria into numerical standards for permits. See *American Paper Inst. v. EPA*, 996 F.2d 346 (D.C.Cir.1993). See also, *American Iron & Steel Inst. v. EPA*, 115 F.3d 979 (D.C.Cir. 1997) (complaining that petitioner's brief on this highly technical issue would be comprehensible only to "those thoroughly versed in the intricacies of the Clean Water Act, in its regulatory jargon, in mathematics, in toxicology, in biology and so forth"—adding, "Too bad AISA did not take the trouble to educate the courts").

4. EPA has been criticized for falling behind in issuance of water quality criteria. See GAO, *EPA Needs to Set Priorities for Water Quality Criteria Issues* (June 1994). It also failed to require some states to set maximum daily loads until required to do so by court order. See *Alaska Center for the Environment v. Browner*, 20 F.3d 981 (9th Cir.1994). The plans themselves have also been criticized: "As anyone who has dealt with state water quality plans knows, they are not 'plans' in a dictionary sense of the word; rather ... they are more of a process composed of criteria/ standards, and abbreviated assessments, some published and some in file drawers, an environment in which site-specific implementation measures can lose their focus, if not simply get lost." Houck, "TMDLs III: A New Framework for the Clean Water Act's Ambient Standards Program," 28 *Env.L.Rep.* 10415, 10420 (1998).

Note on Nonpoint Source Pollution

The permits (and related effluent limitations and water quality requirements) that we have considered so far are required only for point sources. The EPA has concluded that nonpoint source pollution is fast becoming a regulatory priority. Of the water bodies on which EPA had data in 1987, 25% were not fit for their designated uses. In these water bodies, nonpoint sources caused 65% of the stream pollution, 76% of the lake pollution, and 45% of the estuary pollution. *Env.Rep.,* November 13, 1987, at 1740. Agriculture was thought to be the largest single source of unregulated water pollution, including the 3.1 billion tons of topsoil eroded annually. See Malone, "A Historical Essay on the Conservation Provisions of the 1985 Farm Bill: Sodbusting, Swampbusting, and the Conservation Reserve," 34 *U.Kan.L.Rev.* 577, 584–85 (1986). One study indicated that 40% of the total erosion was delivered to waterways. Erosion accounted for about 80% of the total national loadings of phosphorus, 73% of nitrogen, and 99% of total suspended solids; of this total, about a third was from cropland erosion, resulting in about $2.2 billion dollars in nonpoint source pollution damages. Resources for the Future, *Nonpoint Source Pollution: Are Cropland Controls the Answer?* 1–14 (1986).

Section 208 attempted to encourage states to engage in area planning to reduce nonpoint source pollution. It proved ineffective. See Note, "State and Federal Land Use Regulation: An Application to Groundwater and Nonpoint Source Pollution Control," 95 *Yale L.J.* 1433, 1438–39 (1986). In contrast to the "top-down technocratic planning" contemplated by § 208, local governments made most of the actual decisions, and area plans were amended to match. As Howard Latin explained:

> Any community that strenuously objected to a section 208 areawide plan could delay POTW construction for years through recourse to judicial review and political lobbying, which would impede the statutory and EPA goal of achieving rapid water pollution control progress. If EPA found areawide or state plans inadequate, its only enforcement sanction was to withhold federal grants, which would delay pollution control progress and would not penalize the communities that resisted construction of large-scale POTWs.

Latin, "Regulatory Failure, Administrative Incentives, and the New Clean Air Act," 21 *Env.L.* 1647, 1656 (1991).

The 1987 Amendments to the CWA included a renewed attempt to regulate nonpoint source pollution, contained in new § 319. Section 319 provided $400 million for state planning, and required states to develop comprehensive water management plans. This provision was part of the reason for President Reagan's unsuccessful veto attempt on January 30, 1987:

> This new program threatens to become the ultimate whip hand for Federal regulators. For example, in participating States, if farmers have more run-off from their land than the Environmental Protection Agency decides is right, the Agency will be able to intrude into decisions such as how and where the farmers must plow their fields, what fertilizers they must use, and what kind of cover crops they must plant. To take another example, the Agency will be able to become a major force in local zoning decisions that will determine whether families can do such basic things as build a new home. That is too much power for anyone to have, least of all the Federal Government.

* * * Let me repeat—controlling nonpoint source pollution has the potential to touch, in the most intimate ways, practically all of us as citizens, whether farmers, business people, or homeowners. I do not believe State programs should be subject to Federal control.

The 1987 Amendments included some other changes relating to water quality. Section 302 was amended to allow modifications of the requirements under that section when "there is no reasonable relationship between the economic and social costs and the benefits to be obtained (including attainment of the objective of this Act) from achieving such limitation." Modifications are also allowed for up to five years under terms patterned on § 301(c). Section 303(d) was amended to prohibit any revision of minimum daily loads except where water quality standards have been met or lawfully modified. Section 402 was amended with the addition of an anti-backsliding provision, which prohibits issuance of new permits that are laxer than existing permits for the same facilities, with limited exceptions. Effluent limitations based on water quality cannot be modified on the basis of technical or legal mistakes in the old permit, except when the cumulative result of the alterations is to improve water quality.[1]

To date, progress in controlling nonpoint source pollution remains disappointing. Contrary to President Reagan's dire prediction, § 319 has been said to have "not enough carrot, not enough stick, and too much of the same planning imperatives that characterized § 208." Zaring, "Federal Legislative Solutions to Agricultural Nonpoint Source Pollution," 26 *Env. L.Rep.* 10128, 10132 (1996). Regulation of urban runoff focuses on voluntary municipal plans "plus education, plus monitoring to determine the need for more serious permit requirements in the future." Houck, "TMDLs III: A New Framework for the Clean Water Act's Ambient Standards Program," 28 *Env.L.Rep.* 10415, 10428 (1998).

Will further progress take place? As Oliver Houck puts it, "The answer is, of course, maybe." Id. at 10437.

D. BEYOND REGULATION: ECONOMIC INCENTIVES FOR ENVIRONMENTAL PROTECTION

There are several mechanisms that the governments can use to address pollution problems:

1. *Property rights.* The common law allocation of property rights did give landowners rights against polluters, but as we saw at the beginning of this chapter, those property rights did not provide a basis for effective control of pollution. Economists have suggested some ingenious methods of creating novel property rights, such as marketable permits to pollute, that may provide a firmer basis for pollution control.

2. *Direct regulation.* Beyond the recognition of private property rights, the principal method adopted by government to control external

---

1. For commentary on the 1987 Amendments, see Mandelker, "Controlling Nonpoint Source Water Pollution: Can It be Done?" 65 *Chi.–Kent L.Rev.* 479 (1989); Fentress, "Nonpoint Source Pollution, Groundwater, and the 1987 Water Quality Act: Section 208 Revisited?" 19 *Env.L.* 767 (1989).

costs such as pollution has been to prohibit emissions above prescribed limits. Such prohibitions also could be viewed as mandates to supply collective goods like clean air and water.

3. *Subsidies.* Another approach, frequently used in combination with direct regulation, is for government to pay some or all of the costs of private activities which avoid external costs or produce collective goods. Examples are tax incentives—special deductions and credits—for installation of pollution control equipment, and federal grants to municipalities for construction of sewage treatment facilities.

4. *Charges.* In lieu of or in addition to the foregoing approaches, the government can require payment of penalties or fees for private activities which generate external costs or fail to provide collective goods. Relating the amounts of such charges to the estimated costs (to the producer) or benefits (to the public) can create a simulated market incentive for the producer to alter his activities.

5. *Disclosure.* Another type of economic incentive enlists the assistance of consumers and investors. By mandating or facilitating "green labeling" or other forms of information disclosure, the government may be able to create economic pressure on companies to improve their environmental activities. See, e.g., Grodsky, "Certified Green: The Law and Future of Environmental Labeling," 10 *Yale J. on Rev.* 147 (1993).[m]

We begin by considering economists' criticism of conventional regulatory methods.

ANDERSON, ET AL., "ENVIRONMENTAL IMPROVEMENT THROUGH ECONOMIC INCENTIVES"[n]

12–18 (1977).

* * * The major problem with standards-based regulatory programs is not that they in theory are incapable of achieving cost-effective or economically efficient results, but that in practice they could do so only at enormous administrative costs. Current approaches require setting standards based on careful economic analyses of entire polluting industries, mastering the technologies of production and pollution control in the regulated industries, and elaborately subcategorizing industrial processes which are sufficiently different to merit different pollution control standards. The standards arrived at through these involved procedures are often challenged in court on the grounds that they do not represent the "best practicable control technology currently available" or the appropriate statutory standard. The court tests often bog down in

m. Despite the conceptual distinctness of these categories, in reality they tend to blur together, so that the same program, whatever its label, may contain elements of several categories. See David Dreisen, "Is Emissions Trading an Economic Incentive Program? Replacing the Command and Control/Economic Incentive Dichotomy," 55 *Wash & Lee L. Rev.* 289 (1998).

n. Copyright © 1977 by The Johns Hopkins University Press. Published for Resources for the Future.

debates on arcane technical questions that courts are ill-equipped to resolve. The process of applying the standards to individual sources, as in drafting permits for National Pollution Discharge Emission [sic] System, consumes a great deal of time and administrative resources because it requires negotiation over the specific characteristics of each source. Finally, the standards in the permit must be enforced, another process replete with administrative and legal tangles. All of these tasks are made more difficult by the complexity of the standards and the standard-setting process that is necessary to achieve economic objectives, whether they be minimization of plant closures, achievement of cost effectiveness, or overall market efficiency. Why this is so deserves closer attention.

Standard setting is not simply a process of telling a polluter what emission standards he must meet, and then monitoring his emissions to see if he has complied. As we have said, under most legislative provisions, standards pass through some type of benefit-cost comparison— they must be "practical" or "available," or technically and economically "feasible." These are elastic terms intended to make the environmental control agency justify its standards as technologically proven and non-bankrupting. Naturally, there is considerable room for debate over whether an abatement process is really "feasible," and the burden on the agency is increased still further by the requirement that the standards take into account relevant differences in an industry. Thus, what is a feasible and practicable abatement technique for one firm in an industry may not be so for another plant in the same industry, depending on the plant's technology, its rate of return on investment, and other plant-specific factors.

Data on the abatement alternatives open to a polluter, of course, are best known to the polluter himself in most cases, or at least to the subcontractor hired by him. It is difficult for an outsider to an industry to know what the real possibilities are, because there are often few outsiders doing research into abatement or employing full-scale abatement techniques.

Then, too, even if he performs the research, or depends upon a control technology subindustry, the polluter has every incentive not to share this information with a regulatory agency, for then the agency will augment the standards to reduce discharges further, or be less hesitant about cracking down on violators. There is no incentive to perform research which serves in the end to increase a company's capital outlays, with no increase in profits. As yet, there is little evidence that the subcontractors who build control systems will come forward to share their technological advances.

Without accurate or accurate-appearing information on abatement techniques, a regulatory agency is in a bind. It cannot require an industry or firm to do something that is impossible, yet it does not know the limits of the possible. * * * The control agency cannot be expected to have the best expertise in the country on the technological alternatives facing every firm or industry; polluters will almost always know more about their own operations and alternatives than an environmental agency can ever hope to learn. Yet, under a regulatory system, this is precisely the kind of knowledge an environmental control agency must have in order to enforce standards.

Under a system of monetary charges, after the basic charge rate is decided, the greatest source of continuing debate between polluters and the agency concerns, not the technical alternatives available for abatement, but the devices and procedures used to monitor the quantity and quality of the pollutants discharged. Administrative expertise is directed to monitoring technologies. This is a highly favorable turnabout, because it is much more reasonable to expect the U.S. Environmental Protection Agency (EPA) or a state agency to become the recognized authority on monitoring procedures than to expect it to become knowledgeable about every production and pollution control technology in use or soon to be feasible.

* * *

The imposing requirements for technical information under the regulatory approach might be less troublesome if polluters had some incentive to abate their discharges even before all the information was in; in the absence of such incentives, direct regulation is doubly handicapped. Consider the incentives for a typical polluting firm. On the one hand, if the polluter complies with the applicable standards, he must meet the annualized expenses of installing and operating expensive abatement equipment. He also faces a shift in competitive position that is less easily calculated, for he cannot be sure that his competitors will face the same added abatement costs. On the other hand, if the firm does not comply, it will incur costs only if it is caught by the enforcing agency. The expected value of these costs equals the probability of being singled out for prosecution, times the cost of the ensuing legal and political fight, plus the product of the probability of losing a court case and incurring the sanctions likely to be imposed.

* * *

American legal institutions are usually designed to deal with only a small percentage of potential violators. Voluntary compliance is assumed, and generally forthcoming. Under the regulatory approach, however, the benefits of delay are typically so great in comparison with the costs of complying that there is little incentive for voluntary compliance, and a regulatory agency faces the possibility, not of a handful of violators that it could reasonably and effectively handle, but of tacit noncompliance by large segments of an industry. At this point the regulatory process stalls as the enforcement agency begins to bargain with polluters over what equipment to install and what constitutes compliance, to accept a minimum level of emission reductions, and to celebrate these weak, negotiated standards as proof of agency vigilance and success, rather than admit failure publicly and go to the legislature to seek a more effective solution. The agency is slowly and relentlessly coerced toward industry's standards, rather than its own.

Notes

1. Do the preceding parts of this chapter support Anderson's assertions about the shortcomings of direct regulation? How successful has the regulatory approach been? For some defenses of the conventional regulatory approach, see Mintz, "Economic Reform of Environmental Protection: A Brief Comment on a Recent Debate," 15 *Harv.Env.L.Rev.* 85 (1991); Shapiro & McGarity, "Not So Paradoxical: The Rationale For Technology–Based Regulation," 1991 *Duke L.J.* 729. See also Heinzerling, "Regulatory Costs of Mythic Proportions," 187 *Yale L.J.* 1981 (1998) (arguing that economically oriented critics have used inflated estimates of regulatory costs and seriously underestimated benefits).

For one thoughtful appraisal by an observer who is quite sympathetic to the use of economic incentives, consider the following appraisal of the Clean Air Act:

> Early studies suggested savings from the Clean Air Act of between $5.1 to $15.9 billion as a result of reduced mortality, and of $28.4 to $58.1 billion from reduced morbidity. One study found annual health benefits in 1978 of $5.1 to $16 billion as a result of a 60% reduction in air pollution in urban areas with a total population of 150 million. These studies, now quite old, undoubtedly underestimate the benefits because they disregard the large gains since 1980.

> Although the problems of measurement produce severe methodological difficulties, progress since that time appears to have increased. * * * The national Pollution Standard Index reveals dramatic downward trends in air pollution. These reductions are partly attributable to federal controls on emissions of carbon monoxide from automobiles and pollutants that contribute to ozone. National ambient concentrations of the most serious pollutants have all significantly decreased.

> In 1975, for example, 54.2 million metric tons of carbon monoxide were emitted from highway vehicles, a figure that by 1984 had been reduced * * * to 41.4 million. The aggregate decreases are quite dramatic: total suspended particulate levels decreased 20% between 1975 and 1986, while emissions were reduced by about a third; annual mean sulfur dioxide concentrations have declined 36%, with emissions decreasing by 17%; carbon monoxide emissions have decreased by 25%; nitrogen oxide levels decreased by 10%.

C. Sunstein, *After the Rights Revolution: Reconceiving the Regulatory State* 77 (1990). Might the same results have been achieved at lower cost using techniques other than direct regulation?

2. Another cost-benefit analysis found that the costs of the 1990 CAA Amendments exceeded the benefits by a substantial amount. The cost of the national program of urban ozone reduction was estimated at $8–12 billion annually, with a benefit in the form of acute health improvements of only about $1 billion. The analysis concludes:

It is unpleasant to have to weigh in such a calculating manner the pros and cons of further air pollution control efforts * * *. Because resources are scarce, however, the real cost of air pollution control is represented by the government programs or private expenditures that we forego by putting our resources into reducing VOC [volatile organic chemicals] emissions. In the health area alone, $10 billion invested in smoking cessation programs, radon control, better prenatal and neonatal health care, or similar measures might contribute much more to public health and well-being.

Krupnick and Portney, "Controlling Urban Air Pollution: A Benefit–Cost Assessment," 252 *Science* 522, 526 (1991). For comments on this cost-benefit analysis, see 253 *Science* 606–609 (1991). A more recent OMB analysis found that total regulatory benefits significantly outweighed costs. See 29 *Env.Rep.* 847 (1998).

3. To the extent that current regulations are insufficiently cost-effective, one solution may be to give regulators more flexibility in devising methods of achieving environmental goals. Under the Clinton Administration, EPA has made a controversial effort to "reinvent regulation" through Project XL, which would allow individual sources to negotiate alternative compliance plans. For a sample of the debate about this initiative, see Mank, "The Environmental Protection Agency's Project XL and Other Regulatory Reform Initiatives: The Need for Legislative Authorization," 25 *Ecology L.Q.* 1 (1998); Ginsberg & Cummis, "EPA's Project XL: A Paradigm for Promising Regulatory Reform," 26 *Env.L.Rep.* 10059 (1996); Steinzor, "Regulatory Reinvention and Project XL: Does the Emperor Have Any Clothes?," 26 *Env.L.Rep.* 10527 (1996). Lisa Heinzerling argues that in practice proposals for regulatory reform overlook ecological harms in favor of more readily quantified impacts on publich health. See Heinzerling, "Reductionist Regulatory Reform," 8 *Fordham Env.L.Rev.* 459 (1997). Note that she applies the same critique to cost-benefit analysis.

1. EFFLUENT CHARGES AND REGULATORY PENALTIES

SCHULTZE, ET AL., "SETTING NATIONAL PRIORITIES: THE 1973 BUDGET"

368–73 (Brookings Institution 1972).

Many economists, joined recently by a coalition of conservation groups, have urged that economic incentives be given a major role in controlling pollution through the imposition of "effluence charges" (or taxes) on each unit of pollution released by industry into the air or water. This would provide business firms with an incentive to reduce pollution in order to lower their tax burden.

* * *

[A] tax could be levied on each unit of each kind of pollutant discharged into the air or water. Faced with these taxes or "effluent charges," each firm would find it in its own interest to reduce pollution by an amount related to the cost of reduction and through the use of the least-cost means of doing so. It would compare the cost of paying the effluent charge with the cost of cleaning up pollution, and would choose to remove pollution up to the point where the additional cost of removal was greater than the effluent charge. The larger the effluent charge, the greater the percentage of pollutants a firm would find it advantageous to remove. Firms with low costs of control would remove a larger percentage than would firms with high costs—precisely the situation needed to achieve a least-cost approach to reducing pollution for the economy as a whole. The kinds of products whose manufacture generated a lot of pollution would become more expensive and would carry higher prices than those that generated less, and consumers would be induced to buy more of the latter.

The effluent charge approach has another advantage. In the case of regulations that require the removal of a specific percentage of pollutants, once a firm has achieved that point, it has no incentive to cut pollution further. Indeed it has a positive incentive not to do so, since the additional reduction is costly and lowers profits. With effluent charges, however, firms are taxed for every unit of pollution they have not removed. They would have a continuing incentive to devote research and engineering talent toward finding less costly ways of achieving still further reductions. This continuing incentive is important. The quantity of air and water available to the nation is fixed, roughly speaking. But as economic activity grows over time, the volume of pollution discharged into the air and water will rise unless an ever-increasing percentage of pollutants is removed.

Objections have been raised against the effluent charge approach. Some have called effluent charges "licenses to pollute," since firms paying the charge are not subject to prosecution for causing pollution. But payment of the effluent charge is no more a license to pollute than is a permit or a pollution limit established by a regulatory agency. Effluent charges can be set high enough to reduce overall pollution by whatever degree the nation wants. A regulatory agency can similarly set pollution limits designed to achieve that goal. Under neither approach is pollution likely to be reduced to zero: the costs are too great. In a sense, the remaining pollution does result from a license to pollute. But the license will be there under either method of pollution control.

It has also been argued that large firms with substantial market power would simply pass on the effluent charge to their customers and not make the effort to clean up pollution. This might indeed occur, but there is overwhelming reason to believe that it would not be the response of the majority of firms. Effluent charges can be set high enough that the cost of removing a substantial percentage of pollution is less than the cost of paying the charge. Firms could then reduce costs by reducing pollution, just as they can now lower costs by reducing the amount of labor used per unit of output. Despite the fact that many firms do have substantial market power, the drive to lower costs has produced in the American economy an average increase in productivity that *halves* labor requirements per unit of output every twenty-five years. Firms do not as a rule pass up opportunities to cut production costs. And with a stiff effluent charge, the reduction of pollution becomes a way to cut costs.

In the case of toxic and highly dangerous pollutants, such as mercury, effluent charges are not suitable. Even a small amount of such pollutants causes severe damage, and thus prohibition is in order. But for the vast majority of pollutants, effluent charges offer a means of harnessing self-interest and the profit motive in the direction of environmental control.

Notes

1.   Does Schultze indicate how the level of the charges, per unit of pollution, would be determined? What does he mean when he says that the charges "can be set high enough to reduce overall pollution by whatever degree the nation wants?" For discussion of some of the problems involved in setting such taxes, see Barthold, "Issues in the Design of Environmental Excise Taxes," 8:1 *J.Econ.Persp.* 133 (1994). On the plethora of state-level efforts to use various economic incentives, see "Harnessing the Tax Code for Environmental Protection: A survey of State Initiatives," *State Tax Notes*, Special Supplement (April 20, 1998). Some public utility commissions have engaged in a similar effort to internalize environmental costs when considering applications to build new generating facilities. They have required applicants to include "shadow environmental costs" in their analysis of alternative energy sources. For some sharp criticisms of the methods used to assess these shadow costs, .see Pierce, "Electricity Regulation," 93 *Colum.L.Rev.* 1339, 1423–29 (1993).

2.   For enforcement purposes, how frequently must an individual pollution source be monitored under a system of direct regulation? Under a system of effluent charges? Would self-monitoring and reporting by polluters be reliable?

Are bureaucrats, engineers and lawyers unduly conservative with respect to a charge system, or might economists be overly optimistic about the practicality of "the most theoretically desirable policies" for dealing with pollution? Might the noneconomists' preferences for direct regulation be related to a belief that it is more compatible with objectives other than economic efficiency? Can we still afford those other objectives?

3.   For a thoughtful assessment of the relative merits of regulation and market-based systems, see S. Breyer, *Regulation and its Reform* 261–284 (1984). Judge (now Justice) Breyer concluded:

> A major change from total reliance upon classical standard setting to increased reliance upon incentive mechanisms is *probably* desirable when dealing with a complex spillover problem such as pollution. Given the nature of the standard-setting process, the complex spillover problem, and the incentive-based alternatives, environmental regulation is a candidate for change. To know whether significant improvement is in fact possible requires further exploration. How effective is existing regulation, for example? How clean has the air and water become since 1970? How well do the European incentive systems actually work? How

can the practical difficulties with the details of incentive systems be overcome? Enough has been said, however, to suggest that the present system is far from satisfactory, and that incentive-based reform ought to be possible.

Id. at 284. For information on the use of effluent charges in Europe, see Hahn, "Economic Prescriptions for Environmental Problems: How the Patient Followed the Doctor's Orders," *J.Econ.Persp.* 95, 104–06 (1989).

4. An interesting debate about the desirability of nonregulatory methods of pollution control took place in 1985. Professor Howard Latin opened the debate with an argument that the purported advantages of nonregulatory controls were likely to prove illusory in practice:

> This article contends that the academic literature on "regulatory reform" reflects an excessive preoccupation with theoretical efficiency, while it places inadequate emphasis on actual decisionmaking costs and implementation constraints. Any system for environmental regulation must function despite the presence of pervasive uncertainty, high decisionmaking costs, and manipulative strategic behavior resulting from conflicting private and public interests. Under these conditions, the indisputable fact that uniform standards are inefficient does not prove that any other approach would necessarily perform better. In a "second-best" world, the critical issue is not which regulatory system aspires to ideal "efficiency" but which is most likely to prove effective.

Latin, "Ideal Versus Real Regulatory Efficiency: Implementation of Uniform Standards and 'Fine–Tuning' Regulatory Reforms," 37 *Stan.L.Rev.* 1267, 1270 (1985). In a nutshell, Latin's view was that "[i]n their search for 'optimal' regulation or at least for 'substantial' improvement, most analysts have stressed the virtues of alternative regulatory *theories* without adequate consideration of implementation constraints and party motivations." Id. at 1331 (emphasis in original). See also Pedersen, "The Limits of Market–Based Approaches to Environmental Protection," 24 *Env.L.Rep.* 10173 (1994). Professors Bruce Ackerman and Richard Stewart responded with a defense of nonregulatory controls. Relying primarily on EPA experience with various offset and bubble schemes, they contended that marketable pollution permits would be feasible and would save hundreds of millions if not billions of dollars. Ackerman & Stewart, "Reforming Environmental Law," 37 *Stan.L.Rev.* 1333 (1985).

As far as we can tell, the theoretical debate has not advanced much since 1988. In the remainder of this chapter, we turn from this theoretical debate to actual efforts to implement incentive systems.

Note on the Use of Economic Incentives to Achieve Compliance With Regulatory Limits

Economic incentives can be used in tandem with regulation, rather than as an alternative. In 1977 Congress added § 120 to the Clean Air Act, mandating noncompliance penalties for violations of regulatory standards. Patterned after a Connecticut statute, § 120 is intended to deprive polluters of the economic benefits of delay. In 1980 the EPA promulgated final regulations to implement § 120. The regulations were upheld against a variety of attacks in *Duquesne Light Co. v. EPA,* 698 F.2d 456 (D.C.Cir.

1983). In particular, the court held that technological impossibility is not necessarily a defense to imposition of a penalty.

A conflict in the circuits developed over one aspect of the *Duquesne* holding. The issue was the effect on the noncompliance penalty of EPA delay in processing plan revisions. The lower courts all believed that EPA was required to rule on plan revisions within four months, but they disagreed about the effect of violating the deadline. For example, in *American Cyanamid v. United States EPA,* 810 F.2d 493 (5th Cir.1987), the court held that EPA could not collect noncompliance penalties for the period between the four-month deadline and the time EPA finally got around to disapproving a revision. The conflict ultimately reached the Supreme Court. The Court held that the four-month deadline applied only to the submissions of the original SIPs, not to EPA's action on proposed plan revisions, contrary to the assumption made by the lower courts. Since there was no deadline to violate, the Court did not consider how a deadline violation would have affected the calculations of a penalty. *General Motors Corp. v. United States,* 496 U.S. 530, 110 S.Ct. 2528, 110 L.Ed.2d 480 (1990). (For a discussion of *General Motors* and the lower court rulings, see Comment, *"General Motors Corp. v. United States:* A Boon to Clean Air Act Enforcement," 20 *Env.L.Rptr.* 10471 (1990).)

The 1990 amendments impose new deadlines on EPA responses to plan revisions, thus making the *General Motors* holding irrelevant. See CAA § 110(k)(2). If EPA concludes that the submission does not contain enough information to allow EPA to determine its validity, "the State shall be treated as not having made the submission," which presumably means that submission of the revision does not affect the noncompliance penalty. (Also note that under the anti-backsliding provision of § 193, no pre–1990 control requirement can be modified in any non-attainment area unless the modification ensures "equivalent or greater emission reductions of such air pollutant." Hence, plan revisions will not be able to relax requirements in those areas.)

The 1990 amendments also contain an important provision governing the calculation of administrative and judicial penalties. In any penalty assessed under § 113,

> [T]he Administrator or the court, as appropriate, shall take into consideration (in addition to such other factors as justice may require) the size of the business, the economic impact of the penalty on the business, the violator's full compliance history and good faith efforts to comply, the duration of the violation * * *, payment by the violator of penalties previously assessed for the same violation, the economic benefit of noncompliance, and the seriousness of the violation. (§ 113(e)).

The penalty may include "wrongful profits" that the polluter obtained as a result of its failure to comply. See *United States v. Municipal Authority,* 150 F.3d 259 (3d Cir.1998). The 1987 amendments to Clean Water Act contain a similar provision, where the list of factors includes: "the nature, circumstances, extent and gravity of the violation, or violations, and with respect to the violator, ability to pay, any prior history of such violations, the degree of culpability, economic benefit or savings (if any) resulting from the violation, and such other matters as justice may require." (§ 307(g)(3).) The reasons for the variations in language between the two statutes are unclear. The references to "economic benefit" in both provisions, like § 120, are reminiscent of the effluent charge approach.

The idea of using civil penalties to deprive polluters of the economic benefits of delayed compliance seems sound. Calculation of the penalties, however, is quite complex, and there has been a dispute over the soundness of EPA's computer model, BEN. For example, BEN uses the company's rate of return on equity, rather than its rate of return on all assets, to set the interest rate used in the calculation. Defense lawyers argue that this inflates civil penalties. See, e.g., Fuhrman, "Improving EPA's Civil Penalty Policies—And Its Not–So–Gentle BEN Model," *Env.Rep.,* Sept. 9, 1994, at 874. Another complaint is that the model ignores the higher cost of retro-fitting as opposed to timely compliance. See Singh, "Penalty Calculations," 28 *Env.Rep.* 2704 (1998).

2. MARKETABLE PERMITS, OFFSETS, AND BUBBLES

As pointed out in the materials on the Coase Theorem at the beginning of this chapter, under the right circumstances voluntary exchanges can promote economically efficient control of pollution. A variety of schemes have been proposed to facilitate such transactions. The basic concept is for the government to set a ceiling on the amount of pollution permitted, but allow firms to engage in market transactions to distribute those rights among themselves.

An example may help clarify this concept. Remember the fictional pollutant "kryptonia" discussed earlier in this chapter. Suppose that the government wants to reduce kryptonia levels in the air to a certain level, and that air modeling shows that the way to do so is to reduce the total emissions of kryptonia in a locality to five hundred pounds per day. One way to go about this is to have the state establish an SIP setting emission levels for each source. As an alternative, the government might create "kryptonia allowances," authorizing a source to emit ten pounds of kryptonia per day. (These allowances could be distributed among the existing sources in various ways. One possibility would be an auction; another would be to give the allowances to existing sources in proportion to their current emissions.) Once the allowances were distributed, firms would be allowed to buy and sell them. Firms that can cheaply control their emissions would find it worthwhile to sell their allowances to firms with higher control costs. If Coase is right, the original distribution of allowances shouldn't make much difference: in the end, the allowances will be distributed in the most economically efficient way. If everything works according to plan, the government will attain its air quality goal without having to go through the work of writing an SIP, and compliance will be achieved in the cheapest possible manner.

That is the theory, in any event. As we will see, actual implementation of the theory tends to be more complex. While the marketable permit idea remains controversial, however, it has clearly become a serious policy option, rather than an ivory tower fantasy of economists.

For suggestions on program design, see Ayres, "Developing a Market in Emission Credits Incrementally," 25 *Env. Rep.* 1522 (1994).

Note on Emission "Offsets" to Accommodate Industrial Growth

In the United States today, the best-established system of marketable discharge permits has resulted from operation of the "offset" requirement for introduction of new pollution sources into non-attainment areas, under § 173(1)(A) of the Clean Air Act, added in 1977. The 1990 amendments elaborated on this requirement but did not change the basic structure.

→   The offset requirement was intended to assure that new sources would not impair overall progress toward timely attainment of national ambient air quality standards. Under § 173(1)(A), new sources are allowed in non-attainment areas only if "total allowable emissions" from existing and new sources are "sufficiently less than total emissions from existing sources allowed under the applicable implementation plan" when the permit is sought "so as to represent * * * reasonable progress." Thus total "allowable" emissions of each pollutant in question must be *reduced* even though a new source is added. New source owners receive credit only for reducing emissions which are "allowable" under the SIP, not for reductions already overdue. Under the 1990 Act, offsets must often be even larger. For example, in "serious" ozone areas, a 1.2 to 1 ratio is required. Also, limited use of offsets from other non-attainment areas is now allowed by § 173(c).

→   How the offset requirement works in practice has been described by Professor Currie:[o]

> Suppose the owner of a steel mill presently meeting plan requirements wants to construct a new basic-oxygen furnace on the same site. If the region where the mill is located exceeds ambient particulate standards, the owner may obtain the necessary offset credit by shutting down a set of open-hearth furnaces in the existing mill, or by fitting them with additional control equipment not required by the plan, if the resulting reduction of open-hearth emissions sufficiently exceeds the new basic-oxygen emissions to "represent reasonable further progress" toward achieving the ambient standard. If the new plant is to be built at a considerable distance from the old one, the different impacts of the old and new emissions on ambient quality will have to be taken into account in determining whether "reasonable further progress" is being made.
>
> Even if our steelmaker has no existing emissions of its own that can practicably be reduced, it may benefit from the offset provisions, for the statute does not require that the source reducing its emissions be owned or operated by the person seeking to build the new one. Section 173(1)(A) refers to "total allowable emissions from existing sources in the region," and the EPA's guidelines explicitly allowed offsets based on

---

o. Currie, "Relaxation of Implementation Plans Under the 1977 Clean Air Act Amendments," 78 *Mich.L.Rev.* 155, 198–99 (1979). For an illustrative decision applying the offset provision, see *Citizens Against the Refinery's Effects v. EPA,* 643 F.2d 183 (4th Cir.1981) (upholding an offset plan that required a refinery to incorporate LAER technology and also requiring the state highway department to substitute water-based asphalt for oil-based asphalt in roadway repaving to lower hydrocarbon emissions).

reductions from sources owned by others. The logic of the guidelines is impeccable; as long as net emissions are reduced it is immaterial who reduces them. In this way the statute creates a market in emission rights, making private ingenuity work toward improving the air. Thus our steelmaker, unwilling to retire its own open-hearth furnaces, may be able to pay the owner of a nearby foundry to close down a marginal furnace, to control it beyond plan requirements, or to move to another region. Such a contractual offset was recently reported on a large scale in Long Beach, California: The state agency permitted a corporation to construct a new marine terminal after it agreed to pay $78,000,000 to improve emission control at a neighboring power plant and at a number of dry-cleaning establishments.

did affect overall reduction

Early evidence of the existence of a private market in emission rights was provided by the following advertisement, placed by a woodfinishing plant whose impending closing would reduce air pollution emissions in Chicago by about 1600 tons per year:

> *For Sale: Substantial Hydrocarbon Emission Offset in the Chicago area. For details, contact Box EZ–300,* Wall Street Journal.

It has been estimated that this reduction may have been worth as much as $3000 per ton to someone wishing to construct or expand an industrial facility in Chicago.[p]

Since 1979 the EPA has allowed "banking" of unused emission reduction credits, for offset against future new sources.[q] The Administrator expressly stated that the banking policy reflects the market potential of emission offsets:

> [The banking policy is designed to] establish clearly that clean air (or conversely the right to use it) has direct economic value * * *. The new policy will allow localities to bank reductions * * * which result from firms going out of business. These clean air credits could later be transferred to new firms locating in the community, including the possibility of buying and selling them. This policy could be the forerunner of a futures market for air pollution rights.[r]

The reference in this statement to banking by "localities" suggests some questions. Who owns offsets which are not used immediately? How and by whom should they be allocated among potential new sources? According to EPA, "the State is free to govern ownership, use, sale, and commercial transactions in banked emission offsets as it sees fit."[s]

If parent sources are not allowed complete control over alienation of banked offsets, the state may have some role in allocating them. Concerning this possibility, another writer has said:

p. Comment, "Emission–Offset Banking: Accommodating Industrial Growth with Air–Quality Standards." 128 *U.Pa. L.Rev.* 937 (1980). According to the Washington Post, a firm called AER*X is a nationwide broker of emissions credits. The firm has revenues in excess of $1 million a year. (Wash. Post Nat'l Weekly Ed., Nov. 20–26, 1989, at 9).

q. Emission Offset Ruling, 44 Fed.Reg. 3274, 3285 (1979), codified in 40 CFR 51.

r. 9 *Envir.Rep.* 1708 (1979).

s. 44 Fed.Reg. 3280 (1979).

If the state becomes the "banker" of the emission rights the major problem becomes: who decides between competing interests in the banked emission rights? and how? In other words, if two new sources are interested in purchasing the offsets, how are they to be allocated? → There are several options for the state as banker. (1) *First come—first served:* This system would simply allocate the emission rights according to whomever asks first. A limit could be placed on the amount of emission rights that could be handed out per applicant. The State of Oregon currently employs such a permit system in allocating the remaining available sulfur dioxide and particulate emissions in the Portland, Oregon airshed. Clearly, it works. The question is whether such a system is the most efficient and equitable means of distributing the resource. The major problem is that it gives little control to the state (much less local officials) in planning the economic development of a given area. Development is reduced to a race, with no consideration of secondary impacts on the region. (2) *Employment benefit analysis:* In contrast to the free-for-all nature of the first option, the state could condition the permit approval upon the satisfaction of specified social, employment or tax base criteria. The City of Portland, Oregon, for example, is considering recommending that emission rights be given on the basis of number of employees per ton of pollution. There are other possibilities as well. The point is that the state does have the option of allocating the banked offsets on the basis of some prescribed criteria. (3) *Auction:* A more traditional free market approach would be to sell the offsets in units, say in tons per year, to the highest bidder. EPA is particularly interested in this option * * *.[t]

Because of the increased importance and stringency of offset requirements under the 1990 Amendments, some states have become quite actively involved in fostering trading. See *Env.Rep.,* June 25, 1993, at 365.

This note has been concerned with *inter*-source trade-offs. The following case deals with *intra*-source offsets and the so-called "bubble" concept.

CHEVRON, U.S.A., INC. v. NRDC

Supreme Court of the United States, 1984.
467 U.S. 837, 104 S.Ct. 2778, 81 L.Ed.2d 694.

JUSTICE STEVENS delivered the opinion of the Court:

The question presented by this case is whether EPA's decision to allow States to treat all of the pollution-emitting devices within the same industrial grouping as though they were encased within a single "bubble" is based on a reasonable construction of the statutory term "stationary source." [The court of appeals had held the use of bubbles impermissible for nonattainment areas even though it found no explicit statutory language or legislative history on point.]

* * *

t. Comment, "Who Owns the Air? The Emission Offset Concept and Its Implica-   tions," 9 *Envt'l Law* 575 (1979).

When a court reviews an agency's construction of the statute which it administers, it is confronted with two questions. First, always, is the question whether Congress has directly spoken to the precise question at issue. If the intent of Congress is clear, that is the end of the matter; for the court, as well as the agency, must give effect to the unambiguously expressed intent of Congress. If, however, the court determines Congress has not directly addressed the precise question at issue, the court does not simply impose its own construction on the statute, as would be necessary in the absence of an administrative interpretation. Rather, if the statute is silent or ambiguous with respect to the specific issue, the question for the court is whether the agency's answer is based on a permissible construction of the statute.

In light of these well-settled principles it is clear that the Court of Appeals misconceived the nature of its role in reviewing the regulations at issue. Once it determined, after its own examination of the legislation, that Congress did not actually have an intent regarding the applicability of the bubble concept to the permit program, the question before it was not whether in its view the concept is "inappropriate" in the general context of a program designed to improve air quality, but whether the Administrator's view that it is appropriate in the context of this particular program is a reasonable one. Based on the examination of the legislation and its history which follows, we agree with the Court of Appeals that Congress did not have a specific intention on the applicability of the bubble concept in these cases, and conclude that the EPA's use of that concept here is a reasonable policy choice for the agency to make.

* * *

The Clean Air Act Amendments of 1977 are a lengthy, detailed, technical, complex, and comprehensive response to a major social issue. A small portion of the statute expressly deals with nonattainment areas. The focal point of this controversy is one phrase in that portion of the Amendments.

Basically, the statute required each State in a nonattainment area to prepare and obtain approval of a new SIP by July 1, 1979. In the interim those States were required to comply with the EPA's interpretative Ruling of December 21, 1976. The deadline for attainment of the primary NAAQS's was extended until December 31, 1982, and in some cases until December 31, 1987, but the SIP's were required to contain a number of provisions designed to achieve the goals as expeditiously as possible.

Most significantly for our purposes, the statute provided that each plan shall:

> (6) require permits for the construction and operation of new or modified major stationary sources in accordance with section 173
> * * *.

Before issuing a permit, § 173 requires the state agency to determine that (1) there will be sufficient emissions reductions in the region to offset the emissions from the new source and also to allow for reasonable further progress toward attainment, or that the increased emissions will not exceed an allowance for growth established pursuant to § 172(b)(5), (2) the applicant must certify that his other sources in the State are in compliance with the SIP, (3) the agency must determine that the applicable SIP is otherwise being implemented, and (4) the proposed source complies with the lowest achievable emission rate (LAER).

The 1977 Amendments contain no specific reference to the "bubble concept." Nor do they contain a specific definition of the term "stationary source," though they did not disturb the definition of "stationary source" contained in § 111(a)(3), applicable by the terms of the Act to the NSPS program. Section 302(j), however, defines the term "major stationary source" as follows:

> (j) Except as otherwise expressly provided the terms "major stationary source" and "major emitting facility" mean any stationary facility or source of air pollutants which directly emits, or has the potential to emit, one hundred tons per year or more of any air pollutant (including any major emitting facility or source of fugitive emissions of any such pollutant, as determined by rule by the Administrator).

Statutory Language

The definition of the term stationary source in § 111(a)(3) refers to "any building, structure, facility, or installation" which emits air pollution. This definition is applicable only to the NSPS program by the express terms of the statute; the text of the statute does not make this definition applicable to the permit program. Petitioners therefore maintain that there is no statutory language even relevant to ascertaining the meaning of stationary source in the permit program aside from § 302(j), which defines the term major stationary source. We disagree with petitioners on this point.

The definition in § 302(j) tells us what the word "major" means—a source must emit at least 100 tons of pollution to qualify—but it sheds virtually no light on the meaning of the term "stationary source." It does equate a source with a facility—a "major emitting facility" and a "major stationary source" are synonymous under § 302(j). The ordinary meaning of the term facility is some collection of integrated elements which has been designed and constructed to achieve some purpose. Moreover, it is certainly no affront to common English usage to take a reference to a major facility or a major source to connote an entire plant as opposed to its constituent parts. Basically, however, the language of § 302(j) simply does not compel any given interpretation of the term source.

Respondents recognize that, and hence point to § 111(a)(3). Although the definition in that section is not literally applicable to the permit program, it sheds as much light on the meaning of the word source as anything in the statute. As respondents point out, use of the words "building, structure, facility, or installation," as the definition of

source, could be read to impose the permit conditions on an individual building that is a part of a plant. A "word may have a character of its own not to be submerged by its association." On the other hand, the meaning of a word must be ascertained in the context of achieving particular objectives, and the words associated with it may indicate that the true meaning of the series is to convey a common idea. The language may reasonably be interpreted to impose the requirement on any dis- ←
crete, but integrated, operation which pollutes. This gives meaning to all of the terms—a single building, not part of a larger operation, would be covered if it emits more than 100 tons of pollution, as would any facility, structure, or installation. [Indeed, the language itself implies a bubble concept of sorts: each enumerated item would seem to be treated as if it were encased in a bubble.] While respondents insist that each of these terms must be given a discrete meaning, they also argue that § 111(a)(3) defines "source" as that term is used in § 302(j). The latter section, however, equates a source with a facility, whereas the former defines source as a facility, among other items.

We are not persuaded that parsing of general terms in the text of the statute will reveal an actual intent of Congress. We know full well that this language is not dispositive; the terms are overlapping and the language is not precisely directed to the question of the applicability of a given term in the context of a larger operation. To the extent any congressional "intent" can be discerned from this language, it would appear that the listing of overlapping, illustrative terms was intended to enlarge, rather than to confine, the scope of the agency's power to regulate particular sources in order to effectuate the policies of the Act.

LEGISLATIVE HISTORY

In addition, respondents argue that the legislative history and policies of the Act foreclose the plantwide definition, and that the EPA's interpretation is not entitled to deference because it represents a sharp break with prior interpretations of the Act.

Based on our examination of the legislative history, we agree with the Court of Appeals that it is unilluminating. The general remarks pointed to by respondents "were obviously not made with this narrow issue in mind and they cannot be said to demonstrate a Congressional desire * * *." Respondents' argument based on the legislative history relies heavily on Senator Muskie's observation that a new source is subject to the LAER requirement. But the full statement is ambiguous and like the text of § 173 itself, this comment does not tell us what a new source is, much less that it is to have an inflexible definition. We find that the legislative history as a whole is silent on the precise issue before us. It is, however, consistent with the view that the EPA should have broad discretion in implementing the policies of the 1977 Amendments.

More importantly, that history plainly identifies the policy concerns that motivated the enactment; the plantwide definition is fully consistent with one of those concerns—the allowance of reasonable economic growth—and, whether or not we believe it most effectively implements the other, we must recognize that the EPA has advanced a reasonable explanation for its conclusion that the regulations serve the environmental objectives as well. Indeed, its reasoning is supported by the public record developed in the rulemaking process, as well as by certain private studies.

Our review of the EPA's varying interpretations of the word "source"—both before and after the 1977 Amendments—convince us that the agency primarily responsible for administering this important legislation has consistently interpreted it flexibly—not in a sterile textual vacuum, but in the context of implementing policy decisions in a technical and complex arena. The fact that the agency has from time to time changed its interpretation of the term source does not, as respondents argue, lead us to conclude that no deference should be accorded the agency's interpretation of the statute. An initial agency interpretation is not instantly carved in stone. On the contrary, the agency, to engage in informed rulemaking, must consider varying interpretations and the wisdom of its policy on a continuing basis. Moreover, the fact that the agency has adopted different definitions in different contexts adds force to the argument that the definition itself is flexible, particularly since Congress has never indicated any disapproval of a flexible reading of the statute.

Significantly, it was not the agency in 1980, but rather the Court of Appeals that read the statute inflexibly to command a plantwide definition for programs designed to maintain clean air and to forbid such a definition for programs designed to improve air quality. The distinction the court drew may well be a sensible one, but our labored review of the problem has surely disclosed that it is not a distinction that Congress ever articulated itself, or one that the EPA found in the statute before the courts began to review the legislative work product. We conclude that it was the Court of Appeals, rather than Congress or any of the decisionmakers who are authorized by Congress to administer this legislation, that was primarily responsible for the 1980 position taken by the agency.

POLICY

The arguments over policy that are advanced in the parties' briefs create the impression that respondents are now waging in a judicial forum a specific policy battle which they ultimately lost in the agency and in the 32 jurisdictions opting for the bubble concept, but one which was never waged in the Congress. Such policy arguments are more properly addressed to legislators or administrators, not to judges.[12]

---

12. Respondents point out if a brand new factory that will emit over 100 tons of pollutants is constructed in a nonattainment area, that plant must obtain a permit pursuant to § 172(b)(6) and in order to do so, it must satisfy the § 173 conditions including the LAER requirement. Respondents argue if an old plant containing several large emitting units is to be modernized by the replacement of one or more units emitting over 100 tons of pollutant with a new unit emitting less—but still more than 100 tons—the result should be no different simply because "it happens to be built not

In this case, the Administrator's interpretation represents a reasonable accommodation of manifestly competing interests and is entitled to deference: the regulatory scheme is technical and complex, the agency considered the matter in a detailed and reasoned fashion, and the decision involves reconciling conflicting policies. Congress intended to accommodate both interests, but did not do so itself on the level of specificity presented by this case. Perhaps that body consciously desired the Administrator to strike the balance at this level, thinking that those with great expertise and charged with responsibility for administering the provision would be in a better position to do so; perhaps it simply did not consider the question at this level; and perhaps Congress was unable to forge a coalition on either side of the question, and those on each side decided to take their chances with the scheme devised by the agency. For judicial purposes, it matters not which of these things occurred.

Judges are not experts in the field, and are not part of either political branch of the Government. Courts must, in some cases, reconcile competing political interests, but not on the basis of the judges' personal policy preferences. In contrast, an agency to which Congress has delegated policymaking responsibilities may, within the limits of that delegation, properly rely upon the incumbent administration's views of wise policy to inform its judgments. While agencies are not directly accountable to the people, the Chief Executive is, and it is entirely appropriate for this political branch of the Government to make such policy choices—resolving the competing interests which Congress itself either inadvertently did not resolve, or intentionally left to be resolved by the agency charged with the administration of the statute in light of everyday realities.

[handwritten margin note: agency's reasonable interpretation]

When a challenge to an agency construction of a statutory provision, fairly conceptualized, really centers on the wisdom of the agency's policy, rather than whether it is a reasonable choice within a gap left open by Congress, the challenge must fail. In such a case, federal judges—who have no constituency—have a duty to respect legitimate policy choices made by those who do. The responsibilities for assessing the wisdom of such policy choices and resolving the struggle between competing views of the public interest are not judicial ones: "Our Constitution vests such responsibilities in the political branches" [quoting *TVA v. Hill,* infra page 581].

Notes

1. Does *Chevron* represent an expansion of agency power to construe statutes, as compared with previous cases like *du Pont* ? [supra p. 325] If so, is it a desirable expansion? For a somewhat cynical explanation of the opinion in terms of the Court's conservative policy preferences, see Cohen & Spitzer, "Solving the *Chevron* Puzzle," 57 *L. & Contemp.Probs.* 65 (1994). For evidence that *Chevron* has not actually had the expected effect of increasing the percentage of agency affirmances, see Merrill, "Textualism and the Future of the *Chevron* Doctrine," 72 *Wash.U.L.Q.* 351 (1994).

at a new site, but within a *pre-existing plant."*

2. Does *Chevron* represent a definitive construction of the statute? Under a new Administration, could EPA decide that bubbles should not be permitted under the Act and bar the states from using them?

3. Although the "bubble" concept is related to the "offset" policy, it does not seem to have the same implications in terms of creating marketable rights or positive incentives to reduce pollution. Use of the "bubble," however, clearly can reduce the total cost of abatement (thereby making it economically more efficient) and assist in overcoming technological barriers to uniform reduction of emissions from all sources.

How well have bubbles, offsets, and so forth actually worked? The following article contains a useful appraisal on the eve of the 1990 Amendments.

HAHN AND HESTER, "MARKETABLE PERMITS: LESSONS FOR THEORY AND PRACTICE"[u]

16 *Ecology Law Quarterly* 361 (1989).

Offsets are used by new and modified sources in nonattainment areas and by certain specified sources in attainment areas. The Clean Air Act specifies that no new emission sources would be allowed in areas that did not meet the original 1975 air quality deadlines. Concern that this provision would stifle economic growth prompted EPA to institute the offset rule in 1976. This rule requires new and modified emission sources in these areas to obtain emission credits from sources in the same area to offset their new emissions. The sources are still subject to the most stringent emission limits. Offsets may be obtained through internal or external trades. [O]ffset transactions are controlled at the state level.

Bubbles, first allowed in 1979, are used by existing sources in attainment or nonattainment areas. The name derives from the concept of placing an imaginary bubble over a multi-source plant. The levels of emission controls applied to different sources in a bubble may be adjusted to reduce control costs so long as the aggregate limit is not exceeded. In effect, emission credits are created by some sources within the plant and used by others. Originally, all bubbles had to be submitted by the states to EPA for approval. In 1981 EPA began to approve "generic bubble rules" that enabled states to approve bubbles. Several states now have such rules.

Banking, which was first allowed in 1979, provides a mechanism for firms to save emission credits for future use. EPA has established guidelines for banking programs, but states must set up and administer the rules governing banking.

* * *

[L]evels of activity in the three programs have varied widely. * * * An estimated 2,000 offset transactions have taken place, of which only about ten percent have been external. Fewer than 150 bubbles have been approved, only two of which are known to have involved external trades. About twice as many bubbles have been approved by states under generic rules than have been approved at the federal level. In fact, the general pattern seems to be that programs controlled at the state level are much more active than those controlled at the federal level. Banking, however, was not received well by either state regulators or firms. The figures listed for banking are an estimate of the number of times firms have withdrawn banked credits for sale or use. There has been little such activity.

* * * Federally approved bubbles have resulted in savings estimated at $300 million, while state bubbles have resulted in an estimated $135 million in cost savings.[13] * * * [O]ffsets result in no direct emission control cost savings because the use of offsets does not allow a firm to avoid any emission limits. However, since a firm using offsets is allowed to locate major new emission sources in nonattainment areas, presumably there is some economic advantage to the firm, or it would locate in an attainment area where offsets are not required. The willingness of firms to go to the expense of obtaining offsets indicates that they derive some net gain from doing so, but the extent of this gain cannot be estimated. Cost savings from banking also cannot be estimated, but are necessarily small given the number of transactions that have occurred.

[T]he effects [of trading] on environmental quality have been, on the whole, insignificant. * * * Offsets, which require trading ratios greater than 1:1, will naturally lead to reduced emissions. For bubbles, the lack of systematic data collection leaves the question of effects on environmental quality unresolved, but early reports indicated that aggregate effects may be slightly positive. Emission credits for a few of these transactions have been created by lowering permitted emission levels, but not making any actual reduction in emissions. Such transactions have an adverse environmental effect in the sense that emission reductions that would otherwise have been required were foregone. However, their aggregate effect on air quality in local areas is thought to be inconsequential. Banking has probably had a very slight positive effect, since banked credits represent emission reductions that have not been used to offset emission increases. However, because there has been little banking activity, this effect is also very small.

The performance evaluation of emissions trading activities reveals a mixed bag of accomplishments and disappointments. The program has clearly afforded many firms flexibility in meeting emission limits. This flexibility has resulted in significant aggregate cost savings—in the billions of dollars—without significantly affecting environmental quality.

---

13. All cost savings figures are for the lives of the different programs, and are not adjusted for inflation. It is interesting to note that although more state bubbles have been approved than federal, the average cost savings for federal bubbles is much higher.

However, these cost savings have been realized almost entirely from internal trading. They fall far short of the potential savings that could be realized if there were more external trading.

A variety of factors affect the performance of emissions trading. High transaction costs are the single most important determinant of program performance. A large part of these costs result from regulatory restrictions on trading and from administrative requirements that prolong the approval of trades.

Notes

1. Some environmentalists have complained that bubbles and offsets make little contribution to progress on pollution control. For example, Professor Rodgers notes concerns that many offsets are for improvements already required in SIPs, and offsets are rarely available to new sources but are instead used by the owners of existing sources who wish to expand or build new facilities. W. Rodgers, *Environmental Law* 217–218 (2d ed. 1994). He also provides an example of how offset policy can be manipulated:

> A delightful illustration of the subtleties (artfulness? casuistry?) of offset policymaking arose in Citizens Against the Refinery's Effects, Inc. v. United States EPA [643 F.2d 183 (4th Cir.1981)], where a new refinery was to make an appearance in a region already in violation of the photochemical oxidant standard. The Virginia State Air Pollution Control Board proposed to achieve the required offset by reducing the amount of cutback asphalt used for roadpaving operations in three highway districts representing almost the entire eastern one-third of the state. EPA endorsement of this SIP revision was affirmed, in essentially a soft glance opinion, over objections that (1) the geographic area of the offset was arbitrarily determined, (2) the wrong base year was selected in assessing the amount of the offset, (3) the offset strategy of reducing asphalt usage should have been disapproved because the state was voluntarily cutting back anyhow; and (4) the plan was approved without a definite commitment to the lowest achievable emission rate as required by statute.

Id. at 221.

2. EPA has used regulations not unlike the bubble and offset rules in other contexts. For example, Ackerman and Stewart credit EPA's tradeable permit system among gasoline refiners, used in connection with the phase-down of lead additives, with saving hundreds of millions of dollars. Ackerman & Stewart, "Reforming Environmental Law," 37 *Stan.L.Rev.* 1333, 1348–49 (1985). Similarly, EPA's standards for heavy duty vehicles allowed averaging of various "engine families," rather than requiring each type of engine separately to comply. See *NRDC v. Thomas*, 805 F.2d 410 (D.C.Cir. 1986) (upholding this approach on the ground that nothing in the statutory language or legislative history addressed the problem: "[l]acking any clear congressional prohibition of averaging, the EPA's argument that averaging will allow manufacturers more flexibility in cost allocation while ensuring that a manufacturer's overall fleet still meets the emissions reduction standards makes sense." Id. at 425).

3. EPA has become increasingly interested in effluent trading under the Clean Water Act. An intriguing pilot problem was established in the Tar–Pamlico basin in North Carolina. Because of a pressing need to decrease nutrient levels in the basin, the state set strict nitrogen and phosphorus standards for that area which would have imposed heavy costs on point sources but achieved only small improvements in water quality. Dischargers proposed a nutrient trading program between point source and nonpoint pollution. In order to meet annual levels of nutrient reductions, dischargers can make improvements in their own facilities, trade discharges among themselves, or offset excess discharges by paying a tax which is used to control nonpoint pollution. The tax was initially set at a rate of $56/kg. The first phase of the project succeeded in reducing the nutrient load by 28%. See Segio Borgiotti, "Point/Nonpoint Source Trading: A Solution for Nutrient Pollution," 26 *Env. Rep.* 954 (1995). Note also the possibility of taking into account indirect sources, such as air emissions that contaminate water bodies. See "Cross–Media Pollution and the Chesapeake Bay," *Resources*, Summer 1996, at 20. More recently, EPA allowed a trade between two dischargers to meet copper discharge limits in a municipal treatment system. See 29 *Env.Rep.* 695 (1998).

4. A major experiment in using marketable permits has taken place in California. Known as RECLAIM (from Regional Clean Air Incentives Market), the program covers almost all facilities emitting over four tons per year of nitrogen oxides or sulfur oxides. It was expected to apply initially to about 400 facilities, accounting for between two-thirds and three-quarters of the emissions from stationary sources with permits. These facilities were given initial allowances of RECLAIM Trading Credits (or RTCs), which they were then allowed to trade. From 1995 to 2000, the amount of pollution represented by each RTC will decrease at a steady annual rate, with an acceleration in the rate of decline after 2000. The initial allocation is set based on maximum emissions during 1989–1992, with an adjustment to control the total emissions from all sources. To obtain a new permit, new facilities must use BACT and obtain at least a one year's supply of RTCs. For a detailed description of the program, see Selmi, "Transforming Market Incentives from Theory to Reality," 24 *Env.L.Rep.* 10695 (1994). By 1998, more than $42 million in trades had taken place among the 330 facilities in the program. See Whetzel, "California Air Pollution: Strategy for the Future," 28 *Env.Rep.* 2540, 2541 (1998). As a result of litigation by environmentalists, however, the State has suspended approval of new trading programs. See Cifford, "Approval of Smog Credits Suspended," L.A. Times, Aug. 18, 1997, at A26.

5. In connection with acid rain, the 1990 amendments introduced the most systematic use of marketable permits yet to be seen in federal pollution law, as the following note explains.

Note: Trading Across Borders

As we saw at the end of Chapter III, inter-jurisdictional pollution poses huge problems for regulators. Recently, trading systems have emerged as a possible solution. These systems promise to decrease the total cost of pollution control, making controls more politically appealing, while also helping to defuse the difficult distributional issues posed by inter-jurisdictional regulation.

In the United States, the most notable example is the system of sulfur dioxide allowances created to deal with acid rain. We examined in Chapter III the failure of the Clean Air Act's administrative mechanisms for resolving interstate pollution disputes. During the 1980s, any legislative solution was blocked by the skepticism of the Reagan Administration about the reality of acid rain. The deadlock between Congress and the White House was finally broken with the passage of the 1990 amendments. Title IV of the amendments is devoted to acid rain. It imposes a completely new approach to the problem, which was originally devised by the Bush Administration.

The system is based on a system of allowances that can be banked or sold by emitters. Each allowance is equivalent to one ton of emissions. A utility can emit SO_2 only to the extent permitted by its allowances. The allowances are allocated largely on the basis of past emissions and fuel consumption, but there are extra allowances for a variety of purposes. For example, from 1995 to 1999, an extra 200,000 allowances were allocated to power plants in Illinois, Indiana, and Ohio.

The program is divided into two phases:

1. In Phase I, over one hundred plants (listed in the bill) must meet a standard of 2.5 pounds of SO_2 per million Btus. The 111 utility power plants in question are those that in 1990 emitted more than 2.5 pounds of SO_2 per million Btus. (For example, generator #1 at the Colbert plant in Alabama is given a Phase I allowance of 13,570 tons.) This standard had to be attained by 1995, except that plants using scrubbers to meet the standards had until 1997. (This provision is intended to encourage the use of scrubbers and thereby continue at least part of the market for eastern high-sulfur coal.) The Phase I allowances were expected to reduce SO_2 emissions by about ten million tons per year.

2. Phase II requires utilities to reduce emissions by an additional fifty percent. Large, poorly controlled plants must reduce emissions to 1.2 million lbs/mBtu. A complex formula applies to smaller plants. The deadline for compliance is 2000. Total emissions cannot exceed 8.9 million tons annually, but for the first ten years, EPA will have a half million extra allowances in reserve. A further forty thousand allowances can be given to high-growth states. A four-year extension is available for units that use new clean coal technologies.

In part, the system of allocations embodies the efficiency concerns of economists. The system of allowances seems to have been manipulated, however, in the interests of regional equity, so that utilities that are required to engage in heavy investments will be able to recoup part of their expenses. The initial allocations are large enough that some of these utilities will find it feasible to control emissions more than required to stay within their initial allowance, thereby allowing them to sell excess allowances. At least some of these excess allowances will have to be purchased by new utility plants in order to operate.

According to one economic analyst, affected utilities will have to spend about $4 billion annually once the program is fully operative in the year 2000. He adds that the total would have been $2–3 billion more expensive if Congress had required scrubbers, as it did in the 1977 amendments. Although he is skeptical about the benefits of controlling acid rain, he also points out that SO_2 control will have important human health benefits. He estimates the total benefits of the acid rain provisions at \$2–9 billion annually. Portney, "Economics and the Clean Air Act," 4 *J.Econ.Persp.* 173, 175–76 (1990). This system of marketable allowances has given rise to considerable scholarly commentary. See, e.g., Munton, "Dispelling the Myths of the Acid Rain Story," *Environment*, July/Aug. 1998, at 4; Parker, Poling & Moore, "Clean Air Act Allowance Trading," 21 *Env.L.* 2021 (1991); Van Dyke, "Emissions Trading to Reduce Acid Deposition," 100 *Yale L.J.* 2707 (1991).

According to one early report:

> So far * * * the market is a nonstarter. With the first deadline looming, only a few trades have been announced, and the terms of those have not been made public. As a result, utilities owning more than 15,000 megawatts of coal-fired power stations, nearly 20 percent of the affected total, have decided to build "scrubbers" without a clear idea of how much it would cost to meet their obligations by buying the allowances instead.

Wald, "Risk–Shy Utilities Avoid Trading Emission Credits," *New York Times,* January 25, 1993, at C2. The report attributed the lack of trading to risk aversion on the part of utility managements, who believe that under state utility regulation, "if a trade saves money, electric rates are cut, but if a trade later turns out to have raised costs, shareholders suffer." In general, auction purchases have remained quite limited, partly because of the availability of low-sulfur coal to allow relatively inexpensive compliance with Phase I standards. Trading has also been limited by public utility rules and perhaps by flaws in the implementation of the trading programs. See Dallas Burtraw, "Trading Emissions to Clean the Air: Exchanges Few but Savings Many," *Resources*, Winter 1996 at 3. Intra-company trades, however, have been more common.

→ In the meantime, the program has also been criticized for failing to efficiently allocate pollution on the basis of interstate impacts:

> At best, the acid-rain provisions of the 1990 amendments are an incomplete mechanism for dealing with interstate externalities. They apply to only two pollutants: sulfur dioxide and nitrogen oxides. Furthermore, they apply to only one type of facility: electric utilities.

> Moreover, these provisions are not structured to allocate emissions between upwind and downwind states in a desirable manner. With respect of nitrogen oxides, the provisions set emissions standards for new and existing sources. As discussed above, emissions standards are not a well-targeted means for controlling interstate externalities.

> Although [the mandated] decreases in the allowable emissions of sulfur dioxide are likely to reduce the amount of acid rain, particularly after the year 2000, they make no attempt to allocate emissions between upwind states and downwind states in an optimal way. The acid-rain problem manifests itself primarily in the Northeast, but is caused primarily by emissions from the Midwest. Because the market is nation-

al, Midwestern sources could buy, without restriction, permits from the West and the Northeast. Such trades would have an undesirable impact in the Northeast. In fact, downwind states are attempting to prevent their sources from selling permits to upwind sources, though such measures may well be struck down constitutional grounds.

Richard Revesz, "Federalism and Interstate Environmental Externalities," 155 *U. Pa. L. Rev.* 2341, 2341, 2360–61 (1996). Revesz suggests amending marketable permit schemes so that the amount of emissions allowed by each permit would depend on the impact that its emissions would have on air-quality at affected locations.

Despite these criticisms, EPA considers the program highly successful, with the current allowance price of around $100 representing a large reduction in original estimates of control costs. A study by Resources for the Future found "compelling evidence that the program's benefits far exceed its costs." Indeed, EPA now plans to use the sulfur dioxide program as a model for an emission trading system for NOx, although no specific statutory authorization for this program exists. See Zacarolli, "Nitrogen Oxides Emissions Trading," 29 *Env.Rep.* 194, 195 (1998).

Apart from the various criticisms of the sulfur dioxide trading system itself, the political process behind the 1990 Act has also been sharply criticized. To begin with, Congress never really discussed the level of emissions reduction to seek:

> Review of the history of the 1990 Amendments reveals that reasoned deliberation did not occur. Indeed, in sharp contrast to the expectations of emissions trading proponents, Congress deliberately refused to debate the emissions limitation as the Amendments made their way through the legislature. The legislation, originally proposed by the Bush administration, called for a reduction in sulfur dioxide emissions of approximately ten million tons from 1980 levels. This directive remained unchanged from the time the 1990 Amendments were first proposed to the time they were enacted into law. The Senate did, however, add the 8.9–million-ton cap on emissions, apparently in order to ensure the achievement of the ten-million-ton reduction.

Heinzerling, "Selling Pollution, Forcing Democracy," 14 *Stan. Env. L.J.* 300, 323–24 (1995). This absence of debate was all the more striking because a key study estimated that reducing emissions by eight-million tons would be equally effective and perhaps cost only half as much. Id. at 326.

What Congress did debate was how to allocate the allowances:

> It is difficult to imagine what lies behind these special bonuses and exemptions [under the Act], other than the kind of special interest deal that proponents of emissions trading had hoped their system would preempt. The criteria for special bonuses and exemptions are, indeed, so disparate as to invite the conclusion that the only master strategy at work in the allocation of allowances under the 1990 Amendments was the satisfaction of powerful interests. As two commentators have observed, "It would appear that the Senators saw little distinction between the Clean Air Act and a fight over which defense installation to close, or an appropriation for public works projects. The pork tastes as good,

from whichever barrel it comes." It is easy to see, for example, the hand of the eastern coal industry, which mines mostly high-sulfur coal, in the incentives to install scrubbers and clean-coal technology.

Id. at 330. But see Joskow & Schmalensee, "The Political Economy of Market–Based Environmental Policy: The U.S. Acid Rain Program," 61 *J.L. & Econ.* 37 (1998) (statistical study of voting patterns finding only limited influence by "special interests").

Assuming Heinzerling is correct, might one argue that the allowances program made it politically feasible to address the problem of acid rain by providing a mechanism for working out the difficult distributional problems entailed by control measures? It would be somewhat ironic if the major contribution of a tradeable permit system turns out to be its ability to handle political issues of wealth distribution rather than the efficiency benefits for which it was designed.

The concept of emissions trading is also beginning to emerge at the international level. In 1997, an international conference in Kyoto reached an historic agreement to cooperate in addressing the global greenhouse effect. Forty industrial countries agreed to cut emissions of greenhouse gases (primarily carbon dioxide) by at least five percent below 1990 levels. The agreement contains a commitment to emissions trading among the industrial countries, with the details to be worked out later. The agreement also allows industrialized countries to meet their obligations by purchasing emission reductions from developing countries, which are not themselves subject to the five-percent reduction requirement. See Searles, "Analysis of the Kyoto Protocol to the U.N. Framework Convention on Climate Change," *Int'l Env.Rep.*, Feb. 4, 1998, at 131, 133–34. Active negotiation over the design of the trading system continues, though at this writing it is unclear whether the Senate will ratify the Kyoto treaty. See Campbell & Carpenter, "From Kyoto to Buenos Aires: Implementing the Kyoto Protocol on Climate Change," 21 *Env.Rep.* 748 (1998).

For reflections on the on-going development of market techniques, see Jeremy Hockstein, Robert Stavins, and Bradley Whitehead, "Crafting the Next Generation of Market–Based Environmental Tools," *Environment*, May 1997, at 13; Vivien Foster and Robert Hahn, "Designing More Efficient Markets: Lessons from Los Angeles Smog Control," 38 *J. L. & Econ.* 19 (1995).

Review Problem on Techniques of Air Pollution Control

We have previously considered the fictional pollutant, kryptonia. This set of problems concerns a chemical cousin of kryptonia known as Kryptic Oxide (or KO), which is known to produce damage to flowering plants and exacerbate the problems of individuals with respiratory difficulties (particularly if they also smoke cigarettes). Suppose that there are seven major sources and fifty smaller sources in a municipality. Try to work out the details of the following control techniques.

1. *The Common Law.* Clark Kent, on behalf of himself and all other individuals sensitive to the health effects of Kryptic Oxide, brings a class action against the sources based on nuisance law. This gives rise to a series of subissues for you to consider: (a) Should the suit be allowed to proceed if

an administrative agency has jurisdiction to regulate KO? (b) How should the court handle the large number of defendants? (c) How can the court frame an appropriate remedy, taking into account its need for access to scientific expertise and the complex technical and economic questions that might be raised by the defendants? (d) Should the court award an injunction or merely damages—and if only damages, how should they be calculated, and how should they be distributed? (e) Should the court attempt to force the parties toward a settlement?

2. *Conventional Pollution Control.* Suppose that EPA has classified KO as a criterion pollutant and has issued NAAQS. As counsel for one of the sources, make up a list of all of the requirements that firms will be required to meet, either for existing operations or to expand or open new plants. At what points in the process can firms raise claims of economic or technological feasibility? Do you expect the regulatory process to follow the statutory timetable, or are there likely to be delays (and if so, when?).

3. *Marketable Permits.* Assume that KO has not been subjected to regulation under the Clean Air Act, but that a state agency has decided to create a market for KO allowances. The following questions, among others, then arise: (a) How should the total number of allowances be determined? (b) How should these allowances be distributed among firms? (c) Will banking of allowances be permitted? (d) How will the agency monitor and enforce compliance? Try to put together a detailed plan for the allowance program.

Taking into account environmental values, economics, and political feasibility to the extent you think relevant, which of these techniques seems most promising to you?

Chapter V

RISK MANAGEMENT AND SCIENTIFIC UNCERTAINTY

You will recall that some of the materials in Chapter I stressed the high level of scientific uncertainty surrounding environmental issues. See, for example, the articles by Ruhl and Myers, at pages 10 and 17. The most basic question raised by those materials is this: How can we regulate in a sensible way when we are unsure about the causes of a problem and about the appropriate cure?

This chapter explores the nature and scope of some special problems associated with regulation of hazardous and toxic substances. Primary among these is pervasive scientific uncertainty about long-term human effects of exposure to small amounts of such substances. In the face of uncertainty which no party to a regulatory or judicial proceeding may be able to resolve, rules concerning risk assessment, causation, presumptions, burden of proof, sharing of liability, and scope of judicial review become critically important.

A. INTRODUCTION TO RISK ASSESSMENT AND RISK MANAGEMENT

RUCKELSHAUS, "RISK IN A FREE SOCIETY"[a]

14 *Environmental Law Reporter* 10190 (1984).

* * * Risk assessment is the use of a base of scientific research to define the probability of some harm coming to an individual or a population as a result of exposure to a substance or situation. Risk management, in contrast, is the public process of deciding what to do where risk has been determined to exist. It includes integrating risk assessment with considerations of engineering feasibility and figuring out how to exercise our imperative to reduce risk in the light of social, economic, and political factors.

---

a. Reprinted with permission. Copyright, The Environmental Law Institute, 1984. Mr. Ruckelshaus was Administrator of the U.S. EPA in 1984.

The [National Academy of Sciences has] proposed that these two functions be formally separated within regulatory agencies.[b] I said that this appeared to be a workable idea and that we would try to make it happen at EPA. This notion was attractive because the statutes administered by many federal regulatory agencies typically force some action when scientific inquiry establishes the presence of a risk, as, for example, when a substance present in the environment, or the workplace, or the food chain, is found to cause cancer in animals. The statutes may require the agency to act according to some protective formula: to establish "margins of safety" or "prevent significant risk" or "eliminate the risk."

When the action so forced has dire economic or social consequences, the person who must make the decision may be sorely tempted to ask for a "reinterpretation" of the data. We should remember that risk assessment data can be like a captured spy; if you torture it long enough, it will tell you anything you want to know. So it is good public policy to so structure an agency that such temptation is avoided.

But we have found that separating the assessment of risk from its management is rather more difficult to accomplish in practice. In the first place, values, which are supposed to be safely sequestered in risk management, also appear as important influences on the outcome of risk assessments. For example, let us suppose that a chemical in common use is tested on laboratory animals with the object of determining whether it can cause cancer. At the end of the test a proportion of the animals that have been exposed to the substance show evidence of tumor formation.

Now the problems begin. First, in tests like these, the doses given are extremely high, often close to the level the animal can tolerate for a lifetime without dying from toxic non-cancer effects. Environmental exposures are typically much lower, so in order to determine what the risk of cancer is at such lower exposures—that is, to determine the curve that relates a certain dose to a certain response—we must extrapolate down from the high-dose laboratory data. There are a number of statistical models for doing this, all of which fit the data, and all of which are open to debate. We simply do not *know* what the shape of the dose-response curve is at low doses, in the sense that we know, let us say, what the orbit of a satellite will be when we shoot it off.

Next, we must deal with the uncertainty of extrapolating cancer data from animals to man, for example, determining which of the many different kinds of lesions that may appear in animals is actually indicative of a probability that the substance in question may be a human carcinogen. Cancer is cancer to the public, but not to the pathologist.

Finally, we must deal with uncertainty about exposure. We have to determine, usually on the basis of scant data and elaborate mathematical models, how much of the stuff is being produced; how it is being

b. *See* National Research Council, *Risk Assessment in the Federal Government:* *Managing the Process* (1983).

dispersed, changed, or destroyed by natural processes; and how the actual dose that people get is changed by behavioral or population characteristics.

These uncertainties inherent in risk assessment combine to produce an enormously wide range of risk estimates in most cases. For example, the National Academy of Sciences report on saccharin concluded that over the next 70 years the expected number of cases of human bladder cancer resulting from daily exposure to 120 milligrams of saccharin might range from 0.22 to 1,144,000. This sort of range is of limited use to the policymaker and risk assessment scientists are at some pains to make choices among possibilities so as to produce conclusions that are both scientifically supportable and usable.

Such choices are influenced by values, which may be affected by professional training, or by ideas about what constitutes "good science," and, of course by the same complex of experience and individual traits that gives rise to personal values in all of us. An oncologist, for example, who values highly the ability to distinguish between different sorts of lesions, may discount certain test results as being irrelevant to decisions about human carcinogenicity. A public health epidemiologist may look at the same data and come to quite different conclusions.

Historically at EPA it has been thought prudent to make what have been called conservative assumptions; that is, in a situation of unavoidable uncertainty, *our* values lead us to couch our conclusions in terms of a plausible upper bound. As a result, when we generate a number that expresses the potency of some substance in causing disease, we can state that it is unlikely that the risk projected is any greater.

This conservative approach is fine when the risks projected are vanishingly small; it is always nice to learn that some chemical is *not* a national crisis. But when the risks estimated through such assessments are substantial, so that some action may be in the offing, the stacking of conservative assumptions one on top of another becomes a problem for the policymaker. If I am going to propose controls that may have serious economic and social effects, I need to have some idea how much confidence to place in the estimates of risk that prompted those controls. I need to know how likely *real* damage is to occur in the uncontrolled and partially controlled and fully controlled cases. Only then can I apply the balancing judgments that are the essence of my job. This, of course, tends to insert the policymaker back into the guts of risk assessment, which we had concluded is less than wise.

This is a real quandary. I now believe that the main road out of it lies through a marked improvement in the way we communicate the realities of risk analysis to the public. The goal is public understanding. We will only retain the administrative flexibility we need to effectively protect the public health and welfare if the public believes we are trying to act in the public interest. There is an argument, in contradiction, that the best way to protect lies in increased legislative specificity, in closely directing the Agency as to what to control and how much to control it. If we fail to command public confidence, this argument will prevail, and in my opinion it would be a bad thing if it did. You cannot squeeze the complexity inherent in managing environmental risks between the pages of a statute book.

* * *

. . . Let me now propose some principles for more reasonable discussions about risk.

First, we must insist on risk calculations being expressed as distributions of estimates and not as magic numbers that can be manipulated without regard to what they really mean. We must try to display more realistic estimates of risk to show a range of probabilities. To help do this we need new tools for quantifying and ordering sources of uncertainty and for putting them in perspective.

Second, we must expose to public scrutiny the assumptions that underlie our analysis and management of risk. If we have made a series of conservative assumptions within the risk assessment, so that it represents an upper bound estimate of risk, we should try to communicate this and explain why we did it. Although public health protection is our primary value, any particular action to control a pollutant may have effects on other values, such as community stability, employment, natural resources, or the integrity of the ecosystem. We have to get away from the idea that we do quantitative analysis to find the "right" decision, which we will then be obliged to make if we want to call ourselves rational beings. But we are not clockwork mandarins. The point of such analysis is, in fact, the orderly exposition of the values we hold, and the reasoning that travels from some set of values and measurements to a decision.

* * *

Finally, we should understand the limits of quantification; there are some cherished values that will resist being squeezed into a benefits column, but are no less real because of it. * * *

I suppose that the ultimate goal of this effort is to get the American people to understand the difference between a safe world and a zero-risk world with respect to environmental pollutants. We have to define what safe means in light of our increasing ability to detect minute quantities of substances in the environment and to associate carcinogenesis with an enormous variety of substances in common use.

ROSENTHAL, GRAY & GRAHAM, "LEGISLATING ACCEPTABLE CANCER RISK FROM EXPOSURE TO TOXIC CHEMICALS"[c]
19 *Ecology Law Quarterly* 269, 278–279 (1992).

EPA uses risk assessment to predict the probability of developing cancer as a result of exposure to a particular agent. As currently practiced, risk assessment of a carcinogen takes place in four steps: hazard identification, dose-response evaluation, exposure assessment, and risk characterization.

The first step, hazard identification, is the process of determining whether an "agent" (for example, an industrial chemical, a natural product in the environment, or a particular lifestyle) increases a person's risk of developing cancer. The second step, dose-response evaluation, reveals how the likelihood of cancer changes with the level of exposure. A risk assessor might estimate, for example, how the probability of lung cancer changes with the number of cigarettes smoked. The third step, exposure assessment, quantifies the amount, or dose, of the carcinogen to which people may be exposed. This may be the amount of a chemical in the air near a factory, the concentration of radon in the basement of a home, or the amounts of various foods and beverages which an individual consumes each day.

After these quantitative inputs to a risk assessment have been determined, the numbers are combined to yield an overall estimate of risk, the basic component of the final step, risk characterization. A risk characterization is usually expressed numerically as the incremental lifetime risk of cancer due to a particular agent at a particular level of exposure (also referred to as an incremental risk). * * * Good risk characterizations contain not only a final risk number but also a discussion of the uncertainties in and the assumptions behind the assessment, but unfortunately this step is rarely taken.

Cancer risk estimates are predictions of an unknown future, rather than estimates of the future behavior of a known phenomenon. For this reason, they can be quite difficult to quantify with precision. A comparison of the prediction of car accident rates to that of cancer rates illustrates the difficulty. An estimate of the number of persons who will be killed in car accidents can be based on frequency data—actual counts of automobile fatalities over a number of years. A prediction can thus be based on the past behavior of the system. In contrast, cancer risk predictions are based on extrapolated probabilities, not on past frequencies. There are a number of reasons for this. For example, the causes of cancer are much more complex, because cancer does not develop immediately after exposure to a carcinogen, and because regulators want to know the potential risk of substances to which the public has not yet been exposed in great numbers. As a consequence, predictions of cancer risk cannot be known with similar degrees of precision.

In evaluating the seriousness of incremental cancer risks, it is useful to have a sense of perspective about the frequency of cancer. At current U.S. mortality rates, a baby born today has about a one-in-four, or 0.25, chance of contracting fatal cancer in his or her lifetime. This is the average American's baseline cancer risk from all causes. An incremental risk of one in a million, or $10-6$, the most frequently proposed bright line risk standard, is equivalent to a change in lifetime cancer risk from 0.25 to 0.250001.

Notes

1. For a concise critique of risk assessment in the environmental context, see John Dwyer, "Limits of Environmental Risk Assessment," 116 *J. Energy Engineering,* No. 3 (1990). The author expresses concern over the enormous scientific uncertainties at each stage of risk assessment, which make quantifying risks impossible without value-laden, simplifying assumptions. The result is that numerical risk assessments may be given undue weight at the expense of nonquantifiable considerations, and that pseudo-science in the guise of expertise may substitute for genuine political discourse.

2. A strong critique of risk *management* as practiced by EPA is a book by Judge (now Justice) Stephen Breyer, *Breaking the Vicious Circle: Toward Effective Risk Regulation* (1993). Breyer attacks health regulation which goes too far ("the last 10 percent"): the agency "considers a substance that poses serious risks, at least through long exposure to high doses. It then promulgates standards so stringent * * * that the regulatory action ultimately imposes high costs without achieving significant additional safety benefits." *Id.* at 10–11. Breyer also criticizes "random agenda selection," the failure to utilize *comparative risk analysis* to determine regulatory priorities.

For a vigorous critique of *Breaking the Vicious Circle* see Adam Finkel, "A Second Opinion on an Environmental Misdiagnosis: The Risky Prescriptions of Breaking the Vicious Circle," 3 *N.Y.U. Envt'l L.J.* 295 (1995). Finkel expresses serious doubt not only about the positions taken by Justice Breyer but also about the reliability of risk assessment in the environmental context. Finkel's article is one of several by prominent authors in a symposium on "Risk Assessment in the Federal Government." Other articles include John Graham, "The Risk Not Reduced"; Ellen Silbergeld, "The Risks of Comparing Risks"; and W. Kip Viscusi, "Equivalent Frames of Reference for Judging Risk Regulation Policies."

3. Since EPA embraced risk assessment during Mr. Ruckelshaus' second term as Administrator in the mid–1980s, comparative risk analysis has become the touchstone there for reforming environmental law and policymaking. In 1987 a study group of senior EPA officials surveyed 31 types of environmental problems within the Agency's jurisdiction, used formal assessment techniques to estimate how much "risk" was posed by each type of problem, and concluded that society should reorganize its approach toward environmental protection by shifting resources from those problems that rank fairly low on the risk index to higher-ranked problems. See Office of Policy Analysis, U.S. EPA, *Unfinished Business: A Comparative Assessment of Environmental Problems* 95 (1987). In 1989, EPA commissioned its Science Advisory Board to review this conclusion. The Board offered a qualified endorsement; after noting that the data used by scientists to measure environmental risk can be notoriously spotty and that risk-bearing can involve qualitative elements not easily indexed for comparison, the Board nevertheless supported comparative risk analysis as an "important shift in national environmental policy." See Relative Risk Reduction Strategies Committee, U.S. EPA Science Advisory Board, *Reducing Risk: Setting Priorities and Strategies for Environmental Protection* 7 (1990).

For a detailed analysis of the theoretical limitations of comparative risk analysis, see Hornstein, "Reclaiming Environmental Law: A Normative Critique of Comparative Risk Analysis," 92 *Colum.L.Rev.* 562 (1992). The author believes that comparative risk analysis employs an unduly flattened conception of risk that factors out too many important aspects of risk-bearing. He argues that public perceptions of environmental risk (discussed at length in the following article by Gillette & Krier) deserve more credit than comparative risk analysts admit, and that comparative risk analysis distorts decisionmaking by choosing artificial baselines for comparing risks, and disrupts markets for technological innovations that can reduce risk.

An excellent discussion of comparative risk analysis, by leading proponents and critics, is contained in A. Finkel and D. Golding (eds.), *Worst Things First? The Debate Over Risk–Based National Environmental Priorities* (1994). See also the symposium, "Risk in the Republic: Comparative Risk Analysis and Public Policy," 9 *Duke Envt'l L. & Pub. Pol'y Forum* 1 (1997).

GILLETTE & KRIER, "RISK, COURTS, AND AGENCIES"[d]

138 *University of Pennsylvania Law Review* 1027,
1027–29, 1039, 1071–73, 1076–79 (1990).

Risk inheres in our condition. Whether brought on by nature in such forms as earthquakes and disease, or by humans with mundane machines like the automobile and high technologies like nuclear energy, hazard is ubiquitous and inevitable. Hence selective aversion to certain risks, most particularly to the manmade risks of advanced technologies, can prove to be counterproductive. Selective aversion might foreclose progressive new technologies that are, despite their dangers, on balance beneficial. A world with vaccines and nuclear power plants is not perfectly safe, for example, but might be safer than a world without. In other words, though risk by definition is costly, avoiding risk is costly as well.[1] It entails the costs of controls and other risk-reduction measures, and at times the costs of forgone benefits (a risky new technology might guard against even more threatening natural hazards, such as disease; it might displace the greater risks of a technology already in place, or produce units of output at a lower cost than the existing technology, or both). So the objective of risk management must be not the elimination

1. Technically speaking, "risk" refers only to the probability of an event, with something like "gravity" designating its possible adverse consequences. Moreover, "risk" has classically referred only to probabilities that can be precisely estimated, all other instances being consigned to the realm of "uncertainty." *See, e.g.,* F. Knight, Risk, Uncertainty, and Profit 19–20, 197–232 (1921) (arguing that the crucial difference between risk and uncertainty is that the former is "measurable" while the latter is "immeasurable"). Following current practice, we ignore the foregoing distinctions and use risk *in the technical sense* to mean an expected value arrived at by multiplying the potential adverse consequences of an event—loosely, its costs—by the probability that the event will occur (the probability might be objective or subjective). Later, we introduce and consider the meaning of risk *in the popular sense.*

of risk, but rather the minimization of all risk-related costs.[2]

All of this sounds platitudinous, yet it happens to be extraordinarily controversial—especially in the case of "public risks," a recently coined name for the distinctive hazards of high-tech times. Public risks have been defined as manmade "threats to human health or safety that are centrally or mass-produced, broadly distributed, and largely outside the individual risk bearer's direct understanding and control."[3] "Private risks," in contrast, are either of natural origin or, if manmade, produced in relatively discrete units, with local impacts more or less subject to personal control. In these terms, then, disease is a natural private risk; the hazards of commonplace artifacts like automobiles and wood stoves are manmade private risks. Public risks, on the other hand, originate in new or complex technologies like chemical additives, recombinant DNA, mass-produced vaccines, and nuclear power plants.

The public-private distinction is hardly perfect (consider the pollution pouring into the atmosphere from thousands of automobiles, or from thousands of wood stoves), but it is useful enough, especially for purposes of illuminating a currently important controversy that centers on the idea of cost minimization in the risk context. Public risks are precisely the risks that have recently captured the attention of the legal community and the world at large, in no small part because they give rise to such novel problems for lawyers and such grave apprehensions among lay people. Public risks have moved the legal system to relax doctrines—regarding, for example, standards of causation and culpability, burdens of proof, sharing of liability—that were designed to deal with the private risks that once dominated the landscape. And public risks have moved lay people to intensify their demands for risk control measures. These developments suggest that public risks are subject to especially harsh treatment, yet such treatment might often be contrary to minimizing the sum of all risk-related costs. If some public risks, whatever their dangers, are in fact safer or otherwise more beneficial than the risks they would displace, then cost minimization requires open-minded efforts to encourage many of the very technological threats that current legal and popular opinion would instead deter. As a consequence, the question of what to do about public risk has become a subject of considerable (and sometimes heated) debate.

* * *

2. The objective, in other words, is to minimize the *sum* of the costs of risk and the costs of avoiding risk. *Cf.* G. Calabresi, The Costs of Accidents 26 (1970) (stating "as axiomatic that the principal function of accident law is to reduce the sum of the costs of accidents and the costs of avoiding accidents"). While risk cost minimization is an important end of risk management, it is not the only one. For example, the distribution of risk—demographically, spatially, and temporally—also has to be considered, partly for reasons of justice and partly because distribution has a bearing on the measure of risk costs that one might hope to minimize.

3. Huber *"Safety and the Second Best: The Hazards of Public Risk Management in the Courts,"* 85 Colum.L.Rev. 277, 277 (1985).

* * * Many public risks are latent in their materialization. Adverse effects do not appear until long after exposure.[30] In addition, public risks are often diffuse in their impact, spread over many victims, so the costs to any one victim might be small even though the aggregate cost to the total victim population is very large. Similarly, public risks are by definition probabilistic, and the likelihood that exposure will lead to adverse effects is often remote.[32] The effects themselves might be of dramatic dimension, should they occur, but by virtue of low probabilities their expected costs are nevertheless negligible.

These characteristics skew the incentives of presumably self-interested producers and consumers of public risks. Even assuming some knowledge of risks, for example, consumers (including consumers of jobs—employees) and producers alike will generally discount the information because of long latency, low probability, or both. Where latency periods exceed ten to fifteen years, discounting effectively means ignoring the risk altogether.[33] Where probabilities are low, actors commonly (if inappropriately) ignore potential consequences, notwithstanding their likely magnitude should they materialize.[34] And diffuse effects are, on an individual basis, usually small to begin with, and thus of little interest. * * *

* * *

* * * What does "risk" *mean?* To anticipate our argument, suppose that the concept signifies different things to different people—more particularly, one thing to agency experts and another to the lay public. Suppose, in addition, that while each of these meanings is sensible, the expert definition implies levels of public risk that are, by the lay definition, almost invariably too high. It then follows that a selfless agency, determined and free (because of expansive deference) to assess and manage public risk in accord with its own conception, will end up regulating less than called for from the public's point of view. The resulting contest is, at bottom, one of competing rationalities, and its resolution is a matter of ethics and politics, not technical expertise. Nothing in the training, credentials, or legitimacy of risk assessors or bureaucrats qualifies them to settle the issue. Hence deference to agen-

---

30. Latency may also be a feature of some private risks, such as medical malpractice, but it tends to exist systematically in the case of public risks. *See, e.g.,* Page, *"A Generic View of Toxic Chemicals and Similar Risks",* 7 Ecology L.Q. 207, 213 (1978) (discussing characteristics of environmental risk).

32. *See, e.g.,* Farber, *"Toxic Causation",* 71 Minn.L.Rev. 1219, 1228 (1987).

33. The standard formula for discounting a dollar amount to its present value is $\$\times /(1 + r)$ n(where r = a stated interest rate and n = the number of periods during which the interest rate is earned). Assume a .01 probability that an event will occur in 10 years and that, if it does, there will be a loss of \$100,000,000. The expected value of the loss is \$1,000,000 in 10 years. The present (discounted) value of that loss at an interest rate of 5 percent is \$615,000; at 10 percent it is \$385,000. If the event will materialize, if at all, only in 20 years, then the present value figures are \$375,000 and \$150,000 for 5 and 10 percent respectively.

34. *See* D. Parfit, Reasons and Persons 73–75 (1984) (discussing error inherent in ignoring small chances); Shrader–Frechette, *"Parfit and Mistakes in Moral Mathematics",* 98 Ethics 50, 54–55 (1987) (noting also the difficulty in assessing the causation of consequences).

cies would grant them ground they have no right to claim. Deference would beg a central question in the control of public risk.

* * *

* * * Risk, we suggested, can be seen as the function of expected mortality or morbidity, or what we shall here refer to as expected annual fatalities or "body counts," and in these terms many public risk technologies might indeed seem to be relatively safe. Those who favor modern technological developments do so in part precisely because they, like most experts, gauge risk in just this way. They may disagree about details, such as whether one looks at total expected deaths, deaths per person or per hour of exposure, or loss of life expectancy due to exposure, but generally speaking "experts appear to see riskiness as synonymous with expected annual mortality [and morbidity]."[118] So, for example, when technical experts are asked to rank the risks of various activities and technologies, "their responses correlate highly with technical estimates of annual fatalities."[119] When experts write about relative risk, they implicitly or explicitly use body counts as the relevant measure. And, in a way seemingly consistent with the logic of their method, they insist that a death is a death is a death—1,000 lives lost in a single anticipated annual catastrophe, or through many accidents expected every year, or lost ten-fold but only once every decade on average, or lost in a single community or across the country, are all the same to them.

In the view of experts, then, risk is a one-dimensional phenomenon * * *.

For the lay person, risk is *n*-dimensional, as William Lowrance suggested in an early study. He observed that a variety of considerations in addition to expected fatalities and injuries affect people's judgments about risk: involuntary exposure, delayed effects, scientific uncertainty about the hazard in question, "dreaded" versus common hazards (for example, the threat of death from invisible radiation as opposed to an auto accident), irreversible consequences, and others. Since the time of Lowrance's work, any number of studies have found "that many attributes other than death rates determine judgments of riskiness" by lay people, whose "model of what constitutes risk appears to be much richer than that held by most technical experts." Thus the public is known to be concerned about risks that have catastrophic potential, that are

118. Slovic, *"Perception of Risk,"* 236 Sci. 280, 283 (1983) (citation omitted); *see also* Slovic, Fischhoff & Lichtenstein, *"Facts and Fears: Understanding Perceived Risk,"* in Societal Risk Assessment: How Safe is Safe Enough? 181, 191–92 (R. Schwing & W. Albers, Jr. eds. 1980) (experts view risk as synonymous with technical fatality estimates).

119. Slovic, Fischhoff & Lichtenstein, *"Regulation of Risk: A Psychological Perspective,"* in Regulatory Policy and the Social Sciences 241, 263 (R. Noll ed. 1985)

[hereinafter Slovic, Fischhoff & Lichtenstein, *Regulation of Risk*]; *see also id.* at 266 (Fig. 4) (showing that experts' risk judgments are closely associated with annual fatality rates); Slovic, Fischhoff & Lichtenstein, *Rating the Risks, supra* note 93, at 19 (study results showed that "[t]he experts' mean judgments were so closely related to the statistical or calculated frequencies that it seems reasonable to conclude that they viewed the risk of an activity or technology as synonymous with its annual fatalities").

unfamiliar, uncontrollable, or involuntary, that threaten future generations, that would concentrate fatalities in time or space, that are distinc-
tively threatening as opposed to widespread and shared by the general
population, that are manmade as opposed to natural. * * *

* * *

Return, then, to the public's rich image of risk, and reflect for a
moment on its many dimensions. People have a lower tolerance for
involuntary than for voluntary exposure.[140] Even on its surface, the
concern here is easily understood, and closely related to the dimensions
of uncontrollability and uncertainty. Voluntary exposure presupposes
knowledge. Knowledge coupled with freedom of action facilitates individual choice and efforts to control events bearing on the choice. To be
forced to face a risk, on the other hand, or to be ignorant of it, or to
sense that no one is really in command of it, leaves one's well-being in
the hands of others, or of no one. Either alternative is obviously inferior,
under most circumstances, to being in charge.

Upon deeper examination, this sense of voluntariness might trivial-
ize the true concern. Suppose my situation (say I am an unskilled
worker) "forces" me to "choose" a risky occupation, in exchange for
some wage premium. Is my exposure to the risk "voluntary"? Suppose,
more generally, that I rightly see life as full of difficult choices. Is it
sensible to say that, given my power to choose—given that any choice is
"voluntary"—I should accept without complaint whatever consequences
follow? The answer might be yes if the world were organized in a way
consistent with ideal values and principles, but it is not. Behind the
notion of voluntariness, then, there may lurk more fundamental concerns about autonomy and equality and power among individuals in the
society, for it is the pre-existence of these that lets free choice be morally
interesting. People perhaps are saying that some risks seem consistent
with such ideals and others not, and registering the view by showing a
greater acceptance of risks that they regard as "voluntary" in fundamentally important ways, as opposed to "chosen" in some narrower
sense.

The foregoing account enlightens us about other popular dimensions
of risk, such as the enhanced dislike of delayed (latent) effects, and of
irreversible ones. Latency frustrates knowledge, and irreversibility frustrates control. They make it more difficult for us to govern our own
circumstances—and also to govern our governors. How do we hold
accountable officials whose mistakes or misdeeds manifest themselves
only decades after a term of office? And how do we correct for what they
have done, if what they have done is uncorrectable? Latency and irrever-

---

140. *See* Starr, "*Social Benefit versus Technological Risk: What Is Our Society Willing to Pay for Safety?,*" 165 Sci. 1232, 1237 (1969); *see also* Slovic, *supra* note 118, at 281–83 (discussing Starr's findings). There is some indication that the volun-
tary-involuntary distinction actually serves as a proxy for other concerns, such as cata-
strophic potential, dread, uncontrollability, and like factors * * *.

sibility practically deny us the fruits of trial-and-error, perhaps the best means yet devised by which to resolve uncertainty.

What of the special dislike of manmade as opposed to natural hazards? Once again, a story grows out of what has been said thus far: Humans might treat each other with motives that Nature could never have, and this matters. Mark Sagoff develops this theme in the course of considering why the government should regulate artificial risks more strictly than natural ones, even if they are "no more dangerous" (obviously, in the sense of body counting). First, people are responsible for artificial risks, but not for natural ones, and the government's job is to regulate what people do. Second, only manmade risks can, in any meaningful sense, threaten autonomy, an additional reason to be especially wary of them. Third, the harms we suffer because of the acts of others carry special injury; we mourn the deaths from a natural flood but resent, deeply, the ones from a broken dam. We "are concerned not simply with safety but with responsibility and guilt as well."

These same concerns arise in the case of those manmade risks we and others classify as "public": risks generated by highly centralized high technologies. This is especially so because public risks entail so much uncertainty (given their complexity), imply such considerable power, and are capable of such calamitous effects. The last consideration, in particular, implicates the public's aversion to the possibility of disastrous consequences and brings us to the cluster of factors that enter into what is termed "dread." Dread correlates significantly with some aspects of risk that we have already discussed, such as involuntariness and uncontrollability, but also with such others as inequitable distributions, threats to future generations, and catastrophic potential—each of which speaks almost for itself.

The idea of inequitable distributions, for example, reflects the view that just as a right thinking society should concern itself with the distribution of wealth, so too should it do so with the distribution of risk. For example, risks that might result in death or disease are often considered worth taking because they confer significant benefits not otherwise available. This risk burden may be regarded as equitably distributed only if it is borne by those who simultaneously enjoy the benefits. Burdens imposed on others, or diverted to future generations, generate worries about exploitation. Alternatively, risks concentrated in time and space might be regarded as inequitable or otherwise unacceptable because concentration can result in losses that are avoided by broader distributions. This suggests, then, a link between inequitable distributions and catastrophic potential. Concentrated risks can threaten whole communities, and the loss of a community (think of Love Canal, of Chernobyl) is the loss of a valued thing distinct and apart from the disaggregated bodies of a community's citizens.

Notes

1. Cognitive psychologists in recent years have developed a new descriptive theory of how people make decisions under conditions of risk and

uncertainty. A dominant theme in the theory is that most people do not evaluate risky circumstances in the manner assumed by conventional decision theory: specifically, they do not seek to maximize the expected value of some function when selecting among actions with uncertain outcome. This cognitive theory has implications for regulatory policies designed to control risk to life, health, and the environment. For an interesting discussion of the theory, see Noll and Krier, "Some Implications of Cognitive Psychology for Risk Regulation," 19 *J. Legal Studies* 747 (1990).

2. For more discussion of how and why experts and lay persons assess environmental risks differently, see H. Margolis, *Dealing With Risk: Why the Public and the Experts Disagree on Environmental Issues* (1996); Margolis "A New Account of Expert/Lay Conflicts of Risk Intuition," 8 *Duke Envt'l L. & Pol'y Forum* 115 (1997).

3. In Page, "A Generic View of Toxic Chemicals and Similar Risks," 7 *Ecology L.Q.* 207 (1978), the author discusses common characteristics shared by certain environmental problems such as nuclear power, synthetic chemicals, ozone depletion, and recombinant DNA. Two of the characteristics are the potential for catastrophic costs, and the low "subjective" probability (uncertain because lacking a solid actuarial basis) of the catastrophic outcome. Together, these two characteristics result in what Page calls the "zero-infinity dilemma" for risk managers dealing with such environmental problems. To illuminate this dilemma, he gives the following example:

> [S]uppose that 60 of 10,060 chemicals are highly carcinogenic to humans and that a test has been developed which in the following sense is highly reliable. The test scores positive for carcinogenic chemicals ninety-five percent of the time and scores negative for noncarcinogens ninety-four percent of the time. A chemical, drawn from the 10,060, tests positive. What is the probability that the chemical is carcinogenic? Many people are surprised to learn that the actual probability, which can easily be derived from Bayes' Theorem, is only 0.09. As suggested by Kahneman's research, people often expect too much in the way of proof from present tests and research techniques in problems of environmental risk.

An unfortunate generalization arises directly from the underlying mathematics of this example: as the probability of an environmental effect approaches zero, the probability of a positive test being falsely positive approaches one. In other words, as an environmental risk problem takes on more of the characteristics of a zero-infinity dilemma, the probability of a false positive becomes higher. Simultaneously, the management problem becomes tougher because the more an environmental risk problem exhibits the zero-infinity characteristic, the greater is the need to prevent a false negative—in this instance, the labeling of a guilty chemical as innocent.

SUNSTEIN, "WHICH RISKS FIRST?"[e]

1997 *The University of Chicago Legal Forum* 101, 103–105, 112–114 (1997).

Environmental protection has many purposes in addition to the protection of human life, including prevention of adverse health effects short of mortality, aesthetic goals, recreational goals, and prevention of deaths and adverse health effects in animals and plants. These purposes should also be taken into account in deciding which risks are most serious....

* * *

... Some people think that the government should try to maximize the number of total lives saved.[6] If one program would save one hundred lives, and another eighty, the government should (other things being equal) begin with the first program. But other people, referring to pervasive differences between lay and expert evaluations of risk, reject this idea. They say that lay people have more complex, "richer" judgments about which risks are worst and that these judgments should govern regulatory policy. On this view, there is a danger that expert judgments will hide controversial ideas about rationality behind a technocratic smokescreen.

... I reject both of these views. A basic assumption is that the American constitutional order is a republic, or a deliberative democracy, in which public representatives are not supposed merely to register existing judgments but "to refine and enlarge the public view."[7] If the issue of risk regulation is seen in these terms, representatives should attend to reflective citizen judgments, but they should not treat those judgments uncritically or accept them regardless of the reasons offered on their behalf.... And if we examine the reasons that underlie risk-related judgments, we will conclude that it would be obtuse to say that government should attempt to maximize the number of lives saved, no matter the source and nature of relevant risks. Lives are not fungible with lives; it matters a great deal for what purpose and in what context lives are being put in danger. But it would also be odd to rely entirely on lay judgments, which are frequently based on confusion, ignorance, and selective attention. When those judgments are based on misunderstandings of the facts, they should play no role in policy.

I contend that government should attempt a three-step inquiry. First it should try to estimate *decently-livable life-years saved*, rather than total lives saved. Thus the first step in its analysis should be to see how much aggregate extension of decently-livable years can be brought about by different regulatory initiatives. The second step should incorporate lay judgments to the extent that these are based on reasonable judgments of value rather than factual error or selective attention. In this way, regulators should ask if regulatory priorities should be shifted from the aggregate measure by exploring whether there are important qualities in the context that call for a shift. The key questions here are:

—Is the risk inequitably distributed?

---

6. This is the tendency in Stephen Breyer, *Breaking the Vicious Circle: Toward Effective Risk Regulation* (Harvard 1993).

7. Federalist 10 (Madison), in Max Beloff, ed., *The Federalist* 45 (Basil Blackwell 2d ed. 1987).

—Is it especially dreaded?

—Is it run involuntarily?

—How easily can it be controlled by those exposed?

Answers to these questions may call for an adjustment of the first-stage judgment. As we will see, however, the second two questions raise complex issues, for risks are not "voluntary or not" or "uncontrollable or not," but instead come with small or high costs of avoidance. The ordinary criterion of decently-livable life-years should be adjusted upward when the costs of risk avoidance are especially high, and adjusted downward when the costs of risk avoidance are especially low. The third step consists of an incorporation of effects short of mortality, including (but not limited to) morbidity, adverse effects on aesthetics and recreation, and mortality effects for plants and animals.

* * *

There is considerable crudeness . . . in the idea of "lives saved" as the regulatory maximand. Of course no program "saves lives"; at best it extends them. Compare two regulations. The first extends the lives of one hundred elderly people, but in doing so, it gives them five additional years, accompanied by considerable pain and distress. The second extends the lives of eighty children, and in doing so, it gives each of them a statistical likelihood of fifty or more years of life. The second policy seems preferable to the first along two important dimensions. *First*: Lives are certainly not fungible, but where regulatory resources are limited and where choices have to be made, it makes sense (other things being equal and as an administrable start) to save as many years as possible. Other things being equal, many years should be chosen over few. *Second*: If government has a choice between preserving lives in a way that ensures decently-livable years and preserving lives in a way that ensures a barely functional and extremely painful continued existence, it should choose the former. To someone who has a choice between death and five years of constant and considerable pain, the latter will probably seem a lot better; but for government regulators, it is preferable to provide five good years rather than five difficult ones if there is a choice. We might conclude, then, that government agencies should shift their attention from "lives saved" to "decently-livable life-years saved."

* * *

An especially controversial issue lurks in the background: it is possible that some lives might be considered not decently-livable because of unjust or highly disadvantageous social conditions. Desperately poor people, for example, may lack decent life prospects already, and a small incremental reduction in their health may seem to push them below the relevant "floor." For purposes of regulatory policy, this ought not to be counted. If it did count, regulatory policy would be devoted to the protection of those already well-off and to the neglect of those in desperate conditions; thus one social injustice would be compounded by another. The question is whether the saved years meet a decent floor, and it should be stipulated that this criterion is met by lives filled with extreme difficulty because of social and economic deprivation alone.

Notes

1. Sunstein's proposal has some interesting normative implications. Consider a situation where the government has the choice between saving the lives of one infant (with a life expectancy of 80 years) and seventy elderly people (each with a life expectancy of a year). Under Sunstein's analysis, the seventy elderly people count for less than the one infant. Is this tilt against saving the lives of the elderly normatively appealing as a governmental policy? Do people value their years of remaining life at a constant rate–that is, does a twenty-year old place as much weight on a possible one-year reduction in life-expectancy as a seventy-year old, as the "years of life saved" approach assumes? (On the other hand, isn't Sunstein correct that weighing a risk to an infant and an eighty-year-old equally violates common cultural norms?)

2. What additional information about exposures and latency would be required to operationalize Sunstein's approach? Is this information likely to be available, and would demanding that agencies take this information into account overstrain their ability to make meaningful quantatative estimates?

L. ROBERTS, CANCER TODAY: ORIGINS, PREVENTION, AND TREATMENT[f]

4–11 (1984).

Although the incidence and mortality rates for lung cancer have soared during the last 50 years, the age-adjusted rates for cancers at most other sites have remained steady or declined. For some cancers, this reflects a drop in the incidence, or the number of new cancer cases; for others, the striking improvements in the cure rate for certain cancers.

Cancer takes many forms, striking different types of cells in diverse parts of the body. Each cancer runs its own distinctive course. For instance, although cancer usually appears as a tumor—a visible mass of cancer cells—in leukemia the malignant cells largely remain dispersed throughout the body in the blood and bone marrow.

All of these cancers, however, share the same fundamental properties. Cancer is a breakdown of the orderly process of cell growth and differentiation. It seems to begin with a change in a single cell, presumably a mutation in that cell's genetic apparatus. This change transforms the cell profoundly; it begins to divide without restraint, failing to differentiate into its mature form. Eventually, this altered cell will give rise to billions of other aberrant cells, cancer cells, that invade and destroy nearby tissues. As the colony grows, some of these cells will break off, or metastasize, and be carried by the blood or lymph stream to remote parts of the body where they will invade other tissues as well.

* * *

The Biology of Cancer

In the early 1970s, cancer research was galvanized by the discovery of oncogenes, specific genes that can trigger a cell's unbridled growth. Since that time, close to 30 of these cancer genes have been isolated from both human and animal cells. In laboratory experiments, the activity of a single one of them is often sufficient to transform normal cells to cancer cells.

In the past few years, molecular biologists have been able to decipher the genetic code of these cancer genes. To their surprise, they found that the oncogenes are remarkably similar, if not identical, to benign genes that are normally present within the cell. It now appears that each cell contains certain normal genes that when activated or altered in some way can start the cell on the path to cancer. Many cancer researchers suspect that all agents of cancer—radiation, chemicals, and viruses—act upon these genes, somehow releasing their malignant potential.

* * *

Diet and Cancer

Even before the discovery of oncogenes, it was thought that cancer, at least in some of its manifestations, was the product of the interaction of genes and the environment. Certain agents, such as ultraviolet and ionizing radiation, some chemicals, and some viruses, can initiate cancer, presumably by causing a genetic mutation. From recent work, it is tempting to think that the mutation occurs on an oncogene. Still other external or environmental agents can promote or facilitate the process of carcinogenesis without actually inducing it.

There is now widespread agreement that roughly 85 percent of all cancers are caused by broad environmental factors, including lifestyle patterns. The rest, presumably, have a hereditary basis, or else arise from spontaneous metabolic events. Identifying the environmental factors in cancer, however, has not been easy. At this stage, viruses appear to play only a minor role in human cancers. Occupational chemicals are thought to be responsible for 4 percent of all cancers; environmental chemicals for an estimated 2 percent. Tobacco is by far the largest documented cause of cancer, accounting for roughly 30 percent of all cancers in lungs and some other sites.

Recently, epidemiological studies similar to those that uncovered an association between smoking and cancer have detected a link between the foods that people eat and the cancers that afflict them. Overall, dietary factors are thought to be responsible for another 30 percent of the cancer incidence in the United States, which could mean that a substantial portion of those cancers may be preventable.

With a few exceptions, the studies have not turned up specific culprits—certain foods or constituents of foods that cause cancer. Nor does the major problem appear to be food additives or contaminants. Rather, * * * cancer risk is associated with certain broad dietary patterns and the consumption of major nutrients. Specifically, a diet high in fats and fatty meats seems to carry a risk of cancer. Salt-cured, salt-pickled, and highly spiced foods are also suspect. On the other hand, the consumption of high-fiber grains, vegetables, and fruits seems to protect against cancer. In short, cancer risk appears to be a matter of dietary choice, of the balance and proportion of nutrients in the diet, as well as of methods of food preparation.

The case against diet is still circumstantial. These epidemiological studies have revealed broad associations, not causality. Further laboratory and clinical studies are necessary to determine exactly how diet contributes to cancer. For instance, the specific dietary constituents that may be responsible for observed carcinogenic or protective effects are not known, nor are their mechanisms of action. Nonetheless, several federal agencies have decided that the weight of evidence is strong enough to suggest that the public modify its eating habits in accordance with the findings of these studies.

This is not to imply that a modification in diet would elicit a reduction in cancer incidence similar to the one that would result if smoking were eliminated. Studies to date have made it abundantly clear that the relationship of diet to cancer is exceedingly complex. The risk factors in diet cannot simply be eliminated; some of the dietary constituents that seem to pose greatest cancer risk are essential human nutrients.

In addition, * * * it has become increasingly clear from another line of inquiry that natural mutagens and carcinogens are ubiquitous throughout the human diet, occurring in common vegetables, fruits, meats, nuts, and beverages. Conversely, some natural substances, such as the precursor of vitamin A and the mineral selenium, appear to be anticarcinogens, capable of preventing the process of malignant transformation in laboratory studies.

At this stage, the potency of most of the natural carcinogens and the magnitude of risk they pose to human health have not been determined, nor is it known if and how they might interact with anticarcinogens in the diet. What does seem clear, however, is that it will not be possible to specify a risk-free diet.

Cancer researchers generally agree that adoption of a low-risk diet should help to prevent some cancers. The exact benefit to be gained, however, cannot be predicted until the biological mechanisms underlying the association between diet and cancer are better understood.

* * * Traditionally, the government has acted through its regulatory policies to minimize human exposure to harmful substances in foods. It has set standards for food additives and natural contaminants, as well as for pesticide residues and other industrial chemicals that might enter the food supply. Now that foods themselves, not the substances added to them, appear to pose the greatest cancer risk, this regulatory approach no longer appears sufficient, although it is certainly a vital element of any food safety policy. Indeed, the most effective strategy for preventing cancer may simply be to provide information that will help consumers make intelligent dietary decisions, giving them an increasing share of the responsibility for their own protection.

Notes

1. Roberts' book draws upon the work of other scientists such as Drs. Bruce Ames of Berkeley and Richard Doll and Richard Peto of Oxford University, who since 1980 have come to believe that manmade carcinogens may be responsible for a much smaller percentage of human cancers in the United States than was thought earlier. In a study for the Congressional Office of Technology Assessment, Doll and Peto estimated that two-thirds of all cancer deaths in this country were caused by smoking (30 percent) and dietary factors *other* than chemical additives and pollutants (35 percent), such as natural carcinogens, excess fats that increase production of carcinogens in the body, and lack of fibers to flush potential carcinogens out of the bowels. Doll and Peto concluded that less than 8 percent of the cancer deaths resulted from carcinogens in the workplace, environmental pollution, food additives, and industrial products. Ames has found that natural carcinogens are far more pervasive than manmade ones. See Doll and Peto, "The Causes of Cancer: Quantitative Estimates of Avoidable Risks of Cancer in the United States Today," 66 *J.Nat.Cancer Inst.* 1191 (1981); Boffey, "After Years of Cancer Alarms, Progress Amid the Mistakes," *New York Times,* March 20, 1984, p. 17, c. 2.

2. If indeed almost two-thirds of all cancer deaths in the United States are caused by smoking and by dietary factors other than chemical additives and pollutants, while less than one-tenth of the deaths are caused by carcinogens in the workplace, environmental pollution, food additives, and industrial products, what do these data suggest should be the government's strategy for reducing cancer mortality? As many of the materials in the remainder of this chapter and in Chapter VI indicate, our regulatory efforts (other than required labels warning smokers of health risks) have in fact been directed primarily at the latter four causes.

DONIGER, "FEDERAL REGULATION OF VINYL CHLORIDE: A SHORT COURSE IN THE LAW AND POLICY OF TOXIC SUBSTANCES CONTROL"[g]

7 *Ecology Law Quarterly* 500, 500–02, 508–14 (1978).

I. BASIC POLICY PROBLEMS IN TOXIC SUBSTANCES CONTROL: DECIDING UNDER UNCERTAINTY AND BALANCING INCOMMENSURABLE INTERESTS

Two cardinal problems are endemic to any scheme for regulating substances that cause cancer or other long-term, serious health or environmental effects of relatively low probability. First, all decisions must be made under substantial uncertainty about the medical and ecological risks, technological difficulties, and economic costs associated with different degrees of exposure. Second, all decisions involve tradeoffs among groups with interests that are not readily comparable. * * *

A. The Limits of Cancer Risk Assessment

* * *

* * * Studies of cancer incidence in particular groups have shown strong statistical connections between exposure to certain chemical substances and particular cancers. The connection between tobacco smoke and lung cancer is the most widely known. Markedly elevated cancer rates are also found among certain occupational groups in the United States and in other highly industrialized countries. Cancer rates are elevated where air and drinking water are contaminated with industrial organic chemicals. In general, cancer rates are higher than average in American urbanized areas. * * *

The causal relationships underlying the statistical connections observed in humans have been confirmed for many substances by controlled experiments on animals. With one possible exception [arsenic], all substances related to cancer in humans have been shown to cause cancer in animals. In addition, animal experiments have implicated 1,500–2,000 other chemical substances as potential human carcinogens. Many of these substances are synthetic organic chemicals that have been in commercial use only since the 1930s. Because cancer is a latent disease that typically manifests itself only 15 to 40 years after exposure begins, it is too early to know the effects of chemicals that have been in widespread use for only this short period.

This evidence suggests that cancer rates could be cut significantly by reducing human exposure to the disease's chemical causes. * * * In order to make the best use of the resources available to prevent cancer, precise data on which substances are carcinogenic and on how dangerous they are at various levels of exposure would be helpful. * * * Even where a qualitative relationship is visible, precise quantitative estimates of risks to humans cannot be made reliably, particularly for low risks on the order of one case in 10,000 or more subjects.

In the first place, not enough is known about how chemical carcinogens operate, especially at the cellular level. There is general agreement that the substances cause changes in the genetic material of an individual cell or in the mechanisms through which the genetic material controls a cell's behavior, inducing it to multiply wildly. There is uncertainty and disagreement on whether only one such "hit" need occur or whether a certain sequence of independent hits by the same or different substances is needed. * * * Opinions differ on whether there are chemical reactions that detoxify certain amounts of a carcinogen by converting it into a harmless substance, or that repair genetic changes after they have occurred. The metabolic "pathway" of a substance from its point of entry (*e.g.,* lungs, skin, or digestive system) to its point of damage is also often uncertain.

Whether or not there are defense or repair mechanisms has profound implications for strategies for cancer prevention. If the "one-hit" model is accurate, and if there are no detoxification, repair, or other defense mechanisms, then as little as one molecule of a carcinogenic substance, interacting with the appropriate portion of the susceptible cell, can cause an irreversible cancer. If multiple hits by different substances are needed, any one substance alone may not be carcinogenic (or may be only weakly so) but together these substances may be potent causes of the disease. If detoxification or repair mechanisms or other defenses exist, there may be safe doses—"thresholds"—below which no cancers will be caused. More important than the question of whether a threshold exists is the question of what risks to expect from a range of doses. Different propositions about cancer causation lead to different conclusions about the rate of cancer to expect from each dose.[42]

The second major source of uncertainty is a result of the limitations of available research techniques. Current methods for investigating the carcinogenicity of substances do not permit the verification or disproof of alternative theories of cancer causation. The methods are themselves also the subject of great controversy. Observation from direct human experiences is of limited utility. Purposeful experimentation on humans is ethically unacceptable, since the results often would be fatal. Human evidence of carcinogenesis usually comes from observation of occupational groups exposed, often unwittingly, to chemicals in the industrial economy. Some connections can be drawn in the general population, but

---

42. Some assumptions lead to the conclusion that threshold doses exist and that the risk at doses approaching the threshold declines to zero. Other models decline to decide whether there are thresholds. One major model has dose and response in a logarithmic relationship, with risk declining more rapidly than dose at low doses. This model yields higher risks for given doses than those which posit thresholds.

Other researchers argue that the dose-response relationship at low doses is likely to be linear, *i.e.,* that decreases in risk are probably proportional to reductions of dose. This approach yields a risk for a given dose higher than the risks estimated by the other two approaches at least at low doses.

for the most part humans are exposed to too many different substances at unknown doses for unknown periods to permit statistically reliable conclusions to be drawn. Moreover, there are synergistic and antagonistic interactions between chemicals that drastically complicate drawing conclusions about the effects of each chemical. Finally, because latency periods run 15 to 40 years or longer, definitive studies of effects on humans are impracticable.

Studies on rodents are the major source of data on the carcinogenicity of chemicals. Their response characteristics are considered essentially similar to those of humans, so that a substance carcinogenic to one is likely to be carcinogenic to the other. But although the qualitative inferences are quite sound, there are limitations on the ability of the animal tests to indicate the magnitude of human risks. It is difficult both to detect small risks in test animals and to translate risks for animals into risks for humans.

The difficulty in detecting small risks is statistical in nature. For practical and financial reasons, nearly all experiments on animals involve small numbers of subjects, usually no more than a few hundred. In so small a group, a chemical must cause an effect at a relatively high rate for the relationship to be confidently distinguished from random occurrences of the same event.[49] The dose of a substance that induces cancer at rates detectable in such tests is often far higher than most people experience. The critical question is whether lower doses cause cancer, and at what rates. An effect occurring at a very low rate stands a good chance of not being observed in so small a test group, so that the failure to observe an effect in such a test is not a reliable indication of the substance's safety for a larger population.[51] Thus, no test has confirmed the existence of any threshold or detoxification mechanism or resolved any other basic aspect of the theoretical controversies discussed above.

To investigate the effects of low doses directly would require experiments involving enormous numbers of animals. To demonstrate with 95 percent confidence that a given low dose of just one substance causes fewer than one cancer in a million subjects would require a test involving at least *six million* animals. Such "mega-mouse" experiments generally are considered impracticably expensive and vulnerable to laboratory errors that can destroy the statistical reliability of the results.

Limited to observations at unrealistically high doses in unrealistically low numbers, the scientist's recourse is to use mathematical models of dose-response relationships to extrapolate from experimental results downward to the effects of low doses. However, like the theories on

---

49. For an explanation for laymen of the statistical issues, see W. Lowrance, *Of Acceptable Risk* 60–64 (1976).

51. Three examples illustrate the point. In a test involving 100 animals each in an experimental and a control group, if no tumors are detected in either group, there is a 1.0% chance that the real rate of cancer is as high as 4.5%. With 1,000 animals in each group and no tumors, there remains a 1.0% chance that the real rate is as high as 0.46%, or 4.6 animals out of each 1,000. If only ten animals are used in each group and the results show no tumors, the potential error increases drastically; there is a 1.0% chance that the real rate is as high as 37.0%.

which they are based, the models yield widely divergent estimates of the risk associated with each low dose. The extent of the differences is astounding. For example, the major models differ by a factor of *100,000* on the size of the dose that creates a risk of one cancer in a million subjects. The models do provide credible outer limits for the risk associated with each dose, and they do permit the ranking of carcinogens in rough order of their potency. But they cannot provide the regulator with precise estimates of the risks of low doses.

More uncertainty is added to risk estimates by our ignorance of how to translate dose-response data across species lines. There simply is not enough known to determine if humans are more or less sensitive to a given dose of a carcinogen than the test animals.

Several new techniques for assessing carcinogenicity are developing, but these do not yet hold out the promise of yielding quantitative risk estimates or of answering the basic questions about how cancer is caused. There are "quick" tests—such as the Ames test—of chemicals' abilities to mutate bacteria or other single-celled organisms. There is a high correlation between the ability to cause such mutations and carcinogenicity. Currently, however, the value of the "quick" tests is primarily qualitative; they may be able to distinguish strong from weak carcinogens, but cannot give more precise risk estimates.

One important consequence of the uncertainty about the size of small risks is that a regulatory agency does not know the *marginal* risk at each dose; that is, the agency does not know how great a difference in risk is caused by small changes in dose. * * *

Purely scientific problems of risk assessment are aggravated to some degree for regulatory agencies by their incomplete access to information. Most toxicological research is carried out or sponsored by the industries that make or market the substances being evaluated; industrial researchers have incentives to withhold negative information or to perform poorly designed and executed experiments incapable of revealing negative information. * * *

In sum, because the nature of chemical carcinogenesis is unknown, and because available research techniques are limited in their ability to predict human risks from exposure to carcinogens, the only conclusion that may be drawn with complete certainty is that no level of exposure to a chemical that causes cancer in animals is sure to be safe. Neither experimental nor theoretical analysis can give the agencies precise estimates of the risks associated with low doses of substances that are known to cause cancer in humans or animals at higher doses. Nor can regulators be sure how sensitive risks are to changes in dose. At present, the best available techniques produce only broad estimates of the outer limits of risk.

Note

In 1984 a draft report outlining principles and guidelines to be followed by federal regulatory agencies in assessing the carcinogenicity of chemicals was published by the White House Office of Science and Technology Policy. 49 Fed.Reg. 21594–21661 (May 22, 1984). Written by scientists from nine agencies over a period of two years, the report said that existing models which predict that chemicals will not cause cancer until humans have been exposed to certain threshold levels have failed to gain "universal acceptance within the scientific community," and that in regulating suspected carcinogens, agencies therefore should assume that risk is linear at lower dose levels, i.e., that there is at least some risk associated with any exposure. The report also affirmed that animal studies are good indicators of carcinogenicity. The White House said that the guidelines were intended for use by EPA in assessing the risk of cancer posed by substances regulated under the Clean Air Act, Clean Water Act, Safe Drinking Water Act, RCRA, CERCLA, FIFRA, and TSCA. Other federal agencies directed to use the guidelines were the Occupational Safety and Health Administration and the Food and Drug Administration. See 15 *Envir.Rep.* 145 (1984).

Subsequently in 1984, EPA published Proposed Guidelines for Carcinogen Risk Assessment, 49 Fed.Reg. 46294. This document was the first proposed revision of the Agency's 1976 Interim Procedures and Guidelines for the Health Risk Assessment of Suspected Carcinogens, 41 Fed.Reg. 21402–21405 (1976), and was based on the Office of Science and Technology report discussed in the preceding paragraph. The format was patterned after that proposed in National Research Council, *Risk Assessment in the Federal Government: Managing the Process* (1983). The proposed guidelines provided a detailed analysis of EPA's method of determining a substance's risk, including the first Agency-wide numerical indexing of carcinogenicity. See also four related EPA proposals: Proposed Guidelines for Exposure Assessment, 49 Fed.Reg. 46304 (Nov. 23, 1984); Proposed Guidelines for Mutagenicity Risk Assessment, 49 Fed.Reg. 46314 (Nov. 23, 1984); Proposed Guidelines for the Health Assessment of Suspect Developmental Toxicants, 49 Fed.Reg. 46324 (Nov. 23, 1984); and Proposed Guidelines for the Health Risk Assessment of Chemical Mixtures, 50 Fed.Reg. 1170 (Jan. 9, 1985).

In 1986, EPA issued its final Guidelines for Carcinogen Risk Assessment, 51 Fed.Reg. 33992. The risk assessment practices adopted therein were evaluated in Latin, "Good Science, Bad Regulation, and Toxic Risk Assessment," 5 *Yale J. on Regulation* 89 (1988). Latin concluded that EPA's pursuit of "good science," in an area where scientific conclusions are difficult or impossible to attain, is likely to result in "reduced public protection against potential toxic hazards, increased regulatory decision-making costs, and expanded opportunities for obstructive behavior by Agency bureaucrats or private parties hostile to toxics regulation." Id. at 90.

In 1994, a report by the National Academy of Sciences' Committee on Risk Assessment of Hazardous Air Pollutants (see § 112(*o*) of the Clean Air Act) concluded that EPA's general approach to quantitative risk assessment was sound, though the report recommended some seventy changes in the agency's practices. National Academy of Sciences, Committee on Risk Assessment of Hazardous Air Pollutants, *Science and Judgment in Risk Assessment* (1994). For example, the report called for development of a multilevel approach, first using relatively inexpensive techniques to screen out chemicals that do not pose significant health risks, with other chemicals then undergoing repeated evaluations to allow for better estimates as new data and scientific techniques become available. The report was delayed because of a dispute among committee members about EPA's use of conservative "default assumptions" in risk assessments, and about ways to substitute chemical test data for those assumptions. Default assumptions, which may involve specific numerical values, are used when actual data are not available. Because the committee could not reach consensus on this issue, members supporting opposing views wrote papers which appeared as appendices to the report. See 24 *Envir.Rep.* 1699 (1994).

Subsequently in 1994, in response to the NAS report, EPA said it was moving ahead on twenty initiatives to improve its risk assessment procedures. Among eight areas receiving special priority were risk assessments for hazardous air pollutants, revisions of the 1986 cancer risk assessment guidelines, and assessment of non-cancer risks. See 25 *Envir.Rep.* 476 (1994). Thereafter, EPA released "Draft Revisions to the Guidelines for Carcinogen Risk Assessment," allowing for more flexibility in the use of real data and less rigid reliance on the default assumptions of the 1986 guidelines. See 1 *Risk Policy Report,* No. 1, at 5–6, 17 (Sept. 16, 1994).

In 1996 EPA published "Proposed Guidelines for Ecological Risk Assessments," 61 *Fed. Reg.* 47552 (Sept. 9, 1996). The proposal generally followed recommendations in National Academy of Sciences, Committee on Risk Assessment of Hazardous Air Pollutants, *Science and Judgment in Risk Assessment* (1994). There was a 90–day public review and comment period, during which more than 40 sets of comments were received, and EPA expects to take final action on the proposal in the fall of 1998.

Traditionally, EPA has relied heavily on rodent bioassays to establish whether a particular agent causes cancer. Rats are given a chemical and then watched for two years to see whether tumors develop. In contrast, the proposed guidelines call for using a wider range of information, including genetic data, information on the agent's physical and chemical structure, and testing for biological effects leading up to tumor development. EPA would drop its long-standing scheme for classifying cancer hazards by assigning each substance to one of six categories, starting with Category A for known human carcinogens. Instead, the agent would be classified according to one of three "descriptors" of its human carcinogenic potential: "known/likely", "cannot be determined", and "not likely".

Each substance also would receive a narrative description of its potential to cause cancer under different conditions, as well as a short summary of the animal and human evidence supporting these conclusions. These "weight of evidence" narratives are intended to give risk managers more information than a simple category designation. The proposed guidelines would drop EPA's previous assumption that all dose-response relationships are strictly linear. Risk assessors could use non-linear approaches to estimating toxic effects at low doses, which could lead to known carcinogens being declared safe below certain thresholds. The guidelines also would allow risk assessors to consider different exposure routes—for example, inhalation versus ingestion—as well as effects on different populations, such as children and pregnant women.

B. JUDICIAL VIEWS CONCERNING MANAGEMENT OF UNCERTAIN RISKS

RESERVE MINING CO. v. ENVIRONMENTAL PROTECTION AGENCY

United States Court of Appeals, Eighth Circuit, 1975.
514 F.2d 492.

BRIGHT, CIRCUIT JUDGE.

[Reserve Mining disposed of great quantities of mining by-products by discharging them into Lake Superior. These materials contained asbestos, which is known to be a cause of cancer when inhaled. The district court enjoined further discharges, which meant the closing of the facility. On appeal, the Eighth Circuit began by considering two issues: "first, whether the ingestion of fibers, as compared with their inhalation, poses any danger whatsoever; and second, should ingestion pose a danger, whether the exposure resulting from Reserve's discharge may be said to present a legally cognizable risk to health."]

1. INGESTION OF FIBERS AS A DANGER TO HEALTH

All epidemiological studies which associate asbestos fibers with harm to health are based upon inhalation of these fibers by humans. Thus, although medical opinion agrees that fibers entering the respiratory tract can interact with body tissues and produce disease, it is unknown whether the same can be said of fibers entering the digestive tract. If asbestos fibers do not interact with digestive tissue, they are presumably eliminated as waste without harmful effect upon the body.

The evidence bearing upon possible harm from ingestion of fibers falls into three areas: first, the court-sponsored tissue study, designed to measure whether asbestos fibers are present in the tissues of long-time Duluth residents; second, animal experiments designed to measure whether, as a biological phenomenon, fibers can penetrate the gastrointestinal mucosa and thus interact with body tissues; third, the increased incidence of gastrointestinal cancer among workers occupationally exposed to asbestos, and the hypothesis that this increase may be due to the ingestion of fibers initially inhaled.

a. The Tissue Study

Recognizing the complete lack of any direct evidence (epidemiological or otherwise) on the issue of whether the ingestion of fibers poses a risk, the trial court directed that a tissue study be conducted to determine whether the tissues of long-time Duluth residents contain any residue of asbestoslike fibers.

The study sought to analyze by electron microscope the tissues of recently deceased Duluth residents who had ingested Duluth water for at least 15 years; that is, approximately since the beginning of Reserve's operations. As a "control" check on results, tissue samples were obtained from the deceased residents of Houston, Texas, where the water is free of asbestos fibers. Although this study was necessarily expedited, plaintiffs' principal medical witness, Dr. Selikoff, testified to the sound design of the study and expressed his belief that it would yield significant information.

Dr. Selikoff discovered asbestos is a carcinogen

One of the court-appointed experts, Dr. Frederick Pooley, in explaining the results of the study, stated that he found that the tissues of the Duluth residents were virtually free of any fibers which could be attributed to the Reserve discharge. Dr. Brown said of this study:

> It is my conclusion, from the tissue study, that residents of Duluth have not been found to have asbestiform fibers in their tissues when compared with Houston.

* * *

* * * [P]laintiffs argued, and the district court agreed, that because the specimens of tissue represented only a microscopically minute body area, the actual presence of fibers may have been overlooked.

We note that this limitation had not seemed dispositive prior to the study when Dr. Selikoff commented:

> I would think we should find some fibers there. We're looking for needles in a haystack, but that's all right, we should find needles in the haystack with all the difficulties of the study, the technical difficulties, if we examine sufficiently large numbers of samples in some instances we should find some fibers there.

The district court decided, and we agree, that the study cannot be deemed conclusive in exonerating the ingestion of fibers in Lake Superior water as a hazard. The negative results must, however, be given some weight in assessing the probabilities of harm from Reserve's discharge into water. The results also weigh heavily in indicating that no emergency or imminent hazard to health exists. Thus, while this study crucially bears on the determination of whether it is necessary to close Reserve down immediately, the negative results do not dispose of the broader issue of whether the ingestion of fibers poses some danger to public health justifying abatement on less immediate terms.

b. Animal Studies and Penetration of the Gastrointestinal Mucosa

At a somewhat more theoretical level, the determination of whether ingested fibers can penetrate the gastrointestinal mucosa bears on the issue of harm through ingestion. If penetration is biologically impossible, then presumably the interaction of the fibers with body tissues will not occur.

This medical issue has been investigated through experiments with animals which, unfortunately, have produced conflicting results. For example, Reserve witness Dr. Davis reported on his experiment in feeding crocidolite and chrysotile asbestos to rats for varying periods of up to six months. He killed the rats at the end of the period and examined their gastrointestinal tissues for evidence of fibers. At the time of trial, light and electron microscopy has so far revealed no evidence of fibers in the tissues.

Plaintiffs, however, cited contrary studies. Research by George Westlake, in which rats were fed a diet including chrysotile fibers, indicated that fibers had traveled through the colon wall and accumulated in the area of the mesothelium. Pontrefact, who injected chrysotile fibers into the stomachs of rats, found that fibers had dispersed throughout the body tissues.

On this conflicting scientific evidence, Dr. Brown testified that the Westlake and Pontrefact studies provide some support for the hypothesis that asbestos fibers can penetrate the gastrointestinal mucosa.[46]

c. Excess Gastrointestinal Cancer Among the Occupationally Exposed

The affirmative evidence supporting the proposition that the ingestion of fibers poses a danger to health focuses on the increased rate of gastrointestinal cancer among workers occupationally exposed to asbestos dust. Plaintiffs' experts attribute this excess incidence of gastrointestinal cancer to a theory that the asbestos workers first inhaled the asbestos dust and thereafter coughed up and swallowed the asbestos particles.

The attribution of health harm from ingestion rests upon a theoretical basis. As Dr. Selikoff explained, there are several possible explanations for the increased evidence of gastrointestinal cancer, some of which do not involve ingestion. Moreover, as noted previously, the excess rates of gastrointestinal cancer are generally "modest" and substantially lower than the excess rates of mesothelioma and lung cancer associated with inhalation of asbestos dust. Also, the experts advised that an analysis of a small exposed population may produce statistically "unstable" results.

The existence of an excess rate of gastrointestinal cancer among asbestos workers is a matter of concern. The theory that excess cancers may be attributed to the ingestion of asbestos fibers rests on a tenable medical hypothesis. Indeed, Dr. Selikoff testified that ingestion is the "probable" route accounting for the excess in gastrointestinal cancer.

---

46. We note from the record that while attempts to induce tumors in experimental animals through the inhalation of fibers have succeeded, attempts to induce tumors by ingestion have generally failed. Reserve witness Dr. Smith ventured the opinion, based on such studies, that there is no proof that the ingestion of fibers causes cancer in man. The failure to induce animal tumors by ingestion cannot be dispositive on the issue of whether the ingestion of fibers poses a risk to humans. This is because, as a general matter, animal cancer susceptibility is not directly equivalent to human experience, and, more particularly, because the studies so far undertaken may be criticized for various shortcomings in experimental design. Thus, one of Reserve's own witnesses, Dr. Wright, testified that at least one of the studies may be criticized for using too few animals over too brief an experimental time.

The occupational studies support the proposition that the ingestion of asbestos fibers can result in harm to health.

2. LEVEL OF EXPOSURE VIA INGESTION

The second primary uncertainty with respect to ingestion involves the attempt to assess whether the level of exposure from drinking water is hazardous. Of course, this inquiry is handicapped by the great variation in fiber counts, and Dr. Brown's admonition that only a qualitative, and not a quantitative, statement can be made about the presence of fibers.

In spite of these difficulties, the district court found that the level of exposure resulting from the drinking of Duluth water was "comparable" to that found to cause gastrointestinal cancer in asbestos workers. The court drew this finding from an elaborate calculation by Dr. Nicholson in which he attempted to make a statistical comparison between the fibers probably ingested by an asbestos worker subject to an excess risk of gastrointestinal cancer with the probable number of amphibole fibers ingested by a Duluth resident over a period of 18 years. * * * As is evident, this calculation is beset by several uncertainties. * * * Reserve witness Dr. Gross performed a calculation similar to Dr. Nicholson's, but using somewhat different assumptions, and concluded that Duluth water would have to contain several hundred million fibers/liter and be ingested for 60 years before an exposure comparable with occupational levels would be reached.

The comparison has other weaknesses, for without regard to the comparability of the gross exposure levels, the dynamics of the exposure process are markedly different. The vagaries attendant to the use of assumptions rather than facts result in comparisons which are of dubious accuracy. Thus, Dr. Brown testified that, if Nicholson's calculations were correct, he would conclude only that the risk was non-negligible.

The Nicholson comparison, although evidentially weak, must be considered with other evidence. The record does show that the ingestion of asbestos fibers poses some risk to health, but to an undetermined degree. Given these circumstances, Dr. Brown testified that the possibility of a future excess incidence of cancer attributable to the discharge cannot be ignored:[50]

> * * * I would say that it is conceivable that gastrointestinal cancers can develop from the ingestion of asbestos, and what I don't know, Your Honor, is just how low that level of ingestion must be

---

50. Since Lake Superior affords water supplies to an estimated 200,000 people of Duluth and other North Shore Minnesota municipalities, as well as Superior, Wisconsin, we think it is essential that the facts regarding the present disease effects of the discharge be accurately stated.

As our review below demonstrates, we conclude that there is no evidence on a scientific or medical basis showing that Duluth residents experience an excess rate of cancer attributable to Reserve's discharge.

before the likelihood of GI cancer becomes so remote as to be, for all intents and purposes, ignored as a real live possibility.

* * *

C. CONCLUSION

The preceding extensive discussion of the evidence demonstrates that the medical and scientific conclusions here in dispute clearly lie "on the frontiers of scientific knowledge."

The trial court, not having any proof of actual harm, was faced with a consideration of (1) the probabilities of any health harm and (2) the consequences, if any, should the harm actually occur.

* * *

In assessing probabilities in this case, it cannot be said that the probability of harm is more likely than not. Moreover, the level of probability does not readily convert into a prediction of consequences. On this record it cannot be forecast that the rates of cancer will increase from drinking Lake Superior water or breathing Silver Bay air. The best that can be said is that the existence of this asbestos contaminant in air and water gives rise to a reasonable medical concern for the public health. The public's exposure to asbestos fibers in air and water creates some health risk. Such a contaminant should be removed.

The district court found that Reserve's discharge into Lake Superior violated §§ 1160(c)(5) and (g)(1) of the Federal Water Pollution Control Act (FWPCA). These two provisions authorize an action by the United States to secure abatement of water discharges in interstate waters where the discharges violate state water quality standards and "endanger * * * the health or welfare of persons." § 1160(g)(1).

In the context of this environmental legislation, we believe that Congress used the term "endangering" in a precautionary or preventive sense, and, therefore, evidence of potential harm as well as actual harm comes within the purview of that term. We are fortified in this view by the flexible provisions for injunctive relief which permit a court "to enter such judgment and orders enforcing such judgment as the public interest and the equities of the case may require." 33 U.S.C.A. § 1160(c)(5).

* * *

Concededly, the trial court considered many appropriate factors in arriving at a remedy, such as a) the nature of the anticipated harm, b) the burden on Reserve and its employees from the issuance of the injunction, c) the financial ability of Reserve to convert to other methods of waste disposal, and d) a margin of safety for the public.

An additional crucial element necessary for a proper assessment of the health hazard rests upon a proper analysis of the probabilities of harm.

With respect to the water, these probabilities must be deemed low for they do not rest on a history of past health harm attributable to ingestion but on a medical theory implicating the ingestion of asbestos fibers as a causative factor in increasing the rates of gastrointestinal cancer among asbestos workers. With respect to air, the assessment of the risk of harm rests on a higher degree of proof, a correlation between inhalation of asbestos dust and subsequent illness. But here, too, the hazard cannot be measured in terms of predictability, but the assessment must be made without direct proof. But, the hazard in both the air and water can be measured in only the most general terms as a concern for the public health resting upon a reasonable medical theory. Serious consequences could result if the hypothesis on which it is based should ultimately prove true.

A court is not powerless to act in these circumstances. But an immediate injunction cannot be justified in striking a balance between unpredictable health effects and the clearly predictable social and economic consequences that would follow the plant closing.

In addition to the health risk posed by Reserve's discharges, the district court premised its immediate termination of the discharges upon Reserve's persistent refusal to implement a reasonable alternative plan for on-land disposal of tailings.

During these appeal proceedings, Reserve has indicated its willingness to deposit its tailings on land and to properly filter its air emissions. At oral argument, Reserve advised us of a willingness to spend 243 million dollars in plant alteration and construction to halt its pollution of air and water. Reserve's offer to continue operations and proceed to construction of land disposal facilities for its tailings, if permitted to do so by the State of Minnesota, when viewed in conjunction with the uncertain quality of the health risk created by Reserve's discharges, weighs heavily against a ruling which closes Reserve's plant immediately.

Indeed, the intervening union argues, with some persuasiveness, that ill health effects resulting from the prolonged unemployment of the head of the family on a closing of the Reserve facility may be more certain than the harm from drinking Lake Superior water or breathing Silver Bay air.

Furthermore, Congress has generally geared its national environmental policy to allowing polluting industries a reasonable period of time to make adjustments in their efforts to conform to federal standards.

We believe that on this record the district court abused its discretion by immediately closing this major industrial plant. In this case, the risk of harm to the public is potential, not imminent or certain, and Reserve says it earnestly seeks a practical way to abate the pollution. A remedy should be fashioned which will serve the ultimate public weal by insuring clean air, clean water, and continued jobs in an industry vital to the nation's welfare.

* * *

Reserve shall be given a reasonable time to stop discharging its wastes into Lake Superior. A reasonable time includes the time necessary for Minnesota to act on Reserve's present application to dispose of its tailings at Milepost 7 (Lax Lake site), or to come to agreement on some other site acceptable to both Reserve and the state. Assuming agreement and designation of an appropriate land disposal site, Reserve is entitled to a reasonable turn-around time to construct the necessary facilities and accomplish a changeover in the means of disposing of its taconite wastes.

Notes

1. On the basis of the evidence discussed in the opinion, would a judge (or jury) be justified in finding by the preponderance of the evidence that water-borne asbestos fibers cause cancer? If not, how can the court justify forcing Reserve to spend $243 million to end the problem? For further information on the case, see M. Shapo, *A Nation of Guinea Pigs* 191–217 (1979).

2. Compare EDF v. EPA [heptachlor and chlordane], page 483 infra. Would Judge Leventhal's burden of proof techniques have been helpful in resolving the *Reserve Mining* problem? Since asbestos was known to be a carcinogen when inhaled, would Leventhal have placed the burden on Reserve to prove asbestos was safe when ingested? Would this be a reasonable allocation of the burden of proof? Alternatively, should the burden of proof have shifted back to the EPA under the *International Harvester* theory, page 304 supra, given the negative results of the animal and tissue studies?

3. Since *Reserve Mining,* there has been a great deal of research on the carcinogenic properties of ingested asbestos, but the results remain inconclusive. The increased rate of gastrointestinal cancer among asbestos workers is well-established, and the "coughing up and swallowing" hypothesis remains well-accepted. Also, the most carefully conducted epidemiological study, from the San Francisco Bay Area, did find a significant increase in cancer related to asbestos in the drinking water. Other studies (including a follow up study of Duluth), however, point in the opposite direction.

In 1983, EPA conducted a careful survey of the asbestos research and issued its own assessment of risk. An article converted the EPA assessment into a formula for estimating mortality rates. See Nicholson, "Human Cancer Risk from Ingested Asbestos, A Problem of Uncertainty," 53 *Envtl. Health Persp.* 111 (1983). The EPA estimate was based on lifetime exposure of a city of one million people to 100 million fibers per liter of water. EPA predicted an increased risk of death of 1/300 per person, or a total of 3300 excess deaths. Duluth's population was about 100,000, and a reasonable estimate of fiber density was about 33 million fibers per liter. With these modifications, the formula predicts about one hundred excess deaths from gastrointestinal cancer. Alternatively, this means about 1.5 excess deaths annually.

However, by 1977, a water filtration system had been installed in Duluth which removed 99.9 percent of the asbestos fibers. See Sigurdson, "Observations of Cancer Incidence Surveillance in Duluth, Minnesota," 53 *Envtl. Health Persp.* 61 (1983). This means a reduction in the risk by a factor of one thousand, down to something on the order of one expected death every six hundred years (1.5 deaths per year divided by a thousand). Was it appropriate to require Reserve to spend $200 million for a land disposal facility to eliminate such a risk? Or, in a society that complacently tolerates roughly 120 deaths per year from smoking in a city the size of Duluth, is requiring Reserve to spend a fortune to eliminate such a minuscule risk simply hypocritical? See Farber, "Risk Regulation in Perspective: Reserve Mining Revisited," 21 *Envt'l Law* 1321 (1991). The author reassesses the *Reserve Mining* decision in light of the additional facts described in this note 3, and in light of the Supreme Court's decision in the *Industrial Union Department* case, p. 439 infra. He concludes that the *Reserve Mining* decision is defensible from the perspectives of both "feasibility analysis" and cost-benefit analysis.

4. The *Reserve* decision received strong support from the D.C. Circuit's opinion in *Ethyl Corp. v. EPA,* 541 F.2d 1 (D.C.Cir.1976) (en banc). That case involved section 211(c)(1)(A) of the Clean Air Act, which authorized EPA to regulate gasoline additives whose emission products "will endanger the public health or welfare." Acting pursuant to this power, EPA determined that lead additives in gasoline presented "a significant risk of harm" to the public health and issued orders limiting the use of such additives. As in *Reserve Mining,* the court was faced with a high degree of scientific uncertainty. In this case, however, the uncertainty was not as to the harmfulness of the material. Lead is well known to be toxic and clearly can be absorbed into the body from ambient air. Nevertheless, because human beings are exposed to multiple sources of lead, it was difficult to determine whether the incremental increase in the amount of lead in the environment due to gasoline additives had serious health effects. In upholding the EPA, the court stressed that risk management involves policy judgments rather than simply factual determinations. Thus, the court accorded substantial deference to the EPA's conclusion. As the court explained:

> Questions involving the environment are particularly prone to uncertainty. Technological man has altered his world in ways never before experienced or anticipated. The health effects of such alterations are often unknown, sometimes unknowable. While a concerned Congress has passed legislation providing for protection of the public health against gross environmental modifications, the regulators entrusted with the enforcement of such laws have not thereby been endowed with a prescience that removes all doubt from their decision making. Rather, speculation, conflicts, and theoretical extrapolation typify their every action. How else can they act, given a mandate to protect the public health but only a slight or nonexistent data base upon which to draw?
> * * *
> Undoubtedly, certainty is a scientific ideal—to the extent that even science can be certain of its truth. But certainty in the complexities of environmental medicine may be achievable only after the fact, when scientists have the opportunity for leisurely and isolated scrutiny of an

entire mechanism. Awaiting certainty will often allow for only reactive, not preventive regulation. Petitioners suggest that anything less than certainty, that any speculation, is irresponsible. But when statutes seek to avoid environmental catastrophe, can preventive, albeit uncertain, decisions legitimately be so labeled?

Thus, the court concluded that a rigorous step-by-step proof of cause and effect should not be demanded where a statute is precautionary in nature, the evidence is on the frontiers of scientific knowledge, and regulations are designed to protect the public health. Hence, EPA may apply its expertise to draw conclusions from "suspected, but not completely substantiated" relationships between facts, from trends among facts, from theoretical projections and so forth.

This approach was followed in numerous lower court opinions. For example, in *Lead Industries Association, Inc. v. EPA,* 647 F.2d 1130 (D.C.Cir. 1980), the D.C. Circuit upheld a primary air quality standard for lead which incorporated an "adequate margin of safety." In setting the margin of safety, EPA had given no consideration to feasibility or cost. Moreover, the evidence of harm was unclear. Nevertheless, the court held that feasibility and cost were irrelevant and that EPA had acted properly in setting the margin of safety. As the court explained, use of a margin of safety is an important method of protecting against effects which have not yet been uncovered by research and effects whose medical significance is a matter of disagreement. As the court also explained, "Congress has recently acknowledged that more often than not the 'margins of safety' that are incorporated into air quality standards turn out to be very modest or nonexistent, as new information reveals adverse health effects at pollution levels once thought to be harmless." The court also reiterated the need for deference to EPA's expert judgments on these issues. Finally, the court held that the margin of safety requirement could be fulfilled by making conservative decisions at various points in the regulatory process, rather than by determining a safe level and adding a percentage to that as the "margin of safety."

In general, these lower court decisions demonstrated a high degree of deference to EPA's expert judgment. The lower courts, by and large, gave little weight to questions of cost and feasibility when dealing with toxic chemicals. Finally, these courts recognized that administrative action was justified without a showing that harmful effects were more likely than not. Instead, these courts concluded that regulatory intervention was justified whenever a reasonable likelihood of danger could be found.

5. The Supreme Court did not have occasion to consider the problem of risk management until 1980. It then decided two cases in as many years, never to return to the subject again. Before proceeding to consider these cases, it should be noted that they arise in a somewhat different context from most environmental issues. Both the Supreme Court cases involve protection of workers by the Occupational Safety and Health Administration (OSHA). These cases thus involve a rather special kind of environmental problem, since the environment in question is not one used by the general public.

The policy issues presented in OSHA cases are somewhat different from those in normal environmental cases. First, exposure to the risk is somewhat more voluntary than is exposure to, say, ambient air pollution. Second, negotiations between the source of the hazard and the possible victims are feasible to a much greater extent than in the normal pollution case. This is especially true when the victims of the hazard, the employees, are represented by a union. Thus, the transaction costs of private settlements are sometimes much smaller here. Third, the possible victims of the hazard have a much greater stake in the economic health of the enterprise creating the hazard than is the case generally in environmental disputes. The option of closing the plant down in order to end the hazard is generally not acceptable to the workers, nor are actions which would seriously jeopardize the prospects for continued employment. For all of these reasons, the balance between protection from risks versus economic cost may be somewhat different than in the normal environmental case.

Moreover, the statutory scheme is primarily concerned with quite different problems of worker protection. The only provision dealing expressly with toxic chemicals is section 6(b)(5) of the Act, 29 U.S.C.A. § 655(d)(5). This provision requires the agency to set a standard for any toxic material "which most adequately assures, to the extent feasible, that no employee will suffer material impairment of health or functional capacity * * *." Another section of the Act, section 3(8), 29 U.S.C.A. § 652(8), has been thought to be relevant by at least some members of the Court. This section simply defines an occupational safety and health standard as a regulation setting any one of a variety of requirements "reasonably necessary or appropriate to provide safe or healthful places of employment." These provisions are vaguer and provide less guidance than most of the analogous provisions of the Clean Air Act or Clean Water Act. In short, both the statutory context and the policy choices presented in this area are atypical. It is unfortunate therefore that the only guidance we have had from the Supreme Court has been in this rather abnormal setting. _STOP_

INDUSTRIAL UNION DEPARTMENT, AFL–CIO v. AMERICAN PETROLEUM INSTITUTE

Supreme Court of the United States, 1980.
448 U.S. 607, 100 S.Ct. 2844, 65 L.Ed.2d 1010.

JUSTICE STEVENS announced the judgment of the Court and delivered an opinion in which THE CHIEF JUSTICE and JUSTICE STEWART join and in Parts I, II, III–A–C and E of which JUSTICE POWELL joins.

I.

[In sections I and II of the opinion, Justice Stevens set out the background of the case. The case involved an OSHA regulation governing exposure to benzene. The Secretary of Labor had found that benzene was a carcinogen and that no known safe level existed. Hence, he lowered the permissible exposure level for workers from 10 ppm (parts per million) to 1 ppm, which he considered the lowest feasible level. OSHA (the Occupational Safety and Health Administration, within the Department of Labor) estimated the total costs of compliance as including $266 million in capital investments, $200 million in first-year start-up costs, and $34 million in annual costs. About 35,000 employees would benefit from the regulation. There were two arguably relevant statutory provisions. Section 3(8) of the Act, 29 U.S.C.A. § 652(8), defined an occupational safety and health standard as a standard setting any one of a variety of requirements "reasonably necessary or appropriate to provide safe or healthful employment or places of employment". Section 6(b)(5) of the Act, 29 U.S.C.A. § 655(b)(5), required the Secretary to set a standard for any toxic materials "which most adequately assures, to the extent feasible, that no employee will suffer material impairment of health or functional capacity * * *."]

III.

A.

[This section sets out the statutes and the contentions of the parties. Essentially, industry argued that § 3(8) required a cost-benefit analysis, while the Secretary argued that he was "required to impose standards that either guarantee workplaces that are free from any risk of material health impairment, however small, or that come as close as possible to doing so without ruining entire industries."]

If the purpose of the statute were to eliminate completely and with absolute certainty any risk of serious harm, we would agree that it would be proper for the Secretary to interpret §§ 3(8) and 6(b)(5) in this fashion. But we think it is clear that the statute was not designed to require employers to provide absolutely risk-free workplaces whenever it is technologically feasible to do so, so long as the cost is not great enough to destroy an entire industry. Rather, both the language and structure of the Act, as well as its legislative history, indicate that it was intended to require the elimination, as far as feasible, of significant risks of harm.

B.

By empowering the Secretary to promulgate standards that are "reasonably necessary or appropriate to provide safe or healthful employment and places of employment," the Act implies that, before promulgating any standard, the Secretary must make a finding that the workplaces in question are not safe. But "safe" is not the equivalent of "risk-free." There are many activities that we engage in every day—such as driving a car or even breathing city air—that entail some risk of accident or material health impairment; nevertheless, few people would consider these activities "unsafe." Similarly, a workplace can hardly be considered "unsafe" unless it threatens the workers with a significant risk of harm.

Therefore, before he can promulgate *any* permanent health or safety standard, the Secretary is required to make a threshold finding that a place of employment is unsafe—in the sense that significant risks are present and can be eliminated or lessened by a change in practices. This requirement applies to permanent standards promulgated pursuant to § 6(b)(5), as well as to other types of permanent standards. For there is no reason why § 3(8)'s definition of a standard should not be deemed incorporated by reference into § 6(b)(5). The standards promulgated pursuant to § 6(b)(5) are just one species of the genus of standards governed by the basic requirement. That section repeatedly uses the term "standard" without suggesting any exception from, or qualification of the general definition; on the contrary, it directs the Secretary to select *"the* standard"—that is to say, one of various possible alternatives that satisfy the basic definition in § 3(8)—that is most protective. Moreover, requiring the Secretary to make a threshold finding of significant risk is consistent with the scope of the regulatory power granted to him by § 6(b)(5), which empowers the Secretary to promulgate standards, not for chemical and physical agents generally, but for *"toxic* chemicals" and *"harmful* physical agents."

* * *

In the absence of a clear mandate in the Act, it is unreasonable to assume that Congress intended to give the Secretary the unprecedented power over American industry that would result from the Government's view of §§ 3(8) and 6(b)(5), coupled with OSHA's cancer policy. Expert testimony that a substance is probably a human carcinogen—either because it has caused cancer in animals or because individuals have contracted cancer following extremely high exposures—would justify the conclusion that the substance poses some risk of serious harm no matter how minute the exposure and no matter how many experts testified that they regarded the risk as insignificant. That conclusion would in turn justify pervasive regulation limited only by the constraint of feasibility. In light of the fact that there are literally thousands of substances used in the workplace that have been identified as carcinogens or suspect carcinogens, the Government's theory would give OSHA power to impose enormous costs that might produce little, if any, discernible benefit.

If the Government was correct in arguing that neither § 3(8) nor § 6(b)(5) requires that the risk from a toxic substance be quantified sufficiently to enable the Secretary to characterize it as significant in an understandable way, the statute would make such a "sweeping delegation of legislative power" that it might be unconstitutional under the Court's reasoning in *Schechter Poultry Corp. v. United States,* 295 U.S. 495, 539, 55 S.Ct. 837, 847, 79 L.Ed. 1570, and *Panama Refining Co. v. Ryan,* 293 U.S. 388, 55 S.Ct. 241, 79 L.Ed. 446. A construction of the statute that avoids this kind of open-ended grant should certainly be favored.

C.

[In this section of the opinion, Justice Stevens argues that this construction of the statute is supported by the legislative history.]

D.

Given the conclusion that the Act empowers the Secretary to promulgate health and safety standards only where a significant risk of harm exists, the critical issue becomes how to define and allocate the burden of proving the significance of the risk in a case such as this, where scientific knowledge is imperfect and the precise quantification of risks is therefore impossible. The Agency's position is that there is substantial evidence in the record to support its conclusion that there is no absolutely safe level for a carcinogen and that, therefore, the burden is properly on industry to prove, apparently beyond a shadow of a doubt, that there is a safe level for benzene exposure. The Agency argues that, because of the uncertainties in this area, any other approach would render it helpless, forcing it to wait for the leukemia deaths that it believes are likely to occur before taking any regulatory action.

We disagree. As we read the statute, the burden was on the Agency to show, on the basis of substantial evidence, that it is at least more likely than not that long-term exposure to 10 ppm of benzene presents a significant risk of material health impairment. Ordinarily, it is the proponent of a rule or order who has the burden of proof in administrative proceedings. See 5 U.S.C.A. § 556(d). In some cases involving toxic substances, Congress has shifted the burden of proving that a particular substance is safe onto the party opposing the proposed rule.[61] The fact that Congress did not follow this course in enacting OSHA indicates that it intended the Agency to bear the normal burden of establishing the need for a proposed standard.

In this case OSHA did not even attempt to carry its burden of proof. The closest it came to making a finding that benzene presented a significant risk of harm in the workplace was its statement that the benefits to be derived from lowering the permissible exposure level from 10 to 1 ppm were "likely" to be "appreciable." The Court of Appeals held that this finding was not supported by substantial evidence. Of greater importance, even if it were supported by substantial evidence, such a finding would not be sufficient to satisfy the Agency's obligations under the Act.

The inadequacy of the Agency's findings can perhaps be illustrated best by its rejection of industry testimony that a dose-response curve can be formulated on the basis of current epidemiological evidence and that, even under the most conservative extrapolation theory, current exposure levels would cause at most two deaths out of a population of about 30,000 workers every six years. In rejecting this testimony, OSHA made the following statement:

> In the face of the record evidence of numerous actual deaths attributable to benzene-induced leukemia and other fatal blood diseases, OSHA is unwilling to rely on the hypothesis that at most two cancers every six years would be prevented by the proposed standard. By way of example, the Infante study disclosed seven excess leukemia deaths in a population of about 600 people over a

---

61. See *Environmental Defense Fund, Inc. v. EPA,* 179 U.S.App.D.C. 43, 548 F.2d 998, 1004, 1012–1018 (1976), cert. denied, 431 U.S. 925, 97 S.Ct. 2199, 53 L.Ed.2d 239, where the court rejected the argument that the EPA has the burden of proving that a pesticide is unsafe in order to suspend its registration under the Federal Insecticide, Fungicide and Rodenticide Act. The court noted that Congress had deliberately shifted the ordinary burden of proof under the APA, requiring manufacturers to establish the continued safety of their products.

25–year period. While the Infante study involved higher exposures than those currently encountered, the incidence rates found by Infante, together with the numerous other cases reported in the literature of benzene leukemia and other fatal blood diseases, makes it difficult for OSHA to rely on the [witness'] hypothesis to assure that statutorily mandated protection for employees. In any event, due to the fact that there is no safe level of exposure to benzene and that it is impossible to precisely quantify the anticipated benefits, OSHA must select the level of exposure which is most protective of exposed employees.

There are three possible interpretations of OSHA's stated reason for rejecting the witness' testimony: (1) OSHA considered it probable that a greater number of lives would be saved by lowering the standard from 10 ppm; (2) OSHA thought that saving two lives every six years in a work force of 30,000 persons is a significant savings that makes it reasonable and appropriate to adopt a new standard; or (3) even if the small number is not significant and even if the savings may be even smaller, the Agency nevertheless believed it had a statutory duty to select the level of exposure that is most protective of the exposed employees if it is economically and technologically feasible to do so. Even if the Secretary did not intend to rely entirely on this third theory, his construction of the statute would make it proper for him to do so. Moreover, he made no express findings of fact that would support his 1 ppm standard on any less drastic theory. Under these circumstances, we can hardly agree with the Government that OSHA discharged its duty under the Act.

Contrary to the Government's contentions, imposing a burden on the Agency of demonstrating a significant risk of harm will not strip it of its ability to regulate carcinogens, nor will it require the Agency to wait for deaths to occur before taking any action. First, the requirement that a "significant" risk be identified is not a mathematical straitjacket. It is the Agency's responsibility to determine, in the first instance, what it considers to be a "significant" risk. Some risks are plainly acceptable and others are plainly unacceptable. If, for example, the odds are one in a billion that a person will die from cancer by taking a drink of chlorinated water, the risk clearly could not be considered significant. On the other hand, if the odds are one in a thousand that regular inhalation of gasoline vapors that are two percent benzene will be fatal, a reasonable person might well consider the risk significant and take appropriate steps to decrease or eliminate it. Although the Agency has no duty to calculate the exact probability of harm, it does have an obligation to find that a significant risk is present before it can characterize a place of employment as "unsafe."[62]

62. In his dissenting opinion, Mr. Justice Marshall states that "when the question involves determination of the acceptable level of risk, the ultimate decision must necessarily be based on considerations of policy as well as empirically verifiable facts. Factual determinations can at most define the risk in some statistical way; the judgment whether that risk is tolerable cannot be based solely on a resolution of the facts." We agree. Thus, while the Agency must support its finding that a certain level

Second, OSHA is not required to support its finding that a significant risk exists with anything approaching scientific certainty. Although the Agency's findings must be supported by substantial evidence, 29 U.S.C.A. § 655(f), § 6(b)(5) specifically allows the Secretary to regulate on the basis of the "best available evidence." As several courts of appeals have held, this provision requires a reviewing court to give OSHA some leeway where its findings must be made on the frontiers of scientific knowledge. Thus, so long as they are supported by a body of reputable scientific thought, the Agency is free to use conservative assumptions in interpreting the data with respect to carcinogens, risking error on the side of over-protection rather than under-protection.[63]

Finally, the record in this case and OSHA's own rulings on other carcinogens indicate that there are a number of ways in which the Agency can make a rational judgment about the relative significance of the risks associated with exposure to a particular carcinogen.[64]

* * *

E.

Because our review of this case has involved a more detailed examination of the record than is customary, it must be emphasized that we have neither made any factual determinations of our own, nor have we rejected any factual findings made by the Secretary. We express no opinion on what factual findings this record might support, either on the basis of empirical evidence or on the basis of expert testimony; nor do we express any opinion on the more difficult question of what factual determinations would warrant a conclusion that significant risks are present which make promulgation of a new standard reasonably necessary or appropriate. The standard must, of course, be supported by the findings actually made by the Secretary, not merely by findings that we believe he might have made.

of risk exists by substantial evidence, we recognize that its determination that a particular level of risk is "significant" will be based largely on policy considerations. At this point we have no need to reach the issue of what level of scrutiny a reviewing court should apply to the latter type of determination.

63. Mr. Justice Marshall states that, under our approach, the agency must either wait for deaths to occur or must "deceive the public" by making a basically meaningless determination of significance based on totally inadequate evidence. Mr. Justice Marshall's view, however, rests on the erroneous premise that the only reason OSHA did not attempt to quantify benefits in this case was because it could not do so in any reasonable manner. As the discussion of the Agency's rejection of an industry attempt at formulating a dose-response curve demonstrates, however, the Agency's rejection of methods such as dose-response curves was

based at least in part on its view that nothing less than absolute safety would suffice.

64. For example, in the coke oven emissions standard, OSHA had calculated that 21,000 exposed coke oven workers had an annual excess mortality of over 200 and that the proposed standard might well eliminate the risk entirely.

In other proceedings, the Agency has had a good deal of data from animal experiments on which it could base a conclusion on the significance of the risk. For example, the record on the vinyl chloride standard indicated that a significant number of animals had developed tumors of the liver, lung and skin when they were exposed to 50 ppm of vinyl chloride over a period of 11 months. One hundred out of 200 animals died during that period.

In this case the record makes it perfectly clear that the Secretary relied squarely on a special policy for carcinogens that imposed the burden on industry of proving the existence of a safe level of exposure, thereby avoiding the Secretary's threshold responsibility of establishing the need for more stringent standards. In so interpreting his statutory authority, the Secretary exceeded his power.

IV.

[In this part of the opinion, the court remanded a standard governing skin contact with benzene, for similar reasons.]

The judgment of the Court of Appeals remanding the petition for review to the Secretary for further proceedings is affirmed.

It is so ordered.

CHIEF JUSTICE BURGER, concurring.

This case presses upon the Court difficult unanswered questions on the frontiers of science and medicine. The statute and the legislative history give ambiguous signals as to how the Secretary is directed to operate in this area. The opinion by Mr. Justice Stevens takes on a difficult task to decode the message of the statute as to guidelines for administrative action.

To comply with statutory requirements, the Secretary must bear the burden of "finding" that a proposed health and safety standard is "reasonably necessary or appropriate to provide safe or healthful employment and places of employment." This policy judgment entails the subsidiary finding that the pre-existing standard presents a "significant risk" of material health impairment for a worker who spends his entire employment life in a working environment where exposure remains at maximum permissible levels. The Secretary's factual finding of "risk" must be "quantified sufficiently to enable the Secretary to characterize it as significant in an understandable way." Precisely what this means is difficult to say. But because these mandated findings were not made by the Secretary, I agree that the 1 ppm benzene standard must be invalidated. However, I would stress the differing functions of the courts and the administrative agency with respect to such health and safety regulation.

The Congress is the ultimate regulator and the narrow function of the courts is to discern the meaning of the statute and the implementing regulations with the objective of ensuring that in promulgating health and safety standards the Secretary "has given reasoned consideration to each of the pertinent factors" and has complied with statutory commands. Our holding that the Secretary must retrace his steps with greater care and consideration is not to be taken in derogation of the scope of legitimate agency discretion. When the facts and arguments have been presented and duly considered, the Secretary must make a policy judgment as to whether a specific risk of health impairment is significant in terms of the policy objectives of the statute. When he acts in this capacity, pursuant to the legislative authority delegated by

Congress, he exercises the prerogatives of the legislature—to focus on only one aspect of a larger problem, or to promulgate regulations that, to some, may appear as imprudent policy or inefficient allocation of resources. The judicial function does not extend to substantive revision of regulatory policy. That function lies elsewhere—in Congressional and Executive oversight or amendatory legislation; although to be sure the boundaries are often ill defined and indistinct.

Nevertheless, when discharging his duties under the statute, the Secretary is well admonished to remember that a heavy responsibility burdens his authority. Inherent in this statutory scheme is authority to refrain from regulation of insignificant or *de minimis* risks. * * * When the administrative record reveals only scant or minimal risk of material health impairment, responsible administration calls for avoidance of extravagant, comprehensive regulation. Perfect safety is a chimera; regulation must not strangle human activity in the search for the impossible.

JUSTICE POWELL, concurring in part and in the judgment.

I join Parts I, II, III A–C, and III–E of the plurality opinion.[1] The Occupational Safety and Health Agency relied in large part on its "carcinogen policy"—which had not been adopted formally—in promulgating the benzene exposure and dermal contact regulation at issue in this case. For the reasons stated by the plurality, I agree that §§ 6(b)(5) and 3(8) must be read together. They require OSHA to make a threshold finding that proposed occupational health standards are reasonably necessary to provide safe workplaces. When OSHA acts to reduce existing national consensus standards, therefore, it must find that (i) currently permissible exposure levels create a significant risk of material health impairment; and (ii) a reduction of those levels would significantly reduce the hazard.

Although I would not rule out the possibility that the necessary findings could rest in part on generic policies properly adopted by OSHA, see McGarity, Substantive and Procedural Discretion in Administrative Resolution of Science Policy Questions: Regulating Carcinogens in EPA and OSHA, 67 *Geo.L.J.* 729, 754–759 (1979), no properly supported agency policies are before us in this case.[3] I therefore agree with the

1. These portions of the plurality opinion primarily address OSHA's special carcinogen policy, rather than OSHA's argument that it also made evidentiary findings. I do not necessarily agree with every observation in the plurality opinion concerning the presence or absence of such findings. I also express no view on the question whether a different interpretation of the statute would violate the nondelegation doctrine of *Schechter Poultry Corp. v. United States,* 295 U.S. 495, 55 S.Ct. 837, 79 L.Ed. 1570 (1935), and *Panama Refining Co. v. Ryan,* 293 U.S. 388, 55 S.Ct. 241, 79 L.Ed. 446 (1935).

3. OSHA has adopted a formal policy for regulating carcinogens effective April 12, 1980. 45 Fed.Reg. 5002 (Jan. 22, 1980). But no such policy was in effect when the agency promulgated its benzene regulation. Moreover, neither the factual determinations nor the administrative judgments upon which the policy rests are supported adequately on this record alone. Accordingly, we have no occasion to consider the extent to which valid agency policies may supply a basis for a finding that health risks exist in particular cases.

plurality that the regulation is invalid to the extent it rests upon the assumption that exposure to known carcinogens always should be reduced to a level proven to be safe or, if no such level is found, to the lowest level that the affected industry can achieve with available technology.

[Justice Powell concluded that the agency had failed to carry its burden, and also had failed to give adequate consideration to cost.]

JUSTICE REHNQUIST, concurring in the judgment.

In considering these alternative interpretations, my colleagues manifest a good deal of uncertainty, and ultimately divide over whether the Secretary produced sufficient evidence that the proposed standard for benzene will result in any appreciable benefits at all. This uncertainty, I would suggest, is eminently justified, since I believe that this case presents the Court with what has to be one of the most difficult issues that could confront a decision-maker: whether the statistical possibility of future deaths should ever be disregarded in light of the economic costs of preventing those deaths. I would also suggest that the widely varying positions advanced in the briefs of the parties and in the opinions of Mr. Justice Stevens, The Chief Justice, Mr. Justice Powell, and Mr. Justice Marshall demonstrate, perhaps better than any other fact, that Congress, the governmental body best suited and most obligated to make the choice confronting us in this case, has improperly delegated that choice to the Secretary of Labor and, derivatively, to this Court.

* * *

If we are ever to reshoulder the burden of ensuring that Congress itself make the critical policy decisions, this is surely the case in which to do it. It is difficult to imagine a more obvious example of Congress simply avoiding a choice which was both fundamental for purposes of the statute and yet politically so divisive that the necessary decision or compromise was difficult, if not impossible, to hammer out in the legislative forge. Far from detracting from the substantive authority of Congress, a declaration that the first sentence of § 6(b)(5) of the OSHA constitutes an invalid delegation to the Secretary of Labor would preserve the authority of Congress. If Congress wishes to legislate in an area which it has not previously sought to enter, it will in today's political world undoubtedly run into opposition no matter how the legislation is formulated. But that is the very essence of legislative authority under our system. It is the hard choices, and not the filling in of the blanks, which must be made by the elected representatives of the people. When fundamental policy decisions underlying important legislation about to be enacted are to be made, the buck stops with Congress and the President insofar as he exercises his constitutional role in the legislative process.

I would invalidate the first sentence of § 6(b)(5) of the Occupational Safety and Health Act of 1970 as it applies to any toxic substance or harmful physical agent for which a safe level, that is a level at which "no employee will suffer material impairment of health or functional capacity even if such employee has regular exposure to [that hazard] for the period of his working life[,]'' is, according to the Secretary, unknown or otherwise "infeasible." Absent further congressional action, the Secretary would then have to choose, when acting pursuant to § 6(b)(5), between setting a safe standard or setting no standard at all.[8] Accordingly, for the reasons stated above, I concur in the judgment of the Court affirming the judgment of the Court of Appeals.

JUSTICE MARSHALL, with whom JUSTICE BRENNAN, JUSTICE WHITE, and JUSTICE BLACKMUN join, dissenting.

In cases of statutory construction, this Court's authority is limited. If the statutory language and legislative intent are plain, the judicial inquiry is at an end. Under our jurisprudence, it is presumed that ill-considered or unwise legislation will be corrected through the democratic process; a court is not permitted to distort a statute's meaning in order to make it conform with the Justices' own views of sound social policy. See *TVA v. Hill* [page 581 infra].

Today's decision flagrantly disregards these restrictions on judicial authority. The plurality ignores the plain meaning of the Occupational Safety and Health Act of 1970 in order to bring the authority of the Secretary of Labor in line with the plurality's own views of proper regulatory policy. The unfortunate consequence is that the Federal Government's efforts to protect American workers from cancer and other crippling diseases may be substantially impaired.

The first sentence of § 6(b)(5) of the Act provides:

"The Secretary, in promulgating standards dealing with toxic materials or harmful physical agents under this subsection, shall set the standard which most adequately assures, to the extent feasible, on the basis of the best available evidence, that no employee will suffer material impairment of health or functional capacity even if such employee has regular exposure to the hazard dealt with by such standard for the period of his working life."

In this case the Secretary of Labor found, on the basis of substantial evidence, that (1) exposure to benzene creates a risk of cancer, chromosomal damage, and a variety of nonmalignant but potentially fatal blood disorders, even at the level of 1 ppm; (2) no safe level of exposure has been shown; (3) benefits in the form of saved lives would be derived from the permanent standard; (4) the number of lives that would be saved could turn out to be either substantial or relatively small; (5) under the present state of scientific knowledge, it is impossible to calculate even in a rough way the number of lives that would be saved, at least without making assumptions that would appear absurd to much of the medical community; and (6) the standard would not materially harm the finan-

---

8. This ruling would not have any effect upon standards governing toxic substances or harmful physical agents for which safe levels are feasible, upon extant standards promulgated as "national consensus standards" under § 6(a), nor upon the Secretary's authority to promulgate "emergency temporary standards" under § 6(c).

cial condition of the covered industries. The Court does not set aside any of these findings. Thus, it could not be plainer that the Secretary's decision was fully in accord with his statutory mandate "most adequately [to] assure[ ] * * * that no employee will suffer material impairment of health or functional capacity * * *."

The plurality's conclusion to the contrary is based on its interpretation of [section 3(8)], which defines an occupational safety and health standard as one "which requires conditions * * * reasonably necessary or appropriate to provide safe or healthful employment * * *." According to the plurality, a standard is not "reasonably necessary or appropriate" unless the Secretary is able to show that it is "at least more likely than not" that the risk he seeks to regulate is a "significant" one. Nothing in the statute's language or legislative history, however, indicates that the "reasonably necessary or appropriate" language should be given this meaning. Indeed, both demonstrate that the plurality's standard bears no connection with the acts or intentions of Congress and is based only on the plurality's solicitude for the welfare of regulated industries. And the plurality uses this standard to evaluate not the agency's decision in this case, but a strawman of its own creation.

* * *

The plurality's discussion of the record in this case is both extraordinarily arrogant and extraordinarily unfair. It is arrogant because the plurality presumes to make its own factual findings with respect to a variety of disputed issues relating to carcinogen regulation. It should not be necessary to remind the Members of this Court that they were not appointed to undertake independent review of adequately supported scientific findings made by a technically expert agency. And the plurality's discussion is unfair because its characterization of the Secretary's report bears practically no resemblance to what the Secretary actually did in this case. Contrary to the plurality's suggestion, the Secretary did not rely blindly on some draconian carcinogen "policy." If he had, it would have been sufficient for him to have observed that benzene is a carcinogen, a proposition that respondents do not dispute. Instead, the Secretary gathered over 50 volumes of exhibits and testimony and offered a detailed and evenhanded discussion of the relationship between exposure to benzene at all recorded exposure levels and chromosomal damage, aplastic anemia, and leukemia. In that discussion he evaluated, and took seriously, respondents' evidence of a safe exposure level.

* * *

In recent years there has been increasing recognition that the products of technological development may have harmful effects whose incidence and severity cannot be predicted with certainty. The responsibility to regulate such products has fallen to administrative agencies. Their task is not an enviable one. Frequently no clear causal link can be established between the regulated substance and the harm to be averted. Risks of harm are often uncertain, but inaction has considerable costs of its own. The agency must decide whether to take regulatory action against possibly substantial risks or to wait until more definitive information becomes available—a judgment which by its very nature cannot be based solely on determinations of fact.

Those delegations, in turn, have been made on the understanding that judicial review would be available to ensure that the agency's determinations are supported by substantial evidence and that its actions do not exceed the limits set by Congress. In the Occupational Safety and Health Act, Congress expressed confidence that the courts would carry out this important responsibility. But in this case the plurality has far exceeded its authority. The plurality's "threshold finding" requirement is nowhere to be found in the Act and is antithetical to its basic purposes. "The fundamental policy questions appropriately resolved in Congress * * * are *not* subject to re-examination in the federal courts under the guise of judicial review of agency action." *Vermont Yankee Nuclear Power Corp. v. NRDC,* [page 92 supra]. Surely this is no less true of the decision to ensure safety for the American worker than the decision to proceed with nuclear power.

Because the approach taken by the plurality is so plainly irreconcilable with the Court's proper institutional role, I am certain that it will not stand the test of time. In all likelihood, today's decision will come to be regarded as an extreme reaction to a regulatory scheme that, as the Members of the plurality perceived it, imposed an unduly harsh burden on regulated industries. But as the Constitution "does not enact Mr. Herbert Spencer's Social Statics," *Lochner v. New York,* 198 U.S. 45, 75, 25 S.Ct. 539, 546, 49 L.Ed. 937 (1905) (Holmes, J., dissenting), so the responsibility to scrutinize federal administrative action does not authorize this Court to strike its own balance between the costs and benefits of occupational safety standards. I am confident that the approach taken by the plurality today, like that in *Lochner* itself, will eventually be abandoned, and that the representative branches of government will once again be allowed to determine the level of safety and health protection to be accorded to the American worker.

Notes

1. Note that the plurality said a one in a thousand risk "might well" be considered significant. As applied to the general population, such a risk level would mean approximately 240,000 deaths. How many additional deaths would be required before the plurality would find a risk *clearly* significant? On the other hand, in support of the plurality, couldn't one ask whether any rational person would invest almost a billion dollars to save about one life annually? If spent elsewhere, couldn't that money save many more lives?

Refer back to note 3, pages 436–437 supra, following *Reserve Mining.* Assuming the correctness of EPA's 1983 assessment of cancer risk in Duluth from asbestos in the water supply, is a total of 100 excess deaths, or 1.5 deaths per year, a significant risk? What about 1.0 death every 600 years, after installation of the water filtration system?

2. Much of the disagreement in *Industrial Union Department* seemed to stem from varying concepts of risk. The plurality seemed to identify risk with the actual mortality rate caused by existing conditions. The plurality apparently would require the Secretary to find that it is more likely than not that the mortality rate would be "significant". Justice Marshall, on the other hand, seemed to think of risk as relating to the probability of a significant mortality rate. He would therefore have allowed the Secretary to act if there is a substantial likelihood, even though less than 50%, that the mortality rate caused by existing conditions is significant.

3. The disagreement between Stevens and Marshall can also be viewed as a dispute over burden of proof. Justice Stevens would require the Secretary to establish that present levels are unsafe. On the other hand, Justice Marshall, in effect, would recognize a presumption of danger at present levels once a chemical is shown to be toxic at higher levels. Under the Marshall approach, the Secretary must set a level of exposure at which he can make an affirmative finding of safety. As a result, in the "grey area" where the evidence is too unclear to permit the Secretary to reach a definite conclusion about risk or safety, Marshall would allow regulation but Stevens apparently would not.

4. The OSHA carcinogen policy discussed in Justice Powell's concurring opinion and cited in his footnote 3 was amended after *Industrial Union Department* to incorporate the plurality's "significant risk" standard. 46 Fed.Reg. 4889 (final rule) and 7402 (proposed rule) (1981). In 1984, OSHA was directed to apply new guidelines issued by the White House Office of Science and Technology Policy, 49 Fed.Reg. 21594 (1984), discussed in the note at pages 427–428 supra.

5. In *Gade v. National Solid Wastes Management Association*, 505 U.S. 88, 112 S.Ct. 2374, 120 L.Ed.2d 73 (1992), the Supreme Court in a 5–to–4 decision held that OSHA preempts all non-federally approved state occupational safety and health standards relating to any issue with respect to which a federal standard has been promulgated. Thus, states are not permitted to regulate industrial workplace conditions more stringently so as to reduce health or safety risks to levels lower than those tolerated by federal standards.

[handwritten margin note: federal preempts state statute]

LATIN, "THE 'SIGNIFICANCE' OF TOXIC HEALTH RISKS: AN ESSAY ON LEGAL DECISIONMAKING UNDER UNCERTAINTY"[g]

10 *Ecology Law Quarterly* 339, 339–356, 381–386, 394 (1982).

Courts may employ either of two incompatible approaches to resolve problems of uncertainty. One treatment emphasizes judicial reliance on uniform procedural rules applied in different types of disputes. For example, the common law generally imposes the burden of proof, and hence the risk of uncertainty, on the "moving" party in a controversy. Of greater significance for judicial review of regulatory decisions, the Administrative Procedure Act (APA) assigns the burden of proof to "the proponent of a rule or order." The APA doctrine entails reductionism[5] because only one consideration—the procedural posture of the parties—is material to allocation of the burden of proof. * * * In many cases, however, a reductive treatment of uncertainty may impede achievement of the substantive policies of the organic legislation, a high price to pay for simplicity of judicial administration.

The principal thesis of this Article is that, because legislative choices vary with respect to different regulatory programs and different factual issues, the decisionmaking strategy employed to resolve uncertainty in any given program should correspond with the social policies underlying that particular program. * * *

In *Industrial Union Department, AFL–CIO v. American Petroleum Institute* (the benzene case), the Supreme Court invalidated an Occupational Safety and Health Administration (OSHA) regulation aimed at reducing employee exposure to the toxic substance benzene. The critical uncertainty in that case pertained to the degree of risk posed by prevailing levels of benzene exposure. Because the health hazards at the existing exposure limit could not be determined, the plurality opinion held that OSHA had failed to prove a stricter benzene standard was reasonably necessary. The court reached this conclusion only because it imposed the burden of proof on the Agency; yet that allocation was made with little reference to the purposes of the Occupational Safety and Health Act of 1970 (the OSH Act). The plurality instead relied on the reductive rule in the APA without adequately considering the degree to which its allocational doctrine would frustrate Congress' goal of strict toxic substance control.* * *

* * *

I. OVERVIEW OF THE BENZENE DECISION

* * *

Despite the expansive statement [in section 6(b)(5) of the OSH Act] that "no employee" should suffer material health impairment, the plurality opinion in the benzene case relied on definitional language in section 3(8) of the Act to create a threshold requirement that all OSHA standards, including those for toxic substances, be "reasonably necessary or appropriate to provide safe or healthful employment." * * * The plurality opinion concluded that section 6(b)(5) requires imposition of a highly protective standard, but only when some standard is necessary to avoid a significant risk of material health impairment. * * *

There is, however, a crucial difference between regulating a substance that presents a risk *known to be insignificant* and regulating a carcinogen whose risk at a given level of exposure is *uncertain*. * * *

---

5. "Reductionism" is "any method or theory of reducing data, processes, or statements to seeming equivalents that are less complex or developed." The term is usually used in a disparaging manner. Webster's New World Dictionary of the American Language 1191 (2d ed. 1972).

A. *Allocation of the Burden of Proof*

* * *

The major conflict in the case centered on the degree of risk at particular levels of exposure and the benefits that might result from lowering the permissible exposure limit (PEL). After accumulating evidence on the toxicity of benzene, OSHA promulgated a stringent regulation reducing the existing 10 parts per million (ppm) PEL to 1 ppm. The Agency settled on the 1 ppm limit as the safest standard that could feasibly be imposed on employers and administered by responsible officials. Industry experts contended a threshold level exists below which most people would experience no risk most of the time, but * * * agreed that absolute safety could be achieved only with a zero exposure limit. It follows that *some* risk is present at the existing 10 ppm PEL. The Court of Appeals specifically held this conclusion was supported by substantial evidence. Judge Clark also noted "general agreement in the scientific community" that lower exposure ordinarily entails less risk than higher exposure. He therefore approved the Agency's determination that *some* benefit would result from reducing the permissible limit to 1 ppm.

Justice Stevens did not set aside these *qualitative* findings, but he ruled they were insufficient to meet OSHA's burden of proof. The Supreme Court plurality required that "the risk from a toxic substance be *quantified* sufficiently to enable the Secretary to characterize it as significant in an understandable way * * *." * * * Justice Stevens acknowledged that the definition of a "significant" risk is a policy question within the Agency's discretion, but he held that this latitude does not authorize OSHA to regulate toxic exposures without a supportable estimate of the risks to be avoided. * * *

Although the Court insisted on quantitative estimates of toxic risk levels, it failed to understand that quantitative evidence may be available for some purposes but not for others. Epidemiological information like that submitted in the benzene proceeding is often sufficient to identify *aggregate* health effects, the cumulative effects from all levels of past exposure to a given substance. OSHA relied on quantitative evidence of aggregate health effects to demonstrate that benzene is "toxic" despite uncertainty about what specific levels of exposure had prevailed in the past. However, the plurality's analysis requires quantitative estimates of *disaggregated* health effects, the risks associated with *particular levels* of exposure—the existing 10 ppm PEL and the proposed 1 ppm limit. * * *

[T]he plurality acknowledged that the critical legal issue was how to allocate the burden of proof when scientific knowledge is imperfect. * * *

> As we read the statute, the burden was on the Agency to show, on the basis of substantial evidence, that it is at least more likely than not that long-term exposure to 10 ppm of benzene presents a significant risk of material health impairment.

Despite the introductory phrase in this passage, the plurality did not assign legal responsibility for uncertainty through reference to the OSH Act. Rather, the opinion relied on the APA, which imposes the burden of proof on "the proponent of a rule or order." It is true that the OSH Act does not explicitly allocate the burden of proof, but the question remains whether the statute does so implicitly. Justice Stevens disposed of that possibility in a perfunctory manner by citing another health-oriented statute in which Congress had expressly assigned the burden to industry on the safety issue. He then asserted that the absence of a comparable provision in the OSH Act meant Congress "intended the Agency to bear the normal burden of establishing the need for a proposed standard." Because OSHA conceded the risk of harm from exposure to 10 ppm of benzene was unknown, Justice Stevens held the Agency "did not even attempt" to meet its burden of showing that a stricter standard *more likely than not* is reasonably necessary.

$\rightarrow$ The plurality in the benzene case did not discriminate between controversies where OSHA simply fails to quantify the risk and those where it demonstrates that the risk cannot be quantified. Justice Powell, in his concurring opinion, refused to accept this facet of the plurality's analysis. He read the "best available evidence" provision in section 6(b)(5) to mean that OSHA can rely on qualitative judgments derived from expert opinion once it shows quantitative evidence is inconclusive. He further indicated that nothing in the Act "suggests that OSHA's hands are tied when reasonable quantification cannot be accomplished by any known methods." On that basis, Justice Powell decided OSHA had attempted to prove the risk at 10 ppm was significant. He articulated a two-part test to measure the sufficiency of the Agency's findings on that question: did OSHA show by substantial evidence that a "numerical estimate of risks" was unavailable, and if so, did it show by substantial qualitative evidence that a significant risk exists? Justice Powell concluded that OSHA did not succeed in meeting its burden of proof, without indicating which part or parts of his test the Agency had failed. Evidently, a showing of *some* risk and *some* benefit from reduction of that risk was not sufficient. Yet the discussion below suggests the Agency will rarely be able to make a more definitive determination.

* * *

B. Reductive Treatment of Uncertainty

* * * A reductive approach to legal decisionmaking under uncertainty ignores four important variables * * *: (1) the hierarchy of interests established in particular regulatory statutes; (2) the particular factual issues about which the uncertainty arises; (3) the respective abilities of the parties to resolve particular uncertainties; and (4) the question of what legal outcome is desirable when *no* party can resolve the uncertainty.

1. Differing Legislative Priorities

Regulatory statutes reflect a wide range of legislative purposes and priorities. In one program the legislature may prefer health and safety to economic considerations; in a second, the primary objective may be environmental protection; the predominant goal of a third act may be economic development; and a fourth statute may require a balancing of competing objectives, with no interest clearly favored. Uncertainties that arise in these dissimilar contexts could be resolved through the adoption of generalized procedural rules, but they should not be. When the legislature has expressed a preference for one interest over another, uncertainty should be resolved in a manner that promotes the underlying hierarchy of legislative purposes.

* * *

2. Differing Factual Issues

A reductive treatment of uncertainty does not distinguish between different factual issues that arise in regulatory contexts. * * *

Recent judicial decisions[95] have identified six discrete issues with respect to regulation of toxic substances under the OSH Act: (1) Is the substance under consideration sufficiently dangerous to be classified as toxic? (2) Is occupational exposure present? (3) Does the existing permissible exposure limit pose a significant risk of material health impairment? (4) Will the stricter PEL in OSHA's proposed standard significantly reduce the risk? (5) Is the new PEL technologically feasible, and (6) Is it economically feasible? The burden of proof in the benzene case, however, was imposed on a *party,* the "proponent of a rule or order," not on an issue-by-issue basis. In other words, the plurality relied on the APA to assign the burden of proof to OSHA for *all* factual questions.

* * * OSHA should indeed bear the burden on the preliminary issues of toxicity and occupational exposure. Yet a judicially-imposed allocational doctrine that prevents OSHA from effectively regulating the majority of recognized toxic substances because of uncertainty about the *degree* of toxicity at particular exposure levels is incompatible with the substantive mandate in the OSH Act. The legislative policies underlying the OSH Act would be promoted if the burden of proof were allocated to OSHA for the first two legal issues but not for the issues requiring disaggregated risk estimation. No reductive rule can achieve this degree of discrimination.

3. Differing Capacities of the Parties to Resolve Uncertainties

Another important variable is the comparative abilities of the parties to resolve particular factual uncertainties. In the cotton dust case [*American Textile Manufacturers Institute v. Donovan,* infra page 415] the majority opinion's analysis of economic feasibility illustrates the

---

95. 448 U.S. at 642–45; *American Textile Mfrs. Inst., Inc. v. Donovan,* 452 U.S. 490 (1981); *United Steelworkers v. Mar-* *shall,* 647 F.2d 1189 (D.C.Cir.1980), *cert. denied,* 453 U.S. 913 (1981).

importance of this variable. * * * OSHA had not attempted to determine actual compliance costs of the proposed PEL, and the Agency admitted it relied on cost projections that were very imprecise. Moreover, OSHA never contended it could not acquire better information, but simply that it could not make a more reliable estimate based on data then available. The cotton dust majority acknowledged that a cost estimate based on the promulgated PEL "surely would be preferable," but refused to hold as a matter of law that one was required. Justice Brennan concluded instead that the Agency had "acted reasonably" in light of the information before it. He identified several factors supporting the reasonableness of OSHA's action: (1) the "pre-eminent value" placed on employee protection in the OSH Act, (2) the inclusion in section 6(b)(5) of the "best available evidence" clause, (3) the typical imprecision in estimates of compliance costs, and (4) industry's refusal to provide more descriptive data. Information needed to assess the economic costs of proposed standards ordinarily is more readily available to industry than to OSHA. An allocational doctrine that requires the Agency to use reasonable efforts to collect information and then allows regulatory judgments to be based on available data would not foreclose industry from challenging determinations of economic feasibility. Industry could do so, however, only by providing sufficient economic information to rebut OSHA's initial finding. For courts to rule otherwise would permit industry to frustrate strict control of toxic substances by concealing data, and would make OSHA's task extremely difficult in situations where industry had not even attempted to institute effective protection for employees and there were no data concerning compliance costs.

* * * If judges are to assign the burden of proof for different factual issues partly on the basis of the parties' abilities to resolve uncertainties in each specific area, as the cotton dust opinion implies, the courts must reject the reductive approach of the benzene case.

4. When Uncertainty Cannot Be Resolved

Reductive analysis does not distinguish between cases where factual uncertainties can be resolved and cases where no party can answer the critical factual questions. In *Reserve Mining Co.* [supra page ___], * * * Judge Bright * * * found the plaintiffs had not demonstrated significant harm was "more likely than not" to occur. Nevertheless he held "an acceptable but unproved medical theory" that Reserve's discharges were carcinogenic was sufficient to support "a reasonable medical concern for the public health." He then construed the FWPCA itself, and determined that prevention of harm was the major objective of the statute. In light of this congressional priority, Judge Bright concluded even a "threat" of harm justified reasonable abatement measures. He clearly recognized the inability of parties to resolve the uncertainties in the case, but was unwilling to defer regulation indefinitely until the uncertainty could be resolved. Instead he approved reasonable regulation on the grounds that inaction in the face of uncertainty would be inconsistent with the preventive purpose of the FWPCA. This mode of analysis is clearly incompatible with * * * the reductive approach in the benzene case.

* * *

III. INTERPRETATION OF THE OSH ACT

* * *

A. *Preventative Purpose of the OSH Act*

Congress was aware of the "lamentable lack of knowledge" about toxic health effects when it passed the OSH Act; the inadequacy of information was one of the most frequent observations in the legislative history. * * *

In response to this uncertainty, Congress * * * in section 6(b)(5) expressly allowed OSHA to set toxic substances standards on the basis of the best available evidence. * * *

* * *

The proposition that Congress intended OSHA to postpone regulation indefinitely until the Agency can resolve scientific uncertainty is incompatible with the sense of urgency that prevailed when the OSH Act was passed. * * * The uncertainty associated with the introduction of "literally hundreds of new chemicals" was explicitly cited as a critical problem. If the congressional recognition that toxic substances often have delayed effects is juxtaposed with congressional concern over the dangers of new chemicals, for which long-term epidemiological data could not possibly exist, the section 6(b)(5) mandate that OSHA act on the basis of the best *available* evidence cannot be reconciled with the notion that the Agency should wait until information on disaggregated risks can be collected.

Justice Stevens did not allocate the burden of uncertainty in a manner consistent with the preventive purpose of the OSH Act at least in part because of two erroneous factual assumptions. He thought the Agency often could estimate disaggregated risk levels for carcinogens, and that the consequences of promulgating too lenient a standard would be remediable [because workers who were unusually susceptible to benzene could be removed from exposure before they had suffered any permanent damage].

* * *

Unlike progressive diseases such as byssinosis or nonmalignant blood disorders, cancer formation does not invariably depend on cumulative exposures.[376] Leukemia is not detectable in many cases until years or

---

376. The existence of a dose-response curve simply indicates that the probability of contracting leukemia increases as the exposure is increased. A threshold level for benzene-induced leukemia means only that an individual must be exposed to at least that dose before he is at risk. If the person is exposed only once in his life to a suffi-

decades after the fatal exposure occurs. Moreover, the discovery of occasional instances of leukemia among exposed workers would prove nothing because the disease occurs naturally in some people. Only a controlled long-term epidemiological study covering a large number of employees could identify a statistically valid incidence of excess cancers at an exposure limit that Justice Stevens conceded may be "initially set too high." By the time the results of such a study were available, hundreds of thousands of workers would have been exposed to unnecessarily high levels of benzene. And because no cure is known for leukemia, the consequences of that exposure, whatever they may ultimately prove to be, will be irreversible.

* * *

The plurality's insistence on disaggregated risk estimates leads to an anomalous result. Only a few years before OSHA's benzene proceeding, industry voluntarily accepted a maximum exposure level of 10 ppm.[383] Had industry continued to expose workers to 100 ppm or more of benzene, the Agency could probably have proved the risk was significant; the plurality acknowledged there was abundant evidence of toxicity at exposure levels "well above 10 ppm." The benzene case held that once a significant risk is found, section 6(b)(5) requires imposition of a highly protective standard. If OSHA had met the significance threshold at the 100 ppm level, it could then have required compliance with its stringent 1 ppm standard. Yet the same 1 ppm PEL was rejected by the benzene plurality because OSHA could not meet the significance test at industry's relatively new 10 ppm limit.

Suppose OSHA attempts to conduct epidemiological studies at the current 10 ppm PEL in order to document the need for a more stringent limit. If the long-term study at 10 ppm ultimately reveals a significant risk, then the Agency will be allowed to impose its proposed 1 ppm standard, the safest feasible PEL for benzene. If, a few years hence, industry agrees to reduce exposures to a maximum of 5 ppm, and the Agency chooses to promulgate an interim 5 ppm standard, an entirely new epidemiological study limited to exposures of 5 ppm and below will have to be initiated before the 1 ppm limit could be imposed. Positive results in the original 10 ppm study could not support a finding that 5 ppm presents a significant risk.

* * *

cient dose of benzene and if that exposure initiates neoplastic alteration, leukemia may eventually result even when there are no subsequent periods of exposure. In other words, the degree of carcinogenic exposure is relevant to the incidence of disease, not to its severity once contracted. Implicit in OSHA's adoption of the one-hit theory, is the possibility that some people may die from small and infrequent exposures.

383. Industry adopted a consensus limit of 10 ppm in 1969, and OSHA promulgated a national consensus standard at that level in 1971. However, the plurality acknowledged that some plants may have continued "relatively high exposures through the 1970's." Obviously, epidemiological data on benzene risks at low levels of exposure can only be acquired after industries actually reduce exposures to those levels.

CONCLUSION

The incorrect result in the benzene case stemmed from three analytical deficiencies: failure to distinguish between insignificant health risks and uncertain risks, failure to accept the Agency's determination that it cannot estimate disaggregated risks for benzene and other carcinogens, and failure to allocate the burden of uncertainty in a manner compatible with the legislative policy in the OSH Act.

AMERICAN TEXTILE MANUFACTURERS INSTITUTE, INC. v. DONOVAN

Supreme Court of the United States, 1981.
452 U.S. 490, 101 S.Ct. 2478, 69 L.Ed.2d 185.

[This case involved a disease called byssinosis, more commonly known as "brown lung" disease. The disease is primarily caused by the inhalation of cotton dust, a byproduct of textile manufacturing. One study showed that over 25% of the sample of cotton workers suffered at least some form of the disease, while 35,000 workers suffer from the most disabling form. In a footnote early in the opinion, the Court considered whether OSHA had complied with *Industrial Union Department* in promulgating a standard to govern cotton dust:

OSHA amended its Cancer Policy to "carry out the Court's interpretation of the Occupational Safety and Health Act of 1970 that consideration must be given to the significance of the risk in the issuance of a carcinogen standard and that OSHA must consider all relevant evidence in making these determinations." 46 Fed.Reg. 4889, col. 3 (1981). Previously, although lacking such evidence as dose response data, the Secretary presumed that no safe exposure level existed for carcinogenic substances. Following this Court's decision, OSHA deleted those provisions of the Cancer Policy which required the "automatic setting of the lowest feasible level" without regard to determinations of risk significance.

In distinct contrast with its Cancer Policy, OSHA expressly found that "exposure to cotton dust presents a significant health hazard to employees," and that "cotton dust produced significant health effects at low levels of exposure." In addition, the agency noted that "grade ½ byssinosis and associated pulmonary function decrements are significant health effects in themselves and should be prevented in so far as possible." In making its assessment of significant risk, OSHA relied on dose response curve data (the Merchant Study) showing that 25% of employees suffered at least Grade ½ byssinosis at a 500 ug/m 3PEL, and that 12.7% of all employees would suffer byssinosis at the 200 ug/m 3PEL standard. Examining the Merchant Study in light of other studies in the record, the agency found that "the Merchant study provides a reliable assessment of health risk to cotton textile workers from cotton dust." OSHA concluded that the "prevalence of byssinosis should be significantly reduced" by the 200 ug/m 3PEL. * * * It is difficult to imagine what else the agency could do to comply with this Court's decision in *Industrial Union Department v. American Petroleum Institute.*

452 U.S. at 505–506 n. 25, 101 S.Ct. at 2488–2489 n. 25. Having addressed this preliminary issue, the Court then turned to the primary issue in the case.]

JUSTICE BRENNAN delivered the opinion of the Court.

The principal question presented in this case is whether the Occupational Safety and Health Act requires the Secretary, in promulgating a standard pursuant to § 6(b)(5) of the Act, to determine that the costs of the standard bear a reasonable relationship to its benefits. Relying on §§ 6(b)(5) and 3(8) of the Act, petitioners urge not only that OSHA must show that a standard addresses a significant risk of material health impairment, but also that OSHA must demonstrate that the reduction in risk of material health impairment is significant in light of the costs of attaining that reduction. Respondents on the other hand contend that the Act requires OSHA to promulgate standards that eliminate or reduce such risks "to the extent such protection is technologically and economically feasible."

* * *

The starting point of our analysis is the language of the statute itself. Section 6(b)(5) of the Act provides:

> The Secretary, in promulgating standards dealing with toxic materials or harmful physical agents under this subsection, shall set the standard which most adequately assures, *to the extent feasible,* on the basis of the best available evidence, that no employee will suffer material impairment of health or functional capacity even if such employee has regular exposure to the hazard dealt with by such standard for the period of his working life.

Although their interpretations differ, all parties agree that the phrase "to the extent feasible" contains the critical language in § 6(b)(5) for purposes of this case.

The plain meaning of the word "feasible" supports respondents' interpretation of the statute. According to Webster's Third New International Dictionary of the English Language, "feasible" means "capable of being done, executed, or effected." Accord, The Oxford English Dictionary 116 (1933) ("Capable of being done, accomplished or carried out"); Funk & Wagnalls New "Standard" Dictionary of the English Language 903 (1957) ("That may be done, performed or effected"). Thus, § 6(b)(5) directs the Secretary to issue the standard that "most adequately assures * * * that no employee will suffer material impairment of health," limited only by the extent to which this is "capable of being done." In effect then, as the Court of Appeals held, Congress itself defined the basic relationship between costs and benefits, by placing the "benefit" of worker health above all other considerations save those making attainment of this "benefit" unachievable. Any standard based on a balancing of costs and benefits by the Secretary that strikes a different balance than that struck by Congress would be inconsistent with the command set forth in § 6(b)(5). Thus, cost-benefit analysis by OSHA is not required by the statute because feasibility analysis is.[29]

* * *

Even though the plain language of § 6(b)(5) supports this construction, we must still decide whether § 3(8), the general definition of an occupational safety and health standard, either alone or in tandem with § 6(b)(5), incorporates a cost-benefit requirement for standards dealing with toxic materials or harmful physical agents. Section 3(8) of the Act provides:

> The term "occupational safety and health standard" means a standard which requires conditions, or the adoption or use of one or more practices, means, methods, operations, or processes, *reasonably necessary or appropriate* to provide safe or healthful employment and places of employment.

Taken alone, the phrase "reasonably necessary or appropriate" might be construed to contemplate some balancing of the costs and benefits of a standard. Petitioners urge that, so construed, § 3(8) engrafts a cost-benefit analysis requirement on the issuance of § 6(b)(5) standards, even if § 6(b)(5) itself does not authorize such analysis. We need not decide whether § 3(8), standing alone, would contemplate some form of cost-benefit analysis. For even if it does, Congress specifically chose in § 6(b)(5) to impose separate and additional requirements for issuance of a subcategory of occupational safety and health standards dealing with toxic materials and harmful physical agents; it required that those standards be issued to prevent material impairment of health *to the extent feasible*. Congress could reasonably have concluded that *health* standards should be subject to different criteria than *safety* standards because of the special problems presented in regulating them.

Agreement with petitioners' argument that § 3(8) imposes an additional and overriding requirement of cost-benefit analysis on the issuance of § 6(b)(5) standards would eviscerate the "to the extent feasible" requirement. Standards would inevitably be set at the level indicated by cost-benefit analysis, and not at the level specified by § 6(b)(5). For example, if cost-benefit analysis indicated a protective standard of 1000

---

29. In this case we are faced with the issue whether the Act requires OSHA to balance costs and benefits in promulgating a *single* toxic material and harmful physical agent standard under § 6(b)(5). Petitioners argue that without cost-benefit balancing, the issuance of a single standard might result in a "serious misallocation of the finite resources that are available for the protection of worker safety and health," given the other health hazards in the workplace. This argument is more properly addressed to other provisions of the Act which may authorize OSHA to explore costs and benefits before deciding between issuance of several standards regulating different varieties of health and safety hazards, e.g., § 6(g) of the Act, 29 U.S.C. § 655(g); see *Industrial Union Department v. American Petroleum Institute,* supra, 448 U.S., at 644, 100 S.Ct., at 2865; see also Case Comment, 60 B.U.L.R. 115, 122, n. 52, or for promulgating other types of standards not issued under § 6(b)(5). We express no view on these questions.

ug/m 3PEL, while feasibility analysis indicated a 500 ug/m3 PEL, the agency would be forced by the cost-benefit requirement to choose the less stringent point. We cannot believe that Congress intended the general terms of § 3(8) to countermand the specific feasibility requirement of § 6(b)(5). Adoption of petitioners' interpretation would effectively write § 6(b)(5) out of the Act. We decline to render Congress' decision to include a feasibility requirement nugatory, thereby offending the well-settled rule that all parts of a statute, if possible, are to be given effect. Congress did not contemplate any further balancing by the agency for toxic material and harmful physical agents standards, and we should not "impute to Congress a purpose to paralyze with one hand what it sought to promote with the other."

[In the remaining portions of the opinion, the Court concluded that: (1) its construction of the statute was supported by the legislative history, and (2) the agency's finding that its cotton dust standard was feasible was supported by substantial evidence. Justice Stewart dissented from the substantial evidence holding. Justice Rehnquist, in an opinion joined by Chief Justice Burger, reiterated his view that the "feasibility" standard is no standard at all, and hence is unconstitutional.]

Powell recused himself 5-3 decision

Notes

1. The upshot of the Court's two opinions is that risk and cost are separated: the agency first decides if there is currently a "significant risk" and then regulates to the extent feasible. From an economist's point of view, this leads to odd results, since a minor risk might be worth regulating if eliminating the risk is cheap enough, whereas a major risk might not be worth bothering about if the solution would be disproportionately expensive (even though not enough to bankrupt the industry). From an environmentalist viewpoint, as Professor Latin points out, the result of the Court's decisions is that the final level of environmental quality depends on the current level rather than on the absolute level of risk remaining. But if we think in terms of incentives for regulators and industry, perhaps something can be said for the Court's approach: it screens minor risks out of the regulatory process entirely, thereby saving administrative resources and limiting the possibility of an industry being targeted for purely political reasons, and also gives industry an incentive to reduce risks voluntarily below the "significant" level so as to avoid more onerous regulations later. By using separate qualitative standards to assess risk and cost, rather than demanding calculation of a precise ratio, the Court's approach might also be more responsive to the uncertainties surrounding risk regulation. (Of course, even if the Court's approach does make at least some small sense as a matter of policy, is there any reason to think that this approach is what Congress had in mind? Reread the statutory language.)

2. In J. Mendeloff, *The Dilemma of Toxic Substance Regulation: How Overregulation Causes Underregulation at OSHA* (1988), the author maintains that Congress and the federal courts have overregulated occupational risks from toxic substances by requiring excessively stringent administrative exposure standards. In suppressing consideration of costs and adopting strict exposure limits for only a few workplace chemicals, OSHA has generated

strong resistance to the regulation of hundreds of others. Mendeloff would require OSHA to balance costs and benefits in setting exposure standards, and allow OSHA a relaxed burden of proof when the implementation costs of a standard are small. As a first step toward broader coverage, he would have OSHA adopt, for unregulated and underregulated chemicals, a set of standards that was prepared by a private association of industrial hygienists. For a critique, see Dwyer, "Book Review: Overregulation," 15 *Ecology L.Q.* 719 (1988).

3.   In note 30 of the *American Textile* opinion, the Court said, "In other statutes, Congress has used the phrase 'unreasonable risk,' accompanied by explanation in legislative history, to signify a generalized balancing of costs and benefits." In *Corrosion Proof Fittings v. EPA,* 947 F.2d 1201 (5th Cir.1991), page 501 infra, the court cited note 30 of *American Textile* in holding that "EPA must balance the costs of its regulations against their benefits" under the Toxic Substances Control Act. TSCA § 6(a) provides for regulation of "unreasonable risk[s] of injury to health or the environment."

4.   Because of the multiple opinions in *Industrial Union Department,* and subsequent changes in the makeup of the Court, the meaning of the foregoing OSHA decisions for toxics regulation in general is not entirely clear. The four dissenters in the benzene case endorsed the approach previously taken by lower courts in non-OSHA cases like *Reserve Mining.* The members of the plurality took a more cautious view but did not necessarily indicate that their "significant risk" standard was applicable to toxics regulation under other statutes, such as the Clean Air and Clean Water Acts.

It has been argued that the rationale of the plurality "escaped the context of OSHA and apparently established a presumptive significant risk standard for federal regulation of carcinogens, unless language or legislative history directly contradicted such a standard." Cross, Byrd & Lave, "Discernible Risk—A Proposed Standard for Significant Risk in Carcinogen Regulation," 43 *Admin.L.Rev.* 61, 69 (1991). Further, said those authors, the Court of Appeals for the D.C. Circuit, in the 1987 "vinyl chloride" case (immediately below), "pointedly extended the holdings of the *Benzene* decision beyond [OSHA] to the Clean Air Act and carved out a major role for significant risk analysis in the regulation of hazardous air pollutants." Id. at 70.

NATURAL RESOURCES DEFENSE COUNCIL, INC. v. ENVIRONMENTAL PROTECTION AGENCY

United States Court of Appeals (en banc), District of Columbia Circuit, 1987.
824 F.2d 1146.

BORK, CIRCUIT JUDGE:

I.

Section 112 of the Clean Air Act provides for regulation of hazardous air pollutants, which the statute defines as "air pollutant[s] to which no ambient air quality standard is applicable and which in the judgment of the Administrator cause[ ], or contribute[ ] to, air pollution which may reasonably be anticipated to result in an increase in mortality or an increase in serious irreversible, or incapacitating reversible, illness." The statute requires the Administrator to publish a list containing each hazardous pollutant for which he intends to adopt an emission standard, to publish proposed regulations and a notice of public hearing for each such pollutant, and then, within a specified period, either to promulgate an emission standard or to make a finding that the particular agent is not a hazardous air pollutant. The statute directs the Administrator to set an emission standard promulgated under section 112 "at the level which in his judgment provides an ample margin of safety to protect the public health."

This case concerns vinyl chloride regulations. Vinyl chloride is a gaseous synthetic chemical used in the manufacture of plastics and is a strong carcinogen. In late 1975, the Administrator issued a notice of proposed rulemaking to establish an emission standard for vinyl chloride. In the notice, the EPA asserted that available data linked vinyl chloride to carcinogenic, as well as some noncarcinogenic, disorders and that "[r]easonable extrapolations" from this data suggested "that present ambient levels of vinyl chloride may cause or contribute to * * * [such] disorders." The EPA also noted that vinyl chloride is "an apparent non-threshold pollutant," which means that it appears to create a risk to health at all non-zero levels of emission. Scientific uncertainty, due to the unavailability of dose-response data and the twenty-year latency period between initial exposure to vinyl chloride and the occurrence of disease, makes it impossible to establish any definite threshold level below which there are no adverse effects to human health. The notice also stated the "EPA's position that for a carcinogen it should be assumed, in the absence of strong evidence to the contrary, that there is no atmospheric concentration that poses absolutely no public health risk."

Because of this assumption, the EPA concluded that it was faced with two alternative interpretations of its duty under section 112. First, the EPA determined that section 112 might require a complete prohibition of emissions of non-threshold pollutants because a "zero emission limitation would be the only emission standard which would offer absolute safety from ambient exposure." The EPA found this alternative "neither desirable nor necessary" because "[c]omplete prohibition of all emissions could require closure of an entire industry," a cost the EPA found "extremely high for elimination of a risk to health that is of unknown dimensions."

The EPA stated the second alternative as follows:

An alternative interpretation of section 112 is that it authorizes setting emission standards that require emission reduction to the lowest level achievable by use of the best available control technology in cases involving apparent non-threshold pollutants, where complete emission prohibition would result in widespread industry closure and EPA has determined that the cost of such closure would be grossly disproportionate to the benefits of removing the risk that would remain after imposition of the best available control technology.

The EPA adopted this alternative on the belief that it would "produce the most stringent regulation of hazardous air pollutants short of requiring a complete prohibition in all cases."

On October 21, 1976, the EPA promulgated final emission standards for vinyl chloride which were based solely on the level attainable by the best available control technology. The EPA determined that this standard would reduce unregulated emissions by 95 percent. With respect to the effect of the standard on health, the EPA stated that it had assessed the risk to health at ambient levels of exposure by extrapolating from dose-response data at higher levels of exposure and then made the following findings:

> EPA found that the rate of initiation of liver angiosarcoma among [the 4.6 million] people living around uncontrolled plants is expected to range from less than one to ten cases of liver angiosarcoma per year of exposure to vinyl chloride * * *. Vinyl chloride is also estimated to produce an equal number of primary cancers at other sites, for a total of somewhere between less than one and twenty cases of cancer per year of exposure among residents around plants. The number of these effects is expected to be reduced at least in proportion to the reduction in the ambient annual average vinyl chloride concentration, which is expected to be 5 percent of the uncontrolled levels after the standard is implemented.

The EPA did not state whether this risk to health is significant or not. Nor did the EPA explain the relationship between this risk to health and its duty to set an emission standard which will provide an "ample margin of safety."

The Environmental Defense Fund ("EDF") filed suit challenging the standard on the ground that section 112 requires the Administrator to rely exclusively on health and prohibits consideration of cost and technology. The EDF and the EPA settled the suit, however, upon the EPA's agreement to propose new and more stringent standards for vinyl chloride and to establish an ultimate goal of zero emissions.

The EPA satisfied its obligations under the settlement agreement by proposing new regulations on June 2, 1977. While the proposal sought to impose more strict regulation by requiring sources subject to a 10 parts per million ("ppm") limit to reduce emissions to 5 ppm, and by establishing an aspirational goal of zero emissions, the EPA made it clear that it considered its previous regulations valid and reemphasized its view that the inability scientifically to identify a threshold of adverse effects did not require prohibition of all emissions, but rather permitted regulation at the level of best available technology. The EPA received comments on the proposal, but took no final action for more than seven years. On January 9, 1985, the EPA withdrew the proposal. Noting that certain aspects of the proposed regulations imposed "unreasonable" costs and that no control technology "has been demonstrated to significantly and consistently reduce emissions to a level below that required by the current standard," the EPA concluded that it should abandon the 1977 proposal and propose in its place only minor revisions to the 1976 regulations.

This petition for review followed.

* * *

III.

The NRDC's challenge to the EPA's withdrawal of the 1977 amendments is simple: because the statute adopts an exclusive focus on considerations of health, the Administrator must set a zero level of emissions when he cannot determine that there is a level below which no harm will occur.

We must determine whether the EPA's actions are arbitrary, capricious, an abuse of discretion, or otherwise not in accordance with law. Review begins with the question of whether "Congress has directly spoken to the precise question at issue" and has expressed a clear intent as to its resolution. * * * "[I]f the statute is silent or ambiguous with respect to the specific issue," we must accept an agency interpretation if it is reasonable in light of the language, legislative history, and underlying policies of the statute. We find no support in the text or legislative history for the proposition that Congress intended to require a complete prohibition of emissions whenever the EPA cannot determine a threshold level for a hazardous pollutant. Instead, there is strong evidence that Congress considered such a requirement and rejected it.

Section 112 commands the Administrator to set an "emission standard" for a particular "hazardous air pollutant" which in his "judgment" will provide an "ample margin of safety." Congress' use of the term "ample margin of safety" is inconsistent with the NRDC's position that the Administrator has no discretion in the face of uncertainty. The statute nowhere defines "ample margin of safety." The Senate Report, however, in discussing a similar requirement in the context of setting ambient air standards under section 109 of the Act, explained the purpose of the "margin of safety" standard as one of affording "a *reasonable* degree of protection * * * against hazards which research has not yet identified." S.Rep. No. 1196, 91st Cong., 2d Sess. 10 (1970) (emphasis added). * * *

Congress' use of the word "safety," moreover, is significant evidence that it did not intend to require the Administrator to prohibit all emissions of non-threshold pollutants. As the Supreme Court has recently held, "safe" does not mean "risk-free." *Industrial Union Dep't, AFL–CIO v. American Petroleum Inst.*, 448 U.S. 607, 642, 100 S.Ct. 2844, 2864, 65 L.Ed.2d 1010 (1980). Instead, something is "unsafe" only when it threatens humans with "a significant risk of harm."

Thus, the terms of section 112 provide little support for the NRDC's position. The uncertainty about the effects of a particular carcinogenic pollutant invokes the Administrator's discretion under section 112. In contrast, the NRDC's position would eliminate any discretion and would render the standard "ample margin of safety" meaningless as applied to carcinogenic pollutants.[1] Whenever *any* scientific uncertainty existed about the ill effects of a nonzero level of hazardous air pollutants—and we think it unlikely that science will ever yield *absolute* certainty of safety in an area so complicated and rife with problems of measurement, modeling, long latency, and the like—the Administrator would have no discretion but would be required to prohibit all emissions. Had Congress intended that result, it could very easily have said so by writing a statute that states that no level of emissions shall be allowed as to which there is any uncertainty. But Congress chose instead to deal with the pervasive nature of scientific uncertainty and the inherent limitations of scientific knowledge by vesting in the Administrator the discretion to deal with uncertainty in each case.

The NRDC also argues that the legislative history supports its position. To the contrary, that history strongly suggests that Congress did not require the Administrator to prohibit emissions of all non-threshold pollutants; Congress considered and rejected the option of requiring the Administrator to prohibit all emissions.

* * *

IV.

We turn now to the question whether the Administrator's chosen method for setting emission levels above zero is consistent with congressional intent. The Administrator's position is that he may set an emission level for non-threshold pollutants at the lowest level achievable by best available control technology when that level is anywhere below the level of demonstrated harm and the cost of setting a lower level is grossly disproportionate to the benefits of removing the remaining risk. The NRDC argues that this standard is arbitrary and capricious because the EPA is never permitted to consider cost and technological feasibility under section 112 but instead is limited to consideration of health-based factors. Thus, before addressing the Administrator's method of using cost and technological feasibility in this case, we must determine whether he may consider cost and technological feasibility at all.

On its face, section 112 does not indicate that Congress intended to preclude consideration of any factor. Though the phrase "to protect the public health" evinces an intent to make health the primary consideration, there is no indication of the factors the Administrator may or may

---

1. With the exception of mercury, every pollutant the Administrator has listed or intends to list under § 112 is a non-threshold carcinogen. See 40 C.F.R. § 61.01(a) (1986) (listing asbestos, benzene, beryllium, coke oven emissions, inorganic arsenic, radionuclides, and vinyl chloride); 50 Fed.Reg. 24,317 (June 10, 1985) (chromium); 50 Fed. Reg. 32,621 (Aug. 13, 1985) (carbon tetra-chloride); 50 Fed.Reg. 39,626 (Sept. 27, 1985) (chloroform); 50 Fed.Reg. 40,286 (Oct. 2, 1985) (ethylene oxide); 50 Fed.Reg. 41,466 (Oct. 10, 1985) (1,3–butadiene); 50 Fed.Reg. 41,994 (Oct. 16, 1985) (ethylene dichloride); 50 Fed.Reg. 42,000 (Oct. 16, 1985) (cadmium); 50 Fed.Reg. 52,422 (Dec. 23, 1985) (trichloroethylene); 50 Fed.Reg. 52,880 (Dec. 26, 1985) (perchioroethylene).

not consider in determining, in his "judgment," what level of emissions will provide "an ample margin of safety." Instead, the language used, and the absence of any specific limitation, gives the clear impression that the Administrator has some discretion in determining what, if any, additional factors he will consider in setting an emission standard.

The petitioner argues that the legislative history makes clear Congress' intent to foreclose reliance on non-health-based considerations in setting standards under section 112. We find, however, that the legislative history can be characterized only as ambiguous.

* * *

[W]e cannot find a clear congressional intent in the language, structure, or legislative history of the Act to preclude consideration of cost and technological feasibility under section 112.

The petitioner argues next that a finding that section 112 does not preclude consideration of cost and technological feasibility would render the Clean Air Act structurally incoherent and would be inconsistent with the Supreme Court's interpretation of section 110 of the Act, see *Union Electric Co. v. EPA*, 427 U.S. 246, 96 S.Ct. 2518, 49 L.Ed.2d 474 (1976), and this court's interpretation of section 109 of the Act, *see Lead Indus. Ass'n v. EPA*, 647 F.2d 1130 (D.C.Cir.), cert. denied, 449 U.S. 1042, 101 S.Ct. 621, 66 L.Ed.2d 503 (1980), as precluding consideration of these factors. We do not believe that our decision here is inconsistent with either the holding or the statutory interpretation in either case.

First, as discussed below, the court in each case rejected an argument that the EPA must consider cost and technological feasibility as factors equal in importance to health. We reject the same argument here. In this case, however, we must also address the question of whether the Administrator may consider these factors if necessary to further *protect* the public health. This issue was not addressed in either *Union Electric* or *Lead Industries*.

Second, these decisions do not provide precedential support for the petitioner's position that, as a matter of statutory interpretation, cost and technological feasibility may never be considered under the Clean Air Act unless Congress expressly so provides. In each case there was some indication in the language, structure, or legislative history of the specific provision at issue that Congress intended to preclude consideration of cost and technological feasibility. As discussed above, we find no such indication with respect to section 112.

* * *

V.

Since we cannot discern clear congressional intent to preclude consideration of cost and technological feasibility in setting emission standards under section 112, we necessarily find that the Administrator may consider these factors. We must next determine whether the Administrator's use of these factors in this case is "based on a permissible construction of the statute." We must uphold the Administrator's construction if it represents "a reasonable policy choice for the agency to make." We cannot, however, affirm an agency interpretation found to be "arbitrary, capricious, or manifestly contrary to the statute." Nor can we affirm if "it appears from the statute or its legislative history that the accommodation [chosen] is not one that Congress would have sanctioned."

Our role on review of an action taken pursuant to section 112 is generally a limited one. Because the regulation of carcinogenic agents raises questions "on the frontiers of scientific knowledge," we have recognized that the Administrator's decision in this area "will depend to a greater extent upon policy judgments" to which we must accord considerable deference. * * * Despite this deferential standard, we find that the Administrator has ventured into a zone of impermissible action. The Administrator has not exercised his expertise to determine an acceptable risk to health. To the contrary, in the face of uncertainty about risks to health, he has simply substituted technological feasibility for health as the primary consideration under Section 112. Because this action is contrary to clearly discernible congressional intent, we grant the petition for review.

* * *

We find that the congressional mandate to provide "an ample margin of safety" "to protect the public health" requires the Administrator to make an initial determination of what is "safe." This determination must be based exclusively upon the Administrator's determination of the risk to health at a particular emission level. Because the Administrator in this case did not make any finding of the risk to health, the question of how that determination is to be made is not before us. We do wish to note, however, that the Administrator's decision does not require a finding that "safe" means "risk-free," see *Industrial Union Dep't,* 448 U.S. at 642, 100 S.Ct. at 2864, or a finding that the determination is free from uncertainty. Instead, we find only that the Administrator's decision must be based upon an expert judgment with regard to the level of emission that will result in an "acceptable" risk to health. In this regard, the Administrator must determine what inferences should be drawn from available scientific data and decide what risks are acceptable in the world in which we live. See *Industrial Union Dep't,* 448 U.S. at 642, 100 S.Ct. at 2864 ("There are many activities that we engage in every day—such as driving a car or even breathing city air—that entail some risk of accident or material health impairment; nevertheless, few people would consider those activities 'unsafe.' "). This determination must be based solely upon the risk to health. The Administrator cannot under any circumstances consider cost and technological feasibility at this stage of the analysis. The latter factors have no relevance to the preliminary determination of what is safe. Of course, if the Administrator cannot find that there is an acceptable risk at any level, then the Administrator must set the level at zero.

Congress, however, recognized in section 112 that the determination of what is "safe" will always be marked by scientific uncertainty and thus exhorted the Administrator to set emission standards that will provide an "ample margin" of safety. This language permits the Administrator to take into account scientific uncertainty and to use expert discretion to determine what action should be taken in light of that uncertainty. * * * In determining what is an "ample margin" the Administrator may, and perhaps must, take into account the inherent limitations of risk assessment and the limited scientific knowledge of the effects of exposure to carcinogens at various levels, and may therefore decide to set the level below that previously determined to be "safe." This is especially true when a straight line extrapolation from known risks is used to estimate risks to health at levels of exposure for which no data is available. This method, which is based upon the results of exposure at fairly high levels of the hazardous pollutants, will show some risk at every level because of the rules of arithmetic rather than because of any knowledge. In fact the risk at a certain point on the extrapolated line may have no relationship to reality; there is no particular reason to think that the actual line of the incidence of harm is represented by a straight line. Thus, by its nature the finding of risk is uncertain and the Administrator must use his discretion to meet the statutory mandate. It is only at this point of the regulatory process that the Administrator may set the emission standard at the lowest level that is technologically feasible. In fact, this is, we believe, precisely the type of policy choice that Congress envisioned when it directed the Administrator to provide an "ample margin of safety." Once "safety" is assured, the Administrator should be free to diminish as much of the statistically determined risk as possible by setting the standard at the lowest feasible level. Because consideration of these factors at this stage is clearly intended "to protect the public health," it is fully consistent with the Administrator's mandate under section 112.

Notes

1. Would Latin, page 451 supra, criticize the court's requirement that the Administrator determine the "risk to health at a particular emission level"? Was this an insistence upon impossible "disaggregated risk estimates," or was the requirement less onerous than what the plurality demanded in the benzene case?

2. For an interesting perspective on the statute involved in the principal case, see Dwyer, "The Pathology of Symbolic Legislation," 17 *Ecology L.Q.* 233 (1990).

3. In 1989, EPA published some final and some proposed regulations governing industrial benzene emissions. 54 Fed.Reg. 38044, 38083. These were the first toxic air pollutant standards developed under the two-step procedure ordered by the court of appeals. Concerning "acceptable risk" to health, EPA said it would generally presume that a maximum individual risk

("MIR") no higher than 1 in 10,000 was acceptable, i.e., a person living very near to the pollution source and exposed to the maximum, modeled long-term concentration of the pollutant, 24 hours per day for 70 years, should not face an estimated risk greater than 1 in 10,000 of contracting cancer therefrom. Concerning "ample margin of safety," EPA sought to provide protection to the greatest number of persons possible—estimated at 99 percent of all persons within 50 kilometers of all the emission sources—to an individual lifetime risk level no higher than approximately 1 in 1 million. Id. at 38045. For background information about these regulations, see Note, " 'Acceptable' Risk for Hazardous Air Pollutants," 13 *Harv.Envir.L.Rev.* 535 (1989). See also Note, "Risk Assessment of Hazardous Air Pollutants Under the EPA's Final Benzene Rules and the Clean Air Act Amendments of 1990," 70 *Texas L.Rev.* 427 (1991).

Note on Regulation of Hazardous Air Pollutants Under Section 112 of the Clean Air Act, as Amended in 1990

The Clean Air Act Amendments of 1990 included a totally new section 112, somewhat similar in approach to section 307 of the Clean Water Act, pages 341–342 supra. However, the risk management methodology prescribed in the 1987 vinyl chloride case and employed in EPA's 1989 regulations governing industrial benzene emissions was endorsed by Congress and continues to be important under new section 112.

Section 112(b) now contains an initial list of 189 chemicals to be regulated. For each of two categories of sources, "major" and "area" (non-major), EPA is to promulgate emission standards under section 112(d), requiring installation of maximum achievable control technology (MACT). Standards are to be issued in stages, with the final deadline being in the year 2000. Existing sources are to comply with MACT standards within three years after issuance, unless EPA or a state agency grants a one-year extension. With respect to the distinction between "major" and "area" sources, EPA has defined "major" source to mean "any stationary source or group of stationary sources located within a contiguous area and under common control that emits . . ., in the aggregate, 10 tons per year or more of any hazardous air pollutant or 25 tons per year or more of any combination of hazardous air pollutants. . . . " 40 CFR § 63.2. Various industries challenged EPA's requiring the aggregation of all hazardous air emissions within a plant site, instead of only those emissions from equipment in similar industrial categories. The rule was upheld in *National Mining Ass'n v. EPA*, 59 F.3d 1351 (D.C.Cir.1995). The court noted that EPA's interpretation was "not simply consistent with [section 112(a)(1) but] nearly compelled by the statutory language."

Section 112(i)(5) directs EPA to establish an Early Reduction Program, allowing facilities to extend the MACT compliance deadlines for up to six years in exchange for voluntary early reductions of 90 percent or more of hazardous air pollutant emissions. EPA regulations for the Early Reduction Program, 57 Fed.Reg. 61970 (Dec. 29, 1992), detailed the procedures and requirements with which businesses must comply in seeking to obtain compliance extensions. The reductions required under the Early Reduction Program generally were less stringent than those expected to be required under MACT standards. Under the regulations, emission reductions achieved as far back as 1987, by any means and for any purpose, could be included in calculating a facility's early reductions.

In 1994, EPA issued MACT emission standards for organic hazardous air pollutants from the synthetic organic chemical manufacturing industry. 59 Fed.Reg. 19453 (April 22, 1994), codified at 40 CFR 63.100–63.193. The hazardous organic NESHAP, or HON rule, regulates 111 of the 189 hazardous air pollutants listed in section 112(b), and is expected to affect about 370 facilities in 38 states, largely in Louisiana, New Jersey and Texas. EPA estimated that toxic air emissions from the plants would be reduced by 88 percent, or 506,000 tons annually. See 24 *Envir.Rep.* 1883 (1994). One option by which companies can meet HON requirements involves emission averaging. A facility which does not want to meet the limit at one emission point can make the reduction at another point. However, the resulting total emissions will have to be 10 percent less than would have been required if the company had not chosen to average. While a typical chemical manufacturing facility may have 1,000 emission points, HON limits to 25 the number of points among which averaging may be conducted.

Beyond MACT standards, section 112(f)(2) contemplates subsequent adoption, within 8 years after promulgation of MACT standards for each category of sources, of *more stringent* emission standards where necessary "to provide an ample margin of safety to protect public health in accordance with this section (as in effect before the date of enactment of the Clean Air Act Amendments of 1990) or to prevent, taking into consideration costs, energy, safety, and other relevant factors, an adverse environmental effect." If MACT standards applicable to a "known, probable or possible human carcinogen do not reduce lifetime excess cancer risks to the individual most exposed to emissions from a source * * * to less than one in one million, the Administrator shall promulgate standards under this subsection for such source category." Section 112(f)(2)(B) provides that nothing in section 112 "shall be construed as affecting, or applying to the Administrator's interpretation of this section, as in effect before the date of enactment of [the 1990 amendments] and set forth in [the 1989 industrial benzene emission regulations] (54 Federal Register 38044)."

A Joint Explanatory Statement of the Committee of Conference says that, although section 112(f)(2) contains "a trigger for standards for non-threshold pollutants and * * * is also linked to the recently promulgated NESHAP for benzene which sets out the appropriate policy for regulating non-threshold pollutants[,] the absence of a trigger or policy reference for threshold pollutants shall not be interpreted in any way to preclude regulation of threshold pollutants under such subsection or to suggest that non-threshold pollutants are of a higher priority for regulation." 136 Cong. Record H13198 (Oct. 26, 1990).

For discussion of post-MACT "ample margin of safety" standards under section 112(f)(2), see Mank, "What Comes After Technology: Using an 'Exceptions Process' to Improve Residual Risk Regulation of Hazardous Air Pollutants," 13 *Stan.Envtl.L.J.* 263 (1994).

The 1990 amendments contained several provisions intended to improve risk assessment and risk management related to exposure to hazardous substances. Section 112(*o*) directed the EPA Administrator to arrange for

have become or
subcommittee of EPA
subadvisory board.

the National Academy of Sciences to review EPA's risk assessment methodology for determining the carcinogenic risk associated with exposure to hazardous air pollutants and, to the extent practicable, the risk of adverse human health effects other than cancer, such as inheritable genetic mutations, birth defects, and reproductive dysfunctions. (The report of the NAS Committee on Risk Assessment of Hazardous Air Pollutants is discussed in the note at pages 428–429 supra.) Section 303 of the amendments established a Risk Assessment and Management Commission to make a "full investigation of the policy implications and appropriate uses of risk assessment and risk management in regulatory programs under various Federal laws to prevent cancer and other chronic human health effects which may result from exposure to hazardous substances." Finally, new section 112(f)(1) requires that by 1996 the EPA Administrator shall report to Congress on (A) methods of calculating the risk to public health remaining from sources subject to section 112 after application of MACT standards; (B) the public health significance of such estimated remaining risk and the technologically and commercially available methods and costs of reducing such risks; and (C) the actual health effects with respect to persons living in the vicinity of sources, any uncertainties in risk assessment methodology or other health assessment technique, and any negative health or environmental consequences to the community of efforts to reduce such risks. Note that this report is to precede adoption of standards under section 112(f)(2) to protect public health with an "ample margin of safety."

Two other subjects dealt with by the 1990 amendments deserve mention. New section 112(r) authorizes adoption of regulations and programs to prevent the accidental release, and to minimize the consequences of any such release, of any hazardous substance. This provision seeks to avoid events like the chemical release which killed more than 2,000 persons in Bhopal, India in December 1984. New section 129, added to the Clean Air Act in 1990, directs EPA to establish performance standards for municipal, hospital, and other commercial and industrial incinerators. The standards are to reflect the "maximum degree of reduction in emissions [of hazardous pollutants] that the Administrator, taking into consideration the cost of achieving such emission reduction, and any non-air quality health and environmental impacts and energy requirements, determines is achievable for new or existing units in each category."

Pursuant to section 112(r), the EPA Administrator in 1996 issued a final rule requiring some 66,000 facilities to identify and assess by June 1999 their chemical hazards and carry out activities designed to reduce the likelihood and severity of accidental chemical releases. 61 *Fed. Reg.* 31668 (June 20, 1996). Section 112(r) requires facilities to develop and implement risk management programs that incorporate three elements: a hazard assessment, a prevention program, and an emergency response program. These programs are to be summarized in a risk management plan (RMP) available to state and local government agencies and to the public.

- RMP's are public.
- includes all chem. that are on site, not just those discharged. STOP

• in MI these were reviewed by Fire Marshall instead of DEQ.

Chapter VI

REGULATION OF TOXIC
SUBSTANCES AND
HAZARDOUS WASTES

This chapter examines legislation regulating the sale of toxic chemicals and the management of hazardous wastes, and mandating the disclosure of information related to these activities. Section A deals with the Federal Insecticide, Fungicide and Rodenticide Act (FIFRA) and Toxic Substances Control Act (TSCA), which were intended to prevent commercial distribution of chemicals whose use would pose unreasonable risks to health or the environment. Along with scientific testing requirements, presumptions and burden of proof again are important features of the legal landscape. Section B explores subchapter III of the Resource Conservation and Recovery Act (RCRA), concerning hazardous waste management, and state and local laws concerning the siting of hazardous waste facilities. Section C analyzes relevant disclosure requirements under the Emergency Planning and Community Right-to-Know Act (EPCRA) and the federal securities laws.

A. REGULATING THE SALE
OF TOXIC SUBSTANCES

1. PESTICIDE CONTROL

The earliest toxic chemical problem to receive widespread public attention was that of pesticides, thanks in large part to Rachael Carson's *Silent Spring*. The materials in this section consider the federal regulatory scheme for pesticides.[a] The first part of the following opinion discusses some of the statutory scheme in effect *prior* to a major revision of FIFRA in 1972. The court's treatment of the process for *suspension* of a previous registration remains valid and important today.

a. For additional discussion of the statutory framework see W. Rodgers, *Environ-* *mental Law* 393–487 (2d ed. 1994).

petitioner

ENVIRONMENTAL DEFENSE FUND, INC. v. ENVIRONMENTAL PROTECTION AGENCY

[ALDRIN AND DIELDRIN]

United States Court of Appeals, District of Columbia Circuit, 1972.
465 F.2d 528.

LEVENTHAL, CIRCUIT JUDGE.

On December 3, 1970, petitioner Environmental Defense Fund (EDF), a non-profit New York corporation, petitioned the Environmental Protection Agency (EPA) under the Federal Insecticide, Fungicide and *petition* Rodenticide Act (FIFRA), 7 U.S.C.A. §§ 135–135k, for the immediate suspension and ultimate cancellation of all registered uses of aldrin and dieldrin, two chemically similar chlorinated hydrocarbon pesticides. On March 18, 1971, the Administrator of the EPA announced the issuance of "notices of cancellation" for aldrin and dieldrin because of "a substantial question as to the safety of the registered products which has not been effectively countered by the registrant." He declined to order the interim remedy of suspension, pending final decision on cancellation after completion of the pertinent administrative procedure, in light of his decision that "present uses [of aldrin and dieldrin] do not pose an imminent threat to the public such as to require immediate action." EDF filed this petition to review the EPA's failure to suspend the *issue* registration.

I. SIGNIFICANCE OF EPA'S DECISION ON IMMEDIATE SUSPENSION OF FIFRA REGISTRATION

We begin by reviewing the significance of an EPA decision to issue or withhold an order of immediate suspension of a pesticide registration, pending final administrative consideration.

A. *The Statutory Framework of FIFRA*

Since 1970 the Administrator of the EPA has been charged with administering the two systems provided by Congress to regulate the introduction of potentially harmful pesticides into the environment: the establishment of registration and labeling requirements for "economic poisons" under FIFRA, formerly assigned to the Secretary of Agriculture; and the establishment of tolerance limits for shipment in interstate commerce of crops "adulterated" by pesticide residues, under the Food, Drug and Cosmetic Act, 21 U.S.C.A. 301 et seq., formerly assigned to the Department of Health, Education & Welfare.

Aldrin and dieldrin are "economic poisons" under the definition in § 2 of FIFRA, and hence are required to be registered with EPA before they may be distributed in interstate commerce. An economic poison may lawfully be registered only if it is properly labeled—not "misbranded." Section 2(z) of FIFRA, insofar relevant here, provides that an economic poison is "misbranded"—

> (c) if the labeling accompanying it does not contain directions for use which are necessary and if complied with adequate for the protection of the public;

> (d) if the label does not contain a warning or caution statement which may be necessary and if complied with adequate to prevent injury to living man and other vertebrate animals, vegetation, and useful invertebrate animals;

> * * *

> (g) if in the case of an insecticide, nematocide, fungicide, or herbicide when used as directed or in accordance with commonly recognized practice it shall be injurious to living man or other vertebrate animals, or vegetation, except weeds, to which it is applied, or to the person applying such economic poison.

If an economic poison is such that a label with adequate safeguards cannot be written, it may not be registered or sold in interstate commerce.

The burden of establishing the safety of a product requisite for compliance with the labeling requirements, remains at all times on the applicant and registrant. Whenever it appears that a registered economic poison may be or has become "misbranded," the Administrator is required to issue a notice of cancellation.

In § 4 of FIFRA, Congress has provided extensive safeguards for those whose FIFRA registrations are challenged.

* * *

The elaborate procedural protection against improvident cancellations emphasizes the importance of the immediate suspension provision available under § 4 of FIFRA, for use when appropriate:

> Notwithstanding any other provision of this section, the Administrator may, when he finds that such action is necessary to prevent an imminent hazard to the public, by order, suspend the registration of an economic poison immediately. In such case, he shall give the registrant prompt notice of such action and afford the registrant the opportunity to have the matter submitted to an advisory committee and for an expedited hearing under this section.

Because of the potential for delay, and consequent possibility of serious and irreparable environmental damage from an erroneous decision on suspension, a refusal to suspend is a final order reviewable immediately.

* * *

II.   EPA's Reasons for Declining to Order Immediate
Suspension of Aldrin and Dieldrin Registrations

1.   *The Decisions Taken by the EPA Administrator*

The EPA initiated an administrative investigation into registrations
for aldrin and dieldrin that resulted in cancellation of registrations for
certain uses. On December 2, 1970, the EDF addressed a petition to the
Administrator requesting the suspension and eventual cancellation of
registrations for all products containing aldrin and dieldrin. In order to
expedite the administrative process, and in light of our January 1971
decisions in *EDF v. Ruckelshaus* and *Wellford v. Ruckelshaus,* relating to
DDT, and 2, 4, 5–T, the Administrator consolidated the consideration of
registrations of DDT; 2, 4, 5–T; aldrin and dieldrin. On March 18, 1971,
he issued his Statement of Reasons Underlying the Registration Decisions concerning these products, the decision to issue notices of cancellation for all registrations for those substances, and also the decision not
to order interim suspension of registrations pending administrative
decision.

* * *

2.   *General Approach of EPA Statement of Reasons*

This suffices for an introduction to the Statement of Reasons. We
now examine it with greater care, and begin with the considerations
voiced by the Administrator as defining EPA's general approach.

Statutory Tests

* * *

The EPA points out that the final decision on registration depends
on a balance struck between benefits and dangers to the public health
and welfare from the product's use, and comments that the concept of
safety of the product is under evolution and refinement in the light of
increasing knowledge.

Suspension

[EPA's general criteria for suspension were as follows.]

* * * An "imminent hazard" may be declared at any point in a
chain of events which may ultimately result in harm to the public. It is
not necessary that the final anticipated injury actually have occurred
prior to a determination that an "imminent hazard" exists. In this
connection, significant injury or potential injury to plants or animals
alone could justify a finding of imminent hazard to the public from the
use of an economic poison. The type, extent, probability and duration of
potential or actual injury to man, plants and animals will be measured in
light of the positive benefits accruing from, for example, use of the
responsible economic poison in human or animal disease control or food
production.

General Standards

* * *

* * * EPA cites "dramatic steps in disease control" and the gradual amelioration of "the chronic problem of world hunger" as examples of the kind of beneficial effect to be looked for in balancing benefits against harm for specific substances. But it cautions that "triumphs of public health achieved in the past" will not be permitted to justify future registrations, recognizing that fundamentally different considerations are at work in evaluating use of a dangerous pesticide in a developed country such as the United States rather than in a developing non-industrial nation.

The immense difficulties of achieving a comprehensive solution to pesticide control are manifest from the Administrator's Statement of Reasons. It records that there are nearly 45,000 presently outstanding pesticide registrations for "hundreds" of substances in use over approximately five percent of the total land area of the United States. Available data show wide variety among individual substances both as to effectiveness against target species and as to potential harm to non-target species. Laboratory tests with some substances have raised serious questions regarding carcinogenicity that "deserve particular searching" because carcinogenic effects are generally cumulative and irreversible when discovered. Threats presented by individual substances vary not only as to observed persistence in the environment but also as to environmental mobility—which in turn depends in part on how a particular pesticide is introduced into the environment, either by ground insertion or by dispersal directly into the ambient air or water.

Based on the discussion of these general considerations, the EPA concludes that individual decisions on initial or continued registration must depend on a complex administrative calculus, in which the "nature and magnitude of the foreseeable hazards associated with use of a particular product" is weighed against the "nature of the benefit conferred" by its use.

3. *Discussion of Aldrin and Dieldrin*

The EPA's general analysis for suspension, set forth above, is supplemented in the Statement of Reasons by discussions concerning the particular products. Part IV, Dieldrin and Aldrin, comprises slightly more than two pages of the Statement.

* * *

The Administrator's reasons for denial of suspension, as to aldrin and dieldrin, appear in the following paragraphs of the Statement:

> [B]ecause the vast majority of the present use of these products is restricted to ground insertion, which presents little foreseeable damage from general environmental mobility, because of the pattern of declining gross use, and because of the lower historic introduction

of these products into the environmental residue burden to be faced by man and the other biota, the delay inherent in the administrative process does not present an imminent hazard. Thus the substantial question of the safety of these registrations is primarily raised by theoretical data, while review of the evidence from the ambient environment indicates that such potential hazards are not imminent in light of the present registrations.

It is significant to note that no residues of either aldrin or dieldrin are now permitted on corn, eggs, milk, poultry, or animal fats shipped in interstate commerce. Because of the use patterns of aldrin and dieldrin, these products constitute the major sources whereby these substances would find their way into human food chains. During the pendency of the administrative process hereby initiated, this Agency will take no action to grant any residue tolerances for these foodstuffs pursuant to the Food, Drug and Cosmetic Act, although initial tolerances have been requested by the manufacturer.

III.   THE EDF's CONTENTIONS OF INVALIDITY OF NON-SUSPENSION DECISIONS

* * *

Judicial doctrine teaches that a court must consider possibility of success on the merits, the nature and extent of the damage to each of the parties from the granting or denial of the injunction, and where the public interest lies. It was not inappropriate for the Administrator to have chosen a general approach to suspension that permits analysis of similar factors. By definition, a substantial question of safety exists when notices of cancellation issue. If there is no offsetting claim of any benefit to the public, then the EPA has the burden of showing that the substantial safety question does not pose an "imminent hazard" to the public.

Lack of Discussion of Benefits of Aldrin–Dieldrin

EDF is on sound ground in noting that while the EPA's general approach contemplates a decision as to suspension based on a balance of benefit and harm, the later discussion of aldrin and dieldrin relates only to harm.

The Administrator's mere mention of these products' major uses, emphasized by the EPA, cannot suffice as a discussion of benefits, even though

the data before him * * * reflected the view that aldrin-dieldrin pesticides are the only control presently available for some twenty insects which attack corn and for one pest which poses a real danger to citrus orchards * * *.

Brief for EPA, p. 19. The interests at stake here are too important to permit the decision to be sustained on the basis of speculative inference as to what the Administrator's findings and conclusions might have been regarding benefits. * * *

Our conclusion that a mere recitation of a pesticide's uses does not suffice as an analysis of benefits is fortified where, as here, there was a submission, by EDF, that alternative pest control mechanisms are available for such use. The analysis of benefit requires some consideration of whether such proposed alternatives are available or feasible, or whether such availability is in doubt.

* * *

Flexibility as to Limits

Our concern over EPA's failure to discuss benefits reflects our concern that what is done tacitly or by implication may mean that the agency has not taken into account the possibility of orders falling short of complete suspension. EPA has flexibility not only to confine suspensions to certain uses, but also to order conditional suspensions for uses, available only if certain volumes or limits are not exceeded. EPA apparently assumed certain limits of use would prevail. But if there are dangers, and if the benefits of use may be satisfied within certain limits of use, the EPA should consider whether to exercise its authority to determine that the extent of use permitted pending final determination must be held within announced limits.

Analysis of Limited Short–Run Harm

We do not say there is an absolute need for analysis of benefits. It might have been possible for EPA to say that although there were no significant benefits from aldrin-dieldrin the possibility of harm—though substantial enough to present a long-run danger to the public warranting cancellation proceedings—did not present a serious short-run danger that constituted an imminent hazard. EPA's counsel offers this as a justification for its action.

If this is to be said, it must be said clearly, so that it may be reviewed carefully. Logically, there is room for the concept. But we must caution against any approach to the term "imminent hazard," used in the statute, that restricts it to a concept of crisis. It is enough if there is substantial likelihood that serious harm will be experienced during the year or two required in any realistic projection of the administrative process. It is not good practice for an agency to defend an order on the hypothesis that it is valid even assuming there are no benefits, when the reality is that some conclusion of benefits was visualized by the agency. This kind of abstraction pushes argument—and judicial review—to the wall of extremes, when realism calls for an awareness of middle ground.

Notes

1. As construed by the court, to what extent does the statute permit use of a pesticide which is found to present a substantial health risk?

2. The Court places the burden of proof on the EPA to show the lack of an imminent hazard when there is no offsetting claim of a benefit. What is the source of this allocation of the burden of proof?

3. The following events occurred on remand:

* * * After considering the Report [of an advisory committee] and further public comments, the EPA issued an order on December 7, 1972, which affirmed its previous decisions to issue a notice of intent to cancel, without interim suspension.

Cancellation hearings began before Chief Administrative Law Judge (ALJ) Perlman on August 7, 1973. Twelve months into the hearings, on August 2, 1974, the Administrator issued a notice of intent to suspend on the ground that evidence developed since December 1972 indicated that the continued use of aldrin/dieldrin presented an "imminent hazard" to the public. Shell and USDA requested a public hearing on the suspension question. The hearing began before ALJ Perlman on August 14, 1974, and was concluded on September 12, 1974. ALJ Perlman recommended suspension, and, on October 1, 1974, the Administrator suspended the registrations.

EDF, Inc. v. EPA, 510 F.2d 1292, 1297 (D.C.Cir.1975). The Court of Appeals affirmed, in another opinion by Judge Leventhal. Burden of proof was again a significant part of the decision:

Shell, FCM and the USDA further challenge the Administrator's finding that the benefits derived from the suspended uses of aldrin/dieldrin do not outweigh the harms done.

The responsibility to demonstrate that the benefits outweigh the risks is upon the proponents of continued registration. The statute places a heavy burden on any administrative officer to explain the basis for his decision to permit the continued use of a chemical known to produce cancer in experimental animals.

In our 1972 opinion, Environmental Defense Fund, Inc. v. EPA, supra, we said that "a mere recitation of a pesticide's uses does not suffice as an analysis of benefits" where the EPA has refused to initiate suspension proceedings despite evidence of carcinogenicity and a submission that alternative pest control mechanisms exist. We sought a further "elucidation of basis" from the agency to ensure that the evidence of harm was indeed outweighed by benefits flowing from the continued use of the pesticide. Where, as in that case, the agency declines to act in the face of evidence of carcinogenicity it bears the burden of justifying its lack of action:

By definition, a substantial question of safety exists when notices of cancellation issue. If there is no offsetting claim of any benefit to the public, then the EPA has the burden of showing that the substantial safety question does not pose an "imminent hazard" to the public.

150 U.S.App.D.C. at 359, 465 F.2d at 539. In the present case, in contrast, the agency has decided to act, and the burden is on the registrant to establish that continued registration poses no safety threat.

Id. at 1302. Thus, the EPA decision shifted the burden of proof to the registrant. Has Judge Leventhal created ad hoc burden of proof rules for each case? [Cf. his opinion in *International Harvester,* page 304 supra.] Or is there a coherent underlying rationale? Is it significant that in each case the burden was placed on the party advocating continued registration?

FIFRA / FEPCA

Note on FIFRA Amendments

Congress amended FIFRA in 1972 by enacting the Federal Environmental Pesticide Control Act, 7 U.S.C.A. § 136. Section 136 essentially replaced § 135 with respect to pesticides, and was itself amended in 1975, 1978, 1988, 1990, and 1996. In its present form, FIFRA provides a comprehensive framework for regulating the sale and distribution of pesticides within the United States. Under the statute, EPA may not approve a pesticide's introduction into commerce unless the Administrator finds that the pesticide "will not generally cause unreasonable adverse effects on the environment" when used in accordance with any EPA-imposed restrictions and "with widespread and commonly recognized practice." 7 U.S.C.A. § 136a(5)(D). "Unreasonable adverse effects on the environment" are defined to include "any unreasonable risk to man or the environment, taking into account the economic, social, and environmental costs and benefits of the use of any pesticide." § 136(bb). With few exceptions, FIFRA prohibits the sale, distribution, and professional use of unregistered pesticides. §§ 136a(a) & 136j(a)(1).

Because of the explicit requirement of a cost/benefit analysis, FIFRA's "unreasonable adverse effects" standard is unusual among federal environmental statutes: most others (except the Toxic Substances Control Act) employ risk-based standards softened only by the availability of control technologies. By disregarding the benefits of the regulated substances, these risk-based statutes provide more protection to health and the environment and less protection to industry than do FIFRA and TSCA.

As part of a registration, EPA must classify the pesticide for either "general" or "restricted" use. § 136a(d). Restrictions relate to such factors as methods of application, qualifications of applicators, amounts to be used, geographic areas of use, and species of targeted pests. EPA may "conditionally" register a pesticide if the pesticide and its proposed use are identical or substantially similar to any currently registered pesticide and use thereof, or differ only in ways that would not significantly increase the risk of unreasonable adverse effects on the environment. A pesticide containing an active ingredient not contained in any currently registered pesticide also may be conditionally registered for a period reasonably sufficient for the generation of required data if EPA determines that use of the pesticide during such period will not cause any unreasonable adverse effects on the environment, and that use of the pesticide is in the public interest. § 136a(c)(7).

Once registered, pesticides are still subject to continuing scrutiny by EPA. § 136d. Indeed, section 6 of FIFRA requires EPA to cancel a pesticide's registration after the first five years in which the registration has been effective (and at the conclusion of subsequent five year periods if the registration is renewed) "unless the registrant, or other interested person with the concurrence of the registrant, ... requests ... that the registration be continued in effect." § 136d(a). And at any time, EPA may propose cancellation of a registration and initiate elaborate cancellation proceedings if "it appears to the Administrator that a pesticide ... does not comply with [FIFRA] or ... generally causes unreasonable adverse effects on the environment...." § 136d(b).

During the pendency of cancellation proceedings, the registration remains in effect unless the Administrator "suspend[s] the registration of the pesticide immediately." § 136d(c). But before suspending the Administrator must determine that an "imminent hazard" exists. Even then, FIFRA guarantees registrants the right to an expedited administrative hearing on that issue, and the pesticide's registration remains effective during this latter proceeding. § 136d(c)(2). Only if "the Administrator determines that an emergency exists that does not permit the Administrator to hold a hearing before suspending" may she prohibit commerce in the pesticide in advance of notification to the registrant. § 136d(c)(3).

While commerce in unregistered pesticides is generally prohibited, the Administrator may permit continued sale and use of existing stocks of pesticides whose registrations have been cancelled provided "he determines that such sale or use is not inconsistent with the purposes of this subchapter and will not have unreasonable adverse effects on the environment." § 136d(a)(1).

The 1988 amendments to FIFRA dealt with three problems that had hampered implementation of the act. First, about 50,000 "old" pesticides had been registered under permissive pre–1972 safety and testing requirements. Between 1972 and 1988, EPA had been able to identify data needs on only about 25 of those pesticides each year. The 1988 FIFRA amendments called for re-registration or cancellation of the rest within nine years, shifting many tasks and costs from EPA to the registrants. Second, the amendments shifted from the EPA budget to the Federal Judgment Fund (which relies on general appropriations to pay claims against the government) liability to *indemnify* producers, distributors and others for economic loss when EPA suspends or cancels a registration. Third, the amendments shifted, from EPA to the pesticide industry, responsibility for the costs of *disposing* of cancelled pesticides.

Unlike the preceding case, the next one below was decided after the major amendments of 1972 that resulted in the "new" FIFRA, which, though amended in some respects, remains in effect today.

ENVIRONMENTAL DEFENSE FUND, INC. v. ENVIRONMENTAL PROTECTION AGENCY

[HEPTACHLOR AND CHLORDANE]

United States Court of Appeals, District of Columbia Circuit, 1976.
548 F.2d 998.

LEVENTHAL, CIRCUIT JUDGE.

This case involves the pesticides heptachlor and chlordane. Consolidated petitions seek review of an order of the Environmental Protection Agency (EPA) suspending the registration of those pesticides under the Federal Insecticide, Fungicide and Rodenticide Act (FIFRA) for certain uses. The Administrator of EPA issued an order on December 24, 1975. The order prohibited further production of these pesticides for the suspended uses, but permitted the pesticides' continued production and sale for limited minor uses. Even as to the suspended uses, the Order tempered its impact in certain respects: It delayed until August 1, 1976, the effective date of the prohibition of production for use on corn pests; and it permitted the continued sale and use of existing stocks of registered products formulated prior to July 29, 1975.

One petition to review was filed by Earl L. Butz, Secretary of Agriculture of the United States (U.S.D.A.). Secretary Butz and intervenor Velsicol Chemical Corporation, the sole manufacturer of heptachlor and chlordane, urge that the EPA order as to chlordane be set aside on both substantive and procedural grounds. They contend that substantial evidence does not support the Administrator's conclusion that continued use of chlordane poses an "imminent hazard" to human health, and that the Administrator made critical errors in assessing the burden of proof.

* * *

Velsicol and USDA contend that the laboratory tests on mice and rats do not "conclusively" demonstrate that chlordane is carcinogenic to those animals; that mice are too prone to tumors to be used in carcinogenicity testing in any case; and that human exposure to chlordane is insufficient to create a cancer risk. * * *

[The Court's discussion of the animal tests is deleted.]

Human epidemiology studies so far attempted on chlordane and heptachlor gave no basis for concluding that the two pesticides are safe with respect to the issue of cancer. To conclude that they pose a carcinogenic risk to humans on the basis of such a finding of risk to laboratory animals, the Administrator must show a causal connection between the uses of the pesticides challenged and resultant exposure of humans to those pesticides. He made that link by showing that widespread residues of heptachlor and chlordane are present in the human diet and in human tissues. Their widespread occurrence in the environment and accumulation in the food chain is explained by their chemical properties of persistence, mobility and high solubility in lipids (the fats contained in all organic substances.) Residues of chlordane and heptachlor remain in soils and in air and aquatic ecosystems for long periods of time. They are readily transported by means of vaporization, aerial drift, and runoff of eroding soil particles. The residues have been consistently found in meat, fish, poultry and dairy products monitored in the FDA Market Basket Survey and are also frequent in components of animal feeds. This evidence supports a finding that a major route of human exposure is ingestion of contaminated foodstuffs. EPA's National Human Monitoring Survey data shows that heptachlor epoxide and oxychlordane, the principal metabolites of heptachlor and chlordane respectively, are present in the adipose tissue of over 90% of the U.S. population.

The population's exposure to these pesticides, in large part involuntary, can be divided into agricultural and nonagricultural related routes.

Seven million pounds of heptachlor and chlordane were used as corn soil insecticide in 1975, producing residues which persist in the soil for several years after application. These residues are taken up by such food, feed, and forage crops as soybeans, barley, oats, and hays typically rotated with corn. By volatilization the pesticides contaminate corn and other plant leaves. And root crops like potatoes, carrots and beets directly absorb the pesticides from the soil. Other sources of agricultural-related residues include exposure to contaminated dust particles and agricultural runoff containing eroded soil particles.

Velsicol urges that the dietary exposure resulting from agricultural uses of the pesticides is insignificant, and that current exposure is well below "safe" dose levels as calculated by the Mantel–Bryan formula, or by the World Health Organization's Acceptable Daily Intake figures. Mantel himself criticized the use of the formula for a persistent pesticide, and the Administrator rejected the concept of a "safe" dose level defined by mathematical modeling because of "the incomplete assumptions made by the registrant's witnesses about the sources of human exposure in the environment, the natural variation in human susceptibility to cancer, the lack of any evidence relating the level of human susceptibility to cancer from heptachlor and chlordane as opposed to that of the mouse, and the absence of precise knowledge as to the minimum exposure to a carcinogen necessary to cause cancer." That explanation is within the reasonable bounds of the agency's expertise in evaluating evidence. And it is confirmed by the common sense recognition that reliance on average "safe" dietary levels fail to protect people with dietary patterns based on high proportional consumption of residue-contaminated foods (e.g., children who ingest greater quantities of milk than the general population).

There are several non-agricultural uses which involve a large volume of heptachlor and chlordane as well as significant human exposures. For example, the record shows that approximately six million pounds of chlordane are used annually on home lawns and gardens. The Administrator found that these uses involve high risks of human intake "due to the many avenues which exist for direct exposure, through improper handling and misuse, inhalation, and absorption through the skin from direct contact." Velsicol asserts that the mice studies showing carcinogenic effects after ingestion of chlordane do not warrant an inference about the carcinogenic effects of inhaling it or absorbing it through the skin, and that consequently nonagricultural routes of exposure cannot be considered to present a cancer risk. * * * [T]he FIFRA statutory scheme mandates explicit relief—the suspension of registration—when an unreasonable risk to health is made out. We have previously held that it is not necessary to have evidence on a specific use to be able to conclude that the use of a pesticide in general is hazardous. Once the initial showing of hazard is made for one mode of exposure in a suspension proceeding, and the pesticide is shown to be present in human tissues, the burden shifts to the registrant to rebut the inference that other modes of exposure may also pose a carcinogenic hazard for humans. Velsicol has totally failed to meet that burden here. Although it was put on notice in the Notice to Suspend of EPA's intent to rely on direct inhalation and dermal exposure as reasons to suspend household lawn and turf uses of chlordane, it failed to offer even a medical theory as to why the significant inhalation or dermal exposure associated with such uses would not pose a carcinogenic threat. In view of the general failure to understand the mechanics of carcinogenicity, the lack of hypothetical explanation may be based on Velsicol's own data that exposure to vapors of chlordane and heptachlor in the work place, leads (as dietary exposure leads) to storage of oxychlordane, heptachlor epoxide, and other components in the fat tissue, and to circulation of these compounds in the blood, with consequent exposure to other organs in the body. Nor did Velsicol focus on the individual user's intense inhalation exposure associated with lawn and turf uses in its response to the point made in the EPA Staff's exceptions to the ALJ recommended decision, that the evidence showed that an individual using these chemicals for lawn and turf applications is subjected to a marked intensity of inhalation. Instead Velsicol attacked as inconsistent with the minimal amounts of chlordane and heptachlor normally found in ambient air, the EPA Staff's proposed reliance on inhalation as a major route of human exposure for the general population. However, the Administrator did not proceed on this basis. And if Velsicol hypothesized that chlordane residues are safe so long as they reach the tissue only through inhalation (even intense inhalation) it should have presented witnesses expressing that hypothesis. Instead they argue, in general and procedural terms, that the evidence presented by the Administrator was not sufficient to meet his full burden, and this in our view seeks to impose a broader burden on the Administrator than is appropriate in a suspension proceeding.

[The suspension order was therefore affirmed.]

Notes

1. Note the appearance of another burden of proof rule, this time relating to carcinogens. Is the presumption created by the court reasonable? Suppose the agency rejected the inference that a substance which causes cancer under one mode of exposure probably causes cancer under other modes. Should a court reverse based on its own view as to what presumption should apply?

In a law review article, Judge Leventhal maintained he had used "burden of proof" concepts in a different sense than the conventional usage in civil procedure. Instead, he said, burden of proof was used to refer to the burden of "adducing a reasoned presentation supporting [EPA's conclusions]". Leventhal, "Environmental Decisionmaking and the Role of the Courts", 122 *U.Pa.L.Rev.* 509, 535–536 (1974). He also stated that burden of proof concepts are "nothing more or less than devices for controlling risks of error". Id. Do you find this to be persuasive explanation of the pesticide cases? For further discussion, see Rodgers, "Benefits, Costs, and Risks: Oversight of Health and Environmental Decisionmaking", 4 *Harv. Env.L.Rev.* 191, 219–224 (1980).

Which is preferable: Judge Leventhal's approach to burden of proof, or that of the plurality in the *Benzene* case?

2. On denial of the petition for rehearing, the court issued a lengthy supplemental opinion rejecting the contention that the Administrative Procedure Act placed the burden of proof on the EPA throughout the proceeding. *EDF, Inc. v. EPA*, 548 F.2d 998, 1012–1018 (D.C.Cir.1976).

3. Subsequent federal pesticide litigation has focused largely on deviations from the normal suspension/cancellation process discussed in the preceding cases. See *Love v. Thomas*, 858 F.2d 1347 (9th Cir.1988), cert. denied 490 U.S. 1035, 109 S.Ct. 1932, 104 L.Ed.2d 403 (1989) (right of pesticide users to judicial review of emergency suspension order when no registrant requests a hearing); *National Coalition Against the Misuse of Pesticides v. EPA*, 867 F.2d 636 (D.C.Cir.1989) (authority of EPA to enter into agreement providing for voluntary cancellation of registration but allowing continued sale and use of existing stocks of cancelled pesticide).

[handwritten margin note: this is the definite case on suspension + cancellation of pesticides]

4. Stricter state and local regulation of pesticide use is permitted. In *People v. County of Mendocino*, 36 Cal.3d 476, 204 Cal.Rptr. 897, 683 P.2d 1150 (1984), the Supreme Court of California held that a county initiative ordinance prohibiting aerial application of phenoxy herbicides, including 2, 4, 5–T, Silvex, 2, 4–D and any matter containing dioxin, was not preempted by either state law or FIFRA. The court said that Congress, by providing in section 24(a) for further "State" regulation of federally registered pesticides, did not intend to preclude local regulation authorized under state law.

In *Wisconsin Public Intervenor v. Mortier*, 501 U.S. 597, 111 S.Ct. 2476, 115 L.Ed.2d 532 (1991), the Supreme Court held that FIFRA does not preempt local pesticide-regulation ordinances.

[handwritten margin note: fed + state over state]

5. *Arkansas–Platte & Gulf Partnership v. Van Waters & Rogers, Inc.*, 981 F.2d 1177 (10th Cir.1993), held that FIFRA preempts state tort actions against pesticide manufacturers for inadequate labeling. The court relied, in part, upon the Supreme Court's ruling in *Cipollone v. Liggett Group, Inc.*, 505 U.S. 504, 112 S.Ct. 2608, 120 L.Ed.2d 407 (1992), that the Federal Cigarette Labeling and Advertising Act, as amended by the Public Health Cigarette Smoking Act of 1969, preempts state common law failure-to-warn claims against cigarette manufacturers. (The 1969 amendment provided, "No requirement or prohibition based on smoking and health shall be imposed under State law with respect to the advertising or promotion of any cigarettes the packages of which are labeled in conformity with the provisions of this Act.") Section 136v(b) of FIFRA provides that a state "shall not impose or continue in effect any requirements for labeling or packaging in addition to or different from those required under this subchapter." The Tenth Circuit held that this section expressly preempts state tort claims to the extent that they require a showing that a defendant's labeling and packaging should have included additional, different or alternatively stated warnings from those required under FIFRA. To the same effect is *Papas v. Upjohn Co.*, 985 F.2d 516 (11th Cir.1993).

[handwritten margin note: if it has Fed. approved label then you can't sue for inadequate label.]

The California Safe Drinking Water and Toxic Enforcement Act of 1986 ("Proposition 65") requires California to *list* substances that it determines to be carcinogenic or reproductively toxic. Twelve months after a substance has been listed by the state, the manufacturers of products containing the listed substances must provide adequate *warnings* to the consuming public that their products pose a health risk. In *Chemical Specialties Manufacturers Ass'n v. Allenby,* 958 F.2d 941 (9th Cir.1992), cert. denied 506 U.S. 825, 113 S.Ct. 80, 121 L.Ed.2d 44 (1992), CSMA, a trade association of insecticide, disinfectant, and antimicrobial product manufacturers, contended that the adequate warning requirements of Proposition 65 were preempted as applied to products regulated under FIFRA. Proposition 65 provides that the required "warning" need not be provided separately to each exposed individual and may be provided by general methods "such as labels on consumer products, inclusion of notices in mailings to water customers, posting of notices, placing notices in the public news media, and the like, provided that the warning accomplished is clear and reasonable." West's Ann.Cal.Health & Safety Code § 25249.11(f). Relying on FIFRA's definitions of "label" and "labeling," the court rejected CSMA's position and found that point-of-sale warnings satisfying the requirements of Proposition 65 did not constitute additional labeling.

6. *Safe Alternatives for Fruit Fly Eradication v. Berryhill,* 22 ERC 1036, 1984 WL 178937 (C.D.Cal.1984), held that citizens living or working in the area of aerial spraying of the pesticide Malathion by a *state* agency to control the Mexican fruit fly lacked standing to seek an injunction against the spraying program because (a) FIFRA provided no private right of action, and (b) plaintiffs were foreclosed by the *Sea Clammers* decision, page 248 supra, from enforcing FIFRA rights under the Civil Rights Act of 1864, 42 U.S.C.A. § 1983.

7. Pesticides in and on raw agricultural commodities are regulated under the Federal Food, Drug and Cosmetic Act, 21 U.S.C.A. § 301 et seq. EPA sets *tolerance* levels of pesticide concentrations in or on commodities consumed in the United States; the Food and Drug Administration monitors actual pesticide *content* of commodities and has the authority to confiscate foods containing either excessive concentrations of registered pesticides or unsafe residues of unregistered pesticides. 21 U.S.C.A. §§ 342, 346a. Under § 346a, the EPA Administrator is to consider, when establishing tolerances, "the necessity for the production of an adequate, wholesome, and economical food supply" as well as health effects.

Some foods imported into the United States may contain unsafe pesticide residues, including residues of pesticides not registered here.

The following case considered allowable tolerance levels for pesticides in foods and led to a 1996 amendment to the FFDCA exempting pesticide chemical residues from the "Delaney clause."

LES v. REILLY

United States Court of Appeals, Ninth Circuit, 1992.
968 F.2d 985, cert. denied 507 U.S. 950, 113 S.Ct. 1361, 122 L.Ed.2d 740 (1993).

SCHROEDER, CIRCUIT JUDGE:

Petitioners seek review of a final order of the Environmental Protection Agency permitting the use of four pesticides as food additives although they have been found to induce cancer. Petitioners challenge the final order on the ground that it violates the provisions of the Delaney clause, 21 U.S.C. § 348(c)(3), which prohibits the use of any food additive that is found to induce cancer.

* * *

The Federal Food, Drug, and Cosmetic Act (FFDCA), 21 U.S.C. §§ 301–394 (West 1972 & Supp.1992), is designed to ensure the safety of the food we eat by prohibiting the sale of food that is "adulterated." 21 U.S.C. § 331(a). Adulterated food is in turn defined as food containing any unsafe food "additive." 21 U.S.C. § 342(a)(2)(C). A food "additive" is defined broadly as "any substance the intended use of which results or may reasonably be expected to result ... in its becoming a component ... of any food." 21 U.S.C. § 321(s). A food additive is considered unsafe unless there is a specific exemption for the substance or a regulation prescribing the conditions under which it may be used safely. 21 U.S.C. § 348(a).

* * *

The FFDCA also contains special provisions which regulate the occurrence of pesticide residues on raw agricultural commodities. Section 402 of the FFDCA, 21 U.S.C. § 342(a)(2)(B), provides that a raw food containing a pesticide residue is deemed adulterated unless the residue is authorized under section 408 of the FFDCA, 21 U.S.C. § 346a, which allows tolerance regulations setting maximum permissible levels and also provides for exemption from tolerances under certain circumstances. When a tolerance or an exemption has been established for use of a pesticide on a raw agricultural commodity, then the FFDCA allows for the "flow-through" of such pesticide residue to processed foods, even when the pesticide may be a carcinogen. This flow-through is allowed, however, only to the extent that the concentration of the pesticide in the processed food does not exceed the concentration allowed in the raw food.... 21 U.S.C. § 342(a)(2)(C). It is undisputed that the EPA regulations at issue in this case allow for the concentration of cancer-causing pesticides during processing to levels in excess of those permitted in the raw foods.

* * *

The issue before us is whether the EPA has violated section 409 of the FFDCA, the Delaney clause, by permitting the use of carcinogenic food additives which it finds to present only a de minimis or negligible risk of causing cancer. The Agency acknowledges that its interpretation of the law is a new and changed one. From the initial enactment of the Delaney clause in 1958 to the time of the rulings here in issue, the statute had been strictly and literally enforced. The EPA also acknowledges that the language of the statute itself appears, at first glance, to be clear on its face. ("[S]ection 409 mandates a zero risk standard for carcinogenic pesticides in processed foods in those instances where the pesticide concentrates during processing or is applied during or after processing.")

The language is clear and mandatory. The Delaney clause provides that no additive shall be deemed safe if it induces cancer. 21 U.S.C. § 348(c)(3). The EPA states in its final order that appropriate tests have established that the pesticides at issue here induce cancer in humans or animals. The statute provides that once the finding of carcinogenicity is made, the EPA has no discretion. . . .

* * *

The Agency asks us to look behind the language of the Delaney clause to the overall statutory scheme governing pesticides, which permits the use of carcinogenic pesticides on raw food without regard to the Delaney clause. Yet section 402 of the FFDCA, 21 U.S.C. § 342(a)(2)(C), expressly harmonizes that scheme with the Delaney clause by providing that residues on processed foods may not exceed the tolerance level established for the raw food. The statute unambiguously provides that pesticides which concentrate in processed food are to be treated as food additives, and these are governed by the Delaney food additive provision contained in section 409. If pesticides which concentrate in processed foods induce cancer in humans or animals, they render the food adulterated and must be prohibited.

* * *

The EPA's refusal to revoke regulations permitting the use of benomyl, mancozeb, phosmet and trifluralin as food additives on the ground the cancer risk they pose is de minimis is contrary to the provisions of the Delaney clause prohibiting food additives that induce cancer. The EPA's final order is set aside.

Notes

1. In 1996 Congress amended the Federal Food, Drug and Cosmetic Act to exempt pesticide chemical residues from the Delaney clause. Food Quality Protection Act of 1996, P. L. 104–170, § 405 (Aug. 3, 1996), amending FFDCA § 408, 21 U.S.C. § 346a. For such residues, the Delaney distinction between "carcinogen" and "noncarcinogen" was replaced with a new distinction between "threshold" and "nonthreshold" toxicants. The "general rule," for threshold toxicants, is that the EPA Administrator may establish a tolerance for a residue in or on a food if she determines that the tolerance is "safe," i.e., "that there is a reasonable certainty that no harm will result from aggregate exposure to the pesticide chemical residue, including all anticipated dietary exposures and all other exposures for which there is reliable information." 21 U.S.C. § 346a(b)(2)(A). For nonthreshold ("eligible") toxicants, a tolerance must meet at least one of the conditions described in clause (iii), and both of the conditions described in clause (iv), 21 U.S.C. § 346a(b)(2)(B):

(iii) Conditions regarding use

For purposes of clause (ii), the conditions described in this clause with respect to a tolerance for an eligible pesticide chemical residue are the following:

(I) Use of the pesticide chemical that produces the residue protects consumers from adverse effects on health that would pose a greater risk than the dietary risk from the residue.

(II) Use of the pesticide chemical that produces the residue is necessary to avoid a significant disruption in domestic production of an adequate, wholesome, and economical food supply.

(iv) Conditions regarding risk

For purposes of clause (ii), the conditions described in this clause with respect to a tolerance for an eligible pesticide chemical residue are the following:

(I) The yearly risk associated with the nonthreshold effect from aggregate exposure to the residue does not exceed 10 times the yearly risk that would be allowed under [the "general rule" in] subparagraph (A) for such effect.

(II) The tolerance is limited so as to ensure that the risk over a lifetime associated with the nonthreshold effect from aggregate exposure to the residue is not greater than twice the lifetime risk that would be allowed under subparagraph (A) for such effect.

The amendments also require that, in establishing a tolerance for a pesticide chemical residue, the Administrator (i) shall assess the risk of the residue based on available information about consumption patterns (exposure) among infants and children, and about their special susceptibility to the residue, and (ii) shall ensure that there is a reasonable certainty that no harm will result to infants and children from aggregate exposure to the residue. "In the case of threshold effects, for purposes of clause (ii)(I) an additional tenfold margin of safety for the pesticide chemical residue and other sources of exposure shall be applied for infants and children to take into account potential pre-and post-natal toxicity and completeness of the data with respect to exposure and toxicity to infants and children." 21 U.S.C. § 346a(b)(2)(C).

For a discussion of the continuing effects of the Delaney clause in the FFDCA after the 1996 amendments, see James Turner, "Delaney Lives! Reports of Delaney's Death Are Greatly Exaggerated," 28 *Envt'l L. Rptr.* 10003 (1998).

2. As discussed in Chapter III, GATT trade rules may affect domestic environmental regulations, as applied to imports. Section 346a(b)(2)(B)(iii) makes one of the conditions for a tolerance a finding that use is "necessary to avoid a significant disruption in domestic production." This provision may discriminate against foreign producers claiming a tolerance in order to avoid disruption in their production. Because of this discriminatory feature, the provision may be a prima facie violation of Article III of GATT. Other aspects of the provision, though facially neutral, might be found to have a disparate impact on foreign producers, also causing a potential GATT problem.

3. The following article was published after the decision in *Les v. Reilly* but before enactment of the Food Quality Protection Act of 1996, discussed in note 1 above. Although that act also included some amendments to FIFRA, they did not incorporate the aggressive "alternative framework of

environmental law reform" advocated by Professor Hornstein. As he feared, the opportunity for real change was squandered because congressional debate was framed in terms of "risk" rather than "alternative agriculture."

HORNSTEIN, "LESSONS FROM FEDERAL PESTICIDE REGULATION ON THE PARADIGMS AND POLITICS OF ENVIRONMENTAL LAW REFORM"[b]

10 *Yale Journal on Regulation* 369, 371–372, 380, 392–405, 436–446 (1993).

[O]ne of the first environmental problems to come before the Clinton Administration and the 103rd Congress [is] the reform of federal pesticide policy. The policy debate is now framed as a choice between evaluating pesticide residues on processed foods with modern risk assessment techniques or continuing the blanket prohibition of such residues now found in the so-called "Delaney Clause." Although described as a referendum on "science" versus "politics," the Delaney debate in fact avoids much of the important science governing pest management, ignores virtually all of the economics of pesticide use, and marginalizes many of the public health and environmental values implicated by agricultural chemicals. To avoid being misunderstood, this criticism does not reflect a conviction that Delaney is necessarily good policy. There is plausible evidence that a blanket prohibition on all detectible carcinogenic residues can be counterproductive. But there is also plausible evidence that risk assessments frequently sit atop both suspect data and contentious methodological assumptions. More to the point, the use of risk assessments to discern "reasonable risk" under the Federal Insecticide Fungicide and Rodenticide Act (FIFRA) has arguably led to one of the most colossal regulatory failures in Washington. Yet despite these well-known criticisms, the Delaney debate continues as if the only policy options for sound pesticide policy—and environmental regulation in general—were the status quo or a new regime dominated by scientific risk assessments. * * *

This Article argues for an alternative framework of environmental law reform, one more aggressive in identifying and addressing the causes of environmental problems than either existing regulatory programs or reform proposals that emphasize risk-based priority-setting. This alternative framework would focus especially on the role played by existing economic incentives in causing environmental problems and the role that better-designed incentives can play in solving them. * * *

* * *

As a general matter, cause-oriented reforms focus on reducing human pressures on natural resources, often by encouraging "clean" technologies or changes in consumption and use patterns. Roughly speaking, this approach contrasts with the focus of risk-based reforms on managing environmental effects to some level of acceptable risk. * * *

* * *

For all its complexity, * * * it is important to underscore what pesticide regulation is not: it is not a body of law that addresses in any strategic way the underlying prevalence of pesticides in American agriculture, nor is it a body of law designed to minimize pesticide use. On reflection, this characteristic is especially striking because the impetus for modern pesticide regulation, if not for the modern environmental movement in general, was the argument made in 1962 by Rachel Carson in *Silent Spring* for developing just such a strategic environmental law. * * *

* * *

At the core of any alternative legal framework must be an appreciation of the strengths and limitations of what is typically described as "alternative" agriculture. [T]here are basically four types of alternative measures most commonly in use, and about which a scientific literature has developed or is developing. First, there are "cultural" methods to control insects, weeds, and diseases, such as crop rotations, altered planting dates, cultivation, and the planting of border crops. Second, there are "biological control" methods such as the release of predatory or parasitic insects. Third, there is the deployment of "biorational" pest control measures such as pheromone-baited traps, the release of microbiological pathogens of insects or weeds, and the use of genetically engineered pest control products. Fourth, and probably most importantly, there is the use of "integrated pest management" (IPM), a decisionmaking system designed to use all "suitable" pest control techniques, including chemical pesticides, to keep pest populations below economically injurious levels while satisfying environmental and production objectives.

It is fairly plain that alternative pest controls can impose on farmers two types of costs that are generally not imposed to the same extent by chemical pesticides. First, there are often significant information costs involved with more finely-tailored alternative forms of crop protection—such as the need to "scout" a crop to discern the optimal timing of pesticide applications (perhaps the most common IPM technique) or the need to familiarize oneself with the relative effectiveness of a wide assortment of nonchemical measures or products—that clearly transcend the information costs involved in the more routine spraying of a chemical pesticide that may be "automatically" effective against a broad range of pests. Second, to the extent that pest-specific products are used, they will by definition cost more than products that work against a broader range of pests because the pest-specific user market will be smaller and the producer must charge proportionately higher prices to recoup her investments in research and development.

Alternative pest control can also pose free rider and collective action problems. For example, the release of predatory insects will rarely be in an individual farmer's economic self-interest because they cannot be confined to the farmer's property and thus will become to that extent a public good whose full value cannot be recouped. Conversely, if farmers seek to join in an areawide organization for the purposes of cooperative pest control, they may face "hold outs" who attempt to free-ride on the cooperating farmers' efforts—or, worse, hold-outs whose recalcitrant activities actually undermine the cooperative efforts (say, by maintaining fields which serve as "reservoirs" for common pests or by continuing the use of chemical pesticides that kill predatory insects released by the alternative farmers).

* * *

There are, currently, dozens of policy options to encourage low-input agriculture, ranging from mandated reductions in pesticide use by target dates to pesticide risk taxes to expedited registration of "alternative" pest control products. I endorse none of these specific options here. Rather, I want only to underscore two criteria that should guide the merits of the long-overdue development of a true environmental policy for pesticides.

First, Congress should encourage governmental intervention that addresses the underlying reasons for pesticide overuse. Fitting this criteria would be consideration of two obvious problems for any system of low-input agriculture: risk averse farmers may overuse pesticides as a minimax strategy to avoid catastrophic crop losses, and farmers may overuse pesticides because of their relatively low informational costs. Although the issues have their complexities, the arguments appear strong at least in the near term for public subsidization of "IPM" crop insurance premiums and of significant enhancements for existing "extension" programs that have already been developed to train farmers in the new techniques. * * *

Second, Congress should bypass the risk-dominated structures in EPA's pesticide office and legislate direct disincentives to pesticide use. Such an approach would have the benefit of "locking in" structural incentives for low-input agriculture and avoiding the implementation slippage that has inevitably occurred in pesticide regulation. * * *

* * *

Third, risk analysis offers the conceptual umbrella of "science" under which numerous non-scientific values can take shelter from public scrutiny and yet prolong the longevity of pesticides that may be neither desirable nor needed. Consider, for example, the decidedly nonscientific question of deciding how risk averse to be when evaluating uncertain data. * * *

* * *

Reform of pesticide regulation is in theory, and will probably soon prove to be in practice, a logical starting point for self-conscious attention to cause-oriented reform. FIFRA reform legislation was reported from most of the relevant congressional committees near the close of the 102nd Congress, and has been reintroduced early in the 103rd. Congressional attention to pesticides will be driven by the often-noted implications of the proposed North American Free Trade Agreement for acceptable levels of pesticide residues and the Ninth Circuit's recent holding in *Les v. Reilly,* which will require EPA to revoke tolerances and cancel registrations for some twenty-five or more pesticides unless affected by congressional action. A recently released major study by the National Academy of Sciences has focused attention on the EPA's inadequate attention to the tolerance of children to pesticide residues. * * *

Unfortunately, the expected upsurge in public attention to pesticides will be largely squandered if the congressional debate is framed, as it is likely to be, solely in terms of "risk." By all indications, FIFRA reform will focus on administrative improvements to expedite risk-based decisional processes for reregistration and cancellation. And the debate over food safety legislation may well be dominated by the "Delaney paradox" (claiming that the Delaney Clause increases aggregate carcinogenic risk by prohibiting the registration of new pesticides with safer carcinogenic profiles than older, existing ones that are awaiting reregistration or are otherwise permissible under FFDCA). The Delaney debate can be expected to focus on an esoteric battle between those who prefer a specified one-in-one-million standard of acceptable risk and those who prefer the unspecified requirement of "reasonable risk." Although some discussion of risk methodologies is unavoidable and probably beneficial, there is every reason to hope that the debate can be supplemented by formulation of a concrete, long-overdue framework for reducing inefficient pesticide use.

Notes

1. The Food Quality Protection Act of 1996, discussed in the notes preceding the Hornstein article, did give a nod to adoption of Integrated Pest Management (IPM). The act added to FIFRA this provision, 7 U.S.C. § 136r–1:

The Secretary of Agriculture, in cooperation with the [EPA] Administrator, shall implement research, demonstration, and education programs to support adoption of Integrated Pest Management. [IPM] is a sustainable approach to managing pests by combining biological, cultural, physical, and chemical tools in a way that minimizes economic, health, and environmental risks. The Secretary ... and the Administrator shall make information on [IPM] widely available to pesticide users.... Federal agencies shall use [IPM] techniques in carrying out pest management activities and shall promote [IPM] through procurement and regulatory policies, and other activities.

2. Probably the most threatening aspect of the improvident use of pesticides is widespread contamination of underground water sources, aquifers which are or may be tapped by wells to supply drinking water to individual homes and entire cities. For example, before it was banned in 1977 for causing sterility in humans and cancer in laboratory animals, the

soil fumigant "DBCP" was used widely in California vineyards and orchards to combat root worms. Now, up and down the San Joaquin Valley, more than 100 municipal wells have been shut down because of unsafe levels of DBCP. In 18 California counties, including Los Angeles, Riverside, San Bernardino, Orange, and San Diego, more than 1,700 public and private wells serving 200,000 people now exceed federal standards for exposure to DBCP. Cities are faced with retiring more wells or equipping them with elaborate carbon filtration systems. Between 1980 and 1995 the city of Fresno had to close 29 wells and install five carbon filtration systems at a cost of $800,000 each. See Mark Arax, "Banned DBCP Still Haunts San Joaquin Valley Water," *Los Angeles Times*, June 12, 1995, p. A1.

3. Improvident use of pesticides also poses health risks to farm workers who apply the chemicals or work in affected fields. Since many of the workers are poor immigrants, these risks raise environmental justice issues.

For extreme cases of thousands of farm workers in Latin America becoming sterile from unprotected exposure to pesticides manufactured in the United States and used on plantations owned by subsidiaries of U.S. corporations, see *Dow Chemical Co. v. Castro Alfaro*, 786 S.W.2d 674 (Tex.1990), cert. denied 498 U.S. 1024, 111 S.Ct. 671, 112 L.Ed.2d 663 (1991); Diana Schemo, "Pesticide From U.S. Kills the Hopes of Fruit Pickers in the Third World," *New York Times*, Dec. 6, 1995, p. A8, col. 4.

2.   THE TOXIC SUBSTANCES CONTROL ACT[a]

Congress enacted the Toxic Substances Control Act (TSCA) in 1976 to prevent "unreasonable risks of injury to health or the environment" associated with the manufacture, processing, distribution, use or disposal of chemical substances other than drugs and pesticides. TSCA's emphasis is on regulating products rather than wastes. Today's policy of *pollution prevention*, and of avoiding environmental and health problems by front-end regulation of chemical production and use, is the same policy that underlies TSCA.[b]

The Act as a whole must be read in light of the policy section (§ 2(b)). Three policies are set forth. First, data should be developed on the environmental effects of chemicals; primary responsibility for the development of these data is placed on industry. Second, the government should have adequate authority to prevent unreasonable risks of injury to health or the environment, particularly imminent hazards. Finally, this authority should be exercised so as "not to impede unduly or create unnecessary economic barriers to technological innovation while fulfilling the primary purpose of this Act to assure that * * * such chemical substances * * * do not present an unreasonable risk of injury * * *." (§ 2(b)(3)). Obviously, much depends on the relative weights given to

a. 90 Stat. 2003 (1976), 15 U.S.C.A. § 2601, et seq.

b. For an extended discussion of TSCA and its implementation, see Hathaway,

Hayes and Rawson, "A Practitioner's Guide to the Toxic Substances Control Act," parts I–III, 24 *Envtl.L.Rptr.* 10207, 10285, 10357 (1994).

these conflicting goals of protecting technological development and assuring environmental safety.[c]

The most important substantive provisions of the Act are found in sections 4, 5, and 6. These sections concern testing, premanufacturing clearance, and regulation of manufacturing and distribution. We will consider only the main outlines of these provisions, without too much attention to the innumerable exemptions, exceptions, qualifications and procedural details.

Section 4 relates to testing. It empowers the EPA to adopt rules requiring testing by manufacturers of substances. Such rules must be based on a finding that insufficient data are currently available concerning the substance, and that the substance may "present an unreasonable risk" (§ 4(a)(1)(A)(i)), "enter the environment in substantial quantities" (§ 4(a)(1)(B)(i)(I)), *or* present a likelihood of "substantial human exposure" (§ 4(a)(1)(B)(i)(II)). There are, naturally, a variety of complicated procedural devices set out in exhaustive detail in the remainder of the section. In addition to section 4, the statute contains several other provisions aimed at collection of information.[d]

Section 5 requires a manufacturer to give notice to the EPA before manufacturing a *new* chemical substance.[f] If the substance is covered by a § 4 rule, the § 4 test results must be submitted along with the § 5 notice (§ 5(b)(1)(A)).[g] For substances not covered by § 4, but listed by EPA as possibly hazardous, the manufacturer is to submit data it believes show the absence of any unreasonable risk of injury (§ 5(b)(2)(A), (B)). Normally, the next step would be a § 6 proceeding. But if EPA finds that an unreasonable risk may be presented before a § 6 rule can be promulgated, it can issue a "proposed § 6 rule" which will be immediately effective, issue an administrative order, or seek an injunction (§ 5(f)). Often, EPA will not have sufficient information to make a definite finding about safety. EPA can then make risk or prevalence findings similar to those triggering the § 4 testing rules and issue an administrative order. (If a timely objection to the order is filed, however, EPA must seek injunctive relief (§ 5(a)).

[handwritten margin note: usually includes in vitro test result at the minimum]

Section 6, unlike § 5, applies to all chemicals, not just to new chemicals or new uses. The finding necessary to trigger § 6 is that "there is a reasonable basis to conclude" that the substance "presents or will present an unreasonable risk of injury to health or the environment * * *." Having made such a finding, EPA may by rule apply any of a number of restrictions "to the extent necessary to protect adequately

[handwritten margin note: imminent hazards]

---

c. For a general discussion, see Comment, "Risk–Benefit Analysis and Technology Forcing Under the Toxic Substances Control Act", 62 *Iowa L.Rev.* 942, 945–957 (1977).

d. Section 8 gives EPA far-reaching powers to obtain reports and records. This section was given a broad reading in *Dow Chemical v. EPA,* 605 F.2d 673 (3d Cir. 1979), which upheld extension of the stat-

ute to research and development projects. Section 11 gives EPA inspection and subpoena powers.

f. Or an old substance for a "significant new use" § 5(a)(1)(B).

g. There is a special provision, § 5(b)(1)(B), for persons exempted from § 4.

against such risk using the least burdensome requirements" (§ 6(a)). Obviously, much will depend on whether more weight is given to "protect adequately" or to "least burdensome". In general, EPA is directed to use its regulatory powers under other statutes in preference to § 6 (§ 6(c)). The effective date of a proposed rule may be accelerated if the EPA finds a likelihood of "an unreasonable risk of serious or widespread injury to health or the environment" before the effective date of the final rule. The requirements for acceleration under § 6(d), it should be noted, are somewhat different from those applicable to new chemicals under § 5(f). Finally, § 6 contains a special provision for the phasing out of polychlorinated biphenyls (PCBs).

One other provision which deserves mention is § 7, which allows EPA to obtain emergency judicial relief in case of "imminent hazards". See Walker and Eisenfeld, "How to Handle Difficult Chemicals: The Unused Tool in EPA's Chemical Toolbox—Section 7 of the Toxic Substances Control Act," 24 *Envtl.L.Rptr.* 10015 (1994). The Act also contains the usual panoply of provisions on civil and criminal penalties, judicial enforcement, judicial review, hybrid rule-making, and preemption.

NATURAL RESOURCES DEFENSE COUNCIL, INC. v. ENVIRONMENTAL PROTECTION AGENCY

United States District Court, Southern District of New York, 1984.
595 F.Supp. 1255.

DUFFY, D.J.

[Section 4 of TSCA] provides for EPA issuance of rules requiring testing of chemicals which may present unreasonable risks of injury to human health or the environment. The testing required by such rules is to be carried out and financed by the manufacturers and/or processors of the chemical substances. *See* TSCA, 15 U.S.C. § 2603(b)(3). In section 2603(e) of the Act, Congress established an expert panel of government scientists, known as the "Interagency Testing Committee" ("ITC"). ITC is directed to select and recommend to EPA a list of those chemicals whose potential risks to health and the environment are determined to warrant "priority consideration by the agency for the promulgation of a rule. * * * " Thereafter the EPA is required within twelve months of the date on which the substances are first designated to "either initiate a rulemaking proceeding under subsection (a) * * * or if such a proceeding is not initiated within such period, publish in the Federal Register the [EPA] Administrator's reason for not initiating such a proceeding."

A test rule "shall" be promulgated if EPA finds that [the conditions described in section 2603(a) exist].

The final test rule must identify, *inter alia*, the chemical(s) to be tested, the specific effects for which testing must be done, the test standards or protocols, and the deadlines for test completion and submission of data. *See id.* § 2603(b)(1). To formulate a final rule, EPA is required first to publish proposed rules with these characteristics, soliciting public commentary.

* * *

In late 1981 and early 1982, EPA announced in the *Federal Register* that it would consider accepting voluntary testing programs in certain circumstances. These programs would be negotiated and conducted by manufacturers or processors of ITC designated chemical substances in lieu of initiating a rulemaking proceeding. EPA asserts that it adopted this new policy based upon the belief that such agreements would provide the required health and environmental effect test data in an expeditious manner.

* * *

Plaintiff's first four claims are based on ITC's designation, between November 1980 and May 1982, of four chemicals warranting priority rulemaking consideration and review by EPA. In the two to four years since their designations, EPA has not initiated rulemaking proceedings; rather, within twelve months of each of the designations EPA accepted or tentatively accepted voluntary testing programs negotiated with industry.

* * *

Plaintiffs brought this action pursuant to 15 U.S.C. § 2619(a)(2) which provides that "any person may commence a civil action * * * against the [EPA] Administrator to compel the Administrator to perform any duty under this Act which is not discretionary." EPA contends that it has no mandatory duty to issue test rules and therefore its discretionary acts are not subject to review by a citizen-suit civil action.

... Section 2603(e)(1)(B) provides the agency with a choice of either initiating a rulemaking proceeding or publishing its reasons for not doing so. It is evident, however, that the Administrator's duty to choose either to initiate rulemaking proceedings or to publish its reasons for not doing so is a mandatory choice that it must make. Thus, plaintiffs may invoke section 2619(a)(2) to review whether EPA carried out this nondiscretionary act.

Standing Issue

* * *

Both in the legislative history of TSCA and on the face of the statute, Congress has evinced its intention that chemicals on which there is insufficient data will be tested pursuant to formal rulemaking. * * *

...Section 2603 was promulgated to mandate the testing of potentially dangerous chemicals on which there was insufficient data existing at the present time. EPA's negotiation and acceptance of voluntary testing agreements by the manufacturers obviously reflects EPA's belief that additional data concerning the chemicals in question needs to be developed. The absence of a formal finding of testing necessity cannot hide EPA's evident *de facto* findings of such a necessity. * * *

Furthermore, I can find no support for EPA's decision to utilize negotiated testing agreements instead of the statutorily-prescribed initiation of rulemaking proceedings either on the face of the statute or based on some vague assertion of agency discretion. * * *

* * *

The chemicals * * * were recommended for testing by ITC nearly seven years ago * * *. They were among the first chemicals so designated by ITC. No rulemaking activity concerning these chemicals, however, took place until after NRDC brought a successful action to compel EPA's compliance with TSCA in 1979. Thereafter, pursuant to a stipulated timetable, EPA proposed rules for the * * * chemicals * * *. Since then, there have been three and four years without any formal rulemaking accomplished. In effect, EPA has accepted *de facto* voluntary testing programs in place of rulemaking. Voluntary testing programs, I already have held, are inadequate to fulfill the statutory mandate. * * * Accordingly, I find that defendants have unreasonably delayed agency action * * *.

* * * Plaintiffs' motion for partial summary judgment on the [foregoing issues] is granted * * *.

Notes

1. The foregoing decision resulted in a complete revamping of EPA's procedures for negotiating test rules under § 4 of TSCA. The agency now seeks to make consent agreements enforceable on the same basis as test rules. 40 CFR 790. See W. Rodgers, 3 *Environmental Law: Pesticides and Toxic Substances* 426–429 (1988) concerning EPA procedures related to consent agreements and test rules.

The requirement that EPA issue a rule before requiring testing distinguishes TSCA from food, drug, and pesticide statutes, which mandate production of safety data prior to marketing. It seems that TSCA essentially establishes a presumption of safety, which EPA must overcome before it may require further testing of a chemical. See Lyndon, "Information Economics and Chemical Toxicity: Designing Laws to Produce and Use Data," 87 *Mich.L.Rev.* 1795, 1824 (1989). Because of the elaborate procedural barriers, EPA has promulgated relatively few test rules under TSCA. See Applegate, "The Perils of Unreasonable Risk: Information, Regulatory Policy, and Toxic Substances Control," 91 *Colum.L.Rev.* 261, 318–319 (1991).

Manufacturers sometimes challenge EPA test rules judicially, and the courts review in detail the agency's findings and reasons for demanding tests. See *Chemical Manufacturers Ass'n v. EPA*, 899 F.2d 344 (5th Cir.1990) (rule requiring manufacturers and processors of chemical cumene to perform toxicological testing, remanded for EPA to articulate the standards or criteria on the basis of which it found the quantities of cumene entering the environment from the facilities in question to be "substantial," and the human exposure potentially resulting to be "substantial," under TSCA § 4(a)(1)(B)(i)); *Chemical Manufacturers Ass'n v. EPA*, 919 F.2d 158 (D.C.Cir.1990) (upholding EPA's interpretation of § 4(a)(1)(A)(i) as authorizing issuance of a test rule where there is a "more than theoretical basis" to suspect the presence of unreasonable risk of injury to health, and finding that EPA had presented "substantial evidence" of exposure and toxicity so as to justify a test rule).

2. Section 6(a) of TSCA provides that if the Administrator finds that there is "a reasonable basis to conclude" that the manufacture, processing, distribution in commerce, use, or disposal of a chemical substance or mixture "presents or will present an unreasonable risk of injury to health or the environment," he "shall by rule apply one or more of [seven specific] requirements * * * to the extent necessary to protect adequately against such risk *using the least burdensome requirements*" (emphasis added). The listed requirements include, among others, the prohibition of, or limitations on (e.g., total amount, maximum concentration, permissible uses), the manufacture, processing or distribution of such substance; regulation of the manner or method of use or disposal; and mandatory testing, record-keeping, and issuance of instructions, notices and warnings by manufacturers and processors. Section 6(c) prescribes criteria and procedures for promulgation of "subsection (a) rules."

CORROSION PROOF FITTINGS v. ENVIRONMENTAL PROTECTION AGENCY

United States Court of Appeals, Fifth Circuit, 1991.
947 F.2d 1201.

JERRY E. SMITH, CIRCUIT JUDGE:

The Environmental Protection Agency (EPA) issued a final rule under section 6 of the Toxic Substances Control Act (TSCA) to prohibit the future manufacture, importation, processing, and distribution of asbestos in almost all products. Petitioners claim that the EPA's rule-making procedure was flawed and that the rule was not promulgated on the basis of substantial evidence. * * *

Asbestos is a naturally occurring fibrous material that resists fire and most solvents. Its major uses include heat-resistant insulators, cements, building materials, fireproof gloves and clothing, and motor vehicle brake linings. Asbestos is a toxic material, and occupational exposure to asbestos dust can result in mesothelioma, asbestosis, and lung cancer.

* * *

* * * Finding that asbestos constituted an unreasonable risk to health and the environment, the EPA promulgated a staged ban of most commercial uses of asbestos. The EPA estimates that this rule will save either 202 or 148 lives, depending upon whether the benefits are discounted, at a cost of approximately $450–800 million, depending upon the price of substitutes.

The rule is to take effect in three stages, depending upon the EPA's assessment of how toxic each substance is and how soon adequate substitutes will be available. The rule allows affected persons one more year at each stage to sell existing stocks of prohibited products. The rule also imposes labeling requirements on stage 2 or stage 3 products and allows for exemptions from the rule in certain cases.

* * *

Our inquiry into the legitimacy of the EPA rulemaking begins with a discussion of the standard of review governing this case. EPA's phase-out ban of most commercial uses of asbestos is a TSCA § 6(a) rulemaking. TSCA provides that a reviewing court "shall hold unlawful and set aside" a final rule promulgated under § 6(a) "if the court finds that the rule is not supported by substantial evidence in the rulemaking record ... taken as a whole."

* * *

"Under the substantial evidence standard, a reviewing court must give careful scrutiny to agency findings and, at the same time, accord appropriate deference to administrative decisions that are based on agency experience and expertise." As with consumer product legislation, "Congress put the substantial evidence test in the statute because it wanted the courts to scrutinize the Commission's actions more closely than an 'arbitrary and capricious' standard would allow."

The recent case of *Chemical Mfrs. Ass'n v. EPA,* 899 F.2d 344 (5th Cir.1990), provides our basic framework for reviewing the EPA's actions. In evaluating whether the EPA has presented substantial evidence, we examine (1) whether the quantities of the regulated chemical entering into the environment are "substantial" and (2) whether human exposure to the chemical is "substantial" or "significant." An agency may exercise its judgment without strictly relying upon quantifiable risks, costs, and benefits, but it must "cogently explain why it has exercised its discretion in a given manner" and "must offer a 'rational connection between the facts found and the choice made.' "

We note that in undertaking our review, we give all agency rules a presumption of validity, and it is up to the challenger to any rule to show that the agency action is invalid. The burden remains on the EPA, however, to justify that the products it bans present an unreasonable risk, no matter how regulated. See *Industrial Union Dep't v. American Petroleum Inst.,* 448 U.S. 607, 662, 100 S.Ct. 2844, 2874, 65 L.Ed.2d 1010 (1980). Finally, as we discuss in detail infra, because TSCA instructs the EPA to undertake the least burdensome regulation sufficient to regulate the substance at issue, the agency bears a heavier burden when it seeks a partial or total ban of a substance than when it merely seeks to regulate that product. See 15 U.S.C. § 2605(a).

TSCA provides, in pertinent part, as follows:

(a) Scope of regulation.—If the Administrator finds that there is a *reasonable basis* to conclude that the manufacture, processing, distribution in commerce, use, or disposal of a chemical substance or mixture, or that any combination of such activities, presents or will present an *unreasonable risk of injury* to health or the environment, the Administrator shall by rule apply one or more of the following requirements to such substance or mixture to the extent necessary *to protect adequately* against such risk using the *least burdensome* requirements.

As the highlighted language shows, Congress did not enact TSCA as a zero-risk statute. The EPA, rather, was required to consider both alternatives to a ban and the costs of any proposed actions and to "carry out this chapter in a reasonable and prudent manner [after considering] the environmental, economic, and social impact of any action." 15 U.S.C. § 2601(c).

We conclude that the EPA has presented insufficient evidence to justify its asbestos ban. We base this conclusion upon two grounds: the failure of the EPA to consider all necessary evidence and its failure to give adequate weight to statutory language requiring it to promulgate the least burdensome, reasonable regulation required to protect the environment adequately. Because the EPA failed to address these concerns, and because the EPA is required to articulate a "reasoned basis" for its rules, we are compelled to return the regulation to the agency for reconsideration.

TSCA requires that the EPA use the least burdensome regulation to achieve its goal of minimum reasonable risk. This statutory requirement can create problems in evaluating just what is a "reasonable risk." Congress's rejection of a no-risk policy, however, also means that in certain cases, the least burdensome yet still adequate solution may entail somewhat more risk than would other, known regulations that are far more burdensome on the industry and the economy. The very language of TSCA requires that the EPA, once it has determined what an acceptable level of non-zero risk is, choose the least burdensome method of reaching that level.

In this case, the EPA banned, for all practical purposes, all present and future uses of asbestos—a position the petitioners characterize as the "death penalty alternative," as this is the *most* burdensome of all possible alternatives listed as open to the EPA under TSCA. TSCA not only provides the EPA with a list of alternative actions, but also provides those alternatives in order of how burdensome they are. The regulations [sic] thus provide for EPA regulation ranging from labeling the least toxic chemicals to limiting the total amount of chemicals an industry may use. Total bans head the list as the most burdensome regulatory option.

By choosing the harshest remedy given to it under TSCA, the EPA assigned to itself the toughest burden in satisfying TSCA's requirement that its alternative be the least burdensome of all those offered to it. Since, both by definition and by the terms of TSCA, the complete ban of manufacturing is the most burdensome alternative—for even stringent regulation at least allows a manufacturer the chance to invest and meet the new, higher standard—the EPA's regulation cannot stand if there is any other regulation that would achieve an acceptable level of risk as mandated by TSCA.

* * *

The EPA considered, and rejected, such options as labeling asbestos products, thereby warning users and workers involved in the manufacture of asbestos-containing products of the chemical's dangers, and stricter workplace rules. EPA also rejected controlled use of asbestos in the workplace and deferral to other government agencies charged with worker and consumer exposure to industrial and product hazards, such as OSHA, the CPSC, and the MSHA. The EPA determined that deferral to these other agencies was inappropriate because no one other authority could address all the risks posed "throughout the life cycle" by asbestos, and any action by one or more of the other agencies still would leave an unacceptable residual risk.

Much of the EPA's analysis is correct, and the EPA's basic decision to use TSCA as a comprehensive statute designed to fight a multi-industry problem was a proper one that we uphold today on review. What concerns us, however, is the manner in which the EPA conducted some of its analysis. TSCA requires the EPA to consider, along with the effects of toxic substances on human health and the environment, "the benefits of such substance[s] or mixture[s] for various uses and the availability of substitutes for such uses," as well as "the reasonably ascertainable economic consequences of the rule, after consideration for the effect on the national economy, small business, technological innovation, the environment, and public health." *Id.* § 2605(c)(1)(C–D).

The EPA presented two comparisons in the record: a world with no further regulation under TSCA, and a world in which no manufacture of asbestos takes place. The EPA rejected calculating how many lives a less burdensome regulation would save, and at what cost. Furthermore the EPA, when calculating the benefits of its ban, explicitly refused to compare it to an improved workplace in which currently available control technology is utilized. This decision artificially inflated the purported benefits of the rule by using a baseline comparison substantially lower than what currently available technology could yield.

Under TSCA, the EPA was required to evaluate, rather than ignore, less burdensome regulatory alternatives. TSCA imposes a least-to-most-burdensome hierarchy. In order to impose a regulation at the top of the hierarchy—a total ban of asbestos—the EPA must show not only that its proposed action reduces the risk of the product to an adequate level, but also that the actions Congress identified as less burdensome also would not do the job. The failure of the EPA to do this constitutes a failure to meet its burden of showing that its actions not only reduce the risk but do so in the *least burdensome* fashion.

Thus it was not enough for the EPA to show, as it did in this case, that banning some asbestos products might reduce the harm that could occur from the use of these products. If that were the standard, it would be no standard at all, for few indeed are the products that are so safe that a complete ban of them would not make the world still safer.

This comparison of two static worlds is insufficient to satisfy the dictates of TSCA. While the EPA may have shown that a world with a complete ban of asbestos might be preferable to one in which there is only the current amount of regulation, the EPA has failed to show that there is not some intermediate state of regulation that would be superior to both the currently-regulated and the completely-banned world. Without showing that asbestos regulation would be ineffective, the EPA cannot discharge its TSCA burden of showing that its regulation is the least burdensome available to it.

Upon an initial showing of product danger, the proper course for the EPA to follow is to consider each regulatory option, beginning with the least burdensome, and the costs and benefits of regulation under each option. The EPA cannot simply skip several rungs, as it did in this case, for in doing so, it may skip a less-burdensome alternative mandated by TSCA. Here, although the EPA mentions the problems posed by intermediate levels of regulation, it takes no steps to calculate the costs and benefits of these intermediate levels. Without doing this it is impossible, both for the EPA and for this court on review, to know that none of these alternatives was less burdensome than the ban in fact chosen by the agency.

The EPA's offhand rejection of these intermediate regulatory steps is "not the stuff of which substantial evidence is made." While it is true that the EPA considered five different ban options, these differed solely with respect to their effective dates. The EPA did not calculate the risk levels for intermediate levels of regulation, as it believed that there was no asbestos exposure level for which the risk of injury or death was zero. Reducing risk to zero, however, was not the task that Congress set for the EPA in enacting TSCA. The EPA thus has failed "cogently [to] explain why it has exercised its discretion in a given manner," by failing to explore in more than a cursory way the less burdensome alternatives to a total ban.

* * *

In addition to showing that its regulation is the least burdensome one necessary to protect the environment adequately, the EPA also must show that it has a reasonable basis for the regulation. To some extent, our inquiry in this area mirrors that used above, for many of the methodological problems we have noted also indicate that the EPA did not have a reasonable basis. We here take the opportunity to highlight some areas of additional concern.

Most problematical to us is the EPA's ban of products for which no substitutes presently are available. In these cases, the EPA bears a tough burden indeed to show that under TSCA a ban is the least burdensome alternative, as TSCA explicitly instructs the EPA to consider "the benefits of such substance or mixture for various uses and the availability of substitutes for such uses." These words are particularly appropriate where the EPA actually has decided to ban a product, rather than simply restrict its use, for it is in these cases that the lack of an adequate substitute is most troubling under TSCA.

* * *

We also are concerned with the EPA's evaluation of substitutes even in those instances in which the record shows that they are available. The EPA explicitly rejects considering the harm that may flow from the increased use of products designed to substitute for asbestos, even where the probable substitutes themselves are known carcinogens. The EPA justifies this by stating that it has "more concern about the continued use and exposure to asbestos than it has for the future replacement of asbestos in the products subject to this rule with other fibrous substitutes." The agency thus concludes that any "[r]egulatory decisions about asbestos which poses well-recognized, serious risks should not be delayed until the risks of all replacement materials are fully quantified."

This presents two problems. First, TSCA instructs the EPA to consider the relative merits of its ban, as compared to the economic effects of its actions. The EPA cannot make this calculation if it fails to consider the effects that alternative substitutes will pose after a ban.

Second, the EPA cannot say with any assurance that its regulation will increase workplace safety when it refuses to evaluate the harm that will result from the increased use of substitute products. While the EPA may be correct in its conclusion that the alternate materials pose less risk than asbestos, we cannot say with any more assurance than that flowing from an educated guess that this conclusion is true.

Considering that many of the substitutes that the EPA itself concedes will be used in the place of asbestos have known carcinogenic effects, the EPA not only cannot assure this court that it has taken the least burdensome alternative, but cannot even prove that its regulations will increase workplace safety. Eager to douse the dangers of asbestos, the agency inadvertently actually may increase the risk of injury Americans face. The EPA's explicit failure to consider the toxicity of likely substitutes thus deprives its order of a reasonable basis.

Our opinion should not be construed to state that the EPA has an affirmative duty to seek out and test every workplace substitute for any product it seeks to regulate. TSCA does not place such a burden upon the agency. We do not think it unreasonable, however, once interested parties introduce credible studies and evidence showing the toxicity of workplace substitutes, or the decreased effectiveness of safety alternatives such as non-asbestos brakes, that the EPA then consider whether its regulations are even increasing workplace safety, and whether the increased risk occasioned by dangerous substitutes makes the proposed regulation no longer reasonable. . . .

The final requirement the EPA must satisfy before engaging in any TSCA rulemaking is that it only takes steps designed to prevent "unreasonable" risks. In evaluating what is "unreasonable," the EPA is required to consider the costs of any proposed actions and to "carry out this chapter in a reasonable and prudent manner [after considering] the environmental, economic, and social impact of any action." 15 U.S.C. § 2601(c).

* * *

That the EPA must balance the costs of its regulations against their benefits further is reinforced by the requirement that it seek the least burdensome regulation. While Congress did not dictate that the EPA engage in an exhaustive, full-scale cost-benefit analysis, it did require the EPA to consider both sides of the regulatory equation, and it rejected the notion that the EPA should pursue the reduction of workplace risk at any cost. See *American Textile Mfrs. Inst.*, 452 U.S. at 510 n. 30, 101 S.Ct. at 2491 n. 30 ("unreasonable risk" statutes require "a generalized balancing of costs and benefits")....

"back of the envelope calculation"

Even taking all of the EPA's figures as true, and evaluating them in the light most favorable to the agency's decision (non-discounted benefits, discounted costs, analogous exposure estimates included), the agency's analysis results in figures as high as $74 million per life saved. For example, the EPA states that its ban of asbestos pipe will save three lives over the next thirteen years, at a cost of $128–227 million ($43–76 million per life saved), depending upon the price of substitutes; that its ban of asbestos shingles will cost $23–34 million to save 0.32 statistical lives ($72–106 million per life saved); that its ban of asbestos coatings will cost $46–181 million to save 3.33 lives ($14–54 million per life saved); and that its ban of asbestos paper products will save 0.60 lives at a cost of $4–5 million ($7–8 million per life saved). Were the analogous exposure estimates not included, the cancer risks from substitutes such as ductile iron pipe factored in, and the benefits of the ban appropriately discounted from the time of the manifestation of an injury rather than the time of exposure, the costs would shift even more sharply against the EPA's position.

While we do not sit as a regulatory agency that must make the difficult decision as to what an appropriate expenditure is to prevent someone from incurring the risk of an asbestos-related death, we do note that the EPA, in its zeal to ban any and all asbestos products, basically ignored the cost side of the TSCA equation. The EPA would have this court believe that Congress, when it enacted its requirement that the EPA consider the economic impacts of its regulations, thought that spending $200–300 million to save approximately seven lives (approximately $30–40 million per life) over thirteen years is reasonable.

As we stated in the OSHA context, until an agency "can provide substantial evidence that the benefits to be achieved by [a regulation] bear a reasonable relationship to the costs imposed by the reduction, it cannot show that the standard is reasonably necessary to provide safe or healthful workplaces."

Notes

1. Environmentalists condemned the foregoing decision as a "death knell" for TSCA. One said that "if the agency can't use TSCA to ban asbestos, then it can't use Section 6 [to regulate any chemical] because the data base on adverse health effects of asbestos is one of the best." Another said, "The largely unworkable Section 6, which was unwieldly before, is now even more useless." See 22 *Envir.Rep.* 1607 (1991).

2. Is the regulatory standard prescribed by FIFRA and applied in the cases at pages 475–486 supra different from the TSCA standard applied in *Corrosion Proof Fittings?* See Rosenthal, Gray and Graham, "Legislating Acceptable Cancer Risk from Exposure to Toxic Chemicals," 19 *Ecology L.Q.* 269, 306–307 (1992) ("The narrative ['unreasonable risk'] standard in [TSCA] was modeled after the one in FIFRA, so it is not surprising that EPA decisions to limit production or use of a specific chemical under TSCA involve a similar balancing process. As under FIFRA, [EPA] must consider the economic implications of regulation."). See also Applegate, "The Perils of Unreasonable Risk: Information, Regulatory Policy, and Toxic Substances Control," 91 *Columbia L.Rev.* 261, 267–268 (1991) ("EPA is empowered to regulate the 'life cycle' of toxic chemicals through four major statutes: FIFRA, TSCA, [RCRA and CERCLA]. . . . Although the statutes are phrased in different ways and use different regulatory structures, all adopt a standard that can generically be called unreasonable risk. 'Unreasonable' describes an undefined, nonzero level of risk determined on an ad hoc basis by balancing both health considerations and nonhealth concerns such as technology, feasibility, and cost.").

3. Are the estimated costs per life saved under EPA's asbestos regulations blatantly unreasonable, as the court seems to suggest at the end of the *Corrosion Proof Fittings* opinion? A study by Resources for the Future reviewed economic data used by EPA in support of its asbestos, pesticide, and carcinogenic air pollutant regulations. The study concluded that EPA implicitly had attached a value of $15 million to $45 million to the prevention of one case of cancer, much more than individuals appeared to be willing to spend to reduce their own risks of death. See Van Houtven and Cropper, "When Is a Life Too Costly to Save? The Evidence from Environmental Regulations," *Resources,* Winter 1994, p. 6.

A more recent study of regulatory costs of lives saved casts considerable doubt upon the validity of high estimates like those in *Corrosion Proof Fittings* and in the *Resources* article just cited. Lisa Heinzerling, "Regulatory Costs of Mythic Proportions," 107 *Yale L.J.* 1981 (1998). The author suggests that the same data relied upon in most prior studies indicate "a cost per life saved of less than $5 million" in most cases. "This means that . . . the costs per life saved . . . are below the range of current estimates of the monetary value of a human life based on studies of wage premiums for risky jobs. A figure of about $9 million is commonly reported today to be the preference-based value of life for nonmanual labor; for manual laborers, it is much lower, around $2.5 million. Another frequently cited range for the value of a human life is $3 million to $7 million." Id. at 2038–2040.

4. The court in *Corrosion Proof Fittings* also held that EPA must *discount* future benefits and that EPA's benefit-cost analysis gave too much

weight to future deaths. For an exploration of the complexities of the choice of discount rates, with particular emphasis on the issue of discounting lives, see Farber and Hemmersbaugh, "The Shadow of the Future: Discount Rates, Later Generations, and the Environment," 46 *Vanderbilt L.Rev.* 267 (1993).

Professor Heinzerling, in her article cited in note 3 supra, challenges the propriety of "discounting lives," i.e., lives saved in the future, in estimating the benefits of environmental regulation. She points out that the economic study most cited by persons claiming that regulatory costs are excessive in relation to benefits applied an annual discount rate of 10 percent in reducing lives saved in the future to present terms. Thus, 10 lives saved one year in the future are equivalent to 9 lives saved today, 10 lives saved two years in the future equal 8.3 lives saved today, and 10 lives saved 10 years in the future equal 3.9 lives saved today. Id. at 2018, 2043. Heinzerling argues that while discounting lives may be appropriate "as long as the value of a human life is measured in dollars" (though the proper discount *rate* may not be 10 percent), the case for discounting the future benefits of health regulation is "less straightforward" if one does not assign a monetary value to human life. She states the various arguments in support of such nonmonetary discounting and presents interesting counterarguments. Id. at 2044–2056.

5. Does the principal case indicate that the authority of *Reserve Mining,* page 430 supra, and of the other appellate court decisions cited in note 4 at pages 437–438, now is in serious doubt? Read together with the "vinyl chloride" case, page 463, does the principal case suggest that the Supreme Court's views in the OSHA cases, pages 439 and 459, will be applied in most non-OSHA toxics cases?

KIM, "OUT OF THE LAB AND INTO THE FIELD: HARMONIZATION OF DELIBERATE RELEASE REGULATIONS FOR GENETICALLY MODIFIED ORGANISMS"[h]

16 *Fordham International Law Journal* 1160, 1160–1183 (1993).

Biotechnology has the potential to revolutionize both industrial and agrarian economies. Genetic engineering has produced bacteria capable of digesting petroleum, viruses that act as insecticides, pest-resistant crops, and tomatoes that will stay firm for weeks on the shelf. To develop such technologically advanced products, genetically modified organisms ("GMOs") must be used outside of the laboratory and tested in the field. The introduction of GMOs into the environment is commonly known as the "deliberate release" or "planned introduction" of genetically modified organisms into the environment. The deliberate release of GMOs has given rise to intense debate about the possible risks to human health and the environment. Research, however, has not focused on safety concerns.

Regulators in individual nations, faced with the controversy surrounding the deliberate release of GMOs have responded with different policies. Some nations have very stringent laws prohibiting deliberate releases while other nations have left this area unregulated. * * *

* * *

While the potential and actual benefits of releasing GMOs into the environment are widely acknowledged, there is controversy over the possible adverse effects of such releases. Legitimate concerns exist about the biological and ecological consequences of introducing new or altered organisms into the environment on a large scale. The greatest source of apprehension among ecologists is the potential hazards of introducing non-native organisms into a new environment. For example, the introduction of a non-native or "exotic" species into a new environment sometimes results in the new exotic species displacing the native varieties and dominating the environment. A small fraction of introductions of non-native organisms have caused major ecological disturbances. Even though a naturally occurring exotic species is not directly analogous to GMOs, small genetic alterations may nevertheless create ecologically important changes. Thus, GMOs introduced into new environments may also have ecological impacts similar to those of exotic species.

Genetically engineered microorganisms, once released into the natural environment, theoretically may have a good chance to survive, multiply, and exchange genetic material, or hybridize, with other microorganisms in the environment. Such hybridization between genetically engineered organisms and naturally occurring counterparts may create new hazards. For example, wheat that has been genetically modified to resist pesticides may pass its pesticide-resistant gene on to a weed, creating the risk of disrupting ecological cycles. * * *

* * *

Individual countries have responded in different ways to the problem of safeguarding the environment against possible adverse effects from the deliberate release of GMOs into the environment. Denmark and Germany, for example, have created new laws to deal specifically with biotechnology, while countries such as the United States have interpreted pre-existing laws to regulate the deliberate release of GMOs. The newly enacted laws in Denmark and Germany follow a process-oriented approach. Process-oriented regulations view the technique of genetic engineering itself as a risk and regulate the use of DNA techniques, even if the end-product is not a GMO. In contrast, product-specific regulations are not concerned with the use of biotechnology techniques, but with the use of the GMO end-product, such as foods or pesticides. Under the product-specific approach, GMO end-products are regulated like similar products created by more traditional techniques. * * *

* * *

In 1986, the Office of Science Technology Policy issued a policy statement called the Coordinated Framework for Regulation of Biotechnology (the "Framework").[117] The Framework divided jurisdiction over the environmental regulation of biotechnology among several federal agencies. The Framework applies four general principles. First, the Framework states that existing laws will regulate biotechnology. Second, it provides that the products of biotechnology, rather than the process itself, will be regulated. Third, the safety of a biotechnology product will be determined on an individual, or case-by-case, basis. Last, it provides for a coordinated effort among all the agencies involved in regulating biotechnology.

The Framework gave the Environmental Protection Agency (the "EPA") primary responsibility over the environmental regulation of biotechnology. The EPA's regulation of biotechnology has focused on the introduction of microorganisms into the environment. The EPA derives its specific authority to regulate the release of GMOs from two statutes: the Federal Insecticide, Fungicide and Rodenticide Act ("FIFRA") and the Toxic Substances Control Act ("TSCA").

FIFRA treats biopesticides, microorganisms intended for use as pesticides, as chemical pesticides. All pesticides must be registered with the EPA under FIFRA. FIFRA's provisions also require the EPA to issue a permit before the field testing of any bioengineered pesticide. In order to issue the permit, the EPA must determine that the field test will not cause an "unreasonable adverse effect" on the environment. FIFRA places the burden of proof that the benefits of the product outweigh its risks on the permit applicant.

The TSCA authorizes the EPA to acquire information on chemical substances in order to identify potential hazards and exposures. The manufacturer of a new chemical must submit data on the chemical's safety to the EPA. Unless the chemical presents an unreasonable risk to human health or the environment, the EPA must allow the marketing of the new chemical. Under the TSCA, the EPA treats microorganisms and their DNA molecules as chemical substances subject to the TSCA's provisions. Thus, the TSCA's requirements apply to bioremediation products, bioengineered growth hormones, and other biotechnology products.

The Food and Drug Administration (the "FDA") reviews genetically engineered food products for food safety. The FDA derives its regulatory authority from the Food, Drug, and Cosmetic Act, which requires that the manufacturer or importer of a product establish its safety to the FDA's satisfaction before marketing. The FDA regulates human and animal drugs, medical devices, human and animal foods, food additives, and cosmetics.

---

117. Coordinated Framework for Regulation of Biotechnology, 51 Fed.Reg. 23,301   (1986).

While the FDA regulates the marketing of genetically modified foods, the U.S. Department of Agriculture (the "USDA") regulates the release of genetically modified plants, animals, and microorganisms involved in agricultural biotechnology research.[142] The USDA uses the Federal Plant Pest Act (the "PPA") and the Plant Quarantine Act to regulate the release of genetically engineered microorganisms derived from plant pests.[143] The PPA applies to environmental releases of insects or worms considered to be plant pests or organisms containing genetic material from plant pests.[144] The Animal Plant Health and Inspection Service ("APHIS") is the agency within the USDA responsible for the regulation of genetically engineered plants, microorganisms, and animal biologics. APHIS requires that researchers submit a detailed description of their proposed field test in order to receive a permit. As of September 1991, APHIS has issued 181 permits for small-scale field testing of genetically engineered plants or microorganisms.

In March 1993, APHIS announced regulations for a notification process for the introduction of genetically engineered organisms and products.[148] The regulations also included a petition process allowing for a determination that certain articles are no longer regulated articles.

Note

In 1996 a team of Danish researchers reported that some genetically engineered plants designed to withstand herbicides can pass those new genes to nearby weeds, which in turn become resistant to chemicals meant to eradicate them. The researchers did their experiments with a commercial crop called oilseed rape, which is raised widely in Canada and Europe to produce canola oil, and a closely related weed, *Brassica campestris*. Both plants belong to the mustard family. The researchers found that the two plant varieties spontaneously cross-fertilized each other and, within a few generations, the resulting crossbreeds not only contained the new gene but also were capable of passing on the new trait to subsequent generations. See Robert Hotz, "Engineered Plants Pass New Genes to Weeds, Study Finds," *Los Angeles Times*, Mar. 7, 1996, p. A1, col. 5.

On the other hand, genetic engineering also offers some potential environmental benefits. For instance, pest-resistant plants might reduce the need for pesticides. Should EPA take into account the potential environmental benefits in crafting its regulations? Or should EPA rely on the general principle that novel risks ought to be carefully reviewed, even if there is some chance they will replace older, more risky technologies?

142. *See* Proposed USDA Guidelines for Research Involving the Planned Introduction Into the Environment of Organisms With Deliberately Modified Hereditary Traits, 56 Fed.Reg. 4134 (1991) (proposing USDA guidelines for assessing safety of planned releases of GMOs).

143. Federal Plant Pest Act, 7 U.S.C. § 150aa–150jj (1988 & Supp. III 1991); 7 C.F.R. § 340 (1991). The Plant Quarantine Act can also be used to regulate deliberate releases but has rarely been applied to GMOs. Plant Quarantine Act, 7 U.S.C. § 151–164a, § 166–67 (1988).

144. 7 C.F.R. § 340 (1993).

148. Genetically Engineered Organisms and Products; Notification Procedures for the Introduction of Certain Regulated Articles; and Petition for Nonregulated Status; Final Rule, 58 Fed.Reg. 17044 (1993) (to be codified at 7 C.F.R. § 340).

See generally Mary Angelo, "Genetically Engineered Plant Pesticides: Recent Developments in the EPA's Regulation of Biotechnology," 7 *U. Fla. J. L. & Pub. Pol'y* 257 (1996).

STOP

B. REGULATING THE TREATMENT, STORAGE AND DISPOSAL OF HAZARDOUS WASTES

In August 1978, President Carter declared a state of emergency in the Love Canal area of Niagara Falls, New York. Investigating serious health complaints by residents, the state health department found that toxic chemicals had leaked into the basements of many houses, and into the air, water, and soil. Air pollution levels ranged as high as 5000 times the maximum safe levels. In 1947, an uncompleted waterway had been purchased by Hooker Chemical and Plastics Corporation, which used it as a depository for an estimated 352 million pounds of industrial wastes over the following six years. The land had then been used as a school site and a housing development. As a result, three decades later, over 1000 families were evacuated, $30 million in cleanup costs were required, and over $3 billion in damage claims were filed.[a]

Love Canal was not an isolated incident. In the past, land was regarded as a "safe" repository for wastes that could not be disposed of in the air or water. Decades of uncontrolled dumping have led to contamination of land and of related ground and surface waters. By 1983, EPA had identified more than 17,000 possible waste sites and had placed or proposed to place 539 of them on its National Priorities List of sites requiring prompt cleanup.[b] Most were abandoned sites containing wastes produced by the chemical industry. Some were municipal dumps with concentrations of pesticides and household cleaning solvents. Others contained a variety of industrial wastes. The largest numbers of sites were located in the northeastern industrial states and in California, Florida, Texas and Washington.[c]

The problem is greater than originally suspected. One reason is that more waste is generated than was previously believed. A two-year study by EPA suggested that 290 million tons of hazardous waste were produced in the United States and its territories during 1981, more than six times the prior estimate of 44 million tons.[d] The principal industries

a. These facts are drawn from CEQ, *Environmental Quality: Tenth Annual Report* 176–177 (1979); Worobec, "An Analysis of the Resource Conservation and Recovery Act", 11 *Envir.Rep.* 634–635 (1980).

In 1995, after sixteen years of litigation, the Clinton administration announced that Occidential Chemical Corp. had agreed to pay $129 million to the federal government for its costs of cleaning up the Love Canal neighborhood. $102 million was to go to EPA's Superfund to cover governmental cleanup costs. The other $27 million was to go to the Federal Emergency Management Agency, which undertook the initial evacuation and cleanup. Previously, in 1994, Occidential had entered into a $98 million settlement of claims by the state of New York related to Love Canal. *Los Angeles Times*, Dec. 22, 1995, p. A43, col. 1.

b. CEQ, *Environmental Quality 1983: 14th Annual Report* 60–61 (1984). The latter number now has grown to more than 1,200.

c. Id. at 61.

d. Id. at 62.

generating the wastes were chemicals and petroleum (71%) and metals (22%). The wastes included organic materials from industrial processes (e.g., benzene and PCBs), heavy metals, biological wastes with bacterial and viral contaminants, sludge[e] and mixtures of various chemicals deposited at the sites.

Some of the most serious threats involve disposal or storage of wastes at sites where water contamination may occur, for example, sites located in floodplains, over aquifers unprotected by impervious rock or soil, and in filled wetlands. Water filtering through such sites can leach chemicals into ground water, and runoff from rain and snow melt can carry chemicals to nearby streams and rivers.

Congress was confronted with the dual problems of dealing with the serious threats posed by many existing waste disposal sites, and regulating future disposal activities so as not to multiply such threats. The lawmakers approached both problems by enacting the Resource Conservation and Recovery Act of 1976 (RCRA). Thereafter, the Comprehensive Environmental Response, Compensation, and Liability Act of 1980 (CERCLA, also known as the "superfund" law) was passed to further facilitate cleanup of leaking sites and to discourage the creation of new ones.

RCRA was primarily a forward-looking statute. Most of its provisions were aimed at creating a regulatory program to control future waste treatment, storage and disposal activities. However, it also was retrospective, imposing civil liability upon past contributors to treatment, storage or disposal facilities which present an "imminent and substantial endangerment" to health or the environment.

CERCLA was primarily backward-looking. Its main thrust was to create broad civil liability for cleanup of leaking waste disposal sites, most of which probably were expected to antedate the implementation of RCRA's regulatory program. However, CERCLA also was forward-looking. It contained some regulatory provisions, for example, one requiring that persons in charge of facilities notify EPA of hazardous substance releases; but more importantly, strict liability for cleanup of leaking sites was intended to encourage proper behavior in the future by persons

---

e. Sludge is the solid or semisolid by-product of most air and water pollution control methods. Some sludges have high nutrient value for crops. Other sludges contain high concentrations of hazardous and toxic materials and can have potentially harmful health effects.

There are four main varieties of sludge:

1. Air Pollution Control Sludge— These sludges contain sulfur compounds and unburned particulates collected in scrubbers installed in smokestacks.

2. Industrial Wastewater Sludge—Potential pollutants, removed from industri-al waste streams before discharged into surface waters, are generated by the iron and stell industry, the chemical industry, food product manufacturers, and pulp and paper industries.

3. Sewage Sludge—Organic matter, suspended solids, and heavy metals are contained in the sludge produced by sewage treatment plants.

4. Drinking Water Treatment Sludge—This sludge is produced through the purification of drinking water.

Id. at 66.

involved in the generation, transportation or disposal of hazardous wastes.

1. THE RESOURCE CONSERVATION AND RECOVERY ACT

The hazardous waste provisions of the Act are contained in subtitle C of RCRA.[a] Section 3001 requires EPA to promulgate criteria for "identifying the characteristics" of hazardous waste, and for "listing" hazardous waste, which should be subject to RCRA regulation, "taking into account toxicity, persistence, and degradability in nature, potential for accumulation in tissue," and other hazardous traits such as corrosiveness and flammability. The remaining provisions of subtitle C relate to standards and enforcement.

Standards. Three sets of standards are required, covering generators, transporters, and disposal sites. EPA is given broad authority to prescribe such standards "as may be required to protect human health and environment". Certain specific types of standards are also required. Section 3002 requires standards for generators of hazardous wastes covering record-keeping, reporting, labeling, and use of appropriate containers. Section 3002(5) requires use of a manifest system to ensure that the hazardous waste generated by the source is ultimately processed on-site or at a facility with a § 3005 permit. The manifest system is incorporated into § 3003, which requires standards for transporters. (Transporters are also subject to record-keeping and labeling requirements.[b]) As the last phase of this "cradle to grave" system for hazardous wastes, § 3004 requires standards covering treatment, storage and disposal (TSD) facilities. These standards are also intended to cover compliance with the manifest system and other record-keeping requirements. More importantly, they also cover TSD methods, as well as location, construction, and operation of disposal sites.

Enforcement. A permit system established under § 3005 is the key enforcement provision for TSD facilities. EPA is given broad inspection powers (§ 3007) and the power to issue compliance orders (with violators subject to a civil penalty) or begin civil actions against violators of any requirement (§ 3008). Criminal penalties are also available for violation of the permit requirements or falsification of documents (§ 3008(d)). Finally, RCRA makes careful provision for state regulations. Under a provision modeled on the Clean Water Act, states may assume responsibility for hazardous waste control (§ 3006). State laws less stringent than federal requirements are preempted (§ 3009).

EPA undertook the lengthy task of developing the comprehensive hazardous waste regulations [40 CFR 260–271] in two phases. The first phase consisted of defining "hazardous waste" and establishing various operating requirements for the three categories of hazardous waste handlers: generators; transporters; and treatment, storage, and disposal

---

a. 42 U.S.C.A. § 6921 et seq.

b. Section 3003(b) requires EPA to cooperate with the Department of Transportation in establishing certain standards.

(TSD) facilities. The second phase involved promulgating technical standards which would serve as the basis for issuing permits to the various types of treatment, storage, and disposal facilities.

Regulations promulgated in 1980[c] described the overall hazardous waste management system and provided definitions for terms used in the regulations. EPA identified four characteristics—*ignitability, corrosivity, reactivity, and toxicity*—for determining if a solid waste is a hazardous waste, and listed 96 process wastes and approximately 400 chemicals as hazardous if they are discarded.

Generators are required by the regulations to determine if the waste they produce is hazardous; to package, label, mark, and placard the waste properly for off-site transportation; to prepare a complete manifest to accompany the waste to the off-site facilities; and to comply with various record-keeping and reporting requirements. Transporters are basically required to carry completed manifests identifying the waste being transported and to comply with placarding requirements and spill cleanup procedures.

The 1982 promulgation of technical standards for incinerators and land disposal facilities marked the completion of the core of the RCRA hazardous waste regulations. There were then in effect detailed regulations governing every aspect of hazardous waste management—generation, transportation, storage, treatment, and disposal. EPA and authorized states then began the process of issuing permits to the full range of treatment, storage, and disposal facilities in the country.

The land disposal standards apply to all landfills, surface impoundments, waste piles, and land treatment units, both new and existing, used to treat, store, or dispose of hazardous waste. They consist of two sets of performance standards. The first is a set of design and operating standards—basically requiring liners and leachate collection systems for certain units—intended to ensure that owners or operators minimize the formation of leachate and the migration of leachate to adjacent subsurface soil and to ground water. The second is a set of ground water monitoring and response requirements applicable to all units—a three-stage program to detect, evaluate, and correct ground water contamination—intended to ensure that owners or operators detect any ground water contamination and perform corrective action when such contamination threatens human health and the environment.

In 1984, Congress enacted the Hazardous and Solid Waste Amendments of 1984, Public Law 98–616, 98 Stat. 3221, containing extensive amendments to RCRA. The amendments shifted the focus of hazardous waste management away from land disposal to *treatment* alternatives. They prohibited land disposal of hazardous wastes unless one of two conditions is satisfied: either the waste is treated to comply with standards promulgated by EPA under RCRA § 3004(m), or EPA determines

c. 40 CFR 260–265.

that the hazardous constituents will not "migrate" from the disposal unit. RCRA § 3004(g)(5).

As amended by Public Law 98–616, RCRA for the first time provided for regulation of *underground storage tanks* containing petroleum products and other hazardous liquids such as solvents and pesticides. RCRA §§ 9001–9010. The program is administered by EPA or by states with programs satisfying federal requirements. EPA regulations provide for detection and correction of leaks in existing tanks, and establish performance standards for new tanks. 40 CFR Part 280. The aim is to avoid groundwater pollution. Releases into the air of dangerous chemicals from underground tanks, like that which killed more than 2,000 persons in Bhopal, India in December 1984, are not controlled directly by the 1984 RCRA amendments, which nevertheless may help to prevent such accidents. See 15 *Envir.Rep.* 1375 (1984). Section 112(r) of the Clean Air Act, added in 1990, authorizes EPA regulation of accidental releases of hazardous substances into the air.

1986 amendments to RCRA established a $500 million Leaking Underground Storage Tank Trust Fund, derived from federal taxes on motor fuels and to be used for correction of releases of petroleum where EPA cannot identify a solvent owner or operator of the tank who will undertake action properly. The amendments were contained in The Superfund Amendments and Reauthorization Act of 1986, Pub.L. 99–499 §§ 521–522, 99th Cong., 2d Sess. (1986).

[handwritten margin note: major sources of GW contamination — gasoline taxes go to help w/ the cleanup]

For an overview of the federal UST program and of how to comply with it, see Nagle, "RCRA Subtitle I: The Federal Underground Storage Tank Program," 24 *Envt'l L.Rptr.* 10057 (1994). In November 1994, it was reported that about 400,000 of the 1.3 million regulated USTs, or 31 percent, met the federal upgrade and closure requirements set in 1988. See 25 *Env't. Rptr.* 1384 (1994).

A 1995 industry report estimated that the costs to industry and government of cleaning up then current and future leaking underground storage tanks would be about $35 billion. The report said the remaining cleanup effort would entail remediation for about 356,000 tanks, including some leaks not yet reported. The estimated average cost of cleanup was $100,000 per site. The report took into account 1.41 million regulated operational tanks and 907,000 tanks that had been closed since 1988. 25 *Env't Rptr.* 2290 (1995).

a. *"Solid" and "Hazardous" Waste Defined*

RCRA's coverage extends to all "solid waste." However, the waste need not be in solid form. Section 1003(27) provides:

> The term "solid waste" means any garbage, refuse, sludge from a waste treatment plant, water supply treatment plant, or air pollution control facility and other discarded material, including solid, liquid, semisolid, or contained gaseous material resulting from industrial, commercial, mining, and agricultural operations, and from community activities, but does not include solid or dissolved materi-

al in domestic sewage, or solid or dissolved materials in irrigation return flows or industrial discharges which are point sources subject to permits under [§ 402 of the Clean Water Act], or [certain radioactive wastes regulated under the Atomic Energy Act of 1954].

The statutory exclusions leave large quantities of hazardous materials unregulated by RCRA.

An important issue is the extent to which RCRA covers materials that are *recycled* or held for future recycling. Prior EPA regulations defining "solid waste" provided that materials were solid waste if they were abandoned by being disposed of, burned, or incinerated; or stored, treated, or accumulated before or in lieu of those activities. 50 Fed.Reg. 614 (1985). The regulations also provided that certain materials used in recycling might be covered by RCRA, depending on the nature of the material and the recycling activity. The regulations were challenged by the mining and petroleum industries, which argued that materials intended for reuse were not "wastes." The challenge resulted in the following decision.

AMERICAN MINING CONGRESS v. ENVIRONMENTAL PROTECTION AGENCY

United States Court of Appeals, District of Columbia Circuit, 1987.
824 F.2d 1177.

STARR, CIRCUIT JUDGE:

* * * Petitioners, trade associations representing mining and oil refining interests, challenge regulations promulgated by EPA that amend the definition of "solid waste" to establish and define the agency's authority to regulate secondary materials reused within an industry's ongoing production process. In plain English, petitioners maintain that EPA has exceeded its regulatory authority in seeking to bring materials that are not discarded or otherwise disposed of within the compass of "waste."

RCRA is a comprehensive environmental statute under which EPA is granted authority to regulate solid and hazardous wastes. * * *

Congress' "overriding concern" in enacting RCRA was to establish the framework for a national system to insure the safe management of hazardous waste. * * *

RCRA includes two major parts: one deals with nonhazardous solid waste management and the other with hazardous waste management. Under the latter, EPA is directed to promulgate regulations establishing a comprehensive management system. EPA's authority, however, extends only to the regulation of "hazardous waste." Because "hazardous waste" is defined as a subset of "solid waste," § 6903(5), the scope of EPA's jurisdiction is limited to those materials that constitute "solid waste." That pivotal term is defined by RCRA as any garbage, refuse, sludge from a waste treatment plant, water supply treatment plant, or air pollution control facility *and other discarded material,* including solid, liquid, semisolid or contained gaseous material, resulting from industrial, commercial, mining, and agricultural operations, and from community activities. . . .

42 U.S.C. § 6903(27) (emphasis added). As will become evident, this case turns on the meaning of the phrase, "and other discarded material," contained in the statute's definitional provisions.

EPA's interpretation of "solid waste" has evolved over time. On May 19, 1980, EPA issued interim regulations defining "solid waste" to include a material that is "a manufacturing or mining by-product and sometimes is discarded." 45 Fed.Reg. 33,119 (1980). This definition contained two terms needing elucidation: "by-product" and "sometimes discarded." In its definition of "a manufacturing or mining by-product," EPA expressly *excluded* "an intermediate manufacturing or mining product which results from one of the steps in a manufacturing or mining process and is typically processed through the next step of the process within a short time."

In 1983, the agency proposed narrowing amendments to the 1980 interim rule. The agency showed especial concern over *recycling* activities. In the preamble to the amendments, the agency observed that, in light of RCRA's legislative history, it was clear that "Congress indeed intended that materials being recycled or held for recycling can be wastes, and if hazardous, hazardous wastes." The agency also asserted that "not only can materials destined for recycling or being recycled be solid and hazardous wastes, but the Agency clearly has the authority to regulate recycling activities as hazardous waste management."

While asserting its interest in recycling activities (and materials being held for recycling), EPA's discussion left unclear whether the agency in fact believed its jurisdiction extended to materials recycled in an industry's on-going production processes, or only to materials disposed of and recycled as part of a waste management program. In its preamble, EPA stated that "the revised definition of solid waste sets out the Agency's view of its jurisdiction over the recycling of hazardous waste. . . . Proposed section 261.6 then contains exemptions from regulations for those hazardous waste recycling activities that we do not think require regulation." The amended regulatory description of "solid waste" itself, then, did not include materials "used or reused as effective substitutes for raw materials in processes using raw materials as principal feedstocks." EPA explained the exclusion as follows:

> [These] materials are being used essentially as raw materials and so ordinarily are not appropriate candidates for regulatory control. Moreover, when these materials are used to manufacture new products, the processes generally are normal manufacturing operations. . . . The Agency is reluctant to read the statute as regulating actual manufacturing processes.

This, then, seemed clear: EPA was drawing a line between discarding and ultimate recycling, on the one hand, and a continuous or ongoing manufacturing process with one-site "recycling," on the other. If the activity fell within the latter category, then the materials were not deemed to be "discarded."

After receiving extensive comments, EPA issued its final rule on January 4, 1985. Under the final rule, materials are considered "solid waste" if they are abandoned by being disposed of, burned, or incinerated; or stored, treated, or accumulated before or in lieu of those activities. In addition, certain recycling activities fall within EPA's definition. EPA determines whether a material is a RCRA solid waste when it is recycled by examining both the material or substance itself and the recycling activity involved. The final rule identifies five categories of "secondary materials" (spent materials, sludges, by-products, commercial chemical products, and scrap metal). These "secondary materials" constitute "solid waste" when they are disposed of; burned for energy recovery or used to produce a fuel; reclaimed; or accumulated speculatively.[1] Under the final rule, if a material constitutes "solid waste," it is subject to RCRA regulation *unless* it is directly reused as an ingredient or as an effective substitute for a commercial product, or is returned as a raw material substitute to its original manufacturing process.[2] In the jargon of the trade, the latter category is known as the "closed-loop" exception. In either case, the material must not first be "reclaimed" (processed to recover a usable product or regenerated). EPA exempts these activities "because they are like ordinary usage of commercial products."

Petitioners, American Mining Congress ("AMC") and American Petroleum Institute ("API"), challenge the scope of EPA's final rule. Relying upon the statutory definition of "solid waste," petitioners contend that EPA's authority under RCRA is limited to controlling materials that are *discarded or intended for discard.* They argue that EPA's reuse and recycle rules, as applied to in-process secondary materials, regulate materials that have not been discarded, and therefore exceed EPA's jurisdiction.

[The court then describes how petroleum refineries use a complex retrieval system to recapture escaping hydrocarbons and return them to

---

1. Under the final rule, a "use constituting disposal" is defined as direct placement on land of wastes or products containing or derived from wastes. A material is "accumulated speculatively" if it is accumulated prior to being recycled. If the accumulator can show that the materials feasibly can be recycled, and that during a one-year calendar period the amount of material recycled or transferred for recycling is 75% or more of the amount present at the beginning of the year, the materials are not considered solid wastes. A material is "reclaimed" if it is processed to recover a usable product, or if it is regenerated.

2. Specifically, the final rule excludes materials recycled by being: "(1) [u]sed or reused as ingredients in an industrial process to make a product, *provided the materials are not being reclaimed;* or (2) [u]sed or reused as effective substitutes for commercial products; or (3) [r]eturned to the original process from which they are generated, without first being reclaimed." Id. (emphasis added). In the third category, the material must be returned to the original manufacturing process as a substitute for raw material feedstock, and the process must use raw materials as principal feedstocks.

appropriate parts of the refining process. The court also states that mining facilities reprocess ore and recapture for reuse in the production process metal-and mineral-bearing dusts released during processing. The court notes that the materials recaptured by petroleum refineries and mining facilities are considered "solid waste" under EPA's rule.]

* * *

* * * Congress, it will be recalled, granted EPA power to regulate "solid waste." Congress specifically defined "solid waste" as "discarded material." EPA then defined "discarded material" to include materials destined for reuse in an industry's *ongoing* production processes. The challenge to EPA's jurisdictional reach is founded, again, on the proposition that in-process secondary materials are outside the bounds of EPA's lawful authority. Nothing has been *discarded,* the argument goes, and thus RCRA jurisdiction remains untriggered.

The first step in statutory interpretation is, of course, an analysis of the language itself. In pursuit of Congress' intent, we "start with the assumption that the legislative purpose is expressed by the ordinary meaning of the words used." Here, Congress defined "solid waste" as "discarded material." The ordinary plain-English meaning of the word "discarded" is "disposed of," "thrown away" or "abandoned." Encompassing materials retained for immediate reuse within the scope of "discarded material" strains, to say the least, the everyday usage of that term. * * *

* * *

The question we face, then, is whether, in light of the National Legislature's expressly stated objectives and the underlying problems that motivated it to enact RCRA in the first instance, Congress was using the term "discarded" in its ordinary sense—"disposed of" or "abandoned"—or whether Congress was using it in a much more open-ended way, so as to encompass materials no longer useful in their original capacity though destined for immediate reuse in another phase of the industry's ongoing production process.

For the following reasons, we believe the former to be the case. RCRA was enacted, as the Congressional objectives and findings make clear, in an effort to help States deal with the ever-increasing problem of solid waste *disposal* by encouraging the search for and use of alternatives to existing methods of disposal (including recycling) and protecting health and the environment by regulating hazardous wastes. To fulfill these purposes, it seems clear that EPA need not regulate "spent" materials that are recycled and reused in an *ongoing* manufacturing or industrial process. These materials have not yet become part of the waste disposal problem; rather, *they are destined for beneficial reuse or recycling in a continuous process by the generating industry itself.*

* * *

We are constrained to conclude that, in light of the language and structure of RCRA, the problems animating Congress to enact it, and the relevant portions of the legislative history, Congress clearly and unambiguously expressed its intent that "solid waste" (and therefore EPA's regulatory authority) be limited to materials that are "discarded" by virtue of being disposed of, abandoned, or thrown away. While we do not lightly overturn an agency's reading of its own statute, we are persuaded that by regulating in-process secondary materials, EPA has acted in contravention of Congress' intent. Accordingly, the petition for review is Granted.

Mikva, Circuit Judge, dissenting:

* * * In my opinion, the EPA's interpretation of solid waste is completely reasonable in light of the language, policies, and legislative history of RCRA. Congress had broad remedial objectives in mind when it enacted RCRA, most notably to "regulat[e] the treatment, storage, transportation, and disposal of hazardous wastes which have adverse effects on the environment." The disposal problem Congress was combatting encompassed more than just abandoned materials. RCRA makes this clear with its definition of the central statutory term "disposal":

> the discharge, deposit, injection, dumping, spilling, leaking, or placing of any solid waste or hazardous waste into or on any land or water so that such solid waste or hazardous waste or any constituent thereof may enter the environment or be emitted into the air or discharged into any waters, including ground waters.

42 U.S.C. § 6903(3). This definition clearly encompasses more than the everyday meaning of disposal, which is a "discarding or throwing away." Webster's Third International Dictionary 654 (2d ed. 1981). The definition is *functional:* waste is disposed under this provision if it is put into contact with land or water in such a way as to pose the risks to health and the environment that animated Congress to pass RCRA. Whether the manufacturer subjectively intends to put the material to additional use is irrelevant to this definition, as indeed it should be, because the manufacturer's state of mind bears no necessary relation to the hazards of the industrial processes he employs.

Faithful to RCRA's functional approach, EPA reasonably concluded that regulation of certain in-process secondary materials was necessary to carry out its mandate. The materials at issue in this case can pose the same risks as abandoned wastes, whether or not the manufacturer intends eventually to put them to further beneficial use. As the agency explained, "[s]imply because a waste is likely to be recycled will not ensure that it will not be spilled or leaked before recycling occurs." The storage, transportation, and even recycling of in-process secondary materials can cause severe environmental harm. Indeed, the EPA documented environmental disasters caused by the handling or storage of such materials. It also pointed out the risk of damage from spills or leaks when certain in-process secondary materials are placed on land or in underground product storage. * * *

* * * [I]n this case the EPA has interpreted solid waste in a manner that seems to expand the everyday usage of the word "discarded." Its conclusion, however, is fully supportable in light of the statutory scheme and legislative history of RCRA. The agency concluded that certain on-site recycled materials constitute an integral part of the waste disposal problem. This judgment is grounded in the EPA's technical expertise and is adequately supported by evidence in the record. The majority nevertheless reverses the agency because it believes that the materials at issue "have not yet become part of the waste disposal problem." This declaration is nothing more than a substitution of the majority's own conclusions for the sound technical judgment of the EPA. The EPA's interpretation is a reasonable construction of an ambiguous statutory provision and should be upheld.

Notes

1. Should the definition of "solid waste" be based upon whether materials have become a part of the waste disposal problem? Should the definition depend on whether a substance poses a risk warranting regulation? If such considerations are relevant, who—EPA or the courts—should weigh them and make a decision? Under the *Chevron* case, page 390 supra, did the majority in *AMC* give sufficient deference to EPA's conclusion?

2. After the *AMC* decision, various industries claimed that numerous substances which EPA had regulated under subtitle C of RCRA were not "solid waste." Thus, the American Mining Congress claimed that EPA could not regulate sludge from wastewater, stored in a surface impoundment, if the sludge was to be reprocessed later for metals recovery. In American Mining Congress v. EPA (*AMC II*), 907 F.2d 1179, 1186 (D.C.Cir.1990), the court sided with EPA:

> *AMC*'s holding concerned only materials that are "destined for *immediate reuse* in another phase of the industry's ongoing production process" (emphasis added), and that "have not yet become part of the waste disposal problem." Nothing in *AMC* prevents the agency from treating as "discarded" the wastes at issue in this case, which are managed in land disposal units that *are* part of wastewater treatment systems, which *have* therefore become "part of the waste disposal problem," and which are *not* part of ongoing industrial processes. Indeed, [we have] explicitly rejected the very claim that petitioners assert in this case, * * * namely, that under RCRA, potential reuse of a material prevents the agency from classifying it as "discarded."

3. If materials are in fact recycled, can they be considered wastes at the time of recycling? In reliance upon *AMC*, EPA determined that materials utilized in a metals reclamation process ceased to be solid wastes under RCRA when they arrived at a reclamation facility because they no longer were "discarded material." Environmentalists challenged this interpretation and prevailed in *American Petroleum Institute v. EPA,* 906 F.2d 729, 741 (D.C.Cir.1990):

> *AMC* is by no means dispositive of EPA's authority to regulate K061 slag. Unlike the materials in question in *AMC*, K061 is indisputably "discarded" *before* being subject to metals reclamation. Consequently, it

has "become part of the waste disposal problem"; that is why EPA has the power to require that K061 be subject to mandatory metals reclamation. Nor does anything in *AMC* require EPA to cease treating K061 as "solid waste" once it reaches the metals reclamation facility. K061 is delivered to the facility not as part of an *"ongoing* manufacturing or industrial process" within the generating industry, but as part of a mandatory waste treatment plan prescribed by EPA.

4. Current EPA regulations provide that materials are "solid waste" if they are "recycled—or accumulated, stored, or treated before recycling—as specified in [this subsection]." 40 CFR 261.2(c). Subsection (c) identifies types of materials that are regulated when "used in a manner constituting disposal," "burned for energy recovery," "reclaimed," or "accumulated speculatively."

Subtitle C of RCRA provides for regulation of *hazardous* solid waste, while subtitle D deals with regulation, primarily by states, of *nonhazardous* solid waste. However, RCRA does not indicate precisely how EPA is to determine which solid wastes are hazardous. "Hazardous waste" is defined in § 1004(5):

> The term "hazardous waste" means a solid waste, or combination of solid wastes, which because of its quantity, concentration, or physical, chemical, or infectious characteristics may—
>
> (A) cause, or significantly contribute to an increase in mortality or an increase in serious irreversible, or incapacitating reversible, illness; or
>
> (B) pose a substantial present or potential hazard to human health or the environment when improperly treated, stored, transported, or disposed of, or otherwise managed.

Under § 3001, EPA is to promulgate regulations identifying the *characteristics* of hazardous waste and *listing* particular hazardous wastes to be regulated under subtitle C, "taking into account toxicity, persistence, and degradability in nature, potential for accumulation in tissue, and other related factors such as flammability, corrosiveness, and other hazardous characteristics."

EPA regulations provide two principal ways in which solid waste may deemed to be "hazardous": by exhibiting one of four hazardous characteristics (*"characteristic wastes"*) or by being identified specifically as a hazardous waste by EPA (*"listed wastes"*). 40 CFR 261.3. EPA has established four general categories of listed wastes, the "F," "K," "P," and "U" lists. 40 CFR 261.31–261.32. On the "P" list are acutely hazardous chemical products. The "U" list includes non-acutely hazardous chemical products. The "F" and "K" lists of waste mixtures and combinations include wastes that meet the criteria for the "P" and "U" lists or one of the four "characteristics" (*toxicity, ignitability, corrosivity, and reactivity*).

In *Dithiocarbamate Task Force v. EPA*, 98 F.3d 1394 (D.C.Cir.1996), the court held that EPA had acted arbitrarily and capriciously in listing twenty-eight carbamate compounds as hazardous "U" wastes because (1) applicable regulations, 40 CFR 261.11(a)(3), provided ten factors to be considered in making listing decisions, (2) the language and structure of the regulations generally required consideration of all ten factors, and (3) EPA failed either to consider adequately two of the factors or to find explicitly that they were irrelevant or unimportant in the particular listing. Carbamates and derived products are used as pesticides, herbicides and fungicides, and also are used in various ways by the rubber, wood and textile industries.

To prevent generators from evading hazardous waste regulations by diluting or otherwise changing the composition of listed wastes, EPA has adopted two important rules, the *"mixture"* rule and the *"derived-from"* rule. The former provides that a mixture of a "listed" hazardous waste with another solid waste is also a hazardous waste. 40 CFR 261.3(a)(2)(iii) and (iv). The derived-from rule provides that any solid waste "generated from the treatment, storage, or disposal of a hazardous waste, including any sludge, spill, residue, ash, emission control dust, or leachate (but not including precipitation run-off)," is a hazardous waste. 40 CFR 261.3(c)(2)(i).

The following two cases illustrate the application of these rules for identifying what are hazardous wastes to be regulated under subtitle C of RCRA. The first case involves "listed" wastes and the "derived-from" and "mixture" rules. The second case involves "characteristic" wastes. In both, note the basic concern about "leachate," which can contaminate underground soil and water supplies.

CHEMICAL WASTE MANAGEMENT, INC.
v. ENVIRONMENTAL PROTECTION
AGENCY

United States Court of Appeals, District of Columbia Circuit, 1989.
869 F.2d 1526.

Wald, Chief Judge:

* * *

The RCRA was recently modified by the Hazardous Solid Waste Amendments of 1984, which established sweeping restrictions on the land disposal of hazardous wastes. The EPA was required to establish a schedule dividing the hazardous wastes into "thirds," see 42 U.S.C. § 6924(g)(4); the agency promulgated the schedule in May of 1986. The division of the schedule into thirds was designed as a means of phasing in the land disposal restrictions. By August 8, 1988, the EPA was required to promulgate treatment standards for each of the first-third scheduled wastes; these wastes may not be land disposed unless they have been treated to meet the applicable standards or the disposal unit is one from which there will be no migration of hazardous constituents for as long as the waste remains hazardous. Similar land disposal restrictions for second-third and third-third wastes are scheduled to take effect on June 8, 1989 and May 8, 1990 * * *.

The present dispute concerns the rule-making in which the EPA established treatment standards for first-third wastes. * * * EPA issued treatment standards for the various wastes; in lengthy preambles to the notices, the agency discussed the interpretive principles which would guide its application of the standards. Three such principles merit discussion here.

One of these principles concerns the treatment standards applicable to leachate produced from hazardous waste. Leachate is produced when liquids, such as rainwater, percolate through wastes stored in a landfill. The resulting fluid will contain suspended components drawn from the original waste. Proper leachate management involves the storage of wastes in lined containers so that leachate may be collected before it seeps into soil or groundwater. The leachate will periodically be pumped out of the container and subsequently treated.

An EPA regulation promulgated in 1980, known as the "derived-from rule," provided that "any solid waste generated from the treatment, storage, or disposal of a hazardous waste, including any sludge, spill residue, ash, emission control dust, or leachate (but not including precipitation run-off) is a hazardous waste." Thus, for some years prior to the 1988 rulemaking, it had been understood that leachate derived from a hazardous waste was itself a hazardous waste. In the 1988 preambles, the agency stated that leachate derived from multiple hazardous wastes would be deemed to contain each of the wastes from which it was generated, and that it must therefore be treated to meet the applicable treatment standards for each of the underlying wastes. This is known as the "waste code carry-through" principle.

The second interpretive principle at issue in this proceeding also involves the treatment requirements for hazardous waste leachate. In its preamble to the August rule, the agency stated that "[h]azardous waste listings are retroactive, so that once a particular waste is listed, all wastes meeting that description are hazardous wastes no matter when disposed." The implications of that statement center around wastes which were not deemed hazardous at the time they were disposed but which are subsequently listed as hazardous wastes. The RCRA does not require that such wastes be cleaned up or moved from the landfill, nor does the agency impose any retroactive penalty on the prior disposal of the waste. Under the August rule, however, the agency announced that leachate which is actively managed after the underlying wastes have been listed as hazardous will itself be deemed a hazardous waste and must be treated to the applicable standards. Under this approach, the fact that the original waste was not deemed hazardous at the time of disposal is simply irrelevant in determining the treatment requirements for the leachate.

Finally, the agency discussed the applicability of the treatment standards to contaminated environmental media such as soil and groundwater. The preamble stated that "[i]n these cases, the mixture is deemed to be the listed waste." Thus, when a listed hazardous waste (or hazardous waste leachate) is mixed with soil or groundwater—as may occur, for example, through spills or leaking—the soil or groundwater is subject to all the treatment standards or restrictions that would be applicable to the original waste.

THE PRESENT LITIGATION

* * *

Petitioners in this case raised a host of substantive and procedural challenges to the August rulemaking. * * *

Shortly before oral argument, * * * the parties filed an Emergency Joint Motion to Defer Oral Argument on Certain Leachate–Related Issues. That motion, which was granted by this court, covered the petitioners' challenge to the waste code carry-through principle—the requirement that derived-from wastes such as leachate would be deemed to contain each of the original wastes from which they were generated. * * * The explanation [was] that a negotiated settlement seemed likely on all issues pertaining to the waste code carry-through principle. Under the terms of the proposed settlement, all multiple-waste leachate would be rescheduled to the third-third, and a leachate treatability study would be undertaken so that appropriate treatment standards could be determined.

The issues argued to the court, and the issues that we decide today, are therefore limited to the following. First, did the agency improperly engage in retroactive rulemaking in ordering that its leachate regulations be made applicable to leachate derived from wastes which were not deemed hazardous at the time they were disposed? Second, did the agency act in an arbitrary and capricious manner by mandating that environmental media contaminated by hazardous wastes must themselves be treated as hazardous wastes? * * *

* * *

* * * Petitioners argue that the EPA lacks the authority to promulgate retroactive regulations, and they correctly observe that such regulations are disfavored. In our view, however, the crucial question is not whether the EPA is authorized to promulgate a retroactive rule. Rather, the crucial question is whether the challenged regulation in fact operates retroactively. We conclude that it does not.

* * * The agency has made no effort to impose a legal penalty on the disposal of waste which was not deemed hazardous at the time it was disposed. Nor, in fact, does this regulation require the cleanup of any newly listed hazardous wastes. The preamble to the final rule expressly provides that "these residues could become subject to the land disposal restrictions for the listed waste from which they derive *if they are*

managed actively after the effective date of the land disposal prohibition for the underlying waste." The rule has prospective effect only: treatment or disposal of leachate will be subject to the regulation only if that treatment or disposal occurs after the promulgation of applicable treatment standards.

As a practical matter, of course, a landfill operator has little choice but to collect and manage its leachate. Active management of leachate is sound environmental practice, and a panoply of regulations require it. * * *

Moreover, we find this aspect of the agency's interpretation of the derived-from rule to be eminently reasonable. The derived-from rule establishes a presumption: leachate generated from hazardous waste will be presumed hazardous unless it is proved nonhazardous or treated to applicable standards. The reasonableness of that presumption does not vary depending upon the time when the underlying waste was disposed. * * *

* * *

In reviewing the EPA's application of its 1980 rules to contaminated soil, we are guided by two fundamental principles. The first is that "[a]n agency's interpretation of its own regulations will be accepted unless it is plainly wrong." The second is that on "a highly technical question ... courts necessarily must show considerable deference to an agency's expertise." * * *

The agency's rule, adopted in 1980, provides that "[a] hazardous waste will remain a hazardous waste" until it is delisted. The petitioners argue in essence that an agglomeration of soil and hazardous waste is to be regarded as a new and distinct substance, to which the presumption of hazardousness no longer applies. The agency's position is that hazardous waste cannot be presumed to change character when it is combined with an environmental medium, and that the hazardous waste restrictions therefore continue to apply to waste which is contained in soil or groundwater. * * *

* * *

The EPA's approach to contaminated environmental media is * * * consistent with the derived-from and mixture rules established in 1980. These rules provide that a hazardous waste will continue to be presumed hazardous when it is mixed with a solid waste, or when it is contained in a residue from treatment or disposal. The derived-from and mixture rules do not, it is true, apply by their own terms to contaminated soil or groundwater. They nevertheless demonstrate that the agency's rule on contaminated soil is part of a coherent regulatory framework. It is one application of a general principle, consistently adhered to, that a hazardous waste does not lose its hazardous character simply because it changes form or is combined with other substances. In promulgating the mixture rule, the agency did not presume that every mixture of listed wastes and other wastes would in fact present a hazard. Rather, the agency reasoned that "[b]ecause the potential combinations of listed wastes and other wastes are infinite, we have been unable to devise any workable, broadly applicable formula which would distinguish between those waste mixtures which are and are not hazardous." The EPA therefore concluded that it was fair to shift to the individual operator the burden of establishing (through the delisting process) that its own waste mixture is not hazardous. Precisely the same logic applies to combinations of hazardous waste and soil or groundwater.

* * *

The EPA's interpretation is also buttressed by one provision of the Hazardous Solid Waste Amendments of 1984, 42 U.S.C. § 6924(e). Congress there provided that certain specified solvents and dioxins would be prohibited from land disposal. The statute further provided that, for a two-year period after the effective date of the ban, the prohibition "shall not apply to any disposal of contaminated soil or debris resulting from a response action taken under section 9604 or 9606 of this title or a corrective action required under this subchapter." This statutory exemption would of course have been superfluous unless contaminated soil would otherwise fall within the terms of the ban * * *.

We need not decide whether any of these factors, or all of them taken together, would *compel* the conclusion that soil or groundwater contaminated with hazardous waste is itself a hazardous waste as defined by EPA regulations. We do believe, however, that, given the agency's broad discretion to interpret its own rules, it was entirely reasonable for the EPA to arrive at that conclusion. We therefore must sustain the agency's position.

Notes

1. In its long-delayed decision in *Shell Oil Co. v. EPA*, 950 F.2d 741 (D.C.Cir.1991), the court held that EPA had failed to comply with the Administrative Procedure Act's notice-and-comment requirements when promulgating the mixture and derived-from rules in 1980. The court vacated the rules but suggested that EPA reenact them on an <u>interim basis</u> under the "good cause" exemption of 5 U.S.C.A. § 553(b)(3)(B), pending full notice and opportunity to comment. EPA took the suggestion and reissued the rules in 1992. The reinstated rules were challenged but upheld in *Mobil Oil Corp. v. EPA*, 35 F.3d 579 (D.C.Cir.1994).

[handwritten margin note: 8 mo. period when there were no rules.]

Still somewhat in doubt is whether the rules—or the general principle reflected in them, that a hazardous waste does not lose its hazardous character simply because it changes form or is combined with other substances—can be applied to wastes generated *prior* to the rules' reinstatement in 1992. See Satterfield, "EPA's Mixture Rule: Why the Fuss?", 24 *Envtl. L.Rptr.* 10712 (1994); Van Carson et al., "Rebuttal: The Mixture Rule and the Environmental Code," 25 *Envt'l L. Rptr.* 10244 (1995); James Satterfield, "EPA's Continuing Jurisdiction Regulation: A Response to *The Mixture Rule and the Environmental Code*," 25 *Envt'l L. Rptr.* 10262 (1995); and Aaron Goldberg, "The Federal Hazardous Waste Program: A House of

Cards?", 26 *Env't Rptr.* 365 (1995). In *United States v. Bethlehem Steel Corp.*, 38 F.3d 862 (7th Cir.1994), a criminal prosecution under RCRA, the court "reject[ed] the notion that the policy behind the mixture rule is 'embodied' as a general principle within the definition [of hazardous waste] and that such a principle may operate to reach wastes that would have been covered by the mixture rule, but for its invalidation."

2. Are the mixture and derived-from rules likely to require that *non*-hazardous materials be managed as hazardous wastes? EPA's regulations exempt a mixture which "no longer exhibits any characteristic of hazardous waste identified in subpart C of this part." 40 CFR 261.3(a)(2)(iii). The derived-from regulations are subject to a similar limitation. 40 CFR 261.3(d)(1).

3. In 1995 EPA proposed a new Hazardous Waste Identification Rule (HWIR), 60 *Fed. Reg.* 66344 (Dec. 21, 1995). This rule would replace the 1992 interim regulations which reinstated the mixture and derived-from rules. Although EPA was party to a 1995 consent decree requiring the agency to issue a final HWIR by December 15, 1996, Christina Kaneen of the EPA General Counsel's Office reports that the consent decree was modified on April 11, 1997, to require the agency to issue a revised proposed HWIR by October 31, 1999, and a final HWIR by April 30, 2001. The 1995 proposal is analyzed in Kenneth Kastner and Jack Goldman, "HWIR Could Allow Low–Risk Listed Hazardous Waste to Exit RCRA Regulation, Would 'Cap' Unnecessary Treatment Under Land Disposal Restrictions Program," 26 *Env't Rptr.* 1623 (1996).

4. The next case demonstrates the complexity of formulating and applying rules pertaining to "characteristic" wastes, solid wastes which are not specifically "listed" by EPA as hazardous but which manifest one or more of the four characteristics (toxicity, ignitability, corrosivity, and reactivity) set out in EPA regulations for the purpose of identifying other hazardous wastes.

EDISON ELECTRIC INSTITUTE v. ENVIRONMENTAL PROTECTION AGENCY

United States Court of Appeals, District of Columbia Circuit, 1993.
2 F.3d 438.

Before MIKVA, CHIEF JUDGE, SILBERMAN and D.H. GINSBURG, CIRCUIT JUDGES.

Opinion PER CURIAM.

* * * Congress delegated to the Environmental Protection Agency the duty to "promulgate regulations identifying the characteristics of hazardous waste, and listing particular hazardous wastes ... which shall be subject to the provisions of [Subtitle C]." 42 U.S.C. § 6921(b)(1). Thus, Congress directed the Agency to identify hazardous wastes in two ways: (1) identify certain characteristics which would render a solid waste hazardous, and (2) list specific solid wastes that are, so to speak, *per se* hazardous.

This appeal concerns only the former category of solid wastes, those deemed hazardous by virtue of possessing certain general characteristics. More specifically, the petitioners [challenge] EPA's final rule revising the Toxicity Characteristic ("TC")—one of the four characteristics (the other three are ignitability, corrosivity, and reactivity) set out in EPA regulations for the purpose of identifying hazardous solid wastes. The TC seeks to "identify waste which, if improperly disposed of, may release toxic materials in sufficient amounts to pose a substantial hazard to human health or the environment."

In 1980, EPA established a "protocol" for determining the TC of solid wastes, which it dubbed the "Extraction Procedure" ("EP"). The EP toxicity test is based on a particular mismanagement scenario—"co-disposal of toxic wastes in an actively decomposing municipal landfill which overlies a groundwater aquifer"—and is intended to simulate the actual leaching of wastes that might occur in a municipal solid waste ("MSW") landfill. The test requires a waste generator to mix a representative sample of its waste with an acidic leaching medium for 24 hours, and then to test the resulting liquid waste to see if it contains unsafe levels of any of 14 toxic contaminants identified in the National Interim Primary Drinking Water Standards ("NIPDWS") promulgated pursuant to 42 U.S.C. § 300g–1.

In order to duplicate the attenuation in concentration expected to occur between the point of leachate generation and the point of human or environmental exposure, the EP applies a dilution and attenuation factor ("DAF") of 100 to the concentration of toxic contaminants observed in the test extract. Thus, a waste would be considered hazardous, and subject to RCRA Subtitle C regulation, if the results of the EP toxicity test revealed the presence of any listed contaminant at a level of at least 100 times the applicable NIPDWS.

THE REVISED TOXICITY CHARACTERISTIC

* * *

The 1986 rulemaking to revise the TC was necessitated by two intervening pieces of legislation. First, in 1980, Congress passed the Bevill Amendment, 42 U.S.C. § 6921(b)(3)(A), as part of the Solid Waste Disposal Act Amendments of 1980. The Bevill Amendment exempted from Subtitle C regulation certain waste produced by fossil fuel combustion and mineral processing and directed EPA to study the environmental effects of such wastes and to determine whether special regulations were necessary to govern their disposal. In litigation to compel EPA to meet the statutory deadlines for implementation, this Court found that Congress intended to exempt "only those wastes from processing ores or minerals that [are] 'high volume, low hazard' wastes." *Environmental Defense Fund v. EPA*, 852 F.2d 1316, 1328–29 (D.C.Cir.1988) *("EDF II")* cert. denied, 489 U.S. 1011, 109 S.Ct. 1120, 103 L.Ed.2d 183 (1989). In a subsequent rulemaking, EPA decided to exempt only those high volume, low hazard wastes that fell within the top 5% of the largest individual waste streams managed by Subtitle C facilities.

The second piece of intervening legislation was the Hazardous and Solid Waste Amendments of 1984 ("HSWA"), Pub.L. No. 98–616, 98 Stat. 3221. In one provision of HSWA, Congress expressed concern with the TC and the EP toxicity test and directed the Agency to reevaluate * * *. 42 U.S.C. § 6921(g). The legislative history indicates that Congress believed that EPA's test was deficient because it was underinclusive in identifying hazardous wastes.

In response to HSWA, EPA revised its regulations and adopted a new testing procedure in place of the EP, known as the Toxicity Characteristic Leaching Procedure ("TCLP"). * * *

* * *

The American Mining Congress ("AMC") and the Edison Electric Institute ("EEI") challenge EPA's application of the TCLP generic mismanagement scenario to mineral processing wastes and manufactured gas plant wastes. The parties agree that EPA treats these wastes similarly, and they are hereinafter referred to collectively as "mineral wastes." They do not fall under Bevill Amendment's exemption from Subtitle C regulation, as implemented in EPA's regulations, because individual waste generators do not produce them in sufficient quantities to qualify for the high volume, low hazard exception.

* * *

Statutory Requirement of "Accuracy"

AMC and EEI claim that the application of the TCLP to mineral wastes violates the statutory mandate for a more accurate TCLP, see 42 U.S.C. § 6921(g), because the generic mismanagement scenario is based on factual assumptions that do not apply to mineral wastes. They maintain that it is extremely unlikely that mineral wastes will ever be disposed of in municipal solid waste ("MSW") landfills in light of the extremely large volumes of waste that are generated and the relatively small capacity of MSW landfills. * * *

* * *

Finally, AMC and EEI assert that the inapplicability of the TCLP generic mismanagement scenario to the mining context renders three specific TCLP elements—the aggressiveness of the leaching medium, the particle size reduction requirement, and the assumed DAF of 100—far too severe in predicting the hazardousness of these types of wastes. * * *

* * *

EPA settled on a single mismanagement scenario and rejected a "management-based" approach to identifying hazardous wastes, which would require a separate toxicity test for each category of waste that is typically managed in a particular way. In keeping with the RCRA directive to "promulgate regulations identifying the *characteristics* of hazardous waste," 42 U.S.C. § 6921(b)(1) (emphasis added), EPA decided that "the most effective and appropriate approach [to implementing RCRA] is to ... identify[ ] *properties* of wastes that would pose a threat to human health and the environment if improperly managed." The Agency concluded that a management-based approach would raise complex enforcement problems because of the difficulty in determining beforehand how any particular solid waste will eventually be managed. As we have already stated, nothing in the RCRA mandate of a more accurate TC dictates a management-based approach, and the use of a generic mismanagement scenario is a reasonable interpretation of the statutory language.

EPA selected the specific MSW landfill mismanagement scenario because contamination of groundwater through the leaching of land-disposed wastes is a prevalent environmental hazard that is well-documented in EPA damage files and with which Congress was especially concerned in passing RCRA. In response to comments that industrial solid wastes are not often disposed of in MSW landfills, EPA pointed out that states impose few restrictions on the types of non-hazardous wastes accepted at MSW landfills, and that a substantial quantity of the wastes actually received at MSW landfills are industrial wastes. EPA recognized that MSW landfills generate a more aggressive leachate media than other landfills, but chose to adopt a particularly conservative scenario "in view of the statutory mandate to protect human health and the environment, the broad statutory definition of hazardous waste[,] and also because the phenomenon of long term leaching is only incompletely understood." These choices represent a reasonable interpretation of RCRA.

* * *

REASONABLENESS OF APPLYING THE TCLP MISMANAGEMENT SCENARIO TO MINERAL WASTES

The inquiry is not completed by our conclusion that the TCLP mismanagement scenario represents a permissible construction of RCRA under *Chevron*. In addition, to pass muster under the APA, the TCLP must bear some rational relationship to mineral wastes in order for the Agency to justify the application of the toxicity test to those wastes. *See Motor Vehicle Mfrs. Ass'n v. State Farm*, 463 U.S. 29, 43, 103 S.Ct. 2856, 2866, 77 L.Ed.2d 443 (1983). We hold that EPA has failed to demonstrate any such relationship on the record, and therefore remand to the Agency for further proceedings consistent with this opinion.

* * *

The record evidence on which EPA relies does not demonstrate that low volume mineral wastes have ever been disposed of in MSW landfills. * * *

Even in the absence of evidence that at least some mineral wastes have actually been disposed in MSW landfills, EPA's application of the

TCLP to mineral wastes would nonetheless pass muster if there were evidence on the record that mineral wastes were exposed to conditions similar to those simulated by the TCLP. * * * Again, however, there is no evidence or explanation on the record to justify a conclusion that mineral wastes ever come into contact with any form of acidic leaching medium.

* * * We therefore remand to allow the Agency to provide a fuller and more reasoned explanation for its decision to apply the TCLP to mineral wastes.

Notes

1. In *Columbia Falls Aluminum Co. v. Environmental Protection Agency*, 139 F.3d 914 (D.C.Cir.1998), the court held that EPA's use of the TCLP to determine compliance with its treatment standard was arbitrary and capricious because the TCLP failed to predict the actual behavior of hazardous constituents in the leachate after a certain type of aluminum waste ("spent potliner") was treated and disposed in a "monofill," a landfill dedicated exclusively to this type of waste. Tests of the actual leachate showed concentrations of the hazardous constituents that were "orders of magnitude" different from the concentrations predicted by the TCLP. EPA attributed this discrepancy to the fact that the extreme alkaline pH soil conditions at the monofill site were "not analogous to" conditions simulated by the TCLP.

2. Because landfill space is scarce, many cities have built incinerators to dispose of municipal waste, often generating electricity in the process. Such incinerators generate millions of tons of ash. Ash residues include fly ash captured by emission control equipment, bottom ash, and the products of incomplete combustion. Heavy metals are present in the residues, especially in the fly ash. When tested using EPA's "toxicity characteristic leaching procedure" (TCLP), described in the *Edison Electric* case, fly ash and bottom ash from municipal incinerators frequently contain lead and cadmium at concentrations greater than 5 and 1 milligram per liter cutoff levels for the toxicity characteristic.

Regulations adopted by EPA in 1980 provided that "[h]ousehold waste, including household waste that has been collected, transported, stored, treated, disposed, recovered (e.g., refuse-derived fuel) or reused" was not hazardous waste. Moreover, the preamble to the regulations stated that "residues remaining after treatment (e.g., incineration, thermal treatment) are not subject to regulation as a hazardous waste." 45 Fed.Reg. 33099. The regulations thus provided a "waste stream" exemption for household waste, covering it from generation through treatment to final disposal of residues. The regulations did not, however, exempt municipal incinerator ash from subtitle C coverage if the incinerator burned anything *in addition* to household waste, such as nonhazardous industrial waste. In that case, the facility would qualify as a hazardous waste *generator* if the ash it produced was sufficiently toxic—even though the incinerator still was not considered a subtitle C treatment or disposal facility, since all the waste it took in would be characterized as nonhazardous.

In 1984, as part of the Hazardous and Solid Waste Amendments to RCRA, Congress enacted § 3001(i), "Clarification of Household Waste Exclusion." Section 3001(i) provides that a "resource recovery facility" recovering energy from the burning of municipal solid waste "shall not be deemed to be treating, storing, disposing of, or otherwise managing hazardous wastes" for purposes of regulation under subtitle C, "if [the facility] receives and burns only * * * household waste * * * and solid waste from commercial or industrial sources that does not contain hazardous waste * * *."

City of Chicago v. Environmental Defense Fund, 511 U.S. 328, 114 S.Ct. 1588, 128 L.Ed.2d 302 (1994), was a citizen suit by EDF under RCRA § 7002. Plaintiff alleged that the ash generated by defendant Chicago's incinerator—which burned both household waste and nonhazardous industrial waste—was toxic enough to qualify as "hazardous waste" under EPA's TCLP, and that defendant was not adhering to the requirements of subtitle C in disposing of the ash, which was being sent to landfills licensed to receive only nonhazardous waste. The city and EPA contended that under § 3001(i) the ash was excluded from the category of hazardous waste. (The city also claimed that treating the ash as hazardous waste could increase disposal costs by as much as ten times.) The Supreme Court held that although the *incinerator* was not subject to subtitle C regulation as a facility that treats, stores, disposes of, or manages hazardous waste, § 3001(i) did *not* contain any exclusion for the *ash* itself. The incinerator was a *generator* of hazardous waste; and while § 3001(i) states that the facility "shall not be deemed to be treating, storing, disposing of, or otherwise managing hazardous wastes," it "significantly omits from the catalogue" the word "generating." (Section 1004(7) defines "hazardous waste management" as "the systematic control of the collection, source separation, storage, transportation, processing, treatment, recovery, and disposal of hazardous wastes.") Therefore, Chicago was not entitled to the cost-saving waste stream exemption which it claimed.

A few weeks later, EPA announced new procedures for RCRA permit applications for "facilities managing ash from waste-to-energy facilities," 59 Fed.Reg. 29372. Incinerator ash is to be tested under the TCLP, and EPA said it would promulgate within six months land disposal regulations specific to municipal waste combustion ash.

3. *Must* a solid waste be "listed" as a hazardous waste if it exhibits the "toxicity characteristic" or any of the other "characteristics" of hazardous waste (ignitability, corrosivity, and reactivity)? EPA regulations provide that the Administrator "*shall* list a solid waste as a hazardous waste *only* upon determining that the solid waste meets one of the following criteria: (1) It exhibits any of the [four] characteristics of hazardous waste * * *. (2) It has been found to be fatal to humans in low doses * * *. (3) It contains any of [certain toxic constituents] and, after considering [eleven enumerated] factors, the Administrator concludes that the waste is capable of posing a substantial present or potential hazard to human health or the environment when improperly treated, stored, transported or disposed of, or otherwise managed * * *. 40 CFR 261.11(a) (emphasis added).

In *Natural Resources Defense Council v. EPA,* 25 F.3d 1063 (D.C.Cir. 1994), the court held that nothing in RCRA or the foregoing regulation *required* EPA to list used oils from gasoline engines as a hazardous waste

only 14 wastes were mentioned in RCRA specifically

"merely because they exhibit the toxicity characteristic and were thus *eligible* for listing under 40 CFR 261.11(a)(1)" (emphasis added). Instead, the agency "was free * * * to evaluate all used oils under the balancing test set forth in § 261.11(a)(3), [and its evaluation in this case] was reasonable * * *." In other words, wastes exhibiting one or more of the four hazardous "characteristics" need not necessarily be "listed" but may instead be regulated as "characteristic" wastes.

b. The Land Disposal Ban

When it amended RCRA in 1984, Congress sought to discourage land disposal of hazardous waste. Section 1002(b)(7) announced a new national policy that, "to avoid substantial risk to human health and the environment, reliance on land disposal should be minimized or eliminated, and land disposal, particularly landfill and surface impoundment, should be the least favored method for managing hazardous wastes." Section 3004(d)(1) provided a staged prohibition on land disposal of *untreated* hazardous waste unless the EPA Administrator "determines the prohibition of one or more methods of land disposal of such waste is not required in order to protect human health and the environment for so long as the waste remains hazardous." In making these determinations, EPA was directed to take into account the characteristics of the waste, "the long-term uncertainties associated with land disposal," and the importance of encouraging proper management of hazardous waste initially. However, § 3004(d)(1), (e)(1), and (g)(5) limited EPA's discretion by specifying that a method of land disposal may not be determined to be protective of human health and the environment "unless, upon application by an interested person, it has been demonstrated to the Administrator, to a reasonable degree of certainty, that there will be *no migration* of hazardous constituents from the disposal unit or injection zone for as long as the wastes remain hazardous" (emphasis added).

Congress did not entirely ban the land disposal of wastes unable to meet this standard. It provided an exception for wastes treated to "substantially diminish the toxicity of the waste or substantially reduce the likelihood of migration of hazardous constituents from the waste so that short-term and long-term threats to human health and the environment are minimized." § 3004(m). The statute directed EPA to promulgate treatment standards specifying how waste otherwise subject to the "land ban" could satisfy the standard. Thus, the land disposal ban, in effect, applies to *untreated* hazardous wastes and authorizes EPA to require pre-treatment of wastes that cannot be shown to be capable of safe disposal on land in untreated form.

To prevent generators of hazardous wastes from frustrating the land ban by simply storing waste indefinitely, § 3004(j) prohibits the *storage* of wastes subject to the land disposal ban "unless such storage is solely for the purpose of the accumulation of such quantities of hazardous wastes as are necessary to facilitate proper recovery, treatment or disposal." This language was the subject of the following case.

EDISON ELECTRIC INSTITUTE v. ENVIRONMENTAL PROTECTION AGENCY

United States Court of Appeals, District of Columbia Circuit, 1993.
996 F.2d 326.

BUCKLEY, CIRCUIT JUDGE: Three national electric utility associations and seventy-three individual power companies petition for review of the Environmental Protection Agency's interpretation of section 3004(j) of the Resource Conservation and Recovery Act, a provision that governs the storage of hazardous wastes. The EPA's interpretation renders it unlawful to store wastes for indefinite periods pending the development of adequate treatment techniques or disposal capacity. Petitioners contend that this interpretation is both inconsistent with the statute and unreasonable as applied to generators of wastes containing both hazardous and radioactive components, for which there are currently few lawful treatment or disposal options. Because we find that the EPA's interpretation is not only permissible, but is in fact mandated by the terms of the statute, we deny the petition.

* * *

The EPA issued regulations to implement section 3004(j) in 1986. Reiterating the statutory language, the regulations provided that generators were permitted to store hazardous wastes subject to the LDRs [land disposal restrictions] in "tanks or containers on-site" if such storage was "solely for the purpose of the accumulation of such quantities of hazardous waste as are necessary to facilitate proper recovery, treatment, or disposal...." The regulations also established a burden-shifting scheme for determining when storage would be viewed as "solely for the purpose of the accumulation of such quantities of hazardous waste as are necessary to facilitate proper recovery, treatment, or disposal." Specifically, the regulations provided:

> (b) An owner/operator of a treatment, storage or disposal facility may store such wastes for up to one year unless the Agency can demonstrate that such storage was not solely for the purpose of accumulation of such quantities of hazardous waste as are necessary to facilitate proper recovery, treatment, or disposal.

> (c) A[n] owner/operator of a treatment, storage or disposal facility may store such wastes beyond one year; however, the owner/operator bears the burden of proving that such storage was solely for the purpose of accumulation of such quantities of hazardous waste as are necessary to facilitate proper recovery, treatment, or disposal.

* * *

In the present case, we agree with the EPA that Congress has spoken to the precise question at issue, and that section 3004(j) cannot be read to sanction the indefinite storage of potentially unlimited amounts of mixed wastes while treatment methods or disposal capacity is being developed. Turning first to the statutory language, section 3004(j) provides that storage of hazardous wastes covered by the LDRs is prohibited "unless such storage is solely for the purpose of the accumulation of such quantities of hazardous waste as are necessary to facilitate proper recovery, treatment or disposal." Petitioners argue that this language supports their position by claiming that "when there is no capacity available to recover, treat, or dispose of an LDR waste (as in the case of mixed waste), the *only* means available to 'facilitate proper recovery, treatment or disposal' is to accumulate and store the waste until qualified treatment or disposal capacity becomes available."

The problem with this interpretation is that it effectively reads fifteen words "solely for the purpose of the accumulation of such quantities of hazardous waste as are" out of section 3004(j). We find instead that by linking the "accumulation of such quantities" with the purpose of "facilitat[ing]" proper waste management, the statute authorizes storage only when it is intended to build up an amount of waste that can be readily transported, treated, or disposed as, for example, when storage is used to meet minimum volume requirements imposed by waste transporters or treatment facilities.

To the extent that the statutory language leaves any doubt, it evaporates when one considers the "design of the statute as a whole." In particular, RCRA includes provisions that are specifically intended to deal with the problem of inadequate treatment or disposal capacity. Section 3004(h)(2) of RCRA provides that the EPA may grant national capacity variances under which particular wastes would not be subject to the LDRs for up to two years. In addition, section 3004(h)(3) provides that the EPA may grant further extensions "on a case-by-case basis" from an applicable LDR effective date for up to one year, and may renew these extensions for an additional year. The fact that Congress has explicitly provided a statutory mechanism to deal with the contingency of inadequate treatment or disposal capacity weighs heavily against a reading of section 3004(j) that would permit storage to become an alternative avenue for dealing with such shortages.

More broadly, the EPA's interpretation of section 3004(j) is consistent with RCRA's status as a highly prescriptive, technology-forcing statute. As amended in 1984 by the HSWA, RCRA was clearly intended to provide draconian incentives such as the prohibition of all forms of land disposal for specified wastes for the rapid development of adequate treatment and storage capacity. These incentives would be significantly diminished to the extent that generators could rely on the possibility of storing their wastes indefinitely in the event that capacity was not developed in a timely fashion. Indeed, we find it difficult to imagine that Congress would leave such a glaring loophole in the system of incentives it created to promote the development of new treatment and disposal technologies.

* * *

. . . We wish to emphasize that we are not unsympathetic to the hardships that this decision implies for mixed waste generators. They find themselves in the unenviable position of having no choice but to violate the law. Nevertheless, the possibility that such hardships will occur is inherent in statutes such as RCRA that are expressly designed to force technology by threatening extreme sanctions. Moreover, the fact that technology may not be able to keep up with time-tables established by Congress does not mean that courts are at liberty to ignore them, however burdensome the resulting enforcement. Accordingly, if petitioners are to obtain relief from their present predicament, that relief must come from Congress.

Notes

1.   The court emphasized that RCRA is "a highly prescriptive, technology-forcing statute * * * clearly intended to provide draconian incentives * * * for the rapid development of adequate treatment and storage capacity." If generators of hazardous wastes for which adequate treatment methods have not yet been developed could store those wastes indefinitely, the generators would have an incentive *not* to develop treatment technology—at least if the cost of storage was less than the probable sum of the costs of developing the technology and of treating and then disposing of the wastes. On the other hand, firms other than the generators still would have an economic incentive to devise new treatment methods. Observe in the next case below that the Hazardous Waste Treatment Council, an association representing companies that treat hazardous waste, joined with environmental organizations in pressing for more stringent treatment standards. Lax standards or enforcement serves to retard the growth of this sector of our economy.

2.   In the next case, note also the distinction between technology-based treatment and dilution. The "NRDC petitioners" challenged EPA's decision not to require the use of "best demonstrated available technologies" (BDATs) in all situations, prior to land disposal. "Industry petitioners," on the other hand, were protesting regulations mandating levels of treatment which in some situations went beyond removal of the characteristic (ignitability, corrosivity, reactivity, or toxicity) which led to the waste's classification as hazardous.

CHEMICAL WASTE MANAGEMENT, INC.
v. ENVIRONMENTAL PROTECTION
AGENCY

United States Court of Appeals, District of Columbia Circuit, 1992.
976 F.2d 2, cert. denied 507 U.S. 1057, 113 S.Ct. 1961, 123 L.Ed.2d 664 (1993).

Before EDWARDS, BUCKLEY, and HENDERSON, CIRCUIT JUDGES.

Opinion PER CURIAM.

The Hazardous and Solid Waste Amendments of 1984 instituted a ban on the land disposal of classes of hazardous wastes unless certain conditions are met. Those amendments require the Environmental Protection Agency to follow a phased schedule for implementing the ban. In this case we consider various challenges to regulations implementing the final portion of this program, the so-called "third-third" rule, which largely covers the land disposal of wastes deemed hazardous because they possess certain defined characteristics.

Various petitioners raise multi-faceted challenges. A group of industry trade associations and companies (collectively, "industry petitioners") seek review of regulations mandating levels of treatment before land disposal that go beyond the removal of the attribute that led to the waste's classification as hazardous. These petitioners claim that the EPA lacked authority under the statute to require treatment to such levels. * * *

We deny each of these petitions for review. Sections 3004(g)(5) and (m) of [RCRA] give the EPA the statutory authority to mandate the treatment of wastes to levels beyond those at which the wastes present the characteristics that caused them to be deemed hazardous. * * *

Several environmental organizations, as well as the Hazardous Waste Treatment Council, an association representing companies that treat hazardous waste (collectively, "NRDC petitioners"), present different objections. They assert that (1) the new rule's "deactivation" treatment standard impermissibly allows the dilution, rather than treatment with specified technologies, of many characteristic wastes prior to land disposal; (2) the rule authorizes placement of untreated formerly characteristic wastes in surface impoundments within Clean Water Act treatment systems, or into underground injection wells, in violation of RCRA * * *.

The petitions brought by NRDC petitioners are granted in part and denied in part. Under the statute, dilution of characteristic hazardous wastes may constitute treatment, but only if no hazardous constituents are present following dilution that would endanger human health or the environment. The EPA concedes that dilution will not attain this result for certain characteristic wastes. For others, it has not made clear that dilution will meet the requirements for treatment. The standard is therefore vacated as to those wastes. The dilution of wastes in Clean Water Act facilities is acceptable so long as the toxicity of the waste discharged from the facility is minimized or eliminated consistent with RCRA. Similarly, disposal of wastes in underground injection wells may occur as long as the hazardous characteristics have been eliminated and any health and environmental dangers posed by hazardous constituents of the wastes are minimized.

* * *

I.   STATUTORY AND REGULATORY BACKGROUND

[Under RCRA, wastes] are deemed hazardous in one of two ways: They possess one of the four hazardous characteristics identified by the

EPA ("characteristic wastes"), or have been found to be hazardous as a result of an EPA rulemaking ("listed wastes").

The four characteristics identified as hazardous are ignitability, corrosivity, reactivity, and extraction procedure ("EP") toxicity. * * * Characteristic wastes comprise over fifty percent of all the hazardous wastes generated in the United States each year.

Although the EPA may list a waste if it possesses one of the four characteristics described above, in practice it will only list specific wastes that are either acutely hazardous or possess high levels of toxic constituents. A listed waste loses its hazardous status only after a petition for its "delisting" is approved by the EPA in a notice-and-comment rulemaking.

"Once a waste is listed or identified as hazardous, its subsequent management is regulated" under subtitle C of RCRA. * * * The management of a hazardous waste continues "until such time as it ceases to pose a hazard to the public."

* * * The Hazardous and Solid Waste Amendments of 1984 expressed a general policy preference that "reliance on land disposal should be minimized or eliminated." A prohibition on disposal would apply unless the waste is treated so as to minimize the short-term and long-term threats to human health and the environment posed by toxic and hazardous constituents, or unless the EPA finds that no migration of hazardous constituents from the facility will occur after disposal. * * *

* * *

II. Treatment Standards for Characteristic Wastes

* * *

The EPA determined that for most ICR [ignitable, corrosive and reactive] wastes, treatment to characteristic levels would be sufficient. The Agency found upon review that

> [t]he environmental concerns from the properties of ignitability, corrosivity, and reactivity are different from the environmental concern from EP toxic wastes. Toxic constituents can pose a cumulative impact on land disposal even where waste is below the characteristic level. Where wastes pose an ascertainable toxicity concern ... the Agency has developed treatment standards that address the toxicity concern and (in effect) require treatment below the characteristic level.... Otherwise, treatment that removes the properties of ignitability, corrosivity, and reactivity, fully addresses the environmental concern from the properties themselves.

The EPA also retreated from its emphasis on technology-based treatment in the final regulations, altering its position on the use of dilution as a method of treatment:

In all cases, the Agency has determined that for non-toxic hazardous characteristic wastes, it should not matter how the characteristic property is removed so long as it is removed. Thus, dilution is an acceptable treatment method for such wastes.

* * * Only in three subcategories of ICR wastes did the EPA mandate the use of technological treatment * * *.

Industry petitioners contend that RCRA does not provide authority for the EPA to mandate treatment of characteristic wastes after their ignitability, corrosiveness, reactivity, or EP toxicity has been addressed. They make a straightforward argument: Subtitle C regulations attach to a waste only when it is hazardous. The moment a waste ceases to meet the regulatory definition of a hazardous waste, the EPA loses its authority to regulate further. Thus, in industry petitioners' view, RCRA's cradle-to-grave system covers waste only if it remains hazardous throughout its life and at the moment of its burial.

* * *

* * * EPA reiterates the rationales stated in its final rule: The key provisions of the land-ban program, sections 3004(g)(5) and (m), can be read as allowing the Agency to apply land disposal restrictions at any time it wishes; those provisions at a minimum contemplate activity that occurs before land disposal; section 3004(m)(1) requires treatment to avoid the prohibition on land disposal; and treatment must take place, by definition, before disposal occurs. * * * The Agency reasons that the subtitle C program can attach at the point of generation, and the broad language of section 3004(m)(1) allows additional treatment to remove risks posed by wastes beyond those inherent in the characteristic.

To succeed in their *Chevron* step one argument, industry petitioners must show that Congress "has directly spoken to the precise question at issue" and has "unambiguously expressed [its] intent." We find little support in the statute or our prior decisions for the notion that Congress mandated the line industry petitioners draw. These petitioners believe that the definition of a hazardous waste acts as a revolving regulatory door, allowing continual entrance and egress from RCRA's requirements. The key provisions of the statute support a contrary view—that hazardous waste becomes subject to the land disposal program as soon as it is generated.

* * *

We conclude that, in combination, sections 3004(g)(5) and (m) provide the EPA with authority to bar land disposal of certain wastes unless they have been treated to reduce risks beyond those presented by the characteristics themselves. We also find the Agency's assertion of regulatory authority over the wastes from the moment they are generated to be "based on a permissible construction of the statute." *Chevron.*

NRDC petitioners ask this court to vacate the deactivation treatment standard as applied to ICR wastes because it authorizes the dilution of these wastes to eliminate their ignitability, corrosiveness, or reactivity rather than mandating use of technological treatment. * * * They claim that some form of technology must be used to treat wastes in all instances.

They also contend that dilution fails to satisfy the statutory requirement that treatment minimize short-term and long-term threats to human health and the environment, or to substantially diminish the toxicity of the waste. In their view, the removal of these characteristics through dilution only affects the short-term risk that the waste will manifest that property; it does not address the threats posed by the hazardous organic and inorganic constituents of those wastes. * * *

We believe that dilution can, in principle, constitute an acceptable form of treatment for ICR wastes. We do not read the 1984 Amendments as mandating the use of the best demonstrated available technologies ("BDAT") in all situations. To reiterate, section 3004(m)(1) directs the Administrator to

> specify[ ] those levels or methods of treatment, if any, which substantially diminish the toxicity of the waste or substantially reduce the likelihood of migration of hazardous constituents from the waste so that short-term and long-term threats to human health and the environment are minimized.

* * *

We agree that the section imposes an exacting standard: It requires that treatment prior to land disposal "substantially diminish the toxicity of the waste or substantially reduce the likelihood of migration of hazardous constituents from the waste so that short-term and long-term threats to human health and the environment are minimized." But this provision does not bar dilution as a means of treating ICR wastes; instead, it defines the purposes that a method of treatment must achieve. Any treatment that meets those objectives is permissible. When read against RCRA's broad definition of treatment, we cannot say Congress clearly barred dilution as an acceptable methodology.

* * *

III. THE EPA'S DILUTION RULES

The issues that we next face focus on challenges to the EPA's new dilution permissions, formulated to integrate RCRA requirements with Clean Water Act ("CWA") treatment systems and deep injection wells regulated pursuant to the Safe Drinking Water Act ("SDWA"). Contemporaneously with the promulgation of the third-third rule, the EPA amended a rule that had prohibited dilution of wastes in lieu of treatment. Pursuant to the amended rule, centralized CWA treatment systems may aggregate certain characteristic waste streams; the aggregation results in dilution that purportedly removes the hazardous characteristic without treatment. Under this new rule, dilution is allowed where the EPA has not specified a particular treatment method and where the CWA system includes a treatment protocol addressed to the types of characteristic wastes being aggregated. As a consequence of this rule, CWA treatment facilities may continue to use unlined surface impoundments as part of their treatment trains. The EPA also promulgated a new rule that permits the operators of deep injection wells to dilute all characteristic wastes, in lieu of treatment, prior to underground injection.

NRDC petitioners contend that aggregation and dilution of characteristic wastes in CWA facilities, in lieu of treatment, is inconsistent with the requirements for hazardous waste management under RCRA. According to the NRDC, under RCRA subtitle C, solid waste is subject to RCRA's treatment requirements at the moment it exhibits a hazardous characteristic; and the waste may leave the RCRA system only when treated pursuant to RCRA section 3004(m)(1) or when disposed in a facility meeting the no migration requirement of RCRA section 3004(g). Because surface impoundments are technically "land disposal" facilities, NRDC petitioners argue that placement of "decharacterized" wastes in these CWA impoundments before treatment pursuant to section 3004(m) violates RCRA's land ban. Similarly, NRDC petitioners assert that the rule permitting dilution in lieu of treatment prior to deep well injection violates RCRA because it allows land disposal of untreated hazardous wastes. * * *

* * * We hold that the new CWA dilution permission is valid where the waste is decharacterized prior to placement in a CWA surface impoundment and subsequently treated in full conformity with section 3004(m)(1) standards. Aggregation prior to treatment is not per se unacceptable. Aggregation itself occurs in tanks and is, therefore, not "land disposal"; and RCRA does not *require* treatment before aggregation.

To the extent that aggregation in tanks and dilution results in the removal of the waste's characteristic and the minimization of the toxicity of the constituents as required under section 3004(m), all that RCRA commands has been achieved. However, where aggregation and dilution does not eliminate the characteristic or (more likely) does not minimize the toxicity of the constituents, then RCRA requires further treatment.

In those instances where aggregation and dilution result in the elimination of the characteristic, but the toxicity of the constituents has not been minimized, the required further treatment of the constituents may occur after the waste leaves the CWA tank and enters the surface impoundment. Although a surface impoundment is technically a form of "land disposal," and treatment therein normally would be at odds with the commands of RCRA, this approach is nonetheless acceptable because RCRA [§ 1006(b)(1)] requires some accommodation with CWA. However, in all other respects, treatment of solid wastes in a CWA surface impoundment must meet RCRA requirements prior to ultimate discharge into waters of the United States or publicly owned treatment works ("POTWs"). If the treatment in the CWA surface impoundment succeeds in removing the toxicity to the extent 3004(m)(1) would have required, then RCRA does not require a separate treatment regimen. In other words, what leaves a CWA treatment facility can be no more toxic than if the waste streams were individually treated pursuant to the RCRA treatment standards.

Applying the same principles to the deep injection well rule, we hold that dilution is permissible prior to injection only where dilution itself fully meets the section 3004(m)(1) standards.

Notes

1. Why did EPA decide that "treatment to characteristic levels" would be sufficient for most "ICR wastes" but not for "EP toxic wastes"? How does that degree of treatment differ from treatment involving BDAT? Can the former involve only dilution?

2. Underground injection is used to dispose of a substantial part of the nation's hazardous wastes. Supposedly such disposal is allowed only where the waste will not mix with groundwater, e.g., because they will be separated by impermeable rock or soil.

3. Section 1006(b)(1) of RCRA provides that EPA "shall integrate all provisions of this chapter for purposes of administration and enforcement and shall avoid duplication, to the maximum extent practicable, with the appropriate provisions of" the Clean Water Act and other federal environmental laws. Should this provision justify disposal of EP toxic wastes treated only "to characteristic levels" (without using BDAT) in unlined surface impoundments regulated under the CWA (but not in other "land disposal" facilities)?

Five federal statutes regulate routine releases of toxic and hazardous pollutants from and within industrial facilities: RCRA, the Clean Water Act, the Clean Air Act, the Occupational Safety and Health Act, and the Emergency Planning and Community Right–To–Know Act (EPCRA, discussed at page 558 infra). Each of these statutes centers on a list that specifies which pollutants are subject to regulation, but there are five different lists, not one. For an analysis of the development of and inconsistencies among the lists, and a proposal to harmonize the five regulatory regimes, see John Dernbach, "The Unfocused Regulation of Toxic and Hazardous Pollutants," 21 *Harv. Envt'l L. Rev.* 1 (1997).

4. Section 3008 of RCRA provides that for a violation of any requirement of subchapter III (concerning hazardous waste management), the EPA Administrator may issue a compliance order and assess a penalty which takes into account the seriousness of the violation and any good faith efforts to comply. According to a policy statement by EPA in 1984, such penalties are calculated in part to eliminate the economic benefits of infractions. EPA rates violations according to their seriousness—major, moderate, or minor—based on "extent of deviation" from RCRA requirements and "potential for harm." Enforcement personnel are to calculate any economic gains from noncompliance, factor in the gravity component, and adjust the overall penalty to take into account the violator's past compliance record and good or bad faith. See 15 *Envir.Rep.* 86 (1984).

has been a problem for years.

5. Enforcement of state hazardous waste laws (usually adopted pursuant to authority in RCRA) against federal facilities has been a problem. See Comment, "Lawmaker as Lawbreaker: Assessing Civil Penalties Against Federal Facilities Under RCRA," 57 *U.Chi.L.Rev.* 845 (1990). *Maine v. Navy Department,* 973 F.2d 1007 (1st Cir.1992), held that the state of Maine could not recover civil penalties from the Navy Department for past violations of state hazardous waste laws at a Navy shipyard located in the state, because the Supreme Court previously had ruled in *United States Department of Energy v. Ohio,* 503 U.S. 607, 112 S.Ct. 1627, 118 L.Ed.2d 255 (1992), that RCRA did not waive federal agencies' sovereign immunity from imposition of punitive civil penalties. A few weeks later Congress approved the Federal Facility Compliance Act, Pub.Law 102–386, Oct. 6, 1992, amending section 6001 of RCRA to allow state agencies and EPA to enforce hazardous waste laws at federal facilities. The law clarifies that federal sovereign immunity is waived to allow imposition and collection of civil and administrative penalties and fines, even if punitive or coercive, as well as reasonable, nondiscriminatory service charges for permits, review of plans, and inspection and monitoring of facilities.

6. The following article shows that a RCRA practitioner must know EPA's regulations and enforcement policies and practices in great detail.

STOP

STOLL, "COPING WITH THE RCRA HAZARDOUS WASTE SYSTEM: A FEW PRACTICAL POINTS FOR FUN AND PROFIT"[a]

1 *Environmental Hazards* 6, 6–9 (July 1989).

Subtitle C of [RCRA] establishes the famous "cradle to grave" framework for managing today's hazardous waste activities. Along with EPA's ever-changing and ever-expanding regulations, Subtitle C has probably expedited the trip from cradle to grave for more than one environmental manager.

* * *

In truth, the system can be horrible and most of the fear-mongering is fair. There are paths in the regulations, however, through which manufacturing companies may greatly reduce the pain and save lots of money. I would like to pass on a few hypothetical examples and pointers.

One key theme is that a reasonably logical reading of EPA's regulations might cause one to reject an otherwise attractive option. In some situations, however, happy results and great cost savings can be achieved through a more careful reading of EPA's regulations, an awareness of EPA's rulings (often unpublished) and creative thinking. Before turning to the examples, a few Subtitle C fundamentals should be reviewed.

Exclusions. Statutory and/or regulatory provisions exclude certain materials or practices from Subtitle C jurisdiction. A few of the more notable are materials disposed into a public sewer system; industrial

a. Reprinted from *Environmental Hazards,* July 1989, Volume 1, Number 1, with the permission of Prentice Hall Law & Business.

discharges subject to Clean Water Act permits; residues from fossil fuel combustion; and certain "mining" wastes.

Definitions of "solid waste" and "hazardous waste." A material may be hazardous but not a "waste" or a material may be a waste but not "hazardous." In either case, there would be no Subtitle C jurisdiction. A material must be *both* a waste and hazardous to trigger Subtitle C jurisdiction.

EPA's regulations for determining what is a "waste" contain some of the most puzzling english word patterns ever devised. The regulations endeavor to prescribe tests—based on the type of material and on the type of management activity—for determining whether a material is a product (and therefore exempt from RCRA) or a waste (and therefore covered).

EPA's regulations for determining whether a waste is "hazardous" are somewhat simpler. A waste may be hazardous either because it is on a "list" or because—when tested—it fails one of several hazard "characteristic" protocols.

Vast differences in coverage among types of waste management. The "cradle-to-grave" system regulates the following types of parties involved with hazardous waste: a) generators; b) transporters; and c) owners/operators of treatment, storage, or disposal facilities (TSD facilities). One point cannot be overemphasized: *by several orders of magnitude, the system is much harsher on TSD facilities.* Permits, corrective action, post-closure, financial assurance, and many other burdens are part of the TSD game and do not apply to those who only generate and/or transport.

HYPOTHETICAL EXAMPLES

Below are examples where a plant manager seeks ways to cut costs and/or increase revenues and avoid onerous RCRA burdens. One central theme is a follow-up to the third point above: it is often acceptable to stay in the Subtitle C system so long as TSD status can be avoided, and there are several ways (generally unpublicized) to accomplish this. Another key theme is that important RCRA interpretations appear in strange places.

1. Obtaining Useful Feedstock From Others' Wastes

Alpha Company buys Chemical A at $5.00 per pound for use as a degreasing and cleaning solvent. Once used, their "spent" solvent is a listed RCRA hazardous waste.

The Alpha plant manager develops a plan to save millions of dollars. He would buy others' spent solvents, "regenerate" or "reclaim" the solvents to make virgin-quality Chemical A, and use the reclaimed material as a feedstock. He figures he can obtain spent Chemical A at $1.00 per pound.

He runs this by his environmental people, who find the RCRA regulations quite discouraging for two reasons. a) The spent Chemical A is a "waste." While EPA's regulations provide that certain types of materials are not wastes if they are "reclaimed," they specify that "spent" materials are wastes even if reclaimed. b) The reclamation at Alpha's facility would trigger TSD status because i) the reclamation is "treatment" of hazardous waste, and ii) storage of the spent Chemical A prior to reclamation would independently trigger TSD status.

The plant manager, upon checking with corporate management, is glum. Management has concluded that even the millions in savings are not worth TSD status.

Unfortunately these people do not realize that Alpha can have its cake and eat it too. While part a) of the foregoing analysis is correct (the spent Chemical A must be regarded as a hazardous waste), part b) is based upon a misunderstanding of the regulations and an unnecessary factual assumption. *Even though the spent Chemical A will be a hazardous waste when generated and transported, Alpha may be able to reclaim it without triggering TSD status.*

First, even though the reclamation may be "treatment," it is also "recycling." EPA's regulations specify: "The recycling process itself is exempt from RCRA." (EPA buried this fundamental in a parenthetical near the end of a paragraph dealing with storage.)

Second, Alpha might recycle the spent Chemical A *without first storing it.* EPA's regulations contemplate this, and make clear that engaging in this practice will avoid TSD status. For example, Alpha may arrange a system by which trucks enter its facility, park at the reclamation device, and off-load the spent Chemical A through hoses connected directly from the truck to the reclamation device. EPA has on several occasions affirmed that in such a situation, no "storage" is involved.

If Alpha could accomplish this recycling without storage, it would avoid all of the permitting and other horrors of TSD status. It would only need to file a "notification" of its hazardous waste activity and comply with the manifesting (paper trail) requirements.

2. Reclaiming Feedstock From One's Own Wastes Without a "Closed Loop" System

Beta Company uses Chemical A as a feedstock, and a secondary material from Beta's process is "spent" Chemical A. Spent Chemical A is a listed hazardous waste. Beta must pay $5.00 per pound to purchase virgin Chemical A. Beta has been paying $2.00 per pound to have a commercial incinerator destroy spent Chemical A.

The plant manager would like to save millions of dollars by devising a system to reclaim and reuse her spent Chemical A. With a recycling system, she could both drastically reduce the volume of virgin Chemical A she has to buy and eliminate her off-site disposal costs entirely.

Her environmental people tell her that in EPA's definition of solid waste, there is a "closed loop" exemption which such a recycling practice might fit. If spent material is reclaimed and returned to the original process and the entire process is "closed" through interconnected tubes and pipes, the material will not be a RCRA "waste" at all.

The plant manager is glum. There is only one suitable location on her property for the reclamation process, and it is thousands of yards from the place where the spent Chemical A is generated. Because of the layout of the facility, the costs of such a "closed loop" system would be prohibitive.

Here again, the analysis has been correct, as far as it goes, but the plant people have been overlooking some basic points. Even though Beta cannot avoid being a generator, it can still avoid TSD status.

Beta may be able to collect the spent Chemical A in drums, and, *always within 90 days* of the date of generation, recycle the spent Chemical A. In this manner, no TSD status is triggered. First, as described in the first example, the recycling process is exempt. Second, EPA's regulations have long provided that a generator may accumulate its own hazardous wastes in tanks or containers for up to ninety days without triggering TSD status. Thus, so long as Beta keeps "rotating" drummed waste so that no drum is stored more than ninety days before it is recycled, TSD status can be avoided.

Caution: This result can only be achieved if the storage takes place at the same facility where the waste was generated. For instance, if Beta installed its reclamation device on a nearby but separate parcel of land, it could not store drums at all on the separate parcel without triggering TSD. The ninety-day exemption applies only to the generating facility; once off-site, storage of hazardous waste for *any* period of time will trigger TSD. If the reclamation device were on a separate parcel, Beta could avoid TSD only by some form of direct off-loading from transport vehicles as described in the first example.

3. *Other Treatment Avoiding TSD*

Gamma Company generates a hazardous waste and sends it off-site for treatment at a cost of $2.00 per gallon. The plant manager learns that there is a simple and inexpensive treatment process he could use in tanks at his facility which would render the waste nonhazardous. If he could do this, he could save millions of dollars per year in off-site transport and treatment costs.

His environmental people look for regulatory exemptions under which "treatment" would not trigger TSD status. They find three: 1) where wastes which are hazardous only because they are "corrosive" are being neutralized; 2) where waste waters are being treated as part of a Clean Water Act discharge; and 3) where the treatment is part of a "totally enclosed" recycling system.

The plant manager is glum. His proposal would not fit any of these three narrow exceptions. He drops his idea, because the millions in cost savings will not justify TSD status.

Unfortunately for Gamma, its people missed a paragraph in the middle of a long EPA *Federal Register* preamble on an unrelated topic and were unaware of an EPA letter to a Wisconsin consulting firm. With such inimitable administrative procedure, EPA has ruled that generators may "treat" hazardous waste in containers or tanks for no more than ninety days at the generating facility and not trigger TSD status. Thus, so long as treatment occurs on-site in tanks that are emptied at least every ninety days, millions in off-site disposal costs can be saved and TSD status can be avoided.

4. Recycling One's Own Hazardous Wastewater

Delta Company plans to conduct a chemical tank steam-cleaning operation, and will need a million gallons of water a month. The plant manager would like to save money by reusing the same water after treating it, but does not want to trigger TSD status. She is told by her environmental people that the wastewater would clearly be a RCRA hazardous waste (as it will be mixed with commercial chemicals on EPA's RCRA "lists").

But they read the first three hypotheticals in this article and are now thinking creatively. They develop the following logic: i) always store the hazardous waste in tanks or containers for less than ninety days so "storage" will not trigger TSD, then ii) reclaim the wastewater through treatment into reusable water and this "recycling" of hazardous waste will be exempt from RCRA.

They are further comforted by language in EPA's regulations which says that materials reclaimed beneficially are not thereafter RCRA wastes (unless burned for energy recovery or placed in or on the land). Certainly the reclaimed wastewater fits this description.

At this point, however, a lawyer throws cold water on the idea. She discovers language in EPA's 1985 *Federal Register* preamble to the foregoing regulation which strongly suggests that EPA did not intend for wastewater to be protected by it. At this point, the plant manager is glum.

But then the lawyer uses her head. She figures anything that EPA published as far back as 1985 could be suspect, and phones some EPA people. Lo and behold, she finds that EPA headquarters recently sent a memo to one of EPA's regional offices ruling that wastewater can be protected by the regulatory language.

Again, TSD could be avoided and millions of dollars saved only if one were aware of an unpublished EPA interpretation. EPA's last *Federal Register* words on the subject would in fact have tended to squelch the idea.

QUICK POINTERS

Here are a few other quick pointers for avoiding or curtailing Subtitle C exposure:

Redirect Stream to POTW or NPDES. You may be able to redirect certain RCRA waste streams to a public sewer system and/or a point source discharge to the navigable waters. While this may trigger additional Clean Water Act pretreatment and/or NPDES requirements, such requirements may not be nearly as costly and onerous as RCRA requirements.

Change Manufacturing Process. If you generate a waste that is hazardous because it fails a characteristic (*i.e.,* non-"listed"), you may be able to alter your manufacturing process (through chemical and/or engineering changes) to produce a material that does not fail the characteristic and is therefore no longer hazardous. (This approach would not work for a "listed" waste.)

Delisting. If you generate a "listed" waste, you may be able to secure a "delisting" if you can show EPA that at your particular facility, the waste is not truly hazardous. The delisting process is expensive, time consuming, and involves notice-and-comment rulemaking in the *Federal Register*. Nevertheless, many facilities have successfully utilized this process. While serious delays were prevalent a few years ago, EPA is now usually able to process a delisting petition in about a year.

Export. Many companies have found that they can reduce costs by shipping their wastes to Canada or other countries for ultimate treatment and disposal. EPA regulations expressly allow for such "exports" of hazardous waste. In fact, Canada and the U.S. have a bilateral agreement under which many U.S. companies are now shipping their wastes to Canada.

c.   *Waste Minimization and Pollution Prevention*

The concept of waste reduction, or waste minimization, was incorporated into RCRA by the 1984 amendments. Section 1003(b) declares it to be national policy that "wherever feasible, the generation of hazardous waste is to be reduced or eliminated as expeditiously as possible." Section 1003(a)(6) announces the objective of "minimizing the generation of hazardous waste and the land disposal of hazardous waste by encouraging process substitution, materials recovery, properly conducted recycling and reuse, and treatment." Section 3002(a)(6) requires generators to report "efforts undertaken during the year to reduce the volume and toxicity of waste generated"; section 3002(b) requires generators to certify on their waste manifests that they have in place programs "to reduce the volume or quantity and toxicity of such waste to the degree determined by the generator to be economically practicable"; and § 3005(h) requires the same certification in connection with any new permit issued for the "treatment, storage, or disposal of hazardous waste."

In 1993 EPA announced that some 19,000 hazardous waste generators, including many that used incineration, would be asked to make their waste minimization plans public. See 24 *Envir.Rep.* 728 (1993). The agency also said that it planned to publish a list of the targeted generators, those required to certify on their hazardous wastes manifests that they have waste minimization programs in place. The response was that "industry in general will be unalterably opposed to making waste [minimization] plans public." The industry spokesperson denied any statutory authority for EPA to establish such a requirement.

In May 1994, EPA released an update of its draft waste minimization guidance. See 25 *Envir.Rep.* 147 (1994). The update said that there should be specific waste reduction targets, short-term and long-term, though it did not specify what the percentage reduction rates should be. EPA sought comments on this matter. The agency said its goal was to achieve a national percentage reduction by 1997 of highly toxic and persistent hazardous wastes that are combusted. By the year 2000, EPA's goal was to achieve an overall reduction of RCRA hazardous waste through source reduction and recycling. However, the goals were not to be applied to individual facilities because EPA said it lacked statutory authority to impose such requirements.

In a related law, the *Pollution Prevention Act of 1990*, 42 U.S.C.A. §§ 13101–13109, Congress found that there are "significant opportunities for industry to reduce or prevent pollution at the source through cost-effective changes in production, operation, and raw materials use." Congress further found that opportunities for source reduction are "often not realized because existing regulations, and the industrial resources they require for compliance, focus upon treatment and disposal, rather than source reduction * * *." The Act provided that, as a first step in preventing pollution through source reduction, the EPA should establish a source reduction program which collects and disseminates information and provides financial assistance to states.

Besides providing for EPA matching grants to states for programs to promote the use of source reduction techniques by businesses, the Pollution Prevention Act provides that each owner or operator of a facility required to file an annual toxic chemical release form under the Emergency Planning and Community Right-to-Know Act (see page 558 infra) shall include with each such annual filing a toxic chemical source reduction and recycling report for the preceding calendar year. This report must cover each toxic chemical required to be reported in the annual toxic chemical release form. The toxic chemical source reduction and recycling report must explain, for each toxic chemical, the amount of that chemical which has been recycled; source reduction practices used with respect to that chemical; and the techniques used to identify source reduction opportunities. 42 U.S.C.A. § 13106. However, in 1994 EPA announced that a final rule detailing how companies should report pollution prevention data on the Toxic Release Inventory (TRI) reporting form was "on hold indefinitely," pending possible changes in the definitions of solid waste and other related terms under RCRA. See 25 *Envir.Rep.* 498 (1994).

In its 1991 Pollution Prevention Strategy, 56 Fed.Reg. 7849, EPA said studies have shown that pollution prevention can be "the most effective way to reduce risks by reducing or eliminating pollution at its source; it also is often the most cost-effective option because it reduces raw material losses, the need for expensive 'end-of-pipe' technologies, and long-term liability." In short, "pollution prevention offers the unique advantage of harmonizing environmental protection with economic efficiency." The strategy included a plan for targeting 15 to 20 high-risk chemicals that offered opportunities for prevention, and set a "voluntary goal of reducing total environmental releases of these chemicals by 33 percent by the end of 1992, and at least 50 percent by the end of 1995." (Hence the name "33/50 Program.") The strategy further provided that when EPA determined that specific regulatory actions were needed, it would investigate "flexible, cost-effective regulatory approaches that avoid prescriptive approaches and that rely on market-based incentives where practical and authorized by law."

A 1992 internal memorandum from the Deputy Administrator to all EPA personnel emphasized that "prevention is our first priority within an environmental management hierarchy that includes: 1) prevention, 2) recycling, 3) treatment, and 4) disposal or release." EPA Memorandum on Definition of Pollution Prevention, May 28, 1992, 1 *Envir.Rep.* (Fed.Laws) 21:0261. The memorandum stated that pollution prevention means "source reduction," as defined in the Pollution Prevention Act, and other practices that reduce or eliminate the creation of pollutants through increased efficiency in the use of raw materials, energy, water or other resources, or through protection of natural resources by conservation. The Pollution Prevention Act defines "source reduction" to mean any practice which (i) reduces the amount of any hazardous substance, pollutant, or contaminant entering any waste stream or otherwise released into the environment prior to recycling, treatment, or disposal, and (ii) reduces the hazards to public health and the environment associated with the release of such substance, pollutants, or contaminants. Thus, under the Act, recycling, energy recovery, treatment, and disposal are not included within the definition of pollution prevention. However, some practices commonly described as "in-process recycling" may qualify as pollution prevention.

A 1994 study by a private environmental group concluded that EPA's voluntary pollution prevention program was a failure and should be replaced. The study said that many companies had cut their toxic waste at the source, but that for 83 percent of the projects the efforts already were under way before EPA's program was initiated in 1991. The critics said that EPA's industrial toxics project, the "33/50 Program," was "pollution prevention in name only," since "only under 33/50 are waste incineration, treatment, burning for energy recovery, recycling, and production cutbacks considered pollution prevention." See 25 *Envir.Rep.* 280 (1994).

A slightly more positive evaluation of the 33/50 Program is offered by Eric Orts, "Reflexive Environmental Law," 89 *Nw. U.L.Rev.* 1227, 1284–1287 (1995). As of 1994, EPA had invited over 8,000 companies to participate in the program, and 1,200 had agreed to do so. EPA's interim goal of 33% reductions by 1992 was exceeded: a 40% reduction from 1988 levels was achieved, and participating companies claimed to be on target for 50% reductions by 1995. Another author later reported that "the 1,300 participating facilities largely relied on end-of-pipe controls in successfully meeting the fifty percent reduction goal by 1994—one year earlier than planned." Michele Ochsner, "Pollution Prevention: An Overview of Regulatory Incentives and Barriers," 6 *N.Y.U. Envt'l L.J.* 586, 592 (1998).

For further discussion of waste minimization and pollution prevention, see James Salzman, "Sustainable Consumption and the Law," 27 *Envt'l Law* 1243 (1997); Kurt Strasser, "Preventing Pollution," 8 *Fordham Envt'l L.J.* 1 (1996).

2. STATE AND LOCAL SITING OF HAZARDOUS WASTE FACILITIES

MATA, "HAZARDOUS WASTE FACILITIES AND ENVIRONMENTAL EQUITY: A PROPOSED SITING MODEL"[a]

13 *Virginia Environmental Law Journal* 375, 377, 401–410 (1994).

Health risks and adverse economic consequences associated with hazardous waste facilities complicate the siting of these facilities. * * * Arguably, local opposition to the siting of a hazardous waste facility is a logical response to the imposition of large risks on a small population for the benefit of a much larger population.

* * *

In general, states approach the siting of hazardous waste facilities from one of three approaches: super review, site designation, and local control. Additionally, some states require that developers compensate host communities for accepting facilities. Either way, the statutes assume that facilities are necessary to society and must be sited "with as little social cost (including environmental cost) and disruption as possible."

1. SUPER REVIEW MODEL

The super review approach is the most common. It calls for regulatory agencies to await the filing of permit applications before determining whether a particular site is qualified for the intended use. The petition for permit is evaluated according to a set of rules and either satisfied as filed, satisfied with conditions or denied. Under the super review scheme, if a permitting agency denies a permit on grounds that the site is unsuitable, the developer is compelled to give up or propose another site.

Michigan is an example of one state that utilizes the super review siting model,[153] and its statutory scheme contains characteristics typical of the super review approach. The program calls for an initial review of the permit application by the state environmental protection agency. If the application clears this initial hurdle, it is then reviewed for final determination by a specially created site review board. Public participation is expanded during the time the permit application is under review by the board. The program also provides for the reconciliation of state and local interests in instances where concerns are raised by interested parties.

* * *

2. SITE DESIGNATION MODEL

The selection of preferred sites around the state in advance of project proposals characterizes the site designation approach. In this manner, an inventory of sites is maintained even during periods when no project proposals are submitted by developers. An example of the site designation model is the Minnesota siting program.

Under the Minnesota siting scheme, potential sites are selected in one of two ways. First, a facility operator may propose a candidate site with approval from the owners of the site and the municipal government in which it lies.[177] Second, the state may select potential sites, although it may designate no more than one site per county at a time.

Any county containing a potential site may negotiate a contract with the state's office of waste management once it files a resolution of interest (to host a facility) with the state's waste management board. The county, however, can withdraw the resolution of interest at any time prior to executing a final contract. Contracts are subject to several negotiable terms, as noted in the statute. For example, the state and county can negotiate the procedures pertaining to the evaluation and selection of the site and the construction, operation, and maintenance of a proposed facility. The parties can negotiate guidelines for safe operation of the facility and a compensation package. Finally, the county can negotiate provisions for amending the contract and for resolving disputes.

* * *

3. LOCAL CONTROL MODEL

Under local control siting schemes, state siting programs do not preempt local land use regulations. Thus, a local government can employ tough land use regulations to restrict siting of facilities within its jurisdiction. Colorado is one state with a siting scheme that follows the local control model.[188]

* * *

---

153. Mich.Comp.Laws Ann. §§ 299.517–.520 (West 1984 & Supp.1993).

177. Minn.Stat.Ann.   § 115A.21(1)(a) (West 1987 & Supp.1994).

188. Colo.Rev.Stat.Ann. §§ 25–15–200.1

4. COMPENSATION AND INCENTIVES MECHANISMS

In an effort to eliminate local opposition to hazardous waste facility sitings, some states have incorporated compensation mechanisms into siting laws. Under such schemes, a package of inducements would accompany a proposed facility. The rationale behind the compensation approach is that if incentives to accept the facility outweigh local costs, such as health and environmental risks, a community will be more likely to accept the siting of a facility in its neighborhoods. The provision of compensation and incentives may accompany any of the models previously discussed.

Compensation usually is determined in one of three ways. First, it can be a function of the facility's gross receipts or amount of wastes processed. Alternatively, compensation can be based on a standard tax or fee. Finally, a compensation package can contain a number of inducements agreed upon through negotiations between developers and host communities.

The state of Connecticut, for example, employs a compensation mechanism in which the amount of compensation is based either on a certain monetary value per standard unit of waste,[199] in accordance with predetermined values provided by the statute, or on negotiated incentives. These negotiated incentives may include payment to adjoining landowners for a drop in property values; the purchase of a "green belt buffer" around the proposed facility; provision of open space or recreational facilities for the municipality; purchase of public safety equipment; payment of road repair costs (produced by increased use of local roads); creation of access routes to the proposed facility; or direct financial payments. * * *

* * *

Public Participation and State Siting Schemes

In addition to supplementing siting models with compensation and incentive mechanisms, most state siting schemes include devices to promote public participation. Many state siting programs promote active public participation to better inform host community residents of hazardous waste facility proposals and to reduce local opposition and build consensus. These mechanisms are implemented primarily to engage local residents as opposed to the state-wide public. Public participation also is used to "legitimize" the site selection process in the eyes of the public.

One technique that states may use to enhance public participation is to appoint local residents to temporary positions on a state siting board. Such local membership advances the fairness of the siting process and

to–220 (Bradford 1989 & Supp.1993). Florida also operates a siting program that follows the local control model. Local control, however, is not absolute in Florida because the governor and state cabinet can grant a variance from local ordinances or regulations thereby allowing a facility to be sited. Fla.Stat.Ann. § 403.723 (Harrison 1990 & Supp.1992).

199. Conn.Gen.Stat.Ann.   § 22a–128(b)(1) (West 1985).

mitigates local opposition by giving local communities a voice on the state siting board. Siting programs also engage the public by holding open administrative hearings. The siting authorities are then able to take into account the comments and objections raised at such meetings when making final decisions. In addition, local siting boards may be created to involve local participants within a more formal review structure. Moreover, local siting boards help reduce difficulties related to regulating from greater distances. Local interests can be heard and addressed with greater efficiency and with more reliability at a local board than if the board were based at a state capital perhaps many miles away and with fewer interests in common with the local community.

Yet another way states promote public participation is by providing technical assistance grants. The purpose of these grants is to eliminate financial and technical barriers that would otherwise keep potential host communities from participating meaningfully in the siting process. These grants supply local site review boards and other public officials and interested parties with adequate resources to study siting proposals. With greater access to technical information and expertise, it is more likely that local communities will be able to make informed decisions about proposals to site a hazardous waste facility in their community.

Notes

1. At this point you should review the "environmental justice" materials in Chapter I–D, pages 68–77 supra, especially the Saleem article on siting hazardous waste facilities, and the notes following it.

2. Concerning the form of public participation in siting decisions, one author has suggested that the best procedure–and the one actually used in seeking volunteers for several solid waste facilities–is a referendum of the entire electorate after detailed studies but before the final decision. Michael Gerrard, "Turning NIMBY On Its Head: A Siting Solution Based On Federal Allocation, State Responsibility, and Local Control," 25 *Env't Rptr.* 2257 (1995). The author discusses the appropriate geographic extent of the electorate, saying that the referendum should be required to succeed in both the county and the municipality in which the proposed site would be located. If the proposed site were near a border, people in the adjoining jurisdiction also should have a voice. One method to provide this might be to include in the electorate all voters outside the voting jurisdiction but within a certain radius of the facility. An alternative method would be to draw a radius around the facility and allow only people who live within that radius to vote in the referendum, regardless of their political jurisdiction. Gerrard's proposal would link the referendum to a system for compensation of volunteer communities.

Another author has proposed the use of "risk-based compensation committees." A national or state risk assessment process would be used to set (a) maximum allowable levels of risk within a local area, to prevent exploitation of any community, and (b) the minimum amount of compensation that a developer, owner, or operator must provide to the local community. Then a local risk-based siting committee would (1) determine whether to accept a site and (2) negotiate the amount and distribution of compensation.

The relative representation that nearby residents, residents elsewhere in the city, and regional neighbors would have on the committee would depend on "the relative amount of risk to which individuals are potentially or actually exposed, as determined by the risk assessment process.... To protect the interests of racial minorities and those exposed to higher risks, special voting systems could be used, such as weighted cumulative voting or proportional voting." Bradford Mank, "Environmental Justice and Discriminatory Siting: Risk–Based Representation and Equitable Compensation," 56 *Ohio St.L.J.* 329, 401 (1995).

C. MANDATORY DISCLOSURE OF INFOR-MATION CONCERNING CHEMICAL HAZ-ARDS AND RELATED LIABILITIES

Parts A and B of this chapter, as well as much of Chapters IV and V, have dealt with traditional "command and control" regulation. However, we also have explored, and will explore, alternate regulatory approaches. Chapter IV contains important materials on economic incentive systems, such as effluent charges and marketable discharge permits, used increasingly as complements to traditional pollution regulation. Chapter VII will examine the extensive civil liabilities—another type of economic incentive—created by RCRA, CERCLA, and the common law of "toxic torts." And the NEPA materials in Chapter II involve the most prominent example of mandating disclosure of information as a means of influencing both the behavior of the disclosers and the responses of the public and the political system.

This part of Chapter VI discusses two other important examples of disclosure requirements. The first, arising from enactment in 1986 of the federal Emergency Planning and Community Right-to-Know Act (EP-CRA), involves disclosure of the existence of physical conditions which pose potential chemical hazards. The second, stemming from reporting requirements under the federal securities laws, involves disclosure of potential corporate liabilities, especially liabilities of the types discussed in Chapter VII.

BLOMQUIST, "THE LOGIC AND LIMITS OF PUBLIC INFORMATION MANDATES UNDER FEDERAL HAZ-ARDOUS WASTE LAW: A POLICY ANALYSIS"[a]
14 *Vermont L.Rev.* 559, 571–78 (1990).

The Emergency Planning and Community Right-to-Know Act was passed by Congress as Title III to SARA.[54] The two general objectives of Title III are to encourage and support emergency planning efforts by local governments with regard to chemical hazards, and to provide

a. Copyright 1990 by *Vermont Law Review.* Reprinted by permission.

54. Superfund Amendment and Reauthorization Act of 1986 (SARA), Pub.L. No.

99–499, §§ 301–330, 100 Stat. 1613, 1729 (1986) (codified at 42 U.S.C. §§ 11001–11050 (Supp. V 1987)).

citizens and local governments with information concerning potential community-based chemical hazards. Congress included three provisions within Title III to effectuate these objectives. The first concerns government emergency response planning. The second provision addresses emergency release notification by private industry. The third requires the compilation and reporting of information concerning chemical properties, manufacturing, usage, properties, and release.

The first provision of Title III requires the governors of the various states to have established a state emergency response commission by April 17, 1987. State commissions are also required to have established emergency planning districts no later than July 17, 1987, and to have appointed local emergency planning committees for each district by August 17, 1987.

Each local committee is required to have completed preparation of an emergency response plan, no later than October 17, 1988, containing the following information:

1) facilities within the district at which any one of numerous statutorily designated "extremely hazardous substances" at "threshold planning quantities" are present;

2) methods and procedures for reporting a release of an extremely hazardous substance;

3) names of community and facility coordinators;

4) public notification procedures;

5) methods for determining the occurrence of a release and the geographic area or population likely to be impacted;

6) the available emergency equipment and facilities within the community;

7) training programs; and

8) evacuation plans.

"Congress intended the local planning process to be a truly community-based activity, and not simply an exercise carried out by a few representatives of industry and the government bureaucracy in a back room at city hall."

The second component of Title III—the emergency release notification provisions—requires the owner or operator of a "facility" to provide notification of a hazardous substance release within any affected area to the community emergency coordinator of the local committee and to the affected state's commission.[64] The statute mandates that the notification contain specific information. This information must include data about the chemical released, the estimated quantity of the hazardous substance, "the time and duration of the release," "[a]ny known or antici-

---

64. SARA § 304(b)(1), 42 U.S.C. § 355.40(b)(1) (1988).
§ 11004(b)(1) (Supp. V 1987); 40 C.F.R.

pated acute or chronic health risks associated with the emergency and, where appropriate, advice regarding medical attention necessary for exposed individuals," precautions to be taken in response to the release, and pertinent details regarding the contact person who can provide further information.

The final provision is perhaps the most important public environmental information mandate under Title III. This provision contains reporting requirements for chemical usage, chemical properties, manufacturing, and environmental releases. "In order to inform citizens about chemicals located in their communities, Title III requires the owners and operators of certain facilities to submit three types of information concerning such chemicals to state and local authorities." This information entails: (a) material safety data sheets (MSDS) and hazardous chemical lists; (b) hazardous chemical inventory information; and (c) toxic chemical usage, manufacture, and release information.

All three components of Title III—government emergency response planning, emergency release notification procedures, and chemical inventory and usage reporting—are accessible to the public. Three specific public environmental information policies promote this accessibility: first, public participation requirements for local emergency response committees' formulation of emergency response plans; second, liberal public availability of local facility records (emergency response plans, follow-up emergency release notification, MSDS's, inventory forms, lists of hazardous chemicals, toxic chemical release forms); and, third, the EPA's development of a national computerized toxic chemical inventory database.[77] Moreover, citizen suit provisions create "the possibility of community self-help enforcement of SARA Title III by allowing suits against the facility owners or operators, state and local governments, or the EPA."[78]

* * *

SARA's public information programs, particularly the Title III component, will promote six different policy goals. First, Title III will produce a baseline of

> data [that] can be used to characterize exposure levels, evaluate existing regulatory strategies and develop new ones, focus on specific locations of concern, identify important chemical releases and the types of operations they come from, compare permitted releases to reported releases, and aid in the development of waste minimization strategies.

Second, Title III holds promise for acting as "a valuable mechanism for effective emergency management, protecting environmental con-

---

77. SARA § 313(j), 42 U.S.C. § 11023(j) (Supp. V 1987). *See also* 53 Fed.Reg. 6567 (Mar. 9, 1988) (notice of public meeting to discuss options for making information available).

78. Title III follows the "citizen as prosecutor" model by permitting citizen suits for civil penalties as well as injunctive relief. SARA § 326(c), 42 U.S.C. § 11046(c) (Supp. V 1987).

cerns, offering local citizens the opportunity to have a significant impact on the safety of their community, and for providing a structured forum in which industry, government, and citizens can work collectively on these issues."

Third, Title III should be applauded as "Congress' most significant experiment to involve the private sector and decentralize environmental problem solving.... [C]itizens [must] be informed about hazardous materials being stored, handled, or manufactured in their community, and local communities [must] have a coordinated emergency response plan to respond to chemical emergencies."

Fourth, while the information gathered in the Title III process should be viewed as preliminary, and subject to refinement, this public environmental information law will "provide Americans with at least two powerful pictures of the industries that put them at risk. Total annual discharges from the [*Toxic Release Inventory*, or "TRI"] data will be one picture. Another is the 'plume maps' or 'footprints' of potential chemical gas releases as they travel downwind or downstream." In a related way, the Toxic Release Inventory data generated by the imprimatur of section 313 will promote the better understanding of two major risk management problems: (a) identifying and specifying the "[m]any U.S. chemical plants [that] do not [currently] use the Best Achievable Control Technology (BACT) to minimize chemical discharges"; and (b) developing some rudimentary information "regarding chemical discharges once they have left the plant."

Fifth, the emergence of information regarding toxic chemical releases and mass balance inventories will, no doubt, serve as "strong public educational and motivational tools toward the improvement of chemical safety." Finally, Title III will facilitate the development of comparative emissions statistics of hazardous substances that will spur some industrial firms to take a leadership role by "openly communicating about risks" with the public in meetings that may reflect a "new era, and a new partnership." This industrial leadership has the potential of providing exemplary corporate models that will inspire other companies to respond to the competitive need to match the leaders' efforts.

Notes

1. The data disclosed by industries' annual Toxic Release Inventory (TRI) reports, and the reductions in releases seemingly attributable to EPCRA's disclosure requirements, have been remarkable. In 1988, the first reporting year, 18,500 companies disclosed that they had released 10.4 billion pounds of toxic chemicals in 1987: 3.9 billion into landfills, 3.3 billion to treatment and disposal facilities, 2.7 billion into the air, and 550 million into surface waters. These figures were far beyond EPA's expectations. See Weisskopf, "EPA Finds Pollution 'Unacceptably High'," *Washington Post*, April 13, 1989, p. A33. EPA subsequently revised the total of 10.4 billion pounds downward to 7 billion pounds because some mining companies which had reported were not required to do so. After 1987, reported releases declined to 5.7 billion pounds (by 22,650 facilities) in 1989, and 2.6 billion

pounds (by 27,744 facilities) in 1994. Of the latter year's total, 1.56 billion pounds were released into the air, 349 million pounds were injected into underground wells, 289 million pounds were released to land (including landfills and surface impoundments), and 66 million pounds were released into surface waters. 22 *Env't Rptr.* 223 (1991); 27 *Env't Rptr.* 531 (1996). EPA regulations on toxic chemical release reporting are found at 40.C.F.R. Part 372.

For further discussion of EPCRA, see Abell, "Emergency Planning and Community Right to Know: The Toxics Release Inventory," 47 *SMU L.Rev.* 581 (1994) (student comment); Abrams and Ward, "Prospects for Safer Communities: Emergency Response, Community Right to Know, and Prevention of Chemical Accidents," 14 *Harv.Envt'l L.Rev.* 135 (1990). For overviews not only of EPCRA but of other federal statutes requiring reports of releases of pollutants or contaminants, see Cleary, Gottlieb, Steen & Hamilton, "Release Reporting Requirements Under CERCLA and EPCRA," and "Release Reporting Requirements Under TSCA, FIFRA, OSHA, RCRA, CWA, and CAA," 27 *Env't Rptr.* 1171 and 1250 (1996); Arnold Reitze and Steve Schell, "Reporting Requirements for Nonroutine Hazardous Pollutant Releases Under Federal Environmental Laws," 5 *Envt'l Lawyer* 1 (1998).

2. In *Atlantic States Legal Foundation v. Whiting Roll–Up Door Mfg. Corp.*, 38 ERC 1426, 1994 WL 236473 (W.D.N.Y.1994), plaintiffs brought a citizen's enforcement action under § 326 of EPCRA, alleging that defendant had failed to file timely hazardous chemical information with state and federal authorities under §§ 311–313. Among other forms of relief, plaintiffs sought civil penalties, a permanent injunction prohibiting further EPCRA violations, and attorneys' fees and costs. Under a settlement agreement, plaintiffs were "prevailing parties" within the meaning of § 326(f), and the court therefore awarded them more than $32,000 in attorneys' fees and costs.

However, in *Steel Co. v. Citizens for a Better Environment*, 523 U.S. 83, 118 S.Ct. 1003, 140 L.Ed.2d 210 (1998), supra page 104, the Supreme Court held that an environmental group *lacked standing* to bring a citizen suit under EPCRA for "purely past violations." In 1995, plaintiff sent a notice to defendant, to the EPA, and to Illinois authorities, alleging (accurately) that defendant had failed since 1988 (the first year of EPCRA's filing deadlines) to complete and to submit the requisite hazardous-chemical inventory and toxic-chemical release forms. Upon receiving the notice, defendant filed all of the overdue forms with the relevant agencies. EPA chose not to bring suit, e.g., to recover civil penalties; and when the 60–day, post-notice waiting period expired, plaintiff filed suit in the federal district court. The complaint asked for a declaratory judgment that defendant had violated EPCRA, an order requiring defendant to pay civil penalties of $25,000 per day for each EPCRA violation, and an award of plaintiff's attorney and expert witness fees. The Supreme Court held that the constitutional requirement of "redressability—a likelihood that the requested relief will redress the alleged injury," was not satisfied because none of the items of relief sought "would serve to reimburse [plaintiff] for losses caused by the late reporting, or to eliminate any effects of that late reporting upon [plaintiff]." The penalties would be payable to the government, not to plaintiff, and "plaintiff cannot achieve standing to litigate a substantive issue by bringing suit for the cost of bringing suit."

ROBERTS, "DISCLOSURE OF ENVIRONMENTAL LIABILITIES IN DOCUMENTS FILED WITH THE SECURITIES AND EXCHANGE COMMISSION"[b]

National Environmental Enforcement Journal, March 1994, pp. 3–6.

Awareness is increasing among both investors and the public at large that tremendous environmental liabilities now confront many companies operating in the United States. * * * In an attempt to improve environmental liability disclosure practices, the Securities and Exchange Commission (SEC) has been warning recently that it expects more appropriate accounting treatment and more complete discussions of potential environmental liabilities in the documents required to be filed with the SEC.

* * * U.S. EPA currently assists the SEC in its efforts to monitor environmental disclosures by providing the SEC with lists of all companies that have been named as potentially responsible parties for Superfund hazardous waste sites, as well as with lists of companies subject to clean-up requirements under the Resource Conservation and Recovery Act (RCRA). This information is useful to the SEC's Division of Corporation Finance as it reviews environmental liability disclosures in SEC filings.

* * * The reporting requirements for environmental liabilities are contained in the disclosure provisions of the federal securities laws, in the SEC regulations promulgated thereunder, and in the accounting literature. The SEC has taken steps recently to clarify the appropriate accounting treatment for potential environmental liabilities—specifically, how such liabilities should be presented and quantified in a company's financial statements.

Antifraud Provisions

The general antifraud provisions of the federal securities laws impose liability on persons who make false statements or omissions of material facts in connection with the offer, purchase, or sale of securities.[3] Generally, these antifraud provisions require the reporting of the material adverse effects environmental laws and related potential liabilities may have on a company. A failure to disclose fully and fairly all material environmental risks and liabilities is likely to be viewed as a fraud upon investors trading in securities during the period of the omission. Such a failure could result in the institution of an SEC enforcement action or an investor-generated civil suit.

---

b. Copyright © 1994 by the National Environmental Enforcement Journal. Reprinted with permission. At the time of publication, the author, Richard Y. Roberts, was Commissioner, U.S. Securities and Exchange Commission.

3. *See* section 17(a) of the Securities Act of 1933, 15 U.S.C. § 77(a), section 10(b) of the Securities Exchange Act of 1934, 15 U.S.C. § 77j(b), and the rules promulgated thereunder.

In addition to complying with the general antifraud provisions, companies registering public offerings of securities under the Securities Act of 1933, or filing periodic reports under the Securities Exchange Act of 1934, must comply with the applicable line-item disclosure requirements of Regulation S–K.[4] Disclosure documents incorporating all or portions of Regulation S–K include Annual Reports on Form 10–K, proxy statements, and registration statements, among others. The three areas of Regulation S–K where discussions of the impact of environmental liabilities on a company are specifically required are discussed below.

Item 101—Description of Business

Item 101 of Regulation S–K requires that a company provide a general description of its business, including specific disclosure of the material effects that compliance with federal, state, and local environmental laws may have upon the capital expenditures, earnings, and competitive position of the company and its subsidiaries. Additionally, any material estimated capital expenditures for environmental control facilities must be described.

Item 103—Legal Proceedings

Item 103 requires that the company disclose any material pending legal proceedings, including certain proceedings arising under federal or state environmental laws. Specifically, this item requires the company to report any administrative or judicial action arising under environmental laws if: (a) Such proceeding is material to the business or financial condition of the company; (b) such proceeding includes a claim for damages or costs in an amount exceeding ten percent of current consolidated assets; or (c) a governmental authority is a party to the proceeding, unless any sanctions are reasonably expected to be less than $100,000. It is important to note that any such proceedings *known to be contemplated* by governmental authorities must also be disclosed.

Item 303—Management's Discussion and Analysis (MD & A)

The MD & A item requires management to discuss the company's historical results and its future prospects—it is intended to allow investors to view the company through the eyes of management. The MD & A disclosure and the related financial statements are considered the heart of a company's disclosure documents and receive careful scrutiny when reviewed by the SEC. The SEC has initiated a handful of enforcement actions in the MD & A area recently, and more such enforcement cases are anticipated in the future.

* * * [I]f there is a known trend, demand, commitment, event, or uncertainty, management of a company must make two assessments to determine what prospective information is required.

---

4. 17 C.F.R. Part 229. The provisions of Regulation S–K having particular significance for issuers exposed to environmental risk have been incorporated into new Regulation S–B, which applies to small business issuers, without substantive change. *See* 17 C.F.R. Part 228.

First, management must determine whether the known trend, demand, commitment, event, or uncertainty is reasonably likely to come to fruition. If not, no disclosure is required. If management determines that the event is reasonably likely to occur, however, the second assessment must be made: Would the effect of the event be material to the company's financial condition or results of operations? If so, disclosure is required. * * *

ACCOUNTING RULES AND SAB 92

Assuming that management determines that a potential environmental liability is material and must be disclosed, the next issue is timing. When should the company record the potential exposure in the company's financial statements? Generally accepted accounting principles (GAAP), specifically Financial Accounting Standards Board (FASB) Statement No. 5, entitled "Accounting for Contingencies," indicate that a potential loss must be accrued by a charge to income if it is probable that a liability has been incurred and if the amount of the loss can be reasonably estimated. In an attempt to improve the accounting practices in this area, in June 1993, the SEC staff issued Staff Accounting Bulletin No. 92 (SAB), which set forth the staff's interpretation of GAAP regarding contingent liabilities. * * *

The SAB presents the view of SEC staff regarding: (1) The manner in which a contingent liability and any related asset representing claims for recovery, such as insurance proceeds, should be displayed in a company's financial statements (offsetting); (2) the appropriate discount rate to be used for recognition of a contingent liability stated at its present value to reflect the time value of money (discounting); and (3) the disclosures that are likely to be of particular significance to investors in their assessment of these contingencies. In the staff's view, and consistent with FASB Statement No. 5, where a probable environmental liability exists, the amount of loss may be reasonably estimable and therefore accruable even if quantification uncertainties exist. If the specific amount cannot be reasonably determined, but it can be reasonably determined that the loss falls within a range, then the loss is deemed to be reasonably estimable for purposes of FASB Statement No. 5, and the SAB instructs that the best estimate within that range should be accrued. If no amount within the range represents the best estimate, then the minimum amount of that range should be accrued. The SAB also notes that the minimum amount of the range is unlikely to be zero. The SAB further instructs companies to use the footnotes to the financial statements to ensure that the financial statements are not misleading or do not contain material omissions.

With respect to the issue of offsetting, the SAB indicates that, for the vast majority of situations, presentation in the balance sheet of the gross, rather than net, amount of the liability most fairly presents the potential consequences of the contingent claim on the company's resources. Therefore, as a general proposition, companies should separately display in the balance sheet the estimated liability and the probable insurance recovery. Showing only the *net* figure of the two would rarely be in accordance with GAAP. It is the SEC's view that netting the liability and the potential insurance proceeds may leave investors unaware of the magnitude of the liability and may lull them into a less rigorous consideration of the legal sufficiency of the company's claims for recovery and the credit worthiness of the party from whom recovery is sought.

* * *

A second issue of great significance to companies which is discussed in the SAB is the ability to recognize an estimated liability at its present value rather than at the gross amount expected to be payable. Because the ultimate settlement of environmental liabilities may not occur for many years, the effect of discounting the liability to reflect the time value of money may be quite important to some companies. The SAB indicates that discounting an environmental liability for a specific cleanup site to reflect the time value of money is appropriate only if the aggregate amount of the obligation and the amount and timing of the cash payments are fixed or reliably determinable for that site. The company should use a discount rate that is no higher than the rate on risk-free monetary assets—namely, U.S. Treasury securities. That rate is objectively determinable, which should enhance comparability of financial statements between companies.

Note

Corporate failures to disclose potential environmental liabilities to the SEC may provoke not only enforcement actions by the Commission but also shareholder class-action suits.

Placing a dollar value on potential liability can be difficult. See Wise et al., "Estimating Contingent Environmental Liabilities: An Approach to Achieve SEC Compliance," 24 *Env't Rptr.* 1577 (1993). One tricky matter is that joint and several liability under CERCLA may cause a financially solid company to have to pay more than its fair share of cleanup costs if other legally responsible parties lack the resources to pay their shares in response or contribution actions.

See generally Mark Stach, *Disclosing Environmental Liability Under The Securities Laws* (1997); John Bagby et al., "How Green Was My Balance Sheet?: Corporate Liability and Environmental Disclosure," 14 *Va. Envt'l L. J.* 225 (1995); Robert Feller, "Environmental Disclosure and the Securities Laws," 22 *Boston Coll. Envt'l Aff. L. Rev.* 225 (1995).

Chapter VII

ENVIRONMENTAL LIABILITY
AND ENFORCEMENT

———

Chapters IV through VI were concerned primarily with administrative regulation of air and water pollution, toxic chemicals, and hazardous wastes. Like Chapter II, this chapter focuses on remedies obtained through the courts. We begin by looking at "citizen suits," in which plaintiffs assume the role of "private attorneys general." Then we will consider the circumstances under which environmental plaintiffs may obtain injunctive remedies. Third, we will explore the tort-like liability established, and remedies available, under the "imminent hazard" provisions of RCRA and under CERCLA. Next, we will examine the increasing role of criminal enforcement of environmental laws. Finally, we will review some of the major issues in the field known as "toxic torts," involving common law liability for personal injuries and property damages caused by toxic substances.

A. CITIZEN SUITS

Beginning in 1970 with the Clean Air Act, Congress included citizen suit provisions in most of the major environmental statutes, e.g., § 304 of the Clean Air Act, § 505 of the Clean Water Act, § 18 of TSCA, § 7002 of RCRA, § 326 of the Emergency Planning and Community Right–To–Know Act, § 11(g) of the Endangered Species Act, and § 310 of CERCLA. An exception is FIFRA, which does not authorize citizen suits.

The citizen suit provisions of the environmental laws generally authorize "any person" to commence an action against "any person" alleged to be in violation of the laws. They require plaintiffs to give notice, usually 60 days, to the alleged violator and to federal and state authorities prior to filing suit. (However, the Clean Water Act allows suits alleging violation of new source performance standards or toxic effluent standards to be brought immediately after notice, as does RCRA for violations of subtitle C.) Most of the statutes specify that if federal or state authorities are diligently prosecuting compliance actions, citizen suits are barred, though citizens are authorized to intervene in federal enforcement actions.

Among the persons against whom citizen suits may be brought are federal officials who fail to perform mandatory regulatory duties. For example, the Clean Water Act authorizes citizen suits against the EPA "where there is alleged a failure of the Administrator to perform any act or duty * * * which is not discretionary." This type of provision, found in most of the statutes which establish regulatory programs, has been important in ensuring that EPA issues regulations to implement the statutes.

Citizen suits also may be brought against *state* officials accused of violating federal environmental laws. *Natural Resources Defense Council, Inc. v. California Department of Transportation, 96* F.3d 420 (9th Cir. 1996), held that while the Eleventh Amendment prohibits federal courts from hearing suits by private citizens against a state government or agency without the state's consent, the Eleventh Amendment does not bar suit against a state official acting in violation of federal law. The doctrine of *Ex parte Young,* 209 U.S. 123, 28 S.Ct. 441, 52 L.Ed. 714 (1908), is premised on the notion that a state cannot authorize a state officer to violate the Constitution or laws of the United States. Thus, an action by a state officer which violates federal law is not considered an action of the state. Nevertheless, there are limitations upon *Ex parte Young* suits against state officers. In particular, when a plaintiff brings suit against a state official alleging a violation of federal law, the federal court may award only prospective injunctive relief, not retroactive relief requiring payment of civil penalties or declaratory relief pertaining to past violations.

In the 1980s, when there was significant decline in federal enforcement of the environmental laws under the Reagan administration, more citizen suits were brought (especially by several national environmental organizations) to fill the void. These focused particularly on enforcement of the Clean Water Act because it was easy for plaintiffs to prove violations. Point-source dischargers were required to file discharge monitoring reports which were available to the public and could serve as prima facie evidence of noncompliance with NPDES permits. In addition, remedies available in Clean Water Act suits included not only injunctions against further violations but also the assessment of civil penalties payable to the government.

DUBOFF, "THE 1990 AMENDMENTS AND SECTION 304: THE SPECTER OF INCREASED CITIZEN SUIT ENFORCEMENT"[a]

7 *Natural Resources & Environment* 34, 34–37, 60 (1992).

Environmental enforcement actions by private plaintiffs have taken on far greater dimensions in recent years. This is true in terms of both the frequency of these suits and the severity of the sanctions imposed. This major wave of environmental litigation, referred to as citizen suits, began in the early–to mid–1980s and initially focused on the Clean Water Act. While the Clean Water Act continues to be a major focus, citizen suit enforcement under other federal environmental statutes, such as the Emergency Planning and Community Right to Know Act and the Resource Conservation and Recovery Act, is growing. The pattern followed by the environmental plaintiff has often been to target a number of industrial facilities in a specific state or geographic region and file an essentially simultaneous series of very similar suits using a standard complaint, discovery papers, motions for partial summary judgment, and so forth.

The Clean Air Act's (CAA) citizen suit provision, section 304, has been part of the Act since 1970. The types of violations that are subject to section 304 enforcement are quite broad, including, for example, violations of state implementation plan requirements, new source performance standards, prevention of significant deterioration and nonattainment review permits, and controls regarding motor vehicle fuels and fuel additives. Compared to actions under the Clean Water Act, however, CAA citizen suits have been few in number, due at least in part to differences in compliance reporting and the availability of civil penalties. The Clean Air Act Amendments of 1990 dramatically change this situation by making proof of non-compliance far easier and enabling private plaintiffs to seek civil penalty relief. These changes portend a significant increase in Clean Air Act citizen suits.

IMPACT OF THE 1990 AMENDMENTS ON CITIZEN SUITS

Proving Noncompliance. Proving CAA noncompliance has previously presented several hurdles. In many states, air emissions monitoring and compliance records have not been readily available or in a format that easily identified whether the air emissions source was in compliance with CAA standards. To identify applicable regulatory standards, various and often separate documents and records had to be consulted, including construction permits, state implementation plans, and new source performance standards. Identifying noncompliances often required assembling, correlating and interpreting monitoring data in light of the applicable standards. Developing a basis for alleging noncompliance could be a cumbersome and sometimes uncertain process.

This situation is in sharp contrast to the publicly available discharge monitoring reports (DMRs) required under the Clean Water Act's National Pollutant Discharge Elimination System (NPDES) permit program. DMRs contain in a single, integrated document the applicable regulatory standards and corresponding monitoring results for the discharge covered by the report. Citizen plaintiffs have been generally successful in persuading courts to accept these reports as admissions of liability where non-complying discharges are reported, and, with little if anything more, have been able to obtain partial summary judgment on liability. Not surprisingly, an attorney for a national environmental organization that is a frequent citizen suit plaintiff used the phrase "as easy as shooting fish in a barrel" to describe the citizen suit process under the Clean Water Act in a *Wall Street Journal* interview.

A number of the 1990 amendments to the Clean Air Act will make citizen suits a significantly easier undertaking. The new operating permit provisions of Title V of the 1990 amendments will centralize all pollution control requirements in a single, integrated document and require expanded monitoring and reporting. The legislative history of the 1990 amendments emphasizes that these changes were modeled after the NPDES program * * *.

EPA has recently published final regulations governing the Title V permit program, to be codified at 40 C.F.R. part 70. These regulations will be enforced through state programs that meet the requirements of the EPA regulations. Monitoring reports will have to be filed on a recurring basis (at least every six months); certified by a responsible official as true, accurate and complete; with each deviation from permit requirements identified. 40 C.F.R. § 70.6(a)(3)(iii). In addition, monitoring data will have to be submitted in a format consistent with the underlying standard (e.g., pounds of pollutant emitted per hour) so that complex calculations or conversions of raw monitoring data will not be required in order to determine compliance with the applicable regulatory standards. The monitoring reports will be available to the public. Moreover, under section 114(a) of the Clean Air Act, as amended, EPA must establish enhanced monitoring and compliance certification requirements which will be mandatory for major stationary sources and discretionary for other sources. Compliance certifications will identify the CAA requirements applicable to a source, the testing methodology used to determine compliance, the compliance status of the source, and whether compliance is continuous or intermittent. Like the monitoring reporting required by the permit program regulations, the compliance certifications and enhanced monitoring data will be available (except for trade secrets) to would-be section 304 plaintiffs.

Civil Penalty Relief. Prior to the 1990 amendments, the CAA did not authorize civil penalty relief in citizen enforcement actions. The jurisdiction of federal district courts in section 304(a) citizen suits was limited to injunctive relief—issuing orders to enforce emissions standards and other Clean Air Act requirements. The 1990 amendments, however, authorize the courts to assess civil penalties in citizen suits. This change puts CAA citizen enforcement actions on the same footing as citizen suits under other federal environmental laws. Any civil penalties imposed in section 304 suits will be deposited in a special fund for use by EPA in air compliance and enforcement. EPA is currently drafting regulations regarding the establishment and administration of the penalty fund as well as procedures for EPA intervention in citizen suits.

The availability of punitive monetary sanctions, as opposed to injunctive relief alone, gives private plaintiffs an additional and very potent weapon, and provides a substantially greater dimension to section

304 suits. This increases the incentive to bring the suits, the potential for protracted litigation, the likely size of available attorneys' fees and the plaintiff's settlement leverage. The level of civil penalties imposed in Clean Water Act citizen suits has grown considerably, exceeding $4 million in various individual litigated cases as well as in cases that were settled on relief issues. That upward trend continues. Moreover, a communication several years ago from an environmental organization to its members stated that one of the benefits of bringing a series of environmental citizen suits would be to "steer a significant amount of money to worthwhile environmental projects." The organization's optimism was fully justified—consent decrees have directed civil penalties in amounts exceeding $1 million in each of a number of Clean Water Act citizen suits to environmental organizations and environmental mitigation projects. Although the statutory authority to direct penalties to recipients other than the United States Treasury has been disputed, one of the amendments to section 304 expressly authorizes district courts to order that a portion (up to $100,000) of the civil penalty assessed in any given CAA case be used in a "beneficial mitigation project" to enhance public health or the environment.

In this connection it should also be noted that section 304(d) authorizes courts to award attorneys' fees to the party who prevails, or substantially prevails, on the merits of the suit. That party will have its costs of litigation paid by the non-prevailing party (hence the term "fee shifting"). Considering the strict liability nature of regulatory requirements under the federal environmental laws and the ease with which plaintiffs have used a permittee's monitoring reports to assert liability, citizen suit plaintiffs have had little difficulty achieving some degree of success on the merits, a prerequisite for awarding attorneys' fees. Also, although various courts have expressed concern regarding citizen suit plaintiffs' efforts "to keep the meter running," plaintiffs who achieve at least some degree of success on the merits can proceed without substantial concern that a court will reduce the fees that result from protracted litigation where the civil penalty imposed is substantially below the amount that the plaintiff was seeking. * * * [T]he minimal risk associated with recovery of attorneys' fees serves to increase significantly the plaintiffs' settlement leverage.

One additional point should be noted regarding civil penalty relief newly available under section 304. Unlike other citizen suit statutes that limit the civil penalty relief in such suits to the same basis as that provided for government enforcement actions, section 304 of the CAA simply authorizes "any appropriate civil penalties" without incorporating a specific monetary limit. While this lack of precision is confusing, nothing in the legislative history of the 1990 amendments suggests that Congress intended that "appropriate civil penalties" could be higher in a citizen suit than in a government action. It is expected, accordingly, that section 304(a) will be interpreted consistent with the $25,000 per day civil penalty limit that applies to the government under section 113(b) of the CAA.

Other Aspects of Section 304. For industrial facilities that will have to grapple with increasingly demanding CAA requirements, other aspects of section 304 may present more bad news. The amended section 304 does not include several important features that have restrained citizen suits under other environmental statutes.

For example, one of the most controversial issues has been whether citizen suits are limited to ongoing noncompliance or whether these suits can also be brought for purely past violations (i.e., violations that were abated prior to and independent of the citizen suit). This issue had been extensively litigated under the Clean Water Act, including cases where permit compliance had been achieved for many, if not all, permit parameters, unduly stringent permit limits had been superseded, or a discharge had terminated, all prior to the initiation of the citizen suit.

The Supreme Court addressed these issues in *Gwaltney of Smithfield, Ltd. v. Chesapeake Bay Foundation, Inc.*, 484 U.S. 49 (1987). Relying, among other things, on the emphasis Clean Water Act section 505(a) gives to the present tense (a citizen suit may be brought against facilities alleged "to be in violation" of the Clean Water Act), the Supreme Court ruled that a section 505 suit could not be brought for purely past violations. Subsequent decisions by other courts have ruled that this principle is to be applied on a parameter-by-parameter basis; an ongoing violation of one permit requirement does not authorize a citizen suit for previously abated violations of other permit requirements. The practical effect of the *Gwaltney* decision has been a decline in the frequency of Clean Water Act citizen suits, making suits against dischargers that achieved permit compliance or substantial compliance prior to instigation of a citizen suit less attractive to environmental plaintiffs.

The operative language of CAA section 304(a) was identical to section 505(a) of the Clean Water Act, and objections to the effect of the *Gwaltney* decision were raised during Congress' consideration of the Clean Air Act Amendments of 1990. The result was an amendment to section 304(a). While the amended statute retains the former language authorizing suits in the case of facilities alleged "to be in violation" of CAA requirements, it is now augmented with language authorizing citizen suits against facilities alleged "to have violated" applicable standards "if there is evidence that the alleged violation has been repeated." While litigation over the precise meaning of this amendment can be expected * * *, the policy choice that the Supreme Court found inherent in section 505 of the Clean Water Act is equally applicable to the CAA: to allow a purely punitive citizen suit for wholly past violations where compliance has already been achieved without litigation runs counter to the limited, supplementary role intended for citizen suits. Judicial interpretation of the amended section 304 will likely affect the frequency, scope and purpose of citizen enforcement actions under the CAA as significantly as the *Gwaltney* decision did for Clean Water Act litigation.

Finally, section 304(b) of the CAA requires that EPA and state enforcement agencies (as well as the alleged violator) be given sixty days' written notice of a would-be citizen plaintiff's intent to sue, and bars a citizen suit where government enforcement is commenced during the sixty-day period. Whether the identical statutory bar in section 505(b) of the Clean Water Act is triggered by both judicial and administrative enforcement was the subject of considerable Clean Water Act litigation. Congress added section 309(g)(6) to the Clean Water Act in 1987 to resolve the controversy. In general terms, section 309(g)(6) bars a citizen suit if administrative enforcement regarding the same violations is commenced prior to the would-be citizen plaintiff's notice of intent to sue. Unfortunately, the Clean Air Act Amendments of 1990 do not address this point, and the litigation that highlighted the issue under the Clean Water Act may be replayed under the amended CAA.

RECENT DECISIONS ON STANDING IN CITIZEN SUIT LITIGATION

Under Article III of the Constitution, a private plaintiff who seeks to enforce federal environmental laws (or, for that matter, other federal laws) must demonstrate that it has standing to sue. That requires the plaintiff to show that it has sustained, or will sustain, an injury that is caused by or is fairly traceable to the defendant's unlawful conduct (i.e., injury which results from the action the plaintiff seeks to have the court adjudicate and which will be redressed by the relief the plaintiff seeks).

Those prerequisites—referred to as injury in fact, causation and redressability—are often easier to state as principles than to implement in practice. For example, the Supreme Court's recent decision in *Lujan v. Defenders of Wildlife,* 112 S.Ct. 2130 (1992), a citizen suit under the Endangered Species Act, involved four separate opinions taking varying positions regarding the level of specificity required to demonstrate that the plaintiff had been injured, or would be injured, by the activities at issue. * * *

A principal area of controversy in recent environmental cases on standing has been the causation aspect of the three-part test for standing. Decisions on causation have been very hospitable to plaintiffs. Several federal district courts have ruled in citizen enforcement cases that the causation requirement is satisfied by showing that the defendant violated a federal environmental permit standard, and that it is not necessary for the plaintiff to establish a nexus between the violation and the plaintiff's injury. The Third Circuit adopted essentially the same reasoning in *Public Interest Research Group of New Jersey v. Powell Duffryn Terminals, Inc.,* 913 F.2d 64 (3d Cir.1990), *cert. denied,* 111 S.Ct. 1018 (1991). The court applied the following three-part test for satisfying the causation aspect of standing in Clean Water Act citizen suits: (1) a pollutant discharge in excess of an NPDES permit limit (2) to a waterway in which the plaintiff has an interest that is or may be adversely affected (3) which causes or contributes to "the kinds of injuries" alleged by the plaintiff. Explaining the term "kinds of injuries," the court of appeals said that if the defendant exceeded its permit limit for a pollutant and that pollutant is present in the subject waterway, causation is established. The concurring opinion in *Powell Duffryn* acknowledged that the decision was "most questionable" in view of the plaintiffs' failure to establish a causal link between their alleged injuries and the defendant's actions, but suggested that this bending (or breaking) of the rules for standing was justified because "the evolving precepts of standing are perhaps expanded a bit" in environmental cases.

The implications of that broad interpretation of standing are not limited to the Clean Water Act. Under the Third Circuit's reasoning, an individual located perhaps hundreds of miles from a source of air emissions could be found to have standing to maintain a suit under section 304 of the CAA if the source exceeded an emission limit for a given pollutant which happens to be the same type of pollutant that affects ambient air quality in the plaintiff's locality. It would not matter how far removed the injury and challenged conduct may be from each other in distance and time. The universe of potential plaintiffs would be quite large and it would not matter that the presence of the pollutant of concern in a given plaintiff's locality was not casually related to the defendant's actions. In short, this expansive interpretation of standing has serious implications for private enforcement actions under not only the Clean Water Act, but also the CAA and other federal environmental laws.

ATTORNEYS' FEES

Attorneys' fee litigation in citizen suits can rival or exceed the efforts directed to the underlying environmental enforcement suit. The basic formula for determining attorneys' fees under fee-shifting statutes (including federal environmental statutes) is reasonable hours times a reasonable hourly rate, often referred to as the "lodestar" amount. *Pennsylvania v. Delaware Valley Citizens' Council for Clean Air,* 478 U.S. 546 (1986) (*Delaware Valley I*). Much of the litigation under fee-shifting statutes has involved adjustments to the lodestar to reflect matters such as quality of work, extraordinary success on the merits, or the risk associated with representing an environmental plaintiff on a contingent fee basis. *Delaware Valley I,* interpreting section 304 of the CAA, established a strong presumption that the lodestar amount is itself the reasonable fee. The Court ruled against the plaintiff's request for an upward adjustment to the lodestar to reflect quality of work and extraordinary success on the merits, reasoning that both of those factors were already reflected in the appropriate hourly rate and total hours devoted to the underlying suit. In *Delaware Valley II, Pennsylvania v. Delaware Valley Citizens' Council for Clean Air,* 483 U.S. 711 (1987), the Court rejected on the facts the plaintiff's claim for an upward adjustment to the lodestar to account for the risk that the plaintiff's attorneys accepted in taking the case on a contingent fee basis. The Supreme Court's recent decision in *City of Burlington v. Dague,* 112 S.Ct. 2638 (1992), a citizen suit under the Clean Water Act and the Resource Conservation and Recovery Act, takes the next step and rules that an enhancement for successful contingent fee cases is not permitted under the fee-shifting statutes that govern citizen suit litigation.

Notes

1. Concerning standing to sue under citizen-suit provisions, you should review *Lujan v. Defenders of Wildlife,* page 96 supra, *Steel Co. v. Citizens for a Better Environment*, page 104 supra, and the notes following them.

In part IV of the plurality opinion in *Defenders*, Justice Scalia said that the injury-in-fact requirement could not be satisfied by congressional conferral upon *all* persons of "an abstract, self-contained, noninstrumental 'right' to have the Executive observe the procedures required by law." However, Justices Kennedy and Souter joined part IV subject to the "observation" that "Congress has the power to define injuries and articulate chains of causation that will give rise to a case or controversy where none existed before." (In *Federal Election Com'n v. Akins,* ___ U.S. ___, 118 S.Ct. 1777, 141 L.Ed.2d 10 (1998), the Court firmly rejected Justice Scalia's view that widely shared harms do not qualify as injury-in-fact.)

In *Steel Co.*, the Court relied on the redressability requirement in dismissing a suit under EPCRA for defendant's purely past violations in filing hazardous-chemical inventory and toxic-chemical release forms after the legal deadlines. The Court said that none of the items of relief sought by the plaintiff environmental organization (declaratory judgment, civil penalties payable to the government, and attorney and expert witness fees) "would serve to reimburse [plaintiff] for losses caused by the late reporting, or to eliminate any effects of that late reporting upon [plaintiff]."

Also relevant to standing to sue under citizen-suit provisions is *Bennett v. Spear*, page 113 infra. In *Bennett* the Supreme Court held that the citizen-suit provision of the Endangered Species Act conferred standing upon plaintiffs, irrigation districts and ranchers, whose economic interests were threatened by a designation of critical habitat likely to result in reduced releases of irrigation water from a federal reservoir. The Court reversed the holding of the court of appeals that plaintiffs lacked standing because their economic interests did not lie within the "zone of interests" protected by the ESA.

2. As indicated at the beginning of this section, environmental statutes usually require that notice of intention to sue be given to the EPA, to the state in which the violation occurred, and to the alleged violator, at least 60 days prior to the filing of a citizen suit. In *Hallstrom v. Tillamook County,* 493 U.S. 20, 110 S.Ct. 304, 107 L.Ed.2d 237 (1989), the Supreme Court held that such notice requirements must be strictly interpreted and applied by the courts. *Hallstrom* presented the issue whether full compliance with the notice requirement in § 7002 of RCRA was a mandatory precondition to suit, or whether a failure to comply fully could be disregarded by the trial court at its discretion. Eight federal courts of appeals had divided evenly on this question. Four had interpreted notice provisions as "procedural" requirements that left trial courts flexibility to stay an action or allow it to proceed even though plaintiff had failed to comply with the 60–day requirement. The other four appellate courts took the position that plaintiff's failure to comply with the notice requirement deprived the trial court of jurisdiction to hear the case.

In *Hallstrom,* plaintiffs were concerned that leachate from the defendant county's landfill was causing chemical and bacterial pollution of plaintiffs' soil and groundwater. Plaintiffs gave the defendant proper notice of their intent to sue but did not give notice to the federal EPA or to the state environmental agency until after the suit was filed. The federal district court found that the purpose of the notice requirement was to give the public agencies the opportunity to take over the enforcement of the statute from the private plaintiffs. Since neither EPA nor the state agency showed any interest in taking action against the county, the court found that dismissing the action and forcing plaintiffs to refile would only waste judicial resources. After a trial on the merits, the district court found that defendant had violated RCRA. The county was given two years to take the necessary steps to contain the leachate. Plaintiffs appealed the denial of immediate injunctive relief, and the county cross-appealed from denial of its motion for summary judgment because of plaintiffs' failure to comply with the notice requirement. The Ninth Circuit and the Supreme Court held in favor of the county, rejecting the view that the notice requirement was procedural and therefore subject to waiver or equitable modification. For a critique of *Hallstrom*, see Farber, "Procedural Rigidity," *Trial*, Feb. 1990, at 17.

In *Public Interest Research Group of New Jersey, Inc. v. Hercules, Inc.*, 50 F.3d 1239 (3d Cir.1995), before filing a citizen suit under the Clean Water Act, plaintiffs notified Hercules, EPA, and the New Jersey Department of Environmental Protection and Energy that plaintiffs intended to sue Hercules for alleged violations of its federal and state permits limiting effluent discharges from a certain facility. The notice letter claimed that Hercules had committed 68 discharge violations from April 1985 through February 1989. After waiting sixty days, plaintiffs filed a complaint in the federal district court. Plaintiffs attached to the complaint a list of 87 discharge violations, which omitted several of the originally cited violations and included more than 30 new ones. A majority of the new violations pre-dated the sixty-day notice letter; the remainder post-dated it. Between the time when plaintiffs filed their complaint and the time when they moved for summary judgment, they supplemented the list of alleged permit violations to include a total of 114 discharge violations, 328 monitoring violations, 58 reporting violations, and 228 recordkeeping violations. Plaintiffs did not supply Hercules, EPA, or New Jersey with a new notice letter concerning the additional violations. Hercules contended that plaintiff's sixty-day notice lacked the specificity required by the CWA and EPA's regulation, 40 CFR 135.3(a), prescribing the contents of a notice letter. The regulation provided that the notice "shall include sufficient information to permit the recipient to identify the specific standard, limitation, or order alleged to have been violated, the activity alleged to constitute a violation, the person or persons responsible for the alleged violation, the location of the alleged violation, [and] the date or dates of such violation."

The court in *Hercules* said that *Hallstrom*'s analysis of Congress' intent in crafting the citizen-suit provision made clear that not only is the sixty-day notice before filing suit "a mandatory, not optional, condition precedent for suit," but also that the content of the notice must be adequate for its recipients to identify the bases for the citizen's complaint. The court in *Hercules* held that a notice letter which includes a list of discharge violations, by parameter, provides sufficient information for the recipients to identify violations of the same type (same parameter, same outfall) occurring during and after the period covered by the notice letter. The court also held that, when a parameter violation has been noticed, subsequently discovered and directly related violations of discharge limitations or of monitoring, reporting and recordkeeping requirements for that same parameter at that outfall for that same period may be included in the citizen suit. When plaintiffs noticed the discharge violations, an investigation by Hercules, EPA, or the State of those excess discharges should uncover related violations of monitoring, reporting or recordkeeping requirements involved in tracking those pollutant parameters.

In a somewhat similar case, *Atlantic States Legal Foundation v. Stroh Die Casting Co..*, 116 F.3d 814 (7th Cir.1997), cert. denied ___ U.S. ___, 118 S.Ct. 442, 139 L.Ed.2d 379 (1997), the court held that plaintiff's 60–day notice was adequate even though defendant's ongoing discharge permit violations as alleged in plaintiff's complaint were at an outfall not mentioned in the notice. The court said, "We do not read the Third Circuit [in *Hercules*, cited by defendant] as establishing an inflexible rule that would require outfall-by-outfall notice in all cases. It was not faced with a case where the alleged polluter [Stroh], upon receiving a notice about one offending outfall, simply redirected the stream of contaminated water to another outfall. The key to notice is to give the accused company the opportunity to correct the problem."

3. In *Gwaltney of Smithfield, Ltd. v. Chesapeake Bay Foundation*, 484 U.S. 49, 108 S.Ct. 376, 98 L.Ed.2d 306 (1987), plaintiffs brought a citizen suit under the Clean Water Act. Their complaint alleged that defendant "has violated * * * [and] will continue to violate its NPDES permit." Plaintiffs sought declaratory and injunctive relief, imposition of civil penalties, and attorneys' fees and costs. Defendant moved for dismissal for lack of subject-matter jurisdiction because its last recorded permit violation occurred several weeks before plaintiffs filed their complaint. The district court rejected defendant's argument, concluding that § 505 authorized citizen suits on the basis of wholly past violations. In the alternative, the court held that plaintiffs satisfied the jurisdictional requirements of § 505 because their complaint alleged in good faith that defendant was continuing to violate its permit at the time the suit was filed. The court of appeals affirmed. However, the Supreme Court concluded that § 505 did not permit citizen suits for wholly past violations, and remanded the case for the trial court to decide whether plaintiffs' complaint contained a good faith allegation of an ongoing violation by defendant. The Court indicated that plaintiffs would have to offer evidence in the trial court to support their allegation, at which point the defendant would have an opportunity to demonstrate that the allegations were a sham and raised no genuine issue of fact. The Court further said:

> [Defendant] also worries that our construction of § 505 would permit citizen-plaintiffs, if their allegations of ongoing non-compliance become false at some later point in the litigation because the defendant begins to comply with the Act, to continue nonetheless to press their suit to conclusion. * * * Longstanding principles of mootness, however, prevent the maintenance of suit when "there is no reasonable expectation that the wrong will be repeated." In seeking to have a case dismissed as moot, however, the defendant's burden "is a heavy one."

The defendant must demonstrate that it is *"absolutely clear* that the alleged wrongful behavior could not reasonably be expected to recur." Mootness doctrine thus protects defendants from the maintenance of suit under the Clean Water Act based solely on violations wholly unconnected to any present or future wrongdoing, while it also protects plaintiffs from defendants who seek to evade sanction by predictable "protestations of repentance and reform."

4. In *Atlantic States Legal Foundation, Inc. v. Pan American Tanning Corp.,* 993 F.2d 1017 (2d Cir.1993), the issue was whether a citizen suit for injunctive relief and civil penalties under § 505 of the Clean Water Act was moot when, following a series of admitted violations of the statute that continued past the day on which the complaint was filed, the defendant discharger entered into a settlement with a local enforcement agency, covering *some* (but not all) of the violations, and established that any allegedly wrongful behavior could not reasonably be expected to recur. Citing the above-quoted dicta from *Gwaltney,* defendant argued that plaintiff's *entire* suit should be dismissed as moot if defendant could show that it had come into compliance after the complaint was filed and that the allegedly wrongful behavior could not reasonably be expected to recur. The Second Circuit said that the Supreme Court's discussion of mootness in *Gwaltney* left open the question whether mootness bars only claims for *injunctive relief* or whether it also bars claims for *civil penalties.* "Generally, when a plaintiff seeks both injunctive relief and damages or penalties, the Supreme Court has long directed courts to analyze a mootness claim directed at one form of relief separately from a mootness claim directed at the other." The court of appeals noted that two circuits had held that a citizen suit for civil penalties under the Clean Water Act could survive when post-complaint compliance with the Act renders a suit for injunctive relief moot. The Second Circuit agreed, saying that "[a] rule requiring dismissal of a citizen suit in its entirety based on a defendant's post-complaint compliance appears to conflict with the language of Act. Under such rule, a penalty suit would *always* become moot and a defendant would escape *all* liability if it could show, at any time before judgment, 'that the allegedly wrongful behavior could not reasonably be expected to recur.' "The court said that allowing a discharger to escape all liability by virtue of its post-complaint compliance could not be squared with mandatory language in § 309(d) of the Clean Water Act, that any person who violates effluent limitations or permit conditions *"shall* be subject to a civil penalty."

However, in *Friends of the Earth v. Laidlaw Environmental Services (TOC), Inc.,* 149 F.3d 303 (4th Cir. 1998), the Fourth Circuit dismissed as moot a Clean Water Act citizen suit even though the district court had found both pre- and post-complaint permit violations by defendant and had imposed a $400,000 civil penalty. The district court also found that defendant had been in "substantial compliance" for several years prior to the judgment. Citing *Steel Co.,* page 104 supra, the court of appeals said, "Because Plaintiffs have not appealed the denial of declaratory and injunctive relief, . . . this action is moot because the only remedy currently available to Plaintiffs—civil penalties payable to the government—would not redress any injury Plaintiffs have suffered".

5. In *Washington Public Interest Research Group v. Pendleton Woolen Mills,* 11 F.3d 883 (9th Cir.1993), EPA issued a compliance order in 1988, stating that defendant was in violation of its NPDES permit. The order required Pendleton to prepare a report describing the causes of the violations and identifying the actions necessary to bring it into compliance. The order further required Pendleton to make those physical improvements identified as necessary. An amended compliance order included a threat of a sanction of $25,000 per day if Pendleton violated its terms. In 1990, WashPIRG notified EPA and Pendleton of its intent to bring suit against Pendleton for alleged permit violations. More than 60 days thereafter, WashPIRG filed a complaint seeking (1) a declaration establishing Pendleton's violations, (2) an injunction ordering Pendleton into compliance, and (3) civil penalties for Pendleton's violations from 1985 to the present. The district court entered summary judgment in favor of Pendleton, holding that the existence of EPA's action against Pendleton barred WashPIRG's citizen suit. The court of appeals reversed, holding that § 309(g)(6) of the Clean Water Act precludes citizen suits seeking civil penalties *only* if the EPA is diligently pursuing an administrative penalty action, and that the administrative compliance order which EPA had issued to Pendleton did not seek monetary penalties.

On the other hand, *Arkansas Wildlife Federation v. ICI Americas, Inc.,* 29 F.3d 376 (8th Cir.1994), held that a citizen suit was jurisdictionally barred under the Clean Water Act because the state pollution control agency was diligently prosecuting, against the same defendant, an action under the state pollution control act. The bar to the citizen suit applied to *all* of ICI's past CWA violations, even though the original consent administrative order, which called for ICI to pay a civil penalty and to comply with applicable effluent limitations, did not cover all of ICI's violations. The consent order later was amended to incorporate all of ICI's past violations, but not until after AWF already had given proper notice of its intent to initiate a citizen suit and had filed a complaint alleging ICI's ongoing violation of the act and seeking civil penalties and declaratory and injunctive relief. The basis for the court's action was § 309(g)(6)(A)(ii) of the Clean Water Act, which precludes "a civil penalty action" for a violation "with respect to which a State has commenced and is diligently prosecuting an action under a State law comparable to this subsection." The court found that Arkansas had commenced a comparable action when it issued the original consent administrative order, prior to AWF's notice of intent to sue.

6. A very controversial issue is whether businesses which conduct *voluntary environmental compliance audits* can be compelled to disclose the results in civil enforcement proceedings initiated by private or governmental plaintiffs. As of 1998, nineteen states had enacted laws making information gathered through voluntary environmental audits *privileged* in various types of enforcement proceedings. The federal government opposes state privilege laws and has none of its own. See the "Note on Environmental Audit Privileges" at page 687 infra.

Note on Attorneys' Fees

Much of the most important environmental litigation is brought by public interest groups. Their ability to bring these suits, often as private attorneys general policing agency compliance with federal statutes, is dependent on their access to funding. One of the most important sources of funding for these groups is the award of attorneys' fees authorized by many environmental statutes. The availability of fee awards and their size have been the subject of much litigation, both in the environmental area and elsewhere. Two basic rules are that (a) fees are available only to "prevailing parties," and (b) the fee usually is calculated by multiplying a reasonable hourly rate times the number of hours reasonably invested in the suit.

In *Alyeska Pipeline Service Co. v. Wilderness Society,* 421 U.S. 240, 95 S.Ct. 1612, 44 L.Ed.2d 141 (1975), there was no applicable statute authorizing an award of attorneys' fees to the plaintiff organizations, which had sued to prevent the Secretary of the Interior from issuing permits for construction of the trans-Alaska oil pipeline. Plaintiffs prevailed, and the court of appeals awarded them attorneys' fees based upon the court's equitable powers and the theory that plaintiffs were entitled to fees because they were performing the services of a "private attorney general." The Supreme Court reversed, saying that in the United States a prevailing litigant is ordinarily not entitled to collect a reasonable attorneys' fee from the loser, and that exceptions to this "American Rule" are to be established by Congress and not by the courts.

In *Ruckelshaus v. Sierra Club,* 463 U.S. 680, 103 S.Ct. 3274, 77 L.Ed.2d 938 (1983), the issue was whether it was "appropriate," within the meaning of § 307(f) of the Clean Air Act, to award attorneys' fees to a party that had achieved no success on the merits of its claim. Section 307(f) provided, "In any judicial proceeding under this section, the court may award costs of litigation (including reasonable attorney and expert witness fees) whenever it determines that such an award is appropriate." The Supreme Court held that consistent with the "American Rule," it was "appropriate" for lower courts to award attorneys' fees under this section only to a "prevailing litigant." Four Justices dissented, arguing that § 307(f) deliberately contained language differing from the "prevailing party" standard expressly adopted in the attorney fee provisions of many other federal statutes because Congress intended, as was shown by the legislative history, to give the courts of appeals discretionary authority to award fees and costs to a broader category of parties. The dissenters stressed that the Sierra Club was the only party to brief and advocate opposition to the core concept of the EPA regulation in question, "an issue conceded by EPA to be critically important." For a critique of *Ruckelshaus* see Farber, "Statutory Interpretation and Legislative Supremacy," 78 *Geo.L.J.* 281, 301–302 (1989).

In *Armstrong v. ASARCO, Inc.,* 138 F.3d 382 (8th Cir.1998), plaintiffs filed a citizen suit against ASARCO for discharging pollutants without a Clean Water Act permit. Thereafter, EPA filed suit against ASARCO for the same violations and proposed a consent decree to the court. Plaintiffs opposed the decree and obtained further discovery. As a result of the new information, EPA proposed and obtained court approval (over plaintiffs' continued opposition) of a much more severe consent decree, requiring payment of millions of dollars in penalties. Although plaintiffs did not obtain the injunction or judgment sought in their suit, the court held that they were "prevailing parties" because they "played the roles of catalyst and private attorney general," contributing to the settlement. Plaintiffs were awarded attorney fees incurred up to the date of the final consent decree, but not fees incurred opposing that decree or thereafter.

B. INJUNCTIONS

TVA v. HILL

Supreme Court of the United States, 1978.
437 U.S. 153, 98 S.Ct. 2279, 57 L.Ed.2d 117.

[This case involved the application of the Endangered Species Act of 1973 to a nearly completed dam on the Little Tennessee River. The Act is discussed in more detail in Chapter VIII. Here, the dam would have endangered the survival of the snail darter, a previously unknown species of perch which was discovered after litigation over the dam had already begun. There are approximately 130 known species of darters. The district court declined to enjoin construction of the dam, largely because Congress had continued to appropriate money for the dam despite the snail darter problem, and also because the dam was so near completion. The court of appeals reversed, and the Supreme Court granted the government's petition for certiorari.]

CHIEF JUSTICE BURGER delivered the opinion of the Court.

* * *

It may seem curious to some that the survival of a relatively small number of three-inch fish among all the countless millions of species extant would require the permanent halting of a virtually completed dam for which Congress has expended more than $100 million. The paradox is not minimized by the fact that Congress continued to appropriate large sums of public money for the project, even after congressional appropriations committees were apprised of its apparent impact upon the survival of the snail darter. We conclude, however, that the explicit provisions of the Endangered Species Act require precisely that result.

One would be hard pressed to find a statutory provision whose terms were any plainer than those in § 7 of the Endangered Species Act. Its very words affirmatively command all federal agencies "to *insure* that actions *authorized, funded, or carried out* by them do not *jeopardize* the continued existence" of an endangered species or "*result* in the destruction or modification of habitat of such species * * *." 16 U.S.C.A. § 1536. (Emphasis added.) This language admits of no exception. * * *

Concededly, this view of the Act will produce results requiring the sacrifice of the anticipated benefits of the project and of many millions of dollars in public funds. But examination of the language, history and structure of the legislation under review here indicates beyond doubt that Congress intended endangered species to be afforded the highest of priorities.

[The Court then reviewed the legislative history at length].

Issue

It is against this legislative background[29] that we must measure TVA's claim that the Act was not intended to stop operation of a project which, like Tellico Dam, was near completion when an endangered species was discovered in its path. While there is no discussion in the legislative history of precisely this problem, the totality of congressional action makes it abundantly clear that the result we reach today is wholly in accord with both the words of the statute and the intent of Congress. The plain intent of Congress in enacting this statute was to halt and reverse the trend toward species extinction, whatever the cost. This is reflected not only in the stated policies of the Act, but in literally every section of the statute. All persons, including federal agencies, are specifically instructed not to "take" endangered species, meaning that no one is "to harass, harm, pursue, hunt, shoot, wound, kill, trap, capture, or collect" such life forms. Agencies in particular are directed by §§ 2(c) and 3(2) of the Act to "use *all methods* and procedures which are necessary" to preserve endangered species. In addition, the legislative history undergirding § 7 reveals an explicit congressional decision to require agencies to afford first priority to the declared national policy of saving endangered species. The pointed omission of the type of qualifying language previously included in endangered species legislation reveals a conscious decision by Congress to give endangered species priority over the "primary missions" of federal agencies.

It is not for us to speculate, much less act, on whether Congress would have altered its stance had the specific events of this case been anticipated. In any event, we discern no hint in the deliberations of Congress relating to the 1973 Act that would compel a different result than we reach here. Indeed, the repeated expressions of congressional concern over what it saw as the potentially enormous danger presented by the eradication of *any* endangered species suggests how the balance would have been struck had the issue been presented to Congress in 1973.

* * *

One might dispute the applicability of these examples to the Tellico Dam by saying that in this case the burden on the public through the loss of millions of unrecoverable dollars would greatly outweigh the loss of the snail darter. But neither the Endangered Species Act nor Art. III of the Constitution provides federal courts with authority to make such fine utilitarian calculations. On the contrary, the plain language of the Act, buttressed by its legislative history, shows clearly that Congress viewed the value of endangered species as "incalculable." Quite obviously, it would be difficult for a court to balance the loss of a sum certain— even $100 million—against a congressionally declared "incalculable"

---

29. When confronted with a statute which is plain and unambiguous on its face, we ordinarily do not look to legislative history as a guide to its meaning. Here it is not *necessary* to look beyond the words of the statute. We have undertaken such an analysis only to meet Mr. Justice Powell's suggestion that the "absurd" result reached in this case, is not in accord with congressional intent.

value, even assuming we had the power to engage in such a weighing process, which we emphatically do not.

* * *

Having determined that there is an irreconcilable conflict between operation of the Tellico Dam and the explicit provisions of § 7 of the Endangered Species Act, we must now consider what remedy, if any, is appropriate. It is correct, of course, that a federal judge sitting as a chancellor is not mechanically obligated to grant an injunction for every violation of law. This Court made plain in *Hecht Co. v. Bowles,* 321 U.S. 321, 329, 64 S.Ct. 587, 591, 88 L.Ed. 754 (1944), that "[a] grant of *jurisdiction* to issue compliance orders hardly suggests an absolute duty to do so under any and all circumstances." As a general matter it may be said that "[s]ince all or almost all equitable remedies are discretionary, the balancing of equities and hardships is appropriate in almost any case as a guide to the chancellor's discretion." Dobbs, *Remedies* 52 (1973). Thus, in *Hecht* the Court refused to grant an injunction when it appeared from the District Court findings that "the issuance of an injunction would have 'no effect by way of insuring better compliance in the future' and would [have been] 'unjust' to [the] petitioner and not 'in the public interest.' "

But these principles take a court only so far. Our system of government is, after all, a tripartite one, with each Branch having certain defined functions delegated to it by the Constitution. While "[it] is emphatically the province and duty of the judicial department to say what the law is," *Marbury v. Madison,* 5 U.S. 137, 177, 2 L.Ed. 60 (1803), it is equally—and emphatically—the exclusive province of the Congress not only to formulate legislative policies, mandate programs and projects, but also to establish their relative priority for the Nation. Once Congress, exercising its delegated powers, has decided the order of priorities in a given area, it is for the Executive to administer the laws and for the courts to enforce them when enforcement is sought.

Here we are urged to view the Endangered Species Act "reasonably," and hence shape a remedy "that accords with some modicum of commonsense and the public weal." But is that our function? We have no expert knowledge on the subject of endangered species, much less do we have a mandate from the people to strike a balance of equities on the side of the Tellico Dam. Congress has spoken in the plainest of words, making it abundantly clear that the balance has been struck in favor of affording endangered species the highest of priorities, thereby adopting a policy which it described as "institutionalized caution."

Our individual appraisal of the wisdom or unwisdom of a particular course consciously selected by the Congress is to be put aside in the process of interpreting a statute. Once the meaning of an enactment is discerned and its constitutionality determined, the judicial process comes to an end. We do not sit as a committee of review, nor are we vested with the power of veto. The lines ascribed to Sir Thomas Moore by Robert Bolt are not without relevance here:

The law, Roper, the law. I know what's legal, not what's right. And I'll stick to what's legal * * *. I'm *not* God. The currents and eddies of right and wrong, which you find such plain-sailing, I can't navigate, I'm no voyager. But in the thickets of the law, oh there I'm a forester. * * * What would you do? Cut a great road through the law to get after the Devil? * * * And when the last law was down, and the Devil turned round on you—where would you hide, Roper, the laws all being flat? This country's planted thick with laws from coast to coast—Man's laws, not God's—and if you cut them down * * * d'you really think you could stand upright in the winds that would blow then? Yes, I'd give the Devil benefit of law, for my own safety's sake. Bolt, A Man for All Seasons, Act I, at 147 (Heinemann ed. 1967).

We agree with the Court of Appeals that in our constitutional system the commitment to the separation of powers is too fundamental for us to pre-empt congressional action by judicially decreeing what accords with "commonsense and the public weal." Our Constitution vests such responsibilities in the political Branches.

[Justice Powell, joined by Justice Blackmun, dissented on the ground that the Act applied only to federal "actions" that endanger species, and that "actions" should be construed to refer only to future actions following discovery of the threat to endangered species, rather than to actions which were virtually complete at the time the problem was discovered. Justice Powell noted that under the Court's view of the statute, "[t]he only precondition * * * to thus destroying the usefulness of even the most important federal project in our country would be a finding by the Secretary of the Interior that a continuation of the project would threaten the survival or critical habitat of a newly discovered species of water spider or amoeba". He added that "[U]nder the Court's interpretation, the prospects for such disasters are breathtaking indeed * * * "]

Justice Rehnquist, dissenting.

In light of my Brother Powell's dissenting opinion, I am far less convinced than is the Court that the Endangered Species Act of 1973 was intended to prohibit the completion of the Tellico Dam. But the very difficulty and doubtfulness of the correct answer to this legal question convinces me that the Act did *not* prohibit the District Court from refusing, in the exercise of its traditional equitable powers, to enjoin petitioner from completing the Dam. Section 11(g)(1) of the Act, 16 U.S.C.A. § 1540(g)(1), merely provides that "any person may commence a civil suit on his own behalf to enjoin any person, including the United States and any other governmental instrumentality or agency, who is alleged to be in violation of any provision of this chapter." It also grants the district courts "jurisdiction, without regard to the amount in controversy or the citizenship of the parties, to enforce any such provision."

This Court had occasion in *Hecht Co. v. Bowles,* 321 U.S. 321, 64 S.Ct. 587, 88 L.Ed. 754 (1944), to construe language in an Act of

Congress that lent far greater support to a conclusion that Congress intended an injunction to issue as a matter of right than does the language just quoted. There the Emergency Price Control Act of 1942 provided that:

> * * * Upon a showing by the Administrator that [a] person has engaged or is about to engage in any [acts or practices violative of this Act] a permanent or temporary injunction, restraining order, or other order *shall be granted* without bond. 56 Stat. 23 (emphasis added).

But in *Hecht* this Court refused to find even in such language an intent on the part of Congress to require that a district court issue an injunction as a matter of course without regard to established equitable considerations, saying:

> Only the other day we stated that "an appeal to the equity jurisdiction conferred on federal district courts is an appeal to the sound discretion which guides the determinations of courts of equity." * * * The essence of equity jurisdiction has been the power of the Chancellor to do equity and to mould each decree to the necessities of the particular case. Flexibility rather than rigidity has distinguished it. The qualities of mercy and practicality have made equity the instrument for nice adjustment and reconciliation between the public interest and private needs as well as between competing private claims. We do not believe that such a major departure from that long tradition as is here proposed should be lightly implied. * * * [I]f Congress desired to make such an abrupt departure from traditional equity practice as is suggested, it would have made its desire plain.

Only if we were to sharply retreat from the principle of statutory construction announced in *Hecht* could we agree with the Court of Appeals' holding in this case that the judicial enforcement provisions contained in § 11(g)(1) of the Act require automatic issuance of an injunction by the district courts once a violation is found. We choose to adhere to *Hecht*'s teaching that

> [a] grant of *jurisdiction* to issue compliance orders hardly suggests an absolute duty to do so under any and all circumstances. We cannot but think that if Congress had intended to make such a drastic departure from the traditions of equity practice, an unequivocal statement of its purpose would have been made.

Since the District Court possessed discretion to refuse injunctive relief even though it had found a violation of the Act, the only remaining question is whether this discretion was abused in denying respondents' prayer for an injunction. The District Court denied respondents injunctive relief because of the significant public and social harms that would flow from such relief and because of the demonstrated good faith of petitioner. As the Court recognizes, such factors traditionally have played a central role in the decisions of equity courts whether to deny an injunction. This Court has specifically held that a federal court can refuse to order a federal official to take specific action, even though the action might be required by law, if such an order "would work a public injury or embarrassment" or otherwise "be prejudicial to the public interest." Here the District Court, confronted with conflicting evidence of congressional purpose, was on even stronger ground in refusing the injunction.

Since equity is "the instrument for nice adjustment and reconciliation between the public interest and private needs," *Hecht,* supra, 321 U.S., at 329–330, 64 S.Ct., at 592, a decree in one case will seldom be the exact counterpart of a decree in another. Here the District Court recognized that Congress when it enacted the Endangered Species Act made the preservation of the habitat of the snail darter an important public concern. But it concluded that this interest on one side of the balance was more than outweighed by other equally significant factors. These factors, further elaborated in the dissent of my Brother Powell, satisfy me that the District Court's refusal to issue an injunction was not an abuse of its discretion. I therefore dissent from the Court's opinion holding otherwise.

Notes

1. In *TVA v. Hill,* Justice Rehnquist argued strenuously for the existence of broad judicial discretion. Is this consistent with his strictures in *Vermont Yankee,* page 125 supra, on the limited role of the judiciary in administrative law?

2. The issue in *TVA v. Hill* was whether, after considering the merits, a court may use its equitable discretion to deny a remedy. A related, but conceptually distinct question, is whether a court may exercise its equitable discretion to decline to even consider the merits. One common issue relates to laches—that is, the defense that the plaintiff has delayed too long in bringing a lawsuit, to the defendant's detriment. This and similar defenses are not uncommonly raised in environmental litigation. See, e.g., *Portland Audubon Soc. v. Lujan,* 884 F.2d 1233 (9th Cir.1989); *Preservation Coalition, Inc. v. Pierce,* 667 F.2d 851 (9th Cir.1982); Annot., 63 *ALR Fed.* 18. What policy considerations should guide a court's resolution of such a defense?

3. Does *TVA v. Hill* mean that a federal court can never decide to allow unlawful conduct to continue after balancing the equities? Consider the relevance of the following case to your answer.

WEINBERGER v. ROMERO–BARCELO

Supreme Court of the United States, 1982.
456 U.S. 305, 102 S.Ct. 1798, 72 L.Ed.2d 91.

[In connection with naval exercises, bombs occasionally fell into the waters off the Puerto Rican coasts. The District Court held that the bombs constituted "discharges" of "pollutants" under the Clean Water Act. The Act required the Navy to obtain a permit for such discharges. Absent a Presidential exemption, the permit must require such discharges to comply with state water quality regulations. The question before the Court was whether, given these findings, the District Court had discretion to deny an injunction.]

JUSTICE WHITE delivered the opinion of the Court:

In *TVA v. Hill,* we held that Congress had foreclosed the exercise of the usual discretion possessed by a court of equity. There, we thought that "one would be hard pressed to find a statutory provision whose terms were any plainer" than that before us. The statute involved, the Endangered Species Act, required the district court to enjoin completion of the Tellico Dam in order to preserve the snail darter, a species of perch. The purpose and language of the statute under consideration in *Hill,* not the bare fact of a statutory violation, compelled that conclusion. Section 1536 of the Act requires federal agencies to "insure that actions authorized, funded, or carried out by them do not jeopardize the continued existence of [any] endangered species * * * or result in the destruction or habitat of such species which is determined * * * to be critical." The statute thus contains a flat ban on the destruction of critical habitats.

It was conceded in *Hill* that completion of the dam would eliminate an endangered species by destroying its critical habitat. Refusal to enjoin the action would have ignored the "explicit provisions of the Endangered Species Act." Congress, it appeared to us, had chosen the snail darter over the dam. The purpose and language of the statute limited the remedies available to the district court; only an injunction could vindicate the objectives of the Act.

That is not the case here. An injunction is not the only means of ensuring compliance. The FWPCA itself, for example, provides for fines and criminal penalties. Respondents suggest that failure to enjoin the Navy will undermine the integrity of the permit process by allowing the statutory violation to continue. The integrity of the nation's waters, however, not the permit process, is the purpose of the FWPCA. As Congress explained, the objective of the FWPCA is to "restore and maintain the chemical, physical and biological integrity of the Nation's waters." 33 U.S.C. § 1251(a).

This purpose is to be achieved by compliance with the Act, including compliance with the permit requirements. Here, however, the discharge of ordinance had not polluted the waters, and, although the District Court declined to enjoin the discharges, it neither ignored the statutory violation nor undercut the purpose and function of the permit system. The court ordered the Navy to apply for a permit. It temporarily, not permanently, allowed the Navy to continue its activities without a permit.

In *Hill,* we also noted that none of the limited "hardship exemptions" of the Endangered Species Act would "even remotely apply to the Tellico Project." The prohibition of the FWPCA against discharge of pollutants, in contrast, can be overcome by the very permit the Navy was ordered to seek. The Senate Report to the 1972 Amendments explains that it was enacting the permit program because "the Committee recognizes the impracticality of any effort to halt all pollution immediately." That the scheme as a whole contemplates the exercise of discretion and balancing of equities militates against the conclusion that Congress intended to deny courts their traditional equitable discretion in enforcing the statute.

Other aspects of the statutory scheme also suggests that Congress did not intend to deny courts the discretion to rely on remedies other than an immediate prohibitory injunction. Although the ultimate objective of the FWPCA is to eliminate all discharges of pollutants into the navigable waters by 1985, the statute sets forth a scheme of phased compliance. As enacted, it called for the achievement of the "best practicable control technology currently available" by July 1, 1977 and the "best available technology economically achievable" by July 1, 1983. This scheme of phased compliance further suggests that this is a statute in which Congress envisioned, rather than curtailed, the exercise of discretion.

The FWPCA directs the Administrator of the EPA to seek an injunction to restrain immediately discharges of pollutants he finds to be presenting "an imminent and substantial endangerment of the health of persons or to the welfare of persons." This rule of immediate cessation, however, is limited to the indicated class of violations. For other kinds of violations, the FWPCA authorizes the Administrator of the EPA "to commence a civil action for appropriate relief, including a permanent or temporary injunction, for any violation for which he is authorized to issue a compliance order * * *." The provision makes clear that Congress did not anticipate that all discharges would be immediately enjoined. Consistent with this view, the administrative practice has not been to request immediate cessation orders. "Rather, enforcement actions typically result, by consent or otherwise, in a remedial order setting out a detailed schedule of compliance designed to cure the identified violation of the Act." Brief for United States 17. Here, again, the statutory scheme contemplates equitable consideration.

Both the Court of Appeals and respondents attach particular weight to the provision of the FWPCA permitting the President to exempt Federal facilities from compliance with the permit requirements. They suggest that this provision indicates Congressional intent to limit the court's discretion. According to respondents, the exemption provision evidences Congress' determination that only paramount national interests justify failure to comply and that only the President should make this judgment.

We do not construe the provision so broadly. We read the FWPCA as permitting the exercise of a court's equitable discretion, whether the source of pollution is a private party or a federal agency, to order relief that will achieve *compliance* with the Act. The exemption serves a different and complementary purpose, that of permitting *noncompliance* by federal agencies in extraordinary circumstances. Exec.Order No. 12088, which implements the exemption authority, requires the federal agency requesting such an exemption to certify that it cannot meet the applicable pollution standards. "Exemptions are granted by the President only if the conflict between pollution control standards and crucial federal activities cannot be resolved through the development of a practicable remedial program." Brief for United States 25, n. 30.

Should the Navy receive a permit here, there would be no need to invoke the machinery of the Presidential exemption. If not, this course remains open. The exemption provision would enable the President, believing paramount national interests so require, to authorize discharges which the district court has enjoined. Reading the statute to permit the exercise of a court's equitable discretion in no way eliminates the role of the exemption provision in the statutory scheme.

* * *

This Court explained in *Hecht v. Bowles,* 321 U.S. 321, 64 S.Ct. 587, 88 L.Ed. 754 (1944), that a major departure from the long tradition of equity practice should not be lightly implied. As we did there, we construe the statute at issue "in favor of that interpretation which affords a full opportunity for equity courts to treat enforcement proceedings * * * in accordance with their traditional practices, as conditioned by the necessities of the public interest which Congress has sought to protect." We do not read the FWPCA as foreclosing completely the exercise of the court's discretion. Rather than requiring a District Court to issue an injunction for any and all statutory violations, the FWPCA permits the District Court to order that relief it considers necessary to secure prompt compliance with the Act. That relief can include, but is not limited to, an order of immediate cessation.

The exercise of equitable discretion, which must include the ability to deny as well as grant injunctive relief, can fully protect the range of public interests at issue at this stage in the proceedings. The District Court did not face a situation in which a permit would very likely not issue and the requirements and objective of the statute could therefore not be vindicated if discharges were permitted to continue. Should it become clear that no permit will be issued and that compliance with the FWPCA will not be forthcoming, the statutory scheme and purpose would require the court to reconsider the balance it has struck.

Because Congress, in enacting the FWPCA, has not foreclosed the exercise of equitable discretion, the proper standard for appellate review is whether the district court abused its discretion in denying an immediate cessation order while the Navy applied for a permit. We reverse and remand to Court of Appeals for proceedings consistent with this opinion.

STEVENS, JUSTICE, dissenting.

The appropriate remedy for the violation of a federal statute depends primarily on the terms of the statute and the character of the violation. Unless Congress specifically commands a particular form of relief, the question of remedy remains subject to a court's equitable discretion. Because the Federal Water Pollution Control Act does not specifically command the federal courts to issue an injunction every time an unpermitted discharge of a pollutant occurs, the Court today is obviously correct in asserting that such injunctions should not issue "automatically" or "mechanically" in every case. It is nevertheless equally clear that by enacting the 1972 amendments to the FWPCA Congress channeled the discretion of the federal judiciary much more narrowly than the Court's rather glib opinion suggests. Indeed, although there may well be situations in which the failure to obtain an NPDES permit would not require immediate cessation of all discharges, I am convinced that Congress has circumscribed the district courts' discretion on the question of remedy so narrowly that a general rule of immediate cessation must be applied in all but a narrow category of cases. The Court of Appeals was quite correct in holding that this case does not present the kind of exceptional situation that justifies a departure from the general rule.

The Court's mischaracterization of the Court of Appeals' holding is the premise for its essay on equitable discretion. This essay is analytically flawed because it overlooks the limitations on equitable discretion that apply in cases in which public interests are implicated and the defendant's violation of the law is ongoing. Of greater importance, the Court's opinion grants an open-ended license to federal judges to carve gaping holes in a reticulated statutory scheme designed by Congress to protect a precious natural resource from the consequences of ad hoc judgments about specific discharges of pollutants.

* * *

Under these circumstances—the statutory violation is blatant and not merely technical, and the Navy's predicament was foreseen and accommodated by Congress—the Court of Appeals essentially held that the District Court retained no discretion to deny an injunction. The discretion exercised by the District Court in this case was wholly at odds with the intent of Congress in enacting the FWPCA. In essence, the District Court's remedy was a judicial permit exempting the Navy's operations in Vieques from the statute until such time as it could obtain a permit from the Environmental Protection Agency or a statutory exemption from the President. The two principal bases for the temporary judicial permit were matters that Congress did not commit to judicial discretion. First, the District Court was persuaded that the pollution was not harming the quality of the coastal waters, and second, the court was concerned that compliance with the Act might adversely affect national security. The Court of Appeals correctly noted that the first consideration is the business of the EPA and the second is the business of the President.

* * *

It is true that in *TVA v. Hill* there was no room for compromise between the federal project and the statutory objective to preserve an endangered species; either the snail darter or the completion of the

Tellico Dam had to be sacrificed. In the FWPCA, the Court tells us, the congressional objective is to protect the integrity of the Nation's waters, not to protect the integrity of the permit process. Therefore, the Court continues, a federal court may compromise the process chosen by Congress to protect our waters as long as the court is content that the waters are not actually being harmed by the particular discharge of pollutants.

On analysis, however, this reasoning does not distinguish the two cases. Courts are in no better position to decide whether the permit process is necessary to achieve the objectives of the FWPCA than they are to decide whether the destruction of the snail darter is an acceptable cost of completing the Tellico Dam. Congress has made both decisions, and there is nothing in the respective statutes or legislative histories to suggest that Congress invited the federal courts to second-guess the former decision any more than the latter.

Notes

1. Are you persuaded by the Court's attempt in *Weinberger* to distinguish *TVA v. Hill?* Is it proper for an administrative officer to request judicial approval for a plan to continue violating a statute? Just how much discretion does *Weinberger* give judges in statutory enforcement cases? In particular, can a judge permanently excuse compliance with a statute under *Weinberger?* For a thorough analysis of the issue in the preceding case, see Plater, "Statutory Violations and Equitable Discretion," 70 *Cal.L.Rev.* 524 (1982).

2. Consider the following comment on the statute involved in *Weinberger:*

> The Clean Water Act * * * imposes strict deadlines on the use of certain forms of technology. Flagrant, willful violations may result in criminal penalties. Even those who make good faith attempts to meet deadlines are subject to sanctions such as civil penalties if they fail * * *. In a sense then, their conduct is unlawful * * *. Nevertheless, in pronouncing this conduct unlawful, Congress apparently did not intend to create an absolute duty to avoid it * * *. At least by the time of the 1977 amendments, Congress clearly did not envision widespread plant closings as an acceptable price for clean water. Moreover, there is no indication that Congress regarded plant closing as a desirable *voluntary* means of achieving compliance. In other words, the legal duty created by the Clean Water Act is a qualified one. The duty is something more than a mere use of best efforts, for even individuals who use their best efforts are subject to some sanctions if they fail. Nevertheless, it is also something less than an absolute duty, for Congress did not contemplate the use of all available means (such as plant closings) to avoid noncompliance.

Farber, "Equitable Discretion, Legal Duties, and Environmental Injunctions", 45 *U.Pitt.L.Rev.* 513, 537 (1984). Does the qualified nature of the legal duty created by the Clean Water Act distinguish *Weinberger* from *TVA v. Hill?* Note that the legal duty involved in *Weinberger* was particularly qualified, for while the Navy was legally required to obtain a permit, it was not technically covered by the prohibition in section 301 of the statute against discharging without a permit. See id. at 523–524.

UNITED STATES v. WHEELING–PITTSBURGH STEEL CORP.

United States Court of Appeals, Third Circuit, 1987.
818 F.2d 1077.

[Wheeling operates a sinter windbox in a West Virginia plant. A sinter windbox fuses leftovers from steel production into sinter, which is then recycled through blast furnaces. The sinter plant was admittedly in violation of the SIP. After being sued by EPA, Wheeling entered into a consent decree, which was later amended by agreement with EPA to allow Wheeling until the end of 1985 to comply. In late 1985, Wheeling filed a motion to revise the consent decree again because of its pending Chapter 11 reorganization, a 98–day strike against it in 1985, and a pending bubble application. The district court struck the deadline for installation of $3,500,000 worth of new equipment on the basis of these changed circumstances.]

SLOVITER, CIRCUIT JUDGE:

In the posture of the case before us, we need not decide if the district court has the power to extend a polluter's compliance date beyond that set by the Clean Air Act and incorporated in Wheeling's Consent Decree with the government and affected states. EPA concedes that the district court retains some equitable discretion in this respect but argues that it abused its discretion by amending the Consent Decree to indefinitely stay Wheeling's obligations to comply with the statutory deadline, the West Virginia SIP and the Consent Decree. Wheeling counters that the district court's action was reasonable in light of Wheeling's circumstances.

In *Weinberger v. Romero–Barcelo,* 456 U.S. 305, 102 S.Ct. 1798, 72 L.Ed.2d 91 (1982), a case arising under the Federal Water Pollution Control Act (FWPCA), the Supreme Court held that in light of the purpose and language of the statute and the statutory provisions for fines and criminal penalties to ensure compliance with the FWPCA's prohibition of discharges without an EPA permit, the district court retained the discretion to decline to enjoin discharges by the Navy which had not polluted the waters. The Court relied on the traditional equitable discretion of the federal courts.

The Court recognized that in some statutes "Congress * * * foreclosed the exercise of the usual discretion possessed by a court of equity." It also stated that "Congress may intervene and guide or control the exercise of the courts' discretion." Although the issue before us, that of statutory and consent decree compliance deadlines, is different than that before the Court in *Romero–Barcelo,* we will assume *arguendo* that the district court retains some equitable discretion to modify those deadlines. To determine the limits, if any, on the courts' equitable discretion, we must look to the "purpose and language of the statute."

The language of the SICEA amendments to the Clean Air Act limiting the district court's discretion to extend the deadline is clear. The Act states:

> For a source which receives an extension under this subsection, air pollution requirements specified in Federal judicial decrees entered into or modified under this subsection that involves [sic] such source may not be modified to extend beyond December 31, 1985.

42 U.S.C. § 7413(e)(9); see also 42 U.S.C. § 7413(e)(1) ("The Administrator may, in his discretion * * * consent to * * * the modification of an existing Federal judicial decree * * * establishing a schedule for compliance * * * but ending not later than December 31, 1985").

* * *

Congress' concern with its statutory deadline for compliance in SICEA is consistent with its earlier actions in enacting the 1970 and 1977 amendments to the Clean Air Act which strengthened the provisions of the Act and set mandatory deadlines for developing SIPs and for compliance therewith. In adopting the 1970 Amendments, Congress rejected the terms of the House bill which would have required compliance with primary standards within a "reasonable time" and instead accepted the Senate amendment which required attainment of primary standards within three years. Likewise, when Congress amended the Act in 1977 to provide specific authority for the Administrator to enter into "Delayed Compliance Orders", (DCO), it specifically limited the orders to three years. See 42 U.S.C. § 7413(d)(1)(D). In discussing the need for the DCO provision, the House Report criticized the Administrator's practice of entering into compliance agreements that "as construed and applied by EPA [result in] delays [that] are not limited to any particular date or time period."

It is evident therefore from the language of the statute and its legislative history that Congress placed great significance on the compliance dates and intended to limit, if not entirely eliminate, the district court's equitable discretion to extend compliance.

Even assuming that the courts have some retained equitable discretion, the district court's reliance on the pending "bubble" application as a basis for its order extending Wheeling's compliance requirement contravenes the consistent judicial interpretation of the Act. EPA does not dispute that Wheeling submitted an alternative emission reduction plan for a "bubble" to the West Virginia agency and that the application is still pending before that agency. EPA argues, however, that the pendency of such an application cannot relieve Wheeling of its obligation to meet its compliance deadlines, and that the district court's reliance thereon was an error of law. We agree.

The general principle that the company is not relieved of its legal obligation to attain compliance with statutory, regulatory or judicially imposed obligations during the pendency of an application for relief or a variance was emphatically established in *Train v. Natural Resources Defense Council, Inc.,* 421 U.S. 60, 95 S.Ct. 1470, 43 L.Ed.2d 731 (1975) [page 351 supra]. * * *

* * * Nothing in EPA's Emissions Trading Policy Statement which includes the "bubble" concept suggests that an application will be a basis for relieving a polluter from its previous obligations to meet the NAAQS and the schedules for compliance established in the SIPs and any consent decree. On the contrary, EPA's Policy Statement expressly provides that, "These alternatives do not alter existing air quality requirements."

* * *

* * * Likewise, economic infeasibility is not a proper basis for staying compliance with the Clean Air Act. In *Union Electric Co. v. EPA,* 427 U.S. at 246, 96 S.Ct. at 2520, [page 348 supra], the Court rejected the argument that the Administrator had the authority to disapprove a SIP on the basis of technological or economic infeasibility. * * *

Thus, the district court's order improperly considered Wheeling's economic straits and its recent losses as a basis for extending the compliance requirement beyond the December 31, 1985, deadline. It should be noted in this respect that the original compliance order requiring expenditures for the emission control system was entered in 1979. Wheeling was aware of the need to make the expenditures long before its recent economic problems.

Moreover, as indicated by the legislative history previously referred to, Congress was aware of the financial problems the steel industry was facing, but in enacting SICEA it intended to give the steel companies only a limited time during which they could delay compliance with the Clean Air Act in order to modernize their plants.

The steel companies were required during the "stretch out" period "to make continual progress toward achieving clean air requirements by 1985, and to continue the installation of pollution control technology on all existing sources." Thus, knowing of the financial problems the steel companies were facing, Congress intended that consent decrees entered or modified by SICEA provide for timely installation of pollution control equipment. Wheeling's current financial problems are neither so new or unforeseen as to warrant modifying the consent decree, particularly in the face of clear legislative intent to the contrary.

The district court's Memorandum Opinion also states that "EPA's position would, in all probability, force the closing of the sinter plant." Wheeling concedes before this court that "Operation of the sinter plant is not * * * an essential element of [Wheeling's] steel production facilities." While continued operation of steel facilities may advance a state's economic interest, the Clean Air Act reflects a congressional policy decision that removal of pollutants from the air which endanger the lives and health of the populace is a more compelling public interest. The district court was not authorized to impose its own balancing of policy over that of Congress. In this respect, the language used by the Supreme Court in *TVA v. Hill,* 437 U.S. 153, 98 S.Ct. 2279, 57 L.Ed.2d 117 (1978), where it affirmed an injunction against the operation of the $100 million Tellico Dam because it would lead to the extinction of the snail darter, is instructive:

> Here we are urged to view the Endangered Species Act "reasonably," and hence shape a remedy "that accords with some modicum of common sense and the public weal." * * * But is that our function? We have no expert knowledge on the subject of endangered species, much less do we have a mandate from the people to strike a balance of equities on the side of the Tellico Dam. Congress has spoken in the plainest of words, making it abundantly clear that the balance has been struck in favor of affording endangered species the highest of priorities, thereby adopting a policy which it described as institutionalized caution.

Id. at 194, 98 S.Ct. at 2302. If the courts must defer to Congress' judgment as to the need to preserve the snail darter, surely the district court must defer to Congress' decision to require compliance with the emission limitations no later than December 31, 1985.

Notes

1. The court's strict attitude toward time extensions may be consistent with the statute's policy. Is it also consistent with the enthusiasm about equitable discretion reflected in the *Weinberger* decision? Or is the *Weinberger* holding narrower than some of the language in the opinion might suggest?

2. The Supreme Court revisited the issue of equitable discretion in *Amoco Production Co. v. Village of Gambell, Alaska,* 480 U.S. 531, 107 S.Ct. 1396, 94 L.Ed.2d 542 (1987). *Gambell* involved a grant of oil and gas leases to oil companies. The lease property was offshore, but the effects on Alaskan lands may have required the use of special procedures designed to protect the interests of Alaskan Native landowners. The Court found *Weinberger* controlling because only a procedural violation was involved. It also refused to entertain a presumption that procedural violations constitute irreparable injury justifying a preliminary injunction. The Court did note, however, that if an environmental injury had been likely, the result would probably have been different:

> Environmental injury, by its nature, can seldom be adequately remedied by money damages and is often permanent or at least of long duration, i.e., irreparable. If such injury is sufficiently likely, therefore, the balance of harms will usually favor the issuance of an injunction to protect the environment.

This passage seems to draw back considerably from some of the more open-ended language in *Weinberger.* In *Gambell,* following this passage, the Court stressed that injury to the environment was not likely and that the countervailing interest in oil exploration was not merely a private interest but was itself the goal of another federal statute. On the whole, *Gambell* seems closer in spirit to *TVA v. Hill* than to *Weinberger.* For a discussion of recent developments in this area, see Herrmann, "Injunctions for NEPA Violations: Balancing the Equities," 59 *U.Chi.L.Rev.* 1263 (1992) (student note) (arguing that irreparable harm should be construed to include the increased risk to the environment of allowing a project to continue, including the likelihood that the agency will be unwilling to change course once it has made a substantial investment in a project).

There is currently some dispute about the impact of *Gambell* on NEPA cases. Besides proving a NEPA violation, must the plaintiff in a NEPA case demonstrate a threat to environmental quality to obtain an injunction? Does the lack of an adequate EIS in itself constitute an injury, which should be weighed in the balance when determining whether to issue an injunction? For varying views on these issues, see *Town of Huntington v. Marsh,* 884 F.2d 648 (2d Cir.1989); *Sierra Club v. Marsh,* 872 F.2d 497 (1st Cir.1989); *Northern Cheyenne Tribe v. Hodel,* 851 F.2d 1152 (9th Cir.1988). Does it make any sense to say that (1) Congress mandated the preparation of an adequate EIS before the agency action, but (2) the court has discretion to allow the agency to proceed anyway? Doesn't this essentially mean that the agency is free to disregard NEPA whenever a court thinks that obeying the law is unduly burdensome?

3. The special problems raised by *preliminary injunctions* are explored in the following case.

ADAMS v. VANCE

United States Court of Appeals, District of Columbia Circuit, 1978.
570 F.2d 950.

LEVENTHAL, CIRCUIT JUDGE.

The present controversy is the result of long-standing international concern over the survival of the bowhead whale, *Balaena mysticetus.* Subsistence hunting of the bowhead has been the vital element of a millenia-old Eskimo culture. Such hunting posed no danger to the bowhead during the time when its population was at a natural high level. However, irresponsible commercial whaling in the late nineteenth and early twentieth century drastically reduced the bowhead population. Although the bowhead had been under international protection from commercial whaling for most of the twentieth century, it has failed to proliferate back to its former level. If the bowhead population levels remain low, the species will be vulnerable to extinction by overhunting, oil pollution, or the spontaneous population "crashes" which occur in small populations. Accordingly, with the cooperation of the Eskimos themselves, the United States began steps toward regulation of Eskimo whaling which could protect the bowhead without impairing the unique Eskimo culture.[1]

1. The Secretary of Commerce has power to regulate Eskimo whaling under the   Marine Mammal Protection Act of 1972, 16 U.S.C.A. § 1371(b). Preparation for promul-

Before the United States could complete its domestic efforts at whaling control, the International Whaling Commission (IWC), a regulatory body presently consisting of members from seventeen nations, notified the United States in July, 1977 that it was eliminating the subsistence hunting exemption which had allowed Eskimos to hunt bowheads. The consequences of the IWC action are defined by treaty and statute. Essentially, if the Secretary of State on behalf of the United States objected to the IWC action within 90 days (i.e. by 12:00 G.M.T., October 24, 1977) that IWC action would not become effective against the United States. In the absence of such objection, the IWC action would subject Eskimos who continue to hunt bowheads to criminal prosecution.

The United States prepared an elaborate draft environmental impact statement as a basis for the decision on whether to object, and revised the statement after extensive comment by legal representatives of the Eskimos, Alaskans, environmentalists, scientists, U.S. officials and others. On October 20, the Secretary of State announced that the United States would not object. Instead, he declared he would seek reconsideration of the IWC action at an IWC meeting in December. This course of action was approved by the President.

On October 21, the plaintiffs sued the Secretary of State on behalf of the Eskimos who would lose their freedom to hunt as a result of the failure to object. Plaintiffs noted the long history of statutes and administrative and judicial decisions which clearly recognize Eskimo land, fishing and whaling rights, and claimed the Secretary's decision violated the trust obligation to the Eskimos implicit in those statutes and decisions. They also asserted that the environmental impact statement had failed to analyze important alternatives open to the Secretary. Noting that the deadline for objections was only three days away, plaintiffs asked the District Court to enter forthwith a temporary restraining order that would require the Secretary to file an objection. Such an objection, they contended, would not substantially harm the United States' efforts at international environmental cooperation because the International Whaling Convention of 1946 allows objections to be withdrawn freely any time after they are made.

After a short hearing on the afternoon of October 21, the District Court granted the relief requested, and directed the Secretary to file the objection. The court's order was explicitly premised on its view that "defendants will suffer no substantial harm through the issuance of a temporary restraining order, whereas plaintiffs will suffer the loss of their opportunity to meaningfully present their claims should their application be denied." The Secretary immediately appealed. We heard

---

gation of regulations was proposed last June.

    At present, many whales are struck and wounded or killed without being landed. Regulation of the techniques of whaling which reduced the struck and lost rate might allow the Eskimos to continue to hunt without severe impact on the whale population.

[margin note: Ct of Appeals decision]

oral argument on October 24, a Federal holiday, and entered an order of reversal by 1:00 p.m., E.S.T.

* * *

The District Court treated this application for immediate injunctive relief as an ordinary one. Yet when requested immediate injunctive relief deeply intrudes into the core concerns of the executive branch, a court is "quite wrong in routinely applying to this case the traditional standards governing more orthodox 'stays'." *Sampson v. Murray,* 415 U.S. 61, 83–84, 94 S.Ct. 937, 950, 39 L.Ed.2d 166, 183 (1974). A request for an order directing action by the Secretary of State in foreign affairs plainly constitutes such intrusion. Courts must beware "ignoring the delicacies of diplomatic negotiation, the inevitable bargaining for the best solution of an international conflict, and the scope which in foreign affairs must be allowed to the President," *Mitchell v. Laird,* 159 U.S.App.D.C. 344, 349, 488 F.2d 611, 616 (1973). Courts must take into account that international negotiations have their own distinctive time frames, and must be careful "to avoid a fixing of our government's course" by premature interposition.

This country's interest in regard to foreign affairs and international agreements may depend on the symbolic significance to other countries of various stances and on what is practical with regard to diplomatic interaction and negotiation. Courts are not in a position to exercise a judgment that is fully sensitive to these matters. Accordingly, while we do not determine the justiciability of a request for relief of this kind, we think it clear that if such a request is justiciable, the party seeking this kind of relief would have to make an extraordinarily strong showing to succeed. Plaintiffs here have not made such a showing.

[margin note: test]

In reviewing the District Court's grant of the injunction, we apply the familiar test of *Virginia Petroleum Jobbers Association v. FPC,* 104 U.S.App.D.C. 106, 259 F.2d 921 (1958), as modified by *Washington Metropolitan Area Transit Commission v. Holiday Tours, Inc.,* 182 U.S.App.D.C. 220, 559 F.2d 841 (1977).[10] As to the first prong of that test, the movant's likelihood of success on the merits, there is little dispute that plaintiffs have presented serious questions of law indicating a substantial case on the merits. It is well established that the United States owes trust obligations to native Americans, including Eskimos,

---

10. This test requires the court to consider four factors:

(1) Has the petitioner made a strong showing that it is likely to prevail on the merits of its appeal? Without such a substantial indication of probable success, there would be no justification for the court's intrusion into the ordinary processes of administration and judicial review.

(2) Has the petitioner shown that without such relief, it will be irreparably injured? * * *

(3) Would the issuance of a stay substantially harm other parties interested in the proceedings? * * *

(4) Where lies the public interest? * * *

Holiday Tours, 182 U.S.App.D.C. at 222, 559 F.2d at 843.

* * *

[margin notes: is my injury greater than theirs; maybe included or ignored depending on case; on all civil cases]

which require administrators to give the Eskimos' interests considerable weight in many decisions. The precise application of that principle to this suit presents a serious question. The Eskimo claim that the environmental impact statement failed to consider possible alternatives to the proposed action may also raise a serious issue.

Accordingly, under the *Holiday Tours* test, we may assume that if the case did not touch on any extraordinary considerations, and if the balance of equitable factors favored an injunction which would merely preserve the status quo, injunctive relief would be proper. However, as previously noted, there are special considerations here that require plaintiffs to make an exceptionally strong showing on the relevant factors. Moreover, the order here would not merely be preservative of the status quo.

The District Court misconceived entry of a formal objection to the IWC action here as one which could easily be reversed. The United States has been active in persuading other countries to abide by the restrictions of the whaling agreement, notwithstanding severe impact on their domestic concerns. No other nation has entered an objection to an IWC action since 1973, and the symbolic impact of the United States being the first nation to break that pattern was assessed by cognizant U.S. officials and others as likely to be quite grave. * * * We may presume that an objection to an IWC action which was promptly withdrawn by the United States would have less impact than one which was allowed to stay in effect. Yet it was clear error for the District Court to find that an objection, provisional or otherwise, would not substantially endanger the interests of the United States.

Furthermore, while the ban on whaling may indeed cause irreparable injury to the Eskimos, that injury is by no means certain. Since the fall whaling season is almost over, the IWC's elimination of the exemption allowing Eskimo whaling will have little or no effect until next spring. At an IWC meeting in December 1977, well before the spring whaling season, the U.S. will ask the IWC to reconsider its action, considering the shared concern of all nations for unique native cultures and the United States' steps toward domestic regulation of whaling. If efforts in December come to naught, the Eskimos will be injured by the loss of whaling for one year, but their contingent reserves and assistance from the United States as trustee can mitigate the injury for that year. It would remain open to the United States to object to the quota for bowhead whaling next June, thereby limiting the injury to the Eskimos to a single year. In these ways, the Secretary's refusal to object leaves open avenues for mitigation or complete relief.

Notes

1. After the Court of Appeals had entered its order of reversal, the IWC changed its position to permit subsistence hunting by Alaskan natives. See *Adams v. Vance,* 570 F.2d 950, 952 (D.C.Cir.1978).

2. The propriety of a preliminary injunction is a frequently litigated issue in environmental cases. See, e.g., *Quince Orchard Valley Citizens Ass'n, Inc. v. Hodel,* 872 F.2d 75 (4th Cir.1989); *Cuomo v. United States NRC,* 772 F.2d 972 (D.C.Cir.1985); *Lakeshore Terminal & Pipeline Co. v. Defense Fund Supply Center,* 777 F.2d 1171 (6th Cir.1985); *National Wildlife Federation v. Coston,* 773 F.2d 1513 (9th Cir.1985). Were the plaintiffs in *TVA v. Hill* entitled to a preliminary injunction in their favor to halt further construction of the dam? How, if at all, does this question differ from that decided by the Supreme Court in that case?

Judge Posner has observed that because judicial review of an administrative action is based on the record before the agency, there is no need for a trial. Hence, he argued, an application for a preliminary injunction should be treated as a request for a final injunction, and the court should decide the case on the merits rather than applying the traditional test for a preliminary injunction. Judge Posner then proceeded to discuss some possible exceptions, including complex cases in which the judge cannot review the record in time to prevent irreparable injury, the record is incomplete, or an evidentiary hearing is available. See *Cronin v. U.S. Dept. of Agriculture,* 919 F.2d 439 (7th Cir.1990).

3. Does the "foreign affairs" argument made in *Adams v. Vance* apply equally to all "national security" matters? What are the limits to the court's rationale?

4. Most of a trial court's decisions cannot be appealed until a final judgment has been entered in the case. Preliminary injunctions are an exception to this rule, as the main case indicates. This exception can lead to intricate procedural problems, as parties attempt to use it as a means of obtaining appellate court consideration of otherwise nonappealable issues. See, e.g., *Allegheny County Sanitary Authority v. EPA,* 732 F.2d 1167 (3d Cir.1984).

C. CIVIL LIABILITY UNDER RCRA AND CERCLA

1. LIABILITY UNDER THE "IMMINENT HAZARD" PROVISIONS OF RCRA

Section 7003 of RCRA, as amended in 1984, provides in part as follows:

> Notwithstanding any other provision of this chapter, upon receipt of evidence that the *past or present* handling, storage, treatment, transportation or disposal of any solid waste or hazardous waste *may present* an *imminent and substantial endangerment* to health or the environment, the Administrator may bring suit on behalf of the United States in the appropriate district court against any person (including any past or present generator, past or present transporter, or past or present owner or operator of a treatment, storage, or disposal facility) who has *contributed* or who is contributing to such handling, storage, treatment, transportation or disposal to restrain such person from such handling, storage, treatment,

transportation, or disposal, to order such person to take such other action as may be necessary, or both. [Emphasis added]

As the following decision indicates, the courts have given an expansive interpretation to § 7003's provisions regarding both liability and remedies.

UNITED STATES v. WASTE INDUSTRIES, INC.

United States Court of Appeals, Fourth Circuit, 1984.
734 F.2d 159.

SPROUSE, CIRCUIT JUDGE:

After the Environmental Protection Agency (EPA) investigated the Flemington landfill waste disposal site in New Hanover County, North Carolina (the Flemington landfill) for possible water pollution in the surrounding area, the United States of America for the Administrator of the EPA initiated this action against Waste Industries, Inc.; Waste Industries of New Hanover County, Inc.; the New Hanover County Board of Commissioners; and the individual owner-lessors of land used for the Flemington landfill (all defendants will be referred to collectively as the landfill group). The EPA demanded affirmative action by the landfill group under section 7003 of [RCRA] to abate alleged threats to public health and the environment posed by hazardous chemicals leaking from the Flemington landfill, to monitor the area for further contamination, to reimburse the EPA for money spent on the area, and to provide residents with a permanent potable water supply. The district court granted the landfill group's motion to dismiss under Federal Rule of Civil Procedure 12(b)(6) for failure to state a cause of action and the EPA brought this appeal. We reverse.

I

* * *

[In 1972] the County Board granted Waste Industries, Inc. and Waste Industries of New Hanover County, Inc. (referred to collectively as Waste Industries) an exclusive license to dispose of solid waste generated in the County.

* * *

Before Waste Industries began operating the landfill, the residents of the Flemington community had high quality groundwater. Flemington area residents first noticed a decline in water quality in autumn 1977, when their water became foul in color, taste, and smell. Some residents suffered illnesses or side effects such as blisters, boils, and stomach distress they attribute to their use of well water. * * *

* * *

* * * Analysis of Flemington area groundwater samples taken by the EPA revealed a large number of toxic, organic, and inorganic contaminants, including known carcinogens, resulting from improper

disposal of waste at the Flemington landfill. The contaminants found beneath the landfill and in residential wells include tetrachloroethylene, benzene, trichloroethylene; 1, 2–dichloroethane; vinyl chloride, methylene chloride, and lead. These chemicals, migrating from the Flemington landfill, have been detected in residential wells at levels sufficient to affect adversely human health and the environment. * * *

* * * EPA warned many local residents that continued use of their wells for any purpose would endanger their health, and informed the County that * * * water tanks were needed to meet local residents' needs. The EPA helped the County obtain commitments for three-quarters of the funds needed to install a permanent water system in the Flemington community—half from the federal government and one-quarter from the state of North Carolina. * * * A water system funded with federal, state, and local money is now in operation.

The new water system, however, has not solved the problem of escaping waste. As precipitation infiltrates the landfill waste and transports contaminants through permeable soil, the contaminants reach the local aquifer and move laterally through the aquifer in the direction of groundwater flow to the south and east. Tests indicate that the process of leaching and migration of contaminants will continue indefinitely unless remedial action is taken.

II

The EPA, in its initial complaint, requested preliminary and permanent injunctive relief requiring the appropriate parties: (1) to supply affected residents with a permanent and potable source of water; (2) to develop and implement a plan to prevent further contamination; (3) to restore the groundwater; (4) to monitor the area for further contaminations; and (5) to reimburse the EPA for money spent in connection with the Flemington landfill. The EPA later withdrew its request for preliminary relief when the federal, state, and local governments, as described above, jointly funded the installation of a permanent safe water supply, but it continued to demand in its complaint a plan to prevent further contamination, the restoration of groundwater, site monitoring, and reimbursement.

* * *

III

Section 7003 of the Act provides that [n]otwithstanding any other provision of this chapter, upon receipt of evidence that the handling, storage, treatment, transportation or disposal of any solid waste or hazardous waste may present an imminent and substantial endangerment to health or the environment, the Administrator may bring suit on behalf of the United States in the appropriate District Court to immediately restrain any person contributing to such handling, storage, treatment, transportation or disposal to stop such handling, storage, treatment, transportation, or disposal or to take such other actions as may be necessary.

The landfill group contends, and the district court held, that this section does not authorize an action to correct hazardous conditions because it only regulates the wastes themselves before or as they are produced, not the conditions they later create. The fallacy of that contention is demonstrated by the indication of Congress that section 7003 remedies exist apart from the other provisions in the Act's structure. In addition, section 7003 stands apart from the other sections of the Act defining the EPA's regulatory authority. The regulatory scheme for hazardous wastes appears in subtitle C of the Act; the scheme for solid wastes, in subtitle D. In contrast, section 7003 appears in subtitle G, and it is designed to deal with situations in which the regulatory schemes break down or have been circumvented.

* * *

The operative language of section 7003 authorizes the administrator to bring an action against any person contributing to the alleged disposal to stop such disposal "*or* to take such other action as may be necessary." "Disposal" is defined in 42 U.S.C. § 6903(3) as follows:

> The term "disposal" means the discharge, deposit, injection, dumping, spilling, leaking, or placing of any solid waste or hazardous waste into or on any land or water so that such solid waste or hazardous waste or any constituent thereof may enter the environment or be emitted into the air or discharged into any waters, including ground waters.

The inclusion of "leaking" as one of the diverse definitional components of "disposal" demonstrates that Congress intended "disposal" to have a range of meanings, including conduct, a physical state, and an occurrence. Discharging, dumping, and injection (conduct), hazardous waste reposing (a physical state) and movement of the waste after it has been placed in a state of repose (an occurrence) are all encompassed in the broad definition of disposal. "Leaking" ordinarily occurs when landfills are not constructed soundly or when drums and tank trucks filled with waste materials corrode, rust, or rot. Thus "leaking" is an occurrence included in the meaning of "disposal."

* * *

IV

The landfill group argues that section 7003 was designed to control pollution only in emergency situations. The district court agreed, concluding that it was similar to other statutes designed by Congress solely to eliminate emergency problems. We find this position unsupportable, for the section's language stands in contrast to "emergency" type statutes. The language of section 7003 demonstrates that Congress contemplated circumstances in which the disposal of hazardous waste "*may present* an imminent and substantial endangerment" (emphasis added); therefore, the section's application is not specifically limited to an "emergency."

The Third Circuit, in its recent interpretation of the Act's section 7003, reached the same conclusion. It described section 7003 as having "enhanced the courts' traditional equitable powers by authorizing the issuance of injunctions when there is but a risk of harm, a more lenient standard than the traditional requirement of threatened irreparable harm." *United States v. Price,* 688 F.2d 204, 211 (3d Cir.1982). Thus the Third Circuit's interpretation of section 7003, far from limiting its application to emergency situations, gave full effect to this expansion of the courts' traditional powers.

* * *

VI

The landfill group next contends, and the district court held, that section 7003 is solely jurisdictional, authorizing remedies or proceedings, not creating liabilities. Those liabilities, in this view, come only from the earlier, regulatory, portions of the Act. The district court took this view of the section for various reasons, some of which we have already discussed and discarded, including the location of section 7003 within the Act and its broad wording. Again, we cannot agree.

Congress intended section 7003 to function both as a jurisdictional basis and a source of substantive liability. The Eckhardt Report states:

§ 7003 is essentially a codification of the common law public nuisance * * *.

However, § 7003 should not be construed solely with respect to the common law. Some terms and concepts, such as persons "contributing to" disposal resulting in a substantial endangerment, are meant to be more liberal than their common law counterparts.

Eckhardt Report at 31. Congress's intent, then, was to establish a standard of liability by incorporating and expanding upon the common law.

The landfill group observes that some courts have held, by analogy to *City of Milwaukee v. Illinois,* 451 U.S. 304, 101 S.Ct. 1784, 68 L.Ed.2d 114 (1981), that the regulatory provisions of the Act and CERCLA are the sole source of substantive standards in the field of solid and hazardous waste disposal. If true, this would leave no room for the application of common-law principles. * * * *City of Milwaukee,* however, disapproved only of the *courts'* use of federal common law as a source for setting regulatory standards independent of those established by a comprehensive statutory scheme. The Court did not assail *Congress's* prerogative to empower the courts to apply common-law principles as part of an ongoing regulatory scheme.

* * *

VIII

Contrary to the district court holding, we conclude on the peculiar facts of this case that permanent mandatory injunctive relief is an appropriate remedy. The landfill group argues that no emergency exists and that CERCLA provides an adequate remedy at law. The EPA need not prove that an emergency exists to prevail under section 7003, only that the circumstances may present an imminent and substantial endangerment. It has been alleged that an imminent and substantial endangerment exists. We make no finding on whether the EPA will be able to meet its burden at trial. Since this case came to us in the posture of an appeal from the grant of a Rule 12(b)(6) motion to dismiss, we have viewed all the evidence in the light most favorable to the party opposing the motion, the EPA.

Finally, the landfill group contends that an injunction cannot issue because CERCLA provides an adequate remedy at law. This lawsuit was not brought in common-law equity, however, but pursuant to an express statutory command giving the EPA an injunctive remedy. Congress chose to enhance the courts' traditional equitable powers in order to protect the public and the environment. *United States v. Price,* 688 F.2d at 211. Any other decision would, in effect, interpret CERCLA as repealing the Act—a result obviously not intended by Congress.

Notes

1. Is the decision of the court of appeals consistent with *Weinberger v. Romero–Barcelo?* Is it relevant that the court of appeals said that EPA "need not prove that an emergency exists"?

2. What do you think of the court's interpretation of RCRA's definition of "disposal"? Do you agree that the inclusion of "leaking" in the definition demonstrates that "disposal" encompasses not only "conduct" (discharging, depositing, injecting, dumping, spilling, placing) but also "a physical state, and an occurrence?"

Inclusion of "leaking" in RCRA's definition of "disposal"—which definition is incorporated by reference into CERCLA at § 101(29)—has given rise to the "passive migration" issue under both statutes. For example, if A owned a site and disposed of hazardous wastes there, then sold it to B, who resold it to C, is B liable as a *disposer* (to C, or to a neighbor whose land has become contaminated by the wastes, or upon suit by EPA) if B did nothing to contribute to the problem of the wastes or their migration other than by being a purely passive owner while the wastes were spreading through the soil? In *ABB Industrial Systems, Inc. v. Prime Technology, Inc.,* 120 F.3d 351 (2d Cir.1997), the court held that B was not liable to C, either as a "contributor" under RCRA § 7002(a)(1)(B) or as a person "who at the time of disposal ... owned or operated" the site, under CERCLA § 107(a)(2).

3. Once it is determined by a court or agreed by the parties that a disposal site presents an "imminent and substantial endangerment to health or the environment" under section 7003, a program should be developed for removal of the hazardous materials or containment of the threat which they pose. Frequently such programs are technologically complex as well as

extremely costly. For an illustrative and detailed example of a court-approved cleanup and containment agreement, see *United States v. Hooker Chemicals & Plastics Corp.*, 540 F.Supp. 1067 (W.D.N.Y.1982), discussed in Trilling, "Painstaking Negotiation Leads to Landmark Court Order Approving Settlement Agreement in Hyde Park Hazardous Waste Cleanup Litigation," 12 *ELR* 15013 (1982).

UNITED STATES v. NORTHEASTERN PHARMACEUTICAL & CHEMICAL CO., INC.

United States Court of Appeals, Eighth Circuit, 1986.
810 F.2d 726, cert. denied 484 U.S. 848, 108 S.Ct. 146, 98 L.Ed.2d 102 (1987).

McMILLIAN, CIRCUIT JUDGE:

I. FACTS

* * * In 1974 [NEPACCO's] corporate assets were liquidated, and the proceeds were used to pay corporate debts and then distributed to the shareholders. Michaels formed NEPACCO, was a major shareholder, and was its president. Lee was NEPACCO's vice-president, the supervisor of its manufacturing plant located in Verona, Missouri, and also a shareholder. Mills was employed as shift supervisor at NEPACCO's Verona plant.

From April 1970 to January 1972 NEPACCO manufactured the disinfectant hexachlorophene at its Verona plant. NEPACCO leased the plant from Hoffman–Taff, Inc.; Syntex Agribusiness, Inc. (Syntex), is the successor to Hoffman–Taff. Michaels and Lee knew that NEPACCO's manufacturing process produced various hazardous and toxic by-products, including 2,4,5–trichlorophenol (TCP), 2,3,7,8–tetrachlorodibenzo-p-dioxin (TCDD or dioxin), and toluene. The waste by-products were pumped into a holding tank which was periodically emptied by waste haulers. Occasionally, however, excess waste by-products were sealed in 55–gallon drums and then stored at the plant.

In July 1971 Mills approached NEPACCO plant manager Bill Ray with a proposal to dispose of the waste-filled 55–gallon drums on a farm owned by James Denney located about seven miles south of Verona. Ray visited the Denney farm and discussed the proposal with Lee; Lee approved the use of Mills' services and the Denney farm as a disposal site. In mid-July 1971 Mills and Gerald Lechner dumped approximately 85 of the 55–gallon drums into a large trench on the Denney farm * * *.

* * * During April 1980 the EPA conducted an on-site investigation, exposed and sampled 13 of the 55–gallon drums, which were found to be badly deteriorated, and took water and soil samples. The samples were found to contain "alarmingly" high concentrations of dioxin, TCP and toluene.

* * * In August 1980 the government filed its initial complaint against NEPACCO, the generator of the hazardous substances; Michaels and Lee, the corporate officers responsible for arranging for the disposal

of the hazardous substances; Mills, the transporter of the hazardous substances; and Syntex, the owner and lessor of the Verona plant, seeking injunctive relief and reimbursement of response costs pursuant to RCRA § 7003 * * *.

In the meantime the EPA had been negotiating with Syntex about Syntex's liability for cleanup of the Denney farm site. In September 1980 the government and Syntex entered into a settlement and consent decree. Pursuant to the terms of the settlement, Syntex would pay $100,000 of the government's response costs and handle the removal, storage and permanent disposal of the hazardous substances from the Denney farm site. The EPA approved Syntex's proposed cleanup plan, and in June 1981 Syntex began excavation of the trench. In November 1981 the site was closed. The 55–gallon drums are now stored in a specially constructed concrete bunker on the Denney farm. The drums as stored do not present an imminent and substantial endangerment to health or the environment; however, no plan for permanent disposal has been developed, and the site will continue to require testing and monitoring in the future.

In August 1982 the government filed an amended complaint adding counts for relief pursuant to CERCLA §§ 104, 106, 107 (counts II and III). CERCLA was enacted after the filing of the initial complaint. * * * In September 1983 the district court denied the defense demand for a jury trial, holding the government's request for recovery of its response costs was comparable to restitution and thus an equitable remedy. The trial was conducted during October 1983. * * *

[The portions of the court's opinion dealing with CERCLA appear at page 634 infra.]

* * *

As alternative basis for recovery of the response costs incurred before December 11, 1980, the government argues on cross-appeal that it can also recover its response costs pursuant to RCRA § 7003(a). The district court did not reach the recovery issue because it held that under RCRA § 7003(a) (prior to 1984 amendments discussed below), proof of fault or negligence was required in order to impose liability upon past off-site generators and transporters. Because the government did not allege or prove negligence, the district court found no liability * * *. The government argues that the standard of liability under RCRA § 7003(a), as initially enacted and as amended in 1984, is strict liability, not negligence, and that liability under RCRA can be imposed even though the acts of disposal occurred before RCRA became effective in 1976. We agree.

* * *

The critical issue is the meaning of the phrase "contributing to." Before its amendment in 1984, RCRA § 7003(a), imposed liability upon any person "contributing to" "the handling, storage, treatment, transportation or disposal of any solid or hazardous waste" that "may present an imminent and substantial endangerment to health or the environment." * * *

* * * As amended in 1984, RCRA § 7003(a) (new language underlined; deleted language in brackets), now provides in pertinent part:

> Notwithstanding any other provision of this chapter, upon receipt of evidence that the *past or present* handling, storage, treatment, transportation or disposal of any solid waste or hazardous waste may present an imminent and substantial endangerment to health or the environment, the Administrator may bring suit on behalf of the United States in the appropriate district court [to immediately restrain any person] *against any person (including any past or present generator, past or present transporter, or past or present owner or operator of a treatment, storage, or disposal facility) who has contributed or who is* contributing to such handling, storage, treatment, transportation or disposal [to stop] *to restrain such person from* such handling, storage, treatment, transportation, or disposal [or to take such other action as may be necessary], *to order such person to take such other action as may be necessary, or both.*

* * *

* * * From the legislative history of the 1984 amendments, it is clear that Congress intended RCRA § 7003(a), as initially enacted and as amended, to impose liability without fault or negligence and to apply to the present conditions resulting from past activities. In other words, RCRA § 7003(a), as initially enacted and as amended, applies to past non-negligent off-site generators like NEPACCO and to non-negligent past transporters like Mills.

Appellants argue, however, that the 1984 amendments should not be applied to them because the 1984 amendments are not merely "clarifying" amendments but instead substantively changed the existing law. We disagree. First, Congress itself expressly characterized the 1984 amendments as "clarifying" amendments. Second, as part of the legislative history of the 1984 amendments, Congress expressly stated what its intention had been when it initially passed the RCRA in 1976, even though the 1976 legislative history contained no specific discussion of the standard and scope of liability of § 7003(a). * * * Thus, by passing the 1984 amendments the 98th Congress made clear that the intention of the 94th Congress in enacting the RCRA in 1976 had been to impose liability upon past non-negligent off-site generators and transporters of hazardous waste.

* * *

In summary, we hold that RCRA § 7003(a), as initially enacted and as clarified by the 1984 amendments, imposes strict liability upon past off-site generators of hazardous waste and upon past transporters of hazardous waste. * * *

* * *

The government argues * * * that Lee and Michaels can be held individually liable as "contributors" under RCRA § 7003(a). For the reasons discussed below, we agree with the government's liability arguments.

* * *

RCRA § 7003(a) imposes strict liability upon "any person" who is contributing or who has contributed to the disposal of hazardous substances that may present an imminent and substantial endangerment to health or the environment. As defined by statute, the term "person" includes both individuals and corporations and does not exclude corporate officers and employees. * * * [I]mposing liability upon only the corporation, but not those corporate officers and employees who actually make corporate decisions, would be inconsistent with Congress' intent to impose liability upon the persons who are involved in the handling and disposal of hazardous substances.

* * *

We hold Lee and Michaels are individually liable as "contributors" under RCRA § 7003(a), 42 U.S.C.A. § 6973(a). Lee actually participated in the conduct that violated RCRA; he personally arranged for the transportation and disposal of hazardous substances that presented an imminent and substantial endangerment to health and the environment. Unlike Lee, Michaels was not personally involved in the actual decision to transport and dispose of the hazardous substances. As NEPACCO's corporate president and as a major NEPACCO shareholder, however, Michaels was the individual in charge of and directly responsible for all of NEPACCO's operations, including those at the Verona plant, and he had the ultimate authority to control the disposal of NEPACCO's hazardous substances. Cf. *New York v. Shore Realty Corp.*, 759 F.2d at 1052–53 (shareholder-manager held liable under CERCLA).

* * *

Appellants next argue the district court erred in denying their demand for a jury trial because the government's action for recovery of its response costs under CERCLA and RCRA was essentially a claim for legal damages. We disagree. When the government seeks recovery of its response costs under CERCLA or its abatement costs under RCRA, it is in effect seeking equitable relief in the form of restitution or reimbursement of the costs it expended in order to respond to the health and environmental danger presented by hazardous substances.

Notes

1. What do you think of the court's looking to the legislative history of the 1984 "clarifying" amendments to RCRA for guidance concerning the intended meaning of the original 1976 statute?

2. Is it fair to apply section 7003 to "past [i.e., pre–1976] non-negligent off-site generators and transporters" who acted lawfully at the time they

"contributed" to disposal of the hazardous substances? Do you understand the court's rationale for concluding that this does not constitute "retroactive" application of RCRA? Would it be a denial of due process to apply the statute retroactively?

In *Eastern Enterprises v. Apfel*, ___ U.S. ___, 118 S.Ct. 2131, 141 L.Ed.2d 451 (1998), the Supreme Court found a federal law that imposed on a coal mining company a "severe retroactive liability" to pay health benefits for its former employees to be an unconstitutional "taking" of private property.

3.   How important do you think it is for liability under section 7003 to extend to corporate officers and employees, as well as to the corporation itself?

4.   Issues like those in notes 2 and 3 also arise in connection with CERCLA. Although much of the thrust of RCRA is prospective—directed at regulation of future waste treatment and disposal—section 7003 clearly is retrospective also. Thus it overlaps with CERCLA, which is concerned mainly with cleanups of past disposal sites. It is common for public and private plaintiffs in these kinds of cases to rely on both RCRA and CERCLA.

———

Section 7002 of RCRA authorizes citizen suits. These suits can be brought against any person alleged to be in violation of a RCRA permit or standard, but also against any person "who has contributed or who is contributing to the past or present handling, storage, treatment, transportation, or disposal of any solid or hazardous wastes which may present an imminent and substantial endangerment to health or the environment." The similarity to § 7003 is evident. The following article explores various aspects of the application of § 7002.

STOP

BABICH, "RCRA IMMINENT HAZARD AUTHORITY: A POWERFUL TOOL FOR BUSINESSES, GOVERNMENTS, AND CITIZEN ENFORCERS"[a]

24 *Environmental Law Reporter* 10122, 10122–10136 (1994).

Federal antipollution laws generally provide for only two kinds of citizen enforcement suits: (1) suits against persons who are in violation of statutory provisions, regulations, orders, or permits and (2) suits against EPA for failing to discharge mandatory duties, e.g., failing to promulgate regulations by statutory deadlines. RCRA provides these causes of action in § 7002(a)(1)(A) and (a)(2), respectively. RCRA is unique, however, in providing for a third type of citizen enforcement suit to abate potential imminent hazards.

* * *

RCRA imminent hazard authority is a federal statutory counterpart to the common law of public nuisance. * * *

To be entitled to relief under § 7002(a)(1)(B), a plaintiff must prove (1) the existence of "discarded material," i.e., waste, within the meaning of § 1004(27); (2) that the defendant contributes or contributed to handling, storage, treatment, transportation, or disposal of the waste; and (3) that the situation may present an eventual, significant risk to public health or the environment.

The *only* unique aspect of RCRA's imminent hazard provision is that it provides a cause of action for private and other non-EPA parties. For years, all the major federal antipollution laws have allowed EPA to seek court injunctions under similarly worded, residual imminent hazard provisions *in addition* to regulatory provisions. With its 1984 amendments to RCRA, Congress simply broadened RCRA imminent hazard authority to allow "any person" to seek injunctive relief for potential endangerments. Because the language of § 7002(a)(1)(B) adopts the same standards as EPA's imminent hazard authorities, it is generally subject to the same judicial interpretation. Thus, liability under § 7002(a)(1)(B) is strict, joint, several, and retroactive.

In a variety of contexts, the courts have interpreted the phrase "may present an imminent and substantial endangerment" to refer to a significant, potential risk of eventual environmental harm. This interpretation has carried over to § 7002(a)(1)(B) cases. * * *

* * *

As is generally the case in citizen enforcement lawsuits under antipollution laws, RCRA authorizes awards of litigation costs, including attorneys fees and expert witness fees, to the substantially prevailing party. RCRA § 7002(a) also empowers courts to issue injunctions

> to restrain any person who has contributed or who is contributing to the past or present handling, storage, treatment, transportation, or disposal of any solid or hazardous waste referred to in paragraph (1)(B), [or] to order such person to take *such other action as may be necessary....*

* * *

To date, the courts generally have not permitted recovery of response costs in § 7002(a)(1)(B) actions. Whether this trend will continue, however, is open to question. Federal courts have ruled that restitution of costs *is* an appropriate remedy under RCRA § 7003, EPA's imminent hazard provision. * * * As a general rule—absent express congressional instructions to the contrary—statutes that invoke the equitable jurisdiction of the courts are presumed to empower the courts to exercise their full equitable powers, which include the power to order restitution in appropriate cases. Given the current state of the case law, however, potential plaintiffs would be well-advised to ensure compliance with the national contingency plan, so that they may recover their past costs under CERCLA, while using RCRA § 7002(a)(1)(B) to obtain injunctive relief and litigation costs.

RCRA itself is not limited to any particular media. RCRA regulates emissions to air, water, and soil. Moreover, because § 7002(a)(1)(B) uses the statutory definitions of solid and hazardous waste, the scope of the section's imminent hazard authority reaches well beyond RCRA's Subtitle C regulatory program. Thus, EPA has recognized that RCRA's imminent hazard authority "has no media limitation"—and may be used to address releases to land, water, or air. * * *

RCRA's imminent hazard provision does not regulate or prohibit any particular conduct; instead, like CERCLA § 107, it is primarily a liability provision directed at endangerments that persist despite other environmental regulations. Thus, no allegation of a statutory or regulatory violation is needed to support an imminent hazard lawsuit. * * *

* * *

[F]rom the perspective of the regulated community it is nerve-racking to be subject to a liability provision that is not bound by a defined set of regulations or definitions. On the other hand, the open-ended nature of provisions like § 7002(a)(1)(B) helps fuel private waste minimization efforts which, ultimately, may be a more effective check on pollution than traditional, command-and-control government regulation.

Over time, many members of the regulated community may find § 7002(a)(1)(B)'s disadvantages outweighed by the section's usefulness in shifting responsibility for environmental investigations and cleanups to more culpable parties. If a company owns property that an upgradient neighbor has contaminated or is contaminating with chemicals, options presented by other causes of action are limited. CERCLA is a fine vehicle for recovering past response costs or obtaining declaratory relief, but only if the plaintiff has complied substantially with a fairly detailed set of federal regulations (the national contingency plan), and only if the chemicals at issue meet CERCLA's definition of hazardous substance. More importantly, CERCLA fails to provide for injunctions for private parties, except in suits to enforce site-specific standards that are already in effect, e.g., EPA § 106 orders. The Oil Pollution Act is useful only to address "incidents" that occurred after August 18, 1990, and only for oil pollutants that are exempt from CERCLA. A common-law action may be attractive in theory but, in some jurisdictions, state judges lack the resources to give adequate consideration to the extensive motion practice that environmental lawyers typically use to narrow complex cases. Moreover, as noted above, § 7002(a)(1)(B) allows plaintiffs to recover their attorneys fees, an advantage seldom enjoyed at common law and not necessarily provided by CERCLA.

Note

The Babich article suggested that private plaintiffs might be able to recover response costs under § 7002 (a)(1)(B) of RCRA. In *Meghrig v. KFC Western, Inc.,* 516 U.S. 479, 116 S.Ct. 1251, 134 L.Ed.2d 121 (1996), the court of appeals had held that § 7002 (a)(1)(B) did authorize a private plaintiff to seek restitution for cleanup costs, and that the "imminent and substantial endangerment" need not still exist when the suit was filed. However, the Supreme Court reversed, holding that RCRA's citizen suit provision "is not directed at providing compensation for past cleanup efforts." The Court noted that CERCLA expressly permits recovery of response costs by "any person," indicating that Congress "knew how to provide for the recovery of cleanup costs and that the language used to define the remedies under RCRA does not provide that remedy." The Court also emphasized that the RCRA provision permits a private party to bring suit only upon a showing that the solid or hazardous waste at issue "may present" an imminent and substantial endangerment, "quite clearly exclud[ing] waste that no longer presents such a danger."

For a critique of *Meghrig* and an analysis of its practical consequences, see Jerome Organ, "Advice for Owners of Contaminated Land after *Meghrig v. KFC Western, Inc.,*" 26 *Envt'l L. Rptr.* 10582 (1996).

2. Liability Under CERCLA

U.S. COUNCIL ON ENVIRONMENTAL QUALITY, ENVIRONMENTAL QUALITY 1981: 12TH ANNUAL REPORT

99–101 (1981).

In December of 1980, the Comprehensive Environmental Response, Compensation, and Liability Act of 1980 (CERCLA), was signed into law. The goals of the legislation are to eliminate the threats from uncontrolled hazardous waste sites and to remove hazardous substance threats to public health and the environment in a cost-effective manner.

The act has four basic elements. First, it establishes an information-gathering and analysis system which will enable federal and state governments to characterize chemical dump site problems more accurately and to develop priorities for their investigation and response. Owners of hazardous waste sites were required to notify EPA by June 9, 1981, of the nature of the wastes buried at their sites. This notification data will help form the basis for a national list of uncontrolled sites to be used in planning appropriate responses.

Second, the act establishes federal authority to respond to hazardous substance emergencies and to clean up leaking chemical dump sites. Federal response actions are limited to cases in which the responsible party either cannot be found or does not take the required actions. The *← it is broader in practice* legislation mandates the revision of the National Contingency Plan currently published under Section 311 of the Clean Water Act to serve as a framework for such response actions.

Third, the act creates a hazardous substance response trust fund to pay for the removal, remedy, and cleanup of released hazardous substances and hazardous waste sites. * * * Most of the total * * * will be raised by an industry-based tax on manufacturers of petrochemical feedstocks and toxic organic chemicals, and importers of crude oil. The remaining portion * * * will come from general revenues.

Fourth, the act makes those persons responsible for hazardous substance release liable for cleanup and restitution costs. Thus, it creates a strong incentive both for prevention of releases and voluntary cleanup of releases by responsible parties. Furthermore, it replenishes the fund to assure that adequate response capability is available to mitigate environmental emergencies in the future.

CERCLA identifies two categories of federal response to releases of hazardous substances: removal activities (emergency response) and remedial activities (long-term solution). For a site or spill releasing hazardous substances into the environment, a preliminary assessment is made to determine the source and nature of the problem, the existence of an identifiable responsible party, and the appropriate type of response.

During the 1981 fiscal year, EPA responded to 33 emergency removal situations * * *.

In the remedial action category, EPA has compiled a list of 115 top priority sites that are targeted for Superfund action, i.e., enforcement action and/or federally financed cleanup. These sites will also be candidates for inclusion on the list of * * * national priority "response targets" that the Superfund law requires EPA to identify. * * *

The guiding policy behind these efforts is derived from CERCLA itself; private party cleanup, either voluntary or through enforcement action, is the preferred approach, but federally financed cleanup will be implemented when states and the federal government determine it is appropriate. * * *

* * *

A cornerstone of the CERCLA implementation program is the negotiation of cooperative agreements with the states under which they will take the lead responsibility for cleaning up hazardous waste sites. * * *

Where a responsible party is involved in the release of a hazardous substance, EPA works closely and expeditiously with the states to effect an adequate cleanup by that party. Where the responsible party cannot initially be found or is unable to provide cleanup measures, the Fund can be used to clean up and later recover the costs from the responsible party. In other cases the states, or EPA in consultation with the Department of Justice, will negotiate agreements on the level of cleanup appropriate at a site.

Note on CERCLA Implementation

What "hazardous substances" does CERCLA cover? Section 101(14), which defines the term, incorporates by reference the substances designated as hazardous under section 112 of the Clean Air Act, sections 311(b)(2)(A) and 307(a) of the Clean Water Act, section 3001 of RCRA, and section 7 of TSCA. The term does *not* include *petroleum*; thus CERCLA is not applicable to oil spills, though it may apply to spills of oil contaminated with other hazardous substances. *United States v. Mexico Feed & Seed Co.*, 980 F.2d 478 (8th Cir.1992). For a discussion of statutes which cover oil spills generally, see pages 797–806 infra.

EPA published its original section 105 *National Contingency Plan* (NCP) under court order in 1982. 47 Fed.Reg. 31180 (July 16, 1982). The plan governs the use of superfund monies in responding to hazardous substance spills and waste sites; it provides for determination of appropriate levels of response in individual situations, and for the establishment of priorities among spills and sites. The most recent major revisions to the plan were promulgated by EPA in 1990, 55 Fed.Reg. 8666 (Mar. 8, 1990). The plan appears at 40 CFR Part 300.

Section 101(23) and (24) of CERCLA defines two general types of responses to releases or threats of releases of hazardous substances. *"Removal"* means the short-term cleanup of released substances, usually from the surface of the ground, or necessary actions in cases of threats of releases. *"Remedial action"* means long-term actions "consistent with permanent remedy taken instead of or in addition to removal actions * * *." Section 104 authorizes the President to order such responses—consistent with the National Contingency Plan, and subject to certain conditions—when a release or threatened release "may present an imminent and substantial danger to the public health or welfare."

In February 1998 the *National Priorities List* (NPL) of hazardous waste sites eligible for long term remedial action under CERCLA included 1,350 sites. 28 *Envir.Rep.* 2114 (1998).

There has been controversy over the standards to be applied by EPA in determining whether to include a particular site on the NPL. In several cases, the D.C.Circuit has vacated EPA decisions to add sites to the NPL and remanded to the agency in light of its failure to explain adequately the scientific bases for its decisions and its failure to offer substantial evidence in support of those decisions. See *Tex Tin Corp. v. United States Environmental Protection Agency*, 992 F.2d 353 (D.C.Cir.1993); and *National Gypsum Co. v. United States Environmental Protection Agency*, 968 F.2d 40 (D.C.Cir.1992), which cites three similar decisions of that court in 1991 and 1992. However, *Barmet Aluminum Corp. v. Reilly*, 927 F.2d 289 (6th Cir.1991), held that section 113(h) of CERCLA precluded federal courts from reviewing pre-enforcement challenges to proposed placements of waste sites on the NPL. See note 4, p. 655, infra, concerning section 113(h). EPA's Hazard Ranking System, which is part of the NCP, prescribes risk assessment for determining which sites are included on the NPL. Similarly, risk assessment is used for establishing a baseline for site cleanup, for determining the appropriate range of acceptable risk, and for choosing a response. See Applegate, "The Perils of Unreasonable Risk: Information, Regulatory Policy, and Toxic Substances Control," 91 *Colum.L.Rev.* 261, notes 119, 174 (1991).

CERCLA was amended by the Superfund Amendments and Reauthorization Act of 1986 (SARA), Pub.L. 99–499, 99th Cong., 2d Sess. (1986). New sections 116 and 121 established schedules for response actions, and preferences among types of responses. Section 121 established a preference (in remedial actions under section 104 or 106) for treatment which permanently and significantly reduces the volume, toxicity or mobility of the hazardous substances. Offsite transport and disposal of the hazardous substances or contaminated materials are least favored if "practical [onsite] treatment technologies" are available. Remedial actions are to be "cost-effective," considering total short and long-term costs. The actions taken are to attain a degree of cleanup and control of further releases which, at a minimum, "assures protection" of human health and the environment.

[handwritten margin note: timelines have not worked.]

The total number of NPL sites cleaned up from enactment of CERCLA in 1980 until May 1998 was 511, of which 355 were done during the Clinton administration. 28 *Envir. Rep.* 221 (1998). The General Accounting Office (GAO) has estimated that EPA took an average of 9.4 years to evaluate and process sites (other than federally owned facilities) before adding them to the NPL in 1996, and 10.4 years after NPL listing to conduct and finish cleanups done by 1996. Responsible parties have paid for approximately 70 percent of all long-term cleanups. 28 *Envir. Rep.* 2113–14 (1998).

The special corporate and excise taxes which were bringing $4 million per day into the hazardous substance response trust fund, or *superfund* (which is used to pay for NPL-site cleanups when responsible parties are not available or solvent), expired on December 31, 1995. Through 1998 the fund continued to receive some income, primarily from interest on the unexpended balance and recoveries from private parties who were responsible to reimburse EPA for cleanup costs. Without further appropriations by Congress—which has been unwilling to provide more money except as part of a (long-stalled) comprehensive "reform" of CERCLA—the superfund may run out of money by the end of fiscal year 1999. 29 *Envir. Rep.* 22–23 (1998).

"Response costs" recoverable by EPA under CERCLA § 107(a) include not only expenses incurred by the agency in conducting its own "removal" and "remedial" actions but also *attorney fees* and other costs of obtaining and *monitoring* private-party cleanups. *United States v. Chapman*, 146 F.3d 1166 (9th Cir.1998) (attorney fees); *United States v. Lowe*, 118 F.3d 399 (5th Cir.1997) (monitoring costs). (Private plaintiffs, on the other hand, may not recover attorney fees under § 107. See the discussion of *Key Tronic Corp. v. United States*, 511 U.S. 809, 114 S.Ct. 1960, 128 L.Ed.2d 797 (1994), at page 633 infra.)

a. *Discussion Problem #1 on CERCLA Liability*

Suppose that during the early 1970s each of five industrial firms sent between 100 and 500 drums containing various hazardous wastes to a rural site owned by farmer Fred and leased for $200 per month to Walt, who was doing business as Walt's Waste Handlers. After collecting $10 per drum, Walt simply buried the drums in trenches or left them standing in an open field. Now, more than 25 years later, the drums are leaking and have contaminated the soil and groundwater on Fred's farm. Having learned of this situation and of the federal "superfund," neighboring landowners have demanded that the U.S. EPA take action to clean up the disposal site and prevent the contamination from spreading.

On the basis of the next (*Monsanto*) case, the text after it, and CERCLA §§ 104, 106 and 107, how would you answer the following questions?

1. What types of action is EPA authorized to take? Does it matter that the contamination has not spread beyond the boundaries of Fred's farm? What are the controlling statutory provisions?

2. Assuming that they all can be located and have some assets, which of the firms and individuals mentioned above are potentially responsible parties (PRPs) under CERCLA? Is it important to anyone's liability whether, at the time of disposal, Walt was (a) complying with state and local regulatory requirements applicable to disposal sites or (b) acting reasonably, i.e., non-negligently? Is it relevant that all the disposal activities occurred prior to enactment of RCRA and CERCLA? Why or why not? What are the competing policy considerations?

3. For what portion of a total site cleanup might each party be legally responsible? Could the extent of liability differ depending on the identity of the claimant (EPA or other), or on the type of proceeding? What evidentiary rules, including presumptions and burdens of proof, would apply?

4. Under CERCLA, can the neighboring landowners take action directly against any of the PRPs? Can the neighbors recover for losses in the value of their property, or for the costs of medical monitoring (periodic checkups) to determine whether they are becoming ill from exposure to the contamination?

UNITED STATES v. MONSANTO CO.

United States Court of Appeals, Fourth Circuit, 1988.
858 F.2d 160, cert. denied 490 U.S. 1106, 109
S.Ct. 3156, 104 L.Ed.2d 1019 (1989).

SPROUSE, CIRCUIT JUDGE:

Oscar Seidenberg and Harvey Hutchinson (the site-owners) and Allied Corporation, Monsanto Company, and EM Industries, Inc. (the generator defendants), appeal from the district court's entry of summary judgment holding them liable to the United States and the State of South Carolina (the governments) under section 107(a) of [CERCLA]. The court determined that the defendants were liable jointly and severally for $1,813,624 in response costs accrued from the partial removal of hazardous waste from a disposal facility located near Columbia, South Carolina. * * * We affirm the district court's liability holdings * * *.

[The site-owners had leased rural land to COCC and SCRDI, which between 1976 and 1980 accepted for disposal there 7,000 drums of chemical waste generated by third parties. The governments entered into settlement agreements under which twelve of the generators (but not defendants) paid 75% of the cost of a surface cleanup at the site. The governments paid the other 25% and brought this action for reimbursement.]

owners [margin note]

II.

The site-owners and the generator defendants first contest the imposition of CERCLA liability *vel non*, and they challenge the propriety

claims [margin note]

vel non : or the absence of it [handwritten note at bottom] of summary judgment in light of the evidence presented to the trial court. The site-owners also reassert the "innocent landowner" defense that the district court rejected, and claim that the court erroneously precluded them from presenting evidence of a valid affirmative defense under section 107(b)(3). The generator defendants likewise repeat their arguments based on the governments' failure to establish a nexus between their specific waste and the harm at the site. They also claim that the trial court ignored material factual issues relevant to affirmative defenses to liability. We address these contentions sequentially, but pause briefly to review the structure of CERCLA's liability scheme.

In CERCLA, Congress established "an array of mechanisms to combat the increasingly serious problem of hazardous substance releases." Section 107(a) of the statute sets forth the principal mechanism for recovery of costs expended in the cleanup of waste disposal facilities. At the time the district court entered judgment,[9] section 107(a) provided in pertinent part:

(a) Covered persons; scope

Notwithstanding any other provision or rule of law, and subject only to the defenses set forth in subsection (b) of this section—

. . . .

(2) any person who at the time of disposal of any hazardous substance owned or operated any facility at which such hazardous substances were disposed of, [and]

(3) any person who by contract, agreement, or otherwise arranged for disposal or treatment, or arranged with a transporter for transport for disposal or treatment, of hazardous substances owned or possessed by such person, by any other party or entity, at any facility owned or operated by another party or entity and containing such hazardous substances, and

(4) ... from which there is a release, or a threatened release which causes the incurrence of response costs, of a hazardous substance, shall be liable for—

(A) all costs of removal or remedial action incurred by the United States Government or a State not inconsistent with the national contingency plan.

In our view, the plain language of section 107(a) clearly defines the scope of intended liability under the statute and the elements of proof necessary to establish it. We agree with the overwhelming body of precedent that has interpreted section 107(a) as establishing a strict liability scheme. Further, in light of the evidence presented here, we are persuaded that the district court correctly held that the governments

---

9. Congress amended section 107(a) in 1986, Pub.L. No. 99–499, 100 Stat. 1628–30, 1692, 1693, 1705–06 (1986), but the changes are not material to the issues presented in this part of the appeal.

satisfied all the elements of section 107(a) liability as to both the site-owners and the generator defendants.

A. Site–Owners' Liability

In light of the strict liability imposed by section 107(a), we cannot agree with the site-owners contention that they are not within the class of owners Congress intended to hold liable. The traditional elements of tort culpability on which the site-owners rely simply are absent from the statute. The plain language of section 107(a)(2) extends liability to owners of waste facilities regardless of their degree of participation in the subsequent disposal of hazardous waste.

Under section 107(a)(2), *any* person who owned a facility at a time when hazardous substances were deposited there may be held liable for all costs of removal or remedial action if a release or threatened release[12] of a hazardous substance occurs. The site-owners do not dispute their ownership of the Bluff Road facility, or the fact that releases occurred there during their period of ownership. Under these circumstances, all the prerequisites to section 107(a) liability have been satisfied.[13] *See* [*State of New York v. Shore Realty Corp.,* 759 F.2d 1032 (2d Cir.1985)] (site-owner held liable under CERCLA section 107(a)(1) even though he did not contribute to the presence or cause the release of hazardous substances at the facility).[14]

12. The statute defines "release" to include "any spilling, leaking, pumping, pouring, emitting, emptying, discharging, injecting, escaping, leaching, dumping, or disposing into the environment (including the abandonment or discarding of barrels, containers, and other closed receptacles containing any hazardous substance or pollutant or contaminant)." 42 U.S.C.A. § 9601(22) (West Supp.1987).

13. The site-owners' relative degree of fault would, of course, be relevant in any subsequent action for contribution brought pursuant to 42 U.S.C.A. § 9613(f) (West Supp.1987). Congress, in the Superfund Amendments and Reauthorization Act of 1986, Pub.L. 99–499, § 113, 100 Stat. 1613, 1647 (1986) [hereafter SARA], established a right of contribution in favor of defendants sued under CERCLA section 107(a). Section 113(f)(1) provides:

Any person may seek contribution from any other person who is liable or potentially liable under section 9607(a) of this title, during or following any civil action under section 9606 of this title or under section 9607(a) of this title. Such claims shall be brought in accordance with this section and the Federal Rules of Civil Procedure, and shall be governed by Federal law. In resolving contribution claims,

the court may allocate response costs among liable parties using such equitable factors as the court determines are appropriate. Nothing in this subsection shall diminish the right of any person to bring an action for contribution in the absence of a civil action under section 9606 or section 9607 of this title.

42 U.S.C.A. § 9613(f) (West Supp.1987). The legislative history of this amendment suggests that in arriving at an equitable allocation of costs, a court may consider, among other things, the degree of involvement by parties in the generation, transportation, treatment, storage, or disposal of hazardous substances. H.R.Rep. No. 253(III), 99th Cong., 1st Sess. 19 (1985), *reprinted in* 1986 U.S.Code Cong. & Admin.News 2835, 3038, 3042.

14. Congress, in section 101(35) of SARA, acknowledged that landowners may affirmatively avoid liability if they can prove they did not know and had no reason to know that hazardous substances were disposed of on their land *at the time they acquired title or possession.* 42 U.S.C.A. § 9601(35) (West Supp.1987). This explicitly drafted exception further signals Congress' intent to impose liability on landowners who cannot satisfy its express requirements.

The site-owners nonetheless contend that the district court's grant of summary judgment improperly denied them the opportunity to present an affirmative defense under section 107(b)(3). Section 107(b)(3) sets forth a limited affirmative defense based on the complete absence of causation. *See Shore Realty,* 759 F.2d at 1044. It requires proof that the release or threatened release of hazardous substances and resulting damages were caused solely by "a third party other than . . . one whose act or omission occurs in connection with a contractual relationship, existing directly or indirectly, with the defendant. . . ." A second element of the defense requires proof that the defendant "took precautions against foreseeable acts or omissions of any such third party and the consequences that could foreseeably result from such acts or omissions." We agree with the district court that under no view of the evidence could the site-owners satisfy either of these proof requirements.

First, the site-owners could not establish the absence of a direct or indirect contractual relationship necessary to maintain the affirmative defense. They concede they entered into a lease agreement with COCC. They accepted rent from COCC, and after SCRDI was incorporated, they accepted rent from SCRDI. Second, the site-owners presented no evidence that they took precautionary action against the foreseeable conduct of COCC or SCRDI. They argued to the trial court that, although they were aware COCC was a chemical manufacturing company, they were completely ignorant of all waste disposal activities at Bluff Road before 1977. They maintained that they never inspected the site prior to that time. In our view, the statute does not sanction such willful or negligent blindness on the part of absentee owners. The district court committed no error in entering summary judgment against the site-owners.

B. Generator Defendants' Liability

The generator defendants first contend that the district court misinterpreted section 107(a)(3) because it failed to read into the statute a requirement that the governments prove a nexus between the waste they sent to the site and the resulting environmental harm. They maintain that the statutory phrase "containing such hazardous substances" requires proof that the specific substances they generated and sent to the site were present at the facility at the time of release. The district court held, however, that the statute was satisfied by proof that hazardous substances "like" those contained in the generator defendants' waste were found at the site. We agree with the district court's interpretation.

Reduced of surplus language, sections 107(a)(3) and (4) impose liability on off-site waste generators who:

> "arranged for disposal . . . of hazardous substances . . . at any facility . . . *containing such hazardous substances* . . . from which there is a release . . . of a hazardous substance."

In our view, the plain meaning of the adjective "such" in the phrase "containing such hazardous substances" is "[a]like, similar, of the like kind." *Black's Law Dictionary* 1284 (5th ed. 1979). As used in the statute, the phrase "such hazardous substances" denotes hazardous substances alike, similar, or of a like kind to those that were present in a generator defendant's waste or that could have been produced by the mixture of the defendant's waste with other waste present at the site. It does not mean that the plaintiff must trace the ownership of each generic chemical compound found at a site. Absent proof that a generator defendant's specific waste remained at a facility at the time of release, a showing of chemical similarity between hazardous substances is sufficient.[15]

The overall structure of CERCLA's liability provisions also militates against the generator defendants' "proof of ownership" argument. In *Shore Realty,* the Second Circuit held with respect to site-owners that requiring proof of ownership at any time later than the time of disposal would go far toward rendering the section 107(b) defenses superfluous. *Shore Realty,* 759 F.2d at 1044. We agree with the court's reading of the statute and conclude that its reasoning applies equally to the generator defendants' contentions. As the statute provides—"[n]otwithstanding any other provision or rule of law"—liability under section 107(a) is "subject *only* to the defenses set forth" in section 107(b). Each of the three defenses[16] established in section 107(b) "carves out from liability an exception based on causation." *Shore Realty,* 759 F.2d at 1044. Congress has, therefore, allocated the burden of disproving causation to the defendant who profited from the generation and inexpensive disposal of hazardous waste. We decline to interpret the statute in a way that would neutralize the force of Congress' intent.[17]

Finally, the purpose underlying CERCLA's liability provisions counsels against the generator defendants' argument. Throughout the statute's legislative history, there appears the recurring theme of facilitating prompt action to remedy the environmental blight of unscrupulous waste

15. CERCLA plaintiffs need not perform exhaustive chemical analyses of hazardous substances found at a disposal site. *See SCRDI,* 653 F.Supp. at 993 n. 6. They must, however, present evidence that a generator defendant's waste was shipped to a site and that hazardous substances similar to those contained in the defendant's waste remained present at the time of release. The defendant, of course, may in turn present evidence of an affirmative defense to liability.

16. In addition to the limited third-party defense discussed above, sections 107(b)(1) and (2) respectively allow defendants to avoid liability by proving that the release and resulting damages were "caused solely" by an act of God or an act of war. 42 U.S.C. § 9607(b)(1), (2).

17. In fact, Congress specifically declined to include a similar nexus requirement in CERCLA. As the Second Circuit in *Shore Realty* observed, an early House version of what ultimately became section 107(a) limited liability to "any person who caused or contributed to the release or threatened release." 759 F.2d at 1044 (quoting H.R.Rep. 7020, 96th Cong., 2d Sess. § 307(a) (1980), *reprinted in 2 A Legislative History of the Comprehensive Environmental Response, Compensation and Liability Act of 1980* at 438. As ultimately enacted after House and Senate compromise, however, CERCLA "imposed liability on classes of persons without reference to whether they caused or contributed to the release or threat of release." *Shore Realty,* 759 F.2d at 1044. The legislature thus eliminated the element of causation from the plaintiff's liability case.

disposal.[18] In deleting causation language from section 107(a), we assume as have many other courts, that Congress knew of the synergistic and migratory capacities of leaking chemical waste, and the technological infeasibility of tracing improperly disposed waste to its source. In view of this, we will not frustrate the statute's salutary goals by engrafting a "proof of ownership" requirement, which in practice, would be as onerous as the language Congress saw fit to delete.

* * *

III.

The appellants next challenge the district court's imposition of joint and several liability for the governments' response costs.[22] The court concluded that joint and several liability was appropriate because the environmental harm at Bluff Road was "indivisible" and the appellants had "failed to meet their burden of proving otherwise." We agree with its conclusion.

While CERCLA does not mandate the imposition of joint and several liability, it permits it in cases of indivisible harm. *See Shore Realty,* 759 F.2d at 1042 n. 13; *United States v. Chem-Dyne,* 572 F.Supp. 802, 810–11 (S.D.Ohio 1983). In each case, the court must consider traditional and evolving principles of federal common law,[23] which Congress has left to the courts to supply interstitially.

Under common law rules, when two or more persons act independently to cause a single harm for which there is a reasonable basis of apportionment according to the contribution of each, each is held liable only for the portion of harm that he causes. *Edmonds v. Compagnie Generale Transatlantique,* 443 U.S. 256, 260 n. 8, 99 S.Ct. 2753, 2756 n. 8, 61 L.Ed.2d 521 (1979). When such persons cause a single and indivisible harm, however, they are held liable jointly and severally for the entire harm. *Id.* (citing Restatement (Second) of Torts § 433A (1965)). We think these principles, as reflected in the Restatement

---

18. The legislative history underlying the Superfund Amendments and Reauthorization Act of 1986 echoed this theme with even greater force than that underlying CERCLA's original enactment in 1980.

22. The site-owners limit their joint and several liability argument to the contention that it is inequitable under the circumstances of this case, *i.e.,* their limited degree of participation in waste disposal activities at Bluff Road. As we have stated, however, such equitable factors are relevant in subsequent actions for contribution. They are not pertinent to the question of joint and several liability, which focuses principally on the divisibility among responsible parties of the harm to the environment.

23. As many courts have noted, a proposed requirement that joint and several

liability be imposed in all CERCLA cases was deleted from the final version of the bill. *See, e.g., Chem–Dyne,* 572 F.Supp. at 806. "The deletion," however, "was not intended as a rejection of joint and several liability," but rather "to have the scope of liability determined under common law principles." *Id.* at 808. We adopt the *Chem–Dyne* court's thorough discussion of CERCLA's legislative history with respect to joint and several liability. We note that the approach taken in *Chem–Dyne* was subsequently confirmed as correct by Congress in its consideration of SARA's contribution provisions. *See* H.R.Rep. No. 253(I), 99th Cong.2d Sess., 79–80 (1985), *reprinted in* 1986 U.S.Code Cong. & Admin.News at 2835, 2861–62.

(Second) of Torts, represent the correct and uniform federal rules applicable to CERCLA cases.

Section 433A of the Restatement provides:

(1) Damages for harm are to be apportioned among two or more causes where

(a) there are distinct harms, or

(b) there is a reasonable basis for determining the contribution of each cause to a single harm.

(2) Damages for any other harm cannot be apportioned among two or more causes.

Restatement (Second) of Torts § 433A (1965).

Placing their argument into the Restatement framework, the generator defendants concede that the environmental damage at Bluff Road constituted a "single harm," but contend that there was a reasonable basis for apportioning the harm. They observe that each of the off-site generators with whom SCRDI contracted sent a potentially identifiable volume of waste to the Bluff Road site, and they maintain that liability should have been apportioned according to the volume they deposited as compared to the total volume disposed of there by all parties. In light of the conditions at Bluff Road, we cannot accept this method as a basis for apportionment.

The generator defendants bore the burden of establishing a reasonable basis for apportioning liability among responsible parties. *Chem–Dyne*, 572 F.Supp. at 810; Restatement (Second) of Torts § 433B (1965).[24] To meet this burden, the generator defendants had to establish that the environmental harm at Bluff Road was divisible among responsible parties. They presented no evidence, however, showing a relationship between waste volume, the release of hazardous substances, and the harm at the site.[25] Further, in light of the commingling of hazardous substances, the district court could not have reasonably apportioned liability without some evidence disclosing the individual and interactive qualities of the substances deposited there. Common sense counsels that a million gallons of certain substances could be mixed together without

---

24. Section 433(B)(2) of the Restatement provides:

Where the tortious conduct of two or more actors has combined to bring about harm to the plaintiff, and one or more of the actors seeks to limit his liability on the ground that the harm is capable of apportionment among them, the burden of proof as to the apportionment is upon each such actor.

Restatement (Second) of Torts § 433(B)(2) (1965).

25. At minimum, such evidence was crucial to demonstrate that a volumetric apportionment scheme was reasonable. The governments presented considerable evidence identifying numerous hazardous substances found at Bluff Road. An EPA investigator reported, for example, that in the first cleanup phase RAD Services encountered substances "in every hazard class, including explosives such as crystalized dynamite and nitroglycerine. Numerous examples were found of oxidizers, flammable and non-flammable liquids, poisons, corrosives, containerized gases, and even a small amount of radioactive material." Under these circumstances, volumetric apportionment based on the overall quantity of waste, as opposed to the quantity and quality of hazardous substances contained in the waste would have made little sense.

significant consequences, whereas a few pints of others improperly mixed could result in disastrous consequences.[26] Under other circumstances proportionate volumes of hazardous substances may well be probative of contributory harm.[27] In this case, however, volume could not establish the effective contribution of each waste generator to the harm at the Bluff Road site.

Although we find no error in the trial court's imposition of joint and several liability, we share the appellants' concern that they not be ultimately responsible for reimbursing more than their just portion of the governments' response costs.[28] In its refusal to apportion liability, the district court likewise recognized the validity of their demand that they not be required to shoulder a disproportionate amount of the costs. It ruled, however, that making the governments whole for response costs was the primary consideration and that cost allocation was a matter "more appropriately considered in an action for contribution between responsible parties after plaintiff has been made whole." Had we sat in place of the district court, we would have ruled as it did on the apportionment issue, but may well have retained the action to dispose of the contribution questions. *See* [CERCLA § 113(f)]. That procedural course, however, was committed to the trial court's discretion and we find no abuse of it. As we have stated, the defendants still have the right to sue responsible parties for contribution, and in that action they may assert both legal and equitable theories of cost allocation.

IV.

The generator defendants raise numerous constitutional challenges to the district court's interpretation and application of CERCLA. * * *

Many courts have concluded that Congress intended CERCLA's liability provisions to apply retroactively to pre-enactment disposal activities of off-site waste generators. They have held uniformly that retroactive operation survives the Supreme Court's tests for due process validity. We agree with their analyses.

* * *

26. We agree with the district court that evidence disclosing the relative toxicity, migratory potential, and synergistic capacity of the hazardous substances at the site would be relevant to establishing divisibility of harm.

27. Volumetric contributions provide a reasonable basis for apportioning liability only if it can be reasonably assumed, or it has been demonstrated, that independent factors had no substantial effect on the harm to the environment. *Cf.* Restatement (Second) of Torts § 433A comment d, illustrations 4, 5 (1965).

28. The final judgment holds the defendants liable for slightly less than half of the total costs incurred in the cleanup, while it appears that the generator defendants col-

lectively produced approximately 22% of the waste that SCRDI handled. Other evidence indicates that agencies of the federal government produced more waste than did generator defendant Monsanto, and suggests that the amounts contributed by the settling parties do not bear a strictly proportionate relationship to the total costs of cleaning the facility. We note, however, that a substantial portion of the final judgment is attributable to litigation costs. We also observe that the EPA has contributed upwards of $50,000 to the Bluff Road cleanup, and that any further claims against the EPA and other responsible government instrumentalities may be resolved in a contribution action pursuant to CERCLA section 113(f).

* * * While the generator defendants profited from inexpensive waste disposal methods that may have been technically "legal" prior to CERCLA's enactment, it was certainly foreseeable at the time that improper disposal could cause enormous damage to the environment. CERCLA operates remedially to spread the costs of responding to improper waste disposal among all parties that played a role in creating the hazardous conditions. * * *

* * *

In view of the above, the judgment of the district court as to the CERCLA liability of the site-owners and generator defendants is affirmed. * * *

WIDENER, CIRCUIT JUDGE, concurring and dissenting:

I concur in the majority opinion in all respects save its decision not to require the district court to treat the issue of allocation of costs of cleanup among the various defendants, and, as to that, I respectfully dissent. While it may be true that a subsequent suit for contribution may adequately apportion the damages among the defendants, I am of opinion that the district court, as a court of equity, is required to retain jurisdiction and answer that question now.

* * *

I see great danger in postponing the ultimate apportioning of the damages to a later day. As an example, a small generator which deposited a few gallons of relatively innocuous waste liquid at a site is jointly and severally liable for the entire cost of cleanup under this decision. And with that I agree. If that generator were readily available and solvent, however, the government might well, and probably would, proceed against him first in collecting its judgment. The vagaries of and delays in his subsequent suit for contribution might result in needless financial disaster. I do not see this as a desired or even permissible result.

The statute involved, 42 U.S.C. 9613(f)(1), provides that "*[a]ny person* may seek contribution from any other person who is liable or potentially liable under section 9607(a) of this title during or following any civil action under section 9606 of this title or under section 9607(a) of this title." (Italics added) Thus, the statute plainly provides that discretion with respect to contribution is not in the district court to consider relief or not as the majority opinion holds; rather, it is in the generator to seek relief, for "any person" certainly includes the generators of the waste. So, since the matter was brought before the district court, that court had no discretion but to decide the question. To repeat, the discretion is in the party to make the claim, not in the district court to defer decision. While I agree that the claims may be asserted in a separate action, if they are asserted in the main case they must be decided.

Note on Allocation of Costs Among Responsible Parties

(i) Apportionment of Damages

In *United States v. A & F Materials Co.*, 578 F.Supp. 1249, 1256 (S.D.Ill.1984), the court concluded that "a rigid application of the Restatement approach to joint and several liability is inappropriate" because such extensive liability would be unfair to a defendant who contributed only a small amount of waste to a site. The court preferred a "moderate approach" under which the court (a) had the *power* to impose joint and several liability whenever a defendant could not prove his contribution to an injury but (b) still could apportion damages according to the following factors contained in an unsuccessful amendment to CERCLA proposed by Representative (now Vice President) Gore (the "Gore factors"):

> (i) the ability of the parties to demonstrate that their contribution to a discharge, release or disposal of a hazardous waste can be distinguished;

> (ii) the amount of the hazardous waste involved;

> (iii) the degree of toxicity of the hazardous waste involved;

> (iv) the degree of involvement by the parties in the generation, transportation, treatment, storage, or disposal of the hazardous waste;

> (v) the degree of care exercised by the parties with respect to the hazardous waste concerned, taking into account the characteristics of such hazardous waste; and

> (vi) the degree of cooperation by the parties with Federal, State, or local officials to prevent any harm to the public health or the environment.

In *United States v. Alcan Aluminum Corp.*, 964 F.2d 252 (3d Cir.1992), Alcan was one of twenty potentially responsible parties from which EPA sought to recover a total of $1.3 million in response costs. All parties other than Alcan settled for a combined total of $828,500. In a motion for summary judgment against Alcan, EPA sought the remaining $473,790 of its response costs. The government argued that Alcan was jointly and severally liable for the cleanup despite Alcan's argument that the only waste it had taken to the site was a non-hazardous, non-toxic emulsion with heavy metal fragments "orders of magnitude below ambient or naturally occurring background levels." The district court granted the government's motion, and Alcan appealed. The court of appeals vacated the judgment and remanded the case for "further factual development concerning the scope of Alcan's liability," citing section 881 of the Restatement (Second) of Torts, which sets forth an affirmative defense based on the divisibility-of-harm rule in section 433A and reiterates that liability is not joint and several when the harm is divisible:

> If two or more persons, acting independently, tortiously cause distinct harms or a single harm for which there is a reasonable basis for division according to the contribution of each, each is subject to liability only for the portion of the total harm that he has himself caused.

Because of the "intensely factual nature of the 'divisibility' issue," the district court erred in granting the United States summary judgment for its full claim against Alcan without benefit of a hearing. *Alcan* recognizes that proving divisibility will require "an assessment of the relative toxicity, migratory potential and synergistic capacity of the hazardous waste at issue."[a]

Some critics have argued that EPA often settles early with large defendants for amounts far below the actual costs incurred in cleaning up the wastes for which those defendants are responsible. Under joint and several liability, defendants that settle late or litigate bear the brunt of the EPA's failure to exact reasonable settlement amounts from the early settlors. *Alcan* is viewed as a vehicle for ameliorating inequitable results in such situations. See Harris and Milan, "Avoiding Joint and Several Liability under CERCLA," 23 *Envir.Rep.* 1726 (1992).

In re Bell Petroleum Services, Inc., 3 F.3d 889 (5th Cir.1993), reversed a district court's judgment imposing joint and several liability upon each of three *successive* owners of a chrome-plating shop. Each owner had discharged rinse water onto the ground, causing the underlying aquifer to become contaminated with chromium. The court of appeals reviewed the *Chem-Dyne*–Restatement approach adopted in *Monsanto,* the "moderate approach" of *A & F Materials,* and the *Alcan* approach:

> The Fourth Circuit [in *Monsanto,* rejected] the *A & F* moderate approach, stating that, while equitable factors are relevant in an action for contribution, "[t]hey are not pertinent to the question of joint and several liability, which focuses principally on the divisibility among responsible parties of the harm to the environment." 858 F.2d at 171 n. 22. Other courts have similarly concluded that equitable factors, such as those listed in the Gore amendment, have no place in making the decision whether to impose joint and several liability, but are appropriate in an action for contribution among jointly and severally liable defendants. *See Alcan,* 964 F.2d at 270 n. 29.

* * *

> * * * Under the *Restatement,* the plaintiff must first prove that the defendant's conduct was a substantial factor in causing the harm; the defendant may limit its liability by proving its contribution to the harm. In contrast, the *Alcan* approach suggests that a defendant may escape liability altogether if it can prove that its waste, even when mixed with other wastes at the site, did not cause the incurrence of response costs.

* * *

a. In another case also involving Alcan, the Second Circuit "essentially adopt[ed] the Third Circuit's reasoning" in a similar situation. *United States v. Alcan Aluminum Corp.,* 990 F.2d 711 (2d Cir.1993). "Alcan may escape liability for response costs if it either succeeds in proving that its oil emulsion, when mixed with other hazardous wastes, did not contribute to the release and the clean-up costs that followed, or contributed at most to only a divisible portion of the harm. Alcan as the polluter bears the ultimate burden of establishing a reasonable basis for apportioning liability." The court acknowledged that Alcan was being allowed to bring the issue of causation back into the case, "through the back-door, after being denied entry at the front-door," but only to escape payment "where its pollutants did not contribute more than background contamination and also cannot concentrate."

Although these approaches are not entirely uniform, certain basic principles emerge. First, joint and several liability is not mandated under CERCLA; Congress intended that the federal courts impose joint and several liability only in appropriate cases, applying common-law principles. Second, all of the cases rely on the *Restatement* in resolving the issues of joint and several liability. The major differences among the cases concern the timing of the resolution of the divisibility question, whether equitable factors should be considered, and whether a defendant can avoid liability for all, or only some portion, of the damages. Third, even where commingled wastes of unknown toxicity, migratory potential, and synergistic effect are present, defendants are allowed an opportunity to attempt to prove that there is a reasonable basis for apportionment (although they rarely succeed); where such factors are not present, volume may be a reasonable means of apportioning liability.

With respect to the timing of the "divisibility" inquiry, we believe that an early resolution is preferable. We agree with the Second Circuit, however, that this is a matter best left to the sound discretion of the district court. We also agree with the majority view that equitable factors, such as those listed in the Gore amendment, are more appropriately considered in actions for contribution among jointly and severally liable parties, than in making the initial determination of whether to impose joint and several liability. We therefore conclude that the *Chem–Dyne* approach is an appropriate framework for resolving issues of joint and several liability in CERCLA cases. Although we express no opinion with respect to the *Alcan* approach, because it is not necessary with respect to the issues we are faced with in this case, we nevertheless recognize that the *Restatement* principles must be adapted, where necessary, to implement congressional intent with respect to liability under the unique statutory scheme of CERCLA.

Applying *Chem–Dyne* to the facts in *Bell,* the Fifth Circuit concluded that defendant Sequa, the last of the three successive owners of the chrome-plating shop, had "met its burden of proving that, as a matter of law, there is a reasonable basis for apportionment." Although it was not possible to determine exactly how much chromium, the sole contaminant involved, each defendant had introduced into the groundwater, there was sufficient evidence (comparative records concerning chrome-flake purchases, sales of finished products, and electrical usage) from which to make a "reasonable and rational approximation" of each firm's contribution to the contamination "on a volumetric basis."

The *Alcan* and *Bell* cases are discussed in Lynda Oswald, "New Directions in Joint and Several Liability under CERCLA?", 28 *U.C. Davis L. Rev.* 299 (1995). See also Richard White and John Butler, "Applying Cost Causation Principles in Superfund Allocation Cases," 28 *Envt'l L. Rptr.* 10067 (1998).

(ii) Contribution

Section 113(f) of CERCLA, concerning contribution, provides in part as follows:

Any person may seek contribution from any other person who is liable or potentially liable under [§ 107(a)], during or following any civil action under [§ 106 or 107(a)]. Such claims * * * shall be governed by Federal law. In resolving contribution claims, the court may allocate response costs among liable parties using such equitable factors as the court determines are appropriate.

The operation of § 113(f) is illustrated by *Environmental Transportation Systems, Inc. v. ENSCO, Inc.,* 969 F.2d 503 (7th Cir.1992). PCB-contaminated waste had been generated by defendant Northern States Power Co., which hired defendant ENSCO to arrange for disposal. ENSCO hired plaintiff Environmental Transportation Systems to transport the waste to a disposal facility. En route, the ETS truck overturned because it was driven at an excessive speed as the driver attempted to negotiate a highway access ramp. ETS paid for the cost of cleanup of the spill and sought contribution from ENSCO and Northern States under section 113(f) of CERCLA. Defendants moved for summary judgment. The district court, after concluding that ETS was responsible for all costs of cleanup because the accident was entirely ETS's fault, granted defendants' motion. The district court held that, although ENSCO and Northern States would have been liable if sued under section 107, such liability does not necessarily lead to mandatory contribution for cleanup costs. The court of appeals affirmed the judgment of the district court, on the ground that Congress' intent in enacting section 113(f) was that the court should "equitably allocate costs of cleanup according to the relative culpability of the parties rather than an automatic equal shares rule." The court of appeals specifically mentioned that the legislative history of section 113(f) cites the *A & F Materials* criteria (the "Gore factors"), supra, as factors which a court may consider in deciding whether to grant apportionment in a contribution action.

Similarly, in *Control Data Corp. v. S.C.S.C. Corp.* 53 F.3d 930 (8th Cir.1995), plaintiff sought contribution under § 113 (f) after having cleaned up contamination caused by both plaintiff and defendant. Citing the "Gore factors," the court allocated one-third of the total cleanup costs to defendant because the chemical released by it—constituting only ten percent of the total contamination by volume—was much more toxic and difficult to remove than was the chemical released by plaintiff.

A contribution-type claim by one PRP against other PRPs can involve three complex and often interrelated issues: (1) May one PRP, as suggested by the district court in the *ENSCO* case, supra, seek reimbursement from other PRPs by suing them under § 107 rather than under § 113(f)? (Section 107 is more favorable in several respects, including the statute of limitations.) (2) In a suit under § 113(f) is the court authorized to find defendants both jointly and severally liable (as under § 107), or only severally liable for their specific shares of the total cleanup costs? (3) May courts under § 113(f) allocate "orphan shares" of CERCLA response costs among the PRP defendants, or is the liability of each such defendant limited to the proportion of the cleanup costs attributable to its own releases?

Consider the basic hypothetical case discussed in William Araiza, "Text, Purpose and Facts: The Relationship Between CERCLA Sections 107 and 113," 72 *Notre Dame L. Rev.* 193 (1996). EPA determines that GM sent large quantities of waste oil, paint and solvents to an abandoned landfill. EPA negotiates a consent decree in which GM, while denying that it is liable under CERCLA, nevertheless agrees to undertake a multi-million dollar cleanup. GM then discovers that Ford and Chrysler disposed of similar materials at the site. GM also discovers that significant contamination was caused by Eastern Airlines, Smith–Corona and Studebaker, all of which subsequently have gone bankrupt, as well as by several other corporations that cannot be identified. GM sues Ford and Chrysler under CERCLA, seeking 100 percent reimbursement of the cleanup costs incurred by GM.

With respect to issue (1) identified above, most if not all courts of appeals that have faced the issue have concluded that a § 107 action for recovery of costs may be brought only by *innocent* parties that have undertaken cleanups. Generally, therefore, an action by a PRP must be a § 113 action for contribution. *Pinal Creek Group v. Newmont Mining Corp.*, 118 F.3d 1298 (9th Cir.1997), cert. denied ___ U.S. ___, 118 S.Ct. 2340, 141 L.Ed.2d 711 (1998); *Rumpke of Indiana, Inc., v. Cummins Engine Co.,* 107 F.3d 1235 (7th Cir.1997); *Akzo Coatings, Inc. v. Aigner Corp.*, 30 F.3d 761 (7th Cir.1994). However, under the so-called *Akzo* exception, a landowner who is technically a PRP may bring a § 107 action to recover for its direct injuries "if the party seeking relief is itself not responsible for having caused any of the hazardous materials to be spilled onto the property."

In *Rumpke*, plaintiff's suit was based on both the cost recovery theory of § 107(a) and the contribution theory of § 113(f). The court said, "The question is whether our *Akzo* exception applies to Rumpke: may a landowner PRP bring a direct liability suit for cost recovery under § 107(a) against other PRPs (in this case "arrangers"), if it contributed nothing to the hazardous conditions at the site, or is the *Akzo* exception available only to a narrower group of parties, such as the landowner who discovers someone surreptitiously dumping wastes on its land?" The court concluded, "If one were to read § 107(a) as implicitly denying standing to sue even to landowners like Rumpke who did not create the hazardous conditions, this would come perilously close to reading § 107(a) itself out of the statute." On the other hand, "If it turns out that Rumpke is not the innocent party it portrays itself to be, then Rumpke will not qualify for the *Akzo* exception. It would still be entitled to seek contribution for its expenses from the other PRPs" under § 113(f).

With respect to issue (2) identified above, contribution liability under CERCLA usually is held to be several, rather than joint and several. *Pinal Creek*, supra, is an example. Thus, a party suing in contribution may only be able to shift to the contribution defendant the share of the joint liability (under § 107) fairly allocable to that defendant. Professor Araiza proposes that courts employ their equitable apportionment powers under § 113 to impose a modified joint and several liability regime, under which the liability of defendants could be joint and several if equitable factors called for such a result.

Issue (3) identified above can be closely related to issue (2). In Araiza's basic hypothetical, supra, an urgent question is who must pay for the "orphan shares" of the bankrupt and unidentified contributors to the hazardous waste site. If GM is indeed innocent as it claims, should it nevertheless—rather than Ford and Chrysler—have to pay for the orphan shares? Suppose that Ford and Chrysler acknowledge that each is responsible for twenty percent of the contamination or cleanup costs. If Ford and Chrysler are jointly as well as severally liable, they would be responsible for the orphan shares. Even without joint liability, a court may have the authority to charge Ford and Chrysler, perhaps along with GM, for at least some of part of the orphan shares. If not, GM, an allegedly innocent party, would be stuck with all of the orphan shares. The Ninth Circuit, in *Pinal Creek*, supra, said, "Under § 113(f)(1), the cost of orphan shares is distributed equitably among all PRPs, just as cleanup costs are." On these matters, in addition to the Araiza article, see Robert Redemann and Michael Smith, "The Evolution of PRP Standing under the Comprehensive Environmental Response, Compensation, and Liability Act of 1980," 21 *Wm. & Mary Envt'l L. & Pol'y Rev.* 300 (1997); William Evans, "The Phantom PRP in CERCLA Contribution Litigation: EPA to The Rescue?", 26 *Env't Rptr.* 2109 (1996).

Note on Alternatives to EPA Suit Under Section 107

(i) EPA Action Under Section 106

Instead of cleaning up an inactive hazardous waste site and seeking to recover response costs under section 107, can the federal government seek a mandatory injunction under section 106 to compel only a few out of many past offsite generators to do the cleanup? *A & F Materials* said yes, because section 106 is "dependent on the liability provisions of" section 107 (though the court acknowledged that mandatory injunctive relief is a harsh remedy, not to be granted lightly). 578 F.Supp. at 1257–1258. However, *United States v. Stringfellow,* 20 ERC 1905, 1910, 1984 WL 3206 (C.D.Cal.1984), held that sections 106 and 107 have "distinct functions in CERCLA" and that the government may not seek through section 106 an alternative means of reimbursement:

> Insofar as plaintiffs may intend to ask the Court to compel certain actions on the part of defendants, i.e., not merely to restrain all defendants but to force the undertaking of positive steps, the Court concludes that such orders would have to state with specificity the steps to be taken and the party to take them. If steps were ordered taken jointly, the Court would have to prescribe the participation of each defendant. These principles would obtain even if plaintiffs were to ask for money. See generally *United States v. Price,* 688 F.2d 204 (3d Cir.1982) (payment of money is possible form of equitable relief). Such equitable relief would be conceptually distinct from damages. In sum, the Court sees no role under section 106(a) of CERCLA for what plaintiffs describe as "joint and several liability to abate."

See also *United States v. Wade,* 546 F.Supp. 785 (E.D.Pa.1982) (government denied injunctive relief under section 106 to compel cleanup by "nonnegligent past off-site generators").

Pursuant to section 106(a) the EPA also may issue administrative orders directing potentially responsible parties ("PRPs") to take actions to protect public health and welfare and the environment from imminent and substantial endangerment. Failure to comply with such an order "without sufficient cause" can result in a fine of up to $25,000 per day under section 106 and,

[handwritten margin note: this is usually only done w/ companies that have w/ resources to do it, gov't still say how & what is to be done. ⟹ controls the clean up.]

under section 107(c)(3), in liability for "punitive damages in an amount at least equal to, and not more than three times, the amount of any costs incurred by the Fund as a result of such failure to take proper action." See Donald, "Defending Against Daily Fines and Punitive Damages under CERCLA: The Meaning of 'Without Sufficient Cause'," 19 *Colum.J.Envtl.L.* 185 (1994). *Solid State Circuits, Inc. v. Environmental Protection Agency,* 812 F.2d 383 (8th Cir.1987), upheld the constitutionality of section 107(c)(3). *United States v. Parsons,* 936 F.2d 526 (11th Cir.1991), held that the federal government could recover *four times* the amount that EPA spent to clean up a site after defendants failed to comply with an administrative order by EPA to perform the cleanup. The government recovered its full response costs under section 107(a) and treble that amount under section 107(c)(3).

(ii) Private Suits Under Section 107

Besides the federal and state governments, who else can recover response costs under section 107(a)? Local governments which conduct cleanups? The private owner of land adjacent to a leaking disposal site? The owner of the leaking disposal site? In *Jones v. Inmont Corp.,* 584 F.Supp. 1425 (S.D.Ohio 1984), the court held that under section 107(a)(4)(B) private parties owning land adjoining an illegal dump site were included within the phrase "any other person" and could recover their response costs from a past generator of hazardous waste deposited there. See also *Pinole Point Properties, Inc. v. Bethlehem Steel Corp.,* 596 F.Supp. 283 (N.D.Cal.1984). In *City of Philadelphia v. Stepan Chemical Co.,* 544 F.Supp. 1135 (E.D.Pa. 1982), it was held that the city, which owned land on which hazardous industrial wastes were dumped illegally without its permission, was not precluded from recovering its actual cleanup costs from defendant generators, even though the city itself, as site owner, might be liable for any response costs later incurred by the state or federal government. The court said that Philadelphia qualified as "any other person" under section 107(a)(4)(B).

[handwritten margin note: need standing so have to have injury in fact.]

Costs recoverable by private plaintiffs do not include compensation for lost property value, income, or medical monitoring. See *Piccolini v. Simon's Wrecking,* 686 F.Supp. 1063 (M.D.Pa.1988); *Lutz v. Chromatex, Inc.,* 718 F.Supp. 413 (M.D.Pa.1989). Plaintiffs in *Daigle v. Shell Oil Co.,* 972 F.2d 1527 (10th Cir.1992), were neighbors of the Rocky Mountain Arsenal, a federal chemical weapons facility generally regarded as one of the worst hazardous waste sites in the United States. Plaintiffs pointed out that CERCLA's definitions of "removal" and "remedial" actions both refer to "monitoring" necessary to protect "public health and welfare." Section 101(23) and (24). Plaintiffs argued that this language supported their claims for the costs of long term "medical monitoring" or "medical surveillance" designed to detect the onset of any latent disease that might be caused by exposure to toxic fumes released during cleanup of the arsenal. The court rejected the argument, saying that the definitions of removal and remedial actions are directed at containing and cleaning up hazardous substance releases. The monitoring contemplated by the statute is intended to prevent contact between contaminants and the public, and does not include long term health monitoring of the sort requested by plaintiffs. To the same effect is *Price v. U.S. Navy,* 39 F.3d 1011 (9th Cir.1994).

In *Key Tronic Corp. v. United States,* 511 U.S. 809, 114 S.Ct. 1960, 128 L.Ed.2d 797 (1994), one of several parties responsible for contaminating a landfill settled a lawsuit filed by EPA and then brought an action against the Air Force and other responsible parties to recover a share of its cleanup costs, including *attorneys' fees* for legal services in connection with (1) the identification of other PRPs, (2) the preparation and negotiation of the consent decree with EPA, and (3) the prosecution of its action against the Air Force. Since CERCLA §§ 107 and 113(f) do not expressly mention attorneys' fees, in contrast to §§ 310(f) (citizen suits) and 106(b)(2)(E) (persons erroneously ordered to pay response costs), the issue was whether attorneys' fees may constitute "necessary costs of response" recoverable under § 107(a)(4)(B). The Court held that under the "American Rule" discussed in the *Alyeska* case, page 580 supra, Key Tronic could not recover attorneys' fees for prosecuting its action against the Air Force. Neither was plaintiff allowed to recover for legal services in connection with the negotiations culminating in the consent decree with EPA. The Court viewed those services as "primarily protecting Key Tronic's interests as a defendant in the proceedings that established the extent of its liability," not as "necessary costs of response." However, "lawyers' work that is closely tied to the actual cleanup may constitute a necessary cost of response in and of itself," and the component of plaintiff's claim that covered work performed in identifying other PRPs was held to fall into this category. "Unlike the litigation services at issue in *Alyeska,* these efforts might well be performed by engineers, chemists, private investigators or other professionals who are not lawyers." (A court of appeals subsequently has held, in *United States v. Chapman*, 146 F.3d 1166 (9th Cir.1998), that response costs recoverable under § 107 by EPA, in contrast to a private plaintiff, may include attorneys' fees for litigation and negotiations.)

b. *Discussion Problem #2 on CERCLA Liability*

In 1970, Chemco, a new and wholly owned subsidiary of Padre Corp., purchased Blackacre (a warehouse on five acres of land) and began manufacturing specialized industrial chemicals there. Smith, an officer of Padre, was president of Chemco, and Jones was vice-president and plant manager.

Initially, toxic wastes generated by Chemco were kept in 55–gallon drums at Blackacre. In 1971, Jones told Smith that the drums were "piling up," and Smith suggested that Jones "find another solution" to the problem. Jones ordered the excavation of a "holding pond" at the rear of Blackacre, into which were placed the contents of the drums and most of the wastes subsequently generated by Chemco until it ceased operations in 1975. By 1979 the contents of the holding pond had seeped into the ground. In anticipation of selling Blackacre, Chemco filled in the former pond, planted grass there, and removed and sold all equipment from the building.

In 1980, Able purchased Blackacre from Chemco without knowledge of the waste disposal that had occurred there, though Able was aware that Chemco had manufactured chemicals at the site. (At that point Chemco was dissolved, and its only assets—the monies received from Able—were distributed to Padre.) Able used the building as a warehouse without any problem until 1990, when she sold Blackacre to Baker. Baker did not know that Blackacre previously had been owned by Chemco or that the building ever had been used for anything other than a warehouse. Baker has continued to use it for that purpose.

Now chemicals from Chemco's prior operations have appeared in the soil and well water of Whiteacre, neighboring land owned by White. White has spent thousands of dollars for soil and water tests and for an alternative water supply. On the basis of the next *(NEPACCO)* case and the text after it, how would you answer the following questions regarding various parties' possible liability to White under § 107 of CERCLA?

1. May Padre be liable as an "owner or operator" under § 107(a)(2)? As a "successor" to Chemco? What kinds of additional facts would be helpful in answering either of these questions?

2. Is either Smith or Jones liable under § 107(a)(2) as an "operator," or under § 107(a)(3) as a person who "arranged for disposal"?

3. Is Able liable under § 107(a)(2) as a person who "at the time of disposal" owned Blackacre?

4. Is Baker liable under § 107(a)(1), or does he have a defense as an "innocent landowner" under §§ 107(b)(3) and 101(35)(A)?

5. May White's recovery rights be limited because of the specific ways in which she has responded to the contamination?

UNITED STATES v. NORTHEASTERN PHARMACEUTICAL & CHEMICAL CO., INC.

United States Court of Appeals, Eighth Circuit, 1986.
810 F.2d 726, cert. denied 484 U.S. 848, 108 S.Ct. 146, 98 L.Ed.2d 102 (1987).

[The portions of the court's opinion discussing the facts and the applicability of RCRA appear at page 606 supra.]

A. LIABILITY UNDER CERCLA § 107(A)(1)

First, appellants argue the district court erred in finding them liable under CERCLA § 107(a)(1) as the "owners and operators" of a "facility" where hazardous substances are located. Appellants argue that, regardless of their relationship to the NEPACCO plant, they neither owned nor operated the Denney farm site, and that it is the Denney farm site, not the NEPACCO plant, that is a "facility" for purposes of "owner and operator" liability under CERCLA § 107(a)(1). We agree.

CERCLA defines the term "facility" in part as "any site or area where a hazardous substance has been deposited, stored, disposed of, or placed, or otherwise come to be located." CERCLA § 101(9)(B); see *New York v. Shore Realty Corp.*, 759 F.2d 1032, 1043 n. 15 (2d Cir.1985). The term "facility" should be construed very broadly to include "virtually any place at which hazardous wastes have been dumped, or otherwise disposed of." *United States v. Ward,* 618 F.Supp. at 895 (definition of "facility" includes roadsides where hazardous waste was dumped); see also *United States v. Conservation Chemical Co.,* 619 F.Supp. at 185 (stereotypical waste disposal facility); *New York v. General Electric Co.,* 592 F.Supp. 291, 296 (N.D.N.Y.1984) (dragstrip); *United States v. Metate Asbestos Corp.,* 584 F.Supp. 1143, 1148 (D.Ariz.1984) (real estate subdivision). In the present case, however, the place where the hazardous substances were disposed of and where the government has concentrated its clean-up efforts is the Denney farm site, not the NEPACCO plant. The Denney farm site is the "facility." Because NEPACCO, Lee and Michaels did not own or operate the Denney farm site, they cannot be held liable as the "owners or operators" of a "facility" where hazardous substances are located under CERCLA § 107(a)(1).

B.   INDIVIDUAL LIABILITY UNDER CERCLA § 107(A)(3)

CERCLA § 107(a)(3) imposes strict liability upon "any person" who arranged for the disposal or transportation for disposal of hazardous substances. As defined by statute, the term "person" includes both individuals and corporations and does not exclude corporate officers or employees. See CERCLA § 101(21). Congress could have limited the statutory definition of "person" but chose not to do so. Moreover, construction of CERCLA to impose liability upon only the corporation and not the individual corporate officers and employees who are responsible for making corporate decisions about the handling and disposal of hazardous substances would open an enormous, and clearly unintended, loophole in the statutory scheme.

First, Lee argues he cannot be held individually liable for having arranged for the transportation and disposal of hazardous substances under CERCLA § 107(a)(3) because he did not personally own or possess the hazardous substances. Lee argues NEPACCO owned or possessed the hazardous substances.

The government argues Lee "possessed" the hazardous substances within the meaning of CERCLA § 107(a)(3) because, as NEPACCO's plant supervisor, Lee had actual "control" over the NEPACCO plant's hazardous substances. We agree. It is the authority to control the handling and disposal of hazardous substances that is critical under the statutory scheme. The district court found that Lee, as plant supervisor, actually knew about, had immediate supervision over, and was directly responsible for arranging for the transportation and disposal of the NEPACCO plant's hazardous substances at the Denney farm site. * * *

* * *

The government argues Lee can be held individually liable, without "piercing the corporate veil," because Lee personally arranged for the disposal of hazardous substances in violation of CERCLA § 107(a)(3). We agree. As discussed below, Lee can be held individually liable because he personally participated in conduct that violated CERCLA; this personal liability is distinct from the derivative liability that results from "piercing the corporate veil." * * *

We now turn to Lee's basic argument. Lee argues that he cannot be held individually liable for NEPACCO's wrongful conduct because he acted solely as a corporate officer or employee on behalf of NEPACCO. The liability imposed upon Lee, however, was not derivative but personal. Liability was not premised solely upon Lee's status as a corporate officer or employee. Rather, Lee is individually liable under CERCLA § 107(a)(3) because he personally arranged for the transportation and disposal of hazardous substances on behalf of NEPACCO and thus actually participated in NEPACCO's CERCLA violations. * * *

* * *

Burden of Proof of Response Costs

The district court found appellants had the burden of proving the government's response costs were inconsistent with the NCP, and that response costs that are not inconsistent with the NCP are conclusively presumed to be reasonable and therefore recoverable. Appellants argue the district court erred in requiring them to prove the response costs were inconsistent with the NCP, not cost-effective or unnecessary. Appellants further argue the district court erred in assuming all costs that are consistent with the NCP are conclusively presumed to be reasonable. Appellants note that the information and facts necessary to establish consistency with the NCP are matters within the possession of the government.

We believe the district court's analysis is correct. CERCLA § 107(a)(4)(A) states that the government may recover from responsible parties "all costs of removal or remedial action * * * not inconsistent with the [NCP]." The statutory language itself establishes an exception for costs that are inconsistent with the NCP, but appellants, as the parties claiming the benefit of the exception, have the burden of proving that certain costs are inconsistent with the NCP and, therefore, not recoverable. Contrary to appellants' argument, "not inconsistent" is not, at least for purposes of statutory construction and not syntax, the same as "consistent."

The statutory scheme also supports allocation of the burden of proof of inconsistency with the NCP upon the defendants when the *government* seeks recovery of its response costs. As noted above, CERCLA § 107(a)(4)(A) provides that the federal government or a state can recover "all costs of removal or remedial action * * * not inconsistent with the [NCP]." In comparison, CERCLA § 107(a)(4)(B) provides that "any other person," referring to any "person" other than the federal government or a state, can recover "any other necessary costs of response * * * consistent with the [NCP]." That statutory language indicates that *non*-governmental entities must prove that their response costs are consistent with the NCP in order to recover them. The statutory scheme thus differentiates between governmental and non-governmental entities in allocating the burden of proof of whether response costs are consistent with the NCP.

The statutory language also supports the district court's reasoning that under CERCLA § 107(a)(4)(A) "all costs" incurred by the government that are not inconsistent with the NCP are conclusively presumed to be reasonable. CERCLA does not refer to "all *reasonable* costs" but simply to "all costs." * * *

Appellants also argue the district court erred in requiring them to establish that the government's cleanup actions were not cost-effective and necessary. This argument challenges the government's choice of a particular cleanup method. We note, however, that CERCLA § 105(3), (7) requires the EPA, as the agency designated by the President, to revise the NCP required by § 311 of the FWPCA, to include the "national hazardous substance response plan," which is specifically required by CERCLA to include "methods and criteria for determining the appropriate extent of removal, remedy, and other measures," and "means of assuring that remedial action measures are cost-effective." Consideration of whether particular action is "necessary" is thus factored into the "cost-effective" equation. The term "cost-effective" is defined by regulation as "the lowest cost alternative that is technologically feasible and reliable and which effectively mitigates and minimizes damage to and provides adequate protection of public health, welfare, or the environment."

Because determining the appropriate removal and remedial action involves specialized knowledge and expertise, the choice of a particular cleanup method is a matter within the discretion of the EPA. The applicable standard of review is whether the agency's choice is arbitrary and capricious. * * *

Here, appellants failed to show that the government's response costs were inconsistent with the NCP. Appellants also failed to show that the EPA acted arbitrarily and capriciously in choosing the particular method it used to clean up the Denney farm site.

Notes on the Identification of Responsible Parties

(i) Arrangers and Transporters

As *NEPACCO* indicates, CERCLA § 107(a)(3) imposes strict liability upon "any person" who "arranged for" disposal or treatment, or transport for disposal or treatment, of hazardous substances "owned or possessed" by such person. Section 107(a)(4) imposes similar liability upon any person who accepted any hazardous substances "for transport to disposal or treatment facilities * * * selected by such person."

Several cases involved arrangements between different companies to handle hazardous substances. In *United States v. Aceto Agricultural Chemicals Corp.*, 872 F.2d 1373 (8th Cir.1989), plaintiffs alleged that defendant pesticide manufacturers contracted with Aidex Corp. (a bankrupt at the time of litigation) for the "formulation" of their technical grade pesticides into commercial grade pesticides; that inherent in the formulation process (involving mixture of the manufacturers' active ingredients with inert materials according to the manufacturers' specifications) was the generation and disposal of wastes containing defendants' hazardous substances; and that defendants retained ownership of their hazardous substances throughout the formulation process. The court held that these allegations were sufficient to establish—for purposes of defeating defendants' motion to dismiss—that defendants "arranged for" disposal of the hazardous waste under CERCLA § 107(a)(3). Defendants unsuccessfully sought to analogize the case to previous ones in which district courts had refused to impose liability where a "useful" substance was sold to another party who then incorporated it into a product which was later disposed of.

In *Catellus Development Corp. v. United States*, 34 F.3d 748 (9th Cir.1994), an auto parts retailer had sold used automobile batteries to another company which reclaimed the lead and then disposed of the contaminated battery casings at what later became a CERCLA site. On appeal from the district court's summary judgment holding that the retailer had not "arranged for disposal" of a hazardous substance, the court of appeals reversed and remanded. Liability turned, said the court of appeals, on whether the used batteries constituted "solid waste," i.e., "discarded material," under RCRA § 1004(27). Under EPA's RCRA regulations, the spent batteries were solid waste, and the retailer "cannot escape having the battery casings defined as a discarded material simply by selling the battery to another party who then disposed of the casings. * * * Requiring continued ownership or control for section 107(a)(3) liability would make it too easy for a party, wishing to dispose of a hazardous substance, to escape by a sale its responsibility to see that the substance is safely disposed of."

Similarly, in *United States v. Cello-Foil Products, Inc.*, 100 F.3d 1227 (6th Cir.1996), defendants purchased industrial solvents from a manufacturer which shipped the solvents in its re-usable drums and charged defendants a deposit. Later an employee of the manufacturer retrieved the used drums when delivering new, full drums. Returned drums were taken to a facility owned by the manufacturer where any remaining contents were emptied onto the ground. The court of appeals reversed a summary judgment for defendants, holding that there were genuine issues of material fact concerning whether defendants "otherwise arranged for disposal" of their unused hazardous solvents through the drum-deposit arrangement. The court of appeals concluded that the requisite inquiry was whether defendants intended to enter into a transaction that included an "arrangement for" the disposal of hazardous substances. The court said, "The intent need not be proven by direct evidence, but can be inferred from the totality of the circumstances."

"Arranger" liability also may be used to reach corporate officers and parent corporations. In *United States v. TIC Investment Corp.*, 68 F.3d 1082 (8th Cir.1995), the questions were whether an officer in, and the corporate parents of, a subsidiary corporation were liable as arrangers for disposal of hazardous wastes. With respect to the corporate officer, the court held that the proper standard imposed direct arranger liability on him if he had the authority to control and did in fact exercise actual or substantial control, directly or indirectly, over the arrangement for disposal, or the off-site disposal of hazardous substances. The court found that the officer did not delegate authority and left no room for others to exercise any decisionmaking authority or judgment in any area of the business, including hazardous waste disposal. Thus, as a matter of law, he was liable as an arranger. With respect to the parent corporations, the court said that in order for them to incur direct arranger liability for a subsidiary's off-site disposal practices, "[T]here must be some causal connection or nexus between the parent corporation's conduct and the subsidiary's arrangement for disposal, or the off-site disposal itself." The court of appeals reversed the summary judgment against the parent corporations, saying that there were genuine issues of material fact concerning whether they not only had the authority to control but also "exercised actual or substantial control, directly or indirectly, over [the subsidiary's] waste disposal arrangement." (Compare the test for "owner and operator" liability, discussed below.)

With respect to *transporter* liability, the principal contested issue has been the meaning of § 107(a)(4)'s requirement that the disposal or treatment facility be "selected by" the transporter. In *Tippins, Inc. v. USX Corp.*, 37 F.3d 87 (3d Cir.1994), the court concluded that a person is liable as a transporter not only if it "ultimately selects" the disposal facility but also when it "actively participates in the disposal decision to the extent of having had substantial input" into which facility was ultimately chosen.

United States v. USX Corp., 68 F.3d 811 (3d Cir. 1995), involved a claim against the principal shareholders and officers of a closely held corporation that transported hazardous substances. The United States argued that § 107(a)(4) was intended to impose liability on those who control the affairs of a responsible corporation, irrespective of whether those in control actually participated in the liability-creating conduct. The court rejected that argument, saying that liability may not be imposed solely on the basis of an officer's or shareholder's active involvement in the corporation's day-to-day affairs. "Instead, there must be a showing that the person sought to be held liable actually participated in the liability-creating conduct." However, liability is not limited to those who personally participate in the transportation of hazardous wastes, nor is it necessary that the officer participate in the selection of the disposal facility. "Liability may be imposed where the officer is aware of the acceptance of materials for transport and of his company's substantial participation in the selection of the disposal facility. An officer who has authority to control disposal decisions should not escape liability under § 107(a)(4) when he or she has actual knowledge that a subordinate has selected a disposal site and, effectively, acquiesces in the subordinate's actions."

(ii) Owners and Operators

Section 107(a)(1) and (2) of CERCLA impose liability on the *current* "owner and operator" of a disposal or treatment facility from which there is a release or threatened *release*, and on "any person who *at the time of disposal* * * * owned or operated" the facility (emphasis added).

In *State of New York v. Shore Realty Corp.*, 759 F.2d 1032 (2d Cir.1985), the state brought suit against Shore and its officer and shareholder, Leo-

Grande, who had incorporated Shore solely for the purpose of purchasing and developing the Shore Road property. At the time of acquisition, Leo-Grande—who directed and controlled all corporate decisions and actions—knew that hazardous waste was stored there, though neither Shore nor LeoGrande had participated in its generation or transportation. The court held that Shore and LeoGrande were jointly and severally liable under CERCLA for the state's response costs, despite the fact that the Shore Road site was not on the EPA's National Priorities List (NPL). In explaining its decision, the court said:

> Instead of distinguishing between the scope of section 9607 and the scope of section 9604, we hold that NPL listing is not a general requirement under the NCP. We see the NPL as a limitation on remedial, or long-term, actions—as opposed to removal, or short-term, actions—particularly federally funded remedial actions. The provisions requiring the establishment of NPL criteria and listing appear to limit their own application to remedial actions. Section 9605(8)(A) requires EPA to include in the NCP "criteria for determining priorities among releases or threatened releases * * * for the purpose of taking remedial action and, to the extent practicable taking into account the potential urgency of such action, for the purpose of taking removal action." And section 9605(8)(B), which requires EPA to draw up the NPL, refers to "priorities for remedial action." And section 9604, which authorizes and governs federal response actions, reveals the special role of the NPL for federally sponsored remedial actions. Section 9604(c)(3) states that federal remedial actions can be taken only if "the State in which the release occurs first enters into a contract or cooperative agreement" with the federal government, thus setting up a joint federal-state cost-sharing and cleanup effort. At the same time, section 9604(d)(1) states that such joint efforts must be taken "in accordance with criteria and priorities established pursuant to section 9605(8)"—the NPL provision. If the NPL criteria and listing were a general requirement for action "consistent with" the NCP, this language would be surplusage. * * *

* * *

Finally, we reject Shore's argument that the State's response costs are not recoverable because the State has failed to comply with the NCP by not obtaining EPA authorization, nor making a firm commitment to provide further funding for remedial implementation nor submitting an estimate of costs. See 40 C.F.R. § 300.62 (1984) (describing the states' role in joint federal-state response actions). EPA designed the regulatory scheme—the NCP—focusing on federal and joint federal-state efforts. See, e.g., id. § 300.6 (defining "lead agency"). Shore apparently is arguing that EPA has ruled that the State cannot act on its own and seek liability under CERCLA. We disagree. Congress envisioned states' using their own resources for cleanup and recovering those costs from polluters under section 9607(a)(4)(A). We read section 9607(a)(4)(A)'s requirement of consistency with the NCP to mean that states cannot recover costs inconsistent with the response methods outlined in the NCP. Moreover, the NCP itself recognizes a role for states in compelling "potentially responsible parties" to undertake response actions independent of EPA and without seeking reimbursement from Superfund. Thus, the NCP's requirements concerning collaboration in a joint federal-state cleanup effort are inapplicable where the State is acting on its own. Indeed, the kind of action taken here is precisely that envisioned by the regulations.

* * *

We hold LeoGrande liable as an "operator" under CERCLA, 42 U.S.C. § 9607, for the State's response costs. Under CERCLA "owner or operator" is defined to mean "any person owning or operating" an onshore facility, id. § 9601(20)(A), and "person" includes individuals as well as corporations, id. § 9601(21). More important, the definition of "owner or operator" excludes "a person, who, without participating in the management of a * * * facility, holds indicia of ownership primarily to protect his security interest in the facility." Id. § 9601(20)(A). The use of this exception implies that an owning stockholder who manages the corporation, such as LeoGrande, is liable under CERCLA as an "owner or operator." That conclusion is consistent with that of other courts that have addressed the issue. In any event, LeoGrande is in charge of the operation of the facility in question, and as such is an "operator" within the meaning of CERCLA.

On the other hand, a "consultant" who also was the corporate secretary and chairman of the board, and who owned 85 percent of the company's stock, was held not to be an owner or operator under section 107 in *Riverside Market Development Corp. v. International Building Products, Inc.,* 931 F.2d 327 (5th Cir.1991), cert. denied 502 U.S. 1004, 112 S.Ct. 636, 116 L.Ed.2d 654 (1991). The court of appeals found that plaintiffs had failed to produce any evidence showing that the individual personally participated in any conduct that violated CERCLA. He lived in New York and visited the New Orleans plant only two to four times a year, and his participation in plant operations was limited to reviewing financial statements and attending meetings of the officers. See generally Heidt, "Liability of Shareholders Under the Comprehensive Environmental Response, Compensation and Liability Act (CERCLA)," 52 *Ohio St. L.J.* 133 (1991); Healy, "Direct Liability for Hazardous Substance Cleanups Under CERCLA: A Comprehensive Approach," 42 *Case Western Res.L.Rev.* 65 (1992).

United States v. Gurley, 43 F.3d 1188 (8th Cir.1994), cert. denied 516 U.S. 817, 116 S.Ct. 73, 133 L.Ed.2d 33 (1995), imposed "operator" liability not only upon the principal shareholder and president of the corporate owner of a disposal site, but also upon his son who was an employee of the corporation. Citing trial court findings that the son "personally participated in the disposal of the hazardous substances" and that he "had extensive authority ... to implement the policies and practices of the corporate entity, which included the disposal of these hazardous substances," the court of appeals concluded that the evidence clearly established that the son "had *authority* to determine [the corporation's] hazardous waste disposal activities and that he actually *exercised* that authority" (emphasis added). (Query: Would the son also be liable as an "arranger"?)

Is a *parent* corporation necessarily the "owner or operator" of a hazardous waste facility owned by its wholly owned subsidiary? In *United States v.*

Bestfoods, ___ U.S. ___, 118 S.Ct. 1876, 141 L.Ed.2d 43 (1998), the Supreme Court said that the issue was "whether a parent corporation that actively participated in, and exercised control over, the operations of a subsidiary may, without more, be held liable as an operator of a polluting facility owned or operated by the subsidiary." The Court then said, "We answer no, unless the corporate veil may be pierced. But a corporate parent that actively participated in, and exercised control over, the operations of the *facility itself* may be held directly liable in its own right [under CERCLA] as an operator of the facility." [Emphasis added.] Under general corporate law, the corporate veil may be pierced and the parent held liable for the subsidiary's conduct when, e.g., the corporate form would otherwise be misused to accomplish wrongful purposes, most notably fraud, on the parent's behalf; or when stock ownership has been resorted to for the purpose of controlling a subsidiary company so that it may be used as a mere agency or instrumentality of the parent company. But under § 107(a) of CERCLA, according to the Court, an "operator" is one who "directs the workings of, manages, or conducts the affairs of a facility." The operator—e.g., a parent corporation acting through an agent who is not an officer of the subsidiary—"must manage, direct, or conduct operations specifically related to pollution, that is, operations having to do with the leakage or disposal of hazardous waste, or decisions about compliance with environmental regulations." The critical question under § 107(a) is "whether, in degree and detail, actions directed to the facility by an agent of the parent alone are eccentric under accepted norms of parental oversight of a subsidiary's facility." Would a parent that satisfied this test also be liable as an "arranger"?

Because section 107(a) extends liability for cleanup costs to all "owners" of contaminated properties, regardless of the circumstances of their ownership, parties who *involuntarily or innocently* acquired former disposal sites have been required to pay for cleanup, even when the cost exceeded the value of the land. Prompted by the perceived unfairness of such results, Congress in 1986 added a new defense to protect "innocent landowners." While section 107(a)'s general liability standard for "owners and operators" was maintained, Congress expanded section 107(b)(3)'s third-party exception by redefining the term "contractual relationship" in section 101(35). Now, "innocent landowners" who acquire property without "reason to know" that hazardous substances have been disposed of there are not liable as owners or operators under section 107. However, section 101(35) provides, "To establish that the defendant had no reason to know . . . , the defendant must have undertaken, at the time of acquisition, all appropriate inquiry into the previous ownership and uses of the property consistent with good commercial or customary practice in an effort to minimize liability." EPA has declined to issue an administrative standard to clarify the meaning of "all appropriate inquiry," though recognizing that this is "a rapidly evolving field" and that potential purchasers have "an interest in a reliable standard." See 24 *Envir.Rep.* 2199 (1994). Concerning the "due care" required of "innocent" landowners, see Robert Hernan, "Due and Don't Care Under CERCLA: An Emerging Standard for Current Owners," 27 *Envt'l L. Rptr.* 10064 (1997) (owner should, inter alia, notify appropriate governmental authorities upon learning of possible contamination and cooperate with them to determine its scope, endeavor to limit its spread, and remain involved in the investigation and remediation). Innocent owners who learn of releases at the site and then transfer ownership without disclosing such information to subsequent purchasers are denied "innocent" status by § 101(35)(C) and thus are fully liable under section 107(a).

What about landowners like Shore Realty who *know* the condition of the site when they acquire ownership, and who then transfer it to another person after *disclosing* the condition? Are such "passive intervening land-owners" liable under section 107(a)(2)? The answer depends on the definition of "disposal" in section 107(a)(2). Section 101(29) states that "disposal" shall have the meaning provided in section 1004(3) of the Solid Waste Disposal Act, which defines it to include "discharge, deposit, injection, dumping, spilling, *leaking,* or placing of . . . hazardous waste into or on any land or water . . ." (emphasis added). See the discussion of this provision in part III of the opinion in *United States v. Waste Industries, Inc.,* page 603 supra, and in note 2 at page 605. The courts have split on the question of CERCLA liability of passive intervening landowners. In *Nurad, Inc. v. William E. Hooper & Sons Co.,* 966 F.2d 837 (4th Cir.1992), cert. denied 506 U.S. 940, 113 S.Ct. 377, 121 L.Ed.2d 288 (1992), the current owner of contaminated property brought an action against previous owners and previous tenants, seeking reimbursement of costs incurred in removing from the property underground storage tanks and their hazardous contents. The court held that section 107(a)(2) imposes liability not only for active involvement in the "dumping" or "placing" of hazardous wastes at the facility, but for ownership of the facility at a time that hazardous waste was "spilling" or "leaking." The previous owners were held liable to plaintiff, but the claims against the tenants were dismissed on the ground that they lacked authority to control the storage tanks and therefore did not "operate" a facility under section 107(a). However, in *United States v. CDMG Realty Co..,* 96 F.3d 706 (3d Cir.1996), the court rejected the view taken in *Waste Industries* and *Nurad* and held that "while 'leaking' and 'spilling' may not require affirmative human conduct, neither word denotes the gradual spreading of contamination." The court said that it is especially unjustified to stretch the meaning of "leaking" and "spilling" to encompass the passive migration that generally occurs in landfills in view of the fact that another word used in CERCLA, "release," shows that Congress "knew precisely how to refer to this spreading of waste." A prior owner who owned a waste site at the time of "disposal" is liable under § 107(a) only in the event of a "release" or "threatened release." § 101(22) defines release as "any spilling, leaking, . . . escaping, leaching. . . ." The court said that "[l]eaching of contaminants from rain and groundwater movement is a principal cause of contaminant movement in landfills," and that "leaching" is the word commonly used in the environmental context to describe the passive migration of contaminants. The court also said that because CERCLA conditions the innocent landowner defense on the defendant's having purchased the property "after the disposal" of hazardous waste there, "disposal" cannot consist of the constant spreading of contaminants. "Otherwise, the defense would almost never apply, as there would generally be no point 'after disposal'." See Michael Caplan, "Escaping CERCLA Liability: The Interim Owner Passive Migration Defense Gains Circuit Recognition," 28 *Envt'l L. Rptr.* 10121 (1998).

(iii) Successors

In *Louisiana–Pacific Corp. v. Asarco, Inc.,* 909 F.2d 1260 (9th Cir.1990), applying *federal* common law, the court held that CERCLA liability may be imposed upon "successors"—companies that purchase the stock or assets of hazardous waste disposers—under the narrow liability rules applied in most *states*. Under those rules an asset purchaser may be liable only if (1) it expressly or impliedly agreed to assume the predecessor's liabilities, (2) the transaction amounted to a "de facto" merger, (3) the successor is "merely a continuation" of the predecessor, or (4) the transaction involved fraud in an attempt to escape liability. The court left open the possible application of two more expansive successor liability rules, the "product line" rule and the "continuing business enterprise" rule. See Janke and Kuryla, "Environmental Liability Risks for Asset Purchasers," 24 *Envir.Rep.* 2237 (1994); Light, " 'Product Line' and 'Continuity of Enterprise' Theories of Corporation Successor Liability Under CERCLA," 11 *Miss.C.L.Rev.* 63 (1990).

Applying "evolving principles of federal common law" the court in *United States v. Carolina Transformer Co.,* 978 F.2d 832 (4th Cir.1992), applied the continuing business enterprise rule (which it called the "continuity of enterprise" or "substantial continuity" rule) in a case that did not come within the "mere continuation" rule because there was no overlap of stock ownership between the seller and the buyer of a transformer construction business. The factors which the court considered in holding the purchaser liable under CERCLA were (1) retention of the same employees, (2) retention of the same supervisory personnel, (3) retention of the same production facilities in the same location, (4) production of the same product, (5) retention of the same name, (6) continuity of assets, (7) continuity of general business operations, and (8) the successor's holding itself out as the continuation of the previous enterprise.

United States v. Mexico Feed & Seed Co., 980 F.2d 478 (8th Cir.1992), held that a firm which purchased the assets of a waste oil company was not liable under CERCLA as a corporate successor because the purchaser was neither a "mere continuation" nor even a "substantial continuation" of the waste oil company. The court found that imposition of successor liability would be improper because (1) the purchaser was a larger, pre-existing company that had been a competitor of the waste oil company, (2) the purchaser had no knowledge of, and did not use, the waste oil storage tanks associated with the contaminated site, and (3) the government did not present sufficient evidence to support its claim that the purchaser qualified as a "substantial continuation" of the waste oil company. In a footnote the court said, "The issue of whether federal or state law should be used in analyzing successor liability was not raised by the parties and we do not decide it. However, considering the national application of CERCLA and fairness to similarly situated parties, the district court was probably correct in applying federal law."

In *Atchison, Topeka & Santa Fe Railway Co. v. Brown & Bryant, Inc.,* 159 F.3d 358 (9th Cir.1998), the Ninth Circuit expressed doubt about the correctness of its earlier view, in *Louisiana-Pacific,* supra, that federal rather than state common law should govern successor liability under CERCLA. Citing intervening decisions by the Supreme Court in *O'Melveny*

& *Myers v. FDIC,* 512 U.S. 79, 114 S.Ct. 2048, 129 L.Ed.2d 67 (1994), and *Atherton v. FDIC,* 519 U.S. 213, 117 S.Ct. 666, 136 L.Ed.2d 656 (1997), neither of which involved CERCLA, the Ninth Circuit said that the Supreme Court had "rejected many of the very arguments that *Louisiana-Pacific* accepted in deciding CERCLA necessitated a set of uniform federal rules for successor liability." The court read *O'Melveny* to mean that when dealing with a "comprehensive and detailed" federal statutory regulation, a court should "presume that matters left unaddressed in such a scheme are subject to state law." Before a court can recognize a federal rule of decision, there must be a "significant conflict between some federal policy or interest and the use of state law." The court noted that the argued "need" for uniformity of successor liability under CERCLA "stems not from disarray among the various states, but from the alleged need for a more expansive view of successor liability than state law currently provides—in other words, the notion that state law on this issue is inadequate for CERCLA's purposes." The court declined to apply the "sustantial continuity" rule of *Carolina Transformer*, supra, saying, "Fortunately, we need not determine whether state law dictates the parameters of successor liability under CERCLA, as we would reach the same result under federal common law. This is true because we choose not to extend the 'mere continuation' exception to include the broader notion of a 'sustantial continuation.' ... Furthermore, we believe ... the broader 'substantial continuation' exception adds little in the end. In cases in which the broader exception has been applied ..., there has usually been some fraudulent intent and collusion present, in which case the purchaser would [be] liable under another traditional exception—the fraudulently-entered transaction exception. *See, e.g., United States v. Carolina Transformer Co.*"

Both federal and state rules concerning the liability of successors may be modified by contract. *Indemnification agreements* are often used in transactions involving the acquisition of property to address environmental and other liabilities related to the assets and business transferred. Two key issues raised by CERCLA's language and judicial decisions concerning the enforceability of indemnification agreements are (1) whether indemnification agreements are barred by § 107(e), and, if not, (2) whether they nevertheless should be construed narrowly. Section 107(e)(1) provides:

> No indemnification, hold harmless, or similar agreement or conveyance shall be effective to transfer from the owner or operator of any vessel or facility or from any person who may be liable for a release or threat of release under this section, to any other person the liability imposed under this section. Nothing in this subsection shall bar any agreement to insure, hold harmless, or indemnify a party to such agreement for any liability under this section.

A majority of federal courts interpret § 107(e) as allowing indemnity agreements. As a result, indemnity agreements have become an integral part of real estate transactions. For example, in *Mardan Corp. v. C.G.C. Music, Ltd.,* 804 F.2d 1454 (9th Cir.1986), a seller sold land on which it had manufactured musical instruments and deposited waste. As part of the sale the purchaser agreed to release the seller from undisclosed environmental liabilities. After EPA brought an enforcement action against the purchaser (which also had deposited waste upon the property), the purchaser sued the seller under § 107 for recovery of its cleanup costs. The court affirmed a summary judgment for the seller, saying:

> Contractual arrangements apportioning CERCLA liabilities between private "responsible parties" are essentially tangential to the enforcement of CERCLA's liability provisions. Such agreements cannot alter or excuse the underlying liability, but can only change who ultimately pays that liability.

In *AM International v. International Forging Equipment Corp.,* 982 F.2d 989 (6th Cir.1993), the court agreed that § 107(e) does not bar indemnification agreements:

> The underlying purpose of the statutory language under scrutiny is to ensure that responsible parties will pay for the cleanup and that they may not avoid liability to the government by transferring this liability to another. However, this purpose is not inconsistent with parties responsible for the cleanup transferring or allocating among themselves the cost associated with this liability, so long as they remain liable to the third party who can demand the cleanup. This is what is permitted by the second sentence—the shifting or allocation of the risk of the cost of liability between potentially responsible persons, without diluting CERCLA liability for the cleanup itself.

Concerning the construction of indemnification agreements, most courts have applied, either explicitly or implicitly, a rule that such arrangements can bar CERCLA liability between the parties only if there is clear language in the agreement anticipating and requiring such a result. That is, in interpreting release and indemnification agreements, courts have been reluctant to apply those agreements to CERCLA liability absent a finding that the agreement expressly provided for a release of such liabilities or, at a minimum, of "CERCLA—like" environmental liabilities. See *Mobay Corp. v. Allied–Signal, Inc.,* 761 F.Supp. 345 (D.N.J.1991); *Southland Corp. v. Ashland Oil, Inc.,* 696 F.Supp. 994 (D.N.J.1988).

(iv) Lenders and Trustees

CERCLA's significance to mortgage lenders became apparent in *United States v. Maryland Bank & Trust Co.,* 632 F.Supp. 573 (D.Md.1986). The bank held a $335,000 purchase-money mortgage on certain land. The buyer defaulted, and the bank instituted a foreclosure suit. After the bank took title to the land, state and federal authorities determined that it was a contaminated waste site requiring cleanup under CERCLA. The bank was held liable for response costs of more than $550,000.

Section 101(20)(A) of CERCLA now excludes from the definition of "owner or operator" any "person, who, without participating in the management of a . . . facility, holds indicia of ownership primarily to protect his security interest in the . . . facility." Financial institutions and other secured creditors were shocked by the decision in *United States v. Fleet Factors Corp.,* 901 F.2d 1550 (11th Cir.1990), cert. denied 498 U.S. 1046, 111 S.Ct. 752, 112 L.Ed.2d 772 (1991), which denied Fleet's motion for summary judgment because Fleet's activities as a secured creditor might make it liable if it participated in the "financial management of a facility to a degree indicating a *capacity* to influence the [bankrupt debtor] corporation's treatment of hazardous wastes" (emphasis added). The court said that it was not necessary, for liability, that the creditor actually involve itself in day-to-day operations of the facility; it was enough if the involvement with management was "sufficiently broad to support the inference that it could affect hazardous waste decisions if it so chose." Prior district court decisions had permitted lenders to participate in the financial affairs of the borrowers without risking CERCLA liability, so long as the lenders did not become too involved in the borrowers' day-to-day operations.

Shortly after *Fleet Factors,* another court of appeals indicated that the mere capacity or right to control facility operations was not enough to void the secured creditor exemption, and suggested that the creditor must participate in the operational management of the facility to lose the benefit of the exemption. *In re Bergsoe Metal Corp.,* 910 F.2d 668 (9th Cir.1990).

Responding to the understandable clamor from the banking community and to the federal government's increasing role as a secured creditor after taking over failed savings and loans, EPA instituted a rulemaking proceeding to define the secured creditor exemption when legislative efforts to amend CERCLA failed. In April 1992, EPA issued the final regulation, which employed a framework of specific tests to provide clearer articulation of a lender's CERCLA liability. 57 Fed.Reg. 18,382, codified at 40 CFR 300.1100. See O'Brien and Gibson, "Final EPA Rule Allows Traditional Lender Activities Without Superfund Liabilities," 23 *Envir.Rep.* 326 (1992). The rule provided an overall standard for judging when a lender's "[p]articipation in [m]anagement" caused the lender to forfeit its exemption. § 300.1100(c)(1). A lender could, without incurring liability, undertake investigatory actions before the creation of a security interest, monitor or inspect the facility, and require that the borrower comply with all environmental standards. § 300.1100(c)(2). When a loan neared default, the rule permitted the lender to engage in work-out negotiations and activities, including ensuring that the collateral facility did not violate environmental laws. § 300.1100(c)(2)(ii)(B). The rule also protected a secured creditor that acquired full title to the collateral property through foreclosure, as long as the creditor did not participate in the facility's management prior to foreclosure and undertook certain diligent efforts to divest itself of the property. § 300.1100(d). Lenders still faced liability under section 107(a)(3) and (4)— as opposed to liability as "owner or operator" under section 107(a)(1) and (2)—if they arranged for the disposal of hazardous substances at a facility or accepted hazardous waste for transportation and disposal. § 300.1100(d)(3).

In *Kelley v. Environmental Protection Agency,* 15 F.3d 1100 (D.C.Cir. 1994), rehearing denied 25 F.3d 1088 (D.C.Cir.1994), *cert. denied* 513 U.S. 1110, 115 S.Ct. 900, 130 L.Ed.2d 784 (1995), the court vacated EPA's rule on lender liability on procedural grounds. But in 1996, Public Law 104–208, the omnibus budget bill, basically reinstated EPA's 1992 lender liability regulation. The law did this by adding to CERCLA § 101(20), defining "owner or operator," a new subsection (E), "Exclusion of Lenders not Participants in Management." The phrase "participate in management" is defined to mean "actually participating in the management or operational affairs" of a facility, and "does not include merely having the capacity to influence, or the unexercised right to control," facility operations.

There also has been controversy and some litigation concerning the possible liability of *trustees* when trust property is contaminated. CERCLA does not specifically address whether trustees may be *personally* liable, *beyond* the extent of the trust assets, for cleanup costs. There is no express exemption for trustees, in contrast to the situation with respect to secured creditors. The leading case is *City of Phoenix v. Garbage Services Co.,* 816 F.Supp. 564 (D.Ariz.1993).

In determining the scope of liability, the *Phoenix* court looked to existing common law on trustee liability, as reflected in sections 264 and 265 of the Restatement (Second) of Trusts. The court said that if a trustee were held liable under CERCLA § 107(a)(1) solely because he was the current owner of a facility, the disposal of hazardous substances having occurred before he obtained legal title, liability would be limited to the amount of the trust assets. By contrast, liability under § 107(a)(2) for a trustee who held title to the facility at the time of disposal would be as follows:

> Where a trustee is held liable under subsection 107(a)(2), but the trustee did not have the power to control the use of trust property, the trustee's liability is limited to the extent that the trust assets are sufficient to indemnify him.

> Where a trustee had the power to control the use of trust property, and knowingly allowed the property to be used for the disposal of hazardous substances, then the trustee is liable under subsection 107(a)(2) to the same extent that he would be liable if he held the property free of trust.

Since the defendant bank had made the decisions to purchase the operating waste disposal site as a trust asset and to continue leasing it for use as a disposal facility for hazardous substances, the bank would be liable under § 107(a)(2), without regard to the amount of trust assets available to indemnify it, if the plaintiff could prove at trial that hazardous substances were disposed of there when the bank held title.

(v) Governmental Entities

Prior to the 1986 amendments to CERCLA, it was held in *United States v. Union Gas Co.,* 792 F.2d 372 (3d Cir.1986), vacated and remanded 479 U.S. 1025, 107 S.Ct. 865, 93 L.Ed.2d 821 (1987), that the Eleventh Amendment to the Constitution barred the imposition of cleanup liability under CERCLA against states because section 107 did not specifically identify states as liable parties. The court of appeals said that in order to overcome the Eleventh Amendment, the statute had to make it clear that Congress consciously and directly focused on the issue of state sovereign immunity and chose to abrogate it. Subsequently, Congress in 1986 amended section 101(20), defining "owner or operator," to provide for state and local governmental liability under section 107. The Supreme Court then concluded that Congress did intend to subject states to suits for response costs if states caused or contributed to hazardous substance releases. *Pennsylvania v. Union Gas Co.,* 491 U.S. 1, 109 S.Ct. 2273, 105 L.Ed.2d 1 (1989). However, in *Seminole Tribe of Florida v. Florida,* 517 U.S. 44, 116 S.Ct. 1114, 134 L.Ed.2d 252 (1996), the Supreme Court overruled its decision in *Pennsylvania v. Union Gas Co.* The Court held that the Commerce Clause does not authorize Congress to abrogate a state's Eleventh Amendment immunity to suit without its consent. (But the Eleventh Amendment does not apply where the suit is brought by the EPA).

There has been much controversy about the CERCLA liability of *municipal* governments, many of which own or operate disposal or treatment facilities, transport wastes to such facilities, or arrange for disposal, treatment or transport. Municipalities, which are not protected by the Eleventh Amendment, hoped that the courts would interpret CERCLA narrowly to exclude them from section 107(a)'s list of "covered persons." However, federal courts consistently have interpreted the law broadly, holding that municipalities may be liable as owners and operators of hazardous waste sites as well as transporters and generators of hazardous waste. See Manko and Cozine, "The Battle Over Municipal Liability Under CERCLA Heats Up: An Analysis of Proposed Congressional Amendments to Superfund," 5 *Vill.Envtl.L.J.* 23 (1994).

The most important case on this subject is *B.F. Goodrich Co. v. Murtha*, 958 F.2d 1192 (2d Cir.1992). In holding that municipalities which send their residents' household waste to landfills can be liable under CERCLA, the court rejected the following arguments by the municipal defendants: (1) that a municipality cannot be liable under CERCLA for the disposal of hazardous substances since it is acting in its sovereign capacity; (2) that CERCLA's silence regarding municipal solid waste is evidence that Congress intended to exclude it from the definition of hazardous substances; (3) that the exemption for household hazardous waste under RCRA is incorporated into CERCLA's definition of hazardous substances; (4) that CERCLA's legislative history evinces an intent to exclude municipalities from liability for the disposal of municipal solid waste; and (5) that EPA interpreted CERCLA as imposing no liability on municipalities for the disposal of municipal waste.

Under its 1989 "Interim Policy on CERCLA Settlements Involving Municipalities and Municipal Wastes," 54 Fed.Reg. 51071, EPA has attempted to ameliorate the perceived harshness of CERCLA as applied to municipalities. (The policy was supplemented by a guidance on "Policy for Municipality and Municipal Solid Waste CERCLA Settlements at NPL Co–Disposal Sites," reprinted at 28 *Env't Rptr.* 2136 (1998).) Under this policy, EPA generally does not pursue municipalities under CERCLA as generators or transporters of municipal solid waste unless the waste contains hazardous substances derived from commercial, institutional or industrial activity. However, the policy does not address the potential liability of municipalities that own or operate landfills, nor does it immunize municipalities from suits for contribution by third parties whom EPA does pursue.

With respect to hazardous waste facilities owned or operated by the *federal* government, section 120 of CERCLA provides that "[e]ach department, agency and instrumentality of the United States * * * shall be subject to * * * this chapter * * * to the same extent * * * as any nongovernmental entity, including liability under section [107]." Federal facilities are included on the National Priorities List, but funds for cleanup must come from the budget of the responsible department or agency, not from the Superfund.

The greatest potential U.S. liability under section 120 appears to stem from contaminated military bases and nuclear weapons facilities. See "Cleaning Up Federal Facilities: Controversy Over an Environmental Peace Dividend," 23 *Envir.Rep.* 2659 (1993). The facilities need not be owned by the federal government. In *FMC Corp. v. Department of Commerce,* 29 F.3d 833 (3d Cir.1994) (en banc), a contribution suit by a private PRP, the court held that section 120 waives the federal government's immunity from

→ CERCLA liability when the government engages in activities that would subject private parties to liability, and that the government therefore was liable under section 107 as "operator" of a private manufacturing facility over which the government "exerted considerable day-to-day control" during World War II to meet production goals for high-tenacity rayon. Rejecting the government's argument for a *"per se* rule that regulatory activities cannot constitute the basis for CERCLA liability," the court said that "the government can be liable when it engages in regulatory activities extensive enough to make it an operator of a facility or an arranger of the disposal of hazardous wastes."

———

c. *Remedy Selection*

Selection of an appropriate remedy for cleaning up a contaminated disposal site often is a difficult process involving strong differences of opinion among federal, state and local officials, private PRPs, and neighboring landowners. The PRPs do not want to pay for excessively elaborate and expensive responses; neighbors may be concerned that the cleanup will be inadequate, or that it will exacerbate the situation by releasing contaminants that pose little current danger, or that it will be too disruptive of their lives for too long a time; state officials may want enforcement of state regulatory standards which are stricter than federal standards but which EPA believes should be waived; and local officials may be concerned about when and whether the site can be redeveloped and again be a source of jobs and tax revenues.

The following article analyzes the legal framework for remedy selection at CERCLA sites.

PADGETT, "SELECTING REMEDIES AT SUPERFUND SITES: HOW SHOULD 'CLEAN' BE DETERMINED?"[a]

18 *Vermont Law Review* 361, 367–370, 381–387, 391–405 (1994).

The original Superfund statute failed to answer the following two questions: how clean is "clean" and how should "clean" be accomplished? Section 121 [enacted in 1986] was the congressional response to its earlier virtual silence on these issues. * * * While filling this void * * *, Congress embedded a fundamental conflict into the foundation of CERCLA's remedy selection process. Remedies selected in accordance

a. Copyright © 1994 by the Vermont Law Review. Reprinted with permission.

with section 121 were required to protect human health and the environment, attain compliance with ARARs, and be both "cost effective" and "permanent" through the use of treatment technologies to the "maximum extent practicable." The conflict inherent in these directives lies in the fact that, at nearly every Superfund site, a remedy that permanently eliminates the risks posed by the hazardous substances through the use of treatment technology will be far more costly than a remedy that reduces risks by containing or limiting human exposure to the hazardous substances.

* * *

Section 121 established four basic objectives to guide the selection of remedial actions at Superfund sites. Remedial actions must:

> protect human health and the environment, attain applicable or relevant and appropriate requirements [ARARs], be cost effective, and utilize permanent solutions, and alternative treatment or resource recovery technologies, to the maximum extent practicable.

Specifically, section 121(b), which identifies "[g]eneral rules" for selecting remedies, provides that "[t]he President shall select a remedial action that is protective of human health and the environment, that is cost effective, and that utilizes permanent solutions and alternative treatment technologies or resource recovery technologies to the maximum extent practicable."

Subsection (d) of section 121, which establishes the "[d]egree of cleanup" required of remedial actions, reiterates the idea that remedial actions "shall attain a degree of cleanup of hazardous substances ... and of control of further release at a minimum which assures protection of human health and the environment." In circumstances where any hazardous substance, pollutant, or contaminant will remain onsite, subsection (d) further specifies that remedial actions also must comply with any ARAR. Specifically, such remedial action must require "a level or standard of control for such hazardous substance or pollutant or contaminant which at least attains such legally applicable or relevant and appropriate standard, requirement, criteria, or limitation."

Although section 121 specifies that the use of treatment to reduce the volume, toxicity, or mobility of hazardous substances is a "preference," remedies which do not utilize such treatment may be selected if the President "publish[es] an explanation as to why a remedial action involving such reductions was not selected." In addition, the requirement that any particular ARAR be attained by a remedy may be waived by EPA under enumerated circumstances.

* * *

Section 300.430 of the NCP establishes the regulatory parameters for identifying, developing, evaluating, and selecting a proposed remedy for cleaning up a CERCLA site. Section 300.430(e) identifies the requirement of a feasibility study ("FS") for developing and evaluating a range of remedial action alternatives. Section 300.430(f) defines the factors to be used in selecting a preferred remedy from among the range of alternatives developed in the FS. Together, these two subsections establish the heart of EPA's regulatory approach to implementing the remedy selection provisions of section 121 * * *.

* * *

* * * EPA translated the statutory requirements and preferences of section 121 into nine criteria for use in evaluating alternative remedies. Remedial alternatives that survive an initial screening are subject to a detailed comparative and objective assessment. Remedies are evaluated based on the following nine criteria:

1. Overall protection of human health and the environment;

2. Compliance with ARARs;

3. Long-term effectiveness and permanence;

4. Reduction of toxicity, mobility, or volume through treatment;

5. Short-term effectiveness;

6. Implementability;

7. Cost;

8. State acceptance; and

9. Community acceptance.

EPA organized these criteria into three categories. The first two criteria, protectiveness and compliance with ARARs, are "[t]hreshold criteria," which an alternative must satisfy to be eligible for selection. The next five criteria are "[p]rimary balancing criteria." The final two criteria, state and community acceptance, are "[m]odifying criteria." * * *

* * *

To determine whether a remedy is cost effective, the NCP instructs:

Cost-effectiveness is determined by evaluating the following three of the five balancing criteria ... to determine *overall effectiveness:* long-term effectiveness and permanence, reduction of toxicity, mobility, or volume through treatment, and short-term effectiveness. *Overall effectiveness is then compared to cost* to ensure that the remedy is cost-effective. A remedy shall be cost-effective if its *costs are proportional to its overall effectiveness.*

In essence, the NCP offers a tautology to define cost effectiveness. A remedy is effective if, overall, it is effective, based on its long-and short-term effectiveness and the reduction of hazards posed by the hazardous substances. Further, the remedy is cost effective if its costs and effectiveness are "proportional."

The NCP defines a process for determining the maximum extent to which permanent treatment technologies are practicable that is similarly circular and ambiguous. The remedy will be found to utilize such treatment technologies to the maximum extent practicable if it

> provides the *best balance of trade-offs among alternatives* in terms of the five primary balancing criteria.... The balancing shall *emphasize* long-term effectiveness and reduction of toxicity, mobility, or volume through treatment. The balancing shall also *consider* the preference for treatment as a principal element and the bias against off-site land disposal of untreated waste.

Thus, pursuant to the NCP, a treatment technology, or remedy which employs such a technology, may be found *impracticable* if the "trade-offs" that arise from a consideration of the five balancing criteria are "worse" than those that arise from another remedy. Conversely, if the trade offs seem "better" than those trade offs posed by other remedial alternatives, a remedy that utilizes a permanent treatment technology may be determined to be practicable. Since the NCP requires that two of the balancing criteria be weighed in the balance initially, as well as given additional emphasis and consideration, remedies that incorporate treatment technologies may be more likely to be considered practicable.

* * *

For the CERCLA remedy selection process to produce results that are better understood and that achieve greater acceptance among stakeholders, EPA or another lead agency should not be expected to balance the many ambiguous and subjective criteria inherent to remedy selection. Instead, a different approach should be developed that more effectively allows those whose interests are at stake to weigh the trade offs and strike the balance among competing objectives.

Notes

1. After the foregoing discussion, the author proposes changes in the EPA's remedy-selection process. The first question he would ask in each case is, "Why do we want to clean up the site?" That is, he believes that site-specific cleanup objectives must be based more explicitly on achieving defined future uses for that site, taking into account the uses and values of surrounding properties and natural resources which have been impacted by the release of hazardous substances at the site. The current EPA remedy-selection process, in contrast, assumes that the future use of, and access to, the site will be unrestricted. The author urges that for the process to be more effective, all the "stakeholders"—the site owner, neighboring property owners, community residents, state and local government representatives, and other parties with a legitimate interest in the cleanup and future use of the site—"must become players in the process, not merely watchdogs over it."

2. *Ohio v. EPA*, 997 F.2d 1520 (D.C.Cir.1993), upheld several provisions of the NCP that had been challenged by various states and private parties as inconsistent with CERCLA. Among the provisions sustained were the definition of applicable or relevant and appropriate requirements (ARARs), various remedy selection provisions, and provisions concerning

both the role of states in CERCLA cleanups and cost allocations between state and federal governments.

The court approved the NCP's restriction of *state* ARARs to "standards [that] are of general applicability and are legally enforceable." Although the Safe Drinking Water Act is cited in CERCLA § 121(d)(2)(A) as one of the *federal* laws containing ARARs for Superfund cleanups, the court upheld EPA's decision that Maximum Contaminant Level Goals ("MCLGs") established under the SDWA do not have to be attained for contaminants whose MCLG has been set at a level of zero. Under the SDWA, MCLGs are generally unenforceable goals that reflect the level for each contaminant at which "no known or anticipated adverse effects on the health of persons occur and which allows an adequate margin of safety." Many MCLGs for carcinogens are set at zero. The second type of standards, Maximum Contaminant Levels ("MCLs")—the actual maximum permissible concentration levels under the SWDA—must be set as close as "feasible" to their corresponding MCLGs, taking into account available technology and cost. While MCLGs are unenforceable under the SWDA, section 121(d)(2)(A) of CERCLA converts them into enforceable limits (ARARs) where they are "relevant and appropriate under the circumstances of the release or threatened release." In essence, EPA made a categorical determination in the NCP that MCLGs set at a level of zero are *never* relevant and appropriate under the circumstances of a release because "it is impossible to detect whether 'true' zero has actually been attained."

Remedy-selection issues in *Ohio v. EPA* concerned the role of cost-benefit analysis in choosing remedies; the NCP's failure to require the selection of "permanent" remedies to the maximum extent practicable; the use of a cancer risk range between 1 in 10,000 and 1 in 1,000,000 (rather than a minimum risk of 1 in 1,000,000); and the requirement of five-year review of certain remedial actions. CERCLA § 121(b)(1) requires the President to select a remedial action "that is protective of human health and the environment, that is cost effective, and that utilizes permanent solutions * * * to the maximum extent practicable." The court upheld the NCP's classification of permanence as one of several "balancing criteria" rather than as "an overarching statutory principle."

→   3. *United States v. Akzo Coatings of America, Inc.*, 949 F.2d 1409 (6th Cir.1991), was an appeal by the state of Michigan from the entry of a consent decree between EPA and twelve PRPs, requiring the defendants to engage in remedial work at a contaminated site. The proposed remedial plan called for the excavation and incineration of surface soils contaminated with PCBs, lead, arsenic and other toxic materials, and the flushing of the subsurface soils contaminated with various volatile and semi-volatile organic compounds. The state challenged the effectiveness of soil flushing at the site in question, and the PRPs cross-appealed the district court's determination that the decree must comply with Michigan's groundwater anti-degradation law. The court held that the record supported EPA's conclusion that the site was conducive to soil flushing; and that Michigan's anti-degradation law was an ARAR because it was "of general applicability" and not too vague or lacking in a quantifiable standard to be "legally enforceable," as required by the NCP, and was "more stringent than any Federal standard, requirement, criteria or limitation," as required by CERCLA § 121(d)(2)(A)(ii).

4. Suppose that EPA, unable to reach a settlement with the PRPs, proposes to implement itself, under CERCLA § 104, a more elaborate and expensive cleanup program than the PRPs believe is necessary. Knowing that EPA will come after them later for reimbursement under § 107, could the PRPs obtain judicial review of EPA's program before it is implemented, as a means of trying to limit their ultimate liability under CERCLA? Before the 1986 amendments to CERCLA, *Lone Pine Steering Committee v. EPA,* 777 F.2d 882 (3d Cir.1985), cert. denied 476 U.S. 1115, 106 S.Ct. 1970, 90 L.Ed.2d 654 (1986), held that the federal district court lacked jurisdiction to review plaintiff's challenge to EPA's method of cleanup until the Agency brings suit to recover its cleanup costs. The court was concerned that such suits would frustrate Congress' intention that EPA act quickly to remedy problems posed by hazardous waste sites.

In SARA, Congress codified in section 113(h) the general denial of access to the courts to obtain <u>pre-enforcement review</u> of remedial action. Congress remained troubled, however, by the effect the rule might have on citizen groups wishing to challenge the *adequacy* of remedial action before cleanup was completed. Therefore, Congress created an exception authorizing the filing of citizen suits after a removal or remedial action has been taken under section 104 or secured under section 106. Congress encouraged liberal construction of the exception by explaining that such suits can be filed after the completion of "distinct and separate phases" of a remedial action, thus indicating that it is not necessary to wait until the entire action has been completed. The intent was to permit judicial review early enough so that the direction of a multi-stage cleanup could be modified, if necessary, prior to completion. See discussion of the conference report and other legislative history in 17 *Envir.Rep.,* No. 42, Part II, "Superfund II: A New Mandate," at 70–71 (1987).

United States v. Colorado, 990 F.2d 1565 (10th Cir.1993), cert. denied 510 U.S. 1092, 114 S.Ct. 922, 127 L.Ed.2d 216 (1994), held that section 113(h) did not preempt or preclude a state, which had been authorized by EPA to "carry out" the state's hazardous waste program "in lieu of" RCRA [see RCRA section 3006(b)], from doing so at a federal facility which EPA had placed on the NPL and at which a CERCLA response action was under way. On the United States' motion to dismiss (after removal to federal court), the Tenth Circuit said that Colorado's state court suit to enjoin violations of the Colorado Hazardous Waste Management Act was "not necessarily" a "challenge" [under section 113(h)] to the federal CERCLA action because Colorado was seeking not to delay the cleanup but merely to ensure that it was in accordance with state laws which EPA had authorized Colorado to enforce under RCRA.

However, in *McClellan Ecological Seepage Situation v. Perry,* 47 F.3d 325 (9th Cir.1995), cert. denied 516 U.S. 807, 116 S.Ct. 51, 133 L.Ed.2d 16 (1995), the court held that private citizens cannot circumvent the bar to judicial review of ongoing cleanups under CERCLA by suing under other federal and state environmental statutes. Hence, a federal district court lacked jurisdiction to hear a citizen suit claiming that the Defense Department's cleanup of an Air Force base violated state and federal environmental statutes, including RCRA and the Clean Water Act.[a] The case is discussed in Marianne Dugan, "Are Citizen Suits CERCLA § 113(h)'s Unintended Victims?", 27 *Envt'l L. Rptr.* 10003 (1997).

Concerning section 113(h) generally, see Healy, "Judicial Review and CERCLA Response Actions: Interpretive Strategies In the Face of Plain Meaning." 17 *Harv.Envtl.L.Rev.* 1 (1993).

d. Settlements

Section 122(a) of CERCLA, added in 1986, directs that "[w]henever practicable and in the public interest," settlement agreements should be sought by the government to expedite effective remedial actions at superfund sites, consistent with the NCP, and to minimize litigation. Among the tools authorized by section 122 to facilitate cost allocations, reduce transaction costs, and otherwise promote settlements, are (1) de minimis settlements—expedited settlements for small-volume waste contributors; (2) nonbinding preliminary allocations of responsibility ("NBARs") for cleanup costs—developed by EPA for PRPs; (3) mixed-funding agreements to share cleanup costs—permitting use of a combination of federal, state and PRP funds; (4) covenants not to sue—protecting PRPs who settle from future liability to the United States related to the hazardous substance release addressed by a remedial action; and (5) alternative dispute resolution—the use of neutral third parties to help resolve liability and cost-allocation problems.[b]

Section 122(d)(1)(A) provides that whenever the President enters into a settlement agreement with a PRP with respect to remedial action under section 106, except as otherwise provided in subsection 122(g) concerning de minimis settlements, "the agreement shall be entered in the appropriate United States district court as a consent decree."

In addition to section 122, another CERCLA provision of great significance to settlements is section 113(f)(2) concerning *contribution:*

> A person who has resolved its liability to the United States or a State in an administrative or judicially approved settlement shall not be liable for claims for contribution regarding matters addressed in the settlement. Such settlement does not discharge any of the other potentially liable persons unless its terms so provide, but it reduces the potential liability of the others by the amount of the settlement.

a. Similarly, in *Boarhead Corp. v. Erickson*, 923 F.2d 1011 (3d Cir.1991), the court held that section 113(h) prevented a federal district court from reviewing a claim that CERCLA-related activities which EPA planned to conduct on a Pennsylvania farm would violate the National Historic Preservation Act. Even though the lack of review might harm native-American artifacts on the farm, the court said that it must follow Congress' will that cleanups not be delayed by pre-enforcement challenges.

b. Through September 1993, EPA had made little use of most of these tools. Out of 1,074 nonfederal sites on the National Priorities List, EPA had completed de minimis settlements at 78 sites, prepared NBARs at 5 sites, used mixed-funding arrangements at 16 sites, and employed ADR at 35 sites. See General Accounting Office, "Reducing Superfund Transaction Costs," GAO/RCED—94–90, at 1 (1994).

The following case is very instructive regarding EPA's conduct of the settlement process. The court was considering objections to a proposed consent decree by seven non-settling PRP defendants. The objectors, who feared that they would be left with a disproportionate share of the total liability for cleanup costs, were seeking, at the least, to protect their rights of contribution against the settling defendants.

UNITED STATES v. CANNONS ENGINEERING CORP.

United States Court of Appeals, First Circuit, 1990.
899 F.2d 79.

SELYA, CIRCUIT JUDGE. "Superfund" sites are those which require priority remedial attention because of the presence, or suspected presence, of a dangerous accumulation of hazardous wastes. Expenditures to clean up such sites are specially authorized pursuant to [CERCLA § 111]. After the federal government, through the United States Environmental Protection Agency (EPA), identified four such sites in Bridgewater, Massachusetts, Plymouth, Massachusetts, Londonderry, New Hampshire, and Nashua, New Hampshire (collectively, the Sites), the EPA undertook an intensive investigation to locate potentially responsible parties (PRPs). In the course of this investigation, the agency created a de minimis classification (DMC), putting in this category persons or firms whose discerned contribution to pollution of the Sites was minimal both in the amount and toxicity of the hazardous wastes involved. The agency staked out the DMC on the basis of volumetric shares, grouping within it entities identifiable as generators of less than one percent of the waste sent to the Sites. To arrive at a PRP's volumetric share, the agency, using estimates, constituted a ratio between the volume of wastes that the PRP sent to the Sites and the total amount of wastes sent there.

The EPA sent notices of possible liability to some 671 PRPs, including generators and nongenerators. Administrative settlements were thereafter achieved with 300 generators (all de minimis PRPs). In short order, the United States and the two host states, Massachusetts and New Hampshire, brought suits in the United States District Court for the District of Massachusetts against 84 of the PRPs who had rejected, or were ineligible for, the administrative settlement. The suits sought recovery of previously incurred cleanup costs and declarations of liability for future remediation under [CERCLA]. The actions were consolidated.

With its complaint, the United States filed two proposed consent decrees. The first (the MP decree) embodied a contemplated settlement with 47 major PRPs, that is, responsible parties who were ineligible for membership in the DMC. This assemblage included certain generators whose volumetric shares exceeded the 1% cutoff point and certain nongenerators (like the owners of the Sites and hazardous waste transporters). The second consent decree (the DMC decree) embodied a contemplated settlement with 12 de minimis PRPs who had eschewed participation in the administrative settlement. As required by statute, notice of the decrees' proposed entry was published in the Federal Register. No comments were received.

The government thereupon moved to enter the decrees. Seven non-settling defendants [de minimis PRPs] objected. After considering written submissions and hearing arguments of counsel, the district court approved both consent decrees and dismissed all cross-claims against the settling defendants. The court proceeded to certify the decrees as final under Fed.R.Civ.P. 54(b). These appeals followed.

I

We approach our task mindful that, on appeal, a district court's approval of a consent decree in CERCLA litigation is encased in a double layer of swaddling. In the first place, it is the policy of the law to encourage settlements. That policy has particular force where, as here, a government actor committed to the protection of the public interest has pulled the laboring oar in constructing the proposed settlement. While "the true measure of the deference due depends on the persuasive power of the agency's proposal and rationale, given whatever practical considerations may impinge and the full panoply of the attendant circumstances," the district court must refrain from second-guessing the Executive Branch.

Respect for the agency's role is heightened in a situation where the cards have been dealt face up and a crew of sophisticated players, with sharply conflicting interests, sit at the table. That so many affected parties, themselves knowledgeable and represented by experienced lawyers, have hammered out an agreement at arm's length and advocate its embodiment in a judicial decree, itself deserves weight in the ensuing balance. The relevant standard, after all, is not whether the settlement is one which the court itself might have fashioned, or considers as ideal, but whether the proposed decree is fair, reasonable, and faithful to the objectives of the governing statute. * * *

The second layer of swaddling derives from the nature of appellate review. Because approval of a consent decree is committed to the trial court's informed discretion, the court of appeals should be reluctant to disturb a reasoned exercise of that discretion. In this context, the test for abuse of discretion is itself a fairly deferential one. * * *

II

* * *

Originally, the EPA extended an open offer to all de minimis PRPs, including five of the six appellants,[3] proposing an administrative settlement based on 160% of each PRP's volumetric share of the total

---

3. Crown was ineligible to receive the initial offer because of its failure to respond to information requests.

projected response cost, that is, the price of remedial actions, past and anticipated. The settlement figure included a 60% premium to cover unexpected costs and/or unforeseen conditions. Settling PRPs paid their shares in cash and were released outright from all liability. They were also exempted from suits for contribution.

Following consummation of the administrative settlement, plaintiffs entered into negotiations with the remaining PRPs. These negotiations resulted in the proposed MP decree (accepted by 47 "major" defendants) and the DMC decree. The latter was modelled upon the administrative settlement, but featured an increased premium: rather than allowing de minimis PRPs to cash out at a 160% level, an eligible generator could resolve its liability only by agreeing to pay 260% of its volumetric share of the total projected response cost. The EPA justified the incremental 100% premium as being in the nature of delay damages.

* * *

III

* * *

Our starting point is well defined. [SARA] authorized a variety of types of settlements which the EPA may utilize in CERCLA actions, including consent decrees providing for PRPs to contribute to cleanup costs and/or to undertake response activities themselves. SARA's legislative history makes pellucid that, when such consent decrees are forged, the trial court's review function is only to "satisfy itself that the settlement is reasonable, fair, and consistent with the purposes that CERCLA is intended to serve." Reasonableness, fairness, and fidelity to the statute are, therefore, the horses which district judges must ride.

* * *

A. *Procedural Fairness.*

We agree with the district court that fairness in the CERCLA settlement context has both procedural and substantive components. To measure procedural fairness, a court should ordinarily look to the negotiation process and attempt to gauge its candor, openness, and bargaining balance.

In this instance, the district court found the proposed decrees to possess the requisite procedural integrity, and appellants have produced no persuasive reason to alter this finding. * * * But their flagship argument—that the procedural integrity of the settlement was ruptured because appellants were neither allowed to join the MP decree nor informed in advance that they would be excluded—requires comment.

Appellants claim that they were relatively close to the 1% cutoff point, and were thus arbitrarily excluded from the major party settlement, avails them naught. Congress intended to give the EPA broad discretion to structure classes of PRPs for settlement purposes. We cannot say that the government acted beyond the scope of that discretion in separating minor and major players in this instance, that is, in determining that generators who had sent less than 1% of the volume of hazardous waste to the Sites would comprise the DMC and those generators who were responsible for a greater percentage would be treated as major PRPs. While the dividing line was only one of many which the agency could have selected, it was well within the universe of plausibility. * * *

Nor can we say that appellants were entitled to more advance warning of the EPA's negotiating strategy than they received. At the time de minimis PRPs were initially invited to participate in the administrative settlement, the EPA, by letter, informed all of them, including appellants, that:

> The government is anxious to achieve a high degree of participation in this *de minimis* settlement. Accordingly, the terms contained in this settlement offer are the most favorable terms that the government intends to make available to parties eligible for *de minimis* settlement in this case.

Appellants knew, early on, that they were within the DMC and could spurn the EPA's proposal only at the risk of paying more at a later time. Although appellants may have assumed that they could ride on the coattails of the major parties and join whatever MP decree emerged—the government had, on other occasions, allowed such cafeteria-style settlements—the agency was neither asked for, nor did it give, any such assurance in this instance. * * *

B. *Substantive Fairness.*

Substantive fairness introduces into the equation concepts of corrective justice and accountability: a party should bear the cost of the harm for which it is legally responsible. *See generally Developments in the Law—Toxic Waste Litigation,* 99 Harv.L.Rev. 1458, 1477 (1986). The logic behind these concepts dictates that settlement terms must be based upon, and roughly correlated with, some acceptable measure of comparative fault, apportioning liability among the settling parties according to rational (if necessarily imprecise) estimates of how much harm each PRP has done.

Even accepting substantive fairness as linked to comparative fault, an important issue still remains as to how comparative fault is to be measured. There is no universally correct approach. It appears very clear to us that what constitutes the best measure of comparative fault at a particular Superfund site under particular factual circumstances should be left largely to the EPA's expertise. Whatever formula or scheme EPA advances for measuring comparative fault and allocating liability should be upheld so long as the agency supplies a plausible explanation for it, welding some reasonable linkage between the factors it includes in its formula or scheme and the proportionate shares of the settling PRPs. Put in slightly different terms, the chosen measure of comparative fault should be upheld unless it is arbitrary, capricious, and devoid of a rational basis.

Not only must the EPA be given leeway to construct the barometer of comparative fault, but the agency must also be accorded flexibility to diverge from an apportionment formula in order to address special factors not conducive to regimented treatment. While the list of possible variables is virtually limitless, two frequently encountered reasons warranting departure from strict formulaic comparability are the uncertainty of future events and the timing of particular settlement decisions. Common sense suggests that a PRP's assumption of open-ended risks may merit a discount on comparative fault, while obtaining a complete release from uncertain future liability may call for a premium. By the same token, the need to encourage (and suitably reward) early, cost-effective settlements, and to account *inter alia* for anticipated savings in transaction costs inuring from celeritous settlement, can affect the construct. Because we are confident that Congress intended EPA to have considerable flexibility in negotiating and structuring settlements, we think reviewing courts should permit the agency to depart from rigid adherence to formulae wherever the agency proffers a reasonable good-faith justification for departure.

We also believe that a district court should give the EPA's expertise the benefit of the doubt when weighing substantive fairness—particularly when the agency, and hence the court, has been confronted by ambiguous, incomplete, or inscrutable information. * * *

In this instance, we agree with the court below that the consent decrees pass muster from a standpoint of substantive fairness. They adhere generally to principles of comparative fault according to a volumetric standard, determining the liability of each PRP according to volumetric contribution. And, to the extent they deviate from this formulaic approach, they do so on the basis of adequate justification. In particular, the premiums charged to de minimis PRPs in the administrative settlement, and the increased premium charged in the DMC decree, seem well warranted.

The argument that the EPA should have used relative toxicity as a determinant of proportionate liability for response costs, instead of a strictly volumetric ranking, is a stalking horse. Having selected a reasonable method of weighing comparative fault, the agency need not show that it is the best, or even the fairest, of all conceivable methods. The choice of the yardstick to be used for allocating liability must be left primarily to the expert discretion of the EPA, particularly when the PRPs involved are numerous and the situation is complex. We cannot reverse the court below for refusing to second-guess the agency on this score.

* * *

The last point which merits discussion under this rubric involves the fact that the agency upped the ante as the game continued, that is, the premium assessed as part of the administrative settlement was increased substantially for purposes of the later DMC decree. Like the district court, we see no unfairness in this approach. For one thing, litigation is expensive—and having called the tune by their refusal to subscribe to the administrative settlement, we think it not unfair that appellants, thereafter, would have to pay the piper. For another thing, rewarding PRPs who settle sooner rather than later is completely consonant with CERCLA's makeup.

* * *

C.   *Reasonableness.*

* * *

D.   *Fidelity to the Statute.*

* * *

We have recently described the two major policy concerns underlying CERCLA:

First, Congress intended that the federal government be immediately given the tools necessary for a prompt and effective response to the problems of national magnitude resulting from hazardous waste disposal. Second, Congress intended that those responsible for problems caused by the disposal of chemical poisons bear the costs and responsibility for remedying the harmful conditions they created.

The district court thought that these concerns were addressed, and assuaged, by the proposed settlements. So do we.

* * *

In the SARA Amendments, Congress explicitly created a statutory framework that left nonsettlors at risk of bearing a disproportionate amount of liability. The statute immunizes settling parties from liability for contribution and provides that only the amount of the settlement—not the pro rata share attributable to the settling party—shall be subtracted from the liability of the nonsettlors. This can prove to be a substantial benefit to settling PRPs—and a corresponding detriment to their more recalcitrant counterparts.

Although such immunity creates a palpable risk of disproportionate liability, that is not to say that the device is forbidden. To the exact contrary, Congress has made its will explicit and the courts must defer. Disproportionate liability, a technique which promotes early settlements and deters litigation for litigation's sake, is an integral part of the statutory plan.

* * *

The CERCLA statutes do not require the agency to open all settlement offers to all PRPs; and we refuse to insert such a requirement into the law by judicial fiat. Under the SARA Amendments, the right to draw fine lines, and to structure the order and pace of settlement negotiations to suit, is an agency prerogative. After all, "divide and conquer" has been a recognized negotiating tactic since the days of the Roman Empire, and in the absence of a congressional directive, we cannot deny the EPA use of so conventional a tool. So long as it operates in good faith, the EPA is at liberty to negotiate and settle with whomever it chooses.

* * *

Affirmed.

Notes

1. As mentioned in the text preceding *Cannons,* section 113(f)(2) provides that a settling PRP shall not be liable for claims for contribution "regarding matters addressed in the settlement." The meaning of this phrase was at issue in *Akzo Coatings, Inc. v. Aigner Corp.,* 30 F.3d 761 (7th Cir.1994). In response to a section 106 administrative order by EPA, Akzo conducted certain "emergency removal activities" at the "Two–Line Road" facility, incurring costs of more than $1.2 million. Meanwhile, more than 200 other PRPs (including Aigner, but not Akzo) entered into a court-approved settlement with EPA concerning subsequent "remedial" activities to be performed by the settlors at the "Fisher–Calo site," of which the Two–Line Road facility was a part. Akzo then brought suit against Aigner, seeking contribution under section 113(f)(1) for the initial cleanup work which Akzo had performed at the behest of EPA as well as voluntary costs incurred in studying the long-term cleanup of the site with other PRPs. The trial court gave summary judgment for Aigner, finding that Akzo sought contribution for a "matter addressed" in the consent decree. In a split decision the Seventh Circuit reversed because Akzo's work "stands apart in kind, context, and time from the work envisioned by the consent decree." Akzo had engaged in "removal" work, while the settlement provided for the kind of "remedial" work needed to accomplish a complete cleanup of the site. The majority of the court perceived "no unfairness to Aigner" because Akzo's work was "over and done with by the time Aigner signed the consent decree." Thus, acknowledging a right to contribution did "not subject a settling PRP like Aigner to open-ended liability for contribution claims based on future, unanticipated remedial work." In a vigorous dissent, Judge Easterbrook said that the majority "plucks some language ["equitable factors"] from § 113(f)(1) and uses this language as a warrant to disregard the scope of the settlement." Easterbrook expressed concern that the "[r]isk that in the name of equity a court will disregard the actual language of the parties' [settlement] bargain will lead potentially responsible parties to fight harder to avoid liability (and to pay less in settlements, reserving the residue to meet contribution claims), undermining the function of § 113(f)(2)."

James Brusslan, "Truth In Superfund Settlements: The Courts Strike Back on 'Matters Addressed' Contribution Protection," 27 *Env't Rptr.* 2522 (1997), discusses the propensity of the government and settling parties to enter into consent decrees that explicitly define the "matters addressed" therein in such a way as to attempt to bar all third-party contribution claims, even for voluntary private party cleanups not addressed in the decrees. The author cites federal district court decisions rejecting the government's authority to bar contribution claims by defining or construing "matters addressed" to include claims beyond those matters actually addressed in the consent decrees.[a]

2.   In *Dravo Corp. v. Zuber,* 13 F.3d 1222 (8th Cir.1994), a contribution suit, defendant PRPs had entered into a de minimis settlement agreement with EPA under CERCLA § 122(g). Paragraph (5) of that subsection provides that a party who "has resolved its liability to the United States under this subsection" shall not be liable for claims of contribution regarding matters addressed in the settlement. Plaintiff, which had incurred response costs, contended that defendants were not protected from contribution claims until after they fulfilled the obligations which they assumed by entering into the settlement agreement. The court held that "[b]ecause Congress clearly * * * expressed its desire to minimize litigation by granting de minimis PRPs protection from contribution actions as soon as possible, and because this agreement expressly incorporates that mandate," defendants "are protected from contribution actions upon signing the agreement and will be protected so long as they comply with the agreement." Further, since section 122(a) says that "a decision of the President to use or not use the procedures in this section is not subject to judicial review," the court denied plaintiff's requests for discovery by which plaintiff wanted to determine whether—contrary to EPA's conclusion—defendants had contributed to contamination of the site in more than a de minimis way. Because the settlement agreement was embodied in an administrative order under section 122(g)(4), rather than being entered as a consent decree, plaintiff's sole opportunity to block the de minimis agreement had been by filing comments with EPA under section 122(i)(2) within 30 days after notice of the proposed settlement was published in the Federal Register.

3.   In 1993, EPA issued a "guidance" on settlements with "de micromis" waste contributors. OSWER Directive #9834.17, July 30, 1993, discussed in Olmstead, "CERCLA Settlements With De Micromis Waste Contributors," 24 *Envir. Rep.* 1939 (1994). The guidance resulted from the increasing number of contribution suits by PRPs against contributors of "extremely small" amounts of hazardous substances at superfund sites. The de micromis settlement is a subset of the section 122(g) de minimis settlement.

The benefits of the de micromis settlement include an immediately effective covenant not to sue for past and future liability, as well as protection from third-party contribution suits. The settlement may be reopened only for new information showing that the party does not qualify for the de micromis settlement. In contrast, traditional de minimis settlements include reopeners for (1) unexpected cost overruns during implementation of the remedy, (2) the performance of supplemental remedies or additional

[handwritten marginal note: subset of de minimis classification does not get reopened.]

a.   For discussion of practical aspects of representing PRPs in the negotiation of CERCLA settlement agreements, see Hapke and Davis, "Negotiating EPA Consent Orders and Consent Decrees: Steering Your Client Through the Shoals," 24 *Envtl. L.Rptr.* 10116 (1994).

EPA has issued model settlement agreements for use in connection with cleanup cost claims under CERCLA. "Revised Model CERCLA RD/RA Consent Decree," 60 *Fed. Reg.* 38817 (July 28, 1995): "Revised Model *De Minimis* Contributor Consent Decree and Administrative Order on Consent," 60 *Fed. Reg.* 62849 (Dec. 7, 1995); "Final Model CERCLA Past Costs Consent Decree and Administrative Agreement," 60 *Fed. Reg.* 62446 (Dec. 6, 1995).

work if the initial remedy is not protective of public health and the environment, and (3) additional information indicating that a party is not de minimis.

[De micromis settlements are offered only to generators and transporters, not to site owners or operators.] The guidance says that such settlements may be especially appropriate for small businesses, non-profit organizations, and other entities that do not manufacture or use large amounts of hazardous substances in their activities.

4.   In the *Cannons* case the objectors to the consent decrees were "non-settling [PRP] defendants." That is, they were named defendants in the cost recovery action brought by the United States. However, if they had not been named as defendants, as PRPs they still would have had an interest in the outcome of the settlement because of (a) its effect on the amount of their liability for the remaining cleanup costs and (b) the statutory restriction on their right of contribution against other settling PRPs.

United States v. Union Electric Co.., 64 F.3d 1152 (8th Cir.1995), raised the procedural question whether non-settling, non-defendant PRPs should be allowed to intervene, in an action by the United States against other PRPs, to oppose a consent decree that the government had reached with settling PRPs. The court held that because CERCLA protects settling PRPs from contribution claims of non-settling PRPs, the latter have a legally protectable interest sufficient to support their intervention of right, under § 113(i), to challenge the consent decree. Section 113(i) provides that in any action commenced under CERCLA in a federal court, "any person may intervene as a matter of right when such person claims an interest relating to the subject of the action and is so situated that the disposition of the action may, as a practical matter, impair or impede the person's ability to protect that interest."

A subsequent decision in the same case, *United States v. Union Electric Co..*, 132 F.3d 422 (8th Cir.1997), held that the non-settling intervenor-PRPs would not be bound by a cost-allocation formula set forth in the consent decree and therefore could not block approval of the decree by objecting to the formula. The formula apportioned the liability of settling PRPs who had sent transformer oil to the site, on the basis of the volume of oil sent, unless a PRP could prove its oil could not have contained more than 2 parts per billion PCBs.

STOP.

e. *Discussion Problem on Remedy Selection and Settlements*

You are counsel for Medlab, Inc. which operates a small medical testing laboratory. Mary Mecco is the President and sole stockholder. She is interested in selling Medlab (either her stock or the firm's assets), and has been talking with two potential buyers. One is a wealthy individual, and the other is a pharmaceutical company.

On two or three occasions in the past, when her usual waste disposal company could not provide service, Mecco arranged for several gallons of hazardous waste to be taken from Medlab to a large disposal facility operated by Chemwaste Corporation. Unfortunately, that facility now is a superfund site (on the NPL), and Chemwaste is insolvent.

EPA has identified more than one hundred generators which contributed hazardous substances, in various amounts and of varying degrees of toxicity, to the Chemwaste site. Medlab's contributions were among the smallest on a volumetric basis, but they were more toxic than many others. For that reason, EPA decided to offer Medlab a "de minimis" settlement, but not a "de micromis" settlement, under CERCLA § 122(g). Because EPA's remedial design for the Chemwaste site aims to decontaminate completely all of the soil and groundwater (although the site is in an industrial area and the groundwater is not tapped by any wells), the cost is high. Medlab's share of the total bill will be $50,000 if Mecco decides to accept the settlement offer, which is due to expire in a few days. She thinks this is very unfair in light of Medlab's small contributions to the site and EPA's "unreasonably ambitious" remedial design. She wants to hold out for inclusion in the "de micromis" category, which would reduce Medlab's required payment to $10,000 and would give the firm other advantages provided by EPA's OSWER Directive #9834.17 (see note 3 immediately preceding this problem). In the alternative, she would challenge EPA's choice of remedies and try to get the agency to adopt a more modest response that would reduce the overall cost and Medlab's share by perhaps 50 percent.

What advice would you give to Mecco? In formulating your answer, consider the following questions.

1. What are the risks of rejecting EPA's offer of a de minimis settlement? Is CERCLA § 113(f) relevant?

2. What are the chances of requiring EPA to reclassify Medlab as a de micromis contributor?

3. What are the chances of success in challenging EPA's remedial design? When and how could the challenge be made?

4. How might following Mecco's preferred course of action affect the possible sale of Medlab stock or assets? What might be the concerns of the potential buyers?

5. If Medlab does accept the offer of a de minimis settlement, what protective provisions (e.g., for Mecco and a buyer) should you seek to have included in the settlement agreement?

f. Governmental Recovery of Damages for Injury to Natural Resources

Section 107(a)(4)(C) of CERCLA provides that generators, transporters, and site owners and operators shall be liable for damages for "injury to, destruction of, or loss of natural resources, including the reasonable costs of assessing such injury, destruction, or loss" resulting from releases of hazardous waste. "Natural resources" is defined by section 101(16) to mean "land, fish, wildlife, biota, air, water, ground water, drinking water supplies, and other such resources belonging to, managed by, held in trust by, appertaining to, or otherwise controlled by the United States (including the resources of the fishery conservation zone established by the Magnuson Fishery Conservation and Management Act), any State or local government, any foreign government, any Indian tribe, or, if such resources are subject to a trust restriction on alienation, any member of an Indian tribe."

Under section 107(f), CERCLA liability for injury to natural resources is to the United States government, to any state for resources "within the State or belonging to, managed by, controlled by, or appertaining to such State," and to any Indian tribe in specified situations. The statute creates no private cause of action for natural resource damage. Authority to recover is in the President, for the United States, or the "authorized representative of any State," who "shall act on behalf of the public as trustee of such natural resources." Sums recovered shall be retained by the trustee "for use only to restore, replace, or acquire the equivalent of" the natural resources injured, destroyed or lost.

For what categories of natural resources is recovery likely to be allowed? Section 101(16) speaks of resources "belonging to, managed by, held in trust by, appertaining to, or otherwise controlled by" the government. This language seems to encompass not only resources *owned* by a government but also those subject to the "public trust," such as navigable waters, wetlands, and parklands. Less clear is whether the language also includes resources which are *regulated* by a government for purposes of environmental protection—such as endangered species, coastal zones, aquifers providing public water supplies, and the ambient air—or which *could* be regulated constitutionally. See Breen, "CERCLA's Natural Resource Damage Provisions: What Do We Know So Far?", 14 *ELR* 10304, 10306 (1984).

How are the recoverable damages to be measured? Section 301(c) directs the President to promulgate regulations for "the assessment of damages for injury to, destruction of, or loss of" natural resources:

> (2) Such regulations shall specify (A) standard procedures for simplified assessments requiring minimal field observation, including establishing measures of damages based on units of discharge or release or units of affected area, and (B) alternative protocols for conducting assessments in individual cases to determine the type and extent of short-and long-term injury, destruction, or loss. Such regulations shall identify the best available procedures to determine such damages, including both direct and indirect injury, destruction, or loss and shall take into consideration factors including, but not limited to, replacement value, use value, and ability of the ecosystem or resource to recover.

The "standard procedures" are referred to as "Type A" rules, and the "alternative protocols" as "Type B" rules.

The President assigned responsibility for promulgating the regulations to the Department of Interior. In 1986, the Department belatedly published final regulations containing both Type A and Type B assessment rules. Both rules were challenged in court by state governments, environmental organizations, and industry groups. Type A rules for coastal and marine environments were upheld in part and vacated in part in *State of Colorado v. United States Dept. of Interior,* 880 F.2d 481 (D.C.Cir.1989). In 1996, the Department promulgated further Type A rules, for coastal and marine environments and Great Lakes environments, which were upheld in *National Ass'n of Manufacturers v. Dept. of Interior,* 134 F.3d 1095 (D.C.Cir.1998).

Major portions of the Type B rules were found to violate CERCLA in *Ohio v. United States Dept. of Interior,* 880 F.2d 432 (D.C.Cir.1989). The most significant issue in the *Ohio* case concerned the validity of a provision that damages should be "the *lesser of:* restoration or replacement costs; or diminution of use values" (emphasis added). The DOI rules defined "use value" as

> the value to the public of recreational or other public uses of the resource, as measured by changes in consumer surplus, any fees or other payments collectable by the government or Indian tribe for a private party's use of the natural resource, and any economic rent accruing to a private party because the government or Indian tribe does not charge a fee or price for the use of the resource.

Methods for determining use value are discussed below.

The state and environmental challengers in *Ohio* argued that CERCLA requires damages to be at least sufficient to pay the cost in every case of restoring, replacing or acquiring the equivalent of the damaged resource. Because in many cases lost use values will be lower than the cost of restoration or replacement, the Department's rule would result in damage awards too small to pay for restoration. The court used an example—which may have been inspired by the then recent Exxon Valdez oil spill in Alaska—to illustrate the "enormous practical significance" of the "lesser of" rule:

> [I]magine a hazardous substance spill that kills a rookery of fur seals and destroys a habitat for seabirds at a sealife reserve. The lost use value of the seals and seabird habitat would be measured by the market value of the fur seals' pelts (which would be approximately $15 each)[4] plus the selling price per acre of land comparable in value to that on which the spoiled bird habitat was located. Even if, as likely, that use value turns out to be far less than the cost of restoring the rookery and seabird habitat, it would nonetheless be the only measure of damages eligible for the presumption of recoverability under the Interior rule.

The court held that, under CERCLA, the Department of the Interior was not entitled to treat use value and restoration cost as having "equal presumptive legitimacy" as a measure of damages to natural resources. Primary among the statutory provisions cited by the court was section 107(f)(1), which states that natural resource damages recovered by a

---

4. See U.S. Dept. of the Interior, "Measuring Damages to Coastal and Marine Natural Resources," vol. 1 at p. V–37 (mandating $15 figure for valuation under Type A rules); see also 52 Fed.Reg. 9.092 (1987) (stating that $15 value is consistent with valuation principles of Type B rules).

government trustee are "for use only to restore, replace, or acquire the equivalent of such natural resources," and that the measure of damages "shall not be limited by the sums which can be used to restore or replace such resources." The court concluded that Congress intended a "distinct preference" for restoration cost as the measure of damages.

The Department sought to justify its "lesser of" rule as being economically efficient. The court replied as follows:

> Under DOI's economic efficiency view, making restoration cost the measure of damages would be a waste of money whenever restoration would cost more than the use value of the resource. Its explanation of the proposed rules included the following statement:
>
> > [I]f use value is higher than the cost of restoration or replacement, then it would be more rational for society to be compensated for the cost to restore or replace the lost resource than to be compensated for the lost use. Conversely, if restoration or replacement costs are higher than the value of uses foregone, it is rational for society to compensate individuals for their lost uses rather than the cost to restore or replace the injured natural resource.
>
> 50 Fed.Reg. at 52,141. See also 51 Fed.Reg. at 27,704 ("lesser of" rule "promotes a rational allocation of society's assets").
>
> This is nothing more or less than cost-benefit analysis: Interior's rule attempts to optimize social welfare by restoring an injured resource only when the diminution in the resource's value to society is greater in magnitude than the cost of restoring it. And, acknowledgedly, Congress did intend CERCLA's natural resource provisions to operate efficiently. For one thing, the Act requires that the assessment of damages and the restoration of injured resources take place as cost-effectively as possible. Moreover, as we have indicated, there is some suggestion in the legislative history that Congress intended recovery not to encompass restoration cost where restoration is infeasible or where its cost is grossly disproportionate to use value.
>
> The fatal flaw of Interior's approach, however, is that it assumes that natural resources are fungible goods, just like any other, and that the value to society generated by a particular resource can be accurately measured in every case—assumptions that Congress apparently rejected. As the foregoing examination of CERCLA's text, structure and legislative history illustrates, Congress saw restoration as the presumptively correct remedy for injury to natural resources. To say that Congress placed a thumb on the scales in favor of restoration is not to say that it forswore the goal of efficiency. "Efficiency," standing alone, simply means that the chosen policy will dictate the result that achieves the greatest value to society. Whether a particular choice is efficient depends on *how the various alternatives are valued.* Our reading of CERCLA does not attribute to Congress an irrational dislike of "efficiency"; rather, it

suggests that Congress was skeptical of the ability of human beings to measure the true "value" of a natural resource. Indeed, even the common law recognizes that restoration is the proper remedy for injury to property where measurement of damages by some other method will fail to compensate fully for the injury. Congress' refusal to view use value and restoration cost as having equal presumptive legitimacy merely recognizes that natural resources have value that is not readily measured by traditional means. Congress delegated to Interior the job of deciding at what point the presumption of restoration falls away, but its repeated emphasis on the primacy of restoration rejected the underlying premise of Interior's rule, which is that restoration is wasteful if its cost exceeds—by even the slightest amount—the diminution in use value of the injured resource.

With respect to the determination of "use value," the DOI regulations had prescribed methods to be employed when the damaged natural resources are not traded in the market. One of these methods is known as "contingent valuation." Some parties in the *Ohio* case challenged DOI's acceptance of "CV" in the regulations. The court rejected the challenge, saying in part:

> The CV process "includes all techniques that set up hypothetical markets to elicit an individual's economic valuation of a natural resource." CV involves a series of interviews with individuals for the purpose of ascertaining the values they respectively attach to particular changes in particular resources. Among the several formats available to an interviewer in developing the hypothetical scenario embodied in a CV survey are direct questioning, by which the interviewer learns how much the interviewee is willing to pay for the resource; bidding formats, for example, the interviewee is asked whether he or she would pay a given amount for a resource and, depending upon the response, the bid is set higher or lower until a final price is derived; and a "take or leave it" format, in which the interviewee decides whether or not he or she is willing to pay a designated amount of money for the resource. CV methodology thus enables ascertainment of individually-expressed values for different levels of quality of resources, and dollar values of individuals' changes in well-being. The regulations also sanction resort to CV methodology in determining "option"[72] and "existence"[73] values.

---

72. Option value is the dollar amount an individual is willing to pay although he or she is not currently using a resource but wishes to reserve the option to use that resource in a certain state of being in the future. For example, an individual who does not plan to use a beach or visit the Grand Canyon may nevertheless place some value on preservation of the resource in its natural state for personal enjoyment in the event of a later change of mind.

73. Existence value is the dollar amount an individual is willing to pay although he or she does not plan to use the resource, either at present or in the future. The payment is for the knowledge that the resource will continue to exist in a given state or being. Though lacking any interest in personally enjoying the resource, an individual may attach some value to it because he or she may wish to have the resource available for others to enjoy.

Industry Petitioners' complaint is limited to DOI's inclusion of CV in its assessment methodology. They claim fatal departures from CERCLA on grounds that CV methodology is inharmonious with common law damage assessment principles, and is considerably less than a "best available procedure." These petitioners further charge that DOI's extension of CERCLA's rebuttable presumption to CV assessments is arbitrary and capricious, and violative of the due process rights of a potentially responsible party. We find none of these challenges persuasive.

Industry Petitioners point out that at common law there can be no recovery for speculative injuries, and they contend that CV methodology is at odds with that principle. CV methodology, they say, is rife with speculation, amounting to no more than ordinary public opinion polling.

We have already noted our disagreement with the proposition that the strictures of the common law apply to CERCLA. That much of industry petitioners' argument to the contrary thus fades away. CERCLA does, however, require utilization of the "best available procedures" for determinations of damages flowing from destruction of or injury to natural resources, and Industry Petitioners insist that CV methodology is too flawed to qualify as such. In their eyes, the CV process is imprecise, is untested, and has a built-in bias and a propensity to produce overestimation.

It cannot be gainsaid that DOI's decision to adopt CV was made intelligently and cautiously. DOI scrutinized a vast array of position papers and discussions addressing the use of CV. It recognized and acknowledged that CV needs to be "properly structured and professionally applied." It eliminated a feature of CV, as originally proposed, that might have resulted in overly high assessments. We find DOI's promulgation of CV methodology reasonable and consistent with congressional intent, and therefore worthy of deference.

In 1994, the Department of the Interior promulgated new regulations on natural resource damage assessments, in response to the *Ohio* decision. 59 Fed.Reg. 14262 (March 25, 1994). These regulations allow "trustee officials to recover the costs of restoration, rehabilitation, replacement, and/or acquisition of equivalent resources in all cases." The 1994 regulations were upheld in almost all respects in *Kennecott Utah Copper Corp. v. Department of the Interior*, 88 F.3d 1191 (D.C.Cir.1996).[a]

a. For further discussion of the valuation of natural resource damages, see Levy and Friedman, "The Revenge of the Redwoods? Reconsidering Property Rights and the Economic Allocation of Natural Resources," 61 *U.Chi.L.Rev.* 493 (1994); Augustyniak, "Economic Valuation of Services Provided by Natural Resources: Putting a Price on the Priceless," 45 *Baylor L.Rev.* 389 (1993). See also Chapter VIII–B infra; R. Kopp and V. Smith (eds.), *Valuing Natural Assets: The Economics of Natural Resource Damage Assessment* (1993); and the symposium on contingent valuation in 34 *Nat.Resources J.,* No. 1 (1994). See also the discussion of oil-spill damages to natural resources in Chapter VIII, pages 797–804 infra.

g. *Legislative and Administrative Efforts to Reform CERC-LA*

In 1994, Congress considered bills to "reform" CERCLA, but pre-election partisan politics finally prevented enactment of any of the proposals. What was unusual was that virtually all of the major interest groups—environmentalists, industrial interests, and insurers—had reached a consensus with the Clinton administration on the need for reform and on its terms.

The need for change stemmed from the slow pace and enormous cost of CERCLA cleanups, and from the inordinate amounts of money consumed by transaction costs, primarily legal fees. The apparent problems were disagreements over how clean sites should be made, and disagreements among PRPs and their insurers over who should pay what portions of the costs. As a result of the disagreements, the entire program had been bogged down in litigation. Only about 200 sites had been cleaned up in fourteen years.

The bill supported by the Clinton administration and the major interest groups would have changed the program in ways that its supporters believed would have simplified and expedited cleanups. It would have (1) set uniform national standards governing how clean sites should be made, based on formulas that, while still complex, would have been more workable than existing standards; (2) related the extent of cleanup to how the particular site is to be used in the future, saving time and expense in some cases; (3) increased the influence of local citizen groups in cleanup decisions; (4) encouraged arbitration rather than litigation by those who would have to pay for cleanups; and (5) increased federal financing of some cleanups by collecting $8 billion over ten years from insurance companies which, in exchange, would have been protected against some liability.

Republican opponents of the bill blocked it in the House of Representatives just before final adjournment by demanding a series of votes on amendments that would have seriously weakened interest-group and Democratic support for the measure. Among other things, the amendments would have relaxed cleanup standards for groundwater contaminated by carcinogenic chemicals, changed how the costs and benefits of cleanups would be weighed and balanced, and removed a provision calling for union wages to be paid in cleanups. If the House had approved the bill, with or without amendments, Senate Republicans would have sought to abolish CERCLA's retroactive liability for pre–1980 disposal activities. See Cushman, "Congress Forgoes Its Bid to Speed Cleanup of Dumps," *New York Times,* Oct. 6, 1994, p. A1, col. 2.

At the end of 1995, authorization for the special taxes which supported the superfund expired. Since that time the only replenishment of the fund has been from interest on monies already on hand, and from reimbursements obtained from private PRPs to repay response costs incurred by EPA. Unless new taxes are authorized, the superfund is expected run dry by the end of fiscal year 1999.

However, through 1998, Congress was unable to agree on either (a) the "comprehensive reform" of CERCLA advocated by many Republicans, or (b) much more modest steps proposed by Democrats. The latter steps would have included an appropriation of $650 million for the superfund, financial assistance (grants, low-interest loans, and tax benefits) to state and local governments and prospective purchasers for cleanup and development of contaminated "brownfields," and limitations on the potential liability of innocent purchasers of such properties. 27 *Env't Rptr.* 1939 (1997). See Charles de Saillan, "Superfund Reauthorization: A More Modest Proposal," 27 *Envt'l L. Rptr.* 10201 (1997). Republicans rejected these limited steps out of concern that their enactment would decrease support for the broader changes they wanted.

The "comprehensive reform" proposed, e.g., in Senate Bill S 8 and House Bill HR 2727, included (in addition to the items mentioned above) elimination of "retroactive" liability for generators and transporters who disposed of waste before 1980; elimination of liability for "small" waste generators and transporters that contribute only small amounts of waste, employ less than 50 people, or have less than $3 million in gross annual revenues; "caps" on the allocation of liability for response costs to a municipal solid waste generator (10%) or a municipal landfill owner or operator (20%); replacement of the broad preference for costly "treatment" remedies at all contaminated sites, with a narrower preference applicable only to "hot spots" posing a "substantial threat to human health and the environment"; limitations on the recovery of damages for injury to "non-use" values of natural resources; restrictions on federal payment of "orphan shares" of response costs; and provision for the "reopening" of consent decrees allocating response costs among private PRPs. See 28 *Env't Rptr.* 2342, 2468 (1998). See also Leslie Turner, "Reforming CERCLA's Natural Resource Damage Provisions: A Challenge to the 105th Congress From the Clinton Administration," 27 *Envt'l L. Rptr.* 10121 (1997); James Hamilton and W. Kip Viscusi, "The Benefits and Costs of Regulatory Reforms for Superfund," 16 *Stan. Envt'l L.J.* 159 (1997).

In the meantime, EPA has attempted to "reform" CERCLA administratively. In 1995, EPA announced a comprehensive program of 20 administrative reforms related to CERCLA and centered on the promise of smarter and more cost-effective cleanups. U.S. EPA, "Superfund Administrative Reforms: Reform Initiatives" (Oct. 2, 1995), discussed in Michael Steinberg and Joshua Swift, "EPA's New National Remedy Review Board Aims to Improve Superfund Decisions," 26 *Env't Rptr.* 2353 (1996), and at 27 *Env't Rptr.* 2641 (1997). One of the most important reforms was creation of a new National Remedy Review Board to help control remedy costs by providing a cross-Regional, management-level review of high cost decisions on a site-specific basis. To be eligible for Board review, a proposed remedial action must meet one of two tests: It must either (1) cost more than $30 million or (2) cost more than $10 million *and* cost 50 percent more than the least costly remedial action alternative that is both protective and ARAR-compliant. The Board has 20 members, all of whom are senior EPA managers or experts on remedy selection, cost effectiveness, and program implementation from both the Regional and D.C. offices.

Another important reform was a policy of updating previous remedy decisions at individual sites. This encourages Regional offices to examine and modify past remedy decisions when significant new factual, scientific, or technological information suggests that the same level of protectiveness of human health and the environment can be achieved at a lower cost. EPA calculated estimated reductions in future cleanup costs at 31 of the 37 reform-related updates during fiscal 1996 and the first quarter of fiscal 1997 to total $284 million. The importance of this reform is emphasized by a district court decision holding that cleanup cost overruns incurred because of EPA's failure to reconsider its selected site remedy, when changed circumstances fundamentally altered the estimated scope and cost of the remedy, were costs "inconsistent with the national contingency plan" for which PRPs were not liable under CERCLA § 107(a). *United States v. Broderick Investment Co.*, 955 F.Supp. 1268 (D.Colo.1997). See Timothy Malloy, "Second–Look Remedies: Strategies for Re–Evaluating Superfund Cleanups," 26 *Env't Rptr.* 1420 (1995).

In 1998, EPA reported that since the inception of its administrative reforms, superfund cleanups had accelerated by 20 percent, resulting in more than twice as many cleanups during 1993–1997 as in the previous 12 years. At almost 90 percent of all sites on the NPL, according to EPA, physical work on the cleanup remedies had been completed or at least begun. The report said that the Review Board so far had reviewed 20 site decisions and saved an estimated $31 million. 28 *Env't Rptr.* 2114 (1998).

Vacant, contaminated, former industrial sites, mostly in the inner cities, are referred to as "*brownfields.*" EPA estimates that there are at least 100,000 brownfield sites nationwide. 28 *Env't Rptr.* 2727 (1998). Many of these sites are well located in relation to highways, rail facilities, public utilities, and workers in need of employment. However, because of potential CERCLA liabilities, businesses which could use these sites are reluctant to acquire and develop them. As a result, opportunities to create jobs and increase property tax revenues in the central cities are lost. City governments are demanding a solution to this problem, and many states have enacted or are considering voluntary cleanup laws or programs to address the brownfields problem. See the state-by-state summaries at 28 *Env't Rptr.* 2086, 2488 (1998). EPA and Congress also are trying to respond.

In 1989, EPA had issued a guidance which authorized, in very limited circumstances, agreements that would provide prospective purchasers of contaminated property with covenants not to sue under CERCLA. EPA, "Guidance on Landowner Liability Under Section 107(a) of CERCLA, De Minimis Settlements under Section 122(g)(1)(B) of CERCLA, and Settlements with Prospective Purchasers of Contaminated Property" (OSWER Directive No. 9835.9), 54 *Fed. Reg.* 34235 (Aug. 18, 1989). The number of prospective purchaser agreements entered into by EPA under the 1989 guidance was quite small. See Karen Wardzinski, "Prospective Purchaser Agreements Under EPA's New Guidance," 10 *SPG Nat. Resources & Env't* 24 (1996). In 1995, EPA issued a new guidance, revising portions of the 1989 guidance dealing with prospective purchaser agreements. 60 *Fed. Reg.* 34792 (July 3, 1995). It was part of the agency's "brownfields initiative." EPA now will accept something less than a commitment for a complete cleanup of a site where redevelopment provides strong, positive economic benefits to the community. Criteria for evaluating prospective purchaser agreements are identified and analyzed in the Wardzinski article.

In 1997, several bills were introduced in Congress, continuing earlier efforts there to facilitate redevelopment of brownfields. These included Senate Bill 235, which would have allowed businesses to deduct from their federal income taxes the cost of brownfields cleanup. However, Senator Chafee, Chair of the Senate Environment and Public Works Committee, was concerned that stand-alone brownfields legislation would undermine the effort to achieve comprehensive CERCLA reform. He had offered a comprehensive reform bill which also dealt with brownfields, Senate Bill 8. None of these bills was enacted into law.

For detailed discussion of brownfields problems and solutions, see William Buzbee, "Brownfields, Environmental Federalism, and Institutional Determinism," 21 *Wm. & Mary Envt'l L. & Pol'y Rev.* 1 (1997); Andrea Rimer, "Environmental Liability and the Brownfields Phenomenon: An Analysis of Federal Options for Redevelopment," 10 *Tulane Envt'l L.J.* 63 (1996).

D. THE ROLE OF FEDERAL BANKRUPTCY LAW

Because remedial actions at disposal sites often are so costly, it is not surprising that efforts to compel private cleanups, or to obtain reimbursement for remedial measures by public agencies, have been met in some instances by defenses based upon federal bankruptcy law.

Suppose, for example, in Discussion Problem #1 on CERCLA Liability, page 616 supra, that farmer Fred, owner of the contaminated site, goes into bankruptcy. Can EPA require participation (financial or otherwise) by him or his estate in the cleanup? If other PRPs, probably the generators or "arrangers," pay for the cleanup, what rights of contribution, if any, do they have against Fred or his estate?

TOPOL, "HAZARDOUS WASTE AND BANKRUPTCY:
CONFRONTING THE UNASKED QUESTIONS"[a]

13 *Virginia Environmental Law Journal* 186, 191–210 (1994).

* * * The harsh consequences of joint and several liability are somewhat tempered by a provision in CERCLA authorizing PRPs to seek contribution from each other. This allows PRPs to attempt to make their liability for a cleanup proportional to the amount of waste they contributed to the site.

* * *

The treatment of environmental claims under bankruptcy law is important for solvent PRPs at a site where other PRPs have filed for bankruptcy because it determines the extent to which the limited funds of the bankrupt estate must be used to pay for environmental liabilities. Every additional dollar that the insolvent PRP expends on environmental cleanup is a dollar less that the other PRPs will have to pay. On the other hand, it is also a dollar less that non-environmental creditors will receive.

Despite the obvious significance of the issue, however, Congress has provided no guidance. Nothing in CERCLA or the Bankruptcy Code speaks to the treatment of the environmental liabilities of bankrupt PRPs. Consequently, bankruptcy courts have been left the task of determining whether environmental liabilities should be afforded special treatment in the bankruptcy process.

* * *

Four major questions repeatedly arise when environmental cleanup costs are at issue in bankruptcy cases: (1) whether the bankrupt estate can abandon land that is polluted; (2) whether the automatic stay that normally operates in bankruptcy applies to environmental litigation; (3) whether environmental claims should be given priority as an administrative expense; and (4) whether bankruptcy discharges a corporation from its environmental liabilities. Underlying each of these four questions lurks a fifth issue, which often goes unrecognized: the effect on and role of PRPs in the bankruptcy process. To what extent does it matter if the party to the litigation is a private party as opposed to a government entity, and to what extent should the effect of the decision on PRPs be considered? * * *

Two points are apparent from examining the cases and literature in these areas. First, the case law is a mess because the courts are divided in their approach to every one of the above stated issues. Second, the reason for this confusion is the failure to address the fundamental issue underlying all of the cases, which is the allocation of cleanup costs among creditors, PRPs and the Superfund. * * *

In considering these issues, it is important to keep in mind a distinction that the Bankruptcy Code makes between prepetition and postpetition actions of the debtor. If a company files for bankruptcy and continues to operate while in bankruptcy, its actions must comport with environmental and other laws.[35] If it fails to do so, any liabilities that result from its postpetition actions will receive special treatment in bankruptcy. For example, while the automatic stay may limit environmental litigation against debtors for prepetition pollution, courts have consistently held that the automatic stay does not limit the government's ability to prohibit postpetition actions by the debtor that violate environmental laws. * * *

The more difficult question, which is the one typically presented under CERCLA, arises when the disposal of the hazardous waste occurs prepetition, but the resultant harms arise postpetition. The paradigmatic example of this would be a twenty-year old hazardous waste site in which some of the drums are leaking toxic chemicals into the ground. * * *

1. ABANDONMENT OF POLLUTED PROPERTY

Section 554 of the Bankruptcy Code permits a bankruptcy trustee to "abandon any property of the estate that is burdensome to the estate or that is of inconsequential value and benefit to the estate." * * * In bankruptcies involving environmental liabilities, however, a debtor may attempt to abandon land that is polluted with hazardous waste and therefore is not merely worthless, but actually has negative value. This raises the question whether the trustee may abandon polluted land and, if it can be abandoned, whether the estate remains liable for the cost of cleaning up the land.

The Supreme Court confronted this question in 1985 in *Midlantic National Bank v. New Jersey Department of Environmental Protection.*[41] The issue before the Court was whether the bankruptcy trustee could abandon property containing 470,000 gallons of PCB-contaminated oil when it would require over $2.5 million to clean up the site. The Court held "that a trustee may not abandon property in contravention of a state statute or regulation that is reasonably designed to protect the public health or safety from identifiable hazards." Although this language suggests that the right to abandon polluted land is limited, the Court then explained in a footnote that this limitation is a narrow one: "The abandonment power is not to be fettered by laws or regulations not reasonably calculated to protect the public health or safety from imminent and identified harm."[44]

---

35. *See, e.g.,* Ohio v. Kovacs, 469 U.S. 274, 285 (1985) (recognizing in dicta that the bankrupt party, the trustee or a later recipient of the property must comply with the environmental laws of Ohio).

41. 474 U.S. 494 (1986).

44. *Id.* at 507 n. 9. The facts of the case were consistent with that limiting language because the hazardous waste was in "un-

The application of *Midlantic* appears to turn on what the court determines to be an "imminent and identifiable harm." * * * Arguably, hazardous waste sites that are in violation of CERCLA necessarily present an imminent danger. That, after all, was the justification for enacting CERCLA. On the other hand, the footnote in *Midlantic* might be read to distinguish between immediate and future threats. Not surprisingly, the ambiguity in *Midlantic* has left lower courts divided over when particular dangers present a significant enough risk to prohibit abandonment.

Some lower courts have held that *Midlantic* creates a very narrow exception to abandonment power. The Fourth Circuit took this position, explaining that "this narrow exception applies where there is a serious health risk, not where the hazards are speculative or may await appropriate action by an environmental agency." The Tenth Circuit concurred, relying on the statement in *Midlantic* that the exception to the abandonment power "is a narrow one." A number of bankruptcy courts have reached the same conclusion and permitted trustees to abandon land without cleaning up hazardous waste as long as necessary steps, such as notifying the relevant government authorities, are taken to prevent immediate harm to the public. * * *

Other lower courts confronting the issue have reached the opposite result and imposed more rigorous restrictions on a trustee's power of abandonment. In [one case] the bankruptcy court reasoned that because Congress passed CERCLA in order to remedy a threat to public welfare, whenever a violation of CERCLA can be shown, a sufficient threat to public safety exists, warranting restriction of the abandonment power. * * *

Approached in this manner, the cases appear to be about whether the hazardous waste sites will be cleaned up. That is not the case, however, because CERCLA ensures that the federal government will be able to respond to such crises, often in ways that are more effective than anything the insolvent debtor could do. In fact, even the decision in *Midlantic* was not necessary to protect the public safety because New York State had already spent $2.5 million to decontaminate the facility at issue.

The critical issue underlying the abandonment cases therefore concerns the allocation of cleanup costs. A bankrupt debtor is motivated to abandon land whenever the costs of cleanup exceed the value of the land since at that point it is no longer beneficial for the estate to pay for the cleanup in order to resell the land. By abandoning the land, the debtor may be able to eliminate some of the estate's liabilities and increase the return paid to the creditors at the expense of PRPs, who will owe that much more. If, on the other hand, the government is able to prevent abandonment, it may then be able to force the estate to expend addition-

guarded, deteriorating containers" which presented risk of "explosion, fire, contamination of water supplies, destruction of natural resources, and injury, genetic damage, or death through personal contact."

al funds to clean up the hazardous waste. This shift of responsibility to the estate will save PRPs and the Superfund some money, depending on the assets of the debtor. Thus, regardless whether the threat is deemed "imminent," CERCLA ensures that a debtor's land containing hazardous waste will be cleaned up. The critical issue is the allocation of those cleanup costs.

2.   THE AUTOMATIC STAY AND GOVERNMENT INJUNCTIONS

The filing of a bankruptcy petition normally triggers the operation of section 362 of the Bankruptcy Code, the automatic stay provision, which immediately halts "the commencement or continuation ... of a judicial, administrative, or other action or proceeding against the debtor that was or could have been commenced" before the petition was filed. Although the automatic stay halts most litigation against debtors, the Code does contain a provision exempting the "continuation of an action or proceeding by a governmental unit to enforce such governmental unit's police or regulatory power." This exemption appears to apply specifically to cleanup orders. Indeed, the legislative history of the section explicitly provides that "where a governmental unit is suing a debtor to prevent or stop violation of fraud, *environmental protection,* consumer protection, safety, or similar police or regulatory laws, or attempting to fix damages for violation of such a law, the action or proceeding is not stayed under the automatic stay."

The exemption in section 362(b)(4) is limited, however, by section 362(b)(5), which prohibits the government from enforcing a money judgment in the exercise of its regulatory power. A money judgment requiring a debtor to pay for a cleanup would certainly seem to be covered by this section and arguably, government injunctions in these cases might also be considered money judgments because an injunction issued under CERCLA ensures that necessary cleanups will occur.

Thus, the critical question facing bankruptcy courts is whether to characterize government litigation pursuant to CERCLA as regulatory or pecuniary. These cases fall into two categories: the first involves government efforts to obtain an injunction requiring the debtor to conduct cleanup activities and the second involves government litigation for monetary damages. In both categories the courts have developed unsound distinctions.

When the government has sought an injunction in the context of a bankruptcy case, the courts have focused on the harm from the pollution and issued an injunction when the hazardous waste site posed an ongoing threat to the environment. The Third Circuit developed a test generally used for making such a determination in the 1984 case of *Penn Terra Ltd. v. Department of Environmental Resources.*[65] The test is based on whether the government "seeks compensation for past damages or prevention of future harm." This past damage/future harm test, which has been widely adopted, focuses on the harm presented by the environ-

65.   733 F.2d 267 (3d Cir.1984).

mental violation, not when the violation occurred. In *Penn Terra,* for example, the court held that the automatic stay did not limit Pennsylvania's attempt to obtain an injunction requiring the debtor to remedy the harms created by prepetition mining operations, even though the debtor had ceased all mining operations and was liquidating under Chapter 7. The court reasoned that the injunction was necessary to prevent future harm to the environment by halting further deterioration in soil conditions that were attributable to the prepetition mining operations.

The past damage/future harm test developed in *Penn Terra* is necessarily a meaningless one, however, because by definition all hazardous waste sites will pose a future threat of harm to the environment. CERCLA, after all, was enacted for the very purpose of cleaning up past pollution in order to prevent future harm to the public. Thus, to allow the government to obtain an injunction whenever the hazardous waste site poses a threat to the environment is to give it carte blanche to do so regardless of whether the debtor is currently polluting. * * *

If instead of issuing a cleanup order, the government conducts the cleanup itself and seeks cost recovery under CERCLA, its success in bankruptcy court will be limited. Although courts have held that the government is permitted to bring suit to establish damages and liability, that right is limited significantly by the courts' holdings that those judgments cannot be enforced. The cases have reasoned that actions to establish liability are brought for regulatory reasons, but efforts to collect on a claim are brought for pecuniary reasons. By bringing the suit for damages the government is, of course, able to establish a claim for the purpose of collecting at the end of the bankruptcy, but if that claim is classified as unsecured, the government will have to share pro rata with other creditors and probably collect only a small portion of the cleanup costs. In contrast, an injunction ordering the debtor to conduct a cleanup forces the debtor to pay all of the costs of cleanup.

* * *

3. ADMINISTRATIVE PRIORITY FOR CLEANUP COST

Another issue that has produced a split in the courts concerns the classification of environmental claims. At the end of the bankruptcy case, when the debtor is prepared to liquidate under Chapter 7 or reorganize under Chapter 11, the Bankruptcy Code establishes an organized system of priorities for distributing the assets. Secured creditors are paid up to the value of their collateral. The next group to be paid are those parties holding priority claims under section 507(a) of the Code. First among the claims in this category are those for administrative expenses, including "the actual, necessary costs and expenses of preserving the estate."[81] Finally, unsecured claims are paid pro rata. Since unsecured claimants are generally paid only a fraction of the value of their claims, environmental creditors, including both the government and PRPs, have argued

---

81. § 503(b)(1)(A).

that their claims should be classified as administrative expenses. [There is no clear Supreme Court authority on this point, and the lower courts are divided.]

* * *

4. DISCHARGE AND ENVIRONMENTAL CLEANUPS

* * *

The question whether environmental liabilities are dischargeable has emerged as an important issue in bankruptcy. Courts have had little difficulty concluding that a monetary debt resulting from a cleanup that was already undertaken is a dischargeable debt.[103] Where the government is seeking an injunction, however, courts have found classification of the obligation to be more difficult. Some courts have concluded that injunctions requiring a debtor to conduct a cleanup arising from the prepetition disposal of hazardous waste—an issue left open in *Kovacs*[104] —are also dischargeable in bankruptcy since compliance with the injunction would require the expenditure of money.[105] Other courts have held that an injunction to respond to an ongoing claim is not dischargeable.[106]

Another difficult question that courts have confronted is the treatment of postpetition environmental obligations. The cases discussed above deal with cleanups begun prior to the filing of a bankruptcy petition. The long time frame for CERCLA cleanups, however, will mean that many companies will file for bankruptcy before the EPA begins to clean up—or even has knowledge of—hazardous waste sites where the debtor is a PRP.

The Second Circuit recently addressed this question in *In re Chateaugay Corp.*, and appeared to adopt a test that is similar to the past damage/future harm test used to determine whether government cleanup orders are exempt from the automatic stay.[107] In *Chateaugay*, the court held that monetary claims for post-petition environmental cleanups are dischargeable so long as they relate to a prepetition release. As for injunctions, the court held that an injunction to clean up a waste site is not discharged in bankruptcy if that site is continuing to deteriorate because while the "EPA is entitled to seek payment if it elects to incur cleanup costs itself, . . . it has no authority to accept a payment from a responsible party as an alternative to continued pollution." Consequent-

---

103. *See Kovacs,* 469 U.S. at 283; *Chateaugay,* 944 F.2d at 1006.

104. 469 U.S. at 283 (noting that the "only performance sought from Kovacs was the payment of money"); *id.* at 284–85 ("[W]e do not hold that . . . any conduct that will contribute to the pollution of the site or the State's waters is dischargeable in bankruptcy.").

105. *See* United States v. Whizco, Inc., 841 F.2d 147 (6th Cir.1988), *In re* Robinson, 46 B.R. 136 (Bankr.M.D.Fla.), *rev'd on*

other grounds, 55 B.R. 355 (M.D.Fla.1985). It is interesting to note that these cases, unlike those involving the automatic stay, recognize that there may be no functional distinction between an injunction and an obligation to pay money.

106. *See In re* Torwico Electronics, Inc., 8 F.3d 146, 149–50 (3d Cir.1993); *In re* CMC Heartland Partners, 966 F.2d 1143, 1146–47 (7th Cir.1992).

107. 944 F.2d 997 (2d Cir.1991).

ly, the court held, cleanup orders are different than money judgments and must survive the conclusion of the bankruptcy case.

* * *

The Seventh and Ninth Circuits have taken a different approach to the issue and adopted a standard for dischargeability based on "fair contemplat[ion]."[114] Under this standard, environmental claims are dischargeable if the costs are fairly contemplated at the time of bankruptcy.[115] In *In re Jensen*, for example, the Ninth Circuit held that California's environmental claims against a debtor were dischargeable because the State had knowledge of the debtor's potential liability before the filing of the bankruptcy petition.

* * *

5. POTENTIALLY RESPONSIBLE PARTIES

* * *

Consideration of the effect of the case law on PRPs leads to three conclusions. First, while the precise extent of the PRPs' legal rights is uncertain (as is the government's), the current framework places PRPs in a position where they will have difficulty forcing the debtor to fulfill its cleanup obligations under CERCLA. Second, because those issues are fundamentally about who bears the costs of cleanup, PRPs will often be left to pay the costs that would have been allocated to the debtor had it not filed for bankruptcy. Finally, the cases create an artificial distinction between PRPs and the government by frequently permitting only the latter into court, even though PRPs and the Superfund ultimately bear the costs of cleaning up hazardous waste in every case.

E. CRIMINAL LIABILITY UNDER FEDERAL ENVIRONMENTAL LAWS

LAZARUS, "ASSIMILATING ENVIRONMENTAL PROTECTION INTO LEGAL RULES AND THE PROBLEM WITH ENVIRONMENTAL CRIME"[a]

27 *Loyola of Los Angeles Law Review* 867, 868–888 (1994).

Until relatively recently, the enforcement of environmental protection laws meant, without more, their *civil* enforcement. Although, historically, there certainly have been instances of criminal prosecutions in which the defendant's unlawful acts included environmental pollution, there was no systematic effort by either federal or state governments to

---

114. *In re* National Gypsum Co., 139 B.R. 397, 408 (N.D.Tex.1992).

115. *See In re* Chicago, Milwaukee, St. Paul & Pac. R.R. Co., 974 F.2d 775, 786 (7th Cir.1992); *In re* Jensen, 995 F.2d 925, 930–31 (9th Cir.1993).

utilize criminal sanctions on behalf of environmental protection goals. Although Congress routinely included criminal sanctions in each of the major environmental laws that it has enacted since the 1970s, the federal environmental criminal enforcement program remained largely moribund prior to the mid–1980s.

* * *

In the mid– to late 1970s, the Department of Justice (Department) undertook a few publicized prosecutions for violations of environmental protection laws in order to establish at least the threat of criminal enforcement. Several years later, the Department commenced a programmatic effort within what was then the Department's Land and Natural Resources Division, now the Environment and Natural Resources Division (Environment Division). The Department did so by creating an Environmental Crimes Unit (now a Section) within the Environment Division, which would be concerned exclusively with criminal prosecutions arising under the federal environmental protection laws. The Environment Division intended lawyers within that Section to possess the expertise in environmental law necessary both to prosecute environmental cases themselves and to assist federal prosecutors in the offices of the United States Attorney interested in such cases.

At the behest of the Environmental Protection Agency (EPA) and the Department, Congress also took a series of deliberate steps designed to promote environmental criminal prosecutions. Congress added new environmental crimes to existing statutes and significantly increased the criminal penalties associated with the violation of federal environmental statutes, partly to send the message to the Federal Bureau of Investigation (FBI) as well as to the regulated communities that environmental crimes were now a priority for federal law enforcement. Congress also conferred new investigatory authorities on the EPA and substantially increased the EPA's related resources for the specific purpose of enhancing the federal criminal prosecution effort.[9]

There have apparently been concrete results. According to the Department, between fiscal years 1983 and 1993, the Department "has recorded environmental criminal indictments against 911 corporations and individuals, and 686 guilty pleas and convictions have been entered. A total of $212,408,903 in criminal penalties has been assessed. More than 388 years of imprisonment have been imposed of which nearly 191 years account for actual confinement."

* * *

Congress responded positively to * * * arguments in favor of criminal sanctions by including criminal sanctions in almost all of the federal environmental protection laws. The response was, however, also indiscriminate: Congress made virtually *all* "knowing" and some "negligent" violations of environmental pollution control standards, limitations, per-

---

9. *See* Pollution Prosecution Act of 1990, §§ 201–205, Pub.L. No. 101–593, 104 Stat. 2954, 2962–63 (codified at 42 U.S.C. § 4321 (Supp. IV 1992)).

mits, and licenses subject to criminal as well as to civil sanctions. Congress made relatively little effort to define thresholds for when a defendant's conduct justified adding the possibility of criminal sanctions to civil penalties. Except for the knowing and negligent mens rea requirements, Congress just assumed that the civil and criminal thresholds should be precisely the same. The problems with such an assumption are several.

First, the environmental standards are not set based on the existence of traditional notions of criminal culpability. Violations of environmental laws may, of course, involve the most serious risks to human health and of catastrophic, irreversible environmental damage. But the standards upon which those statutory violations are in fact based do not depend on the existence of such risks or damage. They are instead set at far more precautionary, risk-averse levels of protection against risks to human health and the environment. The public—this Author included—may believe that such precautionary levels are wise and appropriate, but that presents a far different public policy issue than whether all such violations rise to a level justifying severe criminal as well as civil sanctions. By simply equating the regulatory thresholds for civil and criminal sanctions, however, Congress never directly addressed this issue.

Congress, for the most part, has not been especially discriminating in defining the mens rea requirements for environmental crimes. Instead, consistent with the rationale that criminal sanctions serve regulatory deterrent purposes, Congress sought to maximize their deterrent effect by deemphasizing mens rea elements for the imposition of criminal sanctions. Hence, although the environmental statutes generally require some mens rea for criminal prosecution—they are not simply strict liability offenses—they do not require much at all in terms of the defendant's knowledge of the actual risks of his or her activity.[52] As a result, although persons who violate environmental laws may possess the most venal and reprehensible of states of mind—and thus warrant the most severe criminal sanction—the environmental criminal sanctions do not require such a state of mind.[53]

---

52. *See, e.g.,* M. Diane Barber, *Fair Warning: The Deterioration of Scienter Under Environmental Criminal Statutes,* 26 Loy.L.A.L.Rev. 105, 144–47 (1992); Kevin A. Gaynor et al., *Environmental Criminal Prosecutions: Simple Fixes for a Flawed System,* 3 Vill.Envtl.L.J. 1, 11–21 (1992); R. Christopher Locke, *Environmental Crimes: The Absence of Intent and the Complexities of Compliance,* 16 Colum.J.Envtl.L. 311 (1991); Ruth Ann Weidel et al., *The Erosion of Mens Rea in Environmental Criminal Prosecutions,* 21 Seton Hall L.Rev. 1100 (1991); Lisa Ann Harig, Note, *Ignorance Is Not Bliss: Responsible Corporate Officers Convicted of Environmental Crimes and the Federal Sentencing Guidelines,* 42 Duke L.J.

145 (1992); Michael Vitiello, Note, *Does Culpability Matter?: Statutory Construction Under 42 U.S.C. § 6928,* 6 Tul.Envtl.L.J. 187, 214–29 (1993).

53. To be sure, many of the environmental statutes include a "knowing endangerment" offense, which imposes even greater criminal sanctions on those violators who act with knowledge of the significant risks they impose, *see, e.g.,* Clean Water Act of 1977, 33 U.S.C.A. § 1319(c)(3) (West 1986 & Supp.1993); Resource Conservation and Recovery Act of 1976, 42 U.S.C.A. § 6928(e) (West 1983); Clean Air Act, 42 U.S.C. § 7413(c) (1988 & Supp. III 1992), but the problems that have developed in the prosecution of environmental

What makes such an approach to mens rea particularly problematic in the environmental law context is that environmental standards, unlike most traditional crimes, present questions of degree rather than of kind. Murder, burglary, assault, and embezzlement are simply unlawful. There is no threshold level below which such conduct is acceptable. In contrast, pollution is not unlawful per se: In many circumstances, some pollution is acceptable. It is only pollution that exceeds certain prescribed levels that is unlawful. But, for that very reason, the mens rea element should arguably be a more, not less, critical element in the prosecution of an environmental offense.

Finally, Congress failed to adequately account for the fact that the civil standards are often set at an action-forcing level and are anything but static. The standards do not necessarily reflect standards of performance that are either economically or technologically feasible. They do not reflect existing conduct or long-settled cultural norms. They instead are more likely to reflect policy makers' predictions of what will be possible and the public's aspirations for a cleaner environment. The underlying science is often very uncertain, and the regulations constantly change in response to new information, court challenges, and sweeping statutory amendments.

Full compliance with all applicable environmental laws is consequently the exception rather than the norm. * * *

For that reason, however, there is a danger, indeed a potential impropriety, in Congress's approach to environmental criminal liability. The question whether certain conduct warrants a criminal sanction is far different than whether a civil sanction may be warranted, precisely because the latter is susceptible to being no more than an economic disincentive. Criminal liability standards should be more settled and less dynamic. They should be more reflective of what in fact can be accomplished rather than of the public's aspirations of how, if pushed, the world can change in the future.

* * *

The executive branch, moreover, has further exacerbated the problem in the environmental criminal context. Rather than fill the vacuum left by Congress, the executive branch has failed to develop specific guidance governing the exercise of prosecutorial discretion in the environmental crimes area. Nor has the executive branch otherwise made much effort to explain publicly its decision-making process in any systematic way.

Notes

1. If Congress does not amend the environmental laws to tighten up the requirements for criminal liability, what other solution does Lazarus suggest at the end of the foregoing excerpt?

crimes have generally not resulted from these more demanding provisions. They instead result from the vague delegations of prosecutorial discretion that inhere in those criminal provisions that lack such requirements.

In 1991, the Department of Justice issued a policy statement encouraging corporations to develop and implement voluntary environmental compliance programs as a means of mitigating exposure to criminal prosecution. U.S. Department of Justice, "Factors in Decisions on Criminal Prosecutions for Environmental Violations in the Context of Significant Voluntary Compliance or Disclosure Efforts by the Violator" (July 1, 1991).

2. On January 12, 1994, EPA's Office of Criminal Enforcement issued guidance on the exercise of *investigative discretion* by EPA's criminal investigators. Memorandum from Earl Devaney, Director of EPA's Office of Criminal Enforcement, "The Exercise of Investigative Discretion," discussed in Chester, "An Overview of EPA's Guidance on Criminal Investigative Discretion," 9 *Nat'l Envtl.Enforcement J.*, No. 10, p. 3 (Nov.1994). The memorandum states that it is intended only as internal guidance for EPA and does not create any procedural or substantive rights or benefits in the regulated community, nor does it limit "lawful enforcement prerogatives" of either EPA or the Department of Justice.

The guidance establishes specific criteria which EPA investigators are to consider before initiating a criminal investigation. Case selection is based on two general measures, "significant environmental harm" and "culpable conduct." These measures, in turn, are divided into several factors which serve as indicators that a case is suitable for criminal investigation. Significant environmental harm encompasses four such factors, while culpable conduct consists of five factors. The existence of any one or more of these factors may justify the commencement of a criminal investigation.

Under most environmental statutes and regulations, a violation can be established without proof of environmental harm. However, the guidance reserves criminal investigations to cases of actual or potential harm. The factors identified as possible indicators of environmental harm are (1) actual harm, (2) the threat of significant harm, (3) the failure to report environmental releases, and (4) a trend or common attitude toward noncompliance within the regulated community.

"Culpable conduct" is not an evaluation of criminal intent, since intent may not be evident at the time of case selection. For investigative purposes, culpable conduct is based on (1) a history of repeated violations, (2) deliberate misconduct, (3) concealment of misconduct or falsification of records, (4) tampering with pollution monitoring or control equipment, or (5) conducting pollution-related activities without necessary permits or approvals.

The guidance also mentions several additional factors to be considered when a corporation is a potential target of criminal investigation. Most notable is the presumption of criminal culpability where a company conducts a compliance audit and fails to remedy promptly any violations discovered. On the other hand, the guidance states that a corporation which has a comprehensive self-evaluation program and which voluntarily discloses environmental violations and then fully and promptly remediates them will usually not become the target of a criminal investigation.

3. In a final policy statement issued in 1995, which dealt primarily with self-disclosed *civil* violations, EPA said that it would "generally not recommend *criminal* prosecution" against those who find violations of environmental laws "through an environmental audit" or through "an

objective, documented, systematic procedure or practice reflecting the regulated entity's due diligence in preventing, detecting, and correcting violations." However, a decision not to recommend prosecution also is dependent on prompt disclosure of the violations; correction and remediation; prevention of recurrence; and an absence of prior violations. EPA, "Incentives for Self–Policing: Discovery, Disclosure, Correction and Prevention of Violations," 60 *Fed. Reg.* 66706 (1995).

In a further policy statement contained in a 1997 internal memo regarding self-disclosures of criminal violations, Earl Devaney of EPA said that agency recommendations against prosecutions, of companies that uncover criminal violations through compliance audits and voluntarily fix them, would apply only to the companies and *not* to individual employees who actually commit environmental crimes. 25 *Env't Rptr.* 2170 (1998).

4. For discussion of environmental criminal law generally, see Mary Clifford (ed.), *Environmental Crime: Enforcement, Policy, and Social Responsibility* (1998); Richard Lazarus, "Meeting the Demands of Integration in the Evolution of Environmental Law: Reforming Environmental Criminal Law," 83 *Geo. L.J.* 2407 (1995); Symposium, "Recent Developments in Environmental Crime," 7 *Fordham Envt'l L.J.* 573 (1996).

[Note on Environmental Audit Privileges] *reduce liability*

A very controversial issue is whether businesses which conduct *voluntary internal compliance audits* can be compelled to disclose the results thereof, e.g., in subsequent civil or criminal litigation initiated by private or governmental plaintiffs. The Department of Justice, the EPA, and the U.S. Sentencing Commission all encourage the establishment of voluntary corporate environmental compliance programs, and consider the existence of such programs to be an ameliorating factor in criminal prosecutions and sentencing. EPA also grants civil penalty mitigation to firms that effectively manage their compliance responsibilities and promptly disclose violations. See James Banks, "EPA's New Enforcement Policy: At Last, a Reliable Roadmap to Civil Penalty Mitigation for Self–Disclosed Violations," 26 *Envt'l L.Rptr.* 10227 (1996); "More than 500 Facilities Report Violations Under Agency's Voluntary Audit Policy," 28 *Env't Rprt.* 859 (1997).

[Several states have enacted, and others are considering, legislation making information gathered through voluntary environmental audits privileged, or protected from disclosure, in various types of enforcement proceedings.]See John Lee and Bertram Frey, "Environmental Audit Laws: A State-by-State Comparison," 28 *Env't Rptr.* 331 (1997). However, the U.S. EPA opposes state privilege laws, fearing that it might have to step in and expend federal resources to pursue enforcement actions in cases that would have been a state responsibility absent restrictions preventing the states from acting on audit results. Representatives of business and industry have pressed EPA to change its position. See 25 *Env't Rptr.* 587, 624 (1994).

now 22 states

As of 1998, nineteen states had enacted laws making information gathered through voluntary environmental audits privileged. Thus, the information is not accessible to third parties, including the government, absent a waiver or court order. About half of the laws also provide *immunity* from criminal, civil, or administrative prosecution and penalties with respect to violations that are disclosed voluntarily. Linda Spahr, "Environmental Self–Audit Privilege: The Straw That Breaks the Back of Criminal Prosecutions," 7 *Fordham Envt'l L. J.* 635, 639 (1996). The laws typically define an environmental audit as a systematic review of a facility's practices to determine noncompliance with certain environmental laws. Most specify a variety of documents which may be considered parts of such reports and to which the privilege extends. These include field notes, records of observations, findings, opinions, suggestions, conclusions, drafts, memoranda, photographs, maps, charts, graphs, and surveys. Most of the laws prohibit persons who participated in audits from disclosing, testifying, or being compelled to testify about the audit reports or underlying facts. Included with participants are those who were made privy to audits, those who did any of the work, and those who provided estimates for corrective work resulting from the audit. *Id.* at 640. For a detailed analysis and comparison of these nineteen state laws, see John–Mark Stensvaag, "The Fine Print of State Environmental Audit Privileges," 16 *UCLA J. Envtl. L. & Pol'y* 69 (1997).

EPA has threatened to withdraw or refuse delegations of authority to implement federal environmental laws and programs, for states whose environmental audit laws interfere unduly with the states' enforcement capabilities. 27 *Env't Rptr.* 2176, 2321 (1997). Early in 1997, EPA issued a guidance establishing principles which the agency will use in judging whether state environmental audit laws interfere with the enforcement authority needed to run federally delegated programs. EPA will use the principles when it considers approving new delegated programs or modifications to existing programs in states that have enacted environmental audit laws. *Id.* at 2176.

EPA and the Department of Justice also take the position that they are not bound by state privilege or immunity laws in federal enforcement proceedings. *Id.* at 2322. Concerning this issue, see Christina Austin, "State Environmental Audit Privilege Laws: Can EPA Still Access Environmental Audits in Federal Court?", 26 *Envt'l Law* 1241 (1996).[a]

Nevertheless, as mentioned in notes 1–3 supra, both EPA and the Department of Justice do consider the existence of an effective environmental audit program to be an important ameliorating factor when they are deciding whether to undertake a criminal investigation or prosecution against a corporation for environmental violations. In its 1997 policy memo, EPA said that it may recommend against criminal prosecution if certain criteria are met:

(1) The company must cooperate fully with EPA, giving access to information in the environmental audit or due diligence program and to all employees and other documents requested.

---

a. For further discussion of state environmental audit laws generally, see E. Lynn Grayson and Christina Riewer, "EPA's Audit Policy and State Audit–Privilege Laws: Moving Beyond Command and Control?", 27 *Envt'l L. Rptr.* 10243 (1997); Eric Orts and Paula Murray, "Environmental Disclosure and Evidentiary Privilege," 1997 *U. Ill. L. Rev. 1;* David Chaumette and William Cason, "Auditing Environmental Audit Policies: Has Industry Been Hoisted On Its Own Petard?", 4 *Wis. Envt'l L. J.* 1 (1997); Jack Goldman, "Will Implementing ISO 14001 Destroy the Confidentiality Of Environmental Compliance Audits?", 27 *Env't Rptr.* 426 (1996); Michael Harris, "Promoting Corporate Self–Compliance: An Examination Of The Debate Over Legal Protection For Environmental Audits," 23 *Ecology L. Q.* 663 (1996).

(2) The violation must be discovered through voluntary self-evaluations and the disclosure made before EPA formally opens a criminal investigation.

(3) The disclosure must be made before EPA's Criminal Investigation Division begins pursuing "promising leads" from sources such as whistle-blowers, citizen complaints, or inspections by public officials.

(4) The discovery of the violation must be made through voluntary actions, not through audits or reviews required by law, regulation, permit, or administrative or judicial order.

(5) Disclosure of the violation generally must be made within ten days of discovery.

(6) The company must certify to EPA in writing, within 60 days of the disclosure, that it has remedied any environmental harm caused by the violation, or that more time is required to complete the remedy.

(7) The company must agree in writing to take steps to prevent recurrence of the criminal violation.

(8) The criminal violation must neither repeat a violation within the past three years nor be part of a pattern of noncompliance by the facility's parent organization.

In *Olen Properties Corp. v. Sheldahl, Inc.,* 38 ERC 1887, 1994 WL 212135 (C.D.Cal.1994), a federal court held that environmental audit memoranda prepared by a company supervisor, to assist the firm's attorneys in evaluating compliance with relevant laws and regulations, were protected by the *attorney-client privilege* and could be withheld from discovery in a private response action under CERCLA.

Note

The next two cases invoke what has come to be known as the "public welfare offense" doctrine. The doctrine originated in *United States v. International Minerals & Chem. Corp..,* 402 U.S. 558, 91 S.Ct. 1697, 29 L.Ed.2d 178 (1971), a misdemeanor case. While *mens rea,* or "guilty knowledge," is a required element of most criminal offenses, a distinguishing feature of environmental crimes is that they require minimal proof of knowledge to sustain a conviction. Under the public welfare offense doctrine, courts have interpreted the term "knowingly" to require only general awareness that a defendant was dealing with a substance likely to be regulated and knowledge that the conduct constituting the offense occurred.

For further discussion of the public welfare offense doctrine, see Andrew Turner, "Mens Rea in Environmental Crime Prosecutions: *Ignorantia Juris* and the White Collar Criminal," 23 *Columbia J. Envt'l L.* 217 (1998); John Cooney et al., "Criminal Enforcement of Environmental Laws: Part II—The Knowledge Element in Environmental Crimes," 25 *Envt'l L. Rptr.* 10525 (1995).

UNITED STATES v. LAUGHLIN

United States Court of Appeals, Second Circuit, 1993.
10 F.3d 961, certiorari denied 511 U.S. 1071,
114 S.Ct. 1649, 128 L.Ed.2d 368 (1994).

MINER, CIRCUIT JUDGE:

Defendant-appellant Harris Goldman appeals from a judgment of conviction and sentence entered in the United States District Court for the Northern District of New York after a jury trial, convicting him of knowingly disposing of hazardous waste without a permit, in violation of [RCRA]. The judgment appealed from also convicted Goldman of failing to report the release of a hazardous substance as required by [CERCLA], which requires that notification be given to the National Response Center or other appropriate governmental agency upon the release of a hazardous substance. The district court sentenced Goldman to concurrent prison terms of three-and-one-half years for the RCRA violation and three years for the CERCLA violation. He was further ordered to pay restitution to the United States in the amount of $607,868. Goldman primarily contends on appeal that the district court delivered an improper charge to the jury regarding the RCRA and CERCLA violations. For the reasons that follow, we affirm.

BACKGROUND

In 1983, GCL Tie & Treating, Inc. ("GCL") purchased a railroad tie treating business located in Sidney, New York from the Railcon Corporation ("Railcon"). GCL was owned by Goldman and his business partner, Thomas Cuevas.

The tie treatment process consisted of first placing untreated green ties into a large cylinder and then adding creosote. The creosote then was heated to boiling. As water and natural wood alcohols were drawn out by a vacuum process, the creosote penetrated the ties. The water, wood alcohols and some creosote, collectively referred to in the industry as "bolton water," * * * then was boiled off so that the remaining creosote sludge could be suctioned out and placed into storage for re-use in the treatment process.

* * *

GCL began experiencing financial difficulties in 1987. Its problems were exacerbated when, early in June, GCL's boiler ceased to function properly. Without a properly functioning boiler, GCL could not recover the creosote sludge left over from the treatment process. GCL quickly began to run out of storage space for the bolton water, and GCL employees were directed to put the excess bolton water into a railroad tanker car that had recently delivered a shipment of new creosote. This tanker car remained on the GCL railroad spur and was used to store the bolton water generated by the treatment process.

* * *

Shortly thereafter, Goldman began to demand repeatedly that Laughlin release the contents of the tanker car onto the ground. After Laughlin refused, Goldman informed him that he was going to release the creosote sludge himself. After one unsuccessful nocturnal attempt to release the creosote sludge, Goldman returned a second time, at approximately three o'clock in the morning, and successfully released the entire contents of the tanker car directly onto the ground.

* * *

1. RCRA

Goldman argues that the district court improperly instructed the jury regarding the elements of the RCRA violation. He claims that the Government was required to prove, as essential elements of the violation, that he was aware of the RCRA regulations applicable to creosote sludge and knew GCL had not obtained a permit to dispose of the creosote sludge and that the district court's failure to so instruct the jury was error. * * *

Goldman was convicted of violating 42 U.S.C. § 6928(d)(2)(A) which provides criminal penalties for:

Any person who . . .

(2) knowingly treats, stores, or disposes of any hazardous waste identified or listed under this subchapter—

(A) without a permit under this subchapter. . . .

Appellant contends that the word "knowingly" applies not only to the prohibited act—treatment, storage, or disposal of a hazardous waste— but also to the fact that the hazardous waste has been identified or listed under RCRA and to the fact that a permit was lacking.

The district court instructed the jury that it had to find that the Government had proved the following elements beyond a reasonable doubt:

(1) "the defendant knowingly disposed of or caused others to dispose of creosote sludge on or about the date set forth in the indictment;"

(2) "that pursuant to [RCRA], the creosote sludge was hazardous;"

(3) "the defendant knew creosote sludge had a potential to be harmful to others or the environment or, in other words, it was not a harmless substance like uncontaminated water;" and

(4) "neither defendant nor GCL had obtained a permit or interim status which authorized the disposal of hazardous waste under [RCRA]."

Prior to delivering these instructions, the district court told the jury that creosote sludge was a hazardous waste as defined under RCRA. Appellant makes no objection to this aspect of the jury charge.

When knowledge is an element of a statute intended to regulate hazardous or dangerous substances, the Supreme Court has determined that the knowledge element is satisfied upon a showing that a defendant was aware that he was performing the proscribed acts; knowledge of regulatory requirements is not necessary. See *United States v. International Minerals & Chem. Corp.*, 402 U.S. 558, 563–65, 91 S.Ct. 1697, 1700–1701, 29 L.Ed.2d 178 (1971) (in prosecution for knowingly violating a hazardous materials regulation, Government was not required to prove that the defendant was aware of regulation, but only that he was aware of shipment of the hazardous materials) * * *.

Although this Court never before has been presented with the question of whether 42 U.S.C. § 6928(d)(2)(A) requires that a defendant have knowledge of the lack of a permit for hazardous waste disposal, most of the courts of appeals that have addressed this issue have responded in the negative.

* * * It is also our perception that a defendant's knowledge that a permit is lacking is not an element of the offense defined by 42 U.S.C. § 6928(d)(2)(A). This conclusion is supported not only by the reasoning of *International Minerals* but also by the fact that the word "knowing" is included in paragraphs (B) and (C) of section 6928(d)(2) but notably omitted from paragraph (A), with which we are concerned. With respect to the mens rea required by section 6928(d)(2)(A), the Government need prove only that a defendant was aware of his act of disposing of a substance he knew was hazardous. Proof that a defendant was aware of the lack of a permit is not required. Accordingly, we hold that the district court properly instructed the jury concerning Goldman's violation of section 6928(d)(2)(A).

2. CERCLA

Goldman also challenges the district court's failure to instruct the jury that the Government must prove, as an element of the CERCLA offense, that Goldman knew that his release of creosote sludge violated CERCLA. The reasoning set forth above regarding the RCRA violation applies with equal force to the CERCLA count. Goldman was charged with violating [CERCLA § 103(a)], which provides, in pertinent part:

> Any person in charge of a ... facility shall, as soon as he has knowledge of any release (other than a federally permitted release) of a hazardous substance from such ... facility in quantities equal to or greater than those determined pursuant to section 9602 of this title, immediately notify the National Response Center ... of such release.

* * *

Like RCRA, CERCLA is a regulatory scheme intended to protect the public health and safety. The reporting requirement at issue here insures the Government's ability to "move quickly to check the spread of a hazardous release." In accordance with our interpretation of "knowingly" in RCRA, discussed *supra,* we find that section [103(a)] does not demand knowledge of the regulatory requirements of CERCLA; it demands only that defendant be aware of his acts. * * * Accordingly, we conclude that the district court properly instructed the jury regarding the CERCLA violation.

Notes

1. Many federal environmental statutes provide for criminal as well as civil penalties for violators. Of these provisions, section 3008(d) of RCRA probably has been the most used by prosecutors. Section 3008(d) authorizes criminal sanctions—fines and imprisonment—for any person who

(1) *knowingly* transports or causes to be transported any hazardous waste identified or listed under this subchapter to a facility which does not have a permit under this subchapter . . . ,

(2) *knowingly* treats, stores, or disposes of any hazardous waste identified or listed under this subchapter—

(A) without a permit under this subchapter . . . ; or

(B) in *knowing* violation of any material condition or requirement of such permit. . . . [Emphasis added.]

In numerous cases under this section, as well as in cases under other environmental laws (including section 103(a) of CERCLA, the other provision involved in the *Laughlin* case), the extent of the knowledge required in order for defendants to be found guilty has been a pivotal issue. The omission of "knowingly" from part (A) of section 3008(d)(2) has caused several courts of appeals to decide whether a defendant must have known of the lack of a RCRA permit.

2. *United States v. Johnson & Towers, Inc.,* 741 F.2d 662 (3d Cir.1984), cert. denied 469 U.S. 1208, 105 S.Ct. 1171, 84 L.Ed.2d 321 (1985), held that *employees* of companies which dispose of hazardous wastes without RCRA permits can be held criminally liable under section 3008(d)(2)(A). The district court had reached the opposite conclusion, holding that the criminal penalties apply only to "owners and operators" because only they, and not their employees, are required to obtain RCRA permits. The result of the district court's decision was that lower and middle management personnel (a foreman and a plant supervisor) who actually conducted the dumping were insulated from criminal liability. Justice Department officials believed that the court of appeals' decision would assist not only in obtaining convictions against employees but also in persuading them to testify against facility owners and operators. See 15 *Envir.Rep.* 662 (1984).

To be convicted under section 3008(d)(2)(A), must an employee have *known* that his or her employer had not obtained a permit? *Johnson & Towers* said that such knowledge was necessary, though it could be inferred from circumstantial evidence in that case. The court said the word "knowingly" in section 3008(d)(2) should be read to modify subsection (A) as well as to encompass knowledge that the waste material is hazardous. Other courts of appeals have disagreed, adopting the position taken by the court in *Laughlin.*

3. With respect to section 3008(d)(1), *United States v. Hayes International Corp.,* 786 F.2d 1499 (11th Cir.1986), held that, in order to convict, the jury must find that the defendant knew both that the waste was hazardous and that the disposal site had no permit. The appellate court, after examining the record, found sufficient evidence from which the jury could infer that the individual defendant knew that the disposition of the waste was improper.

4. In *United States v. Goldsmith,* 978 F.2d 643 (11th Cir.1992), the court held that under parts (1) and (2)(A) of section 3008(d), the government was not required to prove that defendant knew a chemical waste had been *listed* as a "hazardous waste" by EPA: "The government need only prove that a defendant had knowledge of 'the general hazardous character' of the chemical."

5. After § 3008(d) of RCRA, the criminal provisions of the Clean Water Act are probably the next most frequently used bases of environmental prosecutions. The next case is an example, again involving the public welfare offense doctrine.

STOP

UNITED STATES v. SINSKEY

United States Court of Appeals, Eighth Circuit, 1997.
119 F.3d 712

MORRIS SHEPPARD ARNOLD, CIRCUIT JUDGE.

The defendants appeal their convictions for criminal violations of the Clean Water Act. We affirm the judgments of the trial court.

I.

In the early 1990s, Timothy Sinskey and Wayne Kumm were, respectively, the plant manager and plant engineer at John Morrell & Co. ("Morrell"), a large meat-packing plant in Sioux Falls, South Dakota. The meat-packing process created a large amount of wastewater, some of which Morrell piped to a municipal treatment plant and the rest of which it treated at its own wastewater treatment plant ("WWTP"). After treating wastewater at the WWTP, Morrell would discharge it into the Big Sioux River.

One of the WWTP's functions was to reduce the amount of ammonia nitrogen in the wastewater discharged into the river, and the Environmental Protection Agency ("EPA") required Morrell to limit that amount to levels specified in a permit issued under the Clean Water Act ("CWA"), see 33 U.S.C. §§ 1251–1387. As well as specifying the acceptable levels of ammonia nitrogen, the permit also required Morrell to perform weekly a series of tests to monitor the amounts of ammonia nitrogen in the discharged water and to file monthly with the EPA a set of reports concerning those results.

In the spring of 1991, Morrell doubled the number of hogs that it slaughtered and processed at the Sioux Falls plant. The resulting increase in wastewater caused the level of ammonia nitrate in the discharged water to be above that allowed by the CWA permit. Ron

Greenwood and Barry Milbauer, the manager and assistant manager, respectively, of the WWTP, manipulated the testing process in two ways so that Morrell would appear not to violate its permit. In the first technique, which the parties frequently refer to as "flow manipulation" or the "flow game," Morrell would discharge extremely low levels of water (and thus low levels of ammonia nitrogen) early in the week, when Greenwood and Milbauer would perform the required tests. After the tests had been performed, Morrell would discharge an exceedingly high level of water (and high levels of ammonia nitrogen) later in the week. The tests would therefore not accurately reflect the overall levels of ammonia nitrogen in the discharged water. In addition to manipulating the flow, Greenwood and Milbauer also engaged in what the parties call "selective sampling," that is, they performed more than the number of tests required by the EPA but reported only the tests showing acceptable levels of ammonia nitrogen. When manipulating the flow and selective sampling failed to yield the required number of tests showing acceptable levels of ammonia nitrogen, the two simply falsified the test results and the monthly EPA reports, which Sinskey then signed and sent to the EPA. Morrell submitted false reports for every month but one from August, 1991, to December, 1992.

. . .[T]he jury found both Sinskey and Kumm guilty of knowingly rendering inaccurate a monitoring method required to be maintained under the CWA, in violation of 33 U.S.C. § 1319(c)(4), and Sinskey guilty of knowingly discharging a pollutant into waters of the United States in amounts exceeding CWA permit limitations, in violation of 33 U.S.C. § 1319(c)(2)(A); see also 33 U.S.C. § 1311(a). Each appeals his conviction.

II.

Sinskey first challenges the jury instructions that the trial court gave with respect to 33 U.S.C. § 1319(c)(2)(A), which, among other things, punishes anyone who "knowingly violates" § 1311 or a condition or limitation contained in a permit that implements § 1311. That section of the CWA prohibits the discharge of pollutants except in compliance with, among other provisions, § 1342, which establishes the National Pollutant Discharge Elimination System ("NPDES"). The NPDES authorizes the EPA to issue permits that allow the discharge of certain pollutants within specified limitations and with specified reporting and monitoring conditions. As applied in this case, § 1319(c)(2)(A) therefore prohibits the discharge of pollutants in amounts exceeding the limitations specified in an NPDES permit.

The trial court gave an instruction, which it incorporated into several substantive charges, that in order for the jury to find Sinskey guilty of acting "knowingly," the proof had to show that he was "aware of the nature of his acts, perform[ed] them intentionally, and [did] not act or fail to act through ignorance, mistake, or accident." The instructions also told the jury that the government was not required to prove that Sinskey knew that his acts violated the CWA or permits issued under that act. Sinskey contests these instructions as applied to 33 U.S.C. § 1319(c)(2)(A), arguing that because the adverb "knowingly" immediately precedes the verb "violates," the government must prove that he knew that his conduct violated either the CWA or the NPDES permit. We disagree.

Although our court has not yet decided whether 33 U.S.C. § 1319(c)(2)(A) requires the government to prove that a defendant knew that he or she was violating either the CWA or the relevant NPDES permit when he or she acted, we are guided in answering this question by the generally accepted construction of the word "knowingly" in criminal statutes, by the CWA's legislative history, and by the decisions of the other courts of appeals that have addressed this issue. In construing other statutes with similar language and structure, that is, statutes in which one provision punishes the "knowing violation" of another provision that defines the illegal conduct, we have repeatedly held that the word "knowingly" modifies the acts constituting the underlying conduct.

In *Farrell*, 69 F.3d at 892–93, for example, we discussed 18 U.S.C. § 924(a)(2), which penalizes anyone who "knowingly violates" § 922(*o*)(1), which in turn prohibits the transfer or possession of a machine gun. In construing the word "knowingly," we held that it applied only to the conduct proscribed in § 922(*o*)(1), that is, the act of transferring or possessing a machine gun, and not to the illegal nature of those actions. A conviction under § 924(a)(2) therefore did not require proof that the defendant knew that his actions violated the law.

We see no reason to depart from that commonly accepted construction in this case, and we therefore believe that in 33 U.S.C. § 1319(c)(2)(A), the word "knowingly" applies to the underlying conduct prohibited by the statute.... The permit is, in essence, another layer of regulation in the nature of a law, in this case, a law that applies only to Morrell. We therefore believe that the underlying conduct of which Sinskey must have had knowledge is the conduct that is prohibited by the permit, for example, that Morrell's discharges of ammonia nitrates were higher than one part per million in the summer of 1992. Given this interpretation of the statute, the government was not required to prove that Sinskey knew that his acts violated either the CWA or the NPDES permit, but merely that he was aware of the conduct that resulted in the permit's violation.

This interpretation comports not only with our legal system's general recognition that ignorance of the law is no excuse, see *Cheek v. United States*, 498 U.S. 192, 199, 111 S.Ct. 604, 609, 112 L.Ed.2d 617 (1991), but also with Supreme Court interpretations of statutes containing similar language and structure. In *United States v. International Minerals & Chemical Corp.*, 402 U.S. 558, 91 S.Ct. 1697, 29 L.Ed.2d 178 (1971), for example, the Court analyzed a statute that punished anyone who "knowingly violate[d]" certain regulations pertaining to the interstate shipment of hazardous materials. In holding that a conviction under the statute at issue did not require knowledge of the pertinent law, the Court reasoned that the statute's language was merely a shorthand designation for punishing anyone who knowingly committed the specific acts or omissions contemplated by the regulations at issue, and that the statute therefore required knowledge of the material facts but not the relevant law. Id. at 562–63, 91 S.Ct. at 1700–01. The Court also focused on the nature of the regulatory scheme at issue, noting that where "dangerous or . . . obnoxious waste materials" are involved, anyone dealing with such materials "must be presumed" to be aware of the existence of the regulations. Id. at 565, 91 S.Ct. at 1701–02. Requiring knowledge only of the underlying actions, and not of the law, would therefore raise no substantial due process concerns. Id. at 564–65, 91 S.Ct. at 1701–02. Such reasoning applies with equal force, we believe, to the CWA, which regulates the discharge into the public's water of such "obnoxious waste materials" as the byproducts of slaughtered animals.

The act's legislative history, moreover, supports our view of the mens rea required for conviction under 33 U.S.C. § 1319(c)(2)(A). In 1987, Congress amended the act, in part to increase deterrence by strengthening the criminal sanctions for its violation. See, e.g., H.R. Conf. Rep. No. 99–1004 at 138 (1986) and S.Rep. No. 99–50 at 29–30 (1985). To that end, Congress changed the term "willfully" to "knowingly" in that section of the act dealing with intentional violations. See 133 Cong. Rec. H131 (daily ed. Jan. 7, 1987) (statement of Rep. J. Howard), reprinted in 1987 U.S.C.C.A.N. 5, 28, and 33 U.S.C. § 1319, historical and statutory notes, 1987 amendment, at 197 (West supp.1997). Although Congress did not explicitly discuss this change, it may logically be viewed as an effort to reduce the mens rea necessary for a conviction, as the word "willfully" generally connotes acting with the knowledge that one's conduct violates the law, while the word "knowingly" normally means acting with an awareness of one's actions. Compare *Cheek*, 498 U.S. at 201, 111 S.Ct. at 610, with *International Minerals*, 402 U.S. at 562–63, 91 S.Ct. at 1700–01. See also *Babbitt v. Sweet Home Chapter of Communities*, 515 U.S. 687, 696–97 n. 9, 115 S.Ct. 2407, 2412 n. 9, 132 L.Ed.2d 597 (1995) (discussing change in Endangered Species Act from "willfully" to "knowingly"), and Hern, 926 F.2d at 767.

Our confidence in this interpretation is increased by decisions of the only other appellate courts to analyze the precise issue presented here. See *United States v. Hopkins*, 53 F.3d 533, 541 (2d Cir.1995), cert. denied, 516 U.S. 1072, 116 S.Ct. 773, 133 L.Ed.2d 725 (1996), and *United States v. Weitzenhoff*, 35 F.3d 1275, 1283–86 (9th Cir.1993), cert. denied, 513 U.S. 1128, 115 S.Ct. 939, 130 L.Ed.2d 884 (1995). Both cases held that 33 U.S.C. § 1319(c)(2)(A) does not require proof that the defendant knew that his or her acts violated the CWA or the NPDES permits at issue.

Contrary to the defendants' assertions, moreover, *United States v. Ahmad*, 101 F.3d 386 (5th Cir.1996), is inapposite. In *Ahmad*, 101 F.3d at 388, a convenience store owner pumped out an underground gasoline storage tank into which some water had leaked, discharging gasoline into city sewer systems and nearby creeks in violation of 33 U.S.C. § 1319(c)(2)(A). At trial, the defendant asserted that he thought that he was discharging water, and that the statute's requirement that he act knowingly required that the government prove not only that he knew that he was discharging something, but also that he knew that he was discharging gasoline. The Fifth Circuit agreed, holding that a defendant does not violate the statute unless he or she acts knowingly with regard to each element of an offense. *Ahmad*, however, involved a classic mistake-of-fact defense, and is not applicable to a mistake-of-law defense such as that asserted by Sinskey and Kumm. Indeed, the Fifth Circuit noted as much, distinguishing *Hopkins*, 53 F.3d at 533, and *Weitzenhoff*, 35 F.3d at 1275, on the grounds that those decisions involved a mistake-of-law defense. See *Ahmad*, 101 F.3d at 390–91.

Sinskey, joined by Kumm, also challenges the trial court's instructions with respect to 33 U.S.C. § 1319(c)(4), arguing that the government should have been required to prove that they knew that their acts were illegal. This argument has even less force with respect to § 1319(c)(4)—which penalizes a person who "knowingly falsifies, tampers with, or renders inaccurate any monitoring device or method required to be maintained" by the CWA—than it does with respect to § 1319(c)(2)(A). In § 1319(c)(4), the adverb "knowingly" precedes and explicitly modifies the verbs that describe the activities that violate the act.

We have repeatedly held that, in other statutes with similar language, the word "knowingly" refers only to knowledge of the relevant activities (in this case, the defendants' knowledge that they were rendering the monitoring methods inaccurate by aiding and abetting in the flow games and selective sampling)....

* * *

III.

Kumm attacks his conviction for violating 33 U.S.C. § 1319(c)(4) on a number of grounds, first among them the sufficiency of the government's evidence. Kumm claims that the government's evidence established only that he failed to stop others from rendering inaccurate Morrell's monitoring methods, not that he affirmatively participated in the deceit either directly or by aiding and abetting those who did....

After a careful review of the record in the light most favorable to the jury's verdict, we believe that the evidence against Kumm, although hardly overwhelming, is not so weak that no reasonable juror could have convicted him. See id. In particular, we believe that the evidence supports a verdict that he aided and abetted the misleading monitoring scheme by encouraging Greenwood to render Morrell's monitoring methods inaccurate and by discouraging him from complaining about it to others at the WWTP.

* * *

Contrary to Kumm's assertions, the government's case did not focus solely on Kumm's role as a supervisor and his failure to report the violations or to intervene. We note at the outset of this discussion that Kumm was neither charged with, nor convicted of, a failure to report CWA permit violations. Instead, he was charged with, and convicted of, "render[ing] inaccurate" the monitoring methods required under Morrell's CWA permit. See 33 U.S.C. § 1319(c)(4). Kumm argues, however, that the testimony of several witnesses and certain portions of the government's closing argument so emphasized his supervisory status and his inaction, that they led the jury to convict him for being an innocent bystander who merely failed to report the violations or to intervene. After a careful review of the statements at issue, in their full context, we disagree.

As we indicated above, the government sufficiently proved that Kumm actively encouraged the flow manipulation and selective sampling, thereby affirmatively participating in the misleading monitoring scheme. Presenting evidence that Kumm was a supervisor, that is, that he was in a position capable of giving rewards and reassurances, was but a necessary part of showing how he was able to encourage Greenwood. Likewise, testimony that Kumm neither reported nor interfered with the permit violations was consistent with the government's claim that Kumm was encouraging illegal activity. Contrary to Kumm's assertions, this evidence did not merely tend to show that Kumm violated some supposed duty to report permit violations; it tended instead to prove acts of concealment on Kumm's part that allowed the selective sampling scheme effectively to camouflage Morrell's violations.

Note

In *Sinskey*, defendant Kumm was the "plant engineer." His conviction was upheld because there was evidence that he aided and abetted the misleading monitoring scheme by "actively encouraging" the flow manipulation and selective sampling.

The following article indicates that higher-ranking corporate officials may be found guilty of environmental crimes even without having actively participated in commission of the acts.

HARTMAN AND DEMONACO, "THE PRESENT USE OF THE RESPONSIBLE CORPORATE OFFICER DOCTRINE IN THE CRIMINAL ENFORCEMENT OF ENVIRONMENTAL LAWS"[b]

23 *Environmental Law Reporter* 10145, 10146–10151 (1993).

The responsible corporate officer doctrine is more than a prosecutorial theory. Consistent with the applicable case law, Congress explicitly incorporated the category of responsible corporate officer into the defini-

---

tion of a "person" in the penalty provisions of the Clean Water Act (CWA) in 1987[43] and the Clean Air Act (CAA) in 1977.[44] * * *

The 1977 amendments to the CAA made it abundantly clear that Congress intended the responsible corporate officer to be subject to criminal penalties. However, at the time of the amendments, the criminal provisions of the CAA called only for misdemeanor sanctions, as did the criminal provisions in § 309(c) of the CWA. It is anything but clear that Congress would have intended to impose felony sanctions, such as were added to the CAA in 1990 and the CWA in 1987, requiring the imposition of substantial periods of incarceration, on any person who did not have actual knowledge of the wrongdoing.

Because of the upgrading to felonies of former misdemeanor violations in most of the environmental statutes, as well as stiff penalties that individuals now face under the U.S. Sentencing Guidelines, it was necessary for the DOJ to reevaluate how the responsible corporate officer doctrine should be applied to be consistent with congressional intent, yet treat each individual with fairness. This intersection of expanded individual criminal liability and fundamental due process warrants the careful exercise of prosecutorial discretion.

Apart from legislative activity, several references to the responsible corporate officer doctrine in criminal prosecutions arose under the Resource Conservation and Recovery Act (RCRA) and the CWA. However, the federal appellate courts did not squarely face the issue in environmental criminal prosecutions until 1991 in *United States v. Brittain*[52] and *United States v. MacDonald and Watson Waste Oil Co.*[53] These cases were decided only 10 days apart, yet arguably reached quite different results.

In *Brittain*, the defendant contended, among other issues, that he was not a "person" subject to criminal prosecution under the CWA, because the government failed to prove that he was a permittee of a wastewater discharge permit or that he was a responsible corporate officer of a discharging permittee. The City of Enid, Oklahoma, the holder of the wastewater permit, was allowed to discharge pollutants from the city's wastewater treatment plant into a nearby creek. Although the original permit provided for two discharge point sources (outfalls 001 and 002), a new permit was issued that only allowed for one discharge point source (outfall 001). The defendant, who held the position of public utilities director, was informed by the plant supervisor that the plant was discharging raw sewage from outfall 002. In fact, the defendant witnessed two such discharges. Although required to report by

43. 33 U.S.C. § 1319(c)(6) (1987). This section provides that "For purposes of this subsection, the term 'person' shall mean, in addition to the definition contained in section 1362(5) of this title, any responsible corporate officer." Under general definitions in 33 U.S.C. § 1362(5) (1987), the term person is defined to mean "an individual, corporation, partnership, association,

State, municipality, commission, or political subdivision of a State, or any interstate body."

44. 42 U.S.C. § 7413(c)(6) (Supp.1992).

52. 931 F.2d 1413 (10th Cir.1991).

53. 933 F.2d 35 (1st Cir.1991).

the terms of the permit, the defendant instructed the plant supervisor not to report these discharges to the U.S. Environmental Protection Agency (EPA). The defendant was convicted of two violations of the CWA and 18 counts of falsely reporting a material fact to a government agency.

The jury was never presented with the responsible corporate officer issue in the context of a jury question, and the government never suggested that it was relying on this theory. Nonetheless, the Tenth Circuit analyzed the term to determine whether the defendant, as an individual, is a "person" subject to liability under the CWA. Judge Baldock began the analysis by stating:

> Section 1319(c)(3) does not define a "responsible corporate officer" and the legislative history is silent regarding Congress's intention in adding the term. The Supreme Court, however, first recognized the concept of "responsible corporate officer" in 1943.... The *Dotterweich* Court held that a corporation's misdemeanor offense under the Federal Food, Drug, and Cosmetic Act of 1938 (FDCA) was committed by all corporate officers "who do have ... a responsible share in the furtherance of the transaction which the statute outlaws ... though consciousness of wrongdoing be totally wanting."

The Tenth Circuit opined that the underlying rationale of the FDCA also applies to the CWA. According to the court, Congress perceived that the public health concerns outweigh the hardship suffered by a criminally responsible corporate officer * * *.

The Tenth Circuit, in accord with the Third Circuit in *Johnson and Towers,* viewed the inclusion of the category of responsible corporate officers in the definition of the term "person" as an expansion of the class of potential criminal defendants rather than a limitation of that class * * *.

The Tenth Circuit suggests that a responsible corporate officer would not have to personally direct, or commit, a violation of the CWA to be criminally liable. There is nothing novel in this approach. However, in a broad interpretation of criminal culpability unnecessary to its holding, the court concludes:

> Under this interpretation, a "responsible corporate officer," to be held criminally liable, would not have to "willfully or negligently" cause a permit violation. *Instead, the willfulness or negligence of the actor would be imputed to him by virtue of his position of responsibility.*

The legal conclusion in this case, that responsible corporate officers may be persons for purposes of criminal prosecution, is clearly called for by the terms of the statute. Since the defendant had actual knowledge of the illegal conduct and directed that it occur and be concealed from the authorities, the court's analysis of the extent to which knowledge may be imputed to a corporate officer, by virtue of his position alone, must be considered dicta. The DOJ has not followed this dicta in subsequent prosecutions.

In contrast to the Tenth Circuit's approach to this theory of criminal liability, the First Circuit adopted an arguably different approach in *United States v. MacDonald and Watson Waste Oil Co.* The company, its president and owner, and two employees of the company were convicted under RCRA § 3008(d)(1) of knowingly transporting and causing the transportation of hazardous waste, namely toluene and soil contaminated with toluene, to a facility which did not have a permit. The president and owner of the company contended that the court's charge to the jury was in error regarding the element of knowledge in the case of a corporate officer. * * * The court held as follows:

> We agree with the decisions discussed above that knowledge may be inferred from circumstantial evidence, including position and responsibility of defendants such as corporate officers, as well as information provided to those defendants on prior occasions. Further, willful blindness to the facts constituting the offense may be sufficient to establish knowledge. However, the district court erred by instructing the jury that proof that a defendant was a responsible corporate officer, as described, would suffice to *conclusively* establish the element of knowledge expressly required under § 3008(d)(1). Simply because a responsible corporate officer believed that on a prior occasion illegal transactions occurred, he did not *necessarily* possess knowledge of the violation charged. In a crime having knowledge as an express element, a mere showing of official responsibility under *Dotterweich* and *Park* is not an adequate substitute for direct or circumstantial proof of knowledge.

In this opinion, the First Circuit stated quite clearly the most fundamental, and often misunderstood, aspect of the responsible corporate officer doctrine. The doctrine expands the definition of "person," but does not eliminate, or even speak to, the applicable statutory requirements for knowledge in criminal litigation. The DOJ has followed the teachings of this decision in its environmental prosecutions.

Notes

1. Federal enforcement officials have targeted high-level officials of corporations, rather than the corporations themselves, in environmental criminal prosecutions. According to Earl Devaney, director of EPA's Office of Criminal Enforcement, Forensics, and Training, 80 percent of the criminal defendants were companies in 1991, but by 1995, 80 percent were individuals. Most of the individuals cited for environmental crimes are in middle to high management positions, "people who knew what they were doing, but it did it anyway." 27 *Env't Rptr.* 1044 (1996).

2. Environmental crimes, in addition to raising difficult liability issues, also present distinctive sentencing problems. See, e.g., *United States v. Rutana*, 18 F.3d 363 (6th Cir.1994). In December 1993, an advisory group to the United States Sentencing Commission published proposed guidelines for sentencing corporations convicted of federal environmental crimes, stating

that the major activity that a corporation could undertake to lessen its exposure is to establish an environmental compliance program. 58 Fed.Reg. 65764 (Dec. 16, 1993), 24 *Envir.Rep.* 1378 (1993). See Woodrow, "The Proposed Federal Environmental Sentencing Guidelines: A model for Corporate Environmental Compliance Programs," 25 *Envir.Rep.* 325 (1994).

In April 1994, the U.S. Sentencing Commission elected not to recommend that Congress amend the U.S. Sentencing Guidelines (U.S.S.G.) to include the corporate environmental sentencing guidelines proposed by its advisory group.

For a lengthy, critical analysis of the proposed sentencing guidelines, and alternate recommendations, see Jason Lemkin, "Deterring Environmental Crime Through Flexible Sentencing: A Proposal for the New Organizational Environmental Sentencing Guidelines," 84 *Calif. L. Rev.* 307 (1996).

Discussion Problem on Criminal Liability

You are an Assistant United States District Attorney considering whether and how to proceed against a corporate polluter and perhaps some of its officers and employees. EPA investigation has revealed that, on several occasions, in violation of the Clean Water Act and regulations thereunder, there have been significant releases of toxic chemicals from the company's manufacturing plant into the adjacent river. The river is used for public water supply and recreation, but the only known injuries to people or wildlife from the releases were two minor fish kills.

After the first release, which was accidental, the foreman in charge of the process from which the release originated reported it to the plant manager, who in turn reported it to the President. The President told the plant manager to "try to avoid further releases" and to "look into establishing an environmental audit program" for the plant. The President did not report the release to state or federal regulatory officials, nor did she hear or do anything further concerning the later releases or an audit program.

Meanwhile, the plant manager told the foreman, "We don't want any more toxic spills. Do whatever is reasonable to prevent them, but let me know if it will be expensive." The foreman interpreted this to mean that he should take precautions that did not involve significant expense, which he did. When he learned that they were not effective to prevent further releases, he did nothing more, nor did he report the additional releases to his superiors. The plant manager took no steps to establish an audit program until he heard that EPA was investigating the releases.

Would you commence a criminal action against any or all of the corporation, the foreman, the plant manager, and the President? Would you grant the foreman immunity in return for his testimony about the releases, the preventive measures taken, and his conversations with the plant manager?

F. COMMON LAW REMEDIES

1. INJUNCTIONS

VILLAGE OF WILSONVILLE v. SCA SERVICES, INC.

Supreme Court of Illinois, 1981.
86 Ill.2d 1, 55 Ill.Dec. 499, 426 N.E.2d 824.

CLARK, JUSTICE:

* * *

The defendant has operated a chemical-waste landfill since 1977. The site comprises approximately 130 acres, 90 of which are within the village limits of the plaintiff village. The remaining 40 acres are adjacent to the village. The defendant enters into agreements with generators of toxic chemical waste to haul the waste away from the generators' locations. The defendant then delivers it to the Wilsonville site, tests random samples of chemical waste, and then deposits the waste in trenches. There are seven trenches at the site. Each one is approximately 15 feet deep, 50 feet wide, and 250 to 350 feet long. Approximately 95% of the waste materials were buried in 55–gallon steel drums, and the remainder is contained in double-wall paper bags. After the materials are deposited in the trenches, uncompacted clay is placed between groups of containers and a minimum of one foot of clay is placed between the top drum and the top clay level of the trench.

The site is bordered on the east, west, and south by farmland and on the north by the village. The entire site, the village, and much of the surrounding area is located above the abandoned Superior Coal Mine No. 4, which operated from 1917 to 1954. The No. 6 seam of the mine was exploited in this area at a depth of 312 feet. The mining method used to extract coal was the room-and-panel method, whereby about 50% of the coal is left in pillars which provide some support for the earth above the mine. There was testimony at trial by Dr. Nolan Augenbaugh, chairman of the Department of Mining, Petroleum and Geological Engineering at the University of Missouri at Rolla, that pillar failure can occur in any mine where there is a readjustment of stress. * * *

* * *

The village * * * water-distribution system is centralized, and water is purchased from Gillespie, Illinois. The system was built in 1952 after the village tried unsuccessfully to find sufficient water by drilling municipal wells in the area. There are still 73 water wells in the village, some of which are used to water gardens or wash cars. At least one well is used to water pets, and another is used for drinking water. * * *

On February 11, 1976, the defendant applied to the [Illinois] EPA for a permit to develop and operate the hazardous-waste landfill. A developmental permit was issued by the IEPA on May 19, 1976. After a preoperation inspection was conducted by the IEPA, an operational permit was issued to the defendant on September 28, 1976. Each delivery of waste material to the site must be accompanied by a supplemental permit issued by the IEPA. A supplemental permit specifies the chemical nature and quantity of the waste to be deposited at the sites. Between November 12, 1976, and June 7, 1977, the first day of trial, the defendant had obtained 185 such permits.

The materials deposited at the site include polychlorinated biphenyls (PCBs), a neurotoxic, possibly carcinogenic chemical which it has been illegal to produce in this country since 1979. * * * Other materials buried at the site in large quantities are solid cyanide, a substance known as $C_{5,\ 6}$, paint sludge, asbestos, pesticides, mercury, and arsenic. Considerable evidence was adduced to show that these and other substances deposited at the site are extremely toxic to human beings. Some of the adverse reactions which could result from exposure to these materials are pulmonary diseases, cancer, brain damage, and birth defects.

[The court proceeded to analyze the testimony of numerous expert witnesses for both sides during the 104–day trial. It declined to disturb the trial court's findings that there was real danger of contamination of groundwater and neighboring land—due to leaking containers, permeable soil, and subsidence below the disposal site—and of explosions from interactions of chemicals buried at the site.]

The trial court herein concluded that defendant's chemical-waste-disposal site constitutes both a private and a public nuisance. * * * It is generally conceded that a nuisance is remediable by injunction or a suit for damages.

The defendant herein argues that "[e]ven if some or all of plaintiffs' evidence is deemed believable, the findings of the courts below that [defendant's] conduct constitutes a prospective nuisance must be reversed for failure to * * * balance the reasonableness and utility of the defendant's conduct, the harm to the plaintiff, and the general societal policy toward risk-taking before [a court may] find an actionable nuisance present." The defendant continues that the law of Illinois requires that the circuit court engage in a balancing process before reaching a conclusion that the waste disposal site presents a prospective nuisance. * * *

[The court concluded that the trial judge did "carefully engage in a balancing process between the site's social utility and the plaintiffs' right to enjoy their property and not suffer deleterious effects from chemical wastes."]

The defendant's next contention is that the courts below were in error when they failed to require a showing of a substantial risk of certain and extreme future harm before enjoining operation of the defendant's site. We deem it necessary to explain that a prospective nuisance is a fit candidate for injunctive relief. * * * The defendant argues that the proper standard to be used is that an injunction is proper only if there is a "dangerous probability" that the threatened or potential injury will occur. (See Restatement (Second) of Torts sec. 933(1), at 561, comment b (1979).) * * *

We agree with the defendant's statement of the law, but not with its urged application to the facts of this case. Again, Professor Prosser has offered a concise commentary. He has stated that "[o]ne distinguishing feature of equitable relief is that it may be granted upon the threat of harm which has not yet occurred. The defendant may be restrained from entering upon an activity where it is highly probable that it will lead to a nuisance, although if the possibility is merely uncertain or contingent he may be left to his remedy after the nuisance has occurred." (Prosser, Torts sec. 90, at 603 (4th ed. 1971).) This view is in accord with Illinois law. * * *

* * *

The defendant next asserts that error occurred in the courts below when they failed to defer to the IEPA and the USEPA, as well as when they failed to give weight to the permits issued by the IEPA. This assertion has no merit, however, because the data relied upon by the IEPA in deciding to issue a permit to the defendant were data collected by the defendant, data which have been proved at trial to be inaccurate. In particular, defendant's experts concluded that any subsidence at the site would be negligible. The IEPA (as well as the USEPA) adopted this inaccurate conclusion in deciding to issue a permit to the defendant.

We also disagree with the defendant that since the plaintiffs could seek review from the IEPA's decision to grant permits to the defendant through the Pollution Control Board they have an adequate remedy at law and are unable to obtain relief in a court of equity. First, the plaintiffs are not seeking a review of the issuance of permits. The plaintiffs seek to enjoin a nuisance, a matter which is properly brought in a court of equity. This court has stated that jurisdiction exists in the circuit court "to abate public nuisances which may endanger the general welfare." * * *

* * *

Therefore, we conclude that in fashioning relief in this case the trial court did balance relative hardship to be caused to the plaintiffs and defendant, and did fashion reasonable relief when it ordered the exhumation of all material from the site and the reclamation of the surrounding area. * * *

We are also cognizant of *amicus* USEPA's suggestion in its brief and affidavits filed which the appellate court which urge that we remand to the circuit court so that alternatives to closure of the site and exhumation of the waste materials may be considered. The USEPA states: "Heavy equipment may damage drums, releasing wastes and possibly causing gaseous emissions, fires, and explosions. Repackaging and transporting damaged drums also risks releasing wastes. Workers performing the exhumation face dangers from contact with or inhalation of wastes;

these risks cannot be completely eliminated with protective clothing and breathing apparatus. Nearby residents may also be endangered." It is ironic that the host of horribles mentioned by the USEPA in support of keeping the site open includes some of the same hazards which the plaintiffs have raised as reasons in favor of closing the site.

* * *

We note, however, that the USEPA does not suggest how the location of the disposal site above an abandoned tunneled mine and the effects of subsidence can be overcome. * * *

Affirmed and remanded.

RYAN, JUSTICE, concurring:

While I agree with both the result reached by the majority and the reasoning employed supporting the opinion, I wish to add a brief comment. * * *

* * * I believe that there are situations where the harm that is potential is so devastating that equity should afford relief even though the possibility of the harmful result occurring is uncertain or contingent. The Restatement's position applicable to preventative injunctive relief in general is that "[t]he more serious the impending harm, the less justification there is for taking the chances that are involved in pronouncing the harm too remote." (Restatement (Second) of Torts sec. 933, at 561, comment *b* (1979).) If the harm that may result is severe, a lesser possibility of it occurring should be required to support injunctive relief. * * *

Although the "dangerous probability" test has certainly been met in this case, I would be willing to enjoin the activity on a showing of probability of occurrence substantially less than that which the facts presented to this court reveal, due to the extremely hazardous nature of the chemicals being dumped and the potentially catastrophic results.

Notes

1. Is the Illinois court's decision consistent with the *Boomer* and *Milwaukee II* decisions, pages 290 and 267 supra? Is Illinois nuisance law preempted by RCRA?

In *Feikema v. Texaco, Inc.,* 16 F.3d 1408 (4th Cir.1994), the U.S. EPA had negotiated a consent order under section 7003 of RCRA requiring Texaco to remove contaminated soil and to take other protective and remedial measures to deal with oil leaking from a petroleum distribution terminal. The order recognized that the prescribed actions might not address all contamination and that additional long-term measures might be necessary. Plaintiff homeowners then filed a diversity suit against Texaco, alleging claims for nuisance and trespass under Virginia common law. The complaint alleged that despite complying with the consent order, Texaco had failed to remedy the leaking, and that plaintiffs continued to be threatened with oil pollution in the soils of the creek on or near their property. Plaintiffs sought permanent injunctive relief for greater remedial measures than those included in the consent order, plus damages. On Texaco's motion to dismiss plaintiffs' complaint, the court held that "when the EPA, acting within valid statutory authority of the RCRA and not arbitrarily, enters into a consent order, that order will also preempt conflicting state regulation, including a federal court order based on state common law. * * * In these circumstances, the injunctive relief requested by the homeowners would conflict with the remedial measures selected and supervised by the EPA." However, the court also held that plaintiffs' damage claims under state law were not preempted by RCRA.

2. The costs of cleaning up the Wilsonville site totaled about $50 million. In addition, the site owner settled a damage action brought by the village's 700 residents: $1 million was divided among those who were landowners, and $1.5 million was divided among all 700 residents. See *New York Times,* June 26, 1987, p. 14, col. 3.

3. Of what value is a complex state regulatory program, authorized by statute and involving the testing, licensing and surveillance of hazardous waste disposal sites by an expert administrative agency, if the agency's decisions can be overturned in this way? The Illinois Environmental Protection Act provides for appeal of IEPA decisions to the Pollution Control Board, a quasi-judicial agency, and then to the state appellate court. Plaintiffs here did not follow that route, preferring to go belatedly before a local trial judge who was up for reelection. See Note, "Hazardous Wastes: Preserving the Nuisance Remedy," 33 *Stan.L.Rev.* 675 (1981), advocating continued availability of common law nuisance remedies, with standards established under RCRA and its state counterparts to serve as minimums.

2. DAMAGES

GRAD, "REMEDIES FOR INJURIES CAUSED BY HAZARDOUS WASTE: THE REPORT AND RECOMMENDATIONS OF THE SUPERFUND 301(E) STUDY GROUP"[b]

14 *Environmental Law Reporter* 10105, 10105–07 (1984).

The Study Group analyzed available common law and statutory remedies in considerable detail, drawing on both federal and state legal sources and authorities. The scope of the Study Group's analysis of the legal remedies was limited to injuries and damage caused by hazardous spills and wastes, which matches the scope of CERCLA.

The Study Group in its discussions and Report first focused on certain recurring problems that face an injured plaintiff regardless of the cause of action he or she has selected. These recurring issues include problems relating to the applicable statute of limitations, apportionment of liability among the parties defendant, joinder of parties plaintiff, and the critical problems relating to proof of causation.

b. Reprinted with permission from *Recovery for Exposure to Hazardous Substances: The Superfund 301(e) Report and* *Beyond* (copyright © American Bar Association 1984).

The statute of limitations is a substantial problem in states that have not developed the discovery rule—i.e., the rule that the action accrues and the statute begins to run when the plaintiff discovers, or reasonably should have discovered, the injury. With latency periods of twenty years or more, the typical three-year statute of limitations running from the moment of exposure will lapse long before the plaintiff knows he or she has been hurt.

A variety of problems relate to the issue of defendant's responsibilities and to the appropriateness of joinder of defendants. Because numerous parties have some connection with a waste site (e.g., multiple waste producers and transporters, previous owners, etc.), apportionment of liability can be an insurmountable barrier to recovery unless the burden of proof is shifted to the defendants to exonerate themselves or to allocate liability.

Joinder of parties plaintiff is not uniformly available in all jurisdictions. Such a device can be essential to sharing the cost burden of securing expert medical and scientific testimony necessary to prove causation.

The major recurring issue, regardless of the particular cause of action, is proof of causation. The plaintiff must prove the causal nexus between the injury and the exposure for which the defendant is allegedly responsible. This proof is hampered by such factors as the variety of wastes disposed at one site from a variety of sources, long latencies of diseases, change in site ownership, and exposure of the plaintiff to other hazardous substances, to name a few. Proof of causation requires sophisticated medical and scientific testimony to show that the duration, frequency and intensity of exposure could or did produce the kind of injury suffered by the plaintiff. Reliance on government documents developed under a variety of federal health and environmental protection laws may eventually be possible as evidence. It is clear that proof of causation is an almost overwhelming barrier to recovery, particularly in smaller cases, regardless of their merit.

Available Statutory and Common Law Causes of Action

The Report of the Study Group examined virtually all available federal and state statutory remedies and all common law tort remedies available in the several states. It found that there are no federal statutes that expressly provide remedies for personal injury due to hazardous waste in non-occupational settings. An examination of state statutes provided only four instances of recent legislation—California, North Carolina, North Dakota and Rhode Island—to establish liability, usually strict liability, for personal injuries resulting from exposure to hazardous waste. None of the states, however, except California, aids the plaintiff in meeting the burden of proof of causation.

In general, it is clear that there is no basis for reliance on implied private right of action derived from federal pollution control statutes and there can be no reliance on the federal common law of nuisance.[5] There is some basis for reliance on a violation of a statutory standard in a negligence action to show a breach of a duty of care—*i.e.,* to establish negligence *per se* or to provide some evidence of negligence. In a few states, some reliance may also be placed on state public nuisance statutes, which sometimes provide for private causes of action for their enforcement. An examination of statutory remedies, however, leads to the conclusion that to recover for hazardous waste injuries a plaintiff must currently rely primarily on tort causes of action.

The Report examined available common law tort actions in several states, including negligence, trespass, and private and public nuisance actions. It found that each of these actions has some useful application in suits for hazardous waste injuries—subject, however, to the usual barriers of proof of causation, statute of limitations, and allocation and apportionment of liability.

The Report also examined the full range of strict liability approaches to hazardous waste injuries. Strict liability for injuries due to hazardous waste appears to be a viable theory because of the dangerous nature of the activity of hazardous waste disposal. Analyzing the various formulations of strict liability under the Restatement and the Restatement (Second) of the Law of Torts, the majority of the Study Group indicated its preference for a formulation of strict liability based on the magnitude of the risk, deemphasizing such elements as the locale of the activity or the foreseeability of harm, which are relied on in alternative formulations of the strict liability doctrine. The Study Group's analysis emphasizes the application of strict liability to spread costs and to impose liability on those who economically benefit from the polluting activity and who are in the best position to reduce or eliminate the risk. The Report notes, however, that strict liability does not resolve the problem of proof of causation so as to link the defendant's dangerous activity with the injury to the plaintiff, and it is not at all clear that all states would impose strict liability for injuries from exposure to hazardous waste.

After its complete review of the law, the Study Group concluded that although causes of action do exist for some plaintiffs under some circumstances, *a private litigant faces substantial substantive and procedural barriers in a personal injury action for hazardous waste exposure, particularly where the individual claims are relatively small.* Plaintiffs willing to undertake the major costs of litigation would be aided substantially by an easing of plaintiffs' burdens in regard to causation, apportionment of damages, and statutes of limitation. Persons with smaller claims, however, would be unlikely to recover at all unless further steps were taken to reduce both legal and economic barriers to their recovery so as to facilitate their assertion of valid but difficult claims.

---

5. *Milwaukee v. Illinois,* 451 U.S. 304, (1981); *Middlesex County Sewerage Auth. v.* *Nat'l Sea Clammers Ass'n,* 453 U.S. 1 (1981).

Notes

1. In 1983 a New York state trial judge dismissed 54 of 91 personal injury actions seeking compensation from Occidental Chemical Corp. for illnesses allegedly caused by exposure to toxic chemicals at Love Canal. The judge held that the actions were barred by New York's statute of limitations because they were filed more than three years after plaintiffs were allegedly exposed to toxic chemicals at that site. The court said that the period of limitations began to run from the date of exposure, not from discovery of the injury. The other 37 plaintiffs were able to show that they were exposed within three years of filing their actions. 14 *Envir.Rep.* 385 (1983). Approximately forty states have rejected the "exposure" rule in favor of the "discovery" rule, taking the position that the period of limitation does not begin to run until plaintiff discovers her illness. See Brennan, "Environmental Torts," 46 *Vanderbilt L.Rev.* 1, 54 (1993).

2. Asbestos-related lawsuits which provoked Johns Manville Corp. to file for protection from creditors under Chapter 11 of the bankruptcy law caused a major controversy within the insurance industry concerning whether insurers' liability began when workers were exposed to asbestos or when resulting disease was discovered or manifested itself. The problem arose because some asbestos manufacturers had different insurers decades ago, at the time of exposure, than they did more recently, when health effects became apparent. Recent insurers asserted the "exposure" theory, while earlier insurers urged a "manifestation" theory. Federal courts of appeals divided over which was the correct view, and the Supreme Court has not faced the issue.

STATE v. VENTRON CORP.

Supreme Court of New Jersey, 1983.
94 N.J. 473, 468 A.2d 150.

POLLOCK, J.

This appeal concerns the responsibility of various corporations for the cost of the cleanup and removal of mercury pollution seeping from a forty-acre tract of land into Berry's Creek, a tidal estuary of the Hackensack River that flows through the Meadowlands. The plaintiff is the State of New Jersey, Department of Environmental Protection (DEP); the primary defendants are Velsicol Chemical Corporation (Velsicol), its former subsidiary, Wood Ridge Chemical Corporation (Wood Ridge), and Ventron Corporation (Ventron), into which Wood Ridge was merged. Other defendants are F.W. Berk and Company, Inc. (Berk), which no longer exists, United States Life Insurance Company, which was dismissed by the lower courts in an unappealed judgment, and Robert M. and Rita W. Wolf (the Wolfs), who purchased part of the polluted property from Ventron.

Beneath its surface, the tract is saturated by an estimated 268 tons of toxic waste, primarily mercury. For a stretch of several thousand feet, the concentration of mercury in Berry's Creek is the highest found in fresh water sediments in the world. The waters of the creek are contaminated by the compound methyl mercury, which continues to be released as the mercury interacts with other elements. Due to depleted oxygen levels, fish no longer inhabit Berry's Creek, but are present only when swept in by the tide and, thus, irreversibly toxified.

The contamination at Berry's Creek results from mercury processing operations carried on at the site for almost fifty years. * * *

* * *

After a fifty-five-day trial, the trial court determined that Berk and Wood Ridge were jointly liable for the cleanup and removal of the mercury; that Velsicol and Ventron were severally liable for half of the costs; that the Wolfs were not liable * * *.

The Appellate Division substantially affirmed the judgment, but modified it in several respects, including the imposition of joint and several liability on Ventron and Velsicol for all costs incurred in the cleanup and removal of the mercury pollution in Berry's Creek. * * *

* * *

I

From 1929 to 1960, first as lessee and then as owner of the entire forty-acre tract, Berk operated a mercury processing plant, dumping untreated waste material and allowing mercury-laden effluent to drain on the tract. Berk continued uninterrupted operations until 1960, at which time it sold its assets to Wood Ridge and ceased its corporate existence.

In 1960, Velsicol formed Wood Ridge as a wholly-owned subsidiary for the sole purpose of purchasing Berk's assets and operating the mercury processing plant. In 1967, Wood Ridge subdivided the tract and declared a thirty-three-acre land dividend to Velsicol, which continued to permit Wood Ridge to dump material on the thirty-three acres. As a Velsicol subsidiary, Wood Ridge continued to operate the processing plant on the 7.1–acre tract from 1960 to 1968, when Velsicol sold Wood Ridge to Ventron.

Although Velsicol created Wood Ridge as a separate corporate entity, the trial court found that Velsicol treated it not as an independent subsidiary, but as a division. * * * Without spelling out all the details, we find that the record amply supports the conclusion of the trial court that "Velsicol personnel, directors, and officers were constantly involved in the day-to-day operations of the business of [Wood Ridge]."

In 1968, Velsicol sold 100% of the Wood Ridge stock to Ventron, which began to consider a course of treatment for plant wastes. * * *

Starting in the mid–1960's, DEP began testing effluent on the tract, but did not take any action against Wood Ridge. The trial court found, in fact, that the defendants were not liable under intentional tort or negligence theories.

Nonetheless, in 1970, the contamination at Berry's Creek came to the attention of the United States Environmental Protection Agency (EPA), which conducted a test of Wood Ridge's waste water. The tests indicated that the effluent carried two to four pounds of mercury into Berry's Creek each day. Later that year, Wood Ridge installed a waste treatment system that abated, but did not altogether halt, the flow of mercury into the creek. The operations of the plant continued until 1974, at which time Wood Ridge merged into Ventron. Consistent with *N.J.S.A.* 14A:10–6(e), the certificate of ownership and merger provided that Ventron would assume the liabilities and obligations of Wood Ridge. Ventron terminated the plant operations and sold the movable operating assets to Troy Chemical Company, not a party to these proceedings.

On February 5, 1974, Wood Ridge granted to Robert Wolf, a commercial real estate developer, an operation to purchase the 7.1–acre tract on which the plant was located, and on May 20, 1974, Ventron conveyed the tract to the Wolfs. The Wolfs planned to demolish the plant and construct a warehousing facility. In the course of the demolition, mercury-contaminated water was used to wet down the structures and allowed to run into the creek. The problem came to the attention of DEP, which ordered a halt to the demolition, pending adequate removal or containment of the contamination. DEP proposed a containment plan, but the Wolfs implemented another plan and proceeded with their project. DEP then instituted this action.

* * *

II

The lower courts imposed strict liability on Wood Ridge under common-law principles for causing a public nuisance and for "unleashing a dangerous substance during non-natural use of the land." In imposing strict liability, those courts relied substantially on the early English decision of *Rylands v. Fletcher, L.R. 1 Ex.* 265 (1866), *aff'd, L.R. 3 H.L.* 330 (1868). An early decision of the former Supreme Court, *Marshall v. Welwood,* 38 *N.J.L.* 339 (Sup.Ct.1876), however, rejected *Rylands v. Fletcher. But see City of Bridgeton v. B.P. Oil, Inc.,* 146 *N.J.Super.* 169, 179, 369 *A.*2d 49 (Law Div.1976) (landowner is liable under *Rylands* for an oil spill).

Twenty-one years ago, without referring to either *Marshall v. Welwood* or *Rylands v. Fletcher,* this Court adopted the proposition that "an ultrahazardous activity which introduces an unusual danger into the community ... should pay its own way in the event it actually causes damage to others." *Berg v. Reaction Motors Div., Thiokol Chem. Corp.,* 37 *N.J.* 396, 410, 181 *A.*2d 487 (1962). Dean Prosser views *Berg* as accepting a statement of principle derived from *Rylands.* W. Prosser, *Law of Torts* § 78 at 509 & n. 7 (4th ed. 1971).

In imposing liability on a landowner for an ultrahazardous activity, *Berg* adopted the test of the *Restatement of the Law of Torts* (1938). See *id.,* §§ 519–20. Since *Berg,* the *Restatement (Second) of the Law of Torts*

(1977) has replaced the "ultrahazardous" standard with one predicated on whether the activity is "abnormally dangerous." Imposition of liability on a landowner for "abnormally dangerous" activities incorporates, in effect, the *Rylands* test. *Restatement (Second)* § 520, comments (d) & (e).

We believe it is time to recognize expressly that the law of liability has evolved so that a landowner is strictly liable to others for harm caused by toxic wastes that are stored on his property and flow onto the property of others. Therefore, we overrule *Marshall v. Welwood* and adopt the principle of liability originally declared in *Rylands v. Fletcher.* The net result is that those who use, or permit others to use, land for the conduct of abnormally dangerous activities are strictly liable for resultant damages. Comprehension of the relevant legal principles, however, requires a more complete explanation of their development.

* * *

The confusion occasioned by the rejection of the *Rylands* principle of liability and the continuing adherence to the imposition of liability for a "nuisance" led to divergent results. *See Majestic Realty Assocs., Inc. v. Toti Contracting Co.,* 30 *N.J.* 425, 433–35, 153 *A.2d* 321 (1959). In *Majestic Realty,* this Court abandoned the term "nuisance *per se,*" and adopted a rule of liability that distinguished between an "ultrahazardous" activity, for which liability is absolute, and an "inherently dangerous" activity, for which liability depends upon proof of negligence. In making that distinction, the Court implicitly adopted the rule of landowner liability advocated by section 519 of the original *Restatement of Torts, supra.*

This rule, while somewhat reducing the confusion that permeated the law of nuisance, presented the further difficulty of determining whether an activity is "ultrahazardous" or "inherently dangerous." Subsequently, in *Berg,* this Court confirmed strict liability of landowners by noting that it was "primarily concerned with the underlying considerations of reasonableness, fairness and morality rather than with the formulary labels to be attached to the plaintiffs' causes of action or the legalistic classifications in which they are to be placed." 37 *N.J.* at 405, 181 *A.2d* 487.

More recently, the *Restatement (Second) of Torts* reformulated the standard of landowner liability, substituting "abnormally dangerous" for "ultrahazardous" and providing a list of elements to consider in applying the new standard. *Id.,* §§ 519–20. As noted, this standard incorporates the theory developed in *Rylands v. Fletcher.* Under the *Restatement* analysis, whether an activity is abnormally dangerous is to be determined on a case-by-case basis, taking all relevant circumstances into consideration. As set forth in the *Restatement:*

In determining whether an activity is abnormally dangerous, the following factors are to be considered:

(a) existence of a high degree of risk of some harm to the person, land or chattels of others;

(b) likelihood that the harm that results from it will be great;

(c) inability to eliminate the risk by the exercise of reasonable care;

(d) extent to which the activity is not a matter of common usage;

(e) inappropriateness of the activity to the place where it is carried on; and

(f) extent to which its value to the community is outweighed by its dangerous attributes.

[*Restatement (Second) of Torts* § 520 (1977)].

* * *

We approve the trial court's finding that Berk, Wood Ridge, Velsicol, and Ventron are liable under common-law principles for the abatement of the resulting nuisance and damage. The courts below found that the Wolfs are not liable for the costs of cleanup and containment. DEP did not petition for certification on that issue, and we do not consider it on this appeal. Berk and Wood Ridge, not Mr. and Mrs. Wolf, polluted the environment. During their ownership, the Wolfs have not continued to dump mercury and they have been responsible for only a minimal aggravation of the underlying hazardous condition.

Note

Branch v. Western Petroleum, Inc., 657 P.2d 267 (Utah 1982), was an action by private plaintiffs for pollution of their water wells by defendant's chemical wastes. Plaintiffs were awarded damages based on theories of strict liability (*Rylands v. Fletcher*), trespass, nuisance, and "mental suffering, discomfort and annoyance." Plaintiffs also received punitive damages.

Branch was not a case involving a long latency period between plaintiffs' exposure to the chemicals and manifestation of the resulting disease. Hence proof of causation was not a serious problem. However, it is quite different where, twenty or thirty years after disposal of hazardous wastes, nearby residents are diagnosed as having cancer at a rate significantly higher than that experienced by the general population.

FARBER, "TOXIC CAUSATION"[c]

71 Minnesota Law Review 1219, 1220–1251 (1987).

* * * Proof that a toxic substance is harmful often involves evidence on the frontiers of science. In many cases, the most that can be said is that exposure to a substance increased the risk that the plaintiff would contract a disease. Epidemiological evidence often can indicate only the probability that the plaintiff's injury was caused by the defendant. The difficult problem of how to handle these cases has given rise to extensive scholarly debate.[8]

c. Copyright 1987 by the *Minnesota Law Review*. Reprinted with permission.

8. *See, e.g.,* Elliott, *Why Courts? Comment on Robinson,* 14 J. Legal Stud. 799 (1985); Mashaw, *A Comment on Causation,*

At present, something of a scholarly consensus exists in favor of making recoveries proportional to the probability of causation.[9] For instance, if there was a thirty percent likelihood that the defendant caused the plaintiff's cancer, the plaintiff would receive thirty percent of his total damages. Proportional recovery spreads compensation over all possible victims, fully compensating no one but paying something even on the weakest claims.

This Article argues that proportional recovery is valid only under limited circumstances. It proposes a new theory (called the MLV or "most likely victim" approach) that is generally more appropriate. Under MLV, those plaintiffs whose injuries were least likely to have been caused by the defendant receive nothing, while those with the highest causation probabilities get full compensation. MLV has the advantage of focusing compensation on those who were most clearly injured by the defendant, while denying compensation to those whose claims are the most speculative. * * *

* * *

I.   THE EMERGING LAW OF TOXIC CAUSATION

* * *

A.   Toxic Torts in a Nutshell

The plaintiff's first problem is to establish that the defendant's conduct met the requisite liability standard. Although many toxic tort plaintiffs have brought actions under products liability theories holding manufacturers strictly liable for defective products, the liability standard is less clear in cases not involving manufacturers. The generally accepted liability test for hazardous waste releases is stated in the Second Restatement of Torts. Under this test, liability exists despite the exercise of

---

Law Reform, and Guerilla Warfare, 73 Geo. L.J. 1393 (1985); Robinson, *Probabilistic Causation and Compensation for Tortious Risk,* 14 J.Legal Stud. 779 (1985); Rosenberg, *The Causal Connection in Mass Exposure Cases: A "Public Law" Vision of the Tort System,* 97 Harv.L.Rev. 849 (1984); Stewart, *The Role of the Courts in Risk Management,* 16 Envtl.L.Rep. (Envtl.L.Inst.) 10,208 (1986); *Developments, supra* note 4, at 1618–24, 1634–53; Note, *Allocating the Costs of Hazardous Waste Disposal,* 94 Harv.L.Rev. 584 (1981).

9. *See, e.g.,* K. Abraham, *supra* note 5, at 57–60 (advocating use of a fund to compensate individuals on a probabilistic basis); Delgado, *Beyond* Sindell: *Relation of Cause-In–Fact Rules for Indeterminate Plaintiffs,* 70 Calif.L.Rev. 881, 899–902 (1982) (proposing that recoveries be shared pro rata among victims); Landes & Posner, *Tort*

Law as a Regulatory Regime for Catastrophic Personal Injuries, 13 J.Legal Stud. 417, 425–31 (1984) (describing a system in which victims are compensated for actual damages discounted by the probability of occurrence); Robinson, *Multiple Causation in Tort Law: Reflections on the DES Cases,* 68 Va.L.Rev. 713, 759–60 (1982) (suggesting a probabilistic approach); Rosenberg, *supra* note 8, at 881–87 (proposing that courts determine causation under a proportionality rule); *Developments, supra* note 4, at 1619–24 (advocating a system of proportional recovery). *See also* Note, *Increased Risk of Harm: A New Standard for Sufficiency of Evidence of Causation in Medical Malpractice,* 65 B.U.L.Rev. 275, 306 (1985) (presenting a similar proposal to resolve uncertainties about causation in malpractice cases).

due care if an activity was "abnormally dangerous." To determine whether an activity is abnormally dangerous, a court must weigh the probability and severity of foreseeable harm, whether the activity is unusual or is in an inappropriate location, and other factors.[17] Thus, fault plays a role in the Restatement assessment. A few courts have rejected this fault element, however, and have begun to move beyond the abnormally dangerous test. In *State v. Ventron Corp.*, the New Jersey Supreme Court imposed strict liability for harm caused by toxic substances escaping from a landowner's property.[21]

17. According to the Second Restatement, the following factors are relevant: (a) existence of a high degree of risk of some harm to the person, land or chattels of others; (b) likelihood that the harm that results from [the activity] will be great; (c) inability to eliminate the risk by the exercise of reasonable care; (d) extent to which the activity is not a matter of common usage; (e) inappropriateness of the activity to the place where it is carried on; and (f) extent to which its value to the community is outweighed by its dangerous attributes. Restatement (Second) of Torts § 520 (1977).

21. More recently, in an action against a township, a lower court rejected claims for damages based on emotional distress and enhanced risk of cancer. Ayers v. Township of Jackson, 189 N.J.Super. 561, 568–72, 461 A.2d 184, 188–90 (Law Div.1983), *aff'd as modified,* 202 N.J.Super. 106, 493 A.2d 1314 (App.Div.), *petition and cross-petition for certification granted,* 102 N.J. 306, 508 A.2d 191 (1985). In another recent decision, the court held that privately owned waste generators were strictly liable for injuries caused by releases, but that waste haulers, public dump owners, and state regulators were not. Kenney v. Scientific, Inc., 204 N.J.Super. 228, 263–64, 497 A.2d 1310, 1328–29 (Law Div.1985). Commentators believe that the New Jersey Supreme Court's ultimate decisions in these cases will have national impact. *See* Comment, *Hazardous Waste and the Common Law: Will New Jersey Clear the Way for Victims to Recover?,* 15 Envtl.L.Rep. (Envtl.L.Inst.) 10,321, 10,324 (1985). The economic literature on standards of liability is discussed in Ulen, Hester & Johnson, *Minnesota's Environmental Response and Liability Act: An Economic Justification,* 15 Envtl.L.Rep. (Envtl.L.Inst.) 10,109, 10,111–12 (1985) (arguing for strict liability).

When a reasonable medical expert would advise increased surveillance because of exposure, it is hard to see why the firm causing this expense should not be liable, even if the additional risk cannot be quantified. *See*

Ayers, 189 N.J.Super. at 572–73, 461 A.2d at 190; Askey v. Occidental Chem. Corp., 102 A.D.2d 130, 135, 477 N.Y.S.2d 242, 246 (N.Y.App.Div.1984). *See generally* Jackson v. Johns–Manville Sales Corp., 727 F.2d 506, 522 (5th Cir.1984) (*Jackson I*) (stating that courts can establish the "reasonable necessity and expense of future medical examinations"), *aff'd in part, rev'd in part,* 750 F.2d 1314 (5th Cir.1985) (en banc) (*Jackson II*), *aff'd on reh'g,* 781 F.2d 394 (5th Cir.) (en banc) (*Jackson III*), *cert. denied,* 106 S.Ct. 3339 (1986). Since the purpose is to finance a means of limiting future injury, this remedy can be considered preventive rather than compensatory.

On the other hand, to allow damages for emotional distress caused by fear of possible future injuries, as one commentator has suggested, could expose companies to unforeseeable and potentially crippling liability even when it was ultimately determined that their conduct had not caused any tangible harm. Bohrer, *Fear and Trembling in the Twentieth Century: Technological Risk, Uncertainty and Emotional Distress,* 1984 Wis.L.Rev. 83, 99. Nevertheless, in an asbestos case, the Fifth Circuit upheld an award of damages for the plaintiff's fear of getting cancer, although the court concluded that there was no proof of a "medical probability" that he actually would get cancer. Dartez v. Fibreboard Corp., 765 F.2d 456, 467 (5th Cir.1985). *See also Jackson III,* 781 F.2d at 413–15 (upholding damages for fear of cancer where plaintiff already had asbestosis and had greater than 50% chance of getting cancer); Anderson v. Welding Testing Lab., Inc., 304 So.2d 351, 353 (La.1974) (fear of cancer from radiation burns was compensable although the actual risk might be minimal). *But see* Payton v. Abbott Labs, 386 Mass. 540, 544–47, 437 N.E.2d 171, 174–76 (1982) (rejecting emotional distress damages in a DES case). Another damages issue that will not be discussed here is the availability of punitive damages. *See Jackson III,* 781 F.2d at 398–409; *Jackson I,* 727 F.2d at 524–30; Fischer v. Johns–Manville Corp., 103 N.J. 643, 512 A.2d 466 (1986).

Even if the defendant's conduct meets the requisite legal standard for liability, several possible barriers may prevent recovery. Statutes of limitations can create major difficulties in some states. * * *

Another problem is establishing a link between the defendant and the release of the substance. For example, many hazardous waste generators may have shipped similar materials to the site in question. It may be quite difficult to establish whose containers leaked or in what quantities. A similar issue can arise in products liability cases. In *Sindell v. Abbott Laboratories,*[26] the plaintiff's mother was administered the drug diethylstilbesterol (DES) during pregnancy. Although DES was routinely given to prevent miscarriage, it is now known to cause a rare form of cancer in some daughters of women who took the drug. After developing such cancer, the plaintiff sued eleven of the more than two hundred manufacturers of DES. Although the plaintiff was unable to identify the manufacturer of the particular DES which her mother took, the court held that she had stated a cause of action against manufacturers of the drug using an identical formula. Resting this holding on a broad social policy, the court noted that the defendants were "better able to bear the cost of injury resulting from the manufacture of a defective product." The *Sindell* court then adopted a novel theory of liability by making each defendant liable for a share of the plaintiff's damages, based on its share of the DES market. Assuming that the *Sindell* theory of one of its variants becomes the norm in products liability litigation,[33] it could be readily adapted to hazardous waste litigation.

B. The Causation Problem

Sindell and related theories address the problem of linking the defendant to the chemical exposure. An even more difficult problem is that of linking the exposure to the plaintiff's injury. It is a commonplace that toxic chemical regulation involves matters at the boundaries of scientific knowledge. This scientific uncertainty causes severe problems for government regulators, but even more serious problems result for private plaintiffs who must establish a defendant's liability by a preponderance of the evidence.

26. 26 Cal.3d 588, 607 P.2d 924, 163 Cal.Rptr. 132, *cert. denied,* 449 U.S. 912 (1980).

33. For recent cases addressing the *Sindell* doctrine, see H. Blackston v. Shook & Fletcher Insulation Co., 764 F.2d 1480, 1483 (11th Cir.1985); Copeland v. Celotex Corp., 447 So.2d 908, 914–15 (Fla.App. 1984), *quashed,* 471 So.2d 533 (1985); Payton v. Abbott Labs, 386 Mass. 540, 572, 437 N.E.2d 171, 189 (1982); Abel v. Eli Lilly & Co., 418 Mich. 311, 336–37, 343 N.W.2d 164, 175–76, *cert. denied,* 469 U.S. 833 (1984); Namm v. Charles E. Frosst & Co., 178 N.J.Super. 19, 28, 427 A.2d 1121, 1125 (App.Div.1981); Ferrigno v. Eli Lilly Co., 175 N.J.Super. 551, 573, 420 A.2d 1305, 1316 (Law Div.1980); Collins v. Eli Lilly Co., 116 Wis.2d 166, 188–90, 342 N.W.2d 37, 48–49, *cert. denied,* 469 U.S. 826 (1984). A good review of the cases can be found in Judge Weinstein's opinion in In re "Agent Orange" Prods.Liab.Litig., 597 F.Supp. 740, 819–28 (E.D.N.Y.1984). Generally, courts have been most willing to apply the doctrine when all the potential defendants were before the court. *Id.* at 826. For incisive commentary on *Sindell,* see Epstein, *Two Fallacies in the Law of Joint Torts,* 73 Geo.L.J. 1377, 1378–82 (1985) (stating that the market-share solution is unworkable); Wright, *Causation in Tort Law,* 73 Calif.L.Rev. 1735, 1819–21 (1985) (stating that the market-share approach overcharges joined defendants).

[Handwritten margin notes: "modified only applies to consumer litigation."; "occurs only in 12 states NJ, Washington, CA"; "hold them liable according to their market share ⇒ enterprise liability"; "only applies in private suits"]

In considering compensation, it is important to keep in mind that there are really two causation problems. One is the problem of establishing that the chemical involved is capable of causing the type of harm from which the plaintiff suffers. This is often difficult because the causation of diseases like cancer is so poorly understood. * * *

The other problem relating to proof of causation is that of establishing, given that the toxic substance in question can cause harm of the type suffered by the plaintiff, that the plaintiff's harm did in fact result from such exposure. A chemical may increase the prevalence of a disease enough to leave no doubt that some members of the exposed population were injured by that chemical. Others, however, may have suffered injuries from independent sources, and the two groups may be impossible to distinguish. The statistical association between exposure and illness may be too weak to justify a finding that a particular plaintiff's disease is causally linked to an exposure to a hazardous substance.

* * *

Litigation about Agent Orange, a defoliant and herbicide used by American forces in the Vietnam War, has provided the most extensive judicial discussion of toxic causation.[65] Numerous lawsuits were filed against the manufacturers by veterans, their families, and others who contended that Agent Orange had caused various illnesses. Ultimately, the litigation was consolidated in Judge Weinstein's court in the Eastern District of New York.[66] The weakness of the plaintiffs' causation evidence persuaded Judge Weinstein to approve a $180 million settlement, which was considered highly favorable to the defendants.

As Judge Weinstein explained, the evidence concerning the possible dangers from Agent Orange would have been enough for a court to uphold an administrative order limiting its use. Emphasizing the distinc-

65. *See* In re "Agent Orange" Prods.Liab.Litig., 597 F.Supp. 740, 775–95 (E.D.N.Y.1984). Another very useful judicial opinion is Allen v. United States, 588 F.Supp. 247, 404–43 (D.Utah 1984) (discussing the question of causation before holding the government liable for 10 cases of cancer in individuals exposed to fallout near a nuclear bomb test site), *rev'd* 816 F.2d 1417 (10th Cir. Apr.20, 1987) (holding that the "discretionary exception" in 28 U.S.C. § 2680(a) precludes government liability).

66. The main class action was filed in 1979, and the class was certified in 1980. In re "Agent Orange" Prods.Liab.Litig., 597 F.Supp. at 750, 752. The size of the class was variously estimated at 600,000 to 2,400,000, of whom 2440 opted out. *Id.* at 756. More than a thousand members of the class were heard from concerning the possible settlement. *Id.* at 764. Notices concerning the settlement were sent to over 400,-000. *Id.* at 763. Discovery involved more

than 200 depositions and "hundreds of thousands of pages of government documents, many of which were formerly considered classified." *Id.* at 757. The final settlement involved a payment of $180 million with interest at the rate of $60,000 per day. *Id.* at 748. Many of the 4500 lawyers who participated have filed appeals. *See* 54 U.S.L.W. 2095 (Aug. 13, 1985). Because of a dispute about the distribution of the settlement proceeds, the judgment was stayed by the Second Circuit. N.Y. Times, Aug. 28, 1986, § A, at 1, col. 3. The fund had grown to $225 million by August, 1986. *Id.,* Aug. 28, 1986, § B, at 12, col. 1. The settlement approved by Judge Weinstein was upheld by the Second Circuit. N.Y. Times, Apr. 21, 1987, at 14, col. 4. A three-judge panel of the Second Circuit handed down nine opinions, all concerning aspects of the Agent Orange cases, on April 21, 1987. In re "Agent Orange" Prods.Liab.Litig. MDL No. 381, slip ops. (2d Cir. Apr. 21, 1987).

tion between preventive regulatory measures and compensatory legal actions, however, Judge Weinstein noted that "[i]n the latter [case], a far higher probability (greater than 50%) is required since the law believes it unfair to require an individual to pay for another's tragedy unless it is shown that it is more likely than not that he caused it." The key flaw in the plaintiffs' case was that government epidemiological studies showed no statistical link between Agent Orange exposure and significant health effects. Studies by the Air Force, the CDC, and the Australian government all had concluded that no health effects had been demonstrated. Hence, Judge Weinstein agreed that a settlement was in the best interests of the class.

In companion cases, involving opt-outs or individuals never included in the class, Judge Weinstein was forced to rule on the merits of the plaintiffs' claims.[72] In these cases, he granted summary judgment for the defendants despite the plaintiffs' tender of expert testimony linking Agent Orange with health effects. * * * Judge Weinstein ruled the plaintiffs' expert testimony inadmissible, and then granted summary judgment because the plaintiffs had no admissible evidence to counter the defendants' epidemiological studies.

* * * The D.C. Circuit, however, has permitted recovery solely on the basis of expert clinical assessments despite a lack of statistical evidence. In *Ferebee v. Chevron Chemical Co.,*[78] the court stated:

> Thus, a cause-effect relationship need not be clearly established by animal or epidemiological studies before a doctor can testify that, in his opinion, such a relationship exists. As long as the basic methodology employed to reach such a conclusion is sound, such as use of tissue samples, standard tests, and patient examination, products liability law does not preclude recovery until a "statistically significant" number of people have been injured or until science has had the time and resources to complete sophisticated laboratory studies of the chemical. In a courtroom, the test for allowing a plaintiff to recover in a tort suit of this type is not scientific certainty but legal sufficiency. . . .

---

72. *See* Lilley v. Dow Chem. Co. (In re "Agent Orange" Prods.Liab.Litig.), 611 F.Supp. 1267 (E.D.N.Y.1985) (granting summary judgment against the wife of a Vietnam veteran who had opted out of class); Hogan v. Dow Chem. Co. (In re "Agent Orange" Prods.Liab.Litig.), 611 F.Supp. 1290 (E.D.N.Y.1985) (civilian claim dismissed on defendants' summary judgment motion); Fraticelli v. Dow Chem. Co. (In re "Agent Orange" Prods.Liab.Litig.), 611 F.Supp. 1285 (E.D.N.Y.1985) (upholding denial of class status to former University of Hawaii employees claiming exposure to Agent Orange during testing and granting defendants' motion for summary judg-

ment because plaintiffs, among other things, failed to show causation); In re "Agent Orange" Prods.Liab.Litig., 611 F.Supp. 1223 (E.D.N.Y.1985) (granting summary judgment against 281 plaintiffs who opted out of the class, because they could not prove causation).

78. 736 F.2d 1529 (D.C.Cir.), *cert. denied,* 469 U.S. 1062 (1984). *Ferebee* was a suit for damages brought by an agricultural worker against an herbicide manufacturer. The proof of causation consisted of testimony by two treating physicians described by the court as "eminent specialists in pulmonary medicine." *Id.* at 1535.

This language, while not inconsistent with Judge Weinstein's rulings, seems more favorable toward the admission of expert testimony.

* * *

II. THEORETICAL PERSPECTIVES ON TOXIC CAUSATION

Even before the courts had begun to come to grips with the toxic causation issue, a large theoretical literature had developed on the subject. Most of this scholarly literature concerns the use of probabilistic evidence of causation. * * *

A. *The Scholarly Debate on Proportional Recovery*

Much of the causation debate has revolved around a single paradigm case.[81] In this paradigm case, a chemical is known to have raised the death rate by some specified amount over the background rate for a particular disease. For example, suppose the normal rate of some variety of cancer among the unexposed public is ten cases per 100,000; among the exposed population, the rate is fifteen per 100,000. Under the "preponderance of the evidence" standard, none of the fifteen cancer victims could recover, because two-thirds of them probably would have gotten the disease anyway (although we do not know which two-thirds). Yet, it seems unjust to relieve the defendant of liability, because the defendant very likely did cause five cancer cases.

Several scholars have argued that these plaintiffs should receive a recovery proportional to the probability that they were harmed by the defendant. If the case is brought after the cancer has developed, this can be done by giving each plaintiff in the above example one-third of her damages. If the cancer threat is known earlier, before actual cancer cases have occurred, the defendant may be required either to pay every person exposed to the chemical an amount compensating for decreased life expectancy, or to provide each person with insurance covering one-third of the damages resulting from this sort of cancer. Regardless of the mechanics, the result is to expand compensation beyond the plaintiffs who actually got cancer from the chemical while correspondingly reducing each plaintiff's recovery.

Powerful arguments have been made in favor of proportional recovery. *Sindell* has already established that a plaintiff may recover without proving a particular defendant was the cause of the injury. Proportional recovery inverts *Sindell,* allowing recovery where the uncertainty concerns the identity of the injured party rather than that of the defendant. A general consensus seems to exist in favor of blurring the causation requirement in the *Sindell* situation of the "indeterminate defendant." It seems but a small additional step to do so here for the "indeterminate plaintiff." Another point in favor of proportional recovery is that it

---

81. *See* Delgado, *supra* note 9, at 884–86; Rosenberg, *supra* note 8, at 855 (In mass exposure cases, "all or at least large and gradable subclasses of those exposed will be similarly situated with regard to their degree of disease risk, their relationship to the firm, and the circumstances surrounding the tortious conduct.").

guarantees that the defendant pays the plaintiffs as a class for the full amount of injury done by the chemical. The defendant is thus given a powerful economic incentive to avoid imposing this harm. Without proportional recovery, the defendant would often escape liability altogether because of the causation problems. Economic theory indicates that requiring defendants to "internalize" these costs increases economic efficiency. Finally, imposing liability serves the goal of "loss spreading" by shifting some of the loss from individuals to firms that can often pass on the cost of insurance to their customers. Thus, the general policies of tort law are advanced by allowing proportional recovery.

* * *

[A]lthough proportional recovery is a substantial deviation from current practice, the theoretical arguments against it are unpersuasive. A more serious question is how often the factual assumptions underlying proportional recovery are valid. The key assumption—the paradigm case—is that the only evidence of causation is a single statistic expressing the increased rate of disease (or death) among the exposed population. As it turns out, this assumption is often false. Normally, at least some additional information is available, and a different solution becomes appropriate.

B. The MLV Remedy: Compensating the Most Likely Victims

Generally, all of those exposed to a toxic chemical are not equally at risk. Although the exact relationship between doses and disease rates is often poorly understood, the risk of disease is normally related to the amount of exposure.[107] The timing of exposure may also be significant; for example, exposure to DES early in pregnancy seems to have been much more dangerous than exposure late in pregnancy. Thus, the assumption of a uniform increase above the background rate is generally unrealistic.

Similarly, the assumption of a uniform background rate is valid only when nothing except the link to chemical exposure is known about a disease. Often, however, at least some knowledge of other risk factors exists. For instance, cigarette smokers are more likely to get lung cancer than nonsmokers, and the difference is even greater among asbestos workers.

Thus, given two individuals who have become ill after exposure to a chemical, some basis often exists for believing that the chemical was more likely to have caused one case than the other. Using a single statistic for the entire group as a basis for proportional recovery thus overcompensates some plaintiffs and undercompensates others. For ex-

107. *See, e.g.,* Finkelstein & Vingilis, *Radiographic Abnormalities among Asbestos–Cement Workers: An Exposure–Response Study,* 129 AM.REV. RESPIRATORY DISEASES 17, 19 (1984); Newhouse, *Epidemiology of Asbestos–Related Tumors,* 8 SEMINARS IN ONCOLOGY 250, 252, 254 (1981); Peto, Seidman & Selikoff, *Mesothelioma Mortality in Asbestos Workers: Implications for Models of Carcinogensis and Risk Assessment,* 45 BRIT.J.CANCER 124, 133 (1982).

ample, suppose the probability of causation is thirty percent for half the group and ten percent for the other half. Giving them all twenty percent of their damages (the average probability for the group as a whole) undercompensates the thirty-percent subgroup and overcompensates the ten-percent subgroup.

One possible solution would be to divide the group into subgroups composed of individuals with comparable risks. As a practical matter, the data may not allow such fine-tuning. There may exist only a qualitative knowledge about the distribution of risk within the group, rather than the quantitative information needed to make each subgroup's recovery proportional to that subgroup's risk. For example, we might know only that the average probability is twenty percent and that the range is about ten to thirty percent. This is not sufficient information to allow the creation of subgroups. More fundamentally, however, proportional recovery is simply inappropriate.

To understand the proper treatment of these cases, it is helpful to begin with a somewhat simplified example. Suppose we have a single defendant D and a group of N exposed individuals, X_1, X_2, ... X_N. Each individual has suffered one unit of damage due to cancer. For the individual X_1, the probability that the defendant caused the individual's cancer is p_1, with $p_1 > p_2$, ... p_N. The total amount of damage actually caused by the defendant is M, with $M < N$.

The first question is how much D should pay in damages. For much the same reasons advanced in favor of proportional recovery, the answer would seem to be M, the total amount of damage caused by the defendant. This amount provides the proper economic deterrent to D's behavior. * * *

Next, who should get the money? The answer depends on our purposes. We might, after all, give it to all the plaintiffs equally, or all disease victims, or perhaps the poor. One commentator argues that the individuals who actually were harmed by D have no better claim to the money than all other individuals suffering from the same disease.[113] This position is, to say the least, at odds with common views of morality. * * *

A more difficult question is presented by the argument that individuals should be compensated for exposure to risk, not merely for the harm that results in some instances.[116] * * *

113. *See* Mashaw, *supra* note 8, at 1394 (stating that the tort system provides no reason to distinguish for purposes of compensation between those who were injured by natural toxins and those injured by manufactured toxins).

116. *See* Landes & Posner, *supra* note 9, at 428–31; Robinson, *supra* note 8, at 796–98. Landes and Posner seem as much concerned about the timing of compensation as who receives it; they favor risk-based compensation largely because it can be determined soon after the defendant's conduct. *See* Landes & Posner, *supra* note 9, at 431. But MLV is not inconsistent with imposing liability before the injury develops if the relevant probabilities are known. Under MLV, the defendant would purchase full insurance coverage for those plaintiffs who are in the "most likely victim" class. Those among this class who ultimately develop illnesses would receive full compensation; others exposed to the toxic substance would not receive compensation. Thus, the question of timing can be separated from the question of how to distribute the fund.

[Under the normal rules of tort law] the goal is to compensate those whose injuries were actually caused by the defendant so that each dollar going to such a plaintiff is counted as a success. We may not begrudge the other plaintiffs their money (after all, they have suffered a serious illness), but we would prefer that the money went to *D*'s "actual victims." * * *

The solution is to give the *M* units of damages to the *M* plaintiffs with the highest probabilities of being actual victims, giving nothing to the remaining plaintiffs. * * * Because the only constraint is that no victim should receive more than a unit of damages, we give one unit to the victim with the highest probability and keep going down the list until we run out of money with victim M + 1. This is the MLV or "most likely victim" approach to compensation.

Obviously, literally ranking all victims is impractical in actual litigation. The MLV solution can be approximated, however, by putting the victims in subgroups, going down the list of subgroups, paying full compensation to each subgroup, until the defendant's total damages have been exhausted. Implementing MLV is more difficult if each plaintiff brings a separate case but the problems do not seem insurmountable * * *.

Notes

1.   In *Ayers v. Township of Jackson,* cited in footnote 21 of the Farber article, the court recognized a cause of action for medical monitoring or surveillance where plaintiff demonstrates through reliable expert testimony (1) the toxicity of the chemicals to which defendant has caused plaintiff to be exposed, (2) the seriousness of the disease to which plaintiff has been placed at risk, (3) the relative increase in the risk of onset of the disease, and (4) the value of early diagnosis.

Subsequently, *In re Paoli R.R. Yard PCB Litigation,* 916 F.2d 829 (3d Cir.1990), held that a medical monitoring claimant must show (1) that she was significantly exposed to a proven hazardous substance through the negligent actions of defendant, (2) that as a proximate result of exposure she suffers an increased risk of contracting a serious latent disease, (3) that the increased risk makes medical examinations reasonably necessary, and (4) that monitoring and testing procedures exist which make early detection and treatment of the disease possible and beneficial.

In most medical monitoring cases plaintiffs have sought or courts have awarded a traditional common-law lump sum of monetary damages. In a few toxic exposure cases, however, litigants have pursued or courts have expressed their preference for periodic payment of future medical surveillance expenses out of a court-supervised trust fund or similar mechanism. See Blumenberg, "Medical Monitoring Funds: The Periodic Payment of Future Medical Surveillance Expenses in Toxic Exposure Litigation," 43 *Hastings L.J.* 661 (1992).

2.   Do you understand the distinction between a cause of action for medical monitoring and one for enhanced risk? See footnote 21 of the Farber article. See also Susan Martin and Jonathan Martin, "Tort Actions for

Medical Monitoring: Warranted or Wasteful?'', 20 *Colum. J. Envt'l L.* 121 (1995); Tamsen Love, "Deterring Irresponsible Use and Disposal of Toxic Substances: The Case for Legislative Recognition of Increased Risk Causes of Action," 49 *Vand. L. Rev.* 789 (1996).

3. In *Potter v. Firestone Tire & Rubber Co.,* 6 Cal.4th 965, 25 Cal. Rptr.2d 550, 863 P.2d 795 (1993), residents living near a landfill brought an action against a company that had dumped toxic wastes there, alleging that their water supply had been contaminated. The court held "with respect to negligent infliction of emotional distress claims" arising out of exposure to carcinogens and/or other toxic substances:

> Unless an express exception to this general rule is recognized, in the absence of a present physical injury or illness, damages for fear of cancer may be recovered only if the plaintiff pleads and proves that (1) as a result of the defendant's negligent breach of a duty owed to the plaintiff, the plaintiff is exposed to a toxic substance which threatens cancer; *and* (2) the plaintiff's fear stems from a knowledge, corroborated by reliable medical or scientific opinion, that it is more likely than not that the plaintiff will develop the cancer in the future due to the toxic exposure.

4. Introduction and evaluation of expert testimony concerning the interpretation of epidemiological data can be exceedingly complex legally. See *DeLuca v. Merrell Dow Pharmaceuticals, Inc.,* 911 F.2d 941 (3d Cir. 1990), in which plaintiff sought to introduce testimony (to the effect that her birth defects were caused by her mother's use of defendant's drug during pregnancy) by a medical doctor who was not an epidemiologist and whose interpretation of statistical data was at odds with prevailing scientific opinion.

In *Daubert v. Merrell Dow Pharmaceuticals, Inc.,* 509 U.S. 579, 113 S.Ct. 2786, 125 L.Ed.2d 469 (1993), the lower courts had ruled (in a suit factually similar to *DeLuca*) that expert testimony which plaintiffs wanted to present to the jury could not be admitted because it did not rely on epidemiological studies and was not "generally accepted" in the scientific community. The Supreme Court remanded, ruling that the "general acceptance" test applied by the lower courts, see *Frye v. United States,* 293 Fed. 1013 (D.C.App.1923), has been supplanted by a broader and more flexible inquiry under the legislatively enacted Federal Rules of Evidence. "[I]n order to qualify [under Rule 702] as 'scientific knowledge,' an inference or assertion must be derived by the scientific method" and must have been tested, said Justice Blackmun. While publication in a journal subject to peer review is not essential, it is a "relevant" factor for a judge to consider in assessing whether a method or technique is valid. The Court "recognize[d] that in practice, a gatekeeping role for the judge, no matter how flexible, inevitably on occasion will prevent the jury from learning of authentic insights and innovations. That, neverthe-less, is the balance that is struck by Rules of Evidence designed not for the exhaustive search for cosmic understanding but for the particularized resolu-tion of legal disputes." The Court rejected plaintiffs' argument that Congress intended to permit juries to resolve scientific disputes through the adversari-al process in the same manner as they resolve disputes about economic theories or other complex subjects. See Symposium, "Scientific Evidence After the Death of *Frye: Daubert* and Its Implications for Toxic Tort,

Pharmaceutical, and Product Liability Cases," 15 *Cardozo L.Rev.* 1745 (1994); Symposium, "The Impact of Science and Technology on the Courts," 43 *Emory L.J.* 853 (1994).

On remand in *Daubert,* the court of appeals again held that plaintiffs' proffered expert testimony was inadmissible. The court emphasized plaintiffs' failure to show either that the testimony grew out of research conducted by the expert prior to and independently of the litigation, or that the research had been subjected to peer review. *Daubert v. Merrell Dow Pharmaceuticals, Inc.,* 43 F.3d 1311 (9th Cir.1995). For discussion about the meaning and application of the case, see Carl Cranor et al., "Judicial Boundary Drawing and the Need for Context-Sensitive Science in Toxic Torts after *Daubert v. Merrell Dow Pharmaceuticals, Inc.,*" 16 *Va. Envt'l L.J.* 1 (1996).

Chapter VIII

PRESERVATION OF NATURAL AREAS

A primary goal of environmental law is to preserve our remaining wilderness and coastal areas in their natural state. For example, NEPA clearly requires consideration of adverse environmental effects on natural areas. Similarly, the CWA aims at a return of the nation's rivers and lakes to their "natural" state. Section 101(a) of the Clean Water Act sets the goal of water quality "which provides for the protection and propagation of fish, shellfish, and wildlife" and the ultimate goal of complete elimination of water pollution. Besides the protection afforded by these general environmental statutes, natural areas are also protected by a variety of direct state and federal restrictions on land use. This chapter will explore the statutory and constitutional dimensions of these restrictions on the use of land.

In our society, basic control over the use of land is allocated by the law of property. It is that law which determines not only the identity of the owner, but the rights that person has over Blackacre. The division of property rights between the government and various private parties can have profound environmental consequences. We will organize our discussion around three categories of real property. The first category is the private property on which first-year Property courses traditionally focus. At a very high level of generality, the traditional rule has been that the private owner has complete authority, subject only to reasonable regulations to prevent harm to others. To the extent our society comes to see a parcel of land as part of an unbroken ecological web, this traditional rule may come under increasing stress. The second category of property straddles the line between public and private. Legal title often remains in the hands of private parties, but the government has a quasi-property interest that vastly expands its regulatory powers. This type of property is typically aquatic, found in lakes, rivers, and coastal areas. In the third form of property, legal title belongs to the government. The question here is the extent to which the government will honor ecological claims over those of development interests and adjacent private landowners.

A. PERSPECTIVES ON ECOLOGY, ECONOMICS, AND PROPERTY

More than other aspects of environmental law, ecological preservation raises basic questions about the proper goals of public policy. Much of environmental law, particularly in the past decade, has focused on the protection of human health. There are considerable difficulties in achieving that goal, as well as questions about how to balance it against other societal needs. The goal itself, however, is relatively clear, and requires little adjustment in traditional ways of thought. In this chapter, however, we will be dealing with a set of goals that until recently have played only a marginal role in American law. For this reason, we begin with an examination of those goals and their relationship to traditional legal and policy analysis.

In this section, we will consider modern views of ecology, and how those views relate to traditional modes of analysis. The first excerpt is a critical yet sympathetic discussion of ecological values. It devotes particular attention to the relationship between ecology and economic analysis, while also touching on the question of public versus private ownership. The second excerpt questions the viability of traditional conceptions of property in light of modern ecological thought.

MEYERS, "AN INTRODUCTION TO ENVIRONMENTAL THOUGHT: SOME SOURCES AND SOME CRITICISMS"

50 *Indiana Law Journal* 426, 427–29, 433–45, 450–53 (1975).

Let us begin with nature and wilderness values. In 1973, *Not Man Apart,* a magazine published by Friends of the Earth, conducted a poll of prominent environmentalists to name the books to enter an Environmental Hall of Fame. *Silent Spring* by Rachel Carson and *A Sand County Almanac* by Aldo Leopold easily led the field. Leopold's classic provides an ideal starting point for a discussion of wilderness values.

Leopold, both scholar and outdoorsman, was a man who learned the value of wilderness through direct experience. Trained as a forester at Yale University, Leopold spent 15 years in the United States Forest Service and the rest of his career at the University of Wisconsin. That blend of experience is reflected in *A Sand County Almanac,* first published in 1948 and still a strong influence on environmental thinking. A collection of essays, the book is at once graceful and exhorting, poetic and gently resigned. Shortly after its publication, Leopold died tragically, fighting a brush fire on a neighbor's land, just a short distance from his beloved farmhouse on the Wisconsin River. In the foreword Leopold writes:

> Conservation is getting nowhere because it is incompatible with our Abrahamic concept of land. We abuse land because we regard it as a commodity belonging to us. When we see land as a community to

which we belong, we may begin to use it with love and respect. * * * That land is a community is the basic concept of ecology, but that land is to be loved and respected is an extension of ethics. That land yields a cultural harvest is a fact long known, but latterly often forgotten.[1]

Leopold celebrates nature and all the little things in it—including man. Leopold is no misanthrope: he assures us that man has his place in nature if only he would keep it. Man keeps his place through ethics, which Leopold terms "a limitation on freedom of action in the struggle for existence."[2] But what values in nature and the wilderness are strong enough to temper man's struggle for existence? Leopold suggests three. There is, first, the value of an experience that recalls to memory our distinctive national origins and history. Leopold calls this the "split-rail value" and points to the Boy Scout who is reminded of Daniel Boone when he ventures into the forest; the Scout is reenacting a small bit of American history. Secondly, the wilderness experience reaffirms man's membership in the ecological chain. Leopold repeatedly emphasizes this theme of the interrelationship of all natural things, insisting that man's efforts must move toward the soil and not away from it. Leopold's third value is the collection of restraints on behavior called "sportsmanship." Wilderness sportsmanship is largely an internal force, for the hunter or angler is solitary—he appeals to no gallery and is applauded by no grandstand. He is dependent, therefore, on his own conscience and his own moral judgment to uphold the ethic. And that ethic teaches self-reliance, hardihood, and thrift.

Of these three values, the first—the "split-rail value"—is the most uniquely American, for American culture has developed, at every stage, with an acute awareness of wilderness—although more often in the direction of clearing the land, rather than saving it. Nevertheless, consciousness of wilderness has been essential to the American character, and a constant source of national pride. * * *

The second of Leopold's values—man's recognition of his place in the ecological chain—is representative of the thinking of many environmentalists and natural philosophers. His analysis is in two parts: the rejection of private property and capitalist institutions, and their replacement with a land ethic based on adherence to belief in the laws of nature. Leopold's condemnation of ownership institutions goes beyond the traditional debate between economists and environmentalists over the sources of human behavior. The economist holds that private ownership protects the land because man is self-interested and will protect what he owns outright, but will not care for what is collectively owned— "The Tragedy of Commons" as it is called by Garret Hardin. Many environmentalists take a sharply different view of human behavior, contending that private ownership fosters greater abuses than does public ownership. Leopold, however, goes further: he suggests that *any*

---

1. A. Leopold, *A Sand County Almanac* viii-ix (1974).   **2.** Id. at 202.

notion of land ownership is abusive. Remember his statement: "We abuse land because we regard it as a commodity belonging to us."[3]

* * *

Undoubtedly, it was Leopold's experience as an outdoorsman that fostered the development of his third set of values—a collection of voluntary limitations on behavior that he calls "sportsmanship."[4] Sportsmanship is voluntary, good behavior deriving from the recognition of one's involvement in the ecological chain. The sportsman's actions are voluntary because he performs without an audience. "Whatever his acts," Leopold stresses, "they are dictated by his own conscience, rather than by a mob of onlookers."[5] Ethical self-dependence teaches self-reliance, hardihood, thrift. It is difficult to exaggerate the importance of these qualities (particularly self-reliance) in the fabric of environmental thought.

These virtues spring from the depths of the American consciousness, for they are closely related to the Jeffersonian ideal of the independent yeoman farmer. Much as Leopold's sportsman must rely on his own sense of values throughout his wilderness sojourn, so must the land-holding yeoman depend on his own conscience concerning the use of his land and its resources. Both the farmer and the sportsman ultimately lack access to outside sources for moral guidance. They stand alone—powerful, and personally responsible for maintaining or violating the stability, integrity, and beauty of the natural community.

In each of the three nature values just discussed one finds a seedbed of another major line of environmental thought—a nostalgia for a simpler life, with fewer people, more wilderness, and less complexity. This longing for simplicity is expressed by many environmentalists as distrust of, if not outright aversion to, two main components of modern civilization: technology and urbanism. * * * For Leopold, the barbarism of civilization consists in thoughtless application of machinery in a wilderness context. He contrasts the pioneer methods of "go light" and "one-bullet-one-buck" with gadgeteering of modern sportsmen. "Gadgets fill * * * the auto-trunk, and also the trailer," Leopold laments.[6] Mechanization debases the wilderness adventure. It deprives us of the primitive, atavistic experience that is necessary to remind us of our national heritage; it separates us from the community of nature; and it erodes our self-reliance. In short, Leopold feels that immoderate use of machinery destroys the cultural values of nature.

* * *

Should we conclude, then, that Leopold and the nature philosophers do no more than express a personal preference for wilderness values over urban values? Do they establish for the rest of us the supremacy of wilderness values? Does the wilderness remind us of our origins and our

3. [Id.] at viii.   **5.** Id.

4. Id.   **6.** [Id.] at 180.

history any more than Shakespeare? Are the ethical restraints of wilderness sportsmanship any more compelling than the moral imperatives of urban life? Leopold and other naturalists have a single vision of man's nature and needs. And in many respects it is an intensely American view, American in feeling a separation from Europe, in celebrating our frontier, in surveying a country of spacious skies, of amber waves of grain, and purple mountains' majesties. But do they not ignore another vision, also widely shared? That other vision appeared in a newspaper in the fall of 1974. The article recounts the arrival of transfer students at Stanford University, a campus of 9000 acres, with spacious skies, some amber fields, and purple hills, if not mountains, of some pretense to majesty. When asked to compare Stanford with City University of New York, one student said, perhaps inelegantly but with obvious deep feeling: "You could stagnate in a college community like this * * * not enough diversity. Where the city is, that's where things are happening."[7]

How do the environmentalists respond to this? A modern answer may be found in the science of ecology and the rules of behavior some commentators have founded upon it. And a contradiction of that answer may be found in the work of neoclassical economists. Those two schools of thought are considered next.

In treating Leopold's *A Sand County Almanac* as the epitome of environmental thinking, we have focused so far on his poetic and instinctive treatment of the values of wilderness experience. But Leopold was a scientist, and his book is permeated with insights from the science of ecology. "Land, then, is not merely soil; it is a fountain of energy flowing through a circuit of soils, plants, and animals," and "When a change occurs in one part of the circuit, many other parts must adjust themselves to it."[8]

* * *

For me, Barry Commoner's collection of essays entitled *The Closing Circle: Nature, Man and Technology* provides the most accessible discourse on the principles of ecology and their relevance to social policy. It is difficult to introduce *The Closing Circle* in a word or two, just as it is difficult to characterize Professor Commoner briefly. He is foremost a scientist—a biological scholar of renown—but he is also a sensitive social philosopher and a colorful and expressive author. All of these facets of the man are reflected in his essays: they are at once vivid, straightforward and moralistic. Commoner constructs hypotheses regarding air pollution, contamination of waters, and threats of atomic radiation—all based on measurable data. He argues in terms of right and wrong with an urgent sense of moral duty. And he adeptly uses metaphors which evoke in us his desired responses. "The environmental crisis is a sign that the finely sculptured fit between life and its surroundings has begun to corrode." And he asks: "Where did the fabric of the ecosphere

7. San Francisco Sunday Examiner & Chronicle, Sept. 8, 1974, § 5, at 5, cols. 1 & 2.

8. A. Leopold, supra, note 1, at 216.

begin to unravel?"[9] But Commoner's central metaphor is "the circle of life."[10] These figures of speech are, of course, more than simple literary devices: they *do* convey the essence of the science of ecology; they *do* remind us of the cyclical flow of energy and life, and of the impact of human activity on this cycle.

However, it is neither Commoner's scientific accomplishment nor his literary style which interests me most. Instead, I will focus on Commoner the social philosopher, the biologist who extracts from scientific principles a code for human conduct. He calls his informal prescriptions the Laws of Ecology[11]; there are four of these:

(1) Everything is connected to everything else;

(2) Everything must go somewhere;

(3) Nature knows best; and

(4) There is no such thing as a free lunch.

Although these prescriptions may be based on scientific principles, they are normative, and therefore debatable, propositions.

The first law states that "everything is connected to everything else." This may seem to be a simple iteration of the observations of Marsh, Leopold, Carson and other ecologists, all of whom believed in an elaborate web of interconnection among all organisms. Commoner, however, analyzes the functioning of this network of interrelationships in greater detail and with the benefit of modern scholarship. He contends that balance within the ecosphere is achieved by dynamic, self-compensatory properties of the system, and he develops several examples of this self-regulatory process. Consider the freshwater ecological cycle: fish—organic waste—bacterial decay—inorganic nutrients—algae—fish. If, due to unusually warm weather, there is a rapid growth of algae, the supply of nutrients becomes depleted so that algae and nutrients are temporarily out of balance. But through self-correction the system reestablishes equilibrium. The surplus algae increase the available food supply for fish; the fish eat the algae, thereby reducing the algae population and in turn increasing their own waste production, which, as the waste decays, leads once again to a higher level of nutrients. Thus, the freshwater ecosystem returns to proper balance.

In such a precariously balanced system there is always danger that the entire chain may collapse if the self-compensating properties of the system come under too much stress. When large amounts of human wastes are introduced into the freshwater system, the bacterial activity and oxygen consumption may increase so disproportionately to the production of oxygen by algae that the oxygen level goes to zero, and the system collapses. In short, the self-correction that normally restores balance cannot occur. Implicit in this law of limited self-regulation and

9. B. Commoner, *The Closing Circle* 11 (1971).

10. Id. at 12, 299.

11. Id. at 33–48.

total interconnection within an ecosystem is a rule of conduct. The lesson to be learned is: "Do not interfere with the system."

In my view, however, a prescription for behavior does not necessarily follow from a description of scientific fact. Even without human intrusion, life systems may strike ecological balances at quite different levels, and sometimes the operation of natural processes may change their basic structures. Both the coming of the Ice Age and its retreat, for example, had enormous impacts on the ecology of North America. Yet, we make no judgments about the quality of the ecosystems before and after the Ice Age; we merely observe that they were different. Thus, the realization that everything is connected with everything else and that intrusion into the life cycle may produce new ecological balance points does not tell society whether, when, or how to act.

* * *

Ecological philosophy, as represented by Commoner, contains two contradictory premises: the first is the value-free proposition that interrelations of nature's organisms may be observed and hypotheses then constructed to allow prediction of the consequences of certain acts. The second proposition is that because there are consequences which have costs, certain acts should be avoided. At some level of cost, we may all agree. But at lower cost levels there is bound to be disagreement. Even if the costs are indisputable, the benefits will be valued differently by different individuals. The value judgment made by Commoner seems to emphasize the costs and minimize the benefits. All four laws of ecology counsel inaction: do not change nature; avoid technological change; nature's way of doing things is best. Yet, when we ask the ecologist, "why?" we seem to be no farther along than we were before the science of ecology arrived.

* * *

While most of the neoclassical economic thinking on environmental issues has been directed toward pollution problems, some economists have considered the significance of wilderness and nature values in formulating sound social policy. Here, too, the gulf between the economist and the natural philosopher is wide. As we have seen, the naturalists' value scheme expresses a preference for natural processes over the artificial, for wilderness over urbanization. The naturalists' reasoning proceeds as follows: an individual is mentally healthier, whether he knows it or not, if he can escape to nature; given such healthy individuals, society will be better off; and even if this is not the case, nature is irreplaceable and the minority who embrace wilderness values are entitled to protection against irreparable loss. The latter argument is usually bolstered by invoking the claims of future generations of nature-lovers—who may or may not be in the minority.

Some economists would scoff at these claims. They proceed from a different set of assumptions—that each individual knows what is best for himself (or at least knows better than anyone else), and that through bargaining and the free exercise of consumer sovereignty, social welfare will be maximized. "Social welfare" in this usage is not an independent value with normative content. It is comprised of the sum of individual preferences, whether they be "good" or "bad" from the standpoint of these economists' personal set of preferences.

Thus, wherever property interests in natural values can be created, these economists would allow the market to allocate the resources. Take the Grand Canyon National Park as an illustration. Assume that exclusive rights of use may be enforced at negligible cost, since access to the park is easily controlled. In such a situation, a traditional economist such as Milton Friedman would propose that the park be sold to the highest bidder.[12] If a power company or Walt Disney Enterprises offers more for the property than the Sierra Club or the Friends of the Earth, it is because the greater social benefit, as perceived by consumers, lies in commercial development of the canyon.

It is not that this economist personally believes that society is better off with a pleasure palace or a power dam at the Grand Canyon; he sees himself as value-free on the question of how the resource is to be used. His value attaches to the process of allocation; he desires a procedure that will allocate the resource in a manner that will produce the greatest net consumer satisfaction. He accepts the results of dollar voting.

Other economists working within the neoclassical tradition strain to avoid conclusions from a theory that calls for the sale of a Grand Canyon.[13] They postulate an option demand—a consumer preference that the Grand Canyon remain unspoiled—for which the consumer will pay even though he never intends to visit the park. Having hypothesized this option demand, these economists can summon the standard analysis of market failure to support government intervention. One can never measure the aggregate value of the option demand because of the free rider problem. Why should I contribute to the preservation of the Grand Canyon if I think others will carry the day and me along with it?

Just how these theorists justify "No Sale" when their theory hypothesizes an inability to determine consumer preference is somewhat obscure. To the lawyer, they appear to be playing the legal game of burden of proof: make no change in the status quo until proponents of change establish their case. But note that the fighting is internecine; both groups of economists work within the constraints of consumer preference. Their disagreement arises over measurement of aggregate demand, not over how to act once demand is established.

The difference between the environmental philosopher and the neoclassical economist are even wider and deeper than I have described so far. They differ not only over the nature of man but over the proper role of government in ordering society. Aldo Leopold represents a long tradition in environmental thought in believing that man is a part of nature, that his physical and mental wellbeing depend on rapport with

12. See M. Friedman, *Capitalism and Freedom* 31 (1962).

13. Krutilla, "Conservation Reconsidered," 57 *Am.Econ.Rev.* 777, 778–80 (1967).

nature. When man seeks to escape the chain of nature, when technology insulates him from primeval pursuits such as fishing, hunting, and farming, he loses a vitality that makes for a healthy man and a good society. The neoclassical economists regard man as both selfish and rational: man seeks to maximize pleasure and minimize pain and has the ability, through the exercise of reason, to make that calculus and to act on its product. And the economists allow for a vast number of different products in the sum of those individual calculations, for one man's pain is another's pleasure.

The difference then between the environmental philosopher and the economist is that the environmentalist discerns in all mankind certain universal traits or common characteristics that lead man to construct a hierarchy of values and that require society to adopt a set of policies to implement those values. While the economist also perceives a basic characteristic in all mankind, self-interest, his perception leads him to adopt not a value hierarchy against which to test public policy, but to devise a process for accommodating a great variety of competing human desires. The environmentalist would base public policy on a set of values he holds to be transcendent and absolute, inherent in the nature of man and therefore ineluctable. The economist rejects absolutes: what is good is what the individual prefers; a good society is one that maximizes freedom of choice. The economists' values speak to the question of *how* society should be organized in order to satisfy individual desires, whatever they may be.

This difference in attitude toward the nature of man and what is good for him produces a fundamental conflict between the two schools of thought over the proper role of government in resource allocation and environmental protection. While Leopold himself may recognize that his cherished wilderness values may not be shared by the majority, and while his writings may constitute an appeal to individuals to know themselves and change their ways, the environmental movement itself would go further to employ government's power to protect society from itself. * * *

I must confess my unease with environmental postulates carried to these conclusions. The result, too often, is the imposition by government of flat rules reflecting absolutist values. The Federal Water Pollution Control Act Amendments of 1972 are an example. The stated national goal, to be achieved by 1985, is the elimination of the discharge of *all* pollutants into the nation's waters. After 100 years of population growth and industrialization, our waters are to be restored to their natural purity in 13 years. The goal is not likely to be achieved, for the cost would run to hundreds of billions of dollars—some part of which many would prefer to remain in the private sector to be spent by individual decision, and the other part of which, the dollars left in the public sector, might bring greater satisfactions if spent on housing, education and jobs.

The economists' model—and of course they neither invented it nor does it belong to them exclusively—seems to me more in keeping with democratic theory in a pluralistic society. I would argue that the proper role of the government in resource allocation and environmental protection is to define property rights, so that market exchanges can occur; to enforce those bargains and protect property rights so defined; and to intervene in the economy when market failure produces external diseconomies such as water and air pollution. But the intervention should not be based on absolutist values of 100 percent pure water and pure air, for some individuals (probably more than a few) would prefer the alternative goods and services that could be produced by the resources that environmentalists would devote to their absolutist goals.

Notes

1. Meyers argued that economics is a better guide to environmental policy-making than ecology. Is this because economics is a more advanced field than ecology? Is understanding the physical consequences of human actions less relevant in some sense than understanding the economic consequences? Was Meyers simply saying that his own normative judgments are closer to those made by most American economists than to those made by many ecologists?

Meyers said approvingly of the economists that their vision of the good society is one that maximizes freedom of choice by individuals and their ability to satisfy their individual desires. This may be an appropriate goal when individual preferences for consumer goods are involved, but is it equally appropriate when we are considering individual preferences concerning the state of the world as a whole? Is the market an appropriate means for deciding issues of long-term global (or even national) policy? Or is that really the role of the political process?

Your view of the appropriate roles of market and government may depend in part on your vision of politics. Recall the discussion of politics in Chapter I. Is the political process dominated by self-interest or is it also a search for some broader "public interest?" At one extreme, some advocates of public choice theory seem to view government as a puppet of special interest groups. At the other, some believers in republicanism portray government as (at least potentially) a disinterested quest for ultimate public values. Which view is more realistic? More appealing? For further discussion, see D. Farber & P. Frickey, *Law and Public Choice: A Critical Introduction* (1991); Williams, "Environmental Law and Democratic Legitimacy," 4 *Duke Env.L. & Pol.F.* 1 (1994).

2. Commoner and Leopold continue to attract the attention of thoughtful analysts. See Krier, "The Political Economy of Barry Commoner," 20 *Env.L.* 11 (1990); Freyfogle, "The Land Ethic and Pilgrim Leopold," 61 *U.Colo.L.Rev.* 217 (1990). Other philosophies of land use are explored in Bosselman, "Four Land Ethics: Order, Reform, Responsibility, Opportunity," 24 *Env.L.* 1439 (1994).

3. The ecologists' values have long enjoyed broad public support. In 1989, eighty percent of the public agreed with the statement, "Protecting the environment is so important that regulations and standards cannot be too high, and continuing environmental improvements must be made regardless of cost." *N.Y. Times,* July 2, 1989, at 1. See also *N.Y. Times,* April 17,

1990, at 1 ("The environment * * * has reached the forefront of American politics, with candidates for one political office after another proclaiming themselves environmentalists.").

4. The science of ecology has not remained static since the preceding 1975 article. In particular, concepts regarding the stability of ecosystems have become much more sophisticated, and it is no longer believed that complex systems are necessarily more stable than simple ones, at least in some respects. See S. Pimm, *The Balance of Nature? Ecological Issues in the Conservation of Species and Communities* (1991). Some recent work questions the old concept of the local ecological community as a tightly unified entity, but continues to stress the importance of biodiversity. See "Ecologists Dare to Ask: How Much Does Diversity Matter?" 264 *Science* 202 (1994); Buzas and Culver, "Species Pool and Dynamics of Marine Paleocommunities," 264 *Science* 1439 (1994).

The impact of the "New Ecology" on environmental regulation and land management is explored in a Symposium, "Beyond the Balance of Nature: Environmental Law Faces the New Ecology," 7 *Duke Env. L. & Pol'y F.* 1 (1996). One writer summarizes the New Ecology as follows:

> The concept of the "Balance of Nature," so politically successful in the late 1960's and early 1970's, has been dismissed by ecological science. The "Balance of Nature" hypothesized that ecosystems would progress to a steady state, at which they could exist perpetually in "balance." Ecosystems are now seen as dynamic and stochastic rather than in equilibrium; anthropogenic actions most often are seen as inescapably intermingled with ecological systems, rather than avoidable. Unfortunately, however, many of the laws designed to regulate ecological resources were passed when the "Balance of Nature" paradigm was king and have not been redrafted to comport with advances in ecology."
>
>   * * *
>
> Human actions are now seen as inextricably intertwined with the operation of ecosystems. * * * Human effects are evident in nearly every natural system. For example, even before the European colonists arrived in America, the forests of southern New England had been shaped by the burning practices of Native Americans. With universal effects such as global warming and the thinning of the ozone layer, no part of the Earth is untouched by human influence. Thus, as we now are properly identified as merely a force among ecosystems, traditional attempts to simply separate ourselves from ecosystems are no longer prudent.
>
> Ecological research has also borne out the hypothesis that ecosystems fluctuate without equilibrium and beyond the capabilities of humans to assess and control them without error. Instead of being a Kodachrome still-life, the environment is "a moving picture show" replete with random events. These random events are often just part of the system.

Timothy Profeta, "Managing Without A Balance: Environmental Regulation in Light of Ecological Advances," 7 *Duke Env. L. & Pol'y F.* 71, 73 (1996).

Note on Economic Analysis and Preservationism

As we saw in Chapter IV, modern economists typically regard the free market as the preferred means of determining resource allocation. Advocates of privatization argue that this model should be extended to wilderness areas, so that, for example, the Grand Canyon would be sold to the highest bidder. If the highest bidder was the Sierra Club, the Canyon would be saved; if the highest bidder was a mining company, the Canyon would be mined. Any attempt to defend wilderness preservation by government must confront this position.

Several economic arguments can be made, however, in favor of wilderness preservation. As we saw earlier, the market mechanism breaks down when public goods or externalities are present. Arguably, both are involved in wilderness preservation. Many individuals may consider preservation of wilderness worthwhile even though they have no present plans to use the wilderness. As Dean Meyers explained, they may be considered as having a so-called "option demand" for wilderness. That is, these individuals would be willing to pay to preserve the option of using the wilderness in the future for themselves and their descendants. More broadly, some individuals who have no desire to use wilderness at any time may nevertheless have a preference for the preservation of wilderness as an ethical value. These individuals' various desires for wilderness preservation convert wilderness areas into public goods. The reason is that if the wilderness is preserved, these individuals cannot be excluded from enjoying the resulting benefit. This "public good" situation is commonly thought to require a non-market solution.

Furthermore, negative externalities are also present. Many biologists would suggest, on the basis of prior studies of ecological changes, that widespread changes in undeveloped areas are likely to have unforeseen negative consequences there and elsewhere. For example, development of estuaries or marsh areas may indirectly affect wildlife and marine life, thereby impinging on the interests of hunters and fishermen. The existence of these externalities may provide a basis for preserving wilderness areas that is not unlike the basis for preventing pollution.

There is also a temporal element to these externalities, for many of the affected individuals belong to future generations. Some economists have argued that these intertemporal effects may be quite large. The future amount of available wilderness probably will be even less than that existing today. As the supply decreases, the price individuals would be willing to pay for the use of any one piece of wilderness will tend to increase. Preservation of wilderness seems to be a "normal" good—that is, a good which is in greater demand as income rises. If we assume that economic growth will continue, the result will be higher individual incomes and therefore a higher demand for wilderness. Hence, future generations may have a stronger demand for wilderness areas than current generations. Ignoring the preferences of future generations could result in greatly distorted resource allocation over time. Thus, even from the perspective of neoclassical economics, a strong argument can be made for wilderness preservation.

It is also important to acknowledge some of the limitations of economic analysis. As a descriptive science, economics can tell us the consequences of a decision but not its desirability.[a] An example may help explain how economic analysis can break down as a method of making social decisions. Consider the decision to destroy a stand of redwoods. If lumber companies have the legal right to harvest the trees, environmentalists might not be willing (or able) to pay the companies enough to get them to stop. A cost-benefit analyst would say that company profits were greater than the externality to the environmentalists, so logging would be economically efficient. Thus, the loggers can claim that their actions meet the "market" test of cost-benefit analysis: in a world of perfect markets, the logging would proceed because its benefits to loggers outweigh the costs to environmentalists.

The loggers' argument assumes, however, that they own the entitlement to control logging. If the environmentalists had the legal right to prevent logging, they might demand a much higher price to sell that right to the lumber companies. One reason for the disparity is that environmentalists are in a sense "wealthier" (they have a legal entitlement they didn't own before). Changes in wealth shift the demand curve. If the environmentalists own the entitlement, the cost-benefit analysis may well show that logging is inefficient. We can't necessarily decide whether the logging is economically efficient until we know who has the entitlement. Thus, economic analysis is indeterminate in this situation until entitlements have been assigned on some other basis. See Levy and Friedman, "The Revenge of the Redwoods? Reconsidering Property and the Economic Allocation of Natural Resources," 61 *U.Chi.L.Rev.* 493 (1994).

None of this is news to economists. Even the most fervent believers in economic efficiency concede that "there is more to justice than economics." R. Posner, *Economic Analysis of Law* 25–26 (3d ed. 1986).[b]

As the logging example illustrates, the assignment of entitlements can be crucial to analyzing the desirability of regulation. The following article explores conflicting conceptions of how to assign entitlements—or, to use a

---

a. Meyers seems to suggest that economics simply shows how individual preferences can be combined to maximize the welfare of society. Thus, under this view, individuals are completely free to have their own value preferences; economics merely shows how these can be combined to maximize the satisfaction of everyone. But as the Nobel Prize-winner Kenneth Arrow showed in his book, *Social Choice and Individual Values,* no system of aggregating individual preferences can lead to a rational decision method. That is, unless some restrictions are placed on which individual preferences are allowed into consideration, it can be mathematically proved that no method of combining those individual preferences can satisfy the customary standards of rationality. (For example, one of these standards of rationality is that if A is preferred to B, and B is preferred to C, then A is preferred to C.) Thus, the market solution cannot be viewed as a completely neutral means of combining individuals' value judgments.

b. For further discussion of environmentalism and economic efficiency, see J. Sax, *Mountains Without Handrails: Reflections on the National Parks* (1980); Tarlock, "A Comment on Meyers' Introduction to Environmental Thought," 50 *Ind.L.J.* 454 (1975); Tribe, "From Environmental Foundations to Constitutional Structures: Learning from Nature's Future," 84 *Yale L.J.* 556 (1975). For a full presentation of the environmentalist position, see M. Sagoff, *The Economy of the Earth: Philosophy, Law, and the Environment* (1988). For critiques of Sagoff's position, see Rose, Book Review, 87 *Mich.L.Rev.* 1631 (1988); Farber, "Review Essay: Environmentalism, Economics, and the Public Interest," 41 *Stan.L.Rev.* 1021 (1989). On a related subject, Merryman, "The Public Interest in Cultural Property," 77 *Cal.L.Rev.* 339 (1989), contains an evocative analysis of the reasons for preserving works of artistic or historical significance.

more familiar term, "ownership" of property. Building on Leopold's views about property and the land ethic, the author presents a counterpoint to the traditional conception of property law.

BYRNE, "GREEN PROPERTY"[c]
7 Constitutional Commentary 239 (1990).

Environmental concerns have become a significant influence on the goals of American land use law. For example, recent critical-areas regulations severely regulate development in areas of sensitive natural value such as coastlines and watersheds. These regulations impose the most extensive controls on development of private land in our history. They do so to safeguard the natural functions of estuaries, coastlines, and wetlands upon which both sustainable economic activity such as fishing, and organic life itself depend. Also, they affirm the intrinsic worth of the Earth and call on us to restrain our cupidity as the minimum condition of self-esteem. Such regulations reduce the market value of affected land by curtailing industrial development, severely restricting residential densities, and imposing new restrictions on agricultural methods. Indeed, conversion of the site from an economic commodity to a functioning part of a healthy environment may be said to be the objective of the regulation.

Regulation so pervasive challenges fundamental assumptions concerning property in land. Our land law has stood on the twin bases that the owner ought to have extensive discretion over the use of land and that land ought to be put to its most profitable use. These potentially contradictory assumptions are reconciled in the person of the hypothetical rational owner whose fate is to pile up wealth tirelessly. American land use law has expressed these ideological assumptions. Courts justified zoning as a means to increase the total market value of a community's land, by eliminating market depressing incompatible uses, and by preserving the right of each owner to develop his parcel of land in a profitable manner. Zoning regulations that failed to protect these interests of the landowner were said to "take" the owner's property.

* * *

[Recent] regulatory and doctrinal developments provide the basis for a green theory of property. Such a theory would seek primarily to give legal effect to the ecological land ethic, as formulated by thinkers such as Aldo Leopold, which emphasize the moral duty of humanity to act as steward of natural life. A regulatory program incorporating this theory might identify land within the jurisdiction of outstanding natural value and subject it to the following:

    1) Any change in the character of land that impairs its natural value would require a permit.

2) No permit would be granted unless the development served a compelling human need.

3) If the development appears to cause some specific harm to the environment not directly forbidden by positive regulations (such as narrowing the habitat of a diminishing species) it can be permitted only if a) it will be accomplished with the minimum of environmental damage, b) the developer will pay in dollars the cost of environmental damage, and c) the human gains from development substantially exceed the environmental harm from the project.

4) Reasonable public access must be permitted over any land designated as having scientific, aesthetic or recreational value.

5) No compensation should be paid landowners for any regulations or denial of permits under the above regulations if such actions are taken in good faith.

This bare statement of regulatory standards does not begin to address the legitimate political concerns about the institutions that would administer this regime nor its collateral effects on harmless economic activity. The sketch is merely given to suggest the shape of laws serving ecological rather than utilitarian ends.

A green theory of property would support a regulatory program of land use serving ecological ends of removing impediments to the exercise of public control. Property law embraces society's allocation of benefits among its members and the boundaries between private and public control of things. These relational rights have changed often to reflect changing visions of social order. Thus, nineteenth century law sought to disentangle absolute ownership of land from the lingering restrictions of a more communal, pre-industrial regime dating back to the medieval manor; the purposes of such reform included stimulation of wealth creation, enhancement of social mobility, and glorification of individual liberty. A green property law must thoroughly subject individual rights in natural resources to the community's need for biological and spiritual vitality; the purposes of such reforms include the preservation of higher forms of life on earth, the inculcation in humans of moral self-restraint in consuming resources or exploiting others, and the enhancement of pleasure and grace from direct experience of the natural world.

It remains a challenge to articulate these principles in legal doctrine. The essence of such doctrinal innovation must be that the individual possessor does not own the right to degrade the natural ecological systems on his land; such a right must be held by the jurisdiction in trust for present and future members of the community. Such trust should reflect a real fiduciary obligation to other species of life. Joined with such public beneficial ownership of natural ecological systems should be a right of reasonable access by the public to worthwhile natural sites. This formula essentially extends the present public trust doctrine to all undeveloped and agricultural land, while severing it from the historical fictions that sometimes have sustained it.

* * *

Greens should attack directly the proposition that owners may exclude the public from proximity to the ocean or other special natural areas. Valuable preparatory work has been accomplished in elaborating the public trust doctrine to deprive owners in several states of the right to exclude the public from the wet sand area of the beach. The courts have contrasted the harmfulness of development of an ocean beach with the desirability of public (non-consumptive) enjoyment of that immensely invigorating location. Greens should argue that experience of ocean shorefront is an inalienable right of all people, surely no less significant than the right to leaflet a shopping center.[14] Without access to nature, humans lose perspective on their limited claims on creation, their duties of nurture, and perhaps on the providence of death. Every inducement should be offered to divert citizens from shopping centers and televisions to woods and shores. Direct knowledge of the natural world will strengthen public support for responsible policies of preservation.

The argument for exclusion rests on inertia and selfishness. Great Britain has retained from the middle ages public rights of way throughout its countryside. We lack such public rights because of the sparseness of early American settlements and because our property law coalesced when land development was the greatest hope for personal wealth and mobility. Much was sacrificed in the name of development. What losses would owners suffer from recognition of publicly regulated rights of access on land and water of special merit? The most persuasive fear is that public access will create a tragic commons, resulting in destruction through overuse of the prized resource. But such harms can be contained through regulation. * * * The owner's pleasure in exclusive dominion itself need not be countenanced. Some loss of tranquility may be suffered, but those who purchase in highly desirable areas cannot expect complete solitude.

[E]cological balance is a good independent of whether it is preferred by the majority: even if a majority of voters would not support the purchase of an ecological balance, it should be done. Indeed, many voters suffer from consciousness "polluted" by the ceaseless manipulation and organized prurience of a consumer media.

Greens have only begun to think about the political institutions that will make these choices. Green groups frequently adopt an internal decisionmaking procedure that emphasizes mutual education and consensus. Greens resist the careerist politics that typify our larger institutions. (Die Grunen has insisted, for example, that parliamentary repre-

---

14. See *PruneYard Shopping Center v. Robins,* 447 U.S. 74 (1980) (California constitutional provision that permits people to distribute pamphlets and solicit signatures on a petition at a shopping center does not take owner's property rights in violation of fourteenth amendment). See also *State ex rel. Thornton v. Hay* [infra p. 787] (upholding public access to beaches based on custom).

sentatives rotate out of office every few years.) Many also have advocated extensive decentralization of government to political units reflecting the boundaries of natural ecosystems (such as the Appalachians), a movement known as bioregionalism. At the same time greens are committed to disarmament and international cooperation.

One might criticize this as a dreamy, short-lived utopianism that threatens to lapse into anarchy or authoritarianism. Yet abandoning the vision of overcoming greed and parochialism leaves us with little hope that we can preserve the earth as sustenance and joy for our children. Science has assembled an impressive array of information about threats from air pollution, toxic waste, climatic change, water pollution, extinction of species, and population growth. Perhaps under the shadow of disaster an informed citizenry can achieve public virtue. Preservation of the prerogatives of property owners will not address these issues.

* * * The law is wedded to a concept of property that gives precedence to a right to change the existing biologic character of land over increases in the owner's individual wealth. The constitutional shibboleths of the Justices could freeze the fluid stream of property law in the posture of acquisitive individualism. The task of green property law is both to find practical mechanisms for utopian aspirations and to criticize those elements of the legal culture that obstruct urgent reforms.

Notes

1. Eric Freyfogle expresses a similar view about the need to revise traditional concepts of property:

> If we merge [traditional] ideas, we produce an image of a physical world divided into pieces and subject to private ownership and control, a countryside populated with castles, each with an owner who controls. This is perhaps the law's dominant image, a carryover from centuries past. It should be quite plain to us upon even brief reflection that this image of ownership and domination stands in the way of environmental progress. It suggests that we may do what we want on the land that we own, that what we do is no business of others, even if it involves destruction, and that what others do is not business of ours.

* * *

> As ecologists have explained, often in delightful detail, the world around us is intricate and intertwined. Each part of nature is attached to each other part, and what we do to one part has effects that spread widely. * * *

> If our legal culture is going to reflect this rich reality, if it is going to incorporate the numerous natural links that bind one acre to all others, ownership norms need to be based on a vision of property as community. The person who becomes owner of a tract must be seen, not as some recluse on an isolated island, but as part of a natural as well as social community, with all of the obligations that accompany that status. People can close their doors and retreat from the rest of humanity. But they cannot cut their land from the rest of the Earth.

Freyfogle, *Justice and the Earth: Images for Our Planetary Survival* 51–53 (1993). See also Freyfogle, "Ethics, Community, and Private Land," 23 *Ecology L.Q.* 631 (1996). How would Meyers respond?

2.   John Sprankling argues that American property law has been molded partly by the desire to encourage land development, and that as a consequence, it contains a number of built-in biases against wilderness. According to Sprankling, the "abundance of wilderness land in the young United States" led an "instrumentalist judiciary" to modify "English property law to encourage the agrarian development, and thus destruction, of privately owned American wilderness." He gives as examples the doctrines of waste, adverse possession, possession as notice to a bona fide purchaser, good faith improver, trespass, and nuisance, all of which he says "reflect this early antiwilderness retooling." He also argues that the modern versions of these doctrines remain "tilted toward wilderness destruction." See Sprankling, "The Antiwilderness Bias in American Property Law," 63 *U. Chi. L. Rev.* 519 (1996).

3.   At the same time that the current property regime has been attacked by critics like Byrne and Freyfogle for insensitivity to ecological values, it has come under fire from the other side as well. Particularly in the West, renewed demands have been heard to strengthen the rights of property owners as against government regulators. Although they perceive the same regulatory trends as Byrne and Freyfogle, they see in these trends a threat to individual liberty. See Lavelle, "The 'Property Rights' Revolt," 15 *National L.J.* 1 (May 10, 1993). In the next section, we will see the Supreme Court's responses to these conflicting views of property.

B.   PRIVATE PROPERTY

1.   THE TAKING PROBLEM

Attempts to prevent development of private land in the name of environmental protection have met with strenuous opposition on constitutional grounds. The taking clause of the Fifth Amendment provides that private property shall not "be taken for public use, without just compensation." This provision applies only to the federal government. The Fourteenth Amendment, which imposes constitutional restrictions on the states, does not contain similar language. The Supreme Court, however, has construed the Fourteenth Amendment as generating a similar requirement by implication from the due process clause. Consequently, courts have not distinguished between the federal and state governments for purposes of takings analysis.

As the Supreme Court itself has admitted, it has not succeeded in constructing clear rules in this area. It is well established that some government activities, falling short of outright condemnation or seizure of land, still may constitute a taking for constitutional purposes. One rationale is that otherwise the government could force private landowners to devote their property entirely to public uses—for example, by constructing a school on the property and providing free education to the public—thereby indirectly converting the property to governmental use without paying just compensation. We begin with a historical review of takings doctrine, before turning to the recent cases.

Note on the Development of Takings Doctrine

The earliest relevant case is *Hadacheck v. Sebastian,* 239 U.S. 394, 36 S.Ct. 143, 60 L.Ed. 348 (1915). *Hadacheck* involved a Los Angeles city ordinance making it unlawful to operate a brickyard in part of the city. The owner of a local brickyard alleged that he had purchased the land when it was well outside the city limits and far from any residential district. He also claimed that he had had no reason to anticipate that the area would ever be juxtaposed to the city, that much of the property had been excavated for clay, that the land was worth $800,000 if used for brick-making purposes but no more than $60,000 otherwise, and that the ordinance would force him out of business. He also alleged, although this allegation was rejected by the state courts, that the operation of his business did not have detrimental effects on adjoining property; the real purpose of the ordinance allegedly was to give other brickyards located elsewhere in the city a monopoly in the brick market. The Supreme Court decisively rejected the attack on the ordinance:

> It is to be remembered that we are dealing with one of the most essential powers of government, one that is the least limitable. It may, indeed, seem harsh in its exercise, usually is on some individual, but the imperative necessity for its existence precludes any limitation upon it when not exerted arbitrarily. A vested interest cannot be asserted against it because of conditions once obtaining. To so hold would preclude development and fix a city forever in its primitive conditions. There must be progress, and if in its march private interests are in the way they must yield to the good of the community.

Note that *Hadacheck* was decided at a time when the Supreme Court was generally much more willing than it is today to strike down state statutes regulating economic activities. Yet, even in that pro-business period, the Court firmly upheld the *Hadacheck* ordinance.

Hadacheck might seem to suggest that the impact of a regulation on private individuals is irrelevant to determining constitutionality. The theory of the case seems to be that if a statute is otherwise legitimately within the police power—that is, if it is reasonably related to the public health, welfare, or morals—then individuals who suffer severe losses because of the regulation have no remedy. Less than a decade after *Hadacheck,* however, the Supreme Court seemingly drew back from this conclusion in *Pennsylvania Coal Co. v. Mahon,* 260 U.S. 393, 43 S.Ct. 158, 67 L.Ed. 322 (1922). This case involved a Pennsylvania statute making it unlawful for coal companies to cause the collapse or subsidence of any public building, any street, or any private residence. The Mahons were bound by a covenant to permit a coal company, which had sold to the Mahons or their predecessor only the surface rights to their lot, to remove all the coal without liability. The effect of the statute was to annul this covenant. Pennsylvania law recognized three separate property rights: the right to use the surface, the ownership of the subsurface minerals, and the right to have the surface supported by the subsurface earth. The coal company claimed that the statute operated as a taking of both the second and third rights, which belonged to them under their deed with the Mahons. In perhaps the most important single decision under the taking clause, Justice Holmes held that the statute was indeed a taking. The heart of the opinion is to be found in the following famous passage:

> Government hardly could go on if to some extent values incident to property could not be diminished without paying for every such change in the general law. As long recognized, some values are enjoyed under an implied limitation and must yield to the police power. But obviously the implied limitation must have its limits, or the contract and due process clauses are gone. One fact for consideration in determining such limits is the extent of the diminution. When it reaches a certain magnitude, in most if not in all cases there must be an exercise of eminent domain and compensation to sustain the act. So the question depends upon the particular facts. The greatest weight is given to the judgment of the legislature, but it always is open to interested parties to contend that the legislature has gone beyond its constitutional power.

In applying this test, the Court stressed that the statute made coal mining in certain areas impractical and thus had "very nearly the same effect for constitutional purposes as appropriating or destroying it." The Court concluded that so long as "private persons or communities have seen fit to take the risk of acquiring only surface rights, we cannot see that the fact that the risk has become a danger warrants the giving to them greater rights than they bought." Justice Brandeis filed a strong dissent.

At the very least, *Pennsylvania Coal* makes it clear that *Hadacheck* cannot be taken to its logical extreme. That is, cases exist in which a regulation has a legitimate purpose but falls too heavily on a single individual, who must be compensated under the taking clause. As the Court says in *Pennsylvania Coal,* this is a matter of degree and therefore difficult to predict in advance.

Soon after *Pennsylvania Coal,* the Court made it clear that even the physical destruction of property may sometimes be permissible without compensation. In *Miller v. Schoene,* 276 U.S. 272, 48 S.Ct. 246, 72 L.Ed. 568 (1928), the Court upheld a Virginia statute authorizing the state entomologist to order the destruction of ornamental red cedar trees. The purpose of the statute was to prevent the transmission of a plant disease to neighboring apple orchards. The Court held that the existence of cedars was incompatible with the existence of the apple trees, so the state was forced to choose which form of property to preserve. As the Court said, "[W]hen forced to such a choice the state does not exceed its constitutional powers by deciding upon the destruction of one class of property in order to save another which, in the judgment of the legislature, is of greater value to the public." After *Miller,* the Court seemed to lose interest in the taking issue for many years, until it returned to the area in the 1970s.

Penn Central Transportation Co. v. New York, 438 U.S. 104, 98 S.Ct. 2646, 57 L.Ed.2d 631 (1978), attempted to provide a synthesis of the case law up to that time. *Penn Central* involved a New York historic preservation ordinance. Under the ordinance a special commission was empowered to designate buildings as landmarks, subject to administrative and judicial review. After designation, the exterior of a building had to be kept in good repair and exterior alterations had to be approved by the Commission. Development rights lost because of the landmark designation could be transferred to nearby plots of land, thereby allowing additional development on that land beyond the normal restrictions of the zoning and building codes. Penn Central owned Grand Central Terminal, a designated landmark. A plan by Penn Central to build a multistory office building perched above the terminal was rejected by the Commission. Penn Central then brought suit claiming that its property had been taken without compensation. It conceded, however, that the transferable development rights had some value and that the terminal was still capable of earning a reasonable return on its initial investment.

The Court began by reviewing the factors that have shaped prior decisions. The Court admitted that it had been unable to develop any "set formula" for determining when compensation was required. Instead, it referred to the prior cases as involving "essentially ad hoc, factual inquiries." The Court did point, however, to several relevant factors. The most important were (1) whether the regulation had "interfered with distinct investment backed expectations," and (2) whether the government had physically invaded the property or instead had simply enacted "some public program adjusting the benefits and burdens of economic life to promote the common good." In reviewing the specific regulation before it, the Court concluded that the purposes of the ordinance were permissible because the ordinance was "expected to produce a widespread public benefit and applicable to all similarly situated property." The Court then held that the regulation passed the *Pennsylvania Coal* test because it did not deprive the company of all use of the property, but instead allowed continuation of a past use, and more importantly, permitted the company to obtain a "reasonable return" on its investment.

In the two years after *Penn Central,* the Supreme Court displayed a continued interest in the taking issue. These cases seemed to confirm the *Penn Central* Court's description of the case law as involving "essentially ad hoc, factual inquiries." The first case, *Andrus v. Allard,* 444 U.S. 51, 100 S.Ct. 318, 62 L.Ed.2d 210 (1979), seemed to retreat from the *Penn Central* test of "reasonable return on investment." *Allard* involved a statute prohibiting commercial transactions in certain "avian artifacts" such as eagle feathers. The plaintiffs owned bird feathers when the statute was passed and were subject to prosecution for selling them. In rejecting a taking claim, the Court stressed that they retained the rights to possess, donate and devise the feathers. The Court noted that the feathers could conceivably be exhibited for a profit, but then went on to add:

> At any rate, loss of future profits—unaccompanied by any physical property restriction—provides a slender reed upon which to rest a takings claim. Prediction of profitability is essentially a matter of reasoned speculation that courts are not especially competent to perform. Further, perhaps because of its uncertainty, the interest in anticipated gains has traditionally been viewed as less compelling than other property-related interests.

The second case, *Kaiser Aetna v. United States,* 444 U.S. 164, 100 S.Ct. 383, 62 L.Ed.2d 332 (1979), involved a private fish pond which the owners connected to the ocean and converted into a "marina-style subdivision community." Although it initially acquiesced in the project, the federal government later contended the marina was subject to a right of public access. The Court held that imposing this right of access would constitute a taking. The opinion does not purport to establish a general test, but instead stresses that the pond was not commercially navigable in its original state, that the government had allowed the marina conversion, and that the right to exclude others is a fundamental element of the property right. A third case contained an even more cursory analysis. *Agins v. City of Tiburon,* 447 U.S. 255, 100 S.Ct. 2138, 65 L.Ed.2d 106 (1980), involved a zoning ordinance which imposed density restrictions on housing on certain land. The Court simply stated that this was not a taking because it did not "prevent the best use of appellants' land * * * nor extinguish a fundamental attribute of 'ownership', and because the owners were 'free to pursue their reasonable investment expectations by submitting a development plan to local officials'."

After *Agins* there was a lull in the Court's taking jurisprudence. This turned out to be the quiet before the storm. As we will see, beginning in the late 1980s, takings law became a focal point of the Supreme Court docket.

KEYSTONE BITUMINOUS COAL ASS'N v. DeBENEDICTIS

Supreme Court of the United States, 1987.
480 U.S. 470, 107 S.Ct. 1232, 94 L.Ed.2d 472.

[This case involved § 4 of Pennsylvania's Bituminous Mine Subsidence and Land Conservation Act, which prohibited coal mining that caused subsidence damage to pre-existing surface structures. Subsidence could cause sinkholes and troughs, interfere with plowing, and cause loss of groundwater and surface ponds, besides damaging buildings. Where § 4 applied, an implementing regulation required 50% of the coal beneath any structure to be kept in place to provide surface support. Even apart from this requirement, however, coal mining operations normally left substantial amounts of coal in the ground to provide support, access, and ventilation for the mines. The plaintiffs (four mining companies and a trade association) filed a federal civil rights action alleging that § 4 constituted a taking. The District Court and Court of Appeals rejected this claim.]

JUSTICE STEVENS delivered the opinion of the Court:

Petitioners assert that disposition of their takings claim calls for no more than a straightforward application of the Court's decision in *Pennsylvania Coal Co. v. Mahon.* Although there are some obvious similarities between the cases, we agree with the Court of Appeals and the District Court that the similarities are far less significant than the differences, and that *Pennsylvania Coal* does not control this case.

* * *

The holdings and assumptions of the Court in *Pennsylvania Coal* provide obvious and necessary reasons for distinguishing *Pennsylvania*

Coal from the case before us today. The two factors that the Court considered relevant have become integral parts of our takings analysis. We have held that land use regulation can effect a taking if it "does not substantially advance legitimate state interests, * * * or denies an owner economically viable use of his land." Application of these tests to petitioners' challenge demonstrates that they have not satisfied their burden of showing that the Subsidence Act constitutes a taking. First, unlike the Kohler Act [in *Pennsylvania Coal*], the character of the governmental action involved here leans heavily against finding a taking; the Commonwealth of Pennsylvania has acted to arrest what it perceives to be a significant threat to the common welfare. Second, there is no record in this case to support a finding, similar to the one the Court made in *Pennsylvania Coal,* that the Subsidence Act makes it impossible for petitioners to profitably engage in their business, or that there has been undue interference with their investment-backed expectations.

* * *

Thus, the Subsidence Act differs from the Kohler Act in critical and dispositive respects. With regard to the Kohler Act, the Court believed that the Commonwealth had acted only to ensure against damage to some private landowners' homes. Justice Holmes stated that if the private individuals needed support for their structures, they should not have "take[n] the risk of acquiring only surface rights." Here, by contrast, the Commonwealth is acting to protect the public interest in health, the environment, and the fiscal integrity of the area. That private individuals erred in taking a risk cannot estop the State from exercising its police power to abate activity akin to a public nuisance. The Subsidence Act is a prime example that "circumstances may so change in time * * * as to clothe with such a [public] interest what at other times * * * would be a matter of purely private concern."

* * *

The second factor that distinguishes this case from *Pennsylvania Coal* is the finding in that case that the Kohler Act made mining of "certain coal" commercially impracticable. In this case, by contrast, petitioners have not shown any deprivation significant enough to satisfy the heavy burden placed upon one alleging a regulatory taking. For this reason, their takings claim must fail.

* * *

The parties have stipulated that enforcement of [the] 50% rule will require petitioners to leave approximately 27 million tons of coal in place. Because they own that coal but cannot mine it, they contend that Pennsylvania has appropriated it for the public purposes described in the Subsidence Act.

This argument fails for the reason explained in *Penn Central* and *Andrus.* The 27 million tons of coal do not constitute a separate segment of property for takings law purposes. Many zoning ordinances place limits on the property owner's right to make profitable use of some segments of his property. A requirement that a building occupy no more than a specified percentage of the lot on which it is located could be characterized as a taking of the vacant area as readily as the requirement that coal pillars be left in place. Similarly, under petitioners' theory one could always argue that a set-back ordinance requiring that no structure be built within a certain distance from the property line constitutes a taking because the footage represents a distinct segment of property for takings law purposes. There is no basis for treating the less than 2% of petitioners' coal as a separate parcel of property.

CHIEF JUSTICE REHNQUIST, with whom JUSTICE POWELL, JUSTICE O'CONNOR, and JUSTICE SCALIA join, dissenting.

In this case, enforcement of the Subsidence Act and its regulations will require petitioners to leave approximately 27 million tons of coal in place. There is no question that this coal is an identifiable and separable property interest. Unlike many property interests, the "bundle" of rights in this coal is sparse. "'For practical purposes, the right to coal consists in the right to mine it.'"[citing *Pennsylvania Coal*] From the relevant perspective—that of the property owners—this interest has been destroyed every bit as much as if the government had proceeded to mine the coal for its own use. The regulation, then, does not merely inhibit one strand in the bundle, but instead destroys completely any interest in a segment of property. In these circumstances, I think it unnecessary to consider whether petitioners may operate individual mines or their overall mining operations profitably, for they have been denied all use of 27 million tons of coal. I would hold that § 4 of the Subsidence Act works a taking of these property interests.

NOLLAN v. CALIFORNIA COASTAL COMMISSION

Supreme Court of the United States, 1987.
483 U.S. 825, 107 S.Ct. 3141, 97 L.Ed.2d 677.

[The Nollans owned a beachfront lot near a public beach. A concrete seawall parallel to the shoreline separated the beach portion of their property from the rest of the lot. They decided to demolish an existing, run-down structure and replace it with a three-bedroom house. The Coastal Commission granted them permission to do so only on condition that they record an easement on behalf of the public to pass along the beach. The Commission reasoned that the new construction would create a "psychological barrier" when combined with other buildings, causing the public to believe that the beach was not open to the public. The Nollans sought judicial review, arguing that the permit condition was an unconstitutional taking. While the litigation was pending, the Nollans tore down the old structure and built their new house without notifying the Commission.]

JUSTICE SCALIA delivered the opinion of the Court.

Had California simply required the Nollans to make an easement across their beachfront available to the public on a permanent basis in order to increase public access to the beach, rather than conditioning their permit to rebuild their house on their agreeing to do so, we have no doubt there would have been a taking. To say that the appropriation of a public easement across a landowner's premises does not constitute the taking of a property interest but rather, (as Justice Brennan contends) "a mere restriction on its use," is to use words in a manner that deprives them of all their ordinary meaning. Indeed, one of the principal uses of the eminent domain power is to assure that the government be able to require conveyance of just such interests, so long as it pays for them. * * *

* * *

The Commission argues that a permit condition that serves the same legitimate police-power purpose as a refusal to issue the permit should not be found to be a taking if the refusal to issue the permit would not constitute a taking. We agree. Thus, if the Commission attached to the permit some condition that would have protected the public's ability to see the beach notwithstanding construction of the new house—for example, a height limitation, a width restriction, or a ban on fences—so long as the Commission could have exercised its police power (as we have assumed it could) to forbid construction of the house altogether, imposition of the condition would also be constitutional. * * *

The evident constitutional propriety disappears, however, if the condition substituted for the prohibition utterly fails to further the end advanced as the justification for the prohibition. When that essential nexus is eliminated, the situation becomes the same as if California law forbade shouting fire in a crowded theater, but granted dispensations to those willing to contribute $100 to the state treasury. While a ban on shouting fire can be a core exercise of the State's police power to protect the public safety, and can thus meet even our stringent standards for regulation of speech, adding the unrelated condition alters the purpose to one which, while it may be legitimate, is inadequate to sustain the ban. Therefore, even though, in a sense, requiring a $100 tax contribution in order to shout fire is a lesser restriction on speech than an outright ban, it would not pass constitutional muster. Similarly here, the lack of nexus between the condition and the original purpose of the building restriction converts that purpose to something other than what it was. The purpose then becomes, quite simply, the obtaining of an easement to serve some valid governmental purpose, but without payment of compensation. Whatever may be the outer limits of "legitimate state interests" in the takings and land use context, this is not one of them. In short, unless the permit condition serves the same governmental purpose as the development ban, the building restriction is not a valid regulation of land use but "an out-and-out plan of extortion."

The Commission claims that it concedes as much, and that we may sustain the condition at issue here by finding that it is reasonably related to the public need or burden that the Nollans' new house creates or to which it contributes. We can accept, for purposes of discussion, the Commission's proposed test as to how close a "fit" between the condition and the burden is required, because we find that this case does not meet even the most untailored standards. The Commission's principal contention to the contrary essentially turns on a play on the word "access." The Nollans' new house, the Commission found, will interfere with "visual access" to the beach. That in turn (along with other shorefront development) will interfere with the desire of people who drive past the Nollans' house to use the beach, thus creating a "psychological barrier" to "access." The Nollans' new house will also, by a process not altogether clear from the Commission's opinion but presumably potent enough to more than offset the effects of the psychological barrier, increase the use of the public beaches, thus creating the need for more "access." These burdens on "access" would be alleviated by a requirement that the Nollans provide "lateral access" to the beach.

Rewriting the argument to eliminate the play on words makes clear that there is nothing to it. It is quite impossible to understand how a requirement that people already on the public beaches be able to walk across the Nollans' property reduces any obstacles to viewing the beach created by the new house. It is also impossible to understand how it lowers any "psychological barrier" to using the public beaches, or how it helps to remedy any additional congestion on them caused by construction of the Nollans' new house. We therefore find that the Commission's imposition of the permit condition cannot be treated as an exercise of its land use power for any of these purposes. Our conclusion on this point is consistent with the approach taken by every other court that has considered the question, with the exception of the California state courts.

JUSTICE BRENNAN, with whom JUSTICE MARSHALL joins, dissenting.

Even if we accept the Court's unusual demand for a precise match between the condition imposed and the specific type of burden on access created by the appellants, the State's action easily satisfies this requirement. First, the lateral access condition serves to dissipate the impression that the beach that lies behind the wall of homes along the shore is for private use only. It requires no exceptional imaginative powers to find plausible the Commission's point that the average person passing along the road in front of a phalanx of imposing permanent residences, including the appellants' new home, is likely to conclude that this particular portion of the shore is not open to the public. If, however, that person can see that numerous people are passing and repassing along the dry sand, this conveys the message that the beach is in fact open for use by the public. Furthermore, those persons who go down to the public beach a quarter-mile away will be able to look down the coastline and see that persons have continuous access to the tidelands, and will observe signs that proclaim the public's right of access over the dry sand. The burden produced by the diminution in visual access—the impression that the beach is not open to the public—is thus directly alleviated by the provision for public access over the dry sand. The Court therefore has an unrealistically limited conception of what measures could reasonably be chosen to mitigate the burden produced by a diminution of visual access.

Notes

1.   Are *DeBenedictis* and *Nollan* consistent with each other? For extensive discussion of these cases, see Kmiec, "The Original Understanding of the Taking Clause is Neither Weak Nor Obtuse," 88 *Colum.L.Rev.* 1630 (1988); Michelman, "Takings, 1987," 88 *Colum.L.Rev.* 1600 (1988). The implications of *Nollan* for land use regulation are explored in Reynolds, Book Review, 11 *Yale J. on Reg.* 507 (1994); Note, "Municipal Development Exactions, the Rational Nexus Test, and the Federal Constitution," 102 *Harv.L.Rev.* 992 (1989).

2.   In *DeBenedictis,* is Justice Stevens persuasive in distinguishing *Pennsylvania Coal?* Or does he really think it was wrongly decided? If, as the dissent argues, the coal left in the ground must be considered a separate segment of property which has been deprived of all use, what about setback requirements? Should the land covered by the setback be considered a separate parcel on which all construction is banned (and if so, wouldn't a taking be found)? Would the dissent reach a different result if state law did not view the coal mining company as having a vested right? See *Collins v. Oxley,* 897 F.2d 456 (10th Cir.1990).

3.   If Justice Scalia is right that the permit condition in *Nollan* must satisfy a nexus test, are you persuaded by Justice Brennan's view that the test is satisfied? Is the nexus test correct? Justice Scalia's argument relies on an analogy to first amendment law: the government can ban certain speech but not (he says) impose a $100 fee for the right to engage in unprotected speech. This appears to mean that the government can ban certain speech but not tax it. (Or would taxing it be permissible if the purpose of the tax is to discourage the speech, but not if it is intended to raise revenue?) Suppose California put a tax on new beachfront construction and used the proceeds to acquire easements by eminent domain. Does *Nollan* imply that this tax would be unconstitutional? Also, even if there was a taking, couldn't the grant of the construction permit be considered "just compensation?" See Sullivan, "Unconstitutional Conditions," 102 *Harv.L.Rev.* 1413, 1505 (1989).

tax would be valid.

4.   The Court decided two other noteworthy takings cases in the 1986 Term. One involved the proper remedy for a taking. *In First English Evangelical Lutheran Church of Glendale v. Los Angeles County, Cal.,* 482 U.S. 304, 107 S.Ct. 2378, 96 L.Ed.2d 250 (1987), the Court held that the government must pay damages for the temporary restriction on property use caused by an unconstitutional regulation prior to the time the regulation is struck down. *First English* greatly increases the risk to the government of attempting to guess the location of the wavering and blurred line between takings and valid regulations.[d] The other case struck down a federal statute relating to the inheritance of Indian lands. *Hodel v. Irving,* 481 U.S. 704, 107

---

d.   Under *First English,* if a statute "over-regulates," the property owner can obtain compensation for the period between the time the regulation is passed and the time the statute is struck down. The government can avoid having the statute struck down, however, by making compensation available for the property's permanent loss of value. See *Preseault v. I.C.C.,* 494 U.S. 1, 110 S.Ct. 914, 108 L.Ed.2d 1 (1990).

Supreme Ct. said yes they deserved compensation for time rights were taken.

You can file suit as soon as they tell you
you can't do something → becomes ripe, eventhough you
can still file for transfering right.

754   **PRESERVATION OF NATURAL AREAS**   Ch. 8

S.Ct. 2076, 95 L.Ed.2d 668 (1987). To prevent land from being owned by such a large group that its management was impaired, the statute terminated at the owner's death any interest less than a 2% share in land. The Court held that this was a taking, because Congress could have obtained its result by narrower means. Notably, Justice Scalia's concurrence argued that the Court had effectively overruled *Allard* (the eagle feathers case discussed supra p. 747). Justice Brennan responded with a concurrence disputing Scalia's argument.

The availability of a damage remedy heightens the importance of takings law for municipalities. Note, however, that state statutes of limitations do apply to takings claims, which means that landowners must act quickly. See *287 Corporate Center Assocs. v. Township of Bridgewater*, 101 F.3d 320 (3d Cir.1996). On the other hand, a claim brought too early will be dismissed as unripe. There must be a definitive government denial of development rights before a federal action can be brought. The Court clarified the ripeness requirement in *Suitum v. Tahoe Regional Planning Agency*, 520 U.S. 725, 117 S.Ct. 1659, 137 L.Ed.2d 980 (1997). The *Suitum* Court held that the landowner could challenge the denial of a building permit without applying for a transfer of development rights, because the economic impact of the permit denial could be assessed without waiting for the transfer. A concurring opinion argued that the economic value of the transfer rights might be an offset to takings damages, but would not be relevant in determining whether a taking had occurred.

Suitum is "unpopular" decision

5.   The Court took *Nollan* one step further in *Dolan v. City of Tigard*, 512 U.S. 374, 114 S.Ct. 2309, 129 L.Ed.2d 304 (1994). As a condition for permission to expand a hardware store and adjacent parking lot, the city required the store owner to dedicate a floodplain area and a 15–foot fringe for use as a "greenspace" and bike path. The Court found *Nollan* easily satisfied, but also added a test of "rough proportionality." The Court required the city to "make some sort of individualized determination that the required dedication is related both in nature and extent to the impact of the proposed development." Although finding the floodplain requirement less problematic, the Court found an inadequate basis for the bike path requirement: "No precise mathematical calculation is required, but the city must make some effort to quantify its findings in support of the dedication for the pedestrian/bicycle pathway beyond the conclusory statement that it could offset some of the traffic demand generated [by the expansion]." For the argument that *Dolan* should replace the *Nollan* test, see W. Fischel, *Regulatory Takings: Law, Economics, and Politics* 349 (1996).

this case seems not to have much influence

LUCAS v. SOUTH CAROLINA COASTAL COUNCIL

Supreme Court of the United States, 1992.
505 U.S. 1003, 112 S.Ct. 2886, 120 L.Ed.2d 798.

JUSTICE SCALIA delivered the opinion of the Court.

In 1986, petitioner David H. Lucas paid $975,000 for two residential lots on the Isle of Palms in Charleston County, South Carolina, on which he intended to build single family homes. In 1988, however, the South Carolina Legislature enacted the Beachfront Management Act, which had the direct effect of barring petitioner from erecting any permanent habitable structures on his two parcels. A state trial court found that this prohibition rendered Lucas's parcels "valueless." This case requires us to decide whether the Act's dramatic effect on the economic value of Lucas's lots accomplished a taking of private property under the Fifth and Fourteenth Amendments requiring the payment of "just compensation."

Issue

* * *

[O]ur decision in *Mahon* offered little insight into when, and under what circumstances, a given regulation would be seen as going "too far" for purposes of the Fifth Amendment. In 70–odd years of succeeding "regulatory takings" jurisprudence, we have generally eschewed any " 'set formula' " for determining how far is too far, preferring to "engag[e] in * * * essentially ad hoc, factual inquiries," [quoting *Penn Central*]. We have, however, described at least two discrete categories of regulatory action as compensable without case-specific inquiry into the public interest advanced in support of the restraint. The first encompasses regulations that compel the property owner to suffer a physical "invasion" of his property. * * *

The second situation in which we have found categorical treatment appropriate is where regulation denies all economically beneficial or productive use of land. As we have said on numerous occasions, the Fifth Amendment is violated when land-use regulation "does not substantially advance legitimate state interests *or denies an owner economically viable use of his land.*"[15]

15. Regrettably, the rhetorical force of our "deprivation of all economically feasible use" rule is greater than its precision, since the rule does not make clear the "property interest" against which the loss of value is to be measured. When, for example, a regulation requires a developer to leave 90% of a rural tract in its natural state, it is unclear whether we would analyze the situation as one in which the owner has been deprived of all economically beneficial use of the burdened portion of the tract, or as one in which the owner has suffered a mere diminution in value of the tract as a whole. (For an extreme—and, we think, unsupportable—view of the relevant calculus, see *Penn Central Transportation Co. v. New York City,* 42 N.Y.2d 324, 333–334, 397 N.Y.S.2d 914, 920, 366 N.E.2d 1271, 1276–1277 (1977), aff'd, 438 U.S. 104, 98 S.Ct. 2646, 57 L.Ed.2d 631 (1978), where the state court examined the diminution in a particular parcel's value produced by a municipal ordinance in light of total value of the taking claimant's other holdings in the vicinity.) Unsurprisingly, this uncertainty regarding the composition of the denomina- tor in our "deprivation" fraction has produced inconsistent pronouncements by the Court. Compare *Pennsylvania Coal Co. v. Mahon,* 260 U.S. 393, 414, 43 S.Ct. 158, 160, 67 L.Ed. 322 (1922) (law restricting subsurface extraction of coal held to effect a taking), with *Keystone Bituminous Coal Assn. v. DeBenedictis,* [supra p. 748] (nearly identical law held not to effect a taking). The answer to this difficult question may lie in how the owner's reasonable expectations have been shaped by the State's law of property—*i.e.,* whether and to what degree the State's law has accorded legal recognition and protection to the particular interest in land with respect to which the takings claimant alleges a diminution in (or elimination of) value. In any event, we avoid this difficulty in the present case, since the "interest in land" that Lucas has pleaded (a fee simple interest) is an estate with a rich tradition of protection at common law, and since the South Carolina Court of Common Pleas found that the Beachfront Management Act left each of Lucas's beachfront lots without economic value.

We have never set forth the justification for this rule. Perhaps it is simply, as Justice Brennan suggested, that total deprivation of beneficial use is, from the landowner's point of view, the equivalent of a physical appropriation. * * * Surely, at least, in the extraordinary circumstance when *no* productive or economically beneficial use of land is permitted, it is less realistic to indulge our usual assumption that the legislature is simply "adjusting the benefits and burdens of economic life," [*Penn Central*], in a manner that secures an "average reciprocity of advantage" to everyone concerned. And the *functional* basis for permitting the government, by regulation, to affect property values without compensation—that "Government hardly could go on if to some extent values incident to property could not be diminished without paying for every such change in the general law"—does not apply to the relatively rare situations where the government has deprived a landowner of all economically beneficial uses.

On the other side of the balance, affirmatively supporting a compensation requirement, is the fact that regulations that leave the owner of land without economically beneficial or productive options for its use— typically, as here, by requiring land to be left substantially in its natural state—carry with them a heightened risk that private property is being pressed into some form of public service under the guise of mitigating serious public harm. See, *e.g.*, *Annicelli v. South Kingstown,* 463 A.2d 133, 140–141 (R.I.1983) (prohibition on construction adjacent to beach justified on twin grounds of safety and "conservation of open space"); *Morris County Land Improvement Co. v. Parsippany–Troy Hills Township,* 40 N.J. 539, 552–553, 193 A.2d 232, 240 (1963) (prohibition on filling marshlands imposed in order to preserve region as water detention basin and create wildlife refuge). As Justice Brennan explained: "From the government's point of view, the benefits flowing to the public from preservation of open space through regulation may be equally great as from creating a wildlife refuge through formal condemnation or increasing electricity production through a dam project that floods private property." The many statutes on the books, both state and federal, that provide for the use of eminent domain to impose servitudes on private scenic lands preventing developmental uses, or to acquire such lands altogether, suggest the practical equivalence in this setting of negative regulation and appropriation.

We think, in short, that there are good reasons for our frequently expressed belief that when the owner of real property has been called upon to sacrifice *all* economically beneficial uses in the name of the common good, that is, to leave his property economically idle, he has suffered a taking.

* * *

It is correct that many of our prior opinions have suggested that "harmful or noxious uses" of property may be proscribed by government regulation without the requirement of compensation. For a number of reasons, however, we think the South Carolina Supreme Court was too quick to conclude that that principle decides the present case. The "harmful or noxious uses" principle was the Court's early attempt to describe in theoretical terms why government may, consistent with the Takings Clause, affect property values by regulation without incurring an obligation to compensate—a reality we nowadays acknowledge explicitly with respect to the full scope of the State's police power. * * *

The transition from our early focus on control of "noxious" uses to our contemporary understanding of the broad realm within which government may regulate without compensation was an easy one, since the distinction between "harm-preventing" and "benefit-conferring" regulation is often in the eye of the beholder. It is quite possible, for example, to describe in *either* fashion the ecological, economic, and aesthetic concerns that inspired the South Carolina legislature in the present case. One could say that imposing a servitude on Lucas's land is necessary in order to prevent his use of it from "harming" South Carolina's ecological resources; or, instead, in order to achieve the "benefits" of an ecological preserve. Whether one or the other of the competing characterizations will come to one's lips in a particular case depends primarily upon one's evaluation of the worth of competing uses of real estate. * * *

Where the State seeks to sustain regulation that deprives land of all economically beneficial use, we think it may resist compensation only if the logically antecedent inquiry into the nature of the owner's estate shows that the proscribed use interests were not part of his title to begin with.[16] This accords, we think, with our "takings" jurisprudence, which has traditionally been guided by the understandings of our citizens regarding the content of, and the State's power over, the "bundle of rights" that they acquire when they obtain title to property. It seems to us that the property owner necessarily expects the uses of his property to be restricted, from time to time, by various measures newly enacted by the State in legitimate exercise of its police powers; "[a]s long recognized, some values are enjoyed under an implied limitation and must yield to the police power." [*Mahon.*] And in the case of personal property, by reason of the State's traditionally high degree of control over commercial dealings, he ought to be aware of the possibility that new regulation might even render his property economically worthless (at least if the property's only economically productive use is sale or manu-

---

16. Drawing on our First Amendment jurisprudence, Justice Stevens would "loo[k] to the *generality* of a regulation of property" to determine whether compensation is owing. The Beachfront Management Act is general, in his view, because it "regulates the use of the coastline of the entire state." There may be some validity to the principle Justice Stevens proposes, but it does not properly apply to the present case. The equivalent of a law of general application that inhibits the practice of religion without being aimed at religion, is a law that destroys the value of land without being aimed at land. Perhaps such a law—the generally applicable criminal prohibition on the manufacturing of alcoholic beverages challenged in *Mugler* [*v. Kansas*, 123 U.S. 623, 8 S.Ct. 273, 31 L.Ed. 205 (1887)] (1887), comes to mind—cannot constitute a compensable taking. But a regulation *specifically directed to land use* no more acquires immunity by plundering landowners generally than does a law specifically directed at religious practice acquire immunity by prohibiting all religions. Justice Stevens' approach renders the Takings Clause little more than a particularized restatement of the Equal Protection Clause.

facture for sale). In the case of land, however, we think the notion pressed by the Council that title is somehow held subject to the "implied limitation" that the State may subsequently eliminate all economically valuable use is inconsistent with the historical compact recorded in the Takings Clause that has become part of our constitutional culture.

* * *

It seems unlikely that common-law principles would have prevented the erection of any habitable or productive improvements on petitioner's land; they rarely support prohibition of the "essential use" of land. The question, however, is one of state law to be dealt with on remand. We emphasize that to win its case South Carolina must do more than proffer the legislature's declaration that the uses Lucas desires are inconsistent with the public interest, or the conclusory assertion that they violate a common-law maxim such as *sic utere tuo ut alienum non laedas.* As we have said, a "State, by *ipse dixit,* may not transform private property into public property without compensation * * *." Instead, as it would be required to do if it sought to restrain Lucas in a common-law action for public nuisance, South Carolina must identify background principles of nuisance and property law that prohibit the uses he now intends in the circumstances in which the property is presently found. Only on this showing can the State fairly claim that, in proscribing all such beneficial uses, the Beachfront Management Act is taking nothing.[17]

JUSTICE KENNEDY, concurring in the judgment.

In my view, reasonable expectations must be understood in light of the whole of our legal tradition. The common law of nuisance is too narrow a confine for the exercise of regulatory power in a complex and interdependent society. The State should not be prevented from enacting new regulatory initiatives in response to changing conditions, and courts must consider all reasonable expectations whatever their source. The Takings Clause does not require a static body of state property law; it protects private expectations to ensure private investment. I agree with the Court that nuisance prevention accords with the most common expectations of property owners who face regulation, but I do not believe this can be the sole source of state authority to impose severe restrictions. Coastal property may present such unique concerns for a fragile land system that the State can go further in regulating its development and use than the common law of nuisance might otherwise permit.

The Supreme Court of South Carolina erred, in my view, by reciting the general purposes for which the state regulations were enacted without a determination that they were in accord with the owner's reasonable expectations and therefore sufficient to support a severe restriction on specific parcels of property. The promotion of tourism, for instance, ought not to suffice to deprive specific property of all value

---

17. * * * We stress that an affirmative decree eliminating all economically beneficial uses may be defended only if an *objectively reasonable application* of relevant precedents would exclude those beneficial uses in the circumstances in which the land is presently found.

without a corresponding duty to compensate. Furthermore, the means as well as the ends of regulation must accord with the owner's reasonable expectations. Here, the State did not act until after the property had been zoned for individual lot development and most other parcels had been improved, throwing the whole burden of the regulation on the remaining lots. This too must be measured in the balance.

JUSTICE BLACKMUN, dissenting.

Petitioner Lucas is a contractor, manager, and part owner of the Wild Dune development on the Isle of Palms. He has lived there since 1978. In December 1986, he purchased two of the last four pieces of vacant property in the development. The area is notoriously unstable. In roughly half of the last 40 years, all or part of petitioner's property was part of the beach or flooded twice daily by the ebb and flow of the tide. Between 1957 and 1963, petitioner's property was under water. Between 1963 and 1973 the shoreline was 100 to 150 feet onto petitioner's property. In 1973 the first line of stable vegetation was about halfway through the property. Between 1981 and 1983, the Isle of Palms issued 12 emergency orders for sandbagging to protect property in the Wild Dune development. Determining that local habitable structures were in imminent danger of collapse, the Council issued permits for two rock revetments to protect condominium developments near petitioner's property from erosion; one of the revetments extends more than halfway onto one of his lots.

* * *

[T]he Court justifies its new rule that the legislature may not deprive a property owner of the only economically valuable use of his land, even if the legislature finds it to be a harmful use, because such action is not part of the "long recognized" "understandings of our citizens." These "understandings" permit such regulation only if the use is a nuisance under the common law. Any other course is "inconsistent with the historical compact recorded in the Takings Clause." It is not clear from the Court's opinion where our "historical compact" or "citizens' understanding" comes from, but it does not appear to be history.

The principle that the State should compensate individuals for property taken for public use was not widely established in America at the time of the Revolution. * * *

Even into the 19th century, state governments often felt free to take property for roads and other public projects without paying compensation to the owners. As one court declared in 1802, citizens "were bound to contribute as much of [land], as by the laws of the country, were deemed necessary for the public convenience." * * *

* * *

In short, I find no clear and accepted "historical compact" or "understanding of our citizens" justifying the Court's new taking doctrine. Instead, the Court seems to treat history as a grab-bag of principles, to be adopted where they support the Court's theory, and ignored where they do not. If the Court decided that the early common law provides the background principles for interpreting the Taking Clause, then regulation, as opposed to physical confiscation, would not be compensable. If the Court decided that the law of a later period provides the background principles, then regulation might be compensable, but the Court would have to confront the fact that legislatures regularly determined which uses were prohibited, independent of the common law, and independent of whether the uses were lawful when the owner purchased. What makes the Court's analysis unworkable is its attempt to package the law of two incompatible eras and peddle it as historical fact.

JUSTICE STEVENS, dissenting.

In considering Lucas' claim, the generality of the Beachfront Management Act is significant. The Act does not target particular landowners, but rather regulates the use of the coastline of the entire State. Indeed, South Carolina's Act is best understood as part of a national effort to protect the coastline, one initiated by the Federal Coastal Zone Management Act of 1972. * * * Moreover, the Act did not single out owners of undeveloped land. The Act also prohibited owners of developed land from rebuilding if their structures were destroyed, and what is equally significant, from repairing erosion control devices, such as seawalls. In addition, in some situations, owners of developed land were required to "renouris[h] the beach * * * on a yearly basis with an amount * * * of sand * * * not * * * less than one and one-half times the yearly volume of sand lost due to erosion." In short, the South Carolina Act imposed substantial burdens on owners of developed and undeveloped land alike. This generality indicates that the Act is not an effort to expropriate owners of undeveloped land.

Admittedly, the economic impact of this regulation is dramatic and petitioner's investment-backed expectations are substantial. Yet, if anything, the costs to and expectations of the owners of developed land are even greater: I doubt, however, that the cost to owners of developed land of renourishing the beach and allowing their seawalls to deteriorate effects a taking. The costs imposed on the owners of undeveloped land, such as petitioner, differ from these costs only in degree, not in kind.

Notes

1. When a regulation forbids all economically viable use of a unit of property, according to the majority, the owner is entitled to compensation unless its property interest never included the right to engage in those uses in the first place. Applying this test will require courts first to define the relevant unit of property, which may be a difficult task, and then to determine the status of the particular uses under prior state law. If prior law was murky, so that a landowner would have been unsure whether it prohibited all use of the property, should the landowner be entitled to compensation?

2. Justice Scalia's reliance on the "historic compact" has been sharply criticized by Frank Michelman:

We need to ask, in the first place, how or why any judge would consider himself licensed for assertion of anything like objective knowledge—safely proof against the judge's own "will"—of such a free-floating sort of historical fact. (I mean *naked* assertion, too, because the *Lucas* opinion refers to no source external to its subscribers for its crucial claim of judicial knowledge.) We need further to keep in mind some other pertinent and, it seems, equally plausible traditions. One thinks of the tradition of free public access to the sea and its environs, today increasingly read by courts all around this country as encompassing public rights of enjoyment of the beach. One thinks of the tradition of legally required regard for other people's interests when you make use of your property. One thinks of the tradition of a dynamically functional law of property, oriented no less to contemporary community goals than to protection of private advantage. One thinks of the "historical tradition in which the common law core of nuisance has been the frequent subject of statutory additions and refinements, providing most of our modern law of land use.

Michelman, "Property, Federalism, and Jurisprudence: A Comment on *Lucas* and Judicial Conservatism," 35 *William & Mary L.Rev.* 301, 322–23 (1993).

3. Justice Stevens' dissent suggests quite a different approach to takings law, in which discrimination would be the key element. Justice Scalia responds that this approach would make the takings clause a "restatement" of the equal protection clause. Stevens could reply, however, that the takings clause came first, and it is not too unreasonable to suppose that the Framers might have enacted some prohibitions on specific forms of discrimination before they added a general prohibition. If Stevens is right to focus on discrimination as a justification for takings law, would it necessarily follow that discrimination should be assessed in each individual case? Might it make sense to carve out classes of cases where the government rarely acts without compensation, and then simply presume that the exceptional failures to compensate are the result of discrimination? If, in fact, the government rarely deprives landowners of all use of their property without compensation, this approach might even support something along the lines of Scalia's categorical test. See Farber, "Public Choice and Just Compensation," 9 *Const.Comm.* 279 (1992).

A more textualist approach to takings also is possible. The Constitution requires compensation when the government "takes" property, but not when it merely regulates its use. Clearly, a taking has occurred when the government seizes part of a homeowner's grounds for a sidewalk or a nature preserve. The government can also accomplish the same goals by simply requiring the landowner to allow public access across a strip of property (as in *Nollan*) or perhaps by ordering the landowner to leave part of the grounds in an untouched natural state. It is not much of a stretch to say that these actions are equivalent to government seizure of land and should be considered "takings." This approach would suggest that the court consider whether a regulation is the functional equivalent of a conventional form of government appropriation. See generally, Humbach, " 'Taking' The Imperial Judiciary Seriously," 42 *Catholic U.L.Rev.* 771, 812–13 (1993); Sax,

"Takings and the Police Power," 44 *Yale L.J.* 36 (1964). How would *Lucas* and *Nollan* be decided under this approach?

4. From the point of view of developers and regulators, the biggest question about *Lucas* is its implications for "non-total" takings. If a regulation reduces the value of land by 75%, for example, does *Lucas* suggest that a taking has occurred? In this situation, should a court use a watered-down version of the *Lucas* test by broadening the nuisance exception to include a broader range of public policies? Or should the court revert to the *Penn Central* analysis?

Justice Scalia does not discuss measurement of damages. Suppose a landowner suffers a 100% loss in value, but that a 70% loss would *not* have been a taking. Should the landowner receive "full" value for her land, or only the 30% increment?

5. One noteworthy aspect of *Lucas* is Justice Scalia's use of a narrowly construed "nuisance exception," at least in total takings cases. (Compare *DeBenedictis,* supra p. 748). This is in sharp contrast to the call by Byrne and others for an expansive new land ethic focusing on ecological interdependency. Justice Scalia's use of nuisance law has attracted attention from commentators, who have suggested that nuisance law has been far more fluid and adaptable than Scalia suggests. For discussion of this aspect of *Lucas,* see Humbach, "Evolving Thresholds of Nuisance and the Takings Clause," 18 *Colum.J.Env.L.* 1 (1993); Lazarus, "Putting the Correct 'Spin' on *Lucas,"* 45 *Stan.L.Rev.* 1411 (1993); Blumm, "Property Myths, Judicial Activism, and the *Lucas* Case," 23 *Env.L.Rep.* 907 (1993); Louis Halper, "Why the Nuisance Knot Can't Undo the Takings Muddle," 28 *Ind. L.J.* 339 (1995). As Lazarus points out, supra at 1426–27, there is some reason to question whether this aspect of *Lucas* will continue to command the support of a majority of the Court.

6. Given the difficulty of applying current doctrine, would legislative clarification of taking law be useful? Numerous proposals have emerged in recent years for federal taking legislation. Typically, the proposals provide for compensation whenever an agency action (sometimes limited to specific arenas such as the ESA or CWA) causes a decline in property value exceeding some specified threshold. For critiques of these proposals, see Joseph Sax, "Takings Legislation: Where It Stands and What is Next," 23 *Ecology L.Q.* 509 (1996); Carol Rose, "A Dozen Propositions on Private Property, Public Rights, and the New Takings Legislation," 53 *Wash. & Lee L. Rev.* 265 (1996). Professor Rose concludes:

> Much of the literature of the takings debate points out the dangers to private owners from uncompensated public appropriations. These dangers are real. Public appropriations can unfairly single out particular private owners to pay for public benefits, and writ large, they mean that we could impoverish ourselves as a nation by discouraging enterprise and undermining commerce. For this reason, we have constitutional judicial oversight of public regulation through the Takings Clause.

> Handouts of public rights to private owners, however, are unfair to the public. They too can impoverish us as a nation because they decimate resources that are diffuse and difficult to turn into private property but that are still immensely valuable to the public as a whole—

now and (it is to be hoped) in the future. Citizens are entitled to expect that their legislatures will safeguard public rights along with private owners and in so doing, uphold the respect for rights—including public rights—that is a necessary part of the moral infrastructure of any property regime and, indeed, of republican government itself.

Id. at 298.

Problems on Property Rights

Drafting Problem. You have been asked to help a "country in transition" draft a constitutional provision relating to property rights. The country in question is one of many in Eastern Europe that are now attempting to move from communism to a market economy and a democratic political regime. On the one hand, the drafters of the new constitution want to make it clear that they have abandoned communism in favor of a market economy. They also want to provide reassurance to urgently needed foreign investors, who may be afraid that their investments will be directly expropriated or regulated into oblivion. On the other hand, as in many formerly communist countries, the drafters are well aware that communism has left as one of its legacies a series of environmental disasters. They have no desire to cripple environmental regulation, nor do they expect their government to have unlimited funds for compensating property owners. Also, they do not want to use vague language and leave the subject to judicial interpretation; instead, they want as much as possible to provide clear constitutional guidelines. Try drafting a concise provision dealing with the subject, along with brief explanatory notes comparing your proposal with U.S. taking law.

Problem on Ambiguous Property Rights. Under a federal statute, unused portions of railroad rights-of-way may be converted to public hiking and bike trails. Typically, railroads acquired these rights-of-way in the late 19th century. State law was not entirely clear about whether these were simply easements or fee interests in the land, but a federal court concluded that they were actually easements (even in one case where the deed purported to transfer a fee simple), and that a change from railroad to bicycle use would not be encompassed within the easement under state law. As the court remarked, it was "compelled to rule on the consequences of a state of facts occurring some years ago, based on the law of Vermont, law that must be extracted from cases none of which are directly on point." Under a series of federal laws, the railroad's use of the right-of-way was intensively regulated, including a requirement of government approval before the railroad line was abandoned, and (under later statute) a requirement that the railroad offer to sell the right-of-way to local governmental authorities for public use. On these facts, should the federal government be required to compensate the current owners of the surrounding land for the use of the bike paths? For conflicting views on this issue, see *Preseault v. United States*, 100 F.3d 1525 (Fed. Cir. 1996). How would you resolve the issues on the basis of current Supreme Court precedent?

As noted just before the beginning of this section, the current property regime has been attacked from both the "ecological" and "property rights" perspectives. So far, the majority of the Court has shown more sympathy for the latter perspective, but has failed to make the fundamental changes in takings law desired by property rights advocates. In the next subsection, we will consider a recurring conflict between property and ecological values. This conflict arises when the federal government blocks development of wetlands in the name of environmental values.

2. DEVELOPMENT RESTRICTIONS ON PRIVATE WETLANDS

Wetlands were once considered worthless swamps. Today, however, they are understood to have many valuable characteristics:

> Variously dry, wet, or anywhere between, wetlands are by their nature protean. Such constant change makes wetlands ecologically rich; they are often as diverse as rain forests. These shallow water-fed systems are central to the life cycle of many plants and animals, some of them endangered. They provide a habitat as well as spawning grounds for an extraordinary variety of creatures and nesting areas for migratory birds. Some wetlands even perform a global function. The northern peat lands of Canada, Alaska and Eurasia, in particular, may help moderate climatic change by serving as a sink for the greenhouse gas carbon dioxide.

> Wetlands also have commercial and utilitarian functions. They are sources of lucrative harvests of wild rice, fur-bearing animals, fish and shellfish. Wetlands limit the damaging effects of waves, convey and store floodwaters, trap sediment and reduce pollution— the last attribute has earned them the sobriquet "nature's kidneys."

Kusler, Mitsch and Larson, "Wetlands," *Scientific American* 64B (January 1994). As a result of this shift in awareness, governmental policy has shifted from encouragement of draining and filling wetlands to support for preservation and restricted development. The federal government has taken the lead in protecting wetlands.

Federal regulation of dredging and filling activities dates back to the Rivers and Harbors Appropriation Act of 1899. Section 13 of the Act prohibits discharge of "any refuse" other than liquid sewage into navigable waters. 33 U.S.C.A. § 407. The Supreme Court later construed this as a ban on water pollution.[e] Section 10 of the Act prohibits the creation of "any obstruction" to navigation, without permission from Congress. 33 U.S.C.A. § 403. At least since the passage of NEPA, issuance of a permit must be based on consideration of a broad range of environmental factors.

e. *United States v. Standard Oil Co.,* 384 U.S. 224, 86 S.Ct. 1427, 16 L.Ed.2d 492 (1966); *United States v. Pennsylvania Industrial Chemical Corp.,* 411 U.S. 655, 93 S.Ct. 1804, 36 L.Ed.2d 567 (1973). Section 402(a)(5) of the Clean Water Act terminates the permit program administered by the Army Corps of Engineers in the wake of these decisions.

The permit program is now part of the Clean Water Act. Section 404 of the Clean Water Act establishes a separate permit system for discharges of dredged or fill materials into navigable waters. (Note that this covers discharges. What about draining? See *United States v. Mango*, 997 F.Supp. 264 (N.D.N.Y.1998) (not covered).) Courts have been vigorous in remedying violations of these provisions, even issuing orders for restoration of areas to their natural states. For a detailed overview of federal wetlands regulation, see Strand, "Federal Wetlands Law: Part I," 23 *Env.L.Rep.* 10185 (1993); "Federal Wetlands Law: Part II," id. at 10284.

There has been considerable controversy about the Clean Water Act's coverage of wetlands. Under the Rivers and Harbors Act, wetlands were not covered. Traditionally, the jurisdiction of the Army Corps of Engineers only extended to navigable waters. But the Clean Water Act is much more expansive. *United States v. Ashland Oil and Transportation Co.*, 504 F.2d 1317 (6th Cir.1974), holds that the Clean Water Act extends to any waters flowing into any navigable stream.[f] The court's discussion of the constitutional issue is noteworthy:

> Obviously water pollution is a health threat to the water supply of the nation. It endangers our agriculture by rendering water unfit for irrigation. It can end the public use and enjoyment of our magnificent rivers and lakes for fishing, for boating, and for swimming. These health and welfare concerns are, of course, proper subjects for Congressional attention because of their many impacts upon interstate commerce generally. But water pollution is also a direct threat to navigation—the first interstate commerce system in this country's history and still a very important one.

> * * *

> We also know (and we take judicial notice) that two of the important rivers of this circuit, the Rouge River in Dearborn, Michigan, and the Cuyahoga River in Cleveland, Ohio, reached a point of pollution by flammable materials in the last ten years that they repeatedly caught fire. Such pollution is an obvious hazard to navigation which Congress has every right to seek to abate under its interstate commerce powers.

> It would, of course, make a mockery of those powers if its authority to control pollution was limited to the bed of the navigable stream itself. The tributaries which join to form the river could then be used as open sewers as far as federal regulation was concerned.

f. The expansion of federal jurisdiction under the Clean Water Act has raised problems concerning the treatment of minor, routine changes in water use. When a farmer digs a ditch which connects to an existing drainage system, must he get a federal permit? The 1977 amendments to the Act exempt a number of "normal farming, silviculture, and ranching activities" from the § 404 permit requirement for dredging and filling, as well as authorizing use of general permits for other activities. Section 404(e)(1), (f)(1). The general permits are not blanket exemptions, but instead contain numerous qualifications and restrictions. See *United States v. Marathon Dev. Corp.*, 867 F.2d 96 (1st Cir.1989).

The navigable part of the river could become a mere conduit for upstream waste.

Such a situation would have vast impact on interstate commerce. States with cities and industries situated upstream on the nonnavigable tributaries of our great rivers could freely use them for dumping raw sewage and noxious industrial wastes upon their downstream neighboring states. There would be great pressure upon the upstream states to allow such usage. Reduced industrial costs and lower taxes thus resulting would tend to place industries, cities and states located on navigable rivers at a considerable competitive disadvantage in interstate commerce. In such a situation industrial frontage on a creek which flowed ultimately into a navigable stream would become valuable as an access point to an effectively unrestricted sewer.

Given this broad interpretation of the Act's coverage, application of the CWA to at least some wetlands was inevitable. During the Reagan Administration, the Corps' expansive jurisdiction over wetlands became a matter of political controversy, causing the Corps to vacillate in its commitment. See Comment, "Corps Recasts § 404 Permit Program, Braces for Political, Legal Skirmishes," 13 *Env.L.Rep.* 10128 (1983). As the next case demonstrates, the controversy spilled over into the courts.

UNITED STATES v. RIVERSIDE BAYVIEW HOMES, INC.

Supreme Court of the United States, 1985.
474 U.S. 121, 106 S.Ct. 455, 88 L.Ed.2d 419.

[A regulation of the Army Corps defines "waters of the United States" to include "freshwater wetlands" that are adjacent to other waters that themselves are subject to the CWA. Wetlands, in turn, are defined to include "those areas that are inundated or saturated by surface or ground water at a frequency and duration sufficient to support, and that under normal circumstances do support, a prevalence of vegetation typically adapted for life in saturated soil conditions." After Riverside Bayview Homes began fill operations on its property near a lake, the Corps filed suit in federal court for an injunction. The Court of Appeals construed the regulation to apply only to wetlands that are flooded by adjacent navigable waters often enough to support aquatic vegetation. The court's rationale was that a broader definition might constitute a taking.]

Justice White delivered the opinion for a unanimous Court.

The question whether the Corps of Engineers may demand that respondent obtain a permit before placing fill material on its property is primarily one of regulatory and statutory interpretation: we must determine whether respondent's property is an "adjacent wetland" within the meaning of the applicable regulation, and, if so, whether the Corps' jurisdiction over "navigable waters" gives it statutory authority to regulate discharges of fill material into such a wetland. In this connection, we first consider the Court of Appeals' position that the Corps' regulatory authority under the statute and its implementing regulations must be narrowly construed to avoid a taking without just compensation in violation of the Fifth Amendment.

We have frequently suggested that governmental land-use regulation may under extreme circumstances amount to a "taking" of the affected property. We have never precisely defined those circumstances, but our general approach was summed up in *Agins v. Tiburon* [summarized on p. 748 supra], where we stated that the application of land-use regulations to a particular piece of property is a taking only "if the ordinance does not substantially advance legitimate state interests * * * or denies an owner economically viable use of his land." Moreover, we have made it quite clear that the mere assertion of regulatory jurisdiction by a governmental body does not constitute a regulatory taking. The reasons are obvious. A requirement that a person obtain a permit before engaging in a certain use of his or her property does not itself "take" the property in any sense: after all, the very existence of a permit system implies that permission may be granted, leaving the landowner free to use the property as desired. Moreover, even if the permit is denied, there may be other viable uses available to the owner. Only when a permit is denied and the effect of the denial is to prevent "economically viable" use of the land in question can it be said that a taking has occurred.

If neither the imposition of the permit requirement itself nor the denial of a permit necessarily constitutes a taking, it follows that the Court of Appeals erred in concluding that a narrow reading of the Corps' regulatory jurisdiction over wetlands was "necessary" to avoid "a serious taking problem." We have held that, in general, "[e]quitable relief is not available to enjoin an alleged taking of private property for a public use, duly authorized by law, when a suit for compensation can be brought against the sovereign subsequent to a taking." This maxim rests on the principle that so long as compensation is available for those whose property is in fact taken, the governmental action is not unconstitutional. For precisely the same reason, the possibility that the application of a regulatory program may in some instances result in the taking of individual pieces of property is no justification for the use of narrowing constructions to curtail the program if compensation will in any event be available in those cases where a taking has occurred. * * *

Purged of its spurious constitutional overtones, the question whether the regulation at issue requires respondent to obtain a permit before filling its property is an easy one. The regulation extends the Corps' authority under § 404 to all wetlands adjacent to navigable or interstate waters and their tributaries. Wetlands, in turn, are defined as lands that are "inundated *or saturated* by surface *or ground water* at a frequency and duration sufficient to support, and that under normal circumstances do support, a prevalence of vegetation typically adapted for life in saturated soil conditions." The plain language of the regulation refutes the Court of Appeals' conclusion that inundation or "frequent flooding" by the adjacent body of water is a *sine qua non* of a wetland under the regulation. Indeed, the regulation could hardly state more clearly that saturation by either surface or ground water is sufficient to bring an area within the category of wetlands, provided that the saturation is sufficient to and does support wetland vegetation.

* * *

On a purely linguistic level, it may appear unreasonable to classify "lands," wet or otherwise, as "waters." Such a simplistic response, however, does justice neither to the problem faced by the Corps in defining the scope of its authority under § 404(a) nor to the realities of the problem of water pollution that the Clean Water Act was intended to combat. In determining the limits of its power to regulate discharges under the Act, the Corps must necessarily choose some point at which water ends and land begins. Our common experience tells us that this is often no easy task: the transition from water to solid ground is not necessarily or even typically an abrupt one. Rather, between open waters and dry land may lie shallows, marshes, mudflats, swamps, bogs—in short, a huge array of areas that are not wholly aquatic but nevertheless fall far short of being dry land. Where on this continuum to find the limit of "waters" is far from obvious.

Faced with such a problem of defining the bounds of its regulatory authority, an agency may appropriately look to the legislative history and underlying policies of its statutory grants of authority. Neither of these sources provides unambiguous guidance for the Corps in this case, but together they do support the reasonableness of the Corps' approach of defining adjacent wetlands as "waters" within the meaning of § 404(a). Section 404 originated as part of the Federal Water Pollution Control Act Amendments of 1972, which constituted a comprehensive legislative attempt "to restore and maintain the chemical, physical, and biological integrity of the Nation's waters." CWA § 101. This objective incorporated a broad, systemic view of the goal of maintaining and improving water quality: as the House Report on the legislation put it, "the word 'integrity' * * * refers to a condition in which the natural structure and function of ecosystems is maintained." Protection of aquatic ecosystems, Congress recognized, demanded broad federal authority to control pollution, for "[w]ater moves in hydrologic cycles and it is essential that discharge of pollutants be controlled at the source."

In keeping with these views, Congress chose to define the waters covered by the Act broadly. Although the Act prohibits discharges into "navigable waters," the Act's definition of "navigable waters" as "the waters of the United States" makes it clear that the term "navigable" as used in the Act is of limited import. In adopting this definition of "navigable waters," Congress evidently intended to repudiate limits that had been placed on federal regulation by earlier water pollution control statutes and to exercise its powers under the Commerce Clause to regulate at least some waters that would not be deemed "navigable" under the classical understanding of that term.

Of course, it is one thing to recognize that Congress intended to allow regulation of waters that might not satisfy traditional tests of navigability; it is another to assert that Congress intended to abandon traditional notions of "waters" and include in that term "wetlands" as well. Nonetheless, the evident breadth of congressional concern for protection of water quality and aquatic ecosystems suggests that it is reasonable for the Corps to interpret the term "waters" to encompass wetlands adjacent to waters as more conventionally defined. Following the lead of the Environmental Protection Agency, the Corps has determined that wetlands adjacent to navigable waters do as a general matter play a key role in protecting and enhancing water quality:

> The regulation of activities that cause water pollution cannot rely on * * * artificial lines * * * but must focus on all waters that together form the entire aquatic system.

> Water moves in hydrologic cycles, and the pollution of this part of the aquatic system, regardless of whether it is above or below an ordinary high water mark, or mean high tide line, will affect the water quality of the other waters within that aquatic system.

> For this reason, the landward limit of Federal jurisdiction under Section 404 must include any adjacent wetlands that form the border of or are in reasonable proximity to other waters of the United States, as these wetlands are part of this aquatic system.

We cannot say that the Corps' conclusion that adjacent wetlands are inseparably bound up with the "waters" of the United States—based as it is on the Corps' and EPA's technical expertise—is unreasonable. In view of the breadth of federal regulatory authority contemplated by the Act itself and the inherent difficulties of defining precise bounds to regulable waters, the Corps' ecological judgment about the relationship between waters and their adjacent wetlands provides an adequate basis for a legal judgment that adjacent wetlands may be defined as waters under the Act.

This holds true even for wetlands that are not the result of flooding or permeation by water having its source in adjacent bodies of open water. The Corps has concluded that wetlands may affect the water quality of adjacent lakes, rivers, and streams even when the waters of those bodies do not actually inundate the wetlands. For example, wetlands that are not flooded by adjacent waters may still tend to drain into those waters. In such circumstances, the Corps has concluded that wetlands may serve to filter and purify water draining into adjacent bodies of water, and to slow the flow of surface runoff into lakes, rivers, and streams and thus prevent flooding and erosion. In addition, adjacent wetlands may "serve significant natural biological functions, including food chain production, general habitat, and nesting, spawning, rearing and resting sites for aquatic * * * species." In short, the Corps has concluded that wetlands adjacent to lakes, rivers, streams, and other bodies of water may function as integral parts of the aquatic environment even when the moisture creating the wetlands does not find its source in the adjacent bodies of water. Again, we cannot say that the Corps' judgment on these matters is unreasonable, and we therefore conclude that a definition of "waters of the United States" encompassing all wetlands adjacent to other bodies of water over which the Corps has jurisdiction is a permissible interpretation of the Act. Because respondent's property is part of a wetland that actually abuts on a navigable waterway, respondent was required to have a permit in this case.[18]

Notes

1. For approving commentary on the main case, see Comment, "The Supreme Court Endorses A Broad Reading of Corps Wetland Jurisdiction Under FWPCA § 404," 16 *Env.L.Rptr.* 10008 (1986). *Bayview* led several lower courts to uphold broad claims of jurisdiction on behalf of the Corps. See *United States v. Banks,* 115 F.3d 916 (11th Cir.1997) (wetlands were "adjacent" despite half-mile gap and debatable hydrological connection); *United States v. Pozsgai,* 999 F.2d 719 (3d Cir.1993) (wetlands covered by CWA because adjacent to tributaries of navigable stream); *Rueth v. U.S. EPA,* 13 F.3d 227 (7th Cir.1993) (wetlands covered because used by migratory birds).

2. Controversy over the scope of § 404 continues. The National Academy of Sciences issued a report in 1995 suggesting a redefinition in terms of wetland hydrology, exhibiting "constant or recurrent, shallow inundation or saturation at or near the surface of the substrate,"with diagnostic features such as hydric soils and hydrophytic vegetation. So far, this proposal has not resulted in any legal changes, although it may have helped block congressional efforts to restrict the definition of wetlands further. See Margaret Strand, "Recent Developments in Federal Wetlands Law: Part I," 26 *Env. L. Rep.* 10283, 10286–87 (1996); Adler, "Two Views of a Swamp," 148 *Science News* 56 (July 22, 1995).

3. Does the *Lopez* decision [supra p. 215] limit federal regulatory authority over wetlands? In *Leslie Salt v. United States,* 55 F.3d 1388 (9th Cir.1995), cert. denied 516 U.S. 955, 116 S.Ct. 407, 133 L.Ed.2d 325 (1995), the court of appeals upheld federal jurisdiction over artificially created ponds that were dry most of the year but were used by large numbers of migratory birds. Dissenting from denial of certiorari, Justice Thomas argued that the Court should distinguish between "items of interstate commerce" and "simply airborne interstate travelers." He added: "that substantial interstate commerce depends on the continued existence of migratory birds does not give the Corps carte blanche authority to regulate every property that migratory birds use or could use as habitat." 116 S.Ct. at 407, 409. See also

[handwritten margin note: San Francisco Bay b/c connected to navigable waters.]

---

18. Of course, it may well be that not every adjacent wetland is of great importance to the environment of adjoining bodies of water. But the existence of such cases does not seriously undermine the Corps' decision to define all adjacent wetlands as "waters." If it is reasonable for the Corps to conclude that in the majority of cases, adjacent wetlands have significant effects on water quality and the aquatic ecosystem, its definition can stand. That the definition may include some wetlands that are not significantly intertwined with the ecosystem of adjacent waterways is of little moment, for where it appears that a wetland covered by the Corps' definition is in fact lacking in importance to the aquatic environment—or where its importance is outweighed by other values—the Corps may always allow development of the wetland for other uses simply by issuing a permit.

United States v. Wilson, 133 F.3d 251 (4th Cir.1997) (holding that Corps exceeded statutory authority in covering all waters that could possibly affect interstate commerce, noting that this regulation was "constitutionally troubling" after *Lopez*).

* * *

The next case explores the factors to be considered in granting a § 404 permit.

SYLVESTER v. UNITED STATES ARMY CORPS OF ENGINEERS

United States Court of Appeals for the Ninth Circuit, 1989.
882 F.2d 407.

[This was a citizen suit against the Corps and a developer, challenging a permit to fill eleven acres of wetlands for a golf course. The golf course was part of a multi-million dollar resort in Squaw Valley, California. The remainder of the resort, consisting of a resort village and ski runs, was to be located on neighboring wetlands. In *Sylvester v. United States Army Corps of Engineers,* 884 F.2d 394 (9th Cir.1989) [*Sylvester I*], the court rejected a NEPA claim, holding that the environmental assessment could be properly limited to the golf course, rather than including the entire project. The court then remanded for consideration of other issues, such as compliance with § 404 of the Clean Water Act. On remand, the district court denied the plaintiff's request for an emergency injunction to halt construction of the golf course, and the plaintiff appealed.]

SNEED, CIRCUIT JUDGE:

First, we turn to Sylvester's claim that the Corps impermissibly accepted Perini's definition of the project as necessitating an on-site, eighteen hole golf course. By accepting this definition, Sylvester contends that the Corps' evaluation of practicable alternatives was skewed in favor of Perini.

The regulations implementing § 404 of the CWA provide that "no discharge of dredged or fill material shall be permitted if there is a *practicable alternative* to the proposed discharge which would have less adverse impact on the aquatic ecosystem, so long as the alternative does not have other significant adverse environmental consequences." The Corps defines a practicable alternative as an alternative that "is available and capable of being done after taking into consideration cost, existing technology, and logistics *in light of overall project purposes.*" [40 C.F.R. § 230.10(a)(2) (emphasis added). Further, because the golf course is not a water dependent activity, the Corps' regulations presume that practicable alternatives are available "unless clearly demonstrated otherwise."

In its Environmental Assessment (EA), the Corps defined the project's purpose as follows:

> To construct an 18–hole, links style, championship golf course and other recreational amenities in conjunction with the development of the proposed Resort at Squaw Creek. Research conducted for the applicant has indicated that a quality 18–hole golf course is an essential element for a successful alpine destination resort.

Sylvester protests that the use of this definition impermissibly skewed the "practicable alternatives" analysis in favor of Perini. Specifically, Sylvester objects to the Corps' failure to consider off-site locations for the golf course, *i.e.,* a site that was not contiguous to the rest of the resort complex. The Corps rejected consideration of such an alternative because it "did not meet [Perini's] basic purpose and need." The Corps did note, however, that two off-site locations were considered but rejected because of insufficient size and the potential for more severe environmental impacts. In evaluating whether a given alternative site is practicable, the Corps may legitimately consider such facts as cost to the applicant and logistics. In addition, the Corps has a duty to consider the applicant's purpose. As the Fifth Circuit observed: "[T]he Corps has a duty to take into account the objectives of the applicant's project. Indeed, it would be bizarre if the Corps were to ignore the purpose for which the applicant seeks a permit and to substitute a purpose it deems more suitable."

Obviously, an applicant cannot define a project in order to preclude the existence of any alternative sites and thus make what is practicable appear impracticable. This court [has] quite properly suggested that the applicant's purpose must be "legitimate." Yet, in determining whether an alternate site is practicable, the Corps is not entitled to reject Perini's genuine and legitimate conclusion that the type of golf course it wishes to construct is economically advantageous to its resort development.

By contrast, an alternative site does not have to accommodate components of a project that are merely incidental to the applicant's *basic* purpose. For example, in *Shoreline Assocs. v. Marsh,* 555 F.Supp. 169, 179 (D.Md.1983), *aff'd,* 725 F.2d 677 (4th Cir.1984), the Corps refused to issue a permit to a developer for building a number of waterfront town houses together with a boat storage and launching facility. The developer argued that the Corps' proposed alternative site for the town houses could not accommodate the boat storage and launch area. The court upheld the Corps' denial of the permit, observing that the boat facilities were merely "incidental" to the town house development.

In this case, it is not the resort buildings that are at issue as were the town houses in *Shoreline.* The location of the resort buildings was fixed by decisions not involving the Corps of Engineers; and we held in *Sylvester I* that the location of the proposed golf course partially on wetlands did not "federalize" the entire development. Rather the issue in this case, *Sylvester II,* is whether this proposed location ignores other reasonable and practicable alternatives, including no golf course at all. Resolution of this issue requires that the relationship of the course to

the entire project be considered. The Corps of Engineers did consider this relationship. Doing so was neither arbitrary nor capricious.   *706 (2)(A)*

In no way does this conclusion conflict with *Sylvester I*. A relationship required to be considered in determining reasonable and practicable alternatives need not be of such significance as would be necessary to "federalize" the entire project. True, the golf course is not incidental to the resort; but then neither is it the compelling force, the centerpiece, of the resort. To illustrate, *Shoreline* would have resembled *Sylvester I* had the only issue been the location of the boat storage and launch sites, the location of the town houses already having been fixed on a site not subject to federal jurisdiction. Obviously the relationship between the town houses and the boat storage and launch sites would be considered in evaluating possible alternative sites of the latter two; equally obvious, this relationship should not "federalize" the entire project.

Notes

1.   There has been considerable dispute about the test to be used for evaluating alternatives under § 404. See Strand, "Federal Wetlands Law: Part II," 23 *Env.L.Rep.* 10284, 10289–91 (1993); Houck, "Hard Choices: The Analysis of Alternatives Under Section 404 of the Clean Water Act and Similar Environmental Laws," 60 *U.Colo.L.Rev.* 773 (1989). See also *Fund for Animals Inc. v. Rice*, 85 F.3d 535 (11th Cir.1996) (Corps. reasonably determined that other sites were environmentally questionable); *Bersani v. United States EPA*, 850 F.2d 36 (2d Cir.1988) (upholding EPA's focus on existence of alternatives at time applicant acquired sites, rather than at time of permit application).

2.   Another important controversy has concerned mitigation measures, and in particular, adoption of a "no-net loss" policy. President Bush endorsed such a policy in his campaign, but later qualified his position. Ultimately, EPA and the Corps entered into an agreement enunciating a goal of "no net loss," though allowing exceptions from the general duty of "compensatory mitigation" under some circumstances. Gardner, "The Army–EPA Mitigation Agreement: No Retreat from Wetlands Protection," 20 *Env.L.Rep.* 10337 (1990). The Clinton administration made revisions in the Bush plan, without completely satisfying environmentalists. See Blumm, "The Clinton Wetlands Plan: No Net Gain in Wetlands Protection," 9 *J.Land Use & Env.L.* 203 (1994). Of particular interest was the adoption of a favorable attitude toward mitigation banking, which allows developers to create or restore wetlands to compensate for future projects that may destroy wetlands. Id. at 226–28.

For an extensive discussion of mitigation, see Gardner, "Banking on Entrepreneurs: Wetlands, Mitigation Banking, and Takings," 81 *Iowa L. Rev.* 527 (1996). Gardner argues that mitigation banking is underused:

> [A] widespread banking system offers a host of possible benefits. First, from an environmental perspective, there is a greater likelihood that the mitigation will be successful. Second, from the regulated community's viewpoint, mitigation banking should offer more certainty in the permit process. Finally, because a mitigation banking system inures value in a

There should be "no net loss" of wetlands Prob. in implementation.

wetland qua wetland, such a system may reduce the extent to which the regulatory scheme interferes with private property rights.

Id. at 532. He argues that the current program fails to provide sufficient encouragement, partly because of burdensome conditions on banking, and partly because entrepreneurial banking efforts must compete with government-financed banks. Id. at 533.

3.   Professor Houck's 1989 article (cited in note 1, above) also contains some useful statistics about the operation of the § 404 program. In 1987, for example, the Corps received approximately 8600 applications, approved 5071 and denied 397 (the remainder were presumably withdrawn or still pending). More than a third contained mitigation measures. Generally, according to a 1988 GAO study, the Corps adopted mitigation measures suggested by EPA or Fish & Wildlife, but ignores their recommendations to deny permits. 60 U.Colo.L.Rev. at 787–88. By 1989, however, there were some indications that the Corps might be developing a more protective attitude toward wetlands. Id. at 795–98.

4.   If the Corps does deny a permit, the government may then be faced with a taking claim, as in the next case.

DELTONA CORP. v. UNITED STATES

United States Court of Claims, 1981.
657 F.2d 1184.

Kunzig, Judge:

In 1964, plaintiff, Deltona, purchased for $7,500,000 a 10,000 acre parcel in the Florida Gulf coast with the intention of developing a water-oriented residential community, Marco Island. The property, then completely undeveloped, lay astride the mean high water mark and contained large areas of dense mangrove vegetation, including wetlands. Deltona's master plan called for more than 12,000 single family tracts, numerous multifamily sites, school and park areas, shopping districts, marinas, beaches and regular utilities. Structurally, the project revolved about the "finger-fill" or "landfinger" concept and would necessitate considerable dredging and filling as well as the permanent destruction of much of the natural mangrove vegetation.

Deltona divided Marco Island into five construction or permit areas to be built consecutively. These five areas, in order of scheduled completion, were Marco River, Roberts Bay, Collier Bay, Barfield Bay and Big Key. Each separate stage would take three to four years to complete. While partitioned for these limited purposes, in operation, the Marco Island community would be a thoroughly integrated, unified whole.

* * *

The crucial factor in this case is that since the late 1960's the regulatory jurisdiction of the Army Corps of Engineers has substantially expanded pursuant to § 404 of the FWPCA and—under the spur of steadily evolving legislation—the Corps has greatly added to the substantive criteria governing the issuance of dredge and fill permits within its

jurisdiction. Recall that when Deltona initially purchased the Marco Island property in 1964, the regulatory jurisdiction of the Corps was limited to "navigable waters of the United States" and the lone substantive criterion for the issuance of Corps dredge and fill permits was the likely adverse impact upon navigation. Pursuant to this relatively undemanding standard, Deltona routinely succeeded in 1964 in obtaining the first permit for which it applied. By 1976, when the Barfield Bay and Big Key applications were denied, the situation had been radically transformed. The Corps' jurisdiction now extended to all "navigable waters" and the substantive criteria for granting permits had been significantly stiffened. Deltona's particular stumbling block, as we have seen, was its inability to satisfy the Corps' recently inaugurated wetlands protection policy. The impact is self-evident. As the result of an unforeseen change in the law, Deltona is no longer able to capitalize upon a reasonable investment-backed expectation which it had every justification to rely upon until the law began to change.

* * *

Although we have accepted that the expansion of the Corps' regulatory jurisdiction and the stiffening of its requirements for granting permits have substantially frustrated Deltona's reasonable investment-backed expectation with respect to Barfield Bay and Big Key, this development neither "extinguish[es] a fundamental attribute of ownership," nor prevents Deltona from deriving many other economically viable uses from its parcel—however delineated. Indeed, the residual economic value of the land is enormous, both proportionately and absolutely. A few statistics will suffice. In the aggregate, Barfield Bay and Big Key contain only 20% of the total acreage of Deltona's original purchase in 1964 and 33% of the developable lots. All the necessary federal permits for the development of the remainder of Marco Island— Marco River, Roberts Bay, and Collier Bay—have been granted. If we focus solely upon the three construction areas which became subject to the new federal restrictions promulgated during the early 1970's— Collier Bay, Barfield Bay, and Big Key—the salient fact emerges that while Deltona has been blocked from going forward at Barfield Bay and Big Key, it has obtained all the necessary clearances for Collier Bay, a tract approximately 25% of the three areas together. Most striking, even within Barfield Bay and Big Key, there are located 111 acres of uplands which can be developed without obtaining a Corps permit and whose total market value is approximately $2.5 million. Deltona only paid $1.24 million for all of Barfield Bay and Big Key in 1964.

* * *

In *Penn Central* [p. 747 supra], the Supreme Court rejected as "quite simply untenable" the contention that property owners "may establish a 'taking' simply by showing that they have been denied the ability to exploit a property interest that they heretofore had believed was available for development * * *." That is precisely this case. Deltona has been denied the ability to exploit its property by constructing a project that it theretofore had believed "was available for development."

While plaintiff may very well be correct in its alternative assertion that it has been denied the highest and best economic use for its property, it is obvious from the Supreme Court tests we have cited that such an occurrence does *not* form a sufficient predicate for a taking. In effect, the "highest and best use" argument is merely another way of saying that there has been some diminution in value, rather than the complete destruction of all economically viable uses of the property. The Court, however, clearly rejects the notion that diminution in value, by itself, can establish a taking. Notwithstanding the changed phraseology, plaintiff's alternative argument fails as a matter of law.

Notes

1. *Deltona* should be contrasted with two more recent opinions, both written by Judge Plager of the Federal Circuit. The first case, *Florida Rock Industries, Inc. v. United States,* 18 F.3d 1560 (Fed.Cir.1994), involved the denial of a permit to mine limestone lying beneath wetlands. The land had originally been acquired in 1972, before the enactment of the Clean Water Act. The court found that all economic value had not been destroyed, so there was no *Lucas*-type taking. The court remanded, however, for a determination of the extent to which the actual diminution of value should be considered a partial taking. In considering this issue, the lower court was given broad instructions to consider whether the government had acted in a responsible way.

The second case, *Loveladies Harbor, Inc. v. United States,* 28 F.3d 1171 (Fed.Cir.1994), involved a permit denial for the final stage of an ongoing real estate development project. The court relied heavily on *Lucas* to conclude that the permit denial was a taking. The court stressed that "nothing in the state's conduct reflected a considered determination that certain defined activities would violate the state's understanding of its nuisance powers. Nor did Loveladies have the opportunity to decide, at the beginning, whether its investment backed expectations could be realized under the regulatory environment the state later attempted to impose."

Note that both of these opinions are in some sense transition cases, involving project planning and investments pre-dating the 1972 Clean Water Act. Presumably, there is a limited stock of such cases. Will post–1972 investments in wetlands development be given less judicial protection? See *Good v. United States,* 39 Fed. Cl. 81, 109–13 (1997) (no "reasonable investment-backed expectations" when investment made after pervasive regulatory scheme in place).

For discussions of the Federal Circuit's approach, see Margaret Strand, "Recent Developments in Federal Wetlands Law: Part III," 26 *Env. L. Rep.* 10399, 10402–03 (1996); Richard Ausness, "Regulatory Takings and Wetlands Protection in the Post–Lucas Era," 30 *Land & Water L. Rev.* 349 (1995); Michael Blumm, "The End of Environmental Law: Libertarian Property, Natural Law, and the Just Compensation Clause in the Federal Circuit," 25 *Env. L.* 171 (1995)(Federal Circuit's decisions "are out of step with Supreme Court precedent, the history and purpose of the Just Compensation Clause, and are extremely destabilizing to all land use and environmental regulation." Id at 197). These taking claims may also have deterred state governments from taking an active role in administering § 404. See Houck and Holland, "Federalism in Wetlands Regulation," 54 *Md.L.Rev.* 1242, 1258 (1995).

2.   One difficult issue raised in *Deltona* is the "denominator" problem: where the tract includes some land covered by the permit denial and some that is not, which area is used to determine if there has been a total taking? The Court of Federal Claims has suggested a multi-part test, including "the degree of contiguity, the acquisition dates, the extent to which the protected lands increase the value of the other lands," and especially "how the economic expectations of the claimant, with respect to the parcel at issue, have shaped the owner's actual and projected use of the property." An owner "who treats a series of parcels as one property for the purposes of development, financing, planning and utilization, cannot then segregate the properties for the purpose of establishing a taking claim." *Forest Properties, Inc. v. United States*, 39 Fed. Cl. 56, 73 (1997). See also Poirier, "Property, Environment, Community," 12 *J.Env.L. & Lit.* 43, 79 (1997) (test should ask whether developer had separated the sensitive lands from the rest of the tract unreasonably or in bad faith).

3.   How would you advise the Corps or a state regulatory commission concerning the constitutionality of denying a permit to develop a given piece of wetland? What factors would you consider in attempting to determine the probable judicial response to a taking claim? How would you try to build a record favorable to your client?

4.   Should we consider other alternatives to the taking/no taking dichotomy? Possibilities might be the use of transferable development rights like those involved in the *Penn Central* case [supra p. 747]; a broader compensatory scheme financed by a fee for wetland development; a tax on wetland development geared to an estimate of the resulting ecological damage; acquisition of easements either voluntarily or through eminent domain before development is imminent; or steps to decrease economic incentives for developing wetlands (for example, denying tax advantages to such projects or to the ultimate users of the land).

C. QUASI–PUBLIC PROPERTY

1. PUBLIC TRUST AND RELATED DOCTRINES

Blackacre, the archetypal form of property in our society (or at least in Property classes), is typically privately owned. On the other hand, different considerations apply to bodies of water. Like streets, water bodies historically have served as major transportation arteries. Richard Epstein has argued that control of such water bodies should not be allowed to fall into private hands, because private ownership in this context is unconducive to efficient use. See Epstein, "The Public Trust Doctrine," 7 *Cato J.* 411 (1987). (For a critique of Epstein's view see Cohen, "The Public Trust Doctrine: An Economic Perspective," 29 *Cal.W.L.Rev.* 239 (1992).) Whether for Epstein's reason or otherwise,

Anglo–American law has traditionally given the sovereign special prerogatives with respect to waterbodies, at the expense of the private parties who nominally hold title. See Lazarus, "Changing Conceptions of Property and Sovereignty in Natural Resources: Questioning the Public Trust Doctrine," 71 *Iowa L.Rev.* 631 (1986). In this subsection, we will explore the legal doctrines that render many bodies of water quasi-public property. We begin with the foundational American case.

ILLINOIS CENTRAL RAILROAD CO. v. ILLINOIS

Supreme Court of the United States, 1892.
146 U.S. 387, 13 S.Ct. 110, 36 L.Ed. 1018.

JUSTICE FIELD delivered the opinion of the court.

[In 1869 the Illinois legislature granted title to certain submerged lands under Lake Michigan to the Illinois Central Railroad. When the bill was introduced, it had conveyed these lands to the City of Chicago, but somehow before final passage the grantee had been changed to the railroad. In 1873, the State repealed the 1869 Act making the grant. Illinois sued to quiet title.]

The question, therefore, to be considered is whether the legislature was competent to thus deprive the State of its ownership of the submerged lands in the harbor of Chicago, and of the consequent control of its waters; or, in other words, whether the railroad corporation can hold the lands and control the waters by the grant, against any future exercise of power over them by the State.

That the State holds the title to the lands under the navigable waters of Lake Michigan, within its limits, in the same manner that the State holds title to soils under tide water, by the common law, we have already shown, and that title necessarily carries with it control over the waters above them whenever the lands are subjected to use. But it is a title different in character from that which the State holds in lands intended for sale. It is different from the title which the United States holds in the public lands which are open to preemption and sale. It is a title held in trust for the people of the State that they may enjoy the navigation of the waters, carry on commerce over them, and have liberty of fishing therein freed from the obstruction or interference of private parties. The interest of the people in the navigation of the waters and in commerce over them may be improved in many instances by the erection of wharves, docks and piers therein, for which purpose the State may grant parcels of the submerged lands; and, so long as their disposition is made for such purpose, no valid objections can be made to the grants. * * * The trust devolving upon the State for the public, and which can only be discharged by the management and control of property in which the public has an interest, cannot be relinquished by a transfer of the property. The control of the State for the purposes of the trust can never be lost, except as to such parcels as are used in promoting the interests of the public therein, or can be disposed of without any substantial impairment of the public interest in the lands and waters remaining.

* * * A grant of all the lands under the navigable waters of a State has never been adjudged to be within the legislative power; and any attempted grant of the kind would be held, if not absolutely void on its face, as subject to revocation. The State can no more abdicate its trust over property in which the whole people are interested, like navigable waters and soils under them, so as to leave them entirely under the use and control of private parties, except in the instance of parcels mentioned for the improvement of the navigation and use of the waters, or when parcels can be disposed of without impairment of the public interest in what remains, than it can abdicate its police powers in the administration of government and the preservation of the peace. In the administration of government the use of such powers may for a limited period be delegated to a municipality or other body, but there always remains with the State the right to revoke those powers and exercise them in a more direct manner, and one more conformable to its wishes. So with trusts connected with public property, or property of a special character, like lands under navigable waters, they cannot be placed entirely beyond the direction and control of the State.

The harbor of Chicago is of immense value to the people of the State of Illinois in the facilities it affords to its vast and constantly increasing commerce; and the idea that its legislature can deprive the State of control over its bed and waters and place the same in the hands of a private corporation created for a different purpose, one limited to transportation of passengers and freight between distant points and the city, is a proposition that cannot be defended.

* * * It is hardly conceivable that the legislature can divest the State of the control and management of this harbor and vest it absolutely in a private corporation.

* * * The position advanced by the railroad company in support of its claim to the ownership of the submerged lands and the right to the erection of wharves, piers and docks at its pleasure, or for its business in the harbor of Chicago, would place every harbor in the country at the mercy of a majority of the legislature of the State in which the harbor is situated.

Notes

1. *Illinois Central* holds that certain lands are held by the state in trust for the people, and that legislative actions are void (or at least voidable) if a court finds they violate the trust. With reference to the federal government, the Supreme Court has adopted only half of this doctrine:

> "All the public lands of the nation are held in trust for the people of the whole country." *United States v. Trinidad Coal & Coking Co.*, 137 U.S. 160, 11 S.Ct. 57, 34 L.Ed. 640 (1890). And it is not for the courts to say how that trust shall be administered. That is for Congress to determine. The courts cannot compel it to set aside the lands for settlement, or to suffer them to be used for agricultural or grazing

[handwritten margin note: non-justiciable / it is a political ques.]

purposes, nor interfere when, in the exercise of its discretion, Congress establishes a forest reserve for what it decides to be national and public purposes. In the same way and in the exercise of the same trust it may disestablish a reserve, and devote the property to some other national and public purpose. These are rights incident to proprietorship, to say nothing of the power of the United States as a sovereign over the property belonging to it.

Light v. United States, 220 U.S. 523, 537, 31 S.Ct. 485, 488, 55 L.Ed. 570 (1911). (Note that Article IV, § 3 of the Constitution is a grant of plenary power to Congress to dispose of public lands.) *Light* implies that Congressional actions that arguably violate the public trust are nevertheless immune from judicial scrutiny. For a thoughtful discussion of whether public trust concepts could inform judicial decisions regarding public land law, see Wilkinson, "The Public Trust Doctrine in Public Land Law," 14 *U.Cal.Davis L.Rev.* 269 (1980).

2. For a critique of *Illinois Central,* see Eric Pearson, "*Illinois Central* and the Public Trust Doctrine in State Law," 15 *Va. Env. L. Rev.* 713 (1996). Pearson argues that the Court underestimated the amount of sovereign control which the state would retain even if title to the lake bed had actually passed to the railroad. He also argues that the state law was actually intended merely to authorize the railroad to operate a wharf, rather than permanently transferring title to property.

3. Note how the public trust doctrine can be used to avoid a "taking" claim. The Illinois Central Railroad cannot claim that its rights in the lake bed have been taken without just compensation, because all the railroad ever had was a revocable title. One important function of the public trust doctrine is thus to eliminate certain taking claims. The Washington Supreme Court has held that a statutory ban on dredging and filling tidelands is not normally a taking, because the owner never had the right to engage in those activities, but that there may be a taking if the ban denies the owner the right to engage in all profitable activities—provided those activities were permissible under the public trust doctrine before the statute was passed. See *Orion Corp. v. State,* 109 Wn.2d 621, 747 P.2d 1062 (1987). See also *Marine One, Inc. v. Manatee County,* 898 F.2d 1490 (11th Cir.1990) (rescission of marine construction permit cannot be considered a taking).

Oddly enough, the *Lucas* decision (supra p. 754) does not mention the public trust doctrine as an exception to the categorical rule that a total deprivation of use entitles the property owner to compensation. However, the logic of Justice Scalia's opinion seems fully applicable here: the landowner is not entitled to compensation because, from the moment of acquisition, certain uses (here, perhaps all uses) were simply never part of the landowner's bundle of rights. The government can't "take" from the private owner what she never owned in the first place. See Babcock, "Has the U.S. Supreme Court Finally Drained the Swamp of Takings Jurisprudence?," 19 *Harv.Env.L.Rev.* 1 (1995).

BOONE v. KINGSBURY

Supreme Court of California, 1928.
206 Cal. 148, 273 P. 797, cert. denied 280 U.S.
517, 50 S.Ct. 66, 74 L.Ed. 587 (1929).

SEAWELL, J.

[The petitioners were applicants for permits to prospect for oil and other minerals on tidal lands near a small cove. The respondent refused to issue permits on the ground that the actions proposed by the petitioners would interfere with fishing and navigation, and that the statute authorizing issuance therefore violated the public trust doctrine.]

We do not deem it necessary to pursue the question of the title to tide-lands to the extent that the subject has been discussed by counsel, for the reason that the act does not purport to divest the state of its title to any part of its tidelands, but merely grants to its permittees a license or privilege of extracting minerals from the soil, the ownership of which is held in its proprietary right, for a term of years, upon an acreage and royalty basis. It is clear that one of the purposes of the Legislature by the enactment of said chapter 303, was to give to the citizens an opportunity to intercept the large volumes of oil gravitating seaward to inextricable depths, and to reduce to useful purposes oil, gas and mineral deposits reposing beneath the ocean's bed. The commercial value of these subterranean products is enormous. The contribution made to commerce and the varied industries of the world and to the comfort of the race by the modern intensive development of the oil and gas industry is not surpassed, if it is equaled, by any other of the natural agencies or physical forces which are contributing to the material welfare of mankind, including electrical energy. * * *

* * *

None of the lands involved in these proceedings front upon any incorporated city, nor are they situated upon a harbor, bay, inlet or estuary. Neither are they within the inhibitions of the distance limitations or the sale and grant clauses of article 15, § 3, state Constitution, which provides: "All tide lands within two miles of any incorporated city or town of this state, and fronting on the waters of any harbor, estuary, bay, or inlet, used for the purposes of navigation, shall be withheld from grant or sale to private persons, partnerships, or corporations."

The license or privilege authorizing the permittee to prospect and mine tidelands is denominated by the act a lease, but in practical effect it strongly partakes of the character of a contract to prospect or mine said tidelands on a share or percentage basis. In no sense does the state part with title to its tidelands. More than this, it expressly "reserves from sale except upon a rental and royalty basis" all coal, oil, oil shale, phosphate, sodium and other mineral deposits in lands belonging to the state, and persons authorized by said act to prospect for, mine and remove such deposits are restricted to as small a portion of the surface area as may be reasonably required for mining and removing such deposits. In this respect the instant case is widely different from *Illinois Central* [supra p. 778].

* * *

With full knowledge of the subject, the Legislature found that there was nothing in the drilling and operation of oil wells conducted in the manner provided by the statute that would substantially impair the paramount public interest in the lands and water remaining, and upon a consideration of the case we find nothing that would justify us in holding that the finding of the Legislature, which is conclusive in such matters is not fully supported by the facts. To justify an interference by courts with the right of the Legislature to alienate tide or submerged lands, it must appear that such grants do or will impair the power of succeeding Legislatures to regulate, protect, improve, or develop the public rights of navigation and fishing. * * *

By the provisions of the act the state reserves a supervisory control over the entire subject-matter and ample provision is made for a cancellation of the lease or privilege upon a violation of any of its numerous terms designed for the protection of the state. But aside from the precautionary steps taken by the state to safeguard the public's interests, the law vouchsafes ample protection to the paramount rights of the public in the absence of express statutory provisions on the subject.

"The words of the Constitution are to be considered as incorporated in the grant or patent [granting tidelands] the same as if inserted therein. They become a part of it and qualify it, so that the estate granted is limited to the permitted uses." *Forestier v. Johnson,* 164 Cal. 24, 127 P. 156. So, in the instant case, should said permittees offer any substantial interference incompatible with navigation, fishing, or commerce, the state and federal government would have the unquestionable right to abate it. * * *

* * *

No uncertainty can exist as to the rights of the state to absolutely alienate its tide and submerged lands when they are unfit for navigation, are useless as aids of commerce and possess no substantial value as fishing grounds. The policy of this state is and has always been to encourage its citizens to devote waste and unused lands to some useful purpose. The power of the state to absolutely alienate lands perpetually covered by water has been upheld by all courts of the nation, state and federal, where the land so covered was severed from the main body by harbor and other improvements in such manner as to leave the remaining waters of no substantial use to navigation or commerce. It is only in those cases where the reduction of the water area amounts to a substantial interference with navigation and commerce or the fisheries that the absolute power of alienation by the sovereign and its control and dominion over said lands can be questioned.

SHENK, J., dissenting.

I dissent. The statute declared valid by the majority opinion throws open the entire sea coast of California (with the exception of limited areas adjacent to municipalities) for exploration and possession for the development of oil and gas by private parties. This means that from Mexico to the Oregon line a strip of tide and submerged land 3 miles in width and nearly 1,200 miles in length, including the tide and submerged lands along the harbors, bays, estuaries, coves, inlets, and navigable streams and surrounding the coastal islands, is made available for one of the purposes contemplated by the statute. In my opinion the act, in its operation as to all of said lands, is inconsistent with the trust on which the state holds title to the same for the benefit of all of the people of the state for navigation and fishery. The effect of the main opinion is to compel the surveyor-general to issue a prospecting permit and subsequent lease to any qualified person, association, or corporation upon compliance with the formalities prescribed in the act.

MARKS v. WHITNEY

Supreme Court of California, In Bank, 1971.
6 Cal.3d 251, 98 Cal.Rptr. 790, 491 P.2d 374.

McCOMB, JUSTICE.

This is a quiet title action to settle a boundary line dispute caused by overlapping and defective surveys and to enjoin defendants (herein "Whitney") from asserting any claim or right in or to the property of plaintiff Marks. The unique feature here is that a part of Marks' property is tidelands acquired under an 1874 patent issued pursuant to the Act of March 28, 1868; a small portion of these tidelands adjoins almost the entire shoreline of Whitney's upland property. Marks asserted complete ownership of the tidelands and the right to fill and develop them. Whitney opposed on the ground that this would cut off his rights as a littoral owner and as a member of the public in these tidelands and the navigable waters covering them. He requested a declaration in the decree that Marks' title was burdened with a public trust easement; also that it was burdened with certain prescriptive rights claimed by Whitney.

* * *

Appearing as *amici curiae* on the appeal are: the Attorney General, on behalf of the State Lands Commission, the Bay Area Conservation and Development Commission (BCDC) and as chief law enforcement officer of the state[19]; Sierra Club; and Westbay Community Associates.

---

19. California holds the state-wide public easement in tidelands and owns the submerged lands abutting the tidelands. The Legislature has vested in the State Lands Commission "All jurisdiction and authority remaining in the State as to tidelands and submerged lands as to which grants have been or may be made" and has given the commission exclusive administration and control of such lands. (Pub.Resources Code, § 6301.) BCDC is charged with specific duties concerning dredging and filling in San Francisco Bay (Gov.Code, §§ 66600–66610). The Attorney General is presently involved in litigation involving lands in San Francisco Bay which were patented under

Questions: First. Are these tidelands subject to the public trust; if so, should the judgment so declare?

Yes. Regardless of the issue of Whitney's standing to raise this issue the court may take judicial notice of public trust burdens in quieting title to tidelands. This matter is of great public importance, particularly in view of population pressures, demands for recreational property, and the increasing development of seashore and waterfront property. A present declaration that the title of Marks in these tidelands is burdened with a public easement may avoid needless future litigation.

[The court then traced the development of the public trust doctrine in California].

The public uses to which tidelands are subject are sufficiently flexible to encompass changing public needs. In administering the trust the state is not burdened with an outmoded classification favoring one mode of utilization over another. There is a growing public recognition that one of the most important public uses of the tidelands—a use encompassed within the tidelands trust—is the preservation of those lands in their natural state, so that they may serve as ecological units for scientific study, as open space, and as environments which provide food and habitat for birds and marine life, and which favorably affect the scenery and climate of the area. It is not necessary to here define precisely all the public uses which encumber tidelands.

* * *

* * * It is within the province of the trier of fact to determine whether any particular use made or asserted by Whitney in or over these tidelands would constitute an infringement either upon the *jus privatum* of Marks or upon the *jus publicum* of the people. It is also within the province of the trier of fact to determine whether any particular use to which Marks wishes to devote his tidelands constitutes an unlawful infringement upon the *jus publicum* therein. It is a political question, within the wisdom and power of the Legislature, acting within the scope of its duties as trustee, to determine whether public trust uses should be modified or extinguished and to take the necessary steps to free them from such burden. In the absence of state or federal action the court may not bar members of the public from lawfully asserting or exercising public trust rights on this privately owned tidelands.

There is absolutely no merit in Marks' contention that as the owner of the *jus privatum* under this patent he may fill and develop his property, whether for navigational purposes or not; nor in his contention that his past and present plan for development of these tidelands as a marina have caused the extinguishment of the public easement. Recla-

the Act of March 23, 1868 and other statutes. The Attorney General asks this court to declare the existence of the public easement and to recognize the right of Whitney as a member of the public and as a littoral owner to have the existence of the easement in these tidelands declared in this action.

mation with or without prior authorization from the state does not *ipso facto* terminate the public trust nor render the issue moot.

* * *

Second: *Does Whitney have "standing" to request the court to recognize and declare the public trust easement on Marks' tidelands?*

Yes. The relief sought by Marks resulted in taking away from Whitney rights to which he is entitled as a member of the general public. It is immaterial that Marks asserted he was not seeking to enjoin the public. The decree as rendered does enjoin a member of the public.

Members of the public have been permitted *to bring* an action to enforce a public right to use a beach access route; *to bring* an action to quiet title to private and public easements in a public beach; and *to bring* an action to restrain improper filling of a bay and secure a general declaration of the rights of the people to the waterways and wildlife areas of the bay. Members of the public have been allowed *to defend* a quiet title action by asserting the right to use a public right of way through private property. They have been allowed to assert the public trust easement for hunting, fishing and navigation in privately owned tidelands *as a defense* in an action to enjoin such use, and to navigate on shallow navigable waters in small boats.

Whitney had standing to raise this issue. The court could have raised this issue on its own.

Notes

1. What does the California Supreme Court mean when it says that the trial court could have raised this issue "on its own?" To what extent should judges act as "private attorneys general" and take an active role in litigation?

2. The court says that the "trier of fact" should determine whether some particular proposed use conflicts with the public trust. Should this "trier of fact" be a judge or jury, or should it be the administrative agency mentioned in note 1 of the opinion? Not all courts have taken such a dynamic view of the public trust. See *Bott v. Natural Res. Comm'n,* 415 Mich. 45, 327 N.W.2d 838 (1982) (public trust does not protect access to recreational waters).

3. A later California Supreme Court case considered the problem of legislative termination of the trust. Overruling two prior decisions, the court held that an 1870 act conveying title to submerged and tidal lands did not extinguish the public trust over those lands. *City of Berkeley v. Superior Court of Alameda County,* 26 Cal.3d 515, 162 Cal.Rptr. 327, 606 P.2d 362 (1980). The court's holding was based on a strong presumption against termination of the trust. The court held, however, that its decision would not apply retroactively to individuals who had already reclaimed their land.

4. What waters are within the scope of the public trust? In *Phillips Petroleum Co. v. Mississippi,* 484 U.S. 469, 108 S.Ct. 791, 98 L.Ed.2d 877 (1988), the Court ruled that the public trust extended to all tidal waters, not

just to navigable waters. The Court rejected the argument that this ruling would upset "settled expectations":

> We have recognized the importance of honoring reasonable expectations in property interests. But such expectations can only be of consequence where they are "reasonable" ones. Here, Mississippi appears to have consistently held that the public trust in lands under water includes "title to all the land under tidewater." Although the Mississippi Supreme Court acknowledged that this case may be the first where it faced the question of the public trust interest in non-navigable tidelands, the clear and unequivocal statements in its earlier opinions should have been ample indication of the State's claim to tidelands. Moreover, cases which have discussed the State's public trust interest in these lands have described uses of them not related to navigability, such as bathing, swimming, recreation, fishing, and mineral development. These statements, too, should have made clear that the State's claims were not limited to lands under navigable waterways. Any contrary expectations cannot be considered reasonable.

The Court observed that even in states where tidelands are privately held, public rights to use tidelands for fishing, hunting, and swimming have long been recognized, and might be undermined by limiting the public trust to navigable waters.[g]

5. One of the most important modern applications of the public trust doctrine is _National Audubon Society v. Superior Court,_ 33 Cal.3d 419, 189 Cal.Rptr. 346, 658 P.2d 709 (1983). At issue was the diversion by the City of Los Angeles of the streams feeding Mono Lake, which threatened to dry up the lake entirely. Under California water law, Los Angeles was entitled to the water as the first appropriator. The California Supreme Court held, however, that this system of prior appropriation must be reconciled with public trust doctrine, and mandated reconsideration of the water allocation in light of its detrimental environmental effects.[h]

For an update on further developments under California water law, see Gregory Weber, "Articulating the Public Trust: Text, Near–Text, and Context," 27 _Ariz. St. L.J._ 1155 (1995):

> While the [California Water Resources Control] Board has sketched a virtually boundless reach for the trust [in terms of scope of application and potential remedies], it simultaneously has limited the doctrine's application pragmatically. Most prominently, the Board has demonstrat-

g. For commentary on _Phillips,_ see Huffman, "_Phillips Petroleum Co. v. Mississippi:_ A Hidden Victory for Private Property?" 19 _Envir.L.Rep._ 10051 (1989); Comment, "_Phillips Petroleum Co. v. Mississippi:_ Is the Public Trust Becoming Synonymous with the Public Interest?" 18 _Envir.L.Rep._ 10200 (1988). On the repercussions of _Phillips_ in other states, see "New Jersey Asserts Its Rights to Tidal Land After Supreme Court Decision," _New York Times,_ February 28, 1988, at 1, col. 1.

h. See Blumm, "Liberty, the New Property, and Environmental Law," 24 _U.S.F.L.Rev._ 385 (1990); Blumm, "Public Property and the Democratization of Western Water Law: A Modern View of the Public Trust Doctrine," 19 _Envir.L.Rep._ 573 (1989); Dunning, "The Mono Lake Decision: Protecting a Common Heritage Resource from Death by Diversion," 13 _Envir.L.Rep._ 10144 (1983). For further discussion of this issue, see Ausness, "Water Rights, The Public Trust Doctrine, and the Protection of Instream Uses," 1986 _U.Ill.L.Rev._ 407.

ed an unwillingness to kowtow to the mere invocation of the trust. Rather, the Board has demonstrated that not all trust-protected resources are equal. Thus, it has prioritized the protection to be given among trust resources in a given ecosystem. * * * In addition, the Board has placed specific evidentiary burdens on persons who would invoke the trust-doctrine. At the very least, such a party bears an initial burden of coming forward with specific evidence to demonstrate harm to trust uses and to sketch a less-harmful alternative accommodation of trust and consumptive uses. * * *

In addition to these practical limitations, the Board has made some accommodations with the needs to divert for consumptive uses. For example, while the Board has not attempted a full accounting of costs and benefits of various trust balances, it has acknowledged that it is inappropriate to dedicate huge amounts of water for little environmental gain. Conversely, if only small amounts of water are needed to bring relatively large environmental gains, the Board likely will require dedication of such flows. Indeed, the Board has been careful not to force dedications of even small flows if such are unlikely to bring much ecological benefit. * * * Finally, the Board has recognized that the quality of water available to a diverter is as legitimate a concern as the quantity available.

Id. at 1229–31.

STATE EX REL. THORNTON v. HAY

Supreme Court of Oregon, 1969.
254 Or. 584, 462 P.2d 671.

GOODWIN, JUSTICE.

William and Georgianna Hay, the owners of a tourist facility at Cannon Beach, appeal from a decree which enjoins them from constructing fences or other improvements in the dry-sand area between the sixteen-foot elevation contour line [which generally coincides with the limits of vegetation on land] and the ordinary high-tide line of the Pacific Ocean.

The issue is whether the state has the power to prevent the defendant landowners from enclosing the dry-sand area contained within the legal description of their oceanfront property.

Issue

* * *

Until very recently, no question concerning the right of the public to enjoy the dry-sand area appears to have been brought before the courts of this state. The public's assumption that the dry sand as well as the foreshore was "public property" had been reinforced by early judicial decisions. See *Shively v. Bowlby,* 152 U.S. 1, 14 S.Ct. 548, 38 L.Ed. 331 (1894), [which] held that landowners claiming under federal patents owned seaward only to the "high-water" line, a line that was then assumed to be the vegetation line.

In 1935, the United States Supreme Court held that a federal patent conveyed title to land farther seaward to the mean high-tide line. *Borax Consolidated, Ltd. v. Los Angeles,* 296 U.S. 10, 56 S.Ct. 23, 80 L.Ed. 9 (1935). While this decision may have expanded seaward the record ownership of upland landowners, it was apparently little noticed by Oregonians. In any event the *Borax* decision had no discernible effect on the actual practices of Oregon beachgoers and upland property owners.

Recently, however, the scarcity of ocean-front building sites has attracted substantial private investments in resort facilities. Resort owners like these defendants now desire to reserve for their paying guests the recreational advantages that accrue to the dry-sand portions of their deeded property. Consequently, in 1967, public debate and political activity resulted in legislative attempts to resolve conflicts between public and private interests in the dry-sand area. [The legislation purported to recognize the existence of a long-standing public right of access or easement.]

* * *

Because many elements of prescription are present in this case, the state has relied upon the doctrine in support of the decree below. We believe, however, that there is a better legal basis for affirming the decree. The most cogent basis for the decision in this case is the English doctrine of custom. Strictly construed, prescription applies only to the specific tract of land before the court, and doubtful prescription cases could fill the courts for years with tract-by-tract litigation. An established custom, on the other hand, can be proven with reference to a larger region. Ocean-front lands from the northern to the southern border of the state ought to be treated uniformly.

The other reason which commends the doctrine of custom over that of prescription as the principal basis for the decision in this case is the unique nature of the lands in question. This case deals solely with the dry-sand area along the Pacific shore, and this land has been used by the public as public recreational land according to an unbroken custom running back in time as long as the land has been inhabited.

* * *

Two arguments have been arrayed against the doctrine of custom as a basis for decision in Oregon. The first argument is that custom is unprecedented in this state, and has only scant adherence elsewhere in the United States. The second argument is that because of the relative brevity of our political history it is inappropriate to rely upon an English doctrine that requires greater antiquity than a newly-settled land can muster. Neither of these arguments is persuasive.

The custom of the people of Oregon to use the dry-sand area of the beaches for public recreational purposes meets every one of Blackstone's requisites. While it is not necessary to rely upon precedent from other states, we are not the first state to recognize custom as a source of law. See *Perley et ux'r v. Langley,* 7 N.H. 233 (1834).

On the score of the brevity of our political history, it is true that the Anglo–American legal system on this continent is relatively new. Its newness has made it possible for government to provide for many of our institutions by written law rather than by customary law.[20] This truism does not, however, militate against the validity of a custom when the custom does in fact exist. If antiquity were the sole test of validity of a custom, Oregonians could satisfy that requirement by recalling that the European settlers were not the first people to use the dry-sand area as public land.

Finally, in support of custom, the record shows that the custom of the inhabitants of Oregon and of visitors in the state to use the dry sand as a public recreation area is so notorious that notice of the custom on the part of persons buying land along the shore must be presumed. In the case at bar, the landowners conceded their actual knowledge of the public's long-standing use of the dry-sand area, and argued that the elements of consent present in the relationship between the landowners and the public precluded the application of the law of prescription. As noted, we are not resting this decision on prescription, and we leave open the effect upon prescription of the type of consent that may have been present in this case. Such elements of consent are, however, wholly consistent with the recognition of public rights derived from custom.

Because so much of our law is the product of legislation, we sometimes lose sight of the importance of custom as a source of law in our society. It seems particularly appropriate in the case at bar to look to an ancient and accepted custom in this state as the source of a rule of law. The rule in this case, based upon custom, is salutary in confirming a public right, and at the same time it takes from no man anything which he has had a legitimate reason to regard as exclusively his.

Notes

1. Suppose that in 1998 the Minnesota Supreme Court decided to follow *Thornton* for the first time. (Presumably, the Minnesota court decided to ignore a later Oregon case, *McDonald v. Halvorson,* 308 Or. 340, 780 P.2d 714 (1989), which limited *Thornton* to ocean beaches). Suit is brought by a private citizen who wants to fence off beach property along Lake Superior. In light of *Lucas* and *Nollan,* is this a taking?

---

20. The English law on customary rights grew up in a small island nation at a time when most inhabitants lived and died without traveling more than a day's walk from their birthplace. Most of the customary rights recorded in English cases are local in scope. The English had many cultural and language groups which eventually merged into a nation. After these groups developed their own unique customs, the unified nation recognized some of them as law. Some American scholars, looking at the vast geography of this continent and the freshness of its civilization, have concluded that there is no need to look to English customary rights as a source of legal rights in this country. Some of the generalizations drawn by the text writers from English cases would tend to limit customary rights to specific usages in English towns and villages. But it does not follow that a custom, established in fact, cannot have regional application and be enjoyed by a larger public than the inhabitants of a single village.

Suppose instead that the *Thornton* rule was adopted by legislation. Does this affect the takings analysis? Imagine that, in upholding the statute, the Minnesota court announces that (even though there was no previous decision on point) *Thornton* was really the law in Minnesota anyway. Would the U.S. Supreme Court be bound by this determination on appeal? [Reread *Lucas* on this issue.]

2.   Putting aside the taking clause, consider what kind of evidence about beach use ought to be considered before a court embraces a finding of custom. As a litigator, how would you go about presenting such evidence? Alternatively, suppose you were a lobbyist seeking beach access legislation. What kinds of arguments would you make, and what kind of testimony would you seek to present?

3.   Apart from the intriguing issues in property law, beach access also raises important questions of equity. Beach owners are often wealthy suburbanites, while those seeking access are from poorer urban areas. Although not always articulated clearly, class and race issues have lurked in the background of disputes over access. See Marc Poirier, "Environmental Justice and the Beach Access Movements of the 1970s in Connecticut and New Jersey: Stories of Property and Civil Rights," 28 *Conn. L. Rev.* 710 (1996).

Note on the Navigational Servitude

Like the states, the federal government has a quasi-property interest in navigable waters. The federal interest is called the navigational servitude. The operation of the servitude is illustrated in *United States v. Rands,* 389 U.S. 121, 88 S.Ct. 265, 19 L.Ed.2d 329 (1967). The issue in *Rands* was whether the condemnation award for land along the Columbia River should include that portion of its market value attributable to potential use as a port site. The Court held that no individual can own a property interest in the use of navigable waters, for such use is always subject to government control. "Thus, without being constitutionally obligated to pay compensation, the United States may change the course of a navigable stream, or otherwise impair or destroy a riparian owner's access to navigable waters, even though the market value of the riparian owner's land is substantially diminished." Indeed, later in the opinion, the Court referred to the "constitutional power of Congress completely to regulate navigable streams to the total exclusion of private power companies or port owners."

The *Rands* case was somewhat limited by *Kaiser Aetna v. United States,* 444 U.S. 164, 100 S.Ct. 383, 62 L.Ed.2d 332 (1979). *Kaiser Aetna* involved the private improvement of a pond which previously was incapable of being used for navigational purposes. As a result of the improvements, the pond was to be used as a private marina. The Court acknowledged that the strict logic of *Rands* and similar cases might allow the government to require public access to the marina, converting it into a public aquatic park. But, the Court concluded, the facts in the *Kaiser Aetna* case were too far removed from previous cases involving navigable waterways. For one thing, the pond was simply too different from the sort of "great navigable stream" that had previously been held "incapable of private ownership." The Court also stressed the government's previous consent to the marina project:

We have not the slightest doubt that the Government could have refused to allow such dredging on the ground that it could have impaired navigation in the bay, or could have conditioned its approval of the dredging on petitioners' agreement to comply with various measures that it deemed appropriate for the promotion of navigation. But what petitioners *now* have is a body of water that was private property under Hawaiian law, linked to navigable water by a channel dredged by them with the consent of the respondent. While the consent of individual officers representing the United States cannot "estop" the United States, it can lead to the fruition of a number of expectancies embodied in the concept of "property,"—expectancies that, if sufficiently important, the Government must condemn and pay for before it takes over the management of the landowner's property. In this case, we hold that the "right to exclude," so universally held to be a fundamental element of the property right, falls within this category of interests that the Government cannot take without compensation. * * * Thus, if the Government wishes to make what was formerly Kuaapa Pond into a public aquatic park after petitioners have proceeded as far as they have here, it may not, without invoking eminent domain power and paying just compensation, require them to allow free access to the dredged pond while petitioners' agreement with their customers calls for an annual $72 regular fee.

This was obviously a guarded holding. Twenty years later, it is still unclear whether *Kaiser Aetna* is anything more than a narrow exception to the *Rands* rule. See *Good v. United States*, 39 Fed. Cl. 81 (1997) (*Rands* rule still valid).

It is important to note that the navigational servitude applies only to waters meeting the traditional test of navigability. While statements of the traditional test vary, the central concern behind these tests relates to potential use for navigational purposes. On the other hand, as we saw earlier, federal regulation has not been limited to this class of waterways. The courts have held, with strong support in the legislative history, that the Clean Water Act extends beyond traditional navigable waters to all bodies of water within the United States. To the extent that Congress has now extended its jurisdictional net beyond the traditional navigable waterways, however, it can no longer claim the protection of the navigational servitude as a defense to taking claims.

Although the courts have never really articulated the justifications for the navigational servitude, some light is shed by *Avenal v. United States*, 100 F.3d 933 (Fed.Cir.1996), in which the court rejected a compensation claim by owners of state leases for water-bottom lands used by oyster growers. The oyster farmers contended that a federal and state freshwater diversion project had diluted salinity levels and caused silt deposits so as to prevent continued oyster cultivation. Judge Plager concluded that they did hold property interests protected by the Fifth Amendment but that no compensation was due:

> The case before us presents a textbook example of a situation in which the plaintiffs, in the face of established public concerns and while governmental efforts to address those concerns were well known, moved

to take advantage of the existing conditions for their own economic benefit. There is nothing wrong with their having done that; the State of Louisiana provided the mechanisms for it, and their own initiative gave them whatever economic advantages the situation afforded. It is hard for them to claim surprise, however, that the pre-existing salinity conditions, created at least in part by earlier government activity, were again tampered with to their (this time) disadvantage.

Id. at 937. In other words, because of the frequency and intensity of government regulation, and the extent to which those currently complaining have reaped the benefits of earlier government actions, those using waterways do not have "reasonable investment-backed expectations" of non-interference by the government.

2. PROTECTING COASTAL WATERS

The same pollution that may devastate a beach may also destroy rich ecological communities offshore. This section focuses on efforts to protect coastal waters and the adjoining lands from ecological damage.

Pollution in coastal waters comes to public attention through beach closings, and through frequent restrictions on shellfish and oyster harvesting. Other damage is less visible:

> Bays and estuaries that are now in jeopardy—Boston Harbor, for example, or even San Francisco Bay—are still delightful to look at from shore. What is happening underwater is quite another matter, and it is not for the squeamish. Scuba divers talk of swimming through clouds of toilet paper and half-dissolved feces, of bay bottoms covered by a foul and toxic combination of sediment, sewage and petrochemical waste appropriately known as "black mayonnaise." Fishermen haul in lobsters and crab covered with mysterious "burn holes" and fish whose fins are rotting off.

Newsweek, Aug. 2, 1988, at 43. See also "The Fringe of the Ocean— Under Siege from Land," 248 Science 163 (1990).

The risk of environmental disaster in coastal waters became utterly unmistakable on March 24, 1989, when the Exxon Valdez ran into a reef, creating the worst oil spill in U.S. history. Over 240,000 barrels of oil were released, with environmental effects lasting for years. Notably, the 1972 EIS for the Alaska oil pipeline had predicted the possibility of a major spill, but the pipeline was approved because of assurances that an effective contingency plan would be established. As it turned out, the "contingency plan" was more contingency than plan. See "Valdez: The Predicted Spill," 244 Science 20 (1989). Much of our focus in this section will be on the risk of oil spills.

Several general federal statutes such as the Clean Water Act and the Endangered Species Act provide some protection to coastal waters. For example, in *NRDC v. United States EPA*, 863 F.2d 1420 (9th Cir.1988), the court partially reversed EPA's CWA regulations dealing with discharges from offshore oil platforms. We have also seen previously that

NEPA can have important applications in coastal waters. [See *NRDC v. Morton*, p. 179 supra.]

Coastal waters are also the subject of several more specialized federal statutes, two of which are particularly important: the Coastal Zone Management Act and the Outer Continental Shelf Lands Act.[i]

The Coastal Zone Management Act. In 1972 Congress enacted the National Coastal Zone Management Act, 16 U.S.C.A. § 1451 *et seq.* State participation in the program is voluntary. States which elect to participate must adopt land development controls to implement their coastal zone plans in order to be eligible for federal financial assistance available under the act. The four principal characteristics of the program were summarized by the first CZMA administrator:

> First, it is voluntary—there are no sanctions involved. * * * Second, it speaks to "process" and not "substance." It sets up Federal requirements with regard to the processes that have to be addressed in a State's management program, but it does not try to second-guess the State with regard to specific land and water use decisions. Third, it is primarily a coastal waters management program, and refers only to the shorelands to the extent that the use of the shorelands affects the coastal waters. Fourth, it recognizes the importance of both economic development as well as conservation-oriented uses. So it's a balanced approach to management, and not solely an environmental measure.[j]

The regulatory system contemplated by the Act includes a management program and an implementation program. The management program is to consist of a "comprehensive statement" setting forth "objectives, policies and standards" to guide public and private uses in the coastal zone. 16 U.S.C.A. § 1453(12). With respect to the implementation program, participating states may act through their own agencies, local governments, or area-wide or similar agencies, and must be authorized "to administer land and water use regulations, control development * * *, and to resolve conflicts among competing uses." They also must have the legal authority to acquire any necessary interest in land "when necessary to achieve conformance with the management program." 16 U.S.C.A. § 1455(d)(10). This language leaves open the distribution of the powers between state and local governments. While other sections call for some legal authority at the state level to regulate land development

---

i. Also significant is the Ocean Dumping Act. The Ocean Dumping Act is Title I of the Marine Protection, Research, and Sanctuaries Act (MPRSA), 33 U.S.C.A. §§ 1401–1445. (Title III of MPRSA establishes marine sanctuaries, which are the oceanic equivalents of wildlife refuges and national parks.) MPRSA § 102 establishes a dumping permit program to be administered by EPA. EPA is directed to establish criteria for dumping, which must balance the need for the proposed dumping against environ-

mental impacts. Permits may not be issued for dumping unless applicable water quality standards are met. Section 104B prohibits ocean dumping of sewage sludge and industrial waste. Another provision, § 103, deals with dumping of dredge and fill materials.

j. Knecht, "Setting the Perspective," in Council of State Governments, *Proceedings of the Conference on Organizing and Managing the Coastal Zone* 9, 11–12 (June 13–14, 1973).

or review local controls in the coastal zone, the nature and scope of such state authority are left rather unclear. For an overview of the CZMA, see Malone, "The Coastal Zone Management Act and the Takings Clause in the 1990's: Making the Case for Federal Land Use to Preserve Coastal Areas," 62 *Colo.L.Rev.* 711 (1991).

In 1981, after completion of various environmental studies by his predecessor, and over the protests of state and local officials in California, Secretary of the Interior Watt announced an OCS lease sale of the entire Santa Maria Basin, offshore from an extraordinarily scenic stretch of coastline extending between Big Sur and Santa Barbara. The State of California promptly sued and obtained an injunction directing that certain tracts within the basin be excluded from the sale. The lower courts held that the final notices of sale were federal activities "directly affecting" the coastal zone of California and therefore, under § 307(c)(1) [16 U.S.C.A. § 1456(c)(1)] of CZMA, were required to be conducted in a manner, "to the maximum extent practicable, consistent with" the state's approved management program. However, the Supreme Court reversed [5–4] in *Secretary of the Interior v. California,* 464 U.S. 312, 104 S.Ct. 656, 78 L.Ed.2d 496 (1984). The Court reasoned that a lease sale authorizes only preliminary exploration and therefore does not "directly affect" the coastal zone.

In response, Congress amended § 307(c)(1) of the CZMA to read as follows:

> Each Federal agency activity within or outside the coastal zone that affects any land or water use or natural resource of the coastal zone shall be carried out in a manner which is consistent to the maximum extent practicable with the enforceable policies of approved State management programs.

Subsection (B) provides for federal exemption if the federal activity is found by the President to be "in the paramount interest of the United States." The legislative history indicates that the amendment was intended to overrule *Secretary of the Interior v. California,* and to make it clear that the statute does apply to OCS lease sales by eliminating the "directly affecting" standard. Congress also rejected the Court's interpretation in two other respects: the geographical scope of the statute was expanded to apply to activities outside the coastal zone itself; and the requirement that a federal activity be "conducted or supported" by the agency was eliminated.

The constitutional limits of state authority to restrict OCS oil development through coastal zone planning are unclear. Oil industry supporters may attack a state coastal zone program by showing an impermissible burden on interstate commerce. Although a Commerce Clause challenge failed in *Norfolk Southern Corp. v. Oberly,* 822 F.2d 388 (3d Cir.1987), the court said that "CZMA does not authorize states to engage in otherwise impermissible regulation." 822 F.2d at 390.

The Outer Continental Shelf Act. Disputes over the exploration and development of offshore oil and gas deposits have multiplied since the disastrous 1969 blowout and spill in California's Santa Barbara channel, which killed birds and marine organisms, damaged beaches and seafront properties, and impaired fishing and recreational activities over a large area. The disputes most frequently have arisen in connection with federal leasing of tracts in the outer continental shelf (OCS). The United States government, rather than the states, exercises sovereign rights over the seabed and subsoil of the continental shelf beyond three miles from the coastline. *United States v. Maine,* 420 U.S. 515, 95 S.Ct. 1155, 43 L.Ed.2d 363 (1975); Outer Continental Shelf Lands Act (OCS-LA), 43 U.S.C.A. § 1331. Acting primarily through the Department of the Interior, the government leases OCS areas to private firms through a competitive bidding process prescribed by OCSLA. Leasing and resultant exploration, development, production and transportation of OCS oil and gas also are subject to the mandates of NEPA—and the Clean Water Act.

Section 18 of OCSLA, 43 U.S.C.A. § 1344, requires the Secretary to establish a five-year OCS leasing program. Each program is to consist of a schedule of proposed lease sales indicating as precisely as possible the size, timing and location of leasing activity which the Secretary determines will best meet national energy needs for the five-year period following approval. The Secretary must prepare and maintain the program consistent with four basic principles:

(1) Management of the OCS shall be conducted in a manner which considers economic, social, and environmental values of renewable and nonrenewable resources, and the potential impact of oil and gas exploration on other resource values and the marine, coastal, and human environments.

(2) Timing and location of exploration, development, and production among the oil and gas-bearing physiographic regions of the OCS shall be based on consideration of an equitable sharing of developmental benefits and environmental risks among the various regions; the location of such regions with respect to, and the relative needs of, regional and national energy markets; the location of such regions with respect to other uses of the sea and seabed, such as fisheries and navigation; the interest of potential oil and gas producers as indicated by exploration or nomination; laws, goals, and policies of affected states which have been specifically identified by their governors for the Secretary's consideration; and the relative environmental sensitivity and marine productivity of different areas of the OCS.

(3) The Secretary shall select the timing and location of leasing, to the maximum extent practicable, so as to obtain a proper balance between the potential for environmental damage, the potential for discovery of oil and gas, and the potential for adverse impact on the coastal zone.

(4) Leasing activities shall be conducted to assure receipt of fair market value for the lands leased and the rights conveyed by the federal government.

Section 18 also establishes a mechanism for state governments to offer suggestions and comments. The Secretary then must submit the proposed program (and any comments received) to Congress and the President at least sixty days before he approves it, indicating why any specific recommendation of a state government was not accepted.

Following approval by the Secretary, a leasing program is subject for sixty days to judicial review exclusively in the D.C. Circuit, upon suit by any person who participated in the administrative proceedings related to the program and is adversely affected or aggrieved by it. 43 U.S.C.A. § 1349. The court of appeals must consider the matter solely on the record before the Secretary, and his findings are conclusive if supported by substantial evidence. See *California v. Watt,* 668 F.2d 1290 (D.C.Cir. 1981) (ordering reconsideration of a five-year plan approved by President Carter's Secretary of the Interior); *California v. Watt,* 712 F.2d 584 (D.C.Cir.1983) (upholding the revised leasing program for the years 1982–87); *NRDC, Inc. v. Hodel,* 865 F.2d 288 (D.C.Cir.1988) (rejecting most challenges to the 1987–92 plan).

Having survived all these hurdles, a leasing program achieves important practical and legal significance. No lease may be issued for any area unless the area is included in the approved leasing program and unless the lease contains provisions consistent with the approved program. The approved program also becomes the basis for future planning by all affected entities, from federal, state and local governments to the oil industry itself.

Problem on Property Rights Under OCSLA

OCSLA and the leases issued by the Secretary of Interior contain provisions intended to protect against damages from oil spills. The Act confirms that Congress intended to exercise both the proprietary powers of a landowner and the police powers of the legislature in regulating leases of publicly owned resources. Safeguards are not limited to those provided by lease covenants; the Secretary may prescribe at any time rules and regulations which he finds "necessary and proper" for the "conservation of natural resources." 43 U.S.C.A. § 1334(a)(1). Rules in effect at the time a lease is executed are part of the lease, and the Secretary may obtain cancellation of the lease if the lessee breaches any such rule. However, violation of rules issued after the lease has been executed does not enable the Secretary to cancel the lease; the property rights of the lessee are determined only by those rules in effect when the lease is executed.

Hexon Oil Company seeks to set aside an order of the Secretary denying permission to construct a drilling platform in the Santa Maria Channel which is allegedly necessary for full exercise of its lease rights. The lease gave Hexon the right to erect floating drilling platforms, subject to the provisions of OCSLA and to "reasonable regulations" not inconsistent with the lease. After a blowout caused an oil spill, the Secretary ordered all activities on this and other leases suspended pending further environmental studies. A few months later he issued a regulation authorizing emergency "suspension" of any operation which threatened immediate, serious or irreparable harm or damage to the environment, and providing that the suspension should continue indefinitely until, in the Secretary's judgment, the threat had terminated. Hexon claims a distinction between suspension and revocation, asserting that the Secretary had not merely suspended their operations, because a suspension by definition was of a "temporary nature."

Is the Secretary's action authorized by OCSLA? Is it a taking of Hexon's rights under its lease?

Note on Statutory Liability for Oil Spills

Despite the best possible efforts at regulation, accidents do happen. What then? Several federal laws impose liability for oil spills. A precursor to CERCLA, the OCSLA amendments of 1978 established liability for clean-up costs and damages resulting from OCS activities and created the Offshore Oil Spill Pollution Fund. The amendments apply to offshore facilities and to vessels carrying oil from such facilities. Strict liability for clean-up costs and damages is imposed jointly and severally on the owner and operator, not to exceed $250,000 in the case of a vessel, or $35 million plus government removal costs in the case of an offshore facility. Such limits, however, are not applicable if an incident is caused by willful misconduct or gross negligence, or by violation of federal safety regulations, "within the privity or knowledge of the owner or operator." The Fund, which is derived from a fee of 3 cents per barrel imposed on the owner of oil obtained from the OCS, is liable for all losses not otherwise compensated.

Until 1990, liability for other spills was imposed by § 311 of the Clean Water Act.[k] It made vessels strictly liable for clean-up costs incurred by the government unless the owner proved that the spill was solely a result of an Act of God, an act of war, an act or omission of a third party, or negligence by the federal government. These exceptions from liability were narrowly construed. See *United States v. West of England Ship Owner's Mut. Protection & Indem. Ass'n,* 872 F.2d 1192 (5th Cir.1989). Owners of onshore and offshore facilities also were strictly liable for government clean-up costs. Section 311 placed limits on liability for spills: $125,000 for inland oil barges, $250,000 (or $150/ton) for other vessels, and $50 million for onshore and offshore facilities. For the Exxon Valdez, the $150/ton figure came to $32 million. However, the limits were not applicable if the government could show that the discharge was due to "willful negligence or willful misconduct within the privity and knowledge of the owner."

The Oil Pollution Act of 1990 replaced the liability provisions of § 311. Section 1002 [33 U.S.C.A. § 2702] imposes liability on "each responsible party" for removal costs, damage to natural resources, damages "for injury to, or economic losses, resulting from destruction of, real or personal property," and lost profits "due to the injury, destruction, or loss of any real

---

k. The Trans–Alaska Pipeline Authorization Act, 43 U.S.C.A. §§ 1651–1655, and the Deepwater Port Act of 1974, 33 U.S.C.A. §§ 1501–1524, also provided for strict liability and for funds to compensate damaged parties. The Trans–Alaska Act covered only vessels transporting Alaskan pipeline oil to U.S. ports, and it did not recognize the defenses of Act of God or act of omission of a third party. The Deepwater Port Act applied to vessel discharges within "a safety zone" of a deepwater port and allowed the same defenses as the Trans–Alaska Act. Both acts set maximum limits on total liability, $100 million for the Trans–Alaska Act and $20 million for the Deepwater Port Act. The Deepwater Port Act was repealed in 1990.

property, personal property, or natural resources, which shall be recoverable by any claimant." "Responsible parties" are defined in § 1001(32) to include the owners and operators of vessels, on-shore facilities, or pipelines. Defenses to liability are modeled on CERCLA § 107. Liability limits for tankers are now at least $10 million for ships weighing 3000 or more gross tons, or $1200 per ton. Owners of offshore facilities are liable for up to $75 million. Like § 311, the new statute provides for unlimited liability if the spill is caused by gross negligence, wilful misconduct, or a safety violation. The statute also tracks CERCLA in establishing an oil spill trust fund ($1 billion), granting the President federal response authority, and requiring the President to issue regulations governing the measurement of damages for injury to natural resources. After a comprehensive review of the 1990 statute, one commentator recently concluded:

> Significantly, the OPA [Oil Pollution Act] increased financial responsibility requirements to the point where some participants simply will be unable to continue doing business in the offshore area. Federal, state, and local governments are currently involved in a massive effort to prepare for oil spill response actions. Privately owned and operated facilities will soon have to expend considerable sums to demonstrate the financial and logistical capability of responding to a worst-case spill. In view of all this, the cost of doing business for those that remain will increase.

Wall, "Federal Oil Pollution Law and Regulatory Developments," 23 *Env. L.Rep.* 10491 (1993).

Although statutes may ease the plaintiff's burden of establishing fault, other limitations on damages may exist. In *Benefiel v. Exxon Corp.*, 959 F.2d 805 (9th Cir.1992), the court held that liability under the Alaska Pipeline Act was subject to the requirement of proximate cause. The plaintiffs were consumers who alleged that the Exxon Valdez oil spill had resulted in higher oil prices. The flaw in their claim was the existence of intervening causes:

> In this case, the spill itself did not directly cause any injury to the appellants. Rather, plaintiffs alleged the spill triggered a series of intervening events, including the decision of the United States Coast Guard to close the Port of Valdez to facilitate clean-up efforts; the alleged decision by refineries in the western United States to raise prices rather than to use their own oil reserves to make up any shortage; and the decision of wholesalers, distributors and retailers to pass on these price increases.

The court concluded that the "plaintiffs themselves alleged the existence of at least one intervening act causing the price hike: the alleged decision of California oil refiners to exploit the supposed shortage." See also *Adkins v. Trans–Alaska Pipeline Liability Fund*, 101 F.3d 86 (9th Cir.1996) (applying *Benefiel* test to lost profit claims by electrical utility, cafe, tourist businesses, and boat repair companies).

Benefiel was only one piece of the massive litigation arising out of the Exxon Valdez spill. More than a hundred law firms were involved in over two hundred suits, involving more than thirty thousand claims. The total damage claims exceeded fifty billion dollars. Although some of these claims were settled or dismissed, over ten thousand remained. The district court held that some of these claims were foreclosed. Claims by Alaska natives for damage to their way of life were held not recoverable under the rule of *Robins Dry Dock & Repair Co. v. Flint,* 275 U.S. 303, 48 S.Ct. 134, 72 L.Ed. 290 (1927), which requires that a person suffer direct physical harm in order to recover economic losses. By analogy, the court believed that *Robins* also foreclosed nonpecuniary damage claims. On the other hand, there is a recognized exception to *Robins* for commercial fishermen. The court held that this exception applied to fisheries that were actually closed to fishing by the spill, including claims that the market value of their later salmon catch was decreased on the Japanese market because of concerns about contamination. For a fuller discussion of the *Robins* rule, see Goldberg, "Recovery for Economic Loss Following the *Exxon Valdez* Spill," 23 *J.Leg.Studies* 1 (1994). The Alaska natives settled their claims against Exxon for loss of subsistence fishing for twenty million dollars.

A federal jury awarded five billion dollars in punitive damages against Exxon, payable to a consolidated group of plaintiffs, including fishermen, property owners, and others. Exxon claimed that the punitive award was unfair in light of the $2.5 billion it had spent for cleanup and compensation, and $1 billion in settlements with the federal and state governments. Appeals are still pending.

A subject of increasing interest is public recovery of damages for injuries to "natural resources." As we have seen, CERCLA provides for recovery of such damages under some circumstances where hazardous wastes are involved, and the 1990 oil spill statute imposes similar liability. The next case, involving a claim for injury to natural resources under the equivalent state law, is especially interesting because of its pioneering discussion of possible measures of damages.

COMMONWEALTH OF PUERTO RICO
v. SS ZOE COLOCOTRONI

United States Court of Appeals, First Circuit, 1980.
628 F.2d 652, cert. denied 450 U.S. 912, 101 S.Ct. 1350, 67 L.Ed.2d 336 (1981).

CAMPBELL, CIRCUIT JUDGE.

In the early morning hours of March 18, 1973, the SS Zoe Colocotroni, a tramp oil tanker, ran aground on a reef three and a half miles off the south coast of Puerto Rico. To refloat the vessel, the captain ordered the dumping of more than 5,000 tons of crude oil into the surrounding waters. An oil slick four miles long, and a tenth of a mile wide, floated towards the coast and came ashore at an isolated peninsula on the southwestern tip of the island—a place called Bahia Sucia. The present appeal concerns an action in admiralty brought by the Commonwealth of Puerto Rico and the local Environmental Quality Board (EQB) to recover damages for harm done to the coastal environment by the spilled oil.

Defendants have raised numerous objections to the district court's judgment awarding plaintiffs $6,164,192.09 in damages for cleanup costs and environmental harm. * * *

* * *

The district court made the following findings on the issue of damages:

1. Plaintiffs' proven claim of damage to marine organisms covers an approximate area of about 20 acres in and around the West Mangrove. The surveys conducted by Plaintiffs reliably establish that there was a decline of approximately 4,605,486 organisms per acre as a direct result of the oil spill. This means that 92,109,720 marine animals were killed by the Colocotroni oil spill. The uncontradicted evidence establishes that there is a ready market with reference to biological supply laboratories, thus allowing a reliable calculation of the cost of replacing these organisms. The lowest possible replacement cost figure is $.06 per animal, with many species selling from $1.00 to $4.50 per individual. Accepting the lowest replacement cost, and attaching damages only to the lost marine animals in the West Mangrove area, we find the damages caused by Defendants to amount to $5,526,583.20.

2. The evidence is overwhelming to the effect that the sediments in and around the West Mangrove continue to be impregnated with oil. The solutions proposed by Plaintiffs to this problem are unacceptable in that they would bring about the total destruction of this environment without any real guarantee of ultimate success. Furthermore, there is substantial scientific evidence to the effect that much of the undesirable effects of the oil in the sediments will be corrected in time by the weathering processes of nature. The most affected spots in the West Mangrove cover an area of approximately 23 acres. It is the Court's opinion that these areas can best be reestablished by the intensive planting of mangrove and restoration of this area to its condition before the oil spill. The evidence shows that the planting of mangrove runs at about $16,500 per acre, thus bringing the cost of replanting 23 acres to $379,500. The evidence further demonstrates that the planting will require a five year monitoring and fertilizing program which will cost $36,000 per year or $180,000 for the five years. The total damages thus suffered by Plaintiffs by reason of the pollution of the mangrove in the West Mangrove amount to $559,500.

3. Plaintiffs incurred cleanup costs in the amount of $78,-108.89 which were not reimbursed from any source, and they are entitled to recover said damages from Defendants.

* * *

Plaintiffs argue that a state regulatory interest in wildlife and other living resources, expressed metaphorically in the state's status as "public trustee" of its natural resources, is sufficient in itself to support an action for damages to those resources. Defendants reply that, absent a proprietary interest in the resource actually damaged, a state's unexercised regulatory authority over wildlife will not support a proper cause of action. We see no need to decide this difficult question in the present case. Here the Commonwealth of Puerto Rico, exercising its undisputed authority to protect and conserve its natural environment, has by statute authorized one of its agencies to maintain actions of this sort. Under the statute, 12 L.P.R.A. § 1131(29), co-plaintiff Environmental Quality Board has, among others, the following duties, powers and functions:

> To bring, represented by the Secretary of Justice, by the Board's attorneys, or by a private attorney contracted for such purpose, civil actions for damages in any court of Puerto Rico or the United States of America to recover the total value of the damages caused to the environment and/or natural resources upon committing any violation of this chapter and its regulations. The amount of any judgment collected to such effect shall be covered into the Special Account of the Board on Environmental Quality.

We read this statute both as creating a cause of action of the type described by its terms and as designating the EQB as the proper party to bring such an action. * * * Whatever might be the case in the absence of such a local statute, we think that where the Commonwealth of Puerto Rico has thus legislatively authorized the bringing of suits for environmental damages, and has ear-marked funds so recovered to a special fund, such an action must be construed as taking the place of any implied common law action the Commonwealth as trustee, might have brought. * * *

* * *

Defendants next argue the district court erred in failing to apply the common law "diminution in value" rule in calculating damages. Under the traditional rule, the measure of damages for tortious injury to real property is the difference in the commercial or market value of the property before and after the event causing injury. Where the property can be restored to its original condition for a sum less than the diminution in value, however, the cost of restoration may be substituted as a measure of damages. Defendants introduced evidence at trial tending to show that the market value of comparable property in the vicinity of Bahia Sucia was less than $5,000 per acre, based on recent sales. Thus, defendants contend, damages here could not have exceeded $5,000 per affected acre even if the land were shown to have lost all value.

We believe that defendants have misconceived the character of the remedy created by § 1131. The EQB is not concerned with any loss in the market or other commercial value of the Commonwealth's land. In point of fact, the EQB concedes the land has no significant commercial or market value. The claim, rather, is for the injury—broadly conceived—that has been caused to the natural environment by the spilled oil. The question before us is not whether in a typical land damage case a claim of this sort could be successfully advanced—we assume it could not—but rather whether Puerto Rico's statute empowering the EQB to proceed in cases such as this envisions the awarding of damages on a different basis than would have been traditionally allowed.

The district court found that the once flourishing natural environment of the West Mangrove had been seriously damaged by the oil, to the point where some of the underlying sediments were no longer capable of supporting any but the most primitive forms of organic life, such as worms. The Puerto Rico statute authorizing this action specifically empowers the EQB to recover "the *total value* of the damages caused to the environment and/or natural resources" upon a violation of the anti-pollution provisions. Implicit in this choice of language, we think, is a determination not to restrict the state to ordinary market damages. Many unspoiled natural areas of considerable ecological value have little or no commercial or market value. Indeed, to the extent such areas have a commercial value, it is logical to assume they will not long remain unspoiled, absent some governmental or philanthropic protection. A strict application of the diminution in value rule would deny the state any right to recover meaningful damages for harm to such areas, and would frustrate appropriate measures to restore or rehabilitate the environment.

* * *

We turn now to whether the damages awarded by the district court were appropriate. To review the court's award, we must ascertain what a fair and equitable damages measure would be in these circumstances, and, to that end, it will be helpful to examine the remedial provisions in recent similar federal statutes. There is a strong emphasis in Congressional oil pollution enactments on the concept of restoration. As discussed earlier, the 1977 Clean Water Act amendments provided that the state's representative, acting as public trustee, could "recover for the costs of replacing or restoring [natural] resources." 33 U.S.C.A. § 1321(f)(5). In accordance with the trust analogy, the statute provided: "Sums recovered shall be used to restore, rehabilitate, or acquire the equivalent of such natural resources by the appropriate agencies * * *." The legislative history further elaborates this standard:

> New subsection (f)(4) and (5) make governmental expenses in connection with damage to or destruction of natural resources a cost of removal which can be recovered from the owner or operator of the discharged source under section 311. For those resources which can be restored or rehabilitated, the measure of liability is the reasonable costs actually incurred by Federal or State authorities in replacing the resources or otherwise mitigating the damage. Where the damaged or destroyed resource is irreplaceable (as an endangered species or an entire fishery), the measure of liability is the reasonable cost of acquiring resources to offset the loss.

Borrowing from the suggestion provided by this federal legislation, we think the appropriate primary standard for determining damages in a case such as this is the cost reasonably to be incurred by the sovereign or its designated agency to restore or rehabilitate the environment in the affected area to [its] pre-existing condition, or as close thereto as is feasible without grossly disproportionate expenditures. The focus in determining such a remedy should be on the steps a reasonable and prudent sovereign or agency would take to mitigate the harm done by the pollution, with attention to such factors as technical feasibility, harmful side effects, compatibility with or duplication of such regeneration as is naturally to be expected, and the extent to which efforts beyond a certain point would become either redundant or disproportionately expensive. Admittedly, such a remedy cannot be calculated with the degree of certainty usually possible when the issue is, for example, damages on a commercial contract. On the other hand, a district court can surely calculate damages under the foregoing standard with as much or more certainty and accuracy as a jury determining damages for pain and suffering or mental anguish.

There may be circumstances where direct restoration of the affected area is either physically impossible or so disproportionately expensive that it would not be reasonable to undertake such a remedy. Some other measure of damages might be reasonable in such cases, at least where the process of natural regeneration will be too slow to ensure restoration within a reasonable period. The legislative history of the Clean Water Act amendments, quoted above, suggests as one possibility "the reasonable cost of acquiring resources to offset the loss." Alternatives might include acquisition of comparable lands for public parks or, as suggested by defendants below, reforestation of a similar proximate site where the presence of oil would not pose the same hazard to ultimate success. As with the remedy of restoration, the damages awarded for such alternative measures should be reasonable and not grossly disproportionate to the harm caused and the ecological values involved. The ultimate purpose of any such remedy should be to protect the public interest in a healthy, functioning environment, and not to provide a windfall to the public treasury. In emphasizing the above measures, we do not mean to rule out others in appropriate circumstances. There may indeed be cases where traditional commercial valuation rules will afford the best yardstick, as where there is a market in which the damaged resource could have been sold that reflects its actual value. Much must necessarily be left to the discretion of courts, especially before a body of precedent has arisen.

But while the district court's discretion is extensive, we are unable to agree with the approach taken by the court here in placing a value on the damaged resources. Plaintiffs presented two principal theories of damages to the court. The first theory was somewhat analogous to the primary standard we have enunciated above, focusing on plaintiffs' plan to remove the damaged mangrove trees and oil-impregnated sediments from a large area and replace them with clean sediment and container-grown mangrove plants. This plan was estimated to cost approximately $7 million. The district court sensibly and correctly rejected this plan as impractical, inordinately expensive, and unjustifiably dangerous to the healthy mangroves and marine animals still present in the area to be restored. We can find no fault with the district court's conclusion that this draconian plan was not a step that a reasonable trustee of the natural environment would be expected to take as a means of protecting the corpus of the trust.

Plaintiffs' second theory, which the court accepted, focused on the supposed replacement value of the living creatures—the epibenthic and infaunal animals—alleged to have been permanently destroyed or damaged by the oil spill. Plaintiffs repeatedly disavowed any connection between this theory and an actual restoration plan. In other words, plaintiffs did not represent that they proposed to purchase 92 million invertebrate animals for actual introduction into the sediments, (which, being contaminated with oil, would hardly support them), but rather wished to use the alleged replacement value of these animals as a yardstick for estimating the quantum of harm caused to the Commonwealth. This theory has no apparent analog in the standards for measuring environmental damages we have discussed above. To be sure, the federal statutes from which we have borrowed speak in places of replacement as a part of the appropriate recovery. See, e.g., 33 U.S.C.A. § 1321(f)(5). But we believe these references, in context, should be interpreted as meaning replacement as a component in a practicable plan for actual restoration. Thus, for example, if a state were seeking to restore a damaged area of forest, a portion of the damages sought might be allocated to replacement of wild birds or game animals or such other creatures as would not be expected to regenerate naturally within a relatively finite period of time even with appropriate restoration. This is a far different matter from permitting the state to recover money damages for the loss of small, commercially valueless creatures which assertedly would perish if returned to the oil-soaked sands, yet probably would replenish themselves naturally if and when restoration—either artificial or natural—took place.

Notes

1. Does the court's measure of damages provide adequate compensation for the harm caused by the spill? Can you suggest a better way of measuring damages?

2. Note that the Puerto Rican statute did not by its terms limit the government's claims to resources to which it had formal legal title. Nevertheless, the government is clearly given some kind of protected legal interest. Is this in reality a "greening" of the property regime?

Note on Natural Resources Damages

Section 1006(d)(1) of the 1990 Oil Pollution Act, 33 U.S.C.A. § 2706, provides that the measure of natural resource damages is:

> (A) the cost of restoring, rehabilitating, replacing, or acquiring the equivalent of, the damaged natural resources;

> (B) the diminution in value of those natural resources pending restoration; plus

> (C) the reasonable cost of assessing those damages.

These costs are to be assessed with respect to restoration plans, which are to be promulgated by federal or state trustees. Double recoveries are precluded by subsection (d)(3). Section 1006(e) requires the President to issue damage assessment regulations; damage determinations pursuant to those regulations will then enjoy a rebuttable presumption of correctness.[l]

One of the components of damages under § 1006 is the cost of restoration. Arguably, only restoration can fully compensate the public for loss of a natural area. See Note, "Restoration As The Economically Efficient Remedy for Damage to Publicly Owned Natural Resources," 91 *Colum.L.Rev.* 430 (1991). Unfortunately, one of the lessons of the Exxon Valdez oil spill is that our technological capabilities in the area of restoration are still quite primitive, and may in fact be counterproductive. See Holloway, "Trends in Environmental Technologies: Soiled Shores," *Scientific American,* October 1991, at 100.

In theory, valuation should include the amount people are willing to pay for the continued existence of a natural resource that they do not currently use and have no immediate plans to use. A method known as "contingent valuation" has been used to assess this "nonuse value" through survey questions. There is considerable controversy about the reliability of this methodology.[m] In *Ohio v. Lujan,* 880 F.2d 432 (D.C.Cir.1989), the court held that the regulations must cover "non-use values," which can only be measured presently using contingent valuation. The Secretary of the Interior has now issued new and more flexible valuation rules for assessing natural resource damages under CERCLA. (For a fuller discussion, see Chapter VII, p. 666 supra.) The National Oceanic and Atmospheric Administration (NOAA) developed parallel rules under the Oil Pollution Act of 1990. These rules were upheld in *General Electric Co. v. United States Dept. of Commerce,* 128 F.3d 767 (D.C.Cir.1997). The court found the *Ohio* ruling decisive regarding the general legitimacy of contingent valuation. Any claims that a particular contingent valuation was performed without adequate safeguards could be addressed in a later enforcement proceeding. Id. at 773–74.

Perhaps as recondite as the calculation of natural resource damages is the question of how to spend the money. In 1992, the federal and state government settled their restoration damage claims against Exxon for over $1 billion to be paid over ten years. The funds are to be controlled by a federal-state Trustee Council. Alaska natives would like the state to use the funds to purchase native lands for wilderness preservation. The federal government has been seeking to use the funds for damage assessment studies, while the governor proposed a highway for development purposes.

---

l. Another issue, not present in the *Exxon* case but likely to be raised in future cases, concerns the allocation of liability between various polluters. See Robert Copple, "Natural Resource Damages Causation, Fault, and the Baseline Concept: A Quandary in Environmental Decisionmaking," 26 *Env. L. Rev.* 10457 (1996).

m. Hanemann, "Valuing the Environment Through Contingent Valuation," 8 *J.Econ.Persp.* 19 (Fall 1994). See Note, " 'Ask A Silly Question ...': Contingent Valuation of Natural Resource Damages," 105 *Harv.L.Rev.* 1981 (1992). See also Rosenthal and Nelson, "Why Existence Value Should *Not* Be Used in Cost–Benefit Analysis," 11 *J.Pol'y Analysis and Manag.* 116 (1992); Kopp, "Why Existence Value *Should* Be Used in Cost–Benefit Analysis," id. at 123.

Beyond the direct economic effects of the spill, are Alaska natives entitled to compensation for the damage caused to their way of life? Apparently not:

> Admittedly, the oil spill affected the communal life of Alaska Natives, but whatever injury they suffered (other than the harvest loss), though potentially different in degree than that suffered by other Alaskans, was not different in kind. We agree with the district court that the right to lead subsistence lifestyles is not limited to Alaska Natives. While the oil spill may have affected Alaska Natives more severely than other members of the public, "the right to obtain and share wild food, enjoy uncontaminated nature, and cultivate traditional, cultural, spiritual, and psychological benefits in pristine natural surroundings" is shared by all Alaskans. The Class [of Alaskan natives] therefore has failed to prove any "special injury" to support a public nuisance action.

In re Exxon Valdez: Alaska Native Class v. Exxon Corp., 104 F.3d 1196, 1198 (9th Cir.1997).

D. PUBLIC PROPERTY

In the previous section, we considered areas in which the state or federal government has traditionally claimed a special quasi-property relationship. Although few individuals in the eastern half of the United States are aware of this fact, the federal government owns vast amounts of land outright. Thus, despite the primacy of private land ownership, public ownership is far from being inconsequential. This section will primarily focus on this huge public domain.

1. INTRODUCTION TO PUBLIC LAND LAWS

In 1989, the public lands were estimated at over 690 million acres, an area nearly the size of India or roughly one-third of the land area in the United States. About half of this land was located in Alaska. The percentage of federally owned lands, excluding Indian reservations, in the western states ranges from about 30% in Washington to almost 90% in Nevada. The average is close to 50%. Thus federal land policy has critical importance to the western states.

Land policy is also of great importance to a number of important economic interests. The public lands contain approximately 20% of the nation's commercial forest land, as well as large amounts of minerals such as copper, mercury, and nickel. In addition, federal lands in 1989 accounted for approximately 14% of the nation's production of oil. Thus, the federal lands also have tremendous economic importance.

Of course, the public lands also have tremendous importance to conservationists. In perhaps the single most important conservation action of this century, Congress in 1980 set aside vast tracts of land in Alaska as national monuments, parks, and wilderness areas. Roughly 30 million acres were added to the national parks system alone. Even before this legislation, more than 180 million acres had been reserved for national forests and parks. (Oddly, or perhaps intriguingly, the result was to preserve about an acre of wilderness for each individual citizen.) It takes little imagination to foresee the possibility of considerable conflict between environmentalists and resource developers.

Until 1970, the developers clearly had the upper hand in this struggle. In the 1970s, the balance of power shifted to the environmentalists. But in the 1980s, a curious political situation developed because the Reagan Administration strongly favored development, while Congress remained pro-environmentalist. The Reagan Administration made frequent proposals for sharp changes in direction regarding resource use, but little new law resulted because of Congressional opposition. Currently, the Administration is environmentalist, but the balance of power seems to remain in equipoise, with pro-development interests having enough power in Congress to block new environmental legislation, while the President can fend off roll-backs of environmental regulation.

In order to understand the environmental aspects of public land law, a basic understanding of the non-environmental aspects is necessary as background. Unfortunately, there is no comprehensive statutory scheme governing federal lands. The numerous existing statutes are complicated and poorly coordinated. We will attempt only to give a basic outline of public land law.

a. The Basic Legal Structure

Until the Twentieth Century, the federal government's main policy with respect to public lands was to dispose of them as quickly as possible. This policy was evidenced by several homestead acts which conveyed large portions of land to farmers and ranchers. The most important survivor from this period is the Mining Law of 1872, 30 U.S.C.A. § 22 et seq. The Act allows private purchase of "all valuable mineral deposits in lands belonging to the United States." (This statute, however, does not apply to certain important substances such as oil, gas, coal and oil shale.) Any individual who discovers a valuable mineral deposit on public lands can obtain a mining claim for that deposit. The locator of the minerals acquires a possessory interest in the claim, which is a form of transferable property. Beginning at the time of location, this property interest gives the holder the right to extract, process and market the minerals. In addition, the holder of the claim has the right to obtain title to the land on which the claim is located at a nominal cost. The locator of the minerals is not required to apply for a government patent to the land, but if it chooses to do so, the Secretary of the Interior has no discretion about issuing the patent. The sole purpose of this statute is to promote mining.

Apart from history, there seems to be little justification for the 1872 Mining Act. See MacDonnell, "Mineral Law in the United States: A Study in Legal Change," in L. MacDonnell & S. Bates, *Natural Resources Policy and Law: Trends and Directions* 66–92 (1993). In 1994, a scandal erupted when a mining company perfected its patent for almost

2000 acres of federal land, including a gold mine thought to be worth billions of dollars. The firm paid about $10,000 for the land. GAO estimates that about $1.7 billion in minerals is being taken from federal lands each year. See Kenworthy, "There's Gold in Them Thar Laws," *Washington Post Weekly Ed.*, Apr. 25–May 1, 1994, at 31. Although both the Senate and House passed amendments to the 1872 Act, reform efforts sputtered to a halt. Public choice theorists might well consider this a classic victory of a concentrated special interest over a more diffuse public interest.

Among its other flaws, the 1872 Act gave the federal government little power to control mining. In 1976, mining activities were finally subjected to some degree of government regulation. As part of the Federal Land Policy and Management Act, Congress provided that in "managing the public lands" the Secretary "shall, by regulation or otherwise, take any action necessary to prevent unnecessary or undue degradation of the lands." 43 U.S.C.A. § 1732(b). The preceding sentence in the statute makes it clear that this provision is applicable to mining. Until this statute was passed, however, the federal government was essentially powerless to deal with environmental problems relating to mining, and even today its power is limited. State governments may also require permits for mining on federal lands. These permit requirements are not preempted if the state is regulating mining methods to limit environmental damage, as opposed to land use regulations prohibiting mining altogether in certain locations. See *California Coastal Commission v. Granite Rock Co.*, 480 U.S. 572, 107 S.Ct. 1419, 94 L.Ed.2d 577 (1987). Distinguishing between "environmental" and "land use" regulations, as the Court attempted to do in *Granite Rock*, may prove difficult in practice.

Regulation of mining has given rise to takings claims, prompted by the special property rights created under the Mining Act. In *Kunkes v. United States*, 78 F.3d 1549 (Fed.Cir.1996), the court upheld a requirement that owners of unpatented claims make cash payments in order to keep the claims alive:

It is important to remember the type of property at issue here. Congress created unpatented mining claims expressly to encourage development and extraction of minerals, i.e., to exploit valuable mineral deposits. It is entirely reasonable for Congress to require a $100 per claim fee in order to assess whether the claim holders believe that the value of the minerals in their claims is sufficiently great to warrant such a payment; and whether claim holders have the resources and desire to develop these claims. * * * If the claim holder cannot pay a $100 per claim fee, it is unlikely that she would be able solely through her own labor to develop the deposits, thereby frustrating the fundamental purpose in creating rights to unpatented mining claims.

Id. at 1556. Other types of taking claims may arise when new regulations make an unpatented mining operation unprofitable. Arguably, the new regulations do not constitute a taking because they invalidate one of the preconditions of the claim itself, which is that a "valuable discovery" of minerals be present. See Michael Graf, "Application of Takings Law to the Regulation of Unpatented Mining Claims," 24 *Ecology L.Q.* 122–24 (1997). For an overview of mining regulations, see Susan Bass, "Tools for Regulating the Environmental Impact of Mining in the United States," 26 *Env. L. Rep.* 10159 (1996). For a historical review, see John Lacy, "The Historical Origins of the U.S. Mining Laws and Proposals for Change," *NR & E*, Summer 1995, at 13.

Some important natural resources such as oil have been exempted from the 1872 statute. Under the Mineral Leasing Act of 1920, the Secretary of the Interior was empowered to issue prospecting permits and leases for certain minerals such as oil and gas. Unlike the limited government role under the Mining Act, the government's powers to control mineral leasing are quite broad because of its discretion over the issuance of permits and leases.

Another major resource use is logging. Beginning in 1891, the President was authorized to set aside land as national forests. Under an 1897 statute, the purposes of establishing national forests were declared to be water control and "a continuous supply of timber." 16 U.S.C.A. § 475. The motivation for the statute was the fear that forest lands might soon disappear, leaving the United States with a shortage of timber and of watersheds needed to control stream flows. The Supreme Court has recently made it clear, as we shall see below, that it regards these as the exclusive purposes of the 1891 and 1897 Acts. In 1960, Congress broadened the purposes of the national forest system by passing the Multiple–Use Sustained Yield Act, 16 U.S.C.A. §§ 528–531. This statute provides that national forests shall be administered for various purposes, including outdoor recreation, timber, and wildlife purposes. Because the Act gave no guidance as to what weight to give these various purposes, the Act was held to leave the administrator almost complete discretion. In 1974 and 1978, Congress called upon the Secretary of Agriculture to establish land management plans for national forests. This legislation also addresses matters such as clearcutting, a logging practice which had previously given rise to considerable controversy. See 16 U.S.C.A. § 1601 et seq. In 1976, the Federal Land Policy and Management Act was passed, which calls for similar planning on the 450 million acres administered by the Bureau of Land Management. See 43 U.S.C.A. §§ 1701–1784. An important implementing regulation requires the Forest Service "to maintain viable populations of existing native" species. 36 C.F.R. § 219.19. See *Oregon Natural Res. Council v. Lowe*, 109 F.3d 521, 527 (9th Cir.1997); Durkin, "High Noon in the National Forests," *The Amicus Journal*, Summer 1996, at 26.

A cynic might characterize our land laws as creating a gigantic federal welfare program for Western economic interests. The Clinton Administration took office with high hopes of instituting "welfare reform" in this area. For example, the novel proposal was made to require ranchers to pay fair market value for the right to graze on public land.

This proposal was scuttled by Western grazing interests. Efforts to require royalty payments for minerals on public lands and to end below-cost timber sales were also frustrated. Apparently there *is* a free lunch, after all.

The struggle over grazing rights illustrates the difficulties of "redistributional" politics. Technically, the lands involved belong to the public, and ranchers have no more than a license which Congress can terminate at any time. See *Alves v. United States*, 133 F.3d 1454 (Fed.Cir.1998) (grazing permits not property under taking clause). But in the ranchers' communities, the grazing rights are a fundamental form of property, and any effort to meddle with those rights is met with fierce resistance. (Similarly, retirees have only an expectation, not a property interest, in their social security payments, legally speaking—but politically speaking, it is a deeply entrenched "right," which seems to encompass not only current payment levels but anticipated COLA increases.) From one point of view, efforts to increase fees and regulate grazing are a defense of public property against pork barrel politics; from another point of view, they are an attack on vital property rights, threatening an established way of life. Little wonder that the debate has been so heated, or that it has proved so difficult to reach an accommodation. See William Riebsame, "Ending the Range Wars?," *Environment*, May 1996 at 3.

b. *Executive Withdrawals*

Historically, resource development on public lands has been the rule rather than the exception. Most public land law was geared toward encouraging resource development, while preservation was an exception. Thus, preservation of public lands usually has taken place when either the executive or the legislature took action to withdraw lands from the "normal" development process.

Presidential authority to withdraw land from development was upheld by the Supreme Court in *United States v. Midwest Oil Co.*, 236 U.S. 459, 35 S.Ct. 309, 59 L.Ed. 673 (1915). Because of the encouragement offered by the public land laws of the time, a race among oil companies arose in California to remove as much oil as possible as quickly as possible, with each company attempting to pump out the oil before owners of nearby wells could do so. In 1909, the Director of the Geological Survey reported that all the oil lands might be in private hands within a few months. This, in turn, might jeopardize the Navy's fuel supply. In response, the President issued an order "in aid of proposed legislation" withdrawing certain public lands from disposal to the public. The oil companies argued strenuously that the President lacked statutory authority to take this action. The Court held, however, that Congress had been aware of numerous prior instances of similar Presidential actions. Because Congress did not repudiate these previous withdrawals and indeed acquiesced in the practice, Congress was held to have impliedly consented to the Executive practice. The Court stressed the need for flexibility in administering the public lands:

These rules or laws [passed by Congress] for the disposal of public land are necessarily general in their nature. Emergencies may occur, or conditions may so change as to require that the agent in charge [the President] should, in the public interest, withhold the land from sale; and while no such expressed authority has been granted, there is nothing in the nature of the power exercised which prevents Congress from granting it by implication just as could be done by any other owner of property under similar conditions.

The Presidential power at issue in *Midwest Oil* was confirmed by the Pickett Act. The Act authorized the President "in his discretion" to "temporarily withdraw from settlement * * * any of the public lands of the United States * * * and reserve the same for water-power sites, irrigation, classification of lands, or other public purposes to be specified in the orders of withdrawal, and such withdrawals shall remain in force until revoked by him or by an Act of Congress." Such withdrawals did not affect the application of the mining laws to metallic minerals on withdrawn land. Despite the use of the word "temporary," a withdrawal remained in effect until expressly revoked, even though the result was that such a "temporary" withdrawal could last 50 years or more, long after its original purpose had ceased. In part, the rationale for this rule was the need for certainty in the determination of property claims with respect to public lands.

In 1976, the Pickett Act was repealed. The power of the Secretary of the Interior to withdraw public lands is now governed by 43 U.S.C.A. § 1714. The goal of this legislation was to give Congress greater control over executive withdrawals. Withdrawals of large tracts of land (over 5,000 acres) can be made only for 20–year periods, subject to a legislative veto by concurrent resolution of both houses. (The constitutionality of this legislative veto provision is open to question.) The Secretary is authorized to make smaller withdrawals for various periods of time, the period varying from 5 years to infinity depending on the reason for the withdrawal. The statute does provide for emergency 3–year withdrawals, which must be made when either the Secretary or the Senate or House Interior Affairs Committee determines that "an emergency situation exists and that extraordinary measures must be taken to preserve values that would otherwise be lost." This provision was utilized on December 1, 1978, to make an emergency withdrawal of 105 million acres in Alaska. The legislative history shows that the 1976 legislation was intended to eliminate the President's implied withdrawal power under the *Midwest Oil* doctrine. The President does retain withdrawal power under certain other statutes, such as the Antiquities Act, 16 U.S.C.A. § 431, which was also used by President Carter with respect to large tracts of land in Alaska.

c. *Legislative Withdrawals*

The most important legislative land withdrawal, apart from the 1980 Alaskan Lands Act, was the Wilderness Act of 1964, 16 U.S.C.A. §§ 1131–1136. This statute created the National Wilderness Preservation System. The Act defines a wilderness as having four characteristics: (1) unnoticeable human impact, (2) outstanding opportunities for solitude or primitive recreation, (3) an area of at least 5,000 acres or a sufficient size to make preservation practicable, and (possibly but not necessarily) (4) ecological, geological, or other value. Section 1132 of the Act designates certain lands as wilderness areas and provides for review of other national forest lands to determine the desirability of further legislation adding them to the wilderness system.

The most important effect of wilderness designation is found in § 1133 of the Act, which sharply restricts the use of wilderness land. Section 1133 makes the agency administering any wilderness area "responsible for preserving the wilderness character of the area" and for insuring that these areas are devoted to "the public purposes of recreational, scenic, scientific, educational, conservational, and historical use." Except where the Act expressly provides otherwise, no commercial enterprise and no permanent roads are allowed in any wilderness area. Mineral use temporarily remained a major exception, with the mining laws having remained applicable to wilderness areas until 1983. One area of uncertainty is the relationship between the Wilderness Act and earlier legislation, since the Act sharply changes the status of these lands but purports not to repeal such previous legislation.

Apart from its impact on land already designated as wilderness, the statute also has some effect on federal land under study for wilderness designation. In *Parker v. United States,* 448 F.2d 793 (10th Cir.1971), cert. denied 405 U.S. 989, 92 S.Ct. 1252, 31 L.Ed.2d 455 (1972), the Tenth Circuit held that timber sales were barred on land of "predominantly wilderness value" adjacent to a designated wilderness area. The court's rationale was that logging activities would irrevocably destroy the land's wilderness nature and thus deprive Congress of the opportunity to consider its inclusion within the wilderness system. The 1976 Federal Land Policy and Management Act required an inventory by 1991 of all roadless areas of 5,000 acres or more outside of the national forest system. The Act codified the *Parker* approach by requiring that, subject to existing rights, areas under study be managed "in a manner so as not to impair the suitability of such areas for preservation as wilderness." This provision was held to apply to mineral leasing, except for activities actually underway when the 1976 Act was passed. *Rocky Mountain Oil & Gas Ass'n v. Watt,* 696 F.2d 734 (10th Cir.1982).

The Alaska National Interest Lands Conservation Act (ANILCA), 16 U.S.C.A. § 3103, passed in the closing days of the Carter Administration, added vast tracts of land to the national park, wilderness, and wildlife preservation systems, more than doubling the size of each system. Over 40 million acres were added to the national park system alone. Some idea of the character of the land can be gained from the statute itself. Section 201(2), for example, created the Bering Land Bridge National Preserve, some 2.4 million acres, which is to be managed for the study of volcanic activity, to provide habitat for internationally migratory birds, to provide for archeological study of migration between North America and Asia, and to provide habitat for marine mammals, brown and grizzly bears, moose and wolves. Other parts of the statute mention caribou, Dall sheep, raptors, trumpeter swans, bald eagles and peregrine falcons, salmon, sea otters, and seals. The statute also added two million acres to the National Forest System, created two new national monuments covering over three million acres, and created a one million acre national recreation area and an equally large national conservation area. Title VII designated roughly 40 million acres within three national parks, wildlife refuges, and national forests as wilderness areas. The statute contains detailed provisions governing the use of these enormous areas, covering issues like oil and gas exploration and timber harvesting.

2. PROTECTION OF PUBLIC LANDS FROM CONFLICTING PRIVATE USES

Preventing mining, forestry, and other commercial activities in a wilderness area is only part of the task of protecting wilderness. It is also necessary to protect these areas from having their water supplies cut off or their air polluted to the point of impairing their wilderness character. The materials in this section explore the methods of protecting public lands from these threats from private landowners. Once again, property concepts are central.

CAPPAERT v. UNITED STATES

Supreme Court of the United States, 1976.
426 U.S. 128, 96 S.Ct. 2062, 48 L.Ed.2d 523.

CHIEF JUSTICE BURGER delivered the opinion of the Court.

The question presented in this litigation is whether the reservation of Devil's Hole as a national monument reserved federal water rights in unappropriated water.

Devil's Hole is a deep limestone cavern in Nevada. Approximately 50 feet below the opening of the cavern is a pool 65 feet long, 10 feet wide, and at least 200 feet deep, although its actual depth is unknown. The pool is a remnant of the prehistoric Death Valley Lake System and is situated on land owned by the United States since the Treaty of Guadalupe Hidalgo in 1848. By the Proclamation of January 17, 1952, President Truman withdrew from the public domain a 40–acre tract of land surrounding Devil's Hole, making it a detached component of the Death Valley National Monument. The Proclamation was issued under the American Antiquities Preservation Act, which authorizes the President to declare as national monuments "objects of historic or scientific interest that are situated upon the lands owned or controlled by the Government of the United States * * *."

The 1952 Proclamation notes that Death Valley was set aside as a national monument "for the preservation of the unusual features of scenic, scientific, and educational interest therein contained." The Proclamation also notes that Devil's Hole is near Death Valley and contains a "remarkable underground pool." Additional preambulary statements in the Proclamation explain why Devil's Hole was being added to the Death Valley National Monument:

* * *

Whereas the geologic evidence that this subterranean pool is an integral part of the hydrographic history of the Death Valley region is further confirmed by the presence in this pool of a peculiar race of desert fish, and zoologists have demonstrated that this race of fish, which is found nowhere else in the world, evolved only after the gradual drying up of the Death Valley Lake System isolated this fish population from the original ancestral stock that in Pleistocene times was common to the entire region; * * *

The Proclamation provides that Devil's Hole should be supervised, managed, and directed by the National Park Service, Department of the Interior. Devil's Hole is fenced off, and only limited access is allowed by the Park Service.

The Cappaert petitioners own a 12,000–acre ranch near Devil's Hole, 4,000 acres of which are used for growing Bermuda grass, alfalfa, wheat, and barley; 1,700 to 1,800 head of cattle are grazed. The ranch represents an investment of more than $7 million; it employs more than 80 people with an annual payroll of more than $340,000.

In 1968 the Cappaerts began pumping groundwater on their ranch on land 2½ miles from Devil's Hole; they were the first to appropriate groundwater. The groundwater comes from an underground basin or aquifer which is also the source of the water in Devil's Hole. After the Cappaerts began pumping from the wells near Devil's Hole, which they do from March to October, the summer water level of the pool in Devil's Hole began to decrease. Since 1962 the level of water in Devil's Hole has been measured with reference to a copper washer installed in one of the walls of the hole by the United States Geological Survey. Until 1968, the water level, with seasonable variations, had been stable at 1.2 feet below the copper marker. In 1969 the water level in Devil's Hole was 2.3 feet below the copper washer; in 1970, 3.17 feet; in 1971, 3.48 feet; and in 1972, 3.93 feet.

When the water is at the lowest levels, a large portion of a rock shelf in Devil's Hole is above water. However, when the water level is at 3.0 feet below the marker or higher, most of the rock shelf is below water, enabling algae to grow on it. This in turn enables the desert fish (*cyprinodon diabolis*, commonly known as Devil's Hole pupfish), referred to in President Truman's Proclamation, to spawn in the spring. As the rock shelf becomes exposed, the spawning area is decreased, reducing the ability of the fish to spawn in sufficient quantities to prevent extinction.

* * *

In determining whether there is a federally reserved water right implicit in a federal reservation of public land, the issue is whether the

Government intended to reserve unappropriated and thus available water. Intent is inferred if the previously unappropriated waters are necessary to accomplish the purposes for which the reservation was created. Both the District Court and the Court of Appeals held that the 1952 Proclamation expressed an intention to reserve unappropriated water, and we agree. The Proclamation discussed the pool in Devil's Hole in four of the five preambles and recited that the "pool * * * should be given special protection." Since a pool is a body of water, the protection contemplated is meaningful only if the water remains; the water right reserved by the 1952 Proclamation was thus explicit, not implied.[n]

* * *

The implied-reservation-of-water doctrine, however, reserves only that amount of water necessary to fulfill the purpose of the reservation, no more. Here the purpose of reserving Devil's Hole Monument is preservation of the pool. Devil's Hole was reserved "for the preservation of the unusual features of scenic, scientific, and educational interest." The Proclamation notes that the pool contains "a peculiar race of desert fish * * * which is found nowhere else in the world" and that the "pool is of * * * outstanding scientific importance * * *." The pool need only be preserved, consistent with the intention expressed in the Proclamation, to the extent necessary to preserve its scientific interest. The fish are one of the features of scientific interest. The preamble noting the scientific interest of the pool follows the preamble describing the fish as unique; the Proclamation must be read in its entirety. Thus, as the District Court has correctly determined, the level of the pool may be permitted to drop to the extent that the drop does not impair the scientific value of the pool as the natural habitat of the species sought to be preserved. The District Court thus tailored its injunction, very appropriately, to minimal need, curtailing pumping only to the extent necessary to preserve an adequate water level at Devil's Hole, thus implementing the stated objectives of the Proclamation.

[In the concluding portions of its opinion, the Court held that the reservation doctrine applied to groundwater, and that the government's water rights were not limited by state law.]

Notes

1. The apparent simplicity of the implied reservation doctrine conceals some difficult problems. The easiest cases are those in states that follow the appropriation doctrine and are subject to the Desert Land Act, 19 Stat. 377, 43 U.S.C.A. § 321. (The Desert Land Act has the effect of acquiescing in state water priority systems. See *California Oregon Power Co. v. Beaver Portland Cement Co.,* 295 U.S. 142, 55 S.Ct. 725, 79 L.Ed. 1356 (1935).) The application of the doctrine under those circumstances is relatively simple. If

n. The 1952 Proclamation forbids unauthorized persons to "appropriate, injure, destroy, or remove any feature" from the reservation. Since water is a "feature" of the reservation, the Cappaerts, by their pumping, are "appropriating" or "removing" this feature in violation of the Proclamation.

X obtained an appropriative right in 1880, the United States made a withdrawal in 1885, and *Y* obtained an appropriative right in 1900, then the order of priority of water rights is first *X* (whose rights are confirmed by the Desert Land Act), then the United States, and finally *Y*. In contrast, under state law, *Y* would typically have priority over the United States if the United States had not actually begun to use the water until some time after 1900. See Meyers, "The Colorado River," 19 *Stan.L.Rev.* 1, 67–69 (1966). On the other hand, there is considerable controversy over whether the doctrine applies at all in non-appropriation states, and if it does, how the water shares are to be determined. Without entering into the murky depths of water law, it may be enough to note that in part the disagreement concerns the source of the implied reservation: Is it an implied term of the federal government's land grant to the current private landowner's predecessor in title, or is it the result of preemption of state water law by the later federal withdrawal? Footnote 6 in *Cappaert* seems to support somewhat the preemption view.

2. The pupfish were said to be important evidence in on-going investigations of the mechanisms by which new species are formed. See *New York Times,* April 20, 1982, at 21. In 1984, 140 pupfish were counted in Devil's Hole. More than 12,000 acres of land surrounding the Hole were owned by a Las Vegas development company, but were to be sold to the Nature Conservancy for ultimate transfer to the Interior Department. *Newsweek,* January 30, 1984 at 7. By 1990, however, the pupfish were in trouble again, endangered by plans to divert water to Las Vegas from rural eastern and central Nevada, which is now the ultimate source of the water flowing into Devil's Hole. L.A. Times, April 29, 1990, at 3, col. 1.

UNITED STATES v. NEW MEXICO

Supreme Court of the United States, 1978.
438 U.S. 696, 98 S.Ct. 3012, 57 L.Ed.2d 1052.

JUSTICE REHNQUIST delivered the opinion of the Court.

The question posed in this case—what quantity of water, if any, the United States reserved out of the Mimbres River when it set aside the Gila National Forest in 1899—is a question of implied intent and not power.

* * *

Recognition of Congress' power to reserve water for land which is itself set apart from the public domain, however, does not answer the question of the amount of water which has been reserved or the purposes for which the water may be used. Substantial portions of the public domain *have* been withdrawn and reserved by the United States for use as Indian reservations, forest reserves, national parks, and national monuments. And water is frequently necessary to achieve the purposes for which these reservations are made. But Congress has seldom expressly reserved water for use on these withdrawn lands. If water were abundant, Congress' silence would pose no problem. In the arid parts of the West, however, claims to water for use on federal reservations inescapably vie with other public and private claims for the limited quantities to be found in the rivers and streams. This competition is compounded by the sheer quantity of reserved lands in the western States, which lands form brightly colored swaths across the maps of these States.[c]

* * * Each time this Court has applied the "implied-reservation-of-water doctrine," it has carefully examined both the asserted water right and the specific purposes for which the land was reserved, and concluded that without the water the purposes of the reservation would be entirely defeated.

This careful examination is required both because the reservation is implied, rather than expressed, and because of the history of congressional intent in the field of federal-state jurisdiction with respect to allocation of water. Where Congress has expressly addressed the question of whether federal entities must abide by state water law, it has almost invariably deferred to the state law. Where water is necessary to fulfill the very purposes for which a federal reservation was created, it is reasonable to conclude, even in the face of Congress' express deference to state water law in other areas, that the United States intended to reserve the necessary water. Where water is only valuable for a secondary use of the reservation, however, there arises the contrary inference that Congress intended, consistent with its other views, that the United States would acquire water in the same manner as any other public or private appropriator.

[The Court next summarized the history of the national forests. The Court concluded that the national forests were intended to serve only two purposes: water control and timber yield.]

Petitioner's claim that Congress intended to reserve water for recreation and wildlife-preservation is not only inconsistent with Congress' failure to recognize these goals as purposes of the national forests, but would also defeat the very purpose for which Congress did create the national forest system. * * * The water that would be "insured" by preservation of the forest was to "be used for domestic, mining, milling, or irrigation purposes, under the laws of the State wherein such national forests are situated, or under the laws of the United States and the rules and regulations established thereunder." Organic Administration Act of 1897, 16 U.S.C.A. § 481. As this provision and its legislative history evidence, Congress authorized the national forest system principally as a means of enhancing the quantity of water that would be available to the settlers of the arid West. Petitioner, however, would have us now believe

c. The percentage of federally owned land (*excluding* Indian reservations and other trust properties) in the western States ranges from 29.5% of the land in the State of Washington to 86.5% of the land in the State of Nevada, an average of about 46%. * * * Because federal reservations are normally found in the heights of the western States rather than the flat lands, the percentage of water flow originating in or flowing through the reservations is even more impressive. More than 60% of the average annual water yield in the 11 western States is from federal reservations. * * *

that Congress intended to partially defeat this goal by reserving significant amounts of water for purposes quite inconsistent with this goal.

In 1960, Congress passed the Multiple–Use Sustained–Yield Act, * * *. The Supreme Court of the State of New Mexico concluded that this Act did not give rise to any reserved rights not previously authorized in the Organic Administration Act of 1897. "The Multiple–Use Sustained–Yield Act of 1960 does not have a retroactive effect nor can it broaden the purposes for which the Gila National Forest was established under the Organic Act of 1897." While we conclude that the Multiple–Use Sustained–Yield Act of 1960 was intended to broaden the purposes for which national forests had previously been administered, we agree that Congress did not intend to thereby expand the reserved rights of the United States.

* * *

* * * As discussed earlier, the "reserved rights doctrine" is a doctrine built on implication and is an exception to Congress' explicit deference to state water law in other areas. Without legislative history to the contrary, we are led to conclude that Congress did not intend in enacting the Multiple–Use Sustained–Yield Act of 1960 to reserve water for the *secondary* purposes there established. A reservation of additional water could mean a substantial loss in the amount of water available for irrigation and domestic use, thereby defeating Congress' principal purpose of securing favorable conditions of water flow. Congress intended the national forests to be administered for broader purposes after 1960 but there is no indication that it believed the new purposes to be so crucial as to require a reservation of additional water. By reaffirming the primacy of a favorable water flow, it indicated the opposite intent.

JUSTICE POWELL, with whom JUSTICE BRENNAN, JUSTICE WHITE, and JUSTICE MARSHALL join, dissenting in part.

I agree with the Court that the implied-reservation doctrine should be applied with sensitivity to its impact upon those who have obtained water rights under state law and to Congress' general policy of deference to state water law. I also agree that the Organic Administration Act of 1897 cannot fairly be read as evidencing an intent to reserve water for recreational or stockwatering purposes in the national forests.

I do not agree, however, that the forests which Congress intended to "improve and protect" are the still, silent, lifeless places envisioned by the Court. In my view, the forests consist of the birds, animals, and fish—the wildlife—that inhabit them, as well as the trees, flowers, shrubs, and grasses. I therefore would hold that the United States is entitled to so much water as is necessary to sustain the wildlife of the forests, as well as the plants. * * *

* * *

One may agree with the Court that Congress did not, by enactment of the Organic Administration Act of 1897, intend to authorize the creation of national forests simply to serve as wildlife preserves. But it does not follow from this that Congress did not consider wildlife to be part of the forest that it wished to "improve and protect" for future generations. It is inconceivable that Congress envisioned the forests it sought to preserve as including only inanimate components such as the timber and flora. Insofar as the Court holds otherwise, the 55th Congress is maligned and the Nation is the poorer, and I dissent.

Notes

1. Note the majority's argument concerning the federal policy of preserving water flow. The dissent argued that this policy was aimed at downstream users, and that these users were not harmed by the federal government's reservation of an instream flow. 438 U.S. at 724, 98 S.Ct. at 3026. Reserving an instream flow obviously injures upstream users, not the downstream users whom Congress was directly attempting to protect. Does this answer the question of the extent to which Congress was willing to injure upstream appropriators to protect downstream users?

2. Was Justice Rehnquist correct in characterizing the Multiple–Use Act as simply adding "secondary" purposes? For a critique of this portion of the opinion as dicta, see Abrams, "Reserved Water Rights, Indian Rights and the Narrowing Scope of Federal Jurisdiction: The Colorado River Decision," 30 *Stan.L.Rev.* 1111, 1136–1137 n. 173, 1138 nn. 175–176 (1978).

3. In a case decided shortly before *New Mexico,* the Idaho Supreme Court made a similar ruling concerning the purposes for which water could be reserved for national forests, but held that the United States could attempt to prove what amount of water was necessary to achieve these results. *Avondale Irrigation District v. North Idaho Properties, Inc.,* 99 Idaho 30, 577 P.2d 9 (1978). Suppose the government introduces expert testimony that wildlife is necessary to preserve the forest ecology and hence is necessary to the goals of water-flow control and timber production. Under *New Mexico,* should this testimony be considered?

4. The Federal Lands Policy and Management Act, 43 U.S.C.A. § 1701, requires land-use planning for federal lands. Does the statute create any reserved water rights in favor of the national government? For a negative answer, see *Sierra Club v. Watt,* 659 F.2d 203 (D.C.Cir.1981).

What about the Wilderness Act? Did it create reserved water rights? In *Sierra Club v. Block,* 622 F.Supp. 842 (D.Colo.1985), and *Sierra Club v. Lyng,* 661 F.Supp. 1490 (D.Colo.1987), the district court held that the statute did create reserved water rights, and directed the government to take steps to protect those rights. On appeal, the Tenth Circuit held that the issue was not ripe for review. *Sierra Club v. Yeutter,* 911 F.2d 1405 (10th Cir.1990). For a thorough discussion of the issue, see Colburn, "The Morality of Wilderness: Federal Reserved Water Rights in Western Wilderness Areas," 6 *Yale L. & Pol.Rev.* 157 (1988).

Even when federal law fails to protect the water needed on government lands, the government still may be able to assert rights as a landowner under state law. See *In re Water of Hallett Creek Stream System,* 44 Cal.3d 448, 243 Cal.Rptr. 887, 749 P.2d 324 (1988). In that case, the California

Supreme Court also ruled that the state water board had broad discretion over what priority to give the federal government's riparian water rights. For a thoughtful commentary on *Hallett Creek* and its broad implications for property law, see Freyfogle, "Context and Accommodation in Modern Property Law," 41 *Stan.L.Rev.* 1529 (1989).

5. The Wild and Scenic Rivers Act of 1968, 16 U.S.C.A. § 1271 et seq., is one of the few express congressional recognitions of the reserved rights doctrine. The Act is primarily aimed at preventing federal agencies from recommending or licensing projects on specified rivers. The statute also attempts to encourage land management planning in the vicinity of the river. Section 13 of the Act, 16 U.S.C.A. § 1284(c), provides that designation of streams as national wild rivers "shall not be construed as a reservation of the waters of such streams for purposes other than those specified in this Act, or in quantities greater than necessary to accomplish these purposes."

6. Besides interfering with necessary supplies of water, private land uses can also impinge on the intended use of public lands by creating air pollution. Along with the general PSD rules discussed in Chapter IV, § 169A of the Clean Air Act provides special protection for visibility in large national parks and wilderness areas. Among the requirements are the use of BART ("best available retrofit technology") for existing sources, along with the usual mandated SIP revisions. In *Central Arizona Water Conserv. Dist. v. U.S. EPA,* 990 F.2d 1531 (9th Cir.1993), the court upheld rigorous EPA regulations designed to improve visibility at the Grand Canyon. The court remarked that the rule was "the result of a site-specific informal rulemaking process that included virtually unprecedented cooperation between the governmental agency and the directly affected parties." Id. at 1545.

3. ENDANGERED SPECIES

We close this book with a return to the subject of biodiversity, which was also discussed in Chapter I. Protection of endangered species raises the full panoply of issues we have discussed in this book: the division of labor between courts, agencies and legislatures; the meaning and validity of environmental values; the necessity or avoidability of trade-offs between environment and economic factors. As we will see, it also raises questions about the rights of governmental and private property owners.

Endangered species receive particularly strong support under U.S. law.[o] The Endangered Species Act (ESA) stems from the same formative period of U.S. environmental law that saw the passage of NEPA and the federal pollution statutes. Section 4 of the Act requires the Secretary of Commerce and Interior to determine whether any species is endangered and to designate critical habitat, based on the best scientific data available. (Because of their implications, listing decisions can be quite controversial. For a discussion of the issues, see Doremus, "Listing Decisions Under the Endangered Species Act: Why Better Science Isn't Always Better Policy," 75 *Wash.U.L.Q.* 1029 (1997).) Section 7, entitled "Interagency Cooperation," requires consultation to ensure that agency

---

o. A useful survey of current federal activities relevant to biodiversity can be found in Karkainien, "Biodiversity and Land," 83 *Cornell L.Rev.* 1 (1997).

actions do not jeopardize any endangered species—the "consultation" has turned out to be less important than the "do not jeopardize." Section 9 of the Act goes on to forbid "taking" any endangered species. The Supreme Court set the pattern for interpreting the statute in the following celebrated case.

TVA v. HILL

[supra p. 581]

Notes

1. In response to *TVA v. Hill,* Congress amended the Endangered Species Act by creating a special Endangered Species Committee, consisting of several cabinet level officers and other high-ranking officials. The Committee may grant an exemption if it determines (by a vote of at least 5 to 2) that there are no reasonable alternatives to the agency action, that the benefits clearly outweigh those of compliance with the Act, and that the action is in the public interest and of at least regional significance. The Committee must also consider mitigation efforts. (These provisions are found in Endangered Species Amendment of 1978, § 7(e), (h), 16 U.S.C.A. § 1536(e), (h).) The Committee unanimously denied an exemption for Tellico Dam, on the ground that reasonable alternatives to completion of the dam were available with acceptable cost-benefit ratios. The Committee also found that, despite the $100 million already invested in the dam, the benefits of completing the dam did not clearly outweigh the benefits of the alternatives. Essentially, the dam could well fail to produce as much economic benefit as the farms it would flood.[p] Congress then passed a bill mandating completion of the dam. Does this further history show that the Supreme Court's decision was an exercise in futility, or does it show on the contrary that the Court was right to "remand" the problem to Congress? Should the Court have given a more "reasonable" interpretation to the ESA? Or would that have been inconsistent with the legislative mandate? See Farber, "Statutory Interpretation and Legislative Supremacy," 78 *Geo.L.J.* 281, 294–98 (1989). For a retrospective view on *TVA v. Hill,* see Plater, "In the Wake of the Snail Darter," 19 *U.Mich.J.L.Ref.* 805 (1986).

2. We discussed the value of biodiversity in Chapter 1. In deleted portions of the opinion, the Court quoted extensively from the legislative history concerning the reasons for protecting endangered species. The scope of the problem was also indicated by the CEQ's *Global 2000* report, issued in 1980:

> At no time in recorded history has the specter of species extinction loomed so ominously. Largely a consequence of deforestation and the "taming" of wild areas, the projected loss over two decades of approximately one-fifth of all species on the planet (at a minimum, roughly 500,000 species of plants and animals) is a prospective loss to the world

p. You may wonder how a dam could ever be approved in the first place if even the relatively small marginal cost of completion was not clearly outweighed by the benefits. For a study of the pathology of government cost-benefit analyses during this period, see Findley, "The Planning of a Corps of Engineers Reservoir Project: Law, Economics and Politics," 3 *Ecology L.Q.* 1 (1973).

that is literally beyond evaluation. The genetic and ecological values of wild or newly identified species continue to be discovered. They represent an irreplaceable evolutionary legacy whose value, particularly the value of the many expected to be lost in the tropics, will certainly increase especially if the earth's climate becomes warmer. The fact that humankind derives most of its food from no more than 15 species of plants masks to some extent the importance of genetic extinction, but not for the plant breeders who rely on the traits of wild progenitors of domestic plants in their continuing battle against pests and disease and in efforts to increase yields.

See also E.O. Wilson, *The Diversity of Life* (1992).

3.   One reason that *TVA v. Hill* was such an "easy" case is that there was seemingly no question from evidence then available (which later proved to be incomplete) that completing the dam would directly destroy the snail darter by totally wiping out its habitat. But what about government actions that pose subtler threats? Consider the following case.

NATIONAL WILDLIFE FEDERATION v. COLEMAN

United States Court of Appeals, Fifth Circuit, 1976.
529 F.2d 359.

SIMPSON, CIRCUIT JUDGE:

I–10, part of the National System of Interstate and Defense Highways, is a limited access highway across the southern United States which when completed will extend from Los Angeles, California, to Jacksonville, Florida. In Mississippi I–10 will be approximately 77.1 miles long traversing Hancock, Harrison, and Jackson Counties, and is being constructed with 90% federal financing pursuant to the Federal–Aid Highway Act. * * * The remaining 18.9 mile segment of I–10 in Mississippi extends from Highway 57 eastward to the Alabama line and contains the 5.7 mile segment in controversy. This 5.7 mile section runs from an interchange at the intersection of I–10 and Highway 57 on the west to the west bank of the Pascagoula River on the east. Within this 5.7 mile segment the plans call for the construction of an interchange at the junction of the Earl Bond Road and I–10. Both the interchange and the 5.7 section of I–10 will transect the habitat of the Mississippi Sandhill Crane, bisecting the eastern unit of a proposed refuge for the crane, and traversing Section 16 land held by the State of Mississippi in trust for the Jackson County School District.

An estimated number of 40 Mississippi Sandhill Cranes[21] still exist, their range being confined to a total area of approximately 40,000 acres

---

21. The Mississippi Sandhill Crane is a sub-species of sandhill cranes. It is the same size as the Florida Sandhill Crane (Grus canadensis pratensis) and prior to 1972 the Mississippi Sandhill Cranes and the Florida Cranes were thought to be of the same sub-species. Aldrich, A New Sub-species of Sandhill Crane in Mississippi, 85 Proceed- ings of the Biological Society of Washington 63 (1972). Mississippi Cranes are distinguishable from other sub-species of sandhill cranes because of darker plumage and the presence of a red tuft on the top of the head. Beginning in 1965 eggs were taken from the nests of the Mississippi Sandhill Crane population in Jackson County for the

in Jackson County, Mississippi. The Department of Interior designated the Mississippi Sandhill Crane an endangered sub-species on June 4, 1973 * * *. The sole natural habitat of the Crane is marked by the Jackson–Harrison County line on the west, the Pascagoula River on the east, United States Highway 90 on the south, and Bluff Creek on the north. For breeding grounds the cranes use only wet, semi-open, and savanna-like lands with marsh areas, with more trees than is typical of the nesting habitat of other sub-species of sandhill cranes. The nests are built in small openings in shallow water from vegetation surrounding the nest. Although the cranes are non-migratory, during the winter months they flock together in a roosting site in the eastern portion of the Pascagoula Marsh.

* * *

The day before the trial of this action, June 25, 1975, the Director of the Fish and Wildlife Service issued pursuant to Section 4(f) of the Endangered Species Act of 1973, an emergency determination of "critical habitat" for the Mississippi Sandhill Crane. The "critical habitat" as delineated in this determination consists of approximately 100,000 acres in Jackson County and includes land transected by the highway project. The designation of "critical habitat" for the cranes became effective on publication. The Fish and Wildlife Service stated that the reasons for the emergency determination were that "(t)he maintenance of significant portions of habitat and the well-being of the crane are threatened by construction of a new segment of Interstate Highway I–10 between Mississippi State Highway 57 and the Pascagoula River," and that "(t)he construction activities, destruction of habitat, incidental intrusions, and subsequent related commercial and residential development of the area all constitute a significant risk to the well-being of the crane."

* * *

Section 7 of the Endangered Species Act of 1973 imposes on Federal agencies the duty to "insure that actions authorized, funded, or carried out" by them do not jeopardize the continued existence of any endangered species or result in the destruction or modification of habitat of such species which the Secretary of Interior determines to be critical. Hence, § 7 imposes on federal agencies the mandatory duty to insure that their actions will not either (i) jeopardize the existence of an endangered species, or (ii) destroy or modify critical habitat of an endangered species. The primary responsibility for implementing § 7 is on the Secretary of Interior. Federal agencies are required to consult and obtain the assistance of the Secretary before taking any actions which may affect endangered species or critical habitat. However, once an agency has had meaningful consultation with the Secretary of Interior concerning actions which may affect an endangered species the final decision of whether or not to proceed with the action lies with the agency

purpose of propagation in captivity. In 1971 eight of the Cranes had been reared to adult plumage at the Patuxent Wildlife Research Center, Laruel, Maryland.

itself. Section 7 does not give the Department of Interior a veto over the actions of other federal agencies, provided that the required consultation has occurred. It follows that after consulting with the Secretary the federal agency involved must determine whether it has taken all necessary action to insure that its actions will not jeopardize the continued existence of an endangered species or destroy or modify habitat critical to the existence of the species. Once that decision is made it is then subject to judicial review to ascertain whether "the decision was based on a consideration of the relevant factors and whether there has been a clear error of judgment."

In the present case the appellants have the burden of proving that the appellees have failed to take the "action necessary to insure" that the 5.7 mile segment of I–10 does not jeopardize the continued existence of the Mississippi Sandhill Crane or will not destroy or modify habitat determined by the Department of Interior to be critical to the cranes' existence. The court below held that the appellants had failed to meet this burden because the evidence showed that "the defendants have adequately considered the effects of this project on the Crane." Further, the district court found that the FEIS and other documents from the administrative records of the appellees which tended to show that I–10 may be a threat to the continued existence of the cranes "merely reflect opinions of the effect of the highway on the Crane without specifying facts upon which they are based." With respect to the appellants' allegation that private development accompanying the construction of I–10 will jeopardize the existence of the cranes and result in the destruction of critical habitat, the district court found that "the record ... is totally devoid of any statement or opinion rising above mere speculation to indicate that such development will occur or is even likely to occur."

* * *

Principal among the indirect effects of the highway on the crane is the residential and commercial development that can be expected to result from the construction of the highway. The district court found that the record contained no statement or opinion rising above "mere speculation" to indicate that such development is likely to occur. We disagree. In addition to the testimony of Valentine and the letters from the Department of Interior and the Fish and Wildlife Service, the FEIS acknowledges in three places that private development always accompanies the construction of a major highway and that this development is the primary effect of I–10 on the crane. Further, the Department of Housing and Urban Development in a letter to the MSHD commenting on the FEIS stated that construction of this segment of I–10 "will bring with it a concentration of urban growth around interchanges and other selected areas." These predictions by the FHWA, the MSHD, and HUD, agencies experienced in highway and urban development, recognize that private development will accompany the construction of I–10 in Jackson County. The fact that the private development surrounding the highway and the Earl Bond Road interchange does not result from direct federal action does not lessen the appellee's duty under § 7. The appellees do control this development to the extent that they control the placement of the highway and interchanges.

The federal appellees contend that the decision to build the highway was made on the assumption that the Fish and Wildlife Service would acquire a refuge for the crane, and that the Gulf Regional Planning Commission had recognized certain areas for conservation in Jackson County. The FHWA believed that these measures would lessen the impact of the highway on the crane. This reliance on the proposed actions of other agencies does not satisfy the FHWA's burden of insuring that its actions will not jeopardize the continued existence of the crane. Further, even if these actions were taken, the Department of Interior has determined that approximately 100,000 acres of habitat in Jackson County is critical within the meaning of § 7, whereas the refuge proposed by the Fish and Wildlife Service contains only 11,300. The appellees argue that their concern for the crane is also demonstrated by the fact that the highway will cross the proposed refuge at its narrowest point. Under § 7, however, the relevant consideration is the area determined by the Secretary of Interior as "critical habitat" for the crane. The Secretary has delineated an area of 100,000 acres in Jackson County as "critical habitat" under § 7 for the Mississippi Sandhill Crane, and the proposed segment of I-10 traverses an extensive portion of this 100,000 acres. The duty of the appellees is to insure that their actions will not destroy or modify this "critical habitat," and not just the area within the habitat of the crane to be set aside as a refuge.

Similarly, the fact that timber management practices have in the past destroyed habitat of the crane does not lessen the duty of the appellees to insure that the highway and the accompanying private development do not jeopardize the existence of the crane or destroy critical habitat. We note that the appellees' FEIS states that at "the present time the greatest threats to the existence of the Mississippi Sandhill Crane are private development and the construction of Interstate Route No. 10." Hence, irrespective of the past actions of others the appellees have a duty to insure that the highway and the development generated by it do not further threaten the crane and its habitat.

Finally, it is beyond question from the record that the excavation of borrow pits within the area determined by the Secretary of Interior to be "critical habitat" for the crane will destroy and modify that habitat, in violation of § 7. The appellees assert that the FEIS recognized the potential danger of borrow pits to the habitat of the crane, and that the contract plans and specifications for the highway prohibit the forming of borrow pits from any land under option by the Nature Conservancy and in Sections 15 and 16, Township 7 South, Range 7 West. The prohibition of borrow pits in these areas, however, does not satisfy the directive of § 7, since it does not prohibit the excavation of borrow pits in the entire 100,000 acres of habitat determined to be "critical" by the Secretary.

* * *

Final decision →

Because the Department of Interior has primary jurisdiction for administering the Endangered Species Act, and the subject matter of this lawsuit is within the specialized field of the Department we defer to its determination of what modifications are necessary to bring the highway project into compliance with § 7. Therefore, we direct the district court on remand to enter its injunctive order restraining and enjoining the appellees as follows:

> (a) From initiating or carrying out any further work or incurring any further contractual obligations with respect to the interchange at the Earl Bond Road;

> (b) From excavating any borrow pits in the area determined to be critical habitat for the Mississippi Sandhill Crane under the notice published on June 30, 1975, at 40 Fed.Reg. 27501–27502.

This injunction is to remain in force until the Secretary of the Department of Interior determines that the necessary modifications are made in the highway project to insure that it will no longer jeopardize the continued existence of the Mississippi Sandhill Crane or destroy or modify critical habitat of the Mississippi Sandhill Crane. We do not reach a decision as to whether the FHWA can be ordered to acquire land to replace that taken by the Highway project, since we are confident that the Secretary of Transportation and the Secretary of Interior will take all actions necessary on remand to protect the continued existence of the Mississippi Sandhill Crane and its habitat.

Notes

1. *Coleman* is typical of the stringent enforcement given the ESA by most courts. It is not hard to imagine judges unsympathetic to the statute holding that the ESA only extends to the "direct effects" of a government action. Have the courts placed too much restriction on agency discretion? Or are they merely implementing the will of Congress?

2. We began our discussion of U.S. environmental law in Chapter II with a case in which Justice Douglas' dissent argued that trees should have standing. In light of *Coleman,* would it be unreasonable to say that 100,000 acres of Jackson County, Mississippi—right in the heart of Faulkner country—are "owned" by the Sandhill Cranes? True, the cranes don't have legal title, but their interests do seem to receive controlling weight. If so, is this a *reductio ad absurdum* of environmentalism or a harbinger of the "green property" hailed by Peter Byrne [supra p. 740]?

3. In the last decade, the most dramatic confrontation over an endangered species involved the Spotted Owl and its habitat in the old-growth forests of the Northwest. Some of the conifers in this forest are 500–1200 years old. The controversy pitted environmentalists against logging interests and thousands of employees who feared for their jobs. The complex proceedings surrounding the owl are discussed in detail in Houck, "The Endangered Species Act and Its Implementation by the U.S. Departments of Interior and Commerce," 64 *Colo.L.Rev.* 277, 333–350 (1993). In the end, Houck reports:

The Endangered Species Committee ruled that thirty-one of the forty-four timber sales did not qualify for exemption, after all, largely on the grounds of available alternatives and the absence of overriding national or regional significance. By a vote of five to two, only thirteen sales were exempted and these with stipulations that required abandonment of the Jamison strategy and consultation in the future on all sales as a whole. That the ultimate decision was so split, in the face of so much political pressure, is clearly less an indication that the proceedings that led up to them lived up to Congress's expectation than of the fact that BLM's case simply didn't belong there.

In retrospect, if the Secretary's purpose in forcing these proceedings was to show the ESA to be an inflexible monster, the ESA flexed instead. If the Secretary's purpose was to exempt forty-four timber sales come hell or high water, thirty-one sales were left behind.

Id. at 344. The Ninth Circuit then upheld a NEPA-based injunction. *Seattle Audubon Soc. v. Espy,* 998 F.2d 699 (9th Cir.1993).

The Clinton Administration attempted to work out a compromise in order to accommodate the needs of the owl with the desire to save thousands of jobs in the Pacific Northwest. See Healy, "U.S. Proposes Cutting Timber Sales 10% More to Save Owls," *L.A. Times,* Feb. 24, 1994, at A3. One lesson of this controversy may be the need to focus on ecosystem preservation rather than exclusively on species preservation. See Flournoy, "Beyond the 'Spotted Owl Problem': Learning from the Old–Growth Controversy," 17 *Harv.Env.L.Rev.* 262 (1993). The trade-off between owls and jobs seemingly has proved less painful than expected. Oregon has not experienced a net loss of jobs, and retraining programs for loggers have been quite successful. See Egan, "Oregon Foils Forecasters, Thrives as It Protects Owls," *N.Y.Times,* Oct. 11, 1994, at 1.

4. *Coleman* and *TVA v. Hill* both involved governmental actions that threatened endangered species, though in *Coleman* at least part of the effect of the government's action was to induce private conduct. The next case considers the extent to which private landowners are required to preserve the habitat of endangered species. By 1994, the government had brought a hundred criminal prosecutions and at least four injunctive actions against state officials or private parties, with jail, fines, and probation resulting in the criminal cases. See GAO, "Information on Species Protection on Nonfederal Lands," at 12–13 (Dec. 1994) (GAO/RCED–95–16).

BABBITT v. SWEET HOME CHAPTER OF COMMUNITIES FOR A GREAT OREGON

Supreme Court of the United States, 1995.
515 U.S. 687, 115 S.Ct. 2407, 132 L.Ed.2d 597.

[The plaintiffs were small landowners, logging companies, and families dependent on the logging industry in the Pacific Northwest and in the Southeast. They brought this action to challenge the Secretary of the Interior's regulation defining the term "take" under § 9 of the ESA. Section 9 makes it unlawful for any person to take endangered or threatened species, and defines "take" to mean "harass, harm, pursue," "wound," or "kill." The regulation further defines "harm" to include "significant habitual modification or degradation where it actually kills or injures wildlife." The plaintiffs alleged that application of the "harm" regulation to the red-cockaded woodpecker, an endangered species, and the northern spotted owl, a threatened species, had injured them economically. In an en banc opinion, the D.C. Circuit held that the word "harm" was limited to the direct application of force, partly because of its concern regarding the implications of the regulation in terms of the resulting extinction of "property rights."]

JUSTICE STEVENS delivered the opinion of the Court.

Because this case was decided on motions for summary judgment, we may appropriately make certain factual assumptions in order to frame the legal issue. First, we assume respondents have no desire to harm either the red-cockaded woodpecker or the spotted owl; they merely wish to continue logging activities that would be entirely proper if not prohibited by the ESA. On the other hand, we must assume arguendo that those activities will have the effect, even though unintended, of detrimentally changing the natural habitat of both listed species and that, as a consequence, members of those species will be killed or injured. Under respondents' view of the law, the Secretary's only means of forestalling that grave result—even when the actor knows it is certain to occur[9]—is to use his § 5 authority to purchase the lands on which the survival of the species depends. The Secretary, on the other hand, submits that the § 9 prohibition on takings, which Congress defined to include "harm," places on respondents a duty to avoid harm that habitat alteration will cause the birds unless respondents first obtain a permit pursuant to § 10.

The text of the Act provides three reasons for concluding that the Secretary's interpretation is reasonable. First, an ordinary understanding of the word "harm" supports it. The dictionary definition of the verb form of "harm" is "to cause hurt or damage to: injure." In the context of the ESA, that definition naturally encompasses habitat modification that results in actual injury or death to members of an endangered or threatened species.

Respondents argue that the Secretary should have limited the purview of "harm" to direct applications of force against protected species, but the dictionary definition does not include the word "directly" or suggest in any way that only direct or willful action that leads to injury constitutes "harm." Moreover, unless the statutory term "harm" encompasses indirect as well as direct injuries, the word has no meaning

---

9. As discussed above, the Secretary's definition of "harm" is limited to "act[s] which actually kil[l] or injur[e] wildlife." * * * We do not agree with the dissent that the regulation covers results that are not "even foreseeable * * * no matter how long the chain of causality between modification and injury." Respondents have suggested no reason why either the "knowingly violates" or the "otherwise violates" provision of the statute—or the "harm" regulation itself—should not be read to incorporate ordinary requirements of proximate causation and foreseeability.

arguendo: for the sake of argument

that does not duplicate the meaning of other words that § 3 uses to define "take." A reluctance to treat statutory terms as surplusage supports the reasonableness of the Secretary's interpretation.

Second, the broad purpose of the ESA supports the Secretary's decision to extend protection against activities that cause the precise harms Congress enacted the statute to avoid. In *TVA v. Hill* [p. 581 supra], we described the Act as "the most comprehensive legislation for the preservation of endangered species ever enacted by any nation." Whereas predecessor statutes enacted in 1966 and 1969 had not contained any sweeping prohibition against the taking of endangered species except on federal lands, the 1973 Act applied to all land in the United States and to the Nation's territorial seas. As stated in § 2 of the Act, among its central purposes is "to provide a means whereby the ecosystems upon which endangered species and threatened species depend may be conserved * * *."

In *Hill*, we construed § 7 as precluding the completion of the Tellico Dam because of its predicted impact on the survival of the snail darter. Both our holding and the language in our opinion stressed the importance of the statutory policy. "The plain intent of Congress in enacting this statute," we recognized, "was to halt and reverse the trend toward species extinction, whatever the cost. This is reflected not only in the stated policies of the Act, but in literally every section of the statute." Although the § 9 "take" prohibition was not at issue in *Hill*, we took note of that prohibition, placing particular emphasis on the Secretary's inclusion of habitat modification in his definition of "harm." In light of that provision for habitat protection, we could "not understand how TVA intends to operate Tellico Dam without 'harming' the snail darter." Congress' intent to provide comprehensive protection for endangered and threatened species supports the permissibility of the Secretary's "harm" regulation.

Respondents advance strong arguments that activities that cause minimal or unforeseeable harm will not violate the Act as construed in the "harm" regulation. Respondents, however, present a facial challenge to the regulation. Thus, they ask us to invalidate the Secretary's understanding of "harm" in every circumstance, even when an actor knows that an activity, such as draining a pond, would actually result in the extinction of a listed species by destroying its habitat. Given Congress' clear expression of the ESA's broad purpose to protect endangered and threatened wildlife, the Secretary's definition of "harm" is reasonable.[23]

23. The dissent incorrectly asserts that the Secretary's regulation (1) "dispenses with the foreseeability of harm" and (2) "fail[s] to require injury to particular animals." As to the first assertion, the regulation merely implements the statute, and it is therefore subject to the statute's "knowingly violates" language, see 16 U.S.C. §§ 1540(a)(1), (b)(1), and ordinary requirements of proximate causation and foreseeability. See n. 9, *supra*. Nothing in the regulation purports to weaken those requirements. To the contrary, the word "actually" in the regulation should be construed to limit the liability about which the dissent appears most concerned, liability under the statute's "otherwise violates" provision. The Secretary did not need to include "actually" to connote "but for" causation, which the other words in the

Third, the fact that Congress in 1982 authorized the Secretary to issue permits for takings that § 9(a)(1)(B) would otherwise prohibit, "if such taking is incidental to, and not the purpose of, the carrying out of an otherwise lawful activity," 16 U.S.C. § 1539(a)(1)(B), strongly suggests that Congress understood § 9(a)(1)(B) to prohibit indirect as well as deliberate takings. The permit process requires the applicant to prepare a "conservation plan" that specifies how he intends to "minimize and mitigate" the "impact" of his activity on endangered and threatened species, 16 U.S.C. § 1539(a)(2)(A), making clear that Congress had in mind foreseeable rather than merely accidental effects on listed species. No one could seriously request an "incidental" take permit to avert § 9 liability for direct, deliberate action against a member of an endangered or threatened species, but respondents would read "harm" so narrowly that the permit procedure would have little more than that absurd purpose. "When Congress acts to amend a statute, we presume it intends its amendment to have real and substantial effect." Congress' addition of the § 10 permit provision supports the Secretary's conclusion that activities not intended to harm an endangered species, such as habitat modification, may constitute unlawful takings under the ESA unless the Secretary permits them.

We need not decide whether the statutory definition of "take" compels the Secretary's interpretation of "harm," because our conclusions that Congress did not unambiguously manifest its intent to adopt respondents' view and that the Secretary's interpretation is reasonable suffice to decide this case. [citing *Chevron*, p. 390 supra]. The latitude the ESA gives the Secretary in enforcing the statute, together with the degree of regulatory expertise necessary to its enforcement, establishes that we owe some degree of deference to the Secretary's reasonable interpretation.

* * *

When it enacted the ESA, Congress delegated broad administrative and interpretive power to the Secretary. The task of defining and listing endangered and threatened species requires an expertise and attention to detail that exceeds the normal province of Congress. Fashioning appropriate standards for issuing permits under § 10 for takings that would otherwise violate § 9 necessarily requires the exercise of broad discretion. The proper interpretation of a term such as "harm" involves a complex policy choice. When Congress has entrusted the Secretary with broad discretion, we are especially reluctant to substitute our views of wise policy for his. In this case, that reluctance accords with our conclusion, based on the text, structure, and legislative history of the ESA, that the Secretary reasonably construed the intent of Congress when he defined "harm" to include "significant habitat modification or degradation that actually kills or injures wildlife."

definition obviously require. As to the dissent's second assertion, every term in the regulation's definition of "harm" is subser-
vient to the phrase "an act which actually kills or injures wildlife."

In the elaboration and enforcement of the ESA, the Secretary and all persons who must comply with the law will confront difficult questions of proximity and degree; for, as all recognize, the Act encompasses a vast range of economic and social enterprises and endeavors. These questions must be addressed in the usual course of the law, through case-by-case resolution and adjudication.

JUSTICE O'CONNOR, concurring.

My agreement with the Court is founded on two understandings. First, the challenged regulation is limited to significant habitat modification that causes actual, as opposed to hypothetical or speculative, death or injury to identifiable protected animals. Second, even setting aside difficult questions of scienter, the regulation's application is limited by ordinary principles of proximate causation, which introduce notions of foreseeability. These limitations, in my view, call into question *Palila v. Hawaii Dept. of Land and Natural Resources*, 852 F.2d 1106 (C.A.9 1988) (Palila II), and with it, many of the applications derided by the dissent. Because there is no need to strike a regulation on a facial challenge out of concern that it is susceptible of erroneous application, however, and because there are many habitat-related circumstances in which the regulation might validly apply, I join the opinion of the Court.

In my view, the regulation is limited by its terms to actions that actually kill or injure individual animals. JUSTICE SCALIA disagrees, arguing that the harm regulation "encompasses injury inflicted, not only upon individual animals, but upon populations of the protected species." At one level, I could not reasonably quarrel with this observation; death to an individual animal always reduces the size of the population in which it lives, and in that sense, "injures" that population. But by its insight, the dissent means something else. Building upon the regulation's use of the word "breeding," JUSTICE SCALIA suggests that the regulation facially bars significant habitat modification that actually kills or injures hypothetical animals (or, perhaps more aptly, causes potential additions to the population not to come into being). Because "[i]mpairment of breeding does not 'injure' living creatures," JUSTICE SCALIA reasons, the regulation must contemplate application to "a population of animals which would otherwise have maintained or increased its numbers."

I disagree. As an initial matter, I do not find it as easy as JUSTICE SCALIA does to dismiss the notion that significant impairment of breeding injures living creatures. To raze the last remaining ground on which the piping plover currently breeds, thereby making it impossible for any piping plovers to reproduce, would obviously injure the population (causing the species' extinction in a generation). But by completely preventing breeding, it would also injure the individual living bird, in the same way that sterilizing the creature injures the individual living bird. To "injure" is, among other things, "to impair." One need not subscribe to theories of "psychic harm," to recognize that to make it impossible for an animal to reproduce is to impair its most essential physical functions and to render that animal, and its genetic material, biologically obsolete. This, in my view, is actual injury.

In any event, even if impairing an animal's ability to breed were not, in and of itself, an injury to that animal, interference with breeding can cause an animal to suffer other, perhaps more obvious, kinds of injury. The regulation has clear application, for example, to significant habitat modification that kills or physically injures animals which, because they are in a vulnerable breeding state, do not or cannot flee or defend themselves, or to environmental pollutants that cause an animal to suffer physical complications during gestation. Breeding, feeding, and sheltering are what animals do. If significant habitat modification, by interfering with these essential behaviors, actually kills or injures an animal protected by the Act, it causes "harm" within the meaning of the regulation. In contrast to JUSTICE SCALIA, I do not read the regulation's "breeding" reference to vitiate or somehow to qualify the clear actual death or injury requirement, or to suggest that the regulation contemplates extension to nonexistent animals.

JUSTICE SCALIA, with whom THE CHIEF JUSTICE and JUSTICE THOMAS join, dissenting.

I think it unmistakably clear that the legislation at issue here (1) forbade the hunting and killing of endangered animals, and (2) provided federal lands and federal funds for the acquisition of private lands, to preserve the habitat of endangered animals. The Court's holding that the hunting and killing prohibition incidentally preserves habitat on private lands imposes unfairness to the point of financial ruin—not just upon the rich, but upon the simplest farmer who finds his land conscripted to national zoological use. I respectfully dissent.

* * *

The regulation has three features which, for reasons I shall discuss at length below, do not comport with the statute. First, it interprets the statute to prohibit habitat modification that is no more than the cause-in-fact of death or injury to wildlife. Any "significant habitat modification" that in fact produces that result by "impairing essential behavioral patterns" is made unlawful, regardless of whether that result is intended or even foreseeable, and no matter how long the chain of causality between modification and injury. See, e.g., *Palila v. Hawaii Dept. of Land and Natural Resources (Palila II)*, 852 F.2d 1106, 1108–1109 (C.A.9 1988) (sheep grazing constituted "taking" of palila birds, since although sheep do not destroy full-grown mamane trees, they do destroy mamane seedlings, which will not grow to full-grown trees, on which the palila feeds and nests).

Second, the regulation does not require an "act": the Secretary's officially stated position is that an omission will do. The previous version of the regulation made this explicit. * * * When the regulation was modified in 1981 the phrase "or omission" was taken out, but only because (as the final publication of the rule advised) "the [Fish and

Wildlife] Service feels that 'act' is inclusive of either commissions or omissions which would be prohibited by section [1538(a)(1)(B)]." In its brief here the Government agrees that the regulation covers omissions (although it argues that "[a]n 'omission' constitutes an 'act' * * * only if there is a legal duty to act").

The third and most important unlawful feature of the regulation is that it encompasses injury inflicted, not only upon individual animals, but upon populations of the protected species. "Injury" in the regulation includes "significantly impairing essential behavioral patterns, including breeding," Impairment of breeding does not "injure" living creatures; it prevents them from propagating, thus "injuring" a population of animals which would otherwise have maintained or increased its numbers. What the face of the regulation shows, the Secretary's official pronouncements confirm. The Final Redefinition of "Harm" accompanying publication of the regulation said that "harm" is not limited to "direct physical injury to an individual member of the wildlife species," and refers to "injury to a population."

None of these three features of the regulation can be found in the statutory provisions supposed to authorize it. The term "harm" in § 1532(19) has no legal force of its own. An indictment or civil complaint that charged the defendant with "harming" an animal protected under the Act would be dismissed as defective, for the only operative term in the statute is to "take." If "take" were not elsewhere defined in the Act, none could dispute what it means, for the term is as old as the law itself. To "take," when applied to wild animals, means to reduce those animals, by killing or capturing, to human control. See, e.g., 11 *Oxford English Dictionary* (1933) ("Take ... To catch, capture (a wild beast, bird, fish, etc.)"); *Webster's New International Dictionary of the English Language* (2d ed. 1949) (take defined as "to catch or capture by trapping, snaring, etc., or as prey"); *Geer v. Connecticut*, 161 U.S. 519, 523, 16 S.Ct. 600, 602, 40 L.Ed. 793 (1896) ("[A]ll the animals which can be taken upon the earth, in the sea, or in the air, that is to say, wild animals, belong to those who take them") (quoting the Digest of Justinian); 2 W. Blackstone, *Commentaries* 411 (1766) ("Every man ... has an equal right of pursuing and taking to his own use all such creatures as are ferae naturae"). This is just the sense in which "take" is used elsewhere in federal legislation and treaty. And that meaning fits neatly with the rest of § 1538(a)(1), which makes it unlawful not only to take protected species, but also to import or export them; to possess, sell, deliver, carry, transport, or ship any taken species; and to transport, sell, or offer to sell them in interstate or foreign commerce. The taking prohibition, in other words, is only part of the regulatory plan of § 1538(a)(1), which covers all the stages of the process by which protected wildlife is reduced to man's dominion and made the object of profit. It is obvious that "take" in this sense—a term of art deeply embedded in the statutory and common law concerning wildlife—describes a class of acts (not omissions) done directly and intentionally (not indirectly and by accident) to particular animals (not populations of animals).

The Act's definition of "take" does expand the word slightly (and not unusually), so as to make clear that it includes not just a completed taking, but the process of taking, and all of the acts that are customarily identified with or accompany that process ("to harass, harm, pursue, hunt, shoot, wound, kill, trap, capture, or collect"); and so as to include attempts. § 1532(19). The tempting fallacy—which the Court commits with abandon—is to assume that once defined, "take" loses any significance, and it is only the definition that matters. The Court treats the statute as though Congress had directly enacted the § 1532(19) definition as a self-executing prohibition, and had not enacted § 1538(a)(1)(B) at all. But § 1538(a)(1)(B) is there, and if the terms contained in the definitional section are susceptible of two readings, one of which comports with the standard meaning of "take" as used in application to wildlife, and one of which does not, an agency regulation that adopts the latter reading is necessarily unreasonable, for it reads the defined term "take"—the only operative term—out of the statute altogether.

* * *

The Endangered Species Act is a carefully considered piece of legislation that forbids all persons to hunt or harm endangered animals, but places upon the public at large, rather than upon fortuitously accountable individual landowners, the cost of preserving the habitat of endangered species. There is neither textual support for, nor even evidence of congressional consideration of, the radically different disposition contained in the regulation that the Court sustains. For these reasons, I respectfully dissent.

Notes

1. Justice Scalia is the primary proponent of "textualism" in statutory interpretation. How persuasive is his argument that the ESA unambiguously precludes the agency's interpretation? The centerpiece of the dissent is his assertion that the word "take" as applied to wildlife, is "as old as the law itself," and means "to reduce those animals, by killing or capturing, to human control." How likely is it that a reasonable member of Congress would have had in mind the meaning of the term "take" in game law? After all, the statute is not an amendment to other game or fishing laws, but instead is an aggressive addition to the corpus of federal environmental law, where the historic meaning of the word "take" might not immediately spring to mind. Moreover, while Scalia is only willing to concede that the statutory definition of a taking "does expand the word slightly," surely a member of Congress who wanted to know what the word meant would have been more likely to look at the plain language of the definition section of the bill than to consult a treatise on game law. Scalia's reading of the statute may not be impermissible, but under the *Chevron* doctrine [p. 390 supra], he had the burden of showing that the agency's contrary interpretation was not merely wrong but unreasonable. Wouldn't it be peculiar to say that Mrs. O'Leary's cow didn't "harm" the people of Chicago when she kicked over the lantern that started the Chicago fire. After all, she "only" modified their habitat!) Similarly, as a matter of ordinary English usage, doesn't someone

who destroys the nesting grounds used by an endangered species or eliminates their food supply thereby harm them? Is Scalia's interpretation really driven by the demands of the statutory text, or is he more motivated by his concern that the agency's interpretation "imposes unfairness to the point of financial ruin not just upon the rich, but upon the simplest farmer who finds his land conscripted to national zoological use"?

2. How much does *Sweet Home* narrow the regulatory definition through concepts such as proximate cause. For instance, if logging removes forest cover that helps protect an endangered bird from raptors, is the logging a proximate cause of harm? See Quarles, MacLeod & Lundquist, "*Sweet Home* and the Narrowing of Wildlife 'Take' Under Section 9 of the Endangered Species Act," 26 *Env.L.Rev.* 10003, 10012 (1996) (arguing against liability).

3. Should a property owner be deprived of the right to modify the habitat of an endangered species without compensation? Consider whether this would be a taking under current Supreme Court doctrine. See *Good v. United States*, 39 Fed. Cl. 81 (1997) (no taking unless all economic value is destroyed). See also Meltz, "Where the Wild Things Are: The Endangered Species Act and Private Property," 24 *Env. L.* 369 (1994). Doesn't this raise rather squarely the conflict between the "private fiefdom" vision of property and the "green property" hailed by Byrne and others? On the other hand, if no compensation is offered, doesn't that give landowners an incentive to develop land quickly, eliminating possible endangered species, before legal restrictions can be imposed? See David Dana, "Natural Preservation and the Race to Develop," 143 *U. Pa. L. Rev.* 655 (1995). For a policy argument in favor of building compensation payments into habitat conservation plans, see Barton Thompson, "The Endangered Species Act: A Case Study in Takings and Incentives," 49 *Stan. L. Rev.* 305 (1997). One possibility is a scheme in which land is assigned values based on its significance for conservation purposes; property owners wishing to develop land must acquire units from other landowners. Id. at 342. (Compare the marketable permit schemes discussed in Chapter 4).

4. The *Sweet Home* opinion mentions the role of habitat conservation plans in connection with "indirect" taxes. Habitat conservation plans have played an increasing role under the ESA:

> By the summer of 1996, 320 HCPs had been adopted or were under development * * * . Irrigation projects on the Umatilla, the Truckee–Carson and the Yakima Rivers were being revised. The Upper Colorado River was deep into a multi-year planning exercise that will inevitably lead to remanagement of water levels and instream flows. The Lower Colorado was embroiled in a similar exercise from Colorado to Mexico, as were users and regulators of the Platte River Basin of Wyoming and Nebraska. Hydropower operations were in question along the length of the Columbia River for the Pacific salmon, and along rivers of the eastern seaboard for the Atlantic salmon, the width of the continent away. An entirely new water management regime had come to the Sacramento delta and to South Florida as well. Coastal Florida counties were beginning to zone development along their beaches and canals, coastal Alabama along its beaches. Massive private forest holdings were

being revamped in Georgia, North Carolina, and across the American South; a plan for 1.6 million acres of state forest lands was adopted in Washington. Central Texas, unable to keep itself from extinguishing its own water supply, was finally being required to think again, as were, to their continuing grief, real estate developers in the hill country around Austin, Texas—each to meet the biological needs of endangered species.

Oliver Houck, "On the Law of Biodiversity and Ecosystem Management," 81 *Minn. L. Rev.* 869, 957–58 (1997).

A related approach is to involve local authorities in habitat preservation. For example, the federal government delegated responsibility to local governments in Southern California to determine how to conserve gnatcatcher habitat, resulting in a massive local planning process covering most of the remaining open space in San Diego, Orange, and Riverside Counties. The fifty-year plan seeks to preserve hundreds of thousands of acres from Los Angeles to Mexico, and will protect over seventy endangered or threatened species of plants and animals. See George Frampton, "Ecosystem Management in the Clinton Administration," 7 *Duke Env. L. & Pol'y F.* 39, 41 (1996); Stevens, "Salvation at Hand for a California Landscape," N.Y. Times, Feb. 27, 1996, at B7. A key step was taken when San Diego approved the plan, since about one-third of the 172,000 acre preserve will be under its control. L.A. Times, March 3, 1997, at A12. One effort is to enlist voluntary participation by landowners by promising some degree of protection from changed future regulations. Frampton, supra, at 45. These plans have been hailed as inauguring an era of eco-system protection. Wheeler, "The Ecosystem Approach: New Departures for Land and Water," 24 *Ecology L.Q.* 623 (1997). Meanwhile, questions have been raised about the legality of some of the plans. Marianne Lavelle, "Feds Settle To Save Act And Species," *National Law Journal*, Dec. 16, 1996, at 1. But administrative efforts to make the statute more flexible have also been applauded. See Ruhl, "Who Needs Congress? An Agenda for Administrative Reform of the Endangered Species Act," 6 *NYU Env.L.J.* 367 (1998).

5. The overall effectiveness of the ESA is controversial. Charles Mann and Mark Plummer argue that it has failed to save endangered species. C. Mann & M. Plummer, *Noah's Choice: The Future of Endangered Species* (1995). But an empirical study found that "[l]isting appears to have turned the fortunes of about half of the species it protects," and "[e]ach year of protection under the Act improves the prospects for listed species." Rachlinski, Book Review, 82 *Cornell L.Rev.* 356–383 (1997).

Endangered Species Negotiating Problem

Consider the following situation, as described by the Secretary of the Interior:

The basic controversy centers around a bird, the golden-cheeked (wood) warbler. These birds are extraordinary critters. They tend to get back into these evolutionary niches where they become dependent on a single tree, a single food source; thus, they are not very movable. The problem in Austin, for those of you who have not been there, is that the highlands to the West—the old "LBJ hill country"—is the most desirable place to live. The birds and the people both want to live in exactly the same place. Go east of Austin and you will find a Siberia or a Sahara where there is nothing but space. The birds and the people both want to go to the hills on the Balcones Escarpment. The question then becomes, can we sort it out?

Babbitt, "The Endangered Species Act and 'Takings': A Call for Innovation Within the Terms of the Act," 24 *Env.L.Rep.* 355, 365 (1994). For later developments, Stevens, "Texas Balancing Act is Succeeding," N.Y. Times, Feb. 27, 1996, at B8.

A Biological Advisory Team [BAT] made up of experts in the field recommended protecting up to 75% of the remaining habitat for the species. To the extent possible, the group recommended avoiding a "patchy" pattern of preserves. Financing sources might include the city or the federal government.

The groups involved are: (1) the federal government, (2) the city, (3) real estate developers, and (4) environmentalists. Developers view the BAT recommendation as far too high, while environmentalists question whether even 75% preservation is enough. The willingness of Austin voters to support city financing is unclear. Try to negotiate a viable solution. To the extent that your information about the problem is incomplete, try to include in your agreement some mechanism for obtaining new information and taking it into account.

———

At this point you have had a general overview of the leading issues in environmental law. In looking back over the materials, these are questions you may want to consider:

(1) Is the current complexity of the numerous applicable statutes really necessary, or could a simpler, more cohesive scheme be devised?

(2) Are the courts playing an appropriate role in environmental law, or should we either (a) give more authority to agencies to make final decisions, (b) expand judicial review by existing courts, or (c) create special environmental or "science" courts?

(3) Does environmental law conflict with other important goals, such as economic growth, federalism, or property rights?

(4) To what extent is environmental law economically rational—and to what extent should it be?

(5) What is the rationale for protecting the environment, and does that rationale have a viable basis?

Index

References are to Pages

†

0–314–23045–9

90000

9 780314 230454